# Fundamental Accounting Principles

# Fundamental Accounting Principles

Kermit D. Larson
*The University of Texas at Austin*

Twelfth Edition

**IRWIN**
Homewood, IL 60430
Boston, MA 02116

Cover photo: *Eric Meola, The Image Bank/Chicago*



Executive editor: *Lew Gossage*
Associate editor: *Sheila Smith*
Developmental editor: *Nancy Lanum*
Project editor: *Margaret Haywood*
Production manager: *Irene H. Sotiroff*
Designer: *Michael Warrell*
Artist: *Precision Graphics*
Compositor: *York Graphic Services, Inc.*
Typeface: *10/12 Times Roman*
Printer: *Von Hoffmann Press, Inc.*

**Library of Congress Cataloging-in-Publication Data**

Larson, Kermit D.
Fundamental accounting principles / Kermit D. Larson.—12th ed.
p. cm.
ISBN 0-256-07342-2
1. Accounting. I. Title.
HF5635.P975 1990 89–15560
657—dc20 CIP

*Printed in the United States of America*
3 4 5 6 7 8 9 0 VH 6 5 4 3 2 1 0

Dedicated to Nancy,
and to Julie, Tim, and Cindy

# About the Author

Kermit D. Larson is the Arthur Andersen & Co. Alumni Professor of Accounting at The University of Texas at Austin, where he has been a member of the faculty since 1966. He served as chairman of the U.T. Department of Accounting from 1971 to 1975 and was Visiting Associate Professor at Tulane University in 1970. His scholarly articles have been published in a variety of journals such as *The Accounting Review, Journal of Accountancy,* and *Abacus*. He is the author of several books, including *Fundamental Accounting Principles* and *Financial Accounting,* and coauthor of *Advanced Accounting,* all published by Richard D. Irwin, Inc.

Professor Larson's professional activities range from service as chairman of the American Accounting Association's Committee on Concepts and Standards, vice president of the American Accounting Association, Southwest regional vice president of the AAA, and director of the AAA Doctoral Consortium, to member of the Constitutional Drafting Committee of the Federation of Schools of Accountancy and member of the Commission on Professional Accounting Education. He has served on the Accounting Accreditation Committee and on the Accounting Standards Committee of the AACSB and has been an expert witness on cases involving mergers, antitrust litigation, and expropriation of assets by foreign governments. Professor Larson has served on the Board of Directors and Executive Committee of Tekcon, Inc. and presently serves on the Strategic Planning Committee of the American Accounting Association and the National Accountant's Advisory Board of Safeguard Business Systems, Inc.

# Preface

*Fundamental Accounting Principles* and its supplements provide a complete, fully integrated teaching and learning system for the first two-semester accounting course at the college and university level. The objectives of this course generally include: (1) developing a general understanding of financial reports and analyses that students will use in their personal affairs regardless of their fields of specialization, (2) providing a strong foundation for future courses in business and finance, and (3) initiating the course work that leads to a career in accounting. *Fundamental Accounting Principles* serves all of these objectives.

The central focus of *Fundamental Accounting Principles* is to explain the development of accounting information for the use of business managers and other parties who are interested in the financial affairs of a business. Underlying this focus is a primary goal of helping students interpret and use accounting information intelligently and effectively. The concepts and principles that govern accounting processes are explained and persistently emphasized so that students will be able to generalize and apply their knowledge to a variety of new situations.

The early chapters of *Fundamental Accounting Principles* use the single proprietorship to illustrate the accounting cycle. However, corporations are gradually introduced through the first four chapters in a manner that does not interrupt or confuse the discussion of the cycle. As a result, students gain a clear understanding of unincorporated entities and are also prepared for the corporate illustrations of Chapter 5. The assignment material for Chapter 5 is divided equally between corporate and proprietorship businesses so instructors can easily move to full reliance on corporate illustrations or defer an emphasis on corporations until the later chapters in the book.

## Learning through Active Student Involvement

The educational philosophy behind the development of *Fundamental Accounting Principles* is that learning occurs most effectively when students are actively involved. Our objective is to have students use as much of their study time as possible in active behavior such as answering questions and solving problems. This means that the use of student time in passive, low-retention behavior such as reading must be held to a minimum. To accomplish this objective, the twelfth edition of *Fundamental Accounting Principles* reflects a concise yet conceptually thorough writing style and provides a rich source of assignment material that includes a wide range of questions, exercises, problems, and provocative problems. In addition, to encourage students to hold a more active, participative mindset, the twelfth edition has been thoroughly rewritten in a more active voice.

Specific features and changes in the twelfth edition that contribute to this process of learning through active student involvement include the following:

**New Introductions.** Each part of the book and each chapter opens with a new introduction that invites personal involvement and generally describes the personal benefit that will result from studying the part or chapter.

**Careful Integration of Concepts and Applications.** Throughout the book, the definitions and explanations of important concepts and principles are presented in close proximity to illustrations and practical applications of those concepts and principles. As a result, students need not hold abstract concepts in limbo before they see how the concepts are applied.

**New Diagrams.** A variety of new illustrative diagrams are intended to maintain interest and to clarify or summarize the relationships between the concepts under discussion.

**New Excerpts of Relevant News Articles.** A carefully selected set of news articles has been excerpted from sources such as *The Wall Street Journal* and *Forbes* and included in the text under the common title "As a matter of fact." These items contribute to a higher level of student interest and show the contemporary importance of the material in the business world.

**New Chapter Summaries.** To help students review their understanding of the topical coverage, each chapter now contains a summary that is organized in terms of the learning objectives.

**New Demonstration Problems in Each Chapter.** Although the twelfth edition continues its tradition of presenting illustrative problems in close proximity to topical explanations, each chapter also concludes with a demonstration problem and solution. These present integrated examples of how the concepts in the chapter are applied in solving problems.

**New Objective Review Questions in Each Chapter.** Following each chapter's glossary, the twelfth edition includes a new section called Objective Review. This contains a series of multiple-choice questions related to the learning objectives. To minimize the tendency to look at the answers prior to making a definite choice, the answers are located in Appendix I at the end of the book.

**Expanded Assignment Material.** There are nearly 750 exercise and problem assignments in the twelfth edition. This expands even further the marked increase in assignment material introduced in the previous edition. All of the assignments have been newly revised, and an increased number are based on facts drawn from real-world companies. A large number have relatively short solution times that give students the positive incentive of quick feedback and frequent encouragement that results from successful completion.

**Annotation of Selected Assignments.** Brief annotations are provided for the exercises and problems so that students can move quickly to the active process of preparing their solutions.

**Unannotated Provocative Problems.** The role of the provocative problems is to challenge students with somewhat more complex situations in which they must take greater responsibility for analyzing the problems and structuring their solutions. To facilitate this, annotations are not provided and working papers are not specifically designed for these problems. Nevertheless, the revised working papers booklets now include a variety of extra forms that students can adapt to these problems. Provocative problems can help instructors challenge their best students and demonstrate to the entire class the contemporary relevance of the course.

**New Comprehensive Review Problems.** To support the integration of topics across several chapters and to provide structured review on a periodic basis, the text now includes four comprehensive assignment problems. They appear after Chapter 4, Chapter 6, Chapter 12, and Chapter 22.

## Reorganized Coverage to Increase Flexibility

Several changes in the twelfth edition give the instructor greater flexibility in selecting and organizing topical coverage. For example, the discussions of stock investments, consolidated statements, and international operations have been moved to a separate chapter (Chapter 19). Also, the book now contains ten appendixes. Some of the topics in these appendixes represent expanded coverage and some represent reorganized coverage. Each of the topical appendixes is supported by separate learning objectives, assignment material, coverage in the *Study Guides,* and the examination bank.

*a.* Appendix A (after Chapter 3) expands the discussion of adjusting entries to include a clearer treatment of items that are originally recorded in expense and revenue accounts.

*b.* Appendix B (after Chapter 4) contains a discussion of reversing entries. This discussion now appears in a more appropriate location in the book and also permits optional coverage of these procedures.

*c.* Appendix C (after Chapter 5) gives a thorough explanation of the adjusting entry approach to accounting for merchandise inventories.

*d.* Appendix D (after Chapter 7) explains the use of vouchers in a manual accounting system.

*e.* Appendix E contains a review of accounting principles and concise coverage of the FASB's conceptual framework. The appendix is located between Chapters 14 and 15 so that it serves as an excellent close to the first half of the book (or opening to the second semester).

*f.* Appendix F (after Chapter 18) explains the indirect method of calculating the cash provided (or used) by operating activities.

*g.* Appendix G (at the end of the book) supplements the present value discussion in Chapter 10 with an expanded analysis of present and future values.

*h.* Given the recent FASB action to make the disclosures on the effect of price changes voluntary, this topic was moved from Chapter 15 to Appendix H.

*i.* Appendix I contains the answers to all of the multiple-choice, Objective Review questions in the book. These answers are placed at the end of the book rather than in the chapters so students will avoid the natural tendency to look for the correct answer before making a personal choice.

*j.* Appendix J contains all of the financial disclosures that appear in the 1988 annual report of Tyler Corporation.

## Other Important Changes that Affect Several Chapters

In addition to the above changes, many specific improvements in the twelfth edition affect several chapters. Some of these are itemized below:

**A New Emphasis on Ethics in Accounting.** The twelfth edition begins with a new prologue on the importance of ethics in accounting. Thereafter, many chapters include brief cases under the common title "As a Matter of Ethics." These cases are intended to encourage student reflection on the ethical issues confronted by accountants and others who use accounting information. The *Instructor's Resource Manual* includes helpful points for discussion related to each ethical case and copies of the ethical codes adopted by the AICPA and the NAA. Some instructors may use these materials in support of class discussions; others may simply post them or distribute them for student use.

**Additional Questions.** Approximately 90 additional questions for class discussion address the conceptual issues explained in the text. Approximately 425 questions are now provided.

**Expanded Glossaries with Page References.** The glossaries now include well over 400 important terms with concise definitions that focus on the conceptual essence of the terms. Where appropriate, the definitions are consistent with the FASB's conceptual framework. Each term in the glossaries is referenced to the pages in the chapter where the term is discussed. The glossaries are located at the end of each chapter so they can be used effectively when students are reviewing the chapter. However, each glossary term is also highlighted in color in the index to the book.

**Integrated Learning Objectives.** Many of the learning objectives that appear at the beginning of each chapter have been rewritten. To support instructional approaches that focus on learning objectives, the twelfth edition integrates these objectives throughout the text and supporting materials. In the text, they are presented in the margins next to relevant topical coverage and next to related problem assignments. The test bank identifies the learning objectives related to each question and provides for random question selection based on learning objectives.

**New Accounting Cycle Illustration with Improved Teaching Features.** A new illustration, Jerry Dow, Attorney, is used throughout Chapters 1–4. This new illustration contains several improvements that make the book more teachable and easier to understand. For example, all of the financial statements introduced in Chapter 1 (including the statement of cash flows) are drawn from this illustration. Also, Chapter 3 presents the unadjusted trial balance, the adjustments, and the adjusted trial balance in a manner that better prepares students for the Chapter 4 discussion of the work sheet. And in Chapter 4, a series of overlay transparencies are used to show much more clearly the process of developing a work sheet. Throughout these chapters, special care has been taken to ensure that problem requirements never precede a thorough explanation of the issues.

**Descriptive Titles of Illustrations.** Many new illustrations have been added to the text. Also, descriptive titles have been given to the illustrations whenever this adds clarity.

**New Treatment of Dividends.** Dividends are now recorded in a Dividends Declared account to make the corporate procedures parallel to the withdrawals accounts used in unincorporated businesses.

**New Real-World Examples.** All of the exercises, problems, and provocative problems have been revised, and the real-world examples and problems were newly selected for the twelfth edition. These have been drawn primarily from the published financial reports of corporations such as American Can Company, Bell & Howell Company, Caterpillar Inc., Chrysler Corporation, The Clorox Company, Dycom Industries Inc., H. J. Heinz Company, W. R. Grace & Co., Textron Inc., and Tyler Corporation.

**Problem Assignments Solvable with New Computer Packages.** A large number of the exercises, problems, provocative problems, and three of the comprehensive problems in the text can be solved using newly developed software packages that accompany the text. Those that can be solved using *General Ledger Applications Software (GLAS)* are identified in the margin with the

symbol shown above. This software package can also be used to solve the first two manual practice sets.

Many additional exercises, problems, and provocative problems can be solved using *Spreadsheet Applications Template Software (SPATS)* developed by Will Garland of Coastal Carolina College. *SPATS* contains innovatively designed templates based on Lotus® 1-2-3® and includes a very effective tutorial for Lotus® 1-2-3®. The exercises and problems solvable with *SPATS* are identified in the margin of the text with the following symbol.

**Expanded Use of Color to Enhance Learning.** The use of color in the twelfth edition has been carefully designed to support and encourage student learning. Financial reports that are the output of the accounting process are identified by their blue background. A bold blue is used to emphasize key terms, titles of statements, and items of special importance in illustrations. Textual headings require a "hot", bold color to draw attention. These are printed in red, which also is used to emphasize alternative points of special importance in illustrations. A noninterruptive, cream color softly highlights the end-of-chapter material where student involvement in the learning process is greatest. Cream also serves as a background for illustrations.

## Improvements in Specific Chapters

Most of the chapters in this edition reflect specific improvements in addition to those described above. These include the following:

- Chapter 1 contains expanded coverage of the institutional environment of financial reporting and its relationship to standards setting. Also, more attention is given to professional certifications in accounting.
- Chapter 3 reflects an improved conceptual discussion of the realization and matching principles and of accrual versus cash basis accounting.
- Overlay transparencies are used in the work sheet illustrations of Chapter 4 to present more effectively the sequence of steps in the preparation of a work sheet.
- New illustrations in Chapter 7 highlight the principles of internal control and diagram the flow of business papers related to purchases when a voucher system is used. The concept of asset liquidity is also explained in this chapter.
- A new discussion of short-term investments and lower of cost or market is provided in Chapter 8.
- The discussion in Chapter 10 has been reorganized to clarify the concept of cost recovery through depreciation and to place less emphasis on accelerated depreciation methods. Also, the discussion of the Modified Accelerated Cost Recovery System has been updated.
- The tax method of accounting for asset exchanges is more precisely explained in Chapter 11.
- In Chapter 12, the criteria for classifying leases as capital or operating leases are more clearly explained.
- Chapter 15 includes a new discussion and illustration of corporate management structures. Also, a reorganized discussion of preferred stock places less emphasis on participating stock and better illustrates dividends to cumulative stock.
- The material on reporting income and retained earnings items is now presented in Chapter 16, as is the explanation of earnings per share. This reorganization provides a more logically connected set of topics in this chapter and makes room for the separate chapter on stock investments, consolidations, and international operations (Chapter 19). Chapter 16 also introduces the now widely used statement of changes in stockholders' equity.

- The statement of cash flows is explained in Chapter 18. The direct approach (recommended by the FASB) is explained in the chapter and the indirect approach is explained in an appendix. Both the T-account and working paper approaches to preparing the statement are explained.
- The discussion of financial statement ratios in Chapter 20 has been reorganized, and includes new coverage of profit margin, total asset turnover, and their relationship to return on total assets. The calculations of all ratios are reviewed at the end of the chapter.
- Several new diagrams are used in Chapter 21 to support improved explanations of product costs versus period costs, the flow of product costs in manufacturing companies, and the relationship between overhead items, the manufacturing statement, and the income statement.
- Chapter 22 contains an improved explanation of over- or underapplied overhead and new diagrams that show the flow of materials in job order manufacturing processes and in process manufacturing operations.
- The revised discussion in Chapter 23 better reflects the use of computers in accounting and provides clearer explanations of controllable versus uncontrollable costs and the financial statement effects of joint cost allocations.
- Just-in-time inventory systems are now explained in Chapter 25, which also reflects a reorganized discussion of the benefits from budgeting.
- The discussion of variances in Chapter 26 has been revised to include algebraic or formula approaches to explaining variances, a better discussion of overhead variances, and a new diagram that clearly shows the cause of a volume variance. The new chapter also includes more complete illustrations of the entries to record standard costs in the accounts.
- Chapter 28 now includes a surprisingly clear introduction to the most important concepts embodied in *SFAS 96,* the FASB's new accounting requirement for income taxes. The revision also reflects all relevant changes in the federal income tax laws.

## Supplements to the Text

### For the Instructor

The support package for *Fundamental Accounting Principles* includes many items to assist the instructor. The instructor's support items are:

- The *Instructor's Integrated Teaching System,* which includes the entire 28-chapter text in a three-ring binder. This system allows the instructor to prepare class presentations that combine text, teaching transparencies, solutions transparencies, and relevant material from the *Instructor's Resource Manual* in a self-contained binder.
- Two *Solutions Manuals* that have more extensive supporting calculations in this edition.
- *Solution Transparencies* that include all exercises and all problems. These transparencies are now printed in boldface in a new, exception-

ally large typeface so that visibility from a distance is strikingly improved.

- An expanded set of *Teaching Transparencies,* many of which are now in color.
- *Computerized Teaching Transparencies* that are designed to support teaching the course using a computer, data display, and an overhead projector.
- *Video tapes* that are available upon adoption. The tapes reinforce important topics and procedures. They may be used in the classroom or media lab.
- *Spreadsheet Applications Template Software (SPATS),* a new software package developed for use with the text by Will Garland of Coastal Carolina College. SPATS includes a Lotus® 1-2-3® tutorial and innovatively designed templates that may be used with Lotus® 1-2-3® to solve many of the exercises and problems in the text. Upon adoption, this package is available to instructors for classroom or laboratory use.
- *Peachtree® Complete III™*. The leading business accounting software is available for site license. The General Store, Inc. and World of Sports practice sets are available with templates that permit their use with Peachtree® Complete III™.
- *Computerized Tutorials for Chapters 1–14* and *Chapters 15–28,* by Leland Mansuetti. These software packages include true/false and multiple-choice questions with explanations for both correct and incorrect answers by students. Upon adoption, these computerized tutorials are available to instructors for classroom or laboratory use.
- A dramatically expanded test bank to accompany the twelfth edition. The new bank includes a much greater variety of multiple-choice and true/false questions. In addition, the new bank contains at least 100% more exercise-type problems. The printed *Examination Materials I* and *II* booklets now contain a complete copy of the computer test bank plus the solutions to the achievement tests.
- *Computest III,* an improved test generator program that allows editing of questions, provides up to 99 different versions of each test, and allows question selection based on type of question, level of difficulty, or learning objectives.
- *Teletest,* which is a system for obtaining laser-printed tests by telephoning the publisher and specifying the questions to be drawn from the test bank.
- *Achievement Tests, Series A, B, and C.* These examinations come in packages of 30 copies each and are free to adopters. Each series is made up of five examinations plus one final examination for Chapters 1–14 and five examinations plus one final examination for Chapters 15–28.
- The *Instructor's Resource Manual* includes sample course syllabi, suggested homework assignments, a series of lecture outlines, demonstration problems, suggested points for emphasis, and background materials for discussions of ethics in accounting.

### For the Student

In addition to the text, the package of support items for the student includes the following:

- The *Student Integrated Learning System—Chapters 1–14* (Volume I) and *Chapters 14–28* (Volume II). This option allows students to purchase either Chapters 1–14 or Chapters 14–28 of the text with the related working papers and study guides in a 3-ring binder. Students benefit by having all three course-related items in a single package and by obtaining a significant cost savings. The text is also available in the conventional 28-chapter hardcover format.
- *Working Papers, Chapters 1–14* and *Chapters 14–28*. These include working papers for the problems, alternate problems, and comprehensive problems, with additional forms that may be adapted for the exercises and provocative problems. To support flexibility of course design, both volumes include working papers for Chapter 14.
- *Study Guides, Chapters 1–14* and *Chapters 14–28*. These volumes, which provide a basis for independent study and review, have been expanded to include multiple-choice and true/false questions as well as several additional problems with solutions for each chapter and appendix. Coverage of Chapter 14 and Appendix E is reproduced in both volumes.
- *Class Notes,* for use with the computerized teaching transparencies. These are designed to help students be actively involved and take effective notes when the computerized transparencies are used to teach the course.
- *Check Figures* for the problems and alternate problems.
- *World of Sports,* a manual, single proprietorship practice set with business papers that may be assigned after Chapter 6.
- *The General Store, Inc.,* a manual practice set that may be assigned after Chapter 8.
- *Freewheel Corporation,* a manual practice set by Christie Johnson that may be assigned after Chapter 20.
- *NewTech Incorporated,* a manual practice set with a narrative of transactions for a manufacturing corporation. This may be assigned after Chapter 21.
- *Kellogg Business Systems, Inc.,* an extended corporate practice set that may be assigned after Chapter 20. Like the other computerized items for students, it can be ordered on either 5¼ or 3½ inch disks.
- *General Ledger Applications Software (GLAS),* newly developed software that can be used with the text to solve a large number of the exercises, problems, and three of the comprehensive problems. This software can also be used to solve the first two manual practice sets. *GLAS* may be ordered with the textbook, or with the *Student Integrated Learning System,* or as a separate item.

- *ESP—Electronic Spreadsheet Program,* a computerized spreadsheet package by John Wanlass and Kermit Larson that can be used to solve many of the problems in the text and is also broad enough to be used in a separate computer accounting course.

Several items listed earlier under the heading "For the Instructor" are intended for student use at the option of the instructor. They include:

- *Spreadsheet Applications Template Software (SPATS).*
- *Peachtree® Complete III™.*
- *Computerized Tutorials for Chapters 1–14.*
- *Computerized Tutorials for Chapters 15–28.*

## Acknowledgments

I am indebted to those who have been the source of many improvements in the book through their thoughtful and insightful reviews. They include:

C. Frank Beigbeder, Rancho Santiago Community College.
Dave Evans, Johnson County Community College.
Daniel J. Galvin, Diablo Valley College.
Robert I. Glover, Loyola University-New Orleans.
Royal E. Knight, University of North Alabama.
Susan A. Lynn, George Mason University.
Timothy D. Miller, El Camino College.
Chandra Schorg, Northwood Institute.
Larry G. Singleton, The George Washington University.
David Skougstad, Metropolitan State College.
James P. Trebby, Marquette University.
James Zellers, West Virginia State College.

In addition, numerous adopters, students, and professional colleagues have made a variety of significant contributions, suggestions, and constructive criticisms. They include:

Amy Bielek, Peat Marwick Main & Co.
William J. Engel, Jr., Longview Community College.
James W. Deitrick, The University of Texas at Austin.
Anna Fowler, The University of Texas at Austin.
Wilbur L. Garland, Coastal Carolina College.
Cynthia Gloria, Ernst & Young.
Michael Haselkorn, Bentley College.
Lisa Kalish, The University of Texas at Austin.
Eric A. Karl, Transportation & Industrial Funding Corporation.
Cathy X. Larson, Middlesex Community College.
Elliott S. Levy, Bentley College.
Leland E. Mansuetti, Sierra College.
Kenneth Miller, San Antonio College.

Paul Miller, University of Colorado-Colorado Springs.
Kathy Morris, Coopers & Lybrand.
Terry Nunley, University of North Carolina-Charlotte.
George Ortleb III, Pace University.
Daniel P. Small, J. Sargeant Reynolds Community College.
Jack E. Terry, Jack E. Terry & Associates.
D. E. Tillotson, Skagit Valley College.
John W. Wanlass, De Anza College.
Dick D. Wasson, Central Washington University.
Bill Wells, Tulsa Junior College.
Robert G. Wrenn, Los Angeles Harbor College.

I especially want to recognize the contribution of Paul Miller, University of Colorado at Colorado Springs, who has provided extremely important consultation in the development of the new edition. Also, Patricia Kardash and Deborah Perry have been of invaluable assistance in preparing the manuscript and maintaining its error-free tradition.

**Kermit D. Larson**

# Contents in Brief

## Part Seven
## Managerial Accounting for Costs 883



## Part Eight
## Planning and Controlling Business Operations 1019



## Part Nine
## Appendixes 1207

# Contents

# Fundamental Accounting Principles

Part One

# Introduction

Accounting in one form or another touches the lives of everyone: young people add and subtract figures to decide how to spend their weekly allowances; newspaper carriers keep payment records of their customers; students determine where the money for their education is coming from and how to spend it; taxpayers account for their taxable deductions; and businesses account for the profits from their operations. All of us use accounting to make economic decisions of one kind or another.

As you study this accounting text, a new world of understanding and knowledge will unfold. You will be better prepared to earn a living and to live on what you earn; newspaper stories of record sales, bankruptcies, and government regulations will have more meaning; and gradually you will come to understand the important role accounting plays in our economic society.

Part One of *Fundamental Accounting Principles* consists of:

# To the Student Reader

*Fundamental Accounting Principles* is designed to get you actively involved in the learning process so that you will learn quickly and more thoroughly. The more time you spend expressing what you are learning, the more effectively you will learn. In accounting, you do this primarily by answering questions and solving problems. However, you can also express your ideas by using the wide margins for taking notes, summarizing a phrase, or writing down a question that remains unanswered in your mind. These notes will assist in your later review of the material, and the simple process of writing them will help you learn.

As you read the text, you will be exposed to many important new terms. The first time a key term is used, it is printed in blue. In addition to being defined and discussed in the chapter, these terms are listed with concise definitions in a glossary at the end of each chapter. The glossary is a good place to begin your review of important concepts. You can also find the key terms in the Index at the back of the book.

As a guide to your study, specific learning objectives are listed at the beginning of each chapter, repeated in the margins next to the related topics throughout the chapter, and used as a basis for summary at the end of the chapter. The exercises and problems are also coded in terms of these objectives.

Other special features of the book include excerpts from news articles entitled "As a Matter of Fact." These relate real-world events to the material in the chapter. You also will discover brief inserts entitled "As a Matter of Ethics." These encourage you to think about the ethical aspects of accounting.

The use of color in the book has been carefully planned to facilitate your learning. Financial reports, which are the output of the accounting process, are printed on a blue background. Blue is also used to emphasize key terms, titles of statements, and items of special importance in illustrations. Red is used for headings and for emphasizing alternative points of special importance in illustrations. A soft, noninterruptive cream color is used as a background in the illustrations and the end-of-chapter material.

In addition to a summary and glossary, each chapter contains a Demonstration Problem and related solution that illustrate many of the issues discussed in the chapter. There is also a short section entitled "Objective Review" that contains a series of multiple-choice questions or problems related to the learning objectives. Answer them as a quick test of your learning. Then check your answers against the correct ones listed in Appendix I. The exercises and first two sets of problems in each chapter have brief annotations. However, to challenge you to identify the topical issues involved, the provocative problems are not annotated.

Prologue

# Ethics: The Most Fundamental Accounting Principle

*"Each person capable of making moral decisions is responsible for making his own decisions. The ultimate locus of moral responsibility is in the individual."*[1]

As college students, you no doubt realize that ethics and ethical behavior are important features of civilized society. Ethical considerations abound in daily life, both privately and professionally. The media often remind us of the importance of ethics to society. These reminders come in the form of news stories about such things as civil rights violations, fraudulent attempts to "rip off" the elderly, credit card scams, parents who failed to make child support payments, children who ignored or abused their elderly parents, politicians who failed to disclose past instances of misconduct, the alleged bribery of government officials, and Wall Street moguls who used inside information for personal gain.

## The Meaning of Ethics

As a discipline of study, ethics deals "with what is good and bad or right and wrong or with moral duty and obligation." In practice, ethics are "principles of conduct that govern an individual or a profession."[2] Some unethical actions are unlawful. Other actions may be within the law but, nevertheless, are widely recognized as being ethically wrong. In addition, some actions are not clearly right or wrong but are ethically questionable.

Many of the issues we face in school, in the workplace, and beyond have ethical dimensions; they are unavoidable aspects of life. How well we deal with ethical matters influences how we feel about ourselves, how we are perceived by others, and in the aggregate, the quality of our society. But why begin an accounting text with a prologue on ethics? How do ethics relate to business, and more specifically, to the discipline of accounting?

## Ethics in Business

To answer the question of why we begin this text with a prologue on ethics, we must recognize that ethical standards in business and accounting are a matter of public concern. In recent years, many people have expressed concern about deteriorating ethical standards in business. Touche Ross, an international

[1] Harold H. Titus and Morris Keeton, *Ethics for Today,* 4th ed. (New York: American Book–Stratford Press, 1966), p. 131.

[2] *Webster's Third New International Dictionary of the English Language, Unabridged* (Springfield, Mass.: G & C Merriam Co., 1971), p. 780.

public accounting firm, recently conducted an opinion survey on business ethics. The survey included over 1,100 business executives, deans of business schools, and members of Congress. Of those in the survey, 94% agree that "the business community is troubled by ethical problems today."[3] Ironically, those surveyed also believe that companies that are successful over the long run seem to have high ethical standards. You may infer from this that "ethics is good business." Ethical business practices can help create loyal customers and suppliers, trustworthy and productive employees, and a solid reputation.

Because of the widespread public interest in business ethics, many banks, insurance companies, and other businesses have recently revised or written new codes of ethics. Others are currently in the process of developing new codes of ethics. Companies generally use these codes as public statements of their commitment to ethical business practices and also as guides for employees to follow.

### Ethics in Accounting

In accounting, many professional organizations such as the American Institute of Certified Public Accountants have had codes of ethics for years. Most of these codes have been reevaluated and revised in recent years. Ethics is important in accounting because accountants often are required to make decisions that have ethical implications. The activities performed by accountants have a profound impact on many individuals, businesses, and other institutions. An accountant's decisions can affect such things as the amount of money a corporation distributes to its stockholders, the price a buyer pays for a business enterprise, the compensation levels of managers and executives, the success or failure of specific products and divisions, and the amount of local, state, and federal taxes paid by an individual or a business.

To see how an accountant's decisions can have an ethical dimension, consider the following example. Assume that Smith and Jones agreed to be partners in a business venture that would last two years. Because the original idea for the business venture was Smith's, they agreed that Smith would receive 75% of the first year's profits and Jones would receive 25%. However, their agreement was that Smith and Jones would split the profits evenly in years after the first year. At the end of the first year, their accountant discovers that there are two alternative methods for recording a recent transaction. If method A is used, a profit of $100,000 will be recognized in year 1. If method B is used, the profit of $100,000 will not be recognized until year 2. Clearly, the accountant's decision about which method should be used will affect each partner's compensation. If method A is used, Smith will receive $75,000 of the profit and Jones will receive $25,000. But if method B is used, each partner will receive $50,000.

In the above example, more information is needed to help the accountant choose between methods A and B. As an ethical matter, however, the accountant's decision should not be influenced by the fact that method A is more favorable to Smith and method B is more favorable to Jones.

---

[3] Touche Ross & Co., *Ethics in American Business* (New York, 1988), pp. 1–2.

The above example is not unusual. Accountants are frequently called on to choose between alternative methods for recognizing profits. These decisions cannot be made lightly because, as the example shows, the decisions may shift wealth from one party to another.

Another aspect of accounting that illustrates the importance of ethical behavior involves the issue of confidentiality. Accountants, by the very nature of their duties, frequently work with private, confidential information. For example, accountants have access to individual salary records, future business plans and budgets, and a variety of information about the financial status of their clients or employers. As an ethical matter, accountants must respect and maintain the confidentiality of this type of information.

### The Ethical Challenge

As you proceed in your study of accounting, you will encounter many other situations in which ethical considerations are important. We encourage you to seek out and explore any ethical issues that may arise. Accounting must be done ethically if it is to be an effective tool in the service of society. This is, perhaps, the most fundamental principle of accounting.

Ethical decisions and the development of ethical standards are areas in your life where you are in control. Each one of us as individuals is free to shape our own moral positions. Adapting a phrase originally spoken by Supreme Court Justice Earl Warren in reference to the law: "In civilized life, [accounting] floats on a sea of ethics." It is your choice how you elect to navigate this sea.

# 1 Accounting: An Introduction to Its Concepts

Your study begins in this chapter with the questions: What is accounting? and, Why study accounting? Many students will follow careers in accounting, and many others will work closely with accountants. As a result, this chapter discusses the accounting profession, the work accountants do, the periodic financial statements that accountants prepare, the general principles that accountants follow in preparing financial statements, and some of the organizations that govern or influence accounting practices. The chapter also describes the different ways a business might be organized and takes an introductory look at how accountants analyze the effects of business transactions.

**Learning Objectives**

*After studying Chapter 1, you should be able to:*

1. Describe the function of accounting and the nature and purpose of the information it provides.
2. List the main fields of accounting employment and the kinds of work carried on in each field.
3. Describe the information contained in the financial statements of a business and be able to prepare simple financial statements.
4. Briefly explain the accounting concepts and principles introduced in the chapter and describe the process by which generally accepted accounting principles are established.
5. Briefly explain the differences between a single proprietorship, a partnership, and a corporation, comparing the differing responsibilities of their owners for the debts of the business.
6. Recognize and be able to indicate the effects of transactions on the elements of an accounting equation.
7. Define or explain the words and phrases listed in the chapter Glossary.

## What Is Accounting?

Describe the function of accounting and the nature and purpose of the information it provides. (L. O. 1)

"Accounting is a service activity. Its function is to provide quantitative information about economic entities. The information is primarily financial in nature and is intended to be useful in making economic decisions."[1] Accounting reports are used in describing the activities and financial status of many different kinds of economic entities. They include hospitals, schools, cities, governmental agencies, and profit-oriented businesses.

In making decisions about an economic entity, individuals generally must begin by asking questions about the entity. The answers to many such questions are found in accounting reports. If, for example, the entity is a business, the managers of the business would look to accounting for answers to questions such as:

What are the resources of the business?
What debts does it owe?
Does it have earnings?
Are expenses too large in relation to sales?
Is too little or too much merchandise being kept?
Are amounts owed by customers being collected rapidly?
Will the business be able to pay its debts as they mature?
Should the plant be expanded?
Should a new product be introduced?
Should selling prices be increased?

In addition, grantors of credit such as banks, wholesale houses, and manufacturers use accounting information in answering such questions as:

Are the customer's earning prospects good?
What is its debt-paying ability?
Has it paid its debts promptly in the past?
Should it be granted additional credit?

Likewise, governmental units use accounting information in regulating businesses and collecting taxes. Labor unions use it in negotiating working conditions and wage agreements. And last but certainly not least among the users of accounting information are individual investors, who make wide use of accounting data in their investment decisions.

### Accounting and Bookkeeping

Many people confuse **accounting** and **bookkeeping** and look on them as one and the same. In effect, they identify the whole with one of its parts. Actually, bookkeeping is only part of accounting, the record-making part. To keep books is to record transactions, and a bookkeeper is one who records transactions either on a computer or manually or with a bookkeeping machine. Accounting includes much more than this. The accountant should have the ability

[1] Accounting Principles Board, "Basic Concepts and Accounting Principles Underlying Financial Statements of Business Enterprises," *APB Statement No. 4* (New York: AICPA, October 1970), par. 9.

to design the accounting system; to analyze and record complex, nonroutine transactions; and to analyze and interpret accounting information.

### Accounting and Computers

Computers are used for many tasks in our modern society, including the processing of accounting data. A computer can accept and store accounting data, sort and rearrange it, perform arithmetic calculations on it, and prepare reports from the data. Furthermore, a computer can perform these functions very rapidly and with little or no human intervention. However, before a computer can do this, a set of detailed instructions must be prepared and entered into the computer to tell it how to process the data. The person who prepares these instructions must have a thorough understanding of accounting procedures and accounting principles. Thus, while computers have had a tremendous impact on accounting, they are not substitutes for understanding the fundamental concepts and principles of accounting.

## Why Study Accounting?

Considering the wide range of questions that are answered by referring to accounting information, perhaps every educated person in our society should be regarded as a user of accounting information. If you are to use accounting information effectively, you must have some understanding of how the data are gathered and the figures are put together. You must appreciate the limitations of the data and the extent to which portions are based on estimates rather than on precise measurements. And, you must understand accounting terms and concepts. Needless to say, this knowledge is gained in a study of accounting.

Another reason to study accounting is to make it one's lifework. A career in accounting can be very interesting and highly rewarding.

## Accountancy as a Profession

Over the past half century, accountancy as a profession has attained a stature comparable with that of law or medicine. All states license *certified public accountants,* or **CPAs,** just as they license doctors and lawyers. The licensing helps ensure a high standard of professional service. Only individuals who have passed a rigorous examination of their accounting and related knowledge, met other education and experience requirements, and received a license may designate themselves as certified public accountants.

The requirements to be licensed as a CPA are not the same in all states. In general, however, an applicant must be a citizen, 21 years of age, of unquestioned moral character, and a college graduate with a major concentration in accounting. Also, the applicant must pass a rigorous examination in accounting theory, accounting practice, auditing, and business law. The 2½-day examination is uniform in all states and is given on the same days in all states. It is prepared by the American Institute of Certified Public Accountants **(AICPA),** which is the national professional organization of CPAs. In addition to the examination, many states require an applicant to have one or more years of work experience in the office of a CPA or the equivalent before the certificate is granted. However, some states do not require the work experience, and some states permit the applicant to substitute one or more years of experience for the college-level education requirement.

In 1969, the Council of the AICPA took the position that at least five years of college study are necessary to obtain the body of knowledge needed to be a CPA. This position has been reaffirmed in recent years by the AICPA's Council and also by the National Association of State Boards of Accountancy **(NASBA)**.[2] A few states have enacted laws that now require or soon will require five years of college education. More will do so in the future. Many accountants expect this requirement to be in effect throughout the United States by the year 2000. In the meantime, you can learn the requirements of your state (or any other state) by writing to the state board of accountancy.

## The Work of an Accountant

Accountants are employed in three broad fields: (1) in public accounting, (2) in private accounting, or (3) in government.

List the main fields of accounting employment and the kinds of work carried on in each field. (L. O. 2)

### Public Accounting

**Auditing.** The principal service offered by certified public accountants is auditing. Banks commonly require an **audit** of the financial statements of companies that apply for a sizable loan. Such audits are performed by CPAs who are not employees of the audited concern but are independent professional persons working for a fee. Also, companies whose securities are offered for sale to the public generally must be audited before their securities may be sold. Thereafter, additional audits must be made periodically if the securities are to continue being traded.

The purpose of an audit is to lend credibility to a company's financial statements. In making the audit, the auditors carefully examine the company's statements and the accounting records from which they were prepared. In the examination, the *auditors seek to determine whether the statements fairly reflect the company's financial position and operating results, in accordance with generally accepted accounting principles*. Based on their examination, the auditors prepare a report that expresses their opinion about the financial statements. The auditors' report is published together with the audited financial statements.

Banks, investors, and other users of financial statements rely on independent auditors to determine that a company's financial statements are fairly presented. The audit gives these financial statement users the confidence to use financial statement information in making loans, in granting credit, and in buying and selling securities.

**Management Advisory Services.** In addition to auditing, public accountants commonly offer **management advisory services**. An accountant gains from an audit an intimate knowledge of the audited company's accounting and operating procedures. Thus, the accountant is in an excellent position to offer constructive suggestions for improving the company's methods of operation. Clients expect these suggestions as a useful audit by-product. They also commonly engage CPAs to conduct additional investigations for the purpose of determining ways in which their operations may be improved.

[2] The Commission on Professional Accounting Education, *A Postbaccalaureate Education Requirement for the CPA Profession*, July 1983, pp. 8, 10.

## AS A MATTER OF FACT

Plaintiffs' lawyers are increasingly turning their attention to finding creative new ways to sue accountants. As a result, accountants are facing the double whammy of higher legal fees and rising insurance rates.

"There are new players in the liability game and they're getting better at finding reasons to sue accountants," says Dan Goldwasser, an attorney who consults on liability matters for the New York Society of Certified Public Accountants.

Some courts are siding with the plaintiffs, making accountants more vulnerable to suits from parties other than their clients. Arthur Young & Co. is currently appealing a 1987 case in which a California state court ruled that the accounting firm was liable for $4.2 million in damages to investors who had relied on unaudited quarterly financial statements of a computer company, which collapsed.

"A jury ruled that, had our firm issued a letter on the material weaknesses of the company's internal controls, management wouldn't have issued the interim financial statements," says Carl Liggio, general counsel of Arthur Young. "The jury decision, in effect, extended our liability to third parties that may not have even seen the (annual) financial statements," which the firm did audit.

Attorneys also say that more courts around the country are holding accounting firms liable for non-audit work they do for client companies. Over the past few years, CPA firms have been performing compilations and reviews of financial data. In a compilation and review, accountants don't provide assurance to users of financial statements that the figures "fairly represent the company's financial condition," according to accountants' professional rules.

But even though such work doesn't entail an audit, says Mr. Liggio, "some courts are ruling that the figures should be accurate."

Source: Lee Berton, "Suits Against CPAs Are More Creative—And More Common," *The Wall Street Journal*, February 8, 1989, p. B8. Reprinted by permission of *The Wall Street Journal*, © Dow Jones & Company, Inc. 1989. ALL RIGHTS RESERVED.

Such investigations and the suggestions growing from them are known as management advisory services.

Management advisory services include the design, installation, and improvement of a client's general accounting system and any related information systems it may have for managing the company. This may involve selecting appropriate computers, developing software, and installing the procedures necessary to bring an information system into effective operating use. Management advisory services may also include financial planning, budgeting, forecasting, and inventory control.

**Tax Services.** In this day of highly complex tax laws and high tax rates, few important business decisions are made without consideration being given to their tax effect. A CPA, through training and experience, is well qualified to render important service in this area. **Tax services** include not only the preparation and filing of tax returns but also advice as to how transactions may be completed so as to incur the smallest tax.

### Private Accounting

Accountants employed by a single enterprise are said to be in private accounting. A small business may employ only one accountant or it may depend on the services of a public accountant and employ none. A large business, on the other hand, may have more than 100 employees in its accounting department.

They commonly work under the supervision of a chief accounting officer called the **controller.** The title *controller* stems from the fact that one of the chief uses of accounting data is to control the operations of a business.

The one accountant of the small business and the accounting department of a large business do a variety of work, including general accounting, cost accounting, budgeting, and internal auditing.

**General Accounting.** The task of recording transactions, processing the recorded data, and preparing financial reports for the use of management, owners, creditors, and governmental agencies is called **general accounting.** Private accountant employees may design a company's accounting information system, perhaps with the help of the company's CPAs. The private accountant employees also supervise the clerical or data processing staff in recording transactions, maintaining financial records, and preparing the company's financial reports.

**Cost Accounting.** The phase of accounting that has to do with determining and controlling costs and assessing the performance of managers who are responsible for costs is called **cost accounting.** This may involve accounting for the costs of producing a given product or service, or the costs of performing some other specific function. A knowledge of costs and controlling costs is vital to good management. Therefore, a large company may have a number of accountants engaged in this activity.

**Budgeting.** The process of developing formal plans for future business activities is called **budgeting.** The objective of budgeting is to provide management with a clear understanding of all the activities that must be undertaken and completed in order to accomplish their objectives for the company. Then, after the budget plan has been put into effect, it provides a basis for evaluating actual accomplishments. Many large companies have a number of people who devote all their time to this phase of accounting.

**Internal Auditing.** In addition to an annual audit by an independent firm of CPAs, many companies maintain a staff of internal auditors. These employees move from one department of the company to another, checking the records and operating procedures of each department. It is the responsibility of **internal auditing** to make sure that established accounting procedures and management directives are being followed throughout the company. Also, internal auditors are often asked to evaluate the operating efficiency of each department.

**Certificate in Management Accounting (CMA) and Certified Internal Auditors (CIA).** Individuals who work as private accountants are not required as a matter of law to be licensed as CPAs. However, you may seek to obtain a Certificate in Management Accounting **(CMA)** and/or to become a Certified Internal Auditor **(CIA)** as evidence of professional-level competence in these areas of work. The CMA and CIA certifications have examination, education, and experience requirements that generally parallel those for the CPA.

### Governmental Accounting

Furnishing governmental services is a vast and complicated operation in which accounting is just as indispensable as in business. Elected and appointed officials must rely on data accumulated by means of accounting if they are to complete their administrative duties effectively. Accountants are responsible for the accumulation of this data. Accountants also review and audit the millions of income, payroll, and sales tax returns that accompany the tax payments on which governmental units depend. Criminal investigation agencies such as the Federal Bureau of Investigation employ accountants to assist in the process of detecting crimes such as fraud. And finally, federal and state agencies, such as the Interstate Commerce Commission, the Securities and Exchange Commission, and state tax collection departments, use accountants in many capacities in their regulation of business.

## Financial Statements

Financial statements are used to communicate accounting information. They are a primary product of the accounting process. As such, they are a good place to begin the study of accounting. Financial statements are used to convey a concise picture of the results of operations and the financial position of a business. We begin by considering two widely used financial statements: the income statement and the balance sheet.

### The Income Statement

Describe the information contained in the financial statements of a business and be able to prepare simple financial statements. (L. O. 3)

Many people would argue that a company's **income statement** (see Illustration 1–1) is the most important financial statement. The income statement shows whether or not the business achieved or failed to achieve one of its primary objectives—earning a profit, or net income. A **net income** is earned when revenues exceed expenses, but a **net loss** is incurred if the expenses exceed the revenues. An income statement is prepared by listing the revenues earned by the business, then listing the expenses incurred in earning the revenues, and finally subtracting the expenses from the revenues to determine if a net income or a net loss was incurred.

**Revenues** are inflows of assets received in exchange for goods or services provided to customers as part of the major or central operations of the business. As an alternative to the inflow of assets, revenues also may take the form of decreases in liabilities.[3] As shown in Illustration 1–1, the business of Jerry Dow, Attorney, had $3,900 of revenues resulting from legal services provided to clients (customers). Other examples of revenues would be product sales, rent earned, dividends earned, and interest earned.

**Expenses** are outflows or the using up of assets as a result of the major or central operations of a business. As an alternative to the outflow of assets, expenses also may result in the incurrence of liabilities.[4] The business, Jerry Dow, Attorney, used up services in the form of office space provided to the business by a landlord. This was reported as office rent expense of $1,000. The

---

[3] FASB, *Statement of Financial Accounting Concepts No. 6,* "Elements of Financial Statements" (Norwalk, Conn., 1985), par. 78.

[4] Ibid., par. 80.

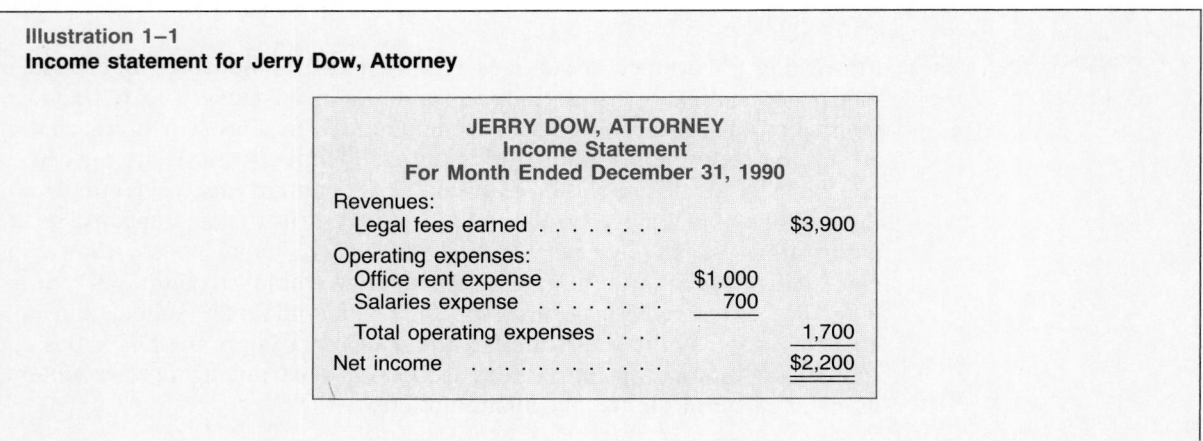

**Illustration 1–1**
**Income statement for Jerry Dow, Attorney**

| JERRY DOW, ATTORNEY<br>Income Statement<br>For Month Ended December 31, 1990 | | |
|---|---|---|
| Revenues: | | |
| Legal fees earned . . . . . . . . | | $3,900 |
| Operating expenses: | | |
| Office rent expense . . . . . . . | $1,000 | |
| Salaries expense . . . . . . . . | 700 | |
| Total operating expenses . . . . | | 1,700 |
| Net income . . . . . . . . . . . . | | $2,200 |

business also used the services of an employee, which was reported as salaries expense of $700.

The heading of an income statement tells the name of the business for which it is prepared and the time period covered by the statement. Both bits of information are important. The time period covered by the statement is extremely important, since the items on the statement must be interpreted in relation to the period of time. For example, the item "Legal fees earned, $3,900" on the income statement of Illustration 1–1 has little significance until it is known that the amount represents one month's legal fees and not the legal fees of a week or a year.

### The Balance Sheet

The purpose of a **balance sheet** is to show the financial position of a business on a specific date. As a matter of fact, the statement is often called a **statement of financial position.** This statement reports the financial position of a business by showing the business's **assets, liabilities,** and **equity.** To begin with, you may think of an asset as a property or property right. Liabilities are debts, and equity is the residual claim of the business's owner or owners. The name of the business and the date are given in the balance sheet heading. It is understood that the amounts shown are as of the close of business on that date.

A balance sheet for Jerry Dow, Attorney, appears in Illustration 1–2. Note that it is dated December 31, 1990. This balance sheet shows that as of the close of business on December 31, the business of Jerry Dow, Attorney, had three different types of assets: cash, law library, and office equipment. The total dollar amount of these assets was $10,860. The statement also shows that the business had one liability, amounting to $760, and the owner's equity in the business amounted to $10,100.

Observe that the two sides of the financial statement are equal. This is where it gets the name *balance sheet*. Its two sides must always be equal because one side shows the resources of the business and the other shows who supplied the resources. For example, the business of Jerry Dow, Attorney, had $10,860 of resources (assets) of which $760 were supplied by its creditors

**Illustration 1–2**
**Balance sheet for Jerry Dow, Attorney**

**JERRY DOW, ATTORNEY**
**Balance Sheet**
**December 31, 1990**

| **Assets** | | **Liabilities** | |
|---|---|---|---|
| Cash | $ 1,100 | Accounts payable | $ 760 |
| Law library | 2,880 | **Owner's Equity** | |
| Office equipment | 6,880 | | |
| | | Jerry Dow, capital | 10,100 |
| Total assets | $10,860 | Total liabilities and owner's equity | $10,860 |

and $10,100 were supplied by its owner. **Creditors** are the individuals or organizations to whom debts are owed. The individuals or organizations who are obligated to pay are called **debtors.**

## Assets, Liabilities, and Owner's Equity

The *assets* of a business are, in general, the properties or economic resources owned by the business. More precisely, assets are "probable future economic benefits obtained or controlled by a particular entity as a result of past transactions or events."[5] Assets include such things as cash, amounts owed to the business by its customers for goods and services sold to them on credit (called **accounts receivable**), merchandise held for sale by the business, supplies, equipment, buildings, and land. Assets may also include such intangible rights as those granted by a patent or copyright.

The *liabilities* of a business are its debts. They are defined more precisely by the FASB as "probable future sacrifices of economic benefits arising from present obligations of a particular entity to transfer assets or provide services to other entities in the future as a result of past transactions or events."[6] Liabilities include obligations such as amounts owed to creditors for goods and services bought on credit (called **accounts payable**), salaries and wages owed employees, taxes payable, notes payable, and interest payable.

The *equity*, or **net assets,** of a business is "the residual interest in the assets of an entity that remains after deducting its liabilities."[7] When a business is owned by one person, the owner's interest or equity is shown on a balance sheet by listing the person's name, followed by the word *capital*, and then the amount of the equity. The use of the word *capital* comes from the idea that the owner has furnished the business with resources or "capital" equal to the amount of the equity.

A liability represents a claim, or right, to be paid. The law recognizes this

[5] FASB, *Statement of Financial Accounting Concepts No. 6*, "Elements of Financial Statements" (Norwalk, Conn., 1985), par. 25. Copyright © by the Financial Accounting Standards Board, Norwalk, Conn. Quoted (or excerpted) with permission. Copies of the complete document are available from the FASB.

[6] Ibid., par. 35.

[7] Ibid., par. 50.

right. If a business fails to pay its creditors, the law gives the creditors the right to force the sale of the assets of the business to secure money to meet creditor claims. Furthermore, if the assets are sold, the creditors are paid first, with any remainder going to the business owner.

Since creditor claims take precedence over those of an owner, an owner's equity in a business is always a residual amount. Creditors recognize this. When they examine the balance sheet of a business, they are always interested in the share of its assets furnished by creditors and the share furnished by its owner or owners. The creditors recognize that if the business must be liquidated and its assets sold, the shrinkage in converting assets into cash must exceed the equity of the owner or owners before the creditors will lose.

## Generally Accepted Accounting Principles (GAAP)

Briefly explain the accounting concepts and principles introduced in the chapter and describe the process by which generally accepted accounting principles are established.
(L. O. 4)

An understanding of financial statement information requires a knowledge of the generally accepted accounting principles that govern the accumulation and presentation of the data appearing on such statements. A common definition of the word *principle* is: "A broad general law or rule adopted or professed as a guide to action; a settled ground or basis of conduct or practice. . . ." Consequently, **generally accepted accounting principles (GAAP)** may be described as broad rules adopted by the accounting profession as guides in measuring, recording, and reporting the financial affairs and activities of a business. They consist of a number of concepts, principles, and procedures that are first discussed at the points shown in the following list. They also are referred to again and again throughout this text in order to increase your understanding of the information conveyed by accounting data.

| | First Introduced | |
|---|---|---|
| | **Chapter** | **Page** |
| **Generally accepted concepts:** | | |
| 1. Business entity concept | 1 | 20 |
| 2. Continuing-concern concept | 1 | 21 |
| 3. Stable-dollar concept | 1 | 21 |
| 4. Time-period concept | 3 | 101 |
| **Generally accepted principles:** | | |
| 1. Cost principle | 1 | 20 |
| 2. Objectivity principle | 1 | 21 |
| 3. Realization principle | 1 | 26 |
| 4. Matching principle | 3 | 112 |
| 5. Materiality principle | 8 | 362 |
| 6. Full-disclosure principle | 8 | 369 |
| 7. Consistency principle | 9 | 400 |
| 8. Conservatism principle | 9 | 403 |
| **Generally accepted procedures:** | | |
| These specify the ways data are processed and reported and are described and discussed throughout the text. | | |

### How Accounting Principles Are Established

Generally accepted accounting principles are not natural laws in the sense of the laws of physics and chemistry. They are man-made rules that depend for their authority on their general acceptance by the accounting profession. They have evolved from the experience and thinking of members of the accounting

Illustration 1–3

**The process of establishing generally accepted accounting principles and its relationship to financial reporting**

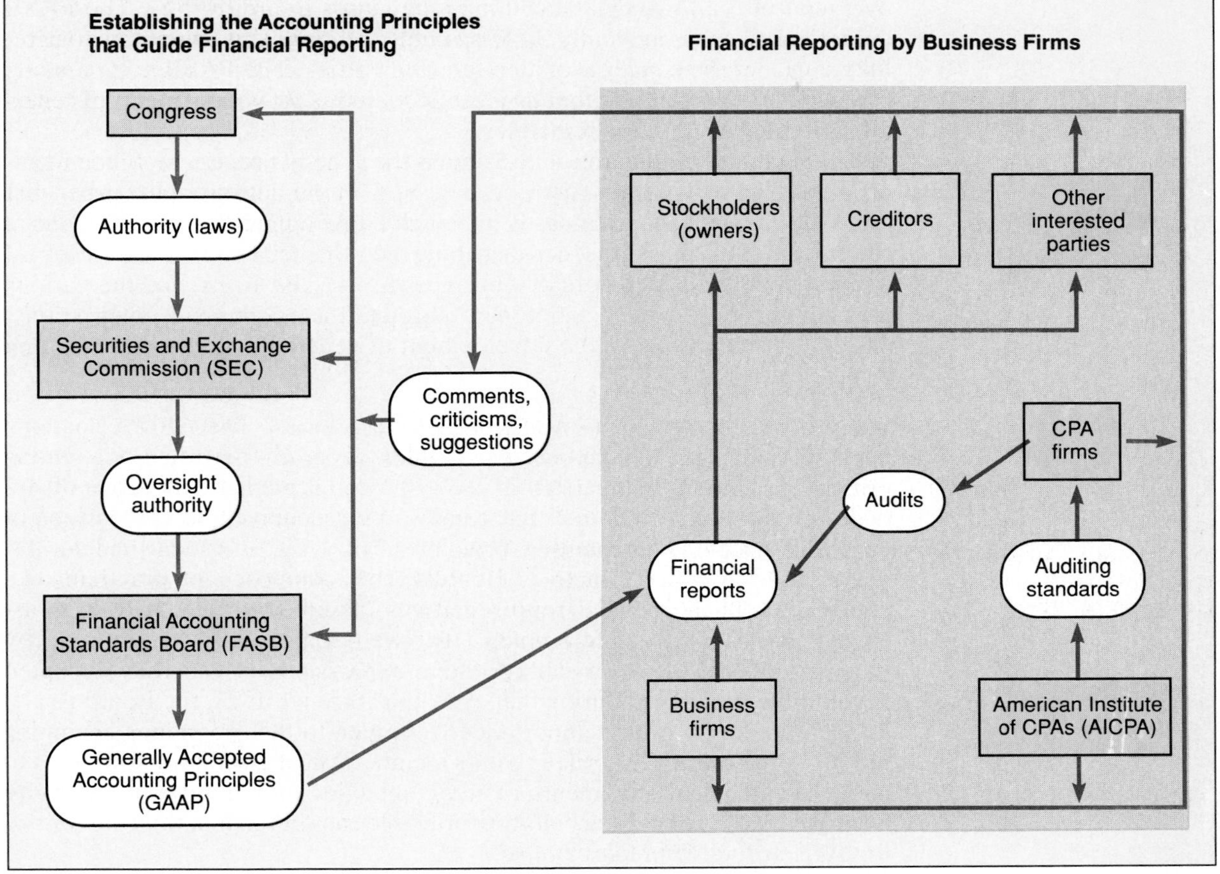


profession, business firms, academic accountants, government agencies, and other interested parties.

The process of establishing generally accepted accounting principles in the United States is closely related to the process of financial reporting to outside parties. (Financial reporting is understood to include financial statements and also other means of communicating information about an enterprise's resources, obligations, earnings, etc.[8]) The two processes of establishing accounting principles and financial reporting are diagrammed in Illustration 1–3.

The left half of Illustration 1–3 shows the general process by which general principles are established. Note that Congress may enact laws that dictate accounting principles. However, Congress has had its greatest impact by es-

[8] FASB, *Statement of Financial Accounting Concepts No. 1,* "Objectives of Financial Reporting by Business Enterprises" (Norwalk, Conn., 1978), par. 7. Copyright © by the Financial Accounting Standards Board, Norwalk, Conn. Quoted (or excerpted) with permission. Copies of the complete document are available from the FASB.

tablishing the Securities and Exchange Commission **(SEC)** and giving it authority over the reporting practices of publicly owned companies. The SEC generally exercises its authority to establish accounting principles through its oversight of the Financial Accounting Standards Board **(FASB)**. The FASB operates quite independently, holding public hearings and attempting to carefully consider the concerns of all interested parties. The FASB's *Statements of Financial Accounting Standards* are accepted as pronouncements of generally accepted accounting principles.

The right half of Illustration 1–3 shows the general process by which financial reporting by business firms occurs. Note in the bottom right corner that the AICPA establishes standards by which CPAs conduct audits of financial statements. Business firms then distribute their financial reports to a variety of interested parties. Also note that business firms, CPA firms, and the various users of accounting information may, through their comments, suggestions, and criticisms, influence the development of generally accepted accounting principles.

**The Role of the AICPA and the Accounting Principles Board.** The AICPA has long been influential in describing and defining generally accepted accounting principles. During the years from 1939 to 1959, it published a series of *Accounting Research Bulletins* that came to be recognized as expressions of generally accepted accounting principles. In 1959, it established an 18-member Accounting Principles Board **(APB)** composed of practicing accountants, educators, and representatives of industry. The APB was assigned the task of issuing opinions that were expected to be regarded by members of the AICPA as authoritative expressions of generally accepted accounting principles. During the years 1962 through 1973, the Board issued 31 such opinions. Added importance was given to these opinions beginning in 1964 when the AICPA ruled that its members must disclose in footnotes to published financial statements of the companies they audit any departure from generally accepted accounting principles as set forth in the *Opinions of the Accounting Principles Board.*

**The Role of the Financial Accounting Standards Board.** In 1973, after 11 years of activity, the APB was terminated. Its place was taken by a seven-member Financial Accounting Standards Board (FASB). The seven members serve full time, receive salaries, and must resign from accounting firms and other employment. They must have a knowledge of accounting, finance, and business, but are not required to be CPAs. This differs from the APB, all members of which were CPAs who served part time, without pay, and continued their affiliations with accounting firms and other employment. The FASB's *Statements of Financial Accounting Standards,* like the APB's *Opinions,* must be considered as authoritative expressions of generally accepted accounting principles. Both the *Statements* and *Opinions* are referred to again and again throughout this text.

**The Role of the Securities and Exchange Commission.** The Securities and Exchange Commission (SEC) plays a prominent role in financial reporting. The SEC is an independent quasi-judicial agency of the federal government. It was established to administer the provisions of various securities and ex-

## AS A MATTER OF FACT

The Securities and Exchange Commission, under pressure from business, is quietly investigating whether the Financial Accounting Standards Board needs an overhaul, accountants and businessmen said.

Since last May individual members of the Business Roundtable, a powerful lobbying group, have been criticizing the FASB in meetings with managing partners of major accounting firms and SEC members. Roundtable members have told the SEC that some rules of the chief rule-making body for accountants aren't effective and are too costly for companies to implement.

In Washington, the SEC's chief accountant's office confirmed that it is reviewing the FASB as part of its oversight responsibilities. The seven-member FASB, based in Norwalk, Conn., derives its power to set standards from the SEC, which under congressional direction must maintain oversight of the body. But business contributes about $3 million a year to a foundation that funds the FASB, whose annual budget is about $11 million, and so has considerable clout in accounting rule-setting.

* * * * *

The SEC review is bound to be looked at closely by Congress. Rep. Ron Wyden, a member of the House Energy and Commerce Committee's oversight and investigations panel, which has held a score of hearings on accounting issues in recent years, said he wasn't familiar with the SEC review of FASB, but added that his prime concern is that the FASB take an aggressive approach to fraud issues. "Nobody wants things that add to business cost, but we certainly want them to be activist on financial fraud," the Oregon Democrat said.

Glen Davison, the SEC's deputy chief accountant, said the SEC is "always overseeing the FASB processes and keeping an eye out for criticisms of standard-setting bodies and ways they can be improved." Mr. Davison said the chief accountant's office is "currently monitoring suggestions raised that the FASB consider changes in the rule-making process."

* * * * *

According to accountants and businessmen, Roundtable members are telling the SEC that some FASB rules use a "cookbook" approach and are so narrow and detailed as to make implementation prohibitively costly.

* * * * *

Dennis Beresford, FASB chairman, said the SEC review is an "internal type of thing that won't result in a report" to the public. As to criticism from the Roundtable, Mr. Beresford said that the FASB "feels pressure from lots of people all the time that suggest changes in the standard-setting procedure. It's a natural creative tension."

But Arthur Wyatt, who quit the rule-making body's board last year because he said he was frustrated over the growing role of business in accounting standard-setting, said that business pressure continues to be a major problem for the FASB.

Source: Lee Berton and Thomas E. Ricks, "SEC, Reportedly Pressed by Business, Studies Need for an Overhaul of FASB," *The Wall Street Journal,* August 3, 1988, p. 22. Reprinted by permission of *The Wall Street Journal,* 

change acts dealing with the distribution and sale of securities. Such securities, to be sold, must be registered with the SEC. This requires the filing of audited financial statements prepared in accordance with the rules of the SEC. Furthermore, the information contained in the statements must be kept current by filing additional audited annual reports. The SEC does not appraise the registered securities. However, it attempts to safeguard investors by requiring that all material facts affecting the worth of the securities be made public and that no important information be withheld. Its rules carry over into the annual reports of large companies and have contributed to the usefulness of these reports. In a real sense, the SEC should be viewed as the dominant authority in the process of establishing accounting principles. To a large extent, however, it has relied on the accounting profession, particularly the FASB and the AICPA, to determine and enforce accepted accounting principles.

**Other Organizations Influence Accounting Principles.** The American Accounting Association (AAA) also has had an influence on the development of generally accepted accounting principles. The AAA is an organization of persons who are interested in accounting. (It is generally identified as the professional association of academic accountants.) It has sponsored a number of research studies and has published many articles dealing with the accounting profession but must depend on the prestige of its authors and the logic of their arguments. Some of the other organizations that influence the development of accounting principles include the Financial Executives Institute (FEI), the National Association of Accountants (NAA), and the Internal Revenue Service (IRS).

## Understanding Generally Accepted Accounting Principles (GAAP)

We believe that an understanding of GAAP is best conveyed with examples illustrating the application of each concept or principle. Consequently, we introduce only three **accounting concepts** and two accounting principles at this point. Discussions of the others are delayed until later in the text when meaningful examples of their application can be developed.

### Business Entity Concept

For accounting purposes, every business is perceived and treated as if it is a separate entity that is distinct from its owner or owners and from every other business. This point of view in accounting is called the **business entity concept.** Businesses are perceived and treated as separate entities because, insofar as a specific business is concerned, the purpose of accounting is to record its transactions and periodically report its financial position and profitability. Consequently, the records and reports of a business should not include either the transactions or assets of another business or the personal assets and transactions of its owner or owners. To include either would distort the financial position and profitability of the business.

### Cost Principle

One of the most fundamental principles in accounting is called the **cost principle.** Under this principle, all goods and services purchased are recorded at cost. For example, if a business pays $50,000 for land to be used in carrying on its operations, the purchase should be recorded at $50,000. It makes no difference if the buyer and several competent outside appraisers think that the land is worth at least $60,000. If the price paid for the land is $50,000, it must be recorded at that amount.

In applying the *cost principle,* costs are measured on a cash or cash-equivalent basis. If the consideration given for an asset or service is cash, cost is measured as the entire cash outlay made to secure the asset or service. If the consideration is something other than cash, cost is measured as the cash-equivalent value of the consideration given or the cash-equivalent value of the asset received, whichever is more clearly evident.[9]

### Objectivity Principle

Why are assets and services recorded at cost rather than some other amount such as estimated market value? The answer is because of the **objectivity principle.** This principle requires that accounting records be based on verifiable events such as business transactions between independent parties. **Business transactions** involve completed exchanges of economic consideration, for example, goods, services, money, or the rights to collect money, between two or more parties. Whims and fancies—for example, management opinion that an asset is "worth more than it cost"—have no place in accounting. To be dependable, accounting information must be based on objective data. As a rule, costs are objective, since they normally are established by buyers and sellers, each striking the best possible bargain for themselves.

### Continuing-Concern Concept

When a business purchases and holds assets for use in its operations, the market values of those assets may change over time. Nevertheless, the accounting records for those assets are not adjusted to reflect market value changes. This is because of the **continuing-concern** or **going-concern concept.** Unless there is strong evidence to the contrary, a balance sheet is prepared under the assumption that the business for which it is prepared will continue in operation. As a continuing or going concern, the assets used in carrying on the operations of the business are not for sale. In fact, they cannot be sold without disrupting the business. Therefore, since the assets are held for use in the business and are not for sale, their current market values are not particularly relevant and need not be shown. Also, without a sale, their current market values usually cannot be objectively established, as is required by the *objectivity principle.*

The *continuing-concern* or *going-concern concept* applies in most situations. However, if a business is about to be sold or liquidated, the *continuing-concern concept* and the *cost principle* do not apply in the preparation of its statements. In such cases, amounts other than costs, such as estimated market values, become more useful and informative.

### The Stable-Dollar Concept

In the United States, accounting transactions are measured, recorded, and reported in terms of dollars. In the measuring, recording, and reporting process, the dollar is treated as a stable unit of measure, like a gallon, an acre, or a mile. However, the dollar, like other currencies, is not a stable unit of measure. When the general price level (the average of all prices) changes, the value of money (its purchasing power) also changes.

Nevertheless, although the instability of the dollar is understood, accountants in their reports continue to add and subtract items acquired in different

---

[9] FASB, *Accounting Standards—Current Text* (Norwalk, Conn., 1988), sec. N35.105. First published as *APB Opinion No. 29,* par. 18.

years with dollars of different sizes. In effect, they ignore changes in the size of the measuring unit. For example, assume a company purchased land some years ago for $10,000 and sold it today for $20,000. If during this period the purchasing power of the dollar declined from 100 cents to 50 cents, it can be said that the company is no better off for having purchased the land for $10,000 and sold it for $20,000 because the $20,000 will buy no more goods and services today than did the $10,000 at the time of the purchase. Yet, using the dollar to measure both transactions, the accountant reports a $10,000 gain from the purchase and sale.

The instability of the dollar as a unit of measure is recognized. However, at the present time, many people do not believe that accounting reports would be more informative if adjustments were made for changes in price levels. Consequently, instead of making such adjustments, accountants rely on the **stable-dollar concept**, which states that accounting reports should be based on the assumption that the value of the dollar does not change.

From the discussions of the *cost principle*, the *continuing-concern concept*, and the *stable-dollar concept*, it should be recognized that in most instances a balance sheet does not show the amounts at which the listed assets can be sold or replaced. Nor does it show the "worth" of the business for which it was prepared, since some of the listed assets may be salable for much more or much less than the dollar amounts at which they are shown.

## Business Organizations

Accounting is applicable to all economic entities such as business concerns, schools, churches, fraternities, and so on. However, this text is focused on accounting for business concerns organized as **single** or **sole proprietorships**, **partnerships**, and **corporations.**

### Single Proprietorships

Briefly explain the differences between a single proprietorship, a partnership, and a corporation, comparing the differing responsibilities of their owners for the debts of the business.
(L. O. 5)

If a business is owned by one person and the business is not organized under state or federal laws as a separate legal entity, the business is called a *single proprietorship*, or *sole proprietorship*. Small retail stores and service enterprises are commonly operated as single proprietorships. There are no legal requirements to be met in starting a single proprietorship business. Furthermore, single proprietorships are the most numerous of all business concerns.

In accounting for a single proprietorship, the *business entity concept* is applied and the business is treated as a separate entity that is distinct from its owner. However, insofar as the debts of the business are concerned, no such legal distinction is made. The owner of a single proprietorship business is personally responsible for its debts. As a result, if the assets of such a business are not sufficient to pay its debts, the personal assets of the proprietor may be taken to satisfy the claims of the business creditors.

### Partnerships

When a business is owned by two or more people (partners) and is not organized as a separate legal entity, it is called a *partnership*. Like a single proprietorship, there are no special legal requirements to be met in starting a partnership business. All that is required is for two or more people to enter into an agreement to operate a business as partners. The agreement becomes a contract and may be either oral or written. However, to avoid disagreements, a written contract is preferred.

For accounting purposes, a partnership business is treated as a separate entity that is distinct from its owners. However, just as with a single proprietorship, no such legal distinction is made insofar as the debts of the business are concerned. A partner is personally responsible for all the debts of the partnership, both his or her own share and the shares of any partners who are unable to pay. Furthermore, the personal assets of a partner may be taken to satisfy all the debts of a partnership if other partners cannot pay.

### Corporations

A *corporation* is formed, or *incorporated,* under the laws of a state or the federal government as a separate legal entity. Unlike a single proprietorship or partnership, a corporation is a separate entity under the law; it is separate and distinct from its owners. The owners of a corporation are called **stockholders** or **shareholders** because their ownership of the corporation's equity is divided into units that are called shares of **stock.** For example, a corporation that has issued 1,000 shares of stock has divided its equity into 1,000 units. A stockholder that owns 500 of these shares would own 50% of the corporation's equity. Such shares of stock may be sold and transferred from one shareholder to another without affecting the operation of the corporation.

Perhaps the most important characteristic of a corporation is its status as a separate legal entity. This characteristic makes a corporation responsible for its own acts and its own debts and relieves its stockholders of liability for either. It enables a corporation to buy, own, and sell property in its own name, to sue and be sued in its own name, and to enter into contracts for which it is solely responsible. In short, the separate legal entity status enables a corporation to conduct its business affairs as a legal person with all the rights, duties, and responsibilities of a person. However, unlike a person, a corporation must act through agents.

A corporation is created by securing a charter from one of the 50 states or the federal government. The requirements for obtaining a charter vary, but in general, they call for filing an application with the proper governmental official and paying certain fees and taxes. If the application complies with the law and all fees and taxes have been paid, the charter is granted and the corporation comes into existence. At that point, the corporation's organizers and perhaps others buy the corporation's stock and become stockholders. Then, the stockholders meet and elect a board of directors. The board then meets, appoints the corporation's president and other officers, and makes them responsible for managing the corporation's business affairs.

Corporations have multiplied, grown, and become the dominant form of business organization in our country. The primary reasons for this have been the lack of stockholder liability and the ease with which stock may be sold and transferred. Nevertheless, the single proprietorship is a simpler form of business. As a result, we begin the study of accounting in the early chapters of this book by focusing primarily on single proprietorships.

## The Balance Sheet Equation

As previously stated, a balance sheet is so called because its two sides must always balance. The sum of the assets shown on the balance sheet must equal the liabilities plus the equity of the owner or owners of the business. This equality may be expressed in equation form as follows:

$$\text{Assets} = \text{Liabilities} + \text{Owner's Equity}$$

When balance sheet equality is expressed in equation form, the resulting equation is called the **balance sheet equation.** It is also known as the **accounting equation,** since all double-entry accounting is based on it. Like any mathematical equation, its elements may be transposed and the equation expressed:

$$\text{Assets} - \text{Liabilities} = \text{Owner's Equity}$$

The equation in this form illustrates the residual nature of the owner's equity. An owner's claims are secondary to the creditors' claims.

## Effects of Transactions on the Accounting Equation

Recognize and be able to indicate the effects of transactions on the elements of an accounting equation.
(L. O. 6)

As mentioned earlier, a *business transaction* is a completed exchange of economic consideration such as goods or services; business transactions affect the elements of the accounting equation. However, regardless of what transactions a business completes, its accounting equation always remains in balance. In other words, the total assets of a business always equal the combined claims of its creditors and the equity of its owner or owners. This may be demonstrated with the following transactions of Jerry Dow's law practice, a single proprietorship business.

On December 1, Jerry Dow began a new law practice by investing $9,000 of his personal cash, which he deposited in a bank account opened in the name of the business, Jerry Dow, Attorney. After the investment, the one asset of the new business and the equity of Dow in the business are shown in the following equation:

$$\underbrace{\text{Assets}}_{\text{Cash, \$9,000}} = \underbrace{\text{Owner's Equity}}_{\text{Jerry Dow, capital, \$9,000}}$$

Observe that after its first transaction, the new business has one asset, cash, $9,000. It has no liabilities, and the equity of Dow in the business is $9,000.

To continue the illustration, after the investment, Dow used $2,500 of the business cash to purchase books for a law library (transaction 2). Next, he used $5,600 of the business cash to buy office equipment (transaction 3). These transactions were exchanges of cash for other assets. Their effects on the accounting equation are shown in color in Illustration 1–4. Observe that the equation remains in balance after each transaction.

Continuing the illustration, assume that Dow needed additional equipment and more library items in the law office. However, the cash balance of the business was not adequate to make these purchases. Consequently, he purchased on credit from Equip-it Company law library items that cost $380 and office equipment that cost $1,280. The effects of this purchase (transaction 4) are shown in Illustration 1–5. Note that the assets were increased by the purchase. However, Dow's equity did not change because Equip-it Company acquired a claim against the assets equal to the increase in the assets. The claim or amount owed Equip-it Company is called an *account payable*.

**Illustration 1–4**
**The effect on the balance sheet equation of asset purchases for cash**

| | Assets | | | | | = | Owner's Equity | |
|---|---|---|---|---|---|---|---|---|
| | Cash | + | Law Library | + | Office Equipment | = | Jerry Dow, Capital | Explanation of Change |
| (1) | $9,000 | | | | | | $9,000 | Investment |
| (2) | −2,500 | | +$2,500 | | | | | |
| Bal. | $6,500 | | $2,500 | | | | $9,000 | |
| (3) | −5,600 | | | | +$5,600 | | | |
| Bal. | $ 900 | + | $2,500 | + | $5,600 | = | $9,000 | |

**Illustration 1–5**
**The effect on the balance sheet equation of asset purchases on credit**

| | Assets | | | | | = | Liabilities | + | Owner's Equity | |
|---|---|---|---|---|---|---|---|---|---|---|
| | Cash | + | Law Library | + | Office Equipment | = | Accounts Payable | + | Jerry Dow, Capital | Explanation of Change |
| Bal. | $900 | | $2,500 | | $5,600 | | | | $9,000 | |
| (4) | | | + 380 | | +1,280 | | +$1,660 | | | |
| Bal. | $900 | + | $2,880 | + | $6,880 | = | $1,660 | + | $9,000 | |

**Illustration 1–6**
**The effect on the balance sheet equation of revenues received in cash and expenses paid in cash**

| | Assets | | | | | = | Liabilities | + | Owner's Equity | |
|---|---|---|---|---|---|---|---|---|---|---|
| | Cash | + | Law Library | + | Office Equipment | = | Accounts Payable | + | Jerry Dow, Capital | Explanation of Change |
| Bal. | $ 900 | | $2,880 | | $6,880 | | $1,660 | | $ 9,000 | |
| (5) | +2,200 | | | | | | | | + 2,200 | Revenue |
| Bal. | $3,100 | | $2,880 | | $6,880 | | $1,660 | | $11,200 | |
| (6) | −1,000 | | | | | | | | − 1,000 | Expense |
| Bal. | $2,100 | | $2,880 | | $6,880 | | $1,660 | | $10,200 | |
| (7) | − 700 | | | | | | | | − 700 | Expense |
| Bal. | $1,400 | + | $2,880 | + | $6,880 | = | $1,660 | + | $ 9,500 | |

A primary objective of a business is to increase the equity of its owner or owners by earning a profit or a net income. Dow's law practice will accomplish this objective by providing legal services to its clients on a fee basis. Of course, the practice will earn a net income only if legal fees earned are greater than the expenses incurred in earning the fees. Legal fees earned and expenses incurred affect the elements of an accounting equation. To illustrate their effects, assume that on December 10, Jerry Dow completed legal work for a client and immediately collected $2,200 in cash for the services rendered (transaction 5). On the same day, he paid $1,000 for the expense of renting office space during December (transaction 6). On December 12, Dow paid the $700 salary of the office secretary (transaction 7). The effects of these transactions are shown in Illustration 1–6.

Observe the effects of the legal fee. The $2,200 fee is a revenue, an inflow of assets from the sale of services. Note that the revenue not only increased assets (cash) but also caused a $2,200 increase in Dow's equity. Dow's equity increased because total assets increased without an increase in liabilities.

Next, observe the effects of paying the $1,000 office rent and the secretary's $700 salary. Both transactions were expenses of the business. Note that the effects are opposite those of a revenue. Simply stated, expenses are outflows or the using up of goods and services in the operation of a business. In the present instance, the business's use of both the office space and the secretary's time may be understood as the using up of services. When the services were paid for, both the assets and Dow's equity in the business decreased. Dow's equity decreased because cash decreased without an increase in other assets or a decrease in liabilities.

Remember that a business earns a net income when its revenues exceed its expenses; and the effect of a net income is to increase the net assets or equity of the owner or owners. (Recall that net assets are the excess of assets over liabilities.) Net assets increase because more assets flow into the business from revenues than are used up or flow out for expenses. The equity of the owner or owners increases as net assets increase. A net loss has the opposite effect.

In this first chapter, to simplify the material and emphasize the effects of revenues and expenses to owner's equity, revenues are added directly to and expenses are deducted from the owner's capital. However, this is not done in actual practice. In actual practice, revenues and expenses are first accumulated in separate categories. They are then combined; and their combined effect, the net income or loss, is added to or deducted from owner's capital. Further discussion of this is deferred to later chapters.

## Realization Principle

In transaction 5, the revenue inflow was in the form of cash. However, revenue inflows are not always in the form of cash. This is because of the **realization principle**, which governs the recognition of revenue. This principle, also called the **recognition principle**, (1) states that the inflow of assets associated with a revenue does not have to be in the form of cash. (2) It requires that the revenue be recognized (entered in the accounting records as revenue) at the time, but not before, it is earned. (Generally, revenue is considered to be earned at the time services are rendered or at the time title to goods sold is transferred.) (3) The principle also requires that the amount of revenue recognized be measured by the cash received plus the cash equivalent (fair value) of any other asset or assets received.

For most businesses, the realization principle is satisfied and revenue is recognized in the accounting records at the time goods are sold to a customer or when services have been performed and are billable.[10] This is known as the *sales basis of revenue recognition*. In many cases, cash is received from the customer at the time the sale is completed. Even if cash is not received, the sale gives the seller the legal right to collect cash in the future. Theoretically,

[10] FASB, *Accounting Standards—Current Text* (Norwalk, Conn., 1988), sec. R/5.101. First published as *APB Opinion No. 10*, par. 12.

**Illustration 1–7**
**The effect on the balance sheet equation of noncash revenues and the later receipt of cash**

| | Assets | | | | | | | = | Liabilities | + | Owner's Equity | |
|---|---|---|---|---|---|---|---|---|---|---|---|---|
| | Cash | + | Accounts Receivable | + | Law Library | + | Office Equipment | = | Accounts Payable | + | Jerry Dow, Capital | Explanation of Change |
| Bal. | $1,400 | | | | $2,880 | | $6,880 | | $1,660 | | $ 9,500 | |
| (8) | | | +$1,700 | | | | | | | | + 1,700 | Revenue |
| Bal. | $1,400 | | $1,700 | | $2,880 | | $6,880 | | $1,660 | | $11,200 | |
| (9) | +1,700 | | −1,700 | | | | | | | | | |
| Bal. | $3,100 | + | $ -0- | + | $2,880 | + | $6,880 | = | $1,660 | + | $11,200 | |

revenue is earned throughout the entire performance of a service or throughout the whole process of securing goods for sale, taking a customer's order, and delivering the goods.[11] Yet, until all steps are completed and there is a right to collect the sales price, the requirements of the *objectivity principle* are not fulfilled and revenue is not recognized.

To demonstrate the recognition of a revenue inflow in a form other than cash, assume that Jerry Dow completed legal work for a client and billed the client $1,700 for the services rendered (transaction 8). Also assume that 10 days later, the client paid in full for the services rendered (transaction 9). The effects of the two transactions are shown in Illustration 1–7.

Observe in transaction 8 that the asset flowing into the business was the right to collect $1,700 from the client, an account receivable. Next observe that the receipt of cash (10 days after the services were rendered) is nothing more than an exchange of assets, cash for the right to collect from the client. Also note that the receipt of cash did not affect Dow's equity because the revenue was recognized in accordance with the *realization principle* and Dow's equity was increased upon completion of the services rendered.

Illustration 1–8 shows all of the previously discussed transactions. It also discloses two additional transactions. The first (transaction 10) occurred on December 24, when Jerry Dow paid Equip-it Company $900. This was in partial settlement of the $1,660 owed for the library and equipment items that had been purchased on credit (transaction 4). The effects of the payment transaction are to reduce in equal amounts both assets and liabilities. As a final transaction, assume that on December 24, Jerry Dow took $1,100 out of the business checking account for his personal use. The effect of this withdrawal by the owner (transaction 11) is to reduce both the assets and the owner's equity in the business.

## Important Transaction Effects

Look at Illustration 1–8 and observe that every transaction affected at least two items in the equation. In each case, after the effects were entered in the columns the equation remained in balance. The accounting system you are beginning to study is called a *double-entry system*. It is based on the fact that every transaction affects two or more items in an accounting equation and

[11] Accounting Principles Board, "Basic Concepts and Accounting Principles Underlying Statements of Business Enterprises," *APB Statement No. 4*, par. 149.

**Illustration 1–8**

**The effect on the balance sheet equation of debt repayments and withdrawals by owner**

| | Assets | | | | | | | = | Liabilities | + | Owner's Equity | |
|---|---|---|---|---|---|---|---|---|---|---|---|---|
| | **Cash** | + | **Accounts Receivable** | + | **Law Library** | + | **Office Equipment** | = | **Accounts Payable** | + | **Jerry Dow, Capital** | **Explanation of Change** |
| (1) | $9,000 | | | | | | | | | | $ 9,000 | Investment |
| (2) | −2,500 | | | | +$2,500 | | | | | | | |
| Bal. | $6,500 | | | | $2,500 | | | | | | $ 9,000 | |
| (3) | −5,600 | | | | | | +$5,600 | | | | | |
| Bal. | $ 900 | | | | $2,500 | | $5,600 | | | | $ 9,000 | |
| (4) | | | | | + 380 | | +1,280 | | +$1,660 | | | |
| Bal. | $ 900 | | | | $2,880 | | $6,880 | | $1,660 | | $ 9,000 | |
| (5) | +2,200 | | | | | | | | | | + 2,200 | Revenue |
| Bal. | $3,100 | | | | $2,880 | | $6,880 | | $1,660 | | $11,200 | |
| (6) | −1,000 | | | | | | | | | | − 1,000 | Expense |
| Bal. | $2,100 | | | | $2,880 | | $6,880 | | $1,660 | | $10,200 | |
| (7) | − 700 | | | | | | | | | | − 700 | Expense |
| Bal. | $1,400 | | | | $2,880 | | $6,880 | | $1,660 | | $ 9,500 | |
| (8) | | | +$1,700 | | | | | | | | + 1,700 | Revenue |
| Bal. | $1,400 | | $1,700 | | $2,880 | | $6,880 | | $1,660 | | $11,200 | |
| (9) | +1,700 | | −1,700 | | | | | | | | | |
| Bal. | $3,100 | | $ -0- | | $2,880 | | $6,880 | | $1,660 | | $11,200 | |
| **(10)** | **− 900** | | | | | | | | **− 900** | | | |
| Bal. | $2,200 | | $ -0- | | $2,880 | | $6,880 | | $ 760 | | $11,200 | |
| **(11)** | **−1,100** | | | | | | | | | | **− 1,100** | **Withdrawal** |
| Bal. | $1,100 | + | $ -0- | + | $2,880 | + | $6,880 | = | $ 760 | + | $10,100 | |

**Illustration 1–9**

**Transactions that affect owner's equity**

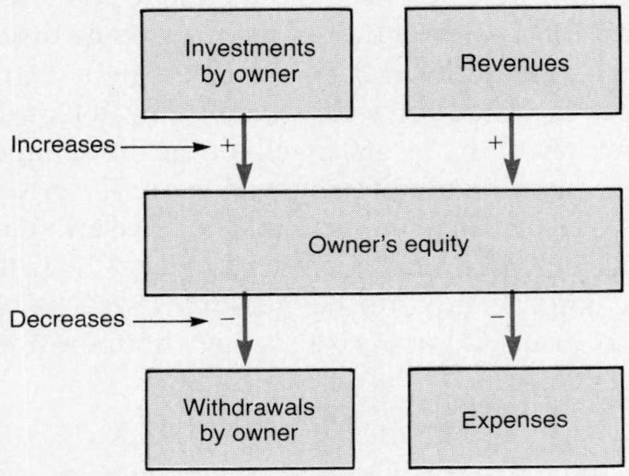


requires a "double entry" or, in other words, entries in two or more places. Also, the fact that the equation remains in balance after each transaction is important in that it helps you discover errors. If the equation does not balance, you know an error has been made.

Also note in Illustration 1–8 the types of transactions that had an effect on

**Illustration 1–10**
**Financial statements for Jerry Dow, Attorney**

**JERRY DOW, ATTORNEY**
**Income Statement**
**For Month Ended December 31, 1990**

| | | |
|---|---|---|
| Revenues: | | |
| Legal fees earned | | $ 3,900 |
| Operating expenses: | | |
| Office rent expense | $1,000 | |
| Salaries expense | 700 | |
| Total operating expenses | | 1,700 |
| Net income | | $ 2,200 |

**JERRY DOW, ATTORNEY**
**Statement of Changes in Owner's Equity**
**For Month Ended December 31, 1990**

| | | |
|---|---|---|
| Jerry Dow, capital, November 30, 1990 | | $ -0- |
| Plus: Investments by owner | $9,000 | |
| Net income | 2,200 | 11,200 |
| Total | | $11,200 |
| Less withdrawals by owner | | 1,100 |
| Jerry Dow, capital, December 31, 1990 | | $10,100 |

**JERRY DOW, ATTORNEY**
**Balance Sheet**
**December 31, 1990**

| **Assets** | | **Liabilities** | |
|---|---|---|---|
| Cash | $ 1,100 | Accounts payable | $ 760 |
| Law library | 2,880 | | |
| Office equipment | 6,880 | **Owner's Equity** | |
| | | Jerry Dow, capital | 10,100 |
| Total assets | $10,860 | Total liabilities and owner's equity | $10,860 |

the owner's equity. They include investments by the owner, revenues, expenses, and withdrawals by the owner. In Illustration 1–9, you may observe that owner's equity is increased as a result of the owner's investments in the business and also by revenues. Owner's equity is decreased as a result of withdrawals by the owner and by expenses.

When financial statements are prepared, these changes in the owner's equity are summarized as shown in Illustration 1–10. Note that the income statement reports the revenues and expenses that were presented in Illustration 1–8. The resulting net income is reported, along with owner's investments and owner's withdrawals, in the **statement of changes in owner's equity.** And the resulting balance in Jerry Dow, Capital is reported in the balance sheet. For purposes of comparison, note that the income statement and balance sheet shown in Illustration 1–10 are the same as those first shown in Illustrations 1–1 and 1–2.

**Illustration 1–11**
**A statement of cash flows for Jerry Dow, Attorney**

**JERRY DOW, ATTORNEY**
**Statement of Cash Flows**
**For Month Ended December 31, 1990**

| | | |
|---|---|---|
| Cash flows from operations: | | |
| Cash received from customers . . . . . . . | +$3,900 | |
| Cash paid for rent . . . . . . . . . . . . . . | −1,000 | |
| Cash paid to employee . . . . . . . . . . . | − 700 | |
| Net cash provided by operating activities . . | | +$2,200 |
| Cash flows from investing activities: | | |
| Purchase of office equipment. . . . . . . . . | −$5,600 | |
| Purchase of law library . . . . . . . . . . . | −2,500 | |
| Net cash used by investing activities . . . . | | −8,100 |
| Cash flows from financing activities: | | |
| Investments by owner . . . . . . . . . . . | +$9,000 | |
| Withdrawals by owner . . . . . . . . . . . | −1,100 | |
| Repayment of debt . . . . . . . . . . . . . | − 900 | |
| Net cash provided by financing activities . . | | +7,000 |
| Net increase in cash . . . . . . . . . . . . . | | $1,100 |
| Cash balance, November 30, 1990. . . . . . . | | -0- |
| Cash balance, December 31, 1990. . . . . . . | | $1,100 |

## Statement of Cash Flows

The financial statements of a business that are presented to its owners and other outside parties include four primary statements. Three of these have already been illustrated. They are the income statement, the balance sheet, and the statement of changes in owner's equity. The fourth financial statement is called the **statement of cash flows.** This statement shows the cash inflows and cash outflows of the business, summarized in three categories. They are cash flows from operations, cash flows from investing activities, and cash flows from financing activities. Observe in Illustration 1–11 the statement of cash flows for Jerry Dow, Attorney. A detailed explanation of the statement of cash flows is presented in Chapter 18.

## Summary of the Chapter in Terms of Learning Objectives

**1.** Accounting provides quantitative information about economic entities that is intended to be useful in making economic decisions. Accounting reports are used to describe the activities and financial status of many different types of economic entities.

**2.** Accountants work in public accounting, private accounting, and government. In public accounting, their work includes auditing, management advisory services, and tax services. In private accounting, their work includes general accounting, cost accounting, budgeting, and internal auditing. Accountants in government work in the same areas as private accounting plus in the areas of crime detection and business regulation.

**3.** The income statement shows revenues, expenses, and net income or net loss. The balance sheet shows assets, liabilities, and owner's equity.

The statement of changes in owner's equity shows the increase in owner's equity from investments by the owner, the decrease from owner withdrawals, and the increase or decrease from net income or net loss. The statement of cash flows shows the cash inflows and outflows from operations, from investing activities, and from financing activities.

**4.** Accounting concepts introduced in this chapter include the business entity concept, the continuing-concern concept, and the stable-dollar concept. The accounting principles introduced in the chapter include the cost principle, the objectivity principle, and the realization principle. Accounting principles in the United States are established primarily by the FASB, under the oversight authority of the SEC.

**5.** A single or sole proprietorship is a business that is owned by one individual and that is not established as a separate entity under the law. A partnership differs from a single proprietorship only in that it has more than one owner. The owner or owners of proprietorships and partnerships are personally liable for the debts of the business. A corporation is established under the law as a separate entity; hence, its owners (stockholders) are not liable for the debts of the corporation.

**6.** Business transactions always affect at least two elements in the accounting equation. After a transaction is recorded, the accounting equation must be in balance.

## Demonstration Problem

After planning for several months, Barbara Schmidt decided to start her own haircutting business called The Cutlery. During its first month of operation, The Cutlery completed the following transactions:

*a.* On August 1, 1990, Schmidt put $2,000 of her savings into a checking account in the name of The Cutlery.

*b.* On August 2, she bought $600 of supplies for the shop.

*c.* On August 3, she paid $500 rent for the month of August for a small store.

*d.* On August 5, she furnished the store, installing new fixtures that the supplier sold to her for $1,200. This amount is to be repaid in three equal payments at the end of August, September, and October.

*e.* The Cutlery opened August 12; and in the first week of business ended August 16, receipts from cash sales amounted to $825.

*f.* On August 17, Schmidt paid $125 to an assistant for working during the business's grand opening.

*g.* Receipts from cash sales during the two-week period ended August 30 amounted to $1,930.

*h.* On August 31, Schmidt paid the first installment on the fixtures.

*i.* On August 31, she withdrew $1,100 cash for her personal expenses.

*Required*

1. Arrange the following asset, liability, and owner's equity titles in an equation like the one in Illustration 1–8: Cash, Store Supplies, Store Equipment (fixtures), Accounts Payable, and Barbara Schmidt, Capital.

Show by additions and subtractions the effects of each of the above transactions on the equation.

2. Prepare an August income statement for The Cutlery.
3. Prepare a statement of changes in owner's equity for August 1990.
4. Prepare a statement of cash flows for August 1990.
5. Prepare an August 31, 1990, balance sheet for the business.

## Solution to Demonstration Problem

1.

| | Assets | | | = Liabilities + | Owner's Equity | |
|---|---|---|---|---|---|---|
| | Cash + | Store Supplies + | Store Equipment = | Accounts Payable + | Barbara Schmidt, Capital | Explanation of Change |
| *a.* | $2,000 | | | | $2,000 | Investment |
| | $2,000 | | | | $2,000 | |
| *b.* | − 600 | +$600 | | | | |
| | $1,400 | $600 | | | $2,000 | |
| *c.* | − 500 | | | | − 500 | Expense |
| | $ 900 | $600 | | | $1,500 | |
| *d.* | | | +$1,200 | +$1,200 | | |
| | $ 900 | $600 | $1,200 | $1,200 | $1,500 | |
| *e.* | + 825 | | | | + 825 | Revenue |
| | $1,725 | $600 | $1,200 | $1,200 | $2,325 | |
| *f.* | − 125 | | | | − 125 | Expense |
| | $1,600 | $600 | $1,200 | $1,200 | $2,200 | |
| *g.* | +1,930 | | | | +1,930 | Revenue |
| | $3,530 | $600 | $1,200 | $1,200 | $4,130 | |
| *h.* | − 400 | | | − 400 | | |
| | $3,130 | $600 | $1,200 | $ 800 | $4,130 | |
| *i.* | −1,100 | | | | −1,100 | Withdrawal |
| | $2,030 + | $600 + | $1,200 = | $ 800 + | $3,030 | |

2.

**THE CUTLERY**
**Income Statement**
**For Month Ended August 31, 1990**

| | | |
|---|---|---|
| Sales . . . . . . . . . . . . . . . . . . . . . . | | $2,755 |
| Expenses: | | |
| Rent. . . . . . . . . . . . . . . . . . . . . . | $(500) | |
| Wages . . . . . . . . . . . . . . . . . . . . | (125) | |
| Total expenses . . . . | | (625) |
| Net income . . . . . . . . . . . . . . . . . . . | | $2,130 |

3.

**THE CUTLERY**
**Statement of Changes in Owner's Equity**
**For Month Ended August 31, 1990**

| | | |
|---|---|---|
| Barbara Schmidt, capital, August 1, 1990 . . | | $ –0– |
| Plus: Investment by owner . . . . . . . . . . | $2,000 | |
| Net income . . . . . . . . . . . . . . | 2,130 | 4,130 |
| Total . . . . . . . . . . . . . . . . . . . . . . | | $ 4,130 |
| Less withdrawal by owner . . . . . . . . . . . | | (1,100) |
| Barbara Schmidt, capital, August 31, 1990 . . | | $ 3,030 |

4.

**THE CUTLERY**
**Statement of Cash Flows**
**For Month Ended August 31, 1990**

| | | |
|---|---|---|
| Cash flows from operations: | | |
| Cash received from customers *(e)* and *(g)* | $ 2,755 | |
| Cash paid for rent *(c)* | (500) | |
| Cash paid for wages *(f)* | (125) | |
| Net cash provided by operations | | $2,130 |
| Cash flows from investing activities: | | |
| Purchase of store supplies *(b)* | | (600) |
| Cash flows from financing activities: | | |
| Investment by owner *(a)* | $ 2,000 | |
| Withdrawal by owner *(i)* | (1,100) | |
| Repayment of debt *(h)* | (400) | |
| Net cash from financing activities | | 500 |
| Net increase in cash | | $2,030 |
| Cash balance, August 1, 1990 | | –0– |
| Cash balance, August 31, 1990 | | $2,030 |

5.

**THE CUTLERY**
**Balance Sheet**
**August 31, 1990**

| **Assets** | | **Liabilities** | |
|---|---|---|---|
| Cash | $2,030 | Accounts payable | $ 800 |
| Store supplies | 600 | **Owner's Equity** | |
| Store equipment | 1,200 | Barbara Schmidt, capital | 3,030 |
| Total assets | $3,830 | Total liabilities and owner's equity | $3,830 |

## Glossary

Define or explain the words and phrases listed in the chapter Glossary. (L. O. 7)

**AAA** the American Accounting Association, an organization of persons interested in accounting; generally identified as the professional association of academic accountants in America. p. 20

**Accounting** a service activity that provides quantitative information about economic entities; the information is primarily financial in nature and is intended to be useful in making economic decisions. p. 8

**Accounting concept** an abstract idea that serves as an important assumption underlying generally accepted accounting principles and procedures. p. 20

**Accounting equation** another name for the *balance sheet equation*. pp. 24–26

**Accounts payable** liabilities resulting from the credit purchase of goods or services. p. 15

**Accounts receivable** amounts owed to a business by its customers for goods or services sold to them on credit. p. 15

**AICPA** American Institute of Certified Public Accountants, the professional association of certified public accountants in the United States. p. 9

**APB** Accounting Principles Board, a committee of the AICPA that was responsible for formulating generally accepted accounting principles prior to the FASB. p. 18

**Assets** probable future economic benefits obtained or controlled by a particular entity as a result of past transactions or events. pp. 14–15

**Audit** a critical examination of an entity's accounting records and statements that is made for the purpose of determining whether the statements fairly reflect the entity's financial position and operating results, in accordance with generally accepted accounting principles. p. 10

**Balance sheet** a financial report showing the assets, liabilities, and equity of an enterprise on a specific date. Also called a *statement of financial position*. pp. 14–15

**Balance sheet equation** an expression in dollar amounts of the equivalency of the assets, liabilities, and equity of an enterprise, usually stated as Assets = Liabilities + Owner's Equity. pp. 24–26

**Bookkeeping** the record-making phase of accounting. p. 8

**Budgeting** the process of developing formal plans for future business activities, which then serve as bases for evaluating actual accomplishments. p. 12

**Business entity concept** the idea that a business is a separate entity that is distinct from its owner or owners and from every other business. p. 20

**Business transaction** a completed exchange of economic consideration, for example, goods, services, money, or the right to collect money, between two or more parties. p. 21

**CIA** Certified Internal Auditor, a certification of an individual's professional level of competence in the field of internal auditing. p. 12

**CMA** Certificate in Management Accounting, a certification of an individual's professional level of competence in management accounting. p. 12

**Continuing-concern concept** the assumption that a business will continue to operate and that the assets held for use in the business will not be sold. p. 21

**Controller** the chief accounting officer of a large business. p. 12

**Corporation** a business that is established under the laws of a state or the federal government as a separate entity. pp. 22–23

**Cost accounting** the phase of accounting that has to do with determining and controlling costs, and assessing the performance of managers who are responsible for costs. p. 12

**Cost principle** the accounting rule that requires assets and services plus any resulting liabilities to be recorded in the accounting records at cost, which is the cash or cash-equivalent amount of the consideration given in exchange for the purchased assets and services. pp. 20–21

**CPA** certified public accountant, an accountant who has met legal requirements as to age, education, experience, residence, and moral character and is licensed to practice public accounting. p. 9

**Creditor** an individual or organization to whom a debt is owed. pp. 14–15

**Debtor** a person or organization that is obligated to pay a liability. p. 15

**Equity** the residual interest in the assets of an entity that remains after deducting its liabilities. Also called *net assets*. pp. 14–16

**Expense** outflows or the using up of assets as a result of the major or central operations of a business; also, the incurrence of liabilities may result as an alternative to outflows of assets. pp. 13–14

**FASB** Financial Accounting Standards Board, the seven-member board that currently has the authority to issue pronouncements of generally accepted accounting principles. p. 18

**FEI** Financial Executives Institute. p. 20

**GAAP** generally accepted accounting principles. p. 16

**General accounting** that phase of accounting dealing primarily with recording transactions, processing the recorded data, and preparing financial statements. p. 12

**Generally accepted accounting principles** broad rules adopted by the accounting profession as guides in measuring, recording, and reporting the financial affairs and activities of a business. p. 16

**Going-concern concept** another name for the *continuing-concern concept*. p. 21

**Income statement** a financial statement showing revenues earned by a business, the expenses incurred in earning the revenues, and the resulting net income or net loss. p. 13

**Internal auditing** the use of a business's own accounting employees to check records and operating procedures for the purpose of making sure that established accounting procedures and management directives are being followed. Also includes evaluations of operating efficiency. p. 12

**IRS** Internal Revenue Service. p. 20

**Liabilities** probable future sacrifices of economic benefits arising from present obligations of a particular entity to transfer assets or provide services to other entities in the future as a result of past transactions or events. pp. 14–16

**Management advisory services** the phase of public accounting dealing with the design, installation, and improvement of a client's accounting system, plus advice on financial planning, budgeting, forecasting, and inventory control. pp. 10–11

**NAA** National Association of Accountants. p. 20

**NASBA** National Association of State Boards of Accountancy. p. 10

**Net assets** another name for *equity,* or the residual interest in the assets of an entity that remains after deducting its liabilities. pp. 15–16

**Net income** the excess of revenues over expenses. p. 13

**Net loss** the excess of expenses over revenues. p. 13

**Objectivity principle** the accounting rule that wherever possible the amounts used in recording transactions be based on verifiable evidence such as business transactions between independent parties. p. 21

**Partnership** a business that is owned by two or more people and that is not organized as a separate legal entity. pp. 22–23

**Realization principle** the accounting rule which states that: (1) the inflow of assets associated with a revenue does not have to be in the form of cash, (2) a revenue should be recorded as a revenue at the time, but not before, it is earned, and (3) the amount of a revenue should be measured in terms of the cash plus cash equivalent amount of other assets received. pp. 26–27

**Recognition principle** another name for the *realization principle*. pp. 26–27

**Revenue** an inflow of assets received in exchange for goods or services provided to customers as part of the major or central operations of the business; may take the form of a decrease in liabilities as well as an inflow of assets. p. 13

**SEC** Securities and Exchange Commission, an agency of the federal government that was established to administer the provisions of various securities and exchange laws. pp. 18–19

**Shareholder** another name for *stockholder*. p. 23

**Single (or sole) proprietorship** a business owned by one individual. p. 22

**Stable-dollar concept** the idea that accounting reports should be based on the assumption that the purchasing power of the unit of measure used in accounting, the dollar, does not change. pp. 21–22

**Statement of cash flows** a financial statement that discloses the inflows and outflows of cash during the period, classified in terms of cash flows from operations, cash flows from investing activities, and cash flows from financing activities. p. 30

**Statement of changes in owner's equity** a financial statement that discloses all changes in owner's equity during the period, including investments by the owner, withdrawals by the owner, and net income or net loss. p. 29

**Statement of financial position** another name for the *balance sheet*. pp. 14–15

**Stock** equity of a corporation that is divided into units or shares. p. 23

**Stockholders** the owners of a corporation; also called *shareholders*. p. 23

**Tax services** the phase of public accounting dealing with the preparation of tax returns and with advice as to how transactions may be completed in a way as to incur the smallest tax liability. p. 11

## Objective Review

Answers to the following questions are listed in Appendix I at the end of the book. Be sure that you decide which is the one best answer to each question *before* you check the answers in the appendix.

1. The primary function of accounting is:
   *a.* To measure the resources owned by economic entities and the financial obligations of the entities.
   *b.* To provide the information that the managers of an entity need to control its operations.
   *c.* To provide quantitative, primarily financial information about economic entities that is useful in making economic decisions.
   *d.* To measure the periodic net income of economic entities.
   *e.* To provide information that the creditors of an entity can use in deciding whether to make additional loans to the entity.
2. Accountants who are employed in public accounting generally work in one or more of the following fields:
   *a.* Internal auditing, tax services, and management advisory services.
   *b.* General accounting, auditing, and budgeting.
   *c.* Governmental accounting, private accounting, and auditing.
   *d.* Tax services, cost accounting, and budgeting.
   *e.* Tax services, management advisory services, and auditing.
3. The financial statements usually presented to the owner of a business and to other outside parties are the:
   *a.* Income statement and balance sheet.
   *b.* Income statement, statement of changes in owner's equity, and balance sheet.
   *c.* Revenues, expenses, assets, liabilities, and owner's equity.
   *d.* Balance sheet, statement of cash flows, income statement, and statement of changes in owner's equity.
   *e.* Income statement, balance sheet, and statement of cash flows.
4. At the present time, generally accepted accounting principles in the United States usually are established by:
   *a.* The U.S. Congress subject to the review of the SEC.
   *b.* The AICPA subject to the oversight authority of the FASB.
   *c.* The FASB subject to the oversight authority of the SEC.
   *d.* The SEC subject to the legal authority of the U.S. Congress.
   *e.* CPA firms subject to the auditing standards established by the AICPA.
5. Compared to a partnership or corporation, the nature of a single proprietorship is that:
   *a.* It is a separate legal entity.
   *b.* Its owner holds all of the shares of stock issued by the business.

*c.* It is not a separate legal entity but is owned by more than one person.
*d.* It is not a separate legal entity and its owner is personally responsible for its debts.
*e.* The debts of the business are the responsibility of the business but not of the owner.

6. A new business has the following transactions: (1) the owner invested $2,500; (2) $1,500 of supplies were purchased for cash; (3) $1,200 was received in payment for services rendered by the business; (4) a salary of $900 was paid to an employee; and (5) $2,000 was borrowed from the bank. After these transactions were completed, the total assets, total liabilities, and total owner's equity of the business are:
*a.* $4,800; $2,000; $2,800.
*b.* $6,300; $3,500; $2,800.
*c.* $4,800; $3,200; $1,600.
*d.* $4,800; $2,300; $2,500.
*e.* $4,800; $–0–; $4,800.

## Questions for Class Discussion

1. What is the nature of accounting and what is its function?
2. What are three or four examples of questions that a business manager might try to answer by looking to accounting information?
3. What is the difference between accounting and bookkeeping?
4. Why is the study of accounting necessary for a person who is responsible for using a computer to process accounting data?
5. Why do the states license certified public accountants?
6. According to the Council of the AICPA, how much education should a person have to enter the accounting profession in the future?
7. What are three broad fields of employment for accountants?
8. What are three types of services typically offered to the public by certified public accountants?
9. What is the purpose of an audit? What do certified public accountants do when they make an audit?
10. What are some examples of the management advisory services typically provided by public accountants?
11. What do the tax services of a public accountant include beyond preparing tax returns?
12. Why is the chief accounting officer of a large company called a controller?
13. What are four broad areas of work performed in private accounting?
14. Government accounting may involve some unique types of work. Give some examples.
15. What does an income statement show?
16. As the words are used in accounting, what is a revenue? An expense?
17. Why is the period of time covered by an income statement of extreme importance?

18. What does a balance sheet show?
19. Does a balance sheet relate to a period of time? Explain.
20. Define *(a)* assets, *(b)* liabilities, *(c)* equity, and *(d)* net assets.
21. Are generally accepted accounting principles natural laws or laws of nature?
22. What are generally accepted accounting principles?
23. Why are the FASB's *Statements of Financial Accounting Standards* and the APB's *Opinions* of importance to accounting students?
24. Why is a business treated as a separate entity for accounting purposes?
25. What is required by the cost principle? Why is such a principle necessary?
26. Why are the balance sheet amounts for assets held for use in a business not changed from time to time to reflect changes in market values?
27. A business shows office stationery on its balance sheet at its $350 cost, although the stationery can be sold for not more than $5 as scrap paper. What accounting principles and concept justify this treatment?
28. In accounting, transactions are measured, recorded, and reported in terms of dollars, and the dollar is assumed to be a stable unit of measure. Is the dollar a stable unit of measure?
29. How does a corporation's status as a separate legal entity affect the responsibility of its stockholders for the debts of the corporation? Does this responsibility or lack of responsibility for the debts of the business apply to the owner or owners of a single proprietorship or partnership business?
30. What is the balance sheet equation? What is its importance to accounting students?
31. Is it possible for a transaction to increase or decrease a single liability without affecting any other asset, liability, or owner's equity item?
32. In accounting, what does the realization principle require?
33. Name four financial statements that businesses present to their owners and other outside parties.

## Exercises

### Exercise 1–1

**Balance sheet for a single proprietorship**
(L. O. 3, 5, 6)

On March 31, 1990, the accounting equation for Rae's Antiques, a single proprietorship, showed the following:

| | |
|---|---|
| Cash | $ 3,000 |
| Other assets | 80,000 |
| Accounts payable | 30,000 |
| Rae Wong, capital | 53,000 |

On that date, Rae Wong sold the "Other assets" for $40,000 in preparation for ending and liquidating the business of Rae's Antiques.

*Required*

1. Prepare a balance sheet for the shop as it would appear immediately after the sale of the assets.

2. Tell how the shop's cash should be distributed in ending the business and why.

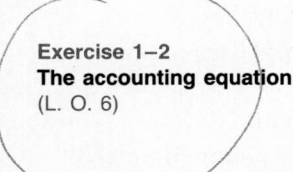

**Exercise 1–2**
**The accounting equation**
(L. O. 6)

Determine the missing amount on each of the following lines:

| | Assets | = Liabilities | + Owner's Equity |
|---|---|---|---|
| *a.* | $46,500 | $9,400 | ? |
| *b.* | 35,600 | ? | $18,600 |
| *c.* | ? | 8,700 | 25,800 |

**Exercise 1–3**
**Effects of transactions on the accounting equation**
(L. O. 6)

The effects of five transactions on the assets, liabilities, and owner's equity of Lee Fox in his dental practice are shown in the following equation with each transaction identified by a letter. Write a short sentence or phrase telling the probable nature of each transaction.

| | Assets | | | | = Liabilities + | Owner's Equity |
|---|---|---|---|---|---|---|
| | Cash + | Accounts Receivable + | Office Supplies + | Land | = Accounts Payable + | Lee Fox, Capital |
| | $11,200 | | $5,250 | $ 2,900 | | $19,350 |
| *a.* | −10,000 | | | +10,000 | | |
| | $ 1,200 | | $5,250 | $12,900 | | $19,350 |
| *b.* | | | + 450 | | +$450 | |
| | $ 1,200 | | $5,700 | $12,900 | $450 | $19,350 |
| *c.* | | +$750 | | | | + 750 |
| | $ 1,200 | $750 | $5,700 | $12,900 | $450 | $20,100 |
| *d.* | − 450 | | | | −450 | |
| | $ 750 | $750 | $5,700 | $12,900 | $-0- | $20,100 |
| *e.* | + 750 | −750 | | | | |
| | $ 1,500 + | $-0- + | $5,700 + | $12,900 = | $-0- + | $20,100 |

**Exercise 1–4**
**Use of the accounting equation**
(L. O. 6)

Determine:

*a.* The equity of the owner in a business having $145,200 of assets and owing $22,800 of liabilities.

*b.* The liabilities of a business having $109,200 of assets and in which the owner has a $77,100 equity.

*c.* The assets of a business with $9,400 of liabilities and in which the owner has a $47,500 equity.

**Exercise 1–5**
**Analyzing the accounting equation**
(L. O. 6)

On September 1, Bob Crane began operating a new real estate agency. After each of the agency's first five transactions, the accounting equation for the agency showed the following balances. Analyze the equations and describe each of the five transactions with their amounts.

| Balances after Transaction | Cash | + Accounts Receivable | + Office Supplies | + Office Furniture | = Accounts Payable | + Bob Crane, Capital |
|---|---|---|---|---|---|---|
| 1 . . . . | $15,000 | $ -0- | $ -0- | $ -0- | $-0- | $15,000 |
| 2 . . . . | 14,600 | -0- | 1,000 | -0- | 600 | 15,000 |
| 3 . . . . | 5,600 | -0- | 1,000 | 9,000 | 600 | 15,000 |
| 4 . . . . | 5,600 | 1,200 | 1,000 | 9,000 | 600 | 16,200 |
| 5 . . . . | 4,100 | 1,200 | 1,700 | 9,800 | 600 | 16,200 |

**Exercise 1–6**
**Determination of net income**
(L. O. 3, 6)

A business had the following assets and liabilities at the beginning and at the end of a year:

| | Assets | Liabilities |
|---|---|---|
| Beginning of the year . . . . | $78,000 | $24,000 |
| End of the year . . . . . . . | 90,000 | 12,000 |

Determine the net income or net loss of the business during the year under each of the following unrelated assumptions:

*a.* The owner of the business made no additional investments in the business and no withdrawals of assets from the business during the year.
*b.* The owner made no additional investments in the business during the year but had withdrawn $1,800 per month to pay personal living expenses.
*c.* During the year, the owner had made no withdrawals but had made a $30,000 additional investment in the business.
*d.* The owner had withdrawn $2,400 from the business each month to pay personal living expenses and near the year-end had invested an additional $12,000 in the business.

**Exercise 1–7**
**Effects of transactions on the accounting equation**
(L. O. 6)

Hannah Neal began the practice of dentistry on December 1, and will prepare financial statements at the end of each month. During December, Ms. Neal completed these transactions:

*a.* Invested $9,600 in cash and dental equipment having a $2,400 fair market (cash equivalent) value.
*b.* Paid the rent on the office space for December, $1,800.
*c.* Purchased additional dental equipment on credit, $6,600.
*d.* Completed dental work for a patient and immediately collected $150 cash for the week.
*e.* Completed dental work for a patient on credit, $1,700.
*f.* Purchased additional dental equipment for cash, $480.
*g.* Paid the dental assistant's wages for December, $1,200.
*h.* Collected $1,000 of the amount owed by the patient of transaction *(e)*.
*i.* Paid for the equipment purchased in transaction *(c)*.

*Required*

Arrange the following asset, liability, and equity titles in an equation form like Illustration 1–8: Cash; Accounts Receivable; Dental Equipment; Accounts Payable; and Hannah Neal, Capital. Then, show by additions and subtractions the effects of the transactions on the elements of the equation. Show new totals after each transaction.

**Exercise 1–8**
**Analysis of transaction effects on the accounting equation**
(L. O. 3)

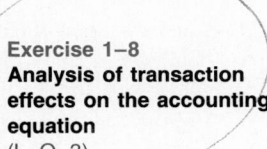

List a transaction for each of the following that will:

*a.* Increase an asset and decrease an asset.
*b.* Increase an asset and increase a liability.
*c.* Decrease an asset and decrease a liability.

*d.* Decrease a liability and increase a liability.
*e.* Increase an asset and increase equity.
*f.* Decrease an asset and decrease equity.

**Exercise 1–9**
**An income statement for a single proprietorship**
(L. O. 3)

On February 1, 1990, Deborah Norris began the practice of law under the name of Deborah Norris, Attorney. On February 28, her records showed the following assets, liabilities, owner's investments, owner's withdrawals, revenues, and expenses.

| | | | |
|---|---|---|---|
| Cash | $ 500 | Owner's withdrawals | $2,000 |
| Accounts receivable | 300 | Legal fees earned | 3,800 |
| Office supplies | 700 | Miscellaneous expense | 50 |
| Law library | 3,000 | Rent expense | 600 |
| Office equipment | 1,500 | Salaries expense | 900 |
| Accounts payable | 1,150 | Telephone expense | 400 |
| Owner's investments | 5,000 | | |

From the information above, prepare a February income statement for the business.

**Exercise 1–10**
**A statement of changes in owner's equity for a single proprietorship**
(L. O. 3)

Based on the facts provided in Exercise 1–9, prepare a February statement of changes in owner's equity for the business of Deborah Norris, Attorney.

**Exercise 1–11**
**A balance sheet for a single proprietorship**
(L. O. 3)

Based on the facts provided in Exercise 1–9, prepare a February 28 balance sheet for the business of Deborah Norris, Attorney.

**Exercise 1–12**
**Identifying the information in each financial statement**
(L. O. 3)

Karen Smith is in the business of managing apartment houses. Examine each of the following items related to the business and state with the appropriate letter (*a, b, c,* or *d*) whether the item should appear on *(a)* an income statement, *(b)* a statement of changes in owner's equity, *(c)* a balance sheet, or *(d)* a statement of cash flows. If an item should appear on two statements, state both letters.

1. Management fees earned.
2. Accounts receivable.
3. Investments of cash by owner.
4. Cash received from customers.
5. Rent expense paid in cash.

6. Cash withdrawals by owner. B
7. Office supplies. C
8. Accounts payable. C

## Problems

**Problem 1–1**
**Effects of transactions on the accounting equation**
(L. O. 6)

Carol Olds, CPA, began a public accounting practice and during a short period completed these transactions:

*a.* Sold for $43,750 a personal investment in General Motors stock and deposited $40,000 of the proceeds in a bank account opened in the name of the practice.

*b.* Purchased for $100,000 a small building to be used as an office. She paid $35,000 in cash and signed a note payable promising to pay the balance over a period of years.

*c.* Took office equipment from home for use in the practice. The equipment had a $500 fair value.

*d.* Purchased office supplies for cash, $350.

*e.* Purchased office equipment on credit, $6,000.

*f.* Completed accounting work for a client and immediately collected $530 for the work done.

*g.* Paid a local newspaper $160 for a notice of the opening of the practice.

*h.* Completed $900 of accounting work for a client on credit.

*i.* Made a $600 installment payment on the equipment purchased in transaction *(e)*.

*j.* The client of transaction *(h)* paid $600 of the amount he owed.

*k.* Paid the office secretary's wages, $550.

*l.* Carol Olds withdrew $300 from the bank account of the practice to pay personal living expenses.

*Required*

1. Arrange the following asset, liability, and owner's equity titles in an equation like Illustration 1–8: Cash; Accounts Receivable; Office Supplies; Office Equipment; Building; Accounts Payable; Notes Payable; and Carol Olds, Capital. Leave space for an Explanation column to the right of Carol Olds, Capital.
2. Show by additions and subtractions the effects of each transaction on the elements of the equation. Show new totals after each addition or subtraction. Next to each change in Carol Olds, Capital, state whether the change was caused by an investment, a revenue, an expense, or a withdrawal.

**Problem 1–2**
**Analyzing transactions and preparing financial statements**
(L. O. 3, 6)

Gary Meyer began a new law practice and completed these transactions during May 1990:

May 1 Transferred $6,000 from his personal savings account to a checking account opened in the name of the law practice, Gary Meyer, Attorney.

May 1 Rented the furnished office of a lawyer who was retiring and paid cash for May's rent, $1,000.
1 Purchased the law library of the retiring lawyer for $4,000, paying $2,000 in cash and agreeing to pay the balance in six months.
2 Purchased office supplies for cash, $200.
7 Completed legal work for a client and immediately collected $680 in cash for the work done.
10 Purchased office equipment on credit, $400.
13 Completed legal work for City National Bank on credit, $1,875.
17 Purchased office supplies on credit, $35.
20 Paid for the office equipment purchased on May 10.
23 Completed legal work for Nash Realty on credit, $1,200.
25 Received $1,875 from City National Bank for the work completed on May 13.
31 Paid the office secretary's salary, $1,300.
31 Paid the monthly utility bills, $125.
31 Gary Meyer took $1,500 out of the business for his personal use.

*Required*

1. Arrange the following asset, liability, and owner's equity titles in an equation like Illustration 1–8: Cash; Accounts Receivable; Office Supplies; Law Library; Office Equipment; Accounts Payable; and Gary Meyer, Capital. Leave space for an Explanation column to the right of Gary Meyer, Capital.
2. Show by additions and subtractions the effects of each transaction on the items of the equation. Show new totals after each transaction. Next to each change in Gary Meyer, Capital, state whether the change was caused by an investment, a revenue, an expense, or a withdrawal.
3. Analyze the increases and decreases in the last column of the equation and prepare a May income statement for the practice.
4. Prepare a May statement of changes in owner's equity.
5. Prepare a May 31 balance sheet.

**Problem 1–3**
**Preparation of balance sheet; calculation of net income**
(L. O. 3, 6)

The records of Bart James, Realtor, show the following assets and liabilities as of the end of 1989 and 1990:

| | December 31 | |
|---|---|---|
| | 1989 | 1990 |
| Cash | $2,300 | $ 500 |
| Accounts receivable | 1,200 | 600 |
| Office supplies | 300 | 150 |
| Automobile | 6,200 | 6,200 |
| For Sale signs | 400 | 400 |
| Office equipment | 2,800 | 6,250 |
| Land | | 37,500 |
| Building | | 127,500 |
| Accounts payable | 750 | 1,050 |
| Notes payable | | 112,500 |

Late in December 1990 (just before the amounts above were calculated), Mr. James purchased in the name of the business, Bart James, Realtor, a small office building and moved the business from rented quarters to the new building. The building and the land cost $165,000. The business paid $52,500 in cash, and a note payable was signed for the balance. Mr. James had to invest an additional $45,000 in the business to enable it to pay the $52,500. The business earned a satisfactory net income during 1990, which enabled Mr. James to withdraw $3,000 per month from the business to pay personal living expenses.

*Required*

1. Prepare two balance sheets for the business, as of the end of 1989 and the end of 1990. (Remember that the owner's equity equals assets less liabilities.)
2. By comparing the owner's equity amounts in the balance sheets and using the additional information presented above, prepare a calculation to show the net income earned by the business during 1990.

**Problem 1–4**
**Preparation of balance sheet and income statement**
(L. O. 3)

Hank Seta graduated from college in May 1990 with a degree in architecture. On June 1, he invested $4,500 in a new business under the name Hank Seta, Architect. Financial statements for the business will be prepared at the end of each month. The following transactions occurred during June:

June 1 Rented the furnished office and equipment of an architect who was retiring, paying $900 cash for June's rent.
1 Purchased drafting supplies for cash, $115.
3 Paid $150 for June's janitorial expense.
6 Completed architectural work for a client and immediately collected $375 cash for the work done.
9 Completed architectural work for Hills Realty on credit, $1,150.
16 Paid the draftsman's salary for the first half of June, $750.
19 Received payment in full for the work completed for Hills Realty on June 9.
21 Completed architectural work for Northern Contractors on credit, $1,200.
22 Purchased additional drafting supplies on credit, $100.
24 Completed architectural work for Ann Trent on credit, $900.
28 Purchased on credit the service of having blueprint copies made; the copies (of architectural plans) were delivered to customers. Cost was $140.
29 Received payment in full from Northern Contractors for the work completed on June 21.
30 Paid for the drafting supplies purchased on June 22.
30 Paid the June telephone bill, $135.
30 Paid the June utilities expense, $95.
30 Paid the draftsman's salary for the second half of June, $750.
30 Purchased insurance protection for the next 12 months (beginning July 1) by paying an $1,800 premium. Since none of this insurance protection had been used up on June 30, it was at that time an asset called Prepaid Insurance.
30 Mr. Seta withdrew $1,000 from the business for his personal use.

*Required*

1. Arrange the following asset, liability, and owner's equity titles in an equation like Illustration 1–8: Cash; Accounts Receivable; Prepaid Insurance; Drafting Supplies; Accounts Payable; and Hank Seta, Capital. Include an Explanation column for changes in owner's equity.
2. Show the effects of the transactions on the elements of the equation by recording increases and decreases in the appropriate columns. Indicate an increase with a + and a decrease with a − before the amount. *Do not determine new totals for the items of the equation after each transaction.*
3. After recording the last transaction, determine and insert on the next line the final total for each item of the equation and determine if the equation is in balance.
4. Analyze the items in the last column of the equation and prepare a June income statement for the practice.
5. Prepare a June statement of changes in owner's equity.
6. Prepare a June 30 balance sheet.

**Problem 1–5**
**Calculating financial statement amounts**
(L. O. 3)

Financial statement information about five unrelated companies is as follows:

| | Company 1 | Company 2 | Company 3 | Company 4 | Company 5 |
|---|---|---|---|---|---|
| December 31, 1989: | | | | | |
| Assets . . . . . . . . | $24,000 | $28,000 | $35,000 | $18,000 | $52,000 |
| Liabilities . . . . . . | 15,000 | 20,000 | 20,000 | 11,000 | ? |
| December 31, 1990: | | | | | |
| Assets . . . . . . . . | 26,000 | 37,000 | 64,000 | ? | 77,000 |
| Liabilities . . . . . . | 12,700 | ? | 27,000 | 16,000 | 30,000 |
| During 1990: | | | | | |
| Net income . . . . . | ? | 5,000 | 10,000 | 9,000 | 12,000 |
| Owner investments . | 3,500 | 6,000 | ? | 12,000 | –0– |
| Owner withdrawals . | 1,000 | 1,500 | 3,000 | 4,000 | 6,000 |

*Required*

1. Answer the following questions about Company 1:
   *a.* What was the owner's equity on December 31, 1989?
   *b.* What was the owner's equity on December 31, 1990?
   *c.* What was the net income for 1990?
2. Answer the following questions about Company 2:
   *a.* What was the owner's equity on December 31, 1989?
   *b.* What was the owner's equity on December 31, 1990?
   *c.* What was the amount of liabilities owed on December 31, 1990?
3. For Company 3, calculate the amount of owner investments during 1990.
4. For Company 4, calculate the amount of assets on December 31, 1990.
5. For Company 5, calculate the amount of liabilities owed on December 31, 1989.

## Alternate Problems

**Problem 1–1A**
**Effects of transactions on the accounting equation**
(L. O. 6)

Carol Olds secured her broker's license and opened a real estate office. During a short period, she completed these transactions:

*a.* Sold for $62,500 a personal investment in General Electric stock, which she had inherited, and deposited $60,000 of the proceeds in a bank account opened in the name of the business, Carol Olds, Realtor.
*b.* Purchased for $150,000 a small building to be used as an office. She paid $45,000 in cash and signed a note payable promising to pay the balance over a period of years.
*c.* Purchased office equipment for cash, $11,600.
*d.* Took from home for use in the business office equipment having a $700 fair value.
*e.* Purchased on credit office supplies, $100, and office equipment, $5,000.
*f.* Paid the local paper $165 for advertising.
*g.* Completed a real estate appraisal for a client on credit and billed the client $250 for the work done.
*h.* Sold a house and collected a $10,000 cash commission on completion of the sale.
*i.* Carol Olds withdrew $2,000 from the business to pay personal expenses.
*j.* The client paid for the appraisal of transaction *(g)*.
*k.* Made a $2,500 installment payment on the amount owed from transaction *(e)*.
*l.* Paid the office secretary's wages, $950.

*Required*

1. Arrange the following asset, liability, and owner's equity titles in an equation like Illustration 1–8: Cash; Accounts Receivable; Office Supplies; Office Equipment; Building; Accounts Payable; Notes Payable; and Carol Olds, Capital. Leave space for an Explanation column to the right of Carol Olds, Capital.
2. Show by additions and subtractions the effects of each transaction on the elements of the equation. Show new totals after each transaction. Next to each change in Carol Olds, Capital, state whether the change was caused by an investment, a revenue, an expense, or a withdrawal.

**Problem 1–2A**
**Analyzing transactions and preparing financial statements**
(L. O. 3, 6)



Gary Meyer graduated from law school in May 1990, and on June 1 began a law practice by investing $5,000 in cash in the practice. He also transferred to the business office equipment having a cash value of $8,500. Then, he completed these additional transactions during June:

June 1 Rented the office of a lawyer who was retiring and paid the rent for June, $800.
1 Moved from home to the law office law books acquired in college.

(In other words, invested the books in the practice.) The books had a $600 fair value.

June 2 Purchased office supplies for cash, $120.

4 Purchased additional law books costing $1,500. Paid $500 in cash and promised to pay the balance within 90 days.

5 Completed legal work for a client and immediately collected $500 for the work done.

10 Completed legal work for Village Bank on credit, $1,500.

15 Purchased additional office supplies on credit, $50.

20 Received $1,500 from Village Bank for the work completed on June 10.

25 Completed legal work for Astor Realty on credit, $1,300.

30 Made a $300 installment payment on the law books purchased on June 4.

30 Paid the June telephone bill, $70.

30 Paid the office secretary's wages, $1,200.

30 Gary Meyer took $1,400 out of the business for his personal use.

*Required*

1. Arrange the following asset, liability, and owner's equity titles in an equation like Illustration 1–8: Cash; Accounts Receivable; Office Supplies; Law Library; Office Equipment; Accounts Payable; and Gary Meyer, Capital. Leave space for an Explanation column to the right of Gary Meyer, Capital.
2. Show by additions and subtractions the effects of each transaction on the elements of the equation. Show new totals after each transaction. Next to each change in Gary Meyer, Capital, state whether the change was caused by an investment, a revenue, an expense, or a withdrawal.
3. Analyze the items in the last column of the equation and prepare a June income statement for the practice.
4. Prepare a June statement of changes in owner's equity.
5. Prepare a June 30 balance sheet.

Problem 1–3A
**Preparation of balance sheet; calculation of net income**
(L. O. 3, 6)

The accounting records of Viola Nunez's medical practice show the following assets and liabilities as of the end of 1989 and 1990:

| | December 31 | |
|---|---|---|
| | **1989** | **1990** |
| Cash | $ 9,600 | $ 1,600 |
| Accounts receivable | 5,700 | 7,000 |
| Office supplies | 1,000 | 800 |
| Automobile | 4,800 | 4,800 |
| Office equipment | 18,500 | 23,200 |
| Land | | 70,000 |
| Building | | 125,000 |
| Accounts payable | 1,400 | 1,600 |
| Notes payable | | 145,000 |

During the last week of December 1990 (just before the amounts above were calculated), Dr. Nunez purchased a small office building in the name of the medical practice, Viola Nunez, M.D., and moved her practice from rented quarters to the new building. The building and the land it occupies cost $195,000; the practice paid $50,000 in cash and signed a note payable for the balance. Dr. Nunez had to invest an additional $40,000 in the practice to enable it to pay the $50,000. The practice earned a satisfactory net income during 1989, which enabled Dr. Nunez to withdraw $3,200 per month from the practice to pay her personal living expenses.

*Required*

1. Prepare two balance sheets for the business, as of the end of 1989 and the end of 1990. (Remember that the owner's equity equals assets less liabilities.)
2. Using the information presented above and by comparing the owner's equity amount in the balance sheets, prepare a calculation to show the net income earned by the business during 1990.

**Problem 1–4A**
**Preparation of balance sheet and income statement**
(L. O. 3)

Hank Seta graduated from college, completed his internship, and on May 1 of the current year began an architectural practice by investing $6,000 in the practice. Financial statements for the business will be prepared at the end of each month. The following transactions occurred during May:

May 1 Rented the office and equipment of an architect who was retiring, paying $1,500 cash for May's rent.
1 Paid $180 for janitorial expense during May.
2 Purchased drafting supplies for cash, $50.
4 Completed an architectural assignment for a client and immediately collected $2,600 cash for the work done.
7 Purchased additional drafting supplies on credit, $160.
9 Completed architectural work for Apex Contractors on credit, $1,500.
15 Paid the draftsman's salary for May 1–15, $800.
16 Paid for the drafting supplies purchased on May 7.
19 Received payment in full from Apex Contractors for the work completed on May 9.
21 Completed architectural work for Wright Realtors on credit, $1,100.
25 Purchased additional drafting supplies on credit, $150.
30 Completed additional architectural work for Apex Contractors on credit, $1,050.
31 Paid the draftsman's salary for May 16–31, $800.
31 Paid the May telephone bill, $50.
31 Paid the May electric bill, $185.
31 Purchased liability insurance protection for the next year (beginning June 1) by paying a premium of $2,000. Since none of this insurance protection had been used up on May 31, it was at that time an asset called Prepaid Insurance.
31 Mr. Seta withdrew $1,700 from the business's checking account to pay for some personal items.

*Required*

1. Arrange the following asset, liability, and owner's equity titles in an equation like Illustration 1–8: Cash; Accounts Receivable; Prepaid Insurance; Drafting Supplies; Accounts Payable; and Hank Seta, Capital. Include an Explanation column for changes in owner's equity.
2. Show the effects of the transactions on the elements of the equation by recording increases and decreases in the appropriate columns. Indicate an increase with a + and a decrease with a − before the amount. *Do not determine new totals for the items of the equation after each transaction.*
3. After recording the last transaction, determine and enter on the next line the final total for each item and determine if the equation is in balance.
4. Analyze the items in the last column of the equation and prepare a May income statement for the practice.
5. Prepare a May statement of changes in owner's equity.
6. Prepare a May 31 balance sheet.

**Problem 1–5A**
**Calculating financial statement amounts**
(L. O. 3)

Financial statement information about five unrelated companies is as follows:

| | Company A | Company B | Company C | Company D | Company E |
|---|---|---|---|---|---|
| December 31, 1989: | | | | | |
| Assets . . . . . . . . | $62,000 | $57,000 | $29,000 | $55,000 | $72,000 |
| Liabilities . . . . . . | 46,000 | 41,000 | 14,000 | 38,000 | ? |
| December 31, 1990: | | | | | |
| Assets . . . . . . . . | 79,000 | 86,000 | ? | 70,000 | 94,000 |
| Liabilities . . . . . . | ? | 59,000 | 18,000 | 32,000 | 49,000 |
| During 1990: | | | | | |
| Net income . . . . . | 13,000 | ? | 7,500 | 15,000 | 18,000 |
| Owner investments . | 7,000 | 10,000 | 10,000 | ? | 12,000 |
| Owner withdrawals . | 2,000 | 4,000 | 2,500 | −0− | 5,000 |

*Required*

1. Answer the following questions about Company A:
   *a.* What was the owner's equity on December 31, 1989?
   *b.* What was the owner's equity on December 31, 1990?
   *c.* What was the amount of liabilities owed on December 31, 1990?
2. Answer the following questions about Company B:
   *a.* What was the owner's equity on December 31, 1989?
   *b.* What was the owner's equity on December 31, 1990?
   *c.* What was the net income for 1990?
3. For Company C, calculate the amount of assets on December 31, 1990.
4. For Company D, calculate the amount of owner investments during 1990.
5. For Company E, calculate the amount of liabilities owed on December 31, 1989.

## Provocative Problems

**Provocative Problem 1–1**
**July Fourth Weekend Fair**
(L. O. 3, 6)

Devon Bailey invested $750 in a short-term enterprise, the sale of soft drinks during the annual July Fourth Weekend Fair in his small rural town. He paid $150 for the right to sell soft drinks in the fairgrounds. He constructed a stand from which to make the sales at a cost of $50 for lumber and crepe paper, none of which had any value at the end of the fair. He bought ice for which he paid $40 and purchased soft drinks costing $750. At this point, he had only $510 in cash and could not pay in full for the drinks. However, since his credit rating was good, the soft drink company accepted $500 in cash and the promise that he would pay the balance the day after the fair ended. During the fair, he collected $1,540 in cash from sales; at the end of the fair, he paid a young man $90 for helping with the sales. He had soft drinks left over that cost $35 and could be returned to the soft drink company. At this point, Devon stopped to decide whether he should cease operations or look for similar opportunities and continue the business.

Assemble the information in such a way that will enable you to prepare an income statement for the three-day period of the fair, which ended on July 5. Also prepare a statement of changes in owner's equity for the three-day period and a balance sheet dated July 6, 1990.

**Provocative Problem 1–2**
**Megan's Delivery Service**
(L. O. 3)

Megan Brinks ran out of money at the end of the first semester of her sophomore year in college. She had to go to work, but she could not find a satisfactory job. However, since she had an automobile, she decided to go into business for herself. Consequently, she began Megan's Delivery Service with no assets other than the automobile, which had a fair market value of $2,400. She kept no accounting records; and now, at the year-end, she has engaged you to determine the net income earned by the service during its first year. You find that the service has a $700 year-end bank balance plus $50 of undeposited cash. Local stores owe the service $125 for delivering packages during the past month. In the last week of the year, Megan sold the automobile for $1,350, and used the cash proceeds to help buy a new delivery truck that cost $6,800. The service still owes a finance company $4,000 as a result of the truck's purchase. Also, when the truck was purchased, Megan borrowed $1,500 from her father to help make the down payment. The loan was made to the delivery service, was interest free, and has not been repaid. Finally, since the service has been profitable from the beginning, Megan has withdrawn $200 of its earnings each week for the 52 weeks of its existence to pay personal living expenses.

Determine and present a calculation to prove the net income earned by the business during the first year of its operations.

**Provocative Problem 1–3**
**WICAT Systems, Inc.**
(L. O. 4)

WICAT Systems manufactures, markets, and services a complete line of computer systems, software, and courseware for training, education, and general-purpose markets. Headquarters for the company are located in Orem, Utah. In the company's 1986 annual report, revenues for the year were reported as

$39,405,000. Net income was $389,000. The notes to the 1986 financial statements included the following comments:

> **Related-Party Transactions**
>
> The Company is affiliated with The WICAT Education Institute, a shareholder, and is the general partner in WISTRAN Partners and BASICS Partnership. The Company has billed The WICAT Education Institute for system sales and services amounting to $291,000, $580,000, and $136,000 for the years ended 1984, 1985, and 1986, respectively. The WICAT Education Institute has billed the Company for services and rent amounting to $75,000, $199,000, and $4,000 for the years ended 1984, 1985, and 1986, respectively.

Why do you think WICAT Systems included the above comments in its annual report? What accounting principle might be compromised by related-party transactions?

Part Two

# Processing Accounting Data

The next five chapters are perhaps more important than any others you will study in your accounting education. In these chapters, we describe the accounting process that starts with an analysis of a business's transactions and ends with the periodic preparation of financial statements. Your careful study of these chapters will pay great dividends. It will make the later parts of the book easier to understand.

Part Two consists of the following chapters:

2. Recording Transactions
3. Adjusting the Accounts and Preparing the Statements
4. The Work Sheet and Closing the Accounts of Proprietorships, Partnerships, and Corporations
5. Accounting for a Merchandising Concern
6. Accounting Systems

# ding Transactions

In Chapter 1, you were introduced to the accounting equation (Assets = Liabilities + Owner's Equity) and the effect of business transactions on the accounting equation. In this chapter, you will learn how the effects of business transactions are recorded and stored in the accounting records. We begin the chapter with a discussion of business papers that provide evidence of transactions and a description of several commonly used accounts in which the effects of the transactions are recorded. Then, we explain the process of recording the effects of transactions. The procedures that you learn in the chapter can be used to record the effects of any type of business transactions you may encounter.

### Learning Objectives

*After studying Chapter 2, you should be able to:*

1. State the names of several commonly used accounts and the nature of the items recorded in those accounts.
2. Explain the mechanics of double-entry accounting and tell why transactions are recorded with equal debits and credits.
3. Apply the rules of debit and credit in recording transactions.
4. Tell the normal balance of any asset, liability, or owner's equity account.
5. Record transactions in a General Journal, post to the ledger accounts, and prepare a trial balance to test the accuracy of the recording and posting.
6. Define or explain the words and phrases listed in the chapter Glossary.

**Illustration 2–1**
**The accounting process**

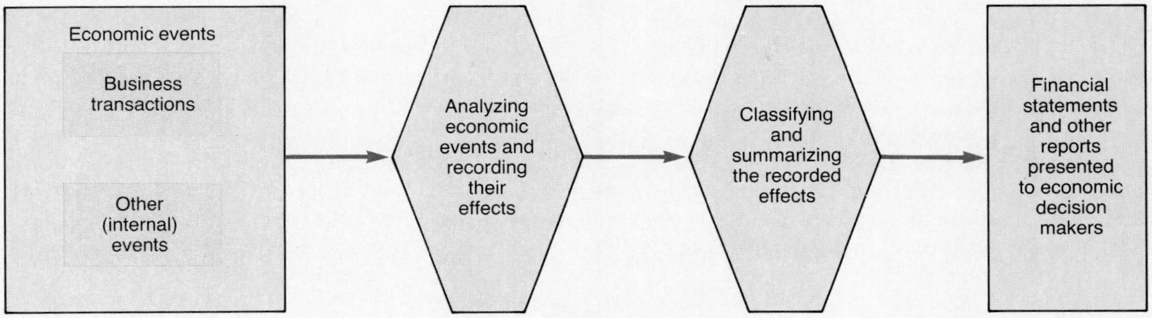


## The Accounting Process Starts by Analyzing Economic Events

In Chapter 1, we said that accounting provides quantitative (primarily financial) information about economic entities. This information is intended to be useful in economic decision making. The accounting process involves (1) analyzing the economic events of an entity and recording the effects of those events, and (2) classifying and summarizing the recorded effects in reports or financial statements that individuals find useful in making economic decisions about the entity. This process is presented graphically in Illustration 2–1.

### Business Transactions

In Illustration 2–1, note that economic events consist of business transactions and other (internal) events. Remember from Chapter 1 that business transactions are completed exchanges of economic consideration between two or more parties. Whenever an entity engages in a business transaction, the transaction will have an effect on the entity's accounting equation. The accounting process begins by analyzing such transactions to determine their effects on the accounting equation. Then, those effects are recorded in the accounting records (the books). Because business transactions are between the entity and some other (outside) party, they are sometimes called *external transactions*.

### Other (Internal) Events

Some economic events have an effect on an entity's accounting equation even though they are not transactions with outside parties. For example, a business uses a machine in its operations. As a result, the remaining usefulness of the machine is decreased. In other words, the economic benefit of the machine is partially used up. The using up of the machine's economic benefit is an economic event that decreases the assets and decreases the owner's equity in the business. Internal economic events of this sort are not transactions between two or more parties. Nevertheless, because they have an effect on the accounting equation, they are sometimes called **internal transactions**. The analysis and recording of internal economic events is the central topic of Chapter 3.

## AS A MATTER OF ETHICS

At a busy fast food restaurant in a food court in a downtown mall, a new employee (who is also an accounting student) received training from the assistant manager. Included in the training were instructions about how to operate the cash register. The assistant manager explained that the formal policy is to ring up every sale when an order is placed and the cash is received. But, because of the pressure of the noon-hour rush, it is easier to accept the cash and make change without ringing up the sales.

The assistant manager explained that it is more important to serve the customers promptly so they won't go to another counter in the food court. Then, after two o'clock, the assistant manager adds up the cash in the drawer and rings up sufficient sales to equal the amount collected. In this way, the tape in the register always comes out right and there are no problems to explain when the manager arrives at four o'clock to handle the dinner traffic.

The new employee sees the advantages in this shortcut, but is wondering whether something is wrong with it.

Many years ago, most companies used pen and ink to manually record and process the data resulting from transactions. Today, only a few, very small companies use this method. Now, large and small companies use computers in recording transactions and in processing the recorded data. A few companies use electric bookkeeping machines, which were developed as an intermediate step in the path of progress from manual to computerized systems.

Nevertheless, you will begin your study of accounting by learning to process accounting data manually. By manually processing the data, you will more readily understand the importance of each step in the accounting process. Also, the general concepts you learn through manual methods will apply equally well to computerized accounting systems.

### Business Papers

The printed documents that businesses use in the process of completing transactions are called **business papers.** They include such things as sales slips or invoices, checks, purchase orders, customer billings, employee earnings records, and bank statements. Because they provide evidence of business transactions and are the basis for accounting entries, business papers are also called **source documents.**

For example, if you buy a tennis racket on credit, two or more copies of an invoice or sales ticket are prepared. One copy is given to you. The other is sent to the store's accounting department and becomes the basis for an entry to record the sale. On the other hand, if you paid cash for the tennis racket and did not buy it on credit, the sale typically would have been "rung up" on a cash register that prints the amount of each sale on a paper tape locked inside the register. At the end of the day, when the proper key is depressed, the register prints on the tape the total cash sales for the day. The tape is then removed and becomes the basis for an entry to record the sales.

Business papers such as a sales invoice often are used by both the seller and the buyer as a basis for recording the transaction in their accounting records. For example, if you bought the tennis racket for use in your business, your copy of the invoice or sales ticket would provide the information you would need to record the transaction in the accounting records of your business.

To summarize, business papers are the starting point in the accounting process. Furthermore, verifiable business papers, particularly those originating outside the business, are also objective evidence of transactions completed and the amounts at which they should be recorded. As you learned in Chapter 1, this type of evidence is important because of the *objectivity principle*.

## Accounts

In accounting for an entity, the different effects of its business transactions must be recorded and stored in separate ''locations'' so that they can be sorted and combined when financial reports are prepared. These locations in the accounting system are called **accounts.** A number of accounts are normally required. A separate account is used for summarizing the increases and decreases in each asset, liability, and owner's equity item appearing on the balance sheet and each revenue and expense item appearing on the income statement.

In its simplest form, an account looks like the letter **T**, is called a **T-account,** and appears as follows:

**(Place for the Name of the Item Recorded in This Account)**

| (Left side) | (Right side) |
|---|---|

Note that the **T** format gives the account a left side, a right side, and a place for the name of the account. The name indicates the type of items or effects to be stored in this particular account. For example, the *Cash* account is the location where all cash increases and decreases are recorded and stored.

When a T-account is used to record increases and decreases in an item, the increases are placed on one side of the account and the decreases on the other. For example, recall the transactions of Jerry Dow's law practice that were discussed in Chapter 1. Many of those transactions affected cash. If the increases and decreases in the cash of Jerry Dow's law practice are recorded in a T-account, they appear as follows:

**Cash**

| | | | |
|---|---|---|---|
| Investment | 9,000 | Purchase of law books | 2,500 |
| Legal fee earned | 2,200 | Purchase of office equipment | 5,600 |
| Collection of account receivable | 1,700 | Rent payment | 1,000 |
| | | Payment of salary | 700 |
| | | Payment of account payable | 900 |
| | | Withdrawal by owner | 1,100 |

### Balance of an Account

The reason for putting the increases on one side and the decreases on the other is that it is easy to add the increases and then add the decreases. The sum of the decreases may then be subtracted from the sum of the increases to determine the remaining balance of the account. Regardless of the type of account, the **account balance** is the difference between its increases and decreases. Also, the balance of an asset account is the amount of that asset owned by the entity on the date the balance is calculated. The balance of a liability account is the amount owed by the entity on the date of the balance.

In the case of the Cash account for Jerry Dow's law practice, the total increases were $12,900, the total decreases were $11,800, and the account balance is $1,100, as shown below.

**Cash**

| | | | |
|---|---|---|---|
| Investment | 9,000 | Purchase of law books | 2,500 |
| Legal fee earned | 2,200 | Purchase of office equipment | 5,600 |
| Collection of account receivable | 1,700 | Rent payment | 1,000 |
| | | Payment of salary | 700 |
| | | Payment of account payable | 900 |
| | | Withdrawal by owner | 1,100 |
| Total increases | **12,900** | Total decreases | **11,800** |
| Less decreases | **−11,800** | | |
| Balance | **1,100** | | |

## Accounts Commonly Used

A business uses a number of accounts to record and store the effects of its transactions. However, the specific accounts a business uses depend on the assets owned, the debts owed, and the information the business needs to obtain from the accounting records. Nevertheless, although there are variations in the accounts different businesses use, the following accounts are common:

### Asset Accounts

State the names of several commonly used accounts and the nature of the items recorded in those accounts.
(L. O. 1)

If the accounting system is to provide useful information about the different assets of a company, you must keep a separate account for each kind of asset owned. Generally, accounts are maintained for the following common assets.

**Cash.** Increases and decreases in cash are recorded in an account called Cash. The cash of a business consists of money or any medium of exchange that a bank will accept at face value for deposit. It includes coins, currency, checks, and postal and bank money orders. The balance of the Cash account shows both the cash on hand in the store or office and that on deposit in the bank.

**Notes Receivable.** A **promissory note** is an unconditional written promise to pay a definite sum of money on demand or at a fixed or determinable future date. When amounts due from others are evidenced by promissory notes, the notes are known as notes receivable and are recorded in a Notes Receivable account.

**Accounts Receivable.** Goods and services are commonly sold to customers on the basis of oral or implied promises of future payment. Such sales are called credit sales or sales on account; and the oral or implied promises to pay are called accounts receivable. Accounts receivable are increased by credit sales and are decreased by customer payments. Since a company must know the amount currently owed by each customer, a separate record must be kept of each customer's purchases and payments. However, we will discuss this separate record in a later chapter. For the present, all increases and decreases in accounts receivable are recorded in a single account called Accounts Receivable.

**Prepaid Insurance.** Fire, liability, and other types of insurance protection are normally paid for in advance. The amount paid is called a premium, which expires as time passes. Many times, an insurance premium gives protection for a long time, perhaps as much as three years. As a result, a large portion of the premium is an asset for a considerable time after payment. When an insurance premium is paid in advance, assets are increased by the amount paid. The increase is normally recorded in an account called Prepaid Insurance. Therefore, whenever financial statements are prepared, the insurance that has expired is calculated and recorded as an expense, and the balance of the Prepaid Insurance account is reduced accordingly.

**Office Supplies.** Stamps, stationery, paper, pencils, and similar items are called office supplies. They are assets when purchased and continue to be assets until used up. As they are used up, the cost of the supplies becomes an expense. Increases and decreases in the asset are commonly recorded in an account called Office Supplies.

**Store Supplies.** Wrapping paper, cartons, bags, string, and similar items used by a store are called store supplies. Increases and decreases in store supplies are recorded in an account of that name.

**Other Prepaid Expenses.** When payments are made for economic benefits that do not expire until some later time, the payments create assets called **prepaid expenses.** Then, as the economic benefits are used up or expire, the assets become expenses. As a practical matter, if a purchased benefit will fully expire before the next income statement is prepared, the payment is generally recorded as an expense. But, when purchased benefits will not be used up or will not fully expire in the current time period, the payments are recorded as prepaid expenses (assets). Examples of prepaid expenses include prepaid insurance, office supplies, and store supplies. Rent that is paid for more than one period in advance is another example. Others include legal fees and management fees when they are paid in advance of receiving the legal or management services. Each type of prepaid expense is accounted for in a separate asset account.

**Equipment.** Increases and decreases in physical assets such as typewriters, desks, chairs, and office machines are commonly recorded in an account called Office Equipment. In a similar manner, physical assets that are used in the selling operations of a store—for example, counters, showcases, and cash registers—are recorded in an account called Store Equipment.

**Buildings.** A building used by a business in carrying on its operations may be a store, garage, warehouse, or factory. Such assets are commonly recorded and accounted for in an account called Buildings. If several buildings are owned, a separate account may be kept for each building.

**Land.** An account called Land is commonly used in recording increases and decreases in the land owned by a business. Land and the buildings placed on it are physically inseparable. Nevertheless, the land and the buildings must be recorded in separate accounts because buildings wear out or depreciate while the land on which they are placed does not.

### Liability Accounts

Recall from Chapter 1 that liabilities are present obligations to transfer assets or provide services to other entities in the future. A business may have several different types of liabilities, each of which requires a separate account. The following are common:

**Notes Payable.** When an entity makes a formal written promise to pay a definite sum of money at a fixed future date, the liability is called a note payable. Increases and decreases in such promissory notes given to creditors are accounted for in an account called Notes Payable.

**Accounts Payable.** When purchases are made on the basis of oral or implied promises to pay, the amounts owed are called accounts payable. The items purchased on credit may be merchandise, supplies, equipment, or services. Since a business must know the amount owed each creditor, an individual record must be kept of the purchases from and the payments to each. However, we will discuss this individual record in a later chapter. For the present, all increases and decreases in accounts payable are recorded in a single Accounts Payable account.

**Unearned Revenue.** As you learned in Chapter 1, the *realization principle* requires that revenue not be recognized until it is earned. Therefore, when a company collects for its products or services before delivery, the amounts collected are received in advance of being earned and are called **unearned revenues.** An unearned revenue is a liability that will be satisfied by delivering the product or service paid for in advance. Examples are subscriptions collected in advance by a magazine publisher, rent collected in advance by a landlord, and legal fees collected in advance by a lawyer. On receipt, the amounts collected are recorded in liability accounts such as Unearned Subscriptions, Unearned Rent, and Unearned Legal Fees. When earned by delivery, the amounts earned are transferred to the revenue accounts: Subscriptions Earned, Rent Earned, and Legal Fees Earned.

**Other Short-Term Payables.** Wages payable, taxes payable, and interest payable are other short-term liabilities, each of which requires a separate account.

### Owner's Equity Accounts

In Chapter 1, we illustrated four different types of transactions that affected the owner's equity in a proprietorship. They are: (1) investments by the owner, (2) withdrawals of cash or other assets by the owner, (3) revenues, and (4) expenses. Recall that in the previous chapter, all such transactions were entered in a column under the name of the owner. This procedure was used to show the effect of transactions on the accounting equation. However, the procedure made it necessary to analyze the items entered in the column in order to prepare an income statement and a statement of changes in owner's equity. Fortunately, such an analysis is not necessary. All that you need is a number of accounts, a separate one for each owner's equity item that appears on the balance sheet and a separate one for each revenue and expense item on the income statement. Then, as each transaction affecting owner's equity is completed, it is recorded in the proper account. The required accounts are as follows:

**Capital Account.** When a person invests in his or her own business, the investment is recorded in an account carrying the owner's name and the word *Capital*. For example, an account called Jerry Dow, Capital is used to record the investment of Jerry Dow in his law practice. In addition to the original investment, the **capital account** is used for any permanent additional increases or decreases in owner's equity.

**Withdrawals Account.** Usually a person invests in a business to earn income. Then, as the business earns income, the net assets of the business increase. From time to time, the owner may withdraw some of the business's assets to pay living expenses or for other personal uses. These withdrawals reduce both assets and owner's equity. To record them, you use an account that has the name of the business owner and the word *Withdrawals*. For example, an account called Jerry Dow, Withdrawals, is used to record the withdrawals of cash by Jerry Dow from his law practice. The **withdrawals account** is also known as the **personal account** or **drawing account**.

An owner of an unincorporated business often withdraws a fixed amount each week or month to pay personal living expenses, and often thinks of these withdrawals as a salary. However, in a legal sense they are not a salary because the owner of an unincorporated business cannot enter into a legally binding contract with himself to hire himself and pay himself a salary. Consequently, by law and by custom, such withdrawals are neither a salary nor an expense of the business. They are simply the opposite of investments by the owner.

**Revenue and Expense Accounts.** When you prepare an income statement for an entity, you need to know the amount of each kind of revenue earned and each kind of expense incurred during the period covered by the statement. To accumulate this information, you need a number of revenue and expense accounts. However, all concerns do not have the same revenues and expenses. Therefore, it is impossible to list all revenue and expense accounts that you might encounter. Nevertheless, common examples of revenue accounts are Revenue from Repairs, Commissions Earned, Legal Fees Earned, Rent Earned, and Interest Earned. Common examples of expense accounts are Advertising Expense, Store Supplies Expense, Office Salaries Expense, Office Supplies Expense, Rent Expense, Utilities Expense, and Insurance Expense. Note that the kind of revenue or expense recorded in each above-mentioned account is evident from its title. This is generally true of such accounts.

## The Ledger

A business may use from two dozen to several thousand accounts to record its transactions. In a computerized system, each account is stored on a disk or on a tape. In a manual system, each account is placed on a separate page in a bound or loose-leaf book, or on a separate card in a tray of cards. If the accounts are kept in a book, the book is called a **ledger.** If they are kept on cards in a file tray, the tray of cards is a ledger. Actually, as used in accounting, the word *ledger* means a group of accounts.

## Debit and Credit

Recall that a T-account has a left side and a right side. However, in accounting, the left side is called the **debit** side, abbreviated "Dr."; and the right side is called the **credit** side, abbreviated "Cr." Also, when amounts are entered on the left side of an account, they are called *debits,* and the account is said to be *debited.* When amounts are entered on the right side, they are called *credits,* and the account is said to be *credited.* The difference between the total debits and the total credits recorded in an account is the *account balance.* The balance may be either a *debit balance* or a *credit balance.* It is a debit balance when the sum of the debits exceeds the sum of the credits. It is a credit balance when the sum of the credits exceeds the sum of the debits.

The words *to debit* and *to credit* should not be confused with *to increase* and *to decrease.* To debit means to enter an amount on the left side of an account. To credit means to enter an amount on the right side. Either may be an increase or a decrease. For example, notice the way in which the investment of Jerry Dow is recorded in the Cash and capital accounts that follow:

**Cash**

| | | | |
|---|---|---|---|
| Investment | 9,000 | | |

**Jerry Dow, Capital**

| | | | |
|---|---|---|---|
| | | Investment | 9,000 |

When Dow invested $9,000 in his law practice, both the cash of the business and Dow's equity increased. Observe in the accounts that the increase in cash is recorded on the left or debit side of the Cash account, while the increase in owner's equity is recorded on the right or credit side. The transaction is recorded in this manner because of the mechanics of **double-entry accounting.**

## Mechanics of Double-Entry Accounting

Explain the mechanics of double-entry accounting and tell why transactions are recorded with equal debits and credits. (L. O. 2)

The mechanics of double-entry accounting are such that every transaction affects and is recorded in two or more accounts with equal debits and credits. One by-product of having equal debits and credits is that many errors are easy to discover. If every transaction is recorded with equal debits and credits, then the debits in the ledger must equal the credits. If you find that the sum of the debits in the ledger does not equal the sum of the credits, you know that an error has been made.

In double-entry accounting, increases in assets are recorded on the debit side of asset accounts. Why do assets have debit balances? There is no good reason; it is simply a matter of convention. However, since assets have debit balances, we can reason that increases in liabilities and owner's equity must be recorded as credits. This results from the accounting equation, A = L + OE, and from the requirement that debits equal credits. In other words, if assets have debit balances, equal debits and credits are possible only if increases in liabilities and owner's equity are recorded on the opposite or credit side. Therefore, increases and decreases in all balance sheet accounts have to be recorded as follows:

| Assets | | = | Liabilities | | + | Owner's Equity | |
|---|---|---|---|---|---|---|---|
| **Debit for** increases | **Credit for** decreases | | **Debit for** decreases | **Credit for** increases | | **Debit for** decreases | **Credit for** increases |

As pictured in these T-accounts, the rules for recording transactions under a double-entry system may be expressed as follows:

1. Increases in assets are debited to asset accounts; therefore, decreases must be credited.
2. Increases in liability and owner's equity items are credited to liability and owner's equity accounts; therefore, decreases must be debited.

Recall from Chapter 1 that owner's equity is increased by the owner's investments and by revenues. Owner's equity is decreased by expenses and by withdrawals. With this recollection, we offer these additional rules:

3. Investments by the owner of a business are credited to the owner's capital account.
4. Since the owner's withdrawals of assets decrease owner's equity, they are debited to the owner's withdrawals account.
5. Since revenues increase owner's equity, they are credited in each case to a revenue account that shows the kind of revenue earned.
6. Since expenses decrease owner's equity, they are debited in each case to an expense account that shows the kind of expense incurred.

At this stage, you will find it helpful to memorize these rules. You will apply them over and over in the course of your study. Eventually, the rules will become second nature to you.

## Transactions Illustrating the Rules of Debit and Credit

The following transactions for Jerry Dow's law practice illustrate how you should apply the rules of debit and credit while recording transactions in the accounts. The number before each transaction is used throughout the illustration so that you can identify the transaction in the accounts. Note that the first 11 transactions are the same ones used in Chapter 1 to illustrate the effects of transactions on the accounting equation. Five additional transactions (12 through 16) are presented in this chapter.

Apply the rules of debit and credit in recording transactions. (L. O. 3)

To record a transaction, you must first analyze it to determine what items were increased or decreased. The rules of debit and credit are then applied to determine the debit and credit effects of the increases or decreases. An analysis of each of the following transactions is given in order to demonstrate the process.

1. On December 1, Jerry Dow invested $9,000 in a new law practice.

**Cash**

| | | | |
|---|---|---|---|
| (1) | 9,000 | | |

**Jerry Dow, Capital**

| | | | |
|---|---|---|---|
| | | (1) | 9,000 |

Analysis of the transaction: The transaction increased the cash of the practice and at the same time it increased Dow's equity in the business. Increases in assets are debited, and increases in owner's equity are credited. Therefore, to record the transaction, Cash should be debited and Jerry Dow, Capital should be credited for $9,000.

2. Purchased books for a law library, paying cash of $2,500.

**Cash**

| | | | |
|---|---|---|---|
| (1) | 9,000 | (2) | 2,500 |

**Law Library**

| | | | |
|---|---|---|---|
| (2) | 2,500 | | |

Analysis of the transaction: The law library is an asset that is increased by the purchase of books; and cash is an asset that is decreased. Increases in assets are debited, and decreases are credited. Therefore, to record the transaction, debit Law Library and credit Cash for $2,500.

3. Purchased office equipment for cash, $5,600.

**Cash**

| | | | |
|---|---|---|---|
| (1) | 9,000 | (2) | 2,500 |
| | | (3) | 5,600 |

**Office Equipment**

| | | | |
|---|---|---|---|
| (3) | 5,600 | | |

Analysis of the transaction: The asset office equipment is increased, and the asset cash is decreased. Debit Office Equipment and credit Cash for $5,600.

4. Purchased on credit from Equip-it Company law library items, $380, and office equipment, $1,280.

**Law Library**

| | | | |
|---|---|---|---|
| (2) | 2,500 | | |
| (4) | 380 | | |

**Office Equipment**

| | | | |
|---|---|---|---|
| (3) | 5,600 | | |
| (4) | 1,280 | | |

**Accounts Payable**

| | | | |
|---|---|---|---|
| | | (4) | 1,660 |

Analysis of the transaction: This transaction increased the assets, law library and office equipment, but it also created a liability. Increases in assets are debits, and increases in liabilities are credits; therefore, debit Law Library for $380 and Office Equipment for $1,280, and credit Accounts Payable for $1,660.

5. Completed legal work for a client and immediately collected a $2,200 fee.

**Cash**

| | | | |
|---|---|---|---|
| (1) | 9,000 | (2) | 2,500 |
| (5) | 2,200 | (3) | 5,600 |

**Legal Fees Earned**

| | | | |
|---|---|---|---|
| | | (5) | 2,200 |

Analysis of the transaction: This revenue transaction increased both assets and owner's equity. Increases in assets are debits, and increases in owner's equity are credits. Since revenues increase owner's equity, revenue accounts are increased with credits. Therefore, debit Cash to record the increase in assets. Credit Legal Fees Earned to increase owner's equity and to accumulate information for the income statement.

6. Paid the office rent for December, $1,000.

**Cash**

| | | | |
|---|---|---|---|
| (1) | 9,000 | (2) | 2,500 |
| (5) | 2,200 | (3) | 5,600 |
| | | (6) | 1,000 |

**Rent Expense**

| | | | |
|---|---|---|---|
| (6) | 1,000 | | |

Analysis of the transaction: The cost of renting the office during December is an expense, the effect of which is to decrease owner's equity. Since decreases in owner's equity are debits, expenses are recorded as debits. Therefore, debit Rent Expense to decrease owner's equity and to accumulate information for the income statement. Also, credit Cash to record the decrease in assets.

7. Paid the secretary's salary for the two weeks ended December 12, $700.

**Cash**

| | | | |
|---|---|---|---|
| (1) | 9,000 | (2) | 2,500 |
| (5) | 2,200 | (3) | 5,600 |
| | | (6) | 1,000 |
| | | (7) | 700 |

**Salaries Expense**

| | | | |
|---|---|---|---|
| (7) | 700 | | |

Analysis of the transaction: The secretary's salary is an expense that decreased owner's equity. Debit Salaries Expense to have the effect of decreasing owner's equity and to accumulate information for the income statement. Also, credit Cash to record the decrease in assets.

8. Completed legal work for a client on credit and billed the client $1,700 for the services rendered.

**Accounts Receivable**

| | | | |
|---|---|---|---|
| (8) | 1,700 | | |

**Legal Fees Earned**

| | | | |
|---|---|---|---|
| | | (5) | 2,200 |
| | | (8) | 1,700 |

Analysis of the transaction: This revenue transaction gave the law practice the right to collect $1,700 from the client, and thus increased assets and owner's equity. Therefore, debit Accounts Receivable for the increase in assets and credit Legal Fees Earned to increase owner's equity and at the same time to accumulate information for the income statement.

9. The client paid the $1,700 legal fee billed in transaction 8.

**Cash**

| | | | |
|---|---|---|---|
| (1) | 9,000 | (2) | 2,500 |
| (5) | 2,200 | (3) | 5,600 |
| (9) | 1,700 | (6) | 1,000 |
| | | (7) | 700 |

**Accounts Receivable**

| | | | |
|---|---|---|---|
| (8) | 1,700 | (9) | 1,700 |

Analysis of the transaction: One asset was increased, and the other decreased. Debit Cash to record the increase in cash, and credit Accounts Receivable to record the decrease in the account receivable, or the decrease in the right to collect from the client.

10. Paid Equip-it Company $900 of the $1,660 owed for the items purchased on credit in transaction 4.

**Cash**

| | | | |
|---|---|---|---|
| (1) | 9,000 | (2) | 2,500 |
| (5) | 2,200 | (3) | 5,600 |
| (9) | 1,700 | (6) | 1,000 |
| | | (7) | 700 |
| | | (10) | 900 |

**Accounts Payable**

| | | | |
|---|---|---|---|
| (10) | 900 | (4) | 1,660 |

Analysis of the transaction: Payments to creditors decrease in equal amounts both assets and liabilities. Decreases in liabilities are debited, and decreases in assets are credited. Debit Accounts Payable and credit Cash.

11. Jerry Dow withdrew $1,100 from the law practice for personal use.

**Cash**

| | | | |
|---|---|---|---|
| (1) | 9,000 | (2) | 2,500 |
| (5) | 2,200 | (3) | 5,600 |
| (9) | 1,700 | (6) | 1,000 |
| | | (7) | 700 |
| | | (10) | 900 |
| | | (11) | 1,100 |

**Jerry Dow, Withdrawals**

| | | | |
|---|---|---|---|
| (11) | 1,100 | | |

Analysis of the transaction: This transaction reduced in equal amounts both assets and owner's equity. Cash is credited to record the asset reduction; and the Jerry Dow, Withdrawals account is debited to decrease owner's equity and to accumulate information for the statement of changes in owner's equity.

12. Signed a contract with Chemical Supply to do its legal work on a fixed-fee basis for $500 per month. Received the fee for the first six months in advance, $3,000.

**Cash**

| | | | |
|---|---|---|---|
| (1) | 9,000 | (2) | 2,500 |
| (5) | 2,200 | (3) | 5,600 |
| (9) | 1,700 | (6) | 1,000 |
| (12) | 3,000 | (7) | 700 |
| | | (10) | 900 |
| | | (11) | 1,100 |

**Unearned Legal Fees**

| | | | |
|---|---|---|---|
| | | (12) | 3,000 |

Analysis of the transaction: The $3,000 receipt of cash increased assets but is not a revenue until earned. Receipt of cash before it is earned creates a liability, which will be satisfied by doing the client's legal work for the next six months. Record the asset increase by debiting Cash. Record the liability increase by crediting Unearned Legal Fees.

13. Paid a $2,400 premium for liability insurance protection that lasts two years.

**Cash**

| | | | |
|---|---|---|---|
| (1) | 9,000 | (2) | 2,500 |
| (5) | 2,200 | (3) | 5,600 |
| (9) | 1,700 | (6) | 1,000 |
| (12) | 3,000 | (7) | 700 |
| | | (10) | 900 |
| | | (11) | 1,100 |
| | | **(13)** | **2,400** |

**Prepaid Insurance**

| | | | |
|---|---|---|---|
| **(13)** | **2,400** | | |

Analysis of the transaction: The advance payment of an insurance premium creates an asset by decreasing another asset. The new asset is recorded with a debit to Prepaid Insurance, and the payment is recorded with a credit to Cash.

14. Purchased office supplies for cash, $120.
15. Paid the December utilities bill for electricity and water, $230.
16. Paid the secretary's salary for the two weeks ended December 26, $700.

**Cash**

| | | | |
|---|---|---|---|
| (1) | 9,000 | (2) | 2,500 |
| (5) | 2,200 | (3) | 5,600 |
| (9) | 1,700 | (6) | 1,000 |
| (12) | 3,000 | (7) | 700 |
| | | (10) | 900 |
| | | (11) | 1,100 |
| | | (13) | 2,400 |
| | | **(14)** | **120** |
| | | **(15)** | **230** |
| | | **(16)** | **700** |

**Office Supplies**

| | | | |
|---|---|---|---|
| **(14)** | **120** | | |

**Utilities Expense**

| | | | |
|---|---|---|---|
| **(15)** | **230** | | |

**Salaries Expense**

| | | | |
|---|---|---|---|
| **(16)** | **700** | | |

Analysis of the transaction: These transactions are alike because each decreased cash; but they differ in that office supplies are assets while the utilities and secretary's services have been used up and are expenses. The cost of the supplies should be debited to an asset account, while the utilities and the salary should be debited to separate expense accounts. Each transaction involves a credit to Cash.

## The Accounts and the Equation

Illustration 2–2 shows the accounts of the Dow law practice after the transactions have been recorded in them. The accounts are classified according to the elements of the accounting equation.

## Preparing a Trial Balance

Recall that in a double-entry accounting system, every transaction is recorded with equal debits and credits. As a result, you know that an error has been made if the total of the debits in the ledger does not equal the total of the credits. Also, when the balances of the accounts are determined, the sum of the debit balances must equal the sum of the credit balances; otherwise, you

Illustration 2–2

**The ledger for Jerry Dow, Attorney**

**Assets = Liabilities + Owner's Equity**

**Assets**

**Cash**

| | | | |
|---|---|---|---|
| (1) | 9,000 | (2) | 2,500 |
| (5) | 2,200 | (3) | 5,600 |
| (9) | 1,700 | (6) | 1,000 |
| (12) | 3,000 | (7) | 700 |
| | | (10) | 900 |
| | | (11) | 1,100 |
| | | (13) | 2,400 |
| | | (14) | 120 |
| | | (15) | 230 |
| | | (16) | 700 |
| Total | 15,900 | Total | 15,250 |
| | −15,250 | | |
| Balance | 650 | | |

**Accounts Receivable**

| | | | |
|---|---|---|---|
| (8) | 1,700 | (9) | 1,700 |

**Prepaid Insurance**

| | | | |
|---|---|---|---|
| (13) | 2,400 | | |

**Office Supplies**

| | | | |
|---|---|---|---|
| (14) | 120 | | |

**Law Library**

| | | | |
|---|---|---|---|
| (2) | 2,500 | | |
| (4) | 380 | | |
| Balance | 2,880 | | |

**Office Equipment**

| | | | |
|---|---|---|---|
| (3) | 5,600 | | |
| (4) | 1,280 | | |
| Balance | 6,880 | | |

**Liabilities**

**Accounts Payable**

| | | | |
|---|---|---|---|
| (10) | 900 | (4) | 1,660 |
| Total | 900 | Total | 1,660 |
| | | | −900 |
| | | Balance | 760 |

**Unearned Legal Fees**

| | | | |
|---|---|---|---|
| | | (12) | 3,000 |

**Owner's Equity**

**Jerry Dow, Capital**

| | | | |
|---|---|---|---|
| | | (1) | 9,000 |

**Jerry Dow, Withdrawals**

| | | | |
|---|---|---|---|
| (11) | 1,100 | | |

**Legal Fees Earned**

| | | | |
|---|---|---|---|
| | | (5) | 2,200 |
| | | (8) | 1,700 |
| | | Balance | 3,900 |

**Rent Expense**

| | | | |
|---|---|---|---|
| (6) | 1,000 | | |

**Salaries Expense**

| | | | |
|---|---|---|---|
| (7) | 700 | | |
| (16) | 700 | | |
| Balance | 1,400 | | |

**Utilities Expense**

| | | | |
|---|---|---|---|
| (15) | 230 | | |

know an error has been made. This equality is tested by preparing a **trial balance.** Preparing a trial balance requires five steps:

1. Determine the balance of each account in the ledger.
2. List the accounts with balances other than zero, with the debit balances in one column and the credit balances in another (see Illustration 2–3).
3. Add the debit balances.

**Illustration 2–3**
**Trial balance drawn from the ledger of Jerry Dow, Attorney**

JERRY DOW, ATTORNEY
Trial Balance
December 31, 1990

| | | |
|---|---|---|
| Cash . . . . . . . . . . . . . . . | $ 650 | |
| Prepaid insurance . . . . . . . | 2,400 | |
| Office supplies . . . . . . . . . | 120 | |
| Law library . . . . . . . . . . . | 2,880 | |
| Office equipment . . . . . . . | 6,880 | |
| Accounts payable . . . . . . | | $ 760 |
| Unearned legal fees . . . . . | | 3,000 |
| Jerry Dow, capital . . . . . . . | | 9,000 |
| Jerry Dow, withdrawals . . . . | 1,100 | |
| Legal fees earned . . . . . . . | | 3,900 |
| Rent expense . . . . . . . . . | 1,000 | |
| Salaries expense . . . . . . . | 1,400 | |
| Utilities expense . . . . . . . . | 230 | |
| Totals . . . . . . . . . . . . . . | $16,660 | $16,660 |

4. Add the credit balances.
5. Compare the sum of the debit balances with the sum of the credit balances.

The trial balance in Illustration 2–3 was prepared from the accounts in Illustration 2–2. Note that its column totals are equal; in other words, the trial balance is in balance. Therefore, debits equal credits in the ledger.

## The Evidence of Accuracy Offered by a Trial Balance

If you prepare a trial balance that does not balance, one or more errors have been made. The error(s) may have been in recording transactions, in determining the account balances, in copying the balances on the trial balance, or in adding the columns of the trial balance. On the other hand, if your trial balance balances, you may assume that the accounts are free of those errors that would cause an inequality in debits and credits.

However, a trial balance that balances is not absolute proof of accuracy. Some errors do not affect the equality of the trial balance columns. For example, you may record a correct debit amount to the wrong account. This error will not cause a trial balance to be out of balance. Another example would be to record, with an equal debit and credit, a wrong amount. Because errors of this sort do not affect the equality of debits and credits, a trial balance that balances does not prove recording accuracy. It does, however, provide evidence that several types of errors have not been made.

## Balance Column Accounts

T-accounts like the ones shown so far are commonly used in textbook illustrations and also in accounting classes for demonstrations. In both cases, their use eliminates details and lets you concentrate on ideas. However, although widely used in textbooks and in teaching, T-accounts are not used in real-world accounting systems. Instead, accounts like the one in Illustration 2–4 are generally used.

Illustration 2–4

**A Cash account formatted as a balance column account**

Cash — Account No. 111

| Date | | Explanation | PR | Debit | Credit | Balance |
|---|---|---|---|---|---|---|
| 1990 Dec. | 1 | | G1 | 9,000 00 | | 9,000 00 |
| | 2 | | G1 | | 2,500 00 | 6,500 00 |
| | 3 | | G1 | | 5,600 00 | 900 00 |
| | 10 | | G1 | 2,200 00 | | 3,100 00 |

The account of Illustration 2–4 is called a **balance column account**. It differs from a T-account in that it has columns for specific information about each debit and credit entered in the account. Also, its Debit and Credit columns are placed side by side, and it has a third, ''Balance,'' column. In this Balance column, the account's new balance is entered each time the account is debited or credited. As a result, the last amount in the column is the account's current balance. For example, on December 1, the illustrated account was debited for the $9,000 investment of Jerry Dow, which caused it to have a $9,000 debit balance. It was then credited for $2,500, and its new $6,500 balance was entered. On December 3, it was credited again for $5,600, which reduced its balance to $900. Then, on December 10, it was debited for $2,200, and its balance was increased to $3,100.

When a balance column account like that of Illustration 2–4 is used, the heading of the Balance column does not tell whether the balance is a debit balance or a credit balance. However, this should not create a problem. You should be able to determine the normal balance of any account by reading the account title and recognizing what type of account it is. These normal balances result from the rules of debit and credit, and are as follows:

Tell the normal balance of any asset, liability, or owner's equity account. (L. O. 4)

| Account Classification | Since Increases Are Recorded as— | The Normal Balance Is— |
|---|---|---|
| Asset | Debits | Debit |
| Liability | Credits | Credit |
| Owner's equity: | | |
| Capital | Credits | Credit |
| Withdrawals | Debits | Debit |
| Revenue | Credits | Credit |
| Expense | Debits | Debit |

When an unusual transaction causes an account to have a balance opposite from its normal kind of balance, this opposite-from-normal kind of balance is indicated in the account by circling the amount or by entering it in red. Also, when a debit or credit entered in an account causes the account to have no

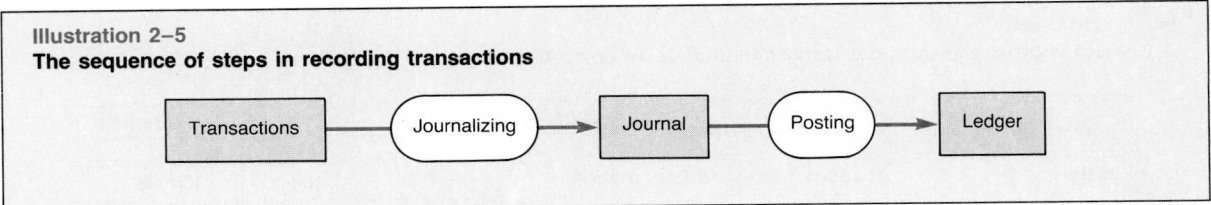

Illustration 2–5
**The sequence of steps in recording transactions**

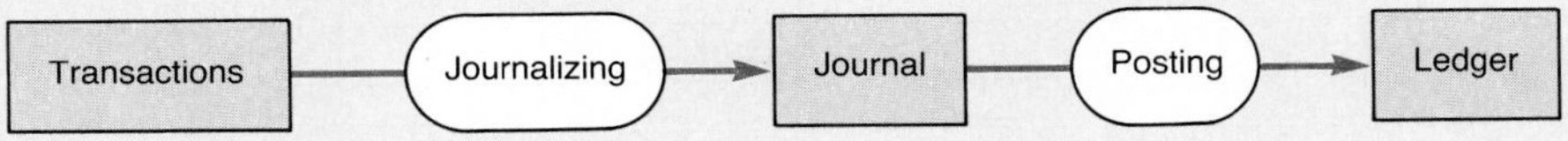


balance, some bookkeepers place a –0– in the Balance column on the line of the entered amount. Others write 0.00 in the column to indicate the account does not have a balance.

## Transactions Should First Be Recorded in a Journal

It is possible to record transactions by entering debits and credits directly in the accounts, as was done earlier in this chapter. However, if you do this and you make an error, the error will be difficult to locate. Even with a transaction that has only one debit and one credit, the debit is entered on one ledger page or card and the credit on another, and there is nothing to link the two together.

Therefore, to link together the debits and credits of each transaction and to provide in one place a complete record of each transaction, it is the universal practice in manual accounting systems to record all transactions first in a **journal**. Then, the debit and credit information about each transaction is copied from the journal to the ledger accounts. These procedures reduce the tendency to make errors in posting. And if errors are made, the journal record makes it possible to trace the debits and credits into the accounts for the purpose of locating the errors.

The process of recording transactions in a journal is called *journalizing transactions*. The process of copying journal entry information from a journal to a ledger is called **posting**. Remember the sequence of these steps, as shown in Illustration 2–5. Since transactions are first journalized and then posted to the ledger, a journal is called a **book of original entry** and a ledger a **book of final entry**.

## The General Journal

The simplest and most flexible type of journal is a **General Journal**. The General Journal is designed so flexibly that it can be used to record any kind of transaction. For each transaction, it provides places for recording (1) the transaction date, (2) the names of the accounts involved, (3) the amount of each debit and credit, and (4) an explanation of the transaction. And when the amounts are copied from the journal to the accounts in the ledger, the General Journal provides (5) a column in which to mark the identifying number of the account to which each debit or credit was copied. Illustration 2–6 shows a typical general journal page on which the first four transactions of the Dow law practice have been recorded.

In Illustration 2–6, the last entry records the credit purchase of law books and office equipment. Note that three accounts are involved. When a transaction involves three or more accounts and is recorded with a general journal entry, a **compound journal entry** is required. A compound journal entry is one that involves three or more accounts.

**Illustration 2–6**
**A General Journal showing four transactions of Jerry Dow, Attorney**

**General Journal** Page 1

| Date | | Account Titles and Explanation | PR | Debit | Credit |
|---|---|---|---|---|---|
| 1990 Dec. | 1 | Cash | | 9,000 00 | |
| | | Jerry Dow, Capital | | | 9,000 00 |
| | | Investment by owner. | | | |
| | | | | | |
| | 2 | Law Library | | 2,500 00 | |
| | | Cash | | | 2,500 00 |
| | | Purchased law books for cash. | | | |
| | | | | | |
| | 3 | Office Equipment | | 5,600 00 | |
| | | Cash | | | 5,600 00 |
| | | Purchased office equipment for cash. | | | |
| | | | | | |
| | 6 | Law Library | | 380 00 | |
| | | Office Equipment | | 1,280 00 | |
| | | Accounts Payable | | | 1,660 00 |
| | | Purchased supplies and equipment on credit. | | | |

## Recording Transactions in a General Journal

Record transactions in a General Journal, post to the ledger accounts, and prepare a trial balance to test the accuracy of the recording and posting. (L. O. 5)

Use the following procedures to record transactions in a General Journal:

1. Write the year in small figures at the top of the first column.
2. Write the month on the first line in the first column. The year and the month are not repeated except at the top of a new page or at the beginning of a new month or year.
3. Write the day of each transaction in the second column on the first line of the transaction.
4. Write the names of the accounts to be debited and credited and an explanation of the transaction in the Account Titles and Explanation column. *The name of the account debited is written first, beginning at the left margin of the column. The name of the account credited is written on the following line, indented about one inch.* The explanation is placed on the next line, indented about a half inch from the left margin. The explanation should be short but sufficient to explain the transaction and set it apart from other transactions.
5. Write the debit amount in the Debit column opposite the name of the

account to be debited. Write the credit amount in the Credit column opposite the account to be credited.

6. Skip a single line between each journal entry to set the entries apart.

At the time transactions are recorded in the General Journal, nothing is entered in the **Posting Reference (PR) column**. However, when the debits and credits are copied from the journal to the ledger, the account numbers of the ledger accounts to which the debits and credits are copied are entered in this column. The Posting Reference column is sometimes called the **Folio column**.

## Posting Transaction Information

The process of posting journal entry information from the journal to the ledger is usually done near the end of a day. All transactions recorded in the journal that day are posted. In the posting procedure, journal debits are copied and become ledger account debits and journal credits are copied and become ledger account credits.

Illustration 2–7 shows the posting procedures for a journal entry. As shown in the illustration, the procedures you should use to post a journal entry are as follows:

For the debit:

1. Find in the ledger the account named in the debit of the entry.
2. Enter in the account the date of the entry as shown in the journal.
3. In the Debit column of the account, write the debit amount shown in the journal.
4. Enter the letter G and the **journal page number** from which the entry is being posted in the posting Reference column of the account. The letter G indicates that the amount was posted from the General Journal. We will discuss other journals later in the text, and each is identified by a letter.
5. Determine the effect of the debit on the account balance and enter the new balance.
6. Enter in the Posting Reference column of the journal the account number of the account to which the amount was posted.

For the credit:

Repeat the above steps. However, the credit amount is entered in the Credit column and has a credit effect on the account balance.

Observe that the last step (step 6) in the posting procedure for either the debit or the credit of an entry is to insert the **account number** in the Posting Reference column of the journal. Inserting the account number in this column serves two purposes: (1) The account number in the journal and the journal page number in the account act as a cross-reference when you want to trace an amount from one record to the other. (2) Writing the account number in the journal as a last step in posting indicates that posting is completed. If posting is interrupted, the bookkeeper, by examining the journal's Posting Reference column, can easily see where posting stopped.

**Illustration 2–7**
**Procedures to follow in posting a general journal entry**

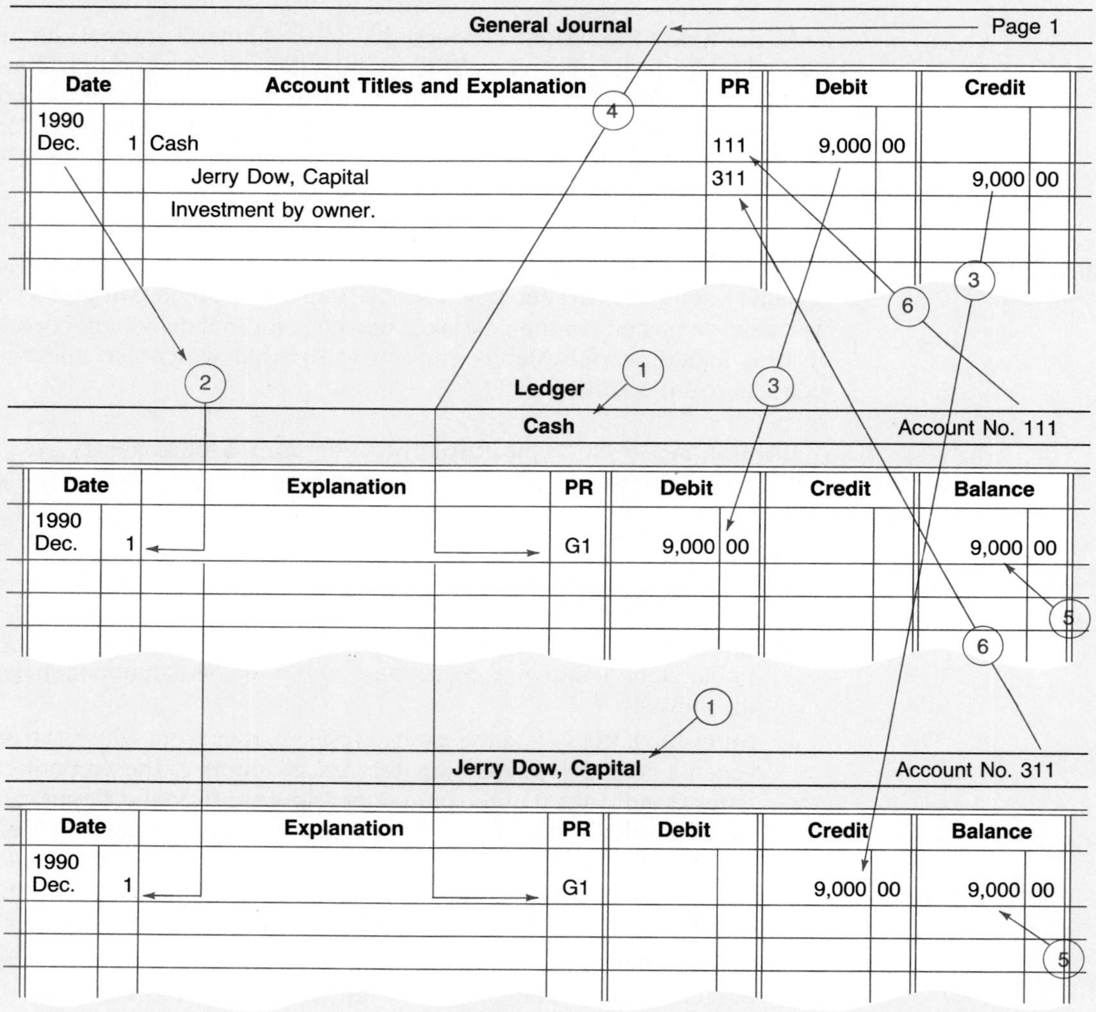


## Account Numbers

All companies should follow a systematic method of assigning identifying numbers to their accounts. A list of all the accounts used by a company, showing the identifying number assigned to each account, is called a **chart of accounts.** One example of a system that service businesses might use in developing a chart of accounts is to assign numbers as follows:

Asset accounts, 111 through 199.
Liability accounts, 211 through 299.
Owner's equity accounts, 311 through 399.

Revenue accounts, 411 through 499.

Operating expense accounts, 511 through 699.

Observe that asset accounts are assigned numbers with first digits of 1, liability accounts are assigned numbers with first digits of 2, and so on. In each case, the first digit of an account's number tells its balance sheet or income statement classification. The second and third digits further identify the account. However, we will describe this type of account numbering system more completely in the next chapter.

## Locating Errors

When a trial balance does not balance, one or more errors have been made. To locate the error or errors, you should check the journalizing, posting, and trial balance preparation steps in their reverse order. First check the addition of the columns in the trial balance to see that no addition errors were made. Then check to see that the account balances were correctly copied from the ledger. Then recalculate the account balances. If at this stage the error or errors are not found, check the posting and then the original journalizing of the transactions.

## Correcting Errors

When an error is discovered in either the journal or the ledger, it must be corrected. Such an error is never erased, for this may indicate an effort to conceal something. However, the method of correction will vary with the nature of the error and the stage in the accounting procedures at which it is discovered.

If an error is discovered in a journal entry before the error is posted, it may be corrected by ruling a single line through the incorrect amount or account name and writing the correct amount or account name above. Likewise, if an incorrect amount was posted to an account, you may correct it in the same manner. However, if an amount was posted to the wrong account, it is best to correct the error with a correcting journal entry. For example, the following journal entry to record the purchase of office supplies was made and posted:

| | | | | |
|---|---|---|---|---|
| Oct. | 14 | Office Furniture and Fixtures . . . . . . . . . . . . . . . . . | 160.00 | |
| | | Cash . . . . . . . . . . . . . . . . . . . . . . . . . . . . | | 160.00 |
| | | To record the purchase of office supplies. | | |

Obviously, the debit of the entry is to the wrong account; therefore, the following entry is needed to correct the error:

| | | | | |
|---|---|---|---|---|
| Oct. | 17 | Office Supplies . . . . . . . . . . . . . . . . . . . . . . . . | 160.00 | |
| | | Office Furniture and Fixtures . . . . . . . . . . . . . . | | 160.00 |
| | | To correct the entry of October 14 in which the Office Furniture and Fixtures account was debited in error for the purchase of office supplies. | | |

The debit of the second entry correctly records the purchase of supplies, and the credit cancels the error of the first entry. Note the full explanation of the correcting entry. Such an explanation should always be full and complete so that anyone can see exactly what occurred.

## Bookkeeping Techniques

When amounts are entered in a journal or a ledger, it is not necessary to use commas indicating thousands of dollars or decimal points to separate dollars and cents. The ruled lines accomplish this. However, when statements are prepared on unruled paper, the decimal points and commas should be used.

Dollar signs are not used in journals or ledgers. However, you should use them on financial reports prepared on unruled paper. On such reports, a dollar sign is placed (1) before the first amount in each column of figures and (2) before the first amount appearing after a ruled line indicates an addition or a subtraction. Examine Illustration 3–5, page 111, for examples of the use of dollar signs on a financial report.

When an amount to be entered in a ledger or a journal is an amount of dollars and no cents, some bookkeepers save time by using a dash in the cents column in the place of two zeros to indicate that there are no cents. However, on financial reports, two zeros are preferred because they are neater in appearance.

In this text, exact dollar amounts are used in order to save space. In such cases, neither zeros nor dashes are used to show that there are no cents involved.

## Summary of the Chapter in Terms of Learning Objectives

**1.** Commonly used asset accounts include Cash, Notes Receivable, Accounts Receivable, Prepaid Insurance, Office Supplies, Store Supplies, Equipment, Buildings, and Land. Commonly used liability accounts include Notes Payable and Accounts Payable, as well as other unearned revenue accounts. The owner's investments in a proprietorship and other relatively permanent changes in the owner's equity are recorded in the owner's capital account. Revenue, expense, and withdrawals accounts are used to accumulate changes in owner's equity.

**2.** In double-entry accounting, every transaction is recorded in two or more accounts with equal debits and credits. Although this procedure does not guarantee accuracy, it provides evidence that several possible errors have not been made.

**3.** Double-entry accounting is based on the accounting equation, A = L + OE. Debits are used to record increases in assets, withdrawals, and expenses. Decreases in liabilities, the owner's capital account, and revenues are also recorded with debits. Credits are used to record increases in liabilities, the owner's capital account, and revenues. Credits are also used to record decreases in assets, withdrawals, and expenses.

**4.** Asset and expense accounts normally have debit balances. Liability, owner's equity, and revenue accounts normally have credit balances.

**5.** The effects of the economic events on an entity's accounting equation are recorded first in a journal such as the General Journal. After they have been journalized, the amounts are copied from the journal to the accounts in the ledger. After the amounts have been posted to the ledger accounts, a trial balance may be prepared to prove that the equality of debits and credits has been maintained.

## Demonstration Problem

*This demonstration problem is based on the same facts as the demonstration problem presented at the end of Chapter 1.* During its first month of operation, Barbara Schmidt's haircutting business (The Cutlery) completed the following transactions:

*a.* On August 1, 1990, Schmidt put $2,000 of her savings into a checking account in the name of The Cutlery.

*b.* On August 2, she bought $600 of supplies for the shop.

*c.* On August 3, she paid $500 rent for the month of August for a small store.

*d.* On August 5, she furnished the store, installing new fixtures which the supplier sold to her for $1,200. This amount was to be repaid in three equal payments at the end of August, September, and October.

*e.* The Cutlery opened August 12, and in the first week of business ended August 16, receipts from cash sales amounted to $825.

*f.* On August 17, Schmidt paid $125 to an assistant for working during the business's grand opening.

*g.* Receipts from cash sales during the two-week period ended August 30 amounted to $1,930.

*h.* On August 31, Schmidt paid the first installment on the fixtures.

*i.* On August 31, she withdrew $1,100 cash for her personal expenses.

*Required*

1. Prepare general journal entries to record the above transactions.
2. Open the following accounts: Cash, 111; Store Supplies, 112; Store Equipment, 131; Accounts Payable, 211; Barbara Schmidt, Capital, 311; Barbara Schmidt, Withdrawals, 312; Sales, 411; Rent Expense, 611; and Wages Expense, 612.
3. Post the journal entries to the proper ledger accounts.
4. Prepare a trial balance for The Cutlery.

## Solution to Demonstration Problem

1.

Page 1

| | Date | | Account Titles and Explanations | PR | Debit | Credit |
|---|---|---|---|---|---|---|
| | 1990 | | | | | |
| *a.* | Aug. | 1 | Cash | 111 | 2,000.00 | |
| | | | Barbara Schmidt, Capital | 311 | | 2,000.00 |
| | | | Invested $2,000 in business. | | | |
| *b.* | | 2 | Store Supplies | 112 | 600.00 | |
| | | | Cash | 111 | | 600.00 |
| | | | Purchased store supplies. | | | |
| *c.* | | 3 | Rent Expense | 611 | 500.00 | |
| | | | Cash | 111 | | 500.00 |
| | | | Paid rent for August. | | | |
| *d.* | | 5 | Store Equipment | 131 | 1,200.00 | |
| | | | Accounts Payable | 211 | | 1,200.00 |
| | | | Purchased fixtures on credit. | | | |
| *e.* | | 16 | Cash | 111 | 825.00 | |
| | | | Sales | 411 | | 825.00 |
| | | | Cash sales to customers. | | | |
| *f.* | | 17 | Wages Expense | 612 | 125.00 | |
| | | | Cash | 111 | | 125.00 |
| | | | Paid wages to assistant. | | | |
| *g.* | | 30 | Cash | 111 | 1,930.00 | |
| | | | Sales | 411 | | 1,930.00 |
| | | | Two weeks' sales to customers. | | | |
| *h.* | | 31 | Accounts Payable | 211 | 400.00 | |
| | | | Cash | 111 | | 400.00 |
| | | | Paid first payment on store equipment purchased on August 5. | | | |
| *i.* | | 31 | Barbara Schmidt, Withdrawals | 312 | 1,100.00 | |
| | | | Cash | 111 | | 1,100.00 |
| | | | Withdrew cash for personal use. | | | |

2., 3.

**Cash** Account No. 111

| Date | | Explanation | PR | Debit | Credit | Balance |
|---|---|---|---|---|---|---|
| 1990 | | | | | | |
| Aug. | 1 | | G1 | 2,000 | | 2,000 |
| | 2 | | G1 | | 600 | 1,400 |
| | 3 | | G1 | | 500 | 900 |
| | 16 | | G1 | 825 | | 1,725 |
| | 17 | | G1 | | 125 | 1,600 |
| | 30 | | G1 | 1,930 | | 3,530 |
| | 31 | | G1 | | 400 | 3,130 |
| | 31 | | G1 | | 1,100 | 2,030 |

**Store Supplies** Account No. 112

| Date | | Explanation | PR | Debit | Credit | Balance |
|---|---|---|---|---|---|---|
| 1990 | | | | | | |
| Aug. | 2 | | G1 | 600 | | 600 |

**Store Equipment** Account No. 131

| Date | | Explanation | PR | Debit | Credit | Balance |
|---|---|---|---|---|---|---|
| 1990 | | | | | | |
| Aug. | 5 | | G1 | 1,200 | | 1,200 |

**Account Payable** Account No. 211

| Date | | Explanation | PR | Debit | Credit | Balance |
|---|---|---|---|---|---|---|
| 1990 | | | | | | |
| Aug. | 5 | | G1 | | 1,200 | 1,200 |
| | 31 | | G1 | 400 | | 800 |

**Barbara Schmidt, Capital** Account No. 311

| Date | | Explanation | PR | Debit | Credit | Balance |
|---|---|---|---|---|---|---|
| 1990 | | | | | | |
| Aug. | 1 | | G1 | | 2,000 | 2,000 |

**Barbara Schmidt, Withdrawals** Account No. 312

| Date | | Explanation | PR | Debit | Credit | Balance |
|---|---|---|---|---|---|---|
| 1990 | | | | | | |
| Aug. | 31 | | G1 | 1,100 | | 1,100 |

**Sales** Account No. 411

| Date | | Explanation | PR | Debit | Credit | Balance |
|---|---|---|---|---|---|---|
| 1990 | | | | | | |
| Aug. | 16 | | G1 | | 825 | 825 |
| | 30 | | G1 | | 1,930 | 2,755 |

**Rent Expense** Account No. 611

| Date | | Explanation | PR | Debit | Credit | Balance |
|---|---|---|---|---|---|---|
| 1990 | | | | | | |
| Aug. | 3 | | G1 | 500 | | 500 |

**Wages Expense** Account No. 612

| Date | | Explanation | PR | Debit | Credit | Balance |
|---|---|---|---|---|---|---|
| 1990 | | | | | | |
| Aug. | 17 | | G1 | 125 | | 125 |

4.

**THE CUTLERY**
**Trial Balance**
**August 31, 1990**

| | | |
|---|---|---|
| Cash | $2,030 | |
| Store supplies | 600 | |
| Store equipment | 1,200 | |
| Accounts payable | | $ 800 |
| Barbara Schmidt, capital | | 2,000 |
| Barbara Schmidt, withdrawals | 1,100 | |
| Sales | | 2,755 |
| Rent expense | 500 | |
| Wages expense | 125 | |
| Totals | $5,555 | $5,555 |

## Glossary

Define or explain the words and phrases listed in the chapter Glossary. (L. O. 6)

**Accounts** separate locations in an accounting system, one of which is used in recording and summarizing the increases and decreases in each type of revenue, expense, asset, liability, or owner's equity item. p. 57

**Account balance** the difference between the increases and decreases recorded in an account. pp. 57–58

**Account number** a unique number that is assigned to an account as a means of identifying that account. pp. 73–74

**Balance column account** an account that has Debit and Credit columns for entering changes in the account and a column for entering the new account balance after each debit or credit is posted to the account. p. 70

**Book of final entry** a ledger to which amounts are posted. p. 71

**Book of original entry** a journal in which transactions are first recorded. p. 71

**Business papers** printed documents that businesses use in the process of completing business transactions and that provide evidence of the transactions; sometimes called *source documents*. pp. 56–57

**Capital account** an account used to record the owner's investments in the business plus any more or less permanent changes in the owner's equity. p. 61

**Chart of accounts** a list of all the accounts used by a company, showing the identifying number assigned to each account. pp. 74–75

**Compound journal entry** a journal entry that has more than one debit or more than one credit. pp. 71–72

**Credit** the right-hand side of a T-account, or entries that decrease assets, or increase liabilities, or increase owner's equity. p. 62

**Debit** the left-hand side of a T-account, or entries that increase assets, or decrease liabilities, or decrease owner's equity. p. 62

**Double-entry accounting** a system of accounting in which each transaction affects and is recorded in two or more accounts with equal debits and credits. p. 62

**Drawing account** another name for the *withdrawals account*. p. 61

**Folio column** another name for the *Posting Reference column*. p. 73

**General Journal** a book of original entry that is designed so flexibly that it can be used to record any type of transaction. pp. 71–72

**Internal transactions** a name sometimes given to economic events that have an effect on an entity's accounting equation but that do not involve transactions with outside parties. p. 55

**Journal** a book of original entry in which a complete record of transactions is first recorded and from which transaction amounts are posted to the ledger accounts. p. 71

**Journal page number** a posting reference number entered in the Posting Reference column of each account to which an amount is posted and which shows the page of the journal from which the amount was posted. p. 73

**Ledger** a group of accounts used by a business in recording its transactions. p. 62

**Personal account** another name for the *withdrawals account*. p. 61

**Posting** transcribing the debit and credit amounts from a journal to the ledger accounts. p. 71

**Posting Reference (PR) column** a column in a journal and in each account that is used for cross-referencing amounts that have been posted from a journal to the account. Also called a *Folio column*. pp. 72–73

**Prepaid expenses** assets created by payments for economic benefits that do not expire until some later time; then, as the benefits expire or are used up, the assets become expenses. p. 59

**Promissory note** a formal written promise to pay a definite sum of money on demand or at a fixed or determinable future date. p. 58

**Source documents** another name for *business papers*. pp. 56–57

**T-account** a simple form of account that is widely used in accounting education to illustrate the debits and credits required in recording a transaction. p. 57

**Trial balance** a list of the accounts that have balances in the ledger, the debit or credit balance of each account, the total of the debit balances, and the total of the credit balances. pp. 68–69

**Unearned revenues** liabilities created by the receipt of cash from customers in payment for products or services that have not yet been delivered to the customers; the liabilities will be satisfied by delivering the product or service. p. 60

**Withdrawals account** the account used to record the transfers of assets from a business to its owner; also known as *personal account* or *drawing account*. p. 61

## Objective Review

Answers to the following questions are listed in Appendix I at the end of the book. Be sure that you decide which is the one best answer to each question *before* you check the answers in the appendix.

1. The following are commonly used accounts: (1) Equipment; (2) Unearned Rent; (3) Store Supplies; (4) Owner, Capital; (5) Accounts Payable; (6) Owner, Withdrawals; and (7) Land. These accounts should be classified as assets, liabilities, or owner's equity as follows:

| | Assets | Liabilities | Owner's Equity |
|---|---|---|---|
| *a.* | 1, 3, 7 | 2, 5 | 4, 6 |
| *b.* | 1, 3, 7 | 2, 5, 6 | 4 |
| *c.* | 1, 3, 7 | 5, 6 | 2, 4 |
| *d.* | 1, 7 | 5, 6 | 2, 3, 4 |
| *e.* | 1, 7 | 2, 5 | 3, 4, 6 |

2. The requirements of double-entry accounting are such that:
   *a.* All transactions that involve debits to asset accounts must also involve credits to liability or owner's equity accounts.

*b.* All transactions are recorded with equal debits and credits.
*c.* The total debits of all recorded transactions will equal the total credits of all recorded transactions.
*d.* The effects on the balance sheet equation of external transactions can be recorded but the effects of other economic events, sometimes called internal transactions, cannot be recorded.
*e.* Both *(b)* and *(c)* are correct.

3. When Lisa Kalish started her business, she invested $5,000 cash plus an automobile that had a fair market value of $12,000. Also, the business assumed responsibility for a note payable of $8,000 that was issued to finance the purchase of the automobile. In recording Lisa's investment:
*a.* The entry will consist of one debit and one credit.
*b.* The entry will consist of two debits and one credit.
*c.* The entry will consist of two debits and two credits.
*d.* The entry will consist of debits that total $17,000 and credits that total $8,000.
*e.* None of the above is correct.

4. The following types of accounts normally have credit balances:
*a.* Revenue, asset, and owner's equity accounts.
*b.* Revenue, expense, and owner's equity accounts.
*c.* Revenue, liability, and owner's equity accounts.
*d.* Liability and expense accounts.
*e.* Asset and expense accounts.

5. The trial balance of a company shows a Wages Expense account with a balance of $700, which resulted from a single transaction. This account:
*a.* Was recorded in the General Journal in the process of journalizing.
*b.* Was journalized when the $700 amount was copied from the General Journal to the ledger account.
*c.* Was posted when the ledger account was listed in the trial balance.
*d.* Represents an increase in owner's equity that resulted from the use of labor.
*e.* Would normally be listed in the trial balance as a credit balance.

## Questions for Class Discussion

1. What are two types of occurrences that affect an entity's accounting equation?
2. What are the two fundamental steps in the accounting process?
3. Why are business papers called source documents?
4. Why is the evidence provided by business papers important to accounting?
5. What is an account? What is a ledger?
6. What determines the number and type of accounts a business will use?
7. What is the difference between a note receivable and an account receivable?
8. What types of transactions increase the owner's equity in a business? What types decrease owner's equity?

9. What are the meanings of the following words and terms: *(a)* debit, *(b)* to debit, *(c)* credit, and *(d)* to credit?
10. Does debit always mean increase and credit always mean decrease?
11. If a transaction has the effect of decreasing an asset, is the decrease recorded as a debit or as a credit? If the transaction has the effect of decreasing a liability, is the decrease recorded as a debit or as a credit?
12. Why are some accounting systems called *double-entry* accounting systems?
13. Given that assets have economic value and that they have debit balances, why do expenses also have debit balances?
14. What entry (debit or credit) would you make to *(a)* increase a revenue, *(b)* decrease an expense, *(c)* record an owner's withdrawals, and *(d)* record an owner's investment?
15. Why are the rules of debit and credit the same for both liability and owner's equity accounts?
16. List the steps in the preparation of a trial balance.
17. Why is a trial balance prepared?
18. What kinds of errors would cause the column totals of a trial balance to be unequal? What are some examples of errors that would not be revealed by a trial balance?
19. Should transactions be recorded first in a journal or first in the ledger? Why?
20. In recording transactions in a General Journal, which is written first, the debit or the credit? Which is indented?
21. What is a compound entry?
22. What kind of transactions can be recorded in a General Journal?
23. What is the purpose of posting reference numbers that are entered in the journal at the time entries are posted to the accounts?
24. What is a chart of accounts?
25. If a wrong amount was journalized and posted to the accounts, how should it be corrected?
26. When are dollar signs used in accounting?
27. Define or describe each of the following:
    *a.* Journal.
    *b.* Ledger.
    *c.* Folio column.
    *d.* Posting.
    *e.* Posting Reference column.

## Exercises

**Exercise 2–1**
**Increases, decreases, and normal balances of accounts**
(L. O. 3, 4)

Prepare the following columnar form. Then enter the word *debit* or *credit* in each of the last three columns to indicate the action necessary to increase the account, the action to decrease the account, and to show the normal balance of the account.

| Kind of Account | Increases | Decreases | Normal Balance |
|---|---|---|---|
| Revenue | Credit | Debit | Credit |
| Asset | Debit | Credit | Debit |
| Owner's withdrawals | Debit | Credit | Debit |
| Liability | Credit | Debit | Credit |
| Expense | Debit | Credit | debit |
| Owner's capital | Credit | Debit | Credit |

**Exercise 2–2**
**Entering transactions in T-accounts**
(L. O. 3)

Place the following T-accounts on a sheet of notebook paper: Cash; Accounts Receivable; Office Supplies; Office Equipment; Accounts Payable; Gae Neff, Capital; Revenue from Services; and Utilities Expense. Then record these transactions by entering debits and credits directly in the accounts. Use the transaction letters to identify amounts entered in the accounts.

*a.* Gae Neff began a service business, called N-E Errands, by investing $5,000 in the business.
*b.* Purchased office supplies for cash, $60.
*c.* Purchased office equipment on credit, $3,000.
*d.* Received $300 cash for services provided to a customer.
*e.* Paid for the office equipment purchased in transaction *(c)*.
*f.* Billed a customer $875 for services provided to the customer.
*g.* Paid the monthly utility bills, $45.
*h.* Collected $350 of the amount owed by the customer of transaction *(f)*.

**Exercise 2–3**
**Preparing a trial balance**
(L. O. 5)

After recording the transactions of Exercise 2–2, prepare a trial balance for N-E Errands. Use the current date.

**Exercise 2–4**
**Analyzing a trial balance**
(L. O. 1, 3, 4)

James Nelson began a real estate agency and completed seven transactions. The transactions included a cash investment by Nelson, a purchase on credit, and other cash transactions. After completing these transactions, he prepared the trial balance that follows. Analyze the trial balance and prepare a list describing each transaction and its amount. (Hint: T-accounts may help.)

**JAMES NELSON, REALTOR**
**Trial Balance**
**November 7, 1990**

| | | |
|---|---|---|
| Cash | $ 5,925 | |
| Office supplies | 225 | |
| Prepaid insurance | 2,700 | |
| Office equipment | 6,000 | |
| Accounts payable | | $ 6,000 |
| James Nelson, capital | | 7,500 |
| James Nelson, withdrawals | 3,000 | |
| Commissions earned | | 4,500 |
| Advertising expense | 150 | |
| Totals | $18,000 | $18,000 |

**Exercise 2-5**
**Trial balance errors**
(L. O. 5)

Prepare a form with the following three column headings: (1) Error, (2) Amount Out of Balance, and (3) Column Having Larger Total. Then for each of the following errors: (1) in the first column list the error by letter, (2) in the second column show the difference in the trial balance column totals that will result from the error, and (3) in the third column indicate which trial balance column (Debit or Credit) will have the larger total as a result of the error. If the error does not affect the trial balance, write "none" in each of the last two columns.

*a.* A $100 debit to Office Supplies was debited to Office Equipment.
*b.* A $135 credit to Office Equipment was credited to Sales.
*c.* A $90 credit to Sales was credited to the Sales account twice.
*d.* A $60 debit to Office Supplies was posted as a $65 debit.
*e.* A $55 debit to Office Supplies was not posted.
*f.* A $22 credit to Sales was posted as a $220 credit.

**Exercise 2-6**
**Analyzing a trial balance error**
(L. O. 5)

A trial balance does not balance. In looking for the error, you notice that Accounts Payable has a credit balance of $6,000. However, you discover that a transaction for the credit purchase of a computer for $525 had been recorded with a $525 debit to Office Equipment and a $525 debit to Accounts Payable. Answer each of the following questions, giving the dollar amount of the misstatement, if any.

*a.* Was the balance of the Office Equipment account overstated, understated, or correctly stated in the trial balance?
*b.* Was the balance of the Accounts Payable account overstated, understated, or correctly stated in the trial balance?
*c.* Was the Debit column total of the trial balance overstated, understated, or correctly stated?
*d.* Was the Credit column total of the trial balance overstated, understated, or correctly stated?
*e.* If the Credit column total of the trial balance was $144,000 before the error was corrected, what was the total of the Debit column?

**Exercise 2-7**
**Preparing a corrected trial balance**
(L. O. 5)

A careless bookkeeper prepared the following trial balance which does not balance, and you have been asked to prepare a corrected trial balance. In examining the records of the concern, you discover the following: (1) The debits to the Cash account total $49,850, and the credits total $45,125. (2) A $115 receipt of cash from a customer in payment of the customer's account was not posted to Accounts Receivable. (3) A $35 purchase of shop supplies on credit was entered in the journal but was not posted to any account. (4) The bookkeeper made a transposition error in copying the balance of the Revenue from Services account in the trial balance. The correct amount was $52,350.

**FRED'S REPAIR SHOP**
**Trial Balance**
**December 31, 1990**

| | | |
|---|---|---|
| Cash . . . . . . . . . . . . . . | $ 4,825 | |
| Accounts receivable . . . . . . | | $ 5,765 |
| Shop supplies . . . . . . . . . | 5,950 | |
| Shop equipment . . . . . . . . | 10,750 | |
| Accounts payable . . . . . . . | 900 | |
| Fred Mason, capital . . . . . . | 12,265 | |
| Fred Mason, withdrawals . . . | 27,000 | |
| Revenue from services . . . . | | 53,250 |
| Rent expense . . . . . . . . . | | 10,800 |
| Advertising expense . . . . . | 640 | |
| Totals . . . . . . . . . . . . . | $62,330 | $69,815 |

**Exercise 2–8**
**Analyzing account entries and balances**
(L. O. 1, 2)

*a.* During the month of July, Ray Company had cash receipts of $12,000 and cash disbursements of $13,500. The July 31 cash balance was $4,200. Calculate the beginning (June 30) cash balance.

*b.* On June 30, Ray Company had an Accounts Receivable balance of $26,000. During the month of July, total credits to Accounts Receivable were $24,000, which resulted from customer payments. The July 31 Accounts Receivable balance was $32,000. Calculate the amount of credit sales during July.

*c.* Earl Ray, the owner of Ray Company, had a capital account balance of $57,500 on June 30 and $74,000 on July 31. Net income for the month of July was $18,000. Calculate the owner's withdrawals during July.

**Exercise 2–9**
**Analyzing transactions from T-accounts**
(L. O. 2, 3)

The following accounts contain seven transactions keyed together with letters. Write a short explanation of each transaction with the amount or amounts involved.

**Cash**

| | | | |
|---|---|---|---|
| (a) | 7,500 | (b) | 2,475 |
| (e) | 450 | (c) | 75 |
| | | (f) | 3,750 |
| | | (g) | 90 |

**Office Equipment**

| | | | |
|---|---|---|---|
| (d) | 11,250 | | |

**Bill Edwards, Capital**

| | | | |
|---|---|---|---|
| | | (a) | 12,000 |

**Office Supplies**

| | | | |
|---|---|---|---|
| (c) | 75 | | |
| (d) | 50 | | |

**Law Library**

| | | | |
|---|---|---|---|
| (a) | 4,500 | | |

**Legal Fees Earned**

| | | | |
|---|---|---|---|
| | | (e) | 450 |

**Prepaid Rent**

| | | | |
|---|---|---|---|
| (b) | 2,475 | | |

**Accounts Payable**

| | | | |
|---|---|---|---|
| (f) | 3,750 | (d) | 11,300 |

**Utilities Expense**

| | | | |
|---|---|---|---|
| (g) | 90 | | |

**Exercise 2–10**
**General journal entries**
(L. O. 1, 3, 5)

Prepare a form like Illustration 2–6 and then prepare general journal entries to record the following transactions. Omit the year in the journal date column.

May 1 Jeff Sims invested $3,000 in cash and an automobile having a $15,000 fair value in a real estate agency he called Sims Realty.
1 Rented furnished office space and paid two months' rent in advance, $1,500.
2 Purchased office supplies for cash, $90.
15 Sold a building lot for a client and collected a $3,750 commission on the sale.
31 Paid for gas and oil used in the agency car during May, $60.

**Exercise 2–11**
**T-accounts and the trial balance**
(L. O. 1, 3, 5)

1. Open T-accounts for each of the following items: Cash; Prepaid Rent; Office Supplies; Automobile; Jeff Sims, Capital; Commissions Earned; and Gas and Oil Expense.
2. Post the transactions of Exercise 2–10 to the T-accounts. Omit posting reference numbers.
3. Prepare a trial balance of the T-accounts.

**Exercise 2–12**
**Analyzing and journalizing revenue transactions**
(L. O. 1, 5)

Examine each of the following transactions and prepare general journal entries to record only the revenue transactions. Explain why the remaining transactions are not revenue transactions.

*a.* Received $800 cash for consulting services provided to customer.
*b.* Received $2,000 cash from Karen Smith, the owner of the business.
*c.* Received $500 from a customer in partial payment of his account receivable.
*d.* Rendered consulting services to a customer on credit, $700.
*e.* Borrowed $4,000 from the bank by signing a promissory note.
*f.* Received $1,000 from a customer in payment for services to be rendered next year.

**Exercise 2–13**
**Analyzing and journalizing expense transactions**
(L. O. 1, 5)

Examine each of the following transactions and prepare general journal entries to record only the expense transactions. Explain why the remaining transactions are not expense transactions.

*a.* Paid $1,000 cash for store equipment.
*b.* Paid $1,400 in partial payment for supplies purchased 30 days previously.
*c.* Paid utility bill of $640.
*d.* Paid $1,200 to owner of the business for his personal use.
*e.* Paid $1,600 salary of office employee.

## Problems

**Problem 2–1**
**Recording transactions in T-accounts; preparing a trial balance**
(L. O. 3, 4, 5)

Carol Blake opened a real estate business and during a short period as an agent completed these business transactions:

*a.* Invested $42,000 in cash and office equipment with a $6,000 fair value in a real estate agency she called Blake Realty.
*b.* Purchased land valued at $30,000 and a small office building valued at $105,000, paying $35,000 cash and signing a note payable to pay the balance over a period of years.
*c.* Purchased office supplies on credit, $60.
*d.* Carol Blake contributed her personal automobile, which had a $7,200 fair value, for exclusive use in the business.
*e.* Purchased additional office equipment on credit, $720.
*f.* Paid the office secretary's salary, $600.
*g.* Sold a house and collected an $8,500 cash commission on the sale.
*h.* Paid $150 for newspaper advertising that had appeared.
*i.* Paid for the supplies purchased on credit in transaction *(c)*.
*j.* Purchased a new typewriter for the business, paying $840 cash plus an old typewriter carried in the accounting records at $140.
*k.* Completed a real estate appraisal on credit and billed the client $210 for the appraisal.
*l.* Paid the secretary's salary, $600.
*m.* Received payment in full for the appraisal of transaction *(k)*.
*n.* Carol Blake withdrew $1,500 from the business to pay personal expenses.

*Required*

1. Open the following T-accounts: Cash; Accounts Receivable; Office Supplies; Office Equipment; Automobile; Land; Building; Accounts Payable; Notes Payable; Carol Blake, Capital; Carol Blake, Withdrawals; Commissions Earned; Appraisal Fees Earned; Office Salaries Expense; and Advertising Expense.
2. Record the transactions by entering debits and credits directly in the accounts. Use the transaction letters to identify each debit and credit amount.
3. Determine the balance of each account in the ledger and prepare a trial balance using the current date and the title Blake, Realty.

**Problem 2–2**
**Posting from general journal entries; preparing a trial balance**
(L. O. 5)

Jack Fish, CPA, completed these transactions during September of the current year:

Sept. 1 Began a public accounting practice by investing $4,200 in cash and office equipment having a $4,800 fair value.

1 Prepaid two months' rent in advance on suitable office space, $1,800.

Sept. 2 Purchased on credit office equipment, $420, and office supplies, $75.
4 Completed accounting work for a client and immediately received payment of $180 cash.
8 Completed accounting work on credit for Frontier Bank, $700.
10 Paid for the items purchased on credit on September 2.
14 Paid the annual $750 premium on an insurance policy.
18 Received payment in full from Frontier Bank for the work completed on September 8.
24 Completed accounting work on credit for Travis Realty, $500.
28 Jack Fish withdrew $300 cash from the practice to pay personal expenses.
29 Purchased additional office supplies on credit, $45.
30 Paid the September utility bills, $165.

*Required*

1. Open the following accounts: Cash; Accounts Receivable; Office Supplies; Prepaid Insurance; Prepaid Rent; Office Equipment; Accounts Payable; Jack Fish, Capital; Jack Fish, Withdrawals; Accounting Fees Earned; and Utilities Expense.
2. Prepare general journal entries to record the transactions.
3. Post to the accounts.
4. Prepare a trial balance. Title the trial balance Jack Fish, CPA.

**Problem 2–3**
**Recording transactions in T-accounts; preparing a trial balance**
(L. O. 3, 5)

Wayne Seale began business as an excavating contractor and during a short period completed these transactions:

*a.* Began business by investing cash, $18,000; office equipment, $1,500; and machinery, $51,000.

*b.* Purchased land for an office site and for parking machinery, $21,000. Paid $6,500 in cash and signed a promissory note payable for the balance.

*c.* Purchased for cash a used prefabricated building and moved it onto the land for use as an office, $6,000.

*d.* Prepaid the annual premium on two insurance policies, $875.

*e.* Completed an excavating job and collected $1,050 cash in full payment.

*f.* Purchased additional machinery costing $8,150. Gave $2,150 in cash and signed a note payable for the balance.

*g.* Completed an excavating job on credit for Northern Contractors, $1,500.

*h.* Purchased additional office equipment on credit, $450.

*i.* Completed an excavating job for Valley Contractors on credit, $1,150.

*j.* Received and recorded as an account payable a bill for rent on a special machine used on the Valley Contractors job, $200.

*k*. Received $1,500 from Northern Contractors for the work of transaction (*g*).

*l*. Paid the wages of the machinery operator, $1,050.

*m*. Paid for the office equipment purchased in transaction (*h*).

*n*. Paid $150 cash for repairs to a machine.

*o*. Wayne Seale wrote a $75 check on the bank account of the business to pay for repairs to his personal automobile. (The car is not used for business purposes.)

*p*. Paid the wages of the machinery operator, $1,100.

*q*. Paid for gas and oil that had been used by the excavating machinery, $250.

*Required*

1. Open the following T-accounts: Cash; Accounts Receivable; Prepaid Insurance; Office Equipment; Machinery; Building; Land; Accounts Payable; Notes Payable; Wayne Seale, Capital; Wayne Seale, Withdrawals; Excavating Revenue; Machinery Repairs Expense; Wages Expense; Machinery Rentals Expense; and Gas and Oil Expense.
2. Record the transactions by entering debits and credits directly in the accounts. Use the transaction letters to identify each debit and credit. Prepare a trial balance using the current date and the title Wayne Seale, Contractor.

**Problem 2–4**
**Journalizing, posting, and preparing a trial balance**
(L. O. 5)

Paula Hill completed these transactions during June of the current year:

June 1 Began an architectural practice by investing cash, $5,500; drafting supplies, $200; and office and drafting equipment, $4,500.

1 Prepaid two months' rent in advance on suitable office space, $1,500.

3 Paid the annual premium on an insurance policy taken out in the name of the practice, $675.

4 Purchased drafting equipment, $575, and drafting supplies, $45, on credit.

9 Delivered a set of plans to a contractor and collected $600 cash in full payment.

15 Paid the draftsman's salary, $780.

16 Completed and delivered a set of plans to Carver Contractors on credit, $850.

18 Purchased drafting supplies on credit, $50.

19 Paid for the equipment and supplies purchased on June 4.

26 Received $850 from Carver Contractors for the plans delivered on June 16.

27 Paula Hill withdrew $250 from the practice for personal use.

28 Paid for the supplies purchased on June 18.

29 Completed architectural work for Blake Realty on credit, $600.

30 Paid the draftsman's salary, $780.

June 30 Paid the June utility bill, $140.
30 Paid the blueprinting expenses incurred in June, $105.

*Required*

1. Open the following accounts: Cash; Accounts Receivable; Prepaid Rent; Prepaid Insurance; Drafting Supplies; Office and Drafting Equipment; Accounts Payable; Paula Hill, Capital; Paula Hill, Withdrawals; Architectural Fees Earned; Salaries Expense; Blueprinting Expense; and Utilities Expense.
2. Prepare and post general journal entries to record the transactions. Prepare a trial balance, titling it Paula Hill, Architect.

**Problem 2–5**
**Journalizing, posting, and preparing financial statements**
(L. O. 5)

Amy Tuck completed these transactions during April of the current year:

Apr. 1 Began a new law practice by investing $3,000 in cash and law books having a $1,500 fair value.
1 Rented the furnished office of a lawyer who was retiring because of illness, and paid the rent (expense) for April, $600.
1 Took out a liability insurance policy giving one year's protection and paid the premium (expense) for the month of April, $45.
3 Purchased office supplies on credit, $50.
9 Completed legal work for a client and immediately collected $300 cash for the work.
13 Paid for the office supplies purchased on April 3.
16 Completed legal work for Knox Realty on credit, $1,000.
23 Completed legal work for National Bank on credit, $900.
26 Received $1,000 from Knox Realty for the work completed on April 16.
28 Amy Tuck wrote a $20 check on the bank account of the legal practice to pay her home telephone bill.
29 Purchased additional office supplies on credit, $54.
30 Paid the April telephone bill of the office, $30.
30 Paid the salary of the office secretary, $1,150.
30 Prepaid the rent on the office for May and June, $1,200.
30 Prepaid the liability insurance premium for the next 11 months, $495.

*Required*

1. Open the following accounts: Cash; Accounts Receivable; Prepaid Rent; Prepaid Insurance; Office Supplies; Law Library; Accounts Payable; Amy Tuck, Capital; Amy Tuck, Withdrawals; Legal Fees Earned; Rent Expense; Salaries Expense; Telephone Expense; and Insurance Expense.
2. Prepare general journal entries to record the transactions, post to the accounts, and prepare a trial balance titled Amy Tuck, Attorney.
3. Prepare an income statement for the month ended April 30.
4. Prepare a statement of changes in owner's equity for the month ended April 30.
5. Prepare a balance sheet dated April 30.

## Alternate Problems

**Problem 2–1A**
**Recording transactions in T-accounts; preparing a trial balance**
(L. O. 3, 4, 5)

Carol Blake completed these transactions during a short period:

*a.* Opened a real estate agency by investing the following assets at their fair values: cash, $4,000; office equipment, $4,500; automobile, $8,000; land, $37,500; and building, $112,500. The business should also assume responsibility for a $90,000 promissory note that was given to the bank to finance the purchase of the land and building.

*b.* Purchased office supplies, $90, and additional office equipment, $525, on credit.

*c.* Collected a $9,500 commission from the sale of property for a client.

*d.* Purchased additional office equipment on credit, $630.

*e.* Paid for advertising that had appeared in the local paper, $190.

*f.* Traded the agency's automobile and $7,000 in cash for a new automobile.

*g.* Paid the office secretary's salary, $785.

*h.* Paid for the supplies and equipment purchased in transaction *(b)*.

*i.* Completed a real estate appraisal for a client on credit, $265.

*j.* Collected a $3,750 commission from the sale of a building lot for a client.

*k.* The client of transaction *(i)* paid $115 of the amount owed.

*l.* Paid the secretary's salary, $785.

*m.* Paid $175 for newspaper advertising that had appeared.

*n.* Carol Blake withdrew $2,500 from the business for personal use.

*Required*

1. Open the following T-accounts: Cash; Accounts Receivable; Office Supplies; Office Equipment; Automobile; Land; Building; Accounts Payable; Notes Payable; Carol Blake, Capital; Carol Blake, Withdrawals; Commissions Earned; Appraisal Fees Earned; Office Salaries Expense; and Advertising Expense.
2. Record the transactions by entering debits and credits directly in the accounts. Use the transaction letters to identify the amounts in the accounts.
3. Determine the balance of each account in the ledger and prepare a trial balance using the current date and the title Blake, Realty.

**Problem 2–2A**
**Posting from general journal entries; preparing a trial balance**
(L. O. 5)

Jack Fish began a public accounting practice and completed these transactions during April of the current year:

Apr. 1 Invested $7,000 in a public accounting practice begun this day.
1 Rented suitable office space and prepaid two months' rent in advance, $2,400.
2 Purchased office supplies, $95, and office equipment, $5,650, on credit.
4 Paid the annual premium on a liability insurance policy, $650.

Apr. 6 Completed accounting work for a client and immediately collected $265 in cash for the work done.
12 Completed accounting work for Heritage Bank on credit, $675.
16 Purchased additional office supplies on credit, $55.
22 Received $675 from Heritage Bank for the work completed on April 12.
25 Jack Fish withdrew $375 from the accounting practice to pay personal expenses.
29 Completed accounting work for Blake Realty on credit, $525.
30 Made an installment payment of $1,245 on the equipment and supplies purchased on April 2.
30 Paid the April utility bills of the accounting practice, $150.

*Required*

1. Open the following accounts: Cash; Accounts Receivable; Office Supplies; Prepaid Insurance; Prepaid Rent; Office Equipment; Accounts Payable; Jack Fish, Capital; Jack Fish, Withdrawals; Accounting Fees Earned; and Utilities Expense.
2. Prepare general journal entries to record the transactions.
3. Post to the accounts.
4. Prepare a trial balance titled Jack Fish, CPA.

**Problem 2–3A**
**Recording transactions in T-accounts; preparing a trial balance**
(L. O. 3, 5)

Wayne Seale completed these transactions during a short period:

*a.* Began business as an excavating contractor by investing cash, $37,500; office equipment, $2,200; and excavating machinery, $67,500.

*b.* Purchased for $37,500 land to be used as an office site and for parking equipment. Paid $15,000 in cash and signed a promissory note payable for the balance.

*c.* Purchased additional excavating machinery costing $32,650. Paid $10,150 in cash and signed a promissory note payable for the balance.

*d.* Paid $6,700 cash for a used prefabricated building and moved it on the land for use as an office.

*e.* Completed an excavating job and immediately collected $1,275 in cash for the work.

*f.* Prepaid the premium on an insurance policy giving one year's protection, $960.

*g.* Completed an $1,875 excavating job for City-Wide Contractors on credit.

*h.* Paid the wages of the equipment operator, $1,200.

*i.* Paid $250 cash for repairs to excavating machinery.

*j.* Received $1,875 from City-Wide Contractors for the work of transaction *(g)*.

*k.* Completed a $1,200 excavating job for SMK Contractors on credit.

*l.* Received and recorded as an account payable a $165 bill for the rent of a special machine used on the SMK Contractors job.

*m*. Purchased additional office equipment on credit, $790.

*n*. Wayne Seale withdrew $750 from the business for personal use.

*o*. Paid the wages of the equipment operator, $1,350.

*p*. Paid the $165 account payable resulting from renting the machine of transaction *(l)*.

*q*. Paid for gas and oil consumed by the excavating machinery, $335.

*Required*

1. Open the following T-accounts: Cash; Accounts Receivable; Prepaid Insurance; Office Equipment; Machinery; Building; Land; Accounts Payable; Notes Payable; Wayne Seale, Capital; Wayne Seale, Withdrawals; Excavating Revenue; Machinery Repairs Expense; Wages Expense; Machinery Rentals Expense; and Gas and Oil Expense.
2. Record the transactions by entering debits and credits directly in the accounts. Use the transaction letters to identify each debit and credit. Prepare a trial balance using the current date and headed Wayne Seale, Contractor.

**Problem 2–4A**
**Journalizing, posting, and preparing a trial balance**
(L. O. 5)

Paula Hill completed these transactions during May of the current year:

May 1 Began an architectural practice by opening a bank account in the name of the practice, Paula Hill, Architect, and deposited $7,500 therein.

1 Rented suitable office space and prepaid two months' rent in advance, $1,500.

2 Purchased for $7,125 office and drafting equipment under an agreement calling for a $1,125 down payment and the balance in monthly installments. Paid the down payment and recorded the account payable.

4 Purchased drafting supplies for cash, $265.

8 Completed and delivered a set of plans to a contractor and immediately received $785 cash in full payment.

12 Paid the annual premium on a liability insurance policy, $720.

14 Purchased on credit additional drafting supplies, $55, and drafting equipment, $175.

15 Paid the salary of the draftsman, $825.

17 Completed and delivered a set of plans to Valley Developers on credit, $1,800.

21 Paid in full for the supplies and equipment purchased on May 14.

25 Completed additional architectural work for Valley Developers on credit, $1,800.

27 Received $1,800 from Valley Developers for the plans delivered on May 17.

28 Paula Hill withdrew $300 cash from the practice to pay personal expenses.

31 Paid the salary of the draftsman, $825.

31 Paid the May utility bills, $120.

31 Paid $200 cash for blueprinting expense.

*Required*

1. Open the following accounts: Cash; Accounts Receivable; Prepaid Rent; Prepaid Insurance; Drafting Supplies; Office and Drafting Equipment; Accounts Payable; Paula Hill, Capital; Paula Hill, Withdrawals; Architectural Fees Earned; Salaries Expense; Blueprinting Expense; and Utilities Expense.
2. Prepare general journal entries to record the transactions, post to the accounts, and prepare a trial balance.

**Problem 2–5A**
**Journalizing, posting, and preparing financial statements**
(L. O. 5)

Amy Tuck graduated from college with a law degree in June of the current year, and during July, she completed these transactions:

July 1 Began the practice of law by investing $3,000 in cash and law books acquired in college and having a $1,200 fair value.
1 Rented the furnished office of a lawyer who was retiring and paid the rent (expense) for July, $725.
2 Purchased law books costing $1,125 under an agreement calling for a $150 down payment and the balance in monthly installments. Paid the down payment and recorded the remaining $975 as an account payable.
5 Purchased office supplies on credit, $70.
6 Took out a liability insurance policy giving one year's protection and paid the premium (expense) for the month of July, $50.
8 Completed legal work for a client and immediately collected $450 for the work done.
12 Paid for the office supplies purchased on credit on July 5.
16 Completed legal work for Lincoln Bank on credit, $1,275.
22 Amy Tuck wrote a $30 check on the bank account of the legal practice to pay her home telephone bill.
24 Received $1,275 from Lincoln Bank for the work completed July 16.
26 Completed legal work for Royal Realty on credit, $900.
30 Paid the telephone bill of the legal practice, $40.
31 Paid the salary of the office secretary, $1,350.
31 Prepaid the rent on the office for August and September, $1,450.
31 Prepaid the liability insurance premium for the next 11 months, $550.

*Required*

1. Open the following accounts: Cash; Accounts Receivable; Prepaid Rent; Prepaid Insurance; Office Supplies; Law Library; Accounts Payable; Amy Tuck, Capital; Amy Tuck, Withdrawals; Legal Fees Earned; Rent Expense; Salaries Expense; Telephone Expense; and Insurance Expense.
2. Prepare general journal entries to record the transactions, post to the accounts, and prepare a trial balance titled Amy Tuck, Attorney.
3. Prepare an income statement for the month ended July 31.
4. Prepare a statement of changes in owner's equity for the month ended July 31.
5. Prepare a balance sheet dated July 31.

## Provocative Problems

**Provocative Problem 2–1**
**Barry Holk, Consultant**
(L. O. 1)

Barry Holk operates an engineering consulting business. Through the month of February, the accounting records for the business had been maintained by a CPA. Those records showed that Holk's February 28 capital balance was $44,600. However, Holk believed that the CPA had overcharged for his work in the past. As a result, Holk decided to keep his own records. At the end of March, he prepared the statements shown below. He was shocked to discover how unprofitable his business had become, and asked you to review the statements. You should prepare new financial statements including a statement of changes in owner's equity.

**BARRY HOLK, CONSULTANT**
**Income Statement**
**For Month Ended March 31, 19—**

| | | |
|---|---|---|
| Revenues: | | |
| Unearned consulting fees | | $12,000 |
| Investments by owner | | 1,000 |
| Total revenues | | $13,000 |
| Operating expenses: | | |
| Rent expense | $1,000 | |
| Telephone expense | 800 | |
| Technical library | 3,500 | |
| Utilities expense | 700 | |
| Withdrawals by owner | 5,000 | |
| Travel and customer entertainment | 4,400 | |
| Insurance expense | 200 | |
| Total operating expenses | | 15,600 |
| Net income (loss) | | $ (2,600) |

**BARRY HOLK, CONSULTANT**
**Balance Sheet**
**March 31, 19—**

| **Assets** | | **Liabilities** | |
|---|---|---|---|
| Cash | $ 5,600 | Accounts payable | $ 1,400 |
| Accounts receivable | 8,800 | Consulting fees earned | 21,700 |
| Prepaid rent | 3,000 | Notes payable | 25,000 |
| Prepaid insurance | 1,200 | Total liabilities | $48,100 |
| Office supplies | 500 | | |
| Land | 18,000 | **Owner's Equity** | |
| Buildings | 47,000 | Barry Holk, capital | 42,000 |
| Salary payments | 6,000 | | |
| Total assets | $90,100 | Total liabilities and owner's equity | $90,100 |

**Provocative Problem 2–2**
**DeShazo's Tennis Camp**
(L. O. 1, 3, 5)

Scott DeShazo opened a new business as a tennis instructor and completed a number of transactions during May, the first month of operation. He recorded all transactions with double entries in just two accounts, Cash and "Income." At the end of the first month, he asks you to review his records and improve his ledger. Based on the following information, you should present a compound general journal entry dated May 31 to show your corrections and improvements.

**Cash** Account No. 111

| Date | | Explanation | PR | Debit | | Credit | | Balance | |
|---|---|---|---|---|---|---|---|---|---|
| May | 1 | Investment by owner | G1 | 3,000 | 00 | | | 3,000 | 00 |
| | 1 | Purchased tennis supplies | G1 | | | 400 | 00 | 2,600 | 00 |
| | 1 | Purchased ball machine | G1 | | | 2,400 | 00 | 200 | 00 |
| | 5 | Signed note payable to bank | G1 | 2,500 | 00 | | | 2,700 | 00 |
| | 11 | Paid for May rental of courts | G1 | | | 800 | 00 | 1,900 | 00 |
| | 14 | Received cash for lessons given | G1 | 1,600 | 00 | | | 3,500 | 00 |
| | 14 | Paid wages of assistants | G1 | | | 700 | 00 | 2,800 | 00 |
| | 27 | Received cash for June lessons | G1 | 1,000 | 00 | | | 3,800 | 00 |
| | 28 | Purchased tennis supplies | G1 | | | 200 | 00 | 3,600 | 00 |
| | 29 | Received cash for lessons given | G1 | 2,300 | 00 | | | 5,900 | 00 |
| | 29 | Paid wages of assistants | G1 | | | 750 | 00 | 5,150 | 00 |
| | 30 | Withdrew cash for personal use | G1 | | | 900 | 00 | 4,250 | 00 |

**Income** Account No. 411

| Date | | Explanation | PR | Debit | | Credit | | Balance | |
|---|---|---|---|---|---|---|---|---|---|
| May | 1 | | G1 | | | 3,000 | 00 | 3,000 | 00 |
| | 1 | | G1 | 400 | 00 | | | 2,600 | 00 |
| | 1 | | G1 | 2,400 | 00 | | | 200 | 00 |
| | 5 | | G1 | | | 2,500 | 00 | 2,700 | 00 |
| | 11 | | G1 | 800 | 00 | | | 1,900 | 00 |
| | 14 | | G1 | | | 1,600 | 00 | 3,500 | 00 |
| | 14 | | G1 | 700 | 00 | | | 2,800 | 00 |
| | 27 | | G1 | | | 1,000 | 00 | 3,800 | 00 |
| | 28 | | G1 | 200 | 00 | | | 3,600 | 00 |
| | 29 | | G1 | | | 2,300 | 00 | 5,900 | 00 |
| | 29 | | G1 | 750 | 00 | | | 5,150 | 00 |
| | 30 | | G1 | 900 | 00 | | | 4,250 | 00 |

**Provocative Problem 2–3**
**Boats and Grub**
(L. O. 3, 5)

Karen Harris, a graduate student, has just completed the first summer's operation of a concession on Green Lake, at which she rents boats and sells sandwiches, soft drinks, and candy. She began the summer's operation with $7,000 in cash and a five-year lease on a boat dock and a small concession building on the lake. The lease requires a $1,200 annual rental, although the concession is open only from June 1 through August 31. On opening day, Karen paid the first year's rent and purchased three boats at $1,250 each, paying cash.

During the summer, she purchased food, soft drinks, and candy costing $6,400, all of which was paid for by summer's end, excepting food costing $340 that was purchased during the last week's operation. By summer's end, she had paid electric bills, $430, and wages of a part-time helper, $1,200. She had also withdrawn $125 of earnings of the concession each week for 12 weeks for personal expenses.

She took in $3,100 in boat rentals during the summer and sold $13,600 of food and drinks, all of which was collected in cash, except $235 owed by Lax Company for food and drinks for an employees' picnic.

On August 31, when she closed for the summer, Karen was able to return to the soft drink company several cases of soft drinks for which she received a $75 cash refund. However, she had to take home for personal consumption a number of candy bars and soft drinks that cost $50 and could have been sold for $100. She then sold the three boats to a used boat dealer for $500 each.

Prepare an income statement showing the results of the summer's operations, a statement of changes in owner's equity, and an August 31 balance sheet. Head the statements Boats and Grub. (T-accounts may be helpful in organizing the data.)

**Provocative Problem 2–4**
**Clay's Lawn Service**
(L. O. 3, 5)

Upon graduation from high school last summer, Clay Stocks needed a job to earn a portion of his first-year college expenses. He was unable to find anything satisfactory and decided to go into the lawn-care business. He had $1,450 in a savings account that he used to buy a lawn mower and other lawn-care tools. However, to haul the tools from job to job, he needed a truck. Consequently, he borrowed $2,800 from a bank by signing a promissory note that had an interest rate of 1% per month in exchange for a secondhand truck.

From the beginning, he had as much work as he could do, and after two months, he repaid the bank loan plus two months' interest. On August 28, he ended the business after exactly three months' operations. Throughout the summer, he followed the practice of depositing in the bank all cash received from customers. An examination of his checkbook record showed he had deposited $4,350. He had written checks to pay $180 for gas, oil, and lubricants used in the truck and mower and a $65 check for mower repairs. A notebook in the truck contained copies of credit card tickets that showed the business owed $90 for additional gas and oil used in the truck and mower. The notebook also showed that customers owed Clay $260 for lawn-care services. He decided to give his lawn-care equipment to his parents, and estimated it had a fair value of $500. He received a good offer on the truck and sold it for $3,100. Under the assumption that Clay had withdrawn $600 from the business during the summer for spending money and to buy clothes, prepare an income statement showing the results of the summer's operations. Also prepare a statement of changes in owner's equity and an August 28 balance sheet. Head the statements Clay's Lawn Service. (T-accounts should be helpful in organizing the data.)

# 3 Adjusting the Accounts and Preparing the Statements

At the beginning of Chapter 2, we recognized that an entity's accounting equation is affected by business transactions and by other (internal) economic events. The primary focus of Chapter 2 was to teach you the double-entry process of recording the effects of business transactions. This process involves journalizing the transactions in a book of original entry and then posting to the accounts. In studying Chapter 3, you will learn that some of the account balances which result from recording business transactions must be adjusted. These adjustments are recorded so that the entity's internal economic events will be reflected in the account balances.

## Learning Objectives

*After studying Chapter 3, you should be able to:*

1. Explain why the life of a business is divided into accounting periods of equal length and why the accounts of a business must be adjusted at the end of each accounting period.
2. Prepare adjusting entries for prepaid expenses, accrued expenses, unearned revenues, accrued revenues, and depreciation.
3. Explain the difference between the cash and accrual bases of accounting.
4. Prepare entries to record cash receipts and cash disbursements of items that were recorded at the end of the previous period as accrued revenues and accrued expenses.
5. Define each asset and liability classification appearing on a balance sheet, classify balance sheet items, and prepare a classified balance sheet.
6. Define or explain the words and phrases listed in the chapter Glossary.

*After studying the appendix to Chapter 3 (Appendix A), you should be able to:*

7. Explain why some companies record prepaid and unearned items in income statement accounts and prepare adjusting entries when this procedure is used.

Explain why the life of a business is divided into accounting periods of equal length and why the accounts of a business must be adjusted at the end of each accounting period.
(L. O. 1)

The life of a business often spans many years, during which its activities go on without interruption. However, decision makers such as managers and investors cannot wait for the business to conclude its operations before they evaluate its financial progress. Instead, they expect a business to provide financial reports periodically. To accomplish this, the accounting process is based on a **time-period concept.** In other words, the activities of a business are identified as occurring during specific time periods such as months, or three-month periods, or years. Then, financial reports that show the results of operations are prepared for each period. Since this division of the life of a business into time periods is done for accounting purposes, the time periods are called **accounting periods.** The primary accounting period used by most businesses is one year, for which they prepare annual financial statements. However, businesses also prepare **interim financial reports** based on one-month or three-month accounting periods.

Businesses do not always adopt the calendar year ending December 31 as the annual accounting period. They may adopt a period of any 12 consecutive months. The specific 12-month period that a business adopts as its annual accounting period is called the **fiscal year** of the business. In choosing a fiscal year, businesses that do not have much seasonal fluctuation in their sales volume often choose the calendar year. Those that have wide fluctuations in volume tend to choose their **natural business year,** which ends when inventories are at their lowest point and business activities are at their lowest ebb. For example, in department stores, the natural business year begins on February 1, after the Christmas and January sales, and ends the following January 31. Therefore, the annual accounting periods of department stores commonly begin on February 1 and end the following January 31.

## Need for Adjustments at the End of an Accounting Period

At the end of an accounting period, after all transactions are recorded, several of the accounts in a company's ledger typically do not show proper end-of-period balances for presentation in the financial statements. This occurs even though all transactions were recorded correctly. The balances are incorrect for statement purposes, not through error, but because internal economic events have occurred and have not yet been recorded. One event of this type involves costs that expire with the passage of time. For example, the second item on the trial balance of Dow's law practice, as prepared in Chapter 2 and reproduced again as Illustration 3–1, is "Prepaid insurance, $2,400." This $2,400 represents the insurance premium for two years. The insurance protection began on December 1. However, by December 31, $2,400 is not the correct balance sheet account for this asset. During December, one month's insurance ($2,400 ÷ 24 = $100) expired and became an expense. Only $2,300, or ($2,400 − $100), remains as an asset. Likewise, the $120 balance in Office Supplies includes the cost of some supplies that have been used up and become an expense during December. Also, the items in the law library have a limited useful life and part of their usefulness expired during December. Therefore, part of the $2,880 cost of the law library should be reported as expense during December. Furthermore, the office equipment has begun to wear out. Because of these events, the balances of the Prepaid Insurance, Office Supplies, Law Library, and Office Equipment accounts are not the proper amounts to

**Illustration 3–1**
**Trial balance drawn from the ledger of Jerry Dow, Attorney**

JERRY DOW, ATTORNEY
Trial Balance
December 31, 1990

| | | |
|---|---|---|
| Cash | $ 650 | |
| Prepaid insurance | 2,400 | |
| Office supplies | 120 | |
| Law library | 2,880 | |
| Office equipment | 6,880 | |
| Accounts payable | | $ 760 |
| Unearned legal fees | | 3,000 |
| Jerry Dow, capital | | 9,000 |
| Jerry Dow, withdrawals | 1,100 | |
| Legal fees earned | | 3,900 |
| Rent expense | 1,000 | |
| Salaries expense | 1,400 | |
| Utilities expense | 230 | |
| Totals | $16,660 | $16,660 |

appear on the December 31 balance sheet. These items must be *adjusted* before financial statements are prepared.

Some of the other accounts in the trial balance of Dow's law practice also must be adjusted before financial statements are prepared. They include Office Salaries Expense, Unearned Legal Fees, and Legal Fees Earned.

## Adjusting the Accounts

Prepare adjusting entries for prepaid expenses, accrued expenses, unearned revenues, accrued revenues, and depreciation. (L. O. 2)

The process of adjusting the accounts is essentially the same as the process of analyzing and recording business transactions. Each account balance and the economic events that affect that account are analyzed to determine whether an adjustment is needed. If an adjustment is required, an **adjusting entry** is prepared to correct the asset or liability account and to correct the related expense or revenue account. After the adjusting entries are journalized, they are posted to the accounts. In the following paragraphs, we will explain why adjusting entries are needed to account for prepaid expenses, **depreciation**, **accrued expenses**, unearned revenues, and **accrued revenues.**

### Prepaid Expenses

As the name implies, a prepaid expense is an economic benefit that has been paid for in advance of its use. At the time of payment, an asset is acquired that will expire or be used up, and as it is used up, it becomes an expense.

For example, during December, the Dow law practice paid a $2,400 premium for liability insurance protection that would last for two years. Although the payment was made on December 26, the policy went into effect on December 1. As each day of December went by, the benefit of insurance protection expired, and a portion of the prepaid insurance became an expense. On December 31, one month's insurance, valued at 1/24 of $2,400, or $100, had expired. Therefore, the following adjusting entry is required so that the accounts will reflect proper asset and expense amounts on December 31:

**Illustration 3–2**
**Allocating the cost of a 24-month insurance policy**

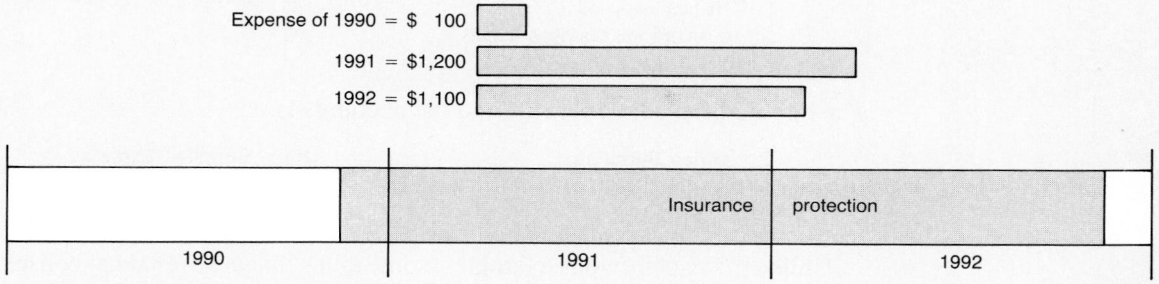


| | | | | |
|---|---|---|---|---|
| | | *Adjustment (a)* | | |
| Dec. | 31 | Insurance Expense . . . . . . . . . . . . . . . . . . . . . . | 100.00 | |
| | | Prepaid Insurance . . . . . . . . . . . . . . . . . . . . | | 100.00 |
| | | To record the expired insurance. | | |

Posting the adjusting entry has the following effect on the accounts:

**Prepaid Insurance**

| | | | |
|---|---|---|---|
| Dec. 26 | 2,400 | Dec. 31 | 100 |

**Insurance Expense**

| | | | |
|---|---|---|---|
| Dec. 31 | 100 | | |

After the entry is posted, the Prepaid Insurance account with a $2,300 balance and the Insurance Expense account with a $100 balance show proper statement amounts.

The allocation of the insurance premium cost to December 1990, to 1991, and to 1992 is shown graphically in Illustration 3–2. In looking at this illustration, you should recognize that adjusting entries will be required to allocate $1,200, or ($2,400 ÷ 24) × 12, to 1991, and to allocate $1,100, or ($2,400 ÷ 24) × 11, to 1992.

To continue, during December, the Dow law practice purchased some office supplies and placed them in the office for use. In the following days, the secretary used some of the supplies. The amount used up was an expense that reduced the supplies on hand. However, the daily reductions were not recognized in the accounts because day-by-day information about amounts used and remaining was not needed. Also, labor is saved by recording only a single amount, the total of all supplies used during the month.

Therefore, for the accounts to reflect proper statement amounts on December 31, the dollar amount of office supplies used during the month must be determined and recorded. To learn the amount used, you must count, or "take an inventory of," the unused supplies remaining. Then, the cost of the remaining supplies is deducted from the cost of the supplies purchased. If, for example, $75 of unused supplies remain, then $45 ($120 − $75 = $45) of supplies were used and became an expense. The following adjusting entry is required to record the using up of the supplies:

| | | | | |
|---|---|---|---|---|
| | | *Adjustment (b)* | | |
| Dec. | 31 | Office Supplies Expense . . . . . . . . . . . . . . . . . . | 45.00 | |
| | | Office Supplies . . . . . . . . . . . . . . . . . . . . . | | 45.00 |
| | | To record the supplies used. | | |

The effect of the adjusting entry on the accounts is:

**Office Supplies**

| | | | |
|---|---|---|---|
| Dec. 26 | 120 | **Dec. 31** | 45 |

**Office Supplies Expense**

| | | | |
|---|---|---|---|
| **Dec. 31** | **45** | | |

Unlike the two previous examples, some items that are prepaid expenses at the time of purchase are both bought and fully used up within a single accounting period. For example, a company might pay its rent in advance on the first day of each month. Each month, the amount paid results in a prepaid expense that fully expires before the month's end and before the end of the accounting period. In such cases, you should ignore the fact that an asset results from each prepayment because an adjustment can be avoided if each prepayment is originally recorded as an expense.

### Depreciation

Tangible, long-lived assets that are held for use in the production or sale of other assets or services are called **plant and equipment.** They include assets such as land, buildings, machines, professional libraries, and automobiles. All items of plant and equipment, except for land, will eventually wear out or lose their usefulness. Therefore, the cost of these assets must be charged off to expense over their useful lives. This process of allocating the cost of these items to expense is called *depreciation*. Depreciation is recorded with adjusting entries similar to those used for prepaid expenses.

For example, the Dow law practice owns a law library that cost $2,880. Dow estimates that the items in this library will be useful for three years, beginning December 1, 1990, after which they will have to be discarded and replaced. Based on this estimate, the depreciation expense for December is calculated as $2,880 ÷ 36 months = $80. You record this expense with the following adjusting entry:

| | | | | |
|---|---|---|---|---|
| | | *Adjustment (c)* | | |
| Dec. | 31 | Depreciation Expense, Law Library . . . . . . . . . . . . . | 80.00 | |
| | | Accumulated Depreciation, Law Library . . . . . . . . | | 80.00 |
| | | To record depreciation for December. | | |

The effect of the entry on the accounts is:

**Law Library**

| | | | |
|---|---|---|---|
| Dec. 2 | 2,500 | | |
| 6 | 380 | | |

**Depreciation Expense, Law Library**

| | | | |
|---|---|---|---|
| **Dec. 31** | **80** | | |

**Accumulated Depreciation, Law Library**

| | | | |
|---|---|---|---|
| | | Dec. 31 | 80 |

After the entry is posted, the Law Library account and its related Accumulated Depreciation, Law Library account together show the December 31 balance sheet amounts for this asset. The Depreciation Expense, Law Library account shows the amount of depreciation expense that should appear on the December income statement.

In most cases, a decrease in an asset is recorded with a credit to the account in which the asset is recorded. However, note in the illustrated accounts that this procedure is not followed in recording depreciation. Rather, depreciation is recorded in a **contra account**, in this case the Accumulated Depreciation, Law Library account. (A contra account is an account the balance of which is subtracted from the balance of an associated account to show a more proper amount for the item recorded in the associated account.)

Why are contra accounts used to record depreciation? The reason is that depreciation entries are not supported by as much objective evidence as are most other entries. Depreciation is only an estimate. You cannot determine the amount of depreciation without estimating how long the asset will last. Contra accounts are used so that readers of a balance sheet can observe both the original cost of the asset and the estimated amount of depreciation that has been charged to expense. For example, the original cost of the law library is shown in the Law Library account to be $2,880. The $80 depreciation that has been charged to expense as of December 31, 1990, is shown in the Accumulated Depreciation, Law Library account.

Note the word *accumulated* in the title of the contra account. This emphasizes the fact that depreciation taken in all prior periods is recorded in this account. For example, if monthly financial statements are prepared for Dow's law practice, the Law Library account and its related accumulated depreciation account at the end of February 1991 will appear as follows:

**Law Library**

| | | | |
|---|---|---|---|
| Dec. 2 | 2,500 | | |
| 6 | 380 | | |

**Accumulated Depreciation, Law Library**

| | | | |
|---|---|---|---|
| | | Dec. 31 | 80 |
| | | Jan. 31 | 80 |
| | | Feb. 28 | 80 |

And the law library's cost and three months' **accumulated depreciation** will be shown on its February 28 balance sheet thus:

| | | |
|---|---|---|
| Law library . . . . . . . . . . . . . . . | $2,880 | |
| Less accumulated depreciation . . . . | 240 | $2,640 |

The office equipment of Dow's law practice is another type of plant and equipment that must be depreciated. Early in December, Dow made two purchases of office equipment for $5,600 and $1,280. For convenience, we will assume that all of the items purchased are estimated to have a four-year useful life. Also, Dow estimates that at the end of the four-year useful life, the business will receive \$880 for the equipment as a trade-in allowance on new equipment. Therefore, the cost that will expire over the 48-month life is \$6,880 − \$880, or \$6,000. Depreciation expense for each month may be calculated as \$6,000 ÷ 48 = \$125, and the entry to record depreciation for December is:

| | | | | |
|---|---|---|---|---|
| | | *Adjustment (d)* | | |
| Dec. | 31 | Depreciation Expense, Office Equipment . . . . . . . . . . | 125.00 | |
| | | Accumulated Depreciation, Office Equipment . . . . . | | 125.00 |
| | | To record depreciation for December. | | |

The effects of posting this entry to the accounts appear as follows:

**Office Equipment**

| Debit | | Credit | |
|---|---|---|---|
| Dec. 3 | 5,600 | | |
| 6 | 1,280 | | |

**Depreciation Expense, Office Equipment**

| Debit | | Credit | |
|---|---|---|---|
| Dec. 31 | 125 | | |

**Accumulated Depreciation, Office Equipment**

| Debit | | Credit | |
|---|---|---|---|
| | | Dec. 31 | 125 |

Accumulated depreciation accounts are sometimes titled *Allowance* for Depreciation. However, the word *Accumulated* is more descriptive of the depreciation procedure.

### Accrued Expenses

Most expenses are recorded at the time they are paid. That is because when the cash payment is recorded, the credit to Cash is balanced by a debit to the expense account. However, at the end of an accounting period, some expenses that were incurred during the period may remain unrecorded because payment is not due. Incurred expenses that are unpaid and therefore unrecorded are called *accrued expenses*. One common example is earned but unpaid wages.

For example, the Dow law practice has a secretary who earns \$70 per day or \$350 per week for a week that begins on Monday and ends on Friday. The secretary's wages are due and payable every two weeks on Friday. During December, these wages were paid on the 12th and 26th and were recorded as follows:

**Cash**

| Debit | | Credit | |
|---|---|---|---|
| | | Dec. 12 | 700 |
| | | 26 | 700 |

**Salaries Expense**

| Debit | | Credit | |
|---|---|---|---|
| Dec. 12 | 700 | | |
| 26 | 700 | | |

If the calendar for December is as shown on the next page and the secretary worked on December 29, 30, and 31, then at the close of business on Wednesday, December 31, the secretary has earned three days' wages that are not paid

| DECEMBER | | | | | | |
|---|---|---|---|---|---|---|
| S | M | T | W | T | F | S |
| | | 1 | 2 | 3 | 4 | 5 | 6 |
| 7 | 8 | 9 | 10 | 11 | 12 | 13 |
| 14 | 15 | 16 | 17 | 18 | 19 | 20 |
| 21 | 22 | 23 | 24 | 25 | 26 | 27 |
| 28 | 29 | 30 | 31 | | | |

and recorded because payment is not due. However, this $210 of earned but unpaid wages is as much a part of the December expenses as the $1,400 of wages that have been paid. Also, on December 31, the unpaid wages are a liability. Therefore, for the accounts to show the correct salary expense for December and all liabilities owed on December 31, you must make an adjusting entry like the following:

| | | | | |
|---|---|---|---|---|
| | | *Adjustment (e)* | | |
| Dec. | 31 | Salaries Expense . . . . . . . . . . . . . . . . . . . . . . | 210.00 | |
| | | Salaries Payable . . . . . . . . . . . . . . . . . . . . | | 210.00 |
| | | To record the accrued wages. | | |

The effect of the entry on the account is:

**Salaries Expense**

| | | | |
|---|---|---|---|
| Dec. 12 | 700 | | |
| 26 | 700 | | |
| 31 | 210 | | |

**Salaries Payable**

| | | | |
|---|---|---|---|
| | | Dec. 31 | 210 |

### Unearned Revenues

An unearned revenue results when payment is received for goods or services in advance of their delivery. For instance, Jerry Dow entered into an agreement with Chemical Supply to do its legal work on a fixed-fee basis of $500 per month, beginning December 15. On December 26, Dow received $3,000 in payment for providing legal services for the six-month period beginning December 15. The fee was recorded with this entry:

| | | | | |
|---|---|---|---|---|
| Dec. | 26 | Cash . . . . . . . . . . . . . . . . . . . . . . . . . . . . | 3,000.00 | |
| | | Unearned Legal Fees . . . . . . . . . . . . . . . . . . | | 3,000.00 |
| | | Received a legal fee in advance. | | |

Receiving the fee in advance increased the cash of the law practice and created a liability, the obligation to do Chemical Supply's legal work for the next six months. However, by December 31, the law practice has discharged $250 of the liability and earned that much revenue, which according to the *realization principle* should appear on the December income statement. Therefore, on December 31, the following adjusting entry is required:

| | | | | |
|---|---|---|---|---|
| | | *Adjustment (f)* | | |
| Dec. | 31 | Unearned Legal Fees . . . . . . . . . . . . . . . . . . . . | 250.00 | |
| | | Legal Fees Earned . . . . . . . . . . . . . . . . . . . . | | 250.00 |
| | | Earned legal fees that had been received in advance. | | |

Posting the entry has this effect on the accounts:

| Unearned Legal Fees | | | |
|---|---|---|---|
| Dec. 31 | 250 | Dec. 26 | 3,000 |

| Legal Fees Earned | | | |
|---|---|---|---|
| | | Dec. 10 | 2,200 |
| | | 12 | 1,700 |
| | | 31 | 250 |

The effect of the entry is to transfer the $250 earned portion of the fee from the liability account to the revenue account. It reduces the liability and records as a revenue the $250 that has been earned.

### Accrued Revenues

Many revenues are recorded when cash is received. Others are recorded at the time the goods or services are sold on credit and a bill is given to the customer. However, at the end of an accounting period, some revenues may remain unrecorded even though they have been earned. Earned revenues that are unrecorded because payment has not been received are called *accrued revenues*. For example, assume that on December 20, Jerry Dow agreed with Guaranty Bank to do its legal work on a fixed-fee basis of $600 per month to be paid at the end of each month's work on the 20th of the month. Under this assumption, by December 31, the law practice has earned one third of a month's fee, or $200. According to the *realization principle,* this revenue should be reported on the December income statement. Therefore, you should make the following adjusting entry:

| | | | | |
|---|---|---|---|---|
| | | *Adjustment (g)* | | |
| Dec. | 31 | Accounts Receivable . . . . . . . . . . . . . . . . . . . . . | 200.00 | |
| | | Legal Fees Earned . . . . . . . . . . . . . . . . . . . . . | | 200.00 |
| | | To record accrued legal fees. | | |

Posting the entry has this effect on the accounts:

| Accounts Receivable | | | |
|---|---|---|---|
| Dec. 12 | 1,700 | Dec. 22 | 1,700 |
| 31 | 200 | | |

| Legal Fees Earned | | | |
|---|---|---|---|
| | | Dec. 10 | 2,200 |
| | | 12 | 1,700 |
| | | 31 | 250 |
| | | 31 | 200 |

## The Adjusted Trial Balance

A trial balance that is prepared before adjustments have been recorded is called an **unadjusted trial balance**. By comparison, an **adjusted trial balance** reflects the effects of the adjustments. Illustration 3–3 shows the December 31, 1990, unadjusted trial balance, the adjustments, and the adjusted trial balance for the law practice of Jerry Dow. Note that in the Adjustments columns, a letter is used to identify each debit and credit with the adjusting entries explained earlier in the chapter.

**Illustration 3–3**

**The December 31, 1990, unadjusted and adjusted trial balances for Jerry Dow, Attorney**

| | Unadjusted Trial Balance | | Adjustments | | Adjusted Trial Balance | |
|---|---|---|---|---|---|---|
| | Dr. | Cr. | Dr. | Cr. | Dr. | Cr. |
| Cash | 650 | | | | 650 | |
| Prepaid insurance | 2,400 | | | *(a)* 100 | 2,300 | |
| Office supplies | 120 | | | *(b)* 45 | 75 | |
| Law library | 2,880 | | | | 2,880 | |
| Office equipment | 6,880 | | | | 6,880 | |
| Accounts payable | | 760 | | | | 760 |
| Unearned legal fees | | 3,000 | *(f)* 250 | | | 2,750 |
| Jerry Dow, capital | | 9,000 | | | | 9,000 |
| Jerry Dow, withdrawals | 1,100 | | | | 1,100 | |
| Legal fees earned | | 3,900 | | *(f)* 250<br>*(g)* 200 | | 4,350 |
| Rent expense | 1,000 | | | | 1,000 | |
| Salaries expense | 1,400 | | *(e)* 210 | | 1,610 | |
| Utilities expense | 230 | | | | 230 | |
| Totals | 16,660 | 16,660 | | | | |
| Insurance expense | | | *(a)* 100 | | 100 | |
| Office supplies expense | | | *(b)* 45 | | 45 | |
| Depreciation expense, law library | | | *(c)* 80 | | 80 | |
| Accumulated depreciation, law library | | | | *(c)* 80 | | 80 |
| Depreciation expense, office equipment | | | *(d)* 125 | | 125 | |
| Accumulated depreciation, office equipment | | | | *(d)* 125 | | 125 |
| Salaries payable | | | | *(e)* 210 | | 210 |
| Accounts receivable | | | *(g)* 200 | | 200 | |
| Totals | | | 1,010 | 1,010 | 17,275 | 17,275 |

## Preparing Statements from the Adjusted Trial Balance

An adjusted trial balance shows proper balance sheet and income statement amounts. Therefore, you can use it to prepare the financial statements. When this is done, the income statement is prepared first because the net income, as calculated on the income statement, is needed to complete the statement of changes in owner's equity.

Illustration 3–4 shows how the revenues and expenses of Dow's law practice are arranged into an income statement and a statement of changes in owner's equity. In preparing the statement of changes in owner's equity, you may have to refer back to the ledger to determine how much of the owner's capital account balance existed at the beginning of the period and how much resulted from the owner's investments during the current period.

Illustration 3–5 shows how the asset, liability, and owner's equity items are drawn from the adjusted trial balance and arranged into a balance sheet. The balance sheet is prepared last, since the owner's equity is calculated in the statement of changes in owner's equity.

Illustration 3–4

**Preparing the income statement and statement of changes in owner's equity from the adjusted trial balance**

**JERRY DOW, ATTORNEY**
**Adjusted Trial Balance**
**December 31, 1990**

| | | |
|---|---|---|
| Cash | $ 650 | |
| Prepaid insurance | 2,300 | |
| Office supplies | 75 | |
| Law library | 2,880 | |
| Office equipment | 6,880 | |
| Accounts payable | | $ 760 |
| Unearned legal fees | | 2,750 |
| Jerry Dow, capital | | 9,000 |
| Jerry Dow, withdrawals | 1,100 | |
| Legal fees earned | | 4,350 |
| Rent expense | 1,000 | |
| Salaries expense | 1,610 | |
| Utilities expense | 230 | |
| Insurance expense | 100 | |
| Office supplies expense | 45 | |
| Depreciation expense, law library | 80 | |
| Accumulated depreciation, law library | | 80 |
| Depreciation expense, office equipment | 125 | |
| Accumulated depreciation, office equipment | | 125 |
| Salaries payable | | 210 |
| Accounts receivable | 200 | |
| Totals | $17,275 | $17,275 |

**JERRY DOW, ATTORNEY**
**Income Statement**
**For the Month Ended December 31, 1990**

| | | |
|---|---|---|
| Revenues: | | |
| Legal fees earned | | $ 4,350 |
| Operating expenses: | | |
| Rent expense | $1,000 | |
| Salaries expense | 1,610 | |
| Utilities expense | 230 | |
| Insurance expense | 100 | |
| Office supplies expense | 45 | |
| Depreciation expense, law library | 80 | |
| Depreciation expense, office equipment | 125 | |
| Total operating expenses | | 3,190 |
| Net income | | $ 1,160 |

**JERRY DOW, ATTORNEY**
**Statement of Changes in Owner's Equity**
**For the Month Ended December 31, 1990**

| | | |
|---|---|---|
| Jerry Dow, capital, November 30, 1990 | | $ –0– |
| Plus: | | |
| Investments by owner | $9,000 | |
| Net income | 1,160 | 10,160 |
| Total | | $10,160 |
| Less: | | |
| Withdrawals by owner | | 1,100 |
| Jerry Dow, capital, December 31, 1990 | | $ 9,060 |

Illustration 3–5

**Preparing the balance sheet from the adjusted trial balance**

JERRY DOW, ATTORNEY
Adjusted Trial Balance
December 31, 1990

| | | |
|---|---|---|
| Cash | $ 650 | |
| Prepaid insurance | 2,300 | |
| Office supplies | 75 | |
| Law library | 2,880 | |
| Office equipment | 6,880 | |
| Accounts payable | | $ 760 |
| Unearned legal fees | | 2,750 |
| Jerry Dow, capital | | 9,000 |
| Jerry Dow, withdrawals | 1,100 | |
| Legal fees earned | | 4,350 |
| Rent expense | 1,000 | |
| Salaries expense | 1,610 | |
| Utilities expense | 230 | |
| Insurance expense | 100 | |
| Office supplies expense | 45 | |
| Depreciation expense, law library | 80 | |
| Accumulated depreciation, law library | | 80 |
| Depreciation expense, office equipment | 125 | |
| Accumulated depreciation, office equipment | | 125 |
| Salaries payable | | 210 |
| Accounts receivable | 200 | |
| Totals | $17,275 | $17,275 |

JERRY DOW, ATTORNEY
Balance Sheet
December 31, 1990

**Assets**

| | | |
|---|---|---|
| Cash | | $ 650 |
| Accounts receivable | | 200 |
| Prepaid insurance | | 2,300 |
| Office supplies | | 75 |
| Law library | $2,880 | |
| Less accumulated depreciation | 80 | 2,800 |
| Office equipment | $6,880 | |
| Less accumulated depreciation | 125 | 6,755 |
| Total assets | | $12,780 |
| **Liabilities** | | |
| Accounts payable | $ 760 | |
| Unearned legal fees | 2,750 | |
| Salaries payable | 210 | |
| Total liabilities | | $ 3,720 |
| **Owner's Equity** | | |
| Jerry Dow, capital, December 31, 1990 | | 9,060 |
| Total liabilities and owner's equity | | $12,780 |

From statement of changes in owner's equity

## The Adjustment Process

The adjustment process is based on two accounting principles, the *realization principle* and the **matching principle.** As explained in Chapter 1, the *realization principle* requires that revenue be reported in the income statement when it is earned, not before and not after. For most firms, revenue is earned at the time a service is rendered or a product is sold to the customer. For example, if a lawyer renders legal services to a client during December, the legal fees are earned during December and must be reported in the December income statement, even though the cash receipt from the client may take place in November or January. In cases such as this, the adjustment process is used to assign the revenue to December, when it was earned.

The *matching principle* requires that expenses be reported on the income statement in the same accounting period as are the revenues that were earned as a result of the expenses. For example, assume that a business uses an office to earn revenues during December. According to the *realization principle,* the revenues must be reported on the December income statement. One expense the business incurred in the pursuit of those December revenues was the December office rent. Therefore, the *matching principle* requires that the rent for December be reported on the December income statement; this must be accomplished even if the December rent was paid in November (or in January). In such cases, the adjustment process is used to match the cost of December's rent with the revenues earned during December.

## Accrual Basis Accounting versus Cash Basis Accounting

Explain the difference between the cash and accrual bases of accounting. (L. O. 3)

When the adjustment process is used to assign revenues to the periods in which they are earned and to match expenses with revenues, the accounting system is described as **accrual basis accounting.** Accrual basis accounting attempts to report revenues and expenses when the economic or financial effects of the transactions impact on the entity. It is based on the understanding that the economic effect of a revenue generally occurs when it is earned, not when cash is received. And the economic effect of an expense is incurred when the benefit expires or is used up, not when cash is paid.

An alternative to accrual basis accounting is the **cash basis of accounting.** Under the cash basis, revenues are reported when cash is received and expenses are reported when cash is paid. No adjustments are made for prepaid, unearned, and accrued items. Since revenues are reported when cash is received and expenses are deducted when cash is paid, net income is calculated as the difference between revenue receipts and expense disbursements.

In discussing the objectives of financial reporting, the FASB concluded that "information about enterprise earnings and its components measured by accrual accounting generally provides a better indication of enterprise performance than information about current cash receipts and payments."[1] Some concerns use a cash basis, but it is acceptable only if the amount of prepaid, unearned, and accrued items is unimportant.

One important benefit of accrual accounting is that it makes the information on accounting statements comparable from period to period. For example, in December 1990, the Dow law practice paid $2,400 for two years of insurance coverage. Under accrual accounting, insurance expense of $100 is reported in

---

[1] *Statement of Financial Accounting Concepts No. 1,* "Objectives of Financial Reporting by Business Enterprises" (Norwalk, Conn., 1978), par. 44.

## AS A MATTER OF ETHICS

At the end of Mystic Company's first business year, its accountant is about to prepare the adjusting entries to record accrued expenses. After discussing these items with the accountant, the company's president instructed the accountant not to make the accruals because the bills will not be received until January or later, and thus should not be included in this year's expenses.

In addition, the president asked how much this year's revenues will be increased by the sales to Brown Company under a contract that was just signed. The accountant explained that there will be no effect on sales until January because Brown Company will not take delivery until after the first of the year. The president was exasperated and told the accountant to record the sales in December because the contract was already signed, and the company is ready to make the deliveries even though the customer does not want to have the items delivered until later.

The combination of not accruing the expenses and recording the sales to Brown Company will substantially increase the company's net income for this year. What should the accountant do? Would your answer be different if the company's statements are or are not to be audited? What if the accountant knows that the president's bonus depends on the amount of income reported in the first year? What if the accountant's job depends on complying with the president's wishes?

the December 1990 income statement, and $100 will be reported as expense each month for the next 23 months. In contrast, a cash basis income statement for December 1990 would show insurance expense of $2,400; and the monthly income statements for the next 23 months would show $–0– expense. When the monthly income statements are compared, the accrual basis correctly shows that all 24 months incurred the expense of insurance coverage. The cash basis would suggest that December 1990 was much less profitable than the following 23 months.

## Disposing of Accrued Items

Prepare entries to record cash receipts and cash disbursements of items that were recorded at the end of the previous period as accrued revenues and accrued expenses. (L. O. 4)

### Accrued Expenses

Earlier in this chapter, the December 29, 30, and 31 accrued wages of the secretary were recorded as follows:

| | | | | |
|---|---|---|---|---|
| Dec. | 31 | Salaries Expense | 210.00 | |
| | | Salaries Payable | | 210.00 |
| | | To record the accrued wages. | | |

When these wages are paid on Friday, January 9, you must make the following entry:

| | | | | |
|---|---|---|---|---|
| Jan. | 9 | Salaries Payable | 210.00 | |
| | | Salaries Expense | 490.00 | |
| | | Cash | | 700.00 |
| | | Paid two weeks' wages. | | |

The first debit in the January 9 entry cancels the liability for the three days' wages accrued on December 31. The second debit records the wages of January's first seven working days as an expense of the January accounting period. The credit records the amount paid to the secretary.

### Accrued Revenues

On December 20, Jerry Dow agreed to do the legal work of Guaranty Bank on a fixed-fee basis for $600 per month. On December 31, the following adjusting entry was made to record one third of a month's revenue earned under this contract.

| | | | | |
|---|---|---|---|---|
| Dec. | 31 | Accounts Receivable . . . . . . . . . . . . . . . . . . . . | 200.00 | |
| | | Legal Fees Earned . . . . . . . . . . . . . . . . . . . . | | 200.00 |
| | | To record the legal fees. | | |

And when payment of the first month's fee is received on January 20, you should make the following entry:

| | | | | |
|---|---|---|---|---|
| Jan. | 20 | Cash . . . . . . . . . . . . . . . . . . . . . . . . . . . . | 600.00 | |
| | | Accounts Receivable . . . . . . . . . . . . . . . . . . . | | 200.00 |
| | | Legal Fees Earned . . . . . . . . . . . . . . . . . . . . | | 400.00 |
| | | Received cash for accrued and earned legal fees. | | |

The first credit in the January 20 entry records the collection of the fee accrued at the end of December. The second credit records as revenue the fee earned during the first 20 days of January.

## Classification of Balance Sheet Items

Define each asset and liability classification appearing on a balance sheet, classify balance sheet items, and prepare a classified balance sheet. (L. O. 5)

The balance sheets that we have presented up to this point (for example, see Illustration 3–5) may be described as **unclassified balance sheets**. This means that no attempt was made to divide the assets or liabilities into classes. However, a balance sheet becomes more useful when you classify its assets and liabilities into meaningful groups. Readers of such **classified balance sheets** can better judge the adequacy of the different kinds of assets used in the business. Also, they can better estimate the probable availability of funds to meet the various liabilities as they become due.

Businesses do not all use the same system of classifying assets and liabilities on their balance sheets. However, most businesses classify them as shown in Illustration 3–6. Assets are classified as (1) current assets, (2) investments, (3) plant and equipment, and (4) intangible assets. Liabilities are classified as (1) current liabilities and (2) long-term liabilities. We explain the nature of these classes in the following paragraphs.

### Current Assets

**Current assets** are defined as cash and other assets that are reasonably expected to be realized in cash or to be sold or consumed within one year or within the normal **operating cycle of the business**, whichever is longer.[2] In addition to cash, current assets typically include temporary investments in market-

[2] FASB, *Accounting Standards—Current Text* (Norwalk, Conn., 1988), sec. B05.105. First published as *Accounting Research Bulletin No. 43*, ch. 3A, par. 4.

**Illustration 3–6**
**A classified balance sheet**

NATIONAL ELECTRICAL SUPPLY
Balance Sheet
December 31, 1990

| | | | |
|---|---|---|---|
| **Assets** | | | |
| **Current assets:** | | | |
| Cash | | $ 1,050 | |
| Temporary investments | | 2,145 | |
| Accounts receivable | | 3,961 | |
| Notes receivable | | 600 | |
| Merchandise inventory | | 10,248 | |
| Prepaid expenses | | 405 | |
| Total current assets | | | $ 18,409 |
| **Investments:** | | | |
| Chrysler Corporation common stock | | $ 2,400 | |
| Land held for future expansion | | 8,000 | |
| Total investments | | | 10,400 |
| **Plant and equipment:** | | | |
| Store equipment | $ 3,200 | | |
| Less accumulated depreciation | 800 | $ 2,400 | |
| Buildings | $70,000 | | |
| Less accumulated depreciation | 18,400 | 51,600 | |
| Land | | 24,200 | |
| Total plant and equipment | | | 78,200 |
| **Intangible assets:** | | | |
| Franchise | | | 10,000 |
| Total assets | | | $117,009 |
| **Liabilities** | | | |
| **Current liabilities:** | | | |
| Accounts payable | $ 2,715 | | |
| Wages payable | 480 | | |
| Notes payable | 3,000 | | |
| Current portion of long-term liabilities | 1,200 | | |
| Total current liabilities | | $ 7,395 | |
| **Long-Term liabilities:** | | | |
| Notes payable | | 48,800 | |
| Total liabilities | | | $56,195 |
| **Owner's Equity** | | | |
| Bruce Brown, capital | | | 60,814 |
| Total liabilities and owner's equity | | | $117,009 |

able securities, accounts receivable, notes receivable, products held for resale (merchandise inventory), and prepaid expenses.

The operating cycle of a business is the average period of time between its acquisition of merchandise or raw materials and the realization of cash from the sale of the merchandise or the sale of the products manufactured from the raw materials. Illustration 3–7 shows a typical operating cycle for a manufacturer. In many companies, this interval is less than one year; as a result, these

Illustration 3–7
**The operating cycle of a manufacturing business**

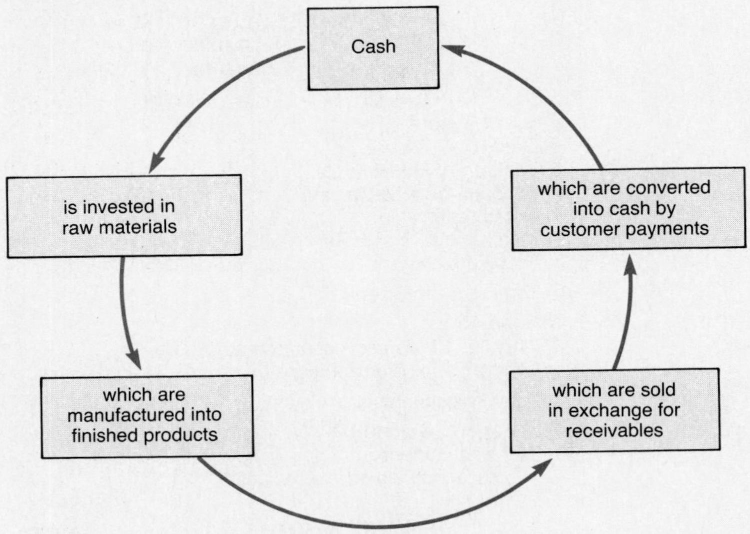


companies use a one-year period in classifying current assets. However, some companies have an operating cycle longer than one year. For example, distilleries must age some products for several years before the products are ready for sale. Consequently, in such companies, inventories or raw materials, manufacturing supplies, and products made from the inventories will not be ready for sale for more than a year.

Return to Illustration 3–6 and note that current assets are listed first. This is because they are more easily converted into cash than are other types of assets. In other words, current assets are said to be more *liquid* than other assets. Also, within the current asset category, the items are listed in the order of their liquidity, the most liquid first and the least liquid last. Note that prepaid expenses are listed last among the current assets. Unlike other current assets, prepaid expenses will not be converted into cash. Nevertheless, prepaid expenses substitute for future cash payments that would be required if the expenses had not been prepaid. Therefore, prepaid expenses are listed as current assets until their benefits expire or they are used up.

The prepaid expenses of a business, as a total, are seldom a major item on its balance sheet. As a result, instead of listing them individually, they are commonly totaled and only the total is shown under the caption "Prepaid expenses." Therefore, the "Prepaid expenses" shown in Illustration 3–6 may include several items such as prepaid insurance, office supplies, and store supplies.

### Investments

The second balance sheet classification is investments. This includes stocks, bonds, and promissory notes that do not qualify as current assets. Generally, this means that they will be held for more than one year or one operating cycle. Investments also include such things as land held for future expansion but not now being used in the business operations. In Illustration 3–6, you should observe that temporary investments of cash are not listed in the Investments category; instead, they are listed as a current asset. We will explain the differences between temporary investments and long-term investments more completely in a later chapter.

### Plant and Equipment

Earlier in this chapter, we described plant and equipment as tangible, long-lived assets that are held for use in the production or sale of other assets or services. Examples include equipment, buildings, and land. The key words in the definition are *long lived* and *held for use in the production or sale of other assets or services*. Land held for future expansion is not a plant asset because it is not being used to produce or sell other assets, goods, or services.

The words *Plant and equipment* are commonly used as a balance sheet caption. Alternative captions are *Property, plant, and equipment* or *Land, buildings, and equipment* or simply *Plant assets*. The order in which plant assets are listed within the balance sheet classification is not uniform.

### Intangible Assets

Economic benefits or resources that do not have a physical substance are called **intangible assets.** Their value stems from the privileges or rights that accrue to their owner. Examples of intangible assets are goodwill, patents, trademarks, copyrights, and franchises.

### Current Liabilities

Obligations that are due to be paid or liquidated within one year or one operating cycle of the business, whichever is longer, are classified as **current liabilities.** Current liabilities usually are satisfied by paying current assets or by incurring new current liabilities. Common current liabilities are accounts payable, notes payable, wages payable, taxes payable, interest payable, and unearned revenues. Also, since long-term liabilities often require periodic payments, the portion of long-term liabilities that comes due within one year or one operating cycle must be classified as a current liability. Illustration 3–6 shows how this item usually is described. The order in which current liability items are listed is not uniform.

Unearned revenues are classified as current liabilities because current assets will normally be required in their liquidation. For example, advance receipts for future delivery of merchandise will be earned and the liability liquidated by delivering merchandise, which is a current asset.

### Long-Term Liabilities

The second liability classification is **long-term liabilities.** Liabilities that are not due and payable within one year or the current operating cycle are listed under this classification. Common long-term liability items are notes payable and bonds payable. Because businesses may owe both long-term notes payable and notes payable that are current liabilities, they sometimes use two different accounts, one called Short-Term Notes Payable and the other Long-Term Notes Payable.

## Owner's Equity on the Balance Sheet

The equity section of a balance sheet differs depending on whether the business is organized as a single proprietorship, a partnership, or a corporation.

### Single Proprietorships and Partnerships

When a business is organized as a single proprietorship, the equity section of the balance sheet is presented as a single line that reports the owner's equity as of the date of the balance sheet. Thus, Illustration 3–5 shows "Jerry Dow, capital, December 31, 1990 . . . . . . . 9,060." In the unusual case where total liabilities exceed total assets, the negative (or debit) equity amount is shown in parentheses and subtracted from total liabilities.

When a business is organized as a partnership, separate capital accounts and withdrawals accounts are maintained for each partner. Changes in the partners' equities are reported in a statement of changes in partners' equities similar to the statement of changes in owner's equity. In the equity section of the balance sheet, the equity of each partner is listed as follows:

**Partner's Equities**

| | | |
|---|---|---|
| Rebecca Matthews, capital . . . . . | $17,300 | |
| Amy Searcy, capital . . . . . . . . . | 24,800 | |
| Total equities of the partners . . . . | | $42,100 |

### Corporations

Corporations are established under the laws of a state or under federal laws. These laws generally distinguish between amounts a corporation receives from its stockholders through investments, and the increase or decrease in stockholders' equity due to net incomes, net losses, and **dividends.** The amounts stockholders have invested are classified as **contributed capital,** or **paid-in capital.** The equity that represents the corporation's cumulative net incomes less net losses and dividends is called **retained earnings.** Therefore, stockholders' equity is shown on a corporation balance sheet as follows:

**Stockholders' Equity**

| | | |
|---|---|---|
| Contributed capital: | | |
| Common stock . . . . . . . . | $400,000 | |
| Retained earnings . . . . . . . . | 124,400 | |
| Total stockholders' equity . . . . | | $524,400 |

If a corporation issues only one kind of stock (others are discussed later), it is called **common stock.** The $400,000 amount shown here for this item is the amount originally contributed to the corporation by its stockholders through the purchase of the corporation's stock. The $124,400 of retained earnings represents the increase in the stockholders' equity resulting from cumulative net incomes that exceeded any net losses and any dividends paid to the stockholders. (A dividend is a distribution, generally of assets, made by a corporation to its stockholders. Such a dividend reduces the assets and the equity of a corporation in the same way a withdrawal reduces the assets and equity of a proprietorship.)

## Alternative Balance Sheet Arrangements

The balance sheet in Illustration 1–2, with the liabilities and owner's equity placed to the right of the assets, is called an **account form balance sheet**. Such an arrangement emphasizes that assets equal liabilities plus owner's equity. Alternatively, when balance sheet items are arranged vertically, such as in Illustration 3–5, the format is called a **report form balance sheet**. Both forms are commonly used, and neither is preferred.

## Identifying Accounts by Number

A typical three-digit account numbering system was introduced in Chapter 2. In such a system, the number assigned to an account usually identifies the account and also identifies the balance sheet or income statement classification of the account. For example, in the following system, the first digit in an account's number tells its primary balance sheet or income statement classification. Account numbers with first digits of 1 are assigned to asset accounts. Liability accounts are assigned numbers with first digits of 2, and the accounts in each balance sheet and income statement classification of a concern selling merchandise are assigned numbers as follows:

111 to 199 are assigned to asset accounts.

211 to 299 are assigned to liability accounts.

311 to 399 are assigned to owner's equity accounts.

411 to 499 are assigned to sales or revenue accounts.

511 to 599 are assigned to cost of goods sold accounts.

611 to 699 are assigned to operating expense accounts.

711 to 799 are assigned to other revenue and expense accounts.

In this system, the second digit of each account number identifies the subclassification of the account, as follows:

- 111 to 199. Asset accounts.
  - 111 to 119. Current asset accounts (second digits of 1).
  - 121 to 129. Long-term investment accounts (second digits of 2).
  - 131 to 139. Plant asset accounts (second digits of 3).
  - 141 to 149. Intangible asset accounts (second digits of 4).
- 211 to 299. Liability accounts.
  - 211 to 219. Current liability accounts (second digits of 1).
  - 221 to 229. Long-term liability accounts (second digits of 2).
- 611 to 699. Operating expense accounts.
  - 611 to 629. Selling expense accounts (second digits of 1 and 2).
  - 631 to 649. General and administrative expense accounts (second digits of 3 and 4).

Finally, each account is assigned a third digit that, within the subclass, is unique to that account. For example, specific current asset accounts might be assigned numbers as follows:

111 to 199. Asset accounts.
  111 to 119. Current asset accounts.
    111. Cash.
    112. Temporary Investments.
    113. Accounts Receivable.
    114. Short-Term Notes Receivable.

The sales and cost of goods sold accounts listed in this account numbering system are discussed in Chapter 5. The division of the operating expense accounts into selling expense accounts and general and administrative expense accounts is also discussed in that chapter. In businesses that sell services rather than tangible products, all expense accounts usually are classified as operating expenses without subdividing them.

## Summary of the Chapter in Terms of Learning Objectives

**1.** The life of a business is divided into accounting periods so that periodic financial reports can be prepared and used to evaluate the financial progress of the business. Adjustments at the end of each period are necessary to correct some of the asset, liability, expense, and revenue accounts and to show the effects of previously unrecorded internal economic events of the business.

**2.** Adjusting entries are used: *(a)* to charge the expired portion of prepaid expenses to expense, *(b)* to charge the expired portion of plant and equipment cost to depreciation expense, *(c)* to accrue expenses and record the related liabilities, *(d)* to recognize as revenues the earned portion of unearned revenue liabilities, and *(e)* to accrue revenues and record the related assets.

**3.** Cash basis accounting does not make adjustments for prepaid expenses, accrued expenses, unearned revenues, and accrued revenues. Revenues are recorded when cash is received, and expenses are recorded when cash is paid. Accrual accounting adjusts for prepaid, unearned, and accrued items; therefore, it reports revenues when earned and expenses when the benefits expire.

**4.** When accrued expenses are paid early in a new accounting period, the entry to record the payment includes a debit to the previously recorded liability and a debit to expense for the portion that expired during the new period. When payment of accrued revenues is received, the entry includes a credit to the previously recorded asset and a credit to revenue for the portion earned during the new period.

**5.** Classified balance sheets usually report four classes of assets: current assets, investments, plant and equipment, and intangible assets. Liabilities are classified as current liabilities and long-term liabilities. The equity of a single proprietorship is reported on one line, while a separate capital account is reported for each partner in a partnership. Corporations report the investments of its stockholders as contributed capital; the equity from net incomes less net losses and dividends is reported as retained earnings.

## Demonstration Problem

The following information relates to Bidder Company on December 31, 1991. The company prepares financial statements annually on a calendar-year basis.

*a.* Bidder Company's weekly payroll is $2,800, paid every Friday for a five-day workweek. At the 1991 year-end, the employees have worked Monday through Wednesday.

*b.* On December 1, 1991, the company borrowed $45,000 from a local bank for 90 days at 12% interest.

*c.* During December, the company advertised in the local paper at a cost of $600, which amount is unpaid and unrecorded.

*d.* Equipment that cost $10,000 and has no salvage value was purchased on July 1, 1990. It has a five-year useful life.

*e.* At the beginning of the year, office supplies amounted to $210. During the year, $650 of supplies were purchased and charged to the asset account. At year-end, there were $280 of supplies on hand.

*f.* On October 1, 1991, Bidder Company contracted to install plumbing for a new housing project. The contract was for $144,000 to install plumbing in 24 new houses. The $144,000 was received on October 1, 1991, and credited to Unearned Plumbing Revenue. As of December 31, 1991, 18 houses have been completed.

*g.* On September 1, 1991, a one-year insurance policy was purchased for $1,200 and was debited to Prepaid Insurance.

*h.* The previous year, on December 1, 1990, the company had purchased a one-year policy for $900. The portion of the cost that relates to 1991 exists in the Prepaid Insurance account.

*Required*

1. Prepare the necessary adjusting journal entries on December 31, 1991.
2. Complete the following schedule:

| Entry | Account | Amount of Adjustment | Amount that Will Appear on Balance Sheet | Classification of Account on Balance Sheet* |
|---|---|---|---|---|
| *a* | Wages payable | $ | $ | |
| *b* | Interest payable | | | |
| *c* | Advertising payable | | | |
| *d* | Accumulated depreciation | | | |
| *e* | Office supplies | | | |
| *f* | Unearned revenues | | | |
| *g* and *h* | Prepaid insurance | | | |

*Indicate whether the account is a current asset, plant and equipment, current liability, or long-term liability.

3. State whether the effect of each adjustment was to increase or decrease or leave unchanged each of the following: net income, total assets, total liabilities.

## Solution to Demonstration Problem

1. Adjusting journal entries.

| | | | | | |
|---|---|---|---|---|---|
| *a.* | Dec. | 31 | Wages Expense . . . . . . . . . . . . . . . . . . | 1,680.00 | |
| | | | Wages Payable . . . . . . . . . . . . . . . . | | 1,680.00 |
| | | | To accrue wages for the last three days of the year ($3/5 \times$ $2,800). | | |
| *b.* | | 31 | Interest Expense . . . . . . . . . . . . . . . . . . | 450.00 | |
| | | | Interest Payable . . . . . . . . . . . . . . . . | | 450.00 |
| | | | To accrue interest for one month ($45,000 $\times$ .12 $\times$ $1/12$). | | |
| *c.* | | 31 | Advertising Expense . . . . . . . . . . . . . . . . . | 600.00 | |
| | | | Advertising Payable . . . . . . . . . . . . . . | | 600.00 |
| | | | To record advertising expense. | | |
| *d.* | | 31 | Depreciation Expense, Equipment . . . . . . . . . | 2,000.00 | |
| | | | Accumulated Depreciation, Equipment . . . . . | | 2,000.00 |
| | | | To record depreciation expense for the year ($10,000 ÷ 5 = $2,000). | | |
| *e.* | | 31 | Office Supplies Expense . . . . . . . . . . . . . . . | 580.00 | |
| | | | Office Supplies . . . . . . . . . . . . . . . . . | | 580.00 |
| | | | To record office supplies used ($210 + $650 − $280). | | |
| *f.* | | 31 | Unearned Plumbing Revenues . . . . . . . . . . . | 108,000.00 | |
| | | | Plumbing Revenues . . . . . . . . . . . . . . . | | 108,000.00 |
| | | | To recognize plumbing revenues earned ($144,000 $\times$ $18/24$). | | |
| *g.* | | 31 | Insurance Expense . . . . . . . . . . . . . . . . . . | 400.00 | |
| | | | Prepaid Insurance . . . . . . . . . . . . . . . . | | 400.00 |
| | | | To adjust for the expired portion of insurance ($1,200 $\times$ $4/12$). | | |
| *h.* | | 31 | Insurance Expense . . . . . . . . . . . . . . . . . . | 825.00 | |
| | | | Prepaid Insurance . . . . . . . . . . . . . . . . | | 825.00 |
| | | | To record the expiration of insurance ($900 $\times$ $11/12$). | | |

2.

| Entry | Account | Amount of Adjustment | Amount that Will Appear on Balance Sheet | Classification of Account on Balance Sheet* |
|---|---|---|---|---|
| *a* | Wages payable | $ 1,680 | $ 1,680 | Current liability |
| *b* | Interest payable | 450 | 450 | Current liability |
| *c* | Advertising payable | 600 | 600 | Current liability |
| *d* | Accumulated depreciation | 2,000 | 3,000 | Plant and equipment |
| *e* | Office supplies | (580) | 280 | Current asset |
| *f* | Unearned revenues | (108,000) | 36,000 | Current liability |
| *g* and *h* | Prepaid insurance | (1,225) | 800* | Current asset |

*$825 + $1,200 − $825 − $400 = $800.

3.

| Entry | Net Income Increase (Decrease) | Total Assets Increase (Decrease) | Total Liabilities Increase (Decrease) |
|---|---|---|---|
| *a* | $ (1,680) | $ –0– | $ 1,680 |
| *b* | (450) | –0– | 450 |
| *c* | (600) | –0– | 600 |
| *d* | (2,000) | (2,000) | –0– |
| *e* | (580) | (580) | –0– |
| *f* | 108,000 | –0– | (108,000) |
| *g* | (400) | (400) | –0– |
| *h* | (825) | (825) | –0– |

## Appendix A

## RECORDING PREPAID AND UNEARNED ITEMS IN INCOME STATEMENT ACCOUNTS

### Prepaid Expenses

Explain why some companies record prepaid and unearned items in income statement accounts and prepare adjusting entries when this procedure is used.
(L. O. 7)

The discussion in Chapter 3 emphasized the fact that prepaid expenses are assets at the time they are purchased. Therefore, at the time of purchase, we recorded prepaid expenses with debits to asset accounts. Then, at the end of the accounting period, adjusting entries were made to transfer the cost that had expired to expense accounts. In the chapter, we also recognized that some prepaid expenses are purchased and will fully expire before the end of the accounting period. When this is expected, it is easier to charge prepaid expenses to expense accounts at the time of purchase. Then, no adjusting entry is necessary.

Some companies follow a practice of recording *all* prepaid expenses with debits to expense accounts. Then, at the end of the accounting period, if any amounts remain unused or unexpired, adjusting entries are made to transfer the cost of the unused portions from the expense accounts to prepaid expense (asset) accounts. This practice is perfectly acceptable. The reported financial statements will be exactly the same under either procedure.

To illustrate the difference between the two procedures, recall that on December 26, the Dow law practice purchased office supplies for $120. That purchase was recorded with a debit to an asset account, but could have been recorded with a debit to an expense account. Both alternatives are shown below:

| | | Purchase Recorded as Asset | | Purchase Recorded as Expense | |
|---|---|---|---|---|---|
| Dec. 26 | Office Supplies . . . . . . . . . . . | 120.00 | | | |
| | Cash . . . . . . . . . . . . . . | | 120.00 | | |
| 26 | Office Supplies Expense . . . . . . | | | 120.00 | |
| | Cash . . . . . . . . . . . . . . | | | | 120.00 |

At the end of the accounting period (December 31), an inventory of the unused office supplies was taken and $75 of supplies were found to be unused. That means \$120 − \$75 = \$45 of office supplies were used and became an expense of December. The required adjusting entry depends on how the original purchase was recorded. The alternative adjusting entries are as follows:

| | | Purchase Recorded as Asset | | Purchase Recorded as Expense | |
|---|---|---|---|---|---|
| Adjusting entries: | | | | | |
| Dec. 31 | Office Supplies Expense . . . . . . | 45.00 | | | |
| | Office Supplies . . . . . . . . | | 45.00 | | |
| 31 | Office Supplies . . . . . . . . . . . | | | 75.00 | |
| | Office Supplies Expense . . . . | | | | 75.00 |

When these entries are posted to the accounts, you can see that the two alternative procedures give the same results. Regardless of which procedure is followed, the December 31 adjusted account balances show office supplies of \$75 and office supplies expense of \$45.

**Purchase Recorded as Asset**

**Office Supplies**

| | | | |
|---|---|---|---|
| Dec. 26 | 120<br>−45 | Dec. 31 | 45 |
| Balance | 75 | | |

**Office Supplies Expense**

| | | | |
|---|---|---|---|
| Dec. 31 | 45 | | |

**Purchase Recorded as Expense**

**Office Supplies**

| | | | |
|---|---|---|---|
| Dec. 31 | 75 | | |

**Office Supplies Expense**

| | | | |
|---|---|---|---|
| Dec. 26 | 120<br>−75 | Dec. 31 | 75 |
| Balance | 45 | | |

To continue the example for another month, assume that during January, Dow's law practice purchased \$150 of supplies; on January 31, an inventory of unused supplies showed \$100 of supplies on hand. As you can see in the above accounts, the December 31 balance in the Office Supplies account was \$75, regardless of which procedure is used. Therefore, the total supplies available for use during January was \$75 + \$150 = \$225. Since \$100 of supplies remain unused on January 31, the adjusting entry on January 31 must be designed to report a supplies asset of \$100 and a supplies expense of \$225 − \$100 = \$125. Depending on how the purchases were recorded, the alternative adjusting entries are:

| | | Purchase Recorded as Asset | | Purchase Recorded as Expense | |
|---|---|---|---|---|---|
| Adjusting entries: | | | | | |
| Jan. 31 | Office Supplies Expense . . . . . . | 125.00 | | | |
| | Office Supplies . . . . . . . . . | | 125.00 | | |
| 31 | Office Supplies. . . . . . . . . . . . | | | 25.00 | |
| | Office Supplies Expense . . . | | | | 25.00 |

Note that if purchases are debited expense accounts, the required adjusting entry increases the Office Supplies account balance \$25, from \$75 to \$100. The credit in the entry reduces the Office Supplies Expense account debit balance from \$150 to \$125.

## Unearned Revenues

The procedures used to record unearned revenues are similar to those used to record prepaid expenses. Receipts of unearned revenues may be recorded with credits to liability accounts (as described in Chapter 3) or they may be recorded with credits to revenue accounts. The adjusting entries at the end of the period will be different, depending on which procedure is followed. Nevertheless, either procedure is acceptable. The amounts reported in the financial statements will be exactly the same, regardless of which procedure is used.

To illustrate the alternative procedures of recording unearned revenues, recall that on December 26, the Dow law practice received $3,000 in payment for legal services to be provided over the six-month period beginning December 15. In Chapter 3, that receipt was recorded with a credit to a liability account. The alternative would be to record it with a credit to a revenue account. Both alternatives are shown below:

| | | Receipt Recorded as a Liability | | Receipt Recorded as a Revenue | |
|---|---|---|---|---|---|
| Dec. 26 | Cash . . . . . . . . . . . . . . . . . . . . | 3,000.00 | | | |
| | Unearned Legal Fees . . . . . . . | | 3,000.00 | | |
| 26 | Cash . . . . . . . . . . . . . . . . . . . . | | | 3,000.00 | |
| | Legal Fees Earned . . . . . . . . | | | | 3,000.00 |

By the end of the accounting period (December 31), the Dow law practice had earned $250 of these legal fees. That means $250 of the liability had been satisfied. Depending on how the original receipt was recorded, the required adjusting entry is as follows:

| | | Receipt Recorded as a Liability | | Receipt Recorded as a Revenue | |
|---|---|---|---|---|---|
| Adjusting entries: | | | | | |
| Dec. 31 | Unearned Legal Fees . . . . . . . . . . | 250.00 | | | |
| | Legal Fees Earned . . . . . . . . | | 250.00 | | |
| 31 | Legal Fees Earned . . . . . . . . . . . | | | 2,750.00 | |
| | Unearned Legal Fees . . . . . . . | | | | 2,750.00 |

Posting these entries shows that the two alternative procedures give the same results. Regardless of which procedure is followed, the December 31 adjusted account balances show unearned legal fees of $2,750 and legal fees earned of $250.

**Receipt Recorded as a Liability**

**Unearned Legal Fees**

| | | | |
|---|---|---|---|
| Dec. 31 | 250 | Dec. 31 | 3,000<br>−250 |
| | | Balance | 2,750 |

**Legal Fees Earned**

| | | | |
|---|---|---|---|
| | | Dec. 31 | 250 |

**Receipt Recorded as a Revenue**

**Unearned Legal Fees**

| | | | |
|---|---|---|---|
| | | Dec. 31 | 2,750 |

**Legal Fees Earned**

| | | | |
|---|---|---|---|
| Dec. 31 | 2,750 | Dec. 26 | 3,000<br>−2,750 |
| | | Balance | 250 |

## Summary of the Appendix in Terms of the Learning Objective

**7.** Because many prepaid expenses expire during the same period they are purchased, some companies choose to charge all prepaid expenses to expense accounts at the time they are purchased. When this is done, end-of-period adjusting entries are required to transfer any unexpired amounts from the expense accounts to appropriate asset accounts. Also, unearned revenues may be credited to revenue accounts at the time cash is received. If so, end-of-period adjusting entries are required to transfer any unearned amounts from the revenue accounts to appropriate unearned revenue accounts.

## Glossary

Define or explain the words and phrases listed in the chapter Glossary. (L. O. 6)

**Account form balance sheet** a balance sheet that is arranged so that the assets are listed on the left and the liability and owner's equity items are listed on the right. p. 119

**Accounting period** the length of time into which the life of a business is divided for the purpose of preparing periodic financial statements. p. 101

**Accrual basis of accounting** a system of accounting in which the adjustment process is used to assign revenues to the periods in which they are earned and to match expenses with revenues. pp. 112–13

**Accrued expenses** expenses that are incurred during an accounting period but that, prior to end-of-period adjustments, remain unrecorded because payment is not due. pp. 102, 106–7

**Accrued revenues** revenues that are earned during an accounting period but that, prior to end-of-period adjustments, remain unrecorded because payment has not been received. pp. 102, 108

**Accumulated depreciation** the total amount of depreciation recorded against an asset or group of assets during the entire period of time the asset or assets have been owned. pp. 104–6

**Adjusted trial balance** a trial balance that shows the account balances after they have been revised to reflect the effects of end-of-period adjustments. pp. 108–9

**Adjusting entry** a journal entry made at the end of an accounting period for the purpose of assigning revenues to the period in which they are earned, assigning expenses to the period in which the expiration of benefit is incurred, and to correct related liability and asset accounts. p. 102

**Cash basis of accounting** an accounting system in which revenues are reported in the income statement when cash is received and expenses are reported when cash is paid; no adjustments are made for prepaid, unearned, and accrued items. pp. 112–13

**Classified balance sheet** a balance sheet that shows assets and liabilities grouped in meaningful subclasses. pp. 114–18

**Common stock** the name given to a corporation's stock when it issues only one kind or class of stock. pp. 118–19

**Contra account** an account the balance of which is subtracted from the balance of an associated account to show a more proper amount for the item recorded in the associated account. p. 105

**Contributed capital** the portion of a corporation's equity that represents investments in the corporation by its stockholders. pp. 118–19

**Current assets** cash or other assets that are reasonably expected to be realized in cash or to be sold or consumed within one year or one operating cycle of the business, whichever is longer. pp. 114–16

**Current liabilities** obligations that are due to be paid or liquidated within one year or one operating cycle of the business, whichever is longer. p. 117

**Depreciation** the expiration of the usefulness of plant and equipment, and the related process of allocating the cost of such assets to expense of the periods during which the assets are used. pp. 102, 104–6

**Dividends** a distribution, generally of assets, made by a corporation to its stockholders. pp. 118–19

**Fiscal year** a period of any 12 consecutive months used by a business as its annual accounting period. p. 101

**Intangible assets** economic benefits or resources without physical substance, the value of which stems from the privileges or rights that accrue to their owner. p. 117

**Interim financial reports** financial reports of a business that are based on one-month or three-month accounting periods. p. 101

**Long-term liabilities** obligations that are not due to be paid within one year or the current operating cycle of the business. p. 118

**Matching principle** the accounting requirement that expenses be reported in the same accounting period as are the revenues that were earned as a result of the expenses. p. 112

**Natural business year** the 12-month period that ends when the activities of a business are at their lowest point. p. 101

**Operating cycle of a business** the average time a business takes to invest cash in merchandise or raw materials that are manufactured into finished products, sell the products, and to convert the receivables (if sales are on credit) back into cash. pp. 114–16

**Paid-in capital** another name for *contributed capital*. pp. 118–19

**Plant and equipment** tangible, long-lived assets that are held for use in the production or sale of other assets or services. p. 104

**Report form balance sheet** a balance sheet with a vertical format that shows the assets above the liabilities and the liabilities above the owner's equity. p. 119

**Retained earnings** the portion of a corporation's equity that represents its cumulative net incomes, less net losses and dividends. pp. 118–19

**Time-period concept** the idea that the life of a business is divisible into time periods of equal length for the purpose of preparing periodic financial reports of the business. p. 101

**Unadjusted trial balance** a trial balance that is prepared before any adjustments have been recorded. p. 108

**Unclassified balance sheet** a balance sheet that presents a single list of assets and a single list of liabilities with no attempt to divide them into classes. p. 114

## Objective Review

Answers to the following questions are listed in Appendix I at the end of the book. Be sure that you decide which is the one best answer to each question *before* you check the answers in the appendix.

1. For purposes of preparing financial statements, the act of dividing the life of a business into equal time periods:
   *a.* Always is done so that the annual accounting period ends at the close of the natural business year.

*b.* Always is done so that the annual accounting period ends at the close of the calendar year.
*c.* Results in an annual accounting period that is called the fiscal year.
*d.* Results in annual financial reports called interim financial reports.
*e.* None of the above are correct.

2. On December 31, 1990, Craft Company failed to make an adjustment for $300 of accrued service revenues earned and also failed to record the expiration of $500 of insurance premiums that had been debited to Prepaid Insurance. As a result of these errors, on the 1990 income statement:
   *a.* Revenues will be overstated $300 and expenses will be understated $500.
   *b.* Revenues will be understated $300 and expenses will be overstated $500.
   *c.* Revenues will be overstated $300 and expenses will be overstated $500.
   *d.* Revenues will be understated $300 and expenses will be understated $500.
   *e.* Net income will be understated by $200.

3. On April 1, 1990, Flay Company paid $3,000 for two years' insurance coverage. In accounting for this item:
   *a.* Under the cash basis of accounting, 1991 insurance expense will be $-0-.
   *b.* Under the cash basis of accounting, 1992 insurance expense will be $375.
   *c.* Under the accrual basis of accounting, 1991 insurance expense will be $1,500.
   *d.* Under the accrual basis of accounting, an adjusting entry for insurance will not be required at the end of 1990.
   *e.* Both *(a)* and *(c)* are correct.

4. On December 31, 1990, Watt Company made an entry to record $400 of accrued salaries. On January 5, the next payment of salaries was $2,000. Related to these transactions only:
   *a.* The entry on January 5 will include a $1,600 credit to Cash.
   *b.* You can be sure that Watt Company is using the cash basis of accounting.
   *c.* The salaries expense charged to 1991 will be $1,600.
   *d.* The salaries expense charged to 1991 will be $2,000.
   *e.* The salaries expense charged to 1990 will be $1,600.

5. A company owns the following items: (1) land used in the operations of the business, (2) office supplies, (3) receivables from customers due in 10 months, (4) a three-year note receivable from the purchaser of land previously owned by the company, (5) the right to receive insurance protection for the next 9 months, (6) land held in case expanded operations require it, (7) trucks used in servicing customers, and (8) trademarks used in selling the company's services. These items should be classified as follows:

| | Current Assets | Investments | Plant and Equipment | Intangible Assets |
|---|---|---|---|---|
| *a.* | 2, 3, 5 | 4 | 1, 6, 7 | 8 |
| *b.* | 2, 3, 5 | 4, 6 | 1, 7 | 8 |
| *c.* | 2, 3 | 4, 6 | 1, 7 | 5, 8 |
| *d.* | 2, 3, 4 | 6 | 1, 7 | 5, 8 |
| *e.* | 2 | 4, 6 | 1, 7 | 3, 5, 8 |

*An asterisk (*) identifies the questions, exercises, and problems that are based on Appendix A at the end of the chapter.*

## Questions for Class Discussion

1. Why is the life of a business divided into time periods of equal length?
2. If a business adopts the calendar year as its annual accounting period, how would you describe financial reports of the business that are based on one-month or three-month accounting periods?
3. Which month would most likely end the natural business year of a business that operates outdoor tennis camps in Minnesota: August or April?
4. In selecting a fiscal year, what type of businesses are most apt to select their natural business year intead of the calendar year?
5. Why would you expect some account balances of a concern to be incorrect for statement purposes at the end of an accounting period even though all transactions were correctly recorded?
6. What purposes are served by making end-of-period adjustments?
7. A prepaid expense is an asset at the time of its purchase or prepayment. When is it best to ignore this and record the prepayment as an expense? Why?
8. What kind of assets require adjusting entries for depreciation?
9. What is a contra account? Give an example.
10. What contra account is used to record depreciation? Why is such an account used?
11. If a building is purchased for $100,000 and depreciation of $2,500 is taken each year, what amount of accumulated depreciation will appear in the balance sheet at the end of five years?
12. What is an accrued expense? Give an example.
13. How does an unearned revenue arise? Give an example of an unearned revenue.
14. What is the balance sheet classification of an unearned revenue?
15. What is an accrued revenue? Give an example.
16. When financial statements are prepared from an adjusted trial balance, why should the income statement be prepared first? What statement is prepared next?
17. Which accounting principles provide the basis for the adjustment process?

18. What is required by the matching principle?
19. Is the cash basis of accounting consistent with the matching principle?
20. What is the difference between the cash and accrual bases of accounting?
21. What are the typical classes of assets and liabilities shown on a classified balance sheet?
22. What are characteristics of a current asset?
23. What is meant by the operating cycle of a business?
24. What are some examples of assets that are shown in the investments category of the balance sheet?
25. What are the characteristics of assets classified as plant and equipment?
26. A local fast-food restaurant paid $20,000 for a franchise that identifies the restaurant as belonging to a nationally recognized chain of restaurants. How should this asset be classified on the local restaurant's balance sheet?
27. What are current liabilities? Long-term liabilities?
28. What are the two classes of equity on the balance sheet of a corporation?

*29. If a company records its prepaid expenses with debits to expense accounts, what type of account does it debit in making end-of-period adjustments for prepaid expenses?

*30. Bee Company records revenues received in advance with credits to liability accounts, while Cee Company records revenues received in advance with credits to revenues accounts. Will these companies have differences in their financial statements as a result of this difference in their procedures? Why or why not?

## Exercises

**Exercise 3–1**
**Adjusting entries for accrued expenses**
(L. O. 2)

A company's two employees earn a total of $225 per day for a five-day week that begins on Monday and ends on Friday. They were paid for the week ended Friday, December 28, and both worked a full day on Monday, December 31. January 1 of the next year was an unpaid holiday, but the employees all worked on Wednesday, Thursday, and Friday, January 2, 3, and 4. Journalize the year-end adjusting entry to record the accrued wages and the entry to pay the employees on January 4.

**Exercise 3–2**
**Adjusting entries for expenses**
(L. O. 2)

Prepare adjusting journal entries on December 31, 1990, prior to the preparation of annual financial statements, for the following independent situations:

*a.* The Shop Supplies account had a $350 debit balance on January 1, 1990; $625 of supplies were purchased during the year; and a year-end inventory showed $180 of supplies on hand.

*b.* The Prepaid Insurance account had a $950 debit balance at the end of the accounting period before adjustment for expired insurance. An examination of insurance policies showed $560 of insurance expired.

*c.* The Prepaid Insurance account had a $780 debit balance at the end of the accounting period before adjustment for expired insurance. An examination of insurance policies showed $375 of unexpired insurance.

*d.* Depreciation on shop equipment was estimated at $1,350 for the accounting period.

*e.* Four months' property taxes, estimated at $848, have accrued but are unrecorded and unpaid at the accounting period end.

**Exercise 3–3**
**Omission of adjusting entries**
(L. O. 1, 2)

Assume that the required adjustments of Exercise 3–2 were not made at the end of the accounting period. For each adjustment, tell the effect of its omission on the income statement and balance sheet prepared at that time.

**Exercise 3–4**
**Missing data in calculations of supplies**
(L. O. 2)

Determine the amounts indicated by the question marks in the columns below. The amounts in each column constitute a separate problem.

| | (a) | (b) | (c) | (d) |
|---|---|---|---|---|
| Supplies on hand on January 1 . . . . . . | $350 | $210 | $560 | $ ? |
| Supplies purchased during the year . . . . | 675 | 795 | ? | 945 |
| Supplies remaining at the year-end . . . . | 250 | ? | 325 | 360 |
| Supplies expense for the year . . . . . . . | ? | 720 | 905 | 840 |

**Exercise 3–5**
**Adjustments and payments of accrued items**
(L. O. 2, 4)

Prepare adjusting journal entries dated April 30 for the following items. Then prepare journal entries to record the May payments.

*a.* Employees are paid total salaries of $2,400 each Friday after they complete a five-day workweek. As of April 30, the employees had worked four days since the last payment. The next payment date is May 1.

*b.* On April 1, the company retained a lawyer at a monthly fee of $250 payable on the 12th of the following month.

*c.* The company owes a $15,000 note payable, which requires that 1% interest be paid each month on the 20th of the month. The interest was paid April 20 and the next payment is due May 20.

**Exercise 3–6**
**Cash basis versus accrual basis expense amounts**
(L. O. 3)

A company paid the $1,080 premium on a three-year insurance policy on October 1, 1990. The policy gave protection beginning on that date.

*a.* Assuming the accrual basis of accounting, how many dollars of the premium will appear as an expense on the annual income statement for 1990? for 1991? for 1992? for 1993?

*b.* Assuming the accrual basis, how many dollars of the premium will appear as an asset on each December 31 balance sheet for 1990? for 1991? for 1992? for 1993?

*c.* Assuming the cash basis of accounting, how many dollars of the premium will appear as an expense on the annual income statement for 1990? for 1991? for 1992? for 1993?

*d.* Assuming the cash basis, how many dollars of the premium will appear as an asset on each December 31 balance sheet for 1990? for 1991? for 1992? for 1993?

**Exercise 3–7**
**Unearned and accrued revenues**
(L. O. 2, 4)

The owner of a building prepares annual financial statements based on a calendar-year accounting period.

*a.* A tenant rented space in the building on November 1 at $450 per month, paying six months' rent in advance. The receipt was credited to Unearned Rent. Give the December 31 adjusting entry of the building owner, prior to the preparation of annual financial statements.

*b.* Another tenant rented space in the building at $525 per month on November 1. The tenant paid the November rent on the first day of November, but by December 31 the December rent had not yet been paid. Give the December 31 adjusting entry of the building owner.

*c.* Assume the tenant in *(b)* paid the rent for December and January on January 3 of the new year. Give the entry to record the receipt of the $1,050.

**Exercise 3–8**
**Classified balance sheet**
(L. O. 5)

The adjusted trial balance that follows was taken from the ledger of Laura Shipley, Attorney. Calculate the amount of owner's equity on December 31, 1990, and prepare a classified year-end balance sheet for the practice.

**LAURA SHIPLEY, ATTORNEY**
**Adjusted Trial Balance**
**December 31, 1990**

| | | |
|---|---|---|
| Cash | $ 2,250 | |
| Accounts receivable | 4,800 | |
| Prepaid insurance | 1,050 | |
| Office supplies | 150 | |
| Investment in X-Ray Corporation common stock | 20,000 | |
| Office equipment | 15,750 | |
| Accumulated depreciation, office equipment | | $ 4,500 |
| Building | 145,000 | |
| Accumulated depreciation, building | | 15,000 |
| Land | 60,000 | |
| Salaries payable | | 300 |
| Unearned legal fees | | 1,200 |
| Long-term notes payable | | 142,500 |
| Laura Shipley, capital | | 72,000 |
| Laura Shipley, withdrawals | 54,000 | |
| Legal fees earned | | 127,500 |
| Operating expenses (combined) | 60,000 | |
| Totals | $363,000 | $363,000 |

**Exercise 3–9**
**Analyzing statements for adjusting entries**
(L. O. 2)

An inexperienced bookkeeper prepared the income statement shown below in columns 1 and 2, but he forgot to adjust the accounts before its preparation. However, the oversight was discovered, and the statement in columns 3 and 4 was prepared. Analyze the statements and prepare the adjusting journal entries that were made between the preparation of the two statements. Assume that one third of the additional property management fees resulted from recognizing accrued fees and two thirds resulted from previously recorded unearned fees that were earned by the date of the statements.

**MASON REALTY**
**Income Statement**
**For Year Ended December 31, 1990**

| | Prepared without Adjustments | | Prepared after Adjustments | |
|---|---|---|---|---|
| Revenues: | | | | |
| Commissions earned | | $82,125 | | $82,125 |
| Property management fees | | 4,500 | | 5,625 |
| Total revenues | | $86,625 | | $87,750 |
| Operating expenses: | | | | |
| Salaries expense | $17,250 | | $18,000 | |
| Rent expense | 13,500 | | 13,500 | |
| Advertising expense | 3,750 | | 3,750 | |
| Gas, oil, and repairs expense | 750 | | 750 | |
| Office supplies expense | | | 150 | |
| Insurance expense | | | 1,350 | |
| Depreciation expense, office equipment | | | 1,500 | |
| Depreciation expense, automobile | | | 3,000 | |
| Total operating expenses | | 35,250 | | 42,000 |
| Net income | | $51,375 | | $45,750 |

**Exercise 3–10**
**Balance sheet equity section for a corporation**
(L. O. 5)

A corporation had $375,000 of common stock issued and outstanding during all of 1990. It began the year with $95,000 of retained earnings, and it declared and paid $30,000 of cash dividends to its stockholders. It also earned a $75,000 net income during 1990. Prepare the equity section of the corporation's year-end balance sheet.

**Exercise 3–11**
**Calculating elements of change in owner's equity**
(Review exercise)

Calculate the missing item in each of the following cases:

| | Case 1 | Case 2 | Case 3 | Case 4 | Case 5 |
|---|---|---|---|---|---|
| The Owner, capital, January 1, 1990 | $95,000 | $76,000 | $ *(c)* | $55,500 | $38,000 |
| Total revenues during 1990 | 84,000 | *(b)* | 65,200 | 67,600 | 46,600 |
| Total expenses during 1990 | 56,500 | 37,200 | 72,000 | *(d)* | 37,500 |
| Withdrawals during the year | 45,000 | 21,000 | 12,800 | 18,000 | *(e)* |
| The Owner, capital, December 31, 1990 | *(a)* | 84,400 | 49,300 | 52,100 | 32,000 |

***Exercise 3–12**
**Adjustments for prepaid items recorded in expense and revenue accounts**
(L. O. 7)

Ace Consulting was organized on December 1 and follows the procedure of debiting expense accounts when it records prepayments of expenses; also, revenue accounts are credited when unearned revenues are received. Prepare adjusting journal entries on December 31 for the following items:

*a.* Shop Supplies were purchased during December for $975. A December 31 inventory showed that $180 of supplies were on hand.

*b.* The company paid insurance premiums of $1,260 during December. On December 31, an examination of the insurance policies showed that $210 of insurance had expired.

*c.* During December, the business received $1,900 from one client for two consulting projects. As of December 31, only one project, for which the client was charged $1,100, had been completed.

*d.* Late in December, the business received $1,500 from a second client for consulting services to be performed in January.

***Exercise 3–13**
**Adjustments for supplies when purchases were recorded as expenses**
(L. O. 7)

Ideas Company prepares monthly financial statements. On June 30, the balance in the Office Supplies account was $400. During July, $740 of supplies were purchased and debited to Office Supplies Expense.

*a.* Prepare an adjusting journal entry on July 31 to account for the supplies, assuming a July 31 inventory of supplies showed that $325 of supplies were on hand.

*b.* Prepare an adjusting journal entry on July 31 to account for the supplies, assuming a July 31 inventory of supplies showed that $500 of supplies were on hand.

## Problems

**Problem 3–1**
**Adjusting journal entries**
(L. O. 2, 4)

The following information for adjustments was available on December 31, 1990, the end of Tuft Company's annual accounting period:

*a.* The Store Supplies account had a $150 debit balance at the beginning of the year, $675 of supplies were purchased during the year, and an inventory of unused supplies at year-end totaled $180.

*b.* An examination of insurance policies showed three policies, as follows:

| Policy | Date of Purchase | Life of Policy | Cost | 1989 | 1990 |
|---|---|---|---|---|---|
| 1 . . . . | September 1, 1989 | 3 years | $2,100 | 233.34 | 700.00 |
| 2 . . . . | March 1, 1990 | 2 years | 840 | | 350.00 |
| 3 . . . . | July 1, 1990 | 1 year | 576 | | 288 |

Prepaid Insurance was debited for the cost of each policy at the time of its purchase. Expired insurance was correctly recorded at the end of 1989.

*c.* The company's two employees earn $60 per day and $70 per day, respectively. They are paid each Friday for a five-day workweek that begins on Monday. This year, December 31 fell on Wednesday, and the employees both worked on Monday, Tuesday, and Wednesday. The next payment for five days' work will be on January 2.

*d.* The company purchased a building on April 1, 1990. The building cost $435,000, has an estimated 25-year life, and is not expected to have any salvage value at the end of that time.

*e.* The company occupies most of the space in its building but it also rents space. One tenant rented a small amount of space on October 1 at $500 per month. The tenant paid the rent on the first day of October and November, and the amounts paid were credited to Rent Earned. However, the tenant did not pay the December rent until January 10, 1991, at which time he also paid the rent for January.

*f.* Another tenant agreed on November 1 to rent a small amount of space at $540 per month, and on that date paid three months' rent in advance. The receipt was credited to Unearned Rent.

*Required*

1. Given the above information, journalize adjusting entries dated December 31, 1990, prior to the preparation of annual financial statements.
2. Prepare journal entries to record the January payments and receipts that involve amounts which were accrued on December 31.

Problem 3–2
**Adjusting entries and the adjusted trial balance**
(L. O. 2, 5)

Century Realty's unadjusted trial balance on December 31, 1990, the end of its annual accounting period, is as follows:

**CENTURY REALTY**
**Trial Balance**
**December 31, 1990**

| | | |
|---|---|---|
| Cash | $ 2,500 | |
| Prepaid insurance | 2,100 | |
| Office supplies | 555 | |
| Office equipment | 7,500 | |
| Accumulated depreciation, office equipment | | $ 2,500 |
| Automobile | 15,350 | |
| Accumulated depreciation, automobile | | 3,000 |
| Accounts payable | | 275 |
| Unearned management fees | | 540 |
| Don Miller, capital | | 15,000 |
| Don Miller, withdrawals | 22,500 | |
| Sales commissions earned | | 49,400 |
| Office salaries expense | 12,360 | |
| Advertising expense | 1,200 | |
| Rent expense | 6,000 | |
| Telephone expense | 650 | |
| Totals | $70,715 | $70,715 |

*Required*

1. Set up accounts for the items in the trial balance plus these additional accounts: Accounts Receivable; Office Salaries Payable; Management Fees Earned; Insurance Expense; Office Supplies Expense; Depreciation Expense, Office Equipment; and Depreciation Expense, Automobile. Enter the trial balance amounts in the accounts.
2. Use the following information to prepare and post adjusting entries:
   *a.* An examination of insurance policies shows $775 of expired insurance.
   *b.* An inventory shows $75 of unused office supplies on hand.
   *c.* Estimated annual depreciation on the office equipment is $935.
   *d.* Estimated annual depreciation on the automobile is $2,100.
   *e.* Century Realty offers property management services. On November 1, the company agreed to manage an office building for a client. The contract calls for a $180 monthly fee, and the client paid the first three months' fees in advance at the time the contract was signed. The amount paid was credited to the Unearned Management Fees account.

*f.* On October 15, the company agreed to manage an apartment building for $120 per month payable at the end of each three-month period. Fees for two and one-half months have accrued.

*g.* The one office employee is paid weekly; and on December 31, three days' wages at $55 per day have accrued.

3. After posting the adjusting entries, prepare an adjusted trial balance, an income statement, a statement of changes in owner's equity, and a classified balance sheet. Miller did not make additional investments in the business during the year.

**Problem 3–3**
**Adjusting entries and the adjusted trial balance**
(L. O. 2, 5)

The unadjusted trial balance of Countrywide Moving and Storage follows:

**COUNTRYWIDE MOVING AND STORAGE**
**Trial Balance**
**December 31, 1990**

| | | |
|---|---|---|
| Cash | $ 2,990 | |
| Accounts receivable | 775 | |
| Prepaid insurance | 4,500 | |
| Office supplies | 485 | |
| Investment in Trail, Inc., common stock | 10,000 | |
| Office equipment | 4,500 | |
| Accumulated depreciation, office equipment | | $ 2,000 |
| Trucks | 54,000 | |
| Accumulated depreciation, trucks | | 14,000 |
| Building | 160,000 | |
| Accumulated depreciation, building | | 35,000 |
| Land | 21,000 | |
| Franchise | 30,000 | |
| Unearned storage fees | | 2,075 |
| Long-term notes payable | | 144,000 |
| Dennis Meade, capital | | 65,000 |
| Dennis Meade, withdrawals | 29,000 | |
| Revenue from moving services | | 110,000 |
| Storage fees earned | | 8,325 |
| Office salaries expense | 13,745 | |
| Drivers' and helpers' wages expense | 32,950 | |
| Gas, oil, and repairs expense | 3,525 | |
| Interest expense | 12,930 | |
| Totals | $380,400 | $380,400 |

*Required*

1. Set up accounts for the items in the trial balance plus these additional accounts: Salaries and Wages Payable; Insurance Expense; Office Supplies Expense; Depreciation Expense, Office Equipment; Depreciation Expense, Trucks; and Depreciation Expense, Building. Enter the trial balance amounts in the accounts.
2. Journalize and post adjusting entries given the following information:
   *a.* Insurance premiums of $2,820 expired during the year.
   *b.* An inventory showed $165 of unused office supplies on hand.
   *c.* Estimated depreciation on the office equipment, $545; *(d)* on the trucks, $5,300; and *(e)* on the building, $6,700.
   *f.* Of the $2,075 credit balance in Unearned Storage Fees, $1,700 was earned by the year-end.
   *g.* Accrued storage fees earned but unrecorded at year-end totaled $315.

*h.* There were $730 of earned but unrecorded drivers' and helpers' wages at the year-end.

3. Prepare an adjusted trial balance, an income statement for the year, a statement of changes in owner's equity, and a classified year-end balance sheet. Meade's capital account balance reflects the December 31, 1989, balance plus a January 1, 1990, investment of $50,000. A $4,800 installment on the note payable is due within one year.

**Problem 3–4**
**Adjusting entries and the adjusted trial balance**
(L. O. 2, 5)

Crestview Trailer Park's unadjusted trial balance is as follows:

**CRESTVIEW TRAILER PARK**
**Trial Balance**
**December 31, 1990**

| | | |
|---|---|---|
| Cash | $ 3,350 | |
| Prepaid insurance | 1,830 | |
| Office supplies | 415 | |
| Office equipment | 2,940 | |
| Accumulated depreciation, office equipment | | $ 975 |
| Buildings and improvements | 110,000 | |
| Accumulated depreciation, buildings and improvements | | 25,620 |
| Land | 114,000 | |
| Unearned rent | | 935 |
| Long-term notes payable | | 142,000 |
| Ida Henry, capital | | 50,100 |
| Ida Henry, withdrawals | 22,000 | |
| Rent earned | | 62,235 |
| Wages expense | 12,200 | |
| Utilities expense | 995 | |
| Property taxes expense | 2,455 | |
| Interest expense | 11,680 | |
| Totals | $281,865 | $281,865 |

*Required*

1. Set up accounts for the items in the trial balance plus these additional accounts: Accounts Receivable; Wages Payable; Property Taxes Payable; Interest Payable; Insurance Expense; Office Supplies Expense; Depreciation Expense, Office Equipment; and Depreciation Expense, Buildings and Improvements. Enter the trial balance amounts in the accounts.
2. Use the following information to prepare and post adjusting journal entries:
   *a.* An insurance policy examination showed $1,400 of expired insurance.
   *b.* An inventory showed $140 of unused office supplies on hand.
   *c.* Estimated depreciation expense on office equipment, $350; and *(d)* on buildings and improvements, $5,500.
   *e.* By year-end, $690 of the Unearned Rent account balance was earned.
   *f.* A tenant is in arrears on rent payments, and this $100 of accrued revenue was unrecorded at the time the trial balance was prepared.

*g.* The one employee of the trailer park works a five-day workweek at $50 per day. The employee was paid last week but has worked three days this week for which he has not been paid.

*h.* Three months' property taxes, totaling $789, have accrued. This additional amount of property taxes expense has not been recorded.

*i.* One month's interest on the note payable, $1,000, has accrued but is unrecorded.

3. Post the adjusting entries and prepare an adjusted trial balance, an income statement for the year, a statement of changes in owner's equity, and a classified balance sheet. Ms. Henry's capital account balance has not been increased by investments during 1990. A $7,200 installment on the note payable is due within one year.

**Problem 3–5**
**Accrual basis income statement**
(L. O. 3, 5)

Lily Kent purchased Pecan Grove, a mobile home park, last September 1, and she has operated it four months without keeping formal accounting records. However, she has deposited all receipts in the bank and has kept an accurate checkbook record of payments. An analysis of the cash receipts and payments follows:

| | | Receipts | Payments |
|---|---|---|---|
| Investment | | $52,000 | |
| Purchased Pecan Grove: | | | |
| Office equipment | $ 1,500 | | |
| Buildings and improvements | 90,000 | | |
| Land | 105,000 | | |
| Total | $196,500 | | |
| Less long-term note payable signed | 145,000 | | |
| Cash paid | | | $51,500 |
| Insurance premium paid | | | 1,140 |
| Office supplies purchased | | | 144 |
| Wages paid | | | 4,000 |
| Utilities paid | | | 450 |
| Property taxes paid | | | 1,500 |
| Owner's withdrawals of cash | | | 4,800 |
| Mobile home space rentals collected | | 19,380 | |
| Totals | | $71,380 | $63,534 |
| Cash balance, December 31 | | | 7,846 |
| Totals | | $71,380 | $71,380 |

Ms. Kent wants you to prepare an accrual basis income statement for the village for the four-month period she has operated the business, a statement of changes in owner's equity, and a December 31 balance sheet. You ascertain the following (T-accounts may be helpful in organizing the data):

The buildings and improvements were estimated to have a 25-year remaining life when purchased and at the end of that time will be wrecked. It is estimated that the sale of salvaged materials will just pay the wrecking costs and the cost of clearing the site. The office equipment is in good condition. At the time of purchase, Ms. Kent estimated she would use the equipment for three years and would then trade it in on new equipment of like kind. She thought

$150 a fair estimate of what she would receive for the old equipment when she traded it in at the end of three years.

The $1,140 payment for insurance was for a policy taken out on September 1. The policy's protection was for one year beginning on that date. Ms. Kent estimates that one third of the office supplies purchased have been used. She also says that the one employee of the park earns $50 per day for a five-day week that ends on Friday. The employee was paid last week but has worked four days, December 28 through 31, for which he has not been paid.

Included in the $19,380 of mobile home rentals collected is $360 received from a tenant for three months' rent beginning on December 1. Also, a tenant has not paid his $120 rent for the month of December.

The long-term note payable requires an annual payment of 12% interest on the beginning principal balance plus a $6,000 annual payment on the principal. The first payment is due next September 1. The property tax payment was for one year's taxes that were paid on October 1 for the tax year beginning on September 1, the day Ms. Kent purchased the business.

***Problem 3–6**
**Recording prepayments and unearned items in income statement accounts**
(L. O. 2, 7)

Setter Company debits expense accounts when recording prepaid expenses; it credits revenue accounts when recording unearned receipts. The following information was available on December 31, 1990, the end of the company's annual accounting period.

*a.* The Store Supplies account had a $340 debit balance at the beginning of the year, $1,250 of supplies were purchased during the year, and an inventory of unused supplies at the year-end totaled $620.

*b.* An examination of insurance policies showed two policies, as follows:

| Policy | Date of Purchase | Life of Policy | Cost |
|---|---|---|---|
| 1 . . . . | May 1, 1988 | 3 years | $2,340 |
| 2 . . . . | October 1, 1990 | 2 years | 2,280 |

Insurance Expense was debited for the cost of each policy at the time of its purchase. However, the correct amount of Prepaid Insurance was recorded during the adjustment processes at the end of 1988 and 1989.

*c.* On October 15, 1990, Setter Company agreed to provide consulting services to a client and received advance payment of $8,500. At year-end, the client agreed that three fourths of the services had been provided.

*d.* The company occupies most of the space in its building but it also rents space to one tenant. The tenant agreed on November 1 to rent a small amount of space at $750 per month, and on that date paid three months' rent in advance.

*e.* The Office Supplies account had a $550 debit balance at the beginning of the year and $750 of supplies were purchased during the year. A year-end inventory of office supplies indicated that supplies amounting to $990 had been used during the year.

*Required*

Prepare adjusting journal entries dated December 31, 1990, prior to the preparation of annual financial statements. For item *(b)*, prepare a separate adjusting entry for each insurance policy.

## Alternate Problems

**Problem 3–1A**
**Adjusting journal entries**
(L. O. 2, 4)

The following information for preparing adjusting entries was available on December 31, 1990, the end of Shiff Company's annual accounting period.

*a.* The Store Supplies account had a $175 debit balance at the beginning of the year, $845 of supplies were purchased during the year, and an inventory of unused supplies at year-end totaled $185.

*b.* An examination of insurance policies showed three policies, as follows:

| Policy | Protection Began on | Life of Policy | Cost |
|---|---|---|---|
| 1 . . . . | March 12, 1989 | 3 years | $1,260 |
| 2 . . . . | May 1, 1990 | 2 years | 810 |
| 3 . . . . | April 1, 1990 | 1 year | 600 |

Prepaid Insurance was debited for the cost of each policy at the time of purchase. Expired insurance was correctly recorded at the end of 1989.

*c.* The company's two employees earn $60 per day and $75 per day, respectively. They are paid each Friday for a five-day workweek that begins on Monday. December 31 fell on Tuesday, and the employees both worked on Monday and Tuesday but have not been paid. The next payment for five days' work will be on January 3.

*d.* The company purchased a building on July 1, 1990. The building cost $675,000, has an estimated 25-year life, and is not expected to have any salvage value at the end of its life.

*e.* The company occupies most of the space in its building, but it also rents space. One tenant rented a small amount of space on September 1 at $300 per month. The tenant paid the rent on the first day of each month, September through November, and the amounts paid were credited to Rent Earned. However, the tenant did not pay the December rent until January 12, at which time he also paid the rent for January.

*f.* Another tenant agreed on November 1 to rent a small amount of space at $335 per month and on that date paid three months' rent in advance. The amount paid was credited to Unearned Rent.

*Required*

1. Given the above information, journalize adjusting entries dated December 31, 1990, prior to the preparation of annual financial statements.
2. Prepare journal entries to record the January payments and receipts that involve amounts which were accrued on December 31.

**Problem 3–2A**
**Adjusting entries and the adjusted trial balance**
(L. O. 2, 5)

Miller Realty's unadjusted trial balance on December 31, 1990, the end of its annual accounting period, is as follows:

**MILLER REALTY**
**Trial Balance**
**December 31, 1990**

| | | |
|---|---|---|
| Cash | $ 2,910 | |
| Prepaid insurance | 1,375 | |
| Office supplies | 435 | |
| Office equipment | 9,375 | |
| Accumulated depreciation, office equipment | | $ 2,880 |
| Automobile | 19,150 | |
| Accumulated depreciation, automobile | | 3,225 |
| Accounts payable | | 335 |
| Unearned management fees | | 675 |
| Don Miller, capital | | 16,700 |
| Don Miller, withdrawals | 27,900 | |
| Sales commissions earned | | 61,920 |
| Office salaries expense | 15,450 | |
| Advertising expense | 1,245 | |
| Rent expense | 7,200 | |
| Telephone expense | 695 | |
| Totals | $85,735 | $85,735 |

*Required*

1. Set up accounts for the items in the trial balance plus these additional accounts: Accounts Receivable; Office Salaries Payable; Management Fees Earned; Insurance Expense; Office Supplies Expense; Depreciation Expense, Office Equipment; and Depreciation Expense, Automobile. Enter the trial balance amounts in the accounts.
2. Use the information that follows to prepare and post adjusting entries:
   *a.* An examination of insurance policies shows $1,085 of expired insurance.
   *b.* An inventory shows $120 of unused office supplies on hand.
   *c.* Estimated annual depreciation on the office equipment is $1,225.
   *d.* Estimated annual depreciation on the automobile is $2,665.
   *e.* The December telephone bill arrived after the trial balance was prepared, and its $60 amount was not included in the trial balance amounts. Also, a $165 bill for newspaper advertising that had appeared in December was not included in the trial balance amounts.
   *f.* A client who was taking a tour around the world signed a contract with Miller Realty for the management of his apartment building. The contract calls for a $225 monthly fee, and management began on December 1. The client paid three months' fees in advance, and the amount paid was credited to the Unearned Management Fees account.
   *g.* Miller Realty agreed to manage the small office building of a second client for $250 per month payable at the end of each three months. The contract was signed on November 15, and one and one-half months' fees have accrued.
   *h.* The one office employee is paid weekly; and on December 31, four days' wages at $60 per day have accrued.
3. After posting the adjusting entries, prepare an adjusted trial balance, an

income statement, a statement of changes in owner's equity, and a classified balance sheet. Miller's capital account balance of $16,700 consists of a $6,700 balance on December 31, 1989, plus a $10,000 investment during 1990.

**Problem 3–3A**
**Adjusting entries and the adjusted trial balance**
(L. O. 2, 5)

The unadjusted trial balance of United Moving and Storage follows:

**UNITED MOVING AND STORAGE**
**Trial Balance**
**December 31, 1990**

| | | |
|---|---|---|
| Cash | $ 3,360 | |
| Accounts receivable | 815 | |
| Prepaid insurance | 5,370 | |
| Office supplies | 480 | |
| Investment in Trail, Inc., common stock | 25,000 | |
| Office equipment | 5,475 | |
| Accumulated depreciation, office equipment | | $ 2,520 |
| Trucks | 66,300 | |
| Accumulated depreciation, trucks | | 17,300 |
| Building | 207,000 | |
| Accumulated depreciation, building | | 42,900 |
| Land | 26,250 | |
| Franchise | 20,000 | |
| Unearned storage fees | | 2,595 |
| Long-term notes payable | | 180,000 |
| Dennis Meade, capital | | 81,170 |
| Dennis Meade, withdrawals | 36,000 | |
| Revenue from moving services | | 135,170 |
| Storage fees earned | | 11,660 |
| Office salaries expense | 17,100 | |
| Drivers' and helpers' wages expense | 39,945 | |
| Gas, oil, and repairs expense | 4,020 | |
| Interest expense | 16,200 | |
| Totals | $473,315 | $473,315 |

*Required*

1. Set up accounts for the items in the trial balance plus these additional accounts: Salaries and Wages Payable; Insurance Expense; Office Supplies Expense; Depreciation Expense, Office Equipment; Depreciation Expense, Trucks; and Depreciation Expense, Building. Enter the trial balance amounts in the accounts.
2. Use the information that follows to prepare and post adjusting entries:
   *a.* Insurance premiums of $4,225 expired during the year.
   *b.* An inventory shows $165 of unused office supplies on hand.
   *c.* Estimated depreciation on the office equipment, $775; *(d)* on the trucks, $8,000; and *(e)* on the building, $9,300.
   *f.* Of the $2,595 balance in the Unearned Storage Fees account, $1,985 was earned by the year-end.
   *g.* Accrued storage fees earned but unrecorded at year-end totaled $515.
   *h.* There were $200 of earned but unrecorded office salaries and $1,135 of earned but unrecorded drivers' and helpers' wages at the year-end.
3. Prepare an adjusted trial balance, an income statement for the year, a

statement of changes in owner's equity, and a classified year-end balance sheet. Meade's $81,170 capital balance reflects the December 31, 1989, balance plus a January 15, 1990, investment of $30,000. A $9,000 installment on the long-term note payable is due within one year.

**Problem 3–4A**
**Adjusting entries and the adjusted trial balance**
(L. O. 2, 5)

Bel-Aire Trailer Park's unadjusted trial balance, at the end of its annual accounting period, follows:

**BEL-AIRE TRAILER PARK**
**Trial Balance**
**December 31, 1990**

| | | |
|---|---|---|
| Cash | $ 3,810 | |
| Prepaid insurance | 2,285 | |
| Office supplies | 390 | |
| Office equipment | 3,675 | |
| Accumulated depreciation, office equipment | | $ 1,225 |
| Buildings and improvements | 138,000 | |
| Accumulated depreciation, buildings and improvements | | 32,025 |
| Land | 142,500 | |
| Unearned rent | | 1,170 |
| Long-term notes payable | | 177,000 |
| Ida Henry, capital | | 62,710 |
| Ida Henry, withdrawals | 27,300 | |
| Rent earned | | 77,800 |
| Wages expense | 15,180 | |
| Utilities expense | 1,240 | |
| Property taxes expense | 2,950 | |
| Interest expense | 14,600 | |
| Totals | $351,930 | $351,930 |

*Required*

1. Set up accounts for the items in the trial balance plus these additional accounts: Accounts Receivable; Wages Payable; Property Taxes Payable; Interest Payable; Insurance Expense; Office Supplies Expense; Depreciation Expense, Office Equipment; and Depreciation Expense, Buildings and Improvements. Enter the trial balance amounts in the accounts.
2. Use the information that follows to prepare and post adjusting journal entries:
   *a.* An insurance policy examination shows $1,850 of expired insurance.
   *b.* An inventory shows $125 of unused office supplies on hand.
   *c.* Estimated depreciation of office equipment, $465; and *(d)* of buildings and improvements, $7,875.
   *e.* An examination reveals that $665 of the Unearned Rent balance was earned by the year-end.
   *f.* One tenant is in arrears on rent payments, and this $150 of accrued revenue was unrecorded at the time the trial balance was prepared.
   *g.* Four months' property taxes expense, estimated at $1,500, has accrued but was not recorded at the time the trial balance was prepared.
   *h.* The one employee of the trailer park works a five-day week at $60 per day. He was paid last week but has worked four days this week for which he has not been paid.

*i.* Three months' interest on the note payable, $4,866, has accrued but is unpaid on the trial balance date.

3. Post the adjusting entries and prepare an adjusted trial balance, an income statement for the year, a statement of changes in owner's equity, and a classified balance sheet. Ms. Henry's capital account balance has not been increased by investments during 1990. An $8,250 payment on the long-term note payable is due within one year.

**Problem 3–5A**
**Accrual basis income statement**
(L. O. 3, 5)

James Piper, a lawyer, has always kept his records on a cash basis; at the end of 1990, he prepared the following cash basis income statement:

**JAMES PIPER, ATTORNEY**
**Income Statement**
**For Year Ended December 31, 1990**

| | |
|---|---|
| Revenues . . . . . . . . . . | 95,500 |
| Expenses . . . . . . . . . . | 40,450 |
| Net income . . . . . . . . . | $55,050 |

In preparing the statement, the following amounts of prepaid, unearned, and accrued items were ignored at the end of 1989 and 1990:

| | End of | |
|---|---|---|
| | **1989** | **1990** |
| Prepaid expenses . . . . . | $2,310 | $1,800 |
| Accrued expenses . . . . | 2,595 | 3,270 |
| Unearned revenues . . . . | 3,300 | 5,430 |
| Accrued revenues . . . . . | 4,550 | 3,660 |

*Required*

Under the assumptions that the 1989 prepaid expenses were consumed or expired in 1990, the 1989 unearned revenues were earned in 1990, and the 1989 accrued items were either paid or received in cash in 1990, prepare a 1990 accrual basis income statement for James Piper's law practice. Attach to your statement calculations showing how you arrived at each 1990 income statement amount.

***Problem 3–6A**
**Recording prepayments and unearned items in income statement accounts**
(L. O. 2, 7)

In recording prepaid expenses and unearned revenues, Nickle Company debits the disbursements to expense accounts and credits the receipts to revenue accounts. The following information was available on December 31, 1990, the end of the Nickle Company's annual accounting period:

*a.* The Store Supplies account had an $880 debit balance at the beginning of the year, $1,790 of supplies were purchased during the year, and an inventory of unused supplies at the year-end totaled $1,320.

*b.* An examination of insurance policies showed two policies, as follows:

| **Policy** | **Date of Purchase** | **Life of Policy** | **Cost** |
|---|---|---|---|
| 1 . . . . | April 1, 1988 | 3 years | $3,528 |
| 2 . . . . | August 1, 1990 | 2 years | 3,408 |

Insurance Expense was debited for the cost of each policy at the time of its purchase. However, the correct amount of Prepaid Insurance was recorded during the adjustment processes at the end of 1988 and 1989.

*c.* On July 20, 1990, Nickle Company agreed to provide consulting services to a client and received advance payment of $12,900. At year-end, the client agreed that two thirds of the services had been provided.

*d.* The company occupies most of the space in its building but it also rents space to one tenant. The tenant agreed on October 1 to rent a small amount of space at $900 per month, and on that date paid four months' rent in advance.

*e.* The Office Supplies account had a $620 debit balance at the beginning of the year and $1,350 of supplies were purchased during the year. A year-end inventory of office supplies indicated that supplies amounting to $1,050 had been used during the year.

*Required*

Prepare adjusting journal entries dated December 31, 1990, prior to the preparation of annual financial statements. For item *(b)*, prepare a separate adjusting entry for each insurance policy.

## Provocative Problems

**Provocative Problem 3–1**
**Kidd Management Services**
(L. O. 3)

The 1989 and 1990 balance sheets of Kidd Management Services show the following assets and liabilities at the end of each of the years:

| | December 31 | |
|---|---|---|
| | **1989** | **1990** |
| Prepaid insurance . . . . . . . . . . . . . . . | $1,580 | $1,140 |
| Property management fees receivable . . . . | 900 | 1,675 |
| Interest payable . . . . . . . . . . . . . . . . | 375 | 310 |
| Unearned property management fees . . . . | 890 | 1,220 |

The concern's records show the following amounts of cash disbursed and received for these items during 1990:

| | |
|---|---|
| Cash disbursed to pay insurance premiums . . | $2,470 |
| Cash disbursed to pay interest . . . . . . . . . | 1,750 |
| Cash received for managing property . . . . . | 9,720 |

Present calculations to show the amounts to be reported on Kidd Management Services' 1990 income statement for *(a)* insurance expense, *(b)* interest expense, and *(c)* property management fees earned.

**Provocative Problem 3–2**
**Field Electrical Service**
(L. O. 3, 5)

Jay Field began Field Electrical Service, a new business, on January 2, 1990. After one year's operations, Jay feels the business has done a lot of work during its first year. However, the bank has begun to dishonor its checks. The company's creditors are dunning it for bills it is unable to pay, and Jay just cannot understand why. Consequently, he has asked your help in determining the results of the first year's operations.

You find that the service's accounting records, such as they are, have been kept by Jay's son, who has no formal training in record-keeping. However, he has prepared for your inspection the following statement of cash receipts and disbursements:

**FIELD ELECTRICAL SERVICE**
**Cash Receipts and Disbursements**
**For Year Ended December 31, 1990**

| | | |
|---|---|---|
| Receipts: | | |
| Owner's investment | $18,000 | |
| Received from customers for services | 53,300 | $71,300 |
| Disbursements: | | |
| Rent expense | $ 4,875 | |
| Repair equipment purchased | 8,100 | |
| Service truck expense | 15,470 | |
| Wages expense | 28,080 | |
| Insurance expense. | 1,905 | |
| Repair parts and supplies | 12,975 | 71,405 |
| Bank overdraft | | $ (105) |

There were no errors in the statement, and you learn these additional facts:

1. The lease contract for the shop space runs for five years and requires rent payments of $375 per month, with the first and last month's rent to be paid in advance. All required payments were made on time.
2. The repair equipment has an estimated six-year life, after which it will be valueless. It has been used a full year.
3. The service truck expense consists of $13,800 paid for the truck on January 2, plus $1,670 paid for gas and oil. Mr. Field expects to use the truck four years, after which he thinks he will get $1,800 for it as a trade-in on a new truck.
4. The wages expense consists of $4,680 paid the service's one employee who was hired on September 1, plus $23,400 of personal withdrawals by Mr. Field. Also, the one employee is owed $150 of earned but unpaid wages.
5. The $1,905 of insurance expense resulted from paying premiums on two insurance policies on January 2. One policy cost $825 and gave protection for one year. The other policy cost $1,080 for two years' protection.
6. In addition to the $12,975 of repair parts and supplies paid for during the year, creditors have billed the business $800 for parts and supplies purchased and delivered but not paid for. Also, an inventory shows $1,430 of unused parts and supplies on hand.
7. Mr. Field reports that the business does most of its work for cash, but customers owe $400 for repair work done on credit.

Prepare an accrual basis income statement for the year, a statement of changes in owner's equity, and a classified balance sheet showing its year-end financial position.

**Provocative Problem 3–3**
**Repairs Fast**
(L. O. 3, 5)

During the first week of January 1990, Ray Slovak began a repair business he calls Repairs Fast. He has kept no accounting records, but he does keep any unpaid invoices in a box near his workbench. He has kept a good record of the year's receipts and payments, which follows:

| | Receipts | Payments |
|---|---|---|
| Investment | $ 7,500 | |
| Shop equipment | | $ 6,000 |
| Repair parts and supplies | | 6,315 |
| Rent payments | | 3,900 |
| Insurance premiums paid | | 1,176 |
| Newspaper advertising paid | | 375 |
| Utility bills paid | | 970 |
| Part-time helper's wages paid | | 9,345 |
| Ray Slovak for personal use | | 22,500 |
| Revenue from repairs | 44,930 | |
| Subtotals | $52,430 | $50,581 |
| Cash balance, December 31, 1990 | | 1,849 |
| Totals | $52,430 | $52,430 |

Ray would like to know how much the business actually earned during its first year. Therefore, he would like for you to prepare an accrual basis income statement, a statement of changes in owner's equity, and a year-end classified balance sheet for the shop.

You learn that the shop equipment has an estimated eight-year life, after which it will be worthless. There is a $475 unpaid invoice in the box near Ray's workbench for supplies received, and an inventory shows $495 of unused supplies on hand. The shop space rents for $300 per month on a five-year lease. The lease contract requires payment of the first and last months' rents in advance, which were paid. The insurance premiums were for two policies taken out on January 2. The first is a one-year policy that cost $360. The second is a two-year policy that cost $816. There are $90 of earned but unpaid wages owed the helper, and customers owe the shop $580 for repair services they have received.

# 4 The Work Sheet and Closing the Accounts of Proprietorships, Partnerships, and Corporations

Your study of Chapter 4 will focus on some of the procedures that are performed at the end of each accounting period. You will learn to use a work sheet to show the effects of the adjustments and to organize the data prior to preparing financial statements. Also, you will learn the necessary steps to get the accounts ready for use in the following accounting period.

**Learning Objectives**

*After studying Chapter 4, you should be able to:*

1. Explain why a work sheet is prepared and be able to prepare a work sheet for a service-type business.
2. Prepare closing entries for a service business and explain why it is necessary to close the temporary accounts at the end of each accounting period.
3. Prepare a post-closing trial balance and explain its purpose.
4. Explain the nature of a corporation's retained earnings and its relationship to the declaration of dividends.
5. Prepare entries to record the declaration and payment of a dividend and to close the temporary accounts of a corporation.
6. List the steps in the accounting cycle in the order in which they are completed and perform each step.
7. Define or explain the words and phrases listed in the chapter Glossary.

*After studying the appendix to Chapter 4 (Appendix B), you should be able to:*

8. Prepare reversing entries and explain when and why they are used.

## Using a Work Sheet at the End of Each Accounting Period

Explain why a work sheet is prepared and be able to prepare a work sheet for a service-type business. (L. O. 1)

In the process of organizing the data that go into the formal financial reports given to managers and other interested parties, accountants prepare numerous memoranda, analyses, and informal papers. These analyses and memoranda, called **working papers**, are invaluable tools of the accountant. One important example of such working papers is the **work sheet** described in this chapter. The work sheet for a business is not given to the owner or manager. It is prepared solely for the accountant's use and is kept by the accountant.

Recall the end-of-period procedures that we discussed in Chapter 3. After all transactions were recorded, an unadjusted trial balance was prepared and adjusting entries were entered in the journal and posted to the accounts. Then, an adjusted trial balance was prepared and used as a basis for preparing the financial statements.

For a very small business, these procedures are satisfactory. However, if a company has more than a few accounts and adjustments, you will make fewer errors if you insert an additional step in the procedures. The additional step is to prepare a work sheet. A work sheet is prepared before the adjusting entries are journalized or posted to the accounts.

On the work sheet, the accountant (1) shows the unadjusted trial balance, (2) shows the effects of the adjustments on the account balances, (3) shows the adjusted trial balance, and (4) sorts the adjusted amounts into columns according to whether the accounts are used in preparing the income statement or the statement of changes in owner's equity or balance sheet. Also, the amount of net income is calculated on the work sheet. After the work sheet is completed, the work sheet information is used to prepare the financial statements and to journalize the adjusting entries and the closing entries. (Closing entries are discussed later in this chapter.)

## Preparing a Work Sheet

Illustration 4–1 shows the multicolumn form that is used to prepare a work sheet. Note that two columns each are provided for the unadjusted trial balance, the adjustments, the adjusted trial balance, the income statement, and the statement of changes in owner's equity or balance sheet. A work sheet could be prepared with two separate columns for the statement of changes in owner's equity and two separate columns for the balance sheet. However, since the statement of changes in owner's equity includes only a few items, this usually is not done. Instead, most work sheets provide only two columns for both statements, as Illustration 4–1 shows.

When a work sheet is used, the unadjusted trial balance is not prepared on a separate form. Instead, the first step in preparing the work sheet is to prepare the unadjusted trial balance in the first two money columns of the work sheet. Turn the first transparency overlay to see Illustration 4–2, which shows this first step in preparing the work sheet for Jerry Dow, Attorney. This is the same example that we used in Chapters 1 through 3.

Remember that Dow's law practice completed a number of transactions during December 1990. The unadjusted trial balance in Illustration 4–2 reflects the account balances after these December transactions were recorded but *before any adjusting entries were journalized or posted.*

In Illustration 4–2, a blank line was left after the Legal Fees Earned account. Based on past experience, the accountant may realize that more than one line will be needed to show the adjustments to a particular account. When you turn the second transparency overlay, you will see in Illustration 4–3 that Legal Fees Earned is an example. Another alternative is to "squeeze" two adjustments on one line or to combine the effects of two or more adjustments in one amount.

The next step in preparing a work sheet is to enter the adjustments in the columns labeled "Adjustments," as in Illustration 4–3. The adjustments in Illustration 4–3 are the same ones that we discussed in Chapter 3. Notice that an identifying letter is used to relate the debit and credit of each adjustment. After you prepare a work sheet, you still have to enter the adjusting entries in the journal and post them to the ledger. At that time, the identifying letters help you to match correctly the debit and credit of each adjusting entry.

Explanations of the adjustments on the illustrated work sheet are as follows:

**Adjustment (*a*):** To adjust for expired insurance.
**Adjustment (*b*):** To adjust for the office supplies used.
**Adjustment (*c*):** To adjust for depreciation of the law library.
**Adjustment (*d*):** To adjust for depreciation of the office equipment.
**Adjustment (*e*):** To adjust for accrued salaries.
**Adjustment (*f*):** To adjust for unearned revenue.
**Adjustment (*g*):** To adjust for accrued revenue.

Most of the adjustments on the illustrated work sheet required one or two additional accounts to be written in below the original trial balance. These accounts did not have balances when the trial balance was prepared. Therefore, they were not listed in the trial balance. However, if you anticipate that additional accounts will be required, you may list them in the process of preparing the unadjusted trial balance.

After the adjustments are entered in the Adjustments columns, the columns are totaled to prove the equality of the debit and credit adjustments. Then you proceed to prepare the adjusted trial balance. To do so, each amount in the Unadjusted Trial Balance columns is combined with its adjustments in the Adjustments columns, if any, and is entered in the Adjusted Trial Balance columns.

For example, in Illustration 4–3, the Prepaid Insurance account has a $2,400 debit balance in the Unadjusted Trial Balance columns. This $2,400 debit is combined with the $100 credit in the Adjustments columns to give Prepaid Insurance a $2,300 debit in the Adjusted Trial Balance columns. Insurance Expense has no balance in the Unadjusted Trial Balance columns, but it has a $100 debit in the Adjustments columns. Therefore, no balance combined with a $100 debit gives Insurance Expense a $100 debit in the Adjusted Trial Balance columns. Cash, Office Equipment, and several other accounts have trial balance amounts but not adjustments, As a result, their unadjusted trial balance amounts are carried unchanged into the Adjusted Trial Balance columns.

After the combined amounts are carried to the Adjusted Trial Balance columns, the Adjusted Trial Balance columns are added to prove their equality. Then, the amounts in these columns are sorted to the financial statement columns, as shown in Illustration 4–4. (Turn the next transparency overlay.) Ex-

Illustration 4–1

**Preparing a worksheet at the end of the accounting period**

The heading should identify the entity, the nature of the document, and the time period

**JERRY DOW, ATTORNEY**
**Work Sheet for Month Ended December 31, 1990**

| | Unadjusted Trial Balance | | Adjustments | | Adjusted Trial Balance | | Income Statement | | Statement of Changes in Owner's Equity or Balance Sheet | |
|---|---|---|---|---|---|---|---|---|---|---|
| Account Titles | Dr. | Cr. | Dr. | Cr. | Dr. | Cr. | Dr. | Cr. | Dr. | Cr. |
| | | | | | | | | | | |

The multicolumn work sheet can be prepared manually or with a computer spreadsheet program

The work sheet collects and summarizes the information used to prepare financial statements and to journalize adjusting and closing entries

**Illustration 4–2**
**The first step is to enter the unadjusted trial balance**

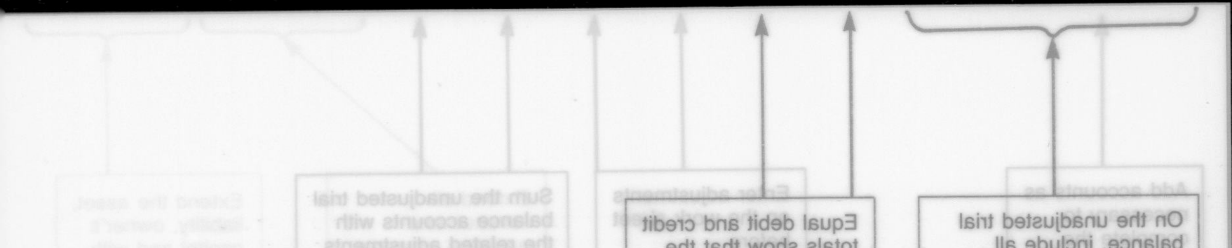

**Illustration 4–5**
**The final step is to enter the net income or loss and balance the financial statement columns**

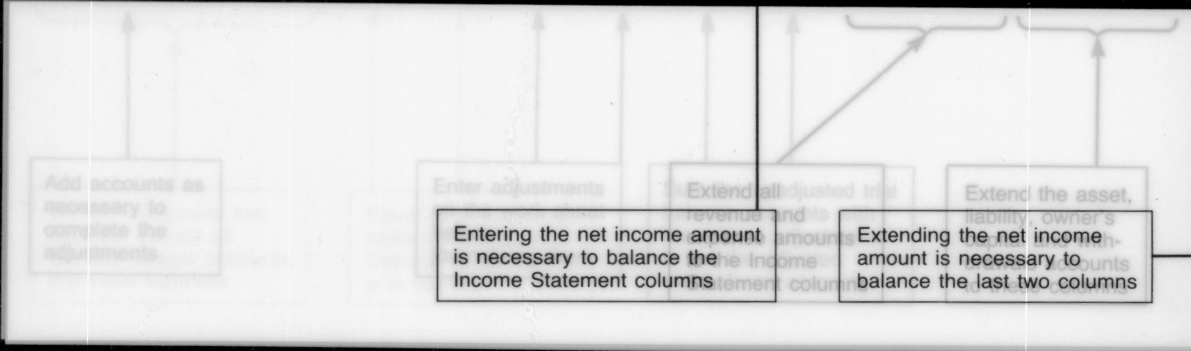

Entering the net income amount is necessary to balance the Income Statement columns
Extending the net income amount is necessary to balance the last two columns

Illustration 4-6

**Financial statements prepared from the worksheet**

**JERRY DOW, ATTORNEY**
**Income Statement**
**For the Month Ended December 31, 1990**

| | | |
|---|---|---|
| Revenues: | | |
| Legal fees earned | | $ 4,350 |
| Operating expenses: | | |
| Rent expense | $1,000 | |
| Salaries expense | 1,610 | |
| Utilities expense | 230 | |
| Insurance expense | 100 | |
| Office supplies expense | 45 | |
| Depreciation expense, law library | 80 | |
| Depreciation expense, office equipment | 125 | |
| Total operating expenses | | 3,190 |
| Net income | | $ 1,160 |

**JERRY DOW, ATTORNEY**
**Statement of Changes in Owner's Equity**
**For the Month Ended December 31, 1990**

| | | |
|---|---|---|
| Jerry Dow, capital, November 30, 1990 | | $ -0- |
| Plus: | | |
| Investments by owner | $9,000 | |
| Net income | 1,160 | 10,160 |
| Total | | $10,160 |
| Less withdrawals by owner | | 1,100 |
| Jerry Dow, capital, December 31, 1990 | | $ 9,060 |

**JERRY DOW, ATTORNEY**
**Balance Sheet**
**December 31, 1990**

**Assets**

| | | |
|---|---|---|
| Cash | | $ 650 |
| Accounts receivable | | 200 |
| Prepaid insurance | | 2,300 |
| Office supplies | | 75 |
| Law library | $2,880 | |
| Less accumulated depreciation | 80 | 2,800 |
| Office equipment | $6,880 | |
| Less accumulated depreciation | 125 | 6,755 |
| Total assets | | $12,780 |

**Liabilities**

| | | |
|---|---|---|
| Accounts payable | $ 760 | |
| Unearned legal fees | 2,750 | |
| Salaries payable | 210 | |
| Total liabilities | | $ 3,720 |

**Owner's Equity**

| | | |
|---|---|---|
| Jerry Dow, capital | | 9,060 |
| Total liabilities and owner's equity | | $12,780 |

penses are sorted to the Income Statement Debit column. Revenues are sorted to the Income Statement Credit column. Assets and the owner's withdrawals are sorted to the Statement of Changes in Owner's Equity or Balance Sheet Debit column. Liability items and the owner's capital account are sorted to the Statement of Changes in Owner's Equity or Balance Sheet Credit column. This task requires answers to only two questions: (1) Is the item to be sorted a debit or a credit? and (2) On which statement does it appear?

After the amounts are sorted to the proper columns, the columns are totaled as shown in Illustration 4–5. (Turn the last transparency overlay.) At this point, the difference between the totals of the Income Statement columns is the net income or loss. The difference is the net income or loss because revenues are entered in the Credit column and expenses in the Debit column. If the Credit column total exceeds the Debit column total, the difference is a net income. If the Debit column total exceeds the Credit column total, the difference is a net loss. In the illustrated work sheet, the Credit column total exceeds the Debit column total, and the result is a $1,160 net income.

After the net income is calculated in the Income Statement columns, it is added to the Statement of Changes in Owner's Equity or Balance Sheet Credit column. In that final column, the balance of the capital account does not yet reflect the increase in capital that resulted from net income. Therefore, adding the net income to this column has the effect of adding it to the capital account.

Had there been a loss, it would have been necessary to add the loss to the Debit column. This is because losses decrease owner's equity, and adding the loss to the Debit column has the effect of subtracting it from the capital account.

When the net income or net loss is added to the appropriate Statement of Changes in Owner's Equity or Balance Sheet column, the totals of the last two columns should balance. If they do not balance, you know that one or more errors were made in constructing the work sheet. The error or errors may have been either mathematical or an amount may have been sorted to a wrong column.

Although balancing the last two columns is done in an effort to discover errors, the fact that they balance is not proof that the work sheet is free from error. These columns will balance even when certain types of errors have been made. For example, if you incorrectly carry an asset amount into the Income Statement Debit column, the columns will still balance. Or, if you carry a liability amount into the Income Statement Credit column, the columns will still balance. Either error will cause the net income amount to be incorrect. But, the columns will be in balance. Therefore, you must exercise care in sorting the adjusted trial balance amounts into the correct financial statement columns.

## Preparing Financial Statements from the Work Sheet

We should emphasize that a work sheet is not a substitute for the financial statements. The work sheet is nothing more than a supporting tool that the accountant uses at the end of an accounting period to help organize the data. However, as soon as it is completed, the accountant uses the work sheet to prepare the financial statements. The items in the Income Statement columns provide the information necessary to prepare the formal income statement.

Next, information is taken from the last two columns to prepare the statement of changes in owner's equity and the balance sheet. The financial statements prepared from the information in Illustration 4–5 are shown in Illustration 4–6.

## Preparing Adjusting Entries from the Work Sheet

Entering the adjustments in the Adjustments columns of a work sheet does not get these adjustments into the ledger accounts. Therefore, after the work sheet is completed, you must prepare adjusting journal entries like the ones described in Chapter 3. The adjusting entries must be entered in the General Journal and posted to the accounts in the ledger. The work sheet makes this easy, because its Adjustments columns provide the information for these entries. All that is needed is an entry for each adjustment. If you prepare adjusting entries from the information in Illustration 4–5, you will see that they are the same adjusting entries we discussed in the last chapter.

## Closing Entries

Prepare closing entries for a service business and explain why it is necessary to close the temporary accounts at the end of each accounting period. (L. O. 2)

After the work sheet and statements are completed and the adjusting entries are recorded, you also must journalize and post **closing entries.** Closing entries are designed to transfer the balances in the revenue accounts, the expense accounts, and the withdrawals account to a balance sheet equity account. In a single proprietorship, they are transferred to the owner's capital account. After the closing entries are posted, the revenue, expense, and withdrawals accounts have zero balances. Thus, these accounts are said to be closed, or cleared.

## Why Closing Entries Are Made

When closing entries are prepared at the end of each accounting period, the revenue and expense accounts are closed by transferring their balances first to a summary account called **Income Summary.** Then, the Income Summary account balance, which is the net income or loss, is transferred in a single proprietorship to the owner's capital account. Finally, the owner's withdrawals account is transferred to the owner's capital account. These transfers, as shown in Illustration 4–7, are necessary because—

*a.* Revenues increase owner's equity, while expenses and withdrawals decrease owner's equity.

*b.* During an accounting period these increases and decreases are temporarily accumulated in revenue, expense, and withdrawals accounts rather than in the owner's capital account.

*c.* Closing entries are needed at the end of each accounting period to transfer the net effect of these increases and decreases out of the revenue, expense, and withdrawals accounts and on to the owner's capital account.

Also, closing entries cause the revenue and expense accounts to begin each new accounting period with zero balances. This is necessary because—

**Illustration 4–7**
**Closing entries**

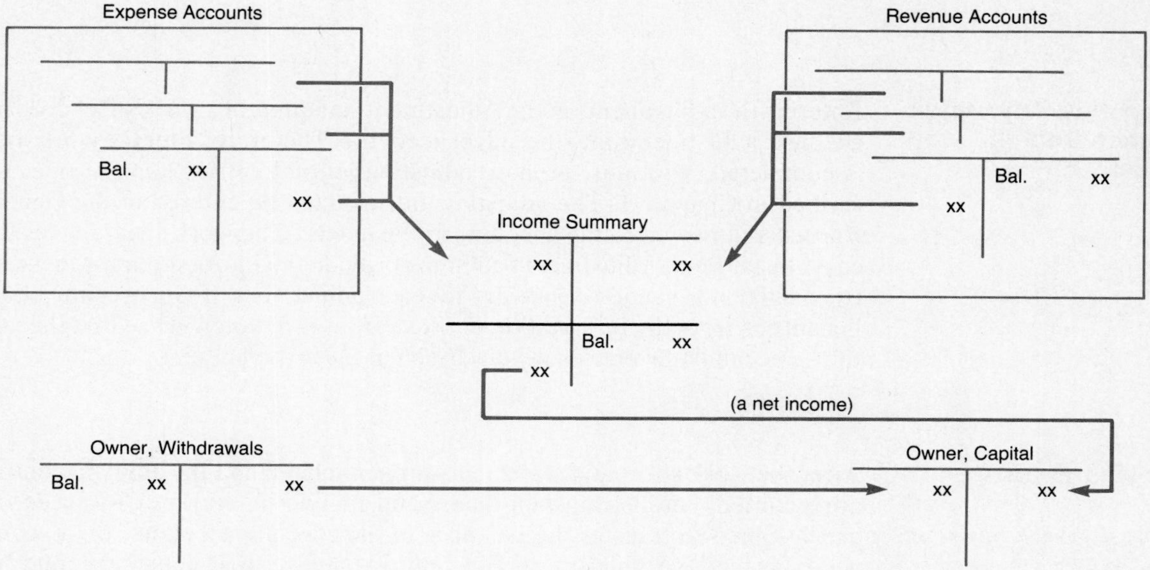


*a.* An income statement reports the revenues earned and expenses incurred during *one accounting period* and is prepared from information recorded in the revenue and expense accounts.

*b.* The revenue and expense accounts are not discarded at the end of each accounting period but are used to record the revenues and expenses of succeeding periods.

*c.* If the balances of these accounts are to reflect only one period's revenues and expenses, the accounts must begin each period with zero balances.

*d.* Since the statement of changes in owner's equity reports the owner's withdrawals during only one period, the withdrawals account must begin each period with a zero balance.

## Closing Entries Illustrated

At the end of December, after its adjusting entries were posted but before its accounts were closed, the revenue, expense, withdrawals, and capital accounts of Dow's law practice had the balances shown in Illustration 4–8. (As a rule, an account's Balance column heading does not tell whether the balance is debit or credit. However, in Illustration 4–8 and in the illustrations that immediately follow, the nature of each account's balance is shown as a study aid.)

In Illustration 4–8, notice that Dow's capital account shows only the $9,000 investment by Dow made on December 1. This is not the amount of Dow's equity on December 31. Closing entries are required to make this account show the December 31 equity.

Illustration 4–8

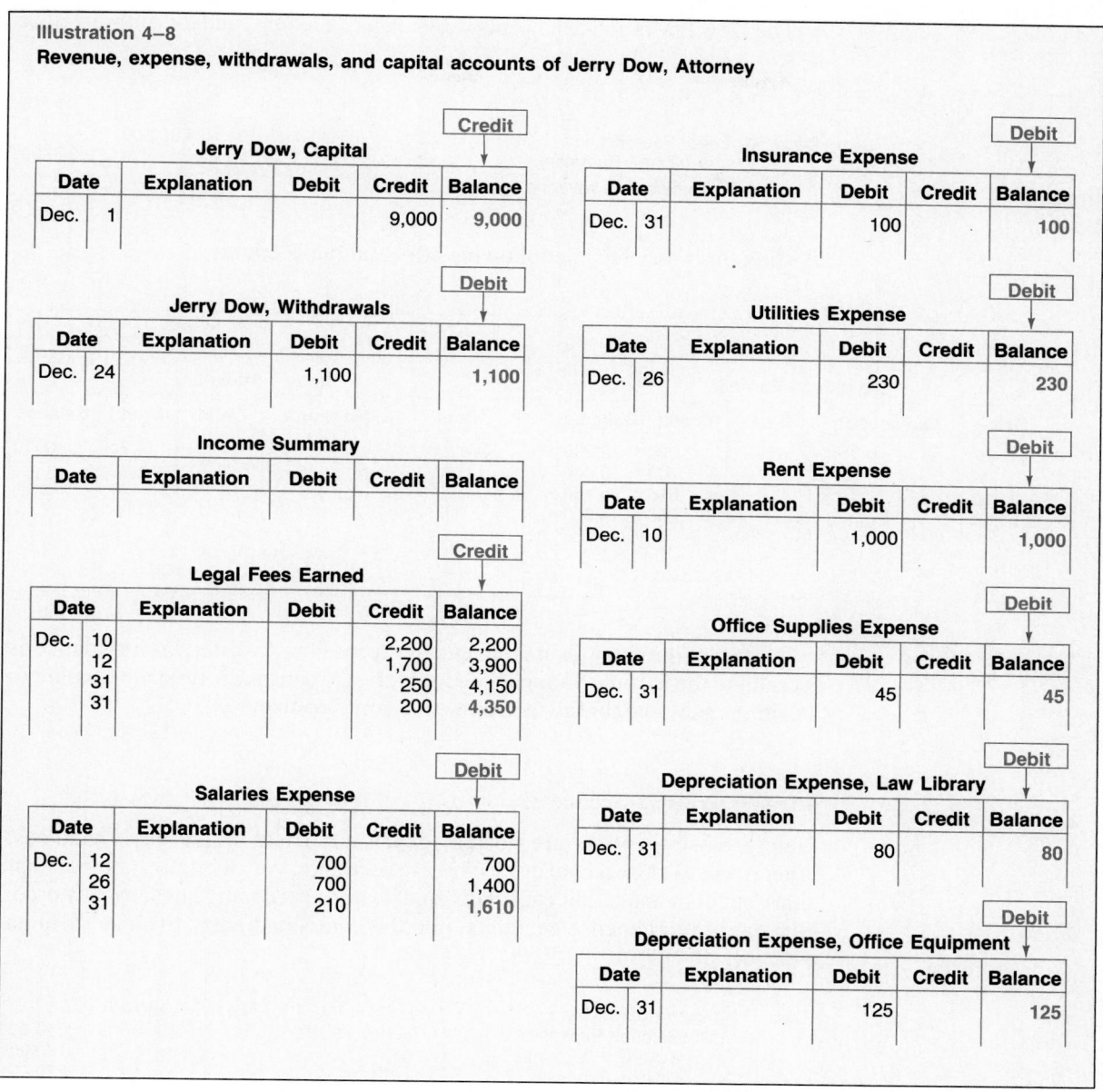

**Revenue, expense, withdrawals, and capital accounts of Jerry Dow, Attorney**

**Jerry Dow, Capital** (Credit balance)

| Date | | Explanation | Debit | Credit | Balance |
|---|---|---|---|---|---|
| Dec. | 1 | | | 9,000 | 9,000 |

**Jerry Dow, Withdrawals** (Debit balance)

| Date | | Explanation | Debit | Credit | Balance |
|---|---|---|---|---|---|
| Dec. | 24 | | 1,100 | | 1,100 |

**Income Summary**

| Date | | Explanation | Debit | Credit | Balance |
|---|---|---|---|---|---|
| | | | | | |

**Legal Fees Earned** (Credit balance)

| Date | | Explanation | Debit | Credit | Balance |
|---|---|---|---|---|---|
| Dec. | 10 | | | 2,200 | 2,200 |
| | 12 | | | 1,700 | 3,900 |
| | 31 | | | 250 | 4,150 |
| | 31 | | | 200 | 4,350 |

**Salaries Expense** (Debit balance)

| Date | | Explanation | Debit | Credit | Balance |
|---|---|---|---|---|---|
| Dec. | 12 | | 700 | | 700 |
| | 26 | | 700 | | 1,400 |
| | 31 | | 210 | | 1,610 |

**Insurance Expense** (Debit balance)

| Date | | Explanation | Debit | Credit | Balance |
|---|---|---|---|---|---|
| Dec. | 31 | | 100 | | 100 |

**Utilities Expense** (Debit balance)

| Date | | Explanation | Debit | Credit | Balance |
|---|---|---|---|---|---|
| Dec. | 26 | | 230 | | 230 |

**Rent Expense** (Debit balance)

| Date | | Explanation | Debit | Credit | Balance |
|---|---|---|---|---|---|
| Dec. | 10 | | 1,000 | | 1,000 |

**Office Supplies Expense** (Debit balance)

| Date | | Explanation | Debit | Credit | Balance |
|---|---|---|---|---|---|
| Dec. | 31 | | 45 | | 45 |

**Depreciation Expense, Law Library** (Debit balance)

| Date | | Explanation | Debit | Credit | Balance |
|---|---|---|---|---|---|
| Dec. | 31 | | 80 | | 80 |

**Depreciation Expense, Office Equipment** (Debit balance)

| Date | | Explanation | Debit | Credit | Balance |
|---|---|---|---|---|---|
| Dec. | 31 | | 125 | | 125 |

Notice also the third account in Illustration 4–8, the Income Summary account. This account is used only at the end of the accounting period to summarize and clear the revenue and expense accounts.

### Closing Revenue Accounts

Before closing entries are posted, revenue accounts have credit balances. Therefore, to close revenue accounts, you must debit each revenue account and credit Income Summary.

The Dow law practice has only one revenue account, and the entry to close it is:

| | | | | |
|---|---|---|---|---|
| Dec. | 31 | Legal Fees Earned | 4,350.00 | |
| | | Income Summary | | 4,350.00 |
| | | To close the revenue account. | | |

Posting this entry has the following effect on the accounts:

**Legal Fees Earned**

| Date | | Explanation | Debit | Credit | Balance |
|---|---|---|---|---|---|
| Dec. | 10 | | | 2,200 | 2,200 |
| | 19 | | | 1,700 | 3,900 |
| | 31 | | | 250 | 4,150 |
| | 31 | | | 200 | 4,350 |
| | 31 | | 4,350 | | -0- |

**Income Summary**

| Date | | Explanation | Debit | Credit | Balance |
|---|---|---|---|---|---|
| Dec. | 31 | | | 4,350 | 4,350 |

Note that the entry clears the revenue account by transferring its balance as a credit to the Income Summary account. It also causes the revenue account to begin the new accounting period with a zero balance.

### Closing Expense Accounts

Before closing entries are posted, expense accounts have debit balances. Therefore, to close a concern's expense accounts, you debit the Income Summary account and credit each individual expense account. The Dow law practice has seven expense accounts, and the compound entry to close them is:

| | | | | |
|---|---|---|---|---|
| Dec. | 31 | Income Summary | 3,190.00 | |
| | | Salaries Expense | | 1,610.00 |
| | | Insurance Expense | | 100.00 |
| | | Utilities Expense | | 230.00 |
| | | Rent Expense | | 1,000.00 |
| | | Office Supplies Expense | | 45.00 |
| | | Depreciation Expense, Law Library | | 80.00 |
| | | Depreciation Expense, Office Equipment | | 125.00 |
| | | To close the expense accounts. | | |

Posting the entry has the effect shown in Illustration 4–9. In that illustration, notice that the entry clears the expense accounts of their balances by transferring the balances in a total as a debit to the Income Summary account. Also, the entry causes the expense accounts to begin the new period with zero balances.

**Illustration 4–9**
**The entry to close the expense accounts**

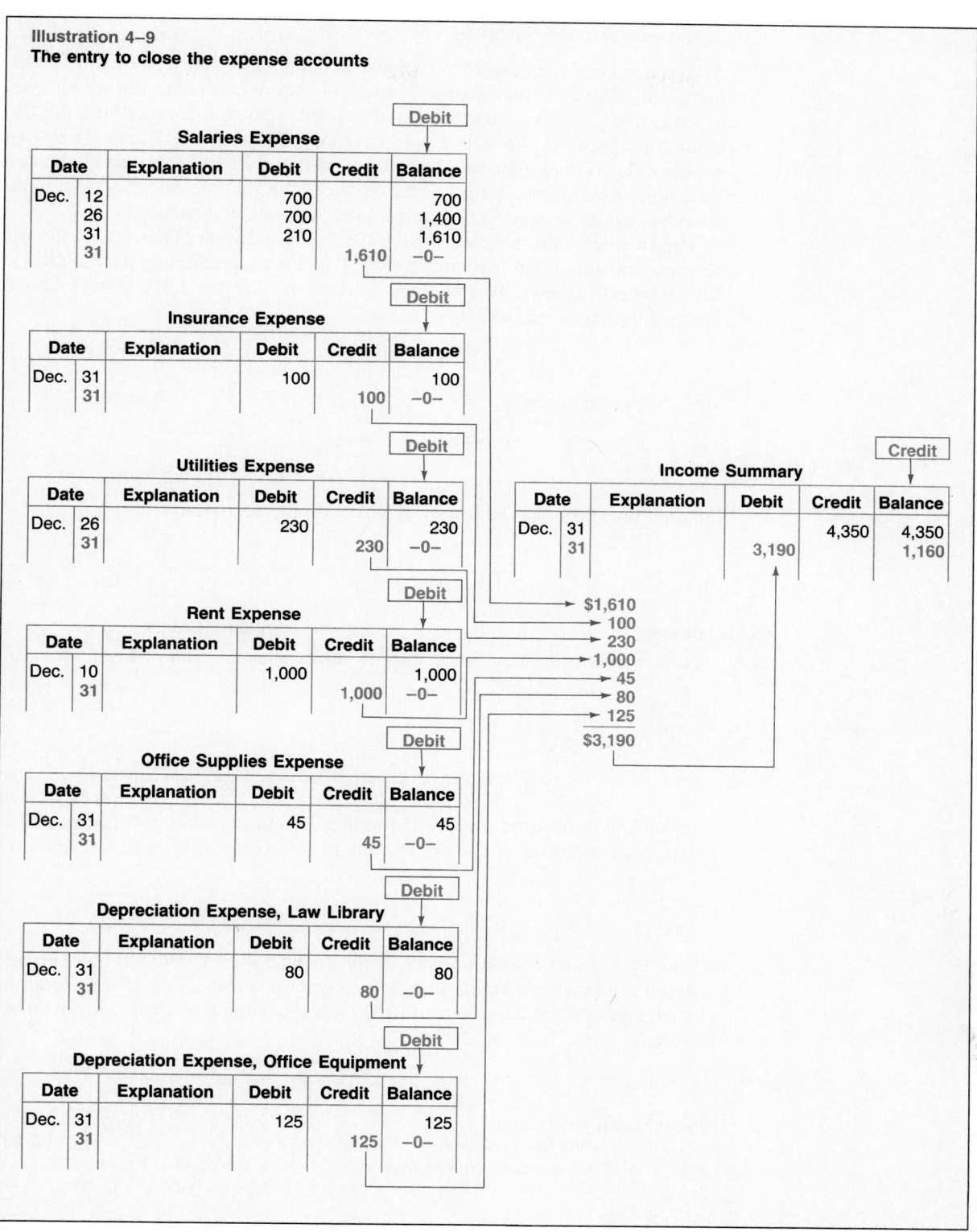

**Salaries Expense**

| Date | | Explanation | Debit | Credit | Balance |
|---|---|---|---|---|---|
| Dec. | 12 | | 700 | | 700 |
| | 26 | | 700 | | 1,400 |
| | 31 | | 210 | | 1,610 |
| | 31 | | | 1,610 | –0– |

**Insurance Expense**

| Date | | Explanation | Debit | Credit | Balance |
|---|---|---|---|---|---|
| Dec. | 31 | | 100 | | 100 |
| | 31 | | | 100 | –0– |

**Utilities Expense**

| Date | | Explanation | Debit | Credit | Balance |
|---|---|---|---|---|---|
| Dec. | 26 | | 230 | | 230 |
| | 31 | | | 230 | –0– |

**Rent Expense**

| Date | | Explanation | Debit | Credit | Balance |
|---|---|---|---|---|---|
| Dec. | 10 | | 1,000 | | 1,000 |
| | 31 | | | 1,000 | –0– |

**Office Supplies Expense**

| Date | | Explanation | Debit | Credit | Balance |
|---|---|---|---|---|---|
| Dec. | 31 | | 45 | | 45 |
| | 31 | | | 45 | –0– |

**Depreciation Expense, Law Library**

| Date | | Explanation | Debit | Credit | Balance |
|---|---|---|---|---|---|
| Dec. | 31 | | 80 | | 80 |
| | 31 | | | 80 | –0– |

**Depreciation Expense, Office Equipment**

| Date | | Explanation | Debit | Credit | Balance |
|---|---|---|---|---|---|
| Dec. | 31 | | 125 | | 125 |
| | 31 | | | 125 | –0– |

$1,610
100
230
1,000
45
80
125
$3,190

**Income Summary**

| Date | | Explanation | Debit | Credit | Balance |
|---|---|---|---|---|---|
| Dec. | 31 | | | 4,350 | 4,350 |
| | 31 | | 3,190 | | 1,160 |

### Closing the Income Summary Account

After a business's revenue and expense accounts are closed to Income Summary, the balance of the Income Summary account is equal to the net income or loss. When revenues exceed expenses, there is a net income, and the Income Summary account has a credit balance. On the other hand, when expenses exceed revenues, there is a loss and the account has a debit balance. But, regardless of the nature of its balance, the Income Summary account must be closed by transferring its balance to the capital account.

The Dow law practice earned $1,160 during December. Therefore, after its revenue and expense accounts are closed, its Income Summary account has a $1,160 credit balance. This balance is transferred to the Jerry Dow, Capital account with an entry like this:

| | | | | |
|---|---|---|---|---|
| Dec. | 31 | Income Summary | 1,160.00 | |
| | | Jerry Dow, Capital | | 1,160.00 |
| | | To close the Income Summary account. | | |

Posting this entry has the following effect on the accounts:

**Income Summary**

| Date | | Explanation | Debit | Credit | Balance |
|---|---|---|---|---|---|
| Dec. | 31 | | | 4,350 | 4,350 |
| | 31 | | 3,190 | | 1,160 |
| | 31 | | 1,160 | | –0– |

**Jerry Dow, Capital**

| Date | | Explanation | Debit | Credit | Balance |
|---|---|---|---|---|---|
| Dec. | 1 | | | 9,000 | 9,000 |
| | 31 | | | 1,160 | 10,160 |

Notice that the entry clears the Income Summary account, transferring its balance, the amount of the net income in this case, to the capital account.

### Closing the Withdrawals Account

At the end of an accounting period, the withdrawals account shows the decrease in the owner's equity due to the owner's withdrawals. The account is closed, and its debit balance is transferred to the capital account with an entry like this:

| | | | | |
|---|---|---|---|---|
| Dec. | 31 | Jerry Dow, Capital | 1,100.00 | |
| | | Jerry Dow, Withdrawals | | 1,100.00 |
| | | To close the withdrawals account. | | |

Posting the entry has this effect on the accounts:

**Jerry Dow, Withdrawals**

| Date | | Explanation | Debit | Credit | Balance |
|---|---|---|---|---|---|
| Dec. | 31 | | 1,100 | | 1,100 |
| | 31 | | | 1,100 | -0- |

**Jerry Dow, Capital**

| Date | | Explanation | Debit | Credit | Balance |
|---|---|---|---|---|---|
| Dec. | 1 | | | 9,000 | 9,000 |
| | 31 | | | 1,160 | 10,160 |
| | 31 | | 1,100 | | 9,060 |

After you post the entry to close the withdrawals account, notice that the two reasons for making closing entries are accomplished: (1) All revenue, expense, and withdrawal accounts have zero balances. (2) The net effect of the period's revenue, expense, and withdrawal transactions on the owner's equity is shown in the capital account.

#### Temporary (Nominal) Accounts and Permanent (Real) Accounts

Revenue accounts, expense accounts, withdrawals accounts, and the Income Summary account are often called **temporary accounts** or **nominal accounts.** These terms are used because amounts are stored in these accounts only temporarily. Such accounts are closed at the end of each accounting period. By contrast, accounts that appear in the balance sheet are often called **permanent accounts** or **real accounts**, because they remain open as long as the asset, liability, or owner's equity items recorded in the accounts continue in existence.

### Sources of Closing Entry Information

Information for closing entries may be taken from the individual revenue and expense accounts. However, the work sheet provides this information in a more convenient form. Look at the work sheet in Illustration 4–5. Every account that has a balance in the Income Statement columns must be closed. In addition, the withdrawals account must be closed.

### The Accounts after Closing

After both adjusting and closing entries are posted, the Dow law practice accounts appear as in Illustration 4–10. Observe that the asset, liability, and owner's capital accounts show their end-of-period balances. Also, note that the revenue and expense accounts have zero balances and are ready to be used when revenues and expenses are recorded in the next accounting period.

### The Post-Closing Trial Balance

Prepare a post-closing trial balance and explain its purpose.
(L. O. 3)

Because errors may have been introduced in the process of adjusting and closing the accounts, a new trial balance is prepared after all adjusting and closing entries have been posted. This **post-closing trial balance** is prepared to retest the equality of the accounts. The post-closing trial balance for Dow's law practice appears in Illustration 4–11.

Illustration 4–10
**The general ledger for Jerry Dow, Attorney**

**Cash** — Account No. 111

| Date | | Explanation | PR | Debit | Credit | Balance |
|---|---|---|---|---|---|---|
| 1990 Dec. | 1 | | G1 | 9,000 00 | | 9,000 00 |
| | 2 | | G1 | | 2,500 00 | 6,500 00 |
| | 3 | | G1 | | 5,600 00 | 900 00 |
| | 10 | | G1 | 2,200 00 | | 3,100 00 |
| | 10 | | G1 | | 1,000 00 | 2,100 00 |
| | 12 | | G1 | | 700 00 | 1,400 00 |
| | 22 | | G1 | 1,700 00 | | 3,100 00 |
| | 24 | | G2 | | 900 00 | 2,200 00 |
| | 24 | | G2 | | 1,100 00 | 1,100 00 |
| | 26 | | G2 | 3,000 00 | | 4,100 00 |
| | 26 | | G2 | | 2,400 00 | 1,700 00 |
| | 26 | | G2 | | 120 00 | 1,580 00 |
| | 26 | | G2 | | 230 00 | 1,350 00 |
| | 26 | | G2 | | 700 00 | 650 00 |

**Accounts Receivable** — Account No. 114

| Date | | Explanation | PR | Debit | Credit | Balance |
|---|---|---|---|---|---|---|
| 1990 Dec. | 12 | | G1 | 1,700 00 | | 1,700 00 |
| | 22 | | G2 | | 1,700 00 | –0– |
| | 31 | | G3 | 200 00 | | 200 00 |

**Prepaid Insurance** — Account No. 115

| Date | | Explanation | PR | Debit | Credit | Balance |
|---|---|---|---|---|---|---|
| 1990 Dec. | 26 | | G2 | 2,400 00 | | 2,400 00 |
| | 31 | | G3 | | 100 00 | 2,300 00 |

**Illustration 4–10 *(continued)***

**Office Supplies** — Account No. 116

| Date | | Explanation | PR | Debit | Credit | Balance |
|---|---|---|---|---|---|---|
| 1990 Dec. | 26 | | G2 | 120 00 | | 120 00 |
| | 31 | | G3 | | 45 00 | 75 00 |

**Law Library** — Account No. 131

| Date | | Explanation | PR | Debit | Credit | Balance |
|---|---|---|---|---|---|---|
| 1990 Dec. | 2 | | G1 | 2,500 00 | | 2,500 00 |
| | 6 | | G1 | 380 00 | | 2,880 00 |

**Office Equipment** — Account No. 132

| Date | | Explanation | PR | Debit | Credit | Balance |
|---|---|---|---|---|---|---|
| 1990 Dec. | 3 | | G1 | 5,600 00 | | 5,600 00 |
| | 6 | | G1 | 1,280 00 | | 6,880 00 |

**Accumulated Depreciation, Law Library** — Account No. 133

| Date | | Explanation | PR | Debit | Credit | Balance |
|---|---|---|---|---|---|---|
| 1990 Dec. | 31 | | G3 | | 80 00 | 80 00 |

**Accumulated Depreciation, Office Equipment** — Account No. 134

| Date | | Explanation | PR | Debit | Credit | Balance |
|---|---|---|---|---|---|---|
| 1990 Dec. | 31 | | G3 | | 125 00 | 125 00 |

Illustration 4–10 *(continued)*

**Accounts Payable** Account No. 212

| Date | | Explanation | PR | Debit | Credit | Balance |
|---|---|---|---|---|---|---|
| 1990 Dec. | 6 | | G1 | | 1,660 00 | 1,660 00 |
| | 24 | | G2 | 900 00 | | 760 00 |

**Salaries Payable** Account No. 213

| Date | | Explanation | PR | Debit | Credit | Balance |
|---|---|---|---|---|---|---|
| 1990 Dec. | 31 | | G3 | | 210 00 | 210 00 |

**Unearned Legal Fees** Account No. 214

| Date | | Explanation | PR | Debit | Credit | Balance |
|---|---|---|---|---|---|---|
| 1990 Dec. | 26 | | G2 | | 3,000 00 | 3,000 00 |
| | 31 | | G3 | 250 00 | | 2,750 00 |

**Jerry Dow, Capital** Account No. 311

| Date | | Explanation | PR | Debit | Credit | Balance |
|---|---|---|---|---|---|---|
| 1990 Dec. | 1 | | G1 | | 9,000 00 | 9,000 00 |
| | 24 | | G2 | 1,100 00 | | 7,900 00 |
| | 31 | | G3 | | 1,160 00 | 9,060 00 |

**Jerry Dow, Withdrawals** Account No. 312

| Date | | Explanation | PR | Debit | Credit | Balance |
|---|---|---|---|---|---|---|
| 1990 Dec. | 24 | | G2 | 1,100 00 | | 1,100 00 |
| | 31 | | G3 | | 1,100 00 | –0– |

**Illustration 4–10 *(continued)***

**Income Summary** Account No. 313

| Date | | Explanation | PR | Debit | Credit | Balance |
|---|---|---|---|---|---|---|
| 1990 Dec. | 31 | | G3 | | 4,350 00 | 4,350 00 |
| | 31 | | G3 | 3,190 00 | | 1,160 00 |
| | 31 | | G3 | 1,160 00 | | –0– |

**Legal Fees Earned** Account No. 411

| Date | | Explanation | PR | Debit | Credit | Balance |
|---|---|---|---|---|---|---|
| 1990 Dec. | 10 | | G1 | | 2,200 00 | 2,200 00 |
| | 12 | | G1 | | 1,700 00 | 3,900 00 |
| | 31 | | G3 | | 250 00 | 4,150 00 |
| | 31 | | G3 | | 200 00 | 4,350 00 |
| | 31 | | G3 | 4,350 00 | | –0– |

**Salaries Expense** Account No. 511

| Date | | Explanation | PR | Debit | Credit | Balance |
|---|---|---|---|---|---|---|
| 1990 Dec. | 12 | | G1 | 700 00 | | 700 00 |
| | 26 | | G2 | 700 00 | | 1,400 00 |
| | 31 | | G3 | 210 00 | | 1,610 00 |
| | 31 | | G3 | | 1,610 00 | –0– |

**Insurance Expense** Account No. 512

| Date | | Explanation | PR | Debit | Credit | Balance |
|---|---|---|---|---|---|---|
| 1990 Dec. | 31 | | G3 | 100 00 | | 100 00 |
| | 31 | | G3 | | 100 00 | –0– |

Illustration 4–10 *(concluded)*

**Utilities Expense** Account No. 513

| Date | | Explanation | PR | Debit | Credit | Balance |
|---|---|---|---|---|---|---|
| 1990 Dec. | 26 | | G2 | 230 00 | | 230 00 |
| | 31 | | G3 | | 230 00 | –0– |

**Rent Expense** Account No. 514

| Date | | Explanation | PR | Debit | Credit | Balance |
|---|---|---|---|---|---|---|
| 1990 Dec. | 10 | | G1 | 1,000 00 | | 1,000 00 |
| | 31 | | G3 | | 1,000 00 | –0– |

**Office Supplies Expense** Account No. 516

| Date | | Explanation | PR | Debit | Credit | Balance |
|---|---|---|---|---|---|---|
| 1990 Dec. | 31 | | G3 | 45 00 | | 45 00 |
| | 31 | | G3 | | 45 00 | –0– |

**Depreciation Expense, Law Library** Account No. 517

| Date | | Explanation | PR | Debit | Credit | Balance |
|---|---|---|---|---|---|---|
| 1990 Dec. | 31 | | G3 | 80 00 | | 80 00 |
| | 31 | | G3 | | 80 00 | –0– |

**Depreciation Expense, Office Equipment** Account No. 518

| Date | | Explanation | PR | Debit | Credit | Balance |
|---|---|---|---|---|---|---|
| 1990 Dec. | 31 | | G3 | 125 00 | | 125 00 |
| | 31 | | G3 | | 125 00 | –0– |

**Illustration 4–11**
**The post-closing trial balance**

JERRY DOW, ATTORNEY
Post-Closing Trial Balance
December 31, 1990

| | | |
|---|---|---|
| Cash | $ 650 | |
| Accounts receivable | 200 | |
| Prepaid insurance | 2,300 | |
| Office supplies | 75 | |
| Law library | 2,880 | |
| Office equipment | 6,880 | |
| Accumulated depreciation, law library | | $ 80 |
| Accumulated depreciation, office equipment | | 125 |
| Accounts payable | | 760 |
| Salaries payable | | 210 |
| Unearned legal fees | | 2,750 |
| Jerry Dow, capital | | 9,060 |
| Totals | $12,985 | $12,985 |

Compare Illustration 4–11 with the accounts that have balances in Illustration 4–10. Note that only asset, liability, and the owner's capital accounts have balances in Illustration 4–10. Note also that these are the only accounts that appear on the post-closing trial balance. The revenue and expense accounts have been cleared and have zero balances at this stage.

## Accounting for Partnerships and Corporations

### Partnership Accounting

Accounting for a partnership is like accounting for a single proprietorship except for transactions that directly affect the partners' capital and withdrawal accounts. For these transactions, you need a capital account and a withdrawals account for each partner. Also, you close the Income Summary account with a compound entry that allocates to each partner his or her share of the net income or loss.

### Corporate Accounting

Explain the nature of a corporation's retained earnings and its relationship to the declaration of dividends. (L. O. 4)

Accounting for a corporation also differs from that of a single proprietorship for transactions that affect the equity accounts of the corporation. The differences occur because accounting principles require a corporation to distinguish between stockholders' equity resulting from amounts invested in the corporation by its stockholders and stockholders' equity resulting from earnings. This distinction is also important because in most states a corporation cannot pay a legal dividend unless it has stockholders' equity resulting from earnings. In making the distinction, two kinds of stockholders' equity accounts are kept: (1) *contributed capital accounts* and (2) *retained earnings accounts*. Amounts invested in a corporation (contributed) by its stockholders are shown in a contributed capital account such as the Common Stock account. Stockholders' equity resulting from earnings is shown in a retained earnings account.

To demonstrate corporate accounting, assume that five persons secured a charter for a new corporation. Each invested $10,000 in the corporation by buying 1,000 shares of its $10 par value common stock. The corporation's entry to record their investments is:

| | | | | |
|---|---|---|---|---|
| Jan. | 5 | Cash . . . . . . . . . . . . . . . . . . . . . . . . . . . . | 50,000.00 | |
| | | Common Stock . . . . . . . . . . . . . . . . . . . . . | | 50,000.00 |
| | | Issued 5,000 shares of $10 par value common stock for cash. | | |

If during its first year the corporation earned $20,000, the entry to close its Income Summary account is:

| | | | | |
|---|---|---|---|---|
| Dec. | 31 | Income Summary . . . . . . . . . . . . . . . . . . . . . | 20,000.00 | |
| | | Retained Earnings . . . . . . . . . . . . . . . . . . . . | | 20,000.00 |
| | | To close the Income Summary account. | | |

If these are the only entries that affected the Common Stock and Retained Earnings accounts during the first year, the corporation's year-end balance sheet will show the stockholders' equity as follows:

| Stockholders' Equity | | |
|---|---|---|
| Common stock, $10 par value, 5,000 shares authorized and outstanding . . . . . . . . | $50,000 | |
| Retained earnings . . . . . . . . . . . . . . | 20,000 | |
| Total stockholder's equity . . . . . . . . . . | | $70,000 |

Since a corporation is a separate legal entity, the names of its stockholders usually are of little interest to a balance sheet reader and are not shown in the equity section. However, in this case, the section does show that the net assets or equity of the corporation's stockholders is $70,000. Of this amount, $50,000 resulted from their purchase of the corporation's stock, and $20,000 was the result of net income that has not been paid out as dividends.

Perhaps the concept of retained earnings would be clearer if the balance sheet item were labeled "Stockholders' equity resulting from earnings." However, the retained earnings caption is commonly used. You should understand that it does not represent a specific amount of cash or any other asset. These are shown in the asset section of the balance sheet. Retained earnings represents nothing more than stockholders' equity resulting from earnings.

To continue, assume that on January 10 of the corporation's second year, its board of directors met and by vote declared a $1 per share dividend payable on February 1 to the January 25 **stockholders of record** (stockholders according to the corporation's records). The entry to record the declaration of the dividend is as follows:

| | | | | |
|---|---|---|---|---|
| Jan. | 10 | Dividends Declared . . . . . . . . . . . . . . . . . . . . . | 5,000.00 | |
| | | Common Dividend Payable . . . . . . . . . . . . . . . | | 5,000.00 |
| | | Declared a $1 per share dividend. | | |

Prepare entries to record the declaration and payment of a dividend and to close the temporary accounts of a corporation. (L. O. 5)

The **Dividends Declared** account is a temporary account that serves the same function for a corporation as does a withdrawals account for a proprietorship. At the end of each period, the Dividends Declared account is closed to Retained Earnings.

The entry to record the payment of the dividend is as follows:

| | | | | |
|---|---|---|---|---|
| Feb. | 1 | Common Dividend Payable . . . . . . . . . . . . . . . . . | 5,000.00 | |
| | | Cash . . . . . . . . . . . . . . . . . . . . . . . . . . . | | 5,000.00 |
| | | Paid the dividend declared on January 10. | | |

Note from the two entries that a dividend declaration and payment reduce the corporation's assets and stockholders' equity just as a withdrawal of cash by the owner of a single proprietorship reduces assets and the owner's equity.

A cash dividend is normally paid by mailing checks to the stockholders. Also, as in this case, three dates are normally involved in a dividend declaration and payment: (1) the **date of declaration**, (2) the **date of record**, and (3) the **date of payment**. Since stockholders may sell their stock to new investors, the three dates give new stockholders an opportunity to have their ownership entered in the corporation's records in time to receive the dividend. Otherwise, the dividend would go to the old stockholders.

A dividend must be formally voted by a corporation's board of directors. Also, courts have generally held that the board is the final judge of when a dividend should be paid. Therefore, stockholders have no right to a dividend until declared. However, as soon as a cash dividend is declared, it becomes a liability of the corporation (normally a current liability) and must be paid. Furthermore, stockholders have the right to sue and force payment of a cash dividend once it is declared.

If during its second year (1991) the corporation suffered a $7,000 net loss, the entries to close its Income Summary and Dividends Declared accounts are:

| | | | | |
|---|---|---|---|---|
| 1991 | | | | |
| Dec. | 31 | Retained Earnings . . . . . . . . . . . . . . . . . . . . . | 7,000.00 | |
| | | Income Summary . . . . . . . . . . . . . . . . . . . . | | 7,000.00 |
| | | To close the Income Summary account. | | |
| | 31 | Retained Earnings . . . . . . . . . . . . . . . . . . . . . | 5,000.00 | |
| | | Dividends Declared . . . . . . . . . . . . . . . . . . . | | 5,000.00 |
| | | To close the Dividends Declared account. | | |

Now assume that during 1992, the corporation paid no dividends but suffered a net loss of $14,000. The entry to close the Income Summary account at the end of 1992 is:

| | | | | |
|---|---|---|---|---|
| 1992 | | | | |
| Dec. | 31 | Retained Earnings . . . . . . . . . . . . . . . . . . . . . | 14,000.00 | |
| | | Income Summary . . . . . . . . . . . . . . . . . . . . | | 14,000.00 |
| | | To close the Income Summary account. | | |

Posting these entries has the following effects on the Retained Earnings account:

**Retained Earnings**

| Date | | Explanation | PR | Debit | Credit | Balance |
|---|---|---|---|---|---|---|
| 1990 | | | | | | |
| Dec. | 31 | Net income | G4 | | 20,000.00 | 20,000.00 |
| 1991 | | | | | | |
| Dec. | 31 | Net loss | G5 | 7,000.00 | | 13,000.00 |
| | 31 | Dividends declared | G7 | 5,000.00 | | 8,000.00 |
| 1992 | | | | | | |
| Dec. | 31 | Net loss | G9 | 14,000.00 | | 6,000.00 |

Due to the dividend and the net losses, the Retained Earnings account has a $6,000 debit balance. A debit balance in a Retained Earnings account indicates a negative amount of retained earnings. A corporation with a negative amount of retained earnings is said to have a **deficit.** A deficit may be shown on a corporation's balance sheet as follows:

**Stockholders' Equity**

| | | |
|---|---|---|
| Common stock, $10 par value, 5,000 shares authorized and outstanding . . . . . . . . | $50,000 | |
| Deduct retained earnings deficit . . . . . . | (6,000) | |
| Total stockholder's equity . . . . . . . . . . | | $44,000 |

In most states, it is illegal for a corporation with a deficit to pay a cash dividend. Such dividends are illegal because as a separate legal entity a corporation is responsible for its own debts. If its creditors are to be paid, they must be paid from the corporation's assets. Therefore, making a dividend illegal when there is a deficit helps prevent a corporation in financial difficulties from paying all of its assets in dividends and leaving nothing for payment of its creditors.

## The Accounting Cycle

In Chapters 2, 3, and 4, we have discussed all of the accounting procedures that must be completed each accounting period, beginning with the recording of transactions in a journal and ending with a post-closing trial balance. Since these steps are repeated each period, they are called the **accounting cycle.** A knowledge of accounting requires that you understand each step and its relation to the others. The steps in the order of their occurrence are as follows:

## AS A MATTER OF FACT

### Corporate Dividend News

#### Dividends Reported February 3

| Company | Period | Amount | Payable date | Record date |
|---|---|---|---|---|
| **REGULAR** | | | | |
| CanadianPacForest . . | Q | b.65 | 4– 3–89 | 3– 3 |
| Commerce Bancshares . | Q | .30 | 3–31–89 | 2–27 |
| Contel Corp . . . . . . | Q | .52 | 2–28–89 | 2–15 |
| Del Labs . . . . . . . . | Q | .10 | 3–24–89 | 2–17 |
| Domtar Inc . . . . . . . | Q | b.12½ | 3–15–89 | 2–15 |
| Du Pont Canada Inc . . | Q | b.15 | 4–28–89 | 4– 3 |
| Franklin Electric . . . . | Q | .16 | 2–24–89 | 2–10 |
| Fremont General Corp . | Q | .15 | 4–28–89 | 3–31 |
| GATX Corp $2.50pf . . | Q | .62½ | 3– 1–89 | 2–15 |
| Golden Poultry Co . . . | Q | .01 | 3– 2–89 | 2–16 |
| Home Group Inc . . . . | Q | .05 | 4– 1–89 | 3– 1 |
| Home Insurance Co pfA | Q | .73¾ | 3– 1–89 | 2–13 |
| Kysor Industrial Corp . | Q | .15 | n4–27–89 | 4–12 |
| n-Corrected payable date. | | | | |
| Marriott Corp . . . . . | Q | .06 | 4–24–89 | 4– 3 |
| Pilgrim's Pride Corp . . | Q | .01½ | 3–31–89 | 3– 9 |
| Southam Inc . . . . . | Q | b.16 | 3–23–89 | 3– 9 |
| Tab Products Co . . . | Q | .05 | 3–15–89 | 2–24 |
| Textl Industries pf '87 . | Q | .27½ | 3– 1–89 | 2–15 |
| Washington Water Pwr . | Q | .62 | 3–15–89 | 2–23 |

* * *

| Company | Period | Amounts New | Amounts Old | Payable Date | Record Date |
|---|---|---|---|---|---|
| **INCREASED** | | | | | |
| Badger Paper Mills . . | Q | .11 | .09 | 3–13–89 | 2–10 |
| Dennison Mfg . . . . | Q | .33 | .32 | 3–10–89 | 2–23 |
| Dofasco Inc . . . . . | Q | b.32 | b.27 | 4– 1–89 | 3–13 |
| Federal Signal . . . . | Q | .21 | .20 | 3– 1–89 | 2–14 |
| GATX Corp . . . . . | Q | .50 | .45 | 3–31–89 | 3–10 |
| Indiana Fed'l Corp . . | Q | .07½ | .05 | 2–28–89 | 2–14 |
| Inland NaturalGas . . | Q | b.18½ | b.17 | 2–28–89 | 2–13 |
| LillyIndCoatcIA . . . | Q | .12 | .11 | 4– 3–89 | 3–13 |
| Olsten Corp . . . . . | Q | .06 | .05 | 3– 1–89 | 2–15 |
| Temple-Inland Inc . . | Q | .29 | .21 | 3–15–89 | 3– 1 |
| Timken Co . . . . . . | Q | .23 | .20 | 3–10–89 | 2–17 |
| US WEST Inc . . . . | Q | .94 | .88 | 5– 1–89 | 4–19 |

* * *

| Company | Period | Amount | Payable Date | Record Date |
|---|---|---|---|---|
| **INITIAL** | | | | |
| Beckman Instruments . . | — | .07 | 3–20–89 | 2–15 |
| Vulcan Materials Co new | Q | .28 | 3–10–89 | 2–24 |

A-Annual; Ac-Accumulation; b-Payable in Canadian funds; F-Final; G-Interim; h-From Income; k-From capital gains; M-Monthly; Q-Quarterly; S-Semi-annual.

* * *

Source: *The Wall Street Journal*, February 6, 1989, p. C9. Reprinted by permission of *The Wall Street Journal*, © Dow Jones & Company, Inc. 1989. ALL RIGHTS RESERVED.

List the steps in the accounting cycle in the order in which they are completed and perform each step.
(L. O. 6)

1. **Journalizing** . . . . . . Analyzing and recording transactions in a journal.
2. **Posting** . . . . . . . . Copying the debits and credits of the journal entries into the ledger accounts.
3. **Preparing an unadjusted trial balance** . Summarizing the ledger accounts and testing the recording accuracy.
4. **Completing the work sheet** . . . . . . . . . Gaining the effects of the adjustments before entering the adjustments in the accounts. Then sorting the account balances into the proper financial statement columns and calculating the net income or net loss.

5. **Preparing the statements** . . . . . . Rearranging the work sheet information onto an income statement, a statement of changes in owner's equity, and a balance sheet.

6. **Adjusting the ledger accounts** . . . . . . . Preparing adjusting journal entries from information in the Adjustments columns of the work sheet and posting the entries in order to bring the account balances up to date.

7. **Closing the temporary accounts** . . . . . . . Preparing and posting entries to close the temporary accounts and to transfer the net income or loss to the capital account or accounts in a single proprietorship or partnership and to the Retained Earnings account in a corporation.

8. **Preparing a post-closing trial balance** . . Proving the accuracy of the adjusting and closing procedures.

## Summary of the Chapter in Terms of Learning Objectives

**1.** A work sheet is a tool the accountant uses at the end of an accounting period to show the effects of the adjustments and to organize the data for use in preparing financial statements and recording the adjusting and closing entries.

**2.** Closing the temporary accounts at the end of each accounting period serves to transfer the effects of these accounts to the proper owner's equity account that appears on the balance sheet. It also gives the revenue, expense, and withdrawals or Dividend Declared accounts' zero balances, preparing them for use in the following period.

**3.** A post-closing trial balance tests the equality of debits and credits in the ledger after the adjusting and closing entries have been posted. It also confirms the fact that all temporary accounts have been closed.

**4.** Retained earnings is the total amount of net incomes a corporation has earned since it was organized, less the total amount of net losses it has incurred and the total amount of dividends it has declared.

**5.** Dividend declarations are recorded with a debit to a temporary account called Dividends Declared and a credit to a liability account. When paid in cash, the liability account is debited and Cash is credited.

**6.** The steps in the accounting cycle are to journalize and post transactions, prepare a trial balance and complete the work sheet, prepare the financial statements, record the adjustments, close the temporary accounts, and prepare a post-closing trial balance.

## Demonstration Problem

The December 31, 1990, adjusted trial balance of The Shoemaker, Inc., is as follows:

| | | |
|---|---|---|
| Cash | $ 83,300 | |
| Prepaid insurance | 19,000 | |
| Prepaid rent | 5,000 | |
| Accounts receivable | 45,000 | |
| Equipment | 165,000 | |
| Accumulated depreciation, equipment | | $ 52,000 |
| Notes receivable | 60,000 | |
| Accounts payable | | 37,000 |
| Notes payable | | 58,000 |
| Income taxes payable | | 21,500 |
| Common stock | | 55,000 |
| Retained earnings | | 99,000 |
| Dividends declared | 75,000 | |
| Sales | | 420,000 |
| Interest earned | | 6,500 |
| Wages expense | 179,000 | |
| Rent expense | 47,000 | |
| Insurance expense | 7,000 | |
| Depreciation expense | 26,000 | |
| Interest expense | 4,700 | |
| Income taxes expense | 33,000 | |
| Totals | $749,000 | $749,000 |

*Required*

1. Prepare closing entries for The Shoemaker, Inc.
2. Prepare a post-closing trial balance for the business.
3. Set up a Retained Earnings account, and post all necessary amounts to the account.

## Solution to Demonstration Problem

1.

**Closing Entries**

| | | | | |
|---|---|---|---|---|
| 1990 | | | | |
| Dec. | 31 | Sales | 420,000.00 | |
| | | Interest Earned | 6,500.00 | |
| | | Income Summary | | 426,500.00 |
| | 31 | Income Summary | 296,700.00 | |
| | | Wages Expense | | 179,000.00 |
| | | Rent Expense | | 47,000.00 |
| | | Insurance Expense | | 7,000.00 |
| | | Depreciation Expense | | 26,000.00 |
| | | Interest Expense | | 4,700.00 |
| | | Income Taxes Expense | | 33,000.00 |
| | 31 | Income Summary | 129,800.00 | |
| | | Retained Earnings | | 129,800.00 |
| | 31 | Retained Earnings | 75,000.00 | |
| | | Dividends Declared | | 75,000.00 |

2.

**THE SHOEMAKER, INC.**
**Post-Closing Trial Balance**
**December 31, 1990**

| | | |
|---|---|---|
| Cash | $ 83,300 | |
| Prepaid insurance | 19,000 | |
| Prepaid rent | 5,000 | |
| Accounts receivable | 45,000 | |
| Equipment | 165,000 | |
| Accumulated depreciation, equipment | | $ 52,000 |
| Notes receivable | 60,000 | |
| Accounts payable | | 37,000 |
| Notes payable | | 58,000 |
| Income taxes payable | | 21,500 |
| Common stock | | 55,000 |
| Retained earnings | | 153,800 |
| Totals | $377,300 | $377,300 |

3.

**Retained Earnings**

| Date | | Explanation | PR | Debit | Credit | Balance |
|---|---|---|---|---|---|---|
| 1990 | | | | | | |
| Jan. | 1 | Beginning balance | | | 99,000 | 99,000 |
| Dec. | 31 | Close Income Summary | | | 129,800 | 228,800 |
| | 31 | Close Dividends Declared | | 75,000 | | 153,800 |

## Appendix B

## REVERSING ENTRIES

Prepare reversing entries and explain when and why they are used. (L. O. 8)

In this appendix, we explain some optional entries accountants may use in accounting for accrued items. These optional entries, called **reversing entries**, are used to make the bookkeeping process easier.

In accounting for Jerry Dow's law practice, the December 31, 1990, adjusting entries included an accrual of the secretary's salary. This entry was as follows:

| | | | | |
|---|---|---|---|---|
| 1990 | | | | |
| Dec. | 31 | Salaries Expense | 210.00 | |
| | | Salaries Payable | | 210.00 |
| | | To record accrued wages. | | |

Then on December 31, the Salaries Expense account was closed to Income Summary.

Since the secretary is paid every two weeks, the next payment is on January 9, and is recorded as follows:

| | | | | |
|---|---|---|---|---|
| Jan. | 9 | Salaries Payable . . . . . . . . . . . . . . . . . . . . . . . | 210.00 | |
| | | Salaries Expense . . . . . . . . . . . . . . . . . . . . . . | 490.00 | |
| | | Cash . . . . . . . . . . . . . . . . . . . . . . . . . . | | 700.00 |
| | | Paid wages for two weeks. | | |

To correctly record a transaction like that of the January 9 entry, a bookkeeper must remember that part of the cash payment is accrued salaries and part is expense of the current period. Since the accrual is easy to forget, you can avoid "the need to remember" by preparing and posting entries to reverse any end-of-period adjustments of accrued items. These reversing entries are made after the adjusting and closing entries are posted and are normally dated the first day of the new accounting period.

Also, when prepaid and unearned items are initially recorded in income statement accounts, the end-of-period adjusting entries transfer the unused or unearned portions to asset and liability accounts. Thereafter, reversing entries may be used to transfer the prepaid asset and unearned liability account balances back into the expense and revenue accounts.

To reverse the accrual of wages, you would make the following entry:

| | | | | |
|---|---|---|---|---|
| Jan. | 1 | Salaries Payable . . . . . . . . . . . . . . . . . . . . . . . | 210.00 | |
| | | Salaries Expense . . . . . . . . . . . . . . . . . . . . | | 210.00 |
| | | To reverse the accrual of salaries. | | |

Observe that the reversing entry is the exact opposite of the original adjusting entry. After the adjusting, closing, and reversing entries are posted, the Salaries Expense and Salaries Payable accounts appear as follows:

**Salaries Expense**

| Date | | Explanation | Dr. | Cr. | Bal. |
|---|---|---|---|---|---|
| Dec. | 12 | Paid wages | 700 | | 700 |
| | 26 | Paid wages | 700 | | 1,400 |
| | 31 | Accrued wages | 210 | | 1,610 |
| | 31 | Closing | | 1,610 | –0– |
| 1991 | | | | | |
| Jan. | 1 | Reversal | | 210 | (210) |

**Salaries Payable**

| Date | | Explanation | Dr. | Cr. | Bal. |
|---|---|---|---|---|---|
| Dec. | 31 | Accrued wages | | 210 | 210 |
| 1991 | | | | | |
| Jan. | 1 | Reversal | 210 | | –0– |

Notice that the reversing entry cancels the $210 of salaries that appeared in the Salaries Payable account. It also causes the accrued salaries to appear in the Salaries Expense account as a $210 credit. (Remember that a circled balance means a balance opposite from normal.) Therefore, due to the reversing entry, when the salaries are paid on January 9, you can record the transaction with this entry:

| | | | | |
|---|---|---|---|---|
| Jan. | 9 | Salaries Expense . . . . . . . . . . . . . . . . . . . . . . | 700.00 | |
| | | Cash . . . . . . . . . . . . . . . . . . . . . . . . . . | | 700.00 |
| | | Paid wages for two weeks. | | |

The entry's $210 debit to Salaries Expense includes both the $210 salary incurred during 1990 and the $490 salary expense incurred during 1991. However, when the entry is posted, because of the previously posted reversing entry, the balance of the Salaries Expense account shows only the $490 expense of the current period, as follows:

**Salaries Expense**

| Date | | Explanation | Dr. | Cr. | Bal. |
|---|---|---|---|---|---|
| Dec. | 12 | Paid wages | 700 | | 700 |
| | 26 | Paid wages | 700 | | 1,400 |
| | 31 | Accrued wages | 210 | | 1,600 |
| | 31 | Closing | | 1,610 | –0– |
| 1991 | | | | | |
| Jan. | 1 | Reversal | | 210 | (210) |
| | 9 | Paid wages | 700 | | 490 |

## Summary of the Appendix in Terms of Learning Objective

**8.** Reversing entries are applicable to all accrued items, such as accrued interest earned, accrued interest expense, accrued taxes, and accrued salaries and wages. Reversing entries are also used for prepaid and unearned items if (and only if) the business records prepaid expenses with debits to expense accounts, and records unearned revenues with credits to revenue accounts. (This practice was explained in Appendix A at the end of Chapter 3.) In any case, however, reversing entries are not required. The financial statements appear exactly the same whether or not reversing entries are used. Reversing entries are used as a convenience in bookkeeping.

## Glossary

Define or explain the words and phrases listed in the chapter Glossary. (L. O. 7)

**Accounting cycle** the recurring accounting steps that are performed each accounting period and that begin with the recording of transactions and proceed through posting the recorded amounts, preparing a trial balance and completing a work sheet, preparing the financial statements, preparing and posting adjusting and closing entries, and preparing a post-closing trial balance. pp. 168–170

**Closing entries** entries made at the end of each accounting period to establish zero balances in the temporary accounts and to transfer the temporary account balances to a capital account or accounts or to the Retained Earnings account. pp. 153–159

**Date of declaration** the date on which a dividend is declared by a corporation's board of directors. p. 167

**Date of payment** the date on which a dividend liability of a corporation is satisfied by mailing checks to the stockholders. p. 167

**Date of record** the date on which the stockholders who are listed in a corporation's records are determined to be those who will receive a dividend. p. 167

**Deficit** a negative amount (debit balance) of retained earnings. p. 168

**Dividends Declared** a temporary account that serves the same function for a corporation as does a withdrawals account for a proprietorship, and which is closed to Retained Earnings at the end of each accounting period. p. 167

**Income Summary** the account used in the closing process to summarize the amounts of revenues and expenses, and from which the amount of the net income or loss is transferred to the owner's capital account in a single proprietorship, the partners' capital accounts in a partnership, or the Retained Earnings account in a corporation. p. 153

**Nominal accounts** another name for *temporary accounts*. p. 159

**Permanent accounts** accounts that remain open as long as the asset, liability, or owner's equity items recorded in the accounts continue in existence; therefore, accounts that appear in the balance sheet. p. 159

**Post-closing trial balance** a trial balance prepared after all adjusting and closing entries have been posted. pp. 159, 165

**Real accounts** another name for *permanent accounts*. p. 159

**Reversing entries** optional entries that transfer the balances in balance sheet accounts which arose as a result of certain adjusting entries (usually accruals) to income statement accounts. p. 172

**Stockholders of record** the stockholders of a corporation as reflected in the records of the corporation. p. 166

**Temporary accounts** accounts that are closed at the end of each accounting period; therefore, the revenue, expense, Income Summary, and withdrawals accounts. p. 159

**Working papers** the memoranda, analyses, and other informal papers prepared by accountants in the process of organizing the data that goes into the formal financial reports given to managers and other interested parties. p. 150

**Work sheet** a working paper on which the accountant shows the unadjusted trial balance, shows the effects of the adjustments on the account balances, calculates the net income or loss, and sorts the adjusted amounts according to the financial statements on which the amounts will appear. p. 150

## Objective Review

Answers to the following questions are listed in Appendix I at the end of the book. Be sure that you decide which is the one best answer to each question *before* you check the answers in the appendix.

1. In preparing a work sheet at the end of the annual accounting period, Fritz Company's accountant incorrectly extended a $6,000 salaries expense amount from the adjusted trial balance to the Statement of Changes in Owner's Equity or Balance Sheet Debit column. As a result of this error:
   *a.* The net income calculated on the work sheet will be understated.
   *b.* On the bottom row of the work sheet, the totals of the last two columns will not be equal.
   *c.* The Adjusted Trial Balance columns will not balance.
   *d.* The net income calculated on the work sheet will be overstated.
   *e.* Both (*a*) and (*b*) are correct.
2. Related to the process of preparing closing entries:
   *a.* All expense accounts are first closed to the revenue accounts, which are then closed to Income Summary.
   *b.* After the process is completed, all temporary accounts will have zero balances.
   *c.* Expenses, revenues, and the withdrawals account are closed to Income Summary.
   *d.* After the process is completed, the Income Summary account balance will equal net income or net loss for the period.
   *e.* None of the above is correct.
3. A post-closing trial balance:
   *a.* Must be prepared as the first step in the end-of-period procedures that lead to the preparation of financial statements.
   *b.* Is one of the important financial statements presented to the owner of a business and other outside parties.
   *c.* Should include only balances of accounts that appear on the balance sheet.
   *d.* Includes the balances of all accounts that appear on the financial statements.
   *e.* Should include only balances of accounts that appear on the statement of changes in owner's equity or on the balance sheet.
4. The retained earnings of a corporation:
   *a.* Include the sum of all past net incomes (less net losses) of the corporation plus any dividends that have been declared but not paid.
   *b.* Represent cash balances the corporation has available to pay dividends.

*c.* Less any contributed capital amounts equal the total stockholders' equity of the corporation.
*d.* Will be reported as a deficit if the sum of all prior net losses plus all dividend declarations exceed the sum of all prior net incomes.
*e.* Will be reported as a positive amount if net income for the current period exceeds dividend declarations during the period.

5. In accounting for dividends that a corporation declares and pays:
*a.* The Dividends Declared account is closed to Income Summary.
*b.* A dividend declaration is debited to Retained Earnings and credited to Dividends Declared.
*c.* A payment of a previously recorded dividend declaration is debited to Dividends Declared and credited to Cash.
*d.* No entry is required on the date of record.
*e.* The Dividends Declared account is reported on the balance sheet as a liability.

6. The steps in the accounting cycle:
*a.* Begin with the preparation of an unadjusted trial balance.
*b.* Are completed once during the life of each business.
*c.* Are concluded with the preparation of a post-closing trial balance.
*d.* Are the eight procedures that are followed in preparing a work sheet.
*e.* All of the above are correct.

*An asterisk (*) identifies the questions, exercises, and problems that are based on Appendix B at the end of the chapter.*

## Questions for Class Discussion

1. What is the difference between working papers and a work sheet?
2. What tasks are performed on a work sheet?
3. Is it possible to complete the statements and adjust and close the accounts without preparing a work sheet? What is gained by preparing a work sheet?
4. At what stage in the accounting process is a work sheet prepared?
5. Where do you obtain the amounts that are entered in the Unadjusted Trial Balance columns of a work sheet?
6. Why are the adjustments in the Adjustments columns of a work sheet keyed together with letters?
7. What is the result of combining the amounts in the Unadjusted Trial Balance columns with the amounts in the Adjustments columns of a work sheet?
8. Why must you exercise care in sorting the items in the Adjusted Trial Balance columns to the proper Income Statement or Balance Sheet columns?
9. In extending the items in the Adjusted Trial Balance columns of a work sheet, what would be the effect on the net income of extending (*a*) an expense into the Statement of Changes in Owner's Equity or Balance Sheet Debit column, (*b*) a liability into the Income Statement Credit

column, and (*c*) a revenue into the Statement of Changes in Owner's Equity or Balance Sheet Debit column? Would each of these errors be detected automatically on the work sheet? Which would be detected automatically? Why?

10. Why are revenue and expense accounts called temporary accounts? Are there any other temporary accounts?
11. What two purposes are accomplished by recording closing entries?
12. What accounts are affected by closing entries? What accounts are not affected?
13. Explain the difference between adjusting and closing entries.
14. What is the purpose of the Income Summary account?
15. Why is a post-closing trial balance prepared?
16. An accounting student listed the item, ''Depreciation expense, building, $1,800,'' on a post-closing trial balance. What did this indicate?
17. What two kinds of accounts are shown in the stockholders' equity section of a corporation's balance sheet?
18. Explain how the retained earnings item found on corporate balance sheets arises.
19. What three dates are normally involved in the declaration and payment of a cash dividend?
20. What is the purpose of using a Dividends Declared account?
21. One corporation uses a Dividends Declared account and another corporation does not. What effect does this difference have on the entries to be made by the corporations?
22. Explain why the payment of a cash dividend by a corporation with a deficit generally is illegal.

*23. If one company uses reversing entries and another does not, what differences between the two companies will show up on the financial statements?

*24. Why do reversing entries make the bookkeeping process easier?

*25. If a company made an adjusting entry to accrue salaries expense of $500 at the end of an accounting period, what reversing entry would be made for this accrual?

*26. At what stage in the accounting cycle are reversing entries recorded? When are they dated?

## Exercises

**Exercise 4–1**
**Sorting account balances on a work sheet**
(L. O. 1)

The balances of the following accounts appeared in the Adjusted Trial Balance columns of a work sheet. Copy the account numbers in a column on a sheet of note paper, and beside each number indicate by letter the Income Statement or Balance Sheet column to which the account's balance would be sorted in completing the work sheet. Use the letter *a* to indicate the Income Statement Debit column, *b* to indicate the Income Statement Credit column, *c* to indicate the Statement of Changes in Owner's Equity or Balance Sheet Debit column, and *d* to indicate the Statement of Changes in Owner's Equity or Balance Sheet Credit column.

1. Cash.
2. Accounts Payable.
3. Accumulated Depreciation, Repair Equipment.
4. Advertising Expense.
5. Leo Walken, Capital.
6. Accounts Receivable.
7. Revenue from Repairs.
8. Leo Walken, Withdrawals.
9. Rent Expense.
10. Repair Equipment.
11. Repair Supplies.
12. Wages Expense.
13. Prepaid Insurance.

**Exercise 4–2**
**Preparing adjusting entries from work sheet information**
(L. O. 1)

The following item amounts are from the Adjustments columns of a work sheet. Use this information to prepare adjusting journal entries dated December 31.

| | Adjustments | |
|---|---|---|
| | **Debit** | **Credit** |
| Prepaid insurance | | (*a*) 1,020 |
| Office supplies | | (*b*) 235 |
| Accumulated depreciation, office equipment | | (*c*) 650 |
| Accumulated depreciation, shop equipment | | (*d*) 4,015 |
| Office salaries expense | (*e*) 65 | |
| Shop wages expense | (*e*) 335 | |
| Insurance expense, office equipment | (*a*) 100 | |
| Insurance expense, shop equipment | (*a*) 920 | |
| Office supplies expense | (*b*) 235 | |
| Depreciation expense, office equipment | (*c*) 650 | |
| Depreciation expense, shop equipment | (*d*) 4,015 | |
| Salaries and wages payable | | (*e*) 400 |
| Totals | 6,320 | 6,320 |

**Exercise 4–3**
**Using T-account information to prepare closing entries**
(L. O. 2)

On a sheet of paper, copy the following T-accounts and their end-of-period balances. Below the accounts, prepare entries to close the accounts. Post to the T-accounts.

**Mac Boss, Capital**

| | | | |
|---|---|---|---|
| | | Dec. 31 | 15,000 |

**Rent Expense**

| | | | |
|---|---|---|---|
| Dec. 31 | 2,800 | | |

**Mac Boss, Withdrawals**

| | | | |
|---|---|---|---|
| Dec. 31 | 18,500 | | |

**Salaries Expense**

| | | | |
|---|---|---|---|
| Dec. 31 | 12,250 | | |

**Income Summary**

| | | | |
|---|---|---|---|
| | | | |

**Insurance Expense**

| | | | |
|---|---|---|---|
| Dec. 31 | 960 | | |

**Commissions Earned**

| | | | |
|---|---|---|---|
| | | Dec. 31 | 39,100 |

**Depreciation Expense, Equipment**

| | | | |
|---|---|---|---|
| Dec. 31 | 600 | | |

**Exercise 4–4**
**Using work sheet information to prepare closing entries**
(L. O. 2)

The following items appeared in the Income Statement columns of a December 31 work sheet prepared for Donald Cole, an attorney. Assume that Mr. Cole withdrew $28,000 from his law practice during the year and prepare entries to close the accounts.

| | Income Statement | |
|---|---|---|
| | Debit | Credit |
| Legal fees earned | | 64,000 |
| Office salaries expense | 15,000 | |
| Rent expense | 7,200 | |
| Insurance expense | 1,500 | |
| Office supplies expense | 350 | |
| Depreciation expense, office equipment | 2,800 | |
| | 26,850 | 64,000 |
| Net income | 37,150 | |
| | 64,000 | 64,000 |

**Exercise 4–5**
**Preparing and posting closing entries for a corporation**
(L. O. 2, 5)

Open the following T-accounts on note paper for a corporation that does repair work for other companies. Below the T-accounts, prepare entries to close the accounts. Post to the T-accounts.

**Common Stock**

| Debit | | Credit | |
|---|---|---|---|
| | | Dec. 31 | 60,000 |

**Rent Expense**

| Debit | | Credit | |
|---|---|---|---|
| Dec. 31 | 7,200 | | |

**Retained Earnings**

| Debit | | Credit | |
|---|---|---|---|
| | | Dec. 31 | 8,400 |

**Salaries Expense**

| Debit | | Credit | |
|---|---|---|---|
| Dec. 31 | 30,000 | | |

**Income Summary**

| Debit | | Credit | |
|---|---|---|---|
| | | | |

**Insurance Expense**

| Debit | | Credit | |
|---|---|---|---|
| Dec. 31 | 1,200 | | |

**Revenue from Repairs**

| Debit | | Credit | |
|---|---|---|---|
| | | Dec. 31 | 60,000 |

**Depreciation Expense, Equipment**

| Debit | | Credit | |
|---|---|---|---|
| Dec. 31 | 4,800 | | |

**Dividends Declared**

| Debit | | Credit | |
|---|---|---|---|
| Nov. 15 | 10,000 | | |

**Exercise 4–6**
**Closing entries for a corporation**
(L. O. 3)

A corporation debited Dividends Declared for $18,000 during the year ended December 31. The items that follow appeared in the Income Statement columns of the work sheet prepared at year-end. Prepare closing journal entries for the corporation.

| | Income Statement | |
|---|---|---|
| | Debit | Credit |
| Revenue from services | | 106,300 |
| Office salaries expense | 32,000 | |
| Rent expense | 15,000 | |
| Insurance expense | 2,100 | |
| Office supplies expense | 500 | |
| Depreciation expense, office equipment | 6,200 | |
| | 55,800 | 106,300 |
| Net income | 50,500 | |
| | 106,300 | 106,300 |

**Exercise 4–7**
**Recording corporate transactions in T-accounts**
(L. O. 4, 5)

1. On a sheet of note paper, open the following T-accounts: Cash, Accounts Receivable, Equipment, Notes Payable, Common Dividend Payable, Common Stock, Retained Earnings, Income Summary, Dividends Declared, Revenue from Services, and Operating Expenses.
2. Record directly in the T-accounts these transactions of a new corporation:
   *a.* Issued common stock for $12,000 cash.
   *b.* Purchased equipment for $10,000 cash.
   *c.* Sold and delivered $30,000 of services on credit.
   *d.* Collected $26,000 of accounts receivable.
   *e.* Paid $20,000 of operating expenses.
   *f.* Declared cash dividends of $4,000.
   *g.* Paid the dividends declared in (*f*).
   *h.* Purchased $6,000 of additional equipment, giving $4,000 in cash and a $2,000 promissory note.
   *i.* Closed the revenue accounts, (*j*) the expense accounts, (*k*) Income Summary, and (*l*) Dividends Declared.
3. Answer these questions:
   *a.* Does the corporation have retained earnings?
   *b.* Does it have any cash?
   *c.* If the corporation has retained earnings, why does it not also have cash?
   *d.* Can the corporation legally declare additional cash dividends?
   *e.* Can it pay additional cash dividends?
   *f.* What does the balance of the Notes Payable account tell the financial statement reader about the makeup of the corporation's assets?
   *g.* Explain what the balance of the Common Stock account represents.
   *h.* Explain what the balance of the Retained Earnings account represents.

**Exercise 4–8**
**Preparing a work sheet**
(L. O. 1)

Following is an alphabetical list of Seeger Company's accounts and their unadjusted balances. All are normal balances. To save you time, the balances are in one- and two-digit numbers.

**Trial Balance Accounts and Balances**

| | | | |
|---|---|---|---|
| Accounts payable | $3 | Rent expense | $ 3 |
| Accounts receivable | 4 | Revenue from repairs | 22 |
| Accumulated depreciation, shop equipment | 3 | Rick Seeger, capital | 13 |
| Cash | 6 | Rick Seeger, withdrawals | 3 |
| Notes payable | 2 | Shop equipment | 8 |
| Prepaid insurance | 4 | Shop supplies | 5 |
| | | Wages expense | 10 |

*Required*

1. Prepare a work sheet form and enter the trial balance accounts and amounts on the work sheet in their alphabetical order.
2. Complete the work sheet using the following information:
   *a.* Estimated depreciation of shop equipment, $2.
   *b.* Expired insurance, $2.
   *c.* Unused shop supplies per inventory, $2.
   *d.* Earned but unpaid wages, $3.

**Exercise 4–9**
**Preparing a work sheet**
(L. O. 1)

The unadjusted trial balance of Medium Company, Inc., as of December 31, 1990, the end of its annual accounting period, follows:

| | | |
|---|---|---|
| Cash | $ 4,500 | |
| Prepaid insurance | 1,500 | |
| Repair supplies | 2,400 | |
| Repair equipment | 18,000 | |
| Accumulated depreciation, repair equipment | | $ 1,200 |
| Common stock | | 17,000 |
| Retained earnings | | 1,800 |
| Dividends declared | 5,000 | |
| Revenue from repairs | | 48,000 |
| Salaries expense | 25,800 | |
| Rent expense | 10,800 | |
| Totals | $68,000 | $68,000 |

*Required*

1. Prepare a work sheet form on note paper and enter the trial balance.
2. Complete the work sheet using the information that follows:
   *a.* Expired insurance, $900.
   *b.* Unused repair supplies per inventory, $400.
   *c.* Estimated depreciation of repair equipment, $2,500.
   *d.* Earned but unpaid salaries, $600.

**Exercise 4–10**
**Adjusting and closing entries**
(L. O. 5)

Prepare adjusting and closing journal entries for the corporation of Exercise 4–9.

**Exercise 4–11**
**The steps in the accounting cycle**
(L. O. 6)

List the letters identifying the following steps in the accounting cycle in the order in which the steps are performed.

*a.* Preparing an unadjusted trial balance.
*b.* Journalizing and posting closing entries.
*c.* Journalizing transactions.
*d.* Preparing a post-closing trial balance.
*e.* Completing the work sheet.
*f.* Posting the entries to record transactions.
*g.* Preparing the financial statements.
*h.* Journalizing and posting adjusting entries.

***Exercise 4–12**
**Reversing entries**
(L. O. 8)

On December 31, adjusting entry information for Janes Company is as follows:

*a.* Depreciation on office equipment, $3,000.
*b.* Four hundred dollars of the Prepaid Insurance balance has expired.
*c.* Employees have earned salaries of $800 that have not been paid.
*d.* The Unearned Service Fees account balance includes $1,000 that has been earned.
*e.* The company has earned $2,400 of service fees that have not been collected or recorded.

*Required*

List the letters that identify adjustments for which reversing entries should be made. Assuming the appropriate adjusting entries have been recorded, prepare the reversing entries.

***Exercise 4–13**
**Reversing entries**
(L. O. 8)

The following information relates to Dawson Company on December 31, 1990, the end of its annual accounting period.

*a.* Dawson rents office space for $2,000 per month. The company failed to pay the rent for December until January 6, at which time it paid the rent for December and January.
*b.* Because Dawson does not use all of its office space, it subleases space to a tenant for $400 per month. The tenant failed to pay the December rent until January 8, at which time it paid the rent for December and January.

*Required*

1. Assuming that Dawson does not use reversing entries, prepare adjusting journal entries dated December 31. Also prepare entries to record Dawson's payment of rent in January and the receipt of rent in January from Dawson's tenant.
2. Assuming that Dawson uses reversing entries, prepare adjusting journal entries dated December 31 and reversing entries dated January 1. Also prepare entries to record Dawson's payment of rent in January and the receipt of rent in January from Dawson's tenant.

## Problems

**Problem 4–1**
**Closing entries for partnerships and corporations**
(L. O. 2, 3, 4, 5)

Roy Red, Ben Blue, and George Green started a business on January 7, 1989, and each invested $45,000 in the business. During 1989, the business lost $11,250; and during 1990, it earned $49,500. On January 5, 1991, the three owners agreed to pay out to themselves $27,000 of the accumulated earnings of the business. On January 9, the $27,000 was paid out.

*Required*

1. Assume that the business is a partnership and the partners share net incomes and net losses equally. Give the entries to record the investments and to close the Income Summary account at the end of 1989 and again at the end of 1990. Also assume that the partners shared equally in the $27,000 of earnings paid out. Give the entry to record the withdrawals.
2. Assume that the business is organized as a corporation and that each owner invested $45,000 in it by buying 4,500 shares of its $10 par value common stock. Give the entry to record the investments. Also, give the entries to close the Income Summary account at the end of 1989 and again at the end of 1990 and to record the declaration and payment of the $2 per share dividend. (Ignore corporate income taxes and assume that the three owners are the corporation's board of directors.)

**Problem 4–2**
**The work sheet; financial statements and closing entries**
(L. O. 1, 2)

At the end of its annual accounting period, a trial balance from the ledger of Rip's Repair Service appeared as follows:

**RIP'S REPAIR SERVICE**
**Unadjusted Trial Balance**
**December 31, 1990**

| | | |
|---|---|---|
| Cash | $ 1,825 | |
| Prepaid insurance | 1,300 | |
| Repair supplies | 4,375 | |
| Repair equipment | 7,860 | |
| Accumulated depreciation, repair equipment | | $ 1,920 |
| Accounts payable | | 295 |
| Rip Horn, capital | | 6,185 |
| Rip Horn, withdrawals | 28,200 | |
| Revenue from repairs | | 55,845 |
| Wages expense | 15,210 | |
| Rent expense | 4,500 | |
| Utilities expense | 975 | |
| Totals | $64,245 | $64,245 |

*Required*

1. Enter the trial balance on a work sheet form and complete the work sheet using the information that follows:
   *a.* Expired insurance, $800.
   *b.* A repair supplies inventory showed $1,160 of unused supplies on hand.
   *c.* Estimated depreciation on repair equipment, $990.
   *d.* Wages earned by the one employee but unpaid and unrecorded, $120.

2. From the work sheet prepare an income statement, a statement of changes in owner's equity, and a classified balance sheet. Mr. Horn did not make additional investments in the business during 1990.
3. Prepare adjusting journal entries and compound closing entries.

**Problem 4–3**
**All steps in the accounting cycle (covers two accounting cycles)**
(L. O. 1, 2, 3, 4, 6)

Tami Martin opened a real estate office she called Martin Realty. During May, she completed these transactions:

| | | |
|---|---|---|
| May | 3 | Invested in the real estate agency $3,000 in cash and an automobile having a $15,000 fair value. |
| | 3 | Rented furnished office space and paid one month's rent, $750. |
| | 4 | Purchased office supplies for cash, $225. |
| | 8 | Paid the premium on a one-year insurance policy, $1,080. |
| | 14 | Paid the salary of the office secretary for two weeks, $600. |
| | 16 | Sold a house and collected an $8,010 commission. |
| | 28 | Paid the salary of the office secretary for two weeks, $600. |
| | 31 | Paid the May telephone bill, $75. |
| | 31 | Paid for gas and oil used in the agency car during May, $90. |

*Required Work for May*

1. Open these accounts: Cash; Prepaid Insurance; Office Supplies; Automobile; Accumulated Depreciation, Automobile; Salaries Payable; Tami Martin, Capital; Tami Martin, Withdrawals; Income Summary; Commissions Earned; Rent Expense; Salaries Expense; Gas, Oil, and Repairs Expense; Telephone Expense; Insurance Expense; Office Supplies Expense; and Depreciation Expense, Automobile.
2. Prepare and post journal entries to record the transactions.
3. Prepare an unadjusted trial balance on a work sheet form and complete the work sheet using the following information:
   *a.* Two thirds of a month's insurance has expired.
   *b.* An inventory shows $185 of unused office supplies remaining.
   *c.* Estimated depreciation on the automobile, $250.
   *d.* Earned but unpaid salary of the office secretary, $60.
4. Prepare an income statement and a statement of changes in owner's equity for May, and prepare a May 31 classified balance sheet.
5. Journalize and post adjusting and closing entries.
6. Prepare a post-closing trial balance.

During June, Tami Martin completed these transactions:

| | | |
|---|---|---|
| June | 1 | Paid the June rent on the office space, $750. |
| | 4 | Purchased additional office supplies for cash, $45. |
| | 11 | Paid the salary of the office secretary for two weeks, $600. |
| | 15 | Tami Martin withdrew $3,000 cash from the business for personal use. |
| | 18 | Sold a building lot and collected a $2,200 commission. |
| | 25 | Paid the salary of the office secretary for two weeks, $600. |
| | 30 | Paid for gas and oil used in the agency car during June, $80. |
| | 30 | Paid the June telephone bill, $65. |

*Required Work for June*

1. Prepare and post journal entries to record the transactions.
2. Prepare an unadjusted trial balance on a work sheet form and complete the work sheet using the following information:
   *a.* One month's insurance has expired.
   *b.* An office supplies inventory shows $185 of unused supplies.
   *c.* Estimated depreciation on the automobile, $250.
   *d.* Earned but unpaid secretary's salary, $180.
3. Prepare an income statement and a statement of changes in owner's equity for June and prepare a June 30 classified balance sheet.
4. Journalize and post adjusting and closing entries.
5. Prepare a post-closing trial balance.

**Problem 4–4**
**End-of-period accounting procedures**
(L. O. 1, 2, 3)

The accounts of Strait Alleys, showing balances as of the end of its annual accounting period, appear in the booklet of working papers that accompanies this text, and a trial balance of its ledger is reproduced on a work sheet form provided there. The trial balance has the items that follow:

**STRAIT ALLEYS**
**Unadjusted Trial Balance**
**December 31, 1990**

| | | |
|---|---|---|
| Cash | $ 1,250 | |
| Bowling supplies | 2,150 | |
| Prepaid insurance | 2,000 | |
| Bowling equipment | 74,325 | |
| Accumulated depreciation, bowling equipment | | $ 11,460 |
| Accounts payable | | 205 |
| Long-term notes payable | | 15,000 |
| Paul Strait, capital | | 31,800 |
| Paul Strait, withdrawals | 23,500 | |
| Bowling revenue | | 81,750 |
| Wages expense | 24,300 | |
| Equipment repairs expense | 630 | |
| Rent expense | 7,200 | |
| Utilities expense | 3,200 | |
| Taxes expense | 760 | |
| Interest expense | 900 | |
| Totals | $140,215 | $140,215 |

*Required*

1. Enter the unadjusted trial balance on a work sheet form and complete the work sheet using the information that follows:
   *a.* Bowling supplies inventory, $315.
   *b.* Expired insurance, $1,680.
   *c.* Estimated depreciation on bowling equipment, $7,125.
   *d.* The December electric bill for the bowling alley arrived in the mail after the trial balance was prepared. Its $330 amount was unrecorded.
   *e.* Wages earned but unpaid and unrecorded, $420.
   *f.* The lease contract on the building calls for an annual rent equal to 10% of the annual bowling revenue, with $600 payable each month on the first day of the month. The $600 was paid each month and debited to the Rent Expense account.

*g.* Personal property taxes on the bowling equipment amounting to $285 have accrued but are unrecorded and unpaid.

*h.* The long-term note payable was signed on September 1, and interest on the debt is at a 12% annual rate or $150 per month. The note calls for payment in advance of $450 interest every three months. Interest payments were made on September 1 and December 1. A $1,500 payment on the note principal is due next September 1.

2. Prepare an income statement, a statement of changes in owner's equity, and a classified balance sheet. Mr. Strait did not make additional investments in the business during 1990.
3. Journalize adjusting and closing entries.
4. Post the adjusting and closing entries and prepare a post-closing trial balance. (Omit this requirement if you are not using the working papers.)

**Problem 4–5**
**End-of-period accounting procedures**
(L. O. 1, 2, 3)

The unadjusted trial balance of Doc's Delivery Service is as follows:

**DOC'S DELIVERY SERVICE**
**Unadjusted Trial Balance**
**December 31, 1990**

| | | |
|---|---|---|
| Cash | $ 785 | |
| Accounts receivable | 1,000 | |
| Prepaid insurance | 3,400 | |
| Office supplies | 365 | |
| Prepaid rent | 375 | |
| Office equipment | 3,690 | |
| Accumulated depreciation, office equipment | | $ 855 |
| Delivery equipment | 22,185 | |
| Accumulated depreciation, delivery equipment | | 4,725 |
| Accounts payable | | 1,335 |
| Unearned delivery service revenue | | 825 |
| Mark Welby, capital | | 34,355 |
| Mark Welby, withdrawals | 18,000 | |
| Delivery service revenue | | 63,085 |
| Rent expense | 4,500 | |
| Telephone expense | 540 | |
| Office salaries expense | 15,090 | |
| Delivery wages expense | 30,480 | |
| Gas, oil, and repairs expense | 4,770 | |
| Totals | $105,180 | $105,180 |

*Required*

1. Enter the unadjusted trial balance on a work sheet form and complete the work sheet using the information that follows:

   *a.* Insurance expired on the office equipment, $150, and on the delivery equipment, $2,835.

   *b.* An inventory showed $165 of unused office supplies on hand.

   *c.* Estimated depreciation on the office equipment, $450.

   *d.* Estimated depreciation on the delivery equipment, $3,625.

   *e.* In December 1989, the company had prepaid the January 1990 rent for garage and office space occupied by the delivery service. This amount appears as the balance of the prepaid Rent account. Rents for February through November were paid each month and debited to the Rent Expense account. Also, $750 was paid for extra space used during the summer. As of the trial balance date, the December rent had not been paid.

*f.* Three stores signed contracts with the delivery service in which they agreed to pay a fixed fee for the delivery of packages. Two of the stores made advance payments on their contracts, and the amounts paid were credited to the Unearned Delivery Service Revenue account. An examination of their contracts shows $420 of the $825 paid was earned by the end of the accounting period. The third store's contract provides for a $300 monthly fee to be paid at the end of each month's service. It was signed on December 15, and one half of a month's revenue has accrued but is unrecorded.

*g.* A $55 December telephone bill and a $90 bill for repairs to a motorcycle used in the business arrived in the mail on December 31. Neither bill was paid or recorded before the trial balance was prepared.

*h.* Office salaries, $120, and delivery wages, $265, have accrued but are unpaid and unrecorded.

2. Prepare an income statement, a statement of changes in owner's equity, and a classified balance sheet. Mr. Welby did not make additional investments in the business during 1990.
3. Journalize adjusting and closing entries.
4. Post the adjusting and closing entries to the accounts and prepare a post-closing trial balance. (If you are not using the working papers, omit this requirement.)

***Problem 4–6**
**Reversing entries**
(L. O. 2, 8)

Windward Service Company's unadjusted trial balance on December 31, 1990, the end of its annual accounting period, is as follows:

**WINDWARD SERVICE COMPANY**
**Unadjusted Trial Balance**
**December 31, 1990**

| | | |
|---|---|---|
| Cash | $ 49,150 | |
| Notes receivable | 25,000 | |
| Office supplies | 2,800 | |
| Land | 30,000 | |
| Unearned service fees | | $ 12,000 |
| Notes payable | | 60,000 |
| J. Cass, capital | | 25,000 |
| J. Cass, withdrawals | 40,000 | |
| Service fees earned | | 178,000 |
| Interest earned | | 1,700 |
| Rent earned | | 8,250 |
| Salaries expense | 129,000 | |
| Insurance expense | 3,300 | |
| Interest expense | 5,700 | |
| Totals | $284,950 | $284,950 |

Information necessary to prepare adjusting entries is as follows:

*a.* Employees, who are paid $5,000 every two weeks, have earned $3,500 since the last payment. The next payment of $5,000 will be on January 4.

*b.* Windward rents office space to a tenant who has paid only $300 of the $750 rent for December. On January 10, the tenant will pay the remainder along with the rent for January.

*c.* An inventory of office supplies discloses $450 of unused supplies.

*d.* Premiums for insurance against injuries to employees are paid monthly. The $300 premium for December will be paid January 12.

*e.* Windward owes $60,000 on a note payable that requires quarterly payments of accrued interest. The quarterly payments of $1,800 each are made on the 15th of January, April, July, and October.

*f.* An analysis of Windward's service contracts with customers shows that $4,200 of the amount customers have prepaid remains unearned.

*g.* Windward has a $25,000 note receivable on which interest of $125 has accrued. On January 20, the note and the total accrued interest of $375 will be repaid to Windward.

*h.* Windward has earned but unrecorded revenue of $5,500 for services provided to a customer that will pay for the work on January 23. At that time, the customer will also pay $2,100 for services Windward will perform in early January.

*Required*

1. Prepare adjusting journal entries.
2. Prepare closing journal entries.
3. Prepare reversing entries.
4. Prepare journal entries to record the January 1991 cash receipts and cash payments identified in the above information.

## Alternate Problems

**Problem 4–1A**
**Closing entries for partnerships and corporations**
(L. O. 2, 3, 4, 5)

On January 5, 1989, Bob Long, Kim Wong, and Phil Song started a business in which Bob Long invested $15,000, Kim Wong invested $30,000, and Phil Song invested $45,000. During 1989, the business lost $4,500; and during 1990, it earned $27,000. On January 5, 1991, the three business owners agreed to pay out to themselves $18,000 of the accumulated earnings of the business; and on January 10, the $18,000 was paid out.

*Required*

1. Assume that the business is a partnership and that the partners share net incomes and net losses in proportion to their investments. Give the entries to record the investments and to close the Income Summary account at the end of 1989 and again at the end of 1990. Also assume that the partners paid out the accumulated earnings in proportion to their investments. Give the entry to record the withdrawals.
2. Assume that the business is organized as a corporation and that the owners invested in the corporation by buying its $10 par value common stock, with Bob Long buying 1,500 shares, Kim Wong buying 3,000

shares, and Phil Song buying 4,500 shares. Give the entry to record the investments. Also give the entries to close the Income Summary account at the end of 1989 and again at the end of 1990. Then give the entries to record the declaration and payment of the $2 per share dividend. (Ignore corporation income taxes and assume the investors are the corporation's board of directors.)

**Problem 4–2A**
**The work sheet; financial statements and closing entries**
(L. O. 1, 2)

A trial balance of the ledger of Ms. Shine Janitorial Service at the end of its annual accounting period appeared as follows:

**MS. SHINE JANITORIAL SERVICE**
**Unadjusted Trial Balance**
**December 31, 1990**

| | | |
|---|---|---|
| Cash | $ 1,600 | |
| Accounts receivable | 320 | |
| Prepaid insurance | 1,980 | |
| Cleaning supplies | 1,225 | |
| Prepaid rent | 450 | |
| Cleaning equipment | 3,915 | |
| Accumulated depreciation, cleaning equipment | | $ 1,710 |
| Trucks | 24,840 | |
| Accumulated depreciation, trucks | | 5,720 |
| Accounts payable | | 965 |
| Unearned janitorial revenue | | 600 |
| Jane Adams, capital | | 17,615 |
| Jane Adams, withdrawals | 23,175 | |
| Janitorial revenue earned | | 51,915 |
| Wages expense | 18,660 | |
| Rent expense | 1,200 | |
| Gas, oil, and repairs expense | 1,160 | |
| Totals | $78,525 | $78,525 |

*Required*

1. Enter the trial balance on a work sheet form and complete the work sheet using the information that follows:
   *a.* Expired insurance, $1,425.
   *b.* An inventory of cleaning supplies showed $185 of unused supplies on hand.
   *c.* The cleaning service rents garage and equipment storage space. At the beginning of the year, three months' rent was prepaid as shown by the debit balance of the Prepaid Rent account. Rents for April through November were paid on the first day of each month and debited to the Rent Expense account. The December rent was unpaid on the trial balance date.
   *d.* Estimated depreciation on the cleaning equipment, $545, and (*e*) on the trucks, $3,255.
   *f.* On November 15, the janitorial service contracted and began cleaning the office of Troy Realty for $300 per month. The realty company paid for two months' service in advance, and the amount paid was credited to the Unearned Janitorial Revenue account. The janitorial service also entered into a contract and began cleaning the office of Knox Insurance Agency on December 15. By the month's end, a half month's revenue, $180, had been earned on this contract but was unrecorded.

*g.* Employee's wages amounting to $270 had accrued but were unrecorded on the trial balance date.

2. Prepare an income statement, a statement of changes in owner's equity, and a classified balance sheet for the business. Ms. Adams did not make additional investments in the business during 1990.
3. Prepare adjusting journal entries and compound closing entries.

**Problem 4–3A**
**All steps in the accounting cycle (covers two accounting cycles)**
(L. O. 1, 2, 3, 4, 6)

Tami Martin started a business she called Martin Realty. During May, she completed the transactions that follow:

May 2 Invested in the real estate agency $3,500 in cash and an automobile having a $12,000 fair value.
2 Rented furnished office space and paid one month's rent, $600.
2 Paid the premium on an insurance policy giving one year's protection, $996.
3 Purchased office supplies for cash, $210.
13 Paid the salary of the office secretary for two weeks, $670.
19 Sold a building lot and collected a $2,400 commission on the sale.
27 Paid the salary of the office secretary for two weeks, $670.
31 Paid the May telephone bill, $65.
31 Paid for gas and oil used in the agency car during May, $70.

*Required Work for May*

1. Open these accounts: Cash; Prepaid Insurance; Office Supplies; Automobile; Accumulated Depreciation, Automobile; Salaries Payable; Tami Martin, Capital; Tami Martin, Withdrawals; Income Summary; Commissions Earned; Rent Expense; Salaries Expense; Gas, Oil, and Repairs Expense; Telephone Expense; Insurance Expense; Office Supplies Expense; and Depreciation Expense, Automobile.
2. Prepare and post journal entries to record the transactions.
3. Prepare an unadjusted trial balance on a work sheet form and complete the work sheet using the information that follows:
   *a.* One month's insurance has expired.
   *b.* An inventory shows $165 of unused office supplies remaining.
   *c.* Estimated depreciation on the automobile, $240.
   *d.* Earned but unpaid wages of the secretary, $134.
4. Prepare an income statement and a statement of changes in owner's equity for May, and prepare a May 31 classified balance sheet.
5. Journalize and post adjusting and closing entries.
6. Prepare a post-closing trial balance.

These transactions were completed by Tami Martin during June:

June 1 Paid the June rent on the office space, $600.
5 Sold a house and collected a $7,275 commission.
7 Tami Martin withdrew $2,250 from the business to pay personal expenses.
10 Paid the salary of the office secretary for two weeks, $670.

June 21 Purchased additional office supplies for cash, $55.
24 Paid the salary of the office secretary for two weeks, $670.
30 Paid the June telephone bill, $60.
30 Paid for gas and oil used in the agency car, $75.

*Required Work for June*

1. Prepare and post journal entries to record the transactions.
2. Prepare an unadjusted trial balance on a work sheet form and complete the work sheet using the information that follows:
   *a.* One month's insurance has expired.
   *b.* An office supplies inventory shows $180 of unused office supplies.
   *c.* Estimated depreciation on the automobile, $240.
   *d.* Earned but unrecorded salary of the secretary, $268.
3. Prepare an income statement and a statement of changes in owner's equity for June, and prepare a June 30 classified balance sheet.
4. Journalize and post adjusting and closing entries.
5. Prepare a post-closing trial balance.

**Problem 4–4A**
**End of period accounting procedures**
(L. O. 1, 2, 3)

The accounts of Strait Alleys, showing the end of its annual accounting period balances, appear in the booklet of working papers that accompanies this text, and a trial balance of the accounts is reproduced on a work sheet form provided there. The trial balance has the items that follow:

**STRAIT ALLEYS**
**Unadjusted Trial Balance**
**December 31, 1990**

| | | |
|---|---|---|
| Cash | $ 1,265 | |
| Bowling supplies | 2,230 | |
| Prepaid insurance | 2,000 | |
| Bowling equipment | 74,295 | |
| Accumulated depreciation, bowling equipment | | $ 11,460 |
| Accounts payable | | 205 |
| Long-term notes payable | | 15,000 |
| Paul Strait, capital | | 32,250 |
| Paul Strait, withdrawals | 23,475 | |
| Bowling revenue | | 81,700 |
| Wages expense | 24,580 | |
| Equipment repairs expense | 690 | |
| Rent expense | 7,200 | |
| Utilities expense | 3,200 | |
| Taxes expense | 780 | |
| Interest expense | 900 | |
| Totals | $140,615 | $140,615 |

*Required*

1. Enter the unadjusted trial balance on a work sheet form and complete the work sheet using the information that follows:
   *a.* Bowling supplies inventory, $270.
   *b.* Expired insurance, $1,795.
   *c.* Estimated depreciation on the bowling equipment, $7,075.
   *d.* A $245 bill for equipment repairs arrived in the mail after the trial balance was prepared. It is unrecorded and unpaid.

*e.* Wages earned but unpaid and unrecorded, $335.

*f.* The lease contract on the bowling alley space calls for an annual rental equal to 11% of the annual bowling revenue, with $600 payable each month on the first day of the month. The $600 was paid each month and debited to the Rent Expense account.

*g.* Personal property taxes on the bowling equipment amounting to $325 have accrued but are unrecorded and unpaid.

*h.* The long-term note payable was signed on August 1. The interest on the debt is at a 12% annual rate or $150 per month. The note requires the payment in advance of $450 interest each three months. Interest was paid on August 1 and November 1. A $3,000 payment on the note principal is due next August 1.

2. Prepare an income statement, a statement of changes in owner's equity, and a classified balance sheet. Mr. Strait did not make any additional investments in the business during 1990.
3. Journalize adjusting and closing entries.
4. Post the adjusting and closing entries and prepare a post-closing trial balance. (Omit this requirement if the working papers are not being used.)

**Problem 4–5A**
**End-of-period accounting procedures**
(L. O. 1, 2, 3)

The unadjusted trial balance of Doc's Delivery Service is as follows:

**DOC'S DELIVERY SERVICE**
**Unadjusted Trial Balance**
**December 31, 1990**

| | | |
|---|---|---|
| Cash | $ 785 | |
| Accounts receivable | 1,000 | |
| Prepaid insurance | 3,415 | |
| Office supplies | 365 | |
| Prepaid rent | 375 | |
| Office equipment | 3,690 | |
| Accumulated depreciation, office equipment | | $ 855 |
| Delivery equipment | 22,185 | |
| Accumulated depreciation, delivery equipment | | 4,725 |
| Accounts payable | | 1,335 |
| Unearned delivery service revenue | | 825 |
| Mark Welby, capital | | 34,355 |
| Mark Welby, withdrawals | 18,000 | |
| Delivery service revenue | | 62,325 |
| Rent expense | 3,750 | |
| Telephone expense | 515 | |
| Office salaries expense | 15,090 | |
| Delivery wages expense | 30,480 | |
| Gas, oil, and repairs expense | 4,770 | |
| Totals | $104,420 | $104,420 |

*Required*

1. Enter the unadjusted trial balance on a work sheet form and complete the work sheet using the information that follows:

   *a.* Expired insurance on the office equipment, $165, and on the delivery equipment, $2,665.

   *b.* An inventory showed $180 of unused office supplies on hand.

*c*. Estimated depreciation on the office equipment, $435, and (*d*) on the delivery equipment, $3,495.

*e*. In December 1989, the company had prepaid the January 1990 rent for garage and office space occupied by the delivery service. This amount appears as the balance of the Prepaid Rent account. Rents for February through November were paid each month and debited to the Rent Expense account. As of December 31, 1990, the December rent had not been paid.

*f*. The delivery service has contracts with three stores for the delivery of packages on a fixed-fee basis. Two of the stores made advance payments on their contracts, and the amounts paid were credited to the Unearned Delivery Service Revenue account. An examination of the contracts shows that $480 of the $825 paid was earned by the end of the accounting period. The third store's contract provides for a $380 monthly fee to be paid at the end of each month's service. One half of a month's revenue has accrued on this contract but it is unrecorded.

*g*. A $125 bill for repairs to a delivery truck during December arrived in the mail after the trial balance was prepared. The bill is unpaid and unrecorded.

*h*. Office salaries, $60, and delivery wages, $145, have accrued but are unpaid and unrecorded.

2. Prepare an income statement, a statement of changes in owner's equity, and a classified balance sheet.
3. Journalize adjusting and closing entries.
4. Post the adjusting and closing entries to the accounts and prepare a post-closing trial balance. (If the working papers are not being used, omit this requirement.)

***Problem 4–6A**
**Reversing entries**
(L. O. 2, 8)

Leeward Service Company's unadjusted trial balance on December 31, 1990, the end of its annual accounting period, is as follows:

**LEEWARD SERVICE COMPANY**
**Unadjusted Trial Balance**
**December 31, 1990**

| | | |
|---|---|---|
| Cash | $ 73,725 | |
| Notes receivable | 37,500 | |
| Office supplies | 4,200 | |
| Land | 45,000 | |
| Unearned service fees | | $ 18,000 |
| Notes payable | | 90,000 |
| Cass, capital | | 37,500 |
| Cass, withdrawals | 60,000 | |
| Service fees earned | | 267,000 |
| Interest earned | | 2,550 |
| Rent earned | | 12,375 |
| Salaries expense | 193,500 | |
| Insurance expense | 4,950 | |
| Interest expense | 8,550 | |
| Totals | $427,425 | $427,425 |

Information necessary to prepare adjusting entries is as follows:

*a.* Employees, who are paid $7,500 every two weeks, have earned $5,250 since the last payment. The next payment of $7,500 will be on January 4.

*b.* Leeward rents office space to a tenant who has paid only $450 of the $1,125 rent for December. On January 12, the tenant will pay the remainder along with the rent for January.

*c.* An inventory of office supplies discloses $675 of unused supplies.

*d.* Premiums for insurance against injuries to employees are paid monthly. The $450 premium for December will be paid January 12.

*e.* Leeward owes $90,000 on a note payable that requires quarterly payments of accrued interest. The quarterly payments of $2,700 each are made on the 15th of January, April, July, and October.

*f.* An analysis of Leeward's service contracts with customers shows that $6,300 of the amount customers have prepaid remains unearned.

*g.* Leeward has a $37,500 note receivable on which interest of $175 has accrued. On January 22, the note and the total accrued interest of $575 will be repaid to Leeward.

*h.* Leeward has earned but unrecorded revenue of $8,250 for services provided to a customer who will pay for the work on January 24. At that time, the customer will also pay $3,100 for services Leeward will perform in early January.

*Required*

1. Prepare adjusting journal entries.
2. Prepare closing journal entries.
3. Prepare reversing entries.
4. Prepare journal entries to record the January 1991 cash receipts and cash payments identified in the above information.

## Provocative Problems

**Provocative Problem 4–1**
**Strongarm Moving Service**
(Review problem)

During his second year in college, Wesley Smith inherited Strongarm Moving Service when his father died. He immediately dropped out of school and took over management of the business. At the time he took over, Wesley recognized he knew little about accounting. However, he reasoned that since the business performed its services strictly for cash, if the cash of the business increased, the business was doing OK. Therefore, he was pleased as he watched the cash balance grow from $2,100 when he took over to $25,715 at year-end. Furthermore, since he had withdrawn $30,000 from the business to buy a new car and to pay personal expenses, he reasoned that the business must have earned $53,615 during the year. He arrived at the $53,615 by adding the $23,615 increase in cash to the $30,000 he had withdrawn from the business. Wesley was shocked when he received the income statement that follows and learned that the business had earned less than the amounts withdrawn.

**STRONGARM MOVING SERVICE**
**Income Statement**
**For Year Ended December 31, 1990**

| | | |
|---|---|---|
| Revenue from moving services | | $120,565 |
| Operating expenses: | | |
| Salaries and wages expense | $54,825 | |
| Gas, oil, and repairs expense | 4,835 | |
| Telephone expense | 525 | |
| Taxes expense | 3,710 | |
| Insurance expense | 3,485 | |
| Office supplies expense | 375 | |
| Depreciation expense, office equipment | 600 | |
| Depreciation expense, trucks | 9,375 | |
| Depreciation expense, building | 7,500 | |
| Total operating expenses | | 85,230 |
| Net income | | $ 35,335 |

After thinking about the statement for several days, Wesley asked you to explain how, in a year in which the cash increased $23,615 and he withdrew $30,000, the business earned only $35,335. In examining the accounts of the business, you note that accrued salaries and wages payable at the beginning of the year were $185 but increased to $575 at year's end. Also, the accrued taxes payable were $675 at the beginning of the year but had increased to $715 at year-end. Also, the balance of the Prepaid Insurance account was $300 less and the balance of the Office Supplies account was $75 less at the end of the year than at the beginning. However, except for the changes in these accounts, the change in cash, and the changes in the balances of the accumulated depreciation accounts, there were no other changes in the balances of the concern's asset and liability accounts between the beginning of the year and the end. Back your explanation with a calculation that accounts for the increase in the business's cash.

**Provocative Problem 4–2**
**Victoria Shaw, Attorney**
(L. O. 2, 6)

During the first year-end closing of the accounts of Victoria Shaw's law practice, the office bookkeeper became seriously ill and entered the hospital, unable to have visitors. Ms. Shaw is certain the bookkeeper prepared a work sheet and complete financial statements, but she has only the income statement and cannot find the work sheet or remaining statements. She does have the unadjusted trial balance. She has asked you to take the information she has and prepare adjusting and closing entries. She also wants you to prepare a statement of changes in owner's equity and a classified balance sheet. She says the $1,800 of unearned legal fees on the trial balance represents a retainer fee paid by Guaranty Bank. The bank retained Victoria Shaw on November 1 to do its legal work, and agreed to pay her $600 per month for her services. She says she has also agreed with Eastside Realty to do its legal work on a fixed-fee basis. The agreement calls for a $450 monthly fee payable at the end of each three months. The agreement was signed on December 1, and one month's fee has accrued but has not been recorded. Ms. Shaw did not make any additional investments in the business during the year.

**VICTORIA SHAW, ATTORNEY**
**Unadjusted Trial Balance**
**December 31, 1990**

| | | |
|---|---|---|
| Cash | $ 1,835 | |
| Legal fees receivable | 2,250 | |
| Office supplies | 490 | |
| Prepaid insurance | 1,350 | |
| Furniture and equipment | 18,750 | |
| Accounts payable | | $ 525 |
| Short-term notes payable | | 7,500 |
| Unearned legal fees | | 1,800 |
| Victoria Shaw, capital | | 11,250 |
| Victoria Shaw, withdrawals | 27,000 | |
| Legal fees earned | | 55,985 |
| Salaries expense | 17,625 | |
| Rent expense | 7,200 | |
| Telephone expense | 560 | |
| Totals | $77,060 | $77,060 |

**VICTORIA SHAW, ATTORNEY**
**Income Statement**
**For Year Ended December 31, 1990**

| | | |
|---|---|---|
| Revenue: | | |
| Legal fees earned | | $57,635 |
| Operating expenses: | | |
| Salaries expense | $18,000 | |
| Rent expense | 7,200 | |
| Telephone expense | 560 | |
| Office supplies expense | 300 | |
| Insurance expense | 1,125 | |
| Depreciation expense, furniture and equipment | 1,800 | |
| Interest expense | 900 | |
| Total operating expenses | | 29,885 |
| Net income | | $27,750 |

**Provocative Problem 4–3**
**Valleyview Realty**
(L. O. 1)

The balance sheet on the next page was prepared for Valleyview Realty at the end of its annual accounting period. After completing the balance sheet, Valleyview Realty's accountant journalized and posted the following adjusting and closing entries for the concern:

| | | | | |
|---|---|---|---|---|
| Dec. | 31 | Insurance Expense | 1,725.00 | |
| | | Prepaid Insurance | | 1,725.00 |
| | 31 | Office Supplies Expense | 315.00 | |
| | | Office Supplies | | 315.00 |
| | 31 | Depreciation Expense, Office Equipment | 960.00 | |
| | | Accumulated Depreciation, Office Equipment | | 960.00 |
| | 31 | Depreciation Expense, Automobile | 3,150.00 | |
| | | Accumulated Depreciation, Automobile | | 3,150.00 |
| | 31 | Unearned Property Management Fees | 750.00 | |
| | | Property Management Fees Earned | | 750.00 |

| | | | | |
|---|---|---|---|---|
| Dec. | 31 | Salaries Expense | 270.00 | |
| | | Salaries Payable | | 270.00 |
| | 31 | Commissions Earned | 74,400.00 | |
| | | Property Management Fees Earned | 2,640.00 | |
| | | Income Summary | | 77,040.00 |
| | 31 | Income Summary | 33,750.00 | |
| | | Salaries Expense | | 16,500.00 |
| | | Rent Expense | | 9,000.00 |
| | | Telephone Expense | | 690.00 |
| | | Gas, Oil, and Repairs Expense | | 1,410.00 |
| | | Insurance Expense | | 1,725.00 |
| | | Office Supplies Expense | | 315.00 |
| | | Depreciation Expense, Office Equipment | | 960.00 |
| | | Depreciation Expense, Automobile | | 3,150.00 |
| | 31 | Income Summary | 43,290.00 | |
| | | Gail Banks, Capital | | 43,290.00 |
| | 31 | Gail Banks, Capital | 36,000.00 | |
| | | Gail Banks, Withdrawals | | 36,000.00 |

**VALLEYVIEW REALTY**
**Balance Sheet**
**December 31, 1990**

**Assets**

| | | | |
|---|---|---|---|
| Current assets: | | | |
| Cash | | $ 2,285 | |
| Prepaid insurance | | 750 | |
| Office supplies | | 165 | |
| Total current assets | | | $ 3,200 |
| Plant and equipment: | | | |
| Office equipment | $ 7,860 | | |
| Less accumulated depreciation | 1,515 | $ 6,345 | |
| Automobile | $18,600 | | |
| Less accumulated depreciation | 4,050 | 14,550 | |
| Total plant and equipment | | | 20,895 |
| Total assets | | | $24,095 |

**Liabilities**

| | | |
|---|---|---|
| Current liabilities: | | |
| Accounts payable | $ 315 | |
| Unearned property management fees | 375 | |
| Salaries payable | 270 | |
| Total liabilities | | $ 960 |

**Owner's Equity**

| | |
|---|---|
| Gail Banks, capital, December 31, 1990 | 23,135 |
| Total liabilities and owner's equity | $24,095 |

Enter the relevant information from the balance sheet and the adjusting and closing entries on a work sheet form and complete the work sheet by working backward to the items that appeared in its Unadjusted Trial Balance columns.

## COMPREHENSIVE PROBLEM

**Satellite Theatre**
(Review of Chapters 1 through 4)

Presented below is the November 30, 1990, unadjusted trial balance of Satellite Theatre, which is owned by J. R. Thompson. The temporary account balances represent the results of entries recorded during the first 11 months of 1990, and the balance in J. R. Thompson's capital account has not changed since December 31, 1989.

**SATELLITE THEATRE**
**Unadjusted Trial Balance**
**November 30, 1990**

| | Acct. No. | Debits | Credits |
|---|---|---|---|
| Cash | 111 | $ 4,000 | |
| Concessions inventory | 112 | 11,200 | |
| Supplies inventory | 113 | 750 | |
| Prepaid movie rental | 114 | 880 | |
| Equipment | 131 | 5,500 | |
| Accumulated depreciation, equipment | 132 | | $ 1,100 |
| Building | 135 | 75,000 | |
| Accumulated depreciation, building | 136 | | 14,500 |
| Accounts payable | 211 | | 1,550 |
| Wages payable | 212 | | –0– |
| Utilities payable | 213 | | 250 |
| Interest payable | 214 | | –0– |
| Long-term notes payable | 231 | | 42,000 |
| J. R. Thompson, capital | 311 | | 14,970 |
| J. R. Thompson, withdrawals | 312 | 8,000 | |
| Income summary | 313 | | –0– |
| Admissions revenue | 411 | | 39,850 |
| Concessions revenue | 412 | | 28,650 |
| Wages expense | 511 | 14,000 | |
| Movie rental expense | 512 | 16,500 | |
| Concessions expense | 513 | –0– | |
| Supplies expense | 514 | –0– | |
| Utilities expense | 515 | 2,800 | |
| Advertising expense | 516 | 3,200 | |
| Maintenance expense | 517 | 1,040 | |
| Depreciation expense, equipment | 518 | –0– | |
| Depreciation expense, building | 519 | –0– | |
| Interest expense | 520 | –0– | |
| Totals | | $142,870 | $142,870 |

The following transactions occurred during the month of December 1990:

Dec. 2 Paid a $250 utility bill that was recorded as accrued on November 30.
5 Paid accounts payable of $950.
6 Paid movie rental of $1,500 in advance.
7 Deposited $1,000 of admissions receipts.
10 Purchased $350 of concessions items on credit.
12 Acquired additional equipment worth $4,000 by paying $500 cash and giving a long-term note payable for the balance.
14 Paid wages of $520 for the period December 1 through 14.
17 Purchased $100 of supplies on credit.

Dec. 21 Deposited $1,750 from concessions sales and $1,660 of admissions receipts.
24 Paid $500 for repairs to roof and marquee for weather damage.
28 Paid wages of $720 for the period December 15 through 28.
30 Paid $400 to newspaper for advertisements that appeared in December.
31 Deposited $2,000 from admissions receipts and $850 from concessions sales.

*Required*

1. Set up accounts for the items listed in the November 30 trial balance, and enter the November 30 balances in them.
2. Prepare and post journal entries to record the December transactions listed above.
3. Prepare a 10-column work sheet and enter the December 31 unadjusted balances from the accounts. Also enter adjusting entries for the following items, and complete the work sheet.
   *a.* Unpaid wages were $160 as of December 31.
   *b.* The December 31 concessions inventory was $960.
   *c.* The supplies inventory was $125 on December 31.
   *d.* The unexpired portion of the prepaid movie rental was $510 as of December 31.
   *e.* Depreciation for the year on the equipment was $1,900.
   *f.* Depreciation for the year on the building was $3,750.
   *g.* Unpaid utilities expense for December was $330.
   *h.* Thompson had withdrawn $1,000 cash on December 30, but he had not taken the time to record it.
   *i.* Interest expense on the note payable for 1990 was $4,300.
4. Prepare an income statement and a statement of changes in owner's equity for the year ended December 31, 1990, and a December 31, 1990, classified balance sheet.
5. Journalize and post the adjusting entries.
6. Journalize and post the closing entries.
7. Prepare a post-closing trial balance.

# 5 Accounting for a Merchandising Concern

The illustrations we have used in previous chapters were of businesses that provided services to their customers: businesses such as law firms, accounting firms, and real estate agencies. In this chapter, we shift our attention to merchandising businesses; they buy goods or products and resell them to their customers. Your study of this chapter will focus on the problem of accounting for the goods that merchandising companies purchase for resale. You will learn to identify the elements of cost of goods sold and to complete the end-of-period procedures that are used to account for merchandising companies, whether they are organized as corporations or as proprietorships.

**Learning Objectives**

*After studying Chapter 5, you should be able to:*

1. Analyze and record transactions that involve the purchase and resale of merchandise.
2. Explain the nature of each item entering into the calculation of cost of goods sold and gross profit from sales.
3. Prepare a work sheet and the financial statements for a merchandising business that uses a periodic inventory system and that is organized as a corporation or as a single proprietorship.
4. Prepare adjusting and closing entries for a merchandising business organized as either a corporation or a single proprietorship.
5. Define or explain the words and phrases listed in the chapter Glossary.

*After studying the appendix to Chapter 5 (Appendix C), you should be able to:*

6. Explain the adjusting entry approach to accounting for inventories and prepare a work sheet, adjusting entries, and closing entries according to the adjusting entry approach.

The accounting records and reports of the Dow law practice, as described in previous chapters, are those of a service enterprise. Other examples of service enterprises are laundries, taxicab companies, hairdressers, theaters, and golf courses. Each performs a service for a commission or fee, and the net income of each is the difference between fees or commissions earned and operating expenses.

A merchandising company, on the other hand, whether a wholesaler or retailer, earns revenue by selling goods or **merchandise.** In such a company, a net income results when revenue from sales exceeds the cost of the goods sold plus operating expenses, as illustrated below:

**EASTSIDE HARDWARE STORE**
**Condensed Income Statement**
**For Month Ended July 31, 1990**

| | |
|---|---|
| Revenue from sales . . . . . . . | $100,000 |
| Less cost of goods sold . . . . | 60,000 |
| Gross profit from sales . . . . . | $ 40,000 |
| Less operating expenses . . . | 25,000 |
| Net income . . . . . . . . . . . . | $ 15,000 |

This income statement shows you that Eastside Hardware Store sold goods to customers for $100,000. The goods that were sold had cost Eastside $60,000. As a result, the company earned a $40,000 **gross profit.** Also, the company incurred operating expenses of $25,000, which resulted in a $15,000 net income for the month.

Gross profit is defined as the amount by which revenue from sales exceeds the cost of goods sold. The elements of this calculation are what make accounting for a merchandising company different from accounting for a service company. To account for a merchandising company, you must understand how to account for the elements of gross profit: for revenue from sales and for cost of goods sold.

## Revenue from Sales

Analyze and record transactions that involve the purchase and resale of merchandise. (L. O. 1)

Revenue from sales consists of gross proceeds from merchandise sales less returns, allowances, and discounts. It may be reported on an income statement as follows:

**IOWA SALES, INCORPORATED**
**Income Statement**
**For Year Ended December 31, 1990**

| | | |
|---|---|---|
| Revenue from sales: | | |
| Gross sales . . . . . . . . . . . . . . . . | | $306,200 |
| Less: Sales returns and allowances . . | 1,900 | |
| Sales discounts . . . . . . . . . | 4,300 | 6,200 |
| Net sales . . . . . . . . . . . . . . . . . . . | | $300,000 |

### Gross Sales

On the partial income statement, the gross sales item is the total cash and credit sales made by the company during the year. Cash sales were "rung up" on the cash register as each sale was completed. At the end of each day, the register total showed the amount of that day's cash sales, which was recorded with an entry like this:

| | | | | |
|---|---|---|---|---|
| Nov. | 3 | Cash . . . . . . . . . . . . . . . . . . . . . . . . . . . . . . | 1,205.00 | |
| | | Sales . . . . . . . . . . . . . . . . . . . . . . . . . . . | | 1,205.00 |
| | | To record the day's cash sales. | | |

Also, the following entry was used to record credit sales:

| | | | | |
|---|---|---|---|---|
| Nov. | 3 | Accounts Receivable . . . . . . . . . . . . . . . . . . . . . | 45.00 | |
| | | Sales . . . . . . . . . . . . . . . . . . . . . . . . . . . | | 45.00 |
| | | Sold merchandise on credit. | | |

### Sales Returns and Allowances

In most stores, customers are allowed to return any unsatisfactory merchandise they bought. Sometimes, customers are allowed to keep the unsatisfactory goods and are given an allowance or an amount off the sales price. Either way, returns and allowances result from dissatisfied customers. Therefore, it is important for management to know the amount of such returns and allowances and their relation to sales. The Sales Returns and Allowances account supplies this information because each return or allowance is recorded as follows:

| | | | | |
|---|---|---|---|---|
| Nov. | 4 | Sales Returns and Allowances . . . . . . . . . . . . . . . | 20.00 | |
| | | Accounts Receivable (or Cash) . . . . . . . . . . . . . | | 20.00 |
| | | Customer returned unsatisfactory merchandise. | | |

### Sales Discounts

When goods are sold on credit, the terms of payment must be stated clearly so there will be no misunderstanding as to the amount and time of payment. These **credit terms** normally appear on the invoice or sales ticket and are part of the sales agreement. Exact terms usually depend on the custom of the trade. In some areas of business, it is customary for invoices to become due and payable 10 days after the end of the month **(EOM)** in which the sale occurred. These credit terms are stated on the sales invoices as "n/10 EOM." In other trades, invoices become due and payable 30 days after the invoice date and carry terms of "n/30." This means that the net amount of the invoice is due 30 days after the invoice date.

When credit periods are long, creditors often grant discounts, called **cash discounts**, for early payments. This reduces the amount invested in accounts receivable, which means that less money is needed to carry on business operations. When discounts for early payment are granted, they are made part of the credit terms and appear on the invoice as, for example, "Terms: 2/10, n/60." Terms of 2/10, n/60 mean that the **credit period** is 60 days but that the debtor may deduct 2% from the invoice amount if payment is made within 10 days after the invoice date. The 10-day period is known as the **discount period.**

At the time of a sale, you do not know if the customer will pay within the discount period and take advantage of a cash discount. As a result, sales discounts usually are not recorded until the customer pays. For example, on November 12, Iowa Sales, Incorporated, sold $100 of merchandise to a customer on credit, terms 2/10, n/60, and recorded the sale as follows:

| | | | | |
|---|---|---|---|---|
| Nov. | 12 | Accounts Receivable | 100.00 | |
| | | Sales | | 100.00 |
| | | Sold merchandise, terms 2/10, n/60. | | |

The customer has two alternative ways to satisfy this $100 obligation. One option is to pay $98 any time on or before November 22. Or, the customer could wait 60 days, until January 11, and pay the full $100. If the customer elects to pay by November 22 and take advantage of the cash discount, Iowa Sales, Incorporated, will record the receipt of the $98 as follows:

| | | | | |
|---|---|---|---|---|
| Nov. | 22 | Cash | 98.00 | |
| | | Sales Discounts | 2.00 | |
| | | Accounts Receivable | | 100.00 |
| | | Received payment for the November 12 sale less the discount. | | |

Cash discounts granted to customers are called **sales discounts**, and are accumulated in the Sales Discounts account until the end of an accounting period. Their total is then deducted from gross sales in calculating net revenue from sales. This is logical. A sales discount is an "amount off" the regular price of goods that is granted for early payment. As a result, it reduces revenue from sales.

## Periodic and Perpetual Inventory Systems

Businesses such as automobile dealers or major appliance stores make a limited number of sales each day. Therefore, they can easily refer to their records at the time of each sale and record the cost of the car or appliance sold. On the other hand, a drugstore or a hardware store may find this difficult. For instance, if a drugstore sells a customer a tube of toothpaste, a box of aspirin, and a magazine, it can easily record with a cash register the sale of these items at marked selling prices. However, with large-volume, low-priced items, it may be quite difficult to determine quickly the cost of each item so that the "cost of goods sold" can be recorded at the time of sale. Some computerized systems allow this to be done. But many stores that sell a large volume of low-priced items often make no effort to record the cost of goods sold at the time of each sale. Rather, they wait until the end of an accounting period, take a physical inventory, and from the inventory and their accounting records determine at that time the cost of all goods sold during the period.

The end-of-period inventories that drug, hardware, grocery, or similar stores take to learn the cost of the goods they have sold are called periodic inventories. Also, the systems such stores use to account for inventories and the cost of goods sold are called **periodic inventory systems.** These systems are described and explained in this chapter. An alternative system of accounting for inventories and cost of goods sold, which involves recording the cost of goods sold each time a sale is made and keeping an up-to-date record of the goods on hand, is called a **perpetual inventory system.** These systems are discussed in Chapter 9.

## Cost of Goods Sold, Periodic Inventory System

Explain the nature of each item entering into the calculation of cost of goods sold and gross profit from sales.
(L. O. 2)

As we mentioned before, a store that uses a periodic inventory system does not record the cost of items sold at the time they are sold. Rather, it waits until the end of an accounting period and determines the cost of all the goods sold during the period. To do this, it must have information about (1) the cost of the merchandise on hand at the beginning of the period, (2) the cost of merchandise purchased during the period, and (3) the cost of unsold goods that remain at the period end. With this information, a store can calculate the cost of goods sold during a period, as follows:

| | |
|---|---|
| Cost of goods on hand at beginning of period . . | $ 19,000 |
| Cost of goods purchased during the period . . . | 232,000 |
| Goods available for sale during the period . . . . | $251,000 |
| Less unsold goods on hand at the period end . . | 21,000 |
| Cost of goods sold during the period . . . . . . . | $230,000 |

In the above calculation, the company had $19,000 of merchandise at the beginning of the accounting period. During the period, it purchased additional merchandise that cost $232,000. Therefore, it had merchandise that cost $251,000 available for sale during the period. However, $21,000 of this merchandise remained on hand (unsold) at the period end. Therefore, the cost of the goods it sold during the period was $230,000.

The following paragraphs explain how you accumulate the information needed to calculate cost of goods sold.

### Merchandise Inventories

The merchandise on hand at the beginning of an accounting period is called the beginning inventory; the merchandise on hand at the end is the ending inventory. Also, since accounting periods follow one after another, the ending inventory of one period is the beginning inventory of the next.

When a periodic inventory system is in use, the dollar amount of the ending inventory is determined by (1) counting the unsold items on the shelves in the store and in the stockroom, (2) multiplying the count for each type of goods by its cost, and (3) adding the costs of the different types of goods.

After the dollar cost of the ending inventory is determined in this manner, it is subtracted from the cost of the goods available for sale to determine cost of goods sold. Also, a journal entry is prepared and posted to record the ending inventory amount in an account called Merchandise Inventory. This ending inventory amount remains as the balance in the Merchandise Inventory account throughout the next accounting period. Thus, throughout the new accounting period, the balance of the Merchandise Inventory account represents the cost of the inventory on hand at the end of the previous period, which also is the beginning inventory of the current period.

We should emphasize the fact that, other than to correct errors, entries are made in the Merchandise Inventory account *only* at the end of each accounting period. As time passes during an accounting period and merchandise is both purchased and sold, neither the purchases nor the cost of goods sold amounts are entered in the Merchandise Inventory account. Therefore, as soon as goods are purchased or sold, the account does not show the dollar amount of merchandise on hand. Rather, the account's balance reflects the beginning inventory of the period.

### Cost of Merchandise Purchased

To determine the cost of merchandise purchased, you must note the invoice price of goods purchased and subtract any discounts, returns, and allowances. Then, you add any freight or other transportation costs incurred by the purchaser to ship the goods from the supplier to the purchaser's place of business. The following paragraphs explain how these amounts are accumulated in the accounts.

Under a periodic inventory system, when merchandise is bought for resale, its cost is debited to an account called Purchases, as follows:

| | | | | |
|---|---|---|---|---|
| Nov. | 5 | Purchases . . . . . . . . . . . . . . . . . . . . . . . . . . | 1,000.00 | |
| | | Accounts Payable . . . . . . . . . . . . . . . . . . . . | | 1,000.00 |
| | | Purchased merchandise on credit, invoice dated November 2, terms 2/10, n/30. | | |

The sole purpose of the Purchases account is to accumulate the cost of all merchandise bought for resale during an accounting period. The account does not at any time show whether the merchandise is on hand or has been disposed of through sale or other means.

If a credit purchase is eligible for a cash discount, payment within the discount period results in a credit to **Purchases Discounts**, as in the following entry:

| | | | | |
|---|---|---|---|---|
| Nov. | 12 | Accounts Payable . . . . . . . . . . . . . . . . . . . . . . | 1,000.00 | |
| | | Purchases Discounts . . . . . . . . . . . . . . . . | | 20.00 |
| | | Cash . . . . . . . . . . . . . . . . . . . . . . . . . . | | 980.00 |
| | | Paid for the purchase of November 5 less the discount. | | |

## AS A MATTER OF ETHICS

Marti Roberts was recently hired to be the accountant for a medium-sized company, and was given responsibility for managing accounts payable. Specifically, she is to assure that the accounts are paid promptly in order to maintain the company's credit standing with its suppliers and to take advantage of all cash discounts. Marti overlapped for several days on the job with Peter Bailey, the outgoing accountant, so that they could spend time together to help her learn the ropes.

Peter told Marti that the system in place has accomplished both goals easily, but has also made another contribution to the company's profits. Because the accounts are always paid, there has been no difficulty with the creditors. However, with respect to the discounts, the system has always been to prepare checks for the "net of discount" amounts and then wait until *after* the end of the discount period before mailing the checks. The checks are dated the last day of the discount period, but are not mailed until five days later. "It's simple," Peter said, "we get the free use of the cash for an extra five days, and who's going to complain? Even if someone gripes, we can always blame the computer or the mail room."

Only a few days later, on March 17, Peter has departed and Marti recognizes that the discount period on a $10,000 payable is about to lapse. The purchase was made on March 8 subject to terms of 2/10, n/30. Marti is trying to decide whether she should pay the bill on March 18 or wait until March 23.

When a supplier offers cash discounts, the total amount to be saved by taking the discounts often is important. Therefore, whenever the invoices offer a discount, many companies take special care to pay within the discount period so that no discounts are lost. On the other hand, good cash management requires that no invoice be paid until the last day of its discount period. To accomplish these objectives, every invoice must be filed in such a way that it automatically comes to the attention of the person responsible for its payment on the last day of its discount period. A simple way to do this is to have a file with 31 folders, one for each day in a month. Then, after an invoice is recorded, it is placed in the file folder of the last day of its discount period. For example, if the last day of an invoice's discount period is November 12, it is filed in folder number 12. Then, on November 12, this invoice, together with any other invoices in the same folder, are removed and paid or refiled for payment without a discount on a later date.

Sometimes, merchandise received from suppliers is not acceptable and must be returned. Or, defective merchandise may be kept by the purchaser because the supplier grants an allowance or reduction in its price. When merchandise is returned, the purchaser "gets its money back." Nevertheless, the process of receiving, inspecting, evaluating, and perhaps returning defective merchandise is costly and should be held to a minimum. As a result, the amount of purchase returns or allowances must be controlled and a purchaser may look for another supplier if purchased merchandise is frequently defective.

An important element in controlling the problem of defective merchandise purchases is to obtain information about the amount of returns and allowances. To gain this information, returns and allowances on purchases are commonly recorded in an account called Purchases Returns and Allowances, as follows:

| | | | | |
|---|---|---|---|---|
| Nov. | 14 | Accounts Payable . . . . . . . . . . . . . . . . . . . . . . . | 65.00 | |
| | | Purchases Returns and Allowances . . . . . . . . . . | | 65.00 |
| | | Returned defective merchandise. | | |

When an invoice for purchased goods is subject to a cash discount and a portion of the goods is returned before the invoice is paid, the discount only applies to the goods kept. For example, assume that you buy merchandise for \$500, subject to a 2% cash discount. Then, you return \$100 of the goods before the invoice is paid. When you pay the amount due before the discount period expires, the discount of 2% applies only to the remaining \$400. In other words, the amount you will pay is $\$400 - (.02 \times \$400) = \$392$.

Sometimes a supplier assumes responsibility for the costs of transporting the sold goods to the customer. When this is the case, the total cost of the goods to the purchaser is the amount the purchaser must pay to the supplier. Other times the purchaser must pay transportation costs. When this occurs, such charges are a proper addition to the cost of the goods purchased and may be recorded with a debit to the Purchases account. However, more complete information is obtained if such costs are debited to an account called **Transportation-In**, as follows:

| | | | | |
|---|---|---|---|---|
| Nov. | 24 | Transportation-In . . . . . . . . . . . . . . . . . . . . . . . | 22.00 | |
| | | Cash . . . . . . . . . . . . . . . . . . . . . . . . . . . . | | 22.00 |
| | | Paid express charges on merchandise purchased. | | |

When there are transportation charges, the buyer and seller must understand which party is responsible for the charges. Normally, in quoting a price, the seller makes this clear by quoting a price of, say \$300, **FOB** factory. FOB factory means free on board or loaded on board the means of transportation at the factory, free of loading charges. The buyer then is responsible for transportation costs from there. Likewise, FOB destination means the seller is responsible for transportation costs to the destination of the goods.

Sometimes, even though the terms are FOB factory, the seller will prepay the transportation costs as a service to the buyer, and add the amount to the invoice. In this case, if the credit terms include a cash discount, the discount does not apply to the transportation charges. In other words, the purchaser must reimburse the seller for 100% of the transportation charges, even if the invoice is paid within the discount period.

At the end of the period, the balances of the Purchases, Purchases Returns and Allowances, Purchases Discounts, and Transportation-In accounts must be combined to determine the cost of the merchandise purchased during the period. This calculation may be shown on the income statement of a merchandising company, as follows:

| | | | |
|---|---|---|---|
| Purchases | | $235,800 | |
| Less: Purchases returns and allowances | $1,200 | | |
| Purchases discounts | 4,100 | 5,300 | |
| Net purchases | | $230,500 | |
| Add transportation-in | | 1,500 | |
| Cost of goods purchased | | | $232,000 |

### Cost of Goods Sold

In the above calculation, the last item is the cost of the merchandise purchased during the accounting period. To calculate cost of goods sold, you must combine this amount with the beginning and ending inventories, as follows:

| | | | | |
|---|---|---|---|---|
| Cost of goods sold: | | | | |
| Merchandise inventory, December 31, 1989 | | | $ 19,000 | |
| Purchases | | $235,800 | | |
| Less: Purchases returns and allowances | $1,200 | | | |
| Purchases discounts | 4,100 | 5,300 | | |
| Net purchases | | $230,500 | | |
| Add transportation-in | | 1,500 | | |
| Cost of goods purchased | | | 232,000 | |
| Goods available for sale | | | $251,000 | |
| Merchandise inventory, December 31, 1990 | | | 21,000 | |
| Cost of goods sold | | | | $230,000 |

### Inventory Losses

Merchandising companies lose merchandise in a variety of ways such as from shrinkage, spoilage, or shoplifting. When merchandise is lost and a periodic inventory system is used, the cost of lost merchandise is automatically included in cost of goods sold. For example, assume a store lost $500 of merchandise to shoplifters during a year. This caused its year-end inventory to be $500 less than it otherwise would have been, since these goods were not available for inclusion in the year-end count. Therefore, since the year-end inventory was $500 smaller because of the loss, the cost of the goods the store sold was $500 greater.

Many merchandisers are troubled with shoplifting or other types of inventory losses. A disadvantage of the periodic inventory system is that it fails to provide clear information about the amount of such losses. Instead, the amount of such losses are "hidden" in the cost of goods sold figure. The perpetual inventory systems described in Chapter 9 provide more complete information about merchandise losses. Chapter 9 also discusses a method of estimating inventory losses when a periodic inventory system is being used.

**Illustration 5–1**
**A classified income statement for a merchandising company**

**IOWA SALES, INCORPORATED**
**Income Statement**
**For Year Ended December 31, 1990**

| | | | | |
|---|---|---|---|---|
| Revenue from sales: | | | | |
| Gross sales | | | | $306,200 |
| Less: Sales returns and allowances | | | $ 1,900 | |
| Sales discounts | | | 4,300 | 6,200 |
| Net sales | | | | $300,000 |
| Cost of goods sold: | | | | |
| Merchandise inventory, December 31, 1989 | | | $ 19,000 | |
| Purchases | | $235,800 | | |
| Less: Purchases returns and allowances | $1,200 | | | |
| Purchases discounts | 4,100 | 5,300 | | |
| Net purchases | | $230,500 | | |
| Add transportation-in | | 1,500 | | |
| Cost of goods purchased | | | 232,000 | |
| Goods available for sale | | | $251,000 | |
| Merchandise inventory, December 31, 1990 | | | 21,000 | |
| Cost of goods sold | | | | 230,000 |
| Gross profit from sales | | | | $ 70,000 |
| Operating expenses: | | | | |
| Selling expenses: | | | | |
| Sales salaries expense | | $ 18,500 | | |
| Rent expense, selling space | | 8,100 | | |
| Advertising expense | | 700 | | |
| Store supplies expense | | 400 | | |
| Depreciation expense, store equipment | | 3,000 | | |
| Total selling expenses | | | $ 30,700 | |
| General and administrative expenses: | | | | |
| Office salaries expense | | $ 25,800 | | |
| Rent expense, office space | | 900 | | |
| Insurance expense | | 600 | | |
| Office supplies expense | | 200 | | |
| Depreciation expense, office equipment | | 700 | | |
| Total general and administrative expenses | | | 28,200 | |
| Total operating expenses | | | | 58,900 |
| Income from operations | | | | $ 11,100 |
| Less income taxes expense | | | | 1,700 |
| Net income | | | | $ 9,400 |

## Income Statement of a Merchandising Company

A classified income statement for a merchandising company has (1) a revenue section, (2) a cost of goods sold section, and (3) an operating expenses section. Note in Illustration 5–1 how the first two sections are brought together to show gross profit from sales.

Also notice in Illustration 5–1 how operating expenses are classified as either "Selling expenses" or "General and administrative expenses." **Selling**

**expenses** include expenses of storing and preparing goods for sale, promoting sales, actually making sales, and delivering goods to customers. **General and administrative expenses** support the overall management and operations of a business. Examples are the central office, accounting, personnel, and credit and collection expenses.

Sometimes an expenditure should be divided or prorated between selling expenses and general and administrative expenses. Iowa Sales, Incorporated, divided the rent on its store building in this manner, as you can see in Illustration 5–1. However, it did not prorate its insurance expense because the amount involved was so small the company felt the extra exactness did not warrant the extra work.

In Illustration 5–1, the last item subtracted is income taxes expense. This income statement was prepared for Iowa Sales, Incorporated, a corporation. Of the three kinds of business organizations, only corporations are subject to the payment of state and federal income taxes. Notice in Illustration 5–1 that the result of subtracting operating expenses from gross profit is called "Income from operations." Income taxes expense is then subtracted to obtain the final net income.

## Work Sheet of a Merchandising Company

Prepare a work sheet and the financial statements for a merchandising business that uses a periodic inventory system and that is organized as a corporation or as a single proprietorship.
(L. O. 3)

In organizing the end-of-period procedures, the work sheet that you use for a merchandising company is just like the work sheet for a service-type company. In both cases, the work sheet serves as a tool to help bring together the end-of-period information needed to prepare the financial statements and prepare the adjusting and closing entries. Illustration 5–2 shows the work sheet for Iowa Sales, Incorporated.

Illustration 5–2 differs from the Chapter 4 work sheet in several ways, the first of which is that it was prepared for a corporation. This is indicated by the word *Incorporated* in the company name. Also, the heading of the last two columns is Retained Earnings Statement or Balance Sheet. Later in this chapter, we will explain how the changes in retained earnings are reported in the retained earnings statement.

In Illustration 5–2, notice the appearance of the Common Stock and Retained Earnings accounts on lines 13 and 14. The balances of these two accounts are carried unchanged from the Unadjusted Trial Balance Credit column into the Retained Earnings Statement or Balance Sheet Credit column.

Illustration 5–2 also differs from the work sheet presented in Chapter 4 in that it does not have any Adjusted Trial Balance columns. Experienced accountants commonly omit these columns from a work sheet in order to reduce the time and effort required in its preparation. They enter the adjustments in the Adjustments columns, combine the adjustments with the unadjusted trial balance amounts, and sort the combined amounts directly to the proper financial statement columns in a single operation. In other words, the adjusted trial balance columns may be omitted in preparing a work sheet.

The remaining similarities and differences of Illustration 5–2 are best described column by column.

**Illustration 5–2**
**A work sheet for a merchandising company**

**IOWA SALES, INCORPORATED**
**Work Sheet**
**For Year Ended December 31, 1990**

| Account Titles | Unadjusted Trial Balance Dr. | Unadjusted Trial Balance Cr. | Adjustments Dr. | Adjustments Cr. | Income Statement Dr. | Income Statement Cr. | Retained Earnings Statement or Balance Sheet Dr. | Retained Earnings Statement or Balance Sheet Cr. |
|---|---|---|---|---|---|---|---|---|
| 1 Cash | 8,200 | | | | | | 8,200 | |
| 2 Accounts receivable | 11,200 | | | | | | 11,200 | |
| 3 Merchandise inventory | 19,000 | | | | 19,000 | 21,000 | 21,000 | |
| 4 Prepaid insurance | 900 | | | (*a*) 600 | | | 300 | |
| 5 Store supplies | 600 | | | (*b*) 400 | | | 200 | |
| 6 Office supplies | 300 | | | (*c*) 200 | | | 100 | |
| 7 Store equipment | 29,100 | | | | | | 29,100 | |
| 8 Accum. depr., store equipment | | 2,500 | | (*d*) 3,000 | | | | 5,500 |
| 9 Office equipment | 4,400 | | | | | | 4,400 | |
| 10 Accum. depr., office equipment | | 600 | | (*e*) 700 | | | | 1,300 |
| 11 Accounts payable | | 3,600 | | | | | | 3,600 |
| 12 Income taxes payable | | | | (*f*) 100 | | | | 100 |
| 13 Common stock | | 50,000 | | | | | | 50,000 |
| 14 Retained earnings | | 8,600 | | | | | | 8,600 |
| 15 Dividends declared | 4,000 | | | | | | 4,000 | |
| 16 Sales | | 306,200 | | | | 306,200 | | |
| 17 Sales returns and allowances | 1,900 | | | | 1,900 | | | |
| 18 Sales discounts | 4,300 | | | | 4,300 | | | |
| 19 Purchases | 235,800 | | | | 235,800 | | | |
| 20 Pur. returns and allowances | | 1,200 | | | | 1,200 | | |
| 21 Purchases discounts | | 4,100 | | | | 4,100 | | |
| 22 Transportation-in | 1,500 | | | | 1,500 | | | |
| 23 Sales salaries expense | 18,500 | | | | 18,500 | | | |
| 24 Rent expense, selling space | 8,100 | | | | 8,100 | | | |
| 25 Advertising expense | 700 | | | | 700 | | | |
| 26 Store supplies expense | | | (*b*) 400 | | 400 | | | |
| 27 Depr. expense, store equipment | | | (*d*) 3,000 | | 3,000 | | | |
| 28 Office salaries expense | 25,800 | | | | 25,800 | | | |
| 29 Rent expense, office space | 900 | | | | 900 | | | |
| 30 Insurance expense | | | (*a*) 600 | | 600 | | | |
| 31 Office supplies expense | | | (*c*) 200 | | 200 | | | |
| 32 Depr. expense, office equipment | | | (*e*) 700 | | 700 | | | |
| 33 Income taxes expense | 1,600 | | (*f*) 100 | | 1,700 | | | |
| 34 | 376,800 | 376,800 | 5,000 | 5,000 | 323,100 | 332,500 | 78,500 | 69,100 |
| 35 Net income | | | | | 9,400 | | | 9,400 |
| 36 | | | | | 332,500 | 332,500 | 78,500 | 78,500 |

### Account Titles Column

In the Account Titles column of the work sheet, several accounts that do not have unadjusted trial balance amounts are listed in the order of their appearance on the financial statements. These accounts are debited and credited in making the adjustments. Entering their names on the work sheet in statement order at the time the work sheet is begun makes later preparation of the statements somewhat easier. If you find that you need accounts that were not listed, they may be entered below the trial balance totals as was done in Chapter 4.

### Unadjusted Trial Balance Columns

In Illustration 5–2, the amounts in the Unadjusted Trial Balance columns are the account balances of Iowa Sales, Incorporated, as of December 31, 1990, the end of its annual accounting period. They were taken from the company's ledger after all transactions were recorded but before any end-of-period adjustments were made.

Note the $19,000 inventory amount that appears in the Unadjusted Trial Balance Debit column on line 3. This is the amount of inventory the company had on December 31, 1989. As the ending inventory for 1989, this amount is also the beginning inventory for 1990. The $19,000 was debited to the Merchandise Inventory account at the end of the previous period and remained in the account as its balance throughout the current accounting period.

### Adjustments Columns

Of the adjustments that appear on the illustrated work sheet, only the adjustment for income taxes is new. A business organized as a corporation is subject to the payment of federal (and perhaps state) income taxes. As to the federal tax, near the beginning of each year a corporation must estimate the amount of income it expects to earn during the year. Then, it must pay, in advance installments, an estimated tax on this income. The advance payments are debited to the Income Taxes Expense account as each installment is paid. Therefore, a corporation that expects to earn a profit normally reaches the end of the year with a debit balance in its Income Taxes Expense account. However, since the balance is an estimate and usually less than the full amount of the tax, an adjustment like that on lines 12 and 33 normally must be made to reflect the additional tax owed.

### Combining and Sorting the Items

After all adjustments are entered and totaled on the work sheet, the amounts in the Unadjusted Trial Balance and Adjustments columns are combined and sorted to the proper financial statement columns. Revenue, cost of goods sold, and expense items go on the income statement and are sorted to the Income Statement columns. Asset, liability, and stockholders' equity items plus Dividends Declared are sorted to the Retained Earnings Statement or Balance Sheet columns.

### Income Statement Columns

Observe in Illustration 5–2 that revenue, cost of goods sold, and expense items maintain their debit and credit positions when sorted to the Income Statement columns. Since sales returns and sales discounts are entered in the Debit column, the effect is to subtract them from sales when the columns are totaled and the net income is determined.

**The Beginning Inventory Amount.** Look at the beginning inventory amount on line 3. Note that the $19,000 unadjusted trial balance amount is sorted to the Income Statement Debit column. It is put in the Income Statement Debit column because, as a debit account balance, it is a positive element in the calculation of cost of goods sold. Recall that on the income statement, the calculation of cost of goods sold begins by adding the beginning inventory plus the net cost of purchases to determine the cost of goods available for sale.

**The Ending Inventory Amount.** Recall that when the periodic inventory system is used, you must take a physical inventory of merchandise on hand at the end of each accounting period. The December 31, 1990, physical inventory of Iowa Sales, Incorporated, showed that it had a $21,000 ending inventory. This amount was determined by counting the items of unsold merchandise and multiplying by the cost of each item.

In preparing a work sheet, after all items are sorted to the proper columns, the ending inventory amount is simply inserted in the Income Statement Credit column and in the Retained Earnings Statement or Balance Sheet Debit column. In Illustration 5–2, note that the $21,000 ending inventory was inserted in these columns on line 3 of the work sheet. The ending inventory amount is placed in the Income Statement Credit column because when cost of goods sold is calculated on the income statement, the ending inventory must be subtracted from cost of goods available for sale.

The ending inventory amount is put in the Retained Earnings Statement or Balance Sheet Debit column because it is an asset that will appear on the balance sheet. (Later in this chapter, we will discuss the journal entry to record the ending inventory in the accounts.)

## Cost of Goods Sold on the Work Sheet

The amounts that enter into the calculation of cost of goods sold are shown in color in the Income Statement columns of Illustration 5–2. The beginning inventory, purchases, and transportation-in amounts appear in the Debit column. The amounts of the ending inventory, purchases returns and allowances, and purchases discounts appear in the Credit column. Note in the following calculations that the sum of the three debit items minus the sum of the three credit items equals the $230,000 cost of goods sold shown in the income statement of Illustration 5–1.

| | | | |
|---|---|---|---|
| Beginning inventory . . . . | $ 19,000 | Ending inventory . . . . . . | $21,000 |
| Purchases . . . . . . . . . | 235,800 | Purchases returns. . . . . . | 1,200 |
| Transportation-in . . . . . | 1,500 | Purchases discounts . . . . | 4,100 |
| Total debits . . . . . . . . | $256,300 | Total credits . . . . . . . . . | $26,300 |
| Less total credits . . . . | (26,300) | | |
| Cost of goods sold . . . . | $230,000 | | |

Therefore, the net effect of putting the six cost of goods sold amounts in the Income Statement columns is to put the $230,000 cost of the goods sold into the columns.

**Illustration 5–3**
**A corporation's retained earnings statement**

**IOWA SALES, INCORPORATED**
**Retained Earnings Statement**
**For Year Ended December 31, 1990**

| | |
|---|---|
| Retained earnings, December 31, 1989 . . | $ 8,600 |
| Add 1990 net income . . . . . . . . . . . . | 9,400 |
| Total . . . . . . . . . . . . . . . . . . . . . . | $18,000 |
| Deduct dividends declared . . . . . . . . | 4,000 |
| Retained earnings, December 31, 1990 . . | $14,000 |

## Completing the Work Sheet and Preparing Financial Statements

After all items are sorted to the proper columns and the ending inventory amount is entered, you complete a work sheet like Illustration 5–2 by adding the columns and determining and adding in the net income or loss, as we explained in the last chapter. When the work sheet for a corporation is completed, it is used to prepare an income statement, a retained earnings statement, and a balance sheet.

### Preparing the Income Statement

After the work sheet is completed, the items in the Income Statement columns are used to prepare a formal income statement. A classified income statement prepared from information in the Income Statement columns of Illustration 5–2 is shown in Illustration 5–1.

### Preparing the Retained Earnings Statement

The **retained earnings statement** reports the changes that have occurred in the corporation's retained earnings during the period. Therefore, the statement accounts for the difference between the retained earnings reported on successive, end-of-period balance sheets.

The information you need to prepare the retained earnings statement is found in the last two columns of the work sheet. The beginning retained earnings balance appears on the line showing the Retained Earnings account. The net income (or net loss) appears on a line near the bottom of the work sheet and the amount of dividends declared also appears on a separate line.

Illustration 5–3 shows the retained earnings statement of Iowa Sales, Incorporated. The statement shows that the company began the year with $8,600 of retained earnings, which is also the amount of retained earnings it reported on its previous year-end balance sheet. Its retained earnings balance was reduced by the declaration of $4,000 of dividends and increased by the $9,400 net income. The result is the final balance of $14,000, which is reported on the December 31, 1990, balance sheet.

Illustration 5–4
**A corporation's classified balance sheet**

IOWA SALES, INCORPORATED
Balance Sheet
December 31, 1990

| | | | |
|---|---|---|---|
| **Assets** | | | |
| Current assets: | | | |
| Cash | | $ 8,200 | |
| Accounts receivable | | 11,200 | |
| Merchandise inventory | | 21,000 | |
| Prepaid expenses | | 600 | |
| Total current assets | | | $41,000 |
| Plant and equipment: | | | |
| Store equipment | $29,100 | | |
| Less accumulated depreciation | 5,500 | $23,600 | |
| Office equipment | $ 4,400 | | |
| Less accumulated depreciation | 1,300 | 3,100 | |
| Total plant and equipment | | | 26,700 |
| Total assets | | | $67,700 |
| **Liabilities** | | | |
| Current liabilities: | | | |
| Accounts payable | | $ 3,600 | |
| Income taxes payable | | 100 | |
| Total liabilities | | | $ 3,700 |
| **Stockholders' Equity** | | | |
| Common stock, $5 par value, 10,000 shares authorized and outstanding | | $50,000 | |
| Retained earnings | | 14,000 | |
| Total stockholders' equity | | | 64,000 |
| Total liabilities and stockholders' equity | | | $67,700 |

**Preparing the Balance Sheet**

The classified balance sheet for Iowa Sales, Incorporated, appears in Illustration 5–4. Since none of the company's prepaid items are material in amount, you will observe that they have been totaled and are shown as a single item on the balance sheet. Also, the $14,000 retained earnings amount on the balance sheet is the final amount that was calculated on the retained earnings statement, as shown in Illustration 5–3.

## Adjusting and Closing Entries

Prepare adjusting and closing entries for a merchandising business organized as either a corporation or a single proprietorship. (L. O. 4)

After the work sheet and statements are completed, you must prepare and post adjusting and closing entries. Illustration 5–5 shows the entries for Iowa Sales, Incorporated. They differ from previously illustrated adjusting and closing entries because an explanation for each entry is not given. Individual explanations may be given but are unnecessary. The words *Adjusting Entries* before the first adjusting entry and *Closing Entries* before the first closing entry are sufficient to explain the entries.

**Illustration 5–5**
**Adjusting and closing entries for a merchandising corporation**

| Date | | Account Titles and Explanation | PR | Debit | Credit |
|---|---|---|---|---|---|
| 1990 | | Adjusting Entries | | | |
| Dec. | 31 | Insurance Expense | | 600.00 | |
| | | Prepaid Insurance | | | 600.00 |
| | 31 | Store Supplies Expense | | 400.00 | |
| | | Store Supplies | | | 400.00 |
| | 31 | Office Supplies Expense | | 200.00 | |
| | | Office Supplies | | | 200.00 |
| | 31 | Depreciation Expense, Store Equipment | | 3,000.00 | |
| | | Accumulated Depreciation, Store Equipment | | | 3,000.00 |
| | 31 | Depreciation Expense, Office Equipment | | 700.00 | |
| | | Accumulated Depreciation, Office Equipment | | | 700.00 |
| | 31 | Income Taxes Expense | | 100.00 | |
| | | Income Taxes Payable | | | 100.00 |
| | | Closing Entries | | | |
| | 31 | Income Summary | | 323,100.00 | |
| | | Merchandise Inventory | | | 19,000.00 |
| | | Sales Returns and Allowances | | | 1,900.00 |
| | | Sales Discounts | | | 4,300.00 |
| | | Purchases | | | 235,800.00 |
| | | Transportation-In | | | 1,500.00 |
| | | Sales Salaries Expense | | | 18,500.00 |
| | | Rent Expense, Selling Space | | | 8,100.00 |
| | | Advertising Expense | | | 700.00 |
| | | Store Supplies Expense | | | 400.00 |
| | | Depreciation Expense, Store Equipment | | | 3,000.00 |
| | | Office Salaries Expense | | | 25,800.00 |
| | | Rent Expense, Office Space | | | 900.00 |
| | | Insurance Expense | | | 600.00 |
| | | Office Supplies Expense | | | 200.00 |
| | | Depreciation Expense, Office Equipment | | | 700.00 |
| | | Income Taxes Expense | | | 1,700.00 |
| | 31 | Merchandise Inventory | | 21,000.00 | |
| | | Sales | | 306,200.00 | |
| | | Purchases Returns and Allowances | | 1,200.00 | |
| | | Purchases Discounts | | 4,100.00 | |
| | | Income Summary | | | 332,500.00 |
| | 31 | Income Summary | | 9,400.00 | |
| | | Retained Earnings | | | 9,400.00 |
| | 31 | Retained Earnings | | 4,000.00 | |
| | | Dividends Declared | | | 4,000.00 |

As we previously explained, the Adjustments columns of its work sheet provide the information you need to prepare a concern's adjusting entries. Each adjustment in the Adjustments columns requires an adjusting entry that is journalized and posted. Compare the adjusting entries in Illustration 5–5 with the adjustments on the work sheet of Illustration 5–2.

A work sheet like Illustration 5–2 also contains the information you need to prepare closing entries. Look at the first closing entry of Illustration 5–5 and the items in the Income Statement Debit column of Illustration 5–2. Note that Income Summary is debited for the column total and each account that has an amount in the column is credited. This entry removes the $19,000 beginning inventory amount from the Merchandise Inventory account. It also closes all the revenue, cost of goods sold, and expense accounts that have debit balances.

Now compare the second closing entry with the items in the Income Statement Credit column of Illustration 5–2. Note that each account which has an amount in the column is debited and the Income Summary account is credited for the column total. This entry closes the revenue and cost of goods sold accounts that have credit balances. It also enters the $21,000 ending inventory amount in the Merchandise Inventory account.

The third closing entry transfers the net income from Income Summary to Retained Earnings, and the fourth closing entry closes the Dividends Declared account by transferring its balance to Retained Earnings.

## Closing Entries and the Inventories

There is nothing especially new about the closing entries of a merchandising company except for the beginning and ending inventory amounts. You need to understand clearly the effect of the closing entries on the Merchandise Inventory account.

Before closing entries were posted, the Merchandise Inventory account of Iowa Sales, Incorporated, showed the $19,000 beginning-of-period inventory as follows:

**Merchandise Inventory** — Account No. 113

| Date | | Explanation | PR | Debit | Credit | Balance |
|---|---|---|---|---|---|---|
| 1989<br>Dec. | 31 | | G10 | 19,000 | | 19,000 |

Then, when the first closing entry is posted, its $19,000 credit to Merchandise Inventory clears the beginning inventory amount from the inventory account as follows:

**Merchandise Inventory** — Account No. 113

| Date | | Explanation | PR | Debit | Credit | Balance |
|---|---|---|---|---|---|---|
| 1989<br>Dec. | 31 | | G10 | 19,000 | | 19,000 |
| 1990<br>Dec. | 31 | | G20 | | 19,000 | –0– |

When the second closing entry is posted, its $21,000 debit to Merchandise Inventory puts the amount of the ending inventory into the inventory account, as follows:

**Illustration 5–6**
**A single-step income statement**

**IOWA SALES, INCORPORATED**
**Income Statement**
**For Year Ended December 31, 1990**

| | | |
|---|---|---|
| Revenue from sales . . . . . . . . . . . . | | $300,000 |
| Expenses: | | |
| Cost of goods sold . . . . . . . . . . . . | $230,000 | |
| Selling expenses . . . . . . . . . . . . . | 30,700 | |
| General and administrative expenses . . | 28,200 | |
| Income taxes expense . . . . . . . . . . | 1,700 | |
| Total expenses. . . . . . . . . . . . . . | | 290,600 |
| Net income . . . . . . . . . . . . . . . . | | $ 9,400 |

**Merchandise Inventory** Account No. 113

| Date | | Explanation | PR | Debit | Credit | Balance |
|---|---|---|---|---|---|---|
| 1989 Dec. | 31 | | G10 | 19,000 | | 19,000 |
| 1990 Dec. | 31 | | G20 | | 19,000 | –0– |
| | 31 | | G23 | 21,000 | | 21,000 |

The $21,000 remains throughout the succeeding year as the debit balance of the inventory account and as a historical record of the amount of inventory at the end of 1990 and the beginning of 1991.

## Other Inventory Methods

There are several ways to handle the inventories in the end-of-period procedures. However, all have the same objectives. These are (1) to remove the beginning inventory amount from the inventory account and to charge (debit) it to Income Summary, and (2) to enter the ending inventory amount in the inventory account and credit it to Income Summary. These objectives may be achieved with closing entries as explained in this chapter. Or, for example, adjusting entries to accomplish the same objectives may be used. Either method is satisfactory. The adjusting entry method is explained in Appendix C at the end of this chapter.

## Multiple-Step and Single-Step Income Statements

The income statement shown in Illustration 5–1 is called a classified income statement because its items are classified in significant groups. It is also a **multiple-step income statement** because cost of goods sold and the expenses are subtracted in steps to get net income. Illustration 5–6 shows another statement format, the **single-step income statement.** Note how cost of goods sold and the expenses are added together in the illustration and are subtracted in "one step" from net sales to get net income. This format is commonly used for

Illustration 5–7
**Combining the income statement and the retained earnings statement**

**IOWA SALES, INCORPORATED**
**Statement of Income and Retained Earnings**
**For Year Ended December 31, 1990**

| | | |
|---|---|---|
| Revenue from sales | | $300,000 |
| Expenses: | | |
| Cost of goods sold | $230,000 | |
| Selling expenses | 30,700 | |
| General and administrative expenses | 28,200 | |
| Income taxes expense | 1,700 | |
| Total expenses | | 290,600 |
| Net income | | $ 9,400 |
| Add retained earnings, December 31, 1989 | | 8,600 |
| Total | | $ 18,000 |
| Deduct dividends declared | | 4,000 |
| Retained earnings, December 31, 1990 | | $ 14,000 |

published statements. Also, note that the information in the income statement is condensed. This is frequently done in published statements.

## Combined Income and Retained Earnings Statement

Many companies combine their income and retained earnings statements into a single statement. Such a statement may be prepared in either single-step or multiple-step form. Illustration 5–7 shows a single-step statement.

## Debit and Credit Memoranda

Merchandise purchased that does not meet specifications, goods received that were not ordered, goods received short of the amount ordered and billed, and invoice errors are matters for adjustment between the buyer and seller. In some cases, the buying company can make the adjustment, for example, when there is an invoice error. If the buying company makes the adjustment, it must notify the seller of its action. It commonly does this by sending a **debit memorandum** or a **credit memorandum.**

A debit memorandum is a business form that has spaces for the name and address of the concern to which it is directed and the printed words, "WE DEBIT YOUR ACCOUNT," followed by space for typing in the reason for the debit. A credit memorandum has the words, "WE CREDIT YOUR ACCOUNT."

To illustrate the use of a debit memorandum, assume that a buyer discovers an invoice error that reduces the invoice total by $10. For such an error, the buyer notifies the seller with a debit memorandum reading: "WE DEBIT YOUR ACCOUNT to correct a $10 error on your November 17 invoice." A debit memorandum is sent because the correction reduces an account payable of the buyer, and a debit is required to reduce an account payable. To record the purchase, the buyer normally marks the correction on the invoice and attaches a copy of the debit memorandum to show that the seller was notified. The buyer then debits Purchases and credits Accounts Payable for the corrected amount.

An adjustment, such as merchandise that does not meet specifications, normally requires negotiations between the buyer and the seller. In such a case, the buyer may debit Purchases for the full invoice amount and then negotiate with the seller for a return or a price adjustment. If the seller agrees to the return or adjustment, the seller notifies the buyer with a credit memorandum. A credit memorandum is used because the return or adjustment reduces an account receivable on the books of the seller, and a credit is required to reduce an account receivable. When the credit memorandum is received, the buyer records it by debiting Accounts Payable and crediting Purchases Returns and Allowances, if the purchase was originally recorded at the full invoice price.

From this discussion you can see that a debit or a credit memorandum may originate with either party to a transaction. The memorandum gets its name from the action of the originator. If the originator debits, the originator sends a debit memorandum. If the originator credits, a credit memorandum is sent.

## Trade Discounts

When a manufacturer or wholesaler prepares a catalog of the items it offers for sale, each item typically is given a **list,** or catalog, **price.** A **trade discount** is a deduction (often as much as 40% or more) from a list (or catalog) price that is used to determine the invoice or sales price of the goods to which it applies. Trade discounts are commonly used by manufacturers and wholesalers to avoid republication of catalogs when selling prices change. If selling prices change, catalog prices can be adjusted simply by issuing a new list of discounts to be applied to the catalog prices.

Understand that trade discounts are quite different from the cash discounts we discussed earlier in this chapter. *Trade discounts are not entered in the accounts by either party to a sale*. Instead, they are used to calculate the sales price. For example, if a manufacturer sells on credit an item listed in its catalog at $100, less a 40% trade discount, it will record the sale as follows:

| | | | | |
|---|---|---|---|---|
| Dec. | 10 | Accounts Receivable [$100 – (.40 × $100)] . . . . . . . . | 60.00 | |
| | | Sales . . . . . . . . . . . . . . . . . . . . . . . . . . . . | | 60.00 |
| | | Sold merchandise on credit. | | |

The buyer will also enter the purchase in its records at $60. Also, if a cash discount is involved, it applies only to the amount of the purchase, $60.

## Summary of the Chapter in Terms of Learning Objectives

**1.** In recording the amount to record as a purchase (or sale), trade discounts are subtracted from list prices to calculate the invoice price, which is debited to Purchases (or credited to Sales). Purchases discounts, purchases returns and allowances, transportation-in, sales discounts, and sales returns and allowances are recorded in separate accounts.

**2.** Sales discounts and sales returns and allowances are subtracted from sales to get net sales. The ending inventory is subtracted from the cost of goods available for sale to get cost of goods sold, which is subtracted from net sales to get gross profit. The beginning inventory plus net purchases equals the cost of goods available for sale.

**3.** When the closing entry approach is used on the work sheet, the beginning inventory is extended to the Income Statement Debit column and the ending inventory is inserted in the Income Statement Credit column and the Statement of Retained Earnings or Balance Sheet Debit column. A corporation's retained earnings statement shows the changes in retained earnings during the period.

**4.** When the closing entry approach is used, the beginning inventory is transferred from Merchandise Inventory to Income Summary in the closing process. Also, the ending inventory is debited to Merchandise Inventory and credited to Income Summary as part of a closing entry.

## Demonstration Problem

Below is a partially completed work sheet prepared for Continental Sales, Inc., as of December 31, 1990, the end of its annual accounting period.

**CONTINENTAL SALES, INC.**
**Work Sheet**
**For Year Ended December 31, 1990**

| Account Titles | Unadjusted Trial Balance Dr. | Unadjusted Trial Balance Cr. | Adjustments Dr. | Adjustments Cr. |
|---|---|---|---|---|
| Cash | 19,000 | | | |
| Merchandise inventory | 52,000 | | | |
| Supplies | 7,000 | | | (*a*) 6,000 |
| Equipment | 40,000 | | | |
| Accumulated depreciation, equipment | | 11,000 | | (*b*) 5,500 |
| Accounts payable | | 3,000 | | |
| Income taxes payable | | 6,000 | | (*c*) 1,000 |
| Common stock | | 50,000 | | |
| Retained earnings | | 19,000 | | |
| Dividends declared | 8,000 | | | |
| Sales | | 320,000 | | |
| Sales discounts | 20,000 | | | |
| Purchases | 147,000 | | | |
| Purchases discounts | | 12,000 | | |
| Transportation-in | 11,000 | | | |
| Salaries expense | 43,000 | | | |
| Rent expense | 24,000 | | | |
| Advertising expense | 21,000 | | | |
| Supplies expense | | | (*a*) 6,000 | |
| Depreciation expense | | | (*b*) 5,500 | |
| Insurance expense | 12,000 | | | |
| Income taxes expense | 17,000 | | (*c*) 1,000 | |
| | 421,000 | 421,000 | 12,500 | 12,500 |

*Required*

1. Complete the work sheet. (Ending inventory is $50,000.)
2. Prepare the 1990 income statement.
3. Prepare the 1990 retained earnings statement.
4. Prepare a balance sheet as of December 31, 1990.
5. Prepare closing entries.

## Solution to Demonstration Problem

1.

**CONTINENTAL SALES, INC.**
**Work Sheet**
**For Year Ended December 31, 1990**

| Account Titles | Unadjusted Trial Balance | | Adjustments | | Income Statement | | Retained Earnings Statement or Balance Sheet | |
|---|---|---|---|---|---|---|---|---|
| | Dr. | Cr. | Dr. | Cr. | Dr. | Cr. | Dr. | Cr. |
| Cash | 19,000 | | | | | | 19,000 | |
| Merchandise inventory | 52,000 | | | | 52,000 | 50,000 | 50,000 | |
| Supplies | 7,000 | | | (*a*) 6,000 | | | 1,000 | |
| Equipment | 40,000 | | | | | | 40,000 | |
| Accumulated depreciation, equipment | | 11,000 | | (*b*) 5,500 | | | | 16,500 |
| Accounts payable | | 3,000 | | | | | | 3,000 |
| Income taxes payable | | 6,000 | | (*c*) 1,000 | | | | 7,000 |
| Common stock | | 50,000 | | | | | | 50,000 |
| Retained earnings | | 19,000 | | | | | | 19,000 |
| Dividends declared | 8,000 | | | | | | 8,000 | |
| Sales | | 320,000 | | | | 320,000 | | |
| Sales discounts | 20,000 | | | | 20,000 | | | |
| Purchases | 147,000 | | | | 147,000 | | | |
| Purchases discounts | | 12,000 | | | | 12,000 | | |
| Transportation-in | 11,000 | | | | 11,000 | | | |
| Salaries expense | 43,000 | | | | 43,000 | | | |
| Rent expense | 24,000 | | | | 24,000 | | | |
| Advertising expense | 21,000 | | | | 21,000 | | | |
| Supplies expense | | | (*a*) 6,000 | | 6,000 | | | |
| Depreciation expense | | | (*b*) 5,500 | | 5,500 | | | |
| Insurance expense | 12,000 | | | | 12,000 | | | |
| Income taxes expense | 17,000 | | (*c*) 1,000 | | 18,000 | | | |
| | 421,000 | 421,000 | 12,500 | 12,500 | 359,500 | 382,000 | 118,000 | 95,500 |
| Net income | | | | | 22,500 | | | 22,500 |
| | | | | | 382,000 | 382,000 | 118,000 | 118,000 |

2.

**CONTINENTAL SALES, INC.**
**Income Statement**
**For Year Ended December 31, 1990**

| | | | |
|---|---|---|---|
| Revenue from sales: | | | |
| Gross sales | | | $320,000 |
| Less: Sales discounts | | | 20,000 |
| Net Sales | | | $300,000 |
| Cost of goods sold: | | | |
| Merchandise inventory, December 31, 1989 | | $ 52,000 | |
| Purchases | $147,000 | | |
| Less: Purchases discounts | 12,000 | | |
| Net purchases | $135,000 | | |
| Plus: Transportation-in | 11,000 | | |
| Cost of goods purchased | | 146,000 | |
| Cost of goods available for sale | | $198,000 | |
| Merchandise inventory, December 31, 1990 | | 50,000 | |
| Cost of goods sold | | | 148,000 |
| Gross profit from sales | | | $152,000 |
| Operating expenses: | | | |
| Salaries expense | | $ 43,000 | |
| Rent expense | | 24,000 | |
| Advertising expense | | 21,000 | |
| Supplies expense | | 6,000 | |
| Depreciation expense | | 5,500 | |
| Insurance expense | | 12,000 | |
| Total operating expenses | | | 111,500 |
| Income from operations | | | 40,500 |
| Less income taxes expense | | | 18,000 |
| Net income | | | $ 22,500 |

3.

**CONTINENTAL SALES, INC.**
**Retained Earnings Statement**
**For Year Ended December 31, 1990**

| | |
|---|---|
| Retained earnings, December 31, 1989 | $19,000 |
| Add 1990 net income | 22,500 |
| Total | $41,500 |
| Deduct dividends declared | 8,000 |
| Retained earnings, December 31, 1990 | $33,500 |

4.

**CONTINENTAL SALES, INC.**
**Balance Sheet**
**December 31, 1990**
**Assets**

| | | |
|---|---|---|
| Current assets: | | |
| Cash | | $19,000 |
| Merchandise inventory | | 50,000 |
| Supplies | | 1,000 |
| Total current assets | | $70,000 |
| Equipment | $40,000 | |
| Less accumulated depreciation | 16,500 | |
| Total equipment | | 23,500 |
| Total assets | | $93,500 |

| | | |
|---|---|---|
| **Liabilities** | | |
| Current liabilities: | | |
| Accounts payable | $ 3,000 | |
| Income taxes payable | 7,000 | |
| Total liabilities | | $10,000 |
| **Stockholders' Equity** | | |
| Common stock | $50,000 | |
| Retained earnings | 33,500 | |
| Total stockholders' equity | | 83,500 |
| Total liabilities and stockholders' equity | | $93,500 |

5.

| | | | | |
|---|---|---|---|---|
| 1990 | | | | |
| Dec. | 31 | Merchandise Inventory | 50,000.00 | |
| | | Sales | 320,000.00 | |
| | | Purchases Discounts | 12,000.00 | |
| | | Income Summary | | 382,000.00 |
| | 31 | Income Summary | 359,500.00 | |
| | | Merchandise Inventory | | 52,000.00 |
| | | Sales Discounts | | 20,000.00 |
| | | Purchases | | 147,000.00 |
| | | Transportation-In | | 11,000.00 |
| | | Salaries Expense | | 43,000.00 |
| | | Rent Expense | | 24,000.00 |
| | | Advertising Expense | | 21,000.00 |
| | | Supplies Expense | | 6,000.00 |
| | | Depreciation Expense | | 5,500.00 |
| | | Insurance Expense | | 12,000.00 |
| | | Income Taxes Expense | | 18,000.00 |
| | 31 | Income Summary | 22,500.00 | |
| | | Retained Earnings | | 22,500.00 |
| | 31 | Retained Earnings | 8,000.00 | |
| | | Dividends Declared | | 8,000.00 |

**Appendix C**

## THE ADJUSTING ENTRY APPROACH TO ACCOUNTING FOR MERCHANDISE INVENTORIES

Explain the adjusting entry approach to accounting for inventories and prepare a work sheet, adjusting entries, and closing entries according to the adjusting entry approach. (L. O. 6)

In Chapter 5, we transferred the beginning inventory to Income Summary in the process of making the closing entries. Also, the ending inventory was recorded in the Merchandise Inventory account as part of a closing entry. An alternative approach is to show these transfers as adjustments on the work sheet and to journalize the transfers as adjusting entries.

Some accountants prefer to use the closing entry approach and others prefer to use the adjusting entry approach. Also, some computerized accounting systems prepare the closing entries automatically. In other words, the person who uses such a system does not prepare closing entries. Instead, a single command "to close" is given, and the computer automatically closes all of the temporary accounts. When such a system is used, you do not have the oppor-

**Illustration C–1**
**Adjusting and closing entries for a merchandising corporation**

| | | Closing Entry Approach | | Adjusting Entry Approach | |
|---|---|---|---|---|---|
| | Adjusting Entries | | | | |
| 1990 | | | | | |
| Dec. 31 | Insurance Expense | 600.00 | | 600.00 | |
| | Prepaid Insurance | | 600.00 | | 600.00 |
| 31 | Store Supplies Expense | 400.00 | | 400.00 | |
| | Store Supplies | | 400.00 | | 400.00 |
| 31 | Office Supplies Expense | 200.00 | | 200.00 | |
| | Office Supplies | | 200.00 | | 200.00 |
| 31 | Depreciation Expense, Store Equipment | 3,000.00 | | 3,000.00 | |
| | Accumulated Depreciation, Store Equipment | | 3,000.00 | | 3,000.00 |
| 31 | Depreciation Expense, Office Equipment | 700.00 | | 700.00 | |
| | Accumulated Depreciation, Office Equipment | | 700.00 | | 700.00 |
| 31 | Income Taxes Expense | 100.00 | | 100.00 | |
| | Income Taxes Payable | | 100.00 | | 100.00 |
| 31 | **Income Summary** | — | | **19,000.00** | |
| | **Merchandise Inventory** | | — | | **19,000.00** |
| 31 | **Merchandise Inventory** | — | | **21,000.00** | |
| | **Income Summary** | | — | | **21,000.00** |
| | Closing Entries | | | | |
| 31 | Income Summary | 323,100.00 | | 304,100.00 | |
| | **Merchandise Inventory** | | **19,000.00** | | — |
| | Sales Returns and Allowances | | 1,900.00 | | 1,900.00 |
| | Sales Discounts | | 4,300.00 | | 4,300.00 |
| | Purchases | | 235,800.00 | | 235,800.00 |
| | Transportation-In | | 1,500.00 | | 1,500.00 |
| | Sales Salaries Expense | | 18,500.00 | | 18,500.00 |
| | Rent Expense, Selling Space | | 8,100.00 | | 8,100.00 |
| | Advertising Expense | | 700.00 | | 700.00 |
| | Store Supplies Expense | | 400.00 | | 400.00 |
| | Depreciation Expense, Store Equipment | | 3,000.00 | | 3,000.00 |
| | Office Salaries Expense | | 25,800.00 | | 25,800.00 |
| | Rent Expense, Office Space | | 900.00 | | 900.00 |
| | Insurance Expense | | 600.00 | | 600.00 |
| | Office Supplies Expense | | 200.00 | | 200.00 |
| | Depreciation Expense, Office Equipment | | 700.00 | | 700.00 |
| | Income Taxes Expense | | 1,700.00 | | 1,700.00 |
| 31 | **Merchandise Inventory** | **21,000.00** | | — | |
| | Sales | 306,200.00 | | 306,200.00 | |
| | Purchases Returns and Allowances | 1,200.00 | | 1,200.00 | |
| | Purchases Discounts | 4,100.00 | | 4,100.00 | |
| | Income Summary | | 332,500.00 | | 311,500.00 |
| 31 | Income Summary | 9,400.00 | | 9,400.00 | |
| | Retained Earnings | | 9,400.00 | | 9,400.00 |
| 31 | Retained Earnings | 4,000.00 | | 4,000.00 | |
| | Dividends Declared | | 4,000.00 | | 4,000.00 |

tunity to insert the beginning and ending inventory amounts in the closing entries. Instead, the adjusting entry approach must be used to bring the Merchandise Inventory account balance up-to-date.

To illustrate the differences between the closing entry approach and the adjusting entry approach, we return to the example of Iowa Sales, Incorporated. In Chapter 5, when the *closing entry approach* was used, the beginning inventory was transferred to Income Summary and the ending inventory was recorded in the Merchandise Inventory account as part of the closing entries. In the *adjusting entry approach,* an adjusting entry is prepared to transfer the beginning inventory from the Merchandise Inventory account to Income Summary. Another adjusting entry records the ending inventory as a debit balance in the Merchandise Inventory account and as a credit in Income Summary. The adjusting and closing entries under both approaches are presented in Illustration C–1.

In Illustration C–1, notice that both approaches accomplish exactly the same changes in the Merchandise Inventory account. The beginning inventory of $19,000 was removed from the account, and the $21,000 ending inventory was recorded in the account.

Also, both approaches result in exactly the same credit balance of $9,400 in the Income Summary account. Under the adjusting entry approach, the effects of the beginning and ending inventories on Income Summary are recorded with adjusting entries. And under the closing entry approach, these effects are recorded with closing entries.

## The Work Sheet under the Adjusting Entry Approach

When the adjusting entry approach is used, the beginning inventory transfer from Merchandise Inventory to Income Summary is entered in the Adjustments columns of the work sheet. Also, the ending inventory amount is debited to Merchandise Inventory and credited to Income Summary in the Adjustments columns. This procedure is followed in Illustration C–2, which shows the work sheet for Iowa Sales, Incorporated.

On line 3 of Illustration C–2, note that the adjustment *(g)* eliminates the beginning inventory from the Merchandise Inventory account. Adjustment *(h)* establishes the ending inventory amount in the account. Because this is an asset on December 31, 1990, the ending amount is carried directly to the Statement of Retained Earnings or Balance Sheet Debit column.

Also in Illustration C–2, you can see that the Income Summary account (line 15) was listed at the time the Unadjusted Trial Balance was first prepared. Note that the debit and credit adjustments to this account are individually carried into the Income Statement columns. Both of these amounts, the beginning inventory and the ending inventory amounts, are used in preparing the income statement. Therefore, you should not subtract one from the other and carry over only the net amount. Rather, the $19,000 beginning inventory is extended to the Income Debit column and the $21,000 ending inventory is extended to the Income Statement Credit column.

The remaining steps to complete the work sheet are exactly the same, whether the adjusting entry approach or the closing entry approach is used. To see the work sheet differences between the two methods, compare Illustration

Illustration C–2
**The work sheet when the adjusting entry approach is used**

**IOWA SALES, INCORPORATED**
**Work Sheet**
**For Year Ended December 31, 1990**

| | Account Titles | Unadjusted Trial Balance | | Adjustments | | Income Statement | | Retained Earnings Statement or Balance Sheet | |
|---|---|---|---|---|---|---|---|---|---|
| | | Dr. | Cr. | Dr. | Cr. | Dr. | Cr. | Dr. | Cr. |
| 1 | Cash | 8,200 | | | | | | 8,200 | |
| 2 | Accounts receivable | 11,200 | | | | | | 11,200 | |
| 3 | Merchandise inventory | 19,000 | | (*h*) **21,000** | (*g*) **19,000** | | | **21,000** | |
| 4 | Prepaid insurance | 900 | | | (*a*) 600 | | | 300 | |
| 5 | Store supplies | 600 | | | (*b*) 400 | | | 200 | |
| 6 | Office supplies | 300 | | | (*c*) 200 | | | 100 | |
| 7 | Store equipment | 29,100 | | | | | | 29,100 | |
| 8 | Accum. depr., store equipment | | 2,500 | | (*d*) 3,000 | | | | 5,500 |
| 9 | Office equipment | 4,400 | | | | | | 4,400 | |
| 10 | Accum. depr., office equipment | | 600 | | (*e*) 700 | | | | 1,300 |
| 11 | Accounts payable | | 3,600 | | | | | | 3,600 |
| 12 | Income taxes payable | | | | (*f*) 100 | | | | 100 |
| 13 | Common stock | | 50,000 | | | | | | 50,000 |
| 14 | Retained earnings | | 8,600 | | | | | | 8,600 |
| 15 | Income summary | | | (*g*) **19,000** | (*h*) **21,000** | **19,000** | **21,000** | | |
| 16 | Dividends declared | 4,000 | | | | | | 4,000 | |
| 17 | Sales | | 306,200 | | | | 306,200 | | |
| 18 | Sales returns and allowances | 1,900 | | | | 1,900 | | | |
| 19 | Sales discounts | 4,300 | | | | 4,300 | | | |
| 20 | Purchases | 235,800 | | | | 235,800 | | | |
| 21 | Purchases returns and allowances | | 1,200 | | | | 1,200 | | |
| 22 | Purchases discounts | | 4,100 | | | | 4,100 | | |
| 23 | Transportation-in | 1,500 | | | | 1,500 | | | |
| 24 | Sales salaries expense | 18,500 | | | | 8,500 | | | |
| 25 | Rent expense, selling space | 8,100 | | | | 8,100 | | | |
| 26 | Advertising expense | 700 | | | | 700 | | | |
| 27 | Store supplies expense | | | (*b*) 400 | | 400 | | | |
| 28 | Depr. expense, store equipment | | | (*d*) 3,000 | | 3,000 | | | |
| 29 | Office salaries expense | 25,800 | | | | 25,800 | | | |
| 30 | Rent expense, office space | 900 | | | | 900 | | | |
| 31 | Insurance expense | | | (*a*) 600 | | 600 | | | |
| 32 | Office supplies expense | | | (*c*) 200 | | 200 | | | |
| 33 | Depr. expense, office equipment | | | (*e*) 700 | | 700 | | | |
| 34 | Income taxes expense | 1,600 | | (*f*) 100 | | 1,700 | | | |
| 35 | | 376,800 | 376,800 | 45,000 | 45,000 | 323,100 | 332,500 | 78,500 | 69,100 |
| 36 | Net income | | | | | 9,400 | | | 9,400 |
| 37 | | | | | | 332,500 | 332,500 | 78,500 | 78,500 |

C–2 (the adjusting entry approach) with Illustration 5–2 on page 212 (the closing entry approach).

## Summary of Appendix C in Terms of the Learning Objective

**6.** When the adjusting entry approach is used, adjusting entries are designed to update the Merchandise Inventory account and to record the beginning and ending inventory elements of cost of goods sold in the Income Summary account. On the work sheet, these adjustments are entered in the Adjustments columns. Then, the ending inventory is extended to the Retained Earnings Statement or Balance sheet Debit column. Both the debit and credit adjustments to Income Summary are individually extended to the Income Statement columns.

## Glossary

Define or explain the words and phrases listed in the chapter Glossary. (L. O. 5)

**Cash discount** a deduction from the invoice price of goods that is granted if payment is made within a specified period of time. p. 204

**Credit memorandum** a memorandum sent to notify its recipient that the business sending the memorandum has in its records credited the account of the recipient. p. 220

**Credit period** the agreed period of time for which credit is granted and at the end of which payment is expected. p. 204

**Credit terms** the specified amounts and timing of payments that a buyer agrees to make in return for being granted credit to purchase goods or services. pp. 203–4

**Debit memorandum** a memorandum sent to notify its recipient that the business sending the memorandum has in its records debited the account of the recipient. p. 220

**Discount period** the period of time during which, if payment is made, a cash discount may be deducted from the invoice price. p. 204

**EOM** an abbreviation for the words *end-of-month* that is sometimes used in expressing the credit terms of a sales agreement. p. 203

**FOB** the abbrevaition for *free on board,* which is used to denote that goods purchased are placed on board the means of transportation at a specified geographic point with all loading and transportation charges to that point to be paid by the seller. p. 208

**General and administrative expenses** expenses to support the management and overall operations of a business, such as central office, accounting, personnel, and credit and collections expenses. p. 211

**Gross profit** net sales minus cost of goods sold. p. 202

**List price** the catalog price of an item from which a trade discount, if offered, is deducted to determine the invoice or gross sales price of the item. p. 221

**Merchandise** assets purchased and held for resale. p. 202

**Multiple-step income statement** an income statement on which cost of goods sold and the expenses are subtracted in steps to get net income. pp. 210, 219

**Periodic inventory system** a method of accounting for inventories in which the inventory account is brought up to date once each period, at the end of the period, by counting the units of each product on hand, multiplying the count for each product by its cost, and adding the costs of the various products. p. 205

**Perpetual inventory system** a method of accounting for inventories in which cost of goods sold is recorded each time a sale is made and an up-to-date record of goods on hand is maintained. p. 205

**Purchases discounts** deductions from the invoice price of purchased items, which are granted by suppliers in return for early payment, i.e., cash discounts from suppliers. p. 206

**Retained earnings statement** a financial statement that reports the changes in a corporation's retained earnings that occurred during an accounting period. p. 215

**Sales discounts** deductions from the invoice price granted to customers in return for early payment, i.e., cash discounts to customers. p. 204

**Selling expenses** the expenses of preparing and storing merchandise for sale, promoting sales, making sales, and delivering goods to customers. pp. 210–11

**Single-step income statement** an income statement on which cost of goods sold and operating expenses are added together and subtracted in one step from net sales to get net income. p. 219

**Trade discount** a deduction from a catalog or list price that is used to determine the invoice price of goods. p. 221

**Transportation-in** costs incurred by a business for transporting merchandise purchases to the business. p. 208

## Objective Review

Answers to the following questions are listed in Appendix I at the end of the book. Be sure that you decide which is the one best answer to each question *before* you check the answers in the appendix.

1. In recording transactions that involve the purchase and resale of merchandise when a periodic inventory system is used:
   *a.* The sales price of merchandise returned by customers is credited to Sales Returns and Allowances.
   *b.* The purchase price of merchandise returned to a supplier is debited to Purchases Returns and Allowances.
   *c.* The Sales account is credited for the cost of merchandise sold to customers.
   *d.* The amount of any sales discounts taken by customers is debited to a Sales Discounts account.
   *e.* The amount of any purchases discounts is debited to a Purchases Discounts account.
2. With a periodic inventory system, cost of goods sold:
   *a.* Is subtracted from the cost of goods available for sale to determine gross profit from sales.
   *b.* Plus the net cost of purchases equals the cost of goods available for sale.
   *c.* Is calculated as the cost of the beginning inventory plus the cost of purchases less the cost of the ending inventory.
   *d.* Is subtracted from gross sales to determine net sales.
   *e.* Includes all operating expenses related to merchandising operations.
3. On the work sheet for a merchandising company that uses the closing entry approach to account for inventories:
   *a.* The beginning inventory is extended from the trial balance to the Income Statement Credit column.
   *b.* The ending inventory is inserted in the Income Statement Debit column and then extended to the Retained Earnings Statement or Balance Sheet Debit column.
   *c.* The amount of cost of goods sold is calculated in the Adjustments columns.

*d.* The beginning inventory and ending inventory amounts appear in the Income Statement Debit and Income Statement Credit columns, respectively.

*e.* The elements that make up the cost of purchases are extended to the Retained Earnings Statement or Balance Sheet Debit column.

4. When closing entries are used to account for merchandise inventories:

*a.* The closing entries include a credit to Merchandise Inventory for the cost of the beginning inventory.

*b.* The closing entries include a debit to Merchandise Inventory for the cost of the ending inventory.

*c.* The cost of goods sold is recorded in a separate Cost of Goods Sold account which is closed to Income Summary.

*d.* Cost of goods sold is calculated as the difference between the beginning and ending merchandise inventory amounts.

*e.* Both (*a*) and (*b*) are correct.

*An asterisk (*) identifies the questions, excercises, and problems that are based on Appendix C at the end of the chapter.*

## Questions for Class Discussion

1. What is gross profit?
2. May a business earn a gross profit on its sales and still suffer a net loss? How?
3. Why should a business be interested in the amount of its sales returns and allowances?
4. Since sales returns and allowances are subtracted from sales on the income statement, why not save the effort of this subtraction by debiting all such returns and allowances directly to the Sales account?
5. What is a cash discount?
6. What is the difference between sales discounts, cash discounts, and purchases discounts?
7. If terms are 2/10, n/60, what is the length of the credit period? What is the length of the discount period?
8. How and when is cost of goods sold determined in a store that uses a periodic inventory system?
9. Which of the following are debited to the Purchases account of a grocery store: (*a*) the purchase of a cash register, (*b*) the purchase of a refrigerated display case, (*c*) the purchase of advertising space in a newspaper, and (*d*) the purchase of a case of tomato soup?
10. If a business is allowed to return all unsatisfactory merchandise purchased and receive full credit for the purchase price, why should it be interested in controlling the amount of its returns?
11. When applied to transportation terms, what do the letters FOB mean? What does FOB destination mean?
12. At the end of an accounting period, which inventory, the beginning

inventory or the ending inventory, appears on the unadjusted trial balance of a company that uses a periodic inventory system?

13. What information appears on a retained earnings statement?
14. What relationship does a retained earnings statement have to the balance sheets at the end of the prior period and at the end of the current period?
15. How does a single-step income statement differ from a multiple-step income statement?
16. During the year, a company purchased merchandise that cost $150,000. What was the company's cost of goods sold if there were: (*a*) no beginning or ending inventories? (*b*) a beginning inventory of $26,000 and no ending inventory? (*c*) a $20,000 beginning inventory and a $32,000 ending inventory? and (*d*) no beginning inventory and an $11,000 ending inventory?
17. In counting the merchandise on hand at the end of an accounting period, a clerk failed to count and consequently omitted from the inventory all the merchandise on one shelf. If the cost of the merchandise on the shelf was $100, what was the effect of the omission on (*a*) the balance sheet and (*b*) the income statement?
18. Suppose that the omission of the $100 from the inventory (question 17) was not discovered. What would be the effect on the balance sheet and income statement prepared at the end of the next accounting period?
19. Distinguish between cash discounts and trade discounts. Is the amount of a trade discount on purchased merchandise credited to the Purchases Discounts account?
20. When a debit memorandum is issued, who debits, the originator of the memorandum or the company receiving it?

*21. Where is the ending inventory entered on the work sheet when the adjusting entry approach to accounting for inventories is used?

*22. What are the procedural differences between the adjusting entry and closing entry approaches to accounting for inventories?

*23. In comparing the adjusting entry and closing entry approaches to accounting for inventories, what effect does the adjusting entry approach have on the reported amount of the ending inventory? What effect does it have on the net income or net loss?

## Exercises

**Exercise 5–1**
**Analyzing and recording purchases and purchases discounts**
(L. O. 1)

Corner Store purchased merchandise having a $6,000 invoice price, terms 2/10, n/60, from a manufacturer and paid for the merchandise within the discount period. (*a*) Give without dates the journal entries made by the store to record the purchase and payment. (*b*) Give without dates the entries made by the manufacturer to record the sale and collection. (*c*) If the store borrowed sufficient money at a 13% annual rate of interest on the last day of the discount period to pay the invoice, how much did the store save by borrowing to take advantage of the discount?

**Exercise 5–2**
**Journalizing merchandise transactions**
(L. O. 1)

Prepare journal entries to record the following transactions of Baird Variety Store.

Jan. 3 Purchased merchandise from West Company subject to the following terms: $500 invoice price, 2/15, n/60, FOB factory.
5 Paid McLean Trucking $45 for shipping charges on purchase of January 3.
7 Returned to West Company unacceptable merchandise with list price of $100.
17 Sent West Company a check to pay for January 3 purchase net of discount and return.
18 Purchased merchandise from North Company subject to the following terms: $800 list price, 2/10, n/30, FOB North Company factory. The invoice showed that North Company had paid a trucking company $60 to ship the merchandise to Baird.
22 After advising North Company that some merchandise was damaged, received a credit memorandum granting Baird a $200 allowance on the January 18 purchase.
28 Paid North Company for the January 18 purchase, net of the allowance, and the shipping charges prepaid by North.

**Exercise 5–3**
**Journal entries for purchases and sales and returns**
(L. O. 1)

On January 5, 1990, Q Company received $6,000 of merchandise and an invoice dated January 4, terms of 2/10, n/30, FOB T Company's factory. On the day the goods were received, Q Company paid Quick Freight Company $180 of shipping charges on the merchandise purchased. The next day, Q Company returned to T Company $500 of the goods that were defective, and on January 14 it mailed T Company a check for the amount owed. Prepare general journal entries to record the foregoing transactions (*a*) on the books of Q Company and (*b*) on the books of T Company. Assume that T Company recorded the return and the check the next day after each was sent.

**Exercise 5–4**
**Calculating expenses and income**
(L. O. 2)

Copy the following tabulation and fill in the missing amounts. Indicate a loss by placing parentheses around the amount. Each horizontal row of figures is a separate problem situation.

| Sales | Beginning Inventory | Purchases | Ending Inventory | Cost of Goods Sold | Gross Profit | Expenses | Net Income or Loss |
|---|---|---|---|---|---|---|---|
| $132,000 | $ 96,000 | $ 84,000 | $ ? | $114,000 | $ ? | $60,000 | $ ? |
| 222,000 | 78,000 | ? | 90,000 | 96,000 | ? | 66,000 | 60,000 |
| 180,000 | 60,000 | ? | 36,000 | ? | 102,000 | 54,000 | 48,000 |
| ? | 90,000 | 132,000 | 72,000 | ? | 120,000 | 48,000 | ? |
| 192,000 | 72,000 | 114,000 | ? | 126,000 | ? | 84,000 | ? |
| 60,000 | 18,000 | ? | 30,000 | 36,000 | ? | ? | 6,000 |
| ? | 138,000 | 264,000 | 156,000 | ? | 168,000 | ? | 60,000 |
| 96,000 | ? | 60,000 | 42,000 | ? | 36,000 | ? | 12,000 |

**Exercise 5–5**
**Multiple-step income statement for a proprietorship**
(L. O. 3)

The Place is a single proprietorship business that ends its annual accounting period on December 31. The Income Statement columns of The Place's December 31, 1990, work sheet appeared as shown below. Use the information in these columns to prepare a 1990 multiple-step income statement for The Place.

| | Income Statement | |
|---|---|---|
| | Debit | Credit |
| Merchandise inventory | 43,000 | 48,000 |
| Sales | | 240,000 |
| Sales returns and allowances | 1,500 | |
| Sales discounts | 1,800 | |
| Purchases | 144,000 | |
| Purchases returns and allowances | | 1,000 |
| Purchases discounts | | 3,000 |
| Transportation-in | 700 | |
| Selling expenses | 36,000 | |
| General and administrative expenses | 25,000 | |
| | 252,000 | 292,000 |
| Net income | 40,000 | |
| | 292,000 | 292,000 |

**Exercise 5–6**
**Preparing and posting proprietorship closing entries**
(L. O. 4)

**Part 1.** Assume that The Place of Exercise 5–5 is owned by Rose Callen and prepare entries to close the temporary accounts of the business.

**Part 2.** Construct a balance column Merchandise Inventory account and enter the $43,000 beginning inventory of Exercise 5–5 as its balance on December 31, 1989. Then post to the account the portions of the closing entries that affect the account.

**Exercise 5–7**
**Preparing an income statement from closing entries**
(L. O. 3, 4)

The following two closing entries (with expenses combined to shorten the exercise) were made by Northwest Sales at the end of its 1990 annual accounting period.

| | | | | |
|---|---|---|---|---|
| Dec. | 31 | Income Summary | 316,800.00 | |
| | | Merchandise Inventory | | 42,000.00 |
| | | Sales Returns and Allowances | | 2,400.00 |
| | | Sales Discounts | | 3,600.00 |
| | | Purchases | | 180,000.00 |
| | | Transportation-In | | 4,800.00 |
| | | Selling Expenses | | 48,000.00 |
| | | General and Administrative Expenses | | 36,000.00 |
| | 31 | Merchandise Inventory | 55,000.00 | |
| | | Sales | 300,000.00 | |
| | | Purchases Returns and Allowances | 1,200.00 | |
| | | Purchases Discounts | 2,400.00 | |
| | | Income Summary | | 358,600.00 |

*Required*

Use the information in the closing entries to prepare an income statement for Northwest Sales.

**Exercise 5–8**
**Multiple-step income statement and retained earnings statement**
(L. O. 3)

The following items, with expenses condensed to conserve space, appeared in the last four columns of a work sheet prepared for Small Shop, Incorporated, as of December 31, 1990, the end of its annual accounting period. Use this information to prepare a 1990 multiple-step income statement and a retained earnings statement for the corporation.

| | Income Statement | | Retained Earnings Statement or Balance Sheet | |
|---|---|---|---|---|
| | **Debit** | **Credit** | **Debit** | **Credit** |
| Merchandise inventory | 48,000 | 60,000 | 60,000 | |
| Other assets | | | 150,000 | |
| Common stock | | | | 75,000 |
| Retained earnings | | | | 107,000 |
| Dividends declared | | | 20,000 | |
| Sales | | 360,000 | | |
| Sales returns and allowances | 1,800 | | | |
| Sales discounts | 3,600 | | | |
| Purchases | 216,000 | | | |
| Purchases returns and allowances | | 1,200 | | |
| Purchases discounts | | 3,000 | | |
| Transportation-in | 600 | | | |
| Selling expenses | 54,000 | | | |
| General and administrative expenses | 42,600 | | | |
| Income taxes expense | 9,600 | | | |
| | 376,200 | 424,200 | 230,000 | 182,000 |
| Net income | 48,000 | | | 48,000 |
| | 424,200 | 424,200 | 230,000 | 230,000 |

**Exercise 5–9**
**Preparing and posting closing entries**
(L. O. 4)

**Part 1.** Prepare entries to close the temporary accounts of Small Shop, Incorporated (Exercise 5–8).

**Part 2.** Construct a Merchandise Inventory account in the form of a balance column account and enter the $48,000 beginning inventory of Exercise 5–8 as its December 31, 1989, balance. Then post to the account the portions of the store's closing entries that affect the account.

**Exercise 5–10**
**Calculating operating expenses and cost of goods sold**
(L. O. 2, 3)

The information that follows was taken from a single proprietorship's income statement.

| | | | |
|---|---|---|---|
| Sales | $180,000 | Purchases returns | $ 600 |
| Sales returns | 1,200 | Purchases discounts | 1,800 |
| Sales discounts | 2,400 | Transportation-in | 3,600 |
| Beginning inventory | 48,000 | Gross profit from sales | 56,400 |
| Purchases | 114,000 | Net loss | 4,800 |

*Required*

Prepare calculations to determine (*a*) total operating expenses, (*b*) cost of goods sold, and (*c*) ending inventory.

**Exercise 5–11**
**Preparing a work sheet for a merchandising corporation**
(L. O. 3)

The trial balance that follows was taken from the ledger of Bexar, Incorporated, at the end of its annual accounting period. (To simplify the problem and to save you time, the account balances are in one- and two-digit numbers.)

**BEXAR, INCORPORATED**
**Unadjusted Trial Balance**
**December 31, 1990**

| | | |
|---|---|---|
| Cash | $ 2 | |
| Accounts receivable | 7 | |
| Merchandise inventory | 6 | |
| Store supplies | 4 | |
| Store equipment | 10 | |
| Accumulated depreciation, store equipment | | $ 3 |
| Accounts payable | | 4 |
| Salaries payable | — | — |
| Common stock, $1 par value | | 12 |
| Retained earnings | | 10 |
| Dividends declared | 1 | |
| Sales | | 42 |
| Sales returns and allowances | 2 | |
| Purchases | 19 | |
| Purchases discounts | | 3 |
| Transportation-in | 2 | |
| Salaries expense | 11 | |
| Rent expense | 7 | |
| Advertising expense | 3 | |
| Depreciation expense, store equipment | — | — |
| Store supplies expense | — | — |
| Totals | $74 | $74 |

*Required*

Prepare a work sheet form (do not include columns for an adjusted trial balance). Copy the unadjusted trial balance onto the work sheet and complete the work sheet using the following information:

*a*. Ending store supplies inventory, $2.

*b*. Estimated depreciation on the store equipment, $4.

*c*. Accrued salaries payable, $2.

*d*. Ending merchandise inventory, $7.

***Exercise 5–12**
**Work sheet for a merchandising corporation; adjusting entry approach**
(L. O. 6)

Use the information in Exercise 5–11 to prepare a work sheet according to the adjusting entry approach to accounting for merchandise inventories.

***Exercise 5–13**
**Updating the Merchandise Inventory account; adjusting entry approach**
(L. O. 6)

Use the adjusting entry approach to accounting for merchandise inventories and prepare adjusting journal entries and closing journal entries for Bexar, Incorporated, the company described in Exercise 5–11.

**Exercise 5–14**
**Preparing a work sheet for a merchandising proprietorship**
(L. O. 3)

The trial balance that follows was taken from the ledger of Linder Sales at the end of its annual accounting period. Bob Linder, the owner of Linder Sales, did not make additional investments in the business during 1990.

**LINDER SALES**
**Unadjusted Trial Balance**
**December 31, 1990**

| | | |
|---|---|---|
| Cash | $ 8 | |
| Accounts receivable | 11 | |
| Merchandise inventory | 16 | |
| Store supplies | 9 | |
| Accounts payable | | $ 19 |
| Salaries payable | — | — |
| Bob Linder, capital | | 26 |
| Bob Linder, withdrawals | 6 | |
| Sales | | 62 |
| Sales returns and allowances | 5 | |
| Purchases | 25 | |
| Purchases discounts | | 4 |
| Transportation-in | 5 | |
| Salaries expense | 19 | |
| Rent expense | 7 | |
| Store supplies expense | — | — |
| Totals | $111 | $111 |

*Required*

Prepare a work sheet form (do not include columns for an adjusted trial balance). Copy the unadjusted trial balance onto the work sheet and complete the work sheet using the following information:

*a.* Ending store supplies inventory, $5.
*b.* Accrued salaries payable, $3.
*c.* Ending merchandise inventory, $21.

**Exercise 5–15**
**Work Sheet for a merchandising proprietorship; adjusting entry approach**
(L. O. 6)

Use the information in Exercise 5–14 to prepare a work sheet according to the adjusting entry approach to accounting for merchandise inventories.

**Exercise 5–16**
**Updating the Merchandise Inventory account; adjusting entry approach**
(L. O. 6)

Use the adjusting entry approach to accounting for merchandise inventories and prepare adjusting journal entries and closing journal entries for Linder Sales, the company described in Exercise 5–14.

## Problems

**Problem 5–1**
**Journal entries for merchandising transactions**
(L. O. 1)

Prepare general journal entries to record the following transactions of Hart Sales Company:

Dec. 1 Purchased merchandise priced at $3,600 on credit, terms 1/15, n/30, FOB the seller's factory.
2 A new computer for office use was purchased on credit for $9,000.
2 Sold merchandise on credit, terms 2/10, 1/30, n/60, $1,800.
3 Paid $115 cash for freight charges on the merchandise shipment of the December 1 transaction.
7 Sold merchandise for cash, $360.
9 Purchased merchandise on credit, terms 2/15, n/30, $1,500.
11 Received a $300 credit memorandum for merchandise purchased on December 9 and returned for credit.
18 Sold merchandise on credit, terms 2/10, n/30, $1,350.
21 Issued a $225 credit memorandum to the customer of December 18 who returned a portion of the merchandise purchased.
22 Purchased office supplies on credit, $185.
23 Received a credit memorandum for unsatisfactory office supplies purchased on December 22 and returned for credit, $60.
24 Paid for the merchandise purchased on December 9, less the return and the discount.
28 The customer who purchased merchandise on December 2 paid for the purchase of that date less the applicable discount.
28 Received payment for the merchandise sold on December 18, less the return and applicable discount.
31 Paid for the merchandise purchased on December 1.

**Problem 5–2**
**Corporate income and retained earnings statements, and closing entries**
(L. O. 2, 3, 4)

On December 31, 1990, the end of Griffin Sales, Inc.'s annual accounting period, the financial statement columns of the company's work sheet were as follows:

| | Income Statement | | Retained Earnings Statement or Balance Sheet | |
|---|---|---|---|---|
| | Debit | Credit | Debit | Credit |
| Merchandise inventory | 33,765 | 35,790 | 35,790 | |
| Other assets | | | 260,000 | |
| Common stock | | | | 100,000 |
| Retained earnings | | | | 186,070 |
| Dividends declared | | | 25,000 | |
| Sales | | 330,510 | | |
| Sales returns and allowances | 1,970 | | | |
| Purchases | 216,765 | | | |
| Purchases returns and allowances | | 780 | | |
| Purchases discounts | | 3,255 | | |
| Transportation-in | 1,405 | | | |
| Sales salaries expense | 32,760 | | | |
| Rent expense, selling space | 16,200 | | | |
| Advertising expense | 1,185 | | | |
| Store supplies expense | 825 | | | |
| Depreciation expense, store equipment | 3,175 | | | |
| Office salaries expense | 15,975 | | | |
| Rent expense, office space | 1,800 | | | |
| Telephone expense | 855 | | | |
| Office supplies expense | 325 | | | |
| Insurance expense | 2,160 | | | |
| Depreciation expense, office equipment | 795 | | | |
| Income taxes expense | 5,655 | | | |
| | 335,615 | 370,335 | 320,790 | 286,070 |
| Net income | 34,720 | | | 34,720 |
| | 370,335 | 370,335 | 320,790 | 320,790 |

*Required*

1. Prepare a 1990 classified, multiple-step income statement for the corporation, showing in detail the expenses and the items that make up cost of goods sold.
2. Prepare a 1990 retained earnings statement.
3. Journalize compound closing entries for the corporation.
4. Open a Merchandise Inventory account and enter a December 31, 1989, balance of $33,765. Then post the portions of the closing entries that affect the account.
5. Prepare a combined, single-step income and retained earnings statement. Condense each revenue and expense category into a single item.

**Problem 5–3**
**Proprietorship work sheet, income statement, and closing entries**
(L. O. 2, 3, 4)

A December 31, 1990, year-end, unadjusted trial balance from the ledger of The Value Store, a single proprietorship, is as follows:

**THE VALUE STORE**
**Unadjusted Trial Balance**
**December 31, 1990**

| | | |
|---|---|---|
| Cash | $ 2,000 | |
| Merchandise inventory | 50,960 | |
| Store supplies | 1,175 | |
| Office supplies | 365 | |
| Prepaid insurance | 2,730 | |
| Store equipment | 31,815 | |
| Accumulated depreciation, store equipment | | $ 12,810 |
| Office equipment | 8,870 | |
| Accumulated depreciation, office equipment | | 3,200 |
| Accounts payable | | 7,305 |
| Don Boise, capital | | 60,450 |
| Don Boise, withdrawals | 27,000 | |
| Sales | | 285,645 |
| Sales returns and allowances | 1,745 | |
| Sales discounts | 3,180 | |
| Purchases | 171,375 | |
| Purchases returns and allowances | | 1,110 |
| Purchases discounts | | 4,410 |
| Transportation-in | 965 | |
| Sales salaries expense | 31,920 | |
| Rent expense, selling space | 19,350 | |
| Advertising expense | 570 | |
| Store supplies expense | –0– | |
| Depreciation expense, store equipment | –0– | |
| Office salaries expense | 18,630 | |
| Rent expense, office space | 2,280 | |
| Office supplies expense | –0– | |
| Insurance expense | –0– | |
| Depreciation expense, office equipment | –0– | |
| Totals | $374,930 | $374,930 |

*Required*

1. Copy the unadjusted trial balance on a work sheet form and complete the work sheet using the following information:
   *a.* Store supplies inventory, $200.
   *b.* Office supplies inventory, $125.
   *c.* Expired insurance, $2,235.
   *d.* Estimated depreciation of store equipment, $3,180.
   *e.* Estimated depreciation of office equipment, $575.
   *f.* Ending merchandise inventory, $52,320.
2. Journalize closing entries for the store.
3. Open a balance column Merchandise Inventory account and enter a December 31, 1989, balance of $50,960. Then post the portions of the closing entries that affect the account.

***Problem 5–4**
**Adjusting entry approach to proprietorship work sheet, adjusting and closing entries**
(L. O. 6)

Use the information presented in Problem 5–3 for The Value Store in solving this problem. However, in satisfying the following requirements, use the adjusting entry approach to accounting for merchandise inventories.

*Required*

1. Copy the unadjusted trial balance on a work sheet form and complete the work sheet. (Note the adjustments information presented in Requirement 1 of Problem 5–3.)
2. Journalize adjusting and closing entries for the store.
3. Open a balance column Merchandise Inventory account and enter a December 31, 1989, balance of $50,960. Then post those portions of the closing entries that affect the account.

**Problem 5–5**
**Corporate work sheet, income and retained earnings statements, and closing entries**
(L. O. 3, 4)

The unadjusted trial balance of Gizmo Shop, Incorporated, on December 31, 1990, the end of the annual accounting period, is as follows:

**GIZMO SHOP, INCORPORATED**
**Unadjusted Trial Balance**
**December 31, 1990**

| | | |
|---|---|---|
| Cash | $ 5,475 | |
| Merchandise inventory | 52,315 | |
| Store supplies | 920 | |
| Office supplies | 475 | |
| Prepaid insurance | 3,165 | |
| Store equipment | 55,795 | |
| Accumulated depreciation, store equipment | | $ 5,310 |
| Office equipment | 12,660 | |
| Accumulated depreciation, office equipment | | 1,385 |
| Accounts payable | | 1,195 |
| Salaries payable | | –0– |
| Income taxes payable | | –0– |
| Common stock, $10 par value | | 60,000 |
| Retained earnings | | 21,825 |
| Dividends declared | 15,000 | |
| Sales | | 412,230 |
| Sales returns and allowances | 2,790 | |
| Purchases | 251,715 | |
| Purchases returns and allowances | | 1,120 |
| Purchases discounts | | 4,385 |
| Transportation-in | 3,275 | |
| Sales salaries expense | 36,975 | |
| Rent expense, selling space | 15,750 | |
| Advertising expense | 5,150 | |
| Store supplies expense | –0– | |
| Depreciation expense, store equipment | –0– | |
| Office salaries expense | 37,740 | |
| Rent expense, office space | 2,250 | |
| Insurance expense | –0– | |
| Office supplies expense | –0– | |
| Depreciation expense, office equipment | –0– | |
| Income taxes expense | 6,000 | |
| Totals | $507,450 | $507,450 |

*Required*

1. Copy the unadjusted trial balance on a work sheet form and complete the work sheet using the information that follows:

*a.* Ending store supplies inventory, $245.
*b.* Ending office supplies inventory, $185.
*c.* Expired insurance, $2,465.
*d.* Depreciation on the store equipment, $5,415.
*e.* Depreciation on the office equipment, $1,485.
*f.* Accrued sales salaries payable, $335; and accrued office salaries payable, $240.
*g.* Additional income taxes expense, $635.
*h.* Ending merchandise inventory, $49,740.

2. Prepare a multiple-step classified income statement showing in detail the expenses and the items that make up cost of goods sold.
3. Prepare a retained earnings statement.
4. Prepare compound closing entries for the corporation.
5. In addition to the foregoing, prepare a single-step statement of income and retained earnings with the items condensed as is commonly done in published statements.

***Problem 5–6**
**Adjusting entry approach to corporate work sheet, income and retained earnings statements, adjusting and closing entries**
(L. O. 6)

Use the information presented in Problem 5–5 for Gizmo Shop, Incorporated, in solving this problem. However, in satisfying the following requirements, use the adjusting entry approach to accounting for merchandise inventories.

*Required*

1. Copy the unadjusted trial balance on a work sheet form and complete the work sheet. (Note the adjustments information presented in Requirement 1 of Problem 5–5.)
2. Prepare a multiple-step classified income statement showing in detail the expenses and the items that make up cost of goods sold.
3. Prepare a retained earnings statement.
4. Prepare adjusting and closing entries for the corporation.
5. In addition to the foregoing, prepare a single-step statement of income and retained earnings with the items condensed as is commonly done in published statements.

**Problem 5–7**
**Proprietorship work sheet, financial statements, and closing entries**
(L. O. 2, 3, 4)

The unadjusted trial balance of Classic Threads on December 31, 1990, the end of the annual accounting period, is as follows:

**CLASSIC THREADS**
**Unadjusted Trial Balance**
**December 31, 1990**

| | | |
|---|---|---|
| Cash | $ 10,275 | |
| Accounts receivable | 22,665 | |
| Merchandise inventory | 51,845 | |
| Store supplies | 2,415 | |
| Office supplies | 775 | |
| Prepaid insurance | 3,255 | |
| Store equipment | 61,980 | |
| Accumulated depreciation, store equipment | | $ 10,830 |
| Office equipment | 12,510 | |
| Accumulated depreciation, office equipment | | 2,825 |
| Accounts payable | | 8,310 |
| Salaries payable | | –0– |
| Sally Fowler, capital | | 106,015 |
| Sally Fowler, withdrawals | 15,000 | |
| Sales | | 562,140 |
| Sales returns and allowances | 5,070 | |
| Purchases | 385,085 | |
| Purchases returns and allowances | | 1,820 |
| Purchases discounts | | 4,710 |
| Transportation-in | 5,125 | |
| Sales salaries expense | 43,220 | |
| Rent expense, selling space | 20,250 | |
| Store supplies expense | –0– | |
| Depreciation expense, store equipment | –0– | |
| Office salaries expense | 48,330 | |
| Rent expense, office space | 8,850 | |
| Office supplies expense | –0– | |
| Insurance expense | –0– | |
| Depreciation expense, office equipment | –0– | |
| Totals | $696,650 | $696,650 |

*Required*

1. Copy the unadjusted trial balance on a work sheet form and complete the work sheet using the information that follows:
   *a.* Ending store supplies inventory, $445.
   *b.* Ending office supplies inventory, $225.
   *c.* Expired insurance, $2,805.
   *d.* Depreciation on the store equipment, $5,415.
   *e.* Depreciation on the office equipment, $1,485.
   *f.* Accrued sales salaries payable, $445; and accrued office salaries payable, $210.
   *g.* Ending merchandise inventory, $54,365.
2. Prepare a multiple-step income statement showing in detail the expenses and the items that make up cost of goods sold.
3. Prepare a statement of changes in owner's equity. On December 31, 1989, the Sally Fowler, Capital account had a balance of $36,015. Early in 1990, Ms. Fowler invested an additional $70,000 in the business.

4. Prepare a year-end classified balance sheet with the prepaid expenses combined.
5. Prepare adjusting and closing entries.

## Alternate Problems

**Problem 5–1A**
**Journal entries for merchandising transactions**
(L. O. 1)

Prepare general journal entries to record the following transactions of Schafer Merchandising:

| | | |
|---|---|---|
| Oct. | 1 | Purchased merchandise on credit, terms 2/10, n/30, $7,200. |
| | 2 | Sold merchandise for cash, $750. |
| | 7 | Purchased merchandise on credit, terms 2/10, n/30, $5,250, FOB the seller's factory. |
| | 7 | Paid $225 cash for freight charges on the merchandise shipment of the previous transaction. |
| | 8 | Purchased delivery equipment on credit, $12,000. |
| | 12 | Sold merchandise on credit, terms 2/15, 1/30, n/60, $3,000. |
| | 13 | Received a $750 credit memorandum for merchandise purchased on October 7 and returned for credit. |
| | 13 | Purchased office supplies on credit, $240, n/30. |
| | 15 | Sold merchandise on credit, terms 2/10, 1/30, n/60, $2,100. |
| | 15 | Paid for the merchandise purchased on October 7, less the return and the discount. |
| | 16 | Received a credit memorandum for unsatisfactory office supplies purchased on October 13 and returned, $60. |
| | 19 | Issued a $210 credit memorandum to the customer who purchased merchandise on October 15 and returned a portion for credit. |
| | 25 | Received payment for the merchandise sold on October 15, less the return and applicable discount. |
| | 27 | The customer of October 12 paid for the purchase of that date, less the applicable discount. |
| | 31 | Paid for the merchandise purchased on October 1. |

**Problem 5–2A**
**Corporate income and retained earnings statements, and closing entries**
(L. O. 2, 3, 4)

On December 31, 1990, the end of Seaside Sales, Inc.'s, annual accounting period, the financial statement columns of its work sheet appeared as follows:

| | Income Statement | | Retained Earnings Statement or Balance Sheet | |
|---|---|---|---|---|
| | Debit | Credit | Debit | Credit |
| Merchandise inventory | 69,330 | 66,545 | 66,545 | |
| Other assets | | | 487,785 | |
| Common stock | | | | 200,000 |
| Retained earnings | | | | 312,370 |
| Dividends declared | | | 50,000 | |
| Sales | | 963,720 | | |
| Sales returns and allowances | 5,715 | | | |
| Sales discounts | 14,580 | | | |
| Purchases | 651,735 | | | |
| Purchases returns and allowances | | 2,730 | | |
| Purchases discounts | | 8,970 | | |
| Transportation-in | 9,205 | | | |
| Sales salaries expense | 70,080 | | | |
| Rent expense, selling space | 33,000 | | | |
| Store supplies expense | 1,620 | | | |
| Depreciation expense, store equipment | 8,910 | | | |
| Office salaries expense | 56,820 | | | |
| Rent expense, office space | 3,000 | | | |
| Office supplies expense | 735 | | | |
| Insurance expense | 3,390 | | | |
| Depreciation expense, office equipment | 2,760 | | | |
| Income taxes expense | 19,125 | | | |
| | 950,005 | 1,041,965 | 604,330 | 512,370 |
| Net income | 91,960 | | | 91,960 |
| | 1,041,965 | 1,041,965 | 604,330 | 604,330 |

*Required*

1. Prepare a 1990 classified, multiple-step income statement for the corporation, showing in detail the expenses and the items that make up cost of goods sold.
2. Prepare a 1990 retained earnings statement.
3. Prepare compound closing entries for the corporation.
4. Open a Merchandise Inventory account and enter a December 31, 1989, balance of $69,330. Then post those portions of the closing entries that affect the account.
5. Prepare a combined, single-step income and retained earnings statement. Condense each revenue and expense category into a single item.

**Problem 5–3A**
**Proprietorship work sheet, income statement, and closing entries**
(L. O. 2, 3, 4)

The December 31, 1990, year-end, unadjusted trial balance of the ledger of Eastman Store, a single proprietorship business, is as follows:

**EASTMAN STORE**
**Unadjusted Trial Balance**
**December 31, 1990**

| | | |
|---|---|---|
| Cash | $ 7,305 | |
| Merchandise inventory | 47,000 | |
| Store supplies | 1,715 | |
| Office supplies | 645 | |
| Prepaid insurance | 3,840 | |
| Store equipment | 57,735 | |
| Accumulated depreciation, store equipment | | $ 9,575 |
| Office equipment | 14,130 | |
| Accumulated depreciation, office equipment | | 3,670 |
| Accounts payable | | 4,680 |
| Bob Eastman, capital | | 93,585 |
| Bob Eastman, withdrawals | 31,500 | |
| Sales | | 478,850 |
| Sales returns and allowances | 3,185 | |
| Sales discounts | 5,190 | |
| Purchases | 331,315 | |
| Purchases returns and allowances | | 1,845 |
| Purchases discounts | | 4,725 |
| Transportation-in | 2,810 | |
| Sales salaries expense | 34,710 | |
| Rent expense, selling space | 24,000 | |
| Advertising expense | 1,220 | |
| Store supplies expense | –0– | |
| Depreciation expense, store equipment | –0– | |
| Office salaries expense | 27,630 | |
| Rent expense, office space | 3,000 | |
| Office supplies expense | –0– | |
| Insurance expense | –0– | |
| Depreciation expense, office equipment | –0– | |
| Totals | $596,930 | $596,930 |

*Required*

1. Copy the unadjusted trial balance on a work sheet form and complete the work sheet using the following information:
   *a.* Store supplies inventory, $385.
   *b.* Office supplies inventory, $180.
   *c.* Expired insurance, $2,765.
   *d.* Depreciation on the store equipment, $5,865.
   *e.* Depreciation on the office equipment, $1,755.
   *f.* Ending merchandise inventory, $48,980.
2. Journalize closing entries for the store.
3. Open a balance column Merchandise Inventory account and enter a December 31, 1989, balance of $47,000. Then post those portions of the closing entries that affect the account.

***Problem 5–4A**
**Adjusting entry approach to proprietorship work sheet, adjusting and closing entries**
(L. O. 6)

Use the information presented in Problem 5–3A for the Eastman Store in solving this problem. However, in satisfying the following requirements, use the adjusting entry approach to accounting for merchandise inventories.

*Required*

1. Copy the unadjusted trial balance on a work sheet form and complete the work sheet. (Note the adjustments information presented in Requirement 1 of Problem 5–3A.)
2. Journalize adjusting and closing entries for the store.
3. Open a balance column Merchandise Inventory account and enter a December 31, 1989, balance of $47,000. Then post those portions of the adjusting entries that affect the account.

**Problem 5–5A**
**Corporate work sheet, income and retained earnings statements, and closing entries**
(L. O. 3, 4)

The unadjusted trial balance of Idaho Sales, Inc., on December 31, 1990, the end of the annual accounting period, is as follows:

**IDAHO SALES, INC.**
**Unadjusted Trial Balance**
**December 31, 1990**

| | | |
|---|---|---|
| Cash | $ 8,835 | |
| Merchandise inventory | 66,810 | |
| Store supplies | 1,460 | |
| Office supplies | 660 | |
| Prepaid insurance | 4,340 | |
| Store equipment | 65,070 | |
| Accumulated depreciation, store equipment | | $ 9,350 |
| Office equipment | 14,505 | |
| Accumulated depreciation, office equipment | | 2,285 |
| Accounts payable | | 3,375 |
| Salaries payable | | –0– |
| Income taxes payable | | –0– |
| Common stock, $10 par value | | 75,000 |
| Retained earnings | | 13,955 |
| Dividends declared | 7,500 | |
| Sales | | 534,810 |
| Sales returns and allowances | 3,180 | |
| Purchases | 352,345 | |
| Purchases returns and allowances | | 2,165 |
| Purchases discounts | | 4,930 |
| Transportation-in | 3,325 | |
| Sales salaries expense | 42,145 | |
| Rent expense, selling space | 19,500 | |
| Advertising expense | 5,495 | |
| Store supplies expense | –0– | |
| Depreciation expense, store equipment | –0– | |
| Office salaries expense | 39,300 | |
| Rent expense, office space | 3,000 | |
| Insurance expense | –0– | |
| Office supplies expense | –0– | |
| Depreciation expense, office equipment | –0– | |
| Income taxes expense | 8,400 | |
| Totals | $645,870 | $645,870 |

*Required*

1. Copy the unadjusted trial balance on a work sheet form and complete the work sheet using the information that follows:

*a.* Ending store supplies inventory, $395.
*b.* Ending office supplies inventory, $185.
*c.* Expired insurance, $3,715.
*d.* Depreciation on the store equipment, $6,390.
*e.* Depreciation on the office equipment, $1,715.
*f.* Accrued sales salaries payable, $515; and accrued office salaries payable, $125.
*g.* Additional income taxes expense, $785.
*h.* Ending merchandise inventory, $64,305.

2. Prepare a multiple-step classified income statement showing in detail the expenses and the items that make up cost of goods sold.
3. Prepare a retained earnings statement.
4. Prepare compound closing entries for the corporation.
5. In addition to the foregoing, prepare a single-step statement of income and retained earnings with the items condensed as is commonly done in published statements.

***Problem 5–6A**
**Adjusting entry approach to corporate work sheet, income and retained earnings statements, adjusting and closing entries**
(L. O. 6)

Use the information presented in Problem 5–5A for Idaho Sales, Inc., in solving this problem. However, in satisfying the following requirements, use the adjusting entry approach to accounting for merchandise inventories.

*Required*

1. Copy the unadjusted trial balance on a work sheet form and complete the work sheet. (Note the adjustments information presented in Requirement 1 of Problem 5–5A.)
2. Prepare a multiple-step classified income statement showing in detail the expenses and the items that make up cost of goods sold.
3. Prepare a retained earnings statement.
4. Prepare adjusting and closing entries for the corporation.
5. In addition to the foregoing, prepare a single-step statement of income and retained earnings with the items condensed as is commonly done in published statements.

**Problem 5–7A**
**Proprietorship work sheet, financial statements, and closing entries**
(L. O. 2, 3, 4)

The unadjusted trial balance of Hanson's Rags on December 31, 1990, the end of the annual accounting period, is as follows:

**HANSON'S RAGS**
**Unadjusted Trial Balance**
**December 31, 1990**

| | | |
|---|---|---|
| Cash | $ 10,170 | |
| Accounts receivable | 23,915 | |
| Merchandise inventory | 51,855 | |
| Store supplies | 2,225 | |
| Office supplies | 840 | |
| Prepaid insurance | 3,570 | |
| Store equipment | 56,280 | |
| Accumulated depreciation, store equipment | | $ 9,170 |
| Office equipment | 11,885 | |
| Accumulated depreciation, office equipment | | 2,750 |
| Accounts payable | | 3,840 |
| Salaries payable | | –0– |
| Bruce Hanson, capital | | 112,840 |
| Bruce Hanson, withdrawals | 25,000 | |
| Sales | | 551,760 |
| Sales returns and allowances | 4,485 | |
| Purchases | 382,020 | |
| Purchases returns and allowances | | 1,920 |
| Purchases discounts | | 4,315 |
| Transportation-in | 4,425 | |
| Sales salaries expense | 39,525 | |
| Rent expense, selling space | 20,250 | |
| Store supplies expense | –0– | |
| Depreciation expense, store equipment | –0– | |
| Office salaries expense | 41,900 | |
| Rent expense, office space | 8,250 | |
| Office supplies expense | –0– | |
| Insurance expense | –0– | |
| Depreciation expense, office equipment | –0– | |
| Totals | $686,595 | $686,595 |

*Required*

1. Copy the unadjusted trial balance on a work sheet form and complete the work sheet using the following information:
   *a.* Ending store supplies inventory, $515.
   *b.* Ending office supplies inventory, $275.
   *c.* Expired insurance, $2,955.
   *d.* Depreciation on the store equipment, $4,965.
   *e.* Depreciation on the office equipment, $1,415.
   *f.* Accrued sales salaries payable, $485; and accrued office salaries payable, $275.
   *g.* Ending merchandise inventory, $53,835.
2. Prepare a multiple-step classified income statement showing in detail the items that make up cost of goods sold and the expense items.
3. Prepare a statement of changes in owner's equity. On December 31, 1989, the Bruce Hanson, Capital account had a balance of $37,840. Early in the year, Mr. Hanson invested an additional $75,000 in the business.
4. Prepare a year-end classified balance sheet with the prepaid expenses combined.
5. Prepare adjusting and closing entries.

## Provocative Problems

**Provocative Problem 5–1**
**Nan's Nursery**
(L. O. 2, 3)

Nan Hall and Mike Linden were partners in a nursery. They disagreed, closed the business, and ended their partnership. In settlement for her partnershp interest, Nan Hall received an inventory of trees, plants, and garden supplies having a $22,500 cost. Since there was nothing practical she could do with the inventory, except to open a new nursery, she did so by investing the inventory and $18,000 in cash. She used $15,000 of the cash to buy equipment, and she opened for business on May 1. During the succeeding eight months, she paid out $63,750 to creditors for additional trees, plants, and garden supplies and $21,000 in operating expenses. She also withdrew $15,000 for personal expenses, and at the year-end, she prepared the balance sheet that follows:

**NAN'S NURSERY**
**Balance Sheet**
**December 31, 1990**

| | | | | |
|---|---|---|---|---|
| Cash | | $ 8,550 | Accounts payable (all for merchandise) | $ 3,300 |
| Merchandise inventory | | 26,650 | Nan Hall, capital | 45,700 |
| Equipment | $15,000 | | | |
| Less depreciation | 1,200 | 13,800 | | |
| Total assets | | $49,000 | Total liabilities and owner's equity | $49,000 |

Based on the information given, prepare calculations to determine the net income earned by the business, the cost of goods sold, and the amount of its sales. Then prepare an income statement showing the result of the nursery's operations during its first eight months.

**Provocative Problem 5–2**
**Westwood Store**
(L. O. 3)

Tony Falk, the owner of Westwood Store, has not maintained an adequate accounting system and has asked you to help him prepare an income statement for the business. Based on information he has provided, the following balance sheet information is now available:

| | December 31 | |
|---|---|---|
| | 1989 | 1990 |
| Cash | $ 3,750 | $12,150 |
| Accounts receivable | 9,300 | 10,950 |
| Merchandise inventory | 45,600 | 42,750 |
| Equipment (net after depreciation) | 37,200 | 30,900 |
| Total assets | $95,850 | $96,750 |
| Accounts payable | $13,950 | $12,300 |
| Accrued wages payable | 450 | 750 |
| Tony Falk, capital | 81,450 | 83,700 |
| Total liabilities and owner's equity | $95,850 | $96,750 |

Also, the store's record of cash receipts and disbursements shows the following:

| | |
|---|---|
| Collection of accounts receivable | $402,600 |
| Payments for: | |
| Accounts payable | 249,300 |
| Employees' wages | 72,150 |
| Other operating expenses | 27,750 |
| Tony Falk, withdrawals | 45,000 |

Under the assumption that the store makes all purchases and sales on credit, prepare calculations to determine the 1990 amounts of its accrual basis sales, purchases, and wages expense. Then prepare an accrual basis income statement for 1990.

**Provocative Problem 5–3**
**Phil's Paints**
(L. O. 3)

Phil Potter worked in the Valley Hills State Bank for 20 years, until his aunt died, leaving him a sizable estate. After sitting around long enough to get bored and see his bank balance dwindle, Phil decided to open a retail paint store. When he started the business on July 1, 1990, Valley Hills had no such store, and it appeared to Phil that the business would succeed.

On July 1, Phil deposited $53,500 in a bank account under the name Phil's Paints. He then paid $12,000 cash for store equipment, which he expected to last 10 years before it became valueless. He also bought merchandise for $37,500 cash, and paid $3,600 in advance for six months' store rent.

Phil estimated that most paint stores marked their goods for sale at prices averaging 35% above cost. In other words, an item that cost $10.00 was marked for sale at $13.50. But to entice customers, he decided to mark his merchandise for sale at 30% above cost. Since his overhead would be low, he thought this would still leave a net income equal to 10% of sales.

On December 31, 1990, six months after opening his store, Phil has come to you for advice. He thinks business has been good. However, he doesn't quite understand why his cash balance has fallen to $1,200.

In talking with Phil and examining his records, you determine that the inventory was replaced three times during the six months, each time at a cost of $37,500. All merchandise suppliers have been paid except for $10,850, which is not yet due. A full stock of merchandise (cost of $37,500) is on hand and customers owe Phil $29,100. In addition to the rent paid in advance, Phil paid $14,700 for other expenses.

Prepare an income statement for the business covering the six-month period ended December 31, a statement of changes in owner's equity, a December 31, 1990, balance sheet, and a statement that explains the $1,200 cash balance by showing the cash receipts and cash disbursements during the six months ended December 31.

# 6 Accounting Systems

Even in small businesses, the quantity of data that is processed through the accounting system is large. As a result, the accounting system should be designed so that the data can be processed efficiently. This chapter explains some general procedures and techniques that you can use in designing an accounting system so that it will efficiently process data.

**Learning Objectives**

*After studying Chapter 6, you should be able to:*

1. Describe the type of transaction that is recorded in each journal when special journals are used and record all types of transactions in an accounting system that uses special journals.
2. Explain how a controlling account and its subsidiary ledger operate and, when special journals are used, post the amounts recorded in the journals to the General Ledger and any subsidiary ledgers.
3. Explain how to test the accuracy of the account balances in the Accounts Receivable and Accounts Payable Ledgers and prepare schedules of the accounts in each subsidiary ledger.
4. Describe how data are processed in computerized accounting systems.
5. Define or explain the words and phrases listed in the chapter Glossary.

## Accounting Systems

An **accounting system** consists of the business papers, records, reports, and procedures that a business uses to record transactions and report their effects. The operation of an accounting system includes three important steps. First, you must capture on business papers or source documents the quantities, dollar amounts, and other important data related to business transactions. Second, you must classify and record in the accounting records the data contained in the source documents. Third, you must summarize in timely reports to management and other interested parties the information contained in the accounting records.

Even in a small business, the quantity of data that is processed through the accounting system is large. As a result, the accounting system should be designed so that the data can be processed efficiently. To help you learn how to accomplish this goal, we begin Chapter 6 with a discussion of techniques that are used primarily in manual accounting systems. You should understand that the basic concepts introduced in this discussion are generally applicable to both manual and computerized accounting systems. Later in the chapter, we turn the discussion specifically to electronic and computerized accounting systems.

## Using Special Journals to Save Labor

Describe the type of transaction that is recorded in each journal when special journals are used and record all types of transactions in an accounting system that uses special journals. (L. O. 1)

The General Journal is a flexible journal in which you can record any transaction. However, each debit and credit entered in a General Journal must be individually posted. As a result, if a General Journal is used to record all the transactions of a business, much time and labor are required to post the individual debits and credits.

One way to reduce the writing and the posting labor is to divide the transactions of a business into groups of similar transactions and to provide a separate **special journal** for recording the transactions in each group. For example, most of the transactions of a merchandising business fall into four groups. These are sales on credit, purchases on credit, cash receipts, and cash disbursements. If a special journal is provided for each group, the journals are:

1. A Sales Journal for recording credit sales.
2. A Purchases Journal for recording credit purchases.
3. A Cash Receipts Journal for recording cash receipts.
4. A Cash Disbursements Journal for recording cash payments.

Also, you must have a General Journal for the miscellaneous transactions that you cannot record in the special journals and also for adjusting, closing, and correcting entries.

The following illustrations show that special journals require less writing in recording transactions than does a General Journal. Also, special journals save posting labor by providing special columns for accumulating the debits and credits of similar transactions. The amounts entered in the special columns are then posted as column totals rather than as individual amounts. For example, if you record credit sales for a month in a Sales Journal like the one at the top of Illustration 6–1, you can save posting labor. To do so, you wait until the end of the month, total the sales recorded in the journal, and then debit Accounts Receivable and credit Sales for the total.

**Illustration 6–1**

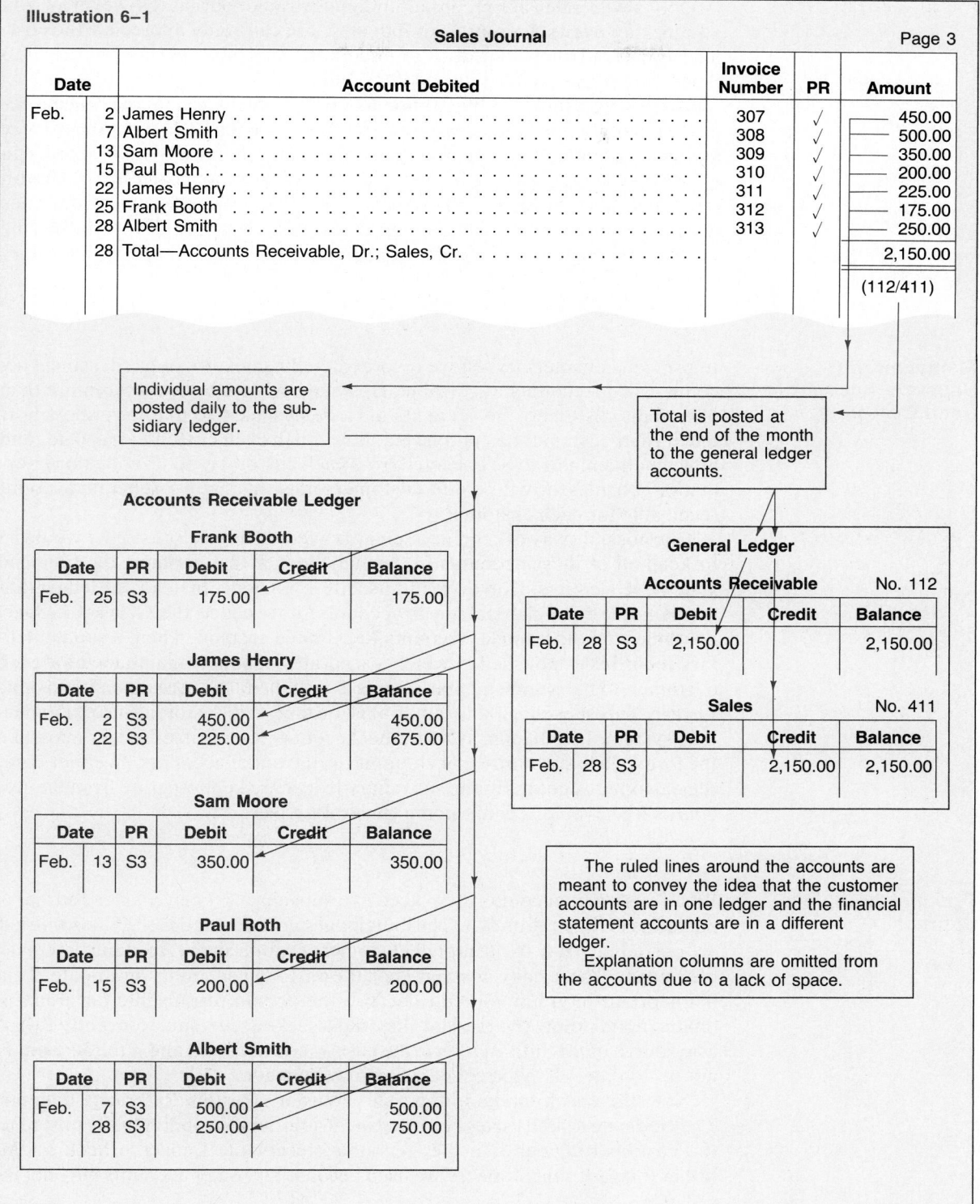

**Sales Journal** — Page 3

| Date | | Account Debited | Invoice Number | PR | Amount |
|---|---|---|---|---|---|
| Feb. | 2 | James Henry | 307 | √ | 450.00 |
| | 7 | Albert Smith | 308 | √ | 500.00 |
| | 13 | Sam Moore | 309 | √ | 350.00 |
| | 15 | Paul Roth | 310 | √ | 200.00 |
| | 22 | James Henry | 311 | √ | 225.00 |
| | 25 | Frank Booth | 312 | √ | 175.00 |
| | 28 | Albert Smith | 313 | √ | 250.00 |
| | 28 | Total—Accounts Receivable, Dr.; Sales, Cr. | | | 2,150.00 |
| | | | | | (112/411) |

Individual amounts are posted daily to the subsidiary ledger.

Total is posted at the end of the month to the general ledger accounts.

**Accounts Receivable Ledger**

**Frank Booth**

| Date | | PR | Debit | Credit | Balance |
|---|---|---|---|---|---|
| Feb. | 25 | S3 | 175.00 | | 175.00 |

**James Henry**

| Date | | PR | Debit | Credit | Balance |
|---|---|---|---|---|---|
| Feb. | 2 | S3 | 450.00 | | 450.00 |
| | 22 | S3 | 225.00 | | 675.00 |

**Sam Moore**

| Date | | PR | Debit | Credit | Balance |
|---|---|---|---|---|---|
| Feb. | 13 | S3 | 350.00 | | 350.00 |

**Paul Roth**

| Date | | PR | Debit | Credit | Balance |
|---|---|---|---|---|---|
| Feb. | 15 | S3 | 200.00 | | 200.00 |

**Albert Smith**

| Date | | PR | Debit | Credit | Balance |
|---|---|---|---|---|---|
| Feb. | 7 | S3 | 500.00 | | 500.00 |
| | 28 | S3 | 250.00 | | 750.00 |

**General Ledger**

**Accounts Receivable** No. 112

| Date | | PR | Debit | Credit | Balance |
|---|---|---|---|---|---|
| Feb. | 28 | S3 | 2,150.00 | | 2,150.00 |

**Sales** No. 411

| Date | | PR | Debit | Credit | Balance |
|---|---|---|---|---|---|
| Feb. | 28 | S3 | | 2,150.00 | 2,150.00 |

The ruled lines around the accounts are meant to convey the idea that the customer accounts are in one ledger and the financial statement accounts are in a different ledger.

Explanation columns are omitted from the accounts due to a lack of space.

Only seven sales are recorded in the illustrated journal. However, if you assume the seven sales represent 700 sales, you can better appreciate the posting labor saved by the one debit to Accounts Receivable and the one credit to Sales, rather than 700 debits and 700 credits.

The special journal in Illustration 6–1 is also called a **columnar journal** because it has columns for recording the date, the customer's name, the invoice number, and the amount of each charge sale. Only charge sales are recorded in it, and they are recorded daily, with the information about each sale placed on a separate line. Normally, the information is taken from a copy of the sales ticket or invoice prepared at the time of the sale. However, before discussing the journal further, you need to understand the role played by **subsidiary ledgers.**

## Maintaining a Separate Account for Each Customer

In previous chapters, when we recorded credit sales, we debited a single account called Accounts Receivable. However, when a business has more than one credit customer, the accounts must be designed so that they show how much each customer has purchased, how much each customer has paid, and how much remains to be collected from each customer. To provide this information, businesses with credit customers must maintain a separate account receivable for each customer.

One possible way of keeping a separate account for each customer would be to keep all of these accounts in the same ledger that contains the financial statement accounts. However, this usually is not done. Instead, the ledger that contains the financial statement accounts, now called the **General Ledger,** continues to hold a single Accounts Receivable account. Then, a supplementary record is established in which a separate account is maintained for each customer. This supplementary record is called the **Accounts Receivable Ledger.** This subsidiary ledger may exist on tape or disk storage in a computerized system. In a manual system, the Accounts Receivable Ledger may take the form of a book or tray that contains the customer accounts. In either case, the customer accounts in the subsidiary ledger are kept separate from the Accounts Receivable account in the General Ledger.

## Posting the Sales Journal

When customer accounts are placed in a subsidiary ledger, a Sales Journal is posted as in Illustration 6–1. The individual sales recorded in the Sales Journal are posted each day to the proper customer accounts in the Accounts Receivable Ledger. These daily postings keep the customer accounts up-to-date. This is important in granting credit because the person responsible for granting credit should know the amount the credit-seeking customer currently owes. The source of this information is the customer's account, and if the account is not up-to-date, an incorrect decision may be made.

Note the check marks in the Sales Journal's Posting Reference column. They indicate that the sales recorded in the journal were individually posted to the customer accounts in the Accounts Receivable Ledger. Check marks rather than account numbers are used because customer accounts may not be numbered. If the accounts are not numbered, they are arranged alphabetically in the Accounts Receivable Ledger so they can be located easily.

In addition to the daily postings to customer accounts, at the end of the month, the Sales Journal's Amount column is totaled. Then, the total is debited to Accounts Receivable and credited to Sales. The credit records the month's revenue from charge sales. The debit records the resulting increase in accounts receivable.

In Illustration 6–1, pay attention to the fact that the individual customer accounts in the subsidiary Accounts Receivable Ledger do not replace the Accounts Receivable account in the General Ledger. The general ledger Accounts Receivable account is maintained because it serves three functions: (1) It shows the total amount owed by all customers. (2) It allows the General Ledger to be a balancing ledger in which debits equal credits. (3) It offers a way of testing the accuracy of the customer accounts in the subsidiary Accounts Receivable Ledger.

## Identifying Posted Amounts

When several journals are posted to ledger accounts, you must indicate in the Posting Reference column before each posted amount the journal and the page number of the journal from which the amount was posted. The journal is indicated by using its initial. Thus, items posted from the Cash Disbursements Journal carry the initial "D" before their journal page numbers in the Posting Reference columns. Likewise, items from the Cash Receipts Journal carry the letter "R." Those from the Sales Journal carry the initial "S." Items from the Purchases Journal carry the initial "P," and from the General Journal, the letter "G."

## Controlling Accounts

You should understand that when debits (or credits) to Accounts Receivable are posted twice (once to Accounts Receivable and once to the customer's account), this does not violate the requirement that debits equal credits. The equality of debits and credits is maintained *in the General Ledger*. The Accounts Receivable Ledger is simply a supplementary record that provides detailed information concerning each customer.

Explain how a controlling account and its subsidiary ledger operate and, when special journals are used, post the amounts recorded in the journals to the General Ledger and any subsidiary ledgers. (L. O. 2)

After all items are posted, the balance in the Accounts Receivable account should be equal to the sum of the balances in the customers' accounts. As a result, the Accounts Receivable account is said to control the Accounts Receivable Ledger and is called a **controlling account.** And since the Accounts Receivable Ledger is a supplementary record that is controlled by an account in the General Ledger, it is called a *subsidiary ledger*. After posting is completed, if the Accounts Receivable balance does not equal the sum of the customer account balances, you know an error has been made.

The Accounts Receivable account and the Accounts Receivable Ledger are not the only examples of controlling accounts and subsidiary ledgers. Most companies buy on credit from several suppliers and must use a controlling account and subsidiary ledger for accounts payable. Another example might be an Office Equipment account, which would control a subsidiary ledger in which each item of equipment is recorded in a separate account.

## Cash Receipts Journal

A Cash Receipts Journal designed to save labor through posting column totals must be a multicolumn journal. A multicolumn journal is necessary because when cash is received from different sources, different accounts are credited. For example, the cash receipts of a store normally fall into three groups: (1) cash from charge customers in payment of their accounts, (2) cash from cash sales, and (3) cash from miscellaneous sources. Note in Illustration 6–2 that a special column is provided for the credits that result when cash is received from each of these sources.

### Cash from Charge Customers

When a Cash Receipts Journal like Illustration 6–2 is used to record cash received in payment of the customer's account, the customer's name is entered in the journal's Account Credited column. The amount credited to the customer's account is entered in the Accounts Receivable Credit column, and the debits to Sales Discounts and Cash are entered in the journal's last two columns.

Look at the Accounts Receivable Credit column. Observe that (1) only credits to customer accounts are entered in this column. (2) The individual credits are posted daily to the customer accounts in the subsidiary Accounts Receivable Ledger. (3) The column total is posted at the end of the month as a credit to the Accounts Receivable controlling account. This is the normal recording and posting procedure when you use special journals and controlling accounts with subsidiary ledgers. Transactions are normally entered in a special journal column. Then, the individual amounts are posted to the subsidiary ledger accounts and the column totals are posted to the general ledger accounts.

### Cash Sales

After cash sales are entered on one or more cash registers and totaled at the end of each day, the daily total is recorded with a debit to Cash and a credit to Sales. When a Cash Receipts Journal like that of Illustration 6–2 is used, the debits to Cash are entered in the Cash Debit column, and the credits are entered in a special column headed Sales Credit. By using a separate Sales Credit column, you can post the total cash sales for a month as a single amount, the column total. (Although cash sales are normally recorded daily from the cash register reading, the cash sales of Illustration 6–2 are recorded only once each week in order to shorten the illustration.)

At the time daily cash sales are recorded in the Cash Receipts Journal, some bookkeepers, as in Illustration 6–2, place a check mark in the Posting Reference (PR) column to indicate that no amount is individually posted from that line of the journal. Other bookkeepers use a double check (√√) to distinguish amounts that are not posted from amounts that are posted to customer accounts.

### Miscellaneous Receipts of Cash

Most cash receipts are from collections of accounts receivable and from cash sales. However, other less frequent sources of cash include borrowing money from a bank or selling unneeded assets. The Other Accounts Credit column is provided for receipts that do not occur often enough to warrant a separate

Illustration 6–2

**Cash Receipts Journal** Page 2

| Date | | Account Credited | Explanation | PR | Other Accounts Credit | Accts. Rec. Credit | Sales Credit | Sales Discounts Debit | Cash Debit |
|---|---|---|---|---|---|---|---|---|---|
| Feb. | 7 | Sales | Cash sales | √ | | | 4,450.00 | | 4,450.00 |
| | 12 | James Henry | Invoice, 2/2 | √ | | 450.00 | | 9.00 | 441.00 |
| | 14 | Sales | Cash sales | √ | | | 3,925.00 | | 3,925.00 |
| | 17 | Albert Smith | Invoice, 2/7 | √ | | 500.00 | | 10.00 | 490.00 |
| | 20 | Notes Payable | Note to bank | 211 | 1,000.00 | | | | 1,000.00 |
| | 21 | Sales | Cash sales | √ | | | 4,700.00 | | 4,700.00 |
| | 23 | Sam Moore | Invoice, 2/13 | √ | | 350.00 | | 7.00 | 343.00 |
| | 25 | Paul Roth | Invoice, 2/15 | √ | | 200.00 | | 4.00 | 196.00 |
| | 28 | Sales | Cash sales | √ | | | 4,225.00 | | 4,225.00 |
| | 28 | Totals | | | 1,000.00 | 1,500.00 | 17,300.00 | 30.00 | 19,770.00 |
| | | | | | (√) | (112) | (411) | (413) | (111) |

Individual amounts in the Other Accounts Credit and Accounts Receivable Credit columns are posted daily.

Total is not posted.

Totals posted at the end of the month.

**Accounts Receivable Ledger**

**Frank Booth**

| Date | | PR | Debit | Credit | Balance |
|---|---|---|---|---|---|
| Feb. | 25 | S3 | 175.00 | | 175.00 |

**James Henry**

| Date | | PR | Debit | Credit | Balance |
|---|---|---|---|---|---|
| Feb. | 2 | S3 | 450.00 | | 450.00 |
| | 12 | R2 | | 450.00 | –0– |
| | 22 | S3 | 225.00 | | 225.00 |

**Sam Moore**

| Date | | PR | Debit | Credit | Balance |
|---|---|---|---|---|---|
| Feb. | 13 | S3 | 350.00 | | 350.00 |
| | 23 | R2 | | 350.00 | –0– |

**Paul Roth**

| Date | | PR | Debit | Credit | Balance |
|---|---|---|---|---|---|
| Feb. | 15 | S3 | 200.00 | | 200.00 |
| | 25 | R2 | | 200.00 | –0– |

**Albert Smith**

| Date | | PR | Debit | Credit | Balance |
|---|---|---|---|---|---|
| Feb. | 7 | S3 | 500.00 | | 500.00 |
| | 17 | R2 | | 500.00 | –0– |
| | 28 | S3 | 250.00 | | 250.00 |

**General Ledger**

**Cash** No. 111

| Date | | PR | Debit | Credit | Balance |
|---|---|---|---|---|---|
| Feb. | 28 | R2 | 19,770.00 | | 19,770.00 |

**Accounts Receivable** No. 112

| Date | | PR | Debit | Credit | Balance |
|---|---|---|---|---|---|
| Feb. | 28 | S3 | 2,150.00 | | 2,150.00 |
| | 28 | R2 | | 1,500.00 | 650.00 |

**Notes Payable** No. 211

| Date | | PR | Debit | Credit | Balance |
|---|---|---|---|---|---|
| Feb. | 20 | R2 | | 1,000.00 | 1,000.00 |

**Sales** No. 411

| Date | | PR | Debit | Credit | Balance |
|---|---|---|---|---|---|
| Feb. | 28 | S3 | | 2,150.00 | 2,150.00 |
| | 28 | R2 | | 17,300.00 | 19,450.00 |

**Sales Discounts** No. 413

| Date | | PR | Debit | Credit | Balance |
|---|---|---|---|---|---|
| Feb. | 28 | R2 | 30.00 | | 30.00 |

column. In an average company, the items entered in this column are few and are posted to a variety of general ledger accounts. As a result, postings are less apt to be omitted if these items are posted daily.

The Cash Receipts Journal's Posting Reference column is used only for daily postings from the Other Accounts and Accounts Receivable columns. The account numbers that appear in the Posting Reference column indicate items that were posted to general ledger accounts. The check marks indicate either that an item like a day's cash sales was not posted or that an item was posted to the subsidiary Accounts Receivable Ledger.

### Month-End Postings

At the end of the month, the amounts in the Accounts Receivable, Sales, Sales Discounts, and Cash columns of the Cash Receipts Journal are posted as column totals. However, the transactions recorded in any journal must result in equal debits and credits to general ledger accounts. Therefore, to be sure that the total debits and credits in a columnar journal are equal, you must **crossfoot** or cross add the column totals before they are posted. To **foot** a column of numbers is to add it. To crossfoot, the Debit column totals are added, the Credit column totals are added, and the two sums are compared for equality. For Illustration 6–2, the two sums appear as follows:

| Debit Columns | | Credit Columns | |
|---|---|---|---|
| Sales discounts debit . . . . . . . | $ 30 | Other accounts credit . . . . . . . | $ 1,000 |
| Cash debit . . . . . . . . . . . . . | 19,770 | Accounts receivable credit . . . | 1,500 |
| | | Sales credit . . . . . . . . . . . | 17,400 |
| Total . . . . . . . . . . . . . . . | $19,800 | Total . . . . . . . . . . . . . . . | $19,800 |

Since the sums are equal, you may assume the debits in the journal equal the credits.

After you crossfoot the journal to show that debits equal credits, the totals of the last four columns are posted as indicated in each column heading. As for the Other Accounts column, since the individual items in this column are posted daily, the column total is not posted. Note in Illustration 6–2 the check mark below the Other Accounts column. The check mark indicates that the column total was not posted. The account numbers of the accounts to which the remaining column totals were posted are shown in parentheses below each column.

Posting items daily from the Other Accounts column with a delayed posting of the offsetting items in the Cash column (total) causes the General Ledger to be out of balance throughout the month. However, this does not matter because before the trial balance is prepared, the offsetting amounts reach the General Ledger in posting the Cash column total.

## Posting Rule

Now that we have illustrated the procedures for posting from two different journals to a subsidiary ledger and its controlling account, the rule that governs all such postings should be clear. The rule is: *In posting to a subsidiary ledger and its controlling account, the controlling account must be debited periodically for an amount or amounts equal to the sum of the debits to the subsidiary ledger, and it must be credited periodically for an amount or amounts equal to the sum of the credits to the subsidiary ledger.*

## Maintaining a Separate Account for Each Creditor

As with accounts receivable, a company must keep a separate account for each creditor. To accomplish this, an Accounts Payable controlling account is maintained in the General Ledger and a separate account for each creditor is maintained in a subsidiary **Accounts Payable Ledger.** Also, the controlling account, subsidiary ledger, and columnar journal techniques demonstrated thus far with accounts receivable apply to the creditor accounts. The only difference is that a Purchases Journal and a Cash Disbursements Journal are used to record most of the transactions that affect these accounts.

## Purchases Journal

A Purchases Journal that has one money column may be used to record purchases of merchandise on credit. However, a Purchases Journal usually is more useful if it is designed as a multicolumn journal in which purchases of both merchandise and supplies can be recorded. Such a journal may have columns like those shown in Illustration 6–3. In the illustrated journal, the invoice date and terms together indicate the date on which payment for each purchase is due. The Accounts Payable Credit column is used to record the amounts credited to each creditor's account. These amounts are posted daily to the individual creditor accounts in the subsidiary Accounts Payable Ledger. At the end of the month, the column total is posted to the Accounts Payable controlling account. The items purchased are recorded in the Debit columns and are posted in the column totals.

## The Cash Disbursements Journal or Check Register

The Cash Disbursements Journal, like the Cash Receipts Journal, has columns so that you can post repetitive debits and credits in column totals. The repetitive cash payments involve debits to the Accounts Payable controlling account and credits to both Purchases Discounts and Cash. In most companies, merchandise is usually purchased on credit. Therefore, a Purchases column is not needed. Instead, the occasional cash purchase is recorded as on line 2 of Illustration 6–4.

Observe that the illustrated journal has a column headed Check Number (Ch. No.). In order to gain control over cash disbursements, all such disbursements, except petty cash disbursements, should be made by check. The checks should be prenumbered by the printer and should be entered in the journal in numerical order with each check's number in the column headed Ch. No. This makes it possible to scan the numbers in the column for omitted checks. When a Cash Disbursements Journal has a column for check numbers, it is often called a **Check Register.**

To post a Cash Disbursements Journal or Check Register like Illustration 6–4, you do the following. Each day, post the individual amounts in the Other Accounts column to the debit of the general ledger accounts named. Also on a daily basis, post the individual amounts in the Accounts Payable column to the subsidiary Accounts Payable Ledger as debits to the named creditors' ac-

**Illustration 6–3**

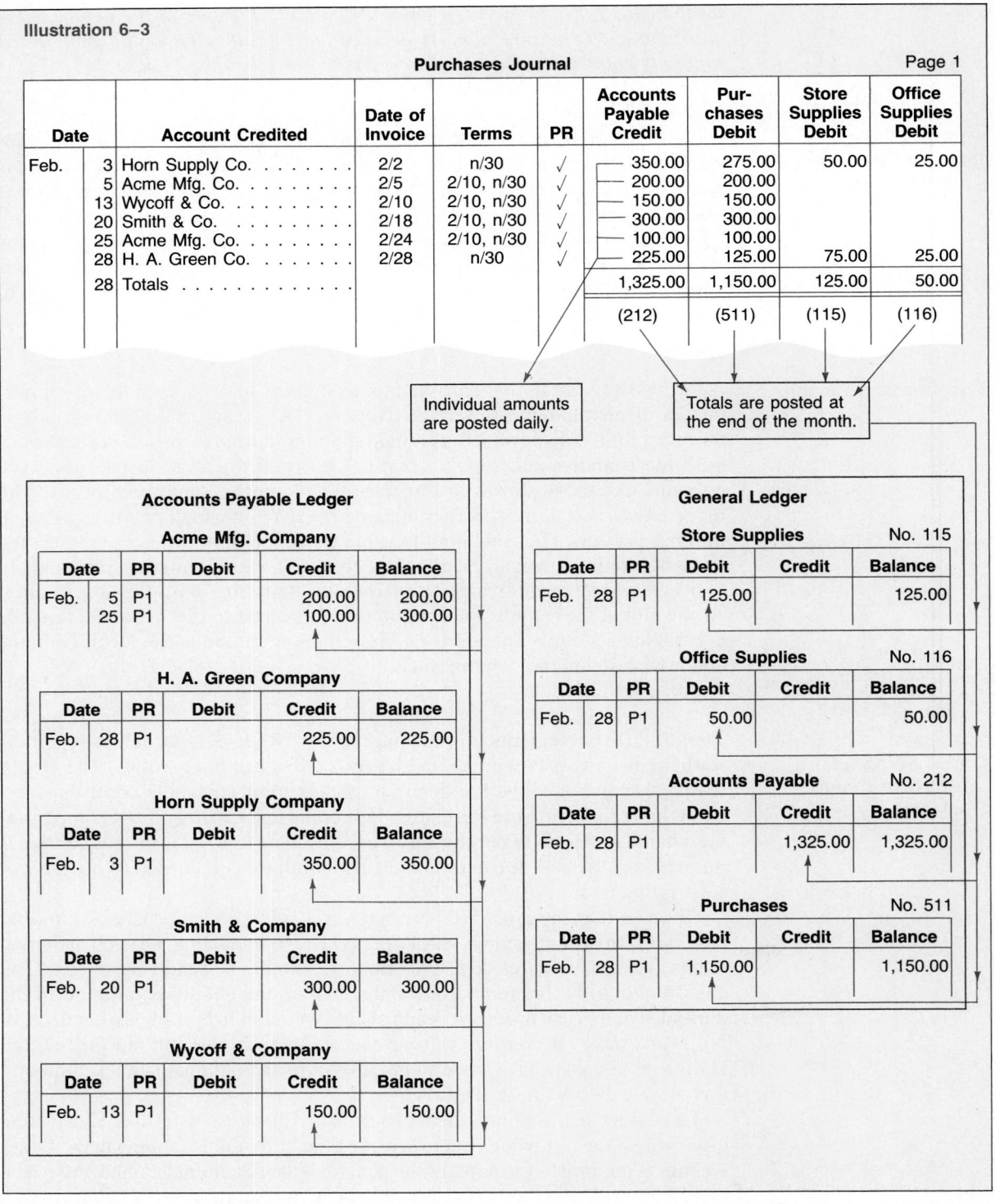

### Purchases Journal

Page 1

| Date | | Account Credited | Date of Invoice | Terms | PR | Accounts Payable Credit | Purchases Debit | Store Supplies Debit | Office Supplies Debit |
|---|---|---|---|---|---|---|---|---|---|
| Feb. | 3 | Horn Supply Co. . . . . . . . . | 2/2 | n/30 | √ | 350.00 | 275.00 | 50.00 | 25.00 |
| | 5 | Acme Mfg. Co. . . . . . . . . | 2/5 | 2/10, n/30 | √ | 200.00 | 200.00 | | |
| | 13 | Wycoff & Co. . . . . . . . . . | 2/10 | 2/10, n/30 | √ | 150.00 | 150.00 | | |
| | 20 | Smith & Co. . . . . . . . . . | 2/18 | 2/10, n/30 | √ | 300.00 | 300.00 | | |
| | 25 | Acme Mfg. Co. . . . . . . . . | 2/24 | 2/10, n/30 | √ | 100.00 | 100.00 | | |
| | 28 | H. A. Green Co. . . . . . . . | 2/28 | n/30 | √ | 225.00 | 125.00 | 75.00 | 25.00 |
| | 28 | Totals . . . . . . . . . . . . . | | | | 1,325.00 | 1,150.00 | 125.00 | 50.00 |
| | | | | | | (212) | (511) | (115) | (116) |

Individual amounts are posted daily.

Totals are posted at the end of the month.

### Accounts Payable Ledger

**Acme Mfg. Company**

| Date | | PR | Debit | Credit | Balance |
|---|---|---|---|---|---|
| Feb. | 5 | P1 | | 200.00 | 200.00 |
| | 25 | P1 | | 100.00 | 300.00 |

**H. A. Green Company**

| Date | | PR | Debit | Credit | Balance |
|---|---|---|---|---|---|
| Feb. | 28 | P1 | | 225.00 | 225.00 |

**Horn Supply Company**

| Date | | PR | Debit | Credit | Balance |
|---|---|---|---|---|---|
| Feb. | 3 | P1 | | 350.00 | 350.00 |

**Smith & Company**

| Date | | PR | Debit | Credit | Balance |
|---|---|---|---|---|---|
| Feb. | 20 | P1 | | 300.00 | 300.00 |

**Wycoff & Company**

| Date | | PR | Debit | Credit | Balance |
|---|---|---|---|---|---|
| Feb. | 13 | P1 | | 150.00 | 150.00 |

### General Ledger

**Store Supplies** No. 115

| Date | | PR | Debit | Credit | Balance |
|---|---|---|---|---|---|
| Feb. | 28 | P1 | 125.00 | | 125.00 |

**Office Supplies** No. 116

| Date | | PR | Debit | Credit | Balance |
|---|---|---|---|---|---|
| Feb. | 28 | P1 | 50.00 | | 50.00 |

**Accounts Payable** No. 212

| Date | | PR | Debit | Credit | Balance |
|---|---|---|---|---|---|
| Feb. | 28 | P1 | | 1,325.00 | 1,325.00 |

**Purchases** No. 511

| Date | | PR | Debit | Credit | Balance |
|---|---|---|---|---|---|
| Feb. | 28 | P1 | 1,150.00 | | 1,150.00 |

Illustration 6–4

**Cash Disbursements Journal** — Page 2

| Date | | Ch. No. | Payee | Account Debited | PR | Other Accounts Debit | Accts. Pay. Debit | Pur. Disc. Credit | Cash Credit |
|---|---|---|---|---|---|---|---|---|---|
| Feb. | 3 | 105 | L. & N. Railroad . . . | Transportation-In . . . | 514 | 15.00 | | | 15.00 |
| | 12 | 106 | East Sales Co. . . . . | Purchases . . . . . . | 511 | 25.00 | | | 25.00 |
| | 15 | 107 | Acme Mfg. Co. . . . . | Acme Mfg. Co. . . . . | √ | | 200.00 | 4.00 | 196.00 |
| | 15 | 108 | Jerry Hale . . . . . . . | Salaries Expense . . . | 611 | 250.00 | | | 250.00 |
| | 20 | 109 | Wycoff & Co. . . . . . | Wycoff & Co. . . . . . | √ | | 150.00 | 3.00 | 147.00 |
| | 28 | 110 | Smith & Co. . . . . . | Smith & Co. . . . . . | √ | | 300.00 | 6.00 | 294.00 |
| | 28 | | Totals . . . . . . . . . | | | 290.00 | 650.00 | 13.00 | 927.00 |
| | | | | | | (√) | (212) | (513) | (111) |

Individual amounts in the Other Accounts Debit column and Accounts Payable Debit column are posted daily.

Totals posted at the end of the month.

**Accounts Payable Ledger**

**Acme Mfg. Company**

| Date | | PR | Debit | Credit | Balance |
|---|---|---|---|---|---|
| Feb. | 5 | P1 | | 200.00 | 200.00 |
| | 15 | D2 | 200.00 | | –0– |
| | 25 | P1 | | 100.00 | 100.00 |

**H. A. Green Company**

| Date | | PR | Debit | Credit | Balance |
|---|---|---|---|---|---|
| Feb. | 28 | P1 | | 225.00 | 225.00 |

**Horn Supply Company**

| Date | | PR | Debit | Credit | Balance |
|---|---|---|---|---|---|
| Feb. | 3 | P1 | | 350.00 | 350.00 |

**Smith & Company**

| Date | | PR | Debit | Credit | Balance |
|---|---|---|---|---|---|
| Feb. | 20 | P1 | | 300.00 | 300.00 |
| | 28 | D2 | 300.00 | | –0– |

**Wycoff & Company**

| Date | | PR | Debit | Credit | Balance |
|---|---|---|---|---|---|
| Feb. | 13 | P1 | | 150.00 | 150.00 |
| | 20 | D2 | 150.00 | | –0– |

**General Ledger**

**Cash** — No. 111

| Date | | PR | Debit | Credit | Balance |
|---|---|---|---|---|---|
| Feb. | 28 | R2 | 19,770.00 | | 19,770.00 |
| | 28 | D2 | | 927.00 | 18,843.00 |

**Accounts Payable** — No. 212

| Date | | PR | Debit | Credit | Balance |
|---|---|---|---|---|---|
| Feb. | 28 | P1 | | 1,325.00 | 1,325.00 |
| | 28 | D2 | 650.00 | | 675.00 |

**Purchases** — No. 511

| Date | | PR | Debit | Credit | Balance |
|---|---|---|---|---|---|
| Feb. | 12 | D2 | 25.00 | | 25.00 |
| | 28 | P1 | 1,150.00 | | 1,175.00 |

**Purchases Discounts** — No. 513

| Date | | PR | Debit | Credit | Balance |
|---|---|---|---|---|---|
| Feb. | 28 | D2 | | 13.00 | 13.00 |

**Transportation-In** — No. 514

| Date | | PR | Debit | Credit | Balance |
|---|---|---|---|---|---|
| Feb. | 3 | D2 | 15.00 | | 15.00 |

**Salaries Expense** — No. 611

| Date | | PR | Debit | Credit | Balance |
|---|---|---|---|---|---|
| Feb. | 15 | D2 | 250.00 | | 250.00 |

Illustration 6–5
**Schedule of accounts payable, December 31, 19—**

| | |
|---|---|
| Acme Mfg. Company . . . . . | $100 |
| H. A. Green Company . . . . | 225 |
| Horn Supply Company . . . . | 350 |
| Total accounts payable . . . . | $675 |

Illustration 6–6

**Sales Journal**

| Date | | Account Debited | Invoice No. | PR | Accounts Receivable Debit | Sales Taxes Payable Credit | Sales Credit |
|---|---|---|---|---|---|---|---|
| Dec. | 1 | D. R. Horn . . . . . . | 7-1698 | | 103.00 | 3.00 | 100.00 |

counts. At the end of the month, after you crossfoot the column totals, post the Accounts Payable column total to the debit of the Accounts Payable controlling account. Then, credit the Purchases Discounts column total to the Purchases Discounts account, and credit the Cash column total to the Cash account. Since the items in the Other Accounts column are posted individually, the column total is not posted.

## Testing the Accuracy of the Ledgers

Explain how to test the accuracy of the account balances in the Accounts Receivable and Accounts Payable Ledgers and prepare schedules of the accounts in each subsidiary ledger. (L. O. 3)

Periodically, after all posting is completed, the account balances in the General Ledger and the subsidiary ledgers should be tested for accuracy. To do this, you first prepare a trial balance of the General Ledger to confirm that debits equal credits. If the trial balance balances, the accounts in the General Ledger, including the controlling accounts, are assumed to be correct. Then you test the subsidiary ledgers by preparing schedules of accounts receivable and accounts payable. To prepare a **schedule of accounts payable,** for example, you list the Accounts Payable Ledger accounts with balances and calculate the sum of the balances. If the total is equal to the balance of the Accounts Payable controlling account, the accounts in the Accounts Payable Ledger are assumed to be correct. Illustration 6–5 shows a schedule of accounts payable drawn from the Accounts Payable Ledger of Illustration 6–4. A **schedule of accounts receivable** is prepared in the same way as a schedule of accounts payable. Also, if its total equals the balance of the Accounts Receivable controlling account, the accounts in the Accounts Receivable Ledger are assumed to be correct.

## Sales Taxes

Many cities and states require retailers to collect sales taxes from their customers and periodically remit these taxes to the city or state treasurer. When a columnar Sales Journal is used, a record of taxes collected can be obtained by adding special columns in the journal as shown in Illustration 6–6.

In posting the journal, the individual amounts in the Accounts Receivable column are posted daily to customer accounts in the Accounts Receivable Ledger. Then, at the end of the month, you post the column total to the Accounts Receivable controlling account. The individual amounts in the Sales Taxes Payable and Sales columns are not posted. Instead, at the end of the month, you credit the total of the Sales Taxes Payable column to the Sales Taxes Payable account, and credit the total of the Sales column to Sales.

A business that collects sales taxes on its cash sales may add a special Sales Taxes Payable column in its Cash Receipts Journal.

## Using Sales Invoices as a Sales Journal

To save labor, you may avoid using a Sales Journal for credit sales. Instead, you can post each sales invoice total directly to the customer's account in a subsidiary Accounts Receivable Ledger. Then, copies of the invoices are bound in numerical order in a binder. At the end of the month, all the invoices of that month are totaled, and you make a general journal entry to debit Accounts Receivable and credit Sales for the total. In effect, the bound invoice copies act as a Sales Journal. Such a procedure is known as direct posting of sales invoices.

## Sales Returns

If a business has only a few sales returns, you may record them in a General Journal with an entry like the following:

| | | | | | |
|---|---|---|---|---|---|
| Oct. | 17 | Sales Returns and Allowances . . . . . . . . . . . | 412 | 17.50 | |
| | | Accounts Receivable—George Ball . . . . . . | 112/√ | | 17.50 |
| | | Customer returned merchandise. | | | |

The debit of the entry is posted to the Sales Returns and Allowances account. The credit is posted to both the Accounts Receivable controlling account and to the customer's account. Note the account number and the check mark, 112/√, in the PR column on the credit line. This indicates that both the Accounts Receivable controlling account in the General Ledger and the George Ball account in the Accounts Receivable Ledger were credited for $17.50.

Companies that have sufficient sales returns can save posting labor by recording them in a special Sales Returns and Allowances Journal like the one in Illustration 6–7. Note that this is in keeping with the idea that a company can design and use a special journal for any group of similar transactions if there are enough transactions to warrant the journal. When a Sales Returns and Allowances Journal is used to record returns, the amounts entered in the journal are posted daily to the customers' accounts. At the end of the month, the journal total is debited to Sales Returns and Allowances and credited to Accounts Receivable.

## General Journal Entries

When special journals are used, a General Journal always is necessary for adjusting, closing, and correcting entries and for a few transactions that cannot be recorded in the special journals. Examples of such transactions would be purchases returns and purchases of plant assets, which would be recorded as follows:

Illustration 6–7

**Sales Returns and Allowances Journal**

| Date | | Account Credited | Explanation | Credit Memo No. | PR | Amount |
|---|---|---|---|---|---|---|
| Oct. | 7 | Robert Moore . . . . . | Defective merchandise . . . | 203 | √ | 10.00 |
| | 14 | James Warren . . . . . | Defective merchandise . . . | 204 | √ | 12.00 |
| | 18 | T. M. Jones . . . . . . . | Not ordered . . . . . . . . . . | 205 | √ | 6.00 |
| | 23 | Sam Smith . . . . . . . | Defective merchandise . . . | 206 | √ | 18.00 |
| | 31 | Sales Returns and Allowances, Dr.; Accounts Receivable, Cr. | | | | 46.00 |
| | | | | | | (412/112) |

| | | | | | |
|---|---|---|---|---|---|
| Oct. | 8 | Accounts Payable—Medford Company . . . . . . | 212/√ | 32.00 | |
| | | Purchases Returns and Allowances . . . . . | 512 | | 32.00 |
| | | Returned defective merchandise. | | | |
| | 11 | Office Equipment . . . . . . . . . . . . . . . . . . . | 133 | 685.00 | |
| | | Accounts Payable—ABC Supply Co. . . . . | 212/√ | | 685.00 |
| | | Purchased a typewriter. | | | |

## Computerized Data Processing

Describe how data are processed in computerized accounting systems. (L. O. 4)

Manual accounting systems like the ones described thus far are used only by small businesses. In fact, even very small businesses now are able to use computers to process their accounting data. Computerized data processing allows data to be entered in the system, classified, stored, and summarized on printed reports with very little human intervention. A computer is capable of—

1. Inputting and storing data.
2. Performing arithmetic calculations on the data.
3. Comparing units of the data to find which are larger or smaller.
4. Sorting or rearranging data.
5. Printing reports from the data stored in the machine.

Computers vary in size and in the speed with which they process data. They range from small desktop microcomputers to machines that with their peripheral equipment occupy a large room. Peripheral equipment includes devices to input or output data and to store data on reels of magnetic tape or on magnetic disks.

Data may be entered into a computer by means of a computer terminal, with previously prepared punched cards, reels of magnetic tape, magnetic disks, and in other ways. For example, one means of entry is to use a laser beam that reads a bar code such as is found on many consumer products.

Inside the computer each alphabetical letter or numerical digit of data becomes a combination of electrical or magnetic states that the computer can manipulate at very high rates of speed. Computers can do thousands or even millions of additions, subtractions, multiplications, and divisions per second, all without error in a predetermined sequence according to instructions stored in the machine.

A computer can do nothing without a previously prepared set of instructions that is entered and stored in the computer. However, with a properly prepared program of instructions, a computer will accept data, store and process the data, and produce the processed results in the form of a report displayed on a monitor, or typed out on an electric typewriter at the rate of approximately 10 characters per second, or printed by a laser printer at up to 2,000 lines per minute.

### The Program

A **computer program** is a set of instructions written in a language the computer "understands." Some of the widely used languages are COBOL, BASIC, RPG, and FORTRAN. The instructions specify each operation a computer is to perform and are entered into the computer before the data to be processed. The program may contain only a few or several thousand detailed instructions. For example, the following shows the steps that must be programmed to have a computer process customers' orders for merchandise.

**Instructions to Be Programmed for Processing Customers' Orders**

1. For the first item on the customer's order, compare the quantity ordered with the quantity on hand as shown by inventory data stored in the computer.
    *a.* If the quantity ordered is not on hand:
        (1) Prepare a back order notifying the customer that the goods are not available but will be shipped as soon as a new supply is received.
        (2) Go to the next item on the customer's order.
    *b.* If the quantity on hand is greater than the amount ordered:
        (1) Deduct the amount ordered from the amount on hand.
        (2) Prepare instructions to ship the goods.
        (3) Compare the amount of the item remaining after filling the customer's order with the reorder point for the item.
            (*a*) If the amount remaining is greater than the reorder point:
                1. Go to the next item on the customer's order.
            (*b*) If the amount remaining is less than the reorder point:
                1. Compute the amount to be purchased and prepare documents for the purchase.
                2. Go to the next item on the customer's order.

In addition to these instructions, a program for processing customer orders would have instructions for preparing invoices, recording sales, and updating customer accounts.

### Designing the Program

Computers have the ability to compare two numbers and decide which is larger. This ability makes it possible for the computer to process data one way or another, depending on the result of the comparison. Note that this ability to compare numbers is essential if the computer is to follow instructions such as those for processing customer orders.

If a computer is to process data correctly, a person (the programmer) must first design a program for the computer to follow. In designing the program, the programmer determines in advance the alternative sets of calculations or processing steps to be made. Then, the programmer must devise the appropriate comparisons that will identify the circumstances under which each particular set of processing steps should be performed. Finally, the programmer must write specific instructions telling the computer how to process the data. A computer can follow through the program's maze of decisions and alternate instructions rapidly and accurately. However, if it encounters an exception not anticipated in the program, it is helpless and can only process the exception incorrectly or stop.

### Modes of Operation

Computers operate in one of two modes: either **batch processing** or **online processing**. In the batch mode, the program and data to be processed are inputted to the computer, processed, and then removed from the computer before another batch is begun. Then, the program for a new job and a new set of data are entered, and the new job is processed. Batch processing may result in customers' orders being processed daily, the payroll being run each week, financial statements being prepared monthly, and the processing of other jobs on a periodic basis. Because transactions are processed in groups or batches, this mode of operation may require less computer capacity, is usually less expensive than online operation, and is used when an immediate processing or an immediate computer response is not required.

In online processing, the program is kept in the computer along with any required data. As new data are entered, they are instantly processed by the computer. For example, in some department stores, the cash registers are connected directly into the store's computer. In addition to cash sales, the registers are used as follows in recording charge sales: After the customer selects merchandise for purchase, the salesperson uses the customer's plastic credit card to print the customer's name on a blank sales ticket. The sales ticket is then placed in the Forms Printer of the cash register, and the sale is recorded. The register prints all pertinent information on the sales ticket and totals it. In order to finalize the sale, controls within the register require that the salesperson depress the proper register keys to record the customer's account number. This, in effect, posts the sale to the customer's account. The salesperson does not actually post to the account. Rather, the data entered with the cash register's keys causes the store's computer to update the customer's account. The computer will also produce the customer's month-end statement, ready for mailing.

Another example of online operation is found in supermarkets, where each item of merchandise is imprinted with a machine-readable inventory tag similar to Illustration 6–8. At one of the store's checkout stands, each item of merchandise selected by a customer is passed over an optical scanner in the countertop, or an optical scanner in a wand is passed over each item's price tag. This actuates the cash register and eliminates the need for handkeying information into the register. It also transmits the sales information to a computer that updates the store's inventory records and prepares orders to a cen-

**Illustration 6–8**
**Machine-readable inventory tag**

tral warehouse to restock any item in low supply. At closing time, the computer prints out detailed summaries of the day's sales and item inventories. It thus provides management with up-to-the-minute information that could not otherwise be obtained.

Other examples of online operations are found in banks, airlines, and factories. However, all have the same results: they reduce human labor, create more accurate records, and provide management with both better and more up-to-date reports. Furthermore, when there are sufficient transactions, they do the work at less cost per transaction.

### Time Sharing

Computer service companies provide computer service to many concerns on a time-sharing basis, using computers that are capable of working on many jobs simultaneously. In providing such service, the computer service company installs an input-output device on the premises of a subscriber to its service. The input-output device is connected to the service company's computer by means of a telephone line. The subscriber uses the input-output device to input data into the service company's computer. The data is held in storage there until processing time is available, usually within a few seconds. The computer then processes the data and transmits the results to the subscriber. For this service the subscriber pays a monthly fee plus a charge for the computer time used.

Through **time sharing**, a growing number of concerns are using computers, even very small businesses. For example, a dentist or a physician practicing alone is a small business. Yet a significant number of such dentists and physicians have their accounts receivable and customer billing done by computer service companies.

### Microcomputers

Another important factor leading to the expanded use of computers is the development of microcomputers. These computers have become less expensive in recent years and are now affordable by very small businesses and individuals. As more and more people become proficient in using these machines, manual accounting systems are being replaced by computerized systems.

## AS A MATTER OF ETHICS

A CPA has a client whose business has grown significantly over the last couple of years and has reached the point where its accounting system has become inadequate for handling both the volume of transactions and management's needs for financial information. The client asks the CPA for advice on which software system would work best for the company.

The CPA has been offered a 10% commission by a software company for each purchase of its system by one of the CPA's clients. The price of one of these systems falls within the range specified by the client. Do you think that the CPA's evaluation of the alternative systems could be affected by this commission arrangement? Should it be? Should the CPA feel compelled to tell the client about the commission arrangement before making a recommendation?

### Recording Actual Transactions

Depending on the accounting system of a business, transactions may be recorded manually in a General Journal or in special journals. Also, if the accounting system is computerized, the recording of transactions must be done in a form that is acceptable to the company's computer. Nevertheless, in the remainder of this text, we use general journal entries to illustrate the recording of most transactions. The general journal entries are intended to show the items increased and decreased by the transactions.

## Summary of the Chapter in Terms of Learning Objectives

**1.** Columnar journals are designed so that repetitive debits to a specific account are entered in a separate column. The same is done for repetitive credits. When special journals are used, all credit sales are entered in a Sales Journal. Credit purchases of merchandise and usually of supplies are entered in a Purchases Journal. All cash receipts are entered in the Cash Receipts Journal, and all cash payments, except for those from petty cash, are entered in the Cash Disbursements Journal (or Check Register). Any transactions that cannot be entered in the special journals are entered in the General Journal.

To enter a transaction when special journals are used, you first decide which journal must be used. Then, the transaction is recorded in accordance with the columns provided in the journal and the nature of the transaction.

**2.** When transactions are posted from special journals to the accounts, individual debits and credits to subsidiary Accounts Receivable and Accounts Payable Ledgers are posted daily. Other amounts that must be posted individually also may be posted daily. Normally, the columns of each special journal are totaled and crossfooted at the end of each month. Then, the column totals are posted to the appropriate general ledger accounts.

**3.** To test the accuracy of a subsidiary ledger after all posting is completed, you prepare a schedule of the accounts in the ledger and compare the total of the account balances with the balance in the related controlling account. If they are not equal, you know an error has been made. If they are equal, you assume the balances are correct.

**4.** In a computerized accounting system, data may be entered in the computer in a variety of ways, such as from a terminal, punched cards, magnetic tape, magnetic disk storage, or laser beam scanners. Following the instructions contained in the computer program, the computer accepts, classifies, and stores the data and prepares summarized reports that may be printed or displayed on a monitor.

## Glossary

Define or explain the words and phrases listed in the chapter Glossary. (L. O. 5)

**Accounting system** the business papers, records, reports, and procedures used by a business in recording transactions and reporting their effects. p. 254

**Accounts Payable Ledger** a subsidiary ledger having an account for each creditor. p. 261

**Accounts Receivable Ledger** a subsidiary ledger having an account for each customer. p. 256

**Batch processing** a mode of computer operation in which a program and data are entered in the computer, processed, and removed from the computer before the next program and data are entered. p. 268

**Check Register** a book of original entry for recording cash payments by check. p. 261

**Columnar journal** a book of original entry having columns, each of which is designated as the place for entering specific data about each transaction of a group of similar transactions. p. 256

**Computer program** a set of instructions that are entered into a computer and that specify the operations the computer is to perform. p. 267

**Controlling account** a general ledger account the balance of which (after posting) equals the sum of the balances of the accounts in a related subsidiary ledger, thereby proving the sum of those subsidiary account balances. p. 257

**Crossfoot** to add the Debit column totals of a journal, add the Credit column totals, and then compare the sums to prove that total debits equal total credits. p. 260

**Foot** to add a column of numbers. p. 260

**General Ledger** the ledger containing the financial statement accounts of a business. p. 256

**Online processing** a mode of computer operation in which the program and required data are maintained in the computer so that as new data are entered, they are processed instantly. p. 268

**Schedule of accounts payable** a list of the balances of all the accounts in the accounts payable ledger that is summed to show the total amount of accounts payable outstanding. p. 264

**Schedule of accounts receivable** a list of the balances of all the accounts in the accounts receivable ledger that is summed to show the total amount of accounts receivable outstanding. p. 264

**Special journal** a book of original entry that is designed and used for recording only a specified type of transaction. p. 254

**Subsidiary ledger** a group of accounts other than general ledger accounts which show the details underlying the balance of a controlling account in the General Ledger. p. 256

**Time sharing** a process by which several users of a computer, each having an input-output device, can input data into a single computer and, as processing time becomes available, have their data processed and transmitted back to their output device. p. 269

## Objective Review

Answers to the following questions are listed in Appendix I at the end of the book. Be sure that you decide which is the one best answer to each question *before* you check the answers in the appendix.

1. When special journals are used:
   *a.* All sales transactions are recorded in the Sales Journal.
   *b.* All purchase transactions are recorded in the Purchases Journal.
   *c.* All cash payments by check are recorded in the Cash Disbursements Journal.
   *d.* All cash receipts except from cash sales of merchandise are recorded in the Cash Receipts Journal.
   *e.* A General Journal is not used.
2. If an accounting system includes an Accounts Receivable controlling account and an Accounts Receivable Ledger:
   *a.* Two accounts are debited when posting sales on credit.
   *b.* The rule that debits must equal credits is not maintained.
   *c.* Two accounts are debited when posting cash sales.
   *d.* Two accounts are credited when posting cash receipts from credit customers.
   *e.* Both *(a)* and *(d)* are correct.
3. When testing the accuracy of the balances in the Accounts Receivable Ledger:
   *a.* You know absolutely that an error has been made if the sum of the customer account balances does not equal the controlling account balance.
   *b.* You can be sure that transactions involving credit customers were correctly journalized if the sum of the customer account balances equals the balance in the controlling account.
   *c.* The sum of the balances in the customer accounts should equal the balance in the Sales account.
   *d.* You can be sure that transactions involving credit customers were correctly posted if the sum of the customer account balances equals the balance in the controlling account.
   *e.* You should foot and crossfoot each of the special journals.
4. In computerized accounting systems:
   *a.* At least five special journals are used.
   *b.* Errors are most often made in the process of posting transactions.
   *c.* A standard computer program is used by all businesses.
   *d.* Cash registers are used to enter all of a business's transactions in the accounting system.
   *e.* Errors in posting and in transferring account balances to financial reports are less apt to occur than they are in manual accounting systems.

## Questions for Class Discussion

1. What are three steps in the operation of an accounting system?
2. How does a columnar journal save posting labor?
3. Most transactions of a merchandising business fall into four groups. What are these four groups?
4. Why should sales to and receipts of cash from charge customers be recorded and posted daily?
5. What functions are served by the Accounts Receivable controlling account?
6. Both credits to customer accounts and credits to miscellaneous accounts are individually posted from a Cash Receipts Journal like that of Illustration 6–2. Why not put both kinds of credits in the same column and thus save journal space?
7. How is a multicolumn journal crossfooted? Why is such a journal crossfooted?
8. How is the equality of a controlling account and its subsidiary ledger accounts maintained?
9. Describe how copies of a company's sales invoices may be used as a Sales Journal.
10. When a general journal entry is used to record a returned charge sale, the credit of the entry must be posted twice. Does this cause the trial balance to be out of balance? Why or why not?
11. How does one tell from which journal a particular amount in a ledger account was posted?
12. How is a schedule of accounts payable prepared? How is it used to prove the balances of the creditor accounts in the Accounts Payable Ledger?
13. After all posting is completed, the balance of the Accounts Receivable controlling account does not agree with the sum of the balances in the Accounts Receivable Ledger. If the trial balance is in balance, where is the error apt to be?
14. Are computerized accounting systems used by small businesses?
15. What are some of the ways data can be entered into a computer?

## Exercises

**Exercise 6–1**
**Special journals**
(L. O. 1)

A company that uses a Sales Journal, a Purchases Journal, a Cash Receipts Journal, a Cash Disbursements Journal, and a General Journal like the ones described in the chapter completed the following transactions. List the transactions by letter and opposite each letter give the name of the journal in which the transaction would be recorded.

*a.* Sold merchandise for cash. Cash Receipts
*b.* Sold merchandise on credit. Sales
*c.* Purchased merchandise on credit. Purchase
*d.* A customer returned merchandise sold for cash; a check was issued.
Cash Disburse

*e.* Paid a creditor.
*f.* Returned merchandise purchased on credit.
*g.* A customer paid for merchandise previously purchased on credit.
*h.* Purchased office supplies on credit.
*i.* Gave a customer credit for merchandise purchased on credit and returned.
*j.* Purchased office equipment on credit.
*k.* Recorded adjusting and closing entries.

**Exercise 6–2**
**The Sales Journal**
(L. O. 1)

A company uses a Sales Journal, a Purchases Journal, a Cash Receipts Journal, a Cash Disbursements Journal, and a General Journal. The following transactions occurred during the month of August:

Aug. 3 Purchased merchandise for $18 on credit from Z Company.
6 Sold merchandise to M. Isak for $35 cash, Invoice No. 15.
10 Sold merchandise to C. Judd for $135, terms 2/15, n/60, Invoice No. 16.
12 Borrowed $25 from the bank by giving a note to the bank.
14 Sold merchandise to S. Clark for $90, terms n/30, Invoice No. 17.
20 Sold used store equipment to G Company for $150.
25 Received $132.30 from C. Judd to pay for the purchase of August 10.
31 Sold merchandise to B. Witten for $115, terms n/30, Invoice No. 18.

*Required*

On a sheet of notebook paper, draw a Sales Journal like the one that appears in Illustration 6–1. Journalize the transactions during August that should be recorded in the Sales Journal.

**Exercise 6–3**
**The Cash Receipts Journal**
(L. O. 1)

A company uses a Sales Journal, a Purchases Journal, a Cash Receipts Journal, a Cash Disbursements Journal, and a General Journal. The following transactions occurred during the month of August:

Aug. 3 L. Fox, the owner of the business, invested $30 in the business.
6 Purchased merchandise for $18 on credit from J Company.
10 Sold merchandise on credit to D. Roy for $12, subject to a $2 sales discount if paid by the end of the month.
12 Borrowed $25 from the bank by giving a note to the bank.
13 Sold merchandise to B. Maddox for $9 cash.
27 Paid J Company $18 for the merchandise purchased on August 6.
28 Received $10 from D. Roy to pay for the purchase of August 10.
31 Paid salaries of $8.

*Required*

1. On a sheet of notebook paper, draw a multicolumn Cash Receipts Journal like the one that appears in Illustration 6–2. (Dollar amounts in this exercise are small so that you may use narrow columns.)
2. Journalize the transactions during August that should be recorded in the Cash Receipts Journal.

**Exercise 6–4**
**The Purchases Journal**
(L. O. 1)

A company uses a Sales Journal, a Purchases Journal, a Cash Receipts Journal, a Cash Disbursements Journal, and a General Journal. The following transactions occurred during the month of August:

Aug. 1 K. Neile, the owner of the business, invested $45 in the business.
3 Purchased merchandise for $21 on credit from F Company, terms n/30.
6 Purchased store supplies from P Company for $5 cash.
8 Sold merchandise on credit to D. Saw for $15, subject to a $2 sales discount if paid by the end of the month.
11 Purchased on credit from P Company office supplies for $6 and store supplies for $10, terms n/30.
18 Sold merchandise to T. Rey for $24 cash.
30 Paid F Company $21 for the merchandise purchased on August 3.

*Required*

1. On a sheet of notebook paper, draw a multicolumn Purchases Journal like the one that appears in Illustration 6–3. (Dollar amounts in this exercise are small so that you may use narrow columns.)
2. Journalize the transactions during August that should be recorded in the Purchases Journal.

**Exercise 6–5**
**The Cash Disbursements Journal**
(L. O. 1)

A company uses a Sales Journal, a Purchases Journal, a Cash Receipts Journal, a Cash Disbursements Journal, and a General Journal. The following transactions occurred during the month of August:

Aug. 1 Purchased merchandise for $60 on credit from Z Company, terms 2/10, n/30.
2 Purchased merchandise for $75 on credit from B Company, terms 2/15, n/60.
5 Issued Check No. 5 to Q Company to buy store supplies for $15.
15 Sold merchandise on credit to F. Hane for $120, terms n/30.
16 Issued Check No. 6 for $55 to repay a note payable to State Bank.
17 Issued Check No. 7 to B Company to pay the amount due for the purchase of August 2, less the discount.
31 Issued Check No. 8 to Z Company to pay the amount due for the purchase of August 1.
31 Paid salary of $30 to D. Jones by issuing Check No. 9.

*Required*

1. On a sheet of notebook paper, draw a multicolumn Cash Disbursements Journal like the one that appears in Illustration 6–4. (Dollar amounts in this exercise are small so that you may use narrow columns.)
2. Journalize the transactions during August that should be recorded in the Cash Disbursements Journal.

**Exercise 6–6**
**General Journal transactions**
(L. O. 1)

A company uses a Sales Journal, a Purchases Journal, a Cash Receipts Journal, a Cash Disbursements Journal, and a General Journal. The following transactions occurred during the month of August:

Aug. 1 N. Fount, the owner of the business, invested $150 in the business.
5 Purchased merchandise for $125 on credit from B Company, terms 2/10, n/30.
11 N. Fount, the owner of the business, contributed an automobile worth $750 to the business.
13 Issued Check No. 5 to G Company to buy store supplies for $15.
15 Sold merchandise on credit to J. Kirk for $120, terms n/30.
16 Returned $35 of defective merchandise to B Company from the purchase on August 5.
19 Issued Check No. 7 to M Company to pay the $225 due for a purchase of July 20.
26 J. Kirk returned $45 of merchandise originally purchased on August 15.
31 Accrued salaries payable were $30.

*Required*
Journalize the transactions during August that should be recorded in the General Journal.

**Exercise 6–7**
**Special journal transactions**
(L. O. 1)

A company uses the following journals: Sales Journal, Purchases Journal, Cash Receipts Journal, Cash Disbursements Journal, and General Journal. On March 15, the company purchased merchandise priced at $15,000, subject to credit terms of 2/10, n/30. On March 25, the company paid the net amount due. However, in journalizing the payment, the bookkeeper debited Accounts Payable for $15,000 and failed to record the cash discount. Cash was credited for the actual amount paid. In what journals would the March 15 and the March 25 transactions have been recorded? What procedure is likely to disclose the error in journalizing the March 25 transaction?

**Exercise 6–8**
**Subsidiary ledger accounts**
(L. O. 2, 3)

At the end of March, the Sales Journal of Crockett Company appeared as follows:

**Sales Journal**

| Date | | Account Debited | Invoice No. | PR | Amount |
|---|---|---|---|---|---|
| Mar. | 4 | Wanda Slater . . . . | 532 | ✓ | 615.00 |
| | 7 | Ted Atkinson . . . . | 533 | ✓ | 1,020.00 |
| | 13 | Hana Moore . . . . . | 534 | ✓ | 855.00 |
| | 22 | Wanda Slater . . . . | 535 | ✓ | 285.00 |
| | 31 | Total . . . . . . . . . | | | 2,775.00 |

The company had also recorded the return of merchandise with the following entry:

| | | | | |
|---|---|---|---|---|
| Mar. | 21 | Sales Returns and Allowances . . . . . . . . . . . . . . . . | 150.00 | |
| | | Accounts Receivable—Hana Moore. . . . . . . . . . . | | 150.00 |
| | | Customer returned merchandise. | | |

*Required*

1. On a sheet of notebook paper, open a subsidiary Accounts Receivable Ledger having a T-account for each customer listed in the Sales Journal. Post to the customer accounts the entries of the Sales Journal and also the portion of the general journal entry that affects a customer's account.
2. Open a General Ledger having T-accounts for Accounts Receivable, Sales, and Sales Returns and Allowances. Post the Sales Journal and the portions of the general journal entry that affect these accounts.
3. Test the accuracy of the subsidiary ledger accounts with a schedule of accounts receivable.

**Exercise 6–9**
**Accounts Receivable Ledger**
(L. O. 2, 3)

Maxmann Company, a company that posts its sales invoices directly and then binds the invoices to make them into a Sales Journal, had the following sales during July:

| | | | |
|---|---|---|---|
| July | 3 | Freida Jenz . . . . | $ 7,200 |
| | 6 | Bob Gibson . . . . | 9,900 |
| | 14 | Earl Waites . . . . | 14,400 |
| | 20 | Bob Gibson . . . . | 15,840 |
| | 22 | Earl Waites . . . . | 6,300 |
| | 30 | Donald Betz . . . . | 13,500 |
| | | Total . . . . . . . . | $67,140 |

*Required*

1. On a sheet of notebook paper, open a subsidiary Accounts Receivable Ledger having a T-account for each customer listed above. Post the invoices to the subsidiary ledger.
2. Give the general journal entry to record the end-of-month total of the Sales Journal.
3. Open an Accounts Receivable controlling account and a Sales account and post the general journal entry.
4. Prove the subsidiary Accounts Receivable Ledger with a schedule of accounts receivable.

**Exercise 6–10**
**Errors related to the Sales Journal**
(L. O. 1, 2, 3)

A company that records credit sales in a Sales Journal and records sales returns in its General Journal made the following errors. List each error by letter, and opposite each letter tell when the error should be discovered:

*a.* Posted a sales return recorded in the General Journal to the Sales Returns and Allowances account and to the Accounts Receivable account but did not post to the customer's account.

*b.* Made an addition error in determining the balance of a customer's account.

*c.* Made an addition error in totaling the Amount column of the Sales Journal.

*d.* Posted a sales return to the Accounts Receivable account and to the customer's account but did not post to the Sales Returns and Allowances account.

*e.* Correctly recorded a $300 sale in the Sales Journal but posted it to the customer's account as a $3,000 sale.

**Exercise 6–11**
**Posting from special journals to T-accounts**
(L. O. 2)

Following are the condensed journals of a merchandising concern. The journal column headings are incomplete in that they do not indicate whether the columns are Debit or Credit columns.

*Required*

1. Prepare T-accounts on a sheet of ordinary notebook paper for the following general ledger and subsidiary ledger accounts. Separate the accounts of each ledger group as follows:

**General Ledger Accounts**
Cash
Accounts Receivable
Prepaid Insurance
Store Equipment
Notes Payable
Accounts Payable
Sales
Sales Returns
Sales Discounts
Purchases
Purchases Returns
Purchases Discounts

**Accounts Receivable Ledger Accounts**
Customer One
Customer Two
Customer Three

**Accounts Payable Ledger Accounts**
Company X
Company Y
Company Z

2. Without referring to any of the illustrations showing complete column headings for the journals, post the following journals to the proper T-accounts.

**Sales Journal**

| Account | Amount |
|---|---|
| Customer One . . . . | 5,250 |
| Customer Two . . . . | 7,800 |
| Customer Three . . . | 10,500 |
| Total. . . . . . . . . . | 23,550 |

**Purchases Journal**

| Account | Amount |
|---|---|
| Company X . . . . . | 6,300 |
| Company Y . . . . . | 7,350 |
| Company Z . . . . . | 8,400 |
| Total . . . . . . . . . | 22,050 |

**General Journal**

| | | | | |
|---|---|---|---|---|
| . . . . . . | . . . | Sales Returns . . . . . . . . . . . . . . . . . . . . . . . . | 1,050.00 | |
| | | Accounts Receivable—Customer Three . . . . . . . | | 1,050.00 |
| | . . . | Accounts Payable—Company Z . . . . . . . . . . . . . . | 1,575.00 | |
| | | Purchases Returns . . . . . . . . . . . . . . . . . . . | | 1,575.00 |

**Cash Receipts Journal**

| Account | Other Accounts | Accounts Receivable | Sales | Sales Discounts | Cash |
|---|---|---|---|---|---|
| Customer One . . . . . . | . . . | 5,250 | . . . | 105 | 5,145 |
| Cash Sales . . . . . . . | . . . | . . . | 7,615 | . . . | 7,615 |
| Notes Payable . . . . . . | 10,000 | . . . | . . . | . . . | 10,000 |
| Cash Sales . . . . . . . | . . . | . . . | 8,665 | . . . | 8,665 |
| Customer Two . . . . . . | . . . | 7,800 | . . . | 156 | 7,644 |
| Store Equipment . . . . | 785 | . . . | . . . | . . . | 785 |
| Totals . . . . . . . . . . | 10,785 | 13,050 | 16,280 | 261 | 39,854 |

**Cash Disbursements Journal**

| Account | Other Accounts | Accounts Payable | Purchases Discounts | Cash |
|---|---|---|---|---|
| Prepaid Insurance . . . . | 525 | . . . | . . . | 525 |
| Company Y . . . . . . . . | . . . | 7,350 | 147 | 7,203 |
| Company Z . . . . . . . . | . . . | 6,825 | 137 | 6,688 |
| Store Equipment . . . . . | 2,625 | . . . | . . . | 2,625 |
| Totals . . . . . . . . . . | 3,150 | 14,175 | 284 | 17,041 |

## Problems

**Problem 6–1**
**Special journals and subsidiary ledgers**
(L. O. 1, 2, 3)

Zenobia Company completed these transactions during April of the current year:

Apr. 2 Purchased merchandise on credit from Barclay Company, invoice dated March 31, terms 2/10, n/60, $5,400.

2 Issued Check No. 660 to *The City Times* for advertising expense, $575.

3 Sold merchandise on credit to Mark Loftis, Invoice No. 742, $9,650. (The terms of all credit sales are 2/10, n/60.)

4 Purchased on credit from Nixen Company merchandise, $7,125; store supplies, $375; and office supplies, $300. Invoice dated April 3, terms n/10 EOM.

6 Received a $75 credit memorandum from Nixen Company for unsatisfactory merchandise received on April 4 and returned for credit.

8 Sold merchandise on credit to Helen Stone, Invoice No. 743, $8,750.

9 Purchased store equipment on credit from Rexor Company, invoice dated April 9, terms n/10 EOM, $13,200.

10 Issued Check No. 661 to Barclay Company in payment of its March 31 invoice, less the discount.

12 Sold merchandise on credit to Regina Niser, Invoice No. 744, $3,450.

13 Received payment from Mark Loftis for the April 3 sale, less the discount.

14 Sold merchandise on credit to Mark Loftis, Invoice No. 745, $4,800.

Apr. 15 Issued Check No. 662, payable to Payroll, in payment of the sales salaries for the first half of the month, $3,345. Cashed the check and paid the employees.

15 Cash sales for the first half of the month, $22,305. (Cash sales are usually recorded daily from the cash register readings. However, they are recorded only twice in this problem to reduce the repetitive transactions.)

18 Received payment from Helen Stone for the April 8 sale, less the discount.

19 Purchased merchandise on credit from Long Company, invoice dated April 18, terms 2/10, n/60, $5,150.

20 Borrowed $18,000 from River City Bank by giving a note payable.

22 Received payment from Regina Niser for the April 12 sale, less the discount.

23 Purchased on credit from Rexor Company merchandise, $1,650; store supplies, $270; and office supplies, $180. Invoice dated April 22, terms n/10 EOM.

24 Received payment from Mark Loftis for the April 14 sale, less the discount.

24 Purchased merchandise on credit from Barclay Company, invoice dated April 23, terms 2/10, n/60, $3,150.

25 Received a $350 credit memorandum from Long Company for defective merchandise received on April 19 and returned.

28 Issued Check No. 663 to Long Company in payment of its April 18 invoice, less the return and the discount.

28 Sold merchandise on credit to Helen Stone, Invoice No. 746, $4,260.

29 Sold merchandise on credit to Regina Niser, Invoice No. 747, $2,475.

30 Issued Check No. 664, payable to Payroll, in payment of the sales salaries for the last half of the month, $3,345.

30 Cash sales for the last half of the month were $23,880.

*Required*

1. Open the following general ledger accounts: Cash, Accounts Receivable, Notes Payable, Sales, and Sales Discounts. Also open subsidiary accounts receivable ledger accounts for Mark Loftis, Regina Niser, and Helen Stone.
2. Prepare a Sales Journal and a Cash Receipts Journal like the ones illustrated in this chapter.
3. Review the transactions of Zenobia Company and enter those transactions that should be journalized in the Sales Journal and those that should be journalized in the Cash Receipts Journal. Ignore any transactions that should be posted in a Purchases Journal, a Cash Disbursements Journal, or a General Journal.
4. Post the items that should be posted as individual amounts from the journals. (Normally, such items are posted daily; but since they are few in number, in this problem you are asked to post them only once.)

5. Foot and crossfoot the journals and make the month-end postings.
6. Prepare a trial balance of the General Ledger and test the accuracy of the subsidiary ledger by preparing a schedule of accounts receivable.

**Problem 6–2**
**Special journals, subsidiary ledgers, schedule of accounts payable**
(L. O. 1, 2, 3)

On March 31, Zenobia Company had a cash balance of $75,000 and a Notes Payable balance of $75,000. The April transactions of Zenobia Company included those listed in Problem 6–1.

*Required*

1. Open the following general ledger accounts: Cash, Store Supplies, Office Supplies, Store Equipment, Notes Payable, Accounts Payable, Purchases, Purchases Returns and Allowances, Purchases Discounts, Advertising Expense, and Sales Salaries Expense. Enter the March 31 balances of Cash and Notes Payable ($75,000 each).
2. Open subsidiary accounts payable ledger accounts for Barclay Company, Long Company, Nixen Company, and Rexor Company.
3. Prepare a General Journal, a Purchases Journal, and a Cash Disbursements Journal like the ones illustrated in this chapter.
4. Review the April transactions of Zenobia Company and enter those transactions that should be journalized in the General Journal, the Purchases Journal, or the Cash Disbursements Journal. Ignore any transactions that should be posted in a Sales Journal or Cash Receipts Journal.
5. Post the items that should be posted as individual amounts from the journals. (Normally, such items are posted daily; but since they are few in number, in this problem you are asked to post them only once.)
6. Foot and crossfoot the journals and make the month-end postings.
7. Prepare a trial balance and a schedule of accounts payable.

**Problem 6–3**
**Special journals, subsidiary ledgers, and a trial balance**
(L. O. 1, 2, 3)

*(If the working papers that accompany this text are not being used, omit this problem.)*

It is January 19, and you have just taken over the accounting work of Webster Company, a concern operating with annual accounting periods that end each January 31. The company's previous accountant journalized its transactions through January 18 and posted all items that required posting as individual amounts, as an examination of the journals and ledgers in the booklet of working papers will show.

The company completed these transactions beginning on January 19:

Jan. 19 Purchased on credit from Reed Suppliers merchandise, $2,450; store supplies, $360; and office supplies, $245. Invoice dated January 19, terms n/10 EOM.

20 Received a $385 credit memorandum from Younger Company for merchandise received on January 17 and returned for credit.

21 Received a $90 credit memorandum from Reed Suppliers for office supplies received on January 19 and returned for credit.

22 Sold merchandise on credit to Brenda Simms, Invoice No. 741, $2,765. (Terms of all credit sales are 2/10, n/60.)

Jan. 23 Issued a credit memorandum to Sam Trent for defective merchandise sold on January 18 and returned for credit, $295.
24 Purchased store equipment on credit from Reed Suppliers, invoice dated January 24, terms n/10 EOM, $3,305.
25 Issued Check No. 450 to Younger Company in payment of its January 15 invoice less the return and the discount.
25 Received payment from Brenda Simms for the January 15 sale less the discount.
26 Issued Check No. 451 to Vax Company in payment of its January 16 invoice less a 2% discount.
27 Sold merchandise on credit to Frank Urich, Invoice No. 742, $3,715.
27 Sold a neighboring merchant a roll of wrapping paper (store supplies) for cash at cost, $135.
28 Received payment from Sam Trent for the January 18 sale less the return and the discount.
29 Received merchandise and an invoice dated January 27, terms 2/10, n/60, from Vax Company, $4,250.
29 Susan Linder, the owner of Webster Company, used Check No. 452 to withdraw $4,500 cash from the business for personal use.
31 Issued Check No. 453 to Max Davis, the company's only sales employee, in payment of his salary for the last half of January, $1,440.
31 Issued Check No. 454 to Central Power Company in payment of the January electric bill, $835.
31 Cash sales for the last half of the month, $44,975. (Cash sales are usually recorded daily but are recorded only twice in this problem in order to reduce the repetitive transactions.)

*Required*

1. Record the transactions in the journals provided.
2. Post to the customer and creditor accounts and also post any amounts that should be posted as individual amounts to the general ledger accounts. (Normally, these amounts are posted daily, but they are posted only once by you in this problem because they are few in number.)
3. Foot and crossfoot the journals and make the month-end postings.
4. Prepare a January 31 trial balance and test the accuracy of the subsidiary ledgers by preparing schedules of accounts receivable and payable.

**Problem 6–4**
**Special journals, preparing and proving the trial balance**
(L. O. 1, 2, 3)

Henderson Company completed these transactions during May of the current year:

May 2 Received merchandise and an invoice dated May 1, terms 2/10, n/60, from Bradley Company, $7,850.
3 Sold merchandise on credit to Omar Hanes, Invoice No. 632, $3,600. (Terms of all credit sales are 2/10, n/60.)
4 Purchased on credit from Abell Company merchandise, $8,345; store supplies, $335; and office supplies, $155. Invoice dated May 2, terms n/10 EOM.
4 Sold merchandise on credit to Leigh Rogers, Invoice No. 633, $5,650.

May 8 Borrowed $25,000 by giving Central National Bank a promissory note payable.

9 Purchased office equipment on credit from Telecore Company, invoice dated May 8, terms n/10 EOM, $2,815.

10 Sent Bradley Company Check No. 282 in payment of its May 1 invoice less the discount.

12 Sold merchandise on credit to Carl Chase, Invoice No. 634, $7,450.

13 Received payment from Omar Hanes for the May 3 sale less the discount.

14 Received payment from Leigh Rogers for the May 4 sale less the discount.

15 Received merchandise and an invoice dated May 14, terms 2/10, n/60, from Thomas Company, $8,935.

15 Issued Check No. 283, payable to Payroll, in payment of sales salaries for the first half of the month, $3,845. Cashed the check and paid the employees.

15 Cash sales for the first half of the month, $83,070. (Normally, cash sales are recorded daily; however, they are recorded only twice in this problem to reduce the number of repetitive entries.)

15 *Post to the customer and creditor accounts and also post any amounts that should be posted as individual amounts to the general ledger accounts. (Normally, such items are posted daily; but you are asked to post them on only two occasions in this problem because they are few in number.)*

18 Purchased on credit from Abell Company merchandise, $1,845; store supplies, $205; and office supplies, $135. Invoice dated May 17, terms n/10 EOM.

18 Received a credit memorandum from Thomas Company for unsatisfactory merchandise received on May 15 and returned for credit, $385.

19 Received a credit memorandum from Telecore Company for office equipment received on May 9 and returned for credit, $585.

22 Received payment from Carl Chase for the sale of May 12 less the discount.

24 Issued Check No. 284 to Thomas Company in payment of its invoice of May 14 less the return and the discount.

25 Sold merchandise on credit to Carl Chase, Invoice No. 635, $3,755.

28 Sold merchandise on credit to Leigh Rogers, Invoice No. 636, $3,485.

29 Issued Check No. 285, payable to Payroll, in payment of sales salaries for the last half of the month, $3,845. Cashed the check and paid the employees.

29 Cash sales for the last half of the month, $90,965.

31 *Post to the customer and creditor accounts and post any amounts that should be posted as individual amounts to general ledger accounts.*

31 *Foot and crossfoot the journals and make the month-end postings.*

*Required*

1. Open the following general ledger accounts: Cash, Accounts Receivable, Store Supplies, Office Supplies, Office Equipment, Notes Payable, Accounts Payable, Sales, Sales Discounts, Purchases, Purchases Returns and Allowances, Purchases Discounts, and Sales Salaries Expense.
2. Open the following accounts receivable ledger accounts: Carl Chase, Omar Hanes, and Leigh Rogers.
3. Open the following accounts payable ledger accounts: Abell Company, Bradley Company, Telecore Company, and Thomas Company.
4. Enter the transactions in a Sales Journal, a Purchases Journal, a Cash Receipts Journal, a Cash Disbursements Journal, and a General Journal similar to the ones illustrated in this chapter. Post when instructed to do so.
5. Prepare a trial balance and test the accuracy of the subsidiary ledgers by preparing schedules of accounts receivable and payable.

**Problem 6–5**
**Special journals, subsidiary ledgers, and the trial balance**
(L. O. 1, 2, 3)

Donnybrook Company completed these transactions during August of the current year:

Aug. 1 Received merchandise and an invoice dated July 31, terms 2/10, n/60, from Lakes Company, $18,900.

1 Purchased store equipment on credit from Barbour Company, invoice dated August 1, terms n/10 EOM, $7,050.

4 Sold merchandise on credit to Robert Sunbeck, Invoice No. 830, $8,250. (Terms of all credit sales are 2/10, n/60.)

6 Sold merchandise on credit to Sheila Jost, Invoice No. 831, $10,650.

8 Cash sales for the week ended August 8, $22,200.

8 *Post to the customer and creditor accounts and also post any amounts that should be posted as individual items to the general ledger accounts. (Normally, such items are posted daily; but to simplify the problem, you are asked to post them only once each week.)*

9 Issued Check No. 940 to The Blue Pages for advertising, $600.

10 Sold merchandise on credit to Kurt Han, Invoice No. 832, $4,800.

10 Issued Check No. 941 to Lakes Company in payment of its July 31 invoice less the discount.

11 Purchased on credit from Outlet Company merchandise, $5,850; store supplies, $555; and office supplies, $390. Invoice dated August 10, terms n/10 EOM.

12 Sold unneeded store equipment at cost for cash, $510.

15 Cash sales for the week ended August 15, $17,250.

15 Received payment from Robert Sunbeck for the sale of August 4 less the discount.

15 Issued Check No. 942, payable to Payroll, in payment of the sales salaries for the first half of the month, $3,900. Cashed the check and paid the employees.

Aug. 15 *Post to the customer and creditor accounts and also post any amounts that should be posted as individual items to the general ledger accounts.*

16 Received payment from Sheila Jost for the sale of August 6 less the discount.

17 Sold merchandise on credit to Kurt Han, Invoice No. 833, $6,525.

18 Sold merchandise on credit to Robert Sunbeck, Invoice No. 834, $3,750.

20 Received merchandise and an invoice dated August 19, terms 2/10, n/60, from Elgin Company, $9,450.

20 Received payment from Kurt Han for the sale of August 10 less the discount.

21 Issued a credit memorandum to Kurt Han for defective merchandise sold on August 17 and returned for credit, $675.

22 Cash sales for the week ended August 22, $20,700.

22 *Post to the customer and creditor accounts and also post any amounts that should be posted as individual items to the general ledger accounts.*

24 Received a $300 credit memorandum from Elgin Company for defective merchandise received on August 20 and returned for credit.

25 Purchased on credit from Outlet Company merchandise, $4,050; store supplies, $450; and office supplies, $225. Invoice dated August 24, terms n/10 EOM.

26 Received merchandise and an invoice dated August 25, terms 2/10, n/60, from Lakes Company, $8,550.

27 Received payment from Kurt Han for the August 17 sale less the return and the discount.

28 Sold merchandise on credit to Sheila Jost, Invoice No. 835, $2,775.

29 Issued Check No. 943 to Elgin Company in payment of its August 19 invoice, less the return and the discount.

29 Issued Check No. 944, payable to Payroll, in payment of the sales salaries for the last half of the month, $3,900.

29 Cash sales for the week ended August 29 were $19,125.

29 *Post to the customer and creditor accounts and also post any amounts that should be posted to the general ledger accounts as individual items.*

31 *Foot and crossfoot the journals and make the month-end postings.*

*Required*

1. Open the following general ledger accounts: Cash, Accounts Receivable, Store Supplies, Office Supplies, Store Equipment, Accounts Payable, Sales, Sales Returns and Allowances, Sales Discounts, Purchases, Purchases Returns and Allowances, Purchases Discounts, Sales Salaries Expense, and Advertising Expense.
2. Open the subsidiary accounts receivable ledger accounts: Kurt Han, Sheila Jost, and Robert Sunbeck.
3. Open these subsidiary accounts payable ledger accounts: Barbour Company, Elgin Company, Lakes Company, and Outlet Company.

4. Prepare a Sales Journal, a Purchases Journal, a Cash Receipts Journal, a Cash Disbursements Journal, and a General Journal like the ones illustrated in this chapter. Enter the transactions in the journals and post when instructed to do so.
5. Prepare a trial balance and test the accuracy of the subsidiary ledgers with schedules of accounts receivable and payable.

## Alternate Problems

**Problem 6–1A**
**Special journals and subsidiary ledgers**
(L. O. 1, 2, 3)

Youngstown Company completed these transactions during May of the current year:

May 1 Issued Check No. 101 to *The Weekly Journal* for advertising expense, $1,080.

2 Purchased merchandise on credit from Barclay Company, invoice dated May 1, terms 2/10, n/60, $6,500.

4 Sold merchandise on credit to Mark Loftis, Invoice No. 203, $6,500. (The terms of all credit sales are 2/10, n/60.)

4 Purchased on credit from Nixen Company merchandise, $7,050; store supplies, $495; and office supplies, $255. Invoice dated May 4, terms n/10 EOM.

5 Sold merchandise on credit to Helen Stone, Invoice No. 204, $12,300.

6 Received a $525 credit memorandum from Nixen Company for unsatisfactory merchandise received on May 4 and returned for credit.

8 Purchased store equipment on credit from Rexor Company, invoice dated May 8, terms n/10 EOM, $17,400.

10 Issued Check No. 102 to Barclay Company in payment of its May 1 invoice, less the discount.

12 Sold merchandise on credit to Regina Niser, Invoice No. 205, $4,650.

14 Received payment from Mark Loftis for the May 4 sale, less the discount.

15 Issued Check No. 103, payable to Payroll, in payment of the sales salaries for the first half of the month, $4,875. Cashed the check and paid the employees.

15 Sold merchandise on credit to Mark Loftis, Invoice No. 206, $7,350.

15 Cash sales for the first half of the month, $14,835. (Cash sales are usually recorded daily from the cash register readings. However, they are recorded only twice in this problem to reduce the repetitive transactions.)

15 Received payment from Helen Stone for the May 5 sale, less the discount.

16 Purchased merchandise on credit from Long Company, invoice dated May 16, terms 2/10, n/60, $8,250.

18 Borrowed $15,000 from Pioneer Trust Bank by giving a note payable.

22 Received payment from Regina Niser for the May 12 sale, less the discount.

May 23 Received a $300 credit memorandum from Long Company for defective merchandise received on May 16 and returned.
24 Purchased on credit from Rexor Company merchandise, $4,410; store supplies, $345; and office supplies, $195. Invoice dated May 23, terms n/10 EOM.
25 Received payment from Mark Loftis for the May 15 sale, less the discount.
26 Purchased merchandise on credit from Barclay Company, invoice dated May 25, terms 2/10, n/60, $3,900.
26 Issued Check No. 104 to Long Company in payment of its May 16 invoice, less the return and the discount.
27 Sold merchandise on credit to Helen Stone, Invoice No. 207, $5,085.
29 Sold merchandise on credit to Regina Niser, Invoice No. 208, $3,495.
31 Issued Check No. 105, payable to Payroll, in payment of the sales salaries for the last half of the month, $4,875.
31 Cash sales for the last half of the month were $20,820.

*Required*

1. Open the following general ledger accounts: Cash, Accounts Receivable, Notes Payable, Sales, and Sales Discounts. Also open subsidiary accounts receivable ledger accounts for Mark Loftis, Regina Niser, and Helen Stone.
2. Prepare a Sales Journal and a Cash Receipts Journal like the ones illustrated in this chapter.
3. Review the transactions of Youngstown Company and enter those transactions that should be journalized in the Sales Journal and those that should be journalized in the Cash Receipts Journal. Ignore any transactions that should be posted in a Purchases Journal, a Cash Disbursements Journal, or a General Journal.
4. Post the items that should be posted as individual amounts from the journals. (Normally, such items are posted daily; but since they are few in number, in this problem you are asked to post them only once.)
5. Foot and crossfoot the journals and make the month-end postings.
6. Prepare a trial balance of the General Ledger and test the accuracy of the subsidiary ledger by preparing a schedule of accounts receivable.

**Problem 6–2A**
**Special journals, subsidiary ledgers, schedule of accounts payable**
(L. O. 1, 2, 3)

On April 30, Youngstown Company had a cash balance of $30,000 and a Notes Payable balance of $30,000. The May transactions of Youngstown Company included those listed in Problem 6–1A.

*Required*

1. Open the following general ledger accounts: Cash, Store Supplies, Office Supplies, Store Equipment, Notes Payable, Accounts Payable, Purchases, Purchases Returns and Allowances, Purchases Discounts, Sales Salaries Expense, and Advertising Expense. Enter the April 30 balances of Cash and Notes Payable ($30,000 each).

2. Open subsidiary accounts payable ledger accounts for Barclay Company, Long Company, Nixen Company, and Rexor Company.
3. Prepare a General Journal, a Purchases Journal, and a Cash Disbursements Journal like the ones illustrated in this chapter.
4. Review the May transactions of Youngstown Company and enter those transactions that should be journalized in the General Journal, the Purchases Journal, or the Cash Disbursements Journal. Ignore any transactions that should be posted in a Sales Journal or Cash Receipts Journal.
5. Post the items that should be posted as individual amounts from the journals. (Normally, such items are posted daily; but since they are few in number, in this problem you are asked to post them only once.)
6. Foot and crossfoot the journals and make the month-end postings.
7. Prepare a trial balance and a schedule of accounts payable.

**Problem 6–3A**
**Special journals, subsidiary ledgers, and a trial balance**
(L. O. 1, 2, 3)

*(If the working papers that accompany this text are not being used, omit this problem.)*

It is January 19, and you have just taken over the accounting work of Crowe Company, a concern operating with annual accounting periods that end each January 31. The company's previous accountant journalized its transactions through January 18 and posted all items that required posting as individual amounts, as an examination of the journals and ledgers in the booklet of working papers will show.

The company completed these transactions beginning on January 19:

Jan. 19 Sold merchandise on credit to Brenda Simms, Invoice No. 741, $8,300. (Terms of all credit sales are 2/10, n/60.)

20 Received a $685 credit memorandum from Younger Company for merchandise received on January 17 and returned for credit.

20 Purchased on credit from Reed Suppliers merchandise, $7,350; store supplies, $1,080; and office supplies, $745. Invoice dated January 19, terms n/10 EOM.

22 Issued a credit memorandum to Sam Trent for defective merchandise sold on January 18 and returned for credit, $445.

23 Received a $270 credit memorandum from Reed Suppliers for office supplies received on January 20 and returned for credit.

23 Purchased store equipment on credit from Reed Suppliers, invoice dated January 22, terms n/10 EOM, $9,925.

24 Sold merchandise on credit to Frank Urich, Invoice No. 742, $11,135.

25 Issued Check No. 450 to Younger Company in payment of its January 15 invoice less the return and the discount.

25 Received payment from Brenda Simms for the January 15 sale less the discount.

26 Issued Check No. 451 to Vax Company in payment of its January 16 invoice less a 2% discount.

28 Received merchandise and an invoice dated January 28, terms 2/10, n/60, from Vax Company, $12,750.

Jan. 28 Received payment from Sam Trent for the January 18 sale less the return and the discount.

30 Sold a neighboring merchant a carton of computer ribbons (store supplies) for cash at cost, $405.

31 Issued Check No. 452 to Valley Power Company in payment of the January electric bill, $2,495.

31 Issued Check No. 453 to Max Davis, the company's only sales employee, in payment of her salary for the last half of January, $1,440.

31 Cash sales for the last half of the month, $54,510. (Cash sales are usually recorded daily but are recorded only twice in this problem in order to reduce the repetitive transactions.)

31 Susan Linder, the owner of Crowe Company, used Check No. 454 to withdraw $7,500 cash from the business for personal use.

*Required*

1. Record the transactions in the journals provided.
2. Post to the customer and creditor accounts and also post any amounts that should be posted as individual amounts to the general ledger accounts. (Normally, these amounts are posted daily, but they are posted only once by you in this problem because they are few in number.)
3. Foot and crossfoot the journals and make the month-end postings.
4. Prepare a January 31 trial balance and test the accuracy of the subsidiary ledgers by preparing schedules of accounts receivable and payable.

**Problem 6–4A**
**Special journals, preparing and proving the trial balance**
(L. O. 1, 2, 3)

Jarrett Company completed these transactions during October of the current year:

Oct. 2 Borrowed $36,000 by giving County Regional Bank a promissory note payable.

3 Received merchandise and an invoice dated October 1, terms 2/10, n/60, from Bradley Company, $12,600.

4 Purchased on credit from Abell Company merchandise, $10,950; store supplies, $450; and office supplies, $225. Invoice dated October 3, terms n/10 EOM.

5 Sold merchandise on credit to Omar Hanes, Invoice No. 520, $9,300. (Terms of all credit sales are 2/10, n/60.)

6 Purchased office equipment on credit from Telecore Company, invoice dated October 5, terms n/10 EOM, $14,550.

9 Sold merchandise on credit to Leigh Rogers, Invoice No. 521, $8,850.

10 Sent Bradley Company Check No. 312 in payment of its October 1 invoice less the discount.

11 Received merchandise and an invoice dated October 10, terms 2/10, n/60, from Thomas Company, $12,900.

15 Received payment from Omar Hanes for the October 5 sale less the discount.

15 Issued Check No. 313, payable to Payroll, in payment of sales salaries for the first half of the month, $7,200. Cashed the check and paid the employees.

Oct. 15 Cash sales for the first half of the month, $44,700. (Normally, cash sales are recorded daily; however, they are recorded only twice in this problem to reduce the number of repetitive entries.)

15 *Post to the customer and creditor accounts and also post any amounts that should be posted as individual amounts to the general ledger accounts. (Normally, such items are posted daily; but you are asked to post them on only two occasions in this problem because they are few in number.)*

16 Sold merchandise on credit to Carl Chase, Invoice No. 522, $10,850.

18 Purchased on credit from Abell Company merchandise, $5,475; store supplies, $525; and office supplies, $420. Invoice dated October 17, terms n/10 EOM.

19 Received payment from Leigh Rogers for the October 9 sale less the discount.

20 Received a credit memorandum from Thomas Company for unsatisfactory merchandise received on October 10 and returned for credit, $1,200.

20 Issued Check No. 314 to Thomas Company in payment of its invoice of October 10 less the return and the discount.

23 Sold merchandise on credit to Carl Chase, Invoice No. 523, $7,050.

26 Received payment from Carl Chase for the sale of October 16 less the discount.

27 Received a credit memorandum from Telecore Company for office equipment received on December 6 and returned for credit, $750.

28 Sold merchandise on credit to Leigh Rogers, Invoice No. 524, $6,150.

31 Issued Check No. 315, payable to Payroll, in payment of sales salaries for the last half of the month, $7,200. Cashed the check and paid the employees.

31 Cash sales for the last half of the month, $50,550.

31 *Post to the customer and creditor accounts and post any amounts that should be posted as individual amounts to general ledger accounts.*

31 *Foot and crossfoot the journals and make the month-end postings.*

*Required*

1. Open the following general ledger accounts: Cash, Accounts Receivable, Store Supplies, Office Supplies, Office Equipment, Notes Payable, Accounts Payable, Sales, Sales Discounts, Purchases, Purchases Returns and Allowances, Purchases Discounts, and Sales Salaries Expense.
2. Open the following accounts receivable ledger accounts: Carl Chase, Omar Hanes, Leigh Rogers.
3. Open the following accounts payable ledger accounts: Abell Company, Bradley Company, Telecore Company, and Thomas Company.
4. Enter the transactions in a Sales Journal, a Purchases Journal, a Cash Receipts Journal, a Cash Disbursements Journal, and a General Journal similar to the ones illustrated in this chapter. Post when instructed to do so.

5. Prepare a trial balance and test the accuracy of the subsidiary ledgers by preparing schedules of accounts receivable and payable.

**Problem 6–5A**
**Special journals, subsidiary ledgers, and the trial balance**
(L. O. 1, 2, 3)

Jocelyn Company completed these transactions during December of the current year:

Dec. 2 Received merchandise and an invoice dated December 1, terms 2/10, n/60, from Lakes Company, $26,850.

3 Sold merchandise on credit to Robert Sunbeck, Invoice No. 825, $12,150. (Terms of all credit sales are 2/10, n/60.)

4 Issued Check No. 240 to *The Weekly Times* for advertising, $2,340.

5 Purchased store equipment on credit from Barbour Company, invoice dated December 4, terms n/10 EOM, $36,300.

6 Sold merchandise on credit to Sheila Jost, Invoice No. 826, $13,950.

7 Cash sales for the week ended December 7, $24,600.

7 *Post to the customer and creditor accounts and also post any amounts that should be posted as individual items to the general ledger accounts. (Normally, such items are posted daily; but to simplify the problem, you are asked to post them only once each week.)*

9 Sold merchandise on credit to Kurt Han, Invoice No. 827, $8,950.

10 Received a credit memorandum from Barbour Company for the return of defective equipment originally purchased on December 5, $1,050.

11 Issued Check No. 241 to Lakes Company in payment of its December 1 invoice less the discount.

12 Sold unneeded store equipment at cost for cash, $720.

13 Received payment from Robert Sunbeck for the sale of December 3 less the discount.

14 Cash sales for the week ended August 14, $22,950.

14 Issued Check No. 242, payable to Payroll, in payment of the sales salaries for the first half of the month, $4,950. Cashed the check and paid the employees.

14 *Post to the customer and creditor accounts and also post any amounts that should be posted as individual items to the general ledger accounts.*

16 Purchased on credit from Outlet Company merchandise, $11,250; store supplies, $930; and office supplies, $570. Invoice dated December 16, terms n/10 EOM.

16 Received payment from Sheila Jost for the sale of December 6 less the discount.

17 Received merchandise and an invoice dated December 17, terms 2/10, n/60, from Elgin Company, $16,650.

17 Sold merchandise on credit to Kurt Han, Invoice No. 828, $13,350.

19 Sold merchandise on credit to Robert Sunbeck, Invoice No. 829, $11,800.

19 Received payment from Kurt Han for the sale of December 9 less the discount.

Dec. 20 Issued a credit memorandum to Kurt Han for defective merchandise sold on December 17 and returned for credit, $150.

21 Cash sales for the week ended December 21, $27,450.

21 *Post to the customer and creditor accounts and also post any amounts that should be posted as individual items to the general ledger accounts.*

22 Received a $450 credit memorandum from Elgin Company for defective merchandise received on December 17 and returned for credit.

23 Purchased on credit from Outlet Company merchandise, $10,200; store supplies, $330; and office supplies, $420. Invoice dated December 22, terms n/10 EOM.

24 Received merchandise and an invoice dated December 23, terms 2/10, n/60, from Lakes Company, $15,300.

27 Received payment from Kurt Han for the December 17 sale less the return and the discount.

27 Issued Check No. 243 to Elgin Company in payment of its December 17 invoice, less the return and the discount.

28 Sold merchandise on credit to Sheila Jost, Invoice No. 830, $8,925.

28 Issued Check No. 244, payable to Payroll, in payment of the sales salaries for the last half of the month, $4,950.

28 Cash sales for the week ended December 28 were $14,625.

31 *Post to the customer and creditor accounts and also post any amounts that should be posted to the general ledger accounts as individual items.*

31 *Foot and crossfoot the journals and make the month-end postings.*

*Required*

1. Open the following general ledger accounts: Cash, Accounts Receivable, Store Supplies, Office Supplies, Store Equipment, Accounts Payable, Sales, Sales Returns and Allowances, Sales Discounts, Purchases, Purchases Returns and Allowances, Purchases Discounts, Sales Salaries Expense, and Advertising Expense.
2. Open the subsidiary accounts receivable ledger accounts: Kurt Han, Sheila Jost, and Robert Sunbeck.
3. Open these subsidiary accounts payable ledger accounts: Barbour Company, Elgin Company, Lakes Company, and Outlet Company.
4. Prepare a Sales Journal, a Purchases Journal, a Cash Receipts Journal, a Cash Disbursements Journal, and a General Journal like the ones illustrated in this chapter. Enter the transactions in the journals and post when instructed to do so.
5. Prepare a trial balance and test the accuracy of the subsidiary ledgers with schedules of accounts receivable and payable.

## COMPREHENSIVE PROBLEM

**Centaur Company**
(Review of Chapters 1 through 6)

*(If the working papers that accompany this text are not being used, omit this problem.)*

Assume it is Monday, March 2, the first business day of the month, and you have just been hired as an accountant by Centaur Company, a company that operates with monthly accounting periods. All of the company's accounting work has been completed through the end of February. Its ledgers show February 28 balances, and you are ready to begin work by recording the following transactions:

Mar. 2 Purchased on credit from Reston Suppliers merchandise, \$5,505; store supplies, \$480; and office supplies, \$165. Invoice dated March 2, terms n/10 EOM.

3 Sold merchandise on credit to Anchor Company, Invoice No. 541, \$5,550. (The terms of all credit sales are 2/10, n/60.)

3 Issued Check No. 320 to District Realty in payment of the March rent, \$2,925. (Use two lines to record the transaction. Charge 80% of the rent to Rent Expense, Selling Space and the balance to Rent Expense, Office Space.)

4 Received a \$390 credit memorandum from Hardman Products for merchandise received on February 27 and returned for credit.

4 Issued a \$225 credit memorandum to Blutex Company for defective merchandise sold on February 28 and returned for credit.

5 Purchased office equipment on credit from Reston Suppliers, invoice dated March 4, terms n/10 EOM, \$5,900.

6 Sold store supplies to the merchant next door at cost for cash, \$35.

6 Issued Check No. 321 to Hardman Products to pay for the \$3,540 of merchandise received on February 27 less the return and a 2% discount.

9 Received payment from Blutex Company for the sale of February 28 less the return and the discount.

11 Received merchandise and an invoice dated March 10, terms 2/10, n/60, from Thomas Brothers, \$6,450.

12 Received a \$260 credit memorandum from Reston Suppliers for defective office equipment received on March 5 and returned for credit.

13 Received payment from Anchor Company for the March 3 sale less the discount.

15 Issued Check No. 322, payable to Payroll, in payment of sales salaries, \$1,315, and office salaries, \$1,125. Cashed the check and paid the employees.

Mar. 15 Cash sales for the first half of the month, $21,435. (Such sales are normally recorded daily. They are recorded only twice in this problem in order to reduce the number of repetitive transactions.)

15 *Post to the customer and creditor accounts and post any amounts that should be posted to the general ledger accounts as individual amounts. (Such items are normally posted daily, but you are asked to post them only twice each month because they are few in number.)*

16 Received merchandise and an invoice dated March 16, terms 2/10, n/60, from Worth Materials, $7,950.

16 Sold merchandise on credit to Pete's Repairs, Invoice No. 542, $4,150.

18 Issued Check No. 323 to Thomas Brothers in payment of its March 10 invoice less the discount.

18 Sold merchandise on credit to Blutex Company, Invoice No. 543, $3,300.

20 Purchased on credit from Reston Suppliers merchandise, $4,995; store supplies, $165; and office supplies, $240. Invoice dated March 19, terms n/10 EOM.

23 Sold merchandise on credit to Maxwell Constructors, Invoice No. 544, $6,245.

24 Issued Check No. 324 to Worth Materials in payment of its March 16 invoice less the discount.

25 Received merchandise and an invoice dated March 25, terms 2/10, n/60, from Thomas Brothers, $4,170.

26 Received payment from Pete's Repairs for the March 16 sale less the discount.

29 Henry Sutton, the owner of Centaur Company, used Check No. 325 to withdraw $2,700 from the business for personal use.

30 Issued Check No. 326, payable to Payroll, in payment of sales salaries, $1,315, and office salaries, $1,125. Cashed the check and paid the employees.

30 Issued Check No. 327 to City Utility in payment of the March electric bill, $745.

30 Cash sales for the last half of the month were $23,415.

31 *Post to the customer and creditor accounts and post any amounts that are posted as individual amounts to the general ledger accounts.*

31 *Foot and crossfoot the journals and make the month-end postings.*

*Required*

1. Enter the transactions in the journals and post when instructed to do so.
2. Prepare a trial balance in the Trial Balance columns of the work sheet

form provided and complete the work sheet using the following information:

*a.* Ending merchandise inventory, $48,660.

*b.* Expired insurance, $510.

*c.* Ending store supplies inventory, $455; and office supplies inventory, $240.

*d.* Estimated depreciation of store equipment, $450; and of office equipment, $300.

3. Prepare a multiple-step classified March income statement, a March 31 classified balance sheet and a March statement of changes in owner's equity.
4. Prepare and post adjusting and closing entries.
5. Prepare a post-closing trial balance and test the accuracy of the subsidiary ledgers with schedules of accounts payable and accounts receivable.

Part Three

# Accounting for Assets

Businesses use many different kinds of assets in carrying on their operations. These include items such as cash, receivables, merchandise inventories, land, buildings, equipment, natural resources, and intangible assets. As you study the next four chapters, you will learn the basic principles of accounting for all these different types of assets. You will see how transactions that involve assets are recorded and how the assets are reported in the financial statements. In addition, you will learn several accounting procedures that help management safeguard and control the assets of the business.

Part Three consists of the following chapters:

# 7 Internal Control and Accounting for Cash

Cash is an asset that every business owns and uses. Cash includes such specific items as currency, coin, demand deposits (or checking accounts), and perhaps savings accounts. In studying this chapter, you will learn the principles of internal control that guide businesses in managing and accounting for cash. The chapter will show you how to establish and use a petty cash fund and how to reconcile a checking account. Also, you will learn a method of accounting for purchases that helps management monitor the extent to which cash discounts are being lost.

**Learning Objectives**

*After studying Chapter 7, you should be able to:*

1. Explain why internal control procedures are needed in a large concern and state the broad principles of internal control.
2. Describe internal control procedures to protect cash received from cash sales, cash received through the mail, and cash disbursements.
3. Explain the operation of a petty cash fund and be able to journalize entries to record petty cash fund transactions.
4. Explain why the bank balance and the book balance of cash are reconciled and be able to prepare such a reconciliation.
5. Tell how recording invoices at net amounts helps gain control over cash discounts taken and be able to account for invoices recorded at net amounts.
6. Define or explain the words and phrases listed in the chapter Glossary.

*After studying the appendix to Chapter 7 (Appendix D), you should be able to:*

7. Explain the use of a Voucher Register and Check Register and prepare entries to record and pay liabilities when these registers are used in a manual accounting system.

**Illustration 7–1**
**Seven principles of good internal control**

1. Clearly establish responsibilities.
2. Maintain adequate records.
3. Insure assets and bond employees.
4. Separate record-keeping and custody over assets.
5. Divide responsibilities for related transactions.
6. Use mechanical devices where practicable.
7. Perform regular and independent reviews.

Cash can be converted into other types of assets or used to buy services or satisfy obligations more easily than any other type of asset. As such, cash is said to be the most **liquid asset**. Because cash has a high degree of **liquidity**, it also is most likely to be the object of fraud or theft. Therefore, in accounting for cash, the procedures for protecting it from theft or other misuse are very important. These *internal control procedures* apply to all assets owned by a business and to all phases of its operations; but they are particularly important with respect to cash.

## Internal Control

Explain why internal control procedures are needed in a large concern and state the broad principles of internal control.
(L. O. 1)

In a small business, the owner-manager often controls the entire operation through personal supervision and direct participation in the activities of the business. For example, he or she commonly buys all the assets and services that are used in the business. Such a manager also hires and supervises all employees, negotiates all contracts, and signs all checks. As a result, the manager knows from personal contact and observation that the business actually received the assets and services for which the checks were written. However, as a business grows, it becomes increasingly difficult to maintain this personal contact. Therefore, at some point the manager must delegate responsibilities and rely on internal control procedures rather than personal contact in controlling the operations of the business.

A properly designed **internal control system** encourages adherence to prescribed managerial policies. It also promotes operational efficiencies; protects the business assets from waste, fraud, and theft; and ensures accurate and reliable accounting data.

Internal control procedures vary from company to company and depend on such factors as the nature of the business and its size. However, the same broad principles of internal control apply to all companies. These broad principles, itemized in Illustration 7–1, are discussed in the following paragraphs.

### Clearly Establish Responsibilities

In order to have good internal control, responsibilities must be clearly established and one person made responsible for each task. When responsibility is shared and something goes wrong, it is difficult to determine who is at fault. For example, when two salesclerks share the same cash drawer and there is a shortage, it is usually impossible to tell which clerk is at fault. Each will tend to blame the other. Neither can prove that he or she is not responsible. To correct this problem, each clerk should have a separate cash drawer, or one of the clerks should be given responsibility for making all change.

### Maintain Adequate Records

To protect assets and assure that employees follow prescribed procedures, good record-keeping is required. Reliable records are also a source of information that management uses to monitor the operations of the business. For example, if detailed records of manufacturing equipment and tools are not maintained, items may disappear without any discrepancy being noticed. And if a comprehensive chart of accounts is not documented carefully and followed precisely, some expenses may be debited to the wrong accounts. As a result, management may never discover that some expenses are excessive.

Numerous forms and internal business papers must be designed and properly used to maintain good internal control. For example, if sales slips are properly designed, sales personnel can record the proper information efficiently and without irritating delays to customers. And if all sales slips are prenumbered and controlled, each salesperson can be held responsible for the sales slips under his or her control. Thus, a salesperson is not apt to make a sale, destroy the sales slip, and pocket the cash.

### Insure Assets and Bond Key Employees

Assets should be covered by adequate casualty insurance, and employees who handle cash and negotiable assets should be bonded. Bonding of employees involves the purchase of an insurance policy against losses from employee theft. Bonding also tends to prevent theft, since bonded employees are less apt to take assets if the employees know a bonding company must be dealt with when the shortage is revealed.

### Separate Record-Keeping and Custody over Assets

A fundamental principle of internal control requires that the person who has access to or is responsible for an asset should not maintain the accounting record for that asset. When this principle is followed, the custodian of an asset, knowing that a record of the asset is being kept by another person, is not likely to misappropriate the asset or waste it; and the record-keeper, who does not have access to the asset, has no reason to falsify the record. Furthermore, if the asset is to be misappropriated and the theft concealed in the records, collusion is necessary.

### Divide Responsibility for Related Transactions

Responsibility for a divisible transaction or a series of related transactions should be divided between individuals or departments so that the work of one acts as a check on that of another. This does not mean there should be duplication of work. Each employee or department should perform an unduplicated portion. For example, responsibility for placing orders, receiving the merchandise, and paying the vendors should not be given to one individual or department. To do so invites laxity in checking the quality and quantity of goods received, and carelessness in verifying the validity and accuracy of invoices. It also invites the purchase of goods for an employee's personal use and the payment of fictitious invoices.

### Use Mechanical Devices Whenever Practicable

Cash registers, check protectors, time clocks, and mechanical counters are examples of control devices that should be used whenever practicable. A cash register with a locked-in tape makes a record of each cash sale. A check protector, by perforating the amount of a check into its face, makes it difficult to change the amount. A time clock registers the exact time an employee arrived on the job and when the employee departed.

### Perform Regular and Independent Reviews

Even if an internal control system is well designed, there is a tendency for it to deteriorate over time. Changes in personnel and the stress of time pressures tend to bring about shortcuts and omissions. Regular reviews of internal control procedures are necessary to be sure that the procedures are being followed. These reviews should be performed by internal auditors who are not directly involved in operations. From this independent perspective, internal auditors can evaluate the overall efficiency of operations as well as the effectiveness of the internal control system.

Many companies also have audits by external CPAs. After testing the company's financial records, the CPAs give an opinion as to whether the company's financial statements are presented fairly in accordance with generally accepted accounting principles. However, before CPAs can decide on how much testing they must do, they first must evaluate the effectiveness of the internal control system.

## Computers and Internal Control

The broad principles of internal control should be followed whether the accounting system is manual or computerized. However, computers have several important effects on internal control. Perhaps the most obvious is that computers provide more rapid access to large quantities of information. As a result, management's ability to monitor and control business operations is greatly improved.

### Computers Reduce Processing Errors

Computers reduce the number of errors in processing information. After the data are entered correctly, the human tendency to make mechanical and mathematical errors is largely eliminated. On the other hand, data entry errors may occur because the process of entering data sometimes appears less logical in a computerized system. Also, the lack of human involvement in later processing may cause data entry errors to go undiscovered.

### Computers Allow More Extensive Testing of Records

The regular review and audit of records can include more extensive testing if a computerized system is used. To reduce the cost of testing when manual methods are used, only small samples of data might be tested. But when computers are used to process data, large samples or even complete data files can be reviewed and analyzed.

### Computerized Systems May Limit Hard Evidence of Processing Steps

Because many data processing steps are performed by the computer, less hard evidence in the form of written forms and analyses may be available for review. Therefore, internal control may depend more on reviews of the design and operation of the computerized processing system and less on reviews of the documents left behind by the system.

### Separation of Duties Must Be Maintained

A common risk with computerized systems is that the separation of critical responsibilities is not maintained. Companies that use computers must have employees with special skills to program and operate the computers. The duties of these employees must be carefully controlled to avoid the risk of fraud. The person who designs and programs the system generally should not also serve as the operator. Control over cash receipts and disbursements should be separated. And check-writing should not be controlled by the computer operator. This problem is particularly difficult in small companies.

## Internal Control for Cash

Describe internal control procedures to protect cash received from cash sales, cash received through the mail, and cash disbursements.
(L. O. 2)

A good system of internal control for cash should provide adequate procedures for protecting both cash receipts and cash disbursements. In the procedures, three basic principles should always be observed. First, there should be a separation of duties so that the people responsible for handling cash and for its custody are not the same people who keep the cash records. Second, all cash receipts should be deposited in the bank, intact, each day. Third, all payments should be made by check. The one exception to the last principle is that small disbursements may be made in cash from a petty cash fund. Petty cash funds are discussed later in this chapter.

The reason for the first principle is that a division of duties necessitates collusion between two or more people if cash is to be embezzled and the theft concealed in the accounting records. The second, requiring that all receipts be deposited intact each day, prevents an employee from making personal use of the money for a few days before depositing it. And if all receipts are deposited intact and all payments are made by check, the bank records provide a separate and external record of all cash transactions. These bank records are used to confirm the accuracy of the company's own records.

The exact procedures used to achieve control over cash vary from company to company. They depend on such things as company size, number of employees, cash sources, and so on. Therefore, you should understand that the procedures described in the following paragraphs are only illustrative of some that are used.

### Cash from Cash Sales

Cash sales should be rung up on a cash register at the time of each sale. To help ensure that correct amounts are rung up, each register should be placed so that customers can see the amounts rung up. Also, the clerks should be required to ring up each sale before wrapping the merchandise. Finally, each cash register should be designed to provide a permanent, locked-in record of each transaction. In some cases, this is accomplished by a direct connection between the register and a computer. The computer is programmed to accept cash register transactions and enter them in the accounting records. In other cases, the register prints a record of each transaction on a paper tape that is locked inside the register.

As we previously stated, custody over cash should be separated from record-keeping for cash. For cash sales, this separation begins with the cash register. The salesclerk who has access to the cash in the register should not have access to its locked-in record. At the end of each day, the salesclerk is usually required to count the cash in the register and to turn the cash and its count over to an employee in the cashier's office. The employee in the cashier's office, like the salesclerk, has access to the cash and should not have access to the computerized accounting records (or the register tape if one is used). A third employee, commonly from the accounting department, examines the computerized record of register transactions (or the register tape) and compares its daily total with the total cash receipts reported by the cashier's office. If a register tape is used, it becomes the basis for the journal entry to record cash sales. The accounting department employee has access to the records for cash but does not have access to the actual cash. The salesclerk and the employee from the cashier's office do not have access to the accounting records and cannot take any cash without the shortage being revealed.

### Cash Received through the Mail

Control of cash that comes in through the mail begins with the person who opens the mail. Preferably, two people should be present when the mail is opened. One of those should make a list in triplicate of the money received. The list should give each sender's name, the purpose for which the money was sent, and the amount. One copy of the list is sent to the cashier with the money. The second copy goes to the bookkeeper. The third copy is kept by the mail clerk. The cashier deposits the money in the bank, and the bookkeeper records the amounts received in the accounting records. Then, if the bank balance is reconciled (discussed later) by a fourth person, errors or fraud by the mail clerk, the cashier, or the bookkeeper will be detected. They will be detected because the cash deposited and the records of three people must agree. Furthermore, fraud is impossible, unless there is collusion. The mail clerk must report all receipts or customers will question their account balances. The cashier must deposit all receipts because the bank balance must agree with the bookkeeper's cash balance. The bookkeeper and the person who reconciles the bank balance do not have access to cash and, therefore, have no opportunity to withhold any.

### Cash Disbursements

It is important to gain control over cash from sales and cash received through the mail. However, most large embezzlements do not involve cash receipts. More often, they are accomplished through the payment of fictitious invoices. Therefore, procedures for controlling cash disbursements are equally as important and sometimes more important than those for cash receipts.

To control cash disbursements, all disbursements should be made by check, except very small payments from petty cash. If authority to sign checks is delegated to some person other than the business owner, that person should not have access to the accounting records. This helps prevent fraudulent disbursements that are concealed in the accounting records.

In a small business, the owner-manager usually signs checks and normally knows from personal contact that the items to be paid for were actually received. However, this is impossible in a large business. In a large business, internal control procedures must be substituted for personal contact. The procedures are designed to tell the check-signer that the obligations for which the checks were written are proper obligations, properly incurred, and should be paid. Often these procedures take the form of a **voucher system.**

## The Voucher System and Control

A voucher system helps gain control over cash disbursements. Such a system: (1) permits only authorized individuals to incur obligations that will result in cash disbursements; (2) establishes procedures for incurring such obligations and for their verification, approval, and recording; (3) permits checks to be issued only in payment of properly verified, approved, and recorded obligations; and (4) requires that every obligation be recorded at the time it is incurred and every purchase be treated as an independent transaction, complete in itself. This is required even though a number of purchases may be made from the same company during a month or other billing period.

When a voucher system is used, control over cash disbursements begins with the incurrence of obligations that will result in cash disbursements. Only specified departments and individuals are authorized to incur such obligations, and the kind each may incur is limited. For example, in a large store, only the purchasing department may incur obligations by purchasing merchandise. However, to gain control, the purchasing, receiving, and paying procedures are divided among several departments. These are the departments that request the purchases, the purchasing department, the receiving department, and the accounting department. To coordinate and control the responsibilities of these departments, several different business papers are used as shown in Illustration 7–2. An explanation of each paper will show you how large companies gain control over cash disbursements for merchandise purchases.

### Purchase Requisition

In a large store, the department managers cannot be allowed to place orders directly with supply sources. If each manager could deal directly with suppliers, the amount of merchandise purchased and the resulting liabilities could not be controlled. Therefore, to gain control over purchases and resulting liabilities, department managers are commonly required to place all orders through the purchasing department. In such cases, the function of the selling department managers in the purchasing procedure is to inform the purchasing department of their needs. Each manager performs this function by preparing in triplicate and signing a business paper called a **purchase requisition.** On the requisition, the manager lists the merchandise needs of his or her department.

**Illustration 7–2**
**Flow of business papers related to purchases when a voucher system is used**

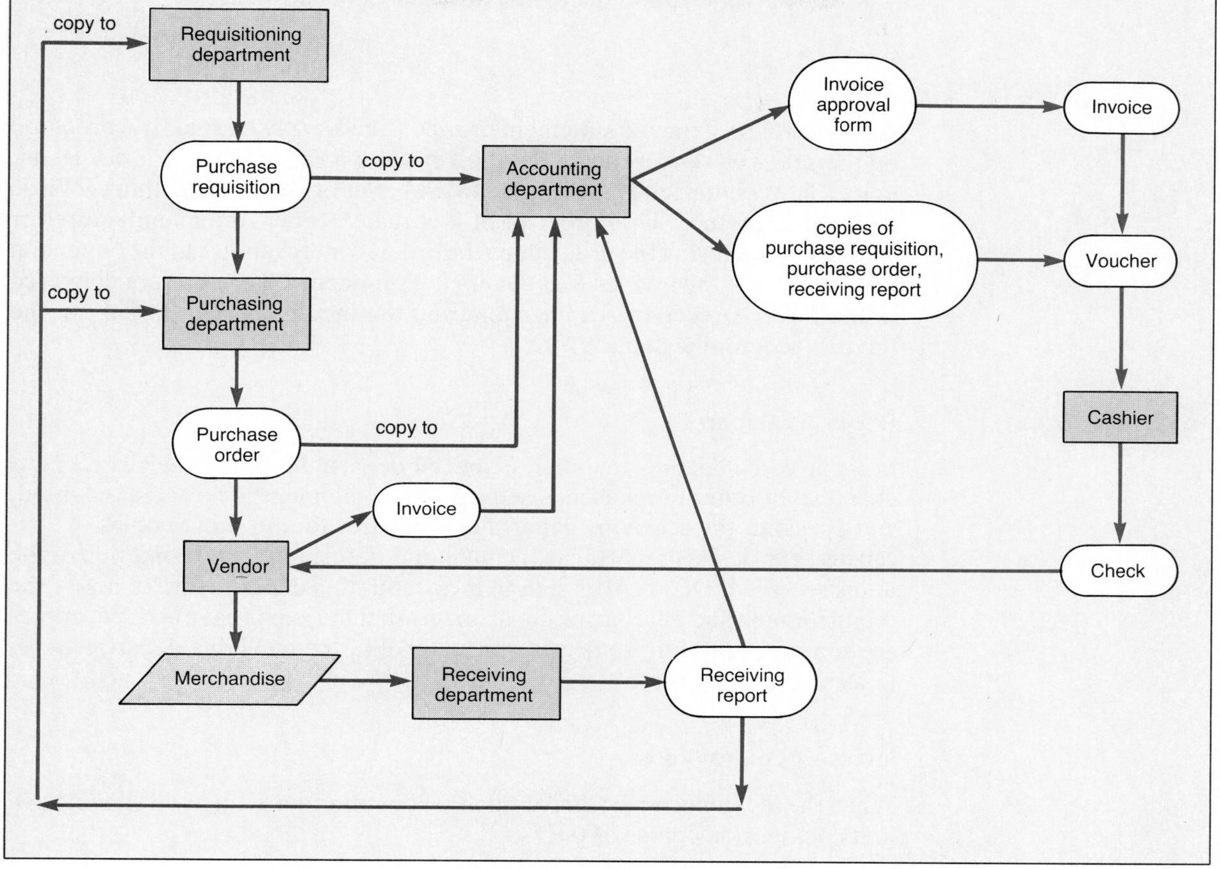


The original and a duplicate copy of the purchase requisition are sent to the purchasing department. The requisitioning department keeps the third copy as a check on the purchasing department.

### Purchase Order

A **purchase order** is a business form used by the purchasing department to place an order with a manufacturer or wholesaler. It authorizes the supplier to ship the merchandise ordered. When a purchase requisition is received from a selling department, the purchasing department prepares four or more copies of the purchase order. The copies are distributed as follows:

**Copy 1,** the original copy, is sent to the supplier as a request to purchase and as authority to ship the merchandise listed.

**Copy 2,** with a copy of the purchase requisition attached, is sent to the accounting department where it will ultimately be used in approving the invoice of the purchase for payment.

**Copy 3** is sent to the department issuing the requisition to acknowledge the requisition and tell the action taken.

**Copy 4** is retained on file by the purchasing department.

### Invoice

An **invoice** is an itemized statement of goods that have been sold. It is prepared by the seller or **vendor**; and from the vendor's point of view, it is a sales invoice. The vendor sends the invoice to the buyer or **vendee**, who thinks of it as a purchase invoice. Upon receipt of a purchase order, the manufacturer or wholesaler receiving the order ships the ordered merchandise to the buyer and mails a copy of the invoice that covers the shipment. The goods are delivered to the buyer's receiving department, and the invoice is sent directly to the buyer's accounting department.

### Receiving Report

Most large companies maintain a special department that receives all merchandise or other purchased assets. As each shipment is received, counted, and checked, the receiving department prepares four or more copies of a **receiving report.** This report lists the quantity, description, and condition of the items received. One copy is sent to the accounting department. To notify the requisitioning and purchasing departments that the goods have arrived, copies are sent to each of those departments. Finally, the receiving department retains a copy in its files.

### Invoice Approval Form

When the receiving report arrives in the accounting department, it should have in its possession copies of the—

1. Requisition listing the items that were to be ordered.
2. Purchase order that lists the merchandise actually ordered.
3. Invoice showing quantity, description, unit price, and total of the goods shipped by the seller.
4. Receiving report that lists quantity and condition of the items received.

With the information on these papers, the accounting department is in a position to approve the invoice for entry on the books and to approve ultimate payment. In approving the invoice, the accounting department checks and compares the information on all the papers. To facilitate the checking procedure and to ensure that no step is omitted, an **invoice approval form** is commonly used. This form may be a separate business paper that is attached to the invoice, or the information shown in Illustration 7–3 may be stamped directly on the invoice with a rubber stamp.

As each step in the checking procedure is finished, the clerk making the check initials the invoice approval form. Initials in each space on the form indicate:

Illustration 7–3
**An invoice approval form**

| | |
|---|---|
| Purchase order number | ________ |
| Requisition check | ________ |
| Purchase order check | ________ |
| Receiving report check | ________ |
| Invoice check: | |
| Price approval | ________ |
| Calculations | ________ |
| Terms | ________ |
| Approved for payment: | ________ |

| | |
|---|---|
| 1. **Requisition check** . . . . . | The items on the invoice agree with the requisition and were requisitioned. |
| 2. **Purchase order check** . . . | The items on the invoice agree with the purchase order and were ordered. |
| 3. **Receiving report check** . . | The items on the invoice agree with the receiving report and were received. |
| 4. **Invoice check:** | |
| **Price approval** . . . . . | The invoice prices are the agreed prices. |
| **Calculations** . . . . . . | The invoice has no mathematical errors. |
| **Terms** . . . . . . . . . . | The terms are the agreed terms. |

### The Voucher

When a voucher system is used, after an invoice is checked and approved, a **voucher** is prepared. A voucher is a business paper on which a transaction is summarized, its correctness certified, and its recording and payment approved. Vouchers vary somewhat from company to company. However, in general, they are designed so that the invoice, bill, or other documents from which they are prepared are attached to and folded inside the voucher. This makes for ease in filing. The inside of a voucher is shown in Illustration 7–4, and the outside in Illustration 7–5. The preparation of a voucher requires only that a clerk enter the required information in the proper blank spaces on a voucher form. The information is taken from the invoice, and its supporting documents are attached to and folded inside the voucher. The voucher is then sent to the desk of the chief clerk or auditor who makes an additional check, approves the accounting distribution (the accounts to be debited), and approves the voucher for recording.

After a voucher is approved and recorded, it is filed until its due date, when it is sent to the office of the company cashier or other disbursing office for payment. Here the person responsible for issuing checks depends on the approved voucher and its signed supporting documents to verify that the obliga-

**Illustration 7–4**
**Inside of a voucher**

VALLEY SUPPLY COMPANY Voucher No. *767*
Eugene, Oregon

Date *Oct. 1, 19--*
Pay to *A. B. Seay Wholesale Company*
City *Salem* State *Oregon*

For the following: (attach all invoices and supporting papers)

| Date of invoice | Terms | Invoice Number and Other Details | Amount |
|---|---|---|---|
| *Sept. 30, 19--* | *2/10, n/60* | *Invoice No. C-11756* | *800.00* |
| | | *Less Discount* | *16.00* |
| | | *Net Amount Payable* | *784.00* |

Payment approved
*N.O. Neal*
Auditor

**Illustration 7–5**
**Outside of a voucher**

ACCOUNTING DISTRIBUTION

| Account Debited | Amount |
|---|---|
| Purchases | *800.00* |
| Transportation-In | |
| Store Supplies | |
| Office Supplies | |
| Sales Salaries | |
| | |
| | |
| | |
| | |
| | |
| Total Vouch. Pay. Cr. | *800.00* |

Voucher No. *767*

Due Date *October 6, 19--*

Pay to *A. B. Seay Wholesale Co.*
City *Salem*
State *Oregon*

Summary of Charges:
Total Charges *800.00*
Discount *16.00*
Net Payment *784.00*

Record of Payment:
Paid
Check No.

tion was properly incurred and should be paid. For example, the purchase requisition and purchase order attached to the voucher confirm that the purchase was authorized. The receiving report shows that the items were received, and the invoice approval form verifies that the invoice was checked for errors. As a result, there is little chance for fraud, unless all the documents were stolen and the signatures forged, or there was collusion.

## The Voucher System and Expenses

Under a voucher system, obligations should be approved for payment and recorded as liabilities when they are incurred, or as soon as possible thereafter. This includes all expenses. For example, when a company receives the monthly telephone bill, the charges, including long-distance calls, should be examined for correctness. A voucher is then prepared, and the telephone bill is attached to and folded inside the voucher. The voucher is then recorded, and a check is issued in its payment, or the voucher is filed for payment at a later date.

The requirement that expenses be approved and recorded when incurred helps ensure that every expense payment is approved when information for its approval is available. However, invoices or statements (bills) for such things as equipment repairs sometimes are not received until weeks after the work is done. If no record of the repairs exists, it is difficult at the time to determine whether the invoice or bill is a correct statement of the amount owed. Also, if no records exist, it is possible for a dishonest employee to arrange with an outsider for more than one payment of an obligation, or for payment of excessive amounts, or for payment for goods and services not received, all with kickbacks to the dishonest employee.

## Recording Vouchers

Normally, a company large enough to use a voucher system will use a computer in recording its transactions. For this reason and also because the primary purpose of this discussion is to describe the control techniques of a voucher system, a manual system of recording vouchers is not described here. However, such a system is described in Appendix D at the end of this chapter.

## The Petty Cash Fund

Explain the operation of a petty cash fund and be able to journalize entries to record petty cash fund transactions.
(L. O. 3)

In controlling cash disbursements, a basic principle is to require that all disbursements be made by check. However, an exception to this rule is made for petty cash disbursements. Every business must make many small payments for items such as postage, express charges, telegrams, and small items of supplies. If such payments are made by check, many checks for immaterial amounts are written. This is both time-consuming and expensive. Therefore, to avoid writing checks for small amounts, you need to establish a petty cash fund and use the money in this fund to make small payments such as those listed above.

To establish a petty cash fund, you should estimate the total amount of small payments likely to be made during a short period, usually not more than a month. Then, a check is drawn for an amount slightly in excess of this estimate. You record the check with a debit to the Petty Cash account and a credit to Cash. The check is cashed, and the money is turned over to a member of the

**Illustration 7–6**
**A petty cash receipt**

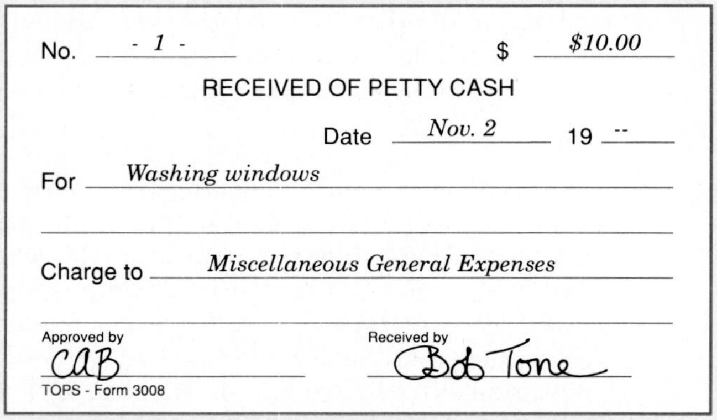
No. - 1 - $ $10.00

RECEIVED OF PETTY CASH

Date Nov. 2 19 --

For Washing windows

Charge to Miscellaneous General Expenses

Approved by CAB Received by Bob Tone

TOPS - Form 3008

office staff who is called the *petty cashier*. This person is responsible for keeping the petty cash and for making payments from this fund.

The petty cashier usually keeps the petty cash in a locked box in the office safe. As each disbursement is made, a *petty cash receipt* (see Illustration 7–6) is signed by the person receiving payment and is placed with the remaining money in the petty cashbox. Under this system, the petty cashbox should always contain paid petty cash receipts and money equal to the amount of the fund.

Each disbursement reduces the money and increases the sum of the receipts in the petty cashbox. When the money is nearly gone, the fund is reimbursed. To reimburse the fund, the petty cashier presents the receipts for petty cash payments to the company cashier. The company cashier stamps each receipt "paid" so that it may not be reused, retains the receipts, and gives the petty cashier a check for their sum. When this check is cashed and the proceeds returned to the petty cashbox, the money in the box is restored to its original amount, and the fund is ready to begin a new cycle of operations.

At the time a check is written to reimburse the petty cash fund, you should sort the paid petty cash receipts into groups according to the expense or other accounts to be debited in recording payments from the fund. Each group is then totaled, and the totals are used in making the reimbursing entry.

## Petty Cash Fund Illustrated

To avoid writing numerous checks for small amounts, a company established a petty cash fund on November 1, designating one of its office clerks, Ned Fox, petty cashier. A $75 check was drawn, cashed, and the proceeds turned over to the clerk. The entry to record the check is shown in Illustration 7–7. The effect of the entry was to transfer $75 from the regular Cash account to the Petty Cash account.

Notice that the entry transfers $75 from the regular Cash account to the Petty Cash account. After the petty cash fund is established, the Petty Cash account is not debited or credited again unless the size of the fund is changed.

**Illustration 7–7**
**Entry to establish the petty cash fund**

**Cash Disbursements Journal**

| Date | | Ch. No. | Payee | Account Debited | PR | Other Accts. Debit | Cash Credit |
|---|---|---|---|---|---|---|---|
| Nov. | 1 | 58 | Ned Fox, Petty Cashier | Petty Cash . . . . . . . . . . | | 75.00 | 75.00 |

**Illustration 7–8**
**Summary of petty cash payments**

| | | |
|---|---|---|
| Miscellaneous general expenses: | | |
| Nov. 2, washing windows . . . . . . . . . . . . | $10.00 | |
| Nov. 17, washing windows . . . . . . . . . . . . | 10.00 | |
| Nov. 27, typewriter repairs . . . . . . . . . . . . | 26.50 | $46.50 |
| Transportation-in: | | |
| Nov. 5, delivery of merchandise purchased . . | $ 6.75 | |
| Nov. 20, delivery of merchandise purchased . . | 8.30 | 15.05 |
| Delivery expense: | | |
| Nov. 18, customer's package delivered . . . . . | | 5.00 |
| Office supplies: | | |
| Nov. 15, purchased paper clips . . . . . . . . . | | 4.75 |
| Total . . . . . . . . . . . . . . . . . . . . . . . . | | $71.30 |

If the fund is exhausted and reimbursements occur too often, the fund should be increased. To record an increase in the size of the fund, debit Petty Cash and credit Cash for the amount of the increase. If the fund is too large, some of the money in the fund should be redeposited in the checking account. Such a reduction in the fund is recorded with a debit to Cash and a credit to Petty Cash.

During November, Ned Fox, the petty cashier, made several payments from the petty cash fund. Each time he asked the person who received payment to sign a receipt. Then, on November 27, after making a $26.50 payment for repairs to an office typewriter, Mr. Fox realized there was not enough cash in the fund for another payment. Therefore, he summarized and totaled the petty cash receipts as shown in Illustration 7–8. The summary and the petty cash receipts were then given to the company cashier in exchange for a $71.30 check to reimburse the fund. Mr. Fox cashed the check, put the $71.30 proceeds in the petty cashbox, and was then ready to make additional payments from the fund.

The reimbursing check was recorded in the Cash Disbursements Journal with the second entry of Illustration 7–9. Information for this entry came from the petty cashier's summary of payments. Note that the debits in the entry record the petty cash payments. Such an entry is necessary to get the debits into the accounts. Therefore, even if the petty cash fund is not low on funds, it

Illustration 7–9
**Entry to reimburse the petty cash fund**

**Cash Disbursements Journal**

| Date | | Ch. No. | Payee | Account Debited | PR | Other Accts. Debit | Cash Credit |
|---|---|---|---|---|---|---|---|
| Nov. | 1 | 58 | Ned Fox, Petty Cashier | Petty Cash . . . . . . . . . | | 75.00 | 75.00 |
| Nov. | 27 | 106 | Ned Fox, Petty Cashier | Transportation-In . . . . . | | 15.05 | |
| | | | | Miscellaneous General Expenses . . . . . . . . | | 46.50 | |
| | | | | Delivery Expense . . . . . | | 5.00 | |
| | | | | Office Supplies . . . . . . | | 4.75 | 71.30 |

should be reimbursed at the end of each accounting period. Otherwise, the financial statements will show an overstated petty cash asset and understated expenses and assets that were paid for out of petty cash.

Occasionally, a petty cashier will forget to get a receipt for a payment. Then, by the time the fund is reimbursed, the petty cashier will have forgotten the expenditure. This causes the fund to be short. If, for whatever reason, the petty cash fund is short at reimbursement time, the shortage is recorded as an expense in the reimbursing entry with a debit to the **Cash Over and Short account.**

## Cash Over and Short

Even though a cashier is careful in making change, customers are sometimes given too much change or are shortchanged. As a result, at the end of a day, the actual cash from a cash register is commonly not equal to the cash sales "rung up" on the register. For example, assume that a cash register shows cash sales of $550 but the actual count of cash in the register is counted as $555. The entry in general journal form to record the cash sales and the overage is:

| | | | | |
|---|---|---|---|---|
| Nov. | 23 | Cash . . . . . . . . . . . . . . . . . . . . . . . . . . . . | 555.00 | |
| | | Cash Over and Short . . . . . . . . . . . . . . . . . | | 5.00 |
| | | Sales . . . . . . . . . . . . . . . . . . . . . . . . . . | | 550.00 |
| | | Day's cash sales and overage. | | |

On the other hand, if there is a shortage of cash in the register on the next day, the entry to record cash sales and the shortage would look like the following:

| | | | | |
|---|---|---|---|---|
| Nov. | 24 | Cash . . . . . . . . . . . . . . . . . . . . . . . . . . . . | 621.00 | |
| | | Cash Over and Short . . . . . . . . . . . . . . . . . . . . . | 4.00 | |
| | | Sales . . . . . . . . . . . . . . . . . . . . . . . . . . | | 625.00 |
| | | Day's cash sales and shortage. | | |

## AS A MATTER OF ETHICS

Nancy Tucker is an internal auditor for a large corporation and is in the process of making surprise counts of several $100 petty cash funds in various offices in the headquarters building. She arrived at the office of one of the fund custodians shortly before lunch while he was on the telephone. Nancy explained the purpose of her visit, and the custodian asked politely that she come back after lunch so that he could finish the business he was conducting by long distance. She agreed and returned about 1:30. The custodian opened the petty cash box and showed her five new $20 bills with consecutive serial numbers. Would you suggest that the auditor take any further action or comment on these events in her report to management?

Normally, customers are more likely to report being shortchanged than being given too much change. As a result, by the end of each accounting period, the Cash Over and Short account usually has a debit balance. If so, the balance represents an expense. You may show this expense on the income statement as a separate item in the general and administrative expense section. Or, if the amount is small, you may combine it with other small expenses and report them as a single item called miscellaneous expenses. If Cash Over and Short has a credit balance at the end of the period, it usually is shown on the income statement as part of the item, miscellaneous revenues.

### Reconciling the Bank Balance

Explain why the bank balance and the book balance of cash are reconciled and be able to prepare such a reconciliation. (L. O. 4)

At least once every month, banks send each commercial depositor a bank statement that shows the activity in the depositor's account during the month. Different banks use a variety of formats for their bank statements. However, all of them include in one place or another: (1) the balance of the depositor's account at the beginning of the month, (2) deposits and any other amounts added to the account, (3) checks and any other amounts deducted from the account, and (4) the account balance at the end of the month, according to the records of the bank. Illustration 7–10 shows a typical bank statement.

Note that the changes in the account are summarized in part A of Illustration 7–10. Specific debits and credits to the account (other than canceled checks) are listed in part B. All canceled checks are listed in numerical order in part C, and the daily account balances are shown in part D.

Banks usually mail the bank statement to the depositor each month. With the statement are the depositor's **canceled checks** and any debit or credit memoranda that have affected the account. These checks are the ones that the bank has paid during the month. They are called canceled checks because they have been stamped or perforated to show that they were paid. Other deductions that may appear on the bank statement include withdrawals through automatic teller machines (ATM withdrawals) and periodic payments arranged in advance by the depositor. Also, the bank may deduct from the depositor's account amounts for service charges and fees, items deposited that are uncollectible, and amounts to correct previous errors. The bank notifies the depositor of each such deduction with a debit memorandum. A copy of each memorandum is sent with the monthly statement.

In addition to deposits made by the depositor, the bank may add amounts to the depositor's account. Examples of additions would be amounts the bank

**Illustration 7–10**
**A typical bank statement**

First City National Bank of Austin P.O. BOX 1727 AUSTIN, TEXAS 78767 512/473-4343

| 01 | ACCOUNT NUMBER | DATE OF THIS STATEMENT | DATE OF LAST STATEMENT | PAGE NO. |
|---|---|---|---|---|
| ☐ | 494 504 2 | 10/31/-- | 9/30/-- | 1 |

FIRSTCITY™
First City National Bank of Austin
Member FDIC

VALLEY COMPANY
1300 FALCON LEDGE
AUSTIN, TEXAS 78746

**A**

| | |
|---|---|
| BALANCE OF PREVIOUS STATEMENT ON 9/30/-- | 1,609.58 |
| 5 DEPOSITS AND OTHER CREDITS TOTALING | 1,155.00 |
| 10 CHECKS AND OTHER DEBITS TOTALING | 723.00 |
| SERVICE CHARGE AMOUNT | .00 |
| INTEREST AMOUNT AT 5.2500% | 8.42 |
| CURRENT BALANCE AS OF THIS STATEMENT | 2,050.00 |
| AVERAGE BALANCE AS OF THIS STATEMENT | 1,924.95 |
| TOTAL INTEREST PAID TO DATE | 124.00 |

**B**

CHECKING ACCOUNT TRANSACTIONS

| DATE | AMOUNT | TRANSACTION DESCRIPTION |
|---|---|---|
| 10/02 | 240.00+ | DEPOSIT |
| 10/09 | 180.00+ | DEPOSIT |
| 10/12 | 23.00− | CHARGE FOR PRINTING NEW CHECKS |
| 10/15 | 100.00+ | DEPOSIT |
| 10/16 | 150.00+ | DEPOSIT |
| 10/23 | 485.00+ | NOTE COLLECTION LESS FEE |
| 10/25 | 30.00− | NSF CHECK AND NSF CHARGE |
| 10/31 | 8.42+ | INTEREST PAID |

**C**

| DATE | CHECK NO | AMOUNT | DATE | CHECK NO | AMOUNT |
|---|---|---|---|---|---|
| 10/03 | 119 | 55.00 | 10/16 | 123 | 25.00 |
| 10/19 | 120 | 200.00 | 10/23 | 125* | 10.00 |
| 10/10 | 121 | 120.00 | 10/26 | 127* | 50.00 |
| 10/14 | 122 | 75.00 | 10/29 | 128 | 135.00 |

*INDICATES A SKIP IN CHECK NUMBER SEQUENCE

**D**

DAILY BALANCE SUMMARY

| DATE | BALANCE | DATE | BALANCE | DATE | BALANCE |
|---|---|---|---|---|---|
| 10/01 | 1,609.58 | 10/12 | 1,831.58 | 10/23 | 2,256.58 |
| 10/02 | 1,849.58 | 10/14 | 1,756.58 | 10/25 | 2,226.58 |
| 10/03 | 1,794.58 | 10/15 | 1,856.58 | 10/26 | 2,176.58 |
| 10/09 | 1,974.58 | 10/16 | 1,981.58 | 10/29 | 2,041.58 |
| 10/10 | 1,854.58 | 10/19 | 1,781.58 | 10/31 | 2,050.00 |

FOR QUESTIONS ON DIRECT DEPOSITS, PLEASE CALL 473-4522, BETWEEN 9:00–4:00 MONDAY-FRIDAY OR WRITE P.O. BOX 1727, AUSTIN, TEXAS 78767.

has collected for the depositor and corrections of previous errors. A credit memorandum is used to notify the depositor of any such additions.

Another addition might be for interest the depositor has earned. Some checking accounts pay the depositor interest based on the average cash balance maintained in the account. The bank calculates the amount of interest earned and credits it to the depositor's account each month. In Illustration 7–10, note that the bank credited $8.42 of interest to the account of Valley Company. The methods used to calculate interest are discussed in the next chapter.

When all receipts are deposited intact and all payments, other than petty cash payments, are drawn from the checking account, the bank statement is a device for proving the accuracy of the depositor's cash records. The proof normally begins by preparing a **bank reconciliation**.

### Need for Reconciling the Bank Balance

Normally, when the bank statement arrives, the balance of cash as shown by the statement does not agree with the balance in the depositor's accounting records. Therefore, in order to prove the accuracy of both the depositor's records and those of the bank, you should **reconcile** the two balances. To reconcile the balances, you must explain or account for the differences between the two balances.

Numerous factors may cause the bank statement balance to differ from the depositor's book balance of cash. Some are:

1. **Outstanding checks.** These are checks that were drawn by the depositor, deducted on the depositor's records, sent to the payees, but have not reached the bank for payment and deduction.
2. **Unrecorded deposits.** Companies often make deposits at the end of each business day, after the bank is closed. These deposits are made in the bank's night depository and are not recorded by the bank until the next business day. Therefore, if a deposit is placed in the night depository the last day of the month, it does not appear on the bank statement for that month.
3. **Charges for uncollectible items and for service.** Sometimes, a company deposits a customer's check that is found to be uncollectible. Usually, the problem is nonsufficient funds in the customer's account to cover the check. Thus, the check is called a nonsufficient funds (NSF) check. The bank first credits the depositor's account for the full amount of the deposit. Then, when the bank learns that the check is uncollectible, it debits the depositor's account for the amount of the check. Also, the bank may charge the depositor a fee for processing the NSF check. The bank notifies the depositor of each such deduction with a debit memorandum. If the item is material in amount, the memorandum is mailed to the depositor on the day of the deduction. Although each deduction should be recorded on the day the memorandum is received, sometimes an entry is not made until the bank reconciliation is prepared. Also, memoranda for small amounts may not be sent to the depositor until the bank statement is mailed.

Other charges to a depositor's account that a bank might report on the bank statement include the printing of new checks. Also, a monthly service charge may be made for processing the checks of the depositor.

4. **Credits for collections and for interest.** Banks often act as collection agents for their depositors, collecting promissory notes and other items. When the bank collects an item, the bank usually deducts a small fee and adds the net proceeds to the depositor's account. It then sends a credit memorandum as notification of the transaction. As soon as the memorandum is received, it should be recorded. However, these items may remain unrecorded until the time of the bank reconciliation.

   Many bank accounts earn interest on the average cash balance in the account during the month. If an account earns interest, the bank statement will include a credit for the amount earned during the past month.
5. **Errors.** Regardless of care and systems of internal control for automatic error detection, both the banks and depositors make errors. Errors by the bank may not be discovered until the depositor completes the bank reconciliation. Also, the depositor's errors often are not discovered until the balance is reconciled.

### Steps in Reconciling the Bank Balance

The steps in reconciling the bank balance are the following:

1. Compare deposits listed on the bank statement with deposits shown in the accounting records. Note any discrepancies and discover which is correct. List any errors or unrecorded items.
2. Examine all other credits to the account shown on the bank statement and determine whether each one was recorded in the books. These items include collections by the bank, correction of previous bank statement errors, and interest earned by the depositor. List any unrecorded items.
3. Compare the list of canceled checks on the bank statement with the actual checks returned with the statement. For each check, make sure that the correct amount was deducted by the bank and that the returned check was properly charged to the company's account. Note any discrepancies or errors.
4. Compare the outstanding checks listed on the previous month's bank reconciliation with the canceled checks listed on the bank statement. Prepare a list of any checks that remain outstanding at the end of the current month.
5. Compare the canceled checks listed on the bank statement with the checks recorded in the books since the last reconciliation. To make this process easier, the bank statement normally lists canceled checks in the same numerical order as the checks are numbered. List any outstanding checks. Although companies with reasonable internal controls would rarely if ever write a check without recording it, an

**Illustration 7–11**
**A typical bank reconciliation**

**VALLEY COMPANY**
**Bank Reconciliation**
**October 31, 1990**

| | | | | | |
|---|---|---|---|---|---|
| Book balance of cash . . . . . | | $1,404.58 | Bank statement balance . . . . | | $2,050.00 |
| Add: | | | Add: | | |
| Proceeds of note less collection fee . . . . . . . . | $485.00 | | Deposit of 10/31 . . . . . . . | | 145.00 |
| Interest earned . . . . . . . . | 8.42 | 493.42 | | | |
| | | $1,898.00 | | | $2,195.00 |
| Deduct: | | | Deduct: | | |
| NSF check plus service charge . . . . . . . | $ 30.00 | | Outstanding checks: | | |
| | | | No. 124 . . . . . . . . . . | $150.00 | |
| Check printing charge . . . . | 23.00 | 53.00 | No. 126 . . . . . . . . . . | 200.00 | 350.00 |
| | | $1,845.00 | | | $1,845.00 |

individual may occasionally write a check and fail to record it in the books. List any canceled checks that are unrecorded in the books.

6. Examine all other debits to the account as shown on the bank statement and determine whether each one was recorded in the books. These include bank charges for newly printed checks, NSF checks, stop payment orders, and monthly service charges.
7. Prepare a reconciliation of the bank statement balance with the book balance of cash. Such a reconciliation is shown in Illustration 7–11.
8. Determine if any debits or credits appearing on the bank statement are unrecorded in the books. Make journal entries to record them.

## Illustration of a Bank Reconciliation

To illustrate a bank reconciliation, assume that in preparing to reconcile its bank balance of October 31, Valley Company discovered the following items. The bank balance as shown by the bank statement was $2,050. However, the cash balance according to the accounting records was $1,404.58. A $145 deposit, placed in the bank's night depository on October 31, was unrecorded by the bank at the time the bank statement was mailed. With the bank statement was a credit memorandum showing that the bank had collected a note receivable for the company on October 23. The note's proceeds of $500 less a $15 collection fee were credited to the company's account. The bank statement also showed a credit of $8.42 for interest earned on the average cash balance in the account. Neither the collection of the note nor the interest had been recorded on the company's books.

A comparison of canceled checks with the company's books showed that two checks were outstanding. Check No. 124 for $150 and Check No. 126 for $200 were outstanding and unpaid by the bank. Other debits on the bank statement that had not been recorded on the books included: (1) a $23 debit memorandum for checks printed by the bank; and (2) an NSF (nonsufficient funds) check for $20 plus related processing fee of $10. The NSF check had been received from a customer, Frank Jones, on October 16, and had been included in that day's deposit.

Illustration 7–11 shows the bank reconciliation that reflects the above items.

A bank reconciliation helps locate any errors made by either the bank or the depositor. It discloses any items that have been entered on the company's books but have not come to the bank's attention. Also, it discloses items that should be recorded on the company's books but are unrecorded on the date of the reconciliation. For example, in Valley Company's reconciliation, the reconciled cash balance, $1,845, is the true cash balance. However, at the time of the reconciliation, Valley Company's accounting records show a $1,404.58 book balance. Therefore, entries must be made to adjust the book balance, increasing it to the true cash balance. This requires four entries. The first is:

| | | | | |
|---|---|---|---|---|
| Nov. | 2 | Cash | 485.00 | |
| | | Collection Expense | 15.00 | |
| | | Notes Receivable | | 500.00 |
| | | To record the collection fee and proceeds of a note collected by the bank. | | |

This entry records the net proceeds of Valley Company's note receivable which had been collected by the bank, the expense of having the bank perform that service, and the reduction in the Notes Receivable account.

The second entry records the interest credited to Valley Company's account by the bank. Interest earned is a revenue, and the entry recognizes both the revenue and the related increase in Cash. As mentioned earlier, interest calculations are discussed in the next chapter. The entry is:

| | | | | |
|---|---|---|---|---|
| Nov. | 2 | Cash | 8.42 | |
| | | Interest Earned | | 8.42 |
| | | To record interest earned on the average cash balance maintained in the checking account. | | |

The third entry is:

| | | | | |
|---|---|---|---|---|
| Nov. | 2 | Accounts Receivable—Frank Jones | 30.00 | |
| | | Cash | | 30.00 |
| | | To charge Frank Jones's account for his NSF check and for the bank's fee. | | |

This entry records the NSF check that was returned as uncollectible. The $20 check was received from Jones in payment of his account and was deposited as cash. The bank, unable to collect the check, charged $10 for handling the NSF check and deducted $30 from the Valley Company account. Therefore, the company must reverse the entry made when the check was received and also record the $10 processing fee. Valley Company charged the $10 fee to Jones's account and will try to collect the entire $30 from Jones.

The fourth entry debits Miscellaneous General Expenses for the check printing charge. The entry is:

| | | | | |
|---|---|---|---|---|
| Nov. | 2 | Miscellaneous General Expense . . . . . . . . . . . . . . . | 23.00 | |
| | | Cash . . . . . . . . . . . . . . . . . . . . . . . . . . . | | 23.00 |
| | | Check printing charge. | | |

## Other Internal Control Procedures

Tell how recording invoices at net amounts helps gain control over cash discounts taken and be able to account for invoices recorded at net amounts. (L. O. 5)

Internal control procedures apply to every phase of a company's operations from purchases through sales, cash receipts, cash disbursements, and the control of plant assets. Many of these procedures are discussed in later chapters. However, a way that a company can gain control over purchases discounts is discussed here, and the technique is illustrated below.

Recall that entries like the following have been used to record the receipt and payment of an invoice for merchandise purchased.

| | | | | |
|---|---|---|---|---|
| Oct. | 2 | Purchases . . . . . . . . . . . . . . . . . . . . . . . . . | 1,000.00 | |
| | | Accounts Payable . . . . . . . . . . . . . . . . . . . | | 1,000.00 |
| | | Purchased merchandise, terms 2/10, n/60. | | |
| | 12 | Accounts Payable . . . . . . . . . . . . . . . . . . . . . . | 1,000.00 | |
| | | Purchases Discounts . . . . . . . . . . . . . . . . . . | | 20.00 |
| | | Cash . . . . . . . . . . . . . . . . . . . . . . . . . . . | | 980.00 |
| | | Paid the invoice of October 2. | | |

These entries reflect the **gross method of recording purchases.** Thus, the invoice was recorded at its gross amount of $1,000. This is the way invoices are recorded in many companies. However, a better method is to record invoices at their **net** (after discount) amounts. To illustrate, a company that records invoices at net amounts purchased merchandise that had a $1,000 invoice price, terms 2/10, n/60. On receipt of the goods, the purchasing company deducted the offered $20 discount from the gross invoice amount and recorded the purchase with this debit and credit:

| | | | | |
|---|---|---|---|---|
| Oct. | 2 | Purchases . . . . . . . . . . . . . . . . . . . . . . . . . | 980.00 | |
| | | Accounts Payable . . . . . . . . . . . . . . . . . . . | | 980.00 |
| | | Purchased merchandise on credit. | | |

If the invoice for this purchase is paid within the discount period, the entry to record the payment has a debit to Accounts Payable and a credit to Cash for $980. However, if payment is not made within the discount period and the discount is *lost*, an entry like the following must be made either before or when the invoice is paid:

| | | | | |
|---|---|---|---|---|
| Dec. | 1 | Discounts Lost . . . . . . . . . . . . . . . . . . . . . . | 20.00 | |
| | | Accounts Payable . . . . . . . . . . . . . . . . . . . | | 20.00 |
| | | To record the discount lost. | | |

A check for the full $1,000 invoice amount is then drawn, recorded, and mailed to the creditor.

**Reporting discounts lost when the net method of recording purchases is used**

XYZ COMPANY
Income Statement
For Year Ended December 31, 1990

| | |
|---|---|
| Sales . . . . . . . . . . . . . . . . . . | $100,000 |
| Cost of goods sold . . . . . . . . . . | 60,000 |
| Gross profit from sales. . . . . . . . . | $ 40,000 |
| Operating expenses . . . . . . . . . . | 28,000 |
| Income from operations . . . . . . . . | $ 12,000 |
| Other revenues and expenses: | |
| Discounts lost. . . . . . . . . . . . . | (150) |
| Net income . . . . . . . . . . . . . . . | $ 11,850 |

### Advantage of the Net Method

When invoices are recorded at gross amounts, the amount of discounts taken is deducted from the balance of the Purchases account on the income statement to arrive at the cost of merchandise purchased. However, when invoices are recorded at gross amounts, the amount of any discounts that are lost does not appear in any account or on the income statement. Therefore, discounts lost may not come to the attention of management. On the other hand, when purchases are recorded at net amounts, the amount of discounts taken does not appear on the income statement. Instead, the amount of **discounts lost** is called to management's attention through the appearance on the income statement of an expense called discounts lost. This is shown in the condensed income statement of Illustration 7–12.

Of the two methods, recording invoices at their net amounts probably supplies management with the more valuable information, the amount of discounts lost through oversight, carelessness, or other cause. It also gives management better control over the work of the people responsible for taking cash discounts. If discounts are lost, someone must explain why. As a result, fewer discounts are lost through carelessness.

## Summary of the Chapter in Terms of Learning Objectives

**1.** Internal control procedures are designed to protect assets against theft or misuse, to promote operational efficiencies, and to encourage adherence to prescribed managerial policies. Principles of good internal control include having clearly established responsibilities, maintaining adequate records, insuring assets and bonding employees, separating record-keeping and custody over assets, dividing responsibilities for related transactions, using mechanical devices where practicable, and regularly performing independent reviews of the internal control practices.

**2.** To maintain control over cash, custody over the assets must be separated from record-keeping for cash. Also, all cash receipts should be deposited in the bank on a daily basis, and all payments, except for minor petty cash payments, should be made by check. A voucher system helps maintain control over cash disbursements.

**3.** The petty cashier, who should be a responsible employee, makes payments from the fund and obtains signed receipts for the payments. The Petty Cash account is debited when the fund is established or increased in size, and petty cash disbursements are recorded whenever the fund is replenished.

**4.** A bank reconciliation is performed to prove the accuracy of the depositor's and the bank's records. When the reconciliation is performed, the bank statement balance is adjusted for such items as outstanding checks and deposits made after banking hours on the day of the bank statement. The records of the depositor are adjusted for such items as service charges, collections the bank has made for the depositor, and interest earned on the average checking account balance.

**5.** When the net method of recording invoices is used, cash discounts lost are reported as an expense in the income statement. By comparison, when the gross method is used, discounts taken are reported as revenues. Therefore, the net method directs management's attention to instances where the company failed to take advantage of discounts.

## Demonstration Problem

Complete the following table for a bank reconciliation as of September 30. Place an "x" in the appropriate columns to indicate whether the item should be added to or deducted from the book or bank balance, or whether it should not appear on the reconciliation. If the book balance is to be adjusted, place a "Dr." or "Cr." in the Must Adjust column to indicate whether the Cash balance should be debited or credited.

| | Book Balance | | | Bank Balance | | Not Shown on the Reconciliation |
|---|---|---|---|---|---|---|
| | Add | Deduct | Must Adjust | Add | Deduct | |
| 1. Interest earned on the account. | | | | | | |
| 2. Deposit made on September 30 after the bank was closed. | | | | | | |
| 3. Checks that were outstanding on August 31 and that cleared the bank in September. | | | | | | |
| 4. NSF check from customer returned on September 15 but not recorded by the company. | | | | | | |
| 5. Checks written and mailed to payees on September 30. | | | | | | |

| | Book Balance | | | Bank Balance | | Not Shown on the Reconciliation |
|---|---|---|---|---|---|---|
| | Add | Deduct | Must Adjust | Add | Deduct | |
| 6. Deposit made on September 5 that was processed on September 8. | | | | | | |
| 7. Unrecorded withdrawal by owner using Automatic Teller Machine. | | | | | | |
| 8. Bank service charge. | | | | | | |
| 9. Checks written and mailed to payees on October 5. | | | | | | |
| 10. Check written by another depositor but charged against the company's account. | | | | | | |
| 11. Principal and interest collected by the bank but not recorded by the company. | | | | | | |
| 12. Special charge for collection of note in No. 11 on company's behalf. | | | | | | |
| 13. Check written against the account and cleared by the bank; erroneously omitted by the bookkeeper. | | | | | | |

## Solution to Demonstration Problem

| | Book Balance | | | Bank Balance | | Not Shown on the Reconciliation |
|---|---|---|---|---|---|---|
| | Add | Deduct | Must Adjust | Add | Deduct | |
| 1. Interest earned on the account. | x | | Dr. | | | |
| 2. Deposit made on September 30 after the bank was closed. | | | | x | | |
| 3. Checks that were outstanding on August 31 and that cleared the bank in September. | | | | | | x |

| | Book Balance | | | Bank Balance | | Not Shown on the Reconciliation |
|---|---|---|---|---|---|---|
| | Add | Deduct | Must Adjust | Add | Deduct | |
| 4. NSF check from customer returned on September 15 but not recorded by the company. | | x | Cr. | | | |
| 5. Checks written and mailed to payees on September 30. | | | | | x | |
| 6. Deposit made on September 5 that was processed on September 8. | | | | | | x |
| 7. Unrecorded withdrawal by owner using Automatic Teller Machine. | | x | Cr. | | | |
| 8. Bank service charge. | | x | Cr. | | | |
| 9. Checks written and mailed to payees on October 5. | | | | | | x |
| 10. Check written by another depositor but charged against the company's account. | | | | x | | |
| 11. Principal and interest collected by the bank but not recorded by the company. | x | | Dr. | | | |
| 12. Special charge for collection of note in No. 11 on company's behalf. | | x | Cr. | | | |
| 13. Check written against the account and cleared by the bank; erroneously omitted by the bookkeeper. | | x | Cr. | | | |

**Appendix D**

## RECORDING VOUCHERS, MANUAL SYSTEM

Explain the use of a Voucher Register and Check Register and prepare entries to record and pay liabilities when these registers are used in a manual accounting system.
(L. O. 7)

When a voucher system is in use, an account called Vouchers Payable replaces the Accounts Payable account described in previous chapters. And for every transaction that will result in a cash disbursement, a voucher is prepared and credited to this account. For example, when merchandise is purchased, the voucher covering the transaction is recorded with a debit to Purchases and a credit to Vouchers Payable. Likewise, when a plant asset is purchased or an

**Illustration D–1**
**A Voucher Register**

Page 32 Voucher

| Date 19— | | Voucher No. | Payee | When and How Paid Date | Check No. | Vouchers Payable Credit | Purchases Debit | Transportation-In Debit | |
|---|---|---|---|---|---|---|---|---|---|
| Oct. | 1 | 767 | A. B. Seay Co. | 10/6 | 733 | 800.00 | 800.00 | | 1 |
| | 1 | 768 | Daily Sentinel | 10/9 | 744 | 53.00 | | | 2 |
| | 2 | 769 | Seaboard Supply Co. | 10/12 | 747 | 235.00 | 155.00 | 10.00 | 3 |
| | 6 | 770 | George Smith | 10/6 | 734 | 85.00 | | | 4 |
| | 6 | 771 | Frank Jones | 10/6 | 735 | 95.00 | | | 5 |
| | 6 | 772 | George Roth | 10/6 | 736 | 95.00 | | | 6 |
| | 30 | 998 | First National Bank | 10/30 | 972 | 505.00 | | | 33 |
| | | | | | | | | | 34 |
| | 30 | 999 | Pacific Telephone Co. | 10/30 | 973 | 18.00 | | | 35 |
| | 31 | 1000 | Tarbell Wholesale Co. | | | 235.00 | 235.00 | | 36 |
| | 31 | 1001 | Office Equipment Co. | 10/31 | 974 | 195.00 | | | 37 |
| | 31 | | Totals | | | 5,079.00 | 2,435.00 | 156.00 | 38 |
| | | | | | | (213) | (511) | (514) | 39 |
| | | | | | | | | | 40 |
| | | | | | | | | | 41 |

expense is incurred, the voucher of the transaction is recorded with a debit to the proper plant asset or expense account and a credit to Vouchers Payable.

In a manual system, vouchers are recorded in a **Voucher Register** similar to Illustration D–1. Such a register has a Vouchers Payable Credit column and a number of debit columns. The exact debit columns vary from company to company, but merchandising concerns always provide a Purchases Debit column. Also, as long as space is available, special debit columns are provided for transactions that occur frequently. In addition, an Other Accounts Debit column is provided for transactions that do not occur often.

In recording vouchers in a register like that of Illustration D–1, all information about each voucher, other than information about its payment, is entered as soon as the voucher is approved for recording. The information as to payment date and the number of the paying check is entered later as each voucher is paid.

In posting a Voucher Register like that in Illustration D–1, the columns are first totaled and crossfooted to prove their equality. The Vouchers Payable column total is then credited to the Vouchers Payable account. The totals of the Purchases, Transportation-In, Sales Salaries Expense, Advertising Expense, Delivery Expense, and Office Salaries Expense columns are debited to these accounts. None of the individual amounts in these columns are posted. However, the individual amounts in the Other Accounts column are posted as individual amounts, and the column total is not posted.

**Register** Page 32

| | Sales Salaries Expense Debit | Adver-tising Expense Debit | Delivery Expense Debit | Office Salaries Expense Debit | Other Accounts Debit | | |
|---|---|---|---|---|---|---|---|
| | | | | | Account Name | PR | Amount Debit |
| 1 | | | | | | | |
| 2 | | 53.00 | | | | | |
| 3 | | | | | Store Supplies . . . . . . . . . . | 117 | 70.00 |
| 4 | | | | 85.00 | | | |
| 5 | 95.00 | | | | | | |
| 6 | 95.00 | | | | | | |
| 33 | | | | | Notes Payable . . . . . . . . . . | 211 | 500.00 |
| 34 | | | | | Interest Expense . . . . . . . . . | 721 | 5.00 |
| 35 | | | | | Telephone Expense . . . . . . . | 655 | 18.00 |
| 36 | | | | | | | |
| 37 | | | | | Office Equipment . . . . . . . . | 134 | 195.00 |
| 38 | 740.00 | 115.00 | 358.00 | 340.00 | | | 935.00 |
| 39 | (611) | (612) | (615) | (615) | | | (√) |
| 40 | | | | | | | |
| 41 | | | | | | | |

## The Unpaid Vouchers File

When a voucher system is in use, some vouchers are paid as soon as they are recorded. Others must be filed until payment is due. As an aid in taking cash discounts, vouchers for which payment is not due are generally filed in an unpaid vouchers file under the dates on which they are to be paid.

The file of unpaid vouchers takes the place of a subsidiary Accounts Payable Ledger. Actually, the file is a subsidiary ledger of amounts owed creditors. Likewise, the Vouchers Payable account is in effect a controlling account controlling the unpaid vouchers file. Therefore, after posting is completed at the end of a month, the balance of the Vouchers Payable account should equal the sum of the unpaid vouchers in the unpaid vouchers file. This is verified each month by preparing a schedule or an adding machine list of the unpaid vouchers in the file and comparing its total with the balance of the Vouchers Payable account. In addition, the unpaid vouchers in the file are compared with the unpaid vouchers shown in the Voucher Register's record of payments column. The number of each paying check and the payment date are entered in the Voucher Register's payments column as each voucher is paid. Therefore, the vouchers in the register without check numbers and payment dates should be the same as those in the unpaid vouchers file.

Illustration D–2
**A Check Register**

**Check Register**

| Date 19— | | Payee | Voucher No. | Check No. | Vouchers Payable Debit | Purchases Discounts Credit | Cash Credit |
|---|---|---|---|---|---|---|---|
| Oct. | 1 | C. B. & Y. RR Co. | 765 | 728 | 14.00 | | 14.00 |
| | 3 | Frank Mills | 766 | 729 | 73.00 | | 73.00 |
| | 3 | Ajax Wholesale Co. | 753 | 730 | 250.00 | 5.00 | 245.00 |
| | 4 | Normal Supply Co. | 747 | 731 | 100.00 | 2.00 | 98.00 |
| | 5 | Office Supply Co. | 763 | 732 | 43.00 | | 43.00 |
| | 6 | A. B. Seay Co. | 767 | 733 | 800.00 | 16.00 | 784.00 |
| | 6 | George Smith | 770 | 734 | 85.00 | | 85.00 |
| | 6 | Frank Jones | 771 | 735 | 95.00 | | 95.00 |
| | 30 | First National Bank | 998 | 972 | 505.00 | | 505.00 |
| | 30 | Pacific Telephone Co. | 999 | 973 | 18.00 | | 18.00 |
| | 31 | Office Equipment Co. | 1001 | 974 | 195.00 | | 195.00 |
| | 31 | Totals | | | 6,468.00 | 28.00 | 6,440.00 |
| | | | | | (213) | (512) | (111) |

## The Voucher System Check Register

In a voucher system, the Cash Disbursements Journal is replaced by a simpler *Check Register*. All checks drawn in payment of vouchers are recorded in the Check Register. No obligation is paid until a voucher covering the payment is prepared and recorded in the Voucher Register. Likewise, no check is drawn except in payment of a specific voucher. Therefore, all checks drawn result in debits to Vouchers Payable and credits to Cash, unless a discount must be recorded. Then, there are credits to both Purchases Discounts and to Cash. A Check Register is shown in Illustration D–2. Note that it has columns for debits to Vouchers Payable and credits to Purchases Discounts and to Cash. In posting, all amounts entered in these columns are posted in the column totals.

## Purchases Returns

Occasionally, an item must be returned after the voucher recording its purchase has been prepared and entered in the Voucher Register. In such cases, the return is recorded with a general journal entry like the following:

| | | | | |
|---|---|---|---|---|
| Nov. | 5 | Vouchers Payable | 15.00 | |
| | | Purchases Returns and Allowances | | 15.00 |
| | | Returned defective merchandise. | | |

In addition to the entry, the amount of the return is deducted on the voucher, and the credit memorandum and other documents verifying the return are attached to the voucher. Then, when the voucher is paid, a check is drawn for its corrected amount.

## Summary of the Appendix in Terms of the Learning Objective

**7.** When a voucher system is used, all transactions that will require payments by check are recorded in a Voucher Register, which serves as a book of original entry. A Purchases Journal is not used. Then, checks drawn in payment of vouchers are recorded in the Check Register, which replaces the Cash Disbursements Journal. The file of unpaid vouchers takes the place of a subsidiary Accounts Payable Ledger.

## Glossary

Define or explain the words and phrases listed in the chapter Glossary. (L. O. 6)

**Bank reconciliation** an analysis that explains the difference between the balance of a checking account as recorded in the depositor's records and the balance as shown on the bank statement. pp. 313–15

**Canceled checks** checks that have been stamped or perforated by the bank to show they have been paid. p. 313

**Cash Over and Short account** an income statement account in which cash overages and cash shortages arising from making change are recorded. pp. 312–13

**Discounts lost** an expense resulting from the failure to take advantage of cash discounts on purchases. p. 320

**Gross method of recording purchases** a method of recording purchases by which offered cash discounts are not deducted from the invoice price in determining the amount to be recorded. p. 319

**Internal control system** the procedures adopted by a business to encourage adherence to prescribed managerial policies, to protect its assets from waste, fraud, and theft, and to ensure accurate and reliable accounting data. pp. 299–301

**Invoice** a document, prepared by a vendor, on which are listed the items sold, the sales prices, the customer's name, and the terms of sale. p. 306

**Invoice approval form** a document on which the accounting department notes that it has performed each step in the process of checking an invoice and approving it for recording and payment. pp. 306–7

**Liquid asset** an asset, such as cash, that can be easily converted into other types of assets or used to buy services or satisfy obligations. p. 299

**Liquidity** a characteristic of an asset indicating how easily the asset can be converted into other types of assets or used to buy services or satisfy obligations. p. 299

**Net method of recording purchases** a method of recording purchases by which offered cash discounts are deducted from the invoice price in determining the amount to be recorded. pp. 319–20

**Outstanding checks** checks that were drawn by the depositor, deducted on the depositor's records, and sent to the payees, but that have not yet reached the depositor's bank for payment and deduction. p. 315

**Purchase order** a business form that is sent to a vendor as a written order for the purchase of goods or services. pp. 305–6

**Purchase requisition** a business form used within a business to ask the purchasing department of the business to buy needed items. pp. 304–5

**Receiving report** a form used within a business to notify the proper persons of the receipt of goods ordered and of the quantities and condition of the goods. p. 306

**Reconcile** to explain or account for the difference between two amounts. p. 315

**Vendee** the purchaser of goods or services. p. 306

**Vendor** the seller of goods or services. p. 306

**Voucher** a business paper used in summarizing a transaction and approving it for recording and payment. pp. 307–9

**Voucher Register** a book of original entry in which approved vouchers are entered. pp. 324–25

**Voucher system** a set of procedures that are designed to control the incurrence of obligations and cash disbursements. p. 304

## Objective Review

Answers to the following questions are listed in Appendix I at the end of the book. Be sure that you decide which is the one best answer to each question *before* you check the answers in the appendix.

1. The broad principles of internal control require that:
   *a.* Responsibility for specific tasks be shared by more than one employee so that one serves as a check on the other.
   *b.* Employees who handle cash and negotiable assets should be bonded.
   *c.* An employee who has custody over an asset should also keep the accounting records for that asset to ensure that the records are kept current.
   *d.* Responsibility for a series of related transactions such as for placing orders for, receiving, and paying for merchandise should be lodged in one person so that responsibility is clearly assigned.
   *e.* All of the above are correct.
2. Regarding internal control procedures for cash receipts:
   *a.* At the end of each day, each salesclerk who receives cash should analyze and correct any errors in the cash register's record of receipts before the records are submitted to the accounting department.
   *b.* An accounting department employee should count the cash received from sales and promptly deposit the cash receipts in the bank.
   *c.* Mail containing cash receipts should be opened by an accounting department employee who is responsible for recording the amount of the receipts and for depositing the receipts in the bank.
   *d.* All cash disbursements, other than from petty cash, should be made by check.
   *e.* All of the above are correct.
3. When a petty cash fund is used:
   *a.* An entry should be prepared to record each payment from the petty cash fund.
   *b.* Payments from the petty cash fund should be recorded with entries that include a credit to the Cash account.
   *c.* Reimbursements of the petty cash fund should be credited to the Cash account.
   *d.* The petty cashier's summary of petty cash payments serves as a journal which is posted to the appropriate General Ledger accounts.

*e.* The balance in the Petty Cash account should be reported in the balance sheet as a long-term investment since this amount is kept in the fund on a long-term basis.

4. Regarding the process of preparing a bank reconciliation at the end of an accounting period:
   *a.* All of the reconciling items shown on a bank reconciliation must be entered in the accounting records after the reconciliation is completed.
   *b.* Items that appear on the reconciliation as corrections to the bank statement balance should be entered in the accounting records.
   *c.* Items that appear on the reconciliation as corrections to the book balance of cash should be entered in the accounting records.
   *d.* Outstanding checks should be subtracted from the book balance of cash.
   *e.* Outstanding checks should be added to the bank balance of cash.
5. When invoices are recorded at net amounts:
   *a.* Purchase discounts taken are recorded in a Purchases Discounts account.
   *b.* The Purchases account is debited for the amount of any purchases discount offered plus the amount to be paid if the purchase discount is taken.
   *c.* The amount of purchases discounts lost is not recorded in a separate account.
   *d.* The amount of purchases discounts taken is not recorded in a separate account.
   *e.* The cash expenditures for purchases will always be less than if the invoices are recorded at gross amounts.

*An asterisk (*) identifies the questions, exercises, and problems that are based on Appendix D at the end of the chapter.*

## Questions for Class Discussion

1. Name the broad principles of internal control.
2. Why should the person who keeps the record of an asset be a different person from the one responsible for custody of the asset?
3. Internal control procedures are important in every business, but at what stage in the development of a business do they become critical?
4. Why should responsibility for a sequence of related transactions be divided among different departments or individuals?
5. In a small business, it is sometimes impossible to separate the functions of record-keeping and asset custody, and it is sometimes impossible to divide responsibilities for related transactions. What should be substituted for these control procedures?
6. Are the principles of internal control for computerized accounting systems different from the principles of internal control for manual accounting systems?

7. What are some of the effects of computers on internal control?
8. What is meant by the phrase *all receipts should be deposited intact*? Why should all receipts be deposited intact on the day of receipt?
9. Why should a company's bookkeeper not be given responsibility for receiving cash for the company nor the responsibility for signing checks or making cash disbursements in any other way?
10. In purchasing merchandise in a large store, why are the department managers not permitted to deal directly with the sources of supply?
11. What are the duties of the selling department managers in the purchasing procedures of a large store?
12. Tell (*a*) who prepares, (*b*) who receives, and (*c*) the purpose of each of the following business papers:

    | | |
    |---|---|
    | Purchase requisition. | Receiving report. |
    | Purchase order. | Invoice approval form. |
    | Invoice. | Voucher. |

13. Do all companies need a voucher system? At what approximate point in a company's growth would you recommend the installation of such a system?
14. When a disbursing officer issues a check in a large business, he or she usually cannot know from personal contact that the assets, goods, or services paid for by the check were received by the business or that the purchase was properly authorized. However, if the company has an internal control system, the officer can depend on the system. Exactly what documents does the officer depend on to tell that the purchase was authorized and properly made and the goods were actually received?
15. Why are some cash payments made from a petty cash fund? Why are not all payments made by check?
16. What is a petty cash receipt? When a petty cash receipt is prepared, who signs it?
17. Explain how a petty cash fund operates.
18. Why should a petty cash fund be reimbursed at the end of each accounting period?
19. What are two results of reimbursing the petty cash fund?
20. What is a bank statement? What kind of information appears on a bank statement?
21. What is the meaning of the phrase *to reconcile a bank balance*?
22. Why should you reconcile the bank statement balance of cash and the depositor's book balance of cash?
23. Which of the following items, disclosed in the process of preparing a bank reconciliation, require entries on the books of the depositor?
    *a*. Outstanding checks.
    *b*. Service charges.
    *c*. Deposits left in the night depository of the bank on the date the bank statement was prepared.
    *d*. Collection by the bank of the depositor's note receivable.

24. What valuable information becomes readily available to management when invoices are recorded at net amounts? Is this information readily available when invoices are recorded at gross amounts?

*25. What kind of transactions are entered in a Voucher Register?

*26. What kind of transactions are entered in a Check Register?

## Exercises

**Exercise 7–1**
**Analyzing internal control**
(L. O. 1, 2)

Roper Company is a young business that has grown rapidly. The company's bookkeeper, who was hired two years ago, left town suddenly after the owner discovered that money had been disappearing over the past 18 months. An audit disclosed that the bookkeeper had written and signed checks made payable to the bookkeeper's cousin, and then recorded the checks as salaries expense. The cousin, who cashed the checks but had never worked for the company, left town with the bookkeeper. As a result, the company incurred a loss of $12,000. Evaluate Roper Company's internal system and indicate which principles of internal control appear to have been ignored in this situation.

**Exercise 7–2**
**Recommending internal control procedures**
(L. O. 1, 2)

What internal control procedures would you recommend in each of the following situations?

*a.* Fox Lunches has one employee that sells sandwiches at a stand next to a college campus. Each day, the employee is given enough sandwiches to last through the lunch period and enough cash to make change. The money is kept in a box at the lunch stand.

*b.* A used goods variety store has one employee that is given cash and sent to garage sales each weekend. The employee pays cash for merchandise to be resold at the variety store.

**Exercise 7–3**
**Petty cash fund**
(L. O. 3)

A company established a $125 petty cash fund on May 1. Two weeks later, on May 15, there was $9.95 in cash in the fund and receipts for these expenditures: postage, $26.40; transportation-in, $20.50; miscellaneous general expenses, $33; and office supplies, $35.15. (*a*) Give in general journal form the entry to establish the fund and (*b*) the entry to reimburse it on May 15. (*c*) Assume that since the fund was exhausted so quickly, it was not only reimbursed on May 15 but also increased in size to $175. Give the entry to reimburse and increase the fund to $175.

**Exercise 7–4**
**Petty cash fund**
(L. O. 3)

A company established a $100 petty cash fund on April 10. On April 30, there was $26.60 in cash in the fund and receipts for these expenditures: transportation-in, $12.25; miscellaneous general expenses, $22.70; and office supplies, $35.45. The petty cashier could not account for the $3 shortage in the fund. Give in general journal form (*a*) the entry to establish the fund and (*b*) the April 30 entry to reimburse the fund and reduce it to $75.

**Exercise 7–5**
**Internal control over cash receipts**
(L. O. 1, 2)

Some of Usher Company's cash receipts from customers are sent to the company in the mail. Usher Company's bookkeeper opens the letters and deposits the cash received each day. What internal control problems are inherent in this arrangement? What changes would you recommend?

**Exercise 7–6**
**Bank reconciliation**
(L. O. 4)

French's Store deposits all receipts intact on the day received and makes all payments by check; and on October 31, after all posting was completed, its Cash account showed a $4,530 debit balance. However, its October 31 bank statement showed only $3,870 on deposit in the bank on that day. Prepare a bank reconciliation for the store, using the following information:

*a*. Outstanding checks, $600.

*b*. Included with the October canceled checks returned by the bank was a $12 debit memorandum for bank services.

*c*. Check No. 426, returned with the canceled checks, was correctly drawn for $36 in payment of the telephone bill and was paid by the bank on October 9, but it had been recorded with a debit to Telephone Expense and a credit to Cash as though it were for $63.

*d*. The October 31 cash receipts, $1,275, were placed in the bank's night depository after banking hours on that date and were unrecorded by the bank at the time the October bank statement was prepared.

**Exercise 7–7**
**Adjusting entries resulting from bank reconciliation**
(L. O. 4)

Give in general journal form any entries that French's Store should make as a result of having prepared the bank reconciliation of the previous exercise.

**Exercise 7–8**
**Recording invoices at gross or net amounts**
(L. O. 5)

Cates Company incurred $42,000 of operating expenses in June, a month in which its sales were $150,000. The company began June with a $78,000 merchandise inventory and ended the month with an $84,000 inventory. During the month, it purchased merchandise having a $96,000 invoice price, all of which was subject to a 2% discount for prompt payment. The company took advantage of the discounts on $66,000 of the purchases; but through an error in filing, it did not earn and could not take the discount on a $30,000 invoice paid on June 30.

*Required*

1. Prepare a June income statement for the company under the assumption that it records invoices at gross amounts.
2. Prepare a second income statement for the company under the assumption that it records invoices at net amounts.

**Exercise 7–9**
**Completion of bank reconciliation**
(L. O. 4)

Complete the following bank reconciliation by filling in the missing amounts:

**NELSON COMPANY**
**Bank Reconciliation**
**March 31, 1990**

| | | | |
|---|---|---|---|
| Book balance of cash | $ ? | Bank statement balance | $4,400 |
| Add: Collection of note | 500 | Add: Deposit of March 31 | ? |
| Interest earned | 15 | Bank error | 30 |
| | $4,715 | | $ ? |
| Deduct: Service charge | ? | Deduct: Outstanding checks | 925 |
| NSF check | 300 | | |
| Reconciled balance | $ ? | Reconciled balance | $4,405 |

## Problems

**Problem 7–1**
**Establishing and reimbursing petty cash fund**
(L. O. 3)

A concern completed the following petty cash transactions during June of the current year:

June 1 Drew a $150 check, cashed it, and gave the proceeds and the petty cashbox to Gus Troy, an office clerk who was to act as petty cashier.
5 Purchased computer paper with petty cash, $28.80.
7 Paid $8.55 COD delivery charges on merchandise purchased for resale.
10 Paid $7.50 parcel post charges on merchandise sold to a customer and delivered by mail.
12 Gave Mr. Hank Bronson, husband of the business owner, $20 from petty cash for cab fare and other personal expenses.
19 Paid $9.25 COD delivery charges on merchandise purchased for resale.
23 Paid a service station attendant $7.50 for washing the personal car of Lil Bronson, the business owner.
24 Paid Ready Delivery Service $15.50 from petty cash to deliver merchandise sold to a customer.
26 Paid $45.50 for minor repairs to an office typewriter.
29 Gus Troy sorted the petty cash receipts by accounts affected and exchanged them for a check to reimburse the fund for expenditures and, since there was only $5.50 in cash in the fund, for the shortage for which he could not account.

*Required*

1. Prepare a general journal entry to record the check establishing the petty cash fund.
2. Prepare a summary of petty cash payments that has these categories: Office supplies, Transportation-in, Delivery expense, Withdrawals, and Miscellaneous expenses. Sort the payments into the appropriate categories, total the expenses in each category, and prepare the general journal entry to reimburse the fund.

**Problem 7–2**
**Establishing, reimbursing, and increasing petty cash fund**
(L. O. 3)

A business completed these transactions:

Aug. 10 Drew a $100 check to establish a petty cash fund, cashed it, and delivered the proceeds and the petty cashbox to Jack Tate, an office secretary who was to act as petty cashier.
15 Paid Sid's Delivery Service $14 to deliver merchandise sold to a customer.
21 Purchased office supplies with petty cash, $24.50.
28 Paid $27 from petty cash to have the office windows washed.
30 Joe Peach, the owner of the business, signed a petty cash receipt and took $12 from petty cash for lunch money.
Sept. 4 Paid $17.25 COD delivery charges on merchandise purchased for resale.
5 Jack Tate noted that there was only $5.25 cash remaining in the fund. Thus, he sorted the paid petty cash receipts by accounts affected and exchanged them for a check to reimburse the fund. However, since the fund had been so rapidly exhausted, the check was made for an amount large enough to increase the size of the fund to $125.
7 Paid Sid's Delivery Service $10.25 to deliver merchandise to a customer.
12 Paid the Eastside Cleaner's delivery person $18.20 on the delivery to the office of clothes Mr. Peach had dropped off at the cleaners.
14 Paid $20.50 COD delivery charges on merchandise purchased for resale.
17 Gave Mrs. Peach, the wife of the business owner, $15 from petty cash for cab fare and other personal expenditures.
21 Paid $35 for minor repairs to an office typewriter.
26 Purchased office supplies with petty cash, $9.90.
29 Paid $8.75 COD delivery charges on merchandise purchased for resale.
30 Jack Tate sorted the petty cash receipts by accounts affected and exchanged them for a check to reimburse the fund for expenditures and, since there was only $5.40 in cash in the fund, for the shortage that he could not explain.

*Required*

1. Prepare a general journal entry to record the check establishing the petty cash fund.
2. Prepare a summary of petty cash payments prior to September 5 that has these categories: Office supplies, Transportation-in, Delivery expense, Withdrawals, and Miscellaneous expenses. Sort the payments into the appropriate categories and total each category. Prepare a similar summary of petty cash payments after September 5.
3. Prepare entries to reimburse the fund and increase its size on September 5 and to reimburse the fund on September 30.

**Problem 7–3**
**Petty cash fund; reimbursement and analysis of errors**
(L. O. 3)

The Hayden Company has only one journal in its accounting system and records all transactions in that General Journal. However, the company recently set up a petty cash fund to facilitate payments of small items. The following transactions involving the petty cash fund were noted by the petty cashier as occurring during April (the last month of the company's fiscal year):

Apr. 2 Received a company check for $75 to establish the petty cash fund.

10 Received a company check to replenish the fund for the following expenditures made since April 1 and to increase the fund to $150.

- *a.* Payment of $10.50 to Ed's Trucking for freight on merchandise delivered to Atkins Company.
- *b.* Purchased postage stamps for $22.
- *c.* Gave Janet Knox, owner of the business, $15 for personal use.
- *d.* Paid $22.75 to Perry Company for repairs of office equipment.
- *e.* Discovered that only $3.25 remained in the petty cash box.

30 Having decided that the April 10 increase in the fund was too large, received a company check to replenish the fund for the following expenditures made since April 10 but allowing the fund to be reduced in size to $100:

- *a.* Payment of $27.50 for emergency repairs to the company's office computer printer.
- *b.* Payment of $25 for janitorial service.
- *c.* Purchased office supplies for $36.75.
- *d.* Payment of $53.20 to King Advertising for a space advertisement in a weekly newsletter.

*Required*

1. Prepare general journal entries to record the establishment of the fund on April 2 and its replenishments on April 10 and on April 30.
2. If Hayden Company had failed to replenish the petty cash fund on April 30, what would have been the effect on net income for the fiscal year ended April 30 and on total assets on April 30? Explain your answer.

**Problem 7–4**
**Preparation of bank reconciliation and recording adjustments**
(L. O. 4)

The following information was available to reconcile Prince Company's book balance of cash with its bank statement balance as of December 31:

- *a.* The December 31 cash balance according to the accounting records was $12,510, and the bank statement balance for that date was $11,939.
- *b.* Two checks, No. 277 for $463 and No. 278 for $418, were outstanding on November 30 when the book and bank statement balances were last reconciled. Check No. 278 was returned with the December canceled checks, but Check No. 277 was not.
- *c.* Check No. 302 for $356 and Check No. 304 for $328, both written and entered in the accounting records in December, were not among the canceled checks returned.

*d.* When the December checks were compared with entries in the accounting records, it was found that Check No. 287 had been correctly drawn for $771 in payment for store supplies but was entered in the accounting records in error as though it were drawn for $717.

*e.* Two debit memoranda and a credit memorandum were included with the returned checks and were unrecorded at the time of the reconciliation. The credit memorandum indicated that the bank had collected a $2,150 note receivable for the company, deducted a $15 collection fee, and credited the balance to the company's account. One of the debit memoranda was for $195 and had attached to it an NSF check in that amount that had been received from a customer, Bob Lasale, in payment of his account. The second debit memorandum was for a special printing of checks and was for $54.

*f.* The December 31 cash receipts, $3,550, had been placed in the bank's night depository after banking hours on that date and did not appear on the bank statement.

*Required*

1. Prepare a December 31 bank reconciliation for the company.
2. Prepare the general journal entries necessary to bring the company's book balance of cash into conformity with the reconciled balance.

**Problem 7–5**
**Preparation of bank reconciliation and recording adjustments**
(L. O. 4)

Norris Company reconciled its book and bank statement balances of cash on February 28 and showed two checks outstanding at that time, No. 371 for $1,000 and No. 374 for $512. The following information was available for the March 31 reconciliation:

*From the March 31 bank statement:*

| | |
|---|---|
| BALANCE OF PREVIOUS STATEMENT ON 2/28/— | 6,886.00 |
| 5 DEPOSITS AND OTHER CREDITS TOTALING | 10,231.00 |
| 9 CHECKS AND OTHER DEBITS TOTALING | 8,693.00 |
| SERVICE CHARGE AMOUNT | 11.00 |
| CURRENT BALANCE AS OF THIS STATEMENT | 8,413.00 |

CHECKING ACCOUNT TRANSACTIONS

| DATE | AMOUNT | TRANSACTION DESCRIPTION |
|---|---|---|
| 3/2 | 1,122.00+ | Deposit |
| 3/12 | 1,984.00+ | Deposit |
| 3/19 | 1,843.00+ | Deposit |
| 3/22 | 1,700.00+ | Deposit |
| 3/28 | 185.00− | NSF check |
| 3/31 | 11.00− | Service charge |
| 3/31 | 3,582.00+ | Credit memorandum |

| DATE | CHECK NO | AMOUNT | DATE | CHECK NO | AMOUNT |
|---|---|---|---|---|---|
| 3/1 | 371 | 1,000.00 | 3/8 | 379 | 2,653.00 |
| 3/2 | 376* | 775.00 | 3/13 | 380 | 475.00 |
| 3/5 | 377 | 1,078.00 | 3/18 | 382* | 1,022.00 |
| 3/11 | 378 | 270.00 | 3/27 | 383 | 1,235.00 |

*Indicates a skip in check sequence.

*From Norris Company's accounting records:*

**Cash Receipts Deposited**

| Date | | | Cash Debit |
|---|---|---|---|
| Mar. | 2 | | 1,122.00 |
| | 12 | | 1,984.00 |
| | 19 | | 1,843.00 |
| | 22 | | 1,700.00 |
| | 31 | | 890.00 |
| | | | 7,539.00 |

**Cash Disbursements**

| Check No. | | Cash Credit |
|---|---|---|
| 376 | | 775.00 |
| 377 | | 1,087.00 |
| 378 | | 270.00 |
| 379 | | 2,653.00 |
| 380 | | 475,00 |
| 381 | | 490.00 |
| 382 | | 1,022.00 |
| 383 | | 1,235.00 |
| 384 | | 172.00 |
| | | 8,179.00 |

**Cash**

| Date | | Explanation | PR | Debit | Credit | Balance |
|---|---|---|---|---|---|---|
| Feb. | 28 | Balance | | | | 5,374.00 |
| Mar. | 31 | Total receipts | R8 | 7,539.00 | | 12,913.00 |
| | 31 | Total disbursements | D9 | | 8,179.00 | 4,734.00 |

Check No. 377 was correctly drawn for $1,078 in payment for office equipment; however, the bookkeeper misread the amount and entered it in the accounting records with a debit to Office Equipment and a credit to Cash as though it were for $1,087.

The NSF check was received from a customer, Pat Slade, in payment of his account. Its return is unrecorded. The credit memorandum resulted from a $3,600 note collected for Norris Company by the bank. The bank had deducted an $18 collection fee. Collection of the note has not been recorded.

*Required*

1. Prepare a March 31 bank reconciliation for the company.
2. Prepare in general journal form the entries needed to adjust the book balance of cash to the reconciled balance.

**Problem 7–6**
**Recording invoices at gross or net amounts**
(L. O. 5)

The July 31 credit balance in the Sales account of Horton Sales showed it had sold $117,000 of merchandise during the month. The concern began July with a $132,100 merchandise inventory and ended the month with a $108,300 inventory. It had incurred $39,000 of operating expenses during the month, and it had also recorded the following transactions:

July 2 Received merchandise purchased at a $12,000 invoice price, invoice dated June 26, terms 2/10, n/30.

4 Received a $1,200 credit memorandum (invoice price) for merchandise received on July 2 and returned for credit.

10 Received merchandise purchased at a $19,000 invoice price, invoice dated July 9, terms 2/10, n/30.

14 Received merchandise purchased at an $18,000 invoice price, invoice dated July 12, terms 2/10, n/30.
18 Paid for the merchandise received on July 10, less the discount.
21 Paid for the merchandise received on July 14, less the discount.
26 After the credit memorandum received on July 4 was attached to the invoice dated June 26, the invoice was mistakenly filed for payment today, which is the last day of its credit period. This caused the discount to be lost. Paid the invoice.

*Required*

1. Assume the concern records invoices at gross amounts. (*a*) Prepare general journal entries to record the transactions. (*b*) Prepare a July income statement for the concern.
2. Assume the concern records invoices at net amounts. (*a*) Prepare general journal entries to record the transactions. (*b*) Prepare a second income statement for the concern under this assumption.

***Problem 7–7**
**Using a voucher system**
(L. O. 7)

Hitchcock Company completed these transactions involving vouchers payable:

Aug. 4 Recorded Voucher No. 524 payable to Evans Company for merchandise having a $3,420 invoice price, invoice dated July 31, terms FOB factory, 2/10, n/30. The vendor had prepaid the freight, $162, adding the amount to the invoice and bringing its total to $3,582.
6 Recorded Voucher No. 525 payable to *The Star* for advertising expense, $396. Issued Check No. 424 in payment of the voucher.
7 Received a credit memorandum for merchandise having a $540 invoice price. The merchandise had been received from Evans Company on August 4, recorded on Voucher No. 524, and later returned for credit.
9 Recorded Voucher No. 526 payable to Western Realty for one month's rent on the space occupied by the store, $1,800. Issued Check No. 425 in payment of the voucher.
11 Recorded Voucher No. 527 payable to North Supply Company for store supplies, $234, terms n/10 EOM.
13 Recorded Voucher No. 528 payable to Rawlins Company for merchandise having a $4,500 invoice price, invoice dated August 11, terms FOB factory, 2/10, n/60. The vendor had prepaid the freight charges, $180, adding the amount to the invoice and bringing its total to $4,680.
14 Recorded Voucher No. 529 payable to Payroll for sales salaries, $1,800, and office salaries, $1,350. Issued Check No. 426 in payment of the voucher. Cashed the check and paid the employees.
18 Recorded Voucher No. 530 payable to Apex Company for merchandise having a $2,700 invoice price, invoice dated August 16, terms 2/10, n/60, FOB factory. The vendor had prepaid the freight charges, $126, adding the amount to the invoice and bringing its total to $2,826.

Aug. 21 Issued Check No. 427 in payment of Voucher No. 528.

25 Recorded Voucher No. 531 payable to Rawlins Company for merchandise having a $5,400 invoice price, invoice dated August 23, terms FOB factory, 2/10, n/60. The vendor had prepaid the freight charges, $252, adding the amount to the invoice and bringing its total to $5,652.

27 Discovered that Voucher No. 524 had been filed in error for payment on the last day of its credit period rather than on the last day of its discount period, causing the discount to be lost. Issued Check No. 428 in payment of the voucher, less the return.

31 Recorded Voucher No. 532 payable to Payroll for sales salaries, $1,800, and office salaries, $1,350. Issued Check No. 429 in payment of the voucher. Cashed the check and paid the employees.

*Required*

1. Assume that Hitchcock Company records vouchers at gross amounts. Prepare a Voucher Register, a Check Register, and a General Journal, and record the transactions.
2. Prepare a Vouchers Payable account and post those portions of the journal and register entries that affect the account.
3. Test the accuracy of the Vouchers Payable account balance by preparing a schedule of vouchers payable.

## Alternate Problems

**Problem 7–1A**
**Establishing and reimbursing petty cash fund**
(L. O. 3)

A concern completed the following petty cash transactions during October of the current year:

Oct. 2 Drew a $125 check, cash it, and turned the proceeds and the petty cashbox over to Norm Bowers, an office clerk who was to act as petty cashier.

5 Paid $9.15 parcel post charges on merchandise sold to a customer and delivered by mail.

8 Purchased office supplies with petty cash, $14.50.

9 Paid $28.35 from petty cash for repairs to an office copier.

12 Paid $10 COD delivery charges on merchandise purchased for resale.

15 Paid Mercury Delivery Service $11.25 to deliver merchandise sold to a customer.

21 Gave Dennis Moore, the owner of the business, $20 from petty cash for personal use.

23 Paid $12.55 COD delivery charges on merchandise purchased for resale.

27 Dennis Moore, owner of the business, signed a petty cash receipt and took $12 from petty cash for lunch money.

30 Norm Bowers exchanged his paid petty cash receipts for a check reimbursing the fund for expenditures and a shortage of cash in the

fund that he could not account for. He reported a cash balance of $2.20 in the fund.

*Required*

1. Prepare a general journal entry to record the check establishing the petty cash fund.
2. Prepare a summary of petty cash payments that has these categories: Office supplies, Transportation-in, Delivery expense, Withdrawals, and Miscellaneous expenses. Sort the payments into the appropriate categories, total the expenses in each category, and prepare the general journal entry to reimburse the fund.

**Problem 7–2A**
**Establishing, reimbursing, and increasing petty cash fund**
(L. O. 3)

A business completed these petty cash transactions:

May 4 Drew a $75 check to establish a petty cash fund, cashed it, and turned the proceeds and the petty cashbox over to Gayle Bates, an office worker who was appointed petty cashier.
6 Paid $12.55 parcel post charges on merchandise sold to a customer and delivered by mail.
8 Paid $14 to have the office windows washed.
11 Purchased office supplies with petty cash, $25.25.
12 Susan Dixon, owner of the business, signed a petty cash receipt and took $8 from petty cash for coffee money.
14 Paid $13.20 COD delivery charges on merchandise purchased for resale.
15 Gayle Bates noted that only $2 remained in the petty cashbox. Thus, she sorted the petty cash receipts in terms of the accounts affected and exchanged the receipts for a check to reimburse the fund. However, since the fund had been exhausted so quickly, the check was made sufficiently large to increase the size of the fund to $150.
18 Paid $35 from petty cash for minor repairs to an office machine.
20 Paid $12.75 COD delivery charges on merchandise purchased for resale.
22 Paid A. M. Delivery Service $15.20 to deliver merchandise sold to a customer.
26 Purchased office supplies with petty cash, $18.
27 Susan Dixon, owner of the business, signed a petty cash receipt and took $15 from petty cash for lunch money.

June 1 Paid $16.50 COD delivery charges on merchandise purchased for resale.
5 Purchased paper clips and pencils with petty cash, $10.80.
10 Paid $18.75 COD delivery charges on merchandise purchased for resale.
12 Gayle Bates sorted the petty cash receipts and exchanged them for a check to replenish the fund for expenditures and, since there was only $1.50 in cash in the fund, for the unexplained shortage.

*Required*

1. Prepare a general journal entry to record the check establishing the petty cash fund.
2. Prepare a summary of petty cash payments prior to May 15 that has these categories: Delivery expense, Office supplies, Miscellaneous expenses, Withdrawals, and Transportation-in. Sort the payments into the appropriate categories and total each category. Prepare a similar summary of petty cash payments after May 15.
3. Prepare entries to reimburse the fund and increase its size on May 15 and to reimburse the fund on June 12.

**Problem 7–3A**
**Petty cash fund; reimbursement and analysis of errors**
(L. O. 3)

The accounting system used by the Franklin Company requires that all entries be journalized in a General Journal. To facilitate payments of small items, Franklin Company recently established a petty cash fund. The following transactions involving the petty cash fund occurred during August (the last month of the company's fiscal year):

Aug. 3 A company check for $200 was drawn and made payable to the petty cashier to establish the petty cash fund.

14 A company check was drawn to replenish the fund for the following expenditures made since August 1 and to increase the fund to $300:

*a.* Purchased postage stamps for $44.

*b.* Payment of $42.30 to Meeks Trucking for delivery of merchandise to customers.

*c.* Gave Beth Rogers, owner of the business, $50 for personal use.

*d.* Paid $60.50 to Appliance Company for repairs of office equipment.

*e.* Discovered that only $1.20 remained in the petty cashbox.

31 The petty cashier noted that $2.60 remained in the fund. Having decided that the August 14 increase in the fund was not large enough, a company check was drawn to replenish the fund for the following expenditures made since August 14 and to increase it to $350:

*a.* Payment of $97.25 for office supplies to support the company's computer.

*b.* Payment of $52.15 for items classified as miscellaneous general expense.

*c.* Payment of $63 for janitorial service.

*d.* Payment of $85 to Southern Advertising Company for a space advertisement in a weekly newsletter.

*Required*

1. Prepare general journal entries to record the establishment of the fund on August 3 and its replenishments on August 14 and on August 31.
2. If Franklin Company had failed to replenish the petty cash fund on August 31, what would have been the effect on net income for the fiscal year ended August 31 and on total assets on August 31? Explain your

answer. (Hint: The amount of Office Supplies to appear on a balance sheet is determined by a physical count of the supplies on hand.)

**Problem 7–4A**
**Preparation of bank reconciliation and recording adjustments**
(L. O. 4)

The following information was available to reconcile Golf Company's book balance of cash with its bank statement balance as of February 28:

*a.* After all posting was completed on February 28, the company's Cash account had a $7,180 debit balance, but its bank statement showed a $9,415 balance.

*b.* Checks No. 217 for $365 and No. 222 for $709 were outstanding on the January 31 bank reconciliation. Check No. 222 was returned with the February canceled checks, but Check No. 217 was not.

*c.* In comparing the canceled checks returned with the bank statement with the entries in the accounting records, it was found that Check No. 297 for the purchase of office equipment was correctly drawn for $724 but was entered in the accounting records as though it were for $742. It was also found that Check No. 331 for $482 and Check No. 333 for $240, both drawn in February, were not among the canceled checks returned with the statement.

*d.* A credit memorandum enclosed with the bank statement indicated that the bank had collected a $3,600 noninterest-bearing note for the concern, deducted a $36 collection fee, and had credited the remainder to the concern's account.

*e.* A debit memorandum for $464 listed a $452 NSF check plus a $12 NSF charge. The check had been received from a customer, Jan Bellors, and was among the canceled checks returned.

*f.* Also among the canceled checks was an $18 debit memorandum for bank services. None of the memoranda had been recorded.

*g.* The February 28 cash receipts, $1,952, were placed in the bank's night depository after banking hours on that date, and their amount did not appear on the bank statement.

*Required*

1. Prepare a bank reconciliation for the company.
2. Prepare entries in general journal form to bring the company's book balance of cash into conformity with the reconciled balance.

**Problem 7–5A**
**Preparation of bank reconciliation and recording adjustments**
(L. O. 4)

Shepard Company reconciled its bank balance on November 30 and showed two checks outstanding at that time, No. 404 for $628 and No. 409 for $124. The following information is available for the December 31 reconciliation:

*From the December 31 bank statement:*

| | |
|---|---|
| BALANCE OF PREVIOUS STATEMENT ON 11/30/— | 4,302.00 |
| 5 DEPOSITS AND OTHER CREDITS TOTALING | 7,344.00 |
| 8 CHECKS AND OTHER DEBITS TOTALING | 5,683.00 |
| SERVICE CHARGE AMOUNT | 7.00 |
| CURRENT BALANCE AS OF THIS STATEMENT | 5,956.00 |

CHECKING ACCOUNT TRANSACTIONS

| DATE | AMOUNT | TRANSACTION DESCRIPTION |
|---|---|---|
| 12/2 | 535.00+ | Deposit |
| 12/11 | 2,268.00+ | Deposit |
| 12/21 | 1,560.00+ | Deposit |
| 12/29 | 1,496.00+ | Deposit |
| 12/30 | 576.00− | NSF check |
| 12/30 | 7.00− | Service charge |
| 12/30 | 1,485.00+ | Credit memorandum |

| DATE | CHECK NO | AMOUNT | DATE | CHECK NO | AMOUNT |
|---|---|---|---|---|---|
| 11/25 | 404 | 628.00 | 12/14 | 413 | 125.00 |
| 12/4 | 410* | 734.00 | 12/16 | 414 | 280.00 |
| 12/2 | 411 | 540.00 | 12/28 | 415 | 770.00 |
| 12/7 | 412 | 2,030.00 | | | |

*Indicates a skip in check sequence.

*From Shepard Company's accounting records:*

**Cash Receipts Deposited**

| Date | | Cash Debit |
|---|---|---|
| Dec. | 2 | 535.00 |
| | 11 | 2,268.00 |
| | 21 | 1,560.00 |
| | 29 | 1,496.00 |
| | 30 | 765.00 |
| | | 6,624.00 |

**Cash Disbursements**

| Check No. | Cash Credit |
|---|---|
| 410 | 734.00 |
| 411 | 540.00 |
| 412 | 2,030.00 |
| 413 | 125.00 |
| 414 | 280.00 |
| 415 | 707.00 |
| 416 | 310.00 |
| 417 | 391.00 |
| | 5,117.00 |

**Cash**

| Date | | Explanation | PR | Debit | Credit | Balance |
|---|---|---|---|---|---|---|
| Nov. | 30 | Balance | | | | 3,550.00 |
| Dec. | 31 | Total receipts | R8 | 6,624.00 | | 10,174.00 |
| | 31 | Total disbursements | D9 | | 5,117.00 | 5,057.00 |

Check No. 415 was correctly drawn for $770 in payment for store equipment; however, the bookkeeper misread the amount and entered it in the accounting records with a debit to Store Equipment and a credit to Cash as though it were for $707. The bank paid and deducted the correct amount.

The NSF check was received from a customer, Fred Gantry, in payment of his account. Its return was unrecorded. The credit memorandum resulted from a $1,500 note which the bank had collected for the company. The bank had deducted a $15 collection fee and deposited the balance in the company's account. Collection of the note has not been recorded.

*Required*

1. Prepare a bank reconciliation for Shepard Company.
2. Prepare in general journal form the entries needed to bring the company's book balance of cash into agreement with the reconciled balance.

**Problem 7–6A**
**Recording invoices at gross or net amounts**
(L. O. 5)

The June 30 credit balance in the Sales account of Crewes Sales showed it had sold $325,000 of merchandise during the month. The concern began June with a $275,000 merchandise inventory and ended the month with a $217,000 inventory. It had incurred $105,000 of operating expenses during the month, and it had also recorded the following transactions:

June 2 Received merchandise purchased at a $36,000 invoice price, invoice dated May 30, terms 2/10, n/30.

8 Received a $6,000 credit memorandum (invoice price) for merchandise received on June 2 and returned for credit.

11 Received merchandise purchased at a $54,000 invoice price, invoice dated June 9, terms 2/10, n/30.

15 Received merchandise purchased at a $63,750 invoice price, invoice dated June 13, terms 2/10, n/30.

19 Paid for the merchandise received on June 11, less the discount.

23 Paid for the merchandise received on June 15, less the discount.

29 After the credit memorandum received on June 8 was attached to the invoice dated May 30, the invoice was mistakenly filed for payment today, which is the last day of its credit period. This caused the discount to be lost. Paid the invoice.

*Required*

1. Assume the concern records invoices at gross amounts. (*a*) Prepare general journal entries to record the transactions. (*b*) Prepare a June income statement for the concern.
2. Assume the concern records invoices at net amounts. (*a*) Prepare general journal entries to record the transactions. (*b*) Prepare a second income statement for the concern under this assumption.

***Problem 7–7A**
**Using a voucher system**
(L. O. 7)

Judd Company completed these transactions involving vouchers payable:

May 1 Recorded Voucher No. 415 payable to Stewart Company for merchandise having a $1,800 invoice price, invoice dated April 28, terms FOB destination, 2/10, n/30.

4 Recorded Voucher No. 416 payable to Johnson Company for merchandise having a $2,800 invoice price, invoice dated May 2, terms FOB factory, 2/10, n/60. The vendor had prepaid the freight charges, $100, adding the amount to the invoice and bringing its total to $2,900.

7 Received a credit memorandum for merchandise having a $600 invoice price. The merchandise was received on May 1. Voucher No. 415, and returned for credit.

12 Issued Check No. 630 in payment of Voucher No. 416.

15 Recorded Voucher No. 417 payable to Payroll for sales salaries, $960, and office salaries, $640. Issued Check No. 631 in payment of the voucher. Cashed the check and paid the employees.

19 Recorded Voucher No. 418 payable to Decor Designers for the purchase of office equipment having a $720 invoice price, terms n/10 EOM.

May 21 Recorded Voucher No. 419 payable to *The SUN* for advertising expense, $300. Issued Check No. 632 in payment of the voucher.

26 Recorded Voucher No. 420 payable to Roxy Company for merchandise having a $2,020 invoice price, invoice dated May 23, terms FOB factory, 2/10, n/60. The vendor had prepaid the freight charges, $80, adding the amount to the invoice and bringing its total to $2,100.

29 Discovered that Voucher No. 415 had been filed in error for payment on the last day of its credit period rather than on the last day of its discount period, causing the discount to be lost. Issued Check No. 633 in payment of the voucher, less the return.

31 Recorded Voucher No. 421 payable to Payroll for sales salaries, $960, and office salaries, $640. Issued Check No. 634 in payment of the voucher. Cashed the check and paid the employees.

*Required*

1. Assume that Judd Company records vouchers at gross amounts. Prepare a Voucher Register, a Check Register, and a General Journal, and record the transactions.
2. Prepare a Vouchers Payable account and post those portions of the journal and register entries that affect the account.
3. Test the accuracy of the Vouchers Payable account balance by preparing a schedule of unpaid vouchers.

## Provocative Problems

**Provocative Problem 7–1**
**The Retiring Employee**
(L. O. 1, 2)

The bookkeeper at Small Company will retire next week after more than 30 years with the store, having been hired by the father of the store's present owner. She has always been a very dependable employee, and as a result has been given more and more responsibilities over the years. Actually, for the past 15 years, she has "run" the store's office, keeping books, verifying invoices, and issuing checks in their payment, which in the absence of the store's owner, Sally Ennis, she could sign. In addition, at the end of each day, the store's salesclerks turn over their daily cash receipts to the bookkeeper. After counting the money and comparing the amounts with the cash register tapes, which she is responsible for removing from the cash registers, she makes the journal entry to record cash sales and then deposits the money in the bank. She also reconciles the bank balance with the book balance of cash each month.

Mrs. Ennis, the store's owner, realizes she cannot expect a new bookkeeper to accomplish as much as the old bookkeeper. And since the store is not large enough to warrant more than one office employee, she recognizes she must take over some of the old bookkeeper's duties when she retires. Mrs. Ennis already places all orders for merchandise and supplies and closely supervises all employees and does not want to add more to her duties than necessary.

Name the internal control principle violated here and tell which of the old bookkeeper's tasks should be taken over by Mrs. Ennis in order to improve the store's internal control over cash.

**Provocative Problem 7–2**
**Sporting Goods Company**
(L. O. 1, 2)

The Sporting Goods Company has enjoyed rapid growth since its beginning several years ago. Last year its sales were in excess of $15 million. However, its purchasing procedures may not have kept pace with its growth. When a plant supervisor or department head needs raw materials, plant assets, or supplies, he or she telephones a request to the purchasing department manager. The purchasing department manager prepares a purchase order in duplicate, sends one copy to the company selling the goods, and keeps the other copy in the files. When the seller's invoice is received, it is sent directly to the purchasing department. When the goods arrive, receiving department personnel count and inspect the items and prepare one copy of a receiving report which is sent to the purchasing department. The purchasing department manager attaches the receiving report and the retained copy of the purchase order to the invoice. If all is in order, the invoice is stamped "approved for payment" and signed by the purchasing department manager. The invoice and its supporting documents are then sent to the accounting department to be recorded and filed until due. On its due date, the invoice and its supporting documents are sent to the office of the company treasurer where a check is prepared and mailed. The number of the paying check is entered on the invoice and the invoice is sent to the accounting department for an entry to record its payment.

Do the procedures of Sporting Goods Company make it fairly easy for someone in the company to institute the payment of fictitious invoices by the company? If so, who is most likely to commit the fraud and what would that person have to do to receive payment of a fictitious invoice? What changes should be made in the company's purchasing procedures, and why should each change be made?

# 8 Short-Term Investments and Receivables

The focus of the last chapter was on accounting for cash, which is the most liquid of all assets. This chapter continues the discussion of liquid assets by focusing on short-term investments of cash, on accounts receivable, and on short-term notes receivable.

**Learning Objectives**

*After studying Chapter 8, you should be able to:*

1. Journalize entries to account for short-term investments; and calculate, record, and report the lower of cost or market of short-term investments in marketable equity securities.
2. Prepare entries to account for credit card sales.
3. Prepare entries to account for credit customers, including allowance method entries and direct write-off method entries to account for bad debts.
4. Calculate the interest on promissory notes and prepare entries to record the receipt of promissory notes and their payment or dishonor.
5. Calculate the discount and proceeds on discounted notes receivable and prepare entries to record the discounting of notes receivable and, if dishonored, their dishonor.
6. Define or explain the words and phrases listed in the chapter Glossary.

Since cash is the typical means by which companies pay their obligations, good management generally requires that companies keep some surplus cash balances. Also, seasonal fluctuations in sales volume often result in surplus cash balances during some months of each year. Rather than leave these surplus cash balances in checking accounts that pay, at best, low rates of interest, many concerns invest their surplus cash in the hope of earning higher returns.

## Short-Term Investments

Journalize entries to account for short-term investments; and calculate, record, and report the lower of cost or market of short-term investments in marketable equity securities. (L. O. 1)

Investments of surplus cash may be in a variety of government or corporate debt obligations or in stocks (equity securities). If the investments can be converted into cash quickly, and if management intends to hold the investments as a source of cash to satisfy the needs of current operations, the investments are called **short-term investments** or **temporary investments.** This means that they are classified on the balance sheet as current assets.[1]

Some investments that are held as a source of cash qualify as current assets because they mature in a short period of time. These include short-term debt obligations of the government or other corporations that mature and will be repaid within one year or the current operating cycle of the business, whichever is longer. Investments in other securities that do not mature in a short period of time can be classified as current assets only if they are marketable. In other words, such securities must be salable without excessive delays. For example, stocks that are actively traded on a stock exchange qualify as marketable.

When short-term investments are purchased, you should record the investments at cost. For example, if Ford Motor Company's short-term notes payable are purchased for $40,000, you record the purchase as follows:

| | | | | |
|---|---|---|---|---|
| Aug. | 16 | Short-Term Investments . . . . . . . . . . . . . . . . . . . | 40,000.00 | |
| | | Cash . . . . . . . . . . . . . . . . . . . . . . . . . | | 40,000.00 |
| | | Bought $40,000 of Ford Motor Company notes due October 16. | | |

Assume that when these notes mature, the cash proceeds are $40,000 plus $800 interest. When the receipt is recorded, the interest is credited to a revenue account, as follows:

| | | | | |
|---|---|---|---|---|
| Oct. | 16 | Cash . . . . . . . . . . . . . . . . . . . . . . . . . . . . | 40,800.00 | |
| | | Short-Term Investments . . . . . . . . . . . . . . . . | | 40,000.00 |
| | | Interest Earned . . . . . . . . . . . . . . . . . . . . | | 800.00 |
| | | Received cash proceeds from mature notes. | | |

When you determine the cost of an investment, you must include any commissions paid. For example, if 1,000 shares of Xerox Corporation common

[1] FASB, *Accounting Standards—Current Text* (Norwalk, Conn., 1988), sec. B05.105. Originally published as *Accounting Research Bulletin No. 43,* chap. 3A, par. 4.

stock are purchased as a short-term investment, at 70⅛ ($70.125 per share)[2] plus a $625 broker's commission, the entry to record the transaction is:

| | | | | |
|---|---|---|---|---|
| Oct. | 15 | Short-Term Investments . . . . . . . . . . . . . . . . . . . | 70,750.00 | |
| | | Cash . . . . . . . . . . . . . . . . . . . . . . . . . . | | 70,750.00 |
| | | Bought 1,000 shares of Xerox stock at $70⅛ plus $625 broker's commission. | | |

If cash dividends are received on stock held as a short-term investment, the dividends are credited to a revenue account, as follows:

| | | | | |
|---|---|---|---|---|
| Dec. | 12 | Cash . . . . . . . . . . . . . . . . . . . . . . . . . . . . | 1,000.00 | |
| | | Dividends Earned . . . . . . . . . . . . . . . . . . . . . | | 1,000.00 |
| | | Received dividend of $1 per share. | | |

When a short-term investment is sold, the difference between the cost of the investment and the cash proceeds from the sale is recorded as a gain or loss. For example, if 500 of the Xerox common shares are sold on December 20 for 69¼ per share less a $350 commission, the sale is recorded as follows:

| | | | | |
|---|---|---|---|---|
| Dec. | 20 | Cash . . . . . . . . . . . . . . . . . . . . . . . . . . . . | 34,275.00 | |
| | | Loss on Sale of Short-Term Investments . . . . . . . . . . | 1,100.00 | |
| | | Short-Term Investments . . . . . . . . . . . . . . . . . | | 35,375.00 |
| | | (500 × $69.25) − $350 = $34,275. $70,750 ÷ 2 = $35,375. | | |

Investments in debt obligations usually are maintained in the accounts at cost until they are sold or mature. However, marketable equity securities are likely to fluctuate in market value. Therefore, short-term investments in marketable equity securities must be reported on the balance sheet at the **lower of cost or market (LCM).**[3]

In calculating the lower of cost or market (LCM), the total cost of all marketable equity securities held as short-term investments is compared with the total market value on the balance sheet date. For example, assume that on December 31, 1990, the company that purchased the Xerox stock has two other short-term investments in marketable equity securities. Lower of cost or market is determined by comparing the total cost and total market of the entire portfolio, as follows:

---

[2] Stocks are quoted on stock exchanges on the basis of dollars and ⅛ dollars per share. For example, a stock quoted at 23⅛ sold for $23.125 per share and one quoted at 36½ sold for $36.50 per share.

[3] FASB, *Accounting Standards—Current Text* (Norwalk, Conn. 1988), sec. I89.102–103. Originally published as *FASB Statement of Financial Accounting Standards No. 12,* par. 8–9.

| Short-Term Investments | Cost | Market | LCM |
|---|---|---|---|
| Johnson & Johnson common stock . . . . | $ 42,600 | $ 43,500 | |
| Polaroid Corporation common stock . . . . | 30,500 | 28,200 | |
| Xerox Corporation common stock . . . . . | 35,375 | 34,000 | |
| Total . . . . . . . . . . . . . . . . . . . . . | $108,475 | $105,700 | $105,700 |

To record the reduction in the value of the short-term investment portfolio, the following entry is made:

| | | | | |
|---|---|---|---|---|
| Dec. | 31 | Loss on Market Decline of Short-Term Investments . . . . | 2,775.00 | |
| | | Allowance to Reduce Short-Term Investments to Market . . . . . . . . . . . . . . . . . . . . . . . | | 2,775.00 |
| | | $108,475 – $105,700 = $2,775. | | |

The Loss on Short-Term Investments account is closed to Income Summary and reported on the income statement. The Allowance to Reduce Short-Term Investments to Market account is a contra asset account. It is subtracted from the cost of the short-term investments so that they are reported in the current asset section of the balance sheet at the lower of cost or market, as follows:

| | |
|---|---|
| Current assets: | |
| Cash . . . . . . . . . . . . . . . . . . . . | xxx |
| Short-term investments, at lower of cost or market (cost is $108,475) . . . . . . . . | 105,700 |

When the market value of short-term investments increases above cost, the increases are not recorded until the investments are sold. However, if short-term investments are written down to a market value below cost, subsequent increases in market value up to the original cost are recorded.

The use of lower of cost or market is often criticized because it is a departure from the *cost principle*. On the other hand, those who support the use of LCM argue that it provides a conservative balance sheet valuation.

In addition to cash and short-term investments, the liquid assets of a business include receivables that result from credit sales to customers. In the following sections of this chapter, we first discuss the procedures used to account for sales when customers use credit cards issued by banks or credit card companies. Then, we focus on accounting for credit sales when a business grants credit to its customers. This involves (1) maintaining a separate account receivable for each customer, (2) accounting for bad debts that result from credit sales, and (3) accounting for notes receivable.

## Credit Card Sales

Prepare entries to account for credit card sales. (L. O. 2)

Many customers use credit cards such as VISA, MasterCard, or American Express to charge purchases from various businesses. This practice gives customers the ability to make purchases without carrying cash or writing checks. Also, customers usually can defer payment to the credit card company. Furthermore, once credit is established with the credit card company, the customer does not have to establish credit with each store. Finally, if customers use a credit card, they can avoid having to make several monthly payments to a variety of creditors.

There are good reasons why businesses allow customers to use credit cards. First, the business does not have to evaluate the credit standing of each customer or make decisions about who should get credit and how much. Second, the business avoids the risk of extending credit to customers who cannot pay. Third, the business often receives cash from the credit card company quicker than it would if customers were granted credit.

With some credit cards, usually those issued by banks, the business deposits a copy of each credit card receipt in its bank account just as it would deposit a customer's check. Thus, the business receives a cash credit immediately upon deposit. With other credit cards, the business sends the appropriate copy of each receipt to the credit card company and then is paid by the company. Until payment is received, the business has an account receivable from the credit card company. In return for the services provided to the business, credit card companies charge a fee ranging from 2% to 5% of credit card sales. This charge is deducted from the cash payment to the business.

Accounting for credit card sales depends on whether cash is received immediately upon deposit or is delayed until paid by the credit card company. If cash is received immediately, the entry to record credit card sales is:

| | | | | |
|---|---|---|---|---|
| Jan. | 25 | Cash | 96.00 | |
| | | Credit Card Expense | 4.00 | |
| | | Sales | | 100.00 |
| | | To record credit card sales less a 4% credit card expense. | | |

If the business must send the receipts to the credit card company and wait for payment, the entry to record credit card sales is:

| | | | | |
|---|---|---|---|---|
| Jan. | 25 | Accounts Receivable, Credit Card Company | 100.00 | |
| | | Sales | | 100.00 |
| | | To record credit card sales. | | |

When cash is received from the credit card company, the entry to record the receipt is:

| | | | | |
|---|---|---|---|---|
| Feb. | 10 | Cash | 96.00 | |
| | | Credit Card Expense | 4.00 | |
| | | Accounts Receivable, Credit Card Company | | 100.00 |
| | | To record cash receipt less 4% credit card expense. | | |

In the above entries, notice that the credit card expense was not recorded until cash was received from the credit card company. This is a matter of convenience. By following this procedure, the business avoids having to calculate the credit card expense each time a sale is recorded. Instead, the expense related to many sales can be calculated once and recorded when cash is received. However, the *matching principle* requires that you report credit card expense in the same period as the sale. Therefore, if the sale and the cash receipt occur in different periods, you must accrue and report the credit card expense in the period of sale.

Credit card expense is sometimes disclosed in the income statement as a type of discount that is deducted from sales to get net sales. Other companies classify it as a selling expense or even as an administrative expense. Arguments can be made for all three alternatives.

## Maintaining a Separate Account for Each Customer

Prepare entries to account for credit customers, including allowance method entries and direct write-off method entries to account for bad debts. (L. O. 3)

In previous chapters, when we recorded credit sales, we debited a single account called Accounts Receivable. However, when a business has more than one credit customer, the accounts must be designed so that they show how much each customer has purchased, how much each customer has paid, and how much remains to be collected from each customer. To provide this information, businesses with credit customers must maintain a separate account receivable for each customer.

One possible way of keeping a separate account for each customer would be to keep all of these accounts in the same ledger that contains the financial statement accounts. However, this usually is not done. Instead, the ledger that contains the financial statement accounts, the **General Ledger,** continues to hold a single Accounts Receivable account. Then, a supplementary record is established in which a separate account is maintained for each customer. This supplementary record is called the **Accounts Receivable Ledger.**

Illustration 8–1 shows the relationship between the Accounts Receivable account in the General Ledger and the individual customer accounts in the Accounts Receivable Ledger. In Illustration 8–1, notice that the sum of the balances in the Accounts Receivable Ledger is equal to the balance of the Accounts Receivable account in the General Ledger. To maintain this relationship, each time credit sales are posted to the Accounts Receivable account, they are also posted to the appropriate customer accounts in the Accounts Receivable Ledger. Also, cash receipts from credit customers must be posted to both the Accounts Receivable account in the General Ledger and to the appropriate customer accounts.

You should understand that when debits (or credits) to Accounts Receivable are posted twice, this does not violate the requirement that debits equal credits. The equality of debits and credits is maintained *in the General Ledger.* The Accounts Receivable Ledger is simply a supplementary record that provides detailed information concerning each customer.

Because the balance in the Accounts Receivable account is always equal to the sum of the balances in the customers' accounts, the Accounts Receivable account is said to control the Accounts Receivable Ledger and is called a **controlling account.** And since the Accounts Receivable Ledger is a supplementary record that is controlled by an account in the General Ledger, it is called a **subsidiary ledger.**

The Accounts Receivable account and the Accounts Receivable Ledger are not the only examples of controlling accounts and subsidiary ledgers. Most

Illustration 8–1
**The Accounts Receivable account and the Accounts Receivable Ledger**

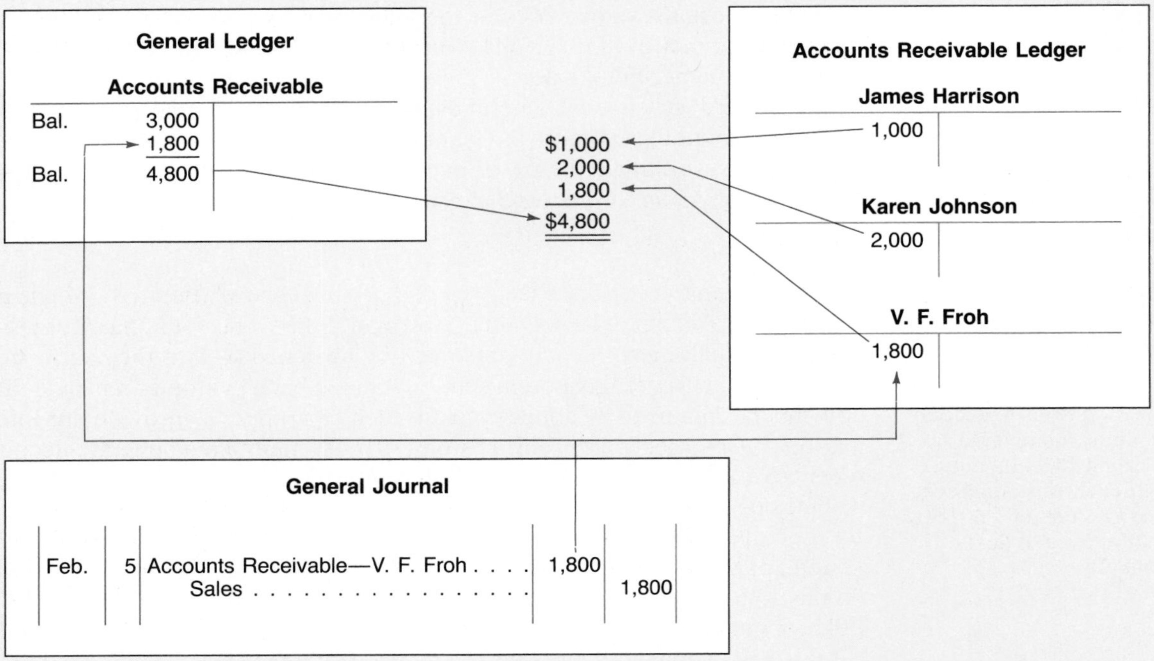


companies buy on credit from several suppliers and must use a controlling account and subsidiary ledger for accounts payable. Another example might be an Office Equipment account, which would control a subsidiary ledger in which each item of equipment is recorded in a separate account.

## Bad Debts

When a company grants credit to its customers, there usually are a few customers who do not pay. The accounts of such customers are called **bad debts** and are an expense of selling on credit.

You might ask: Why do merchants sell on credit if bad debts result? The answer is that they sell on credit to increase sales and profits. They are willing to take a reasonable loss from bad debts to increase sales and profits. Therefore, bad debt losses are an expense of selling on credit, an expense incurred to increase sales.

The reporting of bad debts expenses on the income statement is governed by the *matching principle*. This means that bad debts expenses should be reported in the same accounting period as are the revenues they helped produce.

## Matching Bad Debt Losses with Sales

When credit sales are made, management usually realizes that some portion of those sales will result in bad debts. However, the fact that a credit sale will not be collected often does not become apparent for some time. If a customer fails to pay, most businesses send out several repeat billings. Final acceptance that the customer is not going to pay should wait until every means of collection has been exhausted. Usually, this does not happen until one or more accounting periods after the period in which the sale was made. It may take a year or more. Therefore, to match bad debt losses with the sales they helped produce, they must be matched on an estimated basis. The **allowance method of accounting for bad debts** is designed to accomplish this matching of expenses with revenues.

## Allowance Method of Accounting for Bad Debts

Under the allowance method of accounting for bad debts, at the end of each accounting period, an estimate is made of the total bad debts that are expected to result from the period's sales. An allowance is then provided for the loss. This has two advantages: (1) the estimated loss is charged to the period in which the revenue is recognized; and (2) the accounts receivable are reported on the balance sheet at the amount of cash proceeds that is expected from their collection.

### Recording the Estimated Bad Debts Expense

Under the allowance method of accounting for bad debts, at the end of each accounting period, the estimated bad debts expense is recorded with a work sheet adjustment and an adjusting entry. For example, assume that Fritz Company had charge sales of $300,000 during the first year of its operations. At the end of the year, $20,000 remains uncollected in accounts receivable. Based on these facts, Fritz Company estimates that $1,500 of accounts receivable will be uncollectible. This estimated expense is recorded with an adjusting entry like the following:

| | | | | |
|---|---|---|---|---|
| Dec. | 31 | Bad Debts Expense . . . . . . . . . . . . . . . . . . . . | 1,500.00 | |
| | | Allowance for Doubtful Accounts . . . . . . . . . . . . | | 1,500.00 |
| | | To record the estimated bad debts. | | |

The debit of this entry causes the estimated bad debts expense to appear on the income statement of the year in which the sales were made. As a result, the estimated $1,500 expense of selling on credit is matched with the $300,000 of revenue it helped to produce.

Note that the credit of the entry is to the contra account, **Allowance for Doubtful Accounts.** A contra account must be used because at the time of the adjusting entry, it is not known for certain which customers will not pay. (The total loss from bad debts can be estimated from past experience. However, the exact customers who will not pay cannot be known until every means of collection is exhausted.) Therefore, since the bad accounts are not identifiable at the time of the adjusting entry, they cannot be removed from the subsidiary Accounts Receivable Ledger. As a result, the Allowance for Doubtful Accounts account must be credited instead of the controlling account. If the controlling account were credited, the controlling account balance would no longer equal the sum of the balances in the subsidiary ledger.

### Bad Debts in the Accounts and in the Financial Statements

The process of evaluating customers and approving them for credit usually is not assigned to the selling departments of a business. Otherwise, given their primary objective of increasing sales, selling departments might not use good judgment in approving customers for credit. Because selling departments do not approve customers for credit, bad debts expense normally appears on the income statement as an administrative expense rather than as a selling expense. Since the sales department is not responsible for granting credit, it should not be held responsible for bad debts expense.

Recall that Fritz Company has $20,000 of outstanding accounts receivable at the end of its first year of operations. Thus, after the bad debts adjusting entry is posted, the company's Accounts Receivable and Allowance for Doubtful Accounts accounts show these balances:

| Accounts Receivable | | | | Allowance for Doubtful Accounts | | | |
|---|---|---|---|---|---|---|---|
| Dec. 31 | 20,000 | | | | | Dec. 31 | 1,500 |

The Allowance for Doubtful Accounts credit balance of $1,500 has the effect of reducing accounts receivable (net of the allowance) to their estimated **realizable value.** This term *realizable value* means the expected proceeds from converting the assets into cash. Although $20,000 is legally owed to Fritz Company, only $18,500 is likely to be realized in cash.

When the balance sheet is prepared, the allowance for doubtful accounts is subtracted from the accounts receivable to show the amount that is expected to be realized from the accounts, as follows:

| | | |
|---|---|---|
| Current assets: | | |
| Cash | | $11,300 |
| Short-term investments, at lower of cost or market (cost is $16,000) | | 14,500 |
| Accounts receivable | $20,000 | |
| Less allowance for doubtful accounts | (1,500) | 18,500 |
| Merchandise inventory | | 52,700 |
| Prepaid expenses | | 1,100 |
| Total current assets | | $98,100 |

In the above example, compare the presentations of short-term investments and accounts receivable, and recall that contra accounts are subtracted in both cases. Even though the contra account to the Short-Term Investments account is not shown on the statement, you can easily determine the $1,500 balance of the contra account by comparing the $16,000 cost with the $14,500 net amount. Sometimes, the contra account to Accounts Receivable is presented in a similar fashion, as follows:

| | |
|---|---|
| Accounts receivable (net of $1,500 estimated uncollectible accounts) | 18,500 |

### Writing Off a Bad Debt

When an allowance for doubtful accounts is provided, accounts deemed uncollectible are written off against this allowance. For example, after spending a year trying to collect, Fritz Company finally decided the $100 account of Jack Vale was uncollectible and made the following entry to write it off:

| | | | | |
|---|---|---|---|---|
| Jan. | 23 | Allowance for Doubtful Accounts . . . . . . . . . . . . . . | 100.00 | |
| | | Accounts Receivable—Jack Vale . . . . . . . . . . . | | 100.00 |
| | | To write off an uncollectible account. | | |

Posting the credit of the entry to the Accounts Receivable account removes the amount of the bad debt from the controlling account. Posting it to the Jack Vale account removes the amount of the bad debt from the subsidiary ledger. After the entry is posted, the general ledger accounts appear as follows:

**Accounts Receivable**

| | | | |
|---|---|---|---|
| Dec. 31 | 20,000 | Jan. 23 | 100 |

**Allowance for Doubtful Accounts**

| | | | |
|---|---|---|---|
| Jan. 23 | 100 | Dec. 31 | 1,500 |

Notice two aspects of the entry and the accounts. First, although bad debts are an expense of selling on credit, the allowance account rather than an expense account is debited in the write-off. The allowance account is debited because the expense was recorded at the end of the period in which the sale occurred. At that time, the loss was estimated and the expense was recorded in the bad debts adjusting entry.

Second, although the write-off removed the amount of the account receivable from the ledgers, it did not affect the estimated realizable amount of Fritz Company's accounts receivable, as the following tabulation shows:

| | | |
|---|---|---|
| Accounts receivable . . . . . . . . . . . . . | $20,000 | $19,900 |
| Less allowance for doubtful accounts . . | 1,500 | 1,400 |
| Estimated realizable accounts receivable . . | $18,500 | $18,500 |

### Bad Debt Recoveries

Sometimes, after an account is written off as uncollectible, the customer voluntarily pays all or part of the amount owed. When this happens, the payment should be recorded in the customer's account. This information should be retained in the customer's account for use in future credit evaluations of the customer. When a customer fails to pay and his or her account is written off, the customer's credit standing is impaired. Later, when the customer pays, the payment helps restore the credit standing.

When an account that was previously written off as a bad debt is collected, two entries are made. The first reinstates the customer's account and has the effect of reversing the original write-off. The second entry records the collection of the reinstated account. For example, assume that on August 15 Jack Vale pays in full the account that Fritz Company had previously written off.

The entries to record the bad debt recovery are:

| | | | | |
|---|---|---|---|---|
| Aug. | 15 | Accounts Receivable—Jack Vale . . . . . . . . . . . . . . | 100.00 | |
| | | Allowance for Doubtful Accounts . . . . . . . . . . . . | | 100.00 |
| | | To reinstate the account of Jack Vale written off on January 23. | | |
| | 15 | Cash . . . . . . . . . . . . . . . . . . . . . . . . . . . . . . | 100.00 | |
| | | Accounts Receivable—Jack Vale . . . . . . . . . . . | | 100.00 |
| | | Received full payment of account. | | |

In this case, Jack Vale paid the entire amount previously written off. Sometimes after an account is written off, the customer will pay a portion of the amount owed. The question then arises, should the entire balance of the account be returned to accounts receivable or just the amount paid? The answer is a matter of judgment. If you believe the customer will pay in full, the entire amount owed should be returned. However, only the amount paid should be returned if you believe that no more will be collected.

## Estimating the Amount of Bad Debts Expense

As you already learned, the allowance method of accounting for doubtful accounts requires an adjusting entry at the end of each accounting period to estimate the bad debts expense for the period. That entry takes the following form:

| | | | | |
|---|---|---|---|---|
| Dec. | 31 | Bad Debts Expense . . . . . . . . . . . . . . . . . . . . . | ???? | |
| | | Allowance for Doubtful Accounts . . . . . . . . . . . . | | ???? |

What is the process by which a company estimates the amount to record in this entry? There are two broad alternatives. One is to focus on the income statement relationship between bad debts expense and sales. The other is to focus on the balance sheet relationship between accounts receivable and allowance for doubtful accounts. Both alternatives require a careful analysis of past experience.

### Estimating Bad Debts by Focusing on the Income Statement

The income statement approach to estimating bad debts is based on the idea that some particular percentage of a company's credit sales will become uncollectible. Hence, in the income statement, the amount of bad debts expense should be that same percentage of credit sales.

Suppose, for example, that Baker Company had credit sales of $400,000 in 1990. Based on past experience and the experience of similar companies, Baker Company estimates that 0.6% of credit sales are uncollectible. Using this estimate, Baker Company can expect $2,400 of bad debts expense to result from the year's sales ($400,000 × 0.006 = $2,400). The adjusting entry to record this expense is:

| | | | | |
|---|---|---|---|---|
| Dec. | 31 | Bad Debts Expense . . . . . . . . . . . . . . . . . . . . . . | 2,400.00 | |
| | | Allowance for Doubtful Accounts . . . . . . . . . . . . | | 2,400.00 |

Importantly, this entry *does not* mean the December 31, 1990, balance in Allowance for Doubtful Accounts will be $2,400. For three reasons, it will probably be some other amount.

1. The bad debts percentage (0.6%) is only an estimate. The actual amount of accounts receivable that become uncollectible will likely be larger or smaller than this.
2. Some of the accounts that resulted from 1990 credit sales may have been written off prior to December 31, 1990. If so, the entries to write them off involved debits to Allowance for Doubtful Accounts. Thus, the account balance was increased by the $2,400 estimated expense but also decreased by the amounts previously written off.
3. There probably was a credit balance in the account at the beginning of the year. In each past year, bad debts were estimated at year-end, and accounts that became uncollectible were written off. The balance in Allowance for Doubtful Accounts reflects these events from past years as well as those in the current year.

Often, when the addition to the Allowance for Doubtful Accounts account is based on a percentage of sales, the passage of several accounting periods is required before it becomes apparent that the percentage is either too large or too small. In such cases, when it becomes apparent that the percentage is incorrect, a change in the percentage to be used in future periods should be made.

### Estimating Bad Debts by Focusing on the Balance Sheet

The balance sheet approach to estimating bad debts is based on the idea that some portion of the receivables on the balance sheet date will become uncollectible. Hence, after the bad debts adjusting entry is posted, the Allowance for Doubtful Accounts balance should equal the portion of outstanding accounts receivable estimated to be uncollectible. To obtain this required balance in the Allowance for Doubtful Accounts account, you simply compare the balance before the adjustment with the required balance. The difference between the two is debited to Bad Debts Expense and credited to Allowance for Doubtful Accounts. The balance sheet approach may take two forms: (1) a simplified approach and (2) aging of accounts receivable.

**A Simplified Balance Sheet Approach.** Using the simplified balance sheet approach, a company estimates that a certain percentage of its outstanding receivables will become uncollectible. This estimated percentage is based on past experience and the experience of similar companies. Then, the dollar amount of outstanding receivables is multiplied by the estimated percentage to determine the estimated dollar amount of uncollectible accounts. This amount must appear in the balance sheet as the Allowance for Doubtful Accounts balance. To establish this balance in the account, an adjusting entry is made with a debit to Bad Debts Expense and a credit to Allowance for Doubtful Accounts. The amount of the adjustment is the amount necessary to provide the required balance in Allowance for Doubtful Accounts.

For example, assume that on December 31, 1990, Baker Company of the previous illustration has $50,000 of outstanding accounts receivable. Past experience indicates that 5% of outstanding receivables will become uncollectible. Thus, after the adjusting entry is posted, Allowance for Doubtful Accounts should have a $2,500 credit balance. Assume that before making the necessary adjustment, the account appears as follows:

**Allowance for Doubtful Accounts**

| | | | |
|---|---|---|---|
| Feb. 6 | 800 | Dec. 31 | |
| July 10 | 600 | balance | 2,000 |
| Nov. 20 | 400 | | |

Understand that the $2,000 beginning balance appeared on the December 31, 1989, balance sheet. Then, during 1990, accounts of specific customers were written off on February 6, July 10, and November 20. As a result, the account has a $200 credit balance prior to the December 31, 1990, adjustment. The adjusting entry to give the account the required $2,500 balance is:

| | | | | |
|---|---|---|---|---|
| Dec. | 31 | Bad Debts Expense . . . . . . . . . . . . . . . . . . . . . . | 2,300.00 | |
| | | Allowance for Doubtful Accounts . . . . . . . . . . . . | | 2,300.00 |

**Aging of Accounts Receivable.** Both the income statement approach and the simplified balance sheet approach use the knowledge gained from past experience to estimate bad debts expense. However, neither method of analysis is as refined as the balance sheet approach that involves **aging of accounts receivable.**

With the aging approach, each account is examined in the process of estimating the amount that is uncollectible. Sometimes, the sales and credit department managers have information about specific accounts that allows the managers to decide whether the accounts should be classified as uncollectible. More often, the outstanding receivables are classified in terms of how long they have been outstanding. Then, the estimate of uncollectible accounts is based on the idea that the longer an amount is outstanding, the more likely it will be uncollectible.

To age the accounts receivable outstanding at the end of the period, you must examine each account and classify the outstanding amounts in terms of how long they have been outstanding. After the outstanding amounts have been classified, past experience is used to estimate a percentage of each class that will become uncollectible. These percentages are applied to the amounts in the classes to determine the required allowance for doubtful

**Illustration 8–2**
**Estimating bad debts by aging the accounts**

**BAKER COMPANY**
**Schedule of Accounts Receivable by Age**

| Customer's Name | Not Due | 1 to 30 Days Past Due | 31 to 60 Days Past Due | 61 to 90 Days Past Due | Over 90 Days Past Due |
|---|---|---|---|---|---|
| Charles Abbot . . . . . | $ 450.00 | | | | |
| Frank Allen . . . . . . | 710.00 | | | | |
| George Arden . . . . . | | $ 200.00 | $ 300.00 | | |
| Paul Baum . . . . . . . | | | | | $ 640.00 |
| Totals . . . . . . . . . | $37,000.00 | $6,500.00 | $3,500.00 | $1,900.00 | $1,000.00 |
| | ×2% | ×5% | ×10% | ×25% | ×40% |
| Estimated uncollectible accounts . . . . . . . | $ 740.00 | $ 325.00 | $ 350.00 | $ 475.00 | $ 400.00 |

accounts. This is done by setting up a schedule like the one for Baker Company shown in Illustration 8–2.

The analysis of Illustration 8–2 indicates that the adjusted balance in Baker Company's Allowance for Doubtful Accounts should be $2,290 ($740 + $325 + $350 + $475 + $400 = $2,290). Since the account was previously assumed to have a preadjusted credit balance of $200, the aging of accounts receivable approach requires the following adjusting entry:

| | | | | |
|---|---|---|---|---|
| Dec. | 31 | Bad Debts Expense . . . . . . . . . . . . . . . . . . . . . | 2,090.00 | |
| | | Allowance for Doubtful Accounts . . . . . . . . . . . | | 2,090.00 |

Recall from pages 358–59 that when the income statement approach was used, bad debts expense was estimated to be $2,400. When the simplified balance sheet approach was used (pages 359–60), the estimate was $2,300. And when aging of accounts receivable was used, the estimate was $2,090. It is not surprising that the amounts are different. After all, each approach is only an estimate. However, the aging of accounts receivable allows a more detailed examination of outstanding accounts and is usually most reliable.

## Direct Write-Off Method of Accounting for Bad Debts

The allowance method of accounting for bad debts is designed to satisfy the requirements of the *matching principle*. Therefore, it is the method that should be used in most cases. However, under certain circumstances another method, called the **direct write-off method,** may be acceptable. Under this method, no attempt is made to estimate uncollectible accounts at the end of each period. No adjusting entry is made. Instead, when you decide that an account is uncollectible, it is written off directly to Bad Debts Expense with an entry like this:

| | | | | |
|---|---|---|---|---|
| Nov. | 23 | Bad Debts Expense | 52.00 | |
| | | Accounts Receivable—Dale Hall | | 52.00 |
| | | To write off the uncollectible account. | | |

The debit of the entry charges the bad debt directly to the current year's Bad Debts Expense account. The credit removes the balance of the account from the subsidiary ledger and from the controlling account.

If an account previously written off directly to Bad Debt Expense is later collected in full, you record the recovery with the following entries:

| | | | | |
|---|---|---|---|---|
| Mar. | 11 | Accounts Receivable—Dale Hall | 52.00 | |
| | | Bad Debts Expense | | 52.00 |
| | | To reinstate the account of Dale Hall previously written off. | | |
| | 11 | Cash | 52.00 | |
| | | Accounts Receivable—Dale Hall | | 52.00 |
| | | In full payment of account. | | |

Sometimes a bad debt previously written off directly to the Bad Debts Expense account is recovered in the year following the write-off. If at that time the Bad Debts Expense account has no balance from other write-offs and no write-offs are expected, the credit of the entry recording the recovery can be to a revenue account called Bad Debt Recoveries.

### Direct Write-Off Mismatches Revenues and Expenses

The direct write-off method usually mismatches revenues and expenses. The mismatch occurs because bad debt expenses often are not reported in the same period as the credit sales that become uncollectible. Nevertheless, some small businesses use the direct write-off method when past experience indicates that the amount of bad debts is very small in relation to other financial statement items. For example, the method may be used in a concern where bad debt losses are immaterial in relation to total sales and net income. In such cases, the use of direct write-off comes under the accounting *principle of materiality*.

### The Materiality Principle

The basic idea of the **materiality principle** is that the requirements of any accounting principle may be ignored if the effect on the financial statements is unimportant to financial statement readers. In other words, failure to follow the requirements of an accounting principle is acceptable when the failure does not produce an error or misstatement large enough to influence a financial statement reader's judgment of a given situation.

## Installment Accounts and Notes Receivable

Many companies allow their credit customers to make periodic payments over several months. When this is done, the selling company's asset may be in the form of an installment account receivable or a note receivable. The evidence of an **installment account receivable**, like any other account receivable, includes sales slips or invoices that describe each sales transaction. A note re-

## AS A MATTER OF FACT

New York—Accountants are being sharply criticized by the government for hiding behind outdated professional standards in failing to inform the public about the problems of failing thrifts.

A General Accounting Office report last week alleged that six of 11 audits of collapsed Texas savings associations "did not adequately audit and/or report the S&L's financial or internal control problems."

David L. Clark, an assistant GAO director who helped prepare the report, goes even further. In an interview, he charged that auditors "are hiding behind rhetoric, standards and 10-year-old guidelines that need updating."

* * *

The report accused accountants of making poor evaluations of high-risks loans for real estate and other construction. There was "inadequate evidence in the working papers [of the accountants] to support that [accountants] had properly evaluated loan collectibility," the report said.

* * *

Mr. Clark says that current auditing standards don't force accountants to do enough checking about problem loans. He notes that a 1979 audit guide on thrifts issued by the American Institute of Certified Public Accountants states only that auditors "should consider" visiting construction sites or obtaining independent evaluation of construction completion.

"Since the standards say the auditor 'should consider' this, he can think about it and then not do it," says Mr. Clark. "At the GAO, in the problem audits, we found little evidence that auditors took the extra step. Today they hide in the hazy world of professional judgment."

Thomas P. Kelley, a group vice president of the CPA Institute, notes that while the audit guide hasn't been updated for a decade, new auditing guidelines on thrifts' construction loans have been issued in 1983, 1984, and 1987. "We also plan to issue supplementary guidance throughout 1989," he says.

### Benefit of Hindsight

Mr. Kelley maintains that audits "must be based on professional judgment." He adds: "If the auditor is challenged, he must often defend himself before a jury. The GAO has the benefit of hindsight and its own perspective" in blaming accountants for faulty audits of thrifts.

The GAO's Mr. Clark says that accountants often hide behind "the shield of materiality, claiming that one problem loan isn't material to the thrift's financial condition." Under current audit standards, "materiality" is a loose term often defined as 5% to 10% of profit, assets or net worth.

Mr. Clark says that some accountants say they didn't re-examine some individual loans because they weren't material to the thrift's financial health. "But if we add up several of these loans, they become material," asserts Mr. Clark.

Materiality in auditing "must be considered as cumulative so that the auditors should add up problem loans, not say that one loan doesn't demand more review," says Douglas Carmichael, an accounting professor at Baruch College. Mr. Carmichael is former head of auditing at the CPA Institute.

Defending accountants, Robert Elliott, a partner of Peat Marwick and former member of the institute's auditing standards board, says that CPAs are being "used as a scapegoat for bad laws, poor regulation and incompetent management."

Source: Lee Berton, "GAO Says Accountants Auditing Thrifts Are Hiding Behind Outdated Standards," *The Wall Street Journal*, February 6, 1989, p. C15. Reprinted by permission of *The Wall Street Journal*, 

ceivable, on the other hand, is a written document that promises payment and is signed by the customer. In either case, when payments will be made over several months or if the credit period is long, the customer usually is charged interest. Although the credit period of installment accounts and notes receivable often may be more than one year, they are normally classified as current assets if the company regularly offers customers such terms.

Generally, notes receivable are preferred over accounts receivable when the credit period is long and the receivable relates to a single sale of fairly large

**Illustration 8–3**
**A promissory note**

*$1000.00* *Eugene, Oregon* *March 9, 1990*

*Thirty days* after date *I* promise to pay to the order of *Frank Black*

*One thousand and no / 100* ---------------------------------------- dollars

for value received with interest at *12%*

payable at *First National Bank of Eugene, Oregon*

Hugo Brown

amount. Notes are also used to replace accounts receivable when customers ask for additional time to pay their past-due accounts. In these situations, creditors prefer notes to accounts receivable because the notes may be converted into cash before becoming due by discounting (selling) them to a bank. Also, notes are preferred for legal reasons. If a lawsuit is needed to collect, a note represents written acknowledgment by the debtor of both the debt and its amount.

## Promissory Notes

Calculate the interest on promissory notes and prepare entries to record the receipt of promissory notes and their payment or dishonor.
(L. O. 4)

A promissory note is an unconditional promise in writing to pay on demand or at a fixed or determinable future date a definite sum of money. In the note shown in Illustration 8–3, Hugo Brown promises to pay Frank Black or his order a definite sum of money at a fixed future date. Hugo Brown is the **maker of the note.** Frank Black is the **payee.** To Hugo Brown, the illustrated note is a *note payable,* a liability. To Frank Black, the same note is a *note receivable,* an asset.

The Hugo Brown note bears interest at 12%. Interest is a charge for the use of money. To a borrower, interest is an expense. To a lender, it is a revenue. A note may be interest bearing or it may be noninterest bearing. If a note bears interest, the rate or the amount of interest must be stated on the note.

## Calculating Interest

Unless otherwise stated, the rate of interest on a note is the rate charged for the use of the principal for one year. The formula for calculating interest is:

$$\begin{matrix}\text{Principal} \\ \text{of the} \\ \text{note}\end{matrix} \times \begin{matrix}\text{Annual} \\ \text{rate of} \\ \text{interest}\end{matrix} \times \begin{matrix}\text{Time of the} \\ \text{note expressed} \\ \text{in years}\end{matrix} = \text{Interest}$$

For example, interest on a $1,000, 12%, six-month note is calculated:

$$\$1,000 \times \frac{12}{100} \times .5 = \$60$$

The **maturity date of a note** is the day on which the note must be repaid. Most notes mature in less than a full year, and this period or time of the note often is expressed in days. When the time of a note is expressed in days, the maturity date is the specified number of days after the day the note is dated. As a simple example, a one-day note dated June 15 matures and is due on June 16. Also, a 90-day note dated July 10 matures on October 8. This October 8 due date is calculated as follows:

| | |
|---|---|
| Number of days in July | 31 |
| Minus the date of the note | 10 |
| Gives the number of days the note runs in July | 21 |
| Add the number of days in August | 31 |
| Add the number of days in September | 30 |
| Total through September 30 | 82 |
| Days in October needed to equal the 90-day time of the note, also the maturity date of the note—October | 8 |
| Total time the note runs in days | 90 |

Occasionally, the time of a note is expressed in months. In such cases, the note matures and is payable in the month of its maturity on the same day of the month as its date. For example, a note dated July 10 and payable three months after that date is payable on October 10.

In calculating interest, it was once almost universal practice to treat a year as having just 360 days. This simplified most interest calculations. However, the practice is no longer so common. Nevertheless, to simplify the calculation of interest in assigned problems and to keep the illustrations consistent with the assignments, the practice is continued in this text. It makes the interest calculation on a 90-day, 12%, $1,000 note as follows:

$$\text{Principal} \times \text{Rate} \times \frac{\text{Exact days}}{360} = \text{Interest}$$

or

$$\$1,000 \times \frac{12}{100} \times \frac{90}{360} = \text{Interest}$$

or

$$\overset{10}{\cancel{\$1,000}} \times \frac{\overset{1}{\cancel{12}}}{\underset{1}{\cancel{100}}} \times \frac{90}{\underset{30}{\cancel{360}}} = \$30$$

## Recording the Receipt of a Note

Notes receivable are recorded in a single Notes Receivable account. Each note may be identified in the account by writing the name of the maker in the Explanation column on the line of the entry to record its receipt or payment. Only one account is needed because the individual notes are on hand. Therefore, the maker, rate of interest, due date, and other information may be learned by examining each note.

A note received at the time of a sale is recorded as follows:

| | | | | |
|---|---|---|---|---|
| Dec. | 5 | Notes Receivable . . . . . . . . . . . . . . . . . . . . . | 650.00 | |
| | | Sales. . . . . . . . . . . . . . . . . . . . . . . . . . | | 650.00 |
| | | Sold merchandise, terms six-month, 9% note. | | |

When a business accepts a note as a way of granting a time extension on a past-due account receivable, the business often tries to collect part of the past-due account in cash. This reduces the customer's debt and requires the acceptance of a note for a smaller amount. For example, Symplex Company agrees to accept $232 in cash and a $500, 60-day, 14% note from Joseph Cook to settle his $732 past-due account. When Symplex receives the cash and note, the following entry is made:

| | | | | |
|---|---|---|---|---|
| Oct. | 5 | Cash . . . . . . . . . . . . . . . . . . . . . . . . . . . | 232.00 | |
| | | Notes Receivable . . . . . . . . . . . . . . . . . . . . . | 500.00 | |
| | | Accounts Receivable—Joseph Cook . . . . . . . . . . | | 732.00 |
| | | Received cash and a note in settlement of an account. | | |

When Cook pays the note, the receipt is recorded with this entry:

| | | | | |
|---|---|---|---|---|
| Dec. | 4 | Cash . . . . . . . . . . . . . . . . . . . . . . . . . . . | 511.67 | |
| | | Notes Receivable . . . . . . . . . . . . . . . . . . . | | 500.00 |
| | | Interest Earned . . . . . . . . . . . . . . . . . . . . | | 11.67 |
| | | Collected the Joseph Cook note. $\$500 \times 14\% \times {}^{60}\!/_{360} = \$11.67$. | | |

## Dishonored Notes Receivable

Calculate the discount and proceeds on discounted notes receivable and prepare entries to record the discounting of notes receivable and, if dishonored, their dishonor. (L. O. 5)

Occasionally, the maker of a note either cannot or will not pay the note at maturity. When a note's maker refuses to pay at maturity, the note is said to be dishonored. **Dishonoring a note** does not relieve the maker of the obligation to pay. Furthermore, every legal means should be used to collect. However, collection may require lengthy legal proceedings.

The balance of the Notes Receivable account should show only the amount of notes that have not matured. Therefore, when a note is dishonored, you should remove the amount of the note from the Notes Receivable account and charge it back to the account of its maker. To illustrate, Symplex Company holds an $800, 14%, 60-day note of George Jones. At maturity, Jones dishonors the note. To remove the dishonored note from the Notes Receivable account, the company makes the following entry:

| | | | | |
|---|---|---|---|---|
| Oct. | 14 | Accounts Receivable—George Jones . . . . . . . . . . | 818.67 | |
| | | Interest Earned . . . . . . . . . . . . . . . . . . . . | | 18.67 |
| | | Notes Receivable . . . . . . . . . . . . . . . . . . . | | 800.00 |
| | | To charge the account of George Jones for his dishonored note. | | |

Charging a dishonored note back to the account of its maker serves two purposes. First, it removes the amount of the note from the Notes Receivable account, leaving in the account only notes that have not matured. It also records the dishonored note in the maker's account. The second purpose is important. If in the future the maker of the dishonored note again applies for credit, his or her account will show all past dealings, including the dishonored note.

Note that Jones owes both the principal and the interest. Therefore, the entry records the full amount owed in Jones's account and credits the interest to Interest Earned. This procedure assures that the interest will be included in future efforts to collect from Jones.

## Discounting Notes Receivable

As we previously stated, a note receivable often is preferred to an account receivable. One reason is that the owner of a note can convert the note into cash before it matures by **discounting the note receivable.** In essence, this involves selling the note to a bank or to some other buyer. When a note receivable is discounted, the owner endorses and delivers the note to the bank in exchange for cash. The bank holds the note to maturity and then collects its maturity value from the maker.

To illustrate, assume that on May 28, Symplex Company received a $1,200, 60-day, 12% note dated May 27 from John Owen. It held the note until June 2 and then discounted it at its bank at 14%. Since the maturity date of this note is July 26, the bank must wait 54 days after discounting the note to collect from Owen. These 54 days are called the **discount period** and are calculated as follows:

| | | |
|---|---|---|
| Time of the note in days | | 60 |
| Less time held by Symplex Company: | | |
| Number of days in May | 31 | |
| Less the date of the note | 27 | |
| Days held in May | 4 | |
| Days held in June | 2 | |
| Total days held | | 6 |
| Discount period in days | | 54 |

At the end of the discount period, the bank expects to collect the **maturity value** of this note from Owen. Therefore, as is customary, it bases its discount on the maturity value of the note, which is calculated as follows:

| | |
|---|---|
| Principal of the note | $1,200 |
| Interest on $1,200 for 60 days at 12% | 24 |
| Maturity value | $1,224 |

In this case, the bank's discount rate, or the rate of interest it charges for lending money, is 14%. Therefore, in discounting the note, it will deduct 54 days' interest at 14% from the note's maturity value and will give Symplex

Company the remainder. The amount of interest deducted in advance is called the **bank discount**, and the remainder is called the **proceeds of the discounted note.** The bank discount and the proceeds are calculated as follows:

| | |
|---|---|
| Maturity value of the note | $1,224.00 |
| Less interest on $1,224 for 54 days at 14% | 25.70 |
| Proceeds | $1,198.30 |

In this case, notice that the proceeds, $1,198.30, are $1.70 less than the $1,200 principal amount of the note. Therefore, Symplex will make this entry to record the discount transaction:

| | | | | |
|---|---|---|---|---|
| June | 2 | Cash | 1,198.30 | |
| | | Interest Expense | 1.70 | |
| | | Notes Receivable | | 1,200.00 |
| | | Discounted the John Owen note for 54 days at 14%. | | |

In this entry, notice that the $24 of interest Symplex would have earned by holding the note to maturity is offset against the $25.70 discount charged by the bank. The $1.70 difference is debited to Interest Expense.

In the situation just described, the principal of the discounted note exceeded the proceeds. However, in many cases, the proceeds exceed the principal. When this happens, the difference is credited to Interest Earned. For example, suppose that instead of discounting the John Owen note on June 2, Symplex held the note and discounted it on June 26. If the note is discounted on June 26 at 14%, the discount period is 30 days, the discount is $14.28, and the proceeds of the note are $1,209.72, calculated as follows:

| | |
|---|---|
| Maturity value of the note | $1,224.00 |
| Less interest on $1,224 at 14% for 30 days | 14.28 |
| Proceeds | $1,209.72 |

Since the proceeds exceed the principal, the transaction is recorded as follows:

| | | | | |
|---|---|---|---|---|
| June | 26 | Cash | 1,209.72 | |
| | | Interest Earned | | 9.72 |
| | | Notes Receivable | | 1,200.00 |
| | | Discounted the John Owen note for 30 days at 14%. | | |

### Contingent Liability

A person or company that discounts a note receivable is ordinarily required to endorse the note. This endorsement, unless it is qualified, makes the endorser contingently liable for payment of the note.[4] The **contingent liability** depends

[4] A qualified endorsement is one in which the endorser states in writing that he or she will not be liable for payment.

on the note's dishonor by its maker. If the maker pays, the endorser has no liability. However, if the maker defaults, the endorser's contingent liability becomes an actual liability, and the endorser must pay the note for the maker.

Since it can become an actual liability, a contingent liability may affect the credit standing of the person or concern contingently liable. Therefore, a discounted note should be noted in the Explanation column of the Notes Receivable account. Also, the existence of a contingent liability should be disclosed in the financial statements. For example, assume that Symplex Company holds $500 of notes receivable in addition to the John Owen note. After the entry to record the discounting of John Owen's note is posted, the Notes Receivable account appears as follows:

**Notes Receivable**

| Date | | Explanation | PR | Debit | Credit | Balance |
|---|---|---|---|---|---|---|
| May | 28 | John Owen note | G6 | 1,200.00 | | 1,200.00 |
| June | 7 | Earl Hill note | G6 | 500.00 | | 1,700.00 |
| | 26 | Discounted the John Owen note | G7 | | 1,200.00 | 500.00 |

The contingent liability that results from discounting a note receivable is commonly disclosed in a footnote to the balance sheet. If Symplex Company follows this practice, the company's June 30 balance sheet will show the $500 of notes it has not discounted and the contingent liability that resulted from discounting the John Owen note as follows:

| | |
|---|---|
| Current assets: | |
| Cash . . . . . . . . . . . . . . . . . . . . | $ 5,315 |
| Accounts receivable . . . . . . . . . . . | 21,275 |
| Notes receivable (Footnote 2) . . . . . . | 500 |

Footnote 2: Symplex Company is contingently liable for $1,200 of notes receivable discounted.

### Full-Disclosure Principle

The balance sheet disclosure of contingent liabilities is required by the **full-disclosure principle.** The meaning of this principle is that a concern's financial statements including the footnotes should contain all relevant information about the operations and financial position of the entity. Any data that is important enough to affect a statement reader's evaluation of the concern's operations and financial position should be reported. This does not mean that the concern should report excessive amounts of detail. It simply means that nothing of a significant nature should be withheld and enough information should be provided to make the reports understandable. Examples of items that need to be reported to satisfy the full-disclosure principle include the following:

**Contingent Liabilities.** In addition to discounted notes, a company that is contingently liable due to possible additional tax assessments, pending lawsuits, or product guarantees should disclose these items in its statements.

**Long-Term Commitments under a Contract.** If a company has signed a long-term lease that requires a material annual payment, this should be disclosed even though the liability does not appear in the accounts. Also, if the company has pledged certain of its assets as security for a loan, this should be revealed.

**Accounting Methods Used.** Whenever there are several acceptable accounting methods that may be followed, a company should report in each case the method used, especially when a choice of methods can materially affect reported net income. For example, a company should report by means of financial statement footnotes such items as the inventory method or methods used, depreciation methods used, and the method of recognizing revenue under long-term construction contracts.[5]

## Dishonor of a Discounted Note

A bank always tries to collect a discounted note directly from the maker. If it is able to do so, the one who discounted it will not hear from the bank and will need to do nothing more in regard to the note. However, if a discounted note is dishonored, the bank must promptly notify each endorser of the note if it is to hold the endorsers liable on the note. The process of notifying endorsers that a note has been dishonored is called protesting the note. To protest a note, the bank prepares and mails a **notice of protest** to each endorser. A notice of protest is a statement, usually witnessed by a notary public, that says the note was duly presented to the maker for payment and payment was refused. The cost of protesting a note is called a **protest fee**, and the bank will look to the one who discounted the note for payment of both the note's maturity value and the protest fee.

For example, suppose that instead of paying the $1,200 note previously illustrated, John Owen dishonored it. In such a situation, the bank would immediately notify Symplex Company of the dishonor by mailing a notice of protest and a letter asking payment for the note's maturity value plus the protest fee. If the protest fee is, say, $20, Symplex must pay the bank $1,244. To record the payment, Symplex will charge the $1,244 to the account of John Owen, as follows:

| | | | | |
|---|---|---|---|---|
| July | 27 | Accounts Receivable—John Owen . . . . . . . . . . . . | 1,244.00 | |
| | | Cash . . . . . . . . . . . . . . . . . . . . . . . . . . . | | 1,244.00 |
| | | To charge the account of Owen for the maturity value of his dishonored note plus the protest fee. | | |

[5] FASB, *Accounting Standards—Current Text* (Norwalk, Conn., 1988), sec. A10.105. First published as *APB Opinion No. 22,* pars. 12, 13.

Upon receipt of the $1,244, the bank will deliver the dishonored note to Symplex Company. Symplex will then make every legal effort to collect from Owen, not only the maturity value of the note and protest fee but also interest on both from the date of dishonor until the date of final settlement. However, after exhausting every legal means to collect, it may have to write the account off as a bad debt. Normally, in such cases, no additional interest is taken onto the books before the write-off.

Although dishonored notes often become bad debts, some are also eventually paid by their makers. For example, if 30 days after dishonor, John Owen pays the maturity value of his dishonored note, the protest fee, and interest at 12% on both for 30 days beyond maturity, he will pay the following:

| | |
|---|---|
| Maturity value | $1,224.00 |
| Protest fee | 20.00 |
| Interest on $1,244 at 12% for 30 days | 12.44 |
| Total | $1,256.44 |

Symplex will record receipt as follows:

| | | | | |
|---|---|---|---|---|
| Aug. | 25 | Cash | 1,256.44 | |
| | | Interest Earned | | 12.44 |
| | | Accounts Receivable—John Owen | | 1,244.00 |
| | | Dishonored note and protest fee collected with interest. | | |

## End-of-Period Adjustments

If any notes receivable are outstanding at the end of an accounting period, their accrued interest should be calculated and recorded. For example, on December 16, Perry Company accepted a $3,000, 60-day, 12% note from a customer in granting an extension on a past-due account. When the company's accounting period ends on December 31, the $15 of interest that has accrued on this note is recorded with the following adjusting entry:

| | | | | |
|---|---|---|---|---|
| Dec. | 31 | Interest Receivable | 15.00 | |
| | | Interest Earned | | 15.00 |
| | | To record accrued interest. | | |

The adjusting entry causes the interest earned to appear on the income statement of the period in which it was earned. It also causes the interest receivable to appear on the balance sheet as a current asset.

### Collecting Interest Previously Accrued

When the note is collected, Perry Company's entry to record the receipt is:

| | | | | |
|---|---|---|---|---|
| Feb. | 14 | Cash | 3,060.00 | |
| | | Interest Earned | | 45.00 |
| | | Interest Receivable | | 15.00 |
| | | Notes Receivable | | 3,000.00 |
| | | Received payment of a note and its interest. | | |

The entry's credit to Interest Receivable records collection of the interest accrued at the end of the previous period.

### Recording the Collection When Reversing Entries Are Used

In Appendix B at the end of Chapter 4, we explained how some companies make reversing entries on the first day of a new accounting period. These entries are not necessary but are often used as a bookkeeping convenience. In the above example, if Perry Company had used reversing entries, the December 31 accrual of interest would have been reversed on January 1, as follows:

| | | | | |
|---|---|---|---|---|
| Jan. | 1 | Interest Earned | 15.00 | |
| | | Interest Receivable | | 15.00 |
| | | To reverse accrual of interest. | | |

Since the Interest Earned account was closed to Income Summary on December 31, the above entry would give the Interest Earned account a debit balance of $15. Also, the Interest Receivable balance would be reduced from $15 debit to $0. Then, the cash receipt on February 14 would be recorded as follows:

| | | | | |
|---|---|---|---|---|
| Feb. | 14 | Cash | 3,060.00 | |
| | | Interest Earned | | 60.00 |
| | | Notes Receivable | | 3,000.00 |
| | | Received payment of a note and its interest. | | |

Note that as a result of these two entries, the Interest Earned account balance is $60 − $15, or $45. This balance is exactly the same as when the receipt was recorded without the use of reversing entries (see the February 14 entry at the top of this page).

## Summary of the Chapter in Terms of Learning Objectives

**1.** Short-term investments are recorded at cost; dividends, interest, and gains and losses on the investments are recorded in appropriate income statement accounts. The total cost of the entire portfolio of short-term investments in marketable equity securities is compared with its market value to determine the lower of cost or market. Write-downs to market are credited to a contra account.

**2.** When credit card receipts are deposited in a bank account, the credit card expense is recorded at the time of the deposit. When credit card receipts must be submitted to the credit card company for payment, Accounts Receivable is debited for the sales amount. Then, credit card expense is recorded at the time cash is received from the credit card company. However, credit card expense should be accrued at the end of each accounting period.

**3.** Under the allowance method, bad debts expense is recorded as an adjustment at the end of each accounting period. The amount of the entry is determined either by (*a*) focusing on the income statement relationship between bad debts expense and credit sales or (*b*) focusing on the balance sheet. The later approach may involve aging the accounts or using a percentage relationship between accounts receivable and allowance for doubtful accounts. Then, uncollectible accounts are written off against Allowance for Doubtful Accounts. The direct write-off method charges Bad Debts Expense only when accounts are written off as uncollectible.

**4.** Interest rates are typically stated in annual terms. When a note's time to maturity is more or less than one year, the time must be expressed as a percentage of one year and multiplied by the annual amount of interest to determine the interest on the note. Dishonored notes are credited to Notes Receivable and debited to Accounts Receivable and to the account of the maker.

**5.** The bank's discount rate is applied to the maturity value of a note to determine the discount, which is subtracted from the maturity value to determine the proceeds. If a discounted note receivable is dishonored, the original payee usually becomes liable to pay the note including any protest fee.

## Demonstration Problem

The Garden Company had the following transactions during 1990:

May 8 Purchased 300 shares of Federal Express common stock as a short-term investment. The cost of $40 per share plus $975 in broker's commissions was paid in cash.

July 3 Received $800 in dividends from the Federal Express stock.

14 Wrote off a $750 account receivable from 1989. (Garden Company uses the allowance method.)

26 Bank credit card sales amounted to $15,000. Deposited the sales slips in the local bank, which deducts 5% as its fee.

30 Received $400 in partial settlement of a $2,000 account receivable. The remaining balance was converted to a $1,600, one-year, 12% note receivable.

Aug. 4 Wrote off a $1,100 account receivable arising from a sale earlier in 1990.

15 Accepted a $2,000 down payment and a $10,000 note receivable from a customer in exchange for an inventory item that normally sells for $12,000. The note was dated August 15, bears 12% interest, and matures in six months.

Sept. 2 Sold 100 shares of Federal Express stock at $47 per share, and continued to hold the other 200 shares. The broker's commission on the sale was $225.

Nov. 15 Discounted the $10,000 note (dated August 15) at the local bank at a rate of 16%.

Dec. 2 Purchased 400 shares of McDonald's stock for $60 per share plus $1,600 in commissions. The stock is to be held as a short-term investment.

*Required*

1. Prepare journal entries to record the above transactions on the books of The Garden Company.
2. Prepare adjusting journal entries as of December 31, 1990, for the following items:
   *a.* The market prices of the equity securities held by The Garden Company are: $48 per share for the Federal Express stock, and $55 per share for the McDonald's stock.
   *b.* Bad debts expense is estimated by an aging of accounts receivable. The unadjusted balance of the Allowance for Doubtful Accounts account is a $1,000 debit, while the desired balance is estimated to be a $20,400 credit.
   *c.* Interest is accrued on the note dated July 30, 1990.

## Solution to Demonstration Problem

1.

| | | | | |
|---|---|---|---|---|
| May | 8 | Short-Term Investments | 12,975.00 | |
| | | Cash [(300 × $40) + $975] | | 12,975.00 |
| | | Purchased 300 shares of Federal Express. | | |
| July | 3 | Cash | 800.00 | |
| | | Dividends Earned | | 800.00 |
| | | Received dividends on Federal Express stock. | | |
| | 14 | Allowance for Doubtful Accounts | 750.00 | |
| | | Accounts Receivable | | 750.00 |
| | | Wrote off an uncollectible account. | | |
| | 26 | Cash | 14,250.00 | |
| | | Credit Card Expense | 750.00 | |
| | | Sales | | 15,000.00 |
| | | $15,000 × .05 = $750. | | |
| | 30 | Notes Receivable | 1,600.00 | |
| | | Cash | 400.00 | |
| | | Accounts Receivable | | 2,000.00 |
| | | Accepted a $1,600, one-year, 12% note receivable and $400 in cash in settlement of a customer's account. | | |

| | | | | |
|---|---|---|---|---|
| Aug. | 4 | Allowance for Doubtful Accounts . . . . . . . . . . . . | 1,100.00 | |
| | | Accounts Receivable . . . . . . . . . . . . . . . . . . | | 1,100.00 |
| | | Wrote off an uncollectible account. | | |
| | 15 | Cash . . . . . . . . . . . . . . . . . . . . . . . . . . | 2,000.00 | |
| | | Notes Receivable . . . . . . . . . . . . . . . . . . . . | 10,000.00 | |
| | | Sales . . . . . . . . . . . . . . . . . . . . . . . . . | | 12,000.00 |
| | | Sold merchandise to customer for $2,000 cash and $10,000 note receivable. | | |
| Sept. | 2 | Cash . . . . . . . . . . . . . . . . . . . . . . . . . . | 4,475.00 | |
| | | Gain on Sale of Investment . . . . . . . . . . . . . | | 150.00 |
| | | Short-Term Investments . . . . . . . . . . . . . . . | | 4,325.00 |
| | | Sold 100 shares of Federal Express for $47 per share less a $225 commission. $\$12,975 \times {}^{100}/_{300} = \$4,325$. | | |
| Nov. | 15 | Cash . . . . . . . . . . . . . . . . . . . . . . . . . . | 10,176.00 | |
| | | Interest Earned . . . . . . . . . . . . . . . . . . . . | | 176.00 |
| | | Notes Receivable . . . . . . . . . . . . . . . . . . . | | 10,000.00 |
| | | $\$10,000 + (\$10,000 \times 12\% \times {}^{6}/_{12}) = \$10,600$. $\$10,600 \times 16\% \times {}^{3}/_{12} = \$424$. $\$10,600 - \$424 = \$10,176$. | | |
| Dec. | 2 | Short-Term Investments . . . . . . . . . . . . . . . . . | 25,600.00 | |
| | | Cash . . . . . . . . . . . . . . . . . . . . . . . . . | | 25,600.00 |
| | | Purchased 400 shares of McDonald's for $60 per share plus $1,600 in commissions. | | |

2.

| | | | | |
|---|---|---|---|---|
| 1990 | | | | |
| Dec. | 31 | Loss on Market Decline of Short-Term Investments . . | 2,650.00 | |
| | | Allowance to Reduce Short-Term Investments to Market . . . . . . . . . . . . . . . | | 2,650.00 |
| | | To record the decline in market value of short-term investments. | | |

| Short-Term Investments | Shares | Cost per Share | Total Cost | Value per Share | Total Market | Difference |
|---|---|---|---|---|---|---|
| Federal Express . . | 200 | $43.25 | $ 8,650 | $48.00 | $ 9,600 | |
| McDonald's . . . . | 400 | 64.00 | 25,600 | 55.00 | 22,000 | |
| Total . . . . . . . . | | | $34,250 | | $31,600 | $2,650 |

| | | | | |
|---|---|---|---|---|
| | 31 | Bad Debts Expense . . . . . . . . . . . . . . . . . . . | 21,400.00 | |
| | | Allowance for Doubtful Accounts . . . . . . . . . . | | 21,400.00 |
| | | To adjust the allowance account from $1,000 debit balance to $20,400 credit balance. | | |
| | 31 | Interest Receivable . . . . . . . . . . . . . . . . . . . | 80.00 | |
| | | Interest Earned . . . . . . . . . . . . . . . . . . . . | | 80.00 |
| | | To accrue interest on July 30 note receivable ($\$1,600 \times 12\% \times {}^{5}/_{12}$). | | |

## Glossary

Define or explain the words and phrases listed in the chapter Glossary. (L. O. 6)

**Accounts Receivable Ledger** a subsidiary ledger having an account for each customer. pp. 353–54

**Aging of accounts receivable** a process of classifying accounts receivable in terms of how long they have been outstanding for the purpose of estimating the amount of uncollectible accounts. pp. 360–61

**Allowance for doubtful accounts** the estimated amount of accounts receivable that will be uncollectible. p. 355

**Allowance method of accounting for bad debts** an accounting procedure that (1) estimates the bad debts arising from credit sales and reports bad debt expense during the period of the sales; and (2) reports accounts receivable in the balance sheet net of estimated uncollectibles, which is their estimated realizable value. p. 355

**Bad debt** an uncollectible receivable. p. 354

**Bank discount** the amount of interest charged by a bank when the bank accepts a discounted note from a customer. Also, the interest a bank deducts in advance when making a loan. p. 368

**Contingent liability** a potential liability that will become an actual liability if and only if certain events occur. pp. 368–69

**Controlling account** a general ledger account the balance of which is always equal to the sum of the balances in a related subsidiary ledger. p. 353

**Direct write-off method of accounting for bad debts** a procedure whereby uncollectible accounts are not estimated in advance and are not charged to expense until they prove to be uncollectible. pp. 361–62

**Discount period of a note** the number of days following the date on which a note is discounted at the bank until the maturity date of the note. p. 367

**Discounting a note receivable** selling a note receivable to a bank or other concern, usually with the provision that the seller assumes a contingent liability to pay the note if it is dishonored. p. 367

**Dishonoring a note** refusal of a promissory note's maker to pay the amount due upon maturity of the note. p. 366

**Full-disclosure principle** the accounting requirement that financial statements including the footnotes contain all relevant information about the operations and financial position of the entity and that the information be presented in an understandable manner. p. 369

**General Ledger** the collection of financial statement accounts of a business. p. 353

**Installment accounts receivable** accounts receivable that allow the customer to make periodic payments over several months and which typically earn interest. pp. 362–63

**Lower of cost or market (LCM)** a method of reporting whereby the total cost of the entire portfolio of temporary investments in marketable equity securities is compared to the total market value on the date of the balance sheet and the lesser amount is reported in the balance sheet. pp. 350–51

**Maker of a note** one who signs a note and promises to pay it at maturity. p. 364

**Materiality principle** the idea that the requirements of any accounting principle may be ignored if the effect on the financial statements is unimportant to financial statement readers. p. 362

**Maturity date of a note** the date on which a note and any interest are due and payable. p. 365

**Maturity value of a note** principal of the note plus any interest due on the note's maturity date. p. 367

**Notice of protest** a written statement, usually witnessed by a notary public, that says a note was duly presented to the maker for payment and payment was refused. p. 370

**Payee of a note** the one to whom a promissory note is made payable. p. 364

**Proceeds of a discounted note** the maturity value of a note minus any interest deducted because of its being discounted before maturity. p. 368

**Protest fee** the fee charged for preparing and issuing a notice of protest. p. 370

**Realizable value** the expected proceeds from converting an asset into cash. p. 356

**Short-term investments** investments such as government or corporate debt obligations and marketable equity securities that can be converted into cash quickly and are held as a source of cash to satisfy the needs of current operations. pp. 349–351

**Subsidiary ledger** a collection of accounts other than general ledger accounts which shows the details underlying the balance of a controlling account in the General Ledger. p. 353

**Temporary investments** another name for *short-term investments*. p. 349

## Objective Review

Answers to the following questions are listed in Appendix I at the end of the book. Be sure that you decide which is the one best answer to each question *before* you check the answers in the appendix.

1. In accounting for a portfolio of short-term investments in marketable equity securities:
   *a.* The lower of cost or market of each investment is calculated; then, the lower of cost or market amounts are summed to determine the lower of cost or market for the whole portfolio.
   *b.* The total cost of the investment portfolio is determined and compared to the total market value of the investment portfolio to determine the lower of cost or market of the portfolio.
   *c.* A loss on the market decline of short-term investments is debited to Allowance to Reduce Short-Term Investments to Market.
   *d.* Any cash received as dividends from short-term investments is debited to Dividends Earned.

*e.* Increases in the market value of the short-term portfolio are credited to Gain from Short-Term Investments.

2. In accounting for credit card sales:
*a.* The entry to record credit card sales always includes a debit to Accounts Receivable.
*b.* When the bank credits the seller's checking account immediately upon the seller's deposit of sales receipts, the seller records the credit card sales with a debit to Cash.
*c.* Credit card expense that results from credit sales made in Period One should be reported as expense in Period Two if the cash from the sale is received in Period Two.
*d.* When the bank credits the seller's checking account immediately upon the seller's deposit of sales receipts, the seller does not incur any credit card expense as a result of making credit card sales.
*e.* When the seller must submit accumulated sales receipts to the credit card company and then time passes before cash is received from the credit card company, the seller does not incur any credit card expense as a result of making credit card sales.

3. Just before adjusting entries are made at year-end, Pickle Company's Accounts Receivable balance is $200,000 and Allowance for Doubtful Accounts has a debit balance of $2,000. Credit sales for the year were $1,500,000; the experience of past years suggests that 2% of credit sales prove to be uncollectible. However, an aging of accounts receivable results in a $45,000 estimate of uncollectibles. Using the aging of accounts receivable method, the Bad Debt Expense for the year is:
*a.* $47,000.
*b.* $45,000.
*c.* $43,000.
*d.* $30,000.
*e.* None of the above is correct.

4. Roth Company purchased $6,000 of merchandise from Kraft Company on December 16, 1990. Kraft accepted Roth's $6,000, 90-day, 10% note as payment. Assuming no reversing entries, what entry should Kraft make on March 16, 1991, when the note is paid?

| | | | |
|---|---|---|---|
| a. | Cash | 6,150.00 | |
| | Interest Earned | | 150.00 |
| | Notes Receivable | | 6,000.00 |
| b. | Cash | 6,150.00 | |
| | Notes Receivable | | 6,150.00 |
| c. | Cash | 6,150.00 | |
| | Interest Earned | | 125.00 |
| | Interest Receivable | | 25.00 |
| | Notes Receivable | | 6,000.00 |

| | | | |
|---|---|---|---|
| d. | Cash | 6,125.00 | |
| | Interest Earned | | 125.00 |
| | Notes Receivable | | 6,000.00 |
| e. | None of the above. | | |

5. The proceeds from discounting a $3,000, 10%, 90-day note, if it is discounted 60 days before maturity at 12%, are:
   *a.* $3,075.00.
   *b.* $3,050.00.
   *c.* $3,061.50.
   *d.* $3,013.50.
   *e.* None of the above.

## Questions for Class Discussion

1. Under what conditions should investments be classified as current assets?
2. In a balance sheet, what valuations should be reported for short-term investments in marketable equity securities?
3. What kind of account is credited when you record a loss on market decline of short-term investments?
4. Under what conditions are increases in the market value of short-term investments recorded in the accounts?
5. If 1,000 shares of Bander Corporation common stock are purchased as a short-term investment and the price paid was 67⅜ plus a $400 brokerage commission, what amount should be debited to the Temporary Investments account?
6. If a short-term investment that cost $6,780 was sold for $7,500, how should the difference between the two amounts be recorded?
7. Why do customers often prefer to charge their purchases to credit cards?
8. How do businesses benefit from allowing their customers to use credit cards?
9. Where is credit card expense disclosed on a classified income statement?
10. If a business allows its customers to use a credit card that requires the business to send the credit card receipts to the credit card company and wait to be paid, when is the credit card expense usually recorded?
11. What functions are served by the Accounts Receivable controlling account?
12. How is the equality of a controlling account and its subsidiary ledger maintained?
13. In meeting the requirements of the matching principle, why must bad debts expenses be matched with sales on an estimated basis?

14. What term describes the balance sheet valuation of accounts receivable less allowance for doubtful accounts?
15. What is a contra account? Why is estimated bad debts expense credited to a contra account rather than to the Accounts Receivable controlling account?
16. When bad debts are estimated by the income statement approach, what relationship is the focus of attention?
17. A company had $560,000 of charge sales in a year. How many dollars of bad debts expense may the company expect to experience from these sales if its past bad debts expense has averaged one fourth of 1% of charge sales?
18. Classify the following accounts: (*a*) Accounts Receivable, (*b*) Allowance for Doubtful Accounts, and (*c*) Bad Debts Expense.
19. Explain why writing off a bad debt against the allowance account does not reduce the estimated realizable value of a company's accounts receivable.
20. What are three reasons why Bad Debts Expense usually does not have the same adjusted balance as Allowance for Doubtful Accounts?
21. When bad debts are estimated by the simplified balance sheet approach, what relationship is the focus of attention?
22. Why does the direct write-off method of accounting for bad debts commonly fail in matching revenues and expenses?
23. What is the essence of the accounting principle of materiality?
24. Why might a business prefer a note receivable to an account receivable?
25. Define:
    - *a.* Promissory note.
    - *b.* Payee of a note.
    - *c.* Maturity date.
    - *d.* Dishonored note.
    - *e.* Notice of protest.
    - *f.* Discount period of a note.
    - *g.* Maker of a note.
    - *h.* Principal of a note.
    - *i.* Maturity value.
    - *j.* Contingent liability.
26. What are the due dates of the following notes: (*a*) a 90-day note dated July 10, (*b*) a 60-day note dated April 14, and (*c*) a 90-day note dated November 12?
27. Distinguish between bank discount and cash discount.
28. What does the full-disclosure principle require in a company's accounting statements?

## Exercises

**Exercise 8–1**
**Transactions that involve short-term investments**
(L. O. 1)

Prepare general journal entries to record the following transactions involving Rather Company's short-term investments, all of which occurred during 1990.

*a.* On April 20, paid $50,000 to purchase $50,000 of Chrysler Corporation's short-term (90-day) notes payable, which are dated April 20, and pay interest at a 10% rate.

*b.* On May 15, bought 1,000 shares of General Electric common stock at 56½ plus a $640 brokerage fee.

*c.* On June 1, paid $30,000 to purchase West Corporation's 9% notes payable, $30,000 principal value, due June 15, 1997.

*d.* On July 19, received a check from Chrysler Corporation in payment of the principal and 90 days' interest on the notes purchased in (*a*).

*e.* On October 20, received a $1 per share cash dividend on the General Electric common stock purchased in transaction (*b*).

*f.* On November 5, sold 500 shares of General Electric common stock for $59 per share, less a $375 brokerage fee.

*g.* On December 1, received a check from West Corporation for six months' interest on the notes purchased in (*c*).

**Exercise 8–2**
**Reducing short-term investments to lower of cost or market**
(L. O. 1)

On December 31, 1990, DataFile Corporation owned the following short-term investments in marketable equity securities.

| | Cost | Market Value |
|---|---|---|
| Firestone common stock . . . . . . . . | $12,400 | $13,700 |
| General Tire common stock . . . . . . . | 16,800 | 16,100 |
| Texas Instruments common stock . . . . | 23,200 | 21,300 |
| First Republic common stock . . . . . . . | 28,500 | 28,700 |

DataFile Corporation had no short-term investments prior to 1990. Calculate the lower of cost or market of DataFile Corporation's short-term investments and, if necessary, prepare a general journal entry to record the decline in market value of the investments.

**Exercise 8–3**
**Adjusting the Allowance for Market Decline of Short-Term Investments account**
(L. O. 1)

Hays Company's annual accounting period ends on December 31. The cost and market values of the company's short-term investments in marketable equity securities were as follows on sequential balance sheet dates:

| | Cost | Market Value |
|---|---|---|
| Short-term investments in marketable equity securities: | | |
| On December 31, 1989 . . . . . . . . . . . . . . . . | $15,000 | $14,000 |
| On December 31, 1990 . . . . . . . . . . . . . . . . | 17,000 | 15,500 |

Prepare a general journal entry on December 31, 1990, to adjust the balance in the contra account to Short-Term Investments.

**Exercise 8–4**
**Credit card transactions**
(L. O. 2)

Compton Company allows customers to use two alternative credit cards in charging purchases. With the First Net Bank Card, Compton receives an immediate credit upon depositing sales receipts in its checking account. First Net Bank makes a 3% service charge for credit card sales. The second credit card Compton accepts is American Card. Compton sends the accumulated American Card receipts to the American Company on a weekly basis and is paid by American Company approximately 10 days later. American charges 3.5% of sales for using its card. Prepare entries in general journal form to record the following credit card transactions of Compton Company:

Oct. 1 Sold merchandise for $3,500 on this day, accepting the customers' First Net Bank Card. At the end of the day, the First Net Bank Card receipts were deposited in the company's account at the bank.

2 Sold merchandise for $225, accepting the customer's American Card.
7 Mailed $6,000 of credit card receipts to American Company, requesting payment.
19 Received American Company's check for the October 7 billing, less the normal service charge.

**Exercise 8–5**
**Subsidiary ledger accounts**
(L. O. 3)

Bayfield Company recorded the following transactions during May 1990:

| | | | | |
|---|---|---|---|---|
| May | 4 | Accounts Receivable—Ed Morris | 900.00 | |
| | | Sales | | 900.00 |
| | 8 | Accounts Receivable—Alice Brown | 750.00 | |
| | | Sales | | 750.00 |
| | 19 | Accounts Receivable—Carl Edison | 600.00 | |
| | | Sales | | 600.00 |
| | 20 | Sales Returns and Allowances | 150.00 | |
| | | Accounts Receivable—Carl Edison | | 150.00 |
| | 26 | Accounts Receivable—Ed Morris | 300.00 | |
| | | Sales | | 300.00 |

*Required*

1. Open a General Ledger having T-accounts for Accounts Receivable, Sales, and Sales Returns and Allowances. Also, open a subsidiary Accounts Receivable Ledger having a T-account for each customer. Post the above entries to the customer accounts.
2. List the balances of the accounts in the subsidiary ledger, total the balances, and compare the total with the balance of the Accounts Receivable controlling account.

**Exercise 8–6**
**Allowance for Doubtful Accounts**
(L. O. 3)

On December 31, at the end of its annual accounting period, a company estimated it would lose as bad debts an amount equal to one half of 1% of its $540,000 of charge sales made during the year, and it made an addition to its Allowance for Doubtful Accounts equal to that amount. On the following March 9, it decided the $400 account of Bob Sweete was uncollectible and wrote it off as a bad debt. Two months later, on May 8, Mr. Sweete unexpectedly paid the amount previously written off. Give the required entries in general journal form to record these transactions.

**Exercise 8–7**
**Bad debts expense**
(L. O. 3)

At the end of each year, a company uses the simplified balance sheet approach to estimate bad debts. On December 31, 1990, it has outstanding accounts receivable of $57,000 and estimates that 3% will be uncollectible. *(a)* Give the entry to record bad debts expense for 1990 under the assumption that Allowance for Doubtful Accounts had a $350 credit balance before the adjustment. *(b)* Give the entry under the assumption that Allowance for Doubtful Accounts has a $400 debit balance before the adjustment.

**Exercise 8–8**
**Dishonor of a note**
(L. O. 3)

Prepare general journal entries to record these transactions:

Apr. 6 Accepted a $1,000, 60-day, 12% note dated this day from Mary Greene in granting a time extension on her past-due account.
June 5 Mary Greene dishonored her note when presented for payment.
Dec. 31 After exhausting all legal means of collecting, wrote off the account of Mary Greene against the Allowance for Doubtful Accounts.

**Exercise 8–9**
**Discounting a note receivable**
(L. O. 4, 5)

Prepare general journal entries to record these transactions:

May 11 Sold merchandise to Jack Voit, $2,500, terms 2/10, n/60.
July 11 Received $300 in cash and a $2,200, 90-day, 10% note dated July 11 in granting a time extension on the amount due from Jack Voit.
Aug. 10 Discounted the Jack Voit note at the bank at 12%.
Oct. 9 Since a notice protesting the Jack Voit note had not been received, assumed that it had been paid.

**Exercise 8–10**
**Dishonor of a discounted note**
(L. O. 4, 5)

Prepare general journal entries to record these transactions:

Mar. 6 Accepted a $4,500, 60-day, 12% note dated March 4 from Ronald Becker granting a time extension on his past-due account.
9 Discounted the Ronald Becker note at the bank at 14%.
May 5 Received notice protesting the Ronald Becker note. Paid the bank the maturity value of the note plus a $20 protest fee.
17 Received payment from Ronald Becker of the maturity value of his dishonored note, the protest fee, and interest at 12% on both for 15 days beyond maturity.

**Exercise 8–11**
**Analysis of sales terms and discounted note**
(L. O. 4, 5)

On August 7, Barstow Sales sold Mark Gittes merchandise having a $6,250 catalog list price, less a 20% trade discount, terms 2/10, n/60. (Trade discounts were explained on page 221.) Gittes was unable to pay and was granted a time extension on receipt of his 60-day, 15% note for the amount of the debt, dated October 6. Barstow Sales held the note until October 21, when it discounted the note at its bank at 16%. The note was not protested. Answer these questions:

Journalize all

*a.* How many dollars of trade discount were granted on the sale?
*b.* How many dollars of cash discount could Gittes have earned?
*c.* What was the maturity date of the note?
*d.* How many days were in the note's discount period?
*e.* How much bank discount was deducted by the bank?
*f.* What were the proceeds of the discounted note?

## Problems

**Problem 8–1**
**Accounting for short-term investments**
(L. O. 1)

Solomon Company had no short-term investments on December 31, 1989, but had the following transactions involving short-term investments during 1990:

| | | |
|---|---|---|
| Jan. | 10 | Paid $40,000 to buy six-month U.S. Treasury bills, $40,000 principal amount, 8%, dated January 10. |
| Feb. | 3 | Purchased 600 shares of AT&T common stock at 30½ plus a $300 brokerage fee. |
| | 16 | Purchased 400 shares of Boeing common stock at 43¼ plus a $200 brokerage fee. |
| Mar. | 1 | Paid $30,000 for U.S. Treasury Notes, $30,000 principal amount, 9% dated March 1, 1990, due March 1, 1994. |
| | 28 | Purchased 1,000 shares of Syntex common stock at 45⅛ plus a $675 brokerage fee. |
| June | 1 | Received a $0.30 per share cash dividend on the AT&T common shares. |
| | 17 | Sold 400 shares of AT&T common stock at 32 less a $200 brokerage fee. |
| July | 12 | Received a check for the principal and accrued interest on the U.S. Treasury bills that matured on July 10. |
| Aug. | 14 | Received a $0.35 per share cash dividend on the Boeing common shares. |
| Sept. | 1 | Received a check for six months' interest on the U.S. Treasury Notes purchased on March 1. |
| | 1 | Received a $0.30 per share cash dividend on the remaining AT&T common shares owned by Solomon Company. |
| Nov. | 14 | Received a $0.35 per share cash dividend on the Boeing common shares. |

On December 31, 1990, the market prices of the equity securities held by Solomon Company were: AT&T, 33½; Boeing, 42; and Syntex, 38⅞.

*Required*

1. Prepare general journal entries to record the above transactions.
2. Prepare a schedule to calculate the lower of cost or market of Solomon's short-term investments in marketable equity securities.
3. Prepare adjusting entries, if necessary, to record accrued interest on Solomon Company's investments in debt obligations and to reduce the marketable equity securities to the lower of cost or market.

**Problem 8–2**
**Credit sales and credit card sales**
(L. O. 2, 3)

Barrows Company allows a few customers to make sales on credit. Other customers may use either of two credit cards. The First City Bank makes a 4% service charge for sales on its credit card but immediately credits the checking account of its commercial customers when credit card receipts are deposited. Barrows deposits the First City Bank credit card receipts at the close of each business day.

When customers use the American Credit Card, Barrows Company accumulates the receipts for two or three days and then submits them to the American Credit Company for payment. American makes a 3% service charge and usually pays within one week of being billed.

Barrows Company completed the following transactions:

July 3 Sold merchandise on credit to Bob Jones for $1,170. (Terms of all credit sales are 2/15, n/60.)

4 Sold merchandise for $2,160 to customers who used their First City Bank credit cards. Sold merchandise for $2,400 to customers who used their American credit cards.

5 Sold merchandise for $1,600 to customers who used their American credit cards.

7 Wrote off the account of K. Perry against Allowance for Doubtful Accounts. The $250 balance in Perry's account stemmed from a credit sale in December of last year.

8 The American credit card receipts accumulated since July 3 were submitted to the credit card company for payment.

18 Received Bob Jones's check paying for the purchase of July 3.

19 Received the amount due from American Credit Company.

*Required*

Prepare general journal entries to record the above transactions.

**Problem 8–3**
**Estimating bad debts expense**
(L. O. 3)

On December 31, 1990, Wheaton Company's unadjusted trial balance included the following items:

| | Debit | Credit |
|---|---|---|
| Cash sales | | 150,300 |
| Credit sales | | 308,500 |
| Accounts receivable | 133,400 | |
| Allowance for doubtful accounts | 1,380 | |

*Required*

1. Prepare the adjusting entry on the books of Wheaton Company to estimate bad debts under each of the following independent assumptions:
   *a.* Bad debts are estimated to be 1.5% of total sales.
   *b.* Bad debts are estimated to be 3% of credit sales.
   *c.* An analysis suggests that 7% of outstanding accounts receivable on December 31, 1990, will become uncollectible.
2. Show how Accounts Receivable and Allowance for Doubtful Accounts would appear on the December 31, 1990, balance sheet given the facts in 1. *b* above.
3. Show how Accounts Receivable and Allowance for Doubtful Accounts would appear on the December 31, 1990, balance sheet given the facts in 1. *c* above.

**Problem 8–4**
**Aging accounts receivable**
(L. O. 3)

Miller Corporation had credit sales of $4.2 million in 1990. On December 31, 1990, the company's Allowance for Doubtful Accounts had a credit balance of $4,800. The accountant for Miller Corporation has prepared a schedule of the December 31, 1990, accounts receivable by age, and on the basis of past experience has estimated the percentage of the receivables in each age category that will become uncollectible. This information is summarized as follows:

| December 31, 1990, Accounts Receivable | Age of Accounts Receivable | Uncollectible Percentage Expected |
|---|---|---|
| $420,000 | Not due (under 30 days) | 1.75 |
| 216,000 | 1 to 30 days past due | 3.25 |
| 66,000 | 31 to 60 days past due | 18.00 |
| 42,000 | 61 to 90 days past due | 45.00 |
| 24,000 | over 90 days past due | 75.00 |

*Required*

1. Calculate the amount that should appear in the December 31, 1990, balance sheet as allowance for doubtful accounts.
2. Prepare the general journal entry to record bad debts expense for 1990.
3. On April 2, 1991, Miller Corporation concluded that a customer's $7,800 accounts receivable was uncollectible and that the account should be written off. What effect will this action have on Miller Corporation's 1991 net income? Explain your answer.

**Problem 8–5**
**Recording accounts receivable transactions and bad debt adjustments**
(L. O. 3)

Salinas Company began operations on January 1, 1989. During the next two years, the company completed a number of transactions that involved credit sales, accounts receivable collections, and bad debts. These transactions are summarized as follows:

1989

*a.* Sold merchandise on credit for $174,200, terms n/60.
*b.* Wrote off uncollectible accounts receivable in the amount of $750.
*c.* Received cash of $132,400 in payment of outstanding accounts receivable.
*d.* In adjusting the accounts on December 31, concluded that 2% of the outstanding accounts receivable would become uncollectible.

1990

*a.* Sold merchandise on credit for $238,800, terms n/60.
*b.* Wrote off uncollectible accounts receivable in the amount of $980.
*c.* Received cash of $196,400 in payment of outstanding accounts receivable.
*d.* In adjusting the accounts on December 31, concluded that 2% of the outstanding accounts receivable would become uncollectible.

*Required*

Prepare general journal entries to record the 1989 and 1990 summarized transactions of Salinas Company and the adjusting entries to record bad debts expense at the end of each year.

**Problem 8–6**
**Journalizing notes receivable and bad debts transactions**
(L. O. 3, 4, 5)

Prepare entries in general journal form to record these transactions by Barley Company:

Jan. 5 Accepted a $4,590, 60-day, 10% note dated this day in granting a time extension on the past-due account of Grace Murrow.
Mar. 6 Grace Murrow paid the maturity value of her $4,590 note.
11 Accepted an $1,800, 60-day, 11% note dated this day in granting a time extension on the past-due account of Paul Peters.

May 10 Paul Peters dishonored his note when presented for payment.
14 Accepted a $3,000, 90-day, 13% note dated May 12 in granting a time estension on the past-due account of Ralph Hunter.
22 Discounted the Ralph Hunter note at the bank at 15%.
Aug. 14 Since notice protesting the Ralph Hunter note had not been received, assumed that it had been paid.
16 Accepted a $2,400, 60-day, 11% note dated August 15 in granting a time extension on the past-due account of Elmer Cooper.
Sept. 8 Discounted the Elmer Cooper note at the bank at 13%.
Oct. 15 Received notice protesting the Elmer Cooper note. Paid the bank the maturity value of the note plus a $20 protest fee.
16 Received a $3,600, 60-day, 12% note dated this day from Cathy Reese in granting a time extension on her past-due account.
Nov. 15 Discounted the Cathy Reese note at the bank at 15%.
Dec. 16 Received notice protesting the Cathy Reese note. Paid the bank the maturity value of the note plus a $20 protest fee.
27 Received payment from Cathy Reese of the maturity value of her dishonored note, the protest fee, and interest on both for 12 days beyond maturity at 12%.
31 Wrote off the accounts of Paul Peters and Elmer Cooper against Allowance for Doubtful Accounts.

**Problem 8–7**
**Analysis and journalizing of notes receivable transactions**
(L. O. 4, 5)

Prepare general journal entries to record the following transactions of Crafter Company:

1989
Dec. 14 Accepted a $3,000, 60-day, 12% note dated this day in granting Ed Stafford a time extension on his past-due account.
31 Made an adjusting entry to record the accrued interest on the Ed Stafford note.
31 Closed the Interest Earned account.

1990
Jan. 13 Discounted the Ed Stafford note at the bank at 15%.
Feb. 13 Received notice protesting the Ed Stafford note. Paid the bank the maturity value of the note plus a $20 protest fee.
Mar. 3 Accepted a $2,100, 11%, 60-day note dated this day in granting a time extension on the past-due account of Roy Frix.
27 Discounted the Roy Frix note at the bank at 14%.
May 5 Since notice protesting the Roy Frix note had not been received, assumed that it had been paid.
June 9 Accepted a $2,400, 60-day, 10% note dated this day in granting a time extension on the past-due account of June Quigley.
Aug. 8 Received payment of the maturity value of the June Quigley note.
11 Accepted an $1,800, 60-day, 11% note dated this day in granting Rita Adair a time extension on her past-due account.
31 Discounted the Rita Adair note at the bank at 13%.
Oct. 12 Received notice protesting the Rita Adair note. Paid the bank the maturity value of the note plus a $20 protest fee.

Nov. 9 Received payment from Rita Adair of the maturity value of her dishonored note, the protest fee, and interest on both for 30 days beyond maturity at 11%.

Dec. 27 Wrote off the Ed Stafford account against Allowance for Doubtful Accounts.

## Alternate Problems

**Problem 8–1A**
**Accounting for short-term investments**
(L. O. 1)

Griffen Company had no short-term investments on December 31, 1989, but had the following transactions involving short-term investments during 1990:

Jan. 9 Paid $60,000 to buy six-month U.S. Treasury bills, $60,000 principal amount, 8%, dated January 9.

Feb. 2 Purchased 800 shares of GTE common stock at 35½ plus a $400 brokerage fee.

15 Purchased 600 shares of Aetna common stock at 64¼ plus a $300 brokerage fee.

Mar. 2 Paid $45,000 for U.S. Treasury Notes, $45,000 principal amount, 9%, dated March 2, 1990, due March 2, 1994.

16 Purchased 1,200 shares of Nynex common stock at 55⅛ plus a $975 brokerage fee.

June 2 Received a $0.45 per share cash dividend on the GTE common shares.

16 Sold 600 shares of GTE common stock at 37 less a $300 brokerage fee.

July 11 Received a check for the principal and accrued interest on the U.S. Treasury bills that matured on July 9.

Aug. 13 Received a $0.55 per share cash dividend on the Aetna common shares.

Sept. 2 Received a check for six months' interest on the U.S. Treasury Notes purchased on March 2.

2 Received a $0.45 per share cash dividend on the remaining GTE common shares owned by Griffen Company.

Nov. 13 Received a $0.55 per share cash dividend on the Aetna common shares.

On December 31, 1990, the market prices of the equity securities held by Griffen Company were: GTE, 38½; Aetna, 63; and Nynex, 47⅞.

*Required*

1. Prepare general journal entries to record the above transactions.
2. Prepare a schedule to calculate the lower of cost or market of Griffen's short-term investments in marketable equity securities.
3. Prepare adjusting entries, if necessary, to record accrued interest on Griffen Company's investments in debt obligations and to reduce the marketable equity securities to the lower of cost or market.

**Problem 8–2A**
**Credit sales and credit card sales**
(L. O. 2, 3)

Chilton Company allows a few customers to make sales on credit. Other customers may use either of two credit cards. The American Bank makes a 3% service charge for sales on its credit card but immediately credits the checking account of its commercial customers when credit card receipts are deposited. Chilton deposits the American Bank credit card receipts at the close of each business day.

When customers use the Western Credit Card, Chilton Company accumulates the receipts for two or three days and then submits them to the Western Credit Company for payment. Western makes a 4% service charge and usually pays within one week of being billed.

Chilton Company completed the following transactions:

Apr. 4 Sold merchandise on credit to Joe Blake for $1,750. (Terms of all credit sales are 2/15, n/60.)
5 Sold merchandise for $3,250 to customers who used their American Bank credit cards. Sold merchandise for $3,600 to customers who used their Western credit cards.
6 Sold merchandise for $2,400 to customers who used their Western credit cards.
8 Wrote off the account of T. Kurth against Allowance for Doubtful Accounts. The $500 balance in Kurth's account stemmed from a credit sale in August of last year.
9 The Western credit card receipts accumulated since April 4 were submitted to the credit card company for payment.
19 Received Joe Blake's check paying for the purchase of April 4.
20 Received the amount due from Western Credit Company.

*Required*

Prepare general journal entries to record the above transactions.

**Problem 8–3A**
**Estimating bad debts expense**
(L. O. 3)

On December 31, 1990, Defore Corporation's unadjusted trial balance included the following items:

| | Debit | Credit |
|---|---|---|
| Cash sales | | 360,000 |
| Credit sales | | 585,000 |
| Accounts receivable | 210,000 | |
| Allowance for doubtful accounts | | 200 |

*Required*

1. Prepare the adjusting entry on the books of Defore Corporation to estimate bad debts under each of the following independent assumptions:
   *a.* Bad debts are estimated to be 2% of total sales.
   *b.* Bad debts are estimated to be 3.5% of credit sales.
   *c.* An analysis suggests that 7.5% of outstanding accounts receivable on December 31, 1990, will become uncollectible.

2. Show how Accounts Receivable and Allowance for Doubtful Accounts would appear on the December 31, 1990, balance sheet given the facts in 1. *b* above.
3. Show how Accounts Receivable and Allowance for Doubtful Accounts would appear on the December 31, 1990, balance sheet given the facts in 1. *c* above.

**Problem 8-4A**
**Aging accounts receivable**
(L. O. 3)

Software Corporation had credit sales of $6.5 million in 1990. On December 31, 1990, the company's Allowance for Doubtful Accounts had a debit balance of $7,400. The accountant for Software Corporation has prepared a schedule of the December 31, 1990, accounts receivable by age, and on the basis of past experience has estimated the percentage of the receivables in each age category that will become uncollectible. This information is summarized as follows:

| December 31, 1990, Accounts Receivable | Age of Accounts Receivable | Uncollectible Percentage Expected |
|---|---|---|
| $600,000 | Not due (under 30 days) | 2 |
| 300,000 | 1 to 30 days past due | 3 |
| 70,000 | 31 to 60 days past due | 15 |
| 40,000 | 61 to 90 days past due | 40 |
| 32,000 | over 90 days past due | 80 |

*Required*

1. Calculate the amount that should appear in the December 31, 1990, balance sheet as allowance for doubtful accounts.
2. Prepare the general journal entry to record bad debts expense for 1990.
3. On May 21, 1991, Software Corporation concluded that a customer's $9,600 accounts receivable was uncollectible and that the account should be written off. What effect will this action have on Software Corporation's 1991 net income? Explain your answer.

**Problem 8-5A**
**Recording accounts receivable transactions and bad debt adjustments**
(L. O. 3)

After beginning operations on January 1, 1989, Johanson Company completed a number of transactions during 1989 and 1990 that involved credit sales, accounts receivable collections, and bad debts. These transactions are summarized as follows:

1989

*a.* Sold merchandise on credit for $157,800, terms n/30.
*b.* Received cash of $128,900 in payment of outstanding accounts receivable.
*c.* Wrote off uncollectible accounts receivable in the amount of $300.
*d.* In adjusting the accounts on December 31, concluded that 1.5% of the outstanding accounts receivable would become uncollectible.

1990

*a.* Sold merchandise on credit for $198,800, terms n/30.
*b.* Received cash of $165,300 in payment of outstanding accounts receivable.
*c.* Wrote off uncollectible accounts receivable in the amount of $700.
*d.* In adjusting the accounts on December 31, concluded that 1.5% of the outstanding accounts receivable would become uncollectible.

*Required*

Prepare general journal entries to record the 1989 and 1990 summarized transactions of Johanson Company and the adjusting entries to record bad debts expense at the end of each year.

**Problem 8–6A**
**Journalizing notes receivable and bad debts transactions**
(L. O. 3, 4, 5)

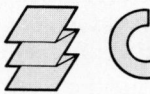

Prepare entries in general journal form to record these transactions by Wheat Company:

Jan. 13 Accepted a $3,000, 60-day, 12% note dated this day in granting a time extension on the past-due account of David Huerta.
Mar. 14 David Huerta dishonored his note when presented for payment.
22 Accepted a $2,100, 90-day, 10% note dated this day in granting a time extension on the past-due account of Rose Jones.
28 Discounted the Rose Jones note at the bank at 16%.
June 26 Since notice protesting the Rose Jones note had not been received, assumed the note had been paid.
28 Accepted $700 in cash and a $1,300, 60-day, 12% note dated this day in granting a time extension on the past-due account of Jake Thomas.
July 22 Discounted the Jake Thomas note at the bank at 14%.
Aug. 29 Received notice protesting the Jake Thomas note. Paid the bank the maturity value of the note plus a $20 protest fee.
Sept. 7 Accepted a $1,500, 60-day, 11% note dated this day in granting a time extension on the past-due account of Ginnie Bauer.
Oct. 13 Discounted the Ginnie Bauer note at the bank at 14%.
Nov. 9 Received notice protesting the Ginnie Bauer note. Paid the bank the maturity value of the note plus a $20 protest fee.
Dec. 6 Received payment from Ginnie Bauer of the maturity value of her dishonored note, the protest fee, and interest at 11% on both for 30 days beyond maturity.
28 Decided the accounts of David Huerta and Jake Thomas were uncollectible and wrote them off against Allowance for Doubtful Accounts.

**Problem 8–7A**
**Analysis and journalizing of notes receivable transactions**
(L. O. 4, 5)

Prepare general journal entries to record the following transactions of Raines Company:

1989
Dec. 9 Accepted a $3,300, 60-day, 12% note dated this day in granting a time extension on the past-due account of Tom Linden.
31 Made an adjusting entry to record the accrued interest on the Tom Linden note.
31 Closed the Interest Earned account.

1990
Jan. 8 Discounted the Tom Linden note at the bank at 14%.
Feb. 10 Since notice protesting the Tom Linden note had not been received, assumed that it had been paid.
Mar. 2 Accepted a $2,000, 90-day, 11% note dated this day in granting a time extension on the past-due account of Lois Goetz.
8 Discounted the Lois Goetz note at the bank at 14%.

June 1 Received notice protesting the Lois Goetz note. Paid the bank the maturity value of the note plus a $25 protest fee.

30 Received payment from Lois Goetz of the maturity value of her dishonored note, the protest fee, and interest on both for 30 days beyond maturity at 11%.

July 3 Accepted a $1,500, 60-day, 10% note dated July 2 in granting a time extension on the past-due account of Janet Casey.

Aug. 31 Janet Casey dishonored her note when presented for payment.

Sept. 1 Accepted $600 in cash and a $1,200, 60-day, 10% note dated this day in granting a time extension on the past-due account of Dick Beaumont.

Oct. 7 Discounted the Dick Beaumont note at the bank at 13%.

Nov. 1 Received notice protesting the Dick Beaumont note. Paid the bank its maturity value plus a $25 protest fee.

Dec. 28 Decided the Janet Casey and Dick Beaumont accounts were uncollectible and wrote them off against Allowance for Doubtful Accounts.

## Provocative Problems

Provocative Problem 8–1
**Personal Sales**
(Review problem)

When his auditor arrived early in January to begin the annual audit, Sam Groves, the owner of Personal Sales, asked that careful attention be given to accounts receivable. Two things caused this request: (1) During the previous week, Mr. Groves had met Bob Peck, a former customer, and had asked him about his account which had recently been written off as uncollectible. Mr. Peck had indignantly replied that he had paid his $425 account in full, and he later produced canceled checks endorsed by Personal Sales to prove it. (2) The income statement prepared for the quarter ended the previous December 31 showed an unusually large volume of sales returns. The bookkeeper who had prepared the statement was a new employee, having begun work on October 1, after being hired on the basis of out-of-town letters of reference. In addition to doing all the record-keeping, the bookkeeper also acts as cashier, receiving and depositing the cash from both cash sales and those received through the mail.

In the process of performing the audit, the auditor prepared from the company's records the following analysis of the accounts receivable for the period October 1 through December 31:

| | Dodd | Reid | Mead | Farr | Soto | Lamb | Teas |
|---|---|---|---|---|---|---|---|
| Balance, October 1 | $ 510 | $300 | $ 820 | $600 | $ 315 | $1,210 | $ 975 |
| Sales | 1,680 | 315 | 1,275 | | 1,580 | 1,000 | 1,450 |
| Total | $2,190 | $615 | $2,095 | $600 | $1,895 | $2,210 | $2,425 |
| Collections | (1,225) | | (950) | | (985) | (1,175) | (1,475) |
| Returns | (205) | (100) | (95) | | (195) | (150) | (60) |
| Bad debts written off | | (515) | | (600) | | | |
| Balance, December 31 | $ 760 | $-0- | $1,050 | $-0- | $ 715 | $ 885 | $ 890 |

The auditor contacted all charge customers and learned that although their account balances as of December 31 agreed with the amounts shown in the company's records, the individual transactions did not. The customers reported credit purchases that totaled $8,150 during the three-month period and returns of $305 for which credit had been granted. Correspondence with Mr. Farr, the customer whose $600 account had been written off, revealed that he had become bankrupt and his creditor claims had been settled by his receiver in bankruptcy at $0.25 on the dollar. The checks had been mailed by his receiver on October 30, and all had been paid and returned by the bank, properly endorsed by the recipients.

Under the assumption the bookkeeper has embezzled cash from the company, determine the total amount he has taken and attempted to conceal with false accounts receivable entries. Account for the deficiency by listing the concealment methods used and the amount he attempted to conceal with each method. Also outline an internal control system that will help protect the company's cash from future embezzlement. Assume the company will hire a new bookkeeper, but that it is small and can have only one office employee who must do all the bookkeeping.

**Provocative Problem 8–2**
**Every-Sport Store**
(L. O. 3)

Dennis Hoover has operated Every-Sport Store for five years. Three years ago, he liberalized the store's credit policy in an effort to increase credit sales. Credit sales have increased, but now Dennis is concerned with the effects of the more liberalized credit policy. Bad debts written off (the store uses the direct write-off method) have increased materially in the last three years, and now Dennis wonders if the increase justifies the substantial bad debt losses which he is certain have resulted from the more liberal credit policy.

An examination of the store's credit sales records, bad debt losses, and accounts receivable for the five years' operations reveal:

| | 1st Year | 2nd Year | 3rd Year | 4th Year | 5th Year |
|---|---|---|---|---|---|
| Credit sales | $180,000 | $198,000 | $270,000 | $325,000 | $360,000 |
| Cost of goods sold | 108,000 | 118,800 | 162,000 | 195,000 | 216,000 |
| Gross profit from credit sales | $ 72,000 | $ 79,200 | $108,000 | $130,000 | $144,000 |
| Expenses other than bad debts | 54,000 | 59,220 | 81,360 | 96,840 | 108,000 |
| Income before bad debts | $ 18,000 | $ 19,980 | $ 26,640 | $ 33,160 | $ 36,000 |
| Bad debts written off | 180 | 790 | 1,350 | 4,210 | 4,300 |
| Income from credit sales | $ 17,820 | $ 19,190 | $ 25,290 | $ 28,950 | $ 31,700 |
| Bad debts by year of sales | $ 720 | $ 595 | $ 3,510 | 3,850 | $ 5,000 |

The last line in the tabulation results from reclassifying bad debt losses so that the losses appear in the same years as do the sales that resulted in the losses. Since some of the fifth-year sales had not been collected at year-end, the $5,000 of fifth-year losses includes $2,845 of estimated bad debts that are still in the accounts receivable.

Prepare a schedule showing in columns by years: income from credit sales before bad debt losses, bad debts incurred, and the resulting income from credit sales. Then, below the income figures show for each year bad debts written off as a percentage of sales followed on the next line by estimated bad debts expense incurred as a percentage of sales. Also prepare a report for Mr. Hoover in which you answer his concern about the new credit policy and recommend any changes you consider desirable in his accounting for bad debts.

# 9 Inventories and Cost of Goods Sold

The operations of merchandising businesses involve the purchase and resale of tangible commodities. In Chapter 5, when we first introduced the topic of accounting for merchandising businesses, we left several important matters for later consideration. In this chapter, we return to the topic and examine the methods businesses use at the end of each period to assign dollar amounts to merchandise inventory and to cost of goods sold. The principles and procedures that are explained in this chapter are used in department stores, grocery stores, automobile dealerships, and any other businesses that purchase goods for resale.

**Learning Objectives**

*After studying Chapter 9, you should be able to:*

1. Calculate the cost of an inventory based on (*a*) specific invoice prices, (*b*) weighted-average cost, (*c*) FIFO, and (*d*) LIFO, and explain the financial statement effects of choosing one method over the others.
2. Calculate the lower-of-cost-or-market amount of an inventory.
3. Explain the effect of an inventory error on the income statements of the current and succeeding years.
4. Prepare entries to record merchandise transactions and maintain subsidiary inventory records under a perpetual inventory system.
5. Estimate an inventory by the retail method and by the gross profit method.
6. Define or explain the words and phrases listed in the chapter Glossary.

The assets that a business purchases and holds for resale are called *merchandise inventory*. As a rule, the items held as merchandise inventory are sold within one year or one operating cycle. Therefore, merchandise inventory is a current asset, usually the largest current asset on the balance sheet of a merchandiser.

## Matching Merchandise Costs with Revenues

Accounting for inventories affects both the balance sheet and the income statement. However, "the major objective in accounting for the goods in the inventory is the matching of appropriate costs against revenues in order that there may be a proper determination of the realized income."[1] The matching process is already a familiar topic. For inventories, it consists of determining how much of the cost of the goods that were available for sale during a period should be deducted from the period's revenue and how much should be carried forward as inventory to be matched against a future period's revenue.

In a periodic inventory system, when the cost of goods available for sale is allocated between cost of goods sold and ending inventory, the key problem is to assign a cost to the ending inventory. However, you should remember that when you assign a cost to the ending inventory, you are also determining cost of goods sold. This is true because the ending inventory is subtracted from the cost of goods available for sale to determine cost of goods sold.

## Items to Include in Merchandise Inventory

The merchandise inventory of a business includes all goods owned by the business and held for sale, regardless of where the goods may be located at the time inventory is counted. In applying this rule, most items present no problem. All that is required is to see that all items are counted, that nothing is omitted, and that nothing is counted more than once. However, goods in transit, goods sold but not delivered, goods on consignment, and obsolete and damaged goods are items that require special attention.

Should merchandise be included in the inventory of a business if the goods are in transit from a supplier to a business on the date the business takes an inventory? The answer to this question depends on whether the rights and risks of ownership have passed from the supplier to the purchasing business. If ownership has passed to the purchaser, they should be included in the purchaser's inventory. Usually, if the buyer is responsible for paying the freight charges, ownership passes as soon as the goods are loaded aboard the means of transportation. (As mentioned in Chapter 5, the terms would be FOB the seller's factory or warehouse.) On the other hand, if the seller is to pay the freight charges, ownership passes when the goods arrive at their destination (FOB destination).

Goods on consignment are goods shipped by their owner (known as the **consignor**) to another person or firm (called the **consignee**) who is to sell the goods for the owner. Consigned goods belong to the consignor and should appear on the consignor's inventory.

---

[1] FASB, *Accounting Standards—Current Text* (Norwalk, Conn., 1988), sec. I78.104. Copyright © by the Financial Accounting Standards Board, Norwalk, Conn. 06856. Quoted with permission. Copies of the complete document are available from the FASB.

Damaged goods and goods that have deteriorated or have become obsolete should not be counted in the inventory if they are not salable. If such goods are salable but at a reduced price, they should be included in the inventory at a conservative estimate of their **net realizable value** (sale price less the cost of making the sale). This causes the accounting period in which the goods deteriorated, were damaged, or became obsolete to suffer the resultant loss.

## Elements of Inventory Cost

As applied to inventories, *cost* means the sum of the applicable expenditures and charges directly or indirectly incurred in bringing an article to its existing condition and location.[2] Therefore, the cost of an inventory item includes the invoice price, less the discount, plus any additional or incidental cost necessary to put the item into place and condition for sale. The additional costs may include import duties, transportation-in, storage, insurance, and any other applicable costs such as those incurred during an aging process (for example, the aging of wine).

If incurred, any of the foregoing enter into the cost of an inventory. However, in pricing an inventory, many concerns do not take into consideration the incidental costs of acquiring merchandise. They price the inventory on the basis of invoice prices only. As a result, the incidental costs are allocated to cost of goods sold during the period in which they are incurred.

In theory, a share of each incidental cost should be assigned to every unit purchased. This causes a portion of each to be carried forward in the inventory to be matched against the revenue of the period in which the inventory is sold. However, the expense of computing costs on such a precise basis may outweigh the benefit from the extra accuracy. Therefore, many businesses take advantage of the *principle of materiality* and charge such costs to cost of goods sold.

## Taking an Ending Inventory

As you learned in Chapter 5, when a **periodic inventory system** is used, the dollar amount of the ending inventory is determined as follows: count the units of each product on hand, multiply the count for each product by its cost, and add the costs for all products. In making the count, items are less likely to be counted twice or omitted from the count if prenumbered **inventory tickets** like the one in Illustration 9–1 are used. Before beginning the inventory count, a sufficient number of the tickets, at least one for each product on hand, is issued to each department in the store. Next, a clerk counts the quantity of each product. From the count and the price tag attached to the merchandise, the clerk fills in the information on the inventory ticket and attaches it to the counted items. After the count is completed, each department is examined for uncounted items. At this stage, inventory tickets are attached to all counted items, and any products without tickets attached are uncounted. After all items are counted and tickets attached, the tickets are removed and sent to the accounting department for completion of the inventory. To ensure that no ticket is lost or left attached to merchandise, all the prenumbered tickets issued are accounted for when the tickets arrive in the accounting department.

---

[2] Ibid., sec. 178.402. Previously published as *Accounting Research Bulletin No. 43*, ch. 4, par. 5.

**Illustration 9–1**
**Inventory ticket used to tag items as they are counted**

| | |
|---|---|
| INVENTORY TICKET no. | *786* |
| Item | |
| Quantity counted | |
| Sales price | $ |
| Cost price | $ |
| Purchase date | |
| Counted by | |
| Checked by | |

In the accounting department, the unit and cost information on the tickets is aggregated by multiplying the number of units of each product by its unit cost. This gives the dollar amount of each product in the inventory, and the total for all the products is the dollar total of the inventory.

## Assigning Costs to Inventory Items

Calculate the cost of an inventory based on (*a*) specific invoice prices, (*b*) weighted-average cost, (*c*) FIFO, and (*d*) LIFO, and explain the financial statement effects of choosing one method over the others. (L. O. 1)

In completing an inventory count, it is necessary to assign costs to the inventory items. When all units are purchased at the same unit cost, this process is easy. However, when identical items were purchased at different costs, a problem arises as to which costs apply to the ending inventory and which apply to the goods sold. There are four commonly used methods of assigning costs to goods in the ending inventory and to goods sold. They are (1) specific invoice prices; (2) weighted-average cost; (3) first-in, first-out; and (4) last-in, first-out. All four methods fall within generally accepted accounting principles.

To illustrate the four methods, assume that at the end of its annual accounting period, a company has on hand 12 units of Product X. Also, assume that the inventory at the beginning of the year and purchases during the year were as follows:

| | | | |
|---|---|---|---|
| Jan. 1 | Beginning inventory . . . . | 10 units @ $100 = | $1,000 |
| Mar. 13 | Purchased . . . . . . . . | 15 units @ $108 = | 1,620 |
| Aug. 17 | Purchased . . . . . . . . | 20 units @ $120 = | 2,400 |
| Nov. 10 | Purchased . . . . . . . . | 10 units @ $125 = | 1,250 |
| Total | . . . . . . . . . . . . . . . . . | 55 units | $6,270 |

### Specific Invoice Prices

When it is possible to identify each item in an inventory with a specific purchase and its invoice, **specific invoice inventory pricing** may be used to assign costs. For example, assume that 6 of the 12 unsold units of Product X were from the November purchase and 6 were from the August purchase. With this information, specific invoice prices can be used to assign cost to the ending inventory and to cost of goods sold as follows:

| | | |
|---|---|---|
| Total cost of 55 units available for sale . . . . . . . . . . . . | | $6,270 |
| Less ending inventory priced by means of specific invoices: | | |
| 6 units from the November purchase at $125 each . . | $750 | |
| 6 units from the August purchase at $120 each . . . . . | 720 | |
| 12 units in the ending inventory . . . . . . . . . . . . . | | 1,470 |
| Cost of goods sold . . . . . . . . . . . . . . . . . . . . . . | | $4,800 |

### Weighted Average

When **weighted-average inventory pricing** is used, the unit prices of the beginning inventory and of each purchase are weighted by the number of units in the beginning inventory and each purchase. The total of these amounts is then divided by the total number of units available for sale to find the weighted-average cost per unit as follows:

| | |
|---|---|
| 10 units @ $100 = | $1,000 |
| 15 units @ $108 = | 1,620 |
| 20 units @ $120 = | 2,400 |
| 10 units @ $125 = | 1,250 |
| 55 | $6,270 |

$6,270 ÷ 55 = $114 weighted-average cost per unit

After the weighted-average cost per unit is determined, this average is used to assign costs to the inventory and the units sold as follows:

| | |
|---|---|
| Total cost of 55 units available for sale . . . . . . . . . . | $6,270 |
| Less ending inventory priced on a weighted-average cost basis: 12 units at $114 each . . . . . . . . . . . | 1,368 |
| Cost of goods sold . . . . . . . . . . . . . . . . . . . . | $4,902 |

### First-In, First-Out

When **first-in, first-out inventory pricing (FIFO)** is used, the items in the beginning inventory are assumed to be sold first. Additional sales are assumed to come in the order in which they were purchased. Thus, the costs of the last items received are assigned to the ending inventory, and the remaining costs are assigned to goods sold. For example, when first-in, first-out is used, the costs of Product X are assigned to the inventory and goods sold as follows:

| | | |
|---|---|---|
| Total cost of 55 units available for sale . . . . . . . . . . . | | $6,270 |
| Less ending inventory priced on a basis of FIFO: | | |
| 10 units from the November purchase at $125 each . . | $1,250 | |
| 2 units from the August purchase at $120 each . . . . | 240 | |
| 12 units in the ending inventory . . . . . . . . . . . . . | | 1,490 |
| Cost of goods sold . . . . . . . . . . . . . . . . . . . . . | | $4,780 |

You need to understand that the use of FIFO is acceptable whether or not the physical flow of goods actually follows a first-in, first-out pattern. The physical flow of products depends on the nature of the product and the way the products are stored. If a product is perishable (for example, fresh tomatoes), the business will attempt to sell them in a first-in, first-out pattern. Other products, for example, bolts or screws that are kept in a large bin, may tend to be sold on a last-in, first-out basis. In either case, the FIFO method of allocating cost may be used.

### Last-In, First-Out

Under the **last-in, first-out inventory pricing (LIFO)** method, the cost of the last goods received are charged to cost of goods sold and matched with revenue from sales. Again, this method is acceptable even though the physical flow of goods may not be on a last-in, first-out basis.

One argument for the use of LIFO is based on the idea that a going concern must replace the inventory items it sells. When goods are sold, replacements are purchased. Thus, it is a sale that causes the replacement of goods. If costs and revenues are then matched, replacement costs should be matched with the sales that induced the acquisitions. Although the costs of the most recent purchases are not quite the same as the costs of the replacements, the costs of the most recent purchases are the most current costs. Thus, the costs of recent purchases closely approximate replacement costs.

Under LIFO, costs are assigned to the 12 remaining units of Product X and to the goods sold as follows:

| | | |
|---|---|---|
| Total cost of 55 units available for sale . . . . . . . . . | | $6,270 |
| Less ending inventory priced on a basis of LIFO: | | |
| 10 units in the beginning inventory at $100 each . . | $1,000 | |
| 2 units from the March purchase at $108 each . . | 216 | |
| 12 units in the ending inventory . . . . . . . . . . . | | 1,216 |
| Cost of goods sold . . . . . . . . . . . . . . . . . . . | | $5,054 |

Notice that when LIFO is used to match costs and revenues, the ending inventory is priced at the cost of the oldest 12 units.

### Comparison of Methods

In a stable market where prices remain unchanged, the choice of an inventory pricing method has little importance. When prices are unchanged over a period of time, all methods give the same cost figures. However, in a changing market where prices are rising or falling, each method may give a different result. These differences are shown in Illustration 9–2, where we assume that Product X sales were $6,000 and operating expenses were $500. In Illustration 9–2, note the differences that resulted from the choice of an inventory pricing method. Since purchase prices were rising throughout the period, FIFO resulted in the lowest cost of goods sold, the highest gross profit, and the highest net income. On the other hand, LIFO resulted in the highest cost of goods sold, the lowest gross profit, and the lowest net income. As you would expect, the results of using the weighted-average method fall between FIFO and LIFO. The results of using specific invoice prices depend entirely on which units were actually sold.

Each of the four pricing methods is generally accepted, and arguments can be made for using each. In one sense, one might argue that specific invoice prices exactly match costs and revenues. However, this method is of practical use only for relatively high-priced items of which only a few units are kept in stock and sold. Weighted-average costs tend to smooth out price fluctuations. FIFO provides an inventory valuation on the balance sheet that most closely approximates current replacement cost. LIFO causes the last costs incurred to be assigned to cost of goods sold. Therefore, it results in a better matching of current costs with revenues on the income statement.

Because the choice of an inventory pricing method often has material effects on the financial statements, the choice of a method should be disclosed in the footnotes to the statements. This information is important to an understanding of the statements and is required by the *full-disclosure principle*.[3]

### Tax Effect of LIFO

The income statements in Illustration 9–2 are assumed to be those of a corporation. Therefore, the income statements include income taxes expense (at an assumed rate of 30%). Note also that because purchase prices were rising, a tax advantage was gained by using LIFO. This advantage arises because when purchase prices are increasing, LIFO assigns the largest dollar amounts to cost of goods sold. As a result, the smallest income is reported when LIFO is used. This in turn results in the smallest income tax expense.

### The Consistency Principle

Since the choice of an inventory pricing method can have a material effect on the financial statements, some companies might be inclined to make a new choice each year. Their objective would be to select whichever method would result in the most favorable financial statements. However, if this were allowed, readers of financial statements would find it extremely difficult to compare the company's financial statements from one year to the next. If income increased, the reader would have difficulty deciding whether the increase resulted from more successful operations or from the change in the accounting method. The *consistency principle* is intended to avoid this problem.

The **consistency principle** requires that a company use the same accounting methods period after period, so that the financial statements of succeeding

---

[3] Ibid., sec. A10.105, 106. First published as *APB Opinion No. 22*, pars. 12, 13.

**Illustration 9–2**
**The income statement effects of alternative inventory pricing methods**

| | Specific Invoice Prices | Weighted Average | FIFO | LIFO |
|---|---|---|---|---|
| Sales | $6,000 | $6,000 | $6,000 | $6,000 |
| Cost of goods sold: | | | | |
| Merchandise inventory, January 1 | $1,000 | $1,000 | $1,000 | $1,000 |
| Purchases | 5,270 | 5,270 | 5,270 | 5,270 |
| Cost of goods available for sale | $6,270 | $6,270 | $6,270 | $6,270 |
| Merchandise inventory, December 31 | 1,470 | 1,368 | 1,490 | 1,216 |
| Cost of goods sold | $4,800 | $4,902 | $4,780 | $5,054 |
| Gross profit | $1,200 | $1,098 | $1,220 | $ 946 |
| Operating expenses | 500 | 500 | 500 | 500 |
| Income before taxes | $ 700 | $ 598 | $ 720 | $ 446 |
| Income taxes expense (30%) | 210 | 179 | 216 | 134 |
| Net income | $ 490 | $ 419 | $ 504 | $ 312 |

periods will be comparable.[4] The *consistency principle* is not limited just to inventory pricing methods. Whenever a company must choose between alternative generally accepted accounting methods, consistency requires that the company continue to use the selected method period after period. As a result, a reader of a company's financial statements may assume that in keeping its records and in preparing its statements, the company used the same procedures employed in previous years. Only on the basis of this assumption can meaningful comparisons be made of the data in a company's statements year after year.

## Changing Accounting Procedures

In achieving comparability, the *consistency principle* does not mean that a company can never change from one accounting method to another. Rather, if a company justifies a different acceptable method or procedure as an improvement in financial reporting, a change may be made. However, when such a change is made, the *full-disclosure principle* requires that the nature of the change, justification for the change, and the effect of the change on net income be disclosed in footnotes to the statements.[5]

## Lower of Cost or Market

Calculate the lower-of-cost-or-market amount of an inventory.
(L. O. 2)

As we have discussed, the *cost* of the ending inventory is determined by using one of the four pricing methods (FIFO, LIFO, weighted average, or specific invoice prices). However, the cost of the inventory is not necessarily the amount that is reported on the balance sheet. Generally accepted accounting principles require that the inventory be reported at market value whenever market is lower than cost. Thus, merchandise inventory is shown on the balance sheet at the *lower of cost or market*.

[4] FASB, *Statement of Financial Accounting Concepts No. 2,* "Qualitative Characteristics of Accounting Information" (Norwalk, Conn., 1980), par. 120.

[5] Ibid., sec. A06.113. First published as *APB Opinion No. 20,* par. 17.

### Market Normally Means Replacement Cost

In applying lower of cost or market to merchandise inventories, what do accountants mean by the term *market?* For the purpose of assigning a value to merchandise inventory, market normally means *replacement cost*. That means the price a company would pay if it bought new items to replace those in its inventory. When the cost to replace merchandise drops below original cost, the sales price of the merchandise also is likely to fall. Therefore, the merchandise is worth less to the company and should be written down to replacement cost (or market).

Lower of cost or market may be applied to merchandise inventory in either of two ways. First, it may be applied to the inventory as a whole. Alternatively, it may be applied separately to each product in the inventory. To illustrate, assume that a company's year-end inventory contains three products (X, Y, and Z) with the following costs and replacement costs:

| Product | Units on Hand | Per Unit Cost | Per Unit Market | Total Cost | Total Market | Lower of Cost or Market (by product) |
|---|---|---|---|---|---|---|
| X . . . . | 20 | $8 | $7 | $160 | $140 | $140 |
| Y . . . . | 10 | 5 | 6 | 50 | 60 | 50 |
| Z . . . . | 5 | 9 | 7 | 45 | 35 | 35 |
| | | | | $255 | | $225 |
| Replacement cost (market) of whole inventory . . | | | | | $235 | |

Note that when the whole inventory is priced at market, the total is $235, which is $20 lower than the $255 cost. Alternatively, when the lower of cost or market is applied separately to each product, the sum is only $225. A company may use either approach to calculate lower of cost or market of merchandise inventory.

Recall from Chapter 8 that lower of cost or market also is used to value a company's short-term investments in marketable equity securities. However, in that case, only one approach is allowed. The total cost and total market value of the entire portfolio of investments is compared to determine the lower of cost or market. Thus, while the lower-of-cost-or-market calculation for merchandise inventory may be done two different ways, the calculation for short-term investments is restricted to one way.

### Inventory Should Never Be Valued at More than Its Net Realizable Value

The idea that *market* is defined as *replacement cost* is subject to an important exception. This exception is that inventory should never be valued at more than its *net realizable value,* which is the expected sales price less additional costs to sell. Understand that merchandise is written down to market because the value of the merchandise to the company has declined. Sometimes, the net realizable value is even less than replacement cost. In that case, the merchandise is worth no more than net realizable value and should be written down to that amount.

For example, assume that merchandise was purchased for $100 and was originally priced to sell for $125. By year-end, a general decline in prices resulted in a replacement cost of $90. However, assume that the merchandise in question has been damaged. Management expects that the merchandise can be sold for $95 if it is first cleaned at a cost of $10. Therefore, net realizable value is $95 − $10, or $85. Since net realizable value ($85) is less than replacement cost ($90), the merchandise should be written down to net realizable value.

### Inventory Should Never Be Valued at Less than Net Realizable Value minus a Normal Profit Margin

A second exception to the idea that *market* means *replacement cost* is that merchandise should never be written down to an amount that is less than net realizable value minus a normal profit margin. To illustrate, suppose that a company normally buys merchandise for $80 and sells it for $100. The gross profit of $20 is 20% of the selling price. Now suppose the selling price falls from $100 to $90. A normal gross profit margin would be $90 × 20% = $18. Therefore, the inventory should not be written down below $90 − $18 = $72, even if replacement cost is less than $72. If the inventory were written down below $72, the income statement of the current period would show an abnormally low gross profit margin. And when the merchandise is sold for $90 the next period, the income statement of that period would show an abnormally high gross profit margin.

## Principle of Conservatism

Generally accepted accounting principles require that inventory be written down to market when market is less than cost. On the other hand, inventory generally cannot be written up to market when market exceeds cost. If writing inventory down to market is justified, why not also write inventory up to market? What is the reason for this apparent inconsistency?

The reason inventory is not written up above cost to a higher market value is that the "gain" from a market value increase is not realized until a sales transaction provides verifiable evidence of the amount of the gain. But why, then, are inventories written down when market is below cost?

Accountants often justify the lower-of-cost-or-market rule by citing the **conservatism principle**. This principle is sometimes expressed simplistically as "recognize all losses but anticipate no profits." More realistically, the principle of conservatism attempts to give the accountant guidance in uncertain situations where amounts must be estimated. In general terms, it implies that when "two estimates of amounts to be received or paid in the future are about equally likely, . . . the less optimistic"[6] should be used. Since the value of inventory is uncertain, writing the inventory down when its market value falls is clearly the less optimistic estimate of the inventory's value to the company.

### Inventory Errors—Periodic System

Explain the effect of an inventory error on the income statements of the current and succeeding years. (L. O. 3)

When the *periodic inventory system* is used, you must be especially careful in taking the end-of-period inventory. If an error is made, it will cause misstatements in cost of goods sold, gross profit, net income, current assets, and owner's equity. Also, the ending inventory of one period is the beginning inventory

[6]FASB, *Statement of Financial Accounting Concept No. 2*, par. 95. Copyright © by the Financial Accounting Standards Board, Norwalk, Conn. 06856. Quoted with permission. Copies of the complete document are available from the FASB.

Illustration 9–3
**Effects of inventory errors—periodic inventory system**

| | 1989 | | 1990 | | 1991 | |
|---|---|---|---|---|---|---|
| Sales | | $100,000 | | $100,000 | | $100,000 |
| Cost of goods sold: | | | | | | |
| Beginning inventory | $20,000 | | $18,000* | | $20,000 | |
| Purchases | 60,000 | | 60,000 | | 60,000 | |
| Goods for sale | $80,000 | | $78,000 | | $80,000 | |
| Ending inventory | 18,000* | | 20,000 | | 20,000 | |
| Cost of goods sold | | 62,000 | | 58,000 | | 60,000 |
| Gross profit | | $ 38,000 | | $ 42,000 | | $ 40,000 |

*Should have been $20,000.

of the next. Therefore, the error will carry forward and cause misstatements in the succeeding period's cost of goods sold, gross profit, and net income. Furthermore, since the amount involved in an inventory often is large, the misstatements can materially damage the usefulness of the financial statements.

To illustrate the effects of an inventory error, assume that in each of the years 1989, 1990, and 1991, a company had $100,000 in sales. If the company maintained a $20,000 inventory throughout the period and made $60,000 in purchases in each of the years, its cost of goods sold each year was $60,000 and its annual gross profit was $40,000. However, assume the company incorrectly calculated its December 31, 1989, inventory at $18,000 rather than $20,000. The error has the effects shown in Illustration 9–3.

Observe in Illustration 9–3 that the $2,000 understatement of the December 31, 1989, inventory caused a $2,000 overstatement in 1989 cost of goods sold and a $2,000 understatement in gross profit and net income. Also, since the ending inventory of 1989 became the beginning inventory of 1990, the error caused an understatement in the 1990 cost of goods sold and a $2,000 overstatement in gross profit and net income. However, by 1991 the error had no effect.

In Illustration 9–3, the December 31, 1989, inventory is understated. Had it been overstated, it would have caused opposite results—the 1989 net income would have been overstated and the 1990 income understated.

Since inventory errors correct themselves by causing offsetting errors in the next period, you might be inclined to think that they are not serious. Do not make this mistake. Management, creditors, and owners base many important decisions on fluctuations in reported net income. Therefore, inventory errors must be avoided.

## Perpetual Inventory Systems

The previous discussion of inventories was focused on the periodic inventory system. Under the periodic system, the Merchandise Inventory account is updated only once each accounting period, at the end of the period. Then, the Merchandise Inventory account reflects the current balance of inventory only until the first purchase or sale in the following period. Thereafter, the Merchandise Inventory account no longer reflects the current balance.

By contrast, the **perpetual inventory system** updates the Merchandise Inventory account after each purchase and each sale. As long as all entries have been posted, the account shows the current amount of inventory on hand. The system takes its name from the fact that the Merchandise Inventory account is "perpetually" up-to-date. When a perpetual inventory system is used, management is able to monitor the inventory on hand on a regular basis. This aids in planning future purchases.

Before computers were widely used in accounting, perpetual inventory systems were limited to companies that sold a limited number of products of relatively high value. The cost and effort of maintaining perpetual inventory records were simply too great for other types of companies. However, since computers have made the record-keeping chore much easier, an increasing number of companies are switching from periodic to perpetual.

## Comparing Journal Entries under Periodic and Perpetual Inventory Systems

Prepare entries to record merchandise transactions and maintain subsidiary inventory records under a perpetual inventory system.
(L. O. 4)

Illustration 9–4 shows in parallel columns the typical journal entries made under periodic and perpetual inventory systems. In Illustration 9–4, observe the entries for the purchase of transaction 1. The perpetual system does not use a Purchases account. Instead, the cost of the items purchased is debited directly to Merchandise Inventory. Also, in transaction 2, the perpetual system credits the cost of purchase returns directly to the Merchandise Inventory account instead of using a Purchases Returns and Allowances account.

Transaction 3 involves the sale of merchandise. Note that the perpetual system requires two entries to record the sale, one to record the revenue and another to record cost of goods sold. Thus, a Cost of Goods Sold account is used in the perpetual system. In the periodic system the elements of cost of goods sold are not transferred to such an account. Instead, they are transferred to Income Summary in the process of recording the closing entries.

The closing entries under the two systems are shown as item 4 in Illustration 9–4. Under the periodic system, all of the cost elements related to inventories are transferred to Income Summary. By comparison, under the perpetual system, those cost elements were already recorded in a Cost of Goods Sold account. Thus, the closing entries simply transfer the balance in the Cost of Goods Sold account to Income Summary. Of course, Sales must be closed under both inventory systems.

In Illustration 9–4, both inventory systems result in the same amounts of sales, cost of goods sold, and end-of-period merchandise inventory.

## Subsidiary Inventory Records—Perpetual System

When a company sells more than one product and uses the perpetual inventory system, the Merchandise Inventory account serves as a controlling account to a subsidiary Merchandise Inventory Ledger. This ledger contains a separate record for each product in stock. This ledger may be computerized or kept on a manual basis. In either case, the record for each product shows the number of units and cost of each purchase, the number of units and cost of each sale, and the resulting balance of product on hand.

Illustration 9–5 shows an example of a subsidiary merchandise inventory record. This particular record is for Product Z, which is stored in Bin 8 of the stockroom. In this case, the record also shows the company's policy of maintaining no more than 25 or no less than 5 units of Product Z on hand.

**Illustration 9–4**

**A comparison of entries under periodic and perpetual inventory systems**

X Company purchases merchandise for $15 per unit and sells it for $25. The company begins the current period with 5 units of product on hand, which cost a total of $75.

| | Periodic | | | Perpetual | | |
|---|---|---|---|---|---|---|
| 1. | Purchased on credit 10 units of merchandise for $15 per unit. | | | | | |
| | Purchases | 150 | | Merchandise Inventory | 150 | |
| | Accounts Payable | | 150 | Accounts Payable | | 150 |
| 2. | Returned 3 units of merchandise originally purchased in (1) above. | | | | | |
| | Accounts Payable | 45 | | Accounts Payable | 45 | |
| | Purchases Returns and Allowances | | 45 | Merchandise Inventory | | 45 |
| 3. | Sold 8 units for $200 cash. | | | | | |
| | Cash | 200 | | Cash | 200 | |
| | Sales | | 200 | Sales | | 200 |
| | | | | Cost of Goods Sold | 120 | |
| | | | | Merchandise Inventory | | 120 |
| 4. | Closing entries: | | | | | |
| | Merchandise Inventory (Ending) | 60 | | Income Summary | 120 | |
| | Sales | 200 | | Cost of Goods Sold | | 120 |
| | Purchases Returns and Allowances | 45 | | | | |
| | Income Summary | | 305 | Sales | 200 | |
| | | | | Income Summary | | 200 |
| | Income Summary | 225 | | | | |
| | Merchandise Inventory (Beginning) | | 75 | | | |
| | Purchases | | 150 | | | |

| | Units | Cost |
|---|---|---|
| Beginning inventory | 5 | $ 75 |
| Purchases | 10 | 150 |
| Purchases returns | (3) | (45) |
| Goods available | 12 | $180 |
| Goods sold | (8) | (120) |
| Ending inventory | 4 | $ 60 |

**First-In, First-Out—Perpetual Inventory System**

In Illustration 9–5, note that the beginning inventory consisted of 10 units that cost $10 each. The first transaction occurred on January 5 and was a sale of 5 units. Next, 20 units were purchased on January 8 at a cost of $10.50 per unit. And on January 10, 3 units were sold. Observe that these 3 units were "costed out" at $10 per unit. This indicates that a first-in, first-out basis is being assumed for this product. The entries to record the sale in the General Journal were the following:

| | | | | |
|---|---|---|---|---|
| Jan. | 10 | Cash (or Accounts Receivable) | xxx | |
| | | Sales | | xxx |
| | 10 | Cost of Goods Sold | 30.00 | |
| | | Merchandise Inventory | | 30.00 |
| | | 3 × $10.00 = $30.00. | | |

**Illustration 9–5**
**First-in, first-out cost flow**

Item *Product Z* Location in stockroom *Bin 8*
Maximum *25* Minimum *5*

| | Received | | | Sold | | | Balance | | |
|---|---|---|---|---|---|---|---|---|---|
| Date | Units | Cost | Total | Units | Cost | Total | Units | Cost | Total |
| 1/1 | | | | | | | 10 | 10.00 | 100.00 |
| 1/5 | | | | 5 | 10.00 | 50.00 | 5 | 10.00 | 50.00 |
| 1/8 | 20 | 10.50 | 210.00 | | | | 5 | 10.00 | |
| | | | | | | | 20 | 10.50 | 260.00 |
| 1/10 | | | | 3 | 10.00 | 30.00 | 2 | 10.00 | |
| | | | | | | | 20 | 10.50 | 230.00 |

**Illustration 9–6**
**Last-in, first-out cost flow**

Item *Product Z* Location in stockroom *Bin 8*
Maximum *25* Minimum *5*

| | Received | | | Sold | | | Balance | | |
|---|---|---|---|---|---|---|---|---|---|
| Date | Units | Cost | Total | Units | Cost | Total | Units | Cost | Total |
| 1/1 | | | | | | | 10 | 10.00 | 100.00 |
| 1/5 | | | | 5 | 10.00 | 50.00 | 5 | 10.00 | 50.00 |
| 1/8 | 20 | 10.50 | 210.00 | | | | 5 | 10.00 | |
| | | | | | | | 20 | 10.50 | 260.00 |
| 1/10 | | | | 3 | 10.50 | 31.50 | 5 | 10.00 | |
| | | | | | | | 17 | 10.50 | 228.50 |

## Last-In, First-Out—Perpetual Inventory System

Perpetual inventories also may be kept on a last-in, first-out basis. When this is done, each sale is recorded as being from the last units received. When these are exhausted, sales are from the next to last, and so on. For example, if LIFO was used for Product Z, the subsidiary merchandise inventory record would appear as in Illustration 9–6.

Compare Illustration 9–6 (LIFO) with Illustration 9–5 (FIFO). Observe that in both illustrations, the sale of 5 units on January 5 is recorded the same way. The cost of these units came from the 10 units in the beginning inventory.

However, the sale of 3 units on January 10 is recorded differently under LIFO than it is under FIFO. Assuming LIFO, as in Illustration 9–6, the January 10 sale is "costed out" at $10.50 per unit. This results in a balance of $228.50, which includes 5 units at $10.00 plus 17 units at $10.50.

The general journal entries to record the January 10 sale, assuming LIFO, are as follows:

| | | | | |
|---|---|---|---|---|
| Jan. | 10 | Cash (or Accounts Receivable) | xxx | |
| | | Sales | | xxx |
| | 10 | Cost of Goods Sold | 31.50 | |
| | | Merchandise Inventory | | 31.50 |
| | | 3 × $10.50 = $31.50. | | |

## The Difference between LIFO (Perpetual) and LIFO (Periodic)

Look again at Illustration 9–6 (LIFO). Note the costs that were assigned to Cost of Goods Sold for the January 5 and January 10 sales. In each case, the costs were taken from the most recent purchase. Thus, the cost of the January 5 sale came from the units in the beginning inventory; they were the only units available on January 5. This means that using LIFO, a perpetual inventory system and a periodic inventory system result in different amounts of cost of goods sold (and ending inventory). With a periodic inventory system, the 8 units sold during the period would come from the last units purchased during the period.

In the case of Product Z, the difference between LIFO (perpetual) and LIFO (periodic) is summarized as follows:

| | LIFO (perpetual) | | LIFO (periodic) | |
|---|---|---|---|---|
| Cost of goods sold: | | | | |
| January 5 sale | 5 × $10.00 = | $ 50.00 | | |
| January 10 sale | 3 × 10.50 = | 31.50 | | |
| Total | | $ 81.50 | 8 × $10.50 = | $ 84.00 |
| Ending inventory: | | | | |
| From beginning inventory | 5 × 10.00 = | $ 50.00 | 10 × 10.00 = | $100.00 |
| From January 8 purchase | 17 × 10.50 = | 178.50 | 12 × 10.50 = | 126.00 |
| Total | | $228.50 | | $226.00 |
| Total goods available | | $310.00 | | $310.00 |

In addition to FIFO and LIFO, perpetual inventory systems can be designed to accommodate an average cost flow assumption. However, illustration of this alternative is deferred for a later course.

## The Retail Method of Estimating Inventories

Estimate an inventory by the retail method and by the gross profit method. (L. O. 5)

Good management requires that income statements be prepared more often than once each year, and inventory information is necessary each time an income statement is prepared. However, taking a physical inventory in a retail store is both time-consuming and expensive. Therefore, many retailers use the so-called **retail inventory method** to estimate inventories without stopping to take a physical count of inventory. Some companies use the retail inventory method to estimate monthly or quarterly statements. Then, they take a physi-

## AS A MATTER OF FACT

Manufactured Homes, Inc. looked like a steady winner for most of 1987. In the first nine months the North Carolina prefab house manufacturer reported pretax earnings of $10.6 million on sales of $148.2 million. But in its fourth quarter the company abruptly booked an enormous $8.5 million loss reserve for credit sales, wiping out those earlier quarterly earnings and ending the year with an anemic pretax $1.6 million.

Was management as surprised as investors? No. Manufactured Homes had been understating its potential credit losses. The outside auditing firm of Peat Marwick Main & Co. believed that to be the case months earlier, and had urged an increase in loss reserves. Management resisted—and management got its way, since corporate quarterly, or 10-Q, reports, unlike annual reports, do not require auditor approval. Come the fourth quarter, the company at last had to bite the bullet. Says Glenn Perry, partner at Peat Marwick, "If we had a requirement to formally review quarterly data, we wouldn't have had a surprise fourth-quarter adjustment."

The situation at Manufactured Homes is not unique. "Misleading quarterly statements have been a persistent problem, particularly among smaller companies," says Glen Davison, deputy chief accountant at the Securities & Exchange Commission. Indeed, last year the SEC took enforcement actions against several companies, including Stereo Village and Cali Computer Systems, largely because of false or misleading quarterly reports.

But these actions were taken after the horse was gone; now the SEC is preparing to close the barn door. In the next month or so the commission is expected to release a proposal requiring that all quarterly reports be "reviewed" on a timely basis by outside auditors. The rule could go into effect as soon as early 1990.

What does the SEC have in mind when it says "review"? As commission officials explain it, outside auditors would check the numbers in quarterly statements and, based on prior auditing experience with the firm, would then question senior management about items that seem out of line. Such problem areas might include unusually large inventories compared with year-ago figures, or steadily increasing accounts receivable. The SEC proposal, in addition, would require the auditors to submit a letter saying that the numbers were reviewed, which would be included on the 10-Q report.

Unlike a full-scale audit, a quarterly review would not require accountants to examine documentation or seek third-party corroboration about management's numbers. Nonetheless, the SEC proposal is an important step in the right direction to tighten lax reporting rules. Currently, only large, actively traded public companies must publish audited quarterly data, and at that, only once a year in their annual 10-K financial reports to shareholders. Gaylen N. Larson, group vice president of Household International, comments: "The key is simply to encourage outside accountants to discuss judgmental issues with senior management."

* * *

Source: Penelope Wang, "Nasty surprises." Excerpted by permission of *Forbes* magazine, January 23, 1989, p. 283, © Forbes Inc., 1989.

cal inventory at the end of each year. These monthly or quarterly statements are called **interim statements**, since they are prepared in between the regular year-end statements. Other companies also use the retail inventory method to prepare the year-end statements. However, all companies must take a physical inventory at least once each year to correct for any errors or shortages.

### Estimating an Ending Inventory by the Retail Method

When the retail method is used to estimate an inventory, a store's records must show the amount of inventory it had at the beginning of the period both *at cost* and *at retail*. You already know what the cost of an inventory is. The retail amount of an inventory simply means the dollar amount of the inventory at the marked selling prices of the inventory items.

Illustration 9–7
**Calculating the ending inventory cost by the retail method**

| | | At Cost | At Retail |
|---|---|---|---|
| (Step 1) | Goods available for sale: | | |
| | Beginning inventory | $20,500 | $ 34,500 |
| | Net Purchases | 39,500 | 65,500 |
| | Goods available for sale | $60,000 | $100,000 |
| (Step 2) | Cost ratio: ($60,000/$100,000) × 100 = 60% | | |
| (Step 3) | Deduct sales at retail | | 70,000 |
| | Ending inventory at retail | | $ 30,000 |
| (Step 4) | Ending inventory at cost ($30,000 × 60%) | $18,000 | |

In addition to the beginning inventory, the accounting records must also show the amount of goods purchased during the period both at cost and at retail. Also, the records must show the amount of net sales at retail. This is the balance of the Sales account less returns and discounts. With this information, the ending inventory is estimated as follows:

**Step 1:** Compute the amount of goods that were for sale during the period both at cost and at retail.

**Step 2:** Divide the goods available "at cost" by the goods available "at retail" to obtain a **retail method cost ratio.**

**Step 3:** Deduct sales (at retail) from goods available for sale (at retail) to determine the ending inventory at retail.

**Step 4:** Multiply the ending inventory at retail by the cost ratio to reduce the inventory to a cost basis.

Illustration 9–7 shows these calculations.

This is the essence of Illustration 9–7: (1) The store had $100,000 of goods (at marked selling prices) for sale during the period. (2) These goods cost 60% of the $100,000 total amount at which they were marked for sale. (3) The store's records (its Sales account) showed that $70,000 of these goods were sold, leaving $30,000 of merchandise unsold and presumably in the ending inventory. Therefore, (4) since cost in this store is 60% of retail, the estimated cost of this ending inventory is $18,000.

An ending inventory calculated as in Illustration 9–7 is an estimate arrived at by deducting sales (goods sold) from goods for sale. As we said before, this method may be used for interim statements or even for year-end statements. However, at least once each year a physical count of the inventory must be taken to correct for any errors or shortages.

### Using the Retail Method to Reduce a Physical Inventory to Cost

In a store, items for sale normally have price tickets attached that show selling prices. So, when a store takes a physical inventory, it commonly takes the inventory at the marked selling prices of the inventoried items. It then reduces the dollar total of this inventory to a cost basis by applying its cost ratio. It does this because the selling prices are readily available and the application of the cost ratio eliminates the need to look up the invoice price of each inventoried item.

For example, assume that the store of Illustration 9–7, in addition to estimating its inventory by the retail method, also takes a physical inventory at the marked selling prices of the inventoried goods. Assume further that the total retail amount of this physical inventory is $29,600. Under these assumptions, the store may calculate the cost for this inventory, without having to look up the cost of each inventoried item, simply by applying its cost ratio to the $29,600 inventory total as follows:

$$\$29{,}600 \times 60\% = \$17{,}760$$

The $17,760 cost figure for this store's ending physical inventory is a satisfactory figure for year-end statement purposes. It is also acceptable to the Internal Revenue Service for tax purposes.

### Inventory Shortage

An inventory determined as in Illustration 9–7 is an estimate of the amount of goods on hand. However, since it is arrived at by deducting sales from goods for sale, it does not reveal any shortages due to breakage, loss, or theft. However, you can estimate the amount of such shortages by comparing the inventory as calculated in Illustration 9–7 with the amount that results from taking a physical inventory.

For example, in Illustration 9–7, we estimated that the ending inventory at retail was $30,000. However, in the previous section, we assumed that this same store took a physical inventory and counted only $29,600 of merchandise on hand (at retail). Therefore, the store must have had an inventory shortage at retail of $30,000 − $29,600 = $400. Stated in terms of cost, the shortage is $400 × 60% = $240.

### Markups and Markdowns

The calculation of a cost ratio often is not as simple as that shown in Illustration 9–7. It is not simple because after merchandise is purchased and marked at retail prices, a store may decide to change the retail prices by marking the goods up or down. When goods are first purchased and marked at selling price, the amount or percentage by which the marked selling prices exceed cost is called a **normal markup.** It is also called a **markon.** For example, if a store's normal markup is 50% on cost and it applies this markup to an item that cost $10, it will mark the item for sale at $15. Normal markups appear in the calculation of a store's cost ratio as the difference between net purchases at cost and at retail.

After goods are first priced to sell at the normal markup, if the prices are increased, the amount of the additional price increases are called **markups.** And if selling prices are decreased, the amounts of the decreases are called **markdowns.** Stores may add markups to the price of goods because the quality or style of the goods make them especially attractive to customers. Goods often are marked down for a clearance sale or whenever the goods are moving slowly.

**Illustration 9–8**
**The effect of markups and markdowns on the retail method**

| | At Cost | At Retail |
|---|---|---|
| Goods available for sale: | | |
| Beginning inventory | $18,000 | $27,800 |
| Net purchases | 34,000 | 50,700 |
| Additional markups | | 1,500 |
| Goods available for sale | $52,000 | $80,000 |
| Cost ratio: ($52,000 ÷ $80,000) × 100 = 65% | | |
| Sales at retail | | $54,000 |
| Markdowns | | 2,000 |
| Total sales and markdowns | | $56,000 |
| Ending inventory at retail ($80,000 less $56,000) | | $24,000 |
| Ending inventory at cost ($24,000 × 65%) | $15,600 | |

When the retail inventory method is used, the store must keep a record of additional markups and markdowns. This information is used in the calculation of the ending inventory as shown in Illustration 9–8.

In Illustration 9–8, notice that the store's $80,000 of goods for sale at retail were reduced $54,000 by sales and $2,000 by markdowns, a total of $56,000. To understand the markdowns, visualize this effect of a markdown. The store had an item for sale during the period at $25. The item did not sell, so the manager marked its price down from $25 to $20. By this act the retail amount of goods for sale in the store was reduced by $5. The total of such markdowns during the year amounted to $2,000.

In the calculations of Illustration 9–8, note that the estimated ending inventory at retail is $24,000. Therefore, since "cost" is 65% of retail, the ending inventory at "cost" is $15,600.

Observe in Illustration 9–8 that markups enter into the calculation of the cost ratio but markdowns do not. Why are markdowns excluded from the cost ratio calculation? The reason for this is that a more conservative figure for the ending inventory results, a figure that approaches "the lower of cost or market." Further discussion of this phase of the retail inventory method is reserved for a more advanced accounting course.

## Gross Profit Method of Estimating Inventories

Sometimes, when a business does not use a perpetual inventory method and does not use the retail method, it still may need to estimate the cost of its inventory. For example, if a fire destroys the inventory or a burglary results in the theft of the inventory, the business must estimate the inventory so that it can file a claim with its insurance company. In cases such as this, the cost of the inventory can be estimated by the **gross profit inventory method**. With this method, a business's historical relationship between cost of goods sold and sales is applied to sales of the current period as a way of estimating cost of goods sold during the current period. Then, cost of goods sold is subtracted from the cost of goods available for sale to get the estimated cost of the ending inventory.

**Illustration 9–9**
**The gross profit method of estimating inventory**

| | | |
|---|---|---|
| Goods available for sale: | | |
| Inventory, January 1, 1990 | | $ 12,000 |
| Net purchases | $20,000 | |
| Add transportation-in | 500 | 20,500 |
| Goods available for sale | | $ 32,500 |
| Less estimated cost of goods sold: | | |
| Sales | $31,500 | |
| Less sales returns | (1,500) | |
| Net sales | $30,000 | |
| Estimated cost of goods sold (70% × $30,000) | | (21,000) |
| Estimated March 27 inventory and inventory loss | | $ 11,500 |

To use the gross profit method, several items of accounting information must be available. This includes information about the normal gross profit margin or rate, the cost of the beginning inventory, the cost of net purchases, transportation-in, and the amount of sales and sales returns.

For example, assume that the inventory of a company was totally destroyed by a fire that occurred on March 27, 1990. The company's average gross profit rate during the past five years has been 30% of net sales. And on the date of the fire, the company's accounts showed the following balances:

| | |
|---|---|
| Sales | $31,500 |
| Sales returns | 1,500 |
| Inventory, January 1, 1990 | 12,000 |
| Net purchases | 20,000 |
| Transportation-in | 500 |

With this information, the gross profit method may be used to estimate the company's inventory loss. To apply the gross profit method, the first step is to recognize that whatever portion of each dollar of net sales was gross profit, the remaining portion was cost of goods sold. Thus, if the company's gross profit rate averages 30%, then 30% of each dollar of net sales was gross profit, and 70% was cost of goods sold. Illustration 9–9 shows how the 70% is used to estimate the inventory that was lost.

To understand Illustration 9–9, recall that in a normal situation an ending inventory is subtracted from goods available for sale to determine the cost of goods sold. Then observe in Illustration 9–9 that the opposite subtraction is made. Estimated cost of goods sold is subtracted from goods for sale to determine the estimated ending inventory.

As we mentioned, the gross profit method often is used to estimate the amount of an insurance claim. Also, it sometimes is used by accountants to see if an inventory amount determined by management's physical count of the items on hand is a reasonable amount.

## Summary of the Chapter in Terms of Learning Objectives

**1.** When specific invoice prices are used to price an inventory, each item in the inventory is identified and the cost of the item is determined by referring to the item's purchase invoice. With weighted-average cost, the total cost of the beginning inventory and of purchases is divided by the number of units available to determine the weighted-average cost per unit. This is multiplied by the number of units in the ending inventory to determine the cost of the inventory. FIFO prices the ending inventory based on the assumption that the first units purchased are the first units sold. LIFO is based on the assumption that the last units purchased are the first units sold. All of these methods are acceptable.

**2.** When lower of cost or market is applied to merchandise inventory, market usually means replacement cost. But market is never higher than net realizable value and never lower than net realizable value minus a normal profit. Lower of cost or market may be applied separately to each product or to the merchandise inventory as a whole.

**3.** When the periodic inventory system is used, an error in counting the ending inventory affects assets (inventory), net income (cost of goods sold), and owner's equity. Since the ending inventory is the beginning inventory of the next period, an error at the end of one period affects the cost of goods sold and the net income of the next period. These next period effects offset the financial statement effects in the previous period.

**4.** Under a perpetual inventory system, purchases and purchases returns are recorded in the Merchandise Inventory account. At the time sales are recorded, the cost of goods sold is credited to Merchandise Inventory. As a result, the Merchandise Inventory is kept up-to-date throughout the accounting period.

**5.** When the retail method is used, sales are subtracted from the retail amount of goods available to determine the ending inventory at retail. This is multiplied by the cost ratio to reduce the inventory amount to cost. To calculate the cost ratio, the cost of goods available is divided by the retail value of goods available (including markups but excluding markdowns).

With the gross profit method, you multiply sales by (1 − the gross profit rate) to estimate cost of goods sold. Then, you subtract the answer from the cost of goods available for sale to estimate the cost of the ending inventory.

## Demonstration Problem

Following is Tale Company's beginning inventory and purchases during 1990:

| | | Item X | | Item Y | |
|---|---|---|---|---|---|
| Date | | Units | Cost per Unit | Units | Cost per Unit |
| 1/1 | Inventory | 400 | $14 | 200 | $11 |
| 3/10 | Purchase | 200 | 15 | 300 | 12 |
| 5/9 | Purchase | 300 | 16 | | |
| 6/17 | Purchase | | | 450 | 18 |
| 9/22 | Purchase | 250 | 20 | | |
| 11/28 | Purchase | 100 | 21 | 110 | 17 |

At December 31, 1990, there were 550 units of X on hand and 320 units of Y.

*Required*

1. Using the above information, apply FIFO inventory pricing and calculate the cost of goods available for sale in 1990, the ending inventory, and the cost of goods sold for each item and for both items combined.
2. In preparing the financial statements for 1990, the bookkeeper misunderstood the instructions and computed the cost of goods sold according to LIFO. Ignore income taxes and determine the size of the misstatement of 1990's income from this error. Assuming that the December 31, 1991, inventory is correctly calculated using FIFO, determine the size of the misstatement of 1991's income. Assume no income taxes.
3. Assume the following additional facts, and use the retail method to estimate the lower of cost or market of the ending inventory:

| | |
|---|---|
| Retail value of the beginning inventory | $13,051 |
| Retail value of purchases | 41,381 |
| Additional markups (at retail) | 3,600 |
| Sales | 33,600 |
| Markdowns | 4,432 |

## Solution to Demonstration Problem

1. FIFO basis:

| | | |
|---|---|---|
| **Item X:** | | |
| 1/1 inventory (400 @ $14) | | $ 5,600 |
| Purchases: | | |
| 3/10 purchase (200 @ $15) | $3,000 | |
| 5/9 purchase (300 @ $16) | 4,800 | |
| 9/22 purchase (250 @ $20) | 5,000 | |
| 11/28 purchase (100 @ $21) | 2,100 | 14,900 |
| Cost of goods available for sale | | $20,500 |
| Ending inventory at FIFO cost: | | |
| 11/28 purchase (100 @ $21) | $2,100 | |
| 9/22 purchase (250 @ $20) | 5,000 | |
| 5/9 purchase (200 @ $16) | 3,200 | |
| Ending inventory | | 10,300 |
| Cost of goods sold | | $10,200 |
| **Item Y:** | | |
| 1/1 inventory (200 @ $11) | | $ 2,200 |
| Purchases: | | |
| 3/10 purchase (300 @ $12) | $3,600 | |
| 6/17 purchase (450 @ $18) | 8,100 | |
| 11/28 purchase (110 @ $17) | 1,870 | 13,570 |
| Cost of goods available for sale | | $15,770 |
| Ending inventory at FIFO cost: | | |
| 11/28 purchase (110 @ $17) | $1,870 | |
| 6/17 purchase (210 @ $18) | 3,780 | |
| Ending inventory | | 5,650 |
| Cost of goods sold | | $10,120 |
| **Combined:** | | |
| Cost of goods available ($20,500 + $15,770) | | $36,270 |
| Cost of ending inventory ($10,300 + $5,650) | | 15,950 |
| Cost of goods sold ($10,200 + $10,120) | | $20,320 |

2. LIFO basis:

| | | |
|---|---|---|
| **Item X:** | | |
| Cost of goods available for sale | | $20,500 |
| Ending inventory at LIFO cost: | | |
| 1/1 inventory (400 @ $14) | $5,600 | |
| 3/10 purchase (150 @ $15) | 2,250 | |
| LIFO cost of ending inventory | | 7,850 |
| Cost of goods sold | | $12,650 |
| **Item Y:** | | |
| Cost of goods available for sale | | $15,770 |
| Ending inventory at LIFO cost: | | |
| 1/1 inventory (200 @ $11) | $2,200 | |
| 3/10 purchase (120 @ $12) | 1,440 | |
| LIFO cost of ending inventory | | 3,640 |
| Cost of goods sold | | $12,130 |
| **Combined:** | | |
| Cost of goods available ($20,500 + $15,770) | | $36,270 |
| Cost of ending inventory ($7,850 + $3,640) | | 11,490 |
| Cost of goods sold | | $24,780 |

If LIFO is mistakenly used when FIFO should have been used, cost of goods sold in 1990 would be overstated by $4,460, which is the difference between the FIFO and LIFO amounts of ending inventory. Income would be understated in 1990 by $4,460. In 1991, income would be overstated by $4,460 because of the understatement of the beginning inventory.

3. Retail method of estimating inventory:

| | At Cost | At Retail |
|---|---|---|
| Goods available for sale: | | |
| Beginning inventory ($5,600 + $2,200 = $7,800) | $ 7,800 | $13,051 |
| Purchases ($14,900 + $13,570 = $28,470) | 28,470 | 41,381 |
| Markups | | 3,600 |
| Goods available for sale | $36,270 | $58,032 |
| Cost ratio: ($36,270 ÷ $58,032) × 100 = 62.5% | | |
| Sales at retail | | $33,600 |
| Markdowns | | 4,432 |
| Total sales and markdowns | | $38,032 |
| Ending inventory at retail ($58,032 − $38,032) | | $20,000 |
| Ending inventory at cost ($20,000 × 62.5%) | $12,500 | |

## Glossary

Define or explain the words and phrases listed in the chapter Glossary. (L. O. 6)

**Conservatism principle** the accounting principle that guides accountants to select the less optimistic estimate when two estimates of amounts to be received or paid are about equally likely. p. 403

**Consignee** one who receives and holds goods owned by another party for the purpose of selling the goods for the owner. p. 395

**Consignor** an owner of goods who ships them to another party who will then sell the goods for the owner. p. 395

**Consistency principle** the accounting requirement that a company use the same accounting methods period after period so that the financial statements of succeeding periods will be comparable. pp. 400–401

**First-in, first-out inventory pricing (FIFO)** the pricing of an inventory under the assumption that the first items received were the first items sold. p. 398

**Gross profit inventory method** a procedure for estimating an ending inventory in which the past gross profit rate is used to estimate cost of goods sold, which is then subtracted from the cost of goods available for sale to determine the estimated ending inventory. pp. 412–414

**Interim statements** monthly or quarterly financial statements prepared in between the regular year-end statements. p. 409

**Inventory ticket** a form attached to the counted items in the process of taking a physical inventory. pp. 396–397

**Last-in, first-out inventory pricing (LIFO)** the pricing of an inventory under the assumption that the last items received were the first items sold. p. 399

**Markdown** a reduction in the marked selling price of merchandise. p. 411

**Markon** the normal amount or percentage of cost that is added to the cost of merchandise to arrive at its selling price. p. 411

**Markup** an increase in the sales price of merchandise above the normal markon given to the goods. p. 411

**Net realizable value** the expected sales price of an item less any additional costs to sell. p. 396

**Normal markup** another name for markon. p. 411

**Periodic inventory system** an accounting system in which the Merchandise Inventory account is updated only once each accounting period, based on a physical count of the inventory. p. 396

**Perpetual inventory system** an inventory system in which cost of goods sold is recorded after each sale and the Merchandise Inventory account is updated after each purchase and each sale. pp. 404–408

**Retail inventory method** a method for estimating an ending inventory based on the ratio of the amount of goods for sale at cost to the amount of goods for sale at marked selling prices. pp. 408–412

**Retail method cost ratio** the ratio of goods available for sale at cost to goods available for sale at retail prices. p. 410

**Specific invoice inventory pricing** the pricing of an inventory where the purchase invoice of each item in the ending inventory is identified and used to determine the cost assigned to the inventory. p. 398

**Weighted-average inventory pricing** an inventory pricing system in which the unit prices of the beginning inventory and of each purchase are weighted by the number of units in the beginning inventory and each purchase. The total of these amounts is then divided by the total number of units available for sale to find the unit cost of the ending inventory and of the units that were sold. p. 398

## Objective Review

Answers to the following questions are listed in Appendix I at the end of the book. Be sure that you decide which is the one best answer to each question *before* you check the answers in the appendix.

1. The following data relate to a single inventory item for Jones Company:

| Date | | Units | Cost per Unit |
|---|---|---|---|
| June 1 | Beginning inventory | 100 | $4 |
| 3 | Purchase | 20 | 5 |
| 15 | Sale | 30 | |
| 18 | Purchase | 40 | 6 |
| 25 | Sale | 25 | |

Using a periodic inventory system and costing inventory by FIFO, the ending inventory is:
*a*. $220.
*b*. $425.
*c*. $450.
*d*. $520.
*e*. $740.

2. Refer to the data about Jones Company in (1) above. Using a perpetual inventory system and costing inventory by LIFO, the ending inventory is:
*a*. $220.
*b*. $425.
*c*. $450.
*d*. $520.
*e*. $740.

3. A company's ending inventory includes the following items:

| Product | Units on Hand | Unit Cost | Market Value per Unit |
|---|---|---|---|
| A . . . . | 10 | $ 5 | $ 4 |
| B . . . . | 30 | 10 | 8 |
| C . . . . | 4 | 15 | 16 |

The inventory's lower of cost or market, applied separately to each product, is:
*a*. $320.
*b*. $340.
*c*. $344.
*d*. $410.
*e*. None of the above.

4. With a perpetual inventory system:
   *a.* A sale of merchandise requires two entries, one to record the revenue and one to record the cost of goods sold.
   *b.* A separate Cost of Goods Sold account is used.
   *c.* The Merchandise Inventory account balance shows the amount of merchandise on hand.
   *d.* Subsidiary inventory records are maintained for each type of product.
   *e.* All of the above are correct.
5. The following data relates to Trenor Company's inventory during the year:

| | Cost | Retail |
|---|---|---|
| Beginning inventory . . . . | $298,000 | $490,000 |
| Purchases . . . . . . . . . | 190,000 | 317,000 |
| Purchases returns . . . . . | 3,200 | 5,000 |
| Markups . . . . . . . . . . | | 6,000 |
| Markdowns . . . . . . . . | | 62,000 |
| Sales . . . . . . . . . . . . | | 270,000 |

   Using the retail method, the estimated cost of the ending inventory is:
   *a.* $152,800.
   *b.* $285,600.
   *c.* $309,400.
   *d.* $476,000.
   *e.* $784,800.
6. The gross profit method:
   *a.* Requires that detailed records be maintained concerning the cost, sales value, markups, and markdowns of inventory items.
   *b.* Is used to estimate the cost of inventory lost in a fire when a perpetual inventory system was used to account for inventory.
   *c.* Is used to estimate the cost of inventory lost in a fire when a periodic inventory system other than the retail method was used to account for inventory.
   *d.* Is used to estimate the cost of inventory lost in a fire when the retail method was used to account for inventory.
   *e.* None of the above is correct.

## Questions for Class Discussion

1. With respect to periodic inventory systems, it has been said that cost of goods sold and ending inventory are opposite sides of the same coin. What is meant by this?
2. Where is merchandise inventory disclosed in the financial statements?
3. If Barnes Company is the consignee and Smith Company is the consignor with respect to goods that are being offered for sale, the goods should show up on the inventory of which company?
4. If Craft sells goods to James, FOB Craft's factory, and the goods are still in transit from Craft to James, which company should include the goods in its physical count of inventory?

5. Of what does the cost of an inventory item consist?
6. Why are incidental costs often ignored in pricing an inventory? Under what accounting principle is this permitted?
7. Give the meanings of the following when applied to inventory: (*a*) FIFO, (*b*) LIFO, (*c*) cost, and (*d*) perpetual inventory.
8. If prices are rising, will the LIFO or the FIFO method of inventory valuation result in the higher gross profit?
9. If prices are falling, will the LIFO or the FIFO method of inventory valuation result in the higher ending inventory?
10. If prices are falling, will the LIFO or the FIFO method of inventory valuation result in the lower cost of goods sold?
11. May a company change its inventory pricing method each accounting period?
12. Does the accounting principle of consistency preclude any changes from one accounting method to another? NO
13. What effect does the full-disclosure principle have if a company changes from one acceptable accounting method to another?
14. What is meant when it is said that under a periodic inventory system, inventory errors "correct themselves"?
15. If inventory errors under a periodic inventory system "correct themselves," why be concerned when such errors are made?
16. What guidance for accountants is provided by the principle of conservatism?
17. What accounts are used in a periodic inventory system but are not used in a perpetual inventory system?
18. What account is used in a perpetual inventory system but is not used in a periodic inventory system.
19. Assuming a last-in, first-out cost flow, why do perpetual inventory systems and periodic inventory systems result in different amounts of cost of goods sold and ending inventory?
20. What is the usual meaning of the word *market* as it is used in determining the lower of cost or market for merchandise inventory?
21. In what way is the use of lower of cost or market with merchandise inventory less restrictive than when it is used with temporary investments in marketable equity securities?
22. In deciding whether to reduce an item of merchandise to the lower of cost or market, what is the importance of the item's net realizable value?
23. Give the meanings of the following when applied in the retail method of estimating an inventory: (*a*) pricing inventory at retail, (*b*) cost ratio, (*c*) normal markup, (*d*) markon, (*e*) additional markup, and (*f*) markdown.
24. A company uses a periodic inventory system, records its merchandise purchases at cost, and assumes a FIFO cost flow. If a fire results in the loss of the company's inventory, what method might the company use to estimate the amount of inventory lost?

## Exercises

**Exercise 9–1**
**Alternative cost flow assumptions, periodic inventory system**
(L. O. 1)

Hoyt Company began a year and purchased merchandise as follows:

| | | | | |
|---|---|---|---|---|
| Jan. 1 | Beginning inventory . . . . | 20 units @ $10.00 = | $ 200 |
| Feb. 9 | Purchased . . . . . . . . . | 100 units @ $11.50 = | 1,150 |
| June 16 | Purchased . . . . . . . . . | 40 units @ $12.50 = | 500 |
| Aug. 22 | Purchased . . . . . . . . . | 80 units @ $14.00 = | 1,120 |
| Dec. 15 | Purchased . . . . . . . . . | 60 units @ $15.00 = | 900 |
| | Total . . . . . . . . . . . . | 300 units | $3,870 |

*Required*

The company uses a periodic inventory system, and the ending inventory consists of 75 units, 25 from each of the last three purchases. Determine the share of the $3,870 cost of the units for sale that should be assigned to the ending inventory and to goods sold under each of the following: (*a*) costs are assigned on the basis of specific invoice prices, (*b*) costs are assigned on a weighted-average cost basis, (*c*) costs are assigned on the basis of FIFO, and (*d*) costs are assigned on the basis of LIFO. Assuming the company has enough income to require that it pay income taxes, which method provides a current tax advantage?

**Exercise 9–2**
**Alternative cost flow assumptions, periodic inventory system**
(L. O. 1)

Higgins Company began a year and purchased merchandise as follows:

| | | | |
|---|---|---|---|
| Jan. 1 | Beginning inventory . . . . | 20 units @ $15.00 = | $ 300 |
| Feb. 9 | Purchased . . . . . . . . . | 100 units @ $14.00 = | 1,400 |
| June 16 | Purchased . . . . . . . . . | 40 units @ $12.50 = | 500 |
| Aug. 22 | Purchased . . . . . . . . . | 80 units @ $11.50 = | 920 |
| Dec. 15 | Purchased . . . . . . . . . | 60 units @ $10.00 = | 600 |
| | Total . . . . . . . . . . . . | 300 units | $3,720 |

*Required*

The company uses a periodic inventory system, and the ending inventory consists of 75 units, 25 from each of the last three purchases. Determine the share of the $3,720 cost of the units for sale that should be assigned to the ending inventory and to goods sold under each of the following: (*a*) costs are assigned on the basis of specific invoice prices, (*b*) costs are assigned on a weighted-average cost basis, (*c*) costs are assigned on the basis of FIFO, and (*d*) costs are assigned on the basis of LIFO. Assuming the company has enough income to require that it pay income taxes, which method provides a current tax advantage?

**Exercise 9–3**
**Lower of cost or market**
(L. O. 2)

Starnes Company's ending inventory includes the following items:

| Product | Units on Hand | Cost per Unit | Replacement Cost per Unit |
|---|---|---|---|
| W . . . . | 15 | $ 8 | $12 |
| X . . . . | 20 | 15 | 12 |
| Y . . . . | 25 | 8 | 7 |
| Z . . . . | 18 | 5 | 5 |

After evaluating each product's selling price and normal profit margin, replacement cost is found to be the best measure of market. Calculate lower of cost or market for the inventory (*a*) as a whole and (*b*) applied separately to each product.

**Exercise 9–4**
**Lower of cost or market**
(L. O. 2)

Calculate the lower of cost or market for the inventory in each of the following independent cases:

1. Toy Company's inventory consists of 60 units of Product P, all of which have been damaged. The company bought the inventory for $12 per unit. Replacement cost is $11 per unit. Expected sales price is $15 per unit, but this can be realized only if $5 additional cost per unit is paid.
2. Doll Company's inventory consists of 110 units of Product Q which were purchased for $30 per unit. Replacement cost is $21 per unit. Expected sales price is $33 per unit, and a normal profit margin based on this price is $10.

**Exercise 9–5**
**Analysis of inventory errors**
(L. O. 3)

Matz Company had $95,000 of sales during each of three consecutive years, and it purchased merchandise costing $70,000 during each of the years. It also maintained a $20,000 inventory from the beginning to the end of the three-year period. However, in accounting under a periodic inventory system, it made an error at the end of year 1 that caused its ending year 1 inventory to appear on its statements at $25,000, rather than the correct $20,000.

*Required*

1. State the actual amount of the company's gross profit in each of the years.
2. Prepare a comparative income statement like the one illustrated in this chapter to show the effect of this error on the shop's cost of goods sold and gross profit in year 1, year 2, and year 3.

**Exercise 9–6**
**Perpetual inventory system—FIFO cost flow**
(L. O. 4)

In its beginning inventory on January 1, 1990, J Company had 30 units of merchandise which had cost $3 per unit. Prepare general journal entries for J Company to record the following transactions during 1990, assuming a perpetual inventory system and a first-in, first-out cost flow:

| | | |
|---|---|---|
| Mar. | 12 | Purchased on credit 120 units of merchandise at $5.25 per unit. |
| | 15 | Returned 20 defective units from the March 12 purchase to the supplier. |
| Sept. | 22 | Purchased for cash 70 units of merchandise at $3.50 per unit. |
| Oct. | 15 | Sold 85 units of merchandise for cash at a price of $5.50 per unit. |
| Dec. | 31 | Prepare entries to close the revenue and expense accounts to Income Summary. |

**Exercise 9–7**
**Perpetual inventory system—LIFO cost system**
(L. O. 6)

In its January 1, 1990, inventory, X Company had 50 units of merchandise which had cost $4 per unit. Prepare general journal entries for X Company to record the following transactions during 1990, assuming a perpetual inventory system and a last-in, first-out cost flow:

| | | |
|---|---|---|
| Mar. | 17 | Purchased on credit 90 units of merchandise at $4.25 per unit. |
| June | 25 | Sold 60 units of merchandise for cash at $8.50 per unit. |
| Aug. | 19 | Purchased for cash 80 units of merchandise at $4.50 per unit. |
| Nov. | 15 | Sold 85 units of merchandise for cash at a price of $8.50 per unit. |

Dec. 31 Prepare entries to close the revenue and expense accounts to Income Summary.

Exercise 9–8
**Estimating ending inventory—retail inventory method**
(L. O. 5)

During an accounting period, Fish Store sold $280,000 of merchandise at marked retail prices. At the period end, the following information was available from its records:

| | At Cost | At Retail |
|---|---|---|
| Beginning inventory . . . . | $ 50,500 | $ 75,000 |
| Net purchases . . . . . . . | 194,500 | 267,000 |
| Additional markups . . . . | | 8,000 |
| Markdowns . . . . . . . . | | 7,200 |

Use the retail method to estimate the store's ending inventory at cost.

Exercise 9–9
**Reducing physical inventory to cost—retail method**
(L. O. 5)

Assume that in addition to estimating its ending inventory by the retail method, Fish Store of Exercise 9–8 also took a physical inventory at the marked selling prices of the inventory items. Assume further that the total of this physical inventory at marked selling prices was $60,200. Then (*a*) determine the amount of this inventory at cost and (*b*) determine the store's inventory shrinkage from breakage, theft, or other cause at retail and at cost.

Exercise 9–10
**Estimating ending inventory—gross profit method**
(L. O. 5)

On January 1, a store had a $51,000 inventory at cost. During the first quarter of the year, it purchased $195,000 of merchandise, returned $1,500, and paid freight charges on merchandise purchased totaling $10,500. During the past several years, the store's gross profit on sales has averaged 35%. Under the assumption the company had $288,000 of sales during the first quarter of the year, use the gross profit method to estimate its end of the first quarter inventory.

## Problems

Problem 9–1
**Alternative cost flows—periodic system**
(L. O. 1)

Crown Company began a year with 850 units of Product A in its inventory that cost $85 each, and it made successive purchases of the product as follows:

| | | |
|---|---|---|
| Apr. | 1 | 1,500 units @ $85 each |
| June | 10 | 1,750 units @ $90 each |
| Aug. | 29 | 1,200 units @ $95 each |
| Nov. | 15 | 1,500 units @ $90 each |

The company uses a periodic inventory system. On December 31, a physical count disclosed that 2,000 units of Product A remained in inventory.

*Required*

1. Prepare a calculation showing the number and total cost of the units that were for sale during the year.
2. Prepare calculations showing the amounts that should be assigned to the ending inventory and to cost of goods sold assuming (*a*) a FIFO basis, (*b*) a LIFO basis, and (*c*) a weighted-average cost basis. Round your calculation of the weighted-average cost per unit to three decimal places.

**Problem 9–2**
**Income statement comparisons and cost flow assumptions**
(L. O. 1)

Breakward Company sold 8,500 units of its product at $25 per unit during 1990. It incurred operating expenses of $4 per unit in selling the units, and it began the year and made successive purchases of the product as follows:

| | |
|---|---|
| January 1 beginning inventory . . . . | 800 units costing $16.00 per unit |
| Purchases: | |
| January 30 . . . . . . . . . . . . . | 1,300 units costing $17.00 per unit |
| April 8 . . . . . . . . . . . . . . . | 2,700 units costing $17.50 per unit |
| July 19 . . . . . . . . . . . . . . | 4,200 units costing $18.25 per unit |
| November 20 . . . . . . . . . . . | 700 units costing $20.00 per unit |

*Required*

Prepare a comparative income statement for the company showing in adjacent columns the net incomes earned from the sale of the product assuming the company uses a periodic inventory system and prices its ending inventory on the basis of: (*a*) FIFO, (*b*) LIFO, and (*c*) weighted-average cost. Round your calculation of the weighted-average cost per unit to three decimal places.

**Problem 9–3**
**Lower of cost or market**
(L. O. 2)

**Case 1:** In this case, an evaluation of the expected selling price and normal profit margin for each product shows that replacement cost is the best measure of market. The inventory includes:

| Product | Units on Hand | Cost | Replacement Cost |
|---|---|---|---|
| X . . . . | 225 | $ 7 | $ 6 |
| Y . . . . | 450 | 12 | 10 |
| Z . . . . | 525 | 35 | 40 |

**Case 2:** In this case, the inventories of Products V and W have been damaged. If $4 additional cost per unit is paid to repackage the Product V units, they can be sold for $45 per unit. The Product W units can be sold for $25 per unit after paying additional cleaning costs of $3 per unit. The inventory includes:

| Product | Units on Hand | Cost | Replacement Cost |
|---|---|---|---|
| V . . . . | 325 | $45 | $42 |
| W . . . . | 150 | 25 | 26 |

**Case 3:** In this case, Product U normally is sold for $70 per unit and has a profit margin of 25%. However, the expected selling price has fallen to $44 per unit. Product T normally is sold for $32 per unit and has a profit margin of 30%. However, the expected selling price of Product T has fallen to $30 per unit. The inventory includes:

| Product | Units on Hand | Cost | Replacement Cost |
|---|---|---|---|
| U . . . . | 200 | $49 | $35 |
| T . . . . | 110 | 24 | 20 |

*Required*

In each of the above independent cases, calculate the lower of cost or market (*a*) for the inventory as a whole and (*b*) for the inventory, applied separately to each product.

**Problem 9–4**
**Analysis of inventory errors**
(L. O. 3)

Smoots Company keeps its inventory records on a periodic basis. The following amounts were reported in the company's financial statements:

| | Financial Statements for Year Ended December 31 | | |
|---|---|---|---|
| | 1989 | 1990 | 1991 |
| (*a*) Cost of goods sold . . . . | $ 48,000 | $ 56,000 | $ 50,000 |
| (*b*) Net income . . . . . . . . | 15,000 | 21,000 | 12,000 |
| (*c*) Total current assets . . . . | 90,000 | 96,000 | 82,000 |
| (*d*) Owners' equity . . . . . . | 102,000 | 110,000 | 100,000 |

In making the physical counts of inventory, the following errors were made:

| | |
|---|---|
| Inventory on December 31, 1989 . . . . | Overstated $5,000 |
| Inventory on December 31, 1990 . . . . | Understated 8,000 |

*Required*

1. For each of the financial statement items listed above as (*a*), (*b*), (*c*), and (*d*), prepare a schedule similar to the following and show the adjustments that would have been necessary to correct the reported amounts.

| | 1989 | 1990 | 1991 |
|---|---|---|---|
| Cost of goods sold: | | | |
| Reported . . . . . . . . . . . . . . . | ______ | ______ | ______ |
| Adjustments: 12/31/89 error . . . . | ______ | ______ | ______ |
| 12/31/90 error . . . . | ______ | ______ | ______ |
| Corrected . . . . . . . . . . . . . . | ______ | ______ | ______ |

2. What is the error in the aggregate net income for the three-year period that resulted from the inventory errors?

**Problem 9–5**
**Inventory records under FIFO and LIFO—perpetual system**
(L. O. 4)

The Wallenby Company sells a product called Walltool and uses a perpetual inventory system to account for its merchandise. The beginning balance of Walltools and transactions during January of this year were as follows:

| | | |
|---|---|---|
| Jan. | 1 | Balance: 18 units costing $11 each. |
| | 8 | Purchased 30 units costing $12 each. |
| | 11 | Sold 12 units. |
| | 17 | Sold 16 units. |
| | 22 | Purchased 24 units costing $14 each. |
| | 28 | Sold 9 units. |
| | 31 | Sold 18 units. |

*Required*

1. Under the assumption the business keeps its records on a FIFO basis, enter the beginning balance and the transactions on a subsidiary inventory record like the one illustrated in this chapter.
2. Under the assumption the business keeps its inventory records on a LIFO basis, enter the beginning inventory and the transactions on a second subsidiary inventory record.
3. Assume the 18 units sold on January 31 were sold on credit to Diane Bay at $21 each and prepare general journal entries to record the sale on a LIFO basis.

**Problem 9–6**
**Retail inventory method**
(L. O. 5)

Tent Store takes a year-end physical inventory at marked selling prices and uses the retail method to reduce the inventory total to a cost basis for statement purposes. It also uses the retail method to estimate the amount of inventory it should have at the end of a year, and by comparison estimates any inventory shortage due to shoplifting or other cause. At the end of last year, its physical inventory at marked selling prices totaled $100,500, and the following information was available from its records:

| | At Cost | At Retail |
|---|---|---|
| Beginning inventory . . . . | $ 58,600 | $ 86,800 |
| Purchases . . . . . . . . . | 400,240 | 575,500 |
| Purchases returns . . . . . | 6,700 | 9,400 |
| Additional markups . . . . | | 12,000 |
| Markdowns . . . . . . . . | | 7,400 |
| Sales . . . . . . . . . . . . | | 563,230 |
| Sales returns . . . . . . . | | 8,900 |

*Required*

1. Use the retail method to estimate the store's year-end inventory at cost.
2. Use the retail method to reduce the store's year-end physical inventory to a cost basis.
3. Prepare a schedule showing the inventory shortage at cost and at retail.

**Problem 9–7**
**Retail inventory method**
(L. O. 5)

The records of Globe Products Company provided the following information for the year ended December 31:

| | At Cost | At Retail |
|---|---|---|
| January 1 beginning inventory . . . . | $ 57,200 | $ 75,200 |
| Purchases . . . . . . . . . . . . . . . | 390,100 | 551,000 |
| Purchases returns . . . . . . . . . . | 5,320 | 7,580 |
| Additional markups . . . . . . . . . | | 11,200 |
| Markdowns . . . . . . . . . . . . . . | | 2,800 |
| Sales . . . . . . . . . . . . . . . . . | | 548,600 |
| Sales returns . . . . . . . . . . . . . | | 6,900 |

*Required*

1. Prepare an estimate of the company's year-end inventory by the retail method.
2. Under the assumption the company took a year-end physical inventory at marked selling prices that totaled $84,250, prepare a schedule showing the store's loss from theft or other cause at cost and at retail.

**Problem 9–8**
**Gross profit method**
(L. O. 5)

When the Southside Store was opened for business on the morning of March 15, it was discovered that thieves had broken in and stolen the store's entire inventory. The following information for the period January 1 through March 15 was available to establish the amount of loss:

| | |
|---|---|
| January 1 merchandise inventory at cost . . . . | $117,000 |
| Purchases . . . . . . . . . . . . . . . . . . . . | 332,300 |
| Purchases returns . . . . . . . . . . . . . . . . | 1,495 |
| Transportation-in . . . . . . . . . . . . . . . . | 2,015 |
| Sales . . . . . . . . . . . . . . . . . . . . . . . | 500,500 |
| Sales returns . . . . . . . . . . . . . . . . . . | 4,950 |

*Required*

Under the assumption the store had earned an average 32% gross profit on sales during the past five years, prepare a statement showing the estimated loss.

**Problem 9–9**
**Gross profit method**
(L. O. 5)

Brader Supply wants to prepare interim financial statements for the first quarter of 1990. The company uses a periodic inventory system but would like to avoid making a physical count of inventory. During the last five years, the company's gross profit rate has averaged 35%; and the following information for the year's first quarter is available from its records:

| | |
|---|---|
| January 1 beginning inventory . . . . | $116,250 |
| Purchases . . . . . . . . . . . . . . . | 275,200 |
| Purchases returns . . . . . . . . . . | 2,550 |
| Transportation-in . . . . . . . . . . | 3,300 |
| Sales . . . . . . . . . . . . . . . . . | 435,500 |
| Sales returns . . . . . . . . . . . . | 6,400 |

*Required*

Use the gross profit method to prepare an estimate of the company's March 31 inventory.

## Alternate Problems

**Problem 9–1A**
**Alternative cost flows—periodic system**
(L. O. 1)

Edgar Company began a year with 1,000 units of Product Z in its inventory that cost $40 each, and it made successive purchases of the product as follows:

| | |
|---|---|
| Mar. 2 | 1,500 units @ $45 each |
| June 19 | 1,550 units @ $50 each |
| Aug. 13 | 1,600 units @ $55 each |
| Nov. 6 | 1,600 units @ $52 each |

The company uses a periodic inventory system. On December 31, a physical count disclosed that 2,000 units of Product Z remained in inventory.

*Required*

1. Prepare a calculation showing the number and total cost of the units that were for sale during the year.
2. Prepare calculations showing the amounts that should be assigned to the ending inventory and to cost of goods sold assuming (*a*) a FIFO basis, (*b*) a LIFO basis, and (*c*) a weighted-average cost basis. Round your calculation of the weighted-average cost per unit to three decimal places.

**Problem 9–2A**
**Income statement comparisons and cost flow assumptions**
(L. O. 1)

Lakewood Company sold 4,500 units of its product at $45 per unit during 1990. It incurred operating expenses of $10 per unit in selling the units, and it began the year and made successive purchases of the product as follows:

| | |
|---|---|
| January 1 beginning inventory . . . . | 600 units costing $15 per unit |
| Purchases: | |
| January 8 . . . . . . . . . . . . | 1,200 units costing $16 per unit |
| April 2 . . . . . . . . . . . . . . | 2,000 units costing $18 per unit |
| July 18 . . . . . . . . . . . . . | 2,500 units costing $20 per unit |
| November 23 . . . . . . . . . . | 1,500 units costing $22 per unit |

*Required*

Prepare a comparative income statement for the company showing in adjacent columns the net incomes earned from the sale of the product assuming the company uses a periodic inventory system and prices its ending inventory on the basis of: (*a*) FIFO, (*b*) LIFO, and (*c*) weighted-average cost. Round your calculation of the weighted-average cost per unit to three decimal places.

Problem 9–3A
**Lower of cost or market**
(L. O. 2)

**Case 1:** In this case, an evaluation of the expected selling price and normal profit margin for each product shows that replacement cost is the best measure of market. The inventory includes:

| Product | Units on Hand | Cost | Replacement Cost |
|---|---|---|---|
| A . . . . | 800 | $20 | $23 |
| B . . . . | 900 | 32 | 29 |
| C . . . . | 400 | 22 | 21 |

**Case 2:** In this case, the inventories of Products D and E have been damaged. If $15 additional cost per unit is paid to repackage the Product D units, they can be sold for $50 per unit. The Product E units can be sold for $70 per unit after paying additional cleaning costs of $18 per unit. The inventory includes:

| Product | Units on Hand | Cost | Replacement Cost |
|---|---|---|---|
| D . . . . | 330 | $44 | $46 |
| E . . . . | 500 | 60 | 55 |

**Case 3:** In this case, Product F normally is sold for $60 per unit and has a profit margin of 30%. However, the expected selling price has fallen to $50 per unit. Product G normally is sold for $75 per unit and has a profit margin of 25%. However, the expected selling price of Product G has fallen to $65 per unit. The inventory includes:

| Product | Units on Hand | Cost | Replacement Cost |
|---|---|---|---|
| F . . . . | 330 | $42 | $30 |
| G . . . . | 190 | 65 | 56 |

*Required*

In each of the above independent cases, calculate the lower of cost or market (*a*) for the inventory as a whole and (*b*) for the inventory, applied separately to each product.

Problem 9–4A
**Analysis of inventory errors**
(L. O. 3)

Milicia Company keeps its inventory records on a periodic basis. The following amounts were reported in the company's financial statements:

| | Financial Statements for Year Ended December 31 | | |
|---|---|---|---|
| | 1989 | 1990 | 1991 |
| (*a*) Cost of goods sold . . . . | $ 67,000 | $ 75,000 | $ 65,000 |
| (*b*) Net income . . . . . . . . | 24,000 | 39,000 | 21,000 |
| (*c*) Total current assets . . . . | 108,000 | 115,000 | 100,000 |
| (*d*) Owners' equity . . . . . . | 144,000 | 157,000 | 162,000 |

In making the physical counts of inventory, the following errors were made:

| | |
|---|---|
| Inventory on December 31, 1989 . . . . | Understated $ 9,000 |
| Inventory on December 31, 1990 . . . . | Overstated 14,000 |

*Required*

1. For each of the financial statement items listed above as (*a*), (*b*), (*c*), and (*d*), prepare a schedule similar to the following and show the adjustments that would have been necessary to correct the reported amounts.

| | 1989 | 1990 | 1991 |
|---|---|---|---|
| Cost of goods sold: | | | |
| Reported | ____ | ____ | ____ |
| Adjustments: 12/31/89 error | ____ | ____ | ____ |
| 12/31/90 error | ____ | ____ | ____ |
| Corrected | ==== | ==== | ==== |

2. What is the error in the aggregate net income for the three-year period that resulted from the inventory errors?

**Problem 9–5A**
**Inventory records under FIFO and LIFO—perpetual system**
(L. O. 4)

The Turner Company sells a product called TurnUp and uses a perpetual inventory system to account for its merchandise. The beginning balance of TurnUps and transactions during January of this year were as follows:

| | | |
|---|---|---|
| Jan. | 1 | Balance: 25 units costing $8 each. |
| | 3 | Purchased 50 units costing $9 each. |
| | 7 | Sold 20 units. |
| | 19 | Sold 15 units. |
| | 21 | Purchased 30 units costing $11 each. |
| | 24 | Sold 15 units. |
| | 29 | Sold 32 units. |

*Required*

1. Under the assumption the concern keeps its records on a FIFO basis, enter the beginning balance and the transactions on a subsidiary inventory record like the one illustrated in this chapter.
2. Under the assumption the concern keeps its inventory records on a LIFO basis, enter the beginning inventory and the transactions on a second subsidiary inventory record.
3. Assume the 32 units sold on January 29 were sold on credit to Sally Rugby at $25 each and prepare general journal entries to record the sale on a LIFO basis.

**Problem 9–6A**
**Retail inventory method**
(L. O. 5)

Calico Stores takes a year-end physical inventory at marked selling prices and uses the retail method to reduce the inventory total to a cost basis for statement purposes. It also uses the retail method to estimate the amount of inventory it should have at the end of a year, and by comparison determines any inventory shortage due to shoplifting or other cause. At the end of last year, its physical inventory at marked selling prices totaled $145,200, and the following information was available from its records:

| | At Cost | At Retail |
|---|---|---|
| Beginning inventory | $ 52,930 | $ 80,200 |
| Purchases | 267,840 | 405,000 |
| Purchases returns | 5,520 | 8,400 |
| Additional markups | | 8,200 |
| Markdowns | | 5,300 |
| Sales | | 340,000 |
| Sales returns | | 4,400 |

*Required*

1. Use the retail method to estimate the store's year-end inventory at cost.
2. Use the retail method to reduce the company's year-end physical inventory to a cost basis.
3. Prepare a schedule showing the inventory overage at cost and at retail.

**Problem 9–7A**
**Retail inventory method**
(L. O. 5)

The records of Ware Products Company provided the following information for the year ended December 31:

| | At Cost | At Retail |
|---|---|---|
| January 1 beginning inventory . . . . | $ 99,000 | $146,100 |
| Purchases . . . . . . . . . . . . . . . | 419,820 | 780,000 |
| Purchases returns . . . . . . . . . . | 8,970 | 17,100 |
| Additional markups . . . . . . . . . | | 18,000 |
| Markdowns . . . . . . . . . . . . . . | | 9,900 |
| Sales . . . . . . . . . . . . . . . . . | | 850,500 |
| Sales returns . . . . . . . . . . . . | | 13,050 |

*Required*

1. Prepare an estimate of the company's year-end inventory by the retail method.
2. Under the assumption the company took a year-end physical inventory at marked selling prices that totaled $77,100, prepare a schedule showing the store's loss from theft or other cause at cost and at retail.

**Problem 9–8A**
**Gross profit method**
(L. O. 5)

When the Accessory Store was opened for business on the morning of March 10, it was discovered that thieves had broken in and stolen the store's entire inventory. The following information for the period January 1 through March 10 was available to establish the amount of loss:

| | |
|---|---|
| January 1 merchandise inventory at cost . . . . | $125,100 |
| Purchases . . . . . . . . . . . . . . . . . . . . | 370,000 |
| Purchases returns . . . . . . . . . . . . . . . | 3,225 |
| Transportation-in . . . . . . . . . . . . . . . | 15,750 |
| Sales . . . . . . . . . . . . . . . . . . . . . . | 720,400 |
| Sales returns . . . . . . . . . . . . . . . . . | 13,200 |

*Required*

Under the assumption the store had earned an average 38% gross profit on sales during the past five years, prepare a statement showing the estimated loss.

**Problem 9–9A**
**Gross profit method**
(L. O. 5)

Hebert Florists wants to prepare interim financial statements for the first quarter of 1990. The company uses a periodic inventory system but would like to avoid making a physical count of inventory. During the last five years, the company's gross profit rate has averaged 30%; and the following information for the year's first quarter is available from its records:

| | |
|---|---|
| January 1 beginning inventory . . . . | $ 70,560 |
| Purchases . . . . . . . . . . . . . . . | 115,240 |
| Purchases returns . . . . . . . . . . | 3,900 |
| Transportation-in . . . . . . . . . . | 9,420 |
| Sales . . . . . . . . . . . . . . . . . | 227,000 |
| Sales returns . . . . . . . . . . . . | 5,040 |

*Required*

Use the gross profit method to prepare an estimate of the company's March 31 inventory.

## Provocative Problems

**Provocative Problem 9–1**
**Caterpillar, Inc.**
(L. O. 1)

Caterpillar, Inc., is a multinational company that designs, manufactures, and markets products in two principal categories: (1) engines and (2) earthmoving, construction, and materials-handling machinery. The company's headquarters are in Peoria, Illinois. In the 1986 annual report of the company, the footnotes to the financial statements included the following:

**Notes**

**8. Inventories**

Reductions in certain LIFO inventories below the preceding year-end levels increased after tax profit for 1986 and 1985 by approximately $38 [million] and $190 [million], respectively ($.39 and $1.94 per share of common stock, respectively) and reduced the after-tax loss for 1984 by approximately $44 [million] ($.46 per share of common stock) . . . .

*Courtesy of Caterpillar, Inc.*

Discuss the financial statement effects of experiencing a reduction in inventory when LIFO is used and explain how this applies to Caterpillar, Inc.

**Provocative Problem 9–2**
**Bell & Howell Company**
(L. O. 1)

Bell & Howell Company has diversified operations that include publishing, document/mail processing, information storage and retrieval, career education, and international marketing services. Its headquarters are located in Skokie, Illinois. The 1986 annual report of Bell & Howell included the following footnote to its financial statements.

**Note A—Significant Accounting Policies:**

**Inventories.** Inventories are valued at cost determined by the last-in, first-out (LIFO) and the first-in, first-out (FIFO) methods as follows: [Dollars in thousands]

| Year end | LIFO | FIFO | Total |
|---|---|---|---|
| 1986 | $84,890 | $52,171 | $137,061 |
| 1985 | 97,498 | 41,042 | 138,540 |

Inventory cost includes material, labor and overhead and is not in excess of market. The company uses the LIFO method of valuing substantially all domestic inventories. If the FIFO method had been used, the LIFO inventories would have been valued $14,409 and $14,348 higher at the end of 1986 and 1985, respectively.

*Courtesy of Bell & Howell Company*

Bell & Howell Company reported a net income of $32,895,000 in 1986. Retained earnings on December 31, 1986, was $244,071,000. If Bell & Howell had used FIFO for all of its inventories and the average income tax rate applicable to the company was 30% in all past years, what would have been reported as total inventories on December 31, 1986, and December 31, 1985? What would have been reported as 1986 net income? What would have been the balance of retained earnings on December 31, 1986?

Comment on Bell & Howell's policy of using FIFO for some inventories and LIFO for other inventories. Is this practice acceptable in light of the consistency principle?

**Provocative Problem 9–3**
**Ft. Worth Boots**
(L. O. 5)

The retail outlet of Ft. Worth Boots suffered extensive smoke and water damage and a small amount of fire damage on September 10. The company carried adequate insurance, and the insurance company's claims adjuster appeared the same day to inspect the damage. After completing his survey, the adjuster agreed with Amy Harris, the store's owner, that the inventory could be sold to a company specializing in fire sales for about one fourth of its cost. The adjuster offered Ms. Harris $112,500 in full settlement for the damage to the inventory. He suggested that the offer be accepted and said he had authority to deliver at once a check for that amount. He also pointed out that a prompt settlement would provide funds to replace the inventory in time for the store to participate in the Christmas shopping season.

Ms. Harris felt the loss might exceed $112,500, but she recognized that a time-consuming count and inspection of each item in the inventory would be required to establish the loss more precisely. She was anxious to get back into business before the Christmas rush, the season making the largest contribution to annual net income, and was reluctant to take the time for the inventory count. Yet, she was also unwilling to take a substantial loss on the insurance settlement.

Ms. Harris asked for and received a one-day period in which to consider the insurance company offer, and immediately went to her records for the following information:

*a.*

| | At Cost | At Retail |
|---|---|---|
| January 1 inventory . . . . . . . . . . . . . . . . . | $ 159,975 | $ 250,200 |
| Purchases, January 1 through September 10 . . | 1,049,625 | 1,638,450 |
| Net sales, January 1 through September 10 . . . | | 1,627,650 |

*b.* On February 15, the remaining inventory of winter footwear was marked down from $72,000 to $54,000 and placed on sale in the annual end-of-the-winter-season sale. Three fourths of the boots were sold. The markdown on the remainder was canceled, and the boots were returned to their regular retail prices. (A markdown cancellation is subtracted from a markdown, and a markup cancellation is subtracted from a markup.)

*c.* In June, a special line of imported Italian boots proved popular, and 84 pairs were marked up from their normal $220.50 retail price to $243.00 per pair. Sixty pairs were sold at the higher price; and on July 20, the markup on the remaining 24 pairs was canceled and they were returned to their regular $220.50 price.

*d.* Between January 1 and September 10, markdowns totaling $8,100 were taken on several odd lots of shoes. Recommend whether or not you think Ms. Harris should accept the insurance company's offer. Back your recommendation with figures.

# 10 Plant and Equipment

In this chapter you will learn how to account for tangible assets that are used in the operations of a business. You will learn how to calculate depreciation on these assets and to account for the costs of repairing and improving them.

### Learning Objectives

*After studying Chapter 10, you should be able to:*

1. Tell what is included in the cost of a plant asset and allocate the cost of lump-sum purchases to the separate assets being purchased.
2. Describe the reasons for depreciation accounting and calculate depreciation by the straight-line and units-of-production methods.
3. Describe how depreciation is disclosed in the financial statements and explain how the original cost of a plant asset is recovered through the sale of the asset's product or service.
4. Describe the use of accelerated depreciation for financial accounting and tax accounting purposes and calculate accelerated depreciation under (*a*) the declining-balance method, (*b*) the sum-of-the-years'-digits method, and (*c*) the Modified Accelerated Cost Recovery System.
5. Explain how subsidiary ledgers and related controlling accounts are used to maintain control over plant assets.
6. Define or explain the words and phrases listed in the chapter Glossary.

Tangible assets that are used in the production or sale of other assets or services and that have a useful life longer than one accounting period are called *plant and equipment* or *plant assets*. In past years, such assets were often described as **fixed assets**. However, the more descriptive terms *plant and equipment* or perhaps *property, plant, and equipment* are now used more often.

The characteristic that distinguishes plant assets from merchandise is that plant assets are held for use while merchandise is held for sale. For example, a typewriter is merchandise to an office equipment business that purchased the typewriter with the intention of selling it. But, if the business owns another typewriter that is used in business operations to prepare correspondence and so forth, this typewriter is classified as plant and equipment.

Plant assets also must be distinguished from long-term investments. Although both are held for more than one accounting period, investments are not used in the principal operations of the business. For example, land that is held for future expansion is classified as a long-term investment. On the other hand, land on which the factory of the business is located is a plant asset. It is classified as a plant asset because it is presently used in business operations. In addition, standby equipment that is held for use in case of a breakdown or during peak periods of production is a plant asset. However, when equipment is removed from service and held for sale, it ceases to be a plant asset.

The characteristic that distinguishes plant assets from tangible current assets such as supplies is that supplies are expected to be used up within one year or the current operating cycle of the business. By comparison, plant assets have longer useful lives that often extend over many accounting periods. Therefore, as the usefulness of plant assets expires over several accounting periods, the cost of plant assets must be allocated to these periods in a systematic and rational manner.[1]

## Cost of a Plant Asset

Tell what is included in the cost of a plant asset and allocate the cost of lump-sum purchases to the separate assets being purchased.
(L. O. 1)

Cost is the basis for recording the acquisition of a plant asset. The cost of a plant asset includes all normal and reasonable expenditures necessary to get the asset in place and ready to use. For example, the cost of a factory machine includes its invoice price, less any cash discount for early payment, plus freight, unpacking, and assembling costs. Cost also includes any expenditures to install the asset such as for a concrete base or foundation, electrical or power connections, and adjustments needed to place the machine in operation. In short, the cost of a plant asset includes all normal, necessary, and reasonable costs incurred in getting the asset in place and ready to produce.

A cost must be normal and reasonable as well as necessary if it is to be properly included in the cost of a plant asset. For example, if a machine is damaged by being dropped during unpacking, repairs should not be added to its cost. They should be charged to an expense account. Also, a fine paid for moving a heavy machine on city streets without proper permits is not part of

[1] See FASB, *Statement of Financial Accounting Concepts No. 3*, "Elements of Financial Statements of Business Enterprises" (Norwalk, Conn., 1985), par. 149.

the cost of the machine. However, if proper permits are obtained, the cost of the permits is included in the cost of the asset.

Sometimes, when a plant asset is purchased, additional costs to repair or remodel the asset must be incurred before the asset meets the needs of the purchaser. In such cases, the repairing or remodeling expenditures should be charged to the asset. Furthermore, depreciation charges should not begin until the asset is put in use.

When a plant asset is constructed by a business for its own use, cost includes material and labor costs plus a reasonable amount of overhead or indirect expenses such as heat, lights, power, and depreciation on the machinery used in constructing the asset. Cost also includes architectural and design fees, building permits, and insurance during construction. However, insurance on the same asset after it has been placed in production is an expense.

When land is purchased for a building site, its cost includes the amount paid for the land plus any real estate commissions. It also includes escrow and legal fees, fees for examining and insuring the title, and any accrued property taxes paid by the purchaser, as well as expenditures for surveying, clearing, grading, draining, and landscaping. All are part of the cost of the land. Furthermore, any assessments incurred at the time of purchase or later for such things as the installation of streets, sewers, and sidewalks should be debited to the Land account since they add a more or less permanent value to the land.

Land purchased as a building site sometimes has an old building that must be removed. In such cases, the entire purchase price, including the amount paid for the building, should be charged to the Land account. Also, the cost of removing the old building, less any amounts recovered through the sale of salvaged materials, should be charged to this account.

Since land has an unlimited life, it is not subject to depreciation. However, **land improvements** such as parking lot surfaces, fences, and lighting systems have limited useful lives. Such costs improve the usefulness of land but must be charged to separate Land Improvement accounts and subjected to depreciation. Finally, a separate Building account must be charged for the cost of purchasing or constructing a building that will be used as a plant asset.

Purchases of land, land improvements, and buildings often are made in a single transaction at a single, lump-sum price. When this occurs, you must apportion the cost of the purchase among the assets, based on the relative market values of the purchased assets. Often, these values must be estimated by appraisal or by using the tax-assessed valuations of the assets.

For example, assume that land appraised at $30,000, land improvements appraised at $10,000, and a building appraised at $60,000 are purchased together for $90,000. The cost may be apportioned on the basis of appraised values as follows:

| | Appraised Value | Percent of Total | Apportioned Cost |
|---|---|---|---|
| Land | $ 30,000 | 30 | $27,000 |
| Land improvements | 10,000 | 10 | 9,000 |
| Building | 60,000 | 60 | 54,000 |
| Totals | $100,000 | 100 | $90,000 |

## Nature of Depreciation

Describe the reasons for depreciation accounting and calculate depreciation by the straight-line and units-of-production methods.
(L. O. 2)

Since plant assets are purchased for use, you may think of a plant asset as a quantity of usefulness that will contribute to the operations of the business throughout the service life of the asset. However, since the life of any plant asset (other than land) is limited, this quantity of usefulness expires as the asset is used. This expiration of a plant asset's quantity of usefulness is generally described as *depreciation;* and in accounting, the term is used to describe the process of allocating and charging the cost of this usefulness to the accounting periods that benefit from the asset's use.

For example, when a company purchases an automobile for use in the business, it purchases a quantity of usefulness, a quantity of transportation. The cost that will expire during the useful life of the car is the cost of the car less the proceeds that will be received when the car is sold or traded in at the end of its service life. This cost that will expire over the useful life of the car must be allocated to the accounting periods that benefit from the car's use; in other words, it must be depreciated. Note that the depreciation process does not measure the decline in the car's market value each period. Nor does it measure the physical deterioration of the car each period. Depreciation is a process of allocating cost.

The foregoing is in line with the current accounting standards which describe depreciation as follows:

> The cost of an [asset] is one of the costs of the services it renders during its useful economic life. Generally accepted accounting principles require that this cost be spread over the expected useful life of the [asset] in such a way as to allocate it as equitably as possible to the periods during which services are obtained from the use of the [asset]. This procedure is known as *depreciation accounting,* a system of accounting that aims to distribute the cost or other basic value of tangible capital assets, less salvage (if any), over the estimated useful life of the unit . . . in a systematic and rational manner. It is a process of allocation, not of valuation.[2]

## Service (Useful) Life of a Plant Asset

The **service life** of a plant asset is the length of time it will be used in the operations of the business. This may not be the same as the asset's potential life. For example, although typewriters have a potential life of six to eight years, a company may plan to trade in its old typewriters on new ones every three years. In this case, the typewriters have a three-year service life. Furthermore, in this company, the cost of the typewriters, less their expected trade-in value, should be charged to depreciation expense over this three-year period.

The service life of a plant asset often is difficult to predict because several factors may be involved. Wear and tear from use determine the useful life of some assets. However, two additional factors, **inadequacy** and **obsolescence**, often need to be considered. Usually, when a business acquires plant assets, it attempts to anticipate how much the business will grow and then acquires assets of a size and capacity to take care of its foreseeable needs. However, if a business grows more rapidly than anticipated, the capacity of the assets may

[2] FASB, *Accounting Standards—Current Text* (Norwalk, Conn., 1988), sec. D40.101. Previously published in *Accounting Research Bulletin No. 43*, ch. 9C, par. 5.

## AS A MATTER OF ETHICS

The economic situation surrounding a company has been quite dismal for a couple of years, and there are no signs of improvement for at least two more years. As a result, net income has been depressed, and the future seems bleak.

A significant item in the calculation of income is the depreciation of factory equipment. Because of frequent product changes, the equipment has been depreciated over only three years. However, in order to improve the income picture, management has instructed Charles Roberts, the company's accountant, to begin using estimated useful lives of six years.

In trying to determine whether to follow management's instructions, Charles is torn between his loyalty to his employer and his responsibility to the public and the stockholders and others who use the company's financial statements. He is also trying to decide what the independent CPA who audits the financial statements will think about the change.

become too small for the productive demands of the business. When this happens, the assets become inadequate.

Obsolescence, like inadequacy, is difficult to anticipate because the exact occurrence of new inventions and improvements normally cannot be predicted. Yet, new inventions and improvements often cause a plant asset to become obsolete and make it wise to discard the obsolete asset long before it wears out.

Many times, a company is able to estimate the service life of a new asset based on its past experience with similar assets. In other cases, when it has no experience with a particular type of asset, a company must depend on the experience of others or on engineering studies and judgment.

### Salvage Value

The total amount of depreciation that should be taken over an asset's service life is the asset's cost minus its estimated **salvage value.** The salvage value of a plant asset is the amount that will be recovered at the end of the asset's service life. Some assets such as typewriters, trucks, and automobiles are traded in on similar new assets at the end of their service lives. The salvage values of such assets are their trade-in values. Other assets may have no trade-in value and little or no salvage value. For example, at the end of its service life, some machinery can be sold only as scrap metal.

The disposal of some plant assets requires the outlay of costs such as the cost to wreck a building. In these cases, the expected salvage value of an asset is the *net* amount to be realized from the sale of the asset. The net amount to be realized is the expected amount to be received for the asset less its disposal cost. In the case of a machine, for example, the cost to remove the machine may equal the amount that can be realized from its sale. In such a case, the machine has no salvage value.

### Allocating Depreciation

Many methods of allocating a plant asset's total depreciation to the several accounting periods in its service life have been suggested and used in past years. However, at the present time, most companies use the *straight-line method* of depreciation in their financial accounting records and on their financial statements. Also, some types of assets are depreciated according to the *units-of-production method*. Later in the chapter, after these two methods are

**Illustration 10–1**
**The financial statement effects of straight-line depreciation**

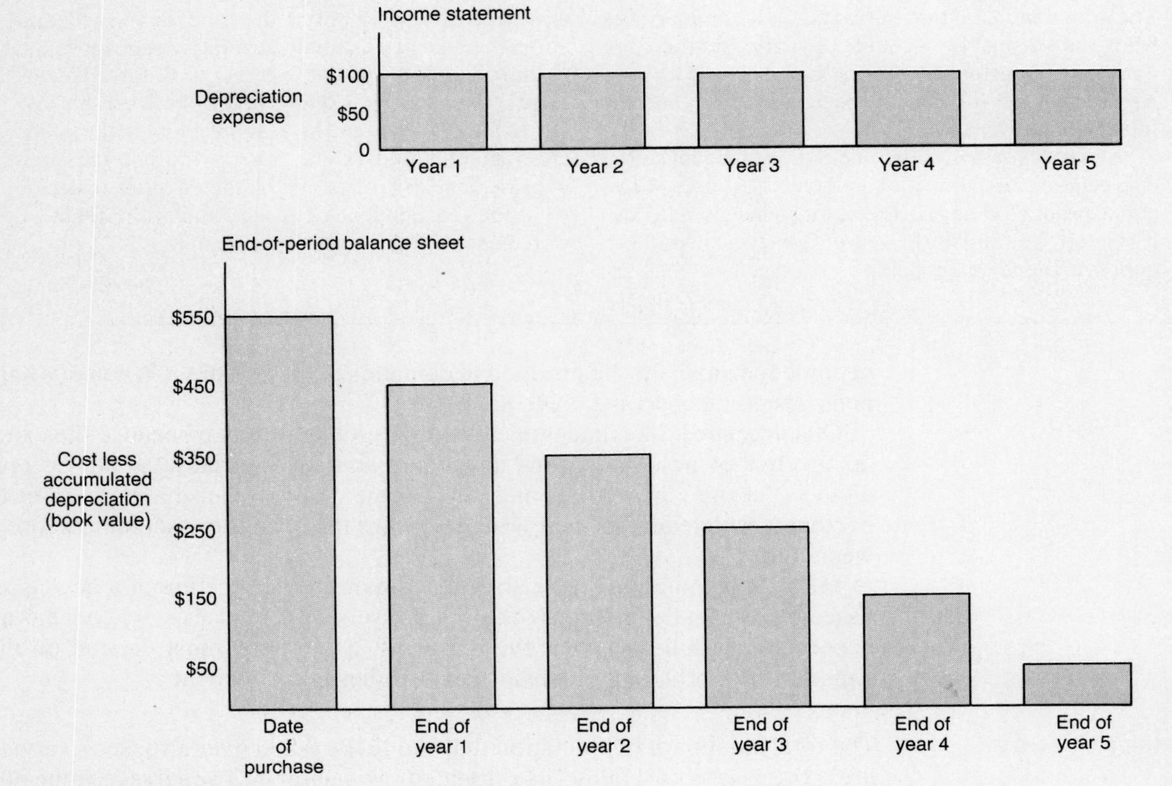


explained, we will discuss some other depreciation methods, which are called *accelerated depreciation methods*.

### Straight-Line Method

When **straight-line depreciation** is used, the cost of the asset minus its estimated salvage value is divided by the estimated number of accounting periods in the asset's service life. The result is the amount of depreciation to be taken each period. For example, if a machine costs $550, has an estimated service life of five years, and an estimated $50 salvage value, its depreciation per year by the straight-line method is $100 and is calculated as follows:

$$\frac{\text{Cost} - \text{Salvage}}{\text{Service life in years}} = \frac{\$550 - \$50}{5} = \$100$$

Note that the straight-line method allocates an equal share of an asset's total depreciation to each accounting period in its life. The financial statement effects of recording straight-line depreciation on the machine are shown in Illustration 10–1.

In Illustration 10–1, note that the cost minus accumulated depreciation, or **book value**, decreases in a straight-line fashion over the five-year life of the asset. (The book value of a plant asset is its cost less accumulated depreciation; it is the net amount shown for the asset on the books and in the balance sheet.) Also, note that the amount of depreciation expense reported in the income statement is the same each period ($100).

### Units-of-Production Method

The purpose of recording depreciation is to charge each accounting period in which an asset is used with a fair share of its cost. The straight-line method charges an equal share to each period; and when plant assets are used about the same amount in each accounting period, this method rather fairly allocates total depreciation. However, in some lines of business, the use of certain plant assets varies greatly from accounting period to accounting period. For example, a contractor may use a particular piece of construction equipment for a month and then not use it again for many months. For such an asset, since its use fluctuates from period to period, **units-of-production depreciation** may provide a better matching of expenses with revenues than straight-line depreciation.

When the units-of-production method is used to depreciate an asset, the cost of an asset minus its estimated salvage value is divided by the estimated units it will produce during its entire service life. This calculation gives depreciation per unit of production. Then, the amount the asset is depreciated in any one accounting period is determined by multiplying the units produced in that period by the depreciation per unit. Units of production often is expressed as units of product. However, units of production also may be measured in terms of units used such as the number of miles driven or hours used.

For example, a truck that cost $24,000 is estimated to have a $4,000 salvage value. Also, the truck's service life in terms of miles is estimated to be 125,000 miles. Therefore, the depreciation per mile, or the depreciation per unit of production, is $0.16 and is calculated as follows:

$$\frac{\text{Cost} - \text{Salvage value}}{\text{Estimated units of production}} = \text{Depreciation per unit of production}$$

or

$$\frac{\$24{,}000 - \$4{,}000}{125{,}000 \text{ miles}} = \$0.16 \text{ per mile}$$

If these estimates are used and the truck is driven 20,000 miles during its first year, depreciation for the first year is $3,200. This is 20,000 miles at $0.16 per mile. If the truck is driven 15,000 miles in the second year, depreciation for the second year is 15,000 times $0.16, or $2,400.

## Depreciation for Partial Years

Plant assets may be purchased or disposed of any time during the year. When an asset is purchased (or disposed of) at some time other than the beginning (or end) of an accounting period, depreciation must be recorded for part of a year. Otherwise, the year of purchase or the year of disposal is not charged with its share of the asset's depreciation.

For example, assume that a machine was purchased and placed in service on October 8, 1991, and the annual accounting period ends on December 31. The machine costs $4,600, has an estimated service life of five years, and an estimated salvage value of $600. Since the machine was purchased and used nearly three months during 1991, the annual income statement should reflect depreciation expense on the machine for part of the year. The amount of depreciation to be reported often is based on the assumption that the machine was purchased on the first of the month nearest the actual date of purchase. Therefore, since the purchase was on October 8, three months' depreciation must be recorded on December 31. If the purchase had been on October 16 or later during October, depreciation would be calculated as if the purchase had been on November 1.

Three months are 3/12 of one year. Therefore, if straight-line depreciation is used, the three months' depreciation is calculated as follows:

$$\frac{\$4{,}600 - \$600}{5} \times \frac{3}{12} = \$200$$

The entry to record depreciation for 1991 on the machine purchased on October 8, 1991, is:

| | | | | |
|---|---|---|---|---|
| Dec. | | Depreciation Expense, Machinery | 200.00 | |
| | | Accumulated Depreciation, Machinery | | 200.00 |
| | | To record depreciation for three months. | | |

On December 31, 1992, and at the end of each of the following three years, a journal entry to record a full year's depreciation on this machine is required. The entry is:

| | | | | |
|---|---|---|---|---|
| Dec. | 31 | Depreciation Expense, Machinery | 800.00 | |
| | | Accumulated Depreciation, Machinery | | 800.00 |
| | | To record depreciation for one year. | | |

After the December 31, 1995, depreciation entry is recorded, the accounts showing the history of this machine appear as follows:

**Machinery**

| | | | |
|---|---|---|---|
| Oct. 8, 1991 | 4,600 | | |

**Accumulated Depreciation Machinery**

| | | | |
|---|---|---|---|
| | | Dec. 31, 1991 | 200 |
| | | Dec. 31, 1992 | 800 |
| | | Dec. 31, 1993 | 800 |
| | | Dec. 31, 1994 | 800 |
| | | Dec. 31, 1995 | 800 |

If this machine is disposed of during 1996, two entries must be made to record the disposal. The first records 1996 depreciation to the date of disposal, and the second records the actual disposal. For example, assume that the machine is sold for $800 on June 24, 1996. To record the disposal, depreciation for six months (depreciation to the nearest full month) must first be recorded. The entry for this is:

| | | | | |
|---|---|---|---|---|
| June | 24 | Depreciation Expense, Machinery . . . . . . . . . . . . . . | 400.00 | |
| | | Accumulated Depreciation, Machinery . . . . . . . . . | | 400.00 |
| | | To record depreciation for one-half year. | | |

After making the entry to record depreciation to the date of sale, a second entry to record the actual sale is made. This entry is:

| | | | | |
|---|---|---|---|---|
| June | 24 | Cash . . . . . . . . . . . . . . . . . . . . . . . . . . . . . | 800.00 | |
| | | Accumulated Depreciation, Machinery . . . . . . . . . . . | 3,800.00 | |
| | | Machinery . . . . . . . . . . . . . . . . . . . . . . . . | | 4,600.00 |
| | | To record sale of machine at book value. | | |

In this instance, the machine was sold for its book value. In the next chapter, you will learn how to account for the more typical situation in which plant assets are sold for more or less than book value.

## Depreciation on the Balance Sheet

Describe how depreciation is disclosed in the financial statements and explain how the original cost of a plant asset is recovered through the sale of the asset's product or service. (L. O. 3)

In presenting information about the plant assets of a business, the *full-disclosure principle* requires that you give a general description of the depreciation method or methods used.[3] Usually, this is presented in a footnote. Also, the financial statements are more informative if you show both the cost and accumulated depreciation of plant assets by major classes. This may be accomplished in the statements or in related footnotes, and might appear as follows:

| | Cost | Accumulated Depreciation | Book Value |
|---|---|---|---|
| Plant assets: | | | |
| Store equipment . . . . | $ 12,400 | $1,500 | $10,900 |
| Office equipment . . . . | 3,600 | 450 | 3,150 |
| Building . . . . . . . . | 72,300 | 7,800 | 64,500 |
| Land . . . . . . . . . . | 15,000 | | 15,000 |
| Totals . . . . . . . . . | $103,300 | $9,750 | $93,550 |

A presentation such as the above provides better information to financial statement readers than would be given if undepreciated costs were the only amounts reported. To illustrate, $50,000 of assets with $40,000 of accumulated depreciation may be quite different than $10,000 of new assets. Yet, the net undepreciated cost is the same in both cases.

[3] Ibid., sec. D40.105. First published in *APB Opinion No. 12*, par. 5.

## Balance Sheet Plant Asset Values

From the discussion so far, you should recognize that the recording of depreciation is not primarily a valuation process. Rather, it is a process of allocating the cost of plant assets to the accounting periods that benefit from their use. Because depreciation is a process of cost allocation rather than valuation, plant assets are reported on balance sheets at their remaining (undepreciated) costs, not at market values.

The fact that balance sheets show undepreciated costs rather than market values may seem to be a failure of accounting. However, plant assets are held for use in the business; they are not held for sale. As a result, many accountants argue that the market values of plant assets are not particularly useful in evaluating the financial position and future prospects of the business. You should understand that a balance sheet is prepared under the assumption the company is a going concern. This means the company is expected to continue in business long enough to recover the original costs of its plant assets through the sale of its products.

The assumption that a company will continue in business long enough to recover its plant asset costs through the sale of its products is known in accounting as the *continuing-concern* or *going-concern concept*. This concept is used to justify carrying plant assets on the balance sheet at cost less accumulated depreciation—in other words, at the share of their cost applicable to future periods. The going-concern concept also explains why an item such as stationery imprinted with the company name is carried at cost even though the stationery is salable only as scrap paper. In all such instances, the intention is to use the assets in carrying on the business operations. They are not for sale, so their market or realizable values are not reported on the balance sheet.

## Recovering the Costs of Plant Assets

An uninformed financial statement reader may make the mistake of thinking that the accumulated depreciation shown on a balance sheet represents funds accumulated to buy new assets when present assets must be replaced. However, an informed reader recognizes that accumulated depreciation represents the portion of an asset's cost that has been charged off to depreciation expense during its life. Accumulated depreciation accounts are contra accounts with credit balances that cannot be used to buy anything. If a business has cash with which to buy assets, it is shown on the balance sheet as a current asset *Cash*, not as accumulated depreciation.

A company that earns a profit or breaks even (neither earns a profit nor suffers a loss) eventually recovers the original cost of its plant assets through the sale of its products. This is best explained with a condensed income statement like that of Illustration 10–2 which shows that Even Steven Company broke even during the year of the illustrated income statement. However, in breaking even, the company also recovered $5,000 of the cost of its plant assets through the sale of its products. It recovered the $5,000 because $100,000 flowed into the company from sales and only $95,000 flowed out to pay for goods sold, rent, and salaries. No funds flowed out for depreciation expense. As a result, the company recovered this $5,000 portion of the cost of its plant assets through the sale of its products. Furthermore, if the company remains in business for the life of its plant assets, either breaking even or earning a profit, it will recover their entire cost in this manner.

At this point you might ask, "Where is the recovered $5,000?" The answer

**Illustration 10–2**
**Recovering the cost of plant assets while breaking even**

EVEN STEVEN COMPANY
Income Statement
For Year Ended December 31, 1991

| | | |
|---|---|---|
| Sales . . . . . . . . . . . . . | | $100,000 |
| Cost of goods sold. . . . . . | $60,000 | |
| Rent expense . . . . . . . . | 10,000 | |
| Salaries expense. . . . . . . | 25,000 | |
| Depreciation expense . . . . | 5,000 | |
| Total. . . . . . . . . . . . . . | | 100,000 |
| Net income . . . . . . . . . | | $ –0– |

is that the company may have the $5,000 in the bank. However, the funds may also have been spent to increase merchandise inventory, to buy additional equipment, to pay off a debt, or they may have been withdrawn from the business by the owner. In short, the funds may still be in the bank or they may have been used for any purpose for which a business uses funds.

## Accelerated Depreciation Methods

Describe the use of accelerated depreciation for financial accounting and tax accounting purposes and calculate accelerated depreciation under (*a*) the declining-balance method, (*b*) the sum-of-the-years'-digits method, and (*c*) the Modified Accelerated Cost Recovery System. (L. O. 4)

Some depreciation methods result in larger depreciation charges during the early years of an asset's life and smaller charges in the later years. These are called **accelerated depreciation** methods. Several years ago, two of these methods, **declining-balance depreciation,** and **sum-of-the-years'-digits depreciation,** were used by many businesses to prepare their income tax returns. The United States tax laws, as codified in the **Internal Revenue Code,** allowed the use of these methods in a variety of situations. Since they were used for tax purposes and also are permitted within generally accepted accounting principles, many businesses used them in their financial accounting records. This made record-keeping easier.

Since December 31, 1980, the tax laws have not allowed the declining-balance or sum-of-the-years'-digits methods to be used for newly purchased assets. As a result, in keeping their financial accounting records, very few companies use either declining balance or sum-of-the-years' digits to depreciate assets purchased since 1980. Nevertheless, many long-lived plant assets purchased prior to 1981 are still being depreciated under one of these methods.

### Declining-Balance Method

Under the declining-balance depreciation method, depreciation of up to twice the straight-line rate, without considering salvage value, may be applied each year to the declining book value of a new plant asset. If this method is followed and twice the straight-line rate is used, depreciation on an asset is determined as follows: (1) calculate a straight-line depreciation rate for the asset; (2) double this rate; and (3) at the end of each year in the asset's life, apply this doubled rate to the asset's remaining book value.

For example, assume that the declining-balance method at twice the straight-line rate is used to calculate depreciation on a $10,000 new asset that has an estimated five-year life and a salvage value of $750. The steps to follow are:

**Step 1:** Divide 100% by 5 (years) to determine the straight-line annual depreciation rate of 20%.
**Step 2:** Double this 20% rate to get a declining-balance rate of 40%.
**Step 3:** Calculate the annual depreciation charges as shown in the following table:

| Year | Annual Depreciation Calculation | Annual Depreciation Expense | End-of-Year Accumulated Depreciation | End-of-Year Book Value |
|---|---|---|---|---|
| 1st year . . . . | 40% of $10,000 | $4,000.00 | $4,000.00 | $6,000.00 |
| 2nd year . . . . | 40% of 6,000 | 2,400.00 | 6,400.00 | 3,600.00 |
| 3rd year . . . . | 40% of 3,600 | 1,440.00 | 7,840.00 | 2,160.00 |
| 4th year . . . . | 40% of 2,160 | 864.00 | 8,704.00 | 1,296.00 |
| 5th year . . . . | 40% of 1,296 | 518.40 | 9,222.40 | 777.60 |

Under the declining-balance method, the book value of a plant asset never reaches zero. Therefore, when the asset is sold, exchanged, or scrapped, any remaining book value is used to determine the gain or loss on the disposal. However, if an asset has a salvage value, the asset may not be depreciated beyond its salvage value. For example, if instead of a $750 salvage value, the foregoing $10,000 asset has an estimated $1,000 salvage value, depreciation for its fifth year is limited to $296. This is the amount required to reduce the asset's book value to its $1,000 salvage value.

### Sum-of-the-Years'-Digits Method

Under the sum-of-the-years'-digits method, the whole numbers from 1 to the number of years in an asset's service life are added. The sum of these numbers becomes the denominator of a series of fractions used to allocate total depreciation to the periods in the asset's service life. The numerators of the fractions are the same whole numbers that represent the years in the asset's life in their reverse order. For example, assume a machine is purchased that costs $7,000, has an estimated five-year life, and has an estimated $1,000 salvage value. The sum-of-the-years'-digits in the asset's life are:

$$1 + 2 + 3 + 4 + 5 = 15$$

and annual depreciation charges are calculated as follows:

| Year | Annual Depreciation Calculation | Annual Depreciation Expense | End-of-Year Accumulated Depreciation | End-of-Year Book Value |
|---|---|---|---|---|
| 1st year . . . . . . . . . | 5/15 of $6,000 | $2,000 | $2,000 | $4,000 |
| 2nd year . . . . . . . . . | 4/15 of 6,000 | 1,600 | 3,600 | 2,400 |
| 3rd year . . . . . . . . . | 3/15 of 6,000 | 1,200 | 4,800 | 1,200 |
| 4th year . . . . . . . . . | 2/15 of 6,000 | 800 | 5,600 | 400 |
| 5th year . . . . . . . . . | 1/15 of 6,000 | 400 | 6,000 | –0– |
| Total depreciation . . . . | | $6,000 | | |

The sum-of-the-years' digits in an asset's life may be calculated by using the formula: $SYD = n[(n + 1)/2]$. For example, sum-of-the-years' digits for a five-year life is:

$$5\left(\frac{5 + 1}{2}\right) = 15$$

### Apporting Accelerated Depreciation

When accelerated depreciation is used and accounting periods do not coincide with the years in an asset's life, depreciation must be apportioned between accounting periods. For example, consider the above case where the sum-of-the-years'-digits method is used to calculate depreciation on a machine. Annual depreciation on the machine is $2,000 during its first year, $1,600 during its second year, and so on for its five-year life. Now assume this machine is placed in use on April 1 and the annual accounting period ends on December 31. As a result, the machine will be in use for three fourths of a year during the first accounting period in its life. Therefore, this period should be charged with $1,500 depreciation ($2,000 × ¾ = $1,500). Likewise, the second accounting period should be charged with $1,700 depreciation [(¼ × $2,000) + (¾ × $1,600) = $1,700]. Similar calculations should be used for the remaining periods in the asset's life.

### Accelerated Depreciation for Tax Purposes

As we stated earlier, U. S. tax laws allow the use of declining-balance and sum-of-the-years'-digits depreciation methods for assets purchased prior to 1981. For assets purchased after 1980 and before 1987, the tax laws allow a different method of accelerated depreciation, which is called the **Accelerated Cost Recovery System (ACRS).** For assets purchased after December 31, 1986, this system was revised and is now called the **Modified Accelerated Cost Recovery System (MACRS).**

As specified in the Tax Reform Act of 1986, depreciable personal property (property other than real estate) purchased after December 31, 1986, is classified into several classes ranging from a 3-year class to a 20-year class. Real property is classified into two classes: the 27½-year class for residential rental property and the 31½-year class for all other real estate. Both classes of real property must be depreciated on a straight-line basis. Personal property may be depreciated on a straight-line basis, but an accelerated method is also available for each class of personal property.

When calculating depreciation for tax purposes, salvage values are ignored for assets purchased after 1980. Also, depreciation methods for personal property are based on the assumption that the asset was purchased half-way through the year. This half-year convention is required regardless of when the asset was actually purchased.[4] Depreciation of real property is based on a half-month convention.

MACRS depreciation is accelerated for two reasons. First, the actual economic lives of the assets in any given class are usually longer than the arbitrary number of years assigned to the class. For example, the five-year class includes assets such as computer equipment, office machinery, and heavy, gen-

[4] Under certain conditions, a half-quarter convention must be used.

**Illustration 10–3**
**Modified Accelerated Cost Recovery System for assets placed in service after December 31, 1986**

| Class Life | |
|---|---|
| 3-year . . . . . | 200% declining balance, switching to straight line |
| 5-year . . . . . | 200% declining balance, switching to straight line |
| 7-year . . . . . | 200% declining balance, switching to straight line |
| 10-year . . . . . | 200% declining balance, switching to straight line |
| 15-year . . . . . | 150% declining balance, switching to straight line |
| 20-year . . . . . | 150% declining balance, switching to straight line |
| 27½-year . . . . | Straight line |
| 31½-year . . . . | Straight line |

eral purpose trucks. Normally, assets such as these would be expected to have useful lives longer than five years. Thus, even when straight-line depreciation is used for tax purposes, the assumed length of life (for tax purposes) may be shorter than the expected service life of the asset (which should be used for financial accounting purposes).

The second reason by MACRS depreciation is accelerated is that MACRS involves using the declining-balance method with a switch to straight line at the point where the switch serves to further accelerate the depreciation. The actual depreciation rates allowed for each class are shown in Illustration 10–3.

To illustrate the MACRS method of switching from declining-balance to straight-line depreciation, assume an asset in the five-year class (for example, a heavy, general purpose truck) is purchased at a cost of $10,000. For declining balance, the depreciation rate is 200% of the straight-line rate. This is (100% ÷ 5) × 2 = 40%. MACRS depreciation is calculated as follows:

| Year | Depreciation for Year | Undepreciated Cost at End of Year | Method Used |
|---|---|---|---|
| 1 . . . . | 20% × $10,000 = $2,000 | $10,000 − $2,000 = $8,000 | Declining balance |
| 2 . . . . | 40% × 8,000 = 3,200 | 8,000 − 3,200 = 4,800 | Declining balance |
| 3 . . . . | 40% × 4,800 = 1,920 | 4,800 − 1,920 = 2,880 | Declining balance |
| 4 . . . . | 40% × 2,880 = 1,152 | 2,880 − 1,152 = 1,728 | Declining balance equals straight line |
| 5 . . . . | $1,728 × (⅔) = 1,152 | 1,728 − 1,152 = 576 | Straight line |
| 6 . . . . | $1,728 × (⅓) = 576 | 576 − 576 = -0- | Straight line |

In this example, declining-balance depreciation for year 4 ($1,152) is exactly the same as straight-line depreciation. To understand this, remember the half-year convention and the fact that the remaining life at the beginning of year 4 is 2½ years, or five 6-month periods. Thus, straight-line depreciation for year 4 would be $2,880 × (⅖) = $1,152, which is the same amount as is calculated under the declining-balance method.

Beginning in year 5, the table shows that depreciation is calculated by the straight-line method. At the beginning of year 5, three 6-month periods remain. Therefore, using the straight-line method, depreciation for year 5 is $1,728 × ⅔ = $1,152, and depreciation for year 6 is $1,728 × ⅓ = $576. The straight-line method is used beginning in year 5 because the switch to straight line has an accelerated effect. To prove this point, if declining-balance depreciation were continued in years 5 and 6, the depreciation would be as follows:

| | | |
|---|---|---|
| Year 5 | Declining-balance depreciation would be . . | 40% × $1,728 = $ 691.20 |
| Year 6 | Depreciate the remaining balance . . . . . | $1,728 − $691.20 = $1,036.80 |

By comparison, the switch to straight-line depreciation resulted in $1,152 depreciation in year 5 and $576 depreciation in year 6.

You should understand that MACRS depreciation generally is not acceptable for use in financial statements. MACRS is not acceptable because it allocates depreciation over a shorter period of time than the estimated service life of the asset.

However, using MACRS depreciation for tax purposes may have an important tax advantage. The tax advantage of using MACRS instead of straight line is that accelerated depreciation *defers* the payment of income taxes from the early years of a plant asset's life until its later years. Taxes are deferred because accelerated depreciation causes larger amounts of depreciation to be charged to the early years. This results in smaller amounts of income and income taxes in these years. However, the taxes are only deferred; they are not avoided. The larger depreciation charges in earlier years are offset by smaller (or even zero) depreciation charges in later years. Thus, larger amounts of income and income taxes are reported and paid in the later years of a plant asset's life.

Special problems in measuring net income may occur when a company uses one depreciation method for financial accounting purposes and another for tax purposes. These problems are discussed in Chapter 28.

## Control of Plant Assets

Explain how subsidiary ledgers and related controlling accounts are used to maintain control over plant assets.
(L. O. 5)

Good internal control requires that each plant asset be separately identified, usually with a serial number that is etched or affixed to the asset. Periodically, an inventory of plant assets should be taken in which the existence and continued use of each asset are verified. Formal records of plant assets on hand should be maintained.

In keeping plant asset records, concerns usually divide their plant assets into functional groups and provide in the General Ledger a separate asset account and accumulated depreciation account for each group. The asset account and related accumulated depreciation account for each group serve as controlling accounts that control detailed subsidiary records. For example, in a store, the Store Equipment account and the Accumulated Depreciation, Store Equipment account control the **Store Equipment Ledger.** This is a subsidiary ledger that has a separate record for each individual item of store equipment. The same is true for the Office Equipment account and the Accumulated Depreciation, Office Equipment account, which control the **Office Equipment Ledger.**

Whether plant asset records are computerized or handwritten, they provide the same basic information. To illustrate plant asset records, assume that a concern's office equipment consists of just one desk and a chair. The general ledger accounts for these assets are Office Equipment and Accumulated Depreciation, Office Equipment. Both are controlling accounts that control sections of the subsidiary record for the desk and chair. The general ledger and subsidiary ledger records of these assets are shown in Illustration 10–4 on pages 448 and 449.

**Illustration 10–4**
**Subsidiary records and controlling accounts for plant assets**

Plant Asset
No. *132-1*

SUBSIDIARY PLANT ASSET AND DEPRECIATION RECORD

Item *Office chair* Account *Office Equipment*
Description *Padded, straight-back, wood*
Mfg. Serial No. ____ Purchased from *Office Equipment Co.*
Where Located *Office*
Person Responsible for the Asset *Office Manager*
Estimated Life *6 years* Estimated Salvage Value *$10.00*
Depreciation per Year *$30.00* per Month *$2.50*

| Date | Explanation | PR | Asset Record Dr. | Asset Record Cr. | Asset Record Bal. | Depreciation Record Dr. | Depreciation Record Cr. | Depreciation Record Bal. |
|---|---|---|---|---|---|---|---|---|
| *July 2, 1989* | | *G1* | *190.00* | | *190.00* | | | |
| *Dec. 31, 1990* | | *G23* | | | | | *15.00* | *15.00* |
| *Dec. 31, 1991* | | *G42* | | | | | *30.00* | *45.00* |
| *Dec. 31, 1992* | | *G65* | | | | | *30.00* | *75.00* |

Final Disposition of the Asset ____

Plant Asset
No. *132-2*

SUBSIDIARY PLANT ASSET AND DEPRECIATION RECORD

Item *Desk* Account *Office Equipment*
Description *Wood, left hand return*
Mfg. Serial No. ____ Purchased from *Office Equipment Co.*
Where Located *Office*
Person Responsible for the Asset *Office Manager*
Estimated Life *6 years* Estimated Salvage Value *$30.00*
Depreciation per Year *$120.00* per Month *$10.00*

| Date | Explanation | PR | Asset Record Dr. | Asset Record Cr. | Asset Record Bal. | Depreciation Record Dr. | Depreciation Record Cr. | Depreciation Record Bal. |
|---|---|---|---|---|---|---|---|---|
| *July 2, 1989* | | *G1* | *750.00* | | *750.00* | | | |
| *Dec. 31, 1990* | | *G23* | | | | | *60.00* | *60.00* |
| *Dec. 31, 1991* | | *G42* | | | | | *120.00* | *180.00* |
| *Dec. 31, 1992* | | *G65* | | | | | *120.00* | *300.00* |

Final Disposition of the Asset ____

**Illustration 10–4 *(concluded)***

**Office Equipment** — **Account No. 132**

| Date | | Explanation | PR | Debit | Credit | Balance |
|---|---|---|---|---|---|---|
| *1989 July* | *2* | *Desk and chair* | *G1* | *940 00* | | *940 00* |

**Accumulated Depreciation, Office Equipment** — **Account No. 133**

| Date | | Explanation | PR | Debit | Credit | Balance |
|---|---|---|---|---|---|---|
| *1989 Dec.* | *31* | | *G23* | | *75 00* | *75 00* |
| *1990 Dec.* | *31* | | *G42* | | *150 00* | *225 00* |
| *1991 Dec.* | *31* | | *G65* | | *150 00* | *375 00* |

At the top of each subsidiary record, observe the plant asset numbers assigned to these two items of office equipment. In each case, the assigned number consists of the number of the Office Equipment account, 132, followed by the asset's number. The remaining information on the subsidiary records is more or less self-evident. Note how the $940 balance of the general ledger account, Office Equipment, is equal to the sum of the $190 and $750 balances in the asset record section of the two subsidiary records. The general ledger account controls this section of the subsidiary ledger. Observe also how the Accumulated Depreciation, Office Equipment account controls the depreciation record section of the subsidiary records. The disposition section at the bottom of the subsidiary records is used to record the final disposal of the asset. When the asset is discarded, sold, or exchanged, a notation telling of the final disposition is entered here. The record is then removed from the subsidiary ledger and filed for future reference.

## Plant Assets of Low Cost

Individual plant asset records are expensive to keep. Therefore, many companies establish a minimum, say, $50 or $100, and do not keep such records for assets costing less than the minimum. Rather, they charge the cost of such assets directly to an expense account at the time of purchase. As long as the amounts are small, this is acceptable under the *materiality principle*.

## Summary of the Chapter in Terms of Learning Objectives

**1.** The cost of plant assets includes all normal and reasonable expenditures necessary to get the assets in place and ready to use. The cost of a lump-sum purchase should be allocated to the individual assets based on their relative market values.

**2.** Plant assets other than land have limited service lives. Therefore, the cost of the assets must be allocated to the accounting periods that benefit from their use. When the allocation is done according to the straight-line method, you divide the cost minus salvage value by the number of periods in the service life of the asset to determine the depreciation expense of each period. Under the units-of-production method, you divide the cost minus salvage value by the estimated number of units the asset will produce to determine the depreciation per unit.

**3.** Financial statements should include a description of the depreciation methods used. Also, financial statements are more informative if cost and accumulated depreciation is reported by major class of asset. When the revenues of a business are large enough to cover all expenses, the cost of depreciation is recovered through revenues.

**4.** For tax purposes, declining-balance and sum-of-the-years' digits depreciation are often used to depreciate assets purchased prior to 1981. From 1981 through 1986, the Accelerated Cost Recovery System was used. And for assets purchased since January 1, 1987, the Modified Accelerated Cost Recovery System is used. Although declining-balance and sum-of-the-years'-digits depreciation are acceptable for financial accounting purposes, they are seldom used. Accelerated depreciation under ACRS or MACRS is not acceptable for financial accounting purposes.

**5.** To maintain control over plant assets, detailed records should be kept. These records usually require the use of subsidiary ledgers that are controlled by asset and accumulated depreciation accounts.

## Demonstration Problem

On July 14, 1990, a company paid $600,000 to acquire a fully equipped factory. The purchase included the following:

| Asset | Appraised Value | Estimated Salvage Value | Estimated Service Life | Depreciation Method |
|---|---|---|---|---|
| Land | $160,000 | | | |
| Land improvements | 80,000 | $ –0– | 10 years | Straight line |
| Building | 320,000 | 100,000 | 10 years | Sum-of-the-years' digits |
| Machinery | 176,000 | 16,000 | 10,000 units | Units of production* |
| Computers | 64,000 | 4,000 | 4 years | Declining balance (at twice the straight-line rate) |
| Total | $800,000 | | | |

*The machinery was used to produce 700 units in 1990 and 1,800 units in 1991.

*Required*

1. Allocate the total $600,000 cost among the five separate assets.
2. Compute the depreciation expense that should be reported for 1990 (half-year) and for 1991.
3. Compute MACRS depreciation for the company's computers for all years from 1990 through 1995, assuming the computers are classified as five-year assets. Round all amounts to the nearest whole dollar and remember to change to straight-line depreciation when it further accelerates the depreciation. Also remember to take one-half year's depreciation in 1990 and in 1995.

## Solution to Demonstration Problem

1.

| Asset | Appraised Value | Percent of Total Value | Allocated Cost |
|---|---|---|---|
| Land | $160,000 | 20 | $120,000 |
| Land improvements | 80,000 | 10 | 60,000 |
| Building | 320,000 | 40 | 240,000 |
| Machinery | 176,000 | 22 | 132,000 |
| Computers | 64,000 | 8 | 48,000 |
| Total | $800,000 | 100 | $600,000 |

2. Depreciation for each asset:

**Land improvements:**

| | | |
|---|---|---|
| Cost | | $60,000 |
| Salvage value | | –0– |
| Net cost | | $60,000 |
| Service life | | 10 years |
| Annual expense | $60,000 ÷ 10 = | $6,000 |
| 1990 depreciation | $6,000 × (½) = | $3,000 |
| 1991 depreciation | | 6,000 |

**Building:**

| | | |
|---|---|---|
| Cost | | $240,000 |
| Salvage value | | 100,000 |
| Net cost | | $140,000 |

Sum-of-the-years' digits = (10 × 11) ÷ 2 = 55

| | | |
|---|---|---|
| 1990 depreciation: | $140,000 × (10/55) × (½) | = $12,727 |
| 1991 depreciation: | $140,000 × (10/55) × (½) | = $12,727 |
| | $140,000 × (9/55) × (½) | = 11,455 |
| Total | | $24,182 |

**Machinery:**

| | |
|---|---|
| Cost | $132,000 |
| Salvage value | 16,000 |
| Net cost | $116,000 |
| Total expected units | 10,000 |
| Expected cost per unit ($116,000 ÷ 10,000) | $11.60 |

| Year | Units × Unit Cost | Depreciation |
|---|---|---|
| 1990 | 700 × $11.60 | $ 8,120 |
| 1991 | 1,800 × $11.60 | 20,880 |

**Computers:**

| | |
|---|---|
| Cost | $48,000 |
| Salvage value | 4,000 |
| Straight-line rate (100%/4 years) | 25% |
| Twice the straight-line rate (25% × 2) | 50% |

| Year | Rate | Beginning Book Value | Depreciation Expense | Accumulated Depreciation | Ending Book Value |
|---|---|---|---|---|---|
| 1990 | 50%/2 | $48,000 | $12,000 | $12,000 | $36,000 |
| 1991 | 50% | 36,000 | 18,000 | 30,000 | 18,000 |

Note: The percentage for 1990 is 50%/2 because the computers were in use for only one half of the year.

3. MACRS depreciation for the computers:

| Year | Rate/ Method | Beginning Book Value | Depreciation Expense | Accumulated Depreciation | Ending Book Value |
|---|---|---|---|---|---|
| 1990 | 20%/DB | $48,000 | $ 9,600 | $ 9,600 | $38,400 |
| 1991 | 40%/DB | 38,400 | 15,360 | 24,960 | 23,040 |
| 1992 | 40%/DB | 23,040 | 9,216 | 34,176 | 13,824 |
| 1993 | 40%/DB | 13,824 | 5,530 | 39,706 | 8,294 |
| 1994 | 1.5 yrs/SL | 8,294 | 5,529* | 45,235 | 2,765 |
| 1995 | 1.5 yrs/SL | 2,765 | 2,765† | 48,000 | –0– |

DB = declining balance.
SL = straight line.
*Beginning 1994 book value divided by 1½ years of remaining life, or $8,294/1.5 years = $5,529 per year.
†One half year's charge $5,529 × (½), rounded to equal the beginning-of-year book value.

## Glossary

Define or explain the words and phrases listed in the chapter Glossary. (L. O. 6)

**Accelerated Cost Recovery System (ACRS)** a unique, accelerated depreciation method prescribed in the tax law for assets placed in service after 1980 and before 1987. p. 445

**Accelerated depreciation** any depreciation method that results in greater amounts of depreciation expense in the early years of a plant asset's life and lesser amounts in later years. p. 443

**Book value** the carrying amount for an item in the accounting records. When applied to a plant asset, it is the cost of the asset minus its accumulated depreciation. p. 439

**Declining-balance depreciation** a depreciation method in which up to twice the straight-line rate of depreciation, without considering salvage value, is applied to the beginning-of-period book value of a plant asset to determine the asset's depreciation charge for the period. pp. 443–444

**Fixed asset** another name for plant asset, no longer widely in use. p. 434

**Inadequacy** a situation in which a plant asset does not produce enough product to meet current needs. pp. 436–437

**Internal Revenue Code** the codification of the United States federal tax laws. p. 443

**Land improvements** assets that improve or increase the usefulness of land but which have a limited useful life and are subject to depreciation. p. 435

**Modified Accelerated Cost Recovery System (MACRS)** the system of depreciation specified in the tax law for assets placed in service after 1986. pp. 445–447

**Obsolescence** a situation in which, because of new inventions and improvements, an old plant asset can no longer produce its product on a competitive basis. pp. 436–437

**Office Equipment Ledger** a subsidiary ledger that contains a separate record for each item of office equipment owned. p. 447

**Salvage value** the portion of a plant asset's cost that will be recovered at the end of its service life through a sale or as a trade-in allowance on a new asset. p. 437

**Service life** the period of time a plant asset is used in the production and sale of other assets or services. p. 436

**Store Equipment Ledger** a subsidiary ledger that contains a separate record for each item of store equipment owned. p. 447

**Straight-line depreciation** a depreciation method that allocates an equal share of the total estimated amount a plant asset will be depreciated during its service life to each accounting period in that life. p. 438

**Sum-of-the-years'-digits depreciation** a depreciation method that allocates depreciation to each year in a plant asset's life on a fractional basis. The denominator of the fractions used is the sum-of-the-years' digits in the estimated service life of the asset, and the numerators are the years' digits in reverse order. pp. 443–444

**Units-of-production depreciation** a depreciation method that allocates depreciation on a plant asset based on the relation of the units of product produced by the asset during a given period to the total units the asset is expected to produce during its entire life. p. 439

## Objective Review

Answers to the following questions are listed in Appendix I at the end of the book. Be sure that you decide which is the one best answer to each question *before* you check the answers in the appendix.

1. Cornwall Company recently purchased a new production machine which involved the following dollar amounts:

| | |
|---|---|
| Gross purchase price | $500,000 |
| Sales tax | 35,000 |
| Freight to move machine to plant | 2,500 |
| Assembly costs | 2,200 |
| Cost of foundation for machine | 1,800 |
| Cost of spare parts to be used in maintenance of the machine | 3,000 |
| Purchase discount taken | 15,000 |

The amount to be recorded as the cost of the machine is:
*a.* $491,500.
*b.* $524,300.
*c.* $520,000.
*d.* $526,500.
*e.* $529,500.

2. Cummins, Inc., recently purchased a new machine for $120,000 on January 1, 1991. Its estimated useful life is five years or 80,000 units of product, and salvage value is $10,000. During 1991, 8,000 units of product were produced. Assuming (1) straight-line depreciation and (2) units-of-production depreciation, respectively, the book value of the machine on December 31, 1991, is:
*a.* $96,000; $108,000.
*b.* $96,000; $ 99,000.
*c.* $88,000; $108,000.
*d.* $98,000; $109,000.
*e.* $22,000; $ 11,000.

3. When disclosing depreciation in the financial statements:
*a.* Depreciation for the current period is subtracted from the asset account balance in the balance sheet.
*b.* Total accumulated depreciation is subtracted as an expense in the income statement.
*c.* Total accumulated depreciation is subtracted from the asset account balance in the balance sheet.
*d.* Depreciation for the current period is subtracted as an expense in the income statement.
*e.* Both (*c*) and (*d*) are correct.

4. Flexoral Industries recently purchased a new machine for $180,000 on January 1, 1990. Its estimated useful life is five years, and salvage value

is $15,000. Depreciation expense for 1991 using (1) double-declining balance and (2) sum-of-the-years'-digits depreciation, respectively, is:

*a.* $28,800; $48,000.
*b.* $39,600; $48,000.
*c.* $39,600; $44,000.
*d.* $43,200; $48,000.
*e.* $43,200; $44,000.

5. In keeping plant asset records:
   *a.* Detailed subsidiary records serve as controlling accounts for the related general ledger account.
   *b.* Computerized records always provide more information than handwritten records.
   *c.* The asset account and related accumulated depreciation account for each group of assets serve as controlling accounts that control detailed subsidiary records.
   *d.* To record a purchase of an office desk, separate general journal entries are made to Office Equipment and to the subsidiary account Office Desk.
   *e.* The Office Equipment Ledger controls the Office Equipment account and the Accumulated Depreciation, Office Equipment account.

## Questions for Class Discussion

1. What are the characteristics of an asset classified as plant and equipment?
2. What is the balance sheet classification of land held for future expansion? Why is such land not classified as a plant asset?
3. What is the difference between land and land improvements?
4. What in general is included in the cost of a plant asset?
5. Tack Company asked for bids from several machine manufacturers for the construction of a special machine. The lowest bid was $37,500. The company decided to build the machine itself and did so at a total cash outlay of $30,000. It then recorded the machine's construction with a debit to Machinery for $37,500, a credit to Cash for $30,000, and a credit to Gain on the Construction of Machinery for $7,500. Was this a proper entry? Discuss.
6. As used in accounting, what is the meaning of the term *depreciation?*
7. Is it possible to keep a plant asset in such an excellent state of repair that recording depreciation is unnecessary?
8. A machine that normally lasts 10 years is purchased even though management knows future growth of the company's operations will require that the machine be replaced in approximately 4 years. What factor in this situation tends to suggest that the machine should be depreciated over 4 years?
9. A company purchases a machine that normally has a service life of 12 years. However, the company's management believes that the devel-

opment of a more efficient machine will make it necessary to replace the machine in 8 years. What period of useful life should be used in calculating depreciation on this machine?

10. A building estimated to have a useful life of 30 years was completed at a cost of $120,000. It was estimated that at the end of the building's life it would be wrecked at a cost of $25,000 and that materials salvaged from the wrecking operation would be sold for $13,000. How much straight-line depreciation should be charged on the building each year?
11. When straight-line depreciation is used, an equal share of the total amount a plant asset is to be depreciated during its life is assigned to each accounting period in that life. Describe a situation in which this may not be a fair basis of allocation. Name a depreciation method that might be fairer in the situation described.
12. Define the following terms as used in accounting for plant assets:
    *a.* Trade-in value. *c.* Book value. *e.* Inadequacy.
    *b.* Market value. *d.* Salvage value. *f.* Obsolescence.
13. What is the sum-of-the-years' digits in the life of a plant asset that will be used for 20 years?
14. Does the recording of depreciation cause a plant asset to appear on the balance sheet at market value? What is accomplished by recording depreciation?
15. Does the balance of the Accumulated Depreciation, Machinery account represent funds accumulated to replace the machinery as it wears out? Describe in your own words what the balance of such an account represents.
16. Why is the Modified Accelerated Cost Recovery System not generally accepted for financial accounting purposes?
17. What is the purpose of periodically taking an inventory of plant assets?
18. What possible justification is there for charging to expense a plant asset that cost $75?
19. What is the implication of the going-concern concept on the valuation of plant assets in the accounting records?
20. Explain how a business that breaks even recovers the cost of its plant assets through the sale of its products. Where are the funds thus recovered?

## Exercises

**Exercise 10–1**
**Cost of a plant asset**
(L. O. 1)

Johnson Corporation purchased a machine for $19,000, terms 2/10, n/60, FOB shipping point. The seller prepaid the freight charges, $1,055, adding the amount to the invoice and bringing its total to $20,055. The machine required a special steel mounting and power connections costing $2,735, and another $2,590 was paid to assemble the machine and get it into operation. In moving the machine onto its steel mounting, it was dropped and damaged. The damages cost $675 to repair, and after being repaired, $280 of raw materials were consumed in adjusting the machine so it would produce a satisfactory product. The adjustments were normal for this type of machine and were not the result of its having been damaged. However, the product produced while the adjustments were being made was not salable. Prepare a calculation to show the cost of this machine for accounting purposes.

**Exercise 10–2**
**Allocating cost between land, land improvements, and buildings**
(L. O. 1)

Charter Company paid $520,000 for real estate plus $10,800 in closing costs. The real estate included land appraised at $160,000, land improvements appraised at $64,000, and a building appraised at $416,000. The plan is to use the building as a factory. Prepare a calculation showing the allocation of cost to the assets purchased and present the journal entry to record the purchase.

**Exercise 10–3**
**Lump-sum purchase of plant assets**
(L. O. 1)

Western Company bought two pickup trucks and a forklift from a financially distressed supplier and had them shipped to the company's plant. The purchase price was $25,000 plus $1,250 that was paid for the shipping charge. The forklift was only half as large as a truck and weighed half as much. Appraised values of the trucks and forklift and costs of initial repairs to get them ready for service were as follows:

| | Truck 1 | Truck 2 | Forklift |
|---|---|---|---|
| Appraised values . . . . | $14,000 | $12,250 | $8,750 |
| Repair costs . . . . . . . | 900 | 600 | 450 |

Determine the cost of each asset for accounting purposes.

**Exercise 10–4**
**Recording the costs of real estate**
(L. O. 1)

After planning to build a new manufacturing plant, Enslow Company purchased a large lot on which a small building was located. The negotiated purchase price of this real estate amounted to $375,000 for the lot plus $450,000 for the building. The company paid $60,000 to have the old building torn down and $75,000 for landscaping of the lot. Finally, it paid $2.7 million construction costs for a new building, which included $120,000 for lighting and paving of a parking lot next to the building. Present a single general journal entry to record the costs incurred by the company, all of which were paid in cash.

**Exercise 10–5**
**Calculating depreciation; four alternative methods**
(L. O. 2, 3)

Barney Company installed a machine in its factory at a $114,000 cost. The machine's useful life was estimated at five years or 36,100 units of product with a $5,700 trade-in value. During its second year, the machine produced 8,600 units of product. Determine the machine's second-year depreciation with depreciation calculated in each of the following ways: (*a*) straight-line rate, (*b*) units-of-production basis, (*c*) declining-balance basis at twice the straight-line rate, and (*d*) sum-of-the-years'-digits basis.

**Exercise 10–6**
**Calculating depreciation; three alternative methods**
(L. O. 2, 3)

On September 1, 1990, Fox Company purchased a machine for $675,000. The machine was expected to last six years and have a salvage value of $45,000. Calculate depreciation expense for 1991, assuming (*a*) straight-line depreciation, (*b*) sum-of-the-years'-digits depreciation, and (*c*) declining-balance depreciation at twice the straight-line rate.

**Exercise 10–7**
**Partial year's depreciation**
(L. O. 2, 5)

Daffy Company purchased and installed a machine on June 2, 1990, at a total cost of $54,000. Straight-line depreciation was taken on December 31 of each year for 1990 through 1993, based on the assumption of a six-year life and no salvage value. Then on August 31, 1994, the company decides to prepare financial statements for the period January through August. Present the entries to record the depreciation on December 31, 1990; December 31, 1991; and August 31, 1994.

**Exercise 10–8**
**MACRS depreciation**
(L. O. 2, 3)

In January 1990, Thompson Company purchased computer equipment for $30,000. The equipment will be used in research and development activities for six years and then sold at an estimated salvage value of $15,000. The equipment is in the five-year class for tax purposes. Prepare a schedule showing each year's depreciation for tax purposes assuming *(a)* five-year straight-line depreciation and *(b)* MACRS depreciation.

**Exercise 10–9**
**Declining-balance depreciation**
(L. O. 3)

Hatfield Company purchased and installed a plant asset that cost $24,000 and was estimated to have a four-year life and a $2,100 trade-in value. Use declining-balance depreciation at twice the straight-line rate to determine the amount of depreciation to be charged against the machine in each of the four years of its life.

**Exercise 10–10**
**Income statement effects of alternative depreciation methods**
(L. O. 2, 3)

Gafford Company recently paid $180,000 for equipment that will last four years and have a salvage value of $30,000. By using the machine in its operations for four years, the company expects to earn $60,000 annually, after deducting all expenses except depreciation. Present a schedule showing income before depreciation, depreciation expense, and net income for each year and the total amounts for the four-year period assuming *(a)* straight-line depreciation, *(b)* sum-of-the-years'-digits depreciation, and *(c)* declining-balance depreciation at twice the straight-line rate.

## Problems

**Problem 10–1**
**Alternative depreciation methods; retirement of plant assets**
(L. O. 2, 3, 5)

**Part 1.** A machine that cost $75,000, has a five-year life, and has an estimated $10,500 salvage value was installed in Blake Company's factory. The factory management estimated the machine would produce 150,000 units of product during its life. It actually produced the following numbers of units: year 1, 21,000; year 2, 33,000; year 3, 30,000; year 4, 28,500; and year 5, 37,500.

*Required*

1. Prepare a calculation showing the number of dollars of this machine's cost that should be charged to depreciation over its five-year life.
2. Prepare a form with the following column headings:

| Year | Straight Line | Units of Production | Declining Balance | Sum-of-the-Years' Digits |
|---|---|---|---|---|
| | | | | |

Then show the depreciation for each year and the total depreciation for the machine under each depreciation method. Use twice the straight-line rate for the declining-balance method.

**Part 2.** Craft Company purchased a used machine for $17,100 on January 3. The next day it was repaired at a cost of $2,025 and was installed on a new platform that cost $1,575. It was estimated the machine would be used for three years and would then have a $2,700 salvage value. Depreciation was to be charged on a straight-line basis. A full year's depreciation was charged on December 31, at the end of the first year of the machine's use; and on September 1, in its second year of use, the machine was retired from service.

*Required*

1. Prepare general journal entries to record the purchase of the machine, the cost of repairing it, and its installation. Assume cash was paid in each case.
2. Prepare entries to record depreciation on the machine on December 31 and on September 1.
3. Prepare entries to record the retirement of the machine under each of the following unrelated assumptions: *(a)* the machine was sold for $12,000; *(b)* it was sold for $6,900; and *(c)* it was destroyed in a fire, and the insurance company paid $6,525 in full settlement of the loss claim.

**Problem 10–2**
**Plant asset records**
(L. O. 2, 4)

Brady Salvage Company completed the following transactions involving plant assets:

1990

Jan. 5 Purchased on credit from Dexter Equipment an electronic scale priced at $3,975. The serial number of the scale was E-56273, its service life was estimated at five years with a trade-in value of $375, and it was assigned plant asset No. 545-1.

Apr. 3 Purchased on credit from Dexter Equipment a Moore mixer priced at $6,141. The serial number of the mixer was M-41652, its service life was estimated at six years with a trade-in value of $525, and it was assigned plant asset No. 556-2.

Dec. 31 Recorded straight-line depreciation on the plant equipment for 1990.

1991

Nov. 4 Sold the Moore mixer to Sharpstowne Steel for $3,750 cash.

4 Purchased a new Master mixer from Penford Equipment for $5,400. The serial number of the mixer was PM-87651, its service life was estimated at eight years with a trade-in value of $720, and it was assigned plant asset No. 556-3.

Dec. 31 Recorded straight-line depreciation on the plant equipment for 1991.

*Required*

1. Open general ledger accounts for Plant Equipment and for Accumulated Depreciation, Plant Equipment. Prepare a subsidiary plant asset record card for each item of equipment purchased.
2. Prepare general journal entries to record the transactions and post to the proper general ledger and subsidiary ledger accounts.

3. Prove the December 31, 1991, balances of the Plant Equipment and Accumulated Depreciation, Plant Equipment accounts by preparing a list showing the cost and accumulated depreciation on each item of plant equipment owned by Brady Salvage Company on that date.

**Problem 10–3**
**Real estate costs and partial year's depreciation**
(L. O. 1, 2, 3)

In early 1991, Angara Company paid $1,207,500 for real estate that included a tract of land on which two buildings were located. The plan was to demolish Building One and build a new store in its place. Building Two was to be used as a company office and was appraised to have a value of $341,250, with a useful life of 15 years and a $26,250 salvage value. A lighted parking lot near Building Two had improvements valued at $136,500 that were expected to last another 10 years and have no salvage value. In its existing condition, the tract of land was estimated to have a value of $887,250.

Angara Company incurred the following additional costs:

| | |
|---|---|
| Cost to demolish Building One . . . . . . . . . . . . . . . | $ 131,250 |
| Cost to landscape new building site . . . . . . . . . . . . | 42,000 |
| Cost to build new building (Building Three), having a useful life of 30 years and a $157,500 salvage value . . . | 1,575,000 |
| Cost of new land improvements near Building Three, which have a 15-year useful life and no salvage value . . | 183,750 |

*Required*

1. Prepare a form having the following column headings: Land, Building Two, Building Three, Land Improvements Two, and Land Improvements Three. Allocate the costs incurred by Angara Company to the appropriate columns and total each column.
2. Prepare a single journal entry dated March 1 to record all of the costs incurred, assuming they were all paid in cash.
3. Prepare December 31 adjusting entries to record depreciation for the 10 months of 1991 during which the assets were in use. Use sum-of-the-years'-digits depreciation for the newly constructed Building Three and Land Improvements Three and straight-line depreciation for Building Two and Land Improvements Two.

**Problem 10–4**
**Plant asset costs and depreciation, including MACRS**
(L. O. 1, 2, 3)

Baku Company recently negotiated a lump-sum purchase of several assets from a bus dealer who was planning to change locations. The purchase was completed on October 31, 1990, at a total cash price of $624,000 and included a garage with land and certain land improvements and a new heavy, general-purpose truck. The estimated market values of the assets were: garage, $429,000; land, $132,000; land improvements, $66,000; and truck, $33,000.

*Required*

1. Prepare a schedule to allocate the lump-sum purchase price to the separate assets that were purchased. Also present the general journal entry to record the purchase.
2. Calculate the 1991 depreciation expense on the garage using the sum-of-the-years'-digits method and assuming a 12-year life and a $21,600 salvage value.

3. Calculate the 1990 depreciation expense on the land improvements assuming a 10-year life and declining-balance depreciation at twice the straight-line rate.
4. The truck is in the five-year class for tax purposes but is expected to last six years and have a salvage value of $2,400. Prepare a schedule showing each year's depreciation on the truck for tax purposes, assuming (*a*) five-year straight-line depreciation and (*b*) MACRS.

**Problem 10–5**
**Recording cost, depreciation, and sale of plant assets**
(L. O. 1, 3, 5)

On October 27, 1988, a company made a lump-sum purchase of two machines from another company that was going out of business. The machines cost $109,350 and were placed in use on November 3, 1988. This additional information about the machines is available:

| Machine No. | Appraised Value | Salvage Value | Estimated Life | Installation Cost | Depreciation Method |
|---|---|---|---|---|---|
| 1 . . . . | $54,000 | $2,700 | 4 years | $1,350 | Sum-of-the-years' digits |
| 2 . . . . | 67,500 | 4,500 | 4 years | 2,250 | Declining balance at twice the straight-line rate |

Depreciation was taken on the machines at the end of 1988, 1989, and 1990; and during the first week in January 1991, the company decided to sell and replace them. Consequently, on January 8, 1991, it sold Machine 1 for $10,500, and on January 9 it sold Machine 2 for $20,250.

*Required*

Prepare a form with the following columnar headings:

| Machine No. | 1988 Depreciation | 1989 Depreciation | 1990 Depreciation | 1991 Depreciation | 1992 Depreciation |
|---|---|---|---|---|---|
| | | | | | |

Enter the machine numbers and the amounts of depreciation that would be taken each calendar year if the machines had been used throughout their four-year useful lives.

## Alternate Problems

**Problem 10–1A**
**Alternative depreciation methods; retirement of plant assets**
(L. O. 2, 3, 5)

**Part 1.** FlatIrons Company purchased and installed a new machine that cost $195,000, had a five-year life, and an estimated $27,300 salvage value. Management estimated that the machine would produce 120,000 units of product during its life. Actual production of units of product was as follows: year 1, 16,800; year 2, 26,400; year 3, 24,000; year 4, 22,800; and year 5, 30,000.

*Required*

1. Prepare a calculation showing the number of dollars of this machine's cost that should be charged to depreciation over its five-year life.
2. Prepare a form with the following column headings:

| Year | Straight Line | Units of Production | Declining Balance | Sum-of-the-Years' Digits |
|---|---|---|---|---|
| | | | | |

Then show the depreciation for each year and the total depreciation for the machine under each depreciation method. Use twice the straight-line rate for the declining-balance method.

**Part 2.** On January 9, Gilman Company purchased a used machine for $68,400. The next day it was repaired at a cost of $8,100 and was mounted on a new cradle that cost $6,300. It was estimated the machine would be used for three years and would then have a $10,800 salvage value. Depreciation was to be charged on a straight-line basis. A full year's depreciation was charged on December 31 of the first and the second years of the machine's use; and on March 29 of its third year of use, the machine was retired from service.

*Required*

1. Prepare general journal entries to record the purchase of the machine, the cost of repairing it, and its installation. Assume cash was paid in each case.
2. Prepare entries to record depreciation on the machine at the end of the first and second years and on March 29 of the third year.
3. Prepare entries to record the retirement of the machine under each of the following unrelated assumptions: (*a*) the machine was sold for $35,250; (*b*) it was sold for $24,150; and (*c*) it was destroyed in a fire, and the insurance company paid $22,050 in full settlement of the loss claim.

**Problem 10–2A**
**Plant asset records**
(L. O. 2, 4)

Parker Lewis Company completed the following transactions involving plant assets:

1990

Jan. 2 Purchased on credit from Southwest Equipment an electric packer priced at $19,875. The serial number of the packer was S-67422, its service life was estimated at five years with a trade-in value of $1,875, and it was assigned plant asset No. 420-1.

Apr. 4 Purchased on credit from Southwest Equipment a Donen vibrator priced at $30,705. The serial number of the vibrator was S-33246, its service life was estimated at six years with a trade-in value of $2,625, and it was assigned plant asset No. 430-2.

Dec. 31 Recorded straight-line depreciation on the plant equipment for 1990.

1991

Nov. 3 Sold the Donen vibrator to Cement Products for $18,750 cash.

7 Purchased a new Supermix vibrator from Stonework Equipment for $27,000. The serial number of the vibrator was CS-83215, its service life was estimated at eight years with a trade-in value of $3,600, and it was assigned plant asset No. 430-3.

Dec. 31 Recorded straight-line depreciation on the plant equipment for 1991.

*Required*

1. Open general ledger accounts for Plant Equipment and for Accumulated Depreciation, Plant Equipment. Prepare a subsidiary plant asset record card for each item of equipment purchased.

2. Prepare general journal entries to record the transactions and post to the proper general ledger and subsidiary ledger accounts.
3. Prove the December 31, 1991, balances of the Plant Equipment and Accumulated Depreciation, Plant Equipment accounts by preparing a list showing the cost and accumulated depreciation on each item of plant equipment owned by Parker Lewis Company on that date.

**Problem 10–3A**
**Real estate costs and partial year's depreciation**
(L. O. 1, 2, 3)

In early 1991, Nobles Company paid $975,000 for real estate that included a tract of land on which two buildings were located. The plan was to demolish Building A and build a new store in its place. Building B was to be used as a company office and was appraised to have a value of $315,000, with a useful life of 20 years and a $45,000 salvage value. A lighted parking lot near Building B had improvements valued at $105,000 that were expected to last another five years and have no salvage value. In its existing condition, the tract of land was estimated to have a value of $630,000.

Nobles Company incurred the following additional costs:

| | |
|---|---|
| Cost to demolish Building A . . . . . . . . . . . . . . . . | $ 71,250 |
| Cost to landscape new building site . . . . . . . . . . . | 81,000 |
| Cost to build new building (Building C), having a useful life of 25 years and a $75,000 salvage value . . . . . | 1,125,000 |
| Cost of new land improvements near Building C, which have an 8-year useful life and no salvage value . . . . | 187,500 |

*Required*

1. Prepare a form having the following column headings: Land, Building B, Building C, Land Improvements B, and Land Improvements C. Allocate the costs incurred by Nobles Company to the appropriate columns and total each column.
2. Prepare a single journal entry dated June 1 to record all of the costs incurred, assuming they were all paid in cash.
3. Prepare December 31 adjusting entries to record depreciation for the seven months of 1991 during which the assets were in use. Use sum-of-the-years'-digits depreciation for the newly constructed Building C and Land Improvements C and straight-line depreciation for Building B and Land Improvements B.

**Problem 10–4A**
**Plant asset costs and depreciation, including MACRS**
(L. O. 1, 2, 3)

Willo Company recently negotiated a lump-sum purchase of several assets from a road equipment dealer who was planning to change locations. The purchase was completed on September 30, 1990, at a total cash price of $870,000 and included a garage with land and certain land improvements and a new heavy, general-purpose truck. The estimated market values of the assets were: sales garage, $552,750; land, $331,650; land improvements, $100,500; and truck, $20,100.

*Required*

1. Prepare a schedule to allocate the lump-sum purchase price to the separate assets that were purchased. Also present the general journal entry to record the purchase.

2. Calculate the 1991 depreciation expense on the garage using the sum-of-the-years'-digits method and assuming a 15-year life and a $37,500 salvage value.
3. Calculate the 1990 depreciation expense on the land improvements assuming an eight-year life and declining-balance depreciation at twice the straight-line rate.
4. The truck is in the five-year class for tax purposes but is expected to last six years and have a salvage value of $2,250. Prepare a schedule showing each year's depreciation on the truck for tax purposes, assuming (*a*) five-year straight-line depreciation and (*b*) MACRS.

**Problem 10–5A**
**Recording cost, depreciation, and sale of plant assets**
(L. O. 1, 3, 5)

On April 3, 1988, Locklin Company made a lump-sum purchase of two machines from another company that was going out of business. The machines cost $328,500 and were placed in use on April 6, 1988. This additional information about the machines is available:

| Machine No. | Appraised Value | Salvage Value | Estimated Life | Installation Cost | Depreciation Method |
|---|---|---|---|---|---|
| 1 . . . . | $160,000 | $ 8,000 | 4 years | $4,000 | Sum-of-the-years' digits |
| 2 . . . . | 200,000 | 12,000 | 4 years | 6,500 | Declining balance at twice the straight-line rate |

Depreciation was taken on the machines at the end of 1988, 1989, and 1990; and during the first week in January 1991, the company decided to sell and replace them. Consequently, on January 5, 1991, it sold Machine 1 for $27,000, and on January 6 it sold Machine 2 for $60,750.

*Required*

Prepare a form with the following columnar headings:

| Machine No. | 1988 Depreciation | 1989 Depreciation | 1990 Depreciation | 1991 Depreciation | 1992 Depreciation |
|---|---|---|---|---|---|
| | | | | | |

Enter the machine numbers and the amounts of depreciation that would be taken each year if the machines had been used throughout their four-year useful lives.

## Provocative Problems

**Provocative Problem 10–1**
**Bell & Howell Company**
(L. O. 2, 3)

Bell & Howell Company's 1986 annual report to its stockholders included financial statements for the year ended December 31, 1986. Those statements showed that Bell & Howell had earned a $32,895,000 net income in 1986. The footnotes to the 1986 financial statements contained the following item:

**Note A**
**Significant Accounting Policies:**

**Property and Depreciation.** Property, plant, and equipment are recorded at cost. In general, the straight-line method of depreciation is used for asset additions since the beginning of 1981 and the double-declining-balance method is used for prior years' assets. Estimated lives range from 5 to 35 years for land improvements, 10 to 50 years for buildings, 2 to 15 years for machinery and equipment and 5 to 15 years for product masters.

Courtesy of Bell & Howell Company

Why might Bell & Howell have chosen to switch from declining-balance depreciation to straight-line depreciation for assets purchased in 1981 and subsequent years? Assuming that the company's total investments in property, plant, and equipment have increased gradually each year, what effect would this change have on comparisons of income earned before and after 1980.

**Provocative Problem 10–2**
**Fizicalle Company**
(L. O. 1)

Fizicalle Company temporarily recorded the costs of a new plant in a summary account called Land and Buildings. Management has now asked you to examine this account and prepare any necessary entries to correct the account balances. In doing so, you find the following debits and credits to the account:

**Debits**

| | | | |
|---|---|---|---|
| Jan. | 4 | Cost of land and buildings acquired for new plant site | $185,500 |
| | 12 | Attorney's fee for title search | 1,775 |
| | 25 | Cost of wrecking old building on plant site | 17,000 |
| Feb. | 3 | Six months' liability and fire insurance on new building | 5,610 |
| June | 30 | Payment to building contractor on completion of building | 705,000 |
| July | 3 | Architect's fee for new building | 50,325 |
| | 7 | City assessment for street improvements | 12,150 |
| | 15 | Cost of landscaping new plant site | 7,500 |
| | | | $984,860 |

**Credits**

| | | | |
|---|---|---|---|
| Jan. | 27 | Proceeds from sale of salvaged materials from old building | $ 3,750 |
| July | 3 | Refund of one month's insurance premium | 935 |
| Dec. | 31 | Depreciation at 2 1/2% per year | 21,000 |
| | 31 | Balance | 959,175 |
| | | | $984,860 |

Your investigation suggests that 40 years is a reasonable life expectancy for a building of the type involved and that an assumption of zero salvage value is reasonable. To summarize your analysis, you decide to prepare a schedule with columns headed Date, Description, Total Amount, Land, Buildings, and Other Accounts and to enter the items found in the Land and Buildings account on the schedule, distributing the amounts to the proper columns. You should show credits on the schedule by enclosing the amounts in parentheses. Realizing that the accounts have not been closed, you should also draft any required correcting entry or entries. Assume that an account called Depreciation Expense, Land and Buildings was debited in recording the $21,000 of depreciation.

**Provocative Problem 10–3**
**Rockwall and Stoneleigh Companies**
(A Review Problem)

Rockwall Company and Stoneleigh Company are almost identical. Each began operations on January 1 of this year with $190,000 of equipment having an eight-year life and a $21,000 salvage value. Each purchased merchandise during the year as follows:

| | | | |
|---|---|---|---|
| Jan. | 1 | 315 units @ $400 per unit = | $126,000 |
| Apr. | 14 | 450 units @ $420 per unit = | 189,000 |
| June | 24 | 675 units @ $435 per unit = | 293,625 |
| Nov. | 6 | 350 units @ $500 per unit = | 175,000 |
| | | | $783,625 |

Now, on December 31 at the end of the first year, each has 440 units of merchandise in its ending inventory. However, Rockwall Company will use straight-line depreciation in arriving at its net income for the year, while Stoneleigh Company will use declining-balance depreciation at twice the straight-line rate. Also, Rockwall Company will use FIFO in costing its ending inventory, and Stoneleigh Company will use LIFO. The December 31 trial balances of the two concerns carried these amounts:

| | Rockwall Company | | Stoneleigh Company | |
|---|---|---|---|---|
| Cash | $ 18,375 | | $ 18,375 | |
| Accounts receivable | 42,000 | | 42,000 | |
| Equipment | 190,000 | | 190,000 | |
| Accounts payable | | $ 96,000 | | $ 96,000 |
| H. Rockwall, capital | | 232,000 | | |
| M. Stoneleigh, capital | | | | 232,000 |
| Sales | | 892,500 | | 892,500 |
| Purchases | 783,625 | | 783,625 | |
| Salaries expense | 78,750 | | 78,750 | |
| Rent expense | 64,050 | | 64,050 | |
| Other cash expenses | 43,700 | | 43,700 | |
| Totals | $1,220,500 | $1,220,500 | $1,220,500 | $1,220,500 |

*Required*

Prepare an income statement for each company and a schedule accounting for the difference in their reported net incomes. Write a short answer to this question: Which, if either, of the companies is the more profitable and why?

# 11 Plant and Equipment, Natural Resources, and Intangible Assets

In this chapter, we continue to examine the accounting issues related to property, plant, and equipment. In studying the chapter, you will learn how to account for disposals of plant assets, how to calculate depreciation when new information causes you to revise depreciation rates, and how to account for the costs of maintaining or improving plant assets. In addition, the chapter introduces you to the issues of accounting for natural resources and intangible assets.

**Learning Objectives**

*After studying Chapter 11, you should be able to:*

1. Prepare entries to record the sale or discarding of a plant asset.
2. Prepare entries to record the exchange of plant assets under accounting rules and under income tax rules and tell which rules should be applied in any given exchange.
3. Make the calculations and prepare the entries to account for revisions in depreciation rates.
4. Make the calculations and prepare the entries to account for plant asset repairs and betterments.
5. Prepare entries to account for natural resources and for intangible assets, including entries to record depletion and amortization.
6. Define or explain the words and phrases listed in the chapter Glossary.

## Plant Asset Disposals

Prepare entries to record the sale or discarding of a plant asset.
(L. O. 1)

Sooner or later, plant assets wear out, become obsolete, or become inadequate. When this occurs, the assets are discarded, sold, or traded in on new assets. The entry to record the disposal of a plant asset depends on which action is taken.

When an asset's accumulated depreciation is equal to its cost, the asset is said to be fully depreciated. If a fully depreciated asset is discarded, the entry to record the disposal is:

| | | | | |
|---|---|---|---|---|
| Jan. | 7 | Accumulated Depreciation, Machinery . . . . . . . . . . . | 1,500.00 | |
| | | Machinery . . . . . . . . . . . . . . . . . . . . . . . . . | | 1,500.00 |
| | | Discarded a fully depreciated machine. | | |

Sometimes a fully depreciated asset is kept in use. In such situations, the asset's cost and accumulated depreciation should not be removed from the accounts; they should remain on the books until the asset is sold, traded, or discarded. Otherwise, the accounts do not show its continued existence. However, no additional depreciation should be recorded, since the reason for recording depreciation is to charge an asset's cost to depreciation expense. The total amount of depreciation expense related to an asset must not exceed the cost of the asset.

Sometimes an asset is discarded before being fully depreciated. For example, suppose an error was made in estimating the service life of a $1,000 machine, and it becomes worthless and is discarded after having only $800 of depreciation recorded against it. In such a situation, there is a loss, and the entry to record the disposal is:

| | | | | |
|---|---|---|---|---|
| Jan. | 10 | Loss on Disposal of Machinery . . . . . . . . . . . . . . . . | 200.00 | |
| | | Accumulated Depreciation, Machinery . . . . . . . . . . . . | 800.00 | |
| | | Machinery . . . . . . . . . . . . . . . . . . . . . . . . . | | 1,000.00 |
| | | Discarded a worthless machine. | | |

### Discarding a Damaged Plant Asset

Occasionally, before the end of its service life, a plant asset is wrecked or destroyed in an accident. For example, a machine that cost $900 and that had been depreciated $400 was totally destroyed in a fire. If the loss was partially covered by insurance and the insurance company paid $350 to settle the loss claim, the entry to record the machine's destruction is:

| | | | | |
|---|---|---|---|---|
| Jan. | 12 | Cash . . . . . . . . . . . . . . . . . . . . . . . . . . . | 350.00 | |
| | | Loss from Fire . . . . . . . . . . . . . . . . . . . . . . . | 150.00 | |
| | | Accumulated Depreciation, Machinery . . . . . . . . . . . . | 400.00 | |
| | | Machinery . . . . . . . . . . . . . . . . . . . . . . . . . | | 900.00 |
| | | To record the destruction of machinery and the receipt of insurance compensation. | | |

If the machine were uninsured, the entry to record its destruction would not have a debit to Cash, and the loss from fire would be $500.

### Selling a Plant Asset

If a plant asset is sold and the selling price exceeds the asset's book value, there is a gain. And if the price is less than book value, there is a loss. For example, assume that a machine that cost $5,000 and had been depreciated $4,000 is sold for a price in excess of its book value, say, for $1,200. In this case, there is a gain, and the entry to record the sale is:

| | | | | |
|---|---|---|---|---|
| Jan. | 4 | Cash | 1,200.00 | |
| | | Accumulated Depreciation, Machinery | 4,000.00 | |
| | | Machinery | | 5,000.00 |
| | | Gain on the Sale of Plant Assets | | 200.00 |
| | | Sold a machine at a price in excess of book value. | | |

However, if the machine is sold for $750, there is a $250 loss. The entry to record the sale is:

| | | | | |
|---|---|---|---|---|
| Jan. | 4 | Cash | 750.00 | |
| | | Loss on the Sale of Plant Assets | 250.00 | |
| | | Accumulated Depreciation, Machinery | 4,000.00 | |
| | | Machinery | | 5,000.00 |
| | | Sold a machine at a price below book value. | | |

## Exchanging Plant Assets

Prepare entries to record the exchange of plant assets under accounting rules and under income tax rules and tell which rules should be applied in any given exchange.
(L. O. 2)

Some plant assets are sold at the end of their useful lives. Others, such as machinery, automobiles, and office equipment, are commonly exchanged for new assets that are similar in purpose. In such exchanges, a trade-in allowance is normally received on the old asset, and the balance is paid in cash. According to generally accepted accounting principles, when a plant asset is exchanged for a similar plant asset and the balance, if any, requires a cash payment, a material book loss should be recognized in the accounts but a book gain should not.[1] A book loss is experienced when the trade-in allowance is less than the book value of the traded asset. A book gain results from a trade-in allowance that exceeds the book value of the traded asset.

### Recognizing a Material Book Loss

To illustrate recognition of a material book loss on an exchange of plant assets, assume that a machine that cost $18,000 and has been depreciated $15,000 is traded in on a new machine that has a $21,000 cash price. A $1,000 trade-in allowance is received, and the $20,000 balance is paid in cash. Under these

[1] Note that the above discussion involves exchanges of similar plant assets when an additional cash *payment* may be required. When exchanges of similar assets involve a cash *receipt*, the accounting rules are more complex. Such cases are explained in more advanced accounting courses. FASB, *Accounting Standards—Current Text* (Norwalk, Conn., 1988), sec. N35.109. First published in *APB Opinion No. 29*, par. 22.

assumptions, the book value of the old machine is $3,000, calculated as follows:

| | |
|---|---|
| Cost of old machine . . . . . . . . . . . . | $18,000 |
| Less accumulated depreciation . . . . | 15,000 |
| Book value . . . . . . . . . . . . . . . . | $ 3,000 |

Since the $1,000 trade-in allowance results in a $2,000 loss on the exchange, the transaction should be recorded as follows:

| | | | | |
|---|---|---|---|---|
| Jan. | 5 | Machinery . . . . . . . . . . . . . . . . . . . . . . . . . . | 21,000.00 | |
| | | Loss on Exchange of Machinery . . . . . . . . . . . . . . | 2,000.00 | |
| | | Accumulated Depreciation, Machinery . . . . . . . . . . . | 15,000.00 | |
| | | Machinery . . . . . . . . . . . . . . . . . . . . . . . . . | | 18,000.00 |
| | | Cash . . . . . . . . . . . . . . . . . . . . . . . . . . . | | 20,000.00 |
| | | Exchanged old machine and cash for a similar machine. | | |

The $21,000 debit to Machinery puts the new machine in the accounts at its cash price. The debit to Loss on Exchange of Machinery records the loss. The old machine is removed from the accounts with the $15,000 debit to Accumulated Depreciation and the $18,000 credit to Machinery.

### Nonrecognition of a Book Gain

When there is a book gain on an exchange of similar plant assets and the balance, if any, involves a cash payment, generally accepted accounting principles require you to record the new asset at the book value of the traded-in asset plus the cash paid. As a result, no gain is recognized. For example, assume that in acquiring the $21,000 machine of the previous section, a $4,500 trade-in allowance, rather than a $1,000 trade-in allowance, is received. The balance to be paid in cash is $16,500. A $4,500 trade-in allowance would result in a book gain. However, when you record the trade, the book gain should not be recognized in the accounts. Rather, it should be absorbed into the cost of the new machine by recording the new machine at an amount equal to the sum of the book value of the old machine plus the cash paid. This is $19,500 and is calculated as follows:

| | |
|---|---|
| Book value of old machine . . . . . . | $ 3,000 |
| Cash given in the exchange . . . . . . | 16,500 |
| Cost basis for the new machine . . . . | $19,500 |

The entry to record the exchange is:

| | | | | |
|---|---|---|---|---|
| Jan. | 5 | Machinery | 19,500.00 | |
| | | Accumulated Depreciation, Machinery | 15,000.00 | |
| | | Machinery | | 18,000.00 |
| | | Cash | | 16,500.00 |
| | | Exchanged old machine and cash for a new machine of like purpose. | | |

Observe that the $19,500 recorded amount for the new machine is equal to its cash price less the $1,500 book gain on the exchange ($21,000 − $1,500 = $19,500). In other words, the $1,500 book gain was absorbed into the amount at which the new machine was recorded. The $19,500 is the *cost basis* of the new machine and is the amount used to record depreciation on the machine or any gain or loss on its sale.

As we have said, when similar plant assets are exchanged and the balance, if any, involves a cash payment, a book gain is not recognized. This rule is based on the opinion that "revenue should not be recognized merely because one productive asset is substituted for a similar productive asset but rather should be considered to flow from the production and sale of the goods or services to which the substituted productive asset is committed."[2] In other words, the gain should be taken in the form of increased net income resulting from smaller depreciation charges on the asset acquired. In this case, depreciation calculated on the recorded $19,500 cost basis of the new machine is less than if calculated on the machine's $21,000 cash price.

### Tax Rules and Plant Asset Exchanges

Depreciation methods for financial statement purposes often are different from those used for tax purposes. As a result, companies usually keep two sets of depreciation records on each asset. Even when the depreciation methods and estimated lives are the same for tax and accounting purposes, two sets of records may be necessary. This is caused by the fact that **income tax rules** and accounting principles do not agree on the treatment of losses on plant asset exchanges. In the case of a gain, the tax rules and accounting principles agree.

According to the Internal Revenue Service, when an old asset is traded in on a similar new asset, both gains and losses must be absorbed into the cost of the new asset. For tax purposes, this cost basis must be used to calculate depreciation on the new asset. Therefore, for tax purposes, it makes no difference whether there is a gain or a loss on the exchange. The cost basis of an

[2] APB, "Accounting for Nonmonetary Transactions," *APB Opinion No. 29* (New York: AICPA, May 1973), par. 16. Copyright © 1973 by the American Institute of Certified Public Accountants, Inc.

asset acquired in an exchange is the sum of the book value of the old asset plus the cash given.

Since accounting principles and tax rules differ in their treatment of a loss on a plant asset exchange, two sets of depreciation records must be kept for the new asset even if the depreciation method and estimated life are the same for tax and accounting purposes. One set must be kept to determine net income for accounting purposes, and the other is kept to determine the depreciation deduction for tax purposes.

Record-keeping is more costly if two sets of records must be maintained. Yet, when an exchange results in a material loss, the loss must be recognized for financial accounting purposes, and keeping two sets of records is necessary. On the other hand, when an exchange results in a loss that is not material, you can appeal to the *materiality principle* and record the new asset on the books at its cost basis for tax purposes. By doing this, you may avoid having to keep two sets of records.

For example, assume that a computer used in the office of a business is traded in on a new computer that has a cash price of $1,800. The purchaser is granted a trade-in allowance of $150 on the old computer and the $1,650 difference is paid in cash. The old computer had cost $1,500 and had been depreciated $1,260 both for tax and accounting purposes. In this case, the old computer's book value is $240, and the trade-in of $150 results in a book loss on the exchange of $90. However, if the $90 loss is assumed to be an immaterial amount, the following method, called the income tax method, may be used to record the exchange:

| | | | | |
|---|---|---|---|---|
| Jan. | 7 | Office Equipment | 1,890.00 | |
| | | Accumulated Depreciation, Office Equipment | 1,260.00 | |
| | | Office Equipment | | 1,500.00 |
| | | Cash | | 1,650.00 |
| | | Traded an old computer and cash for a new computer. | | |

The $1,890 at which the new computer is taken into the accounts by the income tax method is its cost basis for tax purposes and is calculated as follows:

| | |
|---|---|
| Book value of old computer ($1,500 less $1,260) | $ 240 |
| Cash paid ($1,800 less the $150 trade-in allowance) | 1,650 |
| Income tax basis of the new computer | $1,890 |

This income tax method takes the new computer into the accounts at its cost basis for income tax purposes and does not record the loss. As a result, the method violates the rule that a loss on a plant asset exchange should be recorded. However, when the loss is not large enough to affect a financial statement reader's evaluation of the company, the violation is permissible under the *materiality principle*. In this case, we are assuming that the failure to record the $90 loss on the exchange would not materially affect the company's statements.

## Revising Depreciation Rates

Make the calculations and prepare the entries to account for revisions in depreciation rates.
(L. O. 3)

Since depreciation must be based on an asset's useful life, which is an estimate about the future, you should understand that depreciation is an estimate. Furthermore, you should be alert to the possibility that during the life of an asset, new information will show that the original estimate of useful life was wrong. The question that arises is: If your estimate of an asset's useful life changes, what should be done about it? The answer is that the new estimate of useful life should be used to calculate depreciation in the remaining periods of the asset's life. In other words, you correct the estimate by spreading the remaining cost to be depreciated over its remaining (revised) useful life.

For example, assume that seven years ago a machine was purchased at a cost of $10,500. At that time, the machine was estimated to have a 10-year life with a $500 salvage value. Therefore, it was depreciated at the rate of $1,000 per year [($10,500 − $500) ÷ 10 = $1,000]. At the beginning of the asset's eighth year, its book value is $3,500, calculated as follows:

| | |
|---|---|
| Cost | $10,500 |
| Less seven years' accumulated depreciation | 7,000 |
| Book value | $ 3,500 |

Assume that at the beginning of its eighth year, the estimated number of years remaining in this machine's useful life is changed from three to five years with no change in salvage value. Therefore, depreciation for each of the machine's remaining years should be calculated as follows:

$$\frac{\text{Book value} - \text{Salvage value}}{\text{Remaining useful life}} = \frac{\$3{,}500 - \$500}{5 \text{ years}} = \$600 \text{ per year}$$

And $600 of depreciation should be recorded on the machine at the end of the eighth and each succeeding year in its life.

Since this asset was depreciated at the rate of $1,000 per year for the first seven years, you might argue that depreciation expense was overstated during the first seven years. However, depreciation is understood to be an estimate based on the best information available at the time the depreciation is taken.

Changing the useful life of a plant asset is an example of a **change in an accounting estimate.** Such changes result "from new information or subsequent developments and accordingly from better insight or improved judgment." Therefore, generally accepted accounting principles require that changes in accounting estimates, such as this change in estimated useful life, be reflected only in future financial statements, not by attempts to correct past statements.[3]

## Ordinary and Extraordinary Repairs

Make the calculations and prepare the entries to account for plant asset repairs and betterments.
(L. O. 4)

Repairs made to keep an asset in its normal good operating condition are described as **ordinary repairs.** For example, to keep a wood-frame building in good condition, you must periodically have it repainted and have its roof repaired. Also, a machine must be cleaned, oiled, and adjusted, and any worn small parts must be replaced. Such repairs and maintenance are necessary, and their cost should appear on the current income statement as an expense.

[3] FASB, *Accounting Standards—Current Text,* sec. A35.104 and sec. A06.130. First published in *APB Opinion No. 20,* pars. 13 and 31.

**Extraordinary repairs** are major repairs made not to keep an asset in its normal good state of repair but to extend its service life beyond that originally estimated. As a rule, the costs of such repairs are debited to the repaired asset's accumulated depreciation account under the assumption they "make good" past depreciation, add to the asset's useful life, and benefit future periods. For example, a machine was purchased for $8,000 and depreciated under the assumption it would last eight years and have no salvage value. As a result, at the end of the machine's sixth year, its book value is $2,000, calculated as follows:

| | |
|---|---|
| Cost of machine | $8,000 |
| Less six years' accumulated depreciation | 6,000 |
| Book value | $2,000 |

Assume that at the beginning of the machine's seventh year, it is given a major overhaul that extends its estimated useful life three years beyond the eight originally estimated. The $2,100 cost of the overhaul should be recorded as follows:

| | | | | |
|---|---|---|---|---|
| Jan. | 12 | Accumulated Depreciation, Machinery | 2,100.00 | |
| | | Cash (or Accounts Payable) | | 2,100.00 |
| | | To record extraordinary repairs. | | |

In addition, depreciation for each of the five years remaining in the machine's life should be calculated as follows:

| | Before Extraordinary Repairs | Effect of Extraordinary Repairs | After Extraordinary Repairs |
|---|---|---|---|
| Cost | $8,000 | | $8,000 |
| Accumulated depreciation | 6,000 | −$2,100 | 3,900 |
| Book value | $2,000 | + 2,100 | $4,100 |
| Annual depreciation expense for remaining five years ($4,100 ÷ 5) | | | $ 820 |

And, if the machine remains in use for five years after the major overhaul, the five annual depreciation charges of $820 each will exactly write off its new book value, which includes the cost of the extraordinary repairs.

## Betterments

A **betterment** involves modifying an existing plant asset to make it more efficient, usually by replacing part of the asset with an improved or superior part. The result of a betterment is a more efficient or more productive asset, but not necessarily one that has a longer life. For example, if the manual controls on a machine are replaced with automatic controls, the cost of labor may be reduced.

When a betterment is made, its cost should be debited to the improved asset's account, for example, the Machinery account, and depreciated over the remaining service life of the asset. Also, the cost and applicable depreciation of the replaced asset portion should be removed from the accounts.

## Revenue and Capital Expenditures

The value or asset obtained by a **revenue expenditure** expires before the end of the current accounting period. As a result, a revenue expenditure appears on the current income statement as an expense that is deducted from the period's revenues. Expenditures for ordinary repairs, rent, and salaries are examples. Expenditures for betterments and for extraordinary repairs, on the other hand, are examples of what are called **capital expenditures** or **balance sheet expenditures.** They benefit future periods and should appear on the balance sheet as asset increases.

You must be careful to distinguish between capital and revenue expenditures when transactions are recorded because if errors are made, such errors often affect a number of accounting periods. For instance, an expenditure for a betterment initially recorded in error as an expense overstates expenses in the year of the error and understates net income. Also, since the cost of a betterment should be depreciated over the remaining useful life of the bettered asset, depreciation expense of future periods is understated.

## Natural Resources

Prepare entries to account for natural resources and for intangible assets, including entries to record depletion and amortization.
(L. O. 5)

Natural resources such as standing timber, mineral deposits, and oil reserves are known as wasting assets. In their natural state, they represent inventories that will be converted into a product by cutting, mining, or pumping. However, until cut, mined, or pumped, they are noncurrent assets and commonly appear on a balance sheet under captions such as "Timberlands," "Mineral deposits," or "Oil reserves." Sometimes, this caption appears under the "Property, plant, and equipment" category of assets, and sometimes it is shown as a separate category.

Natural resources are accounted for at cost and appear on the balance sheet at cost less accumulated **depletion.** The amount such assets are depleted each year by cutting, mining, or pumping is commonly calculated on a units-of-production basis. For example, if a mineral deposit has an estimated 500,000 tons of available ore and is purchased for $500,000, the depletion charge per ton of ore mined is $1. Furthermore, if 85,000 tons are mined during the first year, the depletion charge for the year is $85,000 and is recorded as follows:

| | | | | |
|---|---|---|---|---|
| Dec. | 31 | Depletion of Mineral Deposit . . . . . . . . . . . . . . . . . | 85,000.00 | |
| | | Accumulated Depletion, Mineral Deposit . . . . . . . . | | 85,000.00 |
| | | To record depletion of the mineral deposit. | | |

On the balance sheet prepared at the end of the first year, the mineral deposit should appear at its $500,000 cost less accumulated depletion of $85,000. If the 85,000 tons of ore are sold by the end of the first year, the entire $85,000 depletion charge reaches the income statement as the depletion cost of the ore mined and sold. However, if a portion remains unsold at the year-end, the depletion cost of the unsold ore is carried forward on the balance sheet as part of the cost of the unsold ore inventory, a current asset.

Often, machinery must be installed or a building constructed in order to exploit a natural resource. The costs of such assets should be depreciated over the life of the natural resource with annual depreciation charges that are in proportion to the annual depletion charges. For example, if a machine is installed in a mine and one eighth of the mine's ore is removed during a year, one eighth of the amount the machine is to be depreciated should be recorded as a cost of the ore mined.

## Intangible Assets

Assets that have no physical existence but that represent certain legal rights and economic relationships beneficial to the owner are called **intangible assets.** Patents, copyrights, leaseholds, goodwill, trademarks, and organization costs are examples. Notes and accounts receivable are also intangible in nature. However, these appear on the balance sheet as current assets rather than under the intangible assets classification.

When an intangible asset is purchased, it is recorded at cost. Thereafter, its cost must be systematically **amortized** or written off to expense over the asset's estimated useful life. However, generally accepted accounting principles require that the amortization period of an intangible asset never be any longer than 40 years.

Amortization of intangible assets is similar to depreciation; both are processes of cost allocation. However, amortization of intangibles is limited to the straight-line method unless it can be demonstrated that another method is more appropriate. Also, while depreciation is recorded in a contra account (Accumulated Depreciation), amortization of intangible asset cost traditionally is credited directly to the asset account. As a result, intangible assets are reported in the balance sheet at that portion of cost not previously written off. Normally, intangible assets are shown in a separate balance section that follows immediately after the plant and equipment section.

### Patents

The federal government grants **patents** to encourage the invention of new machines and mechanical devices. A patent gives its owner the exclusive right to manufacture and sell a patented machine or device for 17 years. When patent rights are purchased, all costs of acquiring the rights may be debited to an account called Patents. Also, the costs of a successful lawsuit in defense of a patent may be debited to this account.

A patent gives its owner exclusive rights to the patented device for 17 years. However, its cost should be amortized or written off over a shorter period if its useful life is estimated to be less than 17 years. For example, if a patent that cost $25,000 has an estimated useful life of 10 years, the following adjusting entry is made at the end of each year in the patent's life to write off 1/10 of its cost:

| | | | | |
|---|---|---|---|---|
| Dec. | 31 | Amortization of Patents . . . . . . . . . . . . . . . . . . . | 2,500.00 | |
| | | Patents . . . . . . . . . . . . . . . . . . . . . . . . . . | | 2,500.00 |
| | | To write off 1/10 of patent costs. | | |

The entry's debit causes $2,500 of patent costs to appear on the annual income statement as one of the costs of the patented product manufactured. The credit directly reduces the balance of the Patents account. Note that the amount of amortization is written off directly to the Patents account.

### Copyrights

A **copyright** is granted by the federal government and in most cases gives its owner the exclusive right to publish and sell a musical, literary, or artistic work for the life of the composer, author, or artist and for 50 years thereafter. Most copyrights actually have value for a much shorter time, and their costs should be amortized over the shorter period. Often, the only cost of a copyright is the fee paid to the Copyright Office. If this fee is not material, it may be charged directly to an expense account. Otherwise, the copyright costs should be capitalized, and the periodic amortization of a copyright should be charged to Amortization Expense, Copyrights.

### Leaseholds

Property is rented under a contract called **lease.** The person or company that owns the property and grants the lease is called the **lessor.** The person or company that secures the right to possess and use the property is called the **lessee.** The rights granted to the lessee under the lease are called **leasehold.**

Some leases require no advance payment from the lessee but do require monthly rent payments. Usually in such cases, a Leasehold account is not needed, and the monthly payments are debited to a Rent Expense account. Sometimes, a long-term lease is written so that the last year's rent must be paid in advance at the time the lease is signed. When this occurs, the last year's advance payment is debited to the Leasehold account. It remains there until the last year of the lease. At that time the Leasehold balance is transferred to Rent Expense.

Often, a long-term lease, one for 20 or 25 years, becomes valuable after a few years because its required rent payments are much less than current rentals for identical property. In such cases, the increase in value of the lease should not be entered on the books since no extra cost was incurred to acquire it. However, if the property is subleased and a cash payment is made for the rights under the old lease, the new tenant should debit the payment to a Leasehold account and write it off as additional rent expense over the remaining life of the lease.

### Leasehold Improvements

Long-term leases often require the lessee to pay for any alterations or improvements to the leased property, such as new partitions and store fronts. Normally, the costs of **leasehold improvements** are debited to an account called Leasehold Improvements. Also, since the improvements become part of the property and revert to the lessor at the end of the lease, you must amortize the cost of the improvements over the life of the lease or the life of the improvements, whichever is shorter. The amortization entry commonly debits Rent Expense and credits Leasehold Improvements.

### Goodwill

The term **goodwill** has a special meaning in accounting. Accountants say that *a business has goodwill when its rate of expected future earnings is greater than the rate of earnings normally realized in its industry*. Above-average earnings and the existence of goodwill may be demonstrated as follows with Companies A and B, both of which are in the same industry:

| | Company A | Company B |
|---|---|---|
| Net assets (other than goodwill) . . . . | $100,000 | $100,000 |
| Normal rate of return in this industry . . | 10% | 10% |
| Normal return on net assets . . . . . . | $ 10,000 | $ 10,000 |
| Expected net income . . . . . . . . . . | 10,000 | 15,000 |
| Expected earnings above average . . . | $ -0- | $ 5,000 |

Company B is expected to have an above-average earnings rate compared to its industry and is said to have goodwill. This goodwill may be the result of excellent customer relations, the location of the business, monopolistic privileges, superior management, or a combination of factors. Furthermore, a prospective investor would normally be willing to pay more for Company B than for Company A if the investor agreed the extra earnings rate should be expected. Thus, goodwill is an asset that has value.

Accountants agree that goodwill should not be recorded unless it is purchased. This normally occurs only when a business is acquired or sold in its entirety. Before a business is to be purchased, the buyer and seller may estimate the amount of goodwill in several different ways. Three examples follow:

1. The buyer and seller may place an arbitrary value on the goodwill of a business being sold. For instance, a seller may be willing to sell a business that has an above-average earnings rate for $115,000, and a buyer may be willing to pay that amount. If they both agree that the net assets of the business other than its goodwill have a $100,000 value, they are arbitrarily valuing the goodwill at $15,000.

## AS A MATTER OF FACT

Under current accounting rules, public companies must amortize goodwill. This seeming technicality may slow—somewhat—the takeover game.

Goodwill arises when a company pays more for an asset than that asset's book value. A brand name may have little or no tangible book value but is nonetheless a valuable asset. A local newspaper can fetch far in excess of the value of its tangible assets. When a brand name or a paper changes hands at more than book value, the excess is booked as "goodwill." This goodwill must be written off over a maximum of 40 years under Financial Accounting Standards Board rules. The writeoffs constitute a charge against reported earnings.

This amortization requirement makes it somewhat difficult for U.S. public companies to buy assets that are encumbered with large amounts of goodwill. Let's say an asset earned $10 million last year after taxes. The property—which has no tangible assets—is for sale at 15 times earnings, or $150 million. If a public company buys that asset, it will have to write off nearly $4 million a year to amortize the goodwill. That would reduce the amount it could report as profits to $6 million and raise the price from 15 times earnings to 25 times—a probably unreasonable amount.

The problem doesn't arise for private companies or leveraged buyouts, financed on cash flow. Since goodwill amortization is a bookkeeping charge rather than a cash charge, it doesn't reduce cash flow.

The same is true for most foreign companies. Unencumbered by U.S. accounting rules, they need not amortize goodwill, or, if they must, they can deduct it from their taxes. At the original price of $60 per share, as Grand Metropolitan initially offered for Pillsbury, goodwill would have been $4 billion. This would have caused a $100 million annual hit to operating earnings for a U.S. company. Why could Grand Met afford it? Because British accounting conventions deduct goodwill straight from equity, without requiring amortization; it affects the balance sheet but not the income statement.

But by making it tough for U.S. public companies to buy, the rule limits the number of potential bidders when a corporate asset goes on the market. The fewer the bidders, the less the final price.

* * *

Source: Laura Jereski, "Ill will." Excerpted by permission of *Forbes* magazine, January 23, 1989, p. 41. © Forbes Inc., 1989.

2. Goodwill may be valued at some multiple of the portion of expected earnings that is above average. For example, if a company is expected to have $5,000 each year in above-average earnings, its goodwill may be valued at, say, four times the portion of its earnings which are above average, or at $20,000. In this case, you may also say that the goodwill is valued at four years' above-average earnings. However, regardless of how it is described, this too is placing an arbitrary value on the goodwill.
3. The portion of a company's earnings that is above average may be capitalized in order to place a value on its goodwill. For example, assume that a business is expected to have earnings each year that are $5,000 above average and the normal rate of return on invested capital in this company's industry is 10%. If the excess earnings are capitalized at 10%, goodwill is valued at $50,000 ($5,000 ÷ 10% = $50,000). Note that this method values the goodwill at the amount that must be invested at the normal rate of return in order to earn the extra $5,000 each year ($50,000 × 10% = $5,000). This is a satisfactory method if the extra earnings are expected to continue for all future periods. However, that may not happen. Therefore, extra earnings are sometimes capitalized at a rate that is higher than the normal

rate of the industry. For example, in the present case, assume a capitalization rate that is twice the normal rate or 20%. If the extra earnings are capitalized at 20%, the goodwill is valued at $25,000 ($5,000 ÷ 20% = $25,000).

There are other ways to think about the amount that should be assigned to goodwill. Nevertheless, in the final analysis, goodwill is always valued at the price a seller is willing to accept and a buyer is willing to pay.

### Trademarks and Trade Names

Companies often design a unique symbol or select a unique name that they use in marketing their products. Sometimes, the ownership and exclusive right to use such a **trademark** or **trade name** can be established simply by demonstrating that the company has used the trademark or trade name before other businesses. However, ownership generally can be established more definitely by registering the trademark or trade name at the U.S. Patent Office. The cost of developing, maintaining, or enhancing the value of a trademark or trade name, perhaps through advertising, should be charged to expense in the period or periods incurred. However, if a trademark or trade name is purchased, the purchase cost should be debited to an asset account and amortized over its estimated useful life.

### Amortization of Intangibles

Some intangibles, such as patents, copyrights, and leaseholds, have limited useful lives that are determined by law, contract, or the nature of the asset. Other intangibles, such as goodwill, trademarks, and trade names, have indeterminable lives. In general, the cost of intangible assets should be amortized over the periods expected to be benefited by their use, which in no case is longer than their legal existence. However, as we stated earlier, generally accepted accounting principles require that the amortization period of intangible assets never be longer than 40 years. This limitation applies even if the life of the asset (for example, goodwill) may continue indefinitely.[4]

## Summary of the Chapter in Terms of Learning Objectives

**1.** When a plant asset is discarded or sold, the cost and accumulated depreciation are removed from the accounts. Any cash proceeds are recorded and compared to the book value at the date of sale or retirement to determine the gain or loss.

**2.** When a plant asset is exchanged for a new asset that is similar in purpose, the book value of the old asset is compared to its market value or trade-in allowance to determine whether the exchange results in a gain or loss. If a material loss occurs, it must be recognized. However, if a gain is indicated, the gain is not recognized. Instead, the new asset account is debited for the book value of the old asset plus any cash paid.

[4] Ibid., sec. 160.110. First published in *APB Opinion No. 17*, par. 29.

When a plant asset and cash are given in exchange for a similar plant asset, neither gains nor losses are recognized for tax purposes. If the loss is not material in amount, this income tax method may also be used for financial accounting purposes.

**3.** When the estimated useful life of a plant asset is changed, the remaining cost to be depreciated is spread over the remaining (revised) useful life of the asset. The remaining cost to be depreciated is the original cost less the accumulated depreciation to date and less the estimated salvage value.

**4.** The cost of ordinary repairs is charged to expense of the current period in which the expense is incurred. Extraordinary repairs extend the useful life of a plant asset and are capitalized by debiting the accumulated depreciation account related to the asset. Betterments make a plant asset more efficient and are debited to the asset account.

**5.** The cost of a natural resource is recorded in an asset account. Then, depletion of the natural resource is recorded by allocating the cost to expense according to a units-of-production basis. The depletion is credited to an accumulated depletion account. Intangible assets are recorded at the cost incurred to purchase the assets. The allocation of intangible asset cost to expense is done on a straight-line basis and is called amortization. Normally, amortization is credited directly to the asset account.

## Demonstration Problem

On January 13, 1987, the Maxwell Company purchased seven identical machines and paid $147,000 cash to the seller. The service life of each machine was predicted to be five years, and the salvage value of each was estimated at $1,000. All seven machines were placed into service at once. Depreciation is based on the assumption that machines are purchased and sold on the first of the month nearest the actual dates of purchase and sale. The straight-line method is used. Prepare entries to record each of the following transactions:

*a.* Machine No. 1 was used until July 7, 1992, when it was retired from service and sold for $1,000 cash. Record depreciation on Machine No. 1 for 1992 and record the sale of the machine.

*b.* Machine No. 2 was used until December 20, 1989, when it was stolen. On December 24, the insurance company paid Maxwell $4,800 cash, which equalled the estimate of the asset's fair value. Record depreciation on Machine No. 2 for 1989 and record the settlement with the insurance company.

*c.* Machine No. 3 was used until January 4, 1990, at which time it was sold for $13,000 cash. Record the sale of Machine No. 3.

*d.* Machine No. 4 was used until December 21, 1990, at which time it was traded in on Machine No. 8, with a cash payment of $20,000. Machine No. 8 had a cash price of $22,000. Record depreciation on Machine No. 4 for 1990 and record the exchange for Machine No. 8.

*e.* Machine No. 5 was used until December 23, 1990, when it was traded in on Machine No. 9, with a cash payment of $18,000. Machine No. 9 had a cash price of $25,500. Record depreciation on Machine No. 5 for 1990 and record the exchange for Machine No. 9.

*f.* Machine No. 6 was used until January 9, 1991, at which time it received a major overhaul which extended its useful life until the end of 1995 and left its expected salvage value at $1,000. The cost of the overhaul was $7,100, which was paid in cash. Record the overhaul, compute the machine's book value after the overhaul, and record depreciation for 1991.

*g.* Machine No. 7 was used only as a backup for the other six machines. Because the machines were more dependable than expected, Machine No. 7 did not deteriorate as quickly as the other machines. Therefore, during 1990, the company manager predicted that its useful life would probably extend until the end of 1994. The estimated salvage value was unchanged. Record depreciation expense on Machine No. 7 for 1990.

## Solution to Demonstration Problem

For Machines Nos. 1–7, the initial cost of each is $147,000 ÷ 7 = $21,000. Annual depreciation for each machine is ($21,000 − $1,000) ÷ 5 = $4,000.

| | | | | | |
|---|---|---|---|---|---|
| *a.* | 1992 | | | | |
| | July | 7 | Cash | 1,000.00 | |
| | | | Accumulated Depreciation, Machine No. 1 | 20,000.00 | |
| | | | Machine No. 1 | | 21,000.00 |
| | | | ($21,000 − $20,000 = $1,000). | | |

Machine No. 1 was fully depreciated before it was retired and was sold for its salvage value. Therefore, there was no gain or loss on the disposal.

| | | | | | |
|---|---|---|---|---|---|
| *b.* | 1989 | | | | |
| | Dec. | 20 | Depreciation Expense | 4,000.00 | |
| | | | Accumulated Depreciation, Machine No. 2 | | 4,000.00 |
| | | 24 | Cash | 4,800.00 | |
| | | | Accumulated Depreciation, Machine No. 2 | 12,000.00 | |
| | | | Loss on Theft | 4,200.00 | |
| | | | Machine No. 2 | | 21,000.00 |
| | | | $21,000 − $12,000 = $9,000. | | |
| | | | $9,000 − $4,800 = $4,200. | | |
| *c.* | 1990 | | | | |
| | Jan. | 4 | Cash | 13,000.00 | |
| | | | Accumulated Depreciation, Machine No. 3 | 12,000.00 | |
| | | | Gain on Disposal | | 4,000.00 |
| | | | Machine No. 3 | | 21,000.00 |
| | | | $21,000 − $12,000 = $9,000. | | |
| | | | $13,000 − $9,000 = $4,000. | | |

*d.*

| | | | | |
|---|---|---|---|---|
| 1990 | | | | |
| Dec. | 21 | Depreciation Expense | 4,000.00 | |
| | | Accumulated Depreciation, Machine No. 4 | | 4,000.00 |
| | 21 | Machine No. 8 | 22,000.00 | |
| | | Accumulated Depreciation, Machine No. 4 | 16,000.00 | |
| | | Loss on Trade | 3,000.00 | |
| | | Cash | | 20,000.00 |
| | | Machine No. 4 | | 21,000.00 |
| | | $4,000 × 4 = $16,000 | | |

*e.*

| | | | | |
|---|---|---|---|---|
| 1990 | | | | |
| Dec. | 23 | Depreciation Expense | 4,000.00 | |
| | | Accumulated Depreciation, Machine No. 5 | | 4,000.00 |
| | 23 | Machine No. 9 | 23,000.00 | |
| | | Accumulated Depreciation, Machine No. 5 | 16,000.00 | |
| | | Cash | | 18,000.00 |
| | | Machine No. 5 | | 21,000.00 |
| | | Machine No. 9 is recorded at less than its cash value in order to avoid reporting a gain on the trade-in. | | |

*f.*

| | | | | |
|---|---|---|---|---|
| 1991 | | | | |
| Jan. | 9 | Accumulated Depreciation, Machine No. 6 | 7,100.00 | |
| | | Cash | | 7,100.00 |

Book value before the overhaul: $21,000 − $16,000 = $5,000.
Book value after the overhaul: $5,000 + $7,100 = $12,100.

| | | | | |
|---|---|---|---|---|
| Dec. | 31 | Depreciation Expense | 2,220.00 | |
| | | Accumulated Depreciation, Machine No. 6 | | 2,220.00 |
| | | ($12,100 − $1,000) ÷ 5 = $2,220. | | |

*g.* Book value at 12/31/89: $21,000 − $12,000 = $9,000.
Revised remaining useful life is from 1/1/90 to 12/31/94, or five years, and the revised annual depreciation charge is: ($9,000 − $1,000) ÷ 5 = $1,600.

| | | | | |
|---|---|---|---|---|
| 1990 | | | | |
| Dec. | 31 | Depreciation Expense | 1,600.00 | |
| | | Accumulated Depreciation, Machine No. 7 | | 1,600.00 |

## Glossary

Define or explain the words and phrases listed in the chapter Glossary. (L. O. 6)

**Amortize** to periodically write off as an expense a share of the cost of an asset, usually an intangible asset. p. 476

**Balance sheet expenditure** another name for *capital expenditure*. p. 475

**Betterment** a modification to an existing plant asset to make it more efficient, usually by replacing part of the asset with an improved or superior part. pp. 474–475

**Capital expenditure** an expenditure that benefits future periods because the value or asset obtained by the expenditure does not fully expire by the end of the current period. Also called a *balance sheet expenditure*. p. 475

**Change in an accounting estimate** a change in a calculated amount to be reported in the financial statements that results from new information or subsequent developments and accordingly from better insight or improved judgment. p. 473

**Copyright** an exclusive right granted by the federal government to publish and sell a musical, literary, or artistic work for a period of years. p. 477

**Depletion** the amount a wasting asset is reduced through cutting, mining, or pumping. pp. 475–476

**Extraordinary repairs** major repairs that extend the service life of a plant asset beyond the number of years originally estimated. p. 474

**Goodwill** that portion of the value of a business that results from the business's expected ability to earn a rate of return greater than the average in its industry. pp. 478–480

**Income tax rules** rules that govern how income for tax purposes and income taxes are to be calculated. p. 471

**Intangible asset** an asset that has no physical existence but has value due to the rights resulting from its ownership and possession. p. 476

**Lease** a contract that grants the right to possess and use property. p. 477

**Leasehold** the rights granted to a lessee under the terms of a lease contract. p. 477

**Leasehold improvements** improvements to leased property made by the lessee. p. 478

**Lessee** an individual or enterprise that has been given possession of property under the terms of a lease contract. p. 477

**Lessor** the individual or enterprise that has given up possession of property under the terms of a lease contract. p. 477

**Ordinary repairs** repairs made to keep a plant asset in its normal good operating condition. p. 473

**Patent** an exclusive right granted by the federal government to manufacture and sell a machine or mechanical device for a period of years. pp. 476–477

**Revenue expenditure** an expenditure that benefits only the current period because the value or asset obtained by the expenditure will fully expire before the end of the current accounting period. p. 475

**Trademark** a unique symbol designed by a company for use in marketing its products or services. p. 480

**Trade name** a unique name selected by a company for use in marketing its products or services. p. 480

## Objective Review

Answers to the following questions are listed in Appendix I at the end of the book. Be sure that you decide which is the one best answer to each question *before* you check the answers in the appendix.

1. On January 1, 1991, Blair Company purchased a computer for $210,000. Estimated useful life is five years, and salvage value is $30,000. The company uses sum-of-the-years'-digits depreciation. If the computer is sold for $100,000 on March 31, 1992, the gain (loss) on the sale will be:
   *a.* $(38,000).
   *b.* $(26,000).
   *c.* $ (8,000).
   *d.* $ 20,000.
   *e.* $ 38,000.
2. Campbell Company traded an old truck for a new one. The original cost of the old truck was $100,000, and its accumulated depreciation is $78,000. The new truck has a cash price of $150,000. However, Campbell received a $10,000 trade-in allowance. Assume any book gain or loss is material. Campbell should record the new truck at:
   *a.* $162,000.
   *b.* $150,000.
   *c.* $140,000.
   *d.* $138,000.
   *e.* $ 22,000.
3. Comfax Company purchased a machine at a cost of $28,400. At that time, the machine was depreciated on a straight-line basis assuming a 9-year life with a $1,400 salvage value. At the beginning of the 7th year, the estimated useful life of the machine is changed from 9 to 10 years with no change in salvage value. Depreciation for each of the machine's remaining years is:
   *a.* $3,000.
   *b.* $2,700.
   *c.* $2,600.
   *d.* $2,250.
   *e.* $1,900.
4. At the beginning of the 5th year of a machine's estimated 7-year useful life, the machine was overhauled, and as a result its estimated useful life was extended to 10 years. The machine originally cost $110,000, and the overhaul cost was $15,000. The cost of the overhaul should be recorded as follows:

| | | | |
|---|---|---|---|
| a. | Machinery | 15,000.00 | |
| | Accumulated Depreciation, Machinery | | 15,000.00 |

| | | | |
|---|---|---|---|
| *b.* | Repairs Expense | 15,000.00 | |
| | Cash | | 15,000.00 |
| *c.* | Accumulated Depreciation, Machinery | 15,000.00 | |
| | Cash | | 15,000.00 |
| *d.* | Accumulated Depreciation, Machinery | 15,000.00 | |
| | Machinery | | 15,000.00 |
| *e.* | Depreciation Expense | 15,000.00 | |
| | Cash | | 15,000.00 |

5. Miller Mines, Inc., paid $500,000 for an ore deposit. The deposit had an estimated 250,000 tons of ore that would be fully mined during the next 10 years. During the current year, 70,000 tons were mined and sold. The amount of depletion expense this year is:
   *a.* $140,000.
   *b.* $120,000.
   *c.* $ 70,000.
   *d.* $ 50,000.
   *e.* $ –0–.

## Questions for Class Discussion

1. If an asset that has been depreciated is sold for cash and the remaining book value of the asset is more than the cash proceeds from the sale, should the difference be debited to depreciation expense? How should the difference be recorded?
2. What is the essential meaning of the accounting principle of materiality?
3. Distinguish between ordinary repairs and extraordinary repairs.
4. How should ordinary repairs to a machine be recorded? How should extraordinary repairs be recorded?
5. What is a betterment? How should a betterment to a machine be recorded?
6. Distinguish between revenue expenditures and capital expenditures and state the difference in how they should be recorded.
7. What is the difference between balance sheet expenditures and capital expenditures?
8. When should a loss on the exchange of a plant asset be recorded? When is it permissible to absorb a loss into the cost basis of the new plant asset? Should a gain on a plant asset exchange be recorded as such?
9. When cash plus a plant asset is exchanged for another asset of similar purpose, what determines the cost basis of the newly acquired asset for federal income tax purposes?
10. When the loss on an exchange of plant assets is immaterial in amount, why might it be convenient to take the newly acquired asset into the accounting records at the amount of its cost basis for tax purposes?

11. When an old plant asset is traded in at a book loss on a new asset of like purpose, the loss is not recognized for tax purposes. In the end, this normally does not reduce the aggregate tax deductions available to the taxpayer. Why?
12. What is the name for the process of allocating the cost of natural resources to expense as the natural resources are used?
13. What are the characteristics of an intangible asset?
14. Is the declining-balance method an acceptable means of calculating depletion of natural resources.
15. What are the general procedures to be followed in accounting for an intangible asset?
16. Define (*a*) lease, (*b*) lessor, (*c*) leasehold, and (*d*) leasehold improvement.
17. In accounting, when is a business said to have goodwill?
18. If at the end of five years it is discovered that a machine that was expected to have a six-year life will actually have an eight-year life, how is this new information reflected in the accounts?
19. X Company bought an established business and paid for goodwill. If X Company plans to incur substantial advertising and promotional costs each year to maintain the value of the goodwill, must the company also amortize the goodwill?

## Exercises

**Exercise 11–1**
**Recording sales of plant assets**
(L. O. 1)

A machine with an expected service life of six years and salvage value of $3,000 was purchased by Aster Company for $39,000. After taking straight-line depreciation for four years, the machine was sold. Present a general journal entry dated December 31 to record the sale assuming the cash proceeds from the sale were: (*a*) $15,000; (*b*) $18,450; and (*c*) $13,750.

**Exercise 11–2**
**Asset disposal in midyear**
(L. O. 1)

Daffy Company purchased and installed a machine on January 2, 1990, at a total cost of $54,000. Straight-line depreciation was taken each year for four years, based on the assumption of a six-year life and no salvage value. The machine was disposed of on August 31, during its fifth year. Present the entries to record the partial year's depreciation on August 31 and to record the disposal under each of the following unrelated assumptions: (*a*) the machine was sold for $20,000; (*b*) it was sold for $8,400; and (*c*) the machine was totally destroyed in a fire, and the insurance company settled the insurance claim for $11,000.

**Exercise 11–3**
**Recording plant asset disposal or trade-in**
(L. O. 1, 2)

On January 4, 1990, Taylor Company disposed of a machine that cost $29,000 and that had been depreciated $18,000. Present without explanations the entries to record the disposal under each of the following unrelated assumptions:

*a*. The machine was sold for $4,300 cash.

*b*. The machine was traded in on a new machine of like purpose having a $32,500 cash price. A $12,500 trade-in allowance was received, and the balance was paid in cash.

*c*. A $4,300 trade-in allowance was received for the machine on a new machine of like purpose having a $32,500 cash price. The balance was paid in cash, and the loss was considered material.

*d*. Transaction (*c*) was recorded by the income tax method because the loss was considered immaterial.

**Exercise 11–4**
**Exchanging plant assets**
(L. O. 2)

Frantz Company traded in its old truck on a new truck, receiving a $16,650 trade-in allowance and paying the remaining $55,350 in cash. The old truck cost $49,500, and straight-line depreciation of $27,000 had been recorded under the assumption it would last five years and have a $4,500 salvage value. Answer the following questions: (*a*) What was the book value of the old truck? (*b*) What is the loss on the exchange? (*c*) Assuming the loss is deemed to be material, what amount should be debited to the New Truck account? (*d*) Assuming the loss is not material and the income tax method is used to record the exchange, what amount should be debited to the New Truck account?

**Exercise 11–5**
**Revising depreciation rates**
(L. O. 3)

Clayton Company depreciated a machine that cost $82,000 on a straight-line basis for five years under the assumption it would have an eight-year life and a $4,800 trade-in value. At that point, Clayton recognized that the machine had five years of remaining useful life, after which it would have an estimated $3,600 trade-in value. (*a*) Determine the machine's book value at the end of its fifth year. (*b*) Determine the amount of depreciation to be charged against the machine during each of the remaining years in its life.

**Exercise 11–6**
**Ordinary repairs, extraordinary repairs, and betterments**
(L. O. 4)

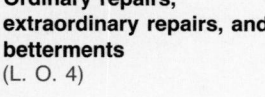

Darnell Company paid $67,500 for a machine that was expected to last six years and have a salvage value of $9,000. Present general journal entries dated December 31 to record the following costs related to the machine:

*a*. During the second year of the machine's life, $1,350 was paid for repairs necessary to keep the machine in good working order.

*b*. During the third year of the machine's life, $6,900 was paid for replacement parts that were expected to increase the machine's productivity by 15% each year.

*c*. During the fourth year of the machine's life, $9,300 was paid for repairs that were expected to increase the service life of the machine from six to eight years.

**Exercise 11–7**
**Extraordinary repairs**
(L. O. 4)

Mather Company owns a building that appeared on its balance sheet at the end of last year at its original $456,000 cost less $328,320 accumulated depreciation. The building has been depreciated on a straight-line basis under the assumption it would have a 25-year life and no salvage value. During the first week in January of the current year, major structural repairs were completed on the building at a $144,000 cost. The repairs did not improve the building's usefulness but they did extend its expected life for 13 years beyond the 25 years originally estimated. *(a)* Determine the building's age on last year's balance sheet date. *(b)* Give the entry to record the cost of the repairs. *(c)* Determine the book value of the building after its repairs were recorded. *(d)* Give the entry to record the current year's depreciation.

**Exercise 11–8**
**Depletion of natural resources**
(L. O. 5)

On January 1, 1990, Bayless Company paid $162,000 for an ore body containing 720,000 tons of ore. The company also installed machinery in the mine that cost $144,000, had an estimated 12-year life and no salvage value, and that was capable of removing the entire ore body in 6 years. The machine will be abandoned when the ore is completely mined. Bayless began mining operations on May 1, and it mined 58,000 tons of ore during the remaining nine months of the year. Give the entries to record the December 31, 1990, depletion of the ore body and the depreciation of the mining machinery.

**Exercise 11–9**
**Amortization of intangible assets**
(L. O. 5)

Marley Company purchased the copyright to a trade manual for $112,500 on January 1, 1990. The copyright legally protects its owner for 25 more years. However, management believes the trade manual can be successfully published and sold for only five more years. Prepare journal entries to record *(a)* the purchase of the copyright and *(b)* annual amortization of the copyright on December 31, 1990.

**Exercise 11–10**
**Calculating goodwill**
(L. O. 5)

J. Klaus has devoted years to building a profitable business that earns an attractive return. Now Klaus is considering the possibility of selling the business and is attempting to estimate the value of goodwill in the business. The recorded net assets of the business (excluding goodwill) amount to $225,000, and in a typical year, net income amounts to $40,500. Most businesses of this type are expected to earn a return of about 15% on net assets. Calculate goodwill assuming *(a)* the amount of goodwill is estimated to be six times the portion of earnings that are above average, and *(b)* the amount of goodwill is estimated by capitalizing above-average earnings at a rate of 12%.

## Problems

**Problem 11–1**
**Purchases, betterments, and sales of plant assets**
(L. O. 2, 4)

The Whitestone Company completed these transactions involving the purchase and operation of delivery trucks:

1989

June 26 Paid cash for a new truck, $34,200 plus $1,710 state and city sales taxes. The truck was estimated to have a four-year life and a $9,000 salvage value.

July 5 Paid $1,890 for special racks and cleats installed in the truck. The racks and cleats did not increase the truck's estimated trade-in value.

Dec. 31 Recorded straight-line depreciation on the truck.

1990

June 25 Paid $2,460 to install an air-conditioning unit in the truck. The unit increased the truck's estimated trade-in value by $300.

Dec. 31 Recorded straight-line depreciation on the truck.

1991

Mar. 15 Paid $330 for repairs to the truck's fender damaged when the driver backed into a loading dock.

Dec. 31 Recorded straight-line depreciation on the truck.

1992

Aug. 31 Traded the old truck and $29,310 in cash for a new truck. The new truck was estimated to have a three-year life and a $9,600 trade-in value, and the invoice for the exchange showed these items:

| | |
|---|---|
| Price of the truck | $37,200 |
| Trade-in allowance granted | (9,000) |
| Balance | $28,200 |
| State and city sales taxes | 1,110 |
| Balance paid in cash | $29,310 |

The loss on the exchange was considered to be material.

Sept. 4 Paid $3,690 for special cleats and racks installed in the truck.

Dec. 31 Recorded straight-line depreciation on the new truck.

*Required*

Prepare general journal entries to record the transactions.

**Problem 11–2**
**Depreciating and exchanging plant assets**
(L. O. 1, 2)

A company completed the following transactions involving machinery:

Machine No. 366-90 was purchased on May 1, 1986, at an installed cost of $48,600. Its useful life was estimated at four years with a $5,400 trade-in value. Straight-line depreciation was recorded on the machine at the end of 1986 and 1987, and on August 5, 1988, it was traded on Machine No. 366-91. A $27,000 trade-in allowance was received, and the balance was paid in cash.

Machine No. 366-91 was purchased on August 5, 1988, at an installed cash price of $63,000, less the trade-in allowance received on Machine No. 366-90. The new machine's life was estimated at five years with a $6,300 trade-in value. Sum-of-the-years'-digits depreciation was recorded on each December 31 of its life; and on January 5, 1993, it was sold for $9,000.

Machine No. 367-10 was purchased on January 6, 1988, at an installed cost of $45,000. Its useful life was estimated at five years, after which it would have a $4,500 trade-in value. Declining-balance depreciation at twice the straight-line rate was recorded on the machine at the end of 1988, 1989, and 1990; and on January 3, 1991, it was traded on Machine No. 367-11. An $8,100 trade-in allowance was received, the balance was paid in cash, the loss was considered immaterial, and the income tax method was used to record the transaction.

Machine No. 367-11 was purchased on January 3, 1991, at an installed cash price of $53,100, less the trade-in allowance received on Machine No. 367-10. It was estimated the new machine would produce 75,000 units of product during its useful life, after which it would have a $5,400 trade-in value. Units-of-production depreciation was recorded on the machine for 1991, a period in which it produced 7,500 units of product. Between January 1 and October 3, 1992, the machine produced 11,250 more units, and on the latter date it was sold for $36,000.

*Required*

Prepare general journal entries to record: (*a*) the purchase of each machine, (*b*) the depreciation recorded on the first December 31 of each machine's life, and (*c*) the disposal of each machine. Treat the entries for the first two machines as one series of transactions and those of the next two machines as an unrelated second series. Only one entry is needed to record the exchange of one machine for another.

**Problem 11–3**
**Intangible assets and natural resources**
(L. O. 5)

**Part 1.** Ten years ago, Domo Products Company leased space in a building for a period of 20 years. The lease contract calls for $67,500 annual rental payments on each January 1 throughout the life of the lease and also provides that the lessee must pay for all additions and improvements to the leased property. Recent construction nearby has made the location more valuable; and on December 28, Domo Products Company subleased the space to Techkon, Inc., for the remaining 10 years of the lease, beginning on the next January 1. Techkon, Inc., paid $150,000 for the privilege of subleasing the property and in addition agreed to assume and pay the building owner the $67,500 annual rental charges. After taking possession of the leased space, Techkon, Inc., paid for remodeling the office portion of the leased space at a cost of $210,000. The remodeled office portion is estimated to have a life equal to the remaining life of the building, 20 years, and was paid for on January 9.

*Required*

Prepare entries for Techkon, Inc., to record: (*a*) Techkon, Inc.'s payment to sublease the building space, (*b*) its payment of the annual rental charge to the building owner, and (*c*) payment for the new office portion. Also, prepare the adjusting entries required at the end of the first year of the sublease to amortize (*d*) a proper share of the $150,000 cost of the sublease and (*e*) a proper share of the office remodeling cost.

**Part 2.** On May 7 of the current year, Vanex Company paid $1,224,000 for mineral land estimated to contain 7,500,000 tons of recoverable ore. It installed machinery costing $216,000, having an 18-year life and no salvage value, and capable of exhausting the mine in 15 years. The machinery was paid for on June 28, three days before mining operations began. During the first six months' operations the company mined 309,375 tons of ore.

*Required*

Prepare entries to record (*a*) the purchase of the mineral land, (*b*) the installation of the machinery, (*c*) the first six months' depletion under the assumption that the land will be valueless after the ore is mined, and (*d*) the first six months' depreciation on the machinery, which will be abandoned after the ore is fully mined.

**Problem 11–4**
**Goodwill**
(L. O. 5)

Excelsior Company's balance sheet on December 31, 1990, is as follows:

| | |
|---|---|
| Cash | $ 94,500 |
| Merchandise inventory | 136,500 |
| Buildings | 420,000 |
| Accumulated depreciation | (110,250) |
| Land | 236,250 |
| Total assets | $ 777,000 |
| Accounts payable | $ 63,000 |
| Long-term note payable | 162,750 |
| Common stock | 393,750 |
| Retained earnings | 157,500 |
| Total liabilities and owners' equity | $ 777,000 |

In Excelsior Company's industry, earnings average 12% of common stockholders' equity. Excelsior Company, however, is expected to earn $110,250 annually. The owners of Excelsior Company believe that the balance sheet amounts are reasonable estimates of fair market values except for goodwill. In discussing a plan to sell the company, they argue that goodwill should be recognized by capitalizing the amount of earnings above average at a rate of 15%. On the other hand, the prospective purchaser argues that goodwill should be valued at five times the earnings above average.

*Required*

1. Calculate the amount of goodwill claimed by Excelsior Company's owners.
2. Calculate the amount of goodwill according to the purchaser.
3. Suppose the purchaser finally agrees to pay the full price requested by Excelsior Company's owners. If the expected earnings level is obtained and the goodwill is amortized over the longest permissible time period, what will be the net income for the first year after the company is purchased?
4. If the purchaser pays the full price requested by Excelsior Company's owners, what percentage of the purchaser's investment will be earned as net income the first year?

**Problem 11–5**
**Depreciation, repairs, and exchanges of plant assets**
(L. O. 1, 2, 3, 4)

**Part 1.** On January 8, 1984, a company purchased and placed in operation a machine estimated to have a 10-year life and no salvage value. The machine cost $135,000 and was depreciated on a straight-line basis. On January 3, 1988, a $5,400 device that increased its output by one fourth was added to the machine. The device did not change the machine's estimated life or its zero salvage value. During the first week of January 1991, the machine was completely overhauled at a $40,500 cost (paid for on January 9). The overhaul added three additional years to the machine's estimated life but did not change its zero salvage value. On June 30, 1992, the machine was destroyed in a fire and the insurance company settled the loss claim for $45,000.

*Required*

Prepare general journal entries to record: (*a*) the purchase of the machine, (*b*) the 1984 depreciation, (*c*) the addition of the new device, (*d*) the 1988 depreciation, (*e*) the machine's overhaul, (*f*) the 1991 depreciation, and (*g*) the insurance settlement.

**Part 2.** A company purchased Machine One at a $55,800 installed cost on January 1, 1986. It was depreciated on a straight-line basis at the end of 1986, 1987, 1988, and 1989 under the assumption it would have a 10-year life and a $10,800 salvage value. After more experience and before recording 1990 depreciation, the company revised its estimate of the machine's remaining years downward from six years to four and revised the estimate of its salvage value downward to $9,000. On April 1, 1992, after recording 1990, 1991, and part of a year's depreciation for 1992, the company traded in Machine One on Machine Two, receiving a $22,500 trade-in allowance. The cash paid for Machine Two was $73,350 less the trade-in allowance. On December 31, 1992, Machine Two was depreciated on a straight-line basis under the assumption it would have a six-year life and a $10,350 salvage value.

*Required*

Prepare entries to record: (*a*) the purchase of Machine One, (*b*) its 1986 depreciation, (*c*) its 1990 depreciation, (*d*) the exchange of the machines, and (*e*) the 1992 depreciation on Machine Two.

## Alternate Problems

**Problem 11–1A**
**Purchases, betterments, and sales of plant assets**
(L. O. 2, 4)

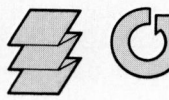

The Franklin Company completed these transactions involving the purchase and operation of delivery vans:

| | |
|---|---|
| 1989 | |
| July 2 | Paid cash for a new van, $27,360 plus $1,360 state and city sales taxes. The van was estimated to have a four-year life and a $7,200 salvage value. |
| July 6 | Paid $1,512 for special racks and cleats installed in the van. The racks and cleats did not increase the van's estimated trade-in value. |
| Dec. 31 | Recorded straight-line depreciation on the van. |
| 1990 | |
| June 26 | Paid $1,968 to install an air-conditioning unit in the van. The unit increased the van's estimated trade-in value by $240. |
| Dec. 31 | Recorded straight-line depreciation on the van. |
| 1991 | |
| May 15 | Paid $285 for repairs to the van's fender damaged when the driver backed into a loading dock. |
| Dec. 31 | Recorded straight-line depreciation on the van. |
| 1992 | |
| Sept. 27 | Traded the old van and $23,448 in cash for a truck. The truck was estimated to have a three-year life and a $7,680 trade-in value, and the invoice for the exchange showed these items: |

| | |
|---|---|
| Price of the truck | $29,760 |
| Trade-in allowance granted | (7,200) |
| Balance | $22,560 |
| State and city sales taxes | 888 |
| Balance paid in cash | $23,448 |

The loss on the exchange was considered to be material.

Oct. 2 Paid $2,952 for special cleats and racks installed in the truck.

Dec. 31 Recorded straight-line depreciation on the truck.

*Required*

Prepare general journal entries to record the transactions.

**Problem 11–2A**
**Depreciation and exchanges of plant assets**
(L. O. 1, 2)

Keto Company completed the following transactions involving machinery:

Machine No. 267-90 was purchased on April 2, 1986, at an installed cost of $77,760. Its useful life was estimated at four years with an $8,640 trade-in value. Straight-line depreciation was recorded on the machine at the end of 1986 and 1987, and on July 3, 1988, it was traded on Machine No. 267-91. A $43,200 trade-in allowance was received, and the balance was paid in cash.

Machine No. 267-91 was purchased on July 3, 1988, at an installed cash price of $100,800, less the trade-in allowance received on Machine No. 267-90. The new machine's life was estimated at five years with a $10,080 trade-in value. Sum-of-the-years'-digits deprecaition was recorded on each December 31 of its life; and on January 7, 1993, it was sold for $14,400.

Machine No. 267-95 was purchased on January 9, 1988, at an installed cost of $72,000. Its useful life was estimated at five years, after which it would have a $7,200 trade-in value. Declining-balance depreciation at twice the straight-line rate was recorded on the machine at the end of 1988, 1989, and 1990; and on January 2, 1991, it was traded on Machine No. 267-96. A $12,960 trade-in allowance was received, the balance was paid in cash, the loss was considered immaterial, and the income tax method was used to record the transaction.

Machine No. 267-96 was purchased on January 2, 1991, at an installed cash price of $84,960, less the trade-in allowance received on Machine No. 267-95. It was estimated the new machine would produce 60,000 units of product during its useful life, after which it would have an $8,640 trade-in value. Units-of-production depreciation was recorded on the machine for 1991, a period in which it produced 6,000 units of product. Between January 1 and October 2, 1992, the machine produced 9,000 more units, and on the latter date it was sold for $57,600.

*Required*

Prepare general journal entries to record: (*a*) the purchase of each machine, (*b*) the depreciation recorded on the first December 31 of each machine's life, and (*c*) the disposal of each machine. Treat the entries for the first two machines as one series of transactions and those of the next two machines as an unrelated second series. Only one entry is needed to record the exchange of one machine for another.

**Problem 11–3A**
**Intangible assets and natural resources**
(L. O. 5)

**Part 1.** Five years ago, D. C. Corporation leased space in a building for a period of 20 years. The lease contract calls for $81,000 annual rental payments on each January 1 throughout the life of the lease and also provides that the lessee must pay for all additions and improvements to the leased property. Recent construction nearby has made the location more valuable; and on December 30, D. C. Corporation subleased the space to T. P., Inc., for the remaining 15 years of the lease, beginning on the next January 1. T. P., Inc., paid

$360,000 for the privilege of subleasing the property and in addition agreed to assume and pay the building owner the $81,000 annual rental charges. After taking possession of the leased space, T. P., Inc., paid for remodeling the office portion of the leased space at a cost of $270,000. The remodeled office portion is estimated to have a life equal to the remaining life of the building, 25 years, and was paid for on January 10.

*Required*

Prepare entries for T. P., Inc., to record: (*a*) T. P., Inc.'s payment to sublease the building space, (*b*) its payment of the annual rental charge to the building owner, and (*c*) payment for the new office portion. Also, prepare the adjusting entries required at the end of the first year of the sublease to amortize (*d*) a proper share of the $360,000 cost of the sublease and (*e*) a proper share of the office remodeling cost.

**Part 2.** On May 8 of the current year, Huber Company paid $1,080,000 for mineral land estimated to contain 9,000,000 tons of recoverable ore. It installed machinery costing $187,500, having an eight-year life and no salvage value, and capable of exhausting the mine in five years. The machinery was paid for on June 28, four days before mining operations began. During the first six months' operations the company mined 720,000 tons of ore.

*Required*

Prepare entries to record (*a*) the purchase of the mineral land, (*b*) the installation of the machinery, (*c*) the first six months' depletion under the assumption that the land will be valueless after the ore is mined, and (*d*) the first six months' depreciation on the machinery, which will be abandoned after the ore is fully mined.

**Problem 11–4A**
**Goodwill**
(L. O. 5)

Batts Company's balance sheet on December 31, 1990, is as follows:

| | |
|---|---|
| Cash | $ 170,100 |
| Merchandise inventory | 245,700 |
| Buildings | 756,000 |
| Accumulated depreciation | (198,450) |
| Land | 425,250 |
| Total assets | $1,398,600 |
| Accounts payable | $ 113,400 |
| Long-term note payable | 295,200 |
| Common stock | 706,500 |
| Retained earnings | 283,500 |
| Total liabilities and owners' equity | $1,398,600 |

In Batts Company's industry, earnings average 11% of common stockholders' equity. Batts Company, however, is expected to earn $198,900 annually. The owners of Batts Company believe that the balance sheet amounts are reasonable estimates of fair market values except for goodwill. In discussing a plan to sell the company, they argue that goodwill should be recognized by capitalizing the amount of earnings above average at a rate of 20%. On the other hand, the prospective purchaser argues that goodwill should be valued at four times the earnings above average.

*Required*

1. Calculate the amount of goodwill claimed by Batts Company's owners.
2. Calculate the amount of goodwill according to the purchaser.
3. Suppose the purchaser finally agrees to pay the full price requested by Batts Company's owners. If the expected earnings level is obtained and the goodwill is amortized over the longest permissible time period, what will be the net income for the first year after the company is purchased?
4. If the purchaser pays the full price requested by Batts Company's owners, what percentage of the purchaser's investment will be earned as net income the first year?

**Problem 11–5A**
**Depreciation, repairs, and exchanges of plant assets**
(L. O. 1, 2, 3, 4)

**Part 1.** On January 6, 1984, Knappe Company purchased a machine estimated to have a 10-year life and no salvage value. The machine cost $216,000 and was depreciated on a straight-line basis. On January 4, 1988, an $8,640 improvement was added to the machine which had the effect of increasing its output by one fourth. The improvement did not change the machine's estimated life or its zero salvage value. On January 8, 1991, the machine was completely overhauled at a $64,800 cost. The overhaul added three additional years to the machine's estimated life but did not change its zero salvage value. On June 30, 1992, the machine was destroyed in a fire and the insurance company settled the loss claim for $72,000.

*Required*

Prepare general journal entries to record: (*a*) the purchase of the machine, (*b*) the 1984 depreciation, (*c*) the addition of the new improvement, (*d*) the 1988 depreciation, (*e*) the machine's overhaul, (*f*) the 1991 depreciation, and (*g*) the insurance settlement.

**Part 2.** A company purchased Machine One at a $139,500 installed cost on January 11, 1986. It was depreciated on a straight-line basis at the end of 1986, 1987, 1988, and 1989 under the assumption it would have a 10-year life and a $27,000 salvage value. After more experience and before recording 1990 depreciation, the company revised its estimate of the machine's remaining years downward from six years to four and revised the estimate of its salvage value downward to $22,500. On April 11, 1992, after recording 1990, 1991, and part of a year's depreciation for 1992, the company traded in Machine One on Machine Two, receiving a $56,250 trade-in allowance. The cash paid for Machine Two was $183,375 less the trade-in allowance. Machine Two was depreciated on a straight-line basis on December 31, 1992, under the assumption it would have a six-year life and a $25,875 salvage value.

*Required*

Prepare entries to record: (*a*) the purchase of Machine One, (*b*) its 1986 depreciation, (*c*) its 1990 depreciation, (*d*) the exchange of the machines, and (*e*) the 1992 depreciation on Machine Two.

## Provocative Problems

**Provocative Problem 11–1**
**Troubled Company**
(L. O. 1, 4)

While examining the accounting records of Troubled Company, you discover two entries during 1991 that appear questionable. The first entry recorded the cash proceeds from an insurance settlement as follows:

| | | | | |
|---|---|---|---|---|
| Nov. | 14 | Cash | 51,000.00 | |
| | | Loss from Fire | 21,000.00 | |
| | | Accumulated Depreciation Machinery | 54,000.00 | |
| | | Machinery | | 126,000.00 |
| | | Received payment of fire loss claim. | | |

Your investigation shows that this entry was intended to record the receipt of an insurance company's $51,000 check to settle a claim resulting from the destruction of a machine in a small plant fire on November 4, 1991. The machine originally cost $108,000 and was put in operation on January 7, 1987. It was depreciated on a straight-line basis for four years under the assumption it would have an eight-year life and no salvage value. During the first week of January 1991, the machine had been overhauled at a cost of $18,000. The overhaul did not increase the machine's capacity or its salvage value. However, it was expected that the overhaul would lengthen the machine's service life two years beyond the eight originally expected.

The second entry that appears questionable was intended to record the receipt of a check from selling a portion of a tract of land. The tract was adjacent to the company's plant and had been purchased the year before. It cost $120,000, and $11,250 was paid for clearing and grading it. Both amounts had been debited to the Factory Land account. The land was to be used for storing finished product; but after the grading was completed, it was obvious the company did not need the entire tract. Troubled Company had received an offer from a purchaser who was willing to pay $67,500 for the east half or $90,000 for the west half. The company decided to sell the west half, and it recorded receipt of the purchaser's check with the following entry:

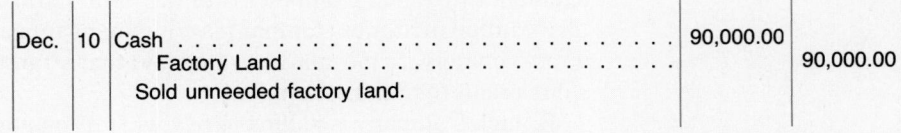

| | | | | |
|---|---|---|---|---|
| Dec. | 10 | Cash | 90,000.00 | |
| | | Factory Land | | 90,000.00 |
| | | Sold unneeded factory land. | | |

Were any errors made in recording these transactions? If so, describe the errors and in each case give an entry or entries that will correct the account balances under the assumption the 1991 revenue and expense accounts have not been closed.

**Provocative Problem 11–2**
**Sticks and Stones Companies**
(A Review Problem)

Sticks Company and Stones Company are similar businesses that sell competing products. Both companies began operations five years ago and are up for sale. Branch Company is considering both Sticks and Stones with the prospect of buying one of them.

In evaluating the two companies, the management of Branch has observed that Sticks Company has reported an average annual net income of $142,020. Stones Company, on the other hand, has reported an average of $171,000. However, the companies have not used the same accounting procedures, and Branch Company management is concerned that the numbers are not comparable. The current balance sheets of the two companies show these items:

| | Sticks Company | Stones Company |
|---|---|---|
| Cash | $ 80,400 | $ 98,400 |
| Accounts receivable | 619,200 | 702,000 |
| Allowance for doubtful accounts | (38,400) | –0– |
| Merchandise inventory | 855,600 | 1,033,200 |
| Store equipment | 345,600 | 307,200 |
| Accumulated depreciation, store equipment | (288,000) | (192,000) |
| Total assets | $1,574,400 | $1,948,800 |
| Current liabilities | $ 748,800 | $ 826,800 |
| Owners' equity | 825,600 | 1,122,000 |
| Total liabilities and owners' equity | $1,574,400 | $1,948,800 |

Sticks Company has used the allowance method in accounting for bad debts and has added to its allowance each year an amount equal to 1% of sales. However, this seems excessive since an examination shows that only $18,000 of its accounts are probably uncollectible. Stones Company has used the direct write-off method but has been slow to write off bad debts. An examination of its accounts shows $36,000 of accounts that are probably uncollectible.

During the past five years, Sticks Company has priced its inventories on a LIFO basis with the result that its current inventory appears on its balance sheet at an amount that is $144,000 below replacement cost. Stones Company has used FIFO, and its ending inventory appears at approximately its replacement cost.

Both companies have assumed eight-year lives and no salvage value in depreciating equipment; however, Sticks Company has used sum-of-the-years'-digits depreciation, while Stones Company has used straight line. The management of Branch Company is of the opinion that straight-line depreciation has resulted in Stones Company's equipment appearing on its balance sheet at approximately its fair market value and that straight-line would have had the same result for Sticks Company.

Branch Company is willing to pay what its management considers fair market value for the assets of either business, not including cash, but including goodwill measured at four times average annual earnings in excess of 15% on the fair market value of the net tangible assets. Branch Company's management defines net tangible assets as all assets other than goodwill, including accounts receivable, minus liabilities. Branch Company will also assume the liabilities of the purchased business, paying its owner the difference between total assets purchased and the liabilities assumed.

*Required*

Prepare the following schedules: (*a*) a schedule showing the net tangible assets of each company at their fair market values according to Branch Company management, (*b*) a schedule showing the revised net incomes of the companies based on FIFO inventories and straight-line depreciation, (*c*) a schedule showing the calculation of each company's goodwill, and (*d*) a schedule showing the amount Branch Company would pay for each business.

**Provocative Problem 11–3**
**Metro Airlines, Inc.**
(L. O. 4)

Metro Airlines, Inc., in a recent annual report to stockholders, included the following footnotes to its consolidated financial statements:

> **Property and equipment, depreciation, and amortization:** Property and equipment are depreciated to residual values over their estimated service lives using the straight-line and declining-balance methods. Upon retirement or sale of property and equipment, the assets and reserve accounts are relieved of the cost and related accumulated depreciation, and the resulting gain or loss is recorded in income.
>
> **Maintenance:** Metroflight charges maintenance expense, on the basis of hours flown, for the estimated costs of Convair aircraft block overhauls. The provision rate per hour is adjusted periodically to reflect actual experience in hours between the block overhauls and in the costs of overhauls. The costs of block overhauls are charged to the reserve for block overhauls when incurred.
>
> Courtesy of Metro Airlines, Inc.

*Required*

1. If Metro uses both straight-line and declining-balance methods to depreciate property and equipment, isn't the company in violation of the consistency principle? Explain.
2. Are the maintenance expenses discussed in the footnote best classified as ordinary repairs or extraordinary repairs?
3. Metro's method of accounting for maintenance expense is different than the normal procedure as described in this chapter. Describe the difference.
4. Why do you think Metro accounts for maintenance expense in the manner described instead of following the procedure described in this chapter?

Part Four

# Liabilities, Partners' Equities, and the Evolving Development of Accounting Principles

Many different kinds of liabilities are incurred by businesses in the process of conducting business operations. These liabilities include short-term obligations such as accounts payable, wages payable, notes payable, unearned revenues, property taxes payable, product warranties, and payroll liabilities. They also include long-term liabilities such as capital leases, and long-term notes payable. You will learn the fundamental principles of accounting for liabilities such as these as you study the next two chapters. Then, in Chapter 14 you will learn about some special accounting issues that relate to partnerships. Finally, we close the first half of the book with a supplement (Appendix E) that summarizes the evolving development of accounting principles.

Part four consists of the following:

# 12 Current and Long-Term Liabilities

You already know that liabilities are one of the three elements in the accounting equation. Some of the liabilities we've discussed in previous chapters include accounts payable, notes payable, wages payable, and unearned revenues. In this chapter, we examine liabilities such as property taxes payable, product warranties, single-payment notes payable, and leases. We also introduce the important concept of present values and reconsider the topic of contingent liabilities. As you study this chapter, you will learn how to define, classify, and measure liabilities.

### Learning Objectives

*After studying Chapter 12, you should be able to:*

1. Explain the difference between current and long-term liabilities.
2. Explain the meaning of definite and estimated liabilities.
3. Record transactions that involve liabilities such as property taxes payable, product warranties, and short-term notes payable.
4. Explain the difference between liabilities and contingent liabilities.
5. Calculate the present value of a sum of money that will be received a number of periods in the future or will be received periodically.
6. Prepare entries to account for long-term noninterest-bearing notes payable and for capital and operating leases.
7. Define or explain the words and phrases listed in the chapter Glossary.

## The Definition and Classification of Liabilities

Liabilities are obligations that require the future payment of assets or performance of services. Not every expected future payment is a liability. To qualify as a liability, the debtor must, as a result of past transactions, be presently obligated to make a future payment. Because liabilities result from past transactions, they normally are enforceable as legal claims against the enterprise.

### Current and Long-Term Liabilities

Explain the difference between current and long-term liabilities. (L. O. 1)

**Current Liabilities.** A business typically has several kinds of liabilities which are classified as either current or long-term liabilities. *Current liabilities* are debts or other obligations the liquidation of which is expected to require the use of existing current assets or the creation of other current liabilities.[1] Current liabilities are due within one year of the balance sheet date or the operating cycle of the business, whichever is longer. Examples of current liabilities are accounts payable, short-term notes payable, wages payable, dividends payable, product warranty liabilities, payroll and other taxes payable, and unearned revenues.

**Long-Term Liabilities.** Obligations that will not require the use of existing current assets because they do not mature within one year (or one operating cycle, whichever is longer) are classified as **long-term liabilities**. Examples of long-term liabilities include leases, long-term notes payable, product warranty liabilities, and bonds payable. However, you should understand that any given liability such as a note payable may be either current or long term. The critical difference is the question of whether or not payment will be made within one year or the current operating cycle of the business, whichever is longer.

### Definite versus Estimated Liabilities

Explain the meaning of definite and estimated liabilities. (L. O. 2)

Three important questions concerning liabilities are: Who will be paid? When is payment due? How much is to be paid? In many situations, the answers to these three questions are determined at the time the liability is incurred. For example, an account payable may be for precisely $100, payable to R. L. Tucker, and due on August 15, 1991. This type of liability is definite with respect to all three questions.

**When the Identity of the Creditor Is Uncertain.** Other types of liabilities may be indefinite with respect to one or more of the three questions. For example, in the case of dividends payable, the amount that will be paid and the due date are definite. The question of who will be paid, however, is not answerable until after the date of record. Even though the identity of the creditor may be uncertain, there is no doubt that the debtor is obligated to pay and a liability should be recognized.

---

[1] FASB, *Accounting Standards—Current Text* (Norwalk, Conn., 1988), sec. B05.402. First published as *Accounting Research Bulletin No. 43,* ch. 3A, par. 7.

**When the Due Date Is Uncertain.** An example of a liability with an uncertain due date is unearned legal fees that a lawyer accepts in return for the obligation to provide services to a client upon call. In this case, the amount of the liability is known. And the client for whom services will be provided is also known. However, the question of when the services will be performed is not definite. Usually, such arrangements are short term and are classified as current liabilities.

**When the Amount to Be Paid Is Uncertain.** When an obligation definitely exists but the amount that will be paid is uncertain, the obligation is called an **estimated liability.** Two important examples of estimated liabilities are property taxes and product warranties.

## Property Taxes Payable

Record transactions that involve liabilities such as property taxes payable, product warranties, and short-term notes payable. (L. O. 3)

Property taxes are levied on an annual basis by a variety of governmental authorities such as counties, cities, and school districts. However, the exact amount of tax to be paid may not become known until the tax year is partially over. For example, the 1991 tax that will be paid on each item of property may not be fixed in amount until September 1991. And the tax may not be due until October 1991. Thus, if financial statements are prepared monthly, the tax expense must be estimated when statements are prepared for January through August.

For example, throughout 1991, a company owns property that has been assessed by the city as having a valuation of $400,000 for property tax purposes. The tax on the property during the previous year (1990) was $11,400. In preparing monthly financial statements during 1991, before the actual tax is known, the company estimates a monthly tax expense of $11,400 ÷ 12 = $950. Until the 1991 tax becomes definite, the company will make monthly adjusting entries as follows:

| | | | | |
|---|---|---|---|---|
| 1991 | | | | |
| Jan. | 31 | Property Taxes Expense . . . . . . . . . . . . . . . . . . . | 950.00 | |
| | | Estimated Property Taxes Payable . . . . . . . . . . . | | 950.00 |
| | | To record estimated property taxes for the month of January. | | |

In September 1991, the city announces that the tax levy for 1991 will be $3 per $100 of assessed value. Now, the company calculates the actual 1991 tax as ($400,000 ÷ $100) × $3 = $12,000, which is $1,000 per month. For the first eight months (January through August), the estimated tax was less than the actual tax by $50 × 8 = $400. This may be recorded at the end of September along with the $1,000 monthly tax, as follows:

| | | | | |
|---|---|---|---|---|
| Sept. | 30 | Property Taxes Expense . . . . . . . . . . . . . . . . . . . | 1,400.00 | |
| | | Estimated Property Taxes Payable . . . . . . . . . . . | | 1,400.00 |
| | | To record property taxes for the month of September and to correct for $50 estimate error during first eight months. | | |

When the annual tax is paid at the end of October 1991, the entry to record the payment is:

| | | | | |
|---|---|---|---|---|
| Oct. | 31 | Property Taxes Expense (October) . . . . . . . . . . . . . . | 1,000.00 | |
| | | Prepaid Property Taxes (November and December) . . . . | 2,000.00 | |
| | | Estimated Property Taxes Payable . . . . . . . . . . . . . | 9,000.00 | |
| | | Cash . . . . . . . . . . . . . . . . . . . . . . . . . . . | | 12,000.00 |
| | | To pay property tax for 1991. | | |

## Product Warranty Liabilities

Product warranty liability is another example of an estimated liability. Most companies provide warranties or guarantees for their products. A **product warranty** is a promise to the customer; the promise obligates the seller or manufacturer for a limited period of time to pay for items such as replacement parts or repair costs if the product breaks or fails to perform. For example, an automobile may be sold with a warranty that covers the mechanical parts for a period of one year or 12,000 miles, whichever comes first. The warranty may also include labor costs to install replacement parts.

When a product with a warranty is sold, the *matching principle* requires that you record all expenses to produce the sale in the same period as the sale. Therefore, the expense of the warranty must be recognized at the time of the sale. Since the exact amount of expense is not known at the time of the sale, the amount must be estimated based on past experience.

For example, a used auto is sold with a one-year or 12,000-mile warranty. The warranty covers mechanical parts, but the customer must pay any labor charges. Suppose the auto was sold on September 1, 1990, at a price of $16,000. Past experience shows that warranty expense is about 2% of the sales price. The entry to record the expense is:

| | | | | |
|---|---|---|---|---|
| Sept. | 1 | Warranty Expense . . . . . . . . . . . . . . . . . . . . . . | 320.00 | |
| | | Estimated Warranty Liability . . . . . . . . . . . . . . . | | 320.00 |
| | | $16,000 × .02 = $320. | | |

Now suppose the customer has a problem with the car and returns it for warranty repairs on January 9, 1991. The auto dealer performs the warranty work by replacing parts that cost $90 and charges the customer $110 for labor. The entry to record the warranty work and the customer's payment is as follows:

| | | | | |
|---|---|---|---|---|
| Jan. | 9 | Cash . . . . . . . . . . . . . . . . . . . . . . . . . . . . | 110.00 | |
| | | Estimated Warranty Liability . . . . . . . . . . . . . . . . | 90.00 | |
| | | Auto Parts Inventory . . . . . . . . . . . . . . . . . . . | | 90.00 |
| | | Service Revenue . . . . . . . . . . . . . . . . . . . . . | | 110.00 |
| | | To record warranty work and service revenue. | | |

What happens if the total warranty costs actually are different from the estimated $320 amount? On any sale, some difference is likely. Over the longer term, management must monitor warranty costs to be sure that 2% is the best estimate. When continued experience shows that warranty costs have changed, the percentage should be modified.

## Contingent Liabilities

We first discussed contingent liabilities in Chapter 8. Discounted notes receivable were presented as an example of contingent liabilities. Contingent liabilities are not existing obligations and, therefore, are not recorded in the books as liabilities. However, the *full-disclosure principle* requires that you disclose contingent liabilities in the financial statements or in footnotes.

### What Distinguishes Liabilities from Contingent Liabilities?

Explain the difference between liabilities and contingent liabilities. (L. O. 4)

Contingent liabilities become definite obligations only if some uncertain event takes place. For example, discounted notes receivable are contingent liabilities that become definite obligations only if the original signers of the notes fail to pay them.

Are product warranties a liability or contingent liability? A product warranty requires service or payment only if the product fails. That sounds like a contingent liability. However, the FASB ruled that *if a contingency is probable and if the liability can be reasonably estimated, it should be recorded in the books as a liability*.[2] Product warranties usually are recorded as liabilities because the failure of some percentage of the products sold is probable and past experience allows a reasonable estimate of the amount of the liability.

### What Are Other Examples of Contingent Liabilities?

**Potential Legal Claims.** In today's legal environment, many companies find themselves being sued for damages for a variety of reasons. The question is should the defendant report a liability or a contingent liability during the time a lawsuit is outstanding and not yet settled? The answer is that unless a payment for damages is probable and can be reasonably estimated, the potential claim of the plaintiff is a contingent liability of the defendant.

**Debt Guaranties.** Sometimes a company will guarantee the payment of a supplier, customer, or other company's debt, usually by cosigning the note payable of the other company. When this is done, the guarantor is contingently liable for the debt of the other company.

## Short-Term Notes Payable

A current liability that requires further attention is short-term notes payable. When a business purchases merchandise on credit and then needs to gain an extension of the credit period, a short-term note payable may be substituted for the account payable. Also, short-term notes payable frequently arise in borrowing from a bank.

[2] Ibid., sec. C59.105. First published as *FASB Statement No. 5*, par. 8.

### Note Given to Secure a Time Extension on an Account

A note payable may be given to secure an extension of time in which to pay an account payable. For example, assume that Brock Company cannot pay its past-due $600 account with Ajax Company. As a result, Ajax Company agrees to accept Brock Company's 60-day, 12%, $600 note in granting an extension on the due date of the debt. Brock Company will record the issuance of the note as follows:

| | | | | |
|---|---|---|---|---|
| Aug. | 23 | Accounts Payable—Ajax Company . . . . . . . . . . . . . | 600.00 | |
| | | Notes Payable . . . . . . . . . . . . . . . . . . . . . . | | 600.00 |
| | | Gave a 60-day, 12% note to extend the due date on the amount owed. | | |

Observe that the note does not pay the debt. Rather, the form of the debt is changed from an account payable to a note payable. Ajax Company should prefer the note to the account because, in case of default and a lawsuit to collect, the note is written evidence of the debt and its amount.

When the note becomes due, Brock Company will give Ajax Company a check for $612 and record the payment of the note and its interest with this entry:

| | | | | |
|---|---|---|---|---|
| Oct. | 22 | Notes Payable . . . . . . . . . . . . . . . . . . . . . . | 600.00 | |
| | | Interest Expense . . . . . . . . . . . . . . . . . . . . . | 12.00 | |
| | | Cash . . . . . . . . . . . . . . . . . . . . . . . . . | | 612.00 |
| | | Paid our note with interest. | | |

### Borrowing from a Bank

In lending money, banks typically require that the borrower sign a promissory note. Oftentimes, the note is written for the amount of money loaned. The customer (debtor) promises to repay the amount of the note plus interest at a specified rate. In this case, the lending transaction is called a *loan*. In other cases, called *discounts,* the note is written for the sum of the amount borrowed plus interest. In other words, with a loan, the bank collects interest when the loan is repaid. With a discount, the bank deducts interest at the time the loan is made. To illustrate loans and discounts, assume that H. A. Green wishes to borrow approximately $2,000 for 60 days at the prevailing 15% rate of interest.

**A Loan.** In a loan transaction, the bank lends Green $2,000 in exchange for a signed promissory note. The note reads: "Sixty days after date I promise to pay $2,000 plus interest at 15%." Green records the transaction as follows:

| | | | | |
|---|---|---|---|---|
| Sept. | 10 | Cash . . . . . . . . . . . . . . . . . . . . . . . . . . | 2,000.00 | |
| | | Notes Payable . . . . . . . . . . . . . . . . . . . . . . | | 2,000.00 |
| | | Gave the bank a 60-day, 15% note. | | |

When the note and interest are paid, Green makes this entry:

| | | | | |
|---|---|---|---|---|
| Nov. | 9 | Notes Payable | 2,000.00 | |
| | | Interest Expense | 50.00 | |
| | | Cash | | 2,050.00 |
| | | Paid our 60-day, 15% note. | | |

Observe that in a loan transaction, the interest is paid at the time the loan is repaid.

**A Discount.** If Green's bank deducts interest at the time a loan is made, the bank will discount Green's $2,000 note. If it discounts the note at 15% for 60 days, it will deduct from the face amount of the note 60 days' interest at 15%, which is $50, and will give Green the difference, $1,950. The $50 deducted interest is called **bank discount.** The net amount received by Green, $1,950, is called the *proceeds* of the discounted note. Green records the transaction as follows:

| | | | | |
|---|---|---|---|---|
| Sept. | 10 | Cash | 1,950.00 | |
| | | Discount on Notes Payable | 50.00 | |
| | | Notes Payable | | 2,000.00 |
| | | Discounted our $2,000 note payable at 15%. | | |

When the note matures, Green is required to pay the bank the face amount of the note, $2,000; Green records the payment like this:

| | | | | |
|---|---|---|---|---|
| Nov. | 9 | Notes Payable | 2,000.00 | |
| | | Cash | | 2,000.00 |
| | | Paid our discounted note payable. | | |

Also, Green must record the interest expense, as follows:

| | | | | |
|---|---|---|---|---|
| Nov. | 9 | Interest Expense | 50.00 | |
| | | Discount on Note Payable | | 50.00 |
| | | To record interest expense. | | |

In this example, note that this last entry could have been avoided if the $50 interest had been debited to Interest Expense in the entry of September 10, as follows:

| | | | | |
|---|---|---|---|---|
| Sept. | 10 | Cash | 1,950.00 | |
| | | Interest Expense | 50.00 | |
| | | Notes Payable | | 2,000.00 |
| | | Discounted our $2,000 note payable at 15%. | | |

As a matter of convenience, when a note is signed and will be due within the same accounting period, many companies use this more efficient procedure.

In a discount transaction, since interest is deducted at the time the loan is made, the note states that only the principal amount is to be repaid at maturity. The note does not call for interest to be paid at maturity. Such a note may read: "Sixty days after date I promise to pay $2,000, with no interest." As a result, this type of note is commonly called a noninterest-bearing note. However, banks are not in business to lend money interest free. Interest is paid in a discount transaction. Since it is deducted at the time the loan is made, the note states that no additional interest will be collected at maturity. Nevertheless, interest is collected in a discount transaction and at a rate slightly higher than in a loan transaction at the same stated interest rate. For example, Green paid $50 for the use of $1,950 for 60 days, so the effective interest rate was a little in excess of 15% on the $1,950 received.

## End-of-Period Adjustments

### Discount on Notes Payable

When a note payable is discounted at a bank, and the note does not become due until the next accounting period, the interest deducted in advance should be debited to Discount on Note Payable. Then, at the end of the period, an adjusting entry is required. For example, on December 11, 1990, a company discounted at 15% its own $6,000, 60-day, noninterest-bearing note payable. It recorded the transaction as follows:

| | | | | |
|---|---|---|---|---|
| 1990 | | | | |
| Dec. | 11 | Cash | 5,850.00 | |
| | | Discount on Notes Payable | 150.00 | |
| | | Notes Payable | | 6,000.00 |
| | | Discounted our noninterest-bearing, 60-day note at 15%. | | |

If this company operates with accounting periods that end each December 31, 20 days' interest on this note, or $50 of the $150 discount, is an expense of the 1990 accounting period. Interest for the remaining 40 days, or $100, is an expense of 1991. Therefore, if revenues and expenses are matched, the company must make the following December 31, 1990, adjusting entry:

| | | | | |
|---|---|---|---|---|
| 1990 | | | | |
| Dec. | 31 | Interest Expense | 50.00 | |
| | | Discount on Notes Payable | | 50.00 |
| | | To record 1990 interest expense. | | |

The adjusting entry removes from the Discount on Notes Payable account the $50 of interest that is applicable to 1990. It leaves in the account the $100 that is an expense of 1991. The $50 then appears on the 1990 income statement as an expense, and the $100 appears on the December 31, 1990, balance sheet.

If this is the only note the company has outstanding, the $100 is deducted on the balance sheet as follows:

| | | |
|---|---|---|
| Current liabilities: | | |
| Notes payable . . . . . . . . . . . . . . . . | $6,000 | |
| Less discount on notes payable . . . . | 100 | $5,900 |

When the adjusted discount on notes payable is subtracted as a contra liability, the net liability on the balance sheet shows the amount received in discounting the note plus the accrued interest on the note to the balance sheet date. In this example, $5,850 was received in discounting the note, and accrued interest on the note is $50. Together they total $5,900, which is the net liability to the bank on December 31.

### Accrued Interest Expense

Interest on an interest-bearing note accrues as time passes. Therefore, if any interest-bearing notes payable are outstanding at the end of an accounting period, the accrued interest should be recorded. For example, a company gave its bank a $4,000, 60-day, 12% note on December 16 to borrow that amount of money. If the company's accounting period ends on December 31, by then 15 days' or $20 interest has accrued on this note. You should record the interest with this adjusting entry:

| | | | | |
|---|---|---|---|---|
| Dec. | 31 | Interest Expense . . . . . . . . . . . . . . . . . . . . . . . | 20.00 | |
| | | Interest Payable . . . . . . . . . . . . . . . . . . . . . | | 20.00 |
| | | To record accrued interest on a note payable. | | |

The adjusting entry causes the $20 accrued interest to appear on the income statement as an expense of the period that benefits from 15 days' use of the money. It also causes the interest payable to appear on the balance sheet as a current liability.

When the note matures in the next accounting period, its payment is recorded as follows:

| | | | | |
|---|---|---|---|---|
| Feb. | 14 | Notes Payable . . . . . . . . . . . . . . . . . . . . . . . | 4,000.00 | |
| | | Interest Payable . . . . . . . . . . . . . . . . . . . . . . . | 20.00 | |
| | | Interest Expense . . . . . . . . . . . . . . . . . . . . . . | 60.00 | |
| | | Cash . . . . . . . . . . . . . . . . . . . . . . . . . . | | 4,080.00 |
| | | Paid a $4,000 note and its interest. | | |

Interest on this note for 60 days is $80. In the illustrated entry, the $80 is divided between the interest accrued at the end of the previous period, $20, and interest applicable to the current period, $60.

## The Concept of Present Value

Calculate the present value of a sum of money that will be received a number of periods in the future or will be received periodically.
(L. O. 5)

The concept of present value enters into many financing and investing decisions and any resulting liabilities. Therefore, an understanding of present value is important for all business students. The concept is based on the idea that the right to receive, say, $1 a year from today is worth less than $1 today. In other words, $1 to be received one year hence has a **present value** of less than $1. How much less depends on how much can be earned on invested funds.

To state the concept in general terms, present value is the amount of money that could be currently invested at a given interest rate to accumulate a total value equal to a given amount to be received or paid at some future date. For example, if a 10% annual return can be earned, the expectation of receiving $1 one year from now has a present value of $0.9091. This can be verified as follows: $0.9091 invested today to earn 10% annually will earn $0.09091 in one year, and when the $0.09091 earned is added to the $0.9091 invested—

| | |
|---|---|
| Investment . . . . | $0.9091 |
| Earnings . . . . . | 0.09091 |
| Total . . . . . . . | $1.00001 |

the investment plus the earnings equal $1.00001, which rounds to the $1 expected.

Likewise, the present value of $1 to be received two years hence is $0.8264 if a 10% compound annual return is expected. This also can be verified as follows: $0.8264 invested to earn 10% compounded annually will earn $0.08264 the first year it is invested, and when the $0.08264 earned is added to the $0.8264 invested—

| | |
|---|---|
| Investment . . . . . . . . . . | $0.8264 |
| First-year earnings . . . . . | 0.08264 |
| End-of-year-1 amount . . . . | $0.90904 |

the investment plus the first year's earnings total $0.90904. During the second year, this $0.90904 will earn $0.090904, which when added to the end-of-year-1 amount—

| | |
|---|---|
| End-of-year-1 amount . . . . | $0.90904 |
| Second-year earnings . . . . | 0.090904 |
| End-of-year-2 amount . . . . | $0.999944 |

equals $0.999944, which rounds to the $1 expected at the end of the second year.

### Present Value Tables

The *present value* of $1 to be received any number of years in the future can be calculated by using the formula, $1/(1 + i)^n$. The $i$ is the interest rate, and $n$ is the number of years to the expected receipt. However, you do not need to use the formula, since there are **present value tables** that show present values com-

**Table 12–1**
**Present Value of $1 at Compound Interest**

| Periods Hence | 4½% | 5% | 6% | 7% | 8% | 9% | 10% | 12% | 14% | 16% |
|---|---|---|---|---|---|---|---|---|---|---|
| 1 | 0.9569 | 0.9524 | 0.9434 | 0.9346 | 0.9259 | 0.9174 | 0.9091 | 0.8929 | 0.8772 | 0.8621 |
| 2 | 0.9157 | 0.9070 | 0.8900 | 0.8734 | 0.8573 | 0.8417 | 0.8264 | 0.7972 | 0.7695 | 0.7432 |
| 3 | 0.8763 | 0.8638 | 0.8396 | 0.8163 | 0.7938 | 0.7722 | 0.7513 | 0.7118 | 0.6750 | 0.6407 |
| 4 | 0.8386 | 0.8227 | 0.7921 | 0.7629 | 0.7350 | 0.7084 | 0.6830 | 0.6355 | 0.5921 | 0.5532 |
| 5 | 0.8025 | 0.7835 | 0.7473 | 0.7130 | 0.6806 | 0.6499 | 0.6209 | 0.5674 | 0.5194 | 0.4761 |
| 6 | 0.7679 | 0.7462 | 0.7050 | 0.6663 | 0.6302 | 0.5963 | 0.5645 | 0.5066 | 0.4556 | 0.4104 |
| 7 | 0.7348 | 0.7107 | 0.6651 | 0.6228 | 0.5835 | 0.5470 | 0.5132 | 0.4523 | 0.3996 | 0.3538 |
| 8 | 0.7032 | 0.6768 | 0.6274 | 0.5820 | 0.5403 | 0.5019 | 0.4665 | 0.4039 | 0.3506 | 0.3050 |
| 9 | 0.6729 | 0.6446 | 0.5919 | 0.5439 | 0.5003 | 0.4604 | 0.4241 | 0.3606 | 0.3075 | 0.2630 |
| 10 | 0.6439 | 0.6139 | 0.5584 | 0.5084 | 0.4632 | 0.4224 | 0.3855 | 0.3220 | 0.2697 | 0.2267 |
| 11 | 0.6162 | 0.5847 | 0.5268 | 0.4751 | 0.4289 | 0.3875 | 0.3505 | 0.2875 | 0.2366 | 0.1954 |
| 12 | 0.5897 | 0.5568 | 0.4970 | 0.4440 | 0.3971 | 0.3555 | 0.3186 | 0.2567 | 0.2076 | 0.1685 |
| 13 | 0.5643 | 0.5303 | 0.4688 | 0.4150 | 0.3677 | 0.3262 | 0.2897 | 0.2292 | 0.1821 | 0.1452 |
| 14 | 0.5400 | 0.5051 | 0.4423 | 0.3878 | 0.3405 | 0.2993 | 0.2633 | 0.2046 | 0.1597 | 0.1252 |
| 15 | 0.5167 | 0.4810 | 0.4173 | 0.3625 | 0.3152 | 0.2745 | 0.2394 | 0.1827 | 0.1401 | 0.1079 |
| 16 | 0.4945 | 0.4581 | 0.3937 | 0.3387 | 0.2919 | 0.2519 | 0.2176 | 0.1631 | 0.1229 | 0.0930 |
| 17 | 0.4732 | 0.4363 | 0.3714 | 0.3166 | 0.2703 | 0.2311 | 0.1978 | 0.1456 | 0.1078 | 0.0802 |
| 18 | 0.4528 | 0.4155 | 0.3503 | 0.2959 | 0.2503 | 0.2120 | 0.1799 | 0.1300 | 0.0946 | 0.0691 |
| 19 | 0.4333 | 0.3957 | 0.3305 | 0.2765 | 0.2317 | 0.1945 | 0.1635 | 0.1161 | 0.0830 | 0.0596 |
| 20 | 0.4146 | 0.3769 | 0.3118 | 0.2584 | 0.2146 | 0.1784 | 0.1486 | 0.1037 | 0.0728 | 0.0514 |

puted with the formula at various interest rates. An example is Table 12–1, which shows the present value amounts rounded to four decimal places. (Four decimal places would not be sufficiently accurate for some uses but will suffice here.)

Observe in Table 12–1 that the first amount in the 10% column is the 0.9091 used in the previous section to introduce the concept of present value. The 0.9091 in the 10% column means that the expectation of receiving $1 one period hence, when discounted at 10%, has a present value of $0.9091. Also note that the second amount in the 10% column is the 0.8264 previously used. This number means that the expectation of receiving $1 two periods hence, discounted at 10%, has a present value of $0.8264.

### Using a Present Value Table

To demonstrate the use of a present value table such as Table 12–1, assume that a company has an opportunity to invest $55,000 in a project. The investment will return $20,000 at the end of the first year, $25,000 at the end of the second year, $30,000 at the end of the third year, and nothing thereafter. Also assume that the company believes the risks of the project justify a 12% return, compounded annually.

Will the project return the original investment plus the 12% demanded? The calculations of Illustration 12–1 indicate that it will. In Illustration 12–1, the expected returns in the second column are multiplied by the present value amounts in the third column to determine the present values in the last column. Since the total of the present values exceeds the required investment by

Illustration 12–1
**Present value of a series of unequal amounts**

| Years Hence | Expected Returns | Present Value of $1 at 12% | Present Value of Expected Returns |
|---|---|---|---|
| 1 . . . . | $20,000 | 0.8929 | $17,858 |
| 2 . . . . | 25,000 | 0.7972 | 19,930 |
| 3 . . . . | 30,000 | 0.7118 | 21,354 |
| Total present value of the returns . . . . . | | | $59,142 |
| Less investment required . . . . . . . . | | | 55,000 |
| Excess over 12% demanded . . . . . . . | | | $ 4,142 |

$4,142, the project will return the $55,000 investment, plus a 12% return thereon, plus an additional $4,142.

In Illustration 12–1, the present value of each year's return was separately calculated. Then, the present values were totaled. When the periodic returns are unequal, as in this example, you must separately calculate the present value of each. However, in cases where the periodic returns are equal, there are shorter ways to calculate the sum of their present values.

For instance, suppose a $17,500 investment will return $5,000 at the end of each year in its five-year life and an investor wants to know the present value of these returns, discounted at 12%. In this case, the periodic returns are equal, and a short way to determine their total present value at 12% is to add the present values of $1 at 12% for periods 1 through 5 (from Table 12–1) as follows—

| |
|---|
| 0.8929 |
| 0.7972 |
| 0.7118 |
| 0.6355 |
| 0.5674 |
| 3.6048 |

and then to multiply $5,000 by the total. The $18,024 result ($5,000 × 3.6048 = $18,024) is the same as would be obtained if you calculate the present value of each year's return and then add the present values. Although the result is the same either way, the method demonstrated here requires four fewer multiplications.

### Present Value of $1 Received Periodically for a Number of Periods

Table 12–2 is based on the idea demonstrated in the above paragraph. To summarize, the present value of a series of equal returns to be received at periodic intervals is nothing more than the sum of the present values of the individual returns. Note the amount on the table's fifth line in the 12% column. It is the same 3.6048 amount that was calculated in the previous paragraph by adding the first five present values of $1 at 12%. All the amounts shown in Table 12–2 could be determined by adding amounts found in Table 12–1. However, there would be some slight variations due to rounding.

Table 12–2
**Present Value of $1 Received Periodically for a Number of Periods**

| Periods Hence | 4½% | 5% | 6% | 7% | 8% | 9% | 10% | 12% | 14% | 16% |
|---|---|---|---|---|---|---|---|---|---|---|
| 1 | 0.9569 | 0.9524 | 0.9434 | 0.9346 | 0.9259 | 0.9174 | 0.9091 | 0.8929 | 0.8772 | 0.8621 |
| 2 | 1.8727 | 1.8594 | 1.8334 | 1.8080 | 1.7833 | 1.7591 | 1.7355 | 1.6901 | 1.6467 | 1.6052 |
| 3 | 2.7490 | 2.7232 | 2.6730 | 2.6243 | 2.5771 | 2.5313 | 2.4869 | 2.4018 | 2.3216 | 2.2459 |
| 4 | 3.5875 | 3.5460 | 3.4651 | 3.3872 | 3.3121 | 3.2397 | 3.1699 | 3.0374 | 2.9137 | 2.7982 |
| 5 | 4.3900 | 4.3295 | 4.2124 | 4.1002 | 3.9927 | 3.8897 | 3.7908 | 3.6048 | 3.4331 | 3.2743 |
| 6 | 5.1579 | 5.0757 | 4.9173 | 4.7665 | 4.6229 | 4.4859 | 4.3553 | 4.1114 | 3.8887 | 3.6847 |
| 7 | 5.8927 | 5.7864 | 5.5824 | 5.3893 | 5.2064 | 5.0330 | 4.8684 | 4.5638 | 4.2883 | 4.0386 |
| 8 | 6.5959 | 6.4632 | 6.2098 | 5.9713 | 5.7466 | 5.5348 | 5.3349 | 4.9676 | 4.6389 | 4.3436 |
| 9 | 7.2688 | 7.1078 | 6.8017 | 6.5152 | 6.2469 | 5.9953 | 5.7590 | 5.3283 | 4.9464 | 4.6065 |
| 10 | 7.9127 | 7.7217 | 7.3601 | 7.0236 | 6.7101 | 6.4177 | 6.1446 | 5.6502 | 5.2161 | 4.8332 |
| 11 | 8.5289 | 8.3064 | 7.8869 | 7.4987 | 7.1390 | 6.8052 | 6.4951 | 5.9377 | 5.4527 | 5.0286 |
| 12 | 9.1186 | 8.8633 | 8.3838 | 7.9427 | 7.5361 | 7.1607 | 6.8137 | 6.1944 | 5.6603 | 5.1971 |
| 13 | 9.6829 | 9.3936 | 8.8527 | 8.3577 | 7.9038 | 7.4869 | 7.1034 | 6.4236 | 5.8424 | 5.3423 |
| 14 | 10.2228 | 9.8986 | 9.2950 | 8.7455 | 8.2442 | 7.7862 | 7.3667 | 6.6282 | 6.0021 | 5.4675 |
| 15 | 10.7395 | 10.3797 | 9.7123 | 9.1079 | 8.5595 | 8.0607 | 7.6061 | 6.8109 | 6.1422 | 5.5755 |
| 16 | 11.2340 | 10.8378 | 10.1059 | 9.4467 | 8.8514 | 8.3126 | 7.8237 | 6.9740 | 6.2651 | 5.6685 |
| 17 | 11.7072 | 11.2741 | 10.4773 | 9.7632 | 9.1216 | 8.5436 | 8.0216 | 7.1196 | 6.3729 | 5.7487 |
| 18 | 12.1600 | 11.6896 | 10.8276 | 10.0591 | 9.3719 | 8.7556 | 8.2014 | 7.2497 | 6.4674 | 5.8179 |
| 19 | 12.5933 | 12.0853 | 11.1581 | 10.3356 | 9.6036 | 8.9501 | 8.3649 | 7.3658 | 6.5504 | 5.8775 |
| 20 | 13.0079 | 12.4622 | 11.4699 | 10.5940 | 9.8182 | 9.1286 | 8.5136 | 7.4694 | 6.6231 | 5.9288 |

A table such as Table 12–2 is used to determine the present value of a series of equal amounts to be received at periodic intervals. For example, what is the present value of a series of ten $1,000 amounts, with one $1,000 amount to be received at the end of each of 10 successive years, discounted at 8%? To determine the answer, look down the 8% column to the amount opposite 10 periods (years in this case). It is 6.7101, and $6.7101 is the present value of $1 to be received annually at the end of each of 10 years, discounted at 8%. Therefore, the present value of the ten $1,000 amounts is $1,000 × 6.7101, or $6,710.10.

## Interest Periods Less than One Year in Length

In the examples so far, the interest rates were applied to time periods that were one year in length. However, interest often is applied to time periods that are shorter than one year. For instance, although interest rates on corporate bonds are usually quoted on an annual basis, the interest on such bonds is normally paid semiannually. As a result, the present value of the interest to be received on such bonds must be based on interest periods that are six months in length.

To illustrate a calculation based on six-month interest periods, assume an investor wants to know the present value of the interest that will be received over a period of five years on some corporation bonds. The bonds have a $10,000 par value, and interest is paid on them every six months at a 14% annual rate. Although the interest rate is stated as an annual rate of 14%, it is actually a rate of 7% per six-month interest period. Therefore, the investor will

## AS A MATTER OF FACT

It is said that accounting, like law, is a profession that has a rule for every situation. If that's true, then why don't accountants have a consistent standard for when, and under what circumstances, to use one of the most fundamental measurements of finance itself—the time value of money?

As anyone who has bought a bank CD knows, the yield on an investment is basically a function of how much money is invested at what rate of return for how long. In theory, both assets and liabilities of corporations can be measured in the same way. For liabilities: How much money would be needed today to pay for an obligation that does not come due for 5 or 10 years—future health obligations of not-yet-retired workers, say, or the projected pension liabilities of a firm 10 or 20 years in the future? For assets: What is the "present value" of a financial asset—a mortgage, say, or a corporate bond—that is due to mature in the year 2013? In both cases, the solution comes from taking the future value or cost of the asset or liability in question, then using an assumed rate of interest over the period of time involved to "discount" it back to its present value.

Unfortunately, the accountants, who actually prepare financial reports have few—and often highly inconsistent—rules for when and how to make those calculations in preparing balance sheets. "Financial statements are becoming irrelevant to business decision making," complains G. Michael Crooch, partner at Arthur Andersen. "We are not measuring items according to their economic value because we're ignoring the time value of money."

Now at last the Financial Accounting Standards Board seems willing to face the problem, by adding a discounting project to its agenda. New rules are years away, but they eventually could have a dramatic effect on corporate financials. Depending upon what FASB finally decides, present value accounting could be used for virtually any transaction that involves a long delay before final settlement. Potential targets for discounting include impaired assets, product and manufacturers' warranties, and loss reserves for property-casualty insurers.

Present value accounting could in some ways be quite a boon to corporations, by reducing the liability side of their balance sheets. How? By recognizing that $1 million payable in 1994 is not as effectively large a liability as $1 million payable in 1989. That's common sense. If you were to take $600,000 and invest it at a relatively modest 10%, it would equal $1 million by the time the liability would need to be paid. Thus the effective liability is not $1 million but $600,000.

* * * * *

In a few cases, present value accounting is already required by FASB. Under a new FASB statement regarding pension accounting, General Electric in 1987 reported only a $15.5 billion liability based on an 8.5% rate of return; without discounting for present value, the liability would have been much greater.

* * * * *

Source: Penelope Wang, "Time is money." Excerpted by permission of *Forbes* magazine, January 9, 1989, p. 300. © Forbes Inc., 1989.

receive $10,000 × 7%, or $700 in interest on these bonds at the end of each six-month interest period. In five years, there are 10 such periods. Therefore, if these 10 receipts of $700 each are discounted at the interest rate of the bonds, to determine their present value, look down the 7% column of Table 12–2 to the amount opposite 10 periods. It is 7.0236, and the present value of the ten $700 semiannual receipts is 7.0236 × $700, or $4,916.52.

*For a more complete discussion of discounting, you should turn to Appendix G at the end of the book. Appendix G expands the discussion of how present value tables are developed and explains the development of future value tables. Large present value and future value tables are included in the appendix, which also has numerous exercises related to discounting.*

## Exchanging a Note for a Plant Asset

When a high-cost asset is purchased, particularly if the credit period is long, a note is sometimes given in exchange for the purchased asset. If the amount of the note is approximately equal to the cash price for the asset and the stated interest rate on the note is approximately the prevailing market rate, the transaction is recorded as follows:

| | | | | |
|---|---|---|---|---|
| Feb. | 12 | Store Equipment | 4,500.00 | |
| | | Notes Payable | | 4,500.00 |
| | | Exchanged a $4,500, three-year, 16% note payable for a refrigerated display case. | | |

A note given in exchange for a plant asset has two elements, which may or may not be stipulated in the note. They are (1) a dollar amount equivalent to the bargained cash price of the asset, and (2) an interest factor to compensate the supplier for the use of the funds that otherwise would have been received in a cash sale. Therefore, when a note is exchanged for a plant asset and the face amount of the note approximately equals the cash price of the asset and the note's interest rate approximates the prevailing market rate, the asset is recorded at the face amount of the note as in the previous illustration.

## Notes that Have an Unreasonable or No Stated Interest Rate

Sometimes no interest rate is stated on a note, or the stated interest rate does not approximate a prevailing market rate. In such cases, the face amount of the note will not be equal to the cash price for the asset. Nevertheless, the asset must be recorded at its cash price or at the present value of the note, whichever is more clearly determinable.[3] To record the asset at the face amount of the note would misstate the asset, liability, and interest expense. Furthermore, these misstatements may be material, especially in case of a long-term note.

To illustrate a situation in which a note with no stated interest rate is exchanged for a plant asset, assume that on January 2, 1991, a noninterest-bearing, five-year, $10,000 note payable is exchanged for a factory machine. Also assume that the cash price of the asset is not readily determinable. If the prevailing market rate of interest on the day of the exchange is 14%, the present value of the note on that day is $5,194. This amount may be calculated by multiplying the face amount of the note by the fifth amount in the 14% column of Table 12–1 ($10,000 × 0.5194 = $5,194). The exchange should be recorded as follows:

| | | | | |
|---|---|---|---|---|
| 1991 | | | | |
| Jan. | 2 | Factory Machinery | 5,194.00 | |
| | | Discount on Notes Payable | 4,806.00 | |
| | | Long-Term Notes Payable | | 10,000.00 |
| | | Exchanged a five-year, noninterest-bearing note for a machine. | | |

[3] Ibid., sec. I69.105. First published as *APB Opinion No. 21*, par. 12.

Illustration 12–2
**Amortization schedule for a five-year, $10,000 note payable, discounted at 14%**

| Year | (a) Face Amount of Note | (b) Unamortized Discount at Beginning of Year | (c) Beginning-of-Year Carrying Amount (a) − (b) | (d) Discount to Be Amortized Each Year (c) × 14% | (e) Unamortized Discount at the End of Year (b) − (d) | (f) End-of-Year Carrying Amount (a) − (e) |
|---|---|---|---|---|---|---|
| 1991 . . . . | $10,000 | $4,806 | $5,194 | $ 727 | $4,079 | $ 5,921 |
| 1992 . . . . | 10,000 | 4,079 | 5,921 | 829 | 3,250 | 6,750 |
| 1993 . . . . | 10,000 | 3,250 | 6,750 | 945 | 2,305 | 7,695 |
| 1994 . . . . | 10,000 | 2,305 | 7,695 | 1,077 | 1,228 | 8,772 |
| 1995 . . . . | 10,000 | 1,228 | 8,772 | 1,228 | −0− | 10,000 |

The $5,194 debit amount in the entry is the present value of the note on the day of the exchange. It is also the cost of the machine and is the amount you must use to calculate depreciation. In the entry, the debit to Discount on Notes Payable and credit to Long-Term Notes Payable together measure the liability that resulted from the transaction. They should appear on a balance sheet prepared immediately after the exchange as follows:

| | | |
|---|---|---|
| Long-term liabilities: | | |
| Long-term notes payable . . . . . . . . . . . . . . . . . . . | $10,000 | |
| Less unamortized discount based on the 14% interest rate prevailing on the date of issue. . . . . . . . . . . . | 4,806 | $5,194 |

### Amortizing the Discount on a Note Payable

The $4,806 discount is a contra liability and is also the interest element of the transaction. Column 3 of Illustration 12–2 shows those parts of the $4,806 that should be amortized and charged to Interest Expense at the end of each of the five years in the life of the note.

The first year's amortization entry is:

| | | | | |
|---|---|---|---|---|
| 1991 Dec. | 31 | Interest Expense. . . . . . . . . . . . . . . . . . . . . . . . | 727.00 | |
| | | Discount on Notes Payable . . . . . . . . . . . . . . . | | 727.00 |
| | | To amortize a portion of the discount on our long-term note. | | |

The $727 amortized is interest at 14% on the note's $5,194 value on the day it was exchanged for the machine. The $727 is rounded to the nearest whole dollar, as are all amounts in Illustration 12–2.

Posting the amortization entry causes the note to appear on the December 31, 1991, balance sheet as follows:

| | | |
|---|---|---|
| Long-term liabilities: | | |
| Long-term notes payable . . . . . . . . . . . . . | $10,000 | |
| Less unamortized discount on the 14% interest rate prevailing on the date of issue . . . . . . | 4,079 | $5,921 |

Compare the net amount at which the note is carried on the December 31, 1991, balance sheet with the net amount shown for the note on the balance sheet prepared on its date of issue. Observe that the **carrying amount of the note** increased $727 between the two dates. (The $727 is the amount of discount amortized and charged to Interest Expense at the end of 1991.)

At the end of 1992 and each succeeding year, the remaining amounts of discount shown in Column (*d*) of Illustration 12–2 should be amortized and charged to Interest Expense. This will cause the carrying amount of the note to increase each year by the amount of discount amortized that year and to reach $10,000, the note's maturity value, at the end of the fifth year. Payment of the note will be recorded as follows:

| | | | | |
|---|---|---|---|---|
| 1996 | | | | |
| Jan. | 2 | Long-Term Notes Payable . . . . . . . . . . . . . . . . . . | 10,000.00 | |
| | | Cash . . . . . . . . . . . . . . . . . . . . . . . . . . . . . | | 10,000.00 |
| | | Paid our long-term noninterest-bearing note. | | |

Look again at Illustration 12–2. Each end-of-year carrying amount in Column (*f*) is determined by subtracting the end-of-year unamortized discount in Column (*e*) from the $10,000 face amount of the note. For example, $10,000 − $4,079 = $5,921. Each beginning-of-year carrying amount is the same as the previous end-of-year amount. In Column (*d*), the amount of discount to be amortized each year is determined by multiplying the beginning-of-year carrying amount in Column (*c*) by the 14% interest rate prevailing at the time of the exchange. For example, $5,921 × 14% = $829 (rounded). Each end-of-year amount of unamortized discount in Column (*e*) is the discount remaining after subtracting the discount amortized that year. For example, $4,806 − $727 = $4,079.

In the balance sheet at the end of each year, the carrying amount of a note payable must be divided into two parts. The portion to be paid during the next year must be shown as a current liability, with the remaining portion shown as a long-term liability.

## Liabilities from Leasing

Prepare entries to account for long-term noninterest-bearing notes payable and for capital and operating leases.
(L. O. 6)

### How to Classify Leases

In recent years, many businesses have chosen to lease plant assets rather than purchase them. By leasing instead of purchasing, a business avoids the immediate cash outflow to pay for the asset. Instead, a lease typically requires a series of payments to be made over the life of the lease.

Although leases require a series of future payments, some leases, which are called **operating leases**, are not recorded as liabilities. In general, the terms of operating leases are such that the lessee does not acquire an ownership interest in the leased property. Because some leases are not recorded as liabilities and therefore do not appear on the balance sheet, leasing is sometimes said to be a form of off-balance sheet financing.

While operating leases generally do not give the lessee the benefits of ownership, other leases have essentially the same economic consequences as if the lessee secured a loan and purchased the leased asset. Such leases are called **capital leases** or **financing leases.** When an asset is leased under a capital lease, the lessee records the asset as if it has been purchased and also records a liability equal to the present value of the future lease payments.

According to the FASB's rules, a lease that meets any one of the following criteria is a capital lease.[4]

1. Ownership of the leased asset is transferred to the lessee at the end of the lease period.
2. The lease gives the lessee the option of purchasing the leased asset at less than fair value at some point during or at the end of the lease period.
3. The period of the lease is 75% or more of the estimated service life of the leased asset.
4. The present value of the minimum lease payments is 90% or more of the fair value of the leased asset.

A lease that does not meet any one of the four criteria is classified as an operating lease.

To illustrate accounting for leases, assume that Alpha Company plans to produce a product that requires the use of a new machine that costs approximately $35,000 and has an estimated 10-year life with no salvage value. Alpha Company does not have $35,000 in available cash and plans to lease the machine as of December 31, 1990. It will lease the machine under one of the following contracts, each of which requires Alpha Company to pay maintenance, taxes, and insurance on the machine: (1) Lease the machine for five years, with annual payments of $7,500 payable at the end of each of the five years. The machine will be returned to the lessor at the end of the lease period. (2) Lease the machine for five years, with annual payments of $10,000 payable at the end of each of the five years. The machine will become the property of Alpha Company at the end of the lease period.

### Accounting for an Operating Lease

The first lease contract does not meet any of the first three criteria of a capital lease. Also, assuming the interest rate available to Alpha Company is 16%, the present value of the lease payments is $7,500 × 3.2743 = $24,557.25, which is less than 90% of $35,000. Therefore, the lease does not meet the fourth criterion of a capital lease. Since the lease does not meet any of the criteria, it must be classified as an operating lease.

---

[4] Ibid., sec. L10.103. First published as *FASB Statement No. 13*, par. 7. Copyright © by the Financial Accounting Standards Board, Norwalk, Conn. 06856, U.S.A. Quoted (or excerpted) with permission. Copies of the complete document are available from the FASB.

If Alpha Company chooses this contract, it should make no entry to record the lease contract. However, each annual rental payment should be recorded as follows:

| | | | | |
|---|---|---|---|---|
| 1991 | | | | |
| Dec. | 31 | Machinery Rentals Expense . . . . . . . . . . . . . . . . . . | 7,500.00 | |
| | | Cash . . . . . . . . . . . . . . . . . . . . . . . . . . . . . | | 7,500.00 |
| | | Paid the annual rent on a leased machine. | | |

Alpha Company should also charge to expense all payments for taxes, insurance, and any repairs to the machine. But, since the leased machine is not recorded as an asset, depreciation expense is not recorded. In addition, Alpha should add a footnote to its income statement that gives a general description of the leasing arrangements.

### Accounting for a Capital Lease

The second lease contract meets the first and fourth criteria of the FASB and is a capital lease. In effect, it is a purchase transaction with the lessor company financing the purchase of the machine for Alpha Company. Therefore, the FASB ruled that the asset and the lease liability should be recorded on the lease date at the present value of the lease payments.

**Recording the Lease Liability.** If Alpha Company chooses the second lease contract and the interest rate available to Alpha on such contracts is 16% annually, it should (based on the fifth amount in the 16% column of Table 12–2) multiply $10,000 by 3.2743 to get a $32,743 present value for the five lease payments. Alpha should then make this entry:

| | | | | |
|---|---|---|---|---|
| 1990 | | | | |
| Dec. | 31 | Machinery . . . . . . . . . . . . . . . . . . . . . . . . . . | 32,743.00 | |
| | | Discount on Lease Financing . . . . . . . . . . . . . . . . | 17,257.00 | |
| | | Long-Term Lease Liability . . . . . . . . . . . . . . . . | | 50,000.00 |
| | | Purchased a machine through a long-term lease contract. | | |

The $32,743 is the cost of the machine. As with any plant asset, it should be charged off to depreciation expense over the machine's expected service life. Note, however, that the expected service life of a leased asset may be limited to the term of the lease. If the lessee does not have the right to ownership at the end of the lease and the lease period is less than the asset's expected life, the lease period becomes the useful life of the asset.

**Reporting a Long-Term Lease Liability on the Balance Sheet.** The $17,257 discount is the interest factor in the transaction. The long-term lease liability less the amount of the discount measures the net liability that results from the pur-

**Illustration 12–3**
**Amortization schedule for a lease liability**

| Year | Beginning-of-Year Lease Liability | Beginning-of-Year Unamortized Discount | Beginning-of-Year Carrying Amount | Discount to Be Amortized (16%) | Unamortized Discount at End of Year | End-of-Year Lease Liability | End-of-Year Carrying Amount |
|---|---|---|---|---|---|---|---|
| 1991 . . . . | $50,000 | $17,257 | $32,743 | $5,239 | $12,018 | $40,000 | $27,982 |
| 1992 . . . . | 40,000 | 12,018 | 27,982 | 4,477 | 7,541 | 30,000 | 22,459 |
| 1993 . . . . | 30,000 | 7,541 | 22,459 | 3,593 | 3,948 | 20,000 | 16,052 |
| 1994 . . . . | 20,000 | 3,948 | 16,052 | 2,568 | 1,380 | 10,000 | 8,620 |
| 1995 . . . . | 10,000 | 1,380 | 8,620 | 1,380* | –0– | –0– | –0– |

*Adjusted for rounding.

chase. The two items should appear on a balance sheet prepared immediately after the transaction as follows:

| | | |
|---|---|---|
| Long-term liabilities: | | |
| Long-term lease liability[5] . . . . . . . . . . . . . . . . . . . | $50,000 | |
| Less unamortized discount based on the 16% interest rate available on the date of the contract . . . . . . . | 17,257 | $32,743 |

**Entries to Record Depreciation, Lease Payments, and Interest.** If Alpha Company plans to depreciate the machine on a straight-line basis over its 10-year life, it should make the following entries at the end of the first year in the life of the lease:

| | | | | |
|---|---|---|---|---|
| 1991 | | | | |
| Dec. | 31 | Depreciation Expense, Machinery . . . . . . . . . . . . . . | 3,274.30 | |
| | | Accumulated Depreciation, Machinery. . . . . . . . . . | | 3,274.30 |
| | | To record depreciation on the machine. | | |
| | 31 | Long-Term Lease Liability. . . . . . . . . . . . . . . . . . . | 10,000.00 | |
| | | Cash . . . . . . . . . . . . . . . . . . . . . . . . . . . | | 10,000.00 |
| | | Made the annual payment on the lease. | | |
| | 31 | Interest Expense. . . . . . . . . . . . . . . . . . . . . . . . | 5,239.00 | |
| | | Discount on Lease Financing . . . . . . . . . . . . . . | | 5,239.00 |
| | | Amortized a portion of the discount on the lease financing. | | |

The first two entries need no comment. The $5,239 amortized in the third entry is interest at 16% for one year on the $32,743 beginning-of-year carrying amount of the lease liability ($\$32,743 \times 16\% = \$5,239$). The $5,239 is rounded to the nearest whole dollar, as are all amounts in Illustration 12–3.

[5] To simplify the illustration, the fact that the first installment on the lease should be classified as a current liability is ignored here and should be ignored in the problems at the end of the chapter.

Posting the entries that record the $10,000 payment and the amortization of the discount causes the **carrying amount of the lease** to appear on the December 31, 1991, balance sheet as follows:

| | | |
|---|---|---|
| Long-term liabilities: | | |
| Long-term lease liability . . . . . . . . . . . . . . . . . . . . | $40,000 | |
| Less unamortized discount based on the 16% interest rate prevailing on the date of the contract . . . . . . . | 12,018 | $27,982 |

At the end of 1992 and each succeeding year, the remaining amounts in Column 5 of Illustration 12–3 should be amortized. This, together with $10,000 annual payments, will reduce the carrying amount of the lease liability to zero by the end of the fifth year.

Return again to Illustration 12–3. To determine the amount of discount to be amortized each year, the beginning-of-year carrying amount of the lease liability was multiplied by 16%. For example, the 1992 amount to be amortized is $4,477 ($27,982 × 16% = $4,477 rounded). Each end-of-year carrying amount was determined by subtracting the end-of-year unamortized discount from the remaining end-of-year lease liability. For example, the December 31, 1992, carrying amount is $30,000 − $7,541 = $22,459.

## Summary of Chapter in Terms of Learning Objectives

**1.** Current liabilities are due within one year of the balance sheet date or within one operating cycle, whichever is longer. The liquidation of current liabilities requires the use of existing assets or the creation of other current liabilities. Long-term liabilities do not have to be paid within one year or one operating cycle.

**2.** A liability is definite when you know the answer to all three of these questions: (*a*) Who will be paid? (*b*) When is payment due? (*c*) How much will be paid? When the amount to be paid is not precisely known, the obligation is called an estimated liability.

**3.** Expenses for property taxes and product warranties often must be recorded before the amounts to be paid are known. Therefore, you must estimate the amounts of the liabilities based on the information currently available. After more information becomes available, the liabilities are corrected with corresponding adjustments to expense. Short-term notes payable are recorded at their face amounts when the stated interest rates of the notes are reasonable approximations of current market rates of interest. When the notes are not interest bearing or the stated rates of interest do not reflect the current market rate, the notes are recorded at their present values.

**4.** An obligation that qualifies as a liability generally does not depend on a future, uncertain event. In contrast, when an economic entity is obligated to make a future payment only if some future event takes place, the potential obligation is called a contingent liability. However, if the future event is probable and the amount of the payment can be reasonably estimated, the obligation qualifies as a liability.

**5.** The present value of an amount to be received or paid in the future is the amount that could be currently invested at the given rate of interest and would accumulate a total value equal to the amount to be received or paid. The present value of a series of equal payments is the sum of the present values of each payment.

**6.** A long-term, noninterest-bearing note must be recorded at its present value. Each period during the life of the note, interest expense is calculated by multiplying the carrying value of the note by the interest rate that was used to discount the note. With a capital lease, you must record the leased asset and the lease liability at the present value of the lease payments. On the other hand, you debit the periodic payments of an operating lease to Rent Expense as they are incurred.

## Demonstration Problem

Prepare journal entries for the 1990 transactions of Kearns Company listed below.

*a.* Kearns accrued estimated property taxes during the first eight months of 1990 at the rate of $20,000 per month. On September 10, Kearns learned that the 1990 tax bill would be $217,200. The due date for these taxes is December 31. Show the property tax entries on September 30 and October 31.

*b.* During September, Kearns sold $140,000 of merchandise under a 180-day warranty. Prior experience shows that the costs of fulfilling the warranty will equal 5% of the selling price. Record the month's warranty expense and liability as a September 30 adjusting entry. Also record an October 8 expenditure of $300 to service an item sold in September.

*c.* On October 10, Kearns arranged with a supplier to pay 25% of Kearns' overdue $10,000 account payable to the supplier. The remaining balance was converted to a $7,500, 90-day note bearing 12% interest.

*d.* On October 15, Kearns borrowed $98,333 by discounting its $100,000, 60-day note to the bank. The discount rate charged by the bank was 10%.

*e.* On December 1, Kearns acquired a machine by giving a $60,000, noninterest-bearing note due in one year. The rate of interest available to Kearns for this type of debt was 12%.

*f.* On December 14, Kearns paid the note described in (*d*).

*g.* On December 31, Kearns accrued the interest on the notes described in (*c*) and (*e*). Show separate adjusting entries, assuming a 360-day year.

In addition to the above transactions, Kearns entered into a three-year lease of machinery on January 1, 1990, and agreed to make three payments on December 31, 1990, 1991, and 1992. Each payment will be $30,158, which will include 10% interest. Title to the machinery will pass to Kearns at the end of the lease, and the lease should be recorded as a capital lease.

*h.* Show the entry to record the lease.

*i.* Prepare a table that shows the interest expense in each year of the lease.

*j.* Show the entries to record the first payment on December 31, 1990, the interest expense for 1990, and the depreciation expense for 1990. The machine's useful life is predicted to be five years, with no salvage value, and straight-line depreciation is used.

*k.* Show how the leased asset and lease liability would appear on the balance sheet as of December 31, 1990.

## Solution to Demonstration Problem

| | | | | | |
|---|---|---|---|---|---|
| *a.* | Sept. | 30 | Property Tax Expense | 2,900.00 | |
| | | | Estimated Property Taxes Payable | | 2,900.00 |

| | |
|---|---|
| Liability on September 30 ($217,200 × 9/12) | $162,900 |
| Recorded liability as of August 31 ($20,000 × 8) | 160,000 |
| Additional liability to record on September 30 | $ 2,900 |

| | | | | | |
|---|---|---|---|---|---|
| | Oct. | 31 | Property Tax Expense | 18,100.00 | |
| | | | Estimated Property Taxes Payable | | 18,100.00 |
| | | | $217,200 ÷ 12 = $18,100. | | |
| *b.* | Sept. | 30 | Warranty Expense | 7,000.00 | |
| | | | Estimated Warranty Liability | | 7,000.00 |
| | | | $140,000 × 5% = $7,000. | | |
| | Oct. | 8 | Estimated Warranty Liability | 300.00 | |
| | | | Cash | | 300.00 |
| *c.* | | 10 | Accounts Payable | 10,000.00 | |
| | | | Cash | | 2,500.00 |
| | | | Notes Payable | | 7,500.00 |
| *d.* | | 15 | Cash | 98,333.00 | |
| | | | Interest Expense | 1,667.00 | |
| | | | Notes Payable | | 100,000.00 |
| *e.* | Dec. | 1 | Machine | 53,574.00 | |
| | | | Discount on Notes Payable | 6,426.00 | |
| | | | Notes Payable | | 60,000.00 |
| | | | $60,000 × .8929 = $53,574. | | |
| *f.* | | 14 | Notes Payable | 100,000.00 | |
| | | | Cash | | 100,000.00 |
| *g.* | | | For the Note in *(c)* | | |
| | | 31 | Interest Expense | 205.00 | |
| | | | Interest Payable | | 205.00 |
| | | | $7,500 × 12% × 82/360 = $205. | | |
| | | | For the Note in *(e)* | | |
| | | 31 | Interest Expense | 535.74 | |
| | | | Discount on Notes Payable | | 535.74 |
| | | | $53,574 × 12% × 30/360 = $535.74. | | |

*h.*

| | | | | |
|---|---|---|---|---|
| Dec. | 31 | Machinery | 75,000.00 | |
| | | Discount on Lease Financing | 15,474.00 | |
| | | Long-Term Lease Liability | | 90,474.00 |
| | | Present value is:<br>$30,158 × 2.4869 = $75,000 (rounded).<br>$30,158 × 3 = $90,474. | | |

*i.*

| Year | Beginning-of-Year Lease Liability | Beginning-of-Year Unamortized Discount | Beginning-of-Year Carrying Amount | Discount to Be Amortized | Unamortized Discount at End of Year | End-of-Year Lease Liability | End-of-Year Carrying Amount |
|---|---|---|---|---|---|---|---|
| 1990 | $90,474 | $15,474 | $75,000 | $7,500 | $7,974 | $60,316 | $52,342 |
| 1991 | 60,316 | 7,974 | 52,342 | 5,234 | 2,740 | 30,158 | 27,418 |
| 1992 | 30,158 | 2,740 | 27,418 | 2,740* | –0– | –0– | –0– |

*Adjusted for rounding.

*j.*

| | | | | |
|---|---|---|---|---|
| Dec. | 31 | Long-Term Lease Liability | 30,158.00 | |
| | | Cash | | 30,158.00 |
| | 31 | Interest Expense | 7,500.00 | |
| | | Discount on Lease Financing | | 7,500.00 |
| | 31 | Depreciation Expense | 15,000.00 | |
| | | Accumulated Depreciation | | 15,000.00 |
| | | $75,000 ÷ 5 = $15,000. | | |

*k.*

| | | |
|---|---|---|
| Long-term liabilities: | | |
| Long-term lease liability | $60,316 | |
| Less unamortized discount based on the 10% interest rate available on the date of the contract | 7,974 | $52,342 |

## Glossary

Define or explain the words and phrases listed in the chapter Glossary. (L. O. 7)

**Bank discount** interest charged and deducted by a bank at the time a loan is made. p. 508

**Capital lease** a lease that meets any of four criteria established by the FASB, the implication of which is that the lease has essentially the same economic consequences as if the lessee had secured a loan and purchased the leased asset. p. 519

**Carrying amount of a lease** the remaining lease liability minus the unamortized discount on the lease financing. p. 522

**Carrying amount of a note** the face amount of a note minus the unamortized discount on the note. p. 518

**Estimated liability** an obligation that definitely exists but for which the amount to be paid is uncertain. p. 504

**Financing lease** another name for a capital lease. p. 519

**Long-term liabilities** obligations that will not require the use of existing current assets in their liquidation because they do not mature within one year or one operating cycle, whichever is longer. p. 503

**Operating lease** a lease that does not meet any of the criteria of the FASB that would make it a capital lease. pp. 518–519

**Present value** the amount of money that could be currently invested at a given interest rate to accumulate a total value equal to a given amount to be received or paid at some future date(s). p. 511

**Present value table** a table that shows the present values of one amount to be received at various future dates when discounted at various interest rates, or that shows the present values of a series of equal payments to be received for a varying number of periods when discounted at various interest rates. pp. 511–514

**Product warranty** a promise to a customer that obligates the seller or manufacturer for a limited period of time to pay for items such as replacement parts or repair costs if the product breaks or fails to perform. p. 505

## Objective Review

Answers to the following questions are listed in Appendix I at the end of the book. Be sure that you decide which is the one best answer to each question *before* you check the answers in the appendix.

1. Which of the following items normally would be classified as a current liability of a company that has a 15-month current operating cycle?
   *a.* Accounts payable due in 13 months.
   *b.* A note payable due in 11 months.
   *c.* Salaries payable.
   *d.* The portion of a long-term lease liability that is due within 15 months.
   *e.* All of the above.

2. Estimated liabilities include:
   *a.* Obligations to pay a specific amount on a specific date when the party to be paid is not known.
   *b.* Obligations to pay a specific amount to a specific person when the due date is not known.
   *c.* Obligations to pay a specific person on a specific date when the amount to be paid is uncertain but can be reasonably estimated.
   *d.* Obligations to pay an amount to an outside party if some uncertain future event occurs.
   *e.* All of the above.
3. A company issued a $12,000, 120-day, noninterest-bearing note by discounting the note at 16% on December 1, 1991. What amount of discount on notes payable should be reported on the December 31, 1991, balance sheet?
   *a.* $1,920.
   *b.* $ 640.
   *c.* $ 480.
   *d.* $ 160.
   *e.* $ –0–.
4. A future payment should be reported on the balance sheet as a liability if:
   *a.* The payment is contingent on a future event that is probable and the amount of the payment is certain.
   *b.* The payment is contingent on a future event that is not probable but the amount of the payment can be reasonably estimated.
   *c.* The payment is contingent on a future event that is probable but the amount of the payment cannot be reasonably estimated.
   *d.* The payment is contingent on a future event that is probable and the amount of the payment can be reasonably estimated.
   *e.* Both (*a*) and (*d*) are correct.
5. A company enters into an agreement whereby the company will make three semiannual payments of $500 each, the first to be made in 6 months, plus an additional $10,000 payment to be made 18 months from now. If the annual rate of interest is 12%, the present value of these payments is:
   *a.* $ 8,318.90.
   *b.* $ 9,732.50.
   *c.* $11,500.00.
   *d.* $12,097.49.
   *e.* $14,257.07.
6. On December 31, 1990, Jacks Company leased for 18 years a building with a fair value of $1,000,000 and an estimated useful life of 25 years. Annual lease payments of $125,522.44 begin on December 31, 1991, and the prevailing interest rate available to Jacks Company was 12%. Which of the following expenses will be recognized on this lease during 1991?
   *a.* Rental expense, $125,522.44.
   *b.* Interest expense, $109,200.00.

*c.* Interest expense, $120,000.00.
*d.* Rental expense, $55,555.56.
*e.* Interest expense, $5,000.00.

## Questions for Class Discussion

1. What is a liability?
2. Are all expected future payments liabilities?
3. Define (*a*) a current liability and (*b*) a long-term liability.
4. If a liability is payable in 15 months, should it be classified as a current liability or as a long-term liability?
5. There are three important questions about which a liability may or may not be definite. What are those questions?
6. What is the nature of an estimated liability?
7. If a company has a definite obligation to pay a given amount of money to an outside party but the date the obligation must be paid is indefinite, should the obligation be reported as a liability on the balance sheet or disclosed as a contingent liability?
8. If a property tax liability is estimated at the end of year 1 and the actual payment of the liability in year 2 turns out to be more than the amount that was estimated, how is the excess accounted for in year 2?
9. What is the difference between a liability and a contingent liability?
10. Under what conditions should a contingency be reported on the balance sheet as a liability?
11. Why are product warranties often recorded as liabilities instead of being disclosed as contingent liabilities?
12. The legal position of a company may be improved by its acceptance of a promissory note in exchange for granting a time extension on the due date of a customer's debt. Why?
13. What is the difference between a loan and a discount as those terms relate to borrowing money from a bank?
14. Which is to the advantage of a bank: (*a*) making a loan to a customer in exchange for the customer's $1,000, 60-day, 9% note or (*b*) making a loan to the customer by discounting the customer's $1,000 noninterest-bearing note for 60 days at 9%? Why?
15. Distinguish between bank discount and cash discount.
16. What determines the present value of $1,000 to be received at some future date?
17. Is $1,000 to be received in one year always worth less than a series of two $500 payments to be received semiannually for the next year?
18. If a $5,000 noninterest-bearing, five-year note is exchanged for a machine, the face amount of the note equals the sum of two different economic costs. What are these two costs?
19. If the Machinery account is debited for $5,000 and Notes Payable is credited for $5,000 in recording the machine of Question 18, what effects will this have on the financial statements?

20. What is the advantage of leasing a plant asset instead of purchasing it?
21. Distinguish between a capital lease and an operating lease. Which causes an asset and a liability to appear on the balance sheet?
22. When a capital lease is to be recorded, how do you determine the amount to be debited to the asset account?

## Exercises

**Exercise 12–1**
**Property tax expense**
(L. O. 3)

Throughout 1991, K Company owned property that was subject to county property taxes and had an assessed valuation for tax purposes of $900,000. The 1990 tax levy was $0.60 per $100 of assessed valuation, and the company expected the 1990 rate to remain unchanged. In early June, the county announced that the 1991 tax levy would be $0.66 per $100 and that taxes would be due July 31, 1991. Prepare entries to record property tax expense for the months of May, June, and July (including the payment of the annual tax on July 31).

**Exercise 12–2**
**Product warranty expense**
(L. O. 3)

Fawn Company manufactures one product for $12 per unit and sells it for $20 per unit. In October, the company sold 150,000 units subject to a one-year warranty. According to the warranty, customers must pay a $2.25 service charge to return a broken unit and have it replaced by a new unit. When a unit under warranty fails, the company simply discards the broken unit and replaces it with a new one. Past experience suggests a 2% failure rate of new products sold, and customers actually returned 1,800 broken units during the month of October. Prepare summary entries for the month of October to record product warranty expense and to record the replacement of 1,800 broken units.

**Exercise 12–3**
**Short-term notes payable**
(L. O. 3)

On December 1, 1990, Blatz Company borrowed $150,000 by giving a 90-day, 12% note payable. The company has an annual, calendar-year accounting period and does not make reversing entries. Prepare general journal entries to record: (*a*) the issuance of the note, (*b*) the required year-end adjusting entry, and (*c*) the entry to pay the note.

**Exercise 12–4**
**Discounted notes payable**
(L. O. 3)

On December 1, 1990, Nozzle Company discounted its own $150,000, 90-day note payable at the bank. The discount rate was 12%. Prepare general journal entries to record: (*a*) the issuance of the note; (*b*) the required December 31, 1990, adjusting entry; (*c*) the payment of the note; and (*d*) the interest expense on the note during 1991.

**Exercise 12–5**
**Present value calculations**
(L. O. 5)

Present calculations to show the following: (*a*) the present value of $30,000 to be received nine years hence, discounted at 16%; (*b*) the total present value of three payments consisting of $35,000 to be received one year hence, $45,000 to be received two years hence, and $60,000 to be received three years hence, all discounted at 14%; and (*c*) the present value of seven payments of $9,000 each, with a payment to be received at the end of each of the next seven years, discounted at 12%.

**Exercise 12–6**
**Present value of investment**
(L. O. 5)

Smith Company is offered a contract whereby it will be paid $12,000 every 6 months for the next 10 years. The first payment would be received six months from today. What will the company be willing to pay for this contract if it expects a 14% annual return on the investment? What if it expects an annual return of only 10%?

**Exercise 12–7**
**Present value of investment**
(L. O. 5)

Titsch Company is offered a contract whereby it will be paid $24,000 annually for the next 10 years. The first payment would be received one year from today. What will the company be willing to pay for this contract if it expects a 14% return on the investment? What if it expects an annual return of only 10%?

**Exercise 12–8**
**Choosing between payment patterns based on present values**
(L. O. 5)

An individual has offered to sell a machine for $13,500. A potential buyer has agreed to purchase the machine for the stated price but, as an alternative, has given the seller the option of receiving 10 annual payments of $2,250 each, the first payment to be one year from now. Assuming the seller expects an annual return of at least 9%, which of the two alternatives should the seller accept?

**Exercise 12–9**
**Exchanging a noninterest-bearing note for a plant asset**
(L. O. 6)

Catter Company purchased equipment on January 1 of the current year. The terms of purchase included $21,000 cash plus a $35,000, noninterest-bearing, five-year note. The available interest rate on this date was 12%. (*a*) Prepare the entry to record the purchase of the machine. (*b*) Show how the liability will appear on a balance sheet prepared on the day of the purchase. (*c*) Prepare the entry to amortize a portion of the discount on the note at the end of its first year.

**Exercise 12–10**
**Liabilities from leasing**
(L. O. 6)

On December 31, 1990, a day when the available interest rate was 12%, Davis Company leased a machine for five years under a contract calling for a $45,000 annual lease payment at the end of each of the next five years, with the machine becoming the property of the lessee at the end of that period. The company decided to lease the machine. Prepare entries to record: (*a*) the leasing of the machine; (*b*) the amortization of the discount on the lease financing at December 31, 1991; and (*c*) the December 31, 1991, payment under the lease.

## Problems

**Problem 12–1**
**Product warranty expense and property tax expense**
(L. O. 2, 3)

**Part 1.** Collie Company sells a single product subject to a six-month warranty that covers replacement parts but not labor. The company uses a periodic inventory system to account for merchandise. Prepare journal entries to record the following transactions completed by the company during the month of April:

Apr. 2 Purchased 1,200 units of merchandise for $30 per unit, paying cash.
3 Purchased $3,900 of spare parts for making repairs to merchandise that is expected to be returned for warranty work.
8 Sold 500 units of merchandise for $60 per unit, receiving cash.
11 Repaired 30 units of merchandise that customers returned under the warranty. Replacement parts cost $750, and the customers paid $570 for labor.
18 Sold 600 units of merchandise for $65 per unit.
21 Repaired 22 units of merchandise under the product warranty. Replacement parts cost $506, and the customers paid $396 for labor.
29 Recorded warranty expense for April. Past experience shows that 4% of the units sold require warranty work, and the average cost of replacement parts is $24 per unit returned. Average labor charges are $18.50.

**Part 2.** Terrapin Company expects to accrue 1991 property taxes at the end of each month using the experience of 1990 as a means of estimating the tax. In January 1990, Terrapin's property was appraised at $900,000. The 1990 tax levy was $2.40 per $100. In January 1991, Terrapin's property was reappraised at $990,000. (The reappraisal was not expected to affect the tax levy of $2.40 per $100.) Early in June 1991, the annual tax levy was set at $2.80 per $100. On November 30, 1991, Terrapin paid the 1991 tax. Complete financial statements are prepared by the company on a monthly basis, and the company does not use reversing entries.

*Required*

Prepare entries at the end of January, June, November, and December 1991 to record property tax expense for each of those months and to record the annual tax payment.

**Problem 12–2**
**Journalizing notes payable transactions**
(L. O. 3)

Prepare general journal entries to record these transactions of Davies Company:

1990
Jan. 8 Purchased merchandise on credit from Grant Company, invoice dated January 7, terms 2/10, n/60, $15,600.
Feb. 5 Borrowed money at First State Bank by discounting our own $25,000 note payable for 60 days at 12%. Since the note matures before the end of the year, the discount should be charged to Interest Expense.
Mar. 10 Gave Grant Company $2,100 cash and a $13,500, 60-day, 12% note to secure an extension on our account that was due.
Apr. 5 Paid the note discounted at First State Bank on February 5.
May 10 Paid the note given Grant Company on March 10.
Nov. 1 Borrowed money at First State Bank by discounting our own $30,000 note payable for 90 days at 14%.
Dec. 16 Borrowed money at InterCity Bank by giving a $25,000, 60-day, 15% note payable.

Dec. 31 Made an adjusting entry to record interest on the November 1 note to First State Bank.

31 Made an adjusting entry to record the accrued interest on the December 16 note to InterCity Bank.

1991

Jan. 30 Paid the November 1 note to First State Bank. Also recorded interest expense related to the note.

Feb. 14 Paid the note given InterCity Bank on December 16.

**Problem 12–3**
**Present values of alternative payment patterns**
(L. O. 5)

Tropical Adventures is negotiating with a naval architect and shipyard in planning the construction of a 90-foot trimaran that Tropical Adventures expects to acquire and place in charter service. The yacht will be completed and ready for service four years hence. If Tropical Adventures pays for the yacht on completion (Payment Plan A), it will cost $500,500. However, two alternative payment plans are available. Plan B would require an immediate payment of $365,650. Plan C would require four annual payments of $105,850, the first of which would be made one year hence. In evaluating the three alternatives, the management of Tropical Adventures has decided to assume an interest rate of 10%.

*Required*

Calculate the present value of each payment and indicate which plan Tropical Adventures should follow.

**Problem 12–4**
**Exchanging a noninterest-bearing note for a plant asset**
(L. O. 6)

On January 2, 1990, a company gave its own $150,000 noninterest-bearing, five-year note payable in exchange for a machine the cash price of which was not readily determinable. The market rate for interest on such notes on the day of the exchange was 8% annually.

*Required*

*(Round all amounts in your answers to the nearest whole dollar.)*

1. Prepare a form with the following column headings and calculate and fill in the required amounts for the five years the note is outstanding.

| Year | Face Amount of Note | Unamortized Discount at Beginning of Year | Beginning-of-Year Carrying Amount | Discount to Be Amortized Each Year | Unamortized Discount at the End of Year | End-of-Year Carrying Amount |
|---|---|---|---|---|---|---|
| | | | | | | |

2. Prepare general journal entries to record: (*a*) the acquisition of the machine, (*b*) the discount amortized at the end of each year, and (*c*) the payment of the note on January 2, 1995.
3. Show how the note should appear on the December 31, 1992, balance sheet.

**Problem 12–5**
**Capital leases and exchanges of plant assets**
(L. O. 6)

Isden Production Company leased a machine on January 1, 1990, under a contract calling for annual payments of $48,000 on December 31 at the end of each of five years, with the machine becoming the property of the lessee company after the fifth $48,000 payment. The machine was estimated to have an eight-year life and no salvage value, and the interest rate available to Isden for equipment loans on the day the lease was signed was 14%. The machine was delivered on January 5, 1990, and was immediately placed in operation. At the beginning of the eighth year in the machine's life, it was overhauled at a $3,060 total cost. The overhaul was paid for on January 10, and it did not increase the machine's efficiency but it did add an additional year to its expected service life. On March 31, during the ninth year in the machine's life, it was traded in on a new machine of like purpose having a $144,000 cash price. A $12,000 trade-in allowance was received, and the balance was paid in cash.

*Required*
*(Round all amounts in your answers to the nearest whole dollar.)*

1. Prepare a schedule with the column headings of Illustration 12–3. Enter the years 1990 through 1994 in the first column and complete the schedule by filling in the proper amounts.
2. Prepare the entry to record the leasing of the machine.
3. Prepare December 31, 1991, entries to record annual depreciation on a straight-line basis, to record the lease payment, and to amortize the discount in the life of the lease. Also show how the machine and the lease liability should appear on the December 31, 1991, balance sheet.
4. Prepare the entries to record the machine's overhaul and the depreciation on the machine at the end of its eighth year.
5. Prepare the March 31, 1998, entries to record the exchange of the machines.

**Problem 12–6**
**Accounting for capital and operating leases**
(L. O. 6)

The Colossal Freight Company needs two new trucks, each of which has an estimated service life of nine years. The trucks could be purchased for $149,000 each, but Colossal does not have enough cash to pay for them. Instead, Colossal agrees to lease Truck 1 for six years, after which the truck remains the property of the lessor. In addition, Colossal agrees to lease Truck 2 for eight years, after which the truck remains the property of the lessor. According to the lease contracts, Colossal must pay $30,000 annually for each truck ($60,000 for two trucks), with the payments to be made at the end of each lease year. Both leases were signed on December 31, 1989, at which time the prevailing interest rate available to Colossal for equipment loans was 12%.

*Required*
*(Round all amounts in your answers to the nearest whole dollar.)*

1. Prepare any required entries to record the lease of *(a)* Truck 1 and *(b)* Truck 2.

2. Prepare the required entries as of the end of the first year in (*a*) the life of Truck 1 and (*b*) the life of Truck 2. Use straight-line depreciation. (Hint: If the length of a capital lease is less than the asset's estimated service life and the asset remains the property of the lessor, depreciation must be taken over the length of the lease.)
3. Truck 1 was returned to the lessor on December 31, 1995, the end of the sixth year. Prepare the required entries as of the end of the sixth year in (*a*) the life of Truck 1 and (*b*) the life of Truck 2.
4. Show how Truck 2 and the lease liability for the truck should appear on the balance sheet as of the end of the sixth year in the life of the lease (after the year-end lease payment).

## Alternate Problems

**Problem 12–1A**
**Product warranty expense and property tax expense**
(L. O. 2, 3)

**Part 1.** Saxon Company sells a single product subject to a one-year warranty that covers replacement parts but not labor. The company uses a periodic inventory system to account for merchandise. Prepare journal entries to record the following transactions completed by the company during the month of September:

| | | |
|---|---|---|
| Sept. | 1 | Purchased 4,500 units of merchandise for $85 per unit, paying cash. |
| | 2 | Purchased $45,600 of spare parts for making repairs to merchandise that is expected to be returned for warranty work. |
| | 5 | Sold 2,500 units of merchandise for $200 per unit, receiving cash. |
| | 10 | Repaired 90 units of merchandise that customers returned under the warranty. Replacement parts cost $5,670, and the customers paid $5,940 for labor. |
| | 17 | Sold 2,000 units of merchandise for $250 per unit. |
| | 22 | Repaired 55 units of merchandise under the product warranty. Replacement parts cost $3,355, and the customers paid $3,520 for labor. |
| | 30 | Recorded warranty expense for September. Past experience shows that 4% of the units sold require warranty work, and the average cost of replacement parts is $62 per unit returned. Average labor charges are $65. |

**Part 2.** Tidwell Company accrues property taxes at the end of each month and uses recent experience as a means of estimating the tax. In early 1990, Tidwell's property was appraised at $700,000. The 1990 tax levy was $1.30 per $100. In January 1991, Tidwell's property was reappraised at $780,000. (The reappraisal was not expected to affect the tax levy of $1.30 per $100.) Early in July 1991, the annual tax levy was set at $1.50 per $100. On October 31, 1991, Tidwell paid the 1990 tax. Complete financial statements are prepared by the company on a monthly basis, and the company does not use reversing entries.

*Required*

Prepare entries at the end of January, July, October, and November 1991 to record property tax expense for each of those months and to record the annual tax payment.

**Problem 12–2A**
**Journalizing notes payable transactions**
(L. O. 3)

Prepare general journal entries to record these transactions:

| | | |
|---|---|---|
| 1990 | | |
| Jan. | 27 | Purchased merchandise on credit,from Haller Company, invoice dated January 7, terms 2/10, n/60, $56,160. |
| Feb. | 18 | Borrowed money at City National Bank by discounting our own $75,000 note payable for 60 days at 12%. Since the note matures before the end of the year, the discount should be charged to Interest Expense. |
| Apr. | 4 | Gave Haller Company $5,160 cash and a $51,000, 60-day, 14% note to secure an extension on our past-due account. |
| | 19 | Paid the note discounted at City National Bank on February 18. |
| June | 3 | Paid the note given Haller Company on April 4. |
| Nov. | 16 | Borrowed money at City National Bank by discounting our own $90,000 note payable for 90 days at 13%. |
| Dec. | 1 | Borrowed money at First State Bank by giving a $60,000, 60-day, 12% note payable. |
| | 31 | Made an adjusting entry to record interest on the November 16 note to City National Bank. |
| | 31 | Made an adjusting entry to record the accrued interest on the December 1 note to First State Bank. |
| 1991 | | |
| Jan. | 30 | Paid the First State Bank note. Also, record interest expense. |
| Feb. | 14 | Paid the November 16 note to City National Bank. |

**Problem 12–3A**
**Present values of alternative payment patterns**
(L. O. 5)

Skylane Airways is negotiating with an airframe outfitter in planning the interior finishings of an eight-passenger turboprop that Skylane Airways expects to acquire and place in charter service. The airplane will be completed and ready for service four years hence. If Skylane pays for the airplane upon completion (Payment Plan A), it will cost $1,895,000. However, two alternative payment plans are available. Plan B would require an immediate payment of $1,422,750. Plan C would require four annual payments of $400,250, the first of which would be made one year hence. In evaluating the three alternatives, the management of Skylane has decided to assume an interest rate of 9%.

*Required*

Calculate the present value of each payment and indicate which plan Skylane should follow.

**Problem 12–4A**
**Exchanging a noninterest-bearing note for a plant asset**
(L. O. 6)

On January 1, 1990, Technic Company gave its own $500,000 noninterest-bearing, six-year note payable in exchange for a machine, the cash price of which was not readily determinable. The market rate for interest on such notes on the day of the exchange was 9% annually.

*Required*

*(Round all amounts in your answers to the nearest whole dollar.)*

1. Prepare a form with the following column headings and calculate and fill in the required amounts for the six years the note is outstanding.

| Year | Face Amount of Note | Unamortized Discount at Beginning of Year | Beginning-of-Year Carrying Amount | Discount to Be Amortized Each Year | Unamortized Discount at the End of Year | End-of-Year Carrying Amount |
|---|---|---|---|---|---|---|
| | | | | | | |

2. Prepare general journal entries to record: (*a*) the acquisition of the machine, (*b*) the discount amortized at the end of each of the first three years, and (*c*) the payment of the note on January 1, 1996.
3. Show how the note should appear on the December 31, 1992, balance sheet.

**Problem 12–5A**
**Capital leases and exchanges of plant assets**
(L. O. 6)

Edenroc Production Company leased a machine on January 2, 1990, under a contract calling for annual payments of $65,000 on December 31 at the end of each of five years, with the machine becoming the property of the lessee company after the fifth $65,000 payment. The machine was estimated to have a six-year life and no salvage value, and the interest rate available to Edenroc for equipment loans on the day the lease was signed was 14%. The machine was delivered on January 4, 1990, and was immediately placed in operation. At the beginning of the sixth year in the machine's life, it was overhauled at an $8,500 total cost. The overhaul was paid for on January 8, and it did not increase the machine's efficiency but it did add an additional two years to its expected service life. On April 30, during the eighth year in the machine's life, it was traded in on a new machine of like purpose having a $275,000 cash price. A $15,000 trade-in allowance was received, and the balance was paid in cash.

*Required*

*(Round all amounts in your answers to the nearest whole dollar.)*

1. Prepare a schedule with the column headings of Illustration 12–3. Enter the years 1990 through 1994 in the first column and complete the schedule by filling in the proper amounts.
2. Prepare the entry to record the leasing of the machine.
3. Prepare December 31, 1991, entries to record annual depreciation on a straight-line basis, to record the lease payment, and to amortize the discount on lease financing. Also show how the machine and the lease liability should appear on the December 31, 1991, balance sheet.
4. Prepare the entries to record the machine's overhaul and the depreciation on the machine at the end of its sixth year.
5. Prepare the April 30, 1997, entries to record the exchange of the machines.

**Problem 12–6A**
**Accounting for capital and operating leases**
(L. O. 6)

The Southwest News Company leased two new printing presses. Each of the presses has an estimated service life of seven years. Press 1 was leased for five years. Press 2 was leased for six years. Each lease agreement calls for $40,000 annual lease payments at the end of the year ($80,000 for both presses). When the period of each lease expires, each press will be returned to the lessor. Both leases were signed on December 31, 1989, at which time the prevailing interest rate available to Southwest News for equipment loans was 9%. Each of the presses could have been purchased for $180,000 cash.

*Required*

*(Round all amounts in your answers to the nearest whole dollar.)*

1. Prepare any required entries to record the lease of (*a*) Press 1 and (*b*) Press 2.
2. Prepare the required entries as of the end of the first year in (*a*) the life of Press 1 and (*b*) the life of Press 2. Use straight-line depreciation. (Hint: If the length of a capital lease is less than the asset's estimated service life and the asset remains the property of the lessor, depreciation must be taken over the length of the lease.)
3. Press 1 was returned to the lessor on December 31, 1994, the end of the fifth year. Prepare the required entries as of the end of the fifth year in (*a*) the life of Press 1 and (*b*) the life of Press 2.
4. Show how Press 2 and the lease liability for the press should appear on the balance sheet as of the end of the fifth year in the life of the lease (after the year-end lease payment).

## Provocative Problems

**Provocative Problem 12–1**
**H. J. Heinz Company**
(L. O. 4)

H. J. Heinz Company is a worldwide provider of processed food products and services. In the company's 1987 annual report, the footnotes to the financial statements included the following item:

> 8. Legal Matters
> Star-Kist Foods, Inc., a wholly-owned subsidiary of the company, and two other tuna canners, Ralston-Purina, Inc., and Castle & Cooke, Inc., are defendants in a suit brought by owners of 21 tuna fishing vessels which was originally filed in February, 1985 in the United States District Court for the Southern District of California in San Diego. The complaint alleges that the defendants have engaged in price fixing and other violations of federal antitrust laws in connection with the purchase of raw tuna from the plaintiffs. Plaintiffs have also asserted in the same litigation, state contract, tort and punitive damage claims. Star-Kist Foods has vigorously defended against this action and in November, 1985, filed its own antitrust and state law counterclaims against the plaintiffs. Most of the plaintiffs have settled with the defendants and settlement negotiations are in progress with the remaining plaintiffs. Management is of the opinion, based on facts presently available, that this action will finally be settled for an amount approximating the amount which has been reserved in the company's 1987 consolidated financial statements. This amount was not material to 1987 results.
> Courtesy of H. J. Heinz Company

Comment on the reasons why the management of H. J. Heinz Company decided to include the above statements among the footnotes to the company's financial statements. Since the legal action against the company had not been resolved when the financial statements were issued, what reasons would have led the company to accrue an expense in the 1987 income statement? Under what circumstances might the company have included a footnote such as the above but avoided reporting an expense on the 1987 income statement?

**Provocative Problem 12–2**
**Lettwinn Corporation**
(L. O. 6)

Lettwinn Corporation is planning to acquire some new equipment from Clifton Company and has asked you to assist in analyzing the situation. The equipment may be purchased for $415,000 and then will be leased by Lettwinn under a 10-year lease contract to a customer for $75,000 payable at the end of each year. After the lease expires, Lettwinn expects to sell the equipment for $115,000.

1. Suppose Lettwinn has $415,000 cash available to buy the equipment and requires a 14% rate of return on its investments. Should the company buy the equipment and lease it to the customer?
2. As an alternative to paying cash, Lettwinn can invest the $415,000 in other operations for five years and earn 14% annually on its investment. If this is done, the equipment may be purchased by signing a $750,000, five-year, noninterest-bearing note payable to Clifton Company. Should Lettwinn pay $415,000 now or sign the $750,000 note?
3. Now suppose Lettwinn does not have the option of signing a $750,000, five-year, noninterest-bearing note. Instead, the company may either pay $415,000 cash or lease the equipment from Clifton Company for eight years, after which the equipment would become the property of Lettwinn. The lease contract would require $93,750 payments at the end of each year. If Lettwinn leases the equipment, it will invest the $415,000 available cash in other operations and earn 14% on the investment. Should Lettwinn pay cash or lease the equipment from Clifton?

## COMPREHENSIVE PROBLEM

**Campbell Stoop Company**
(Review of Chapters 1–12)

Presented below is the December 31, 1990, unadjusted trial balance for the Campbell Stoop Company, which retails doors and related items. Some of these items are manufactured by other companies under patents created by Bill Campbell, the owner of the company. The company is the legal owner of the patents.

**CAMPBELL STOOP COMPANY**
**Unadjusted Trial Balance**
**December 31, 1990**

| | | |
|---|---|---|
| Cash | $ 6,360 | |
| Accounts receivable | 12,000 | |
| Allowance for doubtful accounts | | $ 860 |
| Merchandise inventory | 15,000 | |
| Equipment | 36,000 | |
| Accumulated depreciation, equipment | | 14,200 |
| Building | 75,000 | |
| Accumulated depreciation, building | | 27,000 |
| Patents | 17,500 | |
| Accounts payable | | 9,600 |
| Estimated warranty liability | | 3,900 |
| Interest payable | | –0– |
| Notes payable | | 40,000 |
| Bill Campbell, capital (December 31, 1989, balance) | | 49,623 |
| Bill Campbell, withdrawals | 4,000 | |
| Sales | | 137,500 |
| Interest earned | | 400 |
| Purchases | 70,000 | |
| Depreciation expense, equipment | –0– | |
| Depreciation expense, building | –0– | |
| Wages expense | 22,000 | |
| Bad debts expense | –0– | |
| Patent amortization expense | –0– | |
| Legal expense | 23,000 | |
| Warranty expense | –0– | |
| Interest expense | 2,023 | |
| Miscellaneous expenses | 200 | |
| Totals | $283,083 | $283,083 |

The following additional information is available:

*a.* The process of reconciling the bank statement of December 31, 1990, showed these items:

| | |
|---|---|
| Balance per bank | $5,700 |
| Balance per books | 6,360 |
| Outstanding checks | 725 |
| Deposit in transit | 1,000 |
| Interest earned | 40 |
| Service charges (miscellaneous expense) | 25 |
| Included with the bank statement was a canceled check the company had failed to record. The amount of the check, which was a payment of an account payable, can be determined from the above information | ? |

*b.* An examination of customers' accounts shows that accounts totaling $420 should be written off as uncollectible. In addition, the ending balance of the allowance account should be $990.

*c.* Two items of equipment (No. 3 and No. 5) were purchased two years ago and are being depreciated by the straight-line method. These facts are known about these assets:

| | No. 3 | No. 5 |
|---|---|---|
| Original cost | $20,000 | $16,000 |
| Expected salvage value | 3,600 | 1,000 |
| Useful life | 4 years | 5 years |

*d.* The building was acquired at the beginning of 1986 and is being depreciated under the sum-of-the-years'-digits method. These facts are also known:

| | |
|---|---|
| Original cost | $75,000 |
| Expected salvage value | 20,000 |
| Useful life | 10 years |

*e.* Early in 1990, $20,000 of legal costs were incurred defending the patents against infringement. The bookkeeper had recorded these costs as legal expenses. As of January 1, 1990, the remaining useful life of the patents is expected to be five years.

*f.* The expected cost of servicing items sold this year under warranty is estimated to be 2% of sales. No warranty expense has been recorded for 1990.

*g.* There are two notes payable. The first note is dated January 1, 1990, is not due for several more years, has a principal amount of $15,000, and bears interest at 12% per year. Its terms require Campbell to pay the interest annually on January 1. No interest has yet been recognized for this note in 1990. The second note is paid with installments of $2,821 on March 31 and September 30 of each year. The annual interest rate is 10% (5% semiannual). The $25,000 balance on the books was correctly determined on September 30, 1990, and the $2,023 of interest expense represents the proper total for the first nine months of the year. (In preparing the balance sheet, classify the entire principal of both notes as long-term liabilities; include the interest payable among the current liabilities.)

*h.* In drafting the income statement and preparing the closing entries, a measure of the ending inventory is needed. It is measured with the retail method, and this information is known for 1990:

| | Cost | Retail |
|---|---|---|
| Beginning inventory | $15,000 | $ 27,000 |
| Purchases | 70,000 | 133,000 |
| Additional markups | | 6,666 |
| Markdowns | | 9,068 |
| Sales | | 137,500 |

*Required*

1. Prepare a work sheet for the company using the information below.
2. Journalize entries resulting from the bank reconciliation and journalize the adjusting entries. Also present all calculations that support the entries.
3. Journalize closing entries for the company.
4. Prepare a single step income statement with a supporting calculation of cost of goods sold, a statement of changes in owner's equity, and a balance sheet.

# 13 Payroll Accounting

Wages or salaries generally amount to one of the largest expenses incurred by a business. Accounting for these items involves much more than simply recording liabilities and cash payments to employees. It also includes accounting for: (1) amounts withheld from employees' wages, (2) payroll taxes levied on the employer, and (3) employee (fringe) benefits paid by the employer. As you study this chapter, you will learn the general processes all businesses follow to account for these items.

**Learning Objectives**

*After studying Chapter 13, you should be able to:*

1. List the taxes and other items frequently withheld from employees' wages, make the calculations necessary to prepare a Payroll Register, and prepare the entry to record an accrued payroll.
2. Prepare journal entries to pay employees and explain the operation of a payroll bank account.
3. Calculate the payroll taxes levied on employers and prepare the entries to record the accrual and payment of these taxes.
4. Calculate and record employee fringe benefit costs and show the effect of these items on the total cost of employing labor.
5. Define or explain the words and phrases listed in the chapter Glossary.

Certain federal and state laws directly affect several aspects of payroll accounting. Thus, we begin this chapter with an overview of the more pertinent of these laws.

## The Federal Social Security Act

List the taxes and other items frequently withheld from employees' wages, make the calculations necessary to prepare a Payroll Register, and prepare the entry to record an accrued payroll. (L. O. 1)

The federal Social Security Act provides for a number of programs, two of which materially affect payroll accounting. These are (1) a federal old-age and survivors benefits program with medical care for the aged and (2) a joint federal-state unemployment insurance program.

### Federal Old Age and Survivors Benefits Program

The Social Security Act provides that qualified workers who reach the age of 62 and retire shall receive monthly retirement benefits for the remainder of their lives and certain medical benefits after reaching 65. Covered workers who become disabled also receive benefits as do the families of workers who die either before or after reaching retirement age. The benefits in each case are based on the worker's earnings during the years of employment in covered industries.

In general, any person who works for a covered employer for a sufficient length of time qualifies for benefits. All companies and individuals who employ one or more persons and are not specifically exempted are covered by the law.

### Social Security (FICA) Taxes

Funds for the payment of old-age, survivors, and medical benefits under the Social Security Act come from payroll taxes. The taxes are imposed under a law called the Federal Insurance Contributions Act and are called **FICA taxes.** They are also called social security taxes. These FICA taxes are imposed in equal amounts on covered employers and their employees. At this writing, the act imposes a 1988 tax on both employers and their employees amounting to 7.51% of the first $45,000 paid to each employee. Additional rate increases in the present laws are as follows:

| | Tax on Employees | Tax on Employers |
|---|---|---|
| 1988–89 . . . . . . . | 7.51% | 7.51% |
| 1990 and after . . . . | 7.65 | 7.65 |

The maximum amount of wages subject to FICA taxes is reviewed annually and often is increased (for 1989, the amount is $48,000). Also, Congress may change the rates listed above (probably increasing them) before they become effective. Therefore, since changes are almost certain, you are asked to use an assumed FICA tax rate of 8% on the first $50,000 of wages paid each employee each year in solving the problems at the end of this chapter. Although a few problems may specify some other rate, the 8% rate usually is assumed to simplify calculations. Also, no single rate is likely to be correct for the remaining years this text will be used.

According to the Federal Insurance Contributions Act, each employer must—

1. Withhold from the wages of each employee each payday an amount of FICA tax calculated at the current rate. FICA taxes are withheld from each paycheck during the year until the tax-exempt point is reached.
2. Pay a payroll tax equal to the sum of the FICA taxes withheld from the wages of all employees.
3. Periodically deposit to the credit of the Internal Revenue Service in a bank authorized to receive such deposits (called a **federal depository bank**) both the amounts withheld from the employees' wages and the employer's tax.
4. Within one month after the end of each calendar quarter, file a tax information return known as Employer's Quarterly Federal Tax Return, Form 941. (See Illustration 13–1.)
5. Furnish each employee before January 31 of the following year a Wage and Tax Statement, Form W-2, which tells the employee the amounts of his or her wages that were subject to FICA and federal income taxes and the amounts of such taxes withheld. (A W-2 Form is shown in Illustration 13–2.)
6. Send copies of the W-2 Forms to the Social Security Administration, which posts to each employee's social security account the amount of the employee's wages subject to FICA tax and the FICA tax withheld. These posted amounts become the basis for determining the employee's retirement and survivors benefits. In addition to the posting, the Social Security Administration transmits to the Internal Revenue Service the amount of each employee's wages subject to federal income tax and the amount of such tax withheld.
7. Keep a record for four years for each employee that shows, among other things, wages subject to FICA taxes and the taxes withheld. (The law does not specify the exact form of the record. However, most employers keep individual employee earnings records similar to the one shown later in this chapter.)

In Illustration 13–1, notice the information an employer reports on Form 941. In addition to reporting its employees' and employer's FICA taxes, an employer also reports the amount of its employees' wages that were subject to federal income taxes and the amount of such taxes that were withheld. (We discuss the withholding of employees' federal income taxes later in this chapter.) The amount of employees' wages subject to federal income tax is shown on line 2 of Illustration 13–1, and the amount of tax withheld is reported on lines 3, 4, and 5. The combined amount of the employees' and employer's FICA taxes is reported on line 6 where it says, "Taxable social security wages paid . . ." $34,370.50 × 15.02% = Tax, $5,162.45. The 15.02% is the sum of the (1988) 7.51% tax withheld from the employees' wages plus the 7.51% tax levied on the employer.

The frequency with which an employer must deposit (to the credit of the Internal Revenue Service) the FICA and employees' withheld income taxes

**Illustration 13–1**

**Employer's quarterly report of federal taxes withheld**

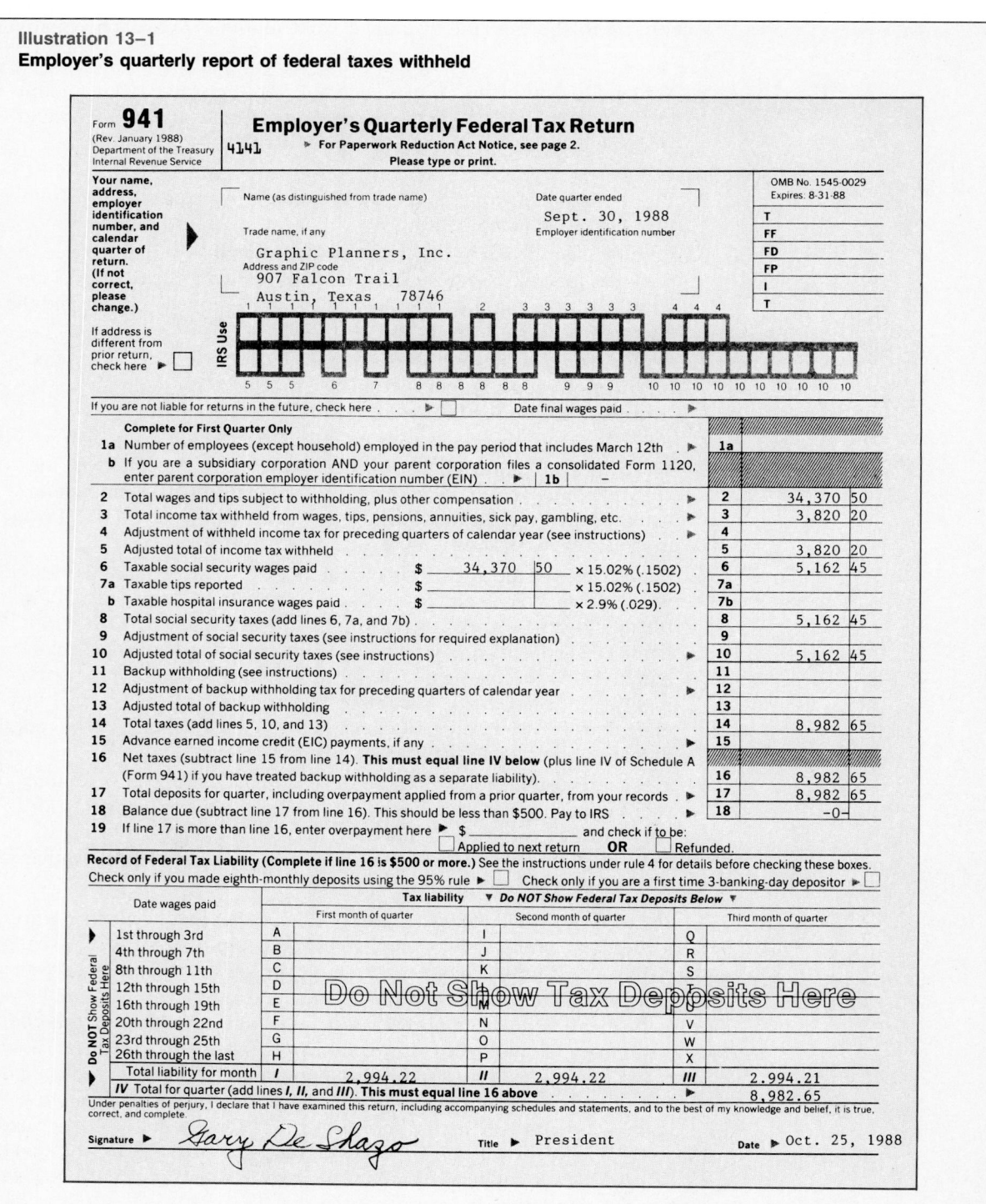

Form **941** (Rev. January 1988) Department of the Treasury Internal Revenue Service 4141

## Employer's Quarterly Federal Tax Return

► For Paperwork Reduction Act Notice, see page 2.

Please type or print.

**Your name, address, employer identification number, and calendar quarter of return. (If not correct, please change.)**

Name (as distinguished from trade name)

Date quarter ended: Sept. 30, 1988

Trade name, if any: Graphic Planners, Inc.

Employer identification number

Address and ZIP code: 907 Falcon Trail, Austin, Texas 78746

OMB No. 1545-0029 Expires: 8-31-88

T / FF / FD / FP / I / T

IRS Use

If address is different from prior return, check here ► ☐

If you are not liable for returns in the future, check here ► ☐ Date final wages paid ►

| | | | |
|---|---|---|---|
| | **Complete for First Quarter Only** | | |
| 1a | Number of employees (except household) employed in the pay period that includes March 12th ► | 1a | |
| b | If you are a subsidiary corporation AND your parent corporation files a consolidated Form 1120, enter parent corporation employer identification number (EIN) ► 1b – | | |
| 2 | Total wages and tips subject to withholding, plus other compensation ► | 2 | 34,370 50 |
| 3 | Total income tax withheld from wages, tips, pensions, annuities, sick pay, gambling, etc. ► | 3 | 3,820 20 |
| 4 | Adjustment of withheld income tax for preceding quarters of calendar year (see instructions) ► | 4 | |
| 5 | Adjusted total of income tax withheld | 5 | 3,820 20 |
| 6 | Taxable social security wages paid $ 34,370 50 × 15.02% (.1502) | 6 | 5,162 45 |
| 7a | Taxable tips reported $ ____ × 15.02% (.1502) | 7a | |
| b | Taxable hospital insurance wages paid $ ____ × 2.9% (.029) | 7b | |
| 8 | Total social security taxes (add lines 6, 7a, and 7b) | 8 | 5,162 45 |
| 9 | Adjustment of social security taxes (see instructions for required explanation) | 9 | |
| 10 | Adjusted total of social security taxes (see instructions) ► | 10 | 5,162 45 |
| 11 | Backup withholding (see instructions) | 11 | |
| 12 | Adjustment of backup withholding tax for preceding quarters of calendar year ► | 12 | |
| 13 | Adjusted total of backup withholding | 13 | |
| 14 | Total taxes (add lines 5, 10, and 13) | 14 | 8,982 65 |
| 15 | Advance earned income credit (EIC) payments, if any ► | 15 | |
| 16 | Net taxes (subtract line 15 from line 14). **This must equal line IV below** (plus line IV of Schedule A (Form 941) if you have treated backup withholding as a separate liability). | 16 | 8,982 65 |
| 17 | Total deposits for quarter, including overpayment applied from a prior quarter, from your records ► | 17 | 8,982 65 |
| 18 | Balance due (subtract line 17 from line 16). This should be less than $500. Pay to IRS ► | 18 | -0- |
| 19 | If line 17 is more than line 16, enter overpayment here ► $ ____ and check if to be: ☐ Applied to next return **OR** ☐ Refunded. | | |

**Record of Federal Tax Liability (Complete if line 16 is $500 or more.)** See the instructions under rule 4 for details before checking these boxes.

Check only if you made eighth-monthly deposits using the 95% rule ► ☐ Check only if you are a first time 3-banking-day depositor ► ☐

Do NOT Show Federal Tax Deposits Here

| Date wages paid | | Tax liability ▼ Do NOT Show Federal Tax Deposits Below ▼ First month of quarter | | Second month of quarter | | Third month of quarter |
|---|---|---|---|---|---|---|
| 1st through 3rd | A | | I | | Q | |
| 4th through 7th | B | | J | | R | |
| 8th through 11th | C | | K | | S | |
| 12th through 15th | D | | L | | T | |
| 16th through 19th | E | | M | | U | |
| 20th through 22nd | F | | N | | V | |
| 23rd through 25th | G | | O | | W | |
| 26th through the last | H | | P | | X | |
| Total liability for month | I | 2,994.22 | II | 2,994.22 | III | 2,994.21 |
| IV Total for quarter (add lines I, II, and III). **This must equal line 16 above** ► | | | | | | 8,982.65 |

Do Not Show Tax Deposits Here

Under penalties of perjury, I declare that I have examined this return, including accompanying schedules and statements, and to the best of my knowledge and belief, it is true, correct, and complete.

Signature ► Gary De Shazo  Title ► President  Date ► Oct. 25, 1988

**Illustration 13–2**
**Reporting an employee's annual wages and taxes**

| | | |
|---|---|---|
| 1 Control number | | OMB No. 1545-0008 |
| 2 Employer's name, address, and ZIP code<br>Graphic Planners, Inc.<br>907 Falcon Trail<br>Austin,Texas 78746 | 3 Employer's identification number<br>74-1633163 | 4 Employer's state I.D. number<br>56-5678 |
| | 5 Statutory employee ☐ Deceased ☐ Pension plan ☐ Legal rep. ☐ | 942 emp. ☐ Subtotal ☐ Deferred compensation ☐ Void ☐ |
| | 6 Allocated tips | 7 Advance EIC payment |
| 8 Employee's social security number 302-02-0222 \| 9 Federal income tax withheld 2,487.20 | 10 Wages, tips, other compensation<br>24,560.60 | 11 Social security tax withheld<br>1,645.56 |
| 12 Employee's name, address, and ZIP code<br>Charles Robert Lusk<br>1310 East 5th Street<br>Austin, Texas 78711 | 13 Social security wages<br>24,560.60 | 14 Social security tips |
| | 16 | 16a Fringe benefits incl. in Box 10 |
| | 17 State income tax \| 18 State wages, tips, etc. | 19 Name of state |
| | 20 Local income tax \| 21 Local wages, tips, etc. | 22 Name of locality |

Form **W-2 Wage and Tax Statement 1988**
This information is being furnished to the Internal Revenue Service.
Copy B To be filed with employee's FEDERAL tax return
Dept. of the Treasury—IRS

depends on the amounts involved. If the sum of the FICA taxes plus the employees' income taxes is less than $500 for a quarter, the taxes may be paid when the employer files an Employer's Quarterly Tax Return, Form 941. This return is due on April 30, July 31, October 31, and January 31 following the end of each calendar quarter. A check for the taxes, if less than $500, may be attached to the return, or the taxes may be deposited in a federal depository bank at the time the return is filed. The check or the deposit is recorded in the same manner as a check paying any other liability.

If the taxes exceed $500 at the end of any month but are less than $3,000, payment must be made within 15 days after the end of the month. Companies with large payrolls may have to make tax payments as often as eight times each month. Note in Illustration 13–1 that each month is divided into eight periods. When the taxes exceed $3,000 at the end of any period, they must be paid within three banking days after the end of that period.

In the example shown in Illustration 13–1, the employer's tax liability exceeded $500 but was less than $3,000 at the end of each month during the quarter. The illustration assumes that the employer paid the amounts due within 15 days after the end of each month.

## Joint Federal-State Unemployment Insurance Program

The federal government participates with the states in a joint federal-state unemployment insurance program. Within this joint program, each state has established and now administers its own unemployment insurance program under which it provides unemployment benefits to insured workers. The federal government approves the state programs and pays a portion of their administrative expenses.

### Federal Unemployment Tax Act

Federal money for administering the state programs is raised by a tax imposed under a law called the Federal Unemployment Tax Act. This act levies a **payroll tax** on employers of one or more people. A payroll tax is levied on an employer and is based on the amount each employee has earned. Note that the federal unemployment tax **(FUTA tax)** is imposed only on employers, not on employees. Also, the money from this tax is used for administrative purposes and not to pay benefits. In periods of high unemployment, however, these funds may also be loaned to states that have temporary fund deficits.

When the Federal Unemployment Tax Act was first passed in 1935, only one state had an unemployment insurance program. At that time, Congress passed certain sections of the Social Security Act and the Federal Unemployment Tax Act with two purposes in view. The first was to encourage the individual states to create satisfactory unemployment insurance programs of their own. The second was to provide funds to be distributed to the states for use in administering the state programs. These acts were successful in accomplishing their first purpose. All states immediately created unemployment benefit programs. Today, the acts remain in effect for their second purpose, to provide funds to be distributed to the states, and also to retain a measure of federal control over the state programs.

### Federal Unemployment Tax

At the time this textbook went to press (1988), the Federal Unemployment Tax Act required employers to:

1. Pay an excise tax (FUTA tax) equal to 6.2% of the first $7,000 in wages paid each employee. However, the federal law grants a maximum credit of 5.4% to employers in a state that has an appropriately designed state unemployment tax program. Since all states have unemployment tax programs, the net federal tax normally is 0.8%.
2. Report the amount of the tax by filing a tax return, called an Employer's Annual Federal Unemployment Tax Return, Form 940. This must be filed on or before January 31 following the end of each tax year. (Ten additional days are allowed for filing if all required tax deposits are made on a timely basis and the full amount of the tax is paid on or before January 31.)
3. Keep records to substantiate the information on the tax return. (In general, the records required by other payroll laws and the regular accounting records satisfy this requirement.)

An employer's federal unemployment tax for the first three quarters of a year must be deposited in a federal depository bank by the last day of the month following each quarter (i.e., on April 30, July 31, and October 31). However, no deposit is required if the tax for a quarter plus the undeposited tax for previous quarters is $100 or less. The tax for the last quarter of a year plus the undeposited tax for previous quarters must be deposited or paid on or before January 31 following the end of the tax year. If the Employer's Annual Federal Unemployment Tax Return is filed on or before that date, a check for the last quarter's tax and any undeposited tax for previous quarters may be attached to the form.

### State Unemployment Insurance Programs

While the various state unemployment insurance programs differ in some respects, all have three common objectives. They are:

1. To pay unemployment benefits for limited periods to unemployed individuals. (To be eligible for benefits, an unemployed individual must have worked for a tax-paying employer covered by the law. In general, the state laws cover all employers who are not specifically exempted.)
2. To encourage the stabilization of employment by covered employers. In all states this is accomplished by a so-called **employer's merit rating** plan. Under a merit rating plan, the tax rate levied on an employer is adjusted to reflect the employer's past record in providing steady employment for employees.
3. To establish and operate employment facilities that assist unemployed individuals in finding suitable employment and assist employers in finding employees.

### State Unemployment Tax

All states support their unemployment insurance programs by placing a payroll tax on employers.[1] The **state unemployment tax** rate may range from 0% up to 9% or more and generally is applied to the first $7,000 earned by each employee. The exact tax rate that must be paid by an employer depends on the employer's merit rating. An employer gains a favorable merit rating by not laying employees off during slack seasons; as a result, the employees do not have to draw unemployment benefits. Clearly, a favorable merit rating offers an important tax savings. For example, if an employer can obtain a merit rating that reduces the tax rate from 5% to 1%, the annual savings is $280 for each employee who earns $7,000 or more per year (4% × $7,000 = $280). If the employer has 100 employees, the annual savings is $28,000.

All states require employers to submit unemployment tax reports. These reports or tax returns usually must be filed with the tax payment within one month after the end of each calendar quarter. Since the benefits paid to unemployed individuals are based on earnings, the tax returns must usually name each employee and summarize the employee's wages.

In addition to reports and payment of taxes, all states require employers to maintain certain payroll records. These generally include a payroll record for each pay period showing the pay period dates, hours worked, and taxable earnings of each employee. An individual earnings record for each employee is also commonly required. The earnings record generally must show about the same information that is required by social security laws. In addition, informa-

[1] States also may levy an unemployment tax on employees.

tion is also commonly required as to (1) the date an employee was hired, rehired, or reinstated after a layoff; (2) the date the employee quit, was discharged, or laid off; and (3) the reason for termination.

## Withholding Employees' Federal Income Taxes

With few exceptions, an employer of one or more persons is required to calculate, withhold, and remit to the Internal Revenue Service the federal income taxes of its employees. The amount of tax to be withheld from each employee's wages is determined by the amount of the wages earned and the number of the employee's personal **withholding allowances.** These withholding allowances generally correspond to the personal exemptions that may be claimed on the employee's tax return. For example, in 1988, each personal exemption allowed the employee to deduct $1,950 from yearly earnings in the process of calculating taxable income. Each employee is allowed one personal exemption plus an exemption for each dependent. Every covered employee is required to furnish his or her employer an employee's withholding allowance certificate, called a Form W-4, on which the employee indicates the number of withholding allowances claimed.

Most employers use a **wage bracket withholding table** similar to the one shown in Illustration 13–3 to determine the federal income taxes to be withheld from each **employee's gross pay.** The illustrated table is for single employees who are paid weekly. Different tables are provided for married employees and for biweekly, semimonthly, and monthly pay periods. Similar tables also are available for determining FICA tax withholdings. Computerized payroll systems calculate the withholdings by formula.

When using the tables to determine the federal income tax to be withheld from an employee's gross wages, you first locate the employee's wage bracket in the first two columns of the appropriate withholding table. Then, on the line of the wage bracket, you find the amount to be withheld by looking in the withholding allowance column that is appropriate for the employee. The column heading numbers refer to the number of withholding allowances claimed by an employee.

In addition to determining and withholding income tax from each employee's wages every payday, employers are required to—

1. Periodically deposit the withheld taxes to the credit of the Internal Revenue Service.
2. Within one month after the end of each calendar quarter, file a report showing the income taxes withheld. This report is the Employer's Quarterly Federal Tax Return, Form 941, discussed previously and shown in Illustration 13–1. It is the same report required for FICA taxes.
3. On or before January 31 of the following year, give each employee a Wage and Tax Statement, Form W-2, which tells the employee (1) his or her total wages for the preceding year, (2) wages subject to FICA taxes, (3) income taxes withheld, and (4) FICA taxes withheld. A copy of this statement must also be given to each terminated employee within 30 days after his or her last wage payment.
4. On or before January 31 following the end of each year, send the So-

**Illustration 13–3**
**A wage bracket withholding table**

**SINGLE** Persons–**WEEKLY** Payroll Period
**(For Wages Paid After December 1987)**

| And the wages are– | | And the number of withholding allowances claimed is– | | | | | | | | | | |
|---|---|---|---|---|---|---|---|---|---|---|---|---|
| At least | But less than | 0 | 1 | 2 | 3 | 4 | 5 | 6 | 7 | 8 | 9 | 10 |
| | | The amount of income tax to be withheld shall be– | | | | | | | | | | |
| $540 | $550 | $102 | $92 | $81 | $71 | $60 | $51 | $45 | $39 | $34 | $28 | $22 |
| 550 | 560 | 105 | 95 | 84 | 74 | 63 | 53 | 46 | 41 | 35 | 30 | 24 |
| 560 | 570 | 108 | 97 | 87 | 76 | 66 | 55 | 48 | 42 | 37 | 31 | 25 |
| 570 | 580 | 111 | 100 | 90 | 79 | 69 | 58 | 49 | 44 | 38 | 33 | 27 |
| 580 | 590 | 114 | 103 | 93 | 82 | 72 | 61 | 51 | 45 | 40 | 34 | 28 |
| 590 | 600 | 116 | 106 | 95 | 85 | 74 | 64 | 53 | 47 | 41 | 36 | 30 |
| 600 | 610 | 119 | 109 | 98 | 88 | 77 | 67 | 56 | 48 | 43 | 37 | 31 |
| 610 | 620 | 122 | 111 | 101 | 90 | 80 | 69 | 59 | 50 | 44 | 39 | 33 |
| 620 | 630 | 125 | 114 | 104 | 93 | 83 | 72 | 62 | 51 | 46 | 40 | 34 |
| 630 | 640 | 128 | 117 | 107 | 96 | 86 | 75 | 65 | 54 | 47 | 42 | 36 |
| 640 | 650 | 130 | 120 | 109 | 99 | 88 | 78 | 67 | 57 | 49 | 43 | 37 |
| 650 | 660 | 133 | 123 | 112 | 102 | 91 | 81 | 70 | 60 | 50 | 45 | 39 |
| 660 | 670 | 136 | 125 | 115 | 104 | 94 | 83 | 73 | 62 | 52 | 46 | 40 |
| 670 | 680 | 139 | 128 | 118 | 107 | 97 | 86 | 76 | 65 | 55 | 48 | 42 |
| 680 | 690 | 142 | 131 | 121 | 110 | 100 | 89 | 79 | 68 | 58 | 49 | 43 |
| 690 | 700 | 144 | 134 | 123 | 113 | 102 | 92 | 81 | 71 | 60 | 51 | 45 |
| 700 | 710 | 147 | 137 | 126 | 116 | 105 | 95 | 84 | 74 | 63 | 53 | 46 |
| 710 | 720 | 150 | 139 | 129 | 118 | 108 | 97 | 87 | 76 | 66 | 55 | 48 |
| 720 | 730 | 153 | 142 | 132 | 121 | 111 | 100 | 90 | 79 | 69 | 58 | 49 |
| 730 | 740 | 156 | 145 | 135 | 124 | 114 | 103 | 93 | 82 | 72 | 61 | 51 |
| 740 | 750 | 158 | 148 | 137 | 127 | 116 | 106 | 95 | 85 | 74 | 64 | 53 |
| 750 | 760 | 161 | 151 | 140 | 130 | 119 | 109 | 98 | 88 | 77 | 67 | 56 |
| 760 | 770 | 164 | 153 | 143 | 132 | 122 | 111 | 101 | 90 | 80 | 69 | 59 |
| 770 | 780 | 167 | 156 | 146 | 135 | 125 | 114 | 104 | 93 | 83 | 72 | 62 |
| 780 | 790 | 170 | 159 | 149 | 138 | 128 | 117 | 107 | 96 | 86 | 75 | 65 |
| 790 | 800 | 172 | 162 | 151 | 141 | 130 | 120 | 109 | 99 | 88 | 78 | 67 |
| 800 | 810 | 175 | 165 | 154 | 144 | 133 | 123 | 112 | 102 | 91 | 81 | 70 |
| 810 | 820 | 178 | 167 | 157 | 146 | 136 | 125 | 115 | 104 | 94 | 83 | 73 |
| 820 | 830 | 181 | 170 | 160 | 149 | 139 | 128 | 118 | 107 | 97 | 86 | 76 |
| 830 | 840 | 184 | 173 | 163 | 152 | 142 | 131 | 121 | 110 | 100 | 89 | 79 |

cial Security Administration copies of all W-2 forms given employees. The Social Security Administration transmits the information as to employees' earnings and withheld taxes to the Internal Revenue Service.

## City and State Income Taxes

In addition to deducting employees' federal income taxes, employers in many cities and in many states also must deduct employees' city and state income taxes. When levied, the city and state taxes are handled in much the same way as federal income taxes.

## Fair Labor Standards Act

The Fair Labor Standards Act, often called the Wages and Hours Law, sets minimum hourly wages and maximum hours of work per week for employees. With certain exceptions, the act covers persons who work for employers engaged directly or indirectly in interstate commerce. In 1988, the law set a $3.35 per hour minimum wage for employees in most occupations and a 40-hour workweek. Also, if covered employees work more than 40 hours in one week, they must be paid for the hours in excess of 40 at their regular pay rate plus an overtime premium of at least one half the regular rate. This gives employees an overtime rate of at least one and one half times their regular pay rate. The act also requires employers to maintain records for each covered employee similar to the Employee's Individual Earnings Record shown later in the chapter (see Illustration 13–8).

## Union Contracts

Employers commonly operate under contracts with their employees' union that provide different terms than the Fair Labor Standards Act. For example, union contracts often provide for time and one half for work in excess of eight hours in any one day, time and one half for work on Saturdays, and double time for Sundays and holidays.

In addition to specifying working hours and wage rates, union contracts often provide for the collection of employees' union dues by the employer. Such a requirement commonly provides that the employer deduct dues from the wages of each employee and remit them to the union. The employer is usually required to remit once each month and to report the name and amount deducted from each employee's pay.

## Other Payroll Deductions

In addition to the payroll deductions we have discussed so far, employees may individually authorize additional deductions, such as deductions to purchase U.S. savings bonds; to pay health, hospital, or life insurance premiums; to repay loans from the employer or the employees' credit union; to pay for donations to charitable organizations; and to pay for merchandise purchased from the employer.

## Timekeeping

Compiling a record of the time worked by each employee is called **timekeeping.** The method used to compile such a record depends on the nature of the company's business and the number of its employees. In a very small business, timekeeping may consist of no more than notations of each employee's working time made in a memorandum book by the manager or owner. In many companies, however, time clocks are used to record on **clock cards** each employee's time of arrival and departure. The time clocks are usually placed near entrances to the office, store, or factory. At the beginning of each payroll period, a clock card for each employee (see Illustration 13–4) is placed in a rack for use by the employee. Upon arriving at work, each employee takes his or her card from the rack and places it in a slot in the time clock. This actuates the clock to stamp the date and arrival time on the card. The employee then returns the card to the rack. Upon leaving the plant, store, or office for lunch or at the end of the day, the procedure is repeated. The employee takes the card from the rack, places it in the clock, and the time of departure is automatically stamped. As a result, at the end of each pay period, the card shows the hours the employee was at work.

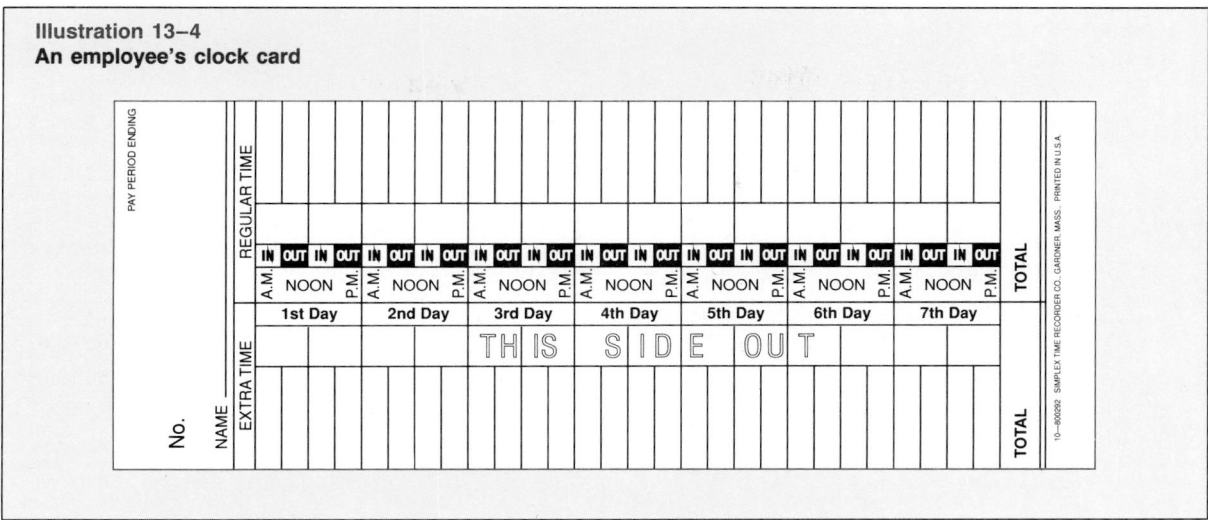

**Illustration 13–4**
**An employee's clock card**

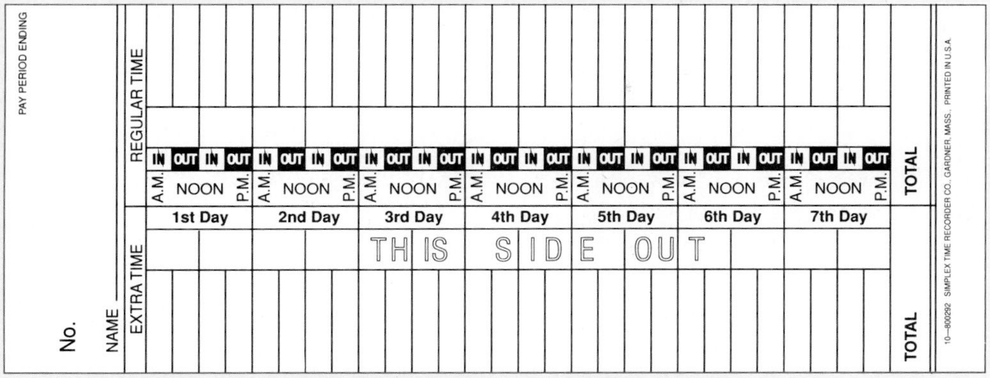


## The Payroll Register

Each pay period the total hours worked as compiled on clock cards or otherwise is summarized in a Payroll Register, an example of which is shown in Illustration 13–5. The illustrated register is for a weekly pay period and shows the payroll data for each employee on a separate line.

In Illustration 13–5, the columns under the heading Daily Time show the hours worked each day by each employee. The total of each employee's hours is entered in the column headed Total Hours. If hours worked include overtime hours, these are entered in the column headed O.T. Hours.

The Reg. Pay Rate column shows the hourly pay rate of each employee. Total hours worked multiplied by the regular pay rate equals regular pay. Overtime hours multiplied by the overtime premium rate (50% in this case) equals overtime premium pay. And, regular pay plus overtime premium pay is the *gross pay* of each employee.

The amounts withheld from each employee's gross pay are recorded in the Deductions columns of the payroll register. For example, you determine the FICA tax deductions by multiplying the gross pay of each employee by the FICA tax rate and then enter the results in the FICA Taxes column. In this and the remaining illustrations of this chapter, we assume that the rate is 8% on the first $50,000 earned by each employee.

As previously stated, the income tax withheld depends on each employee's gross pay and withholding allowances. You can determine these amounts by referring to the appropriate wage bracket withholding tables. You then enter them in the column headed Federal Income Taxes.

The column headed Hosp. Ins. shows the amounts withheld to pay for hospital insurance for the employees and their families. The total withheld from all employees is a current liability of the employer until paid to the insurance company. Likewise, the total withheld for employees' union dues is a current liability until paid to the union. The column marked Union Dues in the illustrated Payroll Register is for this deduction.

Additional columns may be added to the Payroll Register for any other deductions that occur sufficiently often to warrant special columns. For exam-

**Illustration 13–5**
**A Payroll Register**

**Payroll Week Ended**

| Employees | Clock Card No. | Daily Time M | T | W | T | F | S | S | Total Hours | O.T. Hours | Earnings: Regular Pay Rate | Regular Pay | O.T. Premium Pay | Gross Pay |
|---|---|---|---|---|---|---|---|---|---|---|---|---|---|---|
| Robert Austin | 114 | 8 | 8 | 8 | 8 | 8 | | | 40 | | 10.00 | 400.00 | | 400.00 |
| Judy Cross | 102 | 8 | 8 | 8 | 8 | 8 | | | 40 | | 15.00 | 600.00 | | 600.00 |
| John Cruz | 108 | 0 | 8 | 8 | 8 | 8 | 8 | | 40 | | 14.00 | 560.00 | | 560.00 |
| Kay Keife | 109 | 8 | 8 | 8 | 8 | 8 | 8 | | 48 | 8 | 14.00 | 672.00 | 56.00 | 728.00 |
| Lee Miller | 112 | 8 | 8 | 8 | 8 | 0 | | | 32 | | 14.00 | 448.00 | | 448.00 |
| Dale Sears | 103 | 8 | 8 | 8 | 8 | 8 | 4 | | 44 | 4 | 15.00 | 660.00 | 30.00 | 690.00 |
| Totals | | | | | | | | | | | | 3,340.00 | 86.00 | 3,426.00 |

ple, a company that regularly deducts amounts from its employees' pay for U.S. savings bonds may add a special column for this deduction.

An employee's gross pay less total deductions is the **employee's net pay** and is entered in the Net Pay column. The total of this column is the amount the employees are to be paid. The numbers of the checks used to pay the employees are entered in the column headed Check No.

The Distribution columns are used to classify the various salaries in terms of different kinds of expense. Here you enter each employee's gross salary in the proper column according to the type of work performed. The column totals then indicate the amounts to be debited to the salary expense accounts.

## Recording the Payroll

Generally, a Payroll Register such as the one shown is a supplementary memorandum record. As such, you do not post its information directly to the accounts. Instead, you must first record the payroll with a general journal entry, which is then posted to the accounts. The entry to record the payroll shown in Illustration 13–5 is:

| | | | | |
|---|---|---|---|---|
| Mar. | 23 | Sales Salaries Expense | 2,336.00 | |
| | | Office Salaries Expense | 1,090.00 | |
| | | FICA Taxes Payable | | 274.08 |
| | | Employees' Income Taxes Payable | | 558.00 |
| | | Employees' Hospital Insurance Payable | | 320.00 |
| | | Employees' Union Dues Payable | | 40.00 |
| | | Accrued Payroll Payable | | 2,233.92 |
| | | To record the March 23 payroll. | | |

The debits of the entry were taken from the Payroll Register's distribution column totals. They charge the employees' gross earnings to the proper salary expense accounts. The credits to FICA Taxes Payable, Employees' Income Taxes Payable, Employees' Hospital Insurance Payable, and Employees'

**Register**
**March 23, 19—**

| Deductions | | | | | Payment | | Distribution | |
|---|---|---|---|---|---|---|---|---|
| FICA Taxes | Federal Income Taxes | Hosp. Ins. | Union Dues | Total Deductions | Net Pay | Check No. | Sales Salaries | Office Salaries |
| 32.00 | 50.00 | 40.00 | | 122.00 | 278.00 | 893 | | 400.00 |
| 48.00 | 117.00 | 56.00 | 10.00 | 231.00 | 369.00 | 894 | 600.00 | |
| 44.80 | 99.00 | 56.00 | 10.00 | 209.80 | 350.20 | 895 | 560.00 | |
| 58.24 | 120.00 | 56.00 | 10.00 | 244.24 | 483.76 | 896 | 728.00 | |
| 35.84 | 60.00 | 56.00 | 10.00 | 161.84 | 286.16 | 897 | 448.00 | |
| 55.20 | 112.00 | 56.00 | | 223.20 | 466.80 | 898 | | 690.00 |
| 274.08 | 558.00 | 320.00 | 40.00 | 1,192.08 | 2,233.92 | | 2,336.00 | 1,090.00 |

Union Dues Payable record these amounts as current liabilities. The credit to Accrued Payroll Payable records as a liability the net amount to be paid the employees.

## Paying the Employees

Prepare journal entries to pay employees and explain the operation of a payroll bank account.
(L. O. 2)

Almost every business pays its employees with checks. In a company that has few employees, these checks often are drawn on the regular bank account and entered in a Cash Disbursements Journal (or Check Register) like the one described in Chapter 6. Since each check is debited to the Accrued Payroll Payable account, posting labor can be saved by adding an Accrued Payroll Payable column in the journal. If such a column is added, entries to pay the employees of the Illustration 13–5 payroll will appear as in Illustration 13–6

Although not required by law, most employers furnish each employee an earnings statement each payday. The statement gives the employee a record of hours worked, gross pay, deductions, and net pay. The statement often takes the form of a detachable paycheck portion that is removed before the check is cashed. A paycheck with a detachable earnings statement is reproduced in Illustration 13–7.

## Payroll Bank Account

A business with many employees normally uses a special **payroll bank account** to pay its employees. When such an account is used, one check for the total payroll is drawn on the regular bank account and deposited in the special payroll bank account. Then, individual payroll checks are drawn on this special account. Because only one check for the payroll total is drawn on the regular bank account each payday, use of a special payroll bank account simplifies internal control, especially the reconciliation of the regular bank account. It may be reconciled without considering the payroll checks outstanding, and there may be many of these.

When a company uses a special payroll bank account, you must complete the following steps to pay the employees:

Illustration 13–6

**Cash Disbursements Journal**

| Date | | Check No. | Payee | Account Debited | PR | Other Accounts Debit | Accounts Payable Debit | Accrued Payroll Payable Debit | Purchase Discounts Credit | Cash Credit |
|---|---|---|---|---|---|---|---|---|---|---|
| Mar. | 23 | 893 | Robert Austin | Accrued Payroll | | | | 278.00 | | 278.00 |
| | 23 | 894 | Judy Cross | " | | | | 369.00 | | 369.00 |
| | 23 | 895 | John Cruz | " | | | | 350.20 | | 350.20 |
| | 23 | 896 | Kay Keife | " | | | | 483.76 | | 483.76 |
| | 23 | 897 | Lee Miller | " | | | | 286.16 | | 286.16 |
| | 23 | 898 | Dale Sears | " | | | | 466.80 | | 466.80 |

Illustration 13–7
**A payroll check**

| Employee | Total Hours | O.T. Hours | Reg. Pay Rate | Regular Pay | O.T. Prem. Pay | Gross Pay | F.I.C.A. Taxes | Income Taxes | Union Dues | Hosp. Ins. | Total Deductions | Net Pay |
|---|---|---|---|---|---|---|---|---|---|---|---|---|
| *Robert Austin* | *40* | | *10.00* | *400.00* | | *400.00* | *32.00* | *50.00* | | *40.00* | *122.00* | *278.00* |

STATEMENT OF EARNINGS AND DEDUCTIONS FOR EMPLOYEE'S RECORDS—DETACH BEFORE CASHING CHECK

**VALLEY SALES COMPANY**
2590 Chula Vista Street • Eugene, Oregon

**No. 893**

PAY TO THE ORDER OF *Robert Austin* Date *March 23, 19--* $ *278.00*

*Two hundred seventy-eight dollars and no cents* ----------------------------------

Merchants National Bank
Eugene, Oregon

VALLEY SALES COMPANY
*James R. Morris*

1. First, record the information shown on the Payroll Register in the usual manner with a general journal entry similar to the one previously illustrated. This entry causes the sum of the employees' net pay to be credited to the liability account (Accrued Payroll Payable).
2. Next, have a single check written that is payable to Payroll Bank Account for the total amount of the payroll and enter the payment in the Check Register. This requires a debit to Accrued Payroll Payable and a credit to Cash.
3. Next, have the check deposited in the payroll bank account. This transfers an amount of money equal to the payroll total from the regular bank account to the special payroll bank account.
4. Last, have individual payroll checks drawn on the special payroll

**Illustration 13–8**
**Employee's Individual Earnings Record**

Employee's Name Robert Austin S.S. Acct. No. 307-03-2195 Employee No. 114

Home Address 111 South Greenwood Notify in Case of Emergency Margaret Austin Phone No. 964-9834

Employed June 7, 1980 Date of Termination ________ Reason ________

Date of Birth June 6, 1962 Date Becomes 65 June 6, 2027 Male (X) Female ( ) Married (X) Single ( ) Number of Exemptions 1 Pay Rate $10.00

Occupation Clerk Place Office

| Date | | Time Lost | | Time Worked | | | | | | | | | | | | |
|---|---|---|---|---|---|---|---|---|---|---|---|---|---|---|---|---|
| Per. Ends | Paid | Hrs. | Reason | Total | O.T. Hours | Reg. Pay | O.T. Prem. Pay | Gross Pay | FICA Taxes | Fed. Income Taxes | Hosp. Ins. | Union Dues | Total Deductions | Net Pay | Check No. | Cumulative Pay |
| 1/5 | 1/5 | | | 40 | | 400.00 | | 400.00 | 32.00 | 50.00 | 40.00 | | 122.00 | 278.00 | 173 | 400.00 |
| 1/12 | 1/12 | | | 40 | | 400.00 | | 400.00 | 32.00 | 50.00 | 40.00 | | 122.00 | 278.00 | 201 | 800.00 |
| 1/19 | 1/19 | | | 40 | | 400.00 | | 400.00 | 32.00 | 50.00 | 40.00 | | 122.00 | 278.00 | 243 | 1,200.00 |
| 1/26 | 1/26 | 4 | Sick | 36 | | 360.00 | | 360.00 | 28.80 | 43.00 | 40.00 | | 111.80 | 248.20 | 295 | 1,560.00 |
| 2/2 | 2/2 | | | 40 | | 400.00 | | 400.00 | 32.00 | 50.00 | 40.00 | | 122.00 | 278.00 | 339 | 1,960.00 |
| 2/9 | 2/9 | | | 40 | | 400.00 | | 400.00 | 32.00 | 50.00 | 40.00 | | 122.00 | 278.00 | 354 | 2,360.00 |
| 2/16 | 2/16 | | | 40 | | 400.00 | | 400.00 | 32.00 | 50.00 | 40.00 | | 122.00 | 278.00 | 397 | 2,760.00 |
| 2/23 | 2/23 | | | 40 | | 400.00 | | 400.00 | 32.00 | 50.00 | 40.00 | | 122.00 | 278.00 | 446 | 3,160.00 |
| 3/23 | 3/23 | | | 40 | | 400.00 | | 400.00 | 32.00 | 50.00 | 40.00 | | 122.00 | 278.00 | 893 | 4,760.00 |

bank account and delivered to the employees. As soon as all employees cash their checks, the funds in the special account will be exhausted.

A special Payroll Check Register may be used in connection with a payroll bank account. However, most companies do not use such a register. Instead, the payroll check numbers are entered in the Payroll Register so that it serves as a Check Register.

## Employee's Individual Earnings Record

An **Employee's Individual Earnings Record**, as shown in Illustration 13–8, provides for each employee in one record a full year's summary of the employee's working time, gross earnings, deductions, and net pay. In addition, it accumulates information that—

1. Serves as a basis for the employer's state and federal payroll tax returns.
2. Indicates when an employee's earnings have reached the tax-exempt points for FICA and state and federal unemployment taxes.

3. Supplies data for the Wage and Tax Statement, Form W-2, which must be given to the employee at the end of the year.

The payroll information on an Employee's Individual Earnings Record is taken from the Payroll Register. The information as to earnings, deductions, and net pay is first recorded on a single line in the Payroll Register. Then, each pay period, the information is posted from the Payroll Register to the earnings record. Note the last column of the record. It shows an employee's cumulative earnings and is used to determine when the earnings reach the maximum amounts taxed and are no longer subject to the various payroll taxes.

## Payroll Taxes Levied on the Employer

Calculate the payroll taxes levied on employers and prepare the entries to record the accrual and payment of these taxes. (L. O. 3)

As we previously explained, FICA taxes are levied in equal amounts on both covered employers and their employees. In addition, federal unemployment taxes and state unemployment taxes also are levied on the employer. Therefore, each time a payroll is recorded, you must also prepare a general journal entry to record the employer's FICA and state and federal unemployment taxes. For example, the entry to record the employer's *payroll taxes* on the payroll of Illustration 13–5 is:

| | | | | |
|---|---|---|---|---|
| Mar. | 23 | Payroll Taxes Expense | 345.98 | |
| | | FICA Taxes Payable | | 274.08 |
| | | State Unemployment Taxes Payable | | 56.76 |
| | | Federal Unemployment Taxes Payable | | 15.14 |
| | | To record the employer's payroll taxes. | | |

The $345.98 debit of the entry records as an expense the sum of the employer's payroll taxes. The $274.08 credit to FICA Taxes Payable is equal to and matches the FICA taxes deducted from the employees' pay. Note that the employer's portion and the employees' portion are credited to the same FICA Taxes Payable account.

The $56.76 credit to State Unemployment Taxes Payable results from the assumption that the tax rate for this company is 3% and is applied to the first $7,000 earned by each employee. Illustration 13–9 shows the cumulative earnings of each employee prior to this pay period and the resulting amounts from this period that are subject to the various taxes. In Illustration 13–9, notice that Dale Sears has earned more than $7,000. As a result, his current pay is assumed to be exempt from state unemployment tax. Judy Cross has previously earned $6,600, and only the first $400 of her pay is subject to tax. And since Kay Keife has previously earned $6,916, only $84 of her pay is subject to tax. The wages of the remaining employees are taxable in full. Therefore, the $56.76 credit to State Unemployment Taxes Payable in the entry to record the employer's payroll taxes resulted from multiplying the wages subject to tax ($1,892) by the assumed 3% rate.

## Accruing Taxes on Wages

Payroll taxes are levied on wages actually paid. In other words, accrued wages are not subject to payroll taxes until they are paid. Nevertheless, if the requirements of the *matching principle* are to be met, both accrued wages and the accrued taxes on the wages should be recorded at the end of an accounting period. However, since the amounts of such taxes vary little from one ac-

**Illustration 13–9**
**Employees' cumulative earnings through the last pay period and earnings subject to the various taxes**

| Employees | Earnings through Last Pay Period | Earnings This Pay Period | Earnings Subject to— FICA Taxes | State and Federal Unemployment Taxes |
|---|---|---|---|---|
| Robert Austin . . . . | $4,360.00 | $ 400.00 | $ 400.00 | $ 400.00 |
| Judy Cross . . . . . | 6,600.00 | 600.00 | 600.00 | 400.00 |
| John Cruz . . . . . . | 6,160.00 | 560.00 | 560.00 | 560.00 |
| Kay Keife . . . . . . | 6,916.00 | 728.00 | 728.00 | 84.00 |
| Lee Miller . . . . . . | 6,020.00 | 448.00 | 448.00 | 448.00 |
| Dale Sears . . . . . | 7,050.00 | 690.00 | 690.00 | –0– |
| Totals . . . . . . . . | | $3,426.00 | $3,426.00 | $1,892.00 |

counting period to the next and often are small in amount, many employers apply the *materiality principle* and do not accrue payroll taxes.

## Employee (Fringe) Benefit Costs

Calculate and record employee fringe benefit costs and show the effect of these items on the total cost of employing labor. (L. O. 4)

In addition to the wages earned by employees and the related payroll taxes paid by the employer, many companies provide their employees a variety of benefits. Since the costs of these benefits are paid by the employer and the benefits are in addition to the amount of wages earned, they are often called **employee fringe benefits.** For example, an employer may pay for part (or all) of the employees' medical insurance, life insurance, and disability insurance. Another typical employee benefit involves employer contributions to a retirement income plan. Perhaps the most typical employee benefit is vacation pay.

### Employer Contributions to Employee Insurance and Retirement Plans

The entries to record employee benefit costs depend on the nature of the benefit. Some employee retirement plans are quite complicated and involve accounting procedures that are too complex for discussion in this introductory course. In other cases, however, the employer simply makes periodic cash contributions to a retirement fund for each employee and records the amounts contributed as expense. Other employee benefits that require periodic cash payments by the employer include employer payments of insurance premiums for employees.

In the case of employee benefits that simply require the employer to make periodic cash payments, the entries to record the employer's obligations are similar to those used for payroll taxes.[2] For example, assume an employer

[2] Some payments of employee benefits must be added to the gross salary of the employee for the purpose of calculating FICA taxes payable as well as federal and state unemployment taxes payable. However, in this chapter and in the problems at the end of the chapter, the possible effect of employee benefit costs on payroll taxes is ignored to avoid undue complexity in the introductory course.

## AS A MATTER OF FACT

New York—The Financial Accounting Standards Board, as expected, proposed a controversial rule requiring companies to deduct from profits the potential costs of retirees' medical and insurance benefits.

U.S. companies currently deduct such costs from profits as they're paid. Starting with 1992 financial reports, the proposal would require a reserve for such benefits as they're earned by employees from their date of hire to when they become eligible for the benefits, usually at age 55. Small, closely held and foreign companies have until 1994 to begin the reserve.

The rule would require companies to make up for the years in which they haven't already reserved for such potential costs; the proposal would allow them to amortize a portion of such costs over a minimum of 15 years. Benefits analysts estimate the size of this unfunded liability at anywhere from $200 billion to $1 trillion.

Dennis Beresford, chairman of the FASB, said the board knows the proposal upsets many companies because of the size of the obligation. "But our objective is to maintain the integrity of financial statements," he added.

Parties wishing to comment on the proposal have until Aug. 14, the FASB, based in Norwalk, Conn., said. Hearings will be held in New York on Oct. 10, 11 and 12, and in Washington, D.C., on Nov. 2 and 3.

Source: "FASB Proposes Its Rule Requiring Benefits Reserve," *The Wall Street Journal*, February 10, 1989, p. B6. Reprinted by permission of *The Wall Street Journal*, 

with five employees has agreed to pay medical insurance premiums of $100 per month for each employee. The employer also will contribute 10% of each employee's salary to a retirement program. If each employee earns $1,500 per month, the entry to record these employee benefits for the month of March is:

| | | | | |
|---|---|---|---|---|
| Mar. | 31 | Employees' Benefits Expense | 1,250.00 | |
| | | Employees' Medical Insurance Payable | | 500.00 |
| | | Employees' Retirement Program Payable | | 750.00 |
| | | ($1,500 × 5) × 10% = $750. | | |

### Vacation Pay

Nearly all employers promise their employees paid vacation time as a benefit of employment. For example, many employees receive 2 weeks' vacation in return for working 50 weeks each year. The effect of a 2-week vacation is to increase the employer's payroll expenses by 4% (2/50 = .04). However, new employees often do not begin to accrue vacation time until after they've worked for a period of time, perhaps as much as a year. The employment contract may say that no vacation is granted until the employee works one year; but if the first year is completed, the employee receives the full 2 weeks. In this type of situation, the expense associated with vacation pay depends on the employee turnover rate. If the turnover experience of the employer suggests that only 90% of employees actually will be granted vacation time, the additional expense of a 2-week vacation benefit would be 90% of 4%, or 3.6%.

To account for vacation pay, an employer should estimate and record the additional expense during the weeks the employees are working and earning the vacation time. For example, assume that a company with a weekly payroll of $20,000 grants two weeks' vacation after one year's employment. Based on past turnover rates, the employer estimates that 90% of employees actually will be granted vacation time. The entry to record the estimated vacation pay is:

| | | | |
|---|---|---|---|
| Date | Employees' Benefits Expense | 720.00 | |
| | Estimated Vacation Pay Liability | | 720.00 |
| | $20,000 × .04 × .9 = $720. | | |

As employees take their vacations and receive their vacation pay, the entries to record the vacation payroll take the following general form:

| | | | |
|---|---|---|---|
| Date | Estimated Vacation Pay Liability | xxx | |
| | FICA Taxes Payable | | xxx |
| | Employees' Income Taxes Payable | | xxx |
| | Other withholding liability accounts such as Employees' Hospital Insurance Payable | | xxx |
| | Accrued Payroll Payable | | xxx |

Payroll taxes and employee benefits costs are often a major category of expense incurred by a company. They may amount to well over 25% of the salaries earned by employees.

## Computerized Payroll Systems

Manually prepared records like the ones described in this chapter are used in many small companies. However, an increasing number of companies use computers to process their payroll. The computer programs are designed to take advantage of the fact that the same calculations are performed each pay period. Also, much of the same information must be entered for each employee in the Payroll Register, on the employee's earnings record, and on the employee's paycheck. The computers simultaneously store or print the information in all three places.

## Summary of the Chapter in Terms of Learning Objectives

**1.** Taxes withheld from employees' wages include FICA taxes, federal income taxes, and possibly state and local income taxes. Payroll taxes levied on employers include FICA taxes, federal unemployment taxes, and state unemployment taxes.

**2.** An employee's gross pay may be the employee's specified wage rate multiplied by the total hours worked plus an overtime premium rate multiplied by the number of overtime hours worked. Alternatively, it may be the given periodic salary of the employee. Taxes withheld and other deductions for items such as union dues, insurance premiums, and charitable contributions are subtracted from gross pay to determine the net pay.

A payroll bank account is a separate account that is used solely for the purpose of paying employees. Each pay period, an amount equal to the total net pay of all employees is transferred from the regular bank account to the payroll bank account. Then, checks are drawn against the payroll bank account for the net pay of the employees.

**3.** A Payroll Register is used to summarize all employees' hours worked, regular and overtime pay, payroll deductions, net pay, and distribution of gross pay to expense accounts during each pay period. It provides the necessary information for journal entries to record the accrued payroll and to pay the employees.

**4.** When a payroll is accrued at the end of each pay period, payroll taxes also should be accrued with a debit to Payroll Taxes Expense and credits to appropriate liability accounts. Fringe benefit costs that involve simple cash payments by the employee should be accrued with an entry similar to the one used to accrue payroll taxes. To account for the expense associated with vacation pay, you should estimate the expense on an annual basis and allocate the estimated amount to the pay periods during the year. These allocations are recorded with a debit to Employees' Benefits Expense and a credit to Estimated Vacation Pay Liability. Then, payments to employees on vacation are charged to the estimated liability.

## Demonstration Problem

Presented below are various items of information about three employees of the Jasmine Company for the week ending October 20, 1990.

| | Babcock | Dawson | Sanders |
|---|---|---|---|
| Wage rate (per hour) | $10 | $30 | $16 |
| Overtime premium | 50% | 50% | 50% |
| Annual vacation | 2 weeks | 4 weeks | 2 weeks |
| Cumulative wages as of October 13, 1990 | $17,500 | $49,200 | $5,200 |
| **For the week (pay period) ended October 20, 1990:** | | | |
| Hours worked | 46 | 40 | 50 |
| Medical insurance: | | | |
| Jasmine's contribution | $25 | $ 25 | $ 25 |
| Withheld from employee | 15 | 15 | 15 |
| Union dues withheld | 40 | 60 | 40 |
| Federal income tax withheld | 70 | 255 | 120 |
| State income tax withheld | 14 | 51 | 24 |
| **Payroll tax rates:** | | | |
| FICA taxes | 8% on the first $50,000 | | |
| FUTA taxes | 0.8% on the first $7,000 | | |
| State unemployment taxes | 3% on the first $7,000 | | |

*Required*

In solving the following requirements, round all amounts to the nearest whole dollar. Prepare schedules that determine, for each employee and for all employees combined, the following information:

1. Wages earned for the regular 40-hour week, total overtime pay, and gross wages.
2. Vacation pay accrued for the week.
3. Taxes withheld from the employees' wages.
4. Taxes imposed on the employer.
5. Employees' net pay for the week.
6. Employer's total payroll-related cost (wages, taxes, and fringe benefits).

Present journal entries to record the following:

7. Payroll expense.
8. Payroll tax and employees' benefits expense.

## Solution to Demonstration Problem

1. The gross wages (including overtime) for the week.

| | Babcock | Dawson | Sanders | Total |
|---|---|---|---|---|
| Regular wage rate | $ 10 | $ 30 | $ 16 | |
| Regular 40-hour workweek | ×40 | ×40 | ×40 | |
| Regular pay | $400 | $1,200 | $640 | $2,240 |
| Overtime rate | $ 15 | $ 45 | $ 24 | |
| Overtime hours | ×6 | ×–0– | ×10 | |
| Total overtime pay | $ 90 | $ –0– | $240 | 330 |
| Gross wages | $490 | $1,200 | $880 | $2,570 |

2. The vacation pay accrued for the week.

| | Babcock | Dawson | Sanders | Total |
|---|---|---|---|---|
| Annual vacation | 2 weeks | 4 weeks | 2 weeks | |
| Weeks worked in year | 50 weeks | 48 weeks | 50 weeks | |
| Vacation pay as a percentage of regular pay | 4.00% | 8.33% | 4.00% | |
| Regular pay this week | ×$ 400 | ×$1,200 | ×$ 640 | |
| Vacation pay this week | $ 16 | $ 100 | $ 26 | $142 |

The information in the following table is needed for parts 3 and 4:

| Employees | Earnings through October 13 | Earnings This Week | Earnings Subject to FICA | Earnings Subject to Unemployment |
|---|---|---|---|---|
| Babcock | $17,500 | $ 490 | $ 490 | $–0– |
| Dawson | 49,200 | 1,200 | 800 | –0– |
| Sanders | 5,200 | 880 | 880 | 880 |
| Totals | | $2,570 | $2,170 | $880 |

3. The taxes withheld from the employees.

| | Babcock | Dawson | Sanders | Total |
|---|---|---|---|---|
| Federal income tax withholding | $ 70 | $255 | $120 | $445 |
| State income tax withholding | 14 | 51 | 24 | 89 |
| FICA withholding (8%) | 39 | 64 | 70 | 173 |
| Totals | $123 | $370 | $214 | $707 |

4. The taxes imposed on the employer.

| | Babcock | Dawson | Sanders | Total |
|---|---|---|---|---|
| FICA (8%) | $ 39 | $ 64 | $ 70 | $173 |
| FUTA (0.8%) | –0– | –0– | 7 | 7 |
| State unemployment taxes (3%) | –0– | –0– | 26 | 26 |
| Totals | $ 39 | $ 64 | $103 | $206 |

5. The net amount paid to the employees.

| | Babcock | Dawson | Sanders | Total |
|---|---|---|---|---|
| Regular pay | $400 | $1,200 | $640 | $2,240 |
| Overtime pay | 90 | –0– | 240 | 330 |
| Gross pay | $490 | $1,200 | $880 | $2,570 |
| Withholdings: | | | | |
| Federal income tax withholding | $ 70 | $ 255 | $120 | $ 445 |
| State income tax withholding | 14 | 51 | 24 | 89 |
| FICA | 39 | 64 | 70 | 173 |
| Medical insurance | 15 | 15 | 15 | 45 |
| Union dues | 40 | 60 | 40 | 140 |
| Total withholdings | $178 | $ 445 | $269 | $ 892 |
| Net pay to employees | $312 | $ 755 | $611 | $1,678 |

6. The total payroll-related cost to the employer.

| | Babcock | Dawson | Sanders | Total |
|---|---|---|---|---|
| Regular pay | $400 | $1,200 | $ 640 | $2,240 |
| Overtime pay | 90 | –0– | 240 | 330 |
| Gross pay | $490 | $1,200 | $ 880 | $2,570 |
| Taxes and fringe benefits: | | | | |
| FICA tax | $ 39 | $ 64 | $ 70 | $ 173 |
| FUTA tax | –0– | –0– | 7 | 7 |
| State unemployment tax | –0– | –0– | 26 | 26 |
| Vacation pay | 16 | 100 | 26 | 142 |
| Medical insurance | 25 | 25 | 25 | 75 |
| Total taxes and fringe benefits | $ 80 | $ 189 | $ 154 | $ 423 |
| Total payroll related cost | $570 | $1,389 | $1,034 | $2,993 |

7. Journal entry for payroll expense.

| | | | Debit | Credit |
|---|---|---|---|---|
| 1990 | | | | |
| Oct. | 20 | Payroll Expense | 2,570.00 | |
| | | Employees' Federal Taxes Payable | | 445.00 |
| | | Employees' State Taxes Payable | | 89.00 |
| | | FICA Taxes Payable | | 173.00 |
| | | Employees' Medical Insurance Payable | | 45.00 |
| | | Employees' Union Dues Payable | | 140.00 |
| | | Accrued Payroll Payable | | 1,678.00 |
| | | To record payroll expense. | | |

8. Journal entries to record payroll tax and fringe benefit expense.

| | | | Debit | Credit |
|---|---|---|---|---|
| 1990 | | | | |
| Oct. | 20 | Payroll Tax Expense | 206.00 | |
| | | FICA Taxes Payable | | 173.00 |
| | | FUTA Taxes Payable | | 7.00 |
| | | State Unemployment Taxes Payable | | 26.00 |
| | | To record payroll expense. | | |
| | 20 | Employees' Benefits Expense | 217.00 | |
| | | Accrued Vacation Pay | | 142.00 |
| | | Medical Insurance Payable | | 75.00 |
| | | To record fringe benefits expense. | | |

## Glossary

Define or explain the words and phrases listed in the chapter Glossary. (L. O. 5)

**Clock card** a card issued to each employee that the employee inserts in a time clock to record the time of arrival and departure to and from work. p. 550

**Employee fringe benefits** payments by an employer, in addition to wages and salaries, that are made to acquire employee benefits such as insurance coverage and retirement income. pp. 557–559

**Employee's gross pay** the amount an employee earns before any deductions for taxes withheld or other items such as union dues or insurance premiums. p. 548

**Employee's Individual Earnings Record** a record of an employee's hours worked, gross pay, deductions, net pay, and certain personal information about the employee. pp. 555–556

**Employee's net pay** the amount an employee is paid, determined by subtracting from gross pay all deductions for taxes and other items that are withheld from the employee's earnings. p. 552

**Employer's merit rating** an evaluation of an employer by a state, which reflects the employer's experience in maintaining steady employment for its employees or, alternatively, laying them off from time to time. A good rating reduces the employer's unemployment tax rate. p. 547

**Federal depository bank** a bank authorized to receive as deposits amounts of money payable to the federal government. p. 543

**FICA taxes** Federal Insurance Contributions Act taxes, otherwise known as social security taxes, the proceeds of which are used to pay employees' retirement benefits, disability benefits, and certain medical costs after reaching the age of 65. pp. 542–545

**FUTA taxes** federal unemployment taxes levied on employers, the proceeds of which are used primarily to finance administrative expenses of the states' unemployment programs. p. 546

**Payroll bank account** a special bank account a company uses solely for the purpose of paying employees by depositing in the account each pay period an amount equal to the total employees' net pay and drawing the employees' payroll checks on that account. pp. 553–555

**Payroll tax** a tax levied on employers and based on the amount each employee has earned. p. 546

**State unemployment tax** a tax levied by a state on employers, the proceeds of which are used to pay benefits to unemployed workers. p. 547

**Timekeeping** the process of recording the time each employee is on the job. p. 550

**Wage bracket withholding table** a table that shows the amounts of income tax to be withheld from employees' wages at various levels of earnings. pp. 548–549

**Withholding allowance** a number that is used to reduce the amount of federal income tax withheld from an employee's pay, and which corresponds to the personal exemptions the employee is allowed to subtract from annual earnings in calculating taxable income. p. 548

## Objective Review

Answers to the following questions are listed in Appendix I at the end of the book. Be sure that you decide which is the one best answer to each question *before* you check the answers in the appendix.

1. An employee, Rita Ivy, has earnings of $45,000 during the first four months of the year. Her gross salary for May is $11,250. Assume FICA taxes are 8% of the first $50,000, FUTA taxes are 0.8% of the first $7,000, and state unemployment taxes are 3% of the first $7,000. Ms. Ivy has authorized monthly deductions of $110 for medical insurance premiums, which the employer matches with an equal amount. Federal income tax withholding for May is $3,200. Ms. Ivy's net pay for May is:
   *a.* $11,360.00
   *b.* $11,250.00
   *c.* $ 7,940.00
   *d.* $ 7,540.00
   *e.* $ 7,112.50
2. Which of the following steps must be completed when a company uses a special payroll back account?
   *a.* Record the information shown on the Payroll Register with a general journal entry.
   *b.* Write a single check that is payable to Payroll Bank Account for the total amount of the payroll and enter the payment in the Check Register.
   *c.* Deposit a check for the total amount of the payroll in the payroll bank account.
   *d.* Write individual payroll checks to be drawn on the payroll bank account.
   *e.* All of the above.
3. Payroll taxes levied on the employer include:
   *a.* Federal income taxes.
   *b.* State and federal unemployment taxes.
   *c.* FICA taxes applied to all wages earned by each employee.
   *d.* Employer contributions to employee medical insurance.
   *e.* Both (*b*) and (*c*) are correct.
4. Datacom employs two people at $1,800 per month and two people at $4,000 per month. Every employee receives one month's vacation each year. Although no employees took vacation during May, all are expected to take their vacation later this year. In addition, Datacom pays medical insurance premiums of $145 per month per employee and contributes 6% of total salaries to a retirement program. The entry to record these benefits for Datacom employees for the month of May is as follows:

| | | | |
|---|---|---|---|
| *a.* | Employees' Benefits Expense | 2,330.55 | |
| | Estimated Vacation Pay Liability | | 1,054.55 |
| | Employees' Medical Insurance Payable | | 580.00 |
| | Employees' Retirement Program Payable | | 696.00 |

| | | | |
|---|---|---|---|
| b. | Salaries Expense | 11,600.00 | |
| | Estimated Vacation Pay Liability | | 1,054.55 |
| | Employees' Medical Insurance Payable | | 580.00 |
| | Employees' Retirement Program Payable | | 696.00 |
| | Accrued Payroll Payable | | 9,269.45 |
| c. | Estimated Vacation Pay Expense | 1,054.55 | |
| | Employees' Medical Insurance Expense | 580.00 | |
| | Employees' Retirement Program Expense | 696.00 | |
| | Salaries Expense | 11,600.00 | |
| | Accrued Payroll Payable | | 13,930.55 |
| d. | Employees' Benefits Expense | 2,330.55 | |
| | Cash | | 2,330.55 |
| e. | No entry is required. | | |

## Questions for Class Discussion

1. What are FICA taxes? Who pays these taxes and for what purposes are funds from FICA taxes used?
2. What are social security taxes?
3. Fly Company has one employee from whose pay it withholds $40.00 of federal income tax and $21.50 of FICA tax. The employee is paid twice each month. Cast Company has six employees from whose pay it withholds each month a total of $750 of employee FICA taxes and $900 of federal income taxes. When must each of these companies remit these amounts to the Internal Revenue Service?
4. What benefits are paid to unemployed workers from funds raised by the Federal Unemployment Insurance Act? Why was this act passed?
5. Who pays federal unemployment insurance taxes? What is the tax rate?
6. What are the objectives of state unemployment insurance laws? Who pays state unemployment insurance taxes?
7. Why do states assign a merit rating to employers? What is the significance of the rating?
8. What determines the amount that must be deducted from an employee's wages for federal income taxes?
9. What is a wage bracket withholding table?
10. What amount of income tax should be withheld from the salary of a single employee with three withholding allowances who earned $550 in a week? What if the employee earned $660 and had one withholding allowance? (Use the wage bracket withholding table in Illustration 13–3 to find the answers.)
11. What does the Fair Labor Standards Act require of a covered employer?
12. How is a clock card used in recording the time an employee is on the job?
13. How is a special payroll bank account used in paying the wages of employees?

14. At the end of an accounting period, a firm's special payroll bank account has a $685.50 balance because the payroll checks of two employees have not cleared the bank. Should this $685.50 appear on the firm's balance sheet? If so, where?
15. What information is accumulated on an Employee's Individual Earnings Record? Why must this information be accumulated? For what purposes is the information used?
16. What payroll taxes are levied on the employer? What taxes are deducted from the wages of an employee?
17. What are employee fringe benefits? Name some examples.
18. Should the salary of employees while they are on paid vacation be reported as an expense of the period during which they are on vacation? If not, when should the expense be reported?

## Exercises

**Exercise 13–1**
**Calculating gross and net pay**
(L. O. 1)

Terry Rosten, an employee of a company subject to the Fair Labor Standards Act, worked 46 hours during the week ended January 5. Her pay rate is $16 per hour, and her wages are subject to no deductions other than FICA and federal income taxes. She claims two income tax exemptions. Calculate her regular pay, overtime premium pay, gross pay, FICA tax deduction at an assumed 8% rate, income tax deduction (use the wage bracket withholding table of Illustration 13–3), total deductions, and net pay.

**Exercise 13–2**
**Journalizing payroll information**
(L. O. 2)

On January 5, at the end of its first weekly pay period in the year, Clive Company's payroll record showed that its sales employees had earned $3,420 and its office employees had earned $1,800. The employees were to have FICA taxes withheld at an assumed 8% rate plus $738 of federal income taxes, $120 of union dues, and $540 of hospital insurance premiums. Calculate the amount of FICA taxes to be withheld and give the general journal entry to record the payroll.

**Exercise 13–3**
**Calculating payroll deductions and recording the payroll**
(L. O. 1)

The following information as to earnings and deductions for the pay period ended May 12 was taken from a company's payroll records:

| Employees' Names | Gross Pay | Earnings to End of Previous Week | Federal Income Taxes | Health Insurance Deductions |
|---|---|---|---|---|
| Beth Johnson | $ 620 | $ 6,785 | $106.00 | $ 82.00 |
| Dan Tremont | 590 | 6,320 | 81.00 | 82.00 |
| Art Nathan | 500 | 5,500 | 52.00 | 56.50 |
| Sally Becker | 1,500 | 18,200 | 456.00 | 42.50 |
| | $3,210 | | $695.00 | $263.00 |

Calculate the employees' FICA tax withholdings at an assumed 8% rate on the first $50,000 paid each employee and prepare a general journal entry to record the payroll. Assume all employees work in the office.

**Exercise 13–4**
**Calculating and recording payroll taxes**
(L. O. 3)

Use the information provided in Exercise 13–3 to complete the following requirements:

1. Prepare a general journal entry to record the employer's payroll taxes resulting from the payroll. Assume a state unemployment tax rate of 2.1% and a federal unemployment tax of 0.8% on the first $7,000 paid each employee.
2. Prepare a general journal entry to record the following employee benefits incurred by the company: (1) health insurance costs equal to the amounts contributed by each employee and (2) contributions equal to 10% of gross pay for each employee's retirement income program.

**Exercise 13–5**
**Analyzing total labor costs**
(L. O. 4)

Carelli Company's employees earn a gross pay of $20 per hour and work 40 hours each week. The FICA tax rate is 8%, the federal unemployment tax rate is 0.8%, and the state unemployment tax rate is 3.5%. In addition, Carelli Company contributes 10% of gross pay to a retirement program for employees and pays medical insurance premiums of $40 per week per employee. What is Carelli Company's total cost of employing a person for one hour? (Assume that individual wages are less than the $7,000 unemployment tax limit.)

**Exercise 13–6**
**Calculating fringe benefit costs**
(L. O. 4)

Luddite Corporation grants those employees who have worked for the company one complete year vacation time of two weeks. After 10 years of service, employees receive four weeks of vacation. Luddite estimates that 96% of its employees with less than 10 years' service will be granted two weeks' vacation this year, and 99% of those who will have completed 10 or more years of service during the year will be granted four weeks' vacation (1% are expected to resign during their 10th year). The monthly payroll for January includes $160,000 to persons who will not complete 10 years of service this year and $72,000 to persons who, if they do not resign, will have completed 10 years of service by year-end. On January 31, record the January expense arising from the vacation policy of the company.

**Exercise 13–7**
**The cost of FICA tax rate and base changes**
(L. O. 3)

In an effort to reduce the federal government's annual deficit and provide more financial stability to the social security programs of the country, one proposal is to raise FICA tax rates from 7.5% to 10% and to eliminate the $45,000 maximum limitation on the amount of earnings to which the rate applies. What effect would such a proposal have on the total payroll costs of a company with five employees whose salaries are as listed below?

| | |
|---|---|
| A . . . . | $36,700 |
| B . . . . | 45,000 |
| C . . . . | 52,200 |
| D . . . . | 62,200 |
| E . . . . | 79,200 |

**Exercise 13–8**
**Analyzing the cost of payroll taxes and fringe benefits**
(L. O. 3, 4)

Ridder Company's payroll taxes and fringe benefit expenses include unemployment taxes of 0.8% (federal) and 4% (state) on the first $7,000 of each employee's salary, FICA taxes of 8% on the first $50,000, retirement fund contributions of 10% of total earnings, and health insurance premiums of $180 per employee per month. Given the following list of employee salaries, payroll taxes and fringe benefits constitute what percentage of salaries?

| | |
|---|---|
| Belton . . . . . | $31,000 |
| Dirk . . . . . . | 59,700 |
| Hopkins . . . . | 57,500 |
| Jiles . . . . . . | 38,600 |
| Kress . . . . . | 44,200 |

**Exercise 13–9**
**Other payroll deductions**
(L. O. 1)

Curtis Worthington is single, claims four personal exemptions for income tax purposes, and earns a weekly salary of $825. In response to a citywide effort to obtain charitable contributions to the local United Way programs, Worthington has requested that his employer withhold 1% of his salary (net of FICA and income taxes). Assume FICA taxes are 8% of the first $50,000 and use Illustration 13–3 to determine income tax withholdings. Under this program, what will be Worthington's annual contribution to the United Way?

## Problems

**Problem 13–1**
**The Payroll Register and the payroll bank account**
(L. O. 1, 2)

On January 6, at the end of the first weekly pay period of the year, a company's Payroll Register showed that its employees had earned $16,850 of sales salaries and $4,150 of office salaries. Withholdings from the employees' salaries were to include FICA taxes at an assumed rate of 8%, $2,965 of federal income taxes, $840 of hospital insurance, and $275 of union dues.

*Required*

1. Calculate FICA taxes payable and prepare a general journal entry to record the January 6 payroll.
2. Prepare a general journal entry to record the employer's payroll taxes resulting from the January 6 payroll. Assume the company has a merit rating that reduces its state unemployment tax rate to 3.8% of the first $7,000 paid each employee. The federal unemployment tax rate is 0.8%.
3. Under the assumption the company uses a payroll bank account and special payroll checks in paying its employees, give the check register entry (Check No. 542) to transfer funds equal to the payroll from the regular bank account to the payroll bank account.
4. Answer this question: After the check register entry is made and posted, are additional debit and credit entries required to record the payroll checks and pay the employees?

**Problem 13–2**
**The Payroll Register, the payroll bank account, and payroll taxes**
(L. O. 1, 2, 3)

The payroll records of Boutade Corporation provided the following information for the weekly pay period ended December 21:

| Employees | Clock Card No. | Daily Time M | T | W | T | F | S | S | Pay Rate | Federal Income Taxes | Medical Insurance | Union Dues | Earnings to End of Previous Week |
|---|---|---|---|---|---|---|---|---|---|---|---|---|---|
| Paul Lapin | 11 | 8 | 8 | 7 | 7 | 8 | 1 | 0 | $22.00 | $180.00 | $ 50.00 | $15.50 | $40,000 |
| Ruth Moule | 12 | 8 | 7 | 8 | 8 | 8 | 4 | 0 | 18.00 | 150.00 | 50.00 | | 48,000 |
| Carl Simms | 13 | 8 | 8 | 8 | 8 | 8 | 0 | 0 | 20.00 | 120.00 | 50.00 | 15.50 | 5,300 |
| Nick Paxton | 14 | 8 | 8 | 8 | 8 | 8 | 2 | 0 | 24.00 | 117.00 | 45.00 | 15.50 | 35,600 |
| Diana Wood | 15 | 8 | 7 | 8 | 8 | 7 | 3 | 0 | 28.00 | 200.00 | 50.00 | 15.50 | 52,800 |
| | | | | | | | | | | $767.00 | $245.00 | $62.00 | |

*Required*

1. Enter the relevant information in the proper columns of a Payroll Register and complete the register using a FICA tax rate of 8% on the first $50,000 paid each employee. Assume the company is subject to the Fair Labor Standards Act. Charge the wages of Diana Wood to Office Salaries Expense and the wages of the remaining employees to Service Wages Expense.
2. Prepare a general journal entry to record the payroll register information.
3. Make the check register entry (Check No. 399) to transfer funds equal to the payroll from the regular bank account to the payroll bank account under the assumption the company uses special payroll checks and a payroll bank account in paying its employees. Assume the first payroll check is No. 530 and enter the payroll check numbers in the Payroll Register.
4. Prepare a general journal entry to record the employer's payroll taxes resulting from the payroll. Assume the company has a merit rating that reduces its state unemployment tax rate to 4.4% of the first $7,000 paid each employee. The federal unemployment tax rate is 0.8%.

**Problem 13–3**
**The Payroll Register, payroll taxes, and employee fringe benefits**
(L. O. 1, 3, 4)

A company subject to the Fair Labor Standards Act accumulated the following payroll information for the weekly pay period ended December 22:

| Employees | Clock Card No. | Daily Time M | T | W | T | F | S | S | Pay Rate | Income Tax Exemptions | Medical Insurance | Union Dues | Earnings to End of Previous Week |
|---|---|---|---|---|---|---|---|---|---|---|---|---|---|
| Mike Jens | 31 | 7 | 8 | 8 | 8 | 8 | 3 | 0 | $13.00 | 1 | $30.00 | $15.00 | $20,000 |
| Seth Wain | 32 | 8 | 6 | 8 | 8 | 8 | 4 | 0 | 15.50 | 3 | 35.00 | 15.00 | 6,200 |
| Bob Mack | 33 | 8 | 8 | 8 | 8 | 8 | 0 | 0 | 14.50 | 2 | 45.00 | 15.00 | 32,200 |
| Kris Roan | 34 | 8 | 9 | 8 | 8 | 9 | 1 | 0 | 16.00 | 4 | 45.00 | | 5,400 |

*Required*

1. Enter the relevant information in the proper columns of a Payroll Register and complete the register. Assume an 8% FICA tax rate on the first $50,000 of each employee's wages. Use the wage bracket withholding table of Illustration 13–3 to determine the federal income tax to be withheld from the wages of each employee. Assume all employees are single and the first one is a salesperson, the second two work in the shop, and the last one works in the office.
2. Prepare a general journal entry to record the payroll register information.
3. Make the check register entry to transfer funds equal to the payroll from the regular bank account to the payroll bank account (Check No. 522) under the assumption the company uses special payroll checks and a payroll bank account in paying its employees. Assume the first payroll check is No. 230 and enter the payroll check numbers in the Payroll Register.
4. Prepare a general journal entry to record the employer's payroll taxes resulting from the payroll. Assume the company has a merit rating that reduces its state unemployment tax rate to 3.7%. The federal unemployment tax rate is 0.8%.
5. Prepare general journal entries to accrue employee fringe benefit costs for the week. Assume the company matches the employees' payments for medical insurance and contributes an amount equal to 10% of each employee's gross pay to a retirement program. Also, each employee accrues vacation pay at the rate of 5% of the wages and salaries earned. The company estimates that all employees eventually will be paid their vacation pay.

**Problem 13–4**
**General journal entries for payroll transactions**
(L. O. 2)

A company has three employees, each of whom has been employed since January 1, earns $2,000 per month, and is paid on the last day of each month. On March 1, the following accounts and balances appeared in its ledger:

*a.* FICA Taxes Payable, $960. (The balance of this account represents the liability for both the employer and employees' FICA taxes for the February 28 payroll only.)
*b.* Employees' Federal Income Taxes payable, $1,020 (liability for February only).
*c.* Federal Unemployment Taxes Payable, $96 (liability for first two months of the year).
*d.* State Unemployment Taxes Payable, $360 (liability for January and February).
*e.* Employees' Medical Insurance Payable, $1,080 (liability for January and February).

During March and April, the company completed the following transactions related to payroll:

Mar. 11 Issued Check No. 320 payable to East Branch Bank, a federal depository bank authorized to accept employers' payments of FICA taxes and employee income tax withholdings. The $1,980 check was in payment of the February FICA and employee income taxes.

31 Prepared a general journal entry to record the March Payroll Record which had the following column totals:

| FICA Taxes | Federal Income Taxes | Medical Insurance | Total Deductions | Net Pay | Office Salaries | Shop Wages |
|---|---|---|---|---|---|---|
| $480 | $1,020 | $270 | $1,770 | $4,230 | $2,500 | $3,500 |

31 Recorded the employer's $270 liability for its 50% contribution to the medical insurance plan of employees.

31 Issued Check No. 351 payable to Payroll Bank Account in payment of the March payroll. Endorsed the check, deposited it in the payroll bank account, and issued payroll checks to the employees.

31 Prepared a general journal entry to record the employer's payroll taxes resulting from the March payroll. The company has a merit rating that reduces its state unemployment tax rate to 3.0% of the first $7,000 paid each employee. The federal rate is 0.8%.

Apr. 15 Issued Check No. 375 payable to East Branch Bank in payment of the March FICA and employee income taxes.

15 Issued Check No. 376 payable to American Insurance Company in payment of the employee medical insurance premiums for the first quarter.

15 Issued Check No. 377 to the State Tax Commission for the January, February, and March state unemployment taxes. Mailed the check along with the first quarter tax return to the State Tax Commission.

30 Issued Check No. 390 payable to East Branch Bank. The check was in payment of the employer's federal unemployment taxes for the first quarter of the year.

30 Mailed Form 941, reporting the FICA taxes and the employees' federal income tax withholdings for the second quarter.

*Required*

Prepare the necessary check register and general journal entries to record the transactions.

## Alternate Problems

**Problem 13–1A**
**The Payroll Register and the payroll bank account**
(L. O. 1, 2)

Gogol Company's first weekly pay period of the year ended on January 8. On that date, the column totals of the company's Payroll Register indicated its sales employees had earned $19,875, its office employees had earned $9,375, and its delivery employees had earned $2,250. The employees were to have FICA taxes withheld from their wages at an assumed 8% rate plus $3,150 federal income taxes, $1,425 medical insurance deductions, and $340 of union dues.

*Required*

1. Calculate FICA taxes payable and prepare a general journal entry to record the January 8 payroll.
2. Prepare a general journal entry to record the employer's payroll taxes resulting from the January 8 payroll. Assume the company has a merit rating that reduces its state unemployment tax rate to 3.0% of the first $7,000 paid each employee. The federal unemployment tax rate is 0.8%.
3. Under the assumption the company uses a payroll bank account and special payroll checks in paying its employees, give the check register entry (Check No. 378) to transfer funds equal to the payroll from the regular bank account to the payroll bank account.
4. Answer this question: After the check register entry is made and posted, are additional debit and credit entries required to record the payroll checks and pay the employees?

**Problem 13–2A**
**The Payroll Register, the payroll bank account, and payroll taxes**
(L. O. 1, 2, 3)

The following information was taken from the payroll records of Specialty Software Company for the weekly pay period ending December 24:

| Employees | Clock Card No. | Daily Time M | T | W | T | F | S | S | Pay Rate | Federal Income Taxes | Medical Insurance | Union Dues | Earnings to End of Previous Week |
|---|---|---|---|---|---|---|---|---|---|---|---|---|---|
| Lila Tomas | 41 | 8 | 9 | 8 | 8 | 8 | 4 | 0 | $20.00 | $141.00 | $ 35.00 | | $42,500 |
| Mike Lowe | 42 | 7 | 7 | 6 | 8 | 8 | 0 | 0 | 18.00 | 95.00 | 23.00 | $20.00 | 55,800 |
| Rick Corey | 43 | 8 | 8 | 8 | 8 | 8 | 2 | 0 | 22.00 | 107.00 | 46.00 | 20.00 | 6,075 |
| Maria Inez | 44 | 6 | 7 | 8 | 8 | 7 | 2 | 0 | 19.00 | 135.00 | 56.00 | 20.00 | 35,600 |
| James Sun | 45 | 8 | 8 | 8 | 9 | 8 | 0 | 0 | 21.00 | 156.00 | 30.00 | | 49,000 |
| | | | | | | | | | | $634.00 | $190.00 | $60.00 | |

*Required*

1. Enter the relevant information in the proper columns of a Payroll Register and complete the register using an 8% FICA tax rate on the first $50,000 paid each employee. The company pays time and one half for hours in excess of 40 each week. Also, work on Saturdays is paid at time and one half whether the total for the week is over 40 or not. Charge the wages of Lila Tomas to Office Salaries Expense and the wages of the remaining employees to Plant Salaries Expense.
2. Prepare a general journal entry to record the payroll register information.
3. Assume the company uses special payroll checks drawn on a payroll bank account in paying its employees, and make the check register entry (Check No. 484) to transfer funds equal to the payroll from the regular bank account to the payroll bank account. Also assume the first payroll check is No. 631 and enter the payroll check numbers in the Payroll Register.
4. Prepare a general journal entry to record the employer's payroll taxes resulting from the payroll. Assume the company has a merit rating that

reduces its state unemployment tax rate to 3.5% of the first $7,000 paid each employee. The federal unemployment tax rate is 0.8%.

**Problem 13–3A**
**The Payroll Register, payroll taxes, and employee fringe benefits**
(L. O. 1, 3, 4)

The following information for the weekly pay period ended December 10 was taken from the records of a company subject to the Fair Labor Standards Act:

| Employees | Clock Card No. | Daily Time | | | | | | | Pay Rate | Income Tax Exemptions | Medical Insurance | Union Dues | Earnings to End of Previous Week |
|---|---|---|---|---|---|---|---|---|---|---|---|---|---|
| | | M | T | W | T | F | S | S | | | | | |
| Tom Darby | 34 | 7 | 8 | 8 | 7 | 8 | 5 | 0 | $15.00 | 2 | $25.50 | | $25,600 |
| Ed Ward | 35 | 8 | 8 | 7 | 8 | 8 | 3 | 0 | 13.00 | 0 | 18.00 | $15.00 | 6,100 |
| Jill White | 36 | 8 | 8 | 8 | 8 | 7 | 1 | 0 | 14.50 | 3 | 30.50 | | 28,200 |
| Pam Taylor | 37 | 8 | 7 | 9 | 9 | 7 | 4 | 0 | 12.00 | 1 | 22.00 | 15.00 | 6,700 |

*Required*

1. Enter the relevant information in the proper columns of a Payroll Register and complete the register. Use an 8% FICA tax rate to calculate the FICA tax of each employee. Use the wage bracket withholding table of Illustration 13–3 to determine the federal income taxes to be withheld from the wages of each employee. Assume that all employees are single and that the first employee works in the office, the second is a salesperson, and the last two work in the shop.
2. Prepare a general journal entry to record the payroll register information.
3. Make the check register entry (Check No. 389) to transfer funds equal to the payroll from the regular bank account to the payroll bank account. Assume the first payroll check is No. 632 and enter the payroll check numbers in the Payroll Register.
4. Prepare a general journal entry to record the employer's payroll taxes resulting from the payroll. Assume the company has a merit rating that reduces its state unemployment tax rate to 3% of the first $7,000 paid each employee. The federal unemployment tax rate is 0.8%.
5. Prepare a general journal entry to accrue employee fringe benefit costs for the week. Assume the company matches the employees' payments for medical insurance and contributes an amount equal to 10% of each employees' gross pay to a retirement program. Also, Darby and White accrue vacation pay at the rate of 7% of the wages and salaries earned. Ward and Taylor accrue vacation pay at the rate of 5%. The company estimates that all employees eventually will be paid their vacation pay.

**Problem 13–4A**
**General journal entries for payroll transactions**
(L. O. 2)

A company has five employees, each of whom has been employed since January 1, earns $1,200 per month, and is paid on the last day of each month. On June 1, the following accounts and balances appeared on its ledger:

*a.* FICA Taxes Payable, $960. (The balance of this account represents the liability for both the employer and employees' FICA taxes for the May 31 payroll only.)

*b.* Employees' Federal Income Taxes Payable, $1,195 (liability for May only).

*c.* Federal Unemployment Taxes Payable, $96 (liability for April and May only).

*d.* State Unemployment Taxes Payable, $300 (liability for April and May).

*e.* Employees' Medical Insurance Payable, $1,296 (liability for April and May).

During June and July, the company completed the following payroll-related transactions:

June 10 Issued Check No. 726 payable to City State Bank, a federal depository bank authorized to accept employers' payments of FICA taxes and employee income tax withholdings. The $2,155 check was in payment of the May FICA and employee income taxes.

30 Prepared a general journal entry to record the June Payroll Record which had the following column totals:

| FICA Taxes | Federal Income Taxes | Medical Insurance | Total Deductions | Net Pay | Office Salaries | Shop Wages |
|---|---|---|---|---|---|---|
| $480 | $1,195 | $324 | $1,999 | $4,001 | $2,500 | $3,500 |

30 Recorded the employer's $324 liability for its 50% contribution to the medical insurance plan of employees.

30 Issued Check No. 766 payable to Payroll Bank Account in payment of the June payroll. Endorsed the check, deposited it in the payroll bank account, and issued payroll checks to the employees.

30 Prepared a general journal entry to record the employer's payroll taxes resulting from the June payroll. The company has a merit rating that reduces its state unemployment tax rate to 2.5% of the first $7,000 paid each employee. The federal rate is 0.8%.

July 15 Issued Check No. 790 payable to City State Bank in payment of the June FICA and employee income taxes.

15 Issued Check No. 791 payable to Blacke Insurance Company. The check was in payment of the April, May, and June employee health insurance premiums.

15 Issued Check No. 792 to the State Tax Commission for the April, May, and June state unemployment taxes. Mailed the check along with the second quarter tax return to the State Tax Commission.

31 Issued Check No. 801 payable to City State Bank. The check was in payment of the employer's federal unemployment taxes for the second quarter of the year.

31 Mailed Form 941, reporting the FICA taxes and the employees' federal income tax withholdings for the second quarter.

*Required*

Prepare the necessary check register and general journal entries to record the transactions.

## Provocative Problems

**Provocative Problem 13–1**
**Archery Unlimited Company**
(L. O. 1, 3)

Archery Unlimited Company has 80 regular employees, all earning in excess of $7,000 per year. The company's plant and office are located in a state in which the maximum unemployment tax rate is 5.4% of the first $7,000 paid each employee. However, the company has an excellent past unemployment record and a merit rating that reduces its state unemployment tax rate to 3% of the first $7,000 paid each employee.

The company has recently received an order for a line of archery equipment from a chain of department stores. The order should be very profitable and will probably be repeated each year. In filling the order, Archery Unlimited can manufacture the various bows and other supplies with present machines and employees. However, it will have to add 20 persons to its work force for 40 hours per week for 10 weeks to finish the crossbows and pack them for shipment.

The company can hire these workers and add them to its own payroll, or it can secure the services of 20 people through Personnel, Inc. Archery Unlimited will pay Personnel, Inc., $11.75 per hour for each hour worked by each person supplied. The people will be employees of Personnel, Inc., and it will pay their wages and all taxes on the wages. On the other hand, if Archery Unlimited employs the workers and places them on its payroll, it will pay them $10 per hour and will also pay the following payroll taxes on their wages: FICA tax, 8% (assumed rate); federal unemployment tax, 0.8% on the first $7,000 paid each employee; state unemployment tax, 4.5% on the first $7,000 paid each employee. (The state unemployment tax rate will be 4.5% because if the company hires the temporary people and terminates them each year after 10 weeks, it will receive a less favorable merit rating.) The company will also have to pay medical insurance costs of $30 per employee per week.

Should Archery Unlimited place the temporary help on its own payroll, or should it secure their services through Personnel, Inc.? Justify your answer.

**Provocative Problem 13–2**
**Astrolabs Company**
(L. O. 1, 3)

Astrolabs Company employs a scientific specialist at an annual salary of $66,000. The company pays federal unemployment taxes of 0.8% and state unemployment taxes of 3.5% on the first $7,000 of the specialist's salary. FICA taxes are 8% of the first $50,000. The company also pays $150 per month for the employee's medical insurance. Effective June 1, the company agreed to contribute 15% of the specialist's gross pay to a retirement program.

What was the total monthly cost of employing the specialist in January, March, July, and December? Assuming the employee works 180 hours each month, what is the cost per hour in January? If the annual gross salary is increased by $4,000, what will be the increase in the total annual costs of employing the specialist?

# 14 Partnership Accounting

The three common types of business organization, single proprietorships, partnerships, and corporations, were introduced in the early chapters of this book. In this chapter, we look more closely at the partnership form of business organization. The partnership form is widely used, especially in businesses where the owners know each other well. Many professional businesses, including CPA firms, are organized as partnerships.

**Learning Objectives**

*After studying Chapter 14, you should be able to:*

1. List the characteristics of a partnership and explain the importance of mutual agency and unlimited liability to a person about to become a partner.
2. Allocate partnership earnings to partners (*a*) on a stated fractional basis, (*b*) in the partners' capital ratio, and (*c*) through the use of salary and interest allowances.
3. Prepare entries for (*a*) the sale of a partnership interest, (*b*) the admission of a new partner by investment, and (*c*) the retirement of a partner by the withdrawal of partnership assets.
4. Prepare entries required in the liquidation of a partnership.
5. Define or explain the words and phrases listed in the chapter Glossary.

## Characteristics of a Partnership

List the characteristics of a partnership and explain the importance of mutual agency and unlimited liability to a person about to become a partner. (L. O. 1)

A majority of states have adopted the Uniform Partnership Act to govern the formation and operation of partnerships. This act defines a **partnership** as "an association of two or more persons to carry on as co-owners a business for profit." Another definition of a partnership is "an association of two or more competent persons under a contract to combine some or all of their property, labor, and skills in the operation of a business." Both of these definitions say something about the legal nature of a partnership. However, the nature of the partnership form of business becomes clearer when you understand some of the specific features that characterize partnerships.

### A Voluntary Association

A partnership is a voluntary association between the partners. This voluntary nature of a partnership is important because a person assumes some risk by entering a partnership. For example, each partner is responsible for the business acts of his or her partners when the acts are within the scope of the partnership. Also, a partner is personally liable for all of the debts of his or her partnership. As a result, you never have to join a partnership without agreeing who will be the partners. Normally, you should select only financially responsible people who have good judgment.

### Based on a Contract

One advantage of a partnership as a form of business organization is that it is easy to organize. All that is necessary is for two or more legally competent people to agree to become partners. Their agreement becomes a **partnership contract.** This contract should be carefully written so that all anticipated points of future disagreement are covered. However, even if the partners make their agreement orally and fail to put it in writing, the partnership contract is binding.

### Limited Life

The life of a partnership is always limited. Death, bankruptcy, or anything that takes away the ability of one of the partners to contract automatically ends a partnership. In addition, since a partnership is based on a contract, the contract may state a period of time after which the partnership ends. If the contract does not specify a time period, the partnership ends when the business for which it was created is completed. Or, if no time is stated because the business is expected to go on indefinitely, the partnership may be terminated at will by any one of the partners.

### Mutual Agency

In most partnerships, the partners are understood to be mutual agents of the partnership. **Mutual agency** means that every partner can act as an agent of the partnership by committing it to any contract within the apparent scope of its business. For example, a partner in a merchandising business can sign contracts that bind the partnership to buy merchandise, lease a store building, borrow money for the business, or hire employees. These are all within the scope of a merchandising firm. On the other hand, a partner in a law firm, acting alone, cannot contract on behalf of his or her partners to buy merchandise for resale or to rent a store building. These are not within the normal scope of a law firm's business.

Partners may agree to limit the agency powers of any one or more of the partners to negotiate certain contracts for the partnership. Such an agreement is binding on the partners and on outsiders who know of the agreement. However, it is not binding on outsiders who do not know that it exists. Outsiders who are not aware of the agreement have a right to assume that each partner has the normal agency rights of a partner.

Because mutual agency exposes all partners to the actions of any one partner, you should carefully evaluate potential partners before agreeing to join a partnership. The importance of this advice becomes clear when you consider the fact that most partnerships are also characterized by unlimited liability. Mutual agency plus unlimited liability are the reasons most partnerships have only a few partners.

### Unlimited Liability

Normally, when a partnership cannot pay its debts, the creditors may satisfy their claims from the personal assets of the partners. Also, if the property of a partner is insufficient to meet his or her share of the partnership's debts, the creditors may turn to the assets of the remaining partners who are able to pay. Thus, one partner may be called on to pay all the debts of the partnership. This **unlimited liability of partners** is a very important characteristic of partnerships.

Unlimited liability may be illustrated as follows. Ned Albert and Carol Bates each invested $5,000 in a store to be operated as a partnership. They also agreed to share net incomes and losses equally. Albert has no property other than his $5,000 investment. Bates has sizable savings in addition to her investment. After renting a store, the partners bought merchandise for $30,000, paying $10,000 in cash and promising to pay the balance at a later date. However, before the business opened, the store burned and the merchandise was totally destroyed. There was no insurance, and all the partnership assets were lost. Albert has no other assets. Because of unlimited liability, the partnership creditors can collect the full $20,000 of their claims from Bates. However, Bates may look to Albert for payment of half at a later date, if Albert ever is able to pay.

## Limited Partnerships

So far, we have said that all partners normally have unlimited liability. Sometimes, however, a group of individuals want to invest in a partnership but are unwilling to accept the risk of unlimited liability. This can be accomplished by using a unique form of business called a **limited partnership.** A limited partnership has two classes of partners, general partners and limited partners. At least one of the partners, the **general partner(s)** must assume unlimited liability for the debts of the partnership. However, the remaining **limited partners,** have no personal liability beyond the amounts they invest in the business. Usually, a limited partnership is managed by the general partner(s). The limited partners have no active role except for certain major decisions as specified in the partnership agreement. To distinguish limited partnerships from those in which all of the partners have unlimited liability, the latter are often called **general partnerships.**

## Advantages and Disadvantages of a Partnership

Limited life, mutual agency, and unlimited liability are disadvantages of a partnership. Yet, there are other reasons why a partnership may be a preferred form of business organization. A partnership has the advantage of being able to bring together more money and skills than a single proprietorship. A partnership is easier to organize than a corporation. Also, a partnership may escape some of the federal and state regulations and taxes that are imposed on corporations. Finally, partners may act without having to hold stockholders' or directors' meetings, which are required of a corporation.

## Partnership Accounting

Accounting for a partnership is no different than accounting for a single proprietorship except for transactions that directly affect the partners' equities. Because ownership rights in a partnership are divided between two or more partners, there must be:

1. A capital account for each partner.
2. A withdrawals account for each partner.
3. A careful measurement and division of earnings.

When partners invest in a partnership, the capital account of each partner is credited for the amount of that partner's investment. Thereafter, each partner's withdrawals are debited to his or her withdrawals account. And, in the end-of-period closing procedure, a net income is allocated to the partners by crediting each partner's capital account for his or her share. Obviously, these closing procedures are like those you would use for a single proprietorship. The only difference is that separate capital and withdrawals accounts are maintained for each partner. Thus, the closing procedures for a partnership require no further consideration. However, we should examine more carefully the matter of allocating earnings among partners.

## Nature of Partnership Earnings

Partners cannot enter into an employer-employee contractual relationship with themselves. They cannot legally hire themselves and pay themselves a salary. If partners devote their time and services to the affairs of their partnership, they are understood to do so for profit, not for salary. Therefore, when the net income or loss of a partnership is calculated, salary allowances to partners are not deducted as expenses. However, when the net income or loss of the partnership is allocated among the partners, the partners may agree to base part of the allocation on the relative amounts of service provided by the partners.

Just as salary allowances to partners are not expenses of the partnership, neither is interest on the partners' investments. Partners are understood to invest in a partnership for profit, not for interest. Nevertheless, partners may agree that the division of partnership earnings should include a return on invested capital. For example, if one partner contributes five times as much capital as another, fairness would require that this fact be taken into consideration when earnings are allocated among the partners. Likewise, if the services of one partner are more valuable than those of another, some provision should be made for the unequal service contributions.

## Division of Earnings

Allocate partnership earnings to partners (*a*) on a stated fractional basis, (*b*) in the partners' capital ratio, and (*c*) through the use of salary and interest allowances. (L. O. 2)

In the absence of a contrary agreement, the law states that the income or loss of a partnership is shared equally by the partners. However, partners may agree to any method of sharing. If they agree on a method of sharing incomes but say nothing of losses, then losses are shared in the same way as incomes.

Several methods of allocating partnership earnings among the partners are commonly used. Three frequently used methods are to allocate earnings based on: (1) stated fractions assigned to each partner, (2) the ratio of capital investments, or (3) salary and interest allowances and the remainder in a fixed ratio.

## Earnings Allocated on a Stated Fractional Basis

The easiest way to divide partnership earnings is to give each partner a stated fraction of the total. A division on a fractional basis may provide for an equal sharing if service and capital contributions are equal. An equal sharing may also be provided when the greater capital contribution of one partner is offset by a greater service contribution of another. Or, if the service and capital contributions are unequal, a fixed ratio may provide for an unequal sharing. All that is necessary in any case is for the partners to agree as to the fractional share each will receive.

For example, assume that the partnership agreement of Morse and North states that Morse will receive two thirds and North will receive one third of the partnership earnings and the partnership's net income for a year is $30,000. Therefore, after all revenue and expense accounts are closed at the end of the year, the Income Summary account has a $30,000 credit balance. The entry to close the Income Summary account and to allocate the partnership's earnings to the partners is as follows:

| | | | | |
|---|---|---|---|---|
| Dec. | 31 | Income Summary | 30,000.00 | |
| | | A. P. Morse, Capital | | 20,000.00 |
| | | R. G. North, Capital | | 10,000.00 |
| | | To close the Income Summary account and allocate the earnings. | | |

## Division of Earnings Based on the Ratio of Capital Investments

If the nature of a partnership's business is such that earnings are closely related to money invested, a division of earnings based on the ratio of partners' investments offers a fair sharing method. To illustrate this method, assume that Chase, Davis, and Fall have agreed to share earnings in the ratio of their investments. These are Chase, $50,000, Davis, $30,000, and Fall, $40,000. If net income for the year is $48,000, the respective shares of the partners are calculated as follows:

| | | |
|---|---|---|
| **Step 1:** | Chase, capital . . . . | $ 50,000 |
| | Davis, capital. . . . . | 30,000 |
| | Fall, capital . . . . . | 40,000 |
| | Total invested . . . . | $120,000 |

**Step 2:** Share of earnings to Chase: $\frac{\$50,000}{\$120,000} \times \$48,000 = \$20,000$

Share of earnings to Davis: $\frac{\$30,000}{\$120,000} \times \$48,000 = \$12,000$

Share of earnings to Fall: $\frac{\$40,000}{\$120,000} \times \$48,000 = \$16,000$

The entry to allocate the earnings to the partners is then:

| | | | | |
|---|---|---|---|---|
| Dec. | 31 | Income Summary . . . . . . . . . . . . . . . . . . . . . | 48,000.00 | |
| | | T. S. Chase, Capital . . . . . . . . . . . . . . . . . | | 20,000.00 |
| | | S. A. Davis, Capital . . . . . . . . . . . . . . . . . | | 12,000.00 |
| | | R. R. Fall, Capital . . . . . . . . . . . . . . . . . . | | 16,000.00 |
| | | To close the Income Summary account and allocate the earnings. | | |

## Salaries and Interest Allowances

Sometimes partners' service contributions are not equal. Also, the capital contributions of the partners may not be equal. Even in partnerships in which all partners work full time, the services of one partner may be more valuable than the services of another. If the service contributions are not equal, the partners may use salary allowances to compensate for the differences. Or, when capital contributions are not equal, they may allocate part of the earnings in the form of interest to compensate for the unequal investments. When service and investment contributions are both unequal, they may use a combination of salary and interest allowances in an effort to share earnings fairly.

For example, in Hill and Dale's net partnership, Hill is to provide annual services that they agree are worth an annual salary of $36,000. Dale is less experienced in the business, so his service contribution to the business is worth only $24,000. Also, Hill will invest $30,000 in the business, and Dale will invest $10,000. To compensate the partners fairly, given the differences in their service and capital contributions, Hill and Dale agree that they will share incomes or losses as follows:

1. Partners are to be granted annual salary allowances of $36,000 to Hill and $24,000 to Dale.
2. Partners are to be granted an interest allowance equal to 10% of each partner's beginning-of-year capital balance.
3. The remaining balance of income or loss is to be shared equally.

**Illustration 14–1**
**Sharing income when income exceeds interest and salary allowances**

| | Share to Hill | Share to Dale | Totals |
|---|---|---|---|
| Total net income | | | $ 69,000 |
| Allocated as salary allowances: | | | |
| Hill | $36,000 | | |
| Dale | | $24,000 | |
| Total allocated as salary allowances | | | (60,000) |
| Balance of income after salary allowances | | | $ 9,000 |
| Allocated as interest: | | | |
| Hill (10% on $30,000) | 3,000 | | |
| Dale (10% on $10,000) | | 1,000 | |
| Total allocated as interest | | | (4,000) |
| Balance of income after salary and interest allowances | | | $ 5,000 |
| Balance allocated equally: | | | |
| Hill | 2,500 | | |
| Dale | | 2,500 | |
| Total allocated equally | | | (5,000) |
| Balance of income | | | $ -0- |
| Shares of the partners | $41,500 | $27,500 | |

Note that the provisions for salaries and interest in this partnership agreement are called *allowances*. They are called allowances because, in a legal sense, partners do not work for salaries and they do not invest in a partnership to earn interest. They invest and work for earnings. Therefore, when a partnership agreement provides for salaries and interest, these allowances are not reported as salaries and interest expense. They are only a means of sharing income or losses.

Under the Hill and Dale agreement, a first year net income of $69,000 would be shared as in Illustration 14–1.

After the shares in the net income are determined, the following entry is used to close the Income Summary account. Note that the credit amounts in the entry are taken from the first two column totals of the computation shown in Illustration 14–1.

| | | | | |
|---|---|---|---|---|
| Dec. | 31 | Income Summary | 69,000.00 | |
| | | Hill, Capital | | 41,500.00 |
| | | Dale, Capital | | 27,500.00 |
| | | To close the Income Summary account and allocate the earnings. | | |

In Illustration 14–1, the $69,000 net income exceeded the salary and interest allowances of the partners. However, the partners would use the same method to share a loss or to share a net income that was smaller than their salary and interest allowances. For example, assume that Hill and Dale earned only $45,000 during the first year of operations. A $45,000 net income would be shared by the partners as in Illustration 14–2.

**Illustration 14–2**
**Sharing income when interest and salary allowances exceed income**

| | Share to Hill | Share to Dale | Totals |
|---|---|---|---|
| Total net income . . . . . . . . . . . . . . . . . . | | | $ 45,000 |
| Allocated as salary allowances: | | | |
| Hill . . . . . . . . . . . . . . . . . . . . . . . . | $36,000 | | |
| Dale . . . . . . . . . . . . . . . . . . . . . . . . | | $24,000 | |
| Total allocated as salary allowances . . . . | | | (60,000) |
| Balance of income after salary allowances. . . | | | $(15,000) |
| Allocated as interest: | | | |
| Hill (10% on $30,000) . . . . . . . . . . . . | 3,000 | | |
| Dale (10% on $10,000) . . . . . . . . . . . . | | 1,000 | |
| Total allocated as interest . . . . . . . . . . | | | (4,000) |
| Balance of income after salary and interest allowances . . . . . . . . . . . . . . . . . | | | $(19,000) |
| Balance allocated equally: | | | |
| Hill . . . . . . . . . . . . . . . . . . . . . . . . | (9,500) | | |
| Dale . . . . . . . . . . . . . . . . . . . . . . . . | | (9,500) | |
| Total allocated equally . . . . . . . . . . . . . | | | (19,000) |
| Balance of income . . . . . . . . . . . . . . . | | | $ -0- |
| Shares of the partners . . . . . . . . . . . . . | $29,500 | $15,500 | |

The same procedures used to allocate a net income between Hill and Dale would also be used to allocate a net loss. The only difference is that the income-and-loss-sharing procedure would begin with a negative amount of income (a net loss). The amount allocated equally would then be a larger negative amount.

## Partnership Financial Statements

In most respects, partnership financial statements are like those of a single proprietorship. On the balance sheet of a partnership, the owner's equity section often shows the separate capital account balance of each partner. The **statement of changes in partners' equity** shows the total capital balances at the beginning of the period, any additional investments made by the partners, the net income or loss of the partnership, withdrawals by the partners, and the ending capital balances. Usually, this statement shows these changes for each partner's capital account and includes the allocation of income among the partners. For example, recall that Hill and Dale began their partnership by making investments of $30,000 and $10,000, respectively. During the first year of operations, in which the partnership earned $45,000, assume that Hill withdrew $20,000 and Dale withdrew $12,000. The statement of changes in partners' equity appears in Illustration 14–3.

## Withdrawal or Addition of a Partner

A partnership is based on a contract between specific individuals. Therefore, when a partner withdraws from a partnership, the old partnership ceases to exist. Nevertheless, the business may continue to operate as a new partnership among the remaining partners.

The withdrawal of a partner from a partnership may take place two different ways. First, the withdrawing partner may sell his or her interest to another

**Illustration 14–3**
**A statement of changes in partners' equity**

**HILL AND DALE**
**Statement of Changes in Partners' Equity**
**For Year Ended December 31, 19—**

| | Hill | | Dale | | Total |
|---|---|---|---|---|---|
| Beginning capital balances | | $ -0- | | $ -0- | $ -0- |
| Plus: | | | | | |
| Investments by owners | | 30,000 | | 10,000 | 40,000 |
| Net income: | | | | | |
| Salary allowances | $36,000 | | $24,000 | | |
| Interest allowances | 3,000 | | 1,000 | | |
| Balance | (9,500) | | (9,500) | | |
| Total net income | | 29,500 | | 15,500 | 45,000 |
| Total | | $ 59,500 | | $ 25,500 | $ 85,000 |
| Less partners' withdrawals | | (20,000) | | (12,000) | (32,000) |
| Ending capital balances | | $ 39,500 | | $ 13,500 | $ 53,000 |

Prepare entries for (*a*) the sale of a partnership interest, (*b*) the admission of a new partner by investment, and (*c*) the retirement of a partner by the withdrawal of partnership assets. (L. O. 3)

person who pays for the interest by transferring cash or other assets to the withdrawing partner. Second, cash or other assets of the partnership may be distributed to the withdrawing partner in settlement of his or her interest in the partnership.

When a new partner is admitted to a partnership, the old partnership technically ends and is replaced by a new partnership. Similar to the withdrawal of a partner, there are two ways a new partner may be admitted to an existing partnership. First, the new partner may purchase an interest directly from one or more of its partners. In other words, the new partner may pay cash to one or more of the existing partners in exchange for an interest in the partnership. Second, a new partner may join an existing partnership by investing cash or other assets in the business.

## Sale of a Partnership Interest

Exam

Assume that Abbott, Burns, and Camp are partners in a partnership that owes no liabilities and has the following assets and owners' equity:

| Assets | | Owners' Equity | |
|---|---|---|---|
| Cash | $ 3,000 | Abbott, capital | $ 5,000 |
| Other assets | 12,000 | Burns, capital | 5,000 |
| | | Camp, capital | 5,000 |
| Total assets | $15,000 | Total owners' equity | $15,000 |

Camp's equity in this partnership is $5,000. If Camp sells this equity to Davis for $7,000, Camp is selling a $5,000 recorded interest in the partnership assets. The entry on the partnership books to transfer the equity is:

| | | | | |
|---|---|---|---|---|
| Feb. | 4 | Camp, Capital | 5,000.00 | |
| | | Davis, Capital | | 5,000.00 |
| | | To transfer Camp's equity in the partnership to Davis. | | |

After this entry is posted, the assets and owners' equity of the new partnership are:

| Assets | | Owners' Equity | |
|---|---|---|---|
| Cash | $ 3,000 | Abbott, capital | $ 5,000 |
| Other assets | 12,000 | Burns, capital | 5,000 |
| | | Davis, capital | 5,000 |
| Total assets | $15,000 | Total owners' equity | $15,000 |

Two aspects of this transaction are especially important. First, the $7,000 Davis paid to Camp is not recorded in the partnership books. Camp sold and transferred a $5,000 recorded equity in the partnership assets to Davis. The entry that records the transfer is a debit to Camp, Capital and a credit to Davis, Capital for $5,000. Furthermore, the entry is the same whether Davis pays Camp $7,000, or $70,000. The amount is paid directly to Camp. Since the partnership is not a party to the transaction, the assets and the total equity of the partnership are not affected by the transaction.

The second important aspect of this transaction is the question of whether Davis's purchase of Camp's interest qualifies Davis as a new partner. In fact, Abbott and Burns must agree to the sale and transfer if Davis is to become a partner. Abbott and Burns cannot prevent Camp from selling the interest to Davis. But Abbott and Burns do not have to accept Davis as a partner. If Abbott and Burns agree to accept Davis, a new partnership is formed and a new contract with a new income-and-loss-sharing ratio must be drawn.

What if either Abbott or Burns refuses to accept Davis as a partner? Under the Uniform Partnership Act, Davis gets Camp's share of partnership income and losses. And if the partnership is liquidated, Davis gets Camp's share of partnership assets. However, Davis gets no voice in the management of the firm until admitted as a partner.

### Investing Assets in an Existing Partnership

Instead of purchasing the equity of an existing partner, an individual may gain an equity by investing assets in the business. Then, the invested assets become the property of the partnership. For example, assume that the partnership of Evans and Gage has assets and owners' equity as follows:

| Assets | | Owners' Equity | |
|---|---|---|---|
| Cash | $ 3,000 | Evans, capital | $20,000 |
| Other assets | 37,000 | Gage, capital | 20,000 |
| Total assets | $40,000 | Total owners' equity | $40,000 |

Also, assume that Evans and Gage have agreed to accept Hart as a partner with a one-half interest in the business upon his investment of $40,000. The entry to record Hart's investment is:

| | | | | |
|---|---|---|---|---|
| Mar. | 2 | Cash | 40,000.00 | |
| | | Hart, Capital | | 40,000.00 |
| | | To record the investment of Hart. | | |

After the entry is posted, the assets and owners' equity of the new partnership appear as follows:

| Assets | | Owners' Equity | |
|---|---|---|---|
| Cash | $43,000 | Evans, capital | $20,000 |
| Other assets | 37,000 | Gage, capital | 20,000 |
| | | Hart, capital | 40,000 |
| Total assets | $80,000 | Total owners' equity | $80,000 |

In this case, Hart has a 50% equity in the assets of the business. However, he does not necessarily have a right to one half of its net income. The sharing of incomes and losses is a separate matter on which the partners must agree. As you learned earlier in the chapter, the sharing of profits and losses may be in the ratio of the partners' relative capital contributions. However, the method of sharing also may depend on other factors.

### A Bonus to the Old Partners

Sometimes, when the current value of a partnership is greater than the amounts of equity recorded in the accounting records, the partners may require an incoming partner to give a bonus for the privilege of joining the firm. For example, Judd and Kirk operate a partnership business, sharing its earnings equally. The partnership's accounting records show that Judd's recorded equity in the business is $38,000 and Kirk's recorded equity is $32,000. Judd and Kirk agree to accept Lee's $50,000 investment in the business in return for a one-third share of the partnership's earnings and a one-third equity in net assets. Lee's equity is determined with a calculation as follows:

| | |
|---|---|
| Equities of the existing partners ($38,000 + $32,000) | $ 70,000 |
| Investment of the new partner | 50,000 |
| Total partnership equity | $120,000 |
| Equity of Lee (⅓ of total) | $ 40,000 |

Notice that although Lee invested $50,000 in the partnership, his equity in the recorded net assets of the partnership is only $40,000. The $10,000 difference usually is described as a bonus that is allocated to the existing partners (Judd and Kirk). Therefore, the entry to record Lee's investment is:

| | | | | |
|---|---|---|---|---|
| May | 15 | Cash | 50,000.00 | |
| | | Lee, Capital | | 40,000.00 |
| | | Judd, Capital | | 5,000.00 |
| | | Kirk, Capital | | 5,000.00 |
| | | To record the investment of Lee. | | |

Notice that the $10,000 difference between the $50,000 invested by Lee and the $40,000 credited to his capital account is shared by Judd and Kirk according to their income-and-loss-sharing ratio. Such a bonus is always shared by the old partners in their income-and-loss-sharing ratio. This ratio is used because the bonus compensates the old partners for increases in the worth of the partnership that have not yet been recorded as income.

### Recording Goodwill

As discussed above, when a new partner's investment exceeds his or her equity in the partnership's net assets, the entry to record the new partner's admission normally allocates a bonus to the existing partners. Occasionally, however, an alternative method is used to record the admission of a new partner. The alternative method involves recording goodwill on the books of the partnership. The debit to Goodwill is matched with credits that increase the equities of the existing partners.

The goodwill method of recording a new partner's admission would be used only if the evidence indicates that future earnings of the partnership are large enough to justify the increased partnership equity. Evidence of such future earnings might be provided by a historical record of earnings that are consistently in excess of the average for the industry.

In practice, goodwill is seldom recognized upon the admission of a new partner. Instead, the bonus method usually is used.

### Bonus to the New Partner

Sometimes, the members of an existing partnership may be very eager to bring a new partner into their firm. The business may need additional cash or the new partner may have exceptional abilities or business contacts that will increase profits. In such a situation, the old partners may be willing to give the new partner a larger equity in the business than the amount of his or her investment. In this case, the old partners give a bonus to the new partner.

For example, Jay Moss and Mike Owen are partners with capital account balances of $30,000 and $18,000, respectively. They share income and losses in a 2:1 ratio. The partners are anxious to have Kay Pitt join their partnership and will grant her a one-fourth equity in the firm if she will invest $12,000. If Pitt accepts, her equity in the new firm is calculated as follows:

| | |
|---|---|
| Equities of the existing partners ($30,000 + $18,000) . . | $48,000 |
| Investment of the new partner . . . . . . . . . . . . . . | 12,000 |
| Total equities in the new partnership . . . . . . . . . . | $60,000 |
| Equity of Pitt (¼ of total) . . . . . . . . . . . . . . . . . | $15,000 |

And the entry to record Pitt's investment is:

| | | | | |
|---|---|---|---|---|
| June | 1 | Cash . . . . . . . . . . . . . . . . . . . . . . . . . . . | 12,000.00 | |
| | | Moss, Capital ($3,000 × ⅔) . . . . . . . . . . . . . . . | 2,000.00 | |
| | | Owen, Capital ($3,000 × ⅓) . . . . . . . . . . . . . . . | 1,000.00 | |
| | | Pitt, Capital . . . . . . . . . . . . . . . . . . . . . . | | 15,000.00 |
| | | To record the investment of Pitt. | | |

Note that Pitt's bonus is contributed by the old partners in their income-and-loss-sharing ratio. Also remember that Pitt's one-fourth equity does not necessarily entitle her to one fourth of the earnings of the business. The sharing of income and losses is a separate matter for agreement by the partners.

### Withdrawal of a Partner

When a new partnership is formed, the partnership contract should state the procedures to be followed when a partner retires from the partnership. These procedures often state that a withdrawing partner shall withdraw assets equal to the current value of the partner's equity. To accomplish this, the procedures may require an audit of the accounting records and a revaluation of the partnership assets. The revaluation places the assets on the books at current values. It also causes the partners' capital accounts to reflect the current value of their equity.

For example, assume that Blue is retiring from the partnership of Smith, Blue, and Short. The partners have always shared incomes and losses in the ratio of one half to Smith, one fourth to Blue, and one fourth to Short. Their partnership agreement provides for an audit and asset revaluation upon the retirement of a partner. Just prior to the audit and revaluation, their balance sheet shows the following assets and owners' equity:

| Assets | | | Owners' Equity | |
|---|---|---|---|---|
| Cash . . . . . . . . . . . | | $11,000 | Smith, capital . . . . . . . . | $22,000 |
| Merchandise inventory . . | | 16,000 | Blue, capital . . . . . . . . . | 10,000 |
| Equipment . . . . . . . . . | $20,000 | | Short, capital . . . . . . . . | 10,000 |
| Less accum. depr. . . . | 5,000 | 15,000 | | |
| Total assets . . . . . . . . | | $42,000 | Total owners' equity . . . . . | $42,000 |

The audit and appraisal indicate that the merchandise inventory is overvalued by $4,000. Also, due to market changes, the partnership's equipment should be valued at $25,000, less accumulated depreciation of $8,000. The entries to record these revaluations are:

| | | | | |
|---|---|---|---|---|
| Oct. | 31 | Smith, Capital | 2,000.00 | |
| | | Blue, Capital | 1,000.00 | |
| | | Short, Capital | 1,000.00 | |
| | | Merchandise Inventory | | 4,000.00 |
| | | To revalue the inventory. | | |
| | 31 | Equipment | 5,000.00 | |
| | | Accumulated Depreciation, Equipment | | 3,000.00 |
| | | Smith, Capital | | 1,000.00 |
| | | Blue, Capital | | 500.00 |
| | | Short, Capital | | 500.00 |
| | | To revalue the equipment. | | |

Note in the illustrated entries that the partners share the amount of the revaluations in their income-and-loss-sharing ratio. This is fair because revaluations of assets are actually gains and losses. If the partnership were not terminated, these gains and losses would sooner or later show up on the income statement as increases and decreases in net income. The revaluation simply records the effect of the gains and losses earlier than would have occurred.

After the entries revaluing the partnership assets are recorded, the balance sheet for the Smith, Blue, and Short partnership is as follows:

| Assets | | | Owners' Equity | |
|---|---|---|---|---|
| Cash | | $11,000 | Smith, capital | $21,000 |
| Merchandise inventory | | 12,000 | Blue, capital | 9,500 |
| Equipment | $25,000 | | Short, capital | 9,500 |
| Less accum. depr. | 8,000 | 17,000 | | |
| Total assets | | $40,000 | Total owners' equity | $40,000 |

After the revaluation, if Blue retires and takes cash equal to his revalued equity, the entry to record the withdrawal is:

| | | | | |
|---|---|---|---|---|
| Oct. | 31 | Blue, Capital | 9,500.00 | |
| | | Cash | | 9,500.00 |
| | | To record the withdrawal of Blue. | | |

In withdrawing, Blue does not have to take cash in settlement of his equity. He may take any combination of assets to which the partners agree, or he may take the new partnership's promissory note. Also, the withdrawal of Blue generally creates a new partnership between the remaining partners. Therefore, a new partnership contract and a new income-and-loss-sharing agreement may be required.

### Withdrawing Partner Takes Fewer Assets than Recorded Equity

Sometimes, when a partner retires, the remaining partners may not wish to revalue the assets on the books of the partnership. Nevertheless, the current values of the partnership assets must be determined so that the amount of assets to be taken by the retiring partner can be established. For example, the partners may agree that the assets are overvalued. As a result, the retiring partner should be given assets of less value than the book value of his or her equity. Also, even if the assets are not overvalued, a retiring partner may be willing to take less than the current value of his or her equity just to get out of the partnership.

When a partner retires and takes assets of less value than the partner's recorded equity, the partner in effect leaves a portion of the equity in the business. In such cases, the remaining partners share the unwithdrawn equity portion in their income-and-loss-sharing ratio. For example, assume that Black, Brown, and Green are partners who share incomes and losses in a 2:2:1 ratio. Their assets and equities are as follows:

| Assets | | Owners' Equity | |
|---|---|---|---|
| Cash | $ 5,000 | Black, capital | $ 6,000 |
| Merchandise inventory | 9,000 | Brown, capital | 6,000 |
| Store equipment | 4,000 | Green, capital | 6,000 |
| Total assets | $18,000 | Total owners' equity | $18,000 |

Brown is anxious to withdraw from the partnership and offers to take $4,500 in cash in settlement for his equity. Black and Green agree to the $4,500 withdrawal, and Brown retires. The entry to record the retirement is:

| | | | | |
|---|---|---|---|---|
| Mar. | 4 | Brown, Capital | 6,000.00 | |
| | | Cash | | 4,500.00 |
| | | Black, Capital | | 1,000.00 |
| | | Green, Capital | | 500.00 |
| | | To record the withdrawal of Brown. | | |

In retiring, Brown withdrew $1,500 less than his recorded equity. This is divided between Black and Green in their income-and-loss-sharing ratio. The income-and-loss-sharing ratio of the original partnership was Black, 2; Brown, 2; and Green, 1. Therefore, the ratio for sharing between Black and Green was 2:1, and the unwithdrawn book equity of Brown is shared by Black and Green in this ratio.

### Withdrawing Partner Takes More Assets than Recorded Equity

There are two common reasons why a retiring partner might withdraw more assets than his or her recorded equity. First, the partnership assets may be undervalued on the books. Also, the continuing partners may want to encourage the retiring partner to withdraw by giving up assets of greater value than the retiring partner's recorded equity.

When assets are undervalued, the partners may not wish to change the recorded values. If a retiring partner is allowed to withdraw assets of greater value than that partner's recorded equity, the retiring partner is, in effect, withdrawing his or her own equity plus a portion of the continuing partners' equities.

## AS A MATTER OF ETHICS

An accountant has been engaged by the Able, Baker, and Charlie Company to assist in settling the claims of Fran Baker's estate against the partnership following her recent accidental death. Among the records is the partnership agreement, which, unfortunately, has an ambiguous section dealing with settlements in the event of a partner's death. It says that a deceased partner's estate is entitled to the "appropriate share of the partnership assets."

The executor of the estate has suggested that the estate is entitled to one third of the partnership assets' current value. Able, on the other hand, has suggested that the distribution should be based on the book value of the assets, which is only 75% of the current value. Charlie is concerned about the partnership liabilities, which equal 40% of the assets' book value, and 30% of current value, and has felt that the estate is entitled to only one third of the equity. Given their close friendship, the tragedy of Baker's death, and the prosperity of the partnership, none of the three parties will sue to resolve the difference, but they are eager to do what is "right and fair." What should the accountant suggest?

For example, assume that Jones, Thomas, and Finch are partners that share incomes and losses in a 3:2:1 ratio. The assets and owners' equity of the partnership are as follows:

| Assets | | Owners' Equity | |
|---|---|---|---|
| Cash | $ 5,000 | Jones, capital | $ 9,000 |
| Merchandise inventory | 10,000 | Thomas, capital | 6,000 |
| Equipment | 3,000 | Finch, capital | 3,000 |
| Total assets | $18,000 | Total owners' equity | $18,000 |

Finch wishes to withdraw from the partnership. Jones and Thomas plan to continue the business. The partners agree that some of the partnership's assets are undervalued, but they do not wish to increase the recorded values. They further agree that if current values were recorded, the asset total would be increased by $6,000 and the equity of Finch would be increased by $1,000. Therefore, the partners agree that $4,000 is the proper value for Finch's equity and that amount of cash may be withdrawn. The entry to record the withdrawal is:

| | | | | |
|---|---|---|---|---|
| May | 7 | Finch, Capital | 3,000.00 | |
| | | Jones, Capital | 600.00 | |
| | | Thomas, Capital | 400.00 | |
| | | Cash | | 4,000.00 |
| | | To record the withdrawal of Finch. | | |

### Death of a Partner

A partner's death automatically dissolves a partnership. As a result, the deceased partner's estate is entitled to receive the amount of his or her equity. The partnership contract should contain provisions for settlement in case a partner dies. Included should be provisions for (*a*) an immediate closing of the books to determine earnings since the end of the previous accounting period and (*b*) a method for determining and recording current values for the assets and liabilities. After these steps are taken, the remaining partners and the deceased partner's estate must agree to a disposition of the deceased partner's equity. This may involve selling the equity to the remaining partners or to an outsider, or it may involve the withdrawal of assets in settlement. We explained the appropriate entries for both cases in the previous paragraphs.

## Liquidations

Prepare entries required in the liquidation of a partnership. (L. O. 4)

When a partnership is liquidated, its business is ended. The assets are converted into cash, and the creditors are paid. The remaining cash is then distributed to the partners, and the partnership is dissolved. **Partnership liquidations** may follow a variety of different steps. However, we will limit the following discussion to three typical situations.

### All Assets Realized before a Distribution; Assets Are Sold at a Profit

One case involving a partnership liquidation is the situation in which all of the partnership assets are converted into cash at a profit, before any cash is distributed to the partners. The following example shows the necessary accounting entries to be made under these conditions.

Ottis, Skinner, and Parr have operated a partnership for a number of years, sharing incomes and losses in a 3:2:1 ratio. Due to several unsatisfactory conditions, the partners decide to liquidate as of December 31. On that date, the books are closed, and the income from operations is transferred to the partners' capital accounts. Thereafter, the partnership's balance sheet appears as follows:

| Assets | | Liabilities and Owners' Equity | |
|---|---|---|---|
| Cash . . . . . . . . . . . . . . . . | $10,000 | Accounts payable . . . . . . . . . | $ 5,000 |
| Merchandise inventory . . . . . | 15,000 | Ottis, capital . . . . . . . . . . . . | 15,000 |
| Other assets . . . . . . . . . . . | 25,000 | Skinner, capital . . . . . . . . . . | 15,000 |
| | | Parr, capital . . . . . . . . . . . | 15,000 |
| Total assets . . . . . . . . . . . | $50,000 | Total liabilities and owners' equity . . . . . . . . . | $50,000 |

In a liquidation, some gains or losses normally result from the sale of noncash assets. These losses and gains are called "losses and gains from realization." Just like any other net incomes or losses, the losses and gains from realization are shared by the partners in their income-and-loss-sharing ratio. For example, if Ottis, Skinner, and Parr sell their inventory for $12,000 and their other assets for $34,000, the sales and the net gain allocation are recorded as follows:

| | | | | |
|---|---|---|---|---|
| Jan. | 12 | Cash . . . . . . . . . . . . . . . . . . . . . . . . . . . . | 12,000.00 | |
| | | Loss or Gain from Realization . . . . . . . . . . . . . . . | 3,000.00 | |
| | | Merchandise Inventory . . . . . . . . . . . . . . . . . | | 15,000.00 |
| | | Sold the inventory at a loss. | | |

| | | | | |
|---|---|---|---|---|
| Jan. | 15 | Cash | 34,000.00 | |
| | | Other Assets | | 25,000.00 |
| | | Loss or Gain from Realization | | 9,000.00 |
| | | Sold the other assets at a profit. | | |
| | 15 | Loss or Gain from Realization | 6,000.00 | |
| | | Ottis, Capital | | 3,000.00 |
| | | Skinner, Capital | | 2,000.00 |
| | | Parr, Capital | | 1,000.00 |
| | | To allocate the net gain from realization to the partners in their 3:2:1 income-and-loss-sharing ratio. | | |

Notice in the last entry that the losses and gains from realization were shared in the partners' income-and-loss-sharing ratio. In solving liquidation problems, do not make the mistake of allocating the losses and gains in the ratio of the partners' capital balances.

After the merchandise and other assets of Ottis, Skinner, and Parr are sold and the net gain is allocated, a new balance sheet shows the following:

| Assets | | Liabilities and Owners' Equity | |
|---|---|---|---|
| Cash | $56,000 | Accounts payable | $ 5,000 |
| | | Ottis, capital | 18,000 |
| | | Skinner, capital | 17,000 |
| | | Parr, capital | 16,000 |
| Total assets | $56,000 | Total liabilities and owners' equity | $56,000 |

Observe that the one asset, cash, $56,000, exactly equals the sum of the liabilities and the equities of the partners.

After partnership assets are realized and the gain or loss shared, the realized cash is distributed to the proper parties. Since creditors have first claim, they are paid first. After the creditors are paid, the remaining cash is divided among the partners. Each partner has the right to cash equal to his or her equity or, in other words, cash equal to the balance of his or her capital account. The entries to record the final cash payments and distribution to Ottis, Skinner, and Parr are:

| | | | | |
|---|---|---|---|---|
| Jan. | 15 | Accounts Payable | 5,000.00 | |
| | | Cash | | 5,000.00 |
| | | To pay the claims of the creditors. | | |
| | 15 | Ottis, Capital | 18,000.00 | |
| | | Skinner, Capital | 17,000.00 | |
| | | Parr, Capital | 16,000.00 | |
| | | Cash | | 51,000.00 |
| | | To distribute the remaining cash to the partners according to their capital account balances. | | |

Notice that after gains and losses are shared and the creditors are paid, each partner receives cash equal to the balance remaining in his capital account. The partners receive these amounts because a partner's capital account balance represents the partner's equity in the remaining partnership asset, cash. In making the entry to distribute cash to the partners, be sure that you do not make the mistake of distributing it in the partners' income-and-loss-sharing ratio. Gains and losses from realization are allocated according to the income-and-loss-sharing ratio; but cash must be distributed to the partners in relation to their capital account balances.

### All Assets Realized before a Distribution; Assets Sold at a Loss; Each Partner's Capital Account Is Sufficient to Absorb His or Her Share of the Loss

In a partnership liquidation, the assets are sometimes sold at a net loss. For example, assume that the Ottis, Skinner, and Parr partnership does not sell its assets at a profit. Instead, assume that the inventory is sold for $10,000 and the other assets for $12,000. The entries to record the sales and loss allocation are:

| | | | | |
|---|---|---|---|---|
| Jan. | 12 | Cash | 10,000.00 | |
| | | Loss or Gain from Realization | 5,000.00 | |
| | | Merchandise Inventory | | 15,000.00 |
| | | Sold the inventory at a loss. | | |
| | 15 | Cash | 12,000.00 | |
| | | Loss or Gain from Realization | 13,000.00 | |
| | | Other Assets | | 25,000.00 |
| | | Sold the other assets at a loss. | | |
| | 15 | Ottis, Capital | 9,000.00 | |
| | | Skinner, Capital | 6,000.00 | |
| | | Parr, Capital | 3,000.00 | |
| | | Loss or Gain from Realization | | 18,000.00 |
| | | To allocate the loss from realization to the partners in their income-and-loss-sharing ratio. | | |

After the entries are posted, a balance sheet shows that the partnership cash exactly equals the liabilities and the equities of the partners, as follows:

| Assets | | Liabilities and Owners' Equity | |
|---|---|---|---|
| Cash | $32,000 | Accounts payable | $ 5,000 |
| | | Ottis, capital | 6,000 |
| | | Skinner, capital | 9,000 |
| | | Parr, capital | 12,000 |
| Total assets | $32,000 | Total liabilities and owners' equity | $32,000 |

The following entries are required to distribute the cash to the proper parties:

| | | | | |
|---|---|---|---|---|
| Jan. | 15 | Accounts Payable . . . . . . . . . . . . . . . . . . . . . . | 5,000.00 | |
| | | Cash . . . . . . . . . . . . . . . . . . . . . . . . . . | | 5,000.00 |
| | | To pay the partnership creditors. | | |
| | 15 | Ottis, Capital . . . . . . . . . . . . . . . . . . . . . . . . | 6,000.00 | |
| | | Skinner, Capital . . . . . . . . . . . . . . . . . . . . . . | 9,000.00 | |
| | | Parr, Capital . . . . . . . . . . . . . . . . . . . . . . . . | 12,000.00 | |
| | | Cash . . . . . . . . . . . . . . . . . . . . . . . . . . | | 27,000.00 |
| | | To distribute the remaining cash to the partners according to the balances of their capital accounts. | | |

Notice again that after losses are shared and creditors are paid, the remaining cash is distributed to the partners in the ratio of their capital account balances.

#### All Assets Realized before a Distribution; Assets Sold at a Loss; a Partner's Capital Account Is Not Sufficient to Cover His or Her Share of the Loss

Sometimes, the liquidation losses allocated to a partner will exceed that partner's capital account balance. In such cases, the partner must, if possible, cover the deficit by paying cash into the partnership. For example, contrary to the previous illustrations, assume that the Ottis, Skinner, and Parr partnership sells its merchandise for $3,000 and sells its other assets for $4,000. The entries to record the sales and the loss allocation are:

| | | | | |
|---|---|---|---|---|
| Jan. | 12 | Cash . . . . . . . . . . . . . . . . . . . . . . . . . . . . | 3,000.00 | |
| | | Loss or Gain from Realization . . . . . . . . . . . . . . . | 12,000.00 | |
| | | Merchandise Inventory . . . . . . . . . . . . . . . . . . | | 15,000.00 |
| | | Sold the inventory at a loss. | | |
| | 15 | Cash . . . . . . . . . . . . . . . . . . . . . . . . . . . . | 4,000.00 | |
| | | Loss or Gain from Realization . . . . . . . . . . . . . . . | 21,000.00 | |
| | | Other Assets . . . . . . . . . . . . . . . . . . . . . . . | | 25,000.00 |
| | | Sold the other assets at a loss. | | |
| | 15 | Ottis, Capital . . . . . . . . . . . . . . . . . . . . . . . . | 16,500.00 | |
| | | Skinner, Capital . . . . . . . . . . . . . . . . . . . . . . | 11,000.00 | |
| | | Parr, Capital . . . . . . . . . . . . . . . . . . . . . . . . | 5,500.00 | |
| | | Loss or Gain from Realization . . . . . . . . . . . . . | | 33,000.00 |
| | | To allocate the loss from realization to the partners in their income-and-loss-sharing ratio. | | |

After you post the entry to allocate the realization loss, the capital account of Ottis has a $1,500 debit balance and appears as follows:

**Ottis, Capital**

| Date | Explanation | Debit | Credit | Balance |
|---|---|---|---|---|
| Dec. 31 | Balance | | | 15,000.00 |
| Jan. 15 | Share of loss from realization | 16,500.00 | | (1,500.00) |

The partnership agreement states that one half of all losses or gains should be allocated to Ottis. Therefore, since Ottis's capital account balance is not large enough to absorb his share of the loss, he is obligated to pay $1,500 into the partnership to cover the deficit. If Ottis is able to pay, the following entry is made:

| | | | | |
|---|---|---|---|---|
| Jan. | 15 | Cash | 1,500.00 | |
| | | Ottis, Capital | | 1,500.00 |
| | | To record the additional investment of Ottis to cover his share of realization losses. | | |

After the $1,500 is received, the partnership has $18,500 in cash. The following entries are then made to distribute the cash to the proper parties:

| | | | | |
|---|---|---|---|---|
| Jan. | 15 | Accounts Payable | 5,000.00 | |
| | | Cash | | 5,000.000 |
| | | To pay the partnership creditors. | | |
| | 15 | Skinner, Capital | 4,000.00 | |
| | | Parr, Capital | 9,500.00 | |
| | | Cash | | 13,500.00 |
| | | To distribute the remaining cash to the partners according to the balances of their capital accounts. | | |

When a partnership's liquidation losses create a debit balance in one partner's capital account balance, that partner may be unable to make up the deficit. In such cases, since each partner has unlimited liability, the deficit must be borne by the remaining partner or partners. For example, assume that Ottis is unable to pay the $1,500 necessary to cover the deficit in his capital account. If Ottis is unable to pay, his deficit must be shared by Skinner and Parr in their income-and-loss-sharing ratio. The partners share income and losses in the ratio of Ottis, 3; Skinner, 2; and Parr, 1. Therefore, Skinner and Parr share in a 2:1 ratio. This means that Skinner and Parr must share the $1,500 by which Ottis's share of the losses exceeded his capital account balance in a 2:1 ratio. Normally, the defaulting partner's deficit is transferred to the capital accounts of the remaining partners. This is accomplished for Ottis, Skinner, and Parr with the following entry:

| | | | | |
|---|---|---|---|---|
| Jan. | 15 | Skinner, Capital | 1,000.00 | |
| | | Parr, Capital | 500.00 | |
| | | Ottis, Capital | | 1,500.00 |
| | | To transfer the deficit of Ottis to the capital accounts of Skinner and Parr. | | |

After the deficit is transferred, the capital accounts of the partners appear as in Illustration 14–4. The entries to record the final payments to creditors and distribution to the partners are as follows:

**Illustration 14–4**
**Allocating liquidation losses and partner's deficit to capital accounts**

**Ottis, Capital**

| Date | Explanation | Debit | Credit | Balance |
|---|---|---|---|---|
| Dec. 31 | Balance | | | 15,000.00 |
| Jan. 15 | Share of loss from realization | 16,500.00 | | (1,500.00) |
| 15 | Deficit to Skinner and Parr | | 1,500.00 | –0– |

**Skinner, Capital**

| Date | Explanation | Debit | Credit | Balance |
|---|---|---|---|---|
| Dec. 31 | Balance | | | 15,000.00 |
| Jan. 15 | Share of loss from realization | 11,000.00 | | 4,000.00 |
| 15 | Deficit to Skinner and Parr | 1,000.00 | | 3,000.00 |

**Parr, Capital**

| Date | Explanation | Debit | Credit | Balance |
|---|---|---|---|---|
| Dec. 31 | Balance | | | 15,000.00 |
| Jan. 15 | Share of loss from realization | 5,500.00 | | 9,500.00 |
| 15 | Deficit to Skinner and Parr | 500.00 | | 9,000.00 |

| | | | | |
|---|---|---|---|---|
| Jan. | 15 | Accounts Payable | 5,000.00 | |
| | | Cash | | 5,000.00 |
| | | To pay the partnership creditors. | | |
| | 15 | Skinner, Capital | 3,000.00 | |
| | | Parr, Capital | 9,000.00 | |
| | | Cash | | 12,000.00 |
| | | To distribute the remaining cash to the partners according to their capital account balances. | | |

You should understand that the inability of Ottis to meet his loss share at this time does not relieve him of liability. If he becomes able to pay at some future time, Skinner and Parr may collect the full $1,500 from him. Skinner may collect $1,000, and Parr, $500.

## Summary of the Chapter in Terms of Learning Objectives

**1.** A partnership is a voluntary association between the partners that is based on a contract. The life of a partnership is limited by agreement or by the death or incapacity of a partner. Normally, each partner can act as an agent of the other partners and commit the partnership to any contract within the apparent scope of its business. All partners in a general partnership are personally liable for all the debts of the partnership. Limited partnerships include one or more general partners plus one or more (limited) partners whose liabilities are limited to the amount of their investments in the partnership. The risk of becoming a partner results in part from the fact that partnership characteristics include mutual agency and unlimited liability.

**2.** A partnership's net incomes or losses are allocated to the partners according to the partnership agreement. The agreement may specify that each partner will receive a given fraction, or that the allocation of incomes and losses will reflect salary allowances and/or interest allowances. When salary and/or interest allowances are granted, the residual net income or loss usually is allocated equally or on a stated fractional basis.

**3.** When a new partner buys a partnership interest directly from one or more of the existing partners, the amount of cash paid from one partner to another does not affect the total recorded equity of the partnership. The recorded equity of the selling partner(s) is simply transferred to the capital account of the new partner. Alternatively, a new partner may purchase an equity by investing additional assets in the partnership. When this occurs, part of the new partner's investment may be credited as a bonus to the capital accounts of the existing partners. Also, to gain the participation of the new partner, the existing partners may give the new partner a bonus whereby portions of the existing partners' capital balances are transferred to the new partner's capital account. Occasionally, goodwill is recorded when a new partner invests in a partnership.

**4.** When a partnership is liquidated, losses and gains from selling the partnership assets are allocated to the partners according to their income-and-loss-sharing ratio. If a partner's capital account has a deficit balance that the partner cannot pay, the other partners must share the deficit in their relative income-and-loss-sharing ratio.

## Demonstration Problem

The following events affect the partner's capital accounts in several successive partnerships. On a work sheet with six money columns, one for each of five partners and a totals column, show the effects of the following events on the partners' capital accounts:

4/13/88 Kelly and Emerson create K&E Co. Each invests $10,000, and they agree to share profits equally.

12/31/88 K&E Co. earns $15,000 in the year. Kelly withdraws $4,000 from the partnership, and Emerson withdraws $7,000.

1/1/89 Reed is made a partner in KE&R Co. after contributing $12,000 cash. The partners agree that each will get a 10% interest allowance on their beginning capital balances. In addition, Emerson and Reed are to receive $5,000 salary allowances. The remainder of the income is to be divided evenly.

12/31/89 The partnership's income for the year is $40,000, and these withdrawals occur: Kelly, $5,000; Emerson, $12,500; and Reed, $11,000.

1/1/90 For $20,000, Kelly sells her interest to Merritt, who is accepted by Emerson and Reed as a partner in the new ER&M Co. The profits are to be shared equally after Emerson and Reed each receive $25,000 salaries.

12/31/90 The partnership's income for the year is $35,000, and these withdrawals occur: Emerson, $2,500; and Reed, $2,000.

1/1/91 Davis is admitted as a partner after investing $60,000 cash in the new Davis & Associates partnership. Davis is given a 50% interest in capital after the other partners transfer $3,000 to his account from each of theirs. A 20% interest allowance on the beginning-of-year capital balances will be used in sharing profits, but there will be no salaries. Davis will get 40% of the remainder, and the other three partners will each get 20%.

12/31/91 Davis & Associates earns $127,600 for the year, and these withdrawals occur: Emerson, $25,000; Reed, $27,000; Merritt, $15,000; and Davis, $40,000.

1/1/92 Davis buys out Emerson and Reed for the balances of their capital accounts, after a revaluation of the partnership assets. The revaluation gain is $50,000, which is divided in the previous 1:1:1:2 ratio. Davis pays the others from personal funds. Merritt and Davis will share profits on a 1:9 ratio.

2/29/92 The partnership had $10,000 of income since the beginning of the year. Merritt retires and receives partnership cash equal to her capital balance. Davis takes possession of the partnership assets in his own name, and the company is dissolved.

## Solution to Demonstration Problem

| Event | Kelly | Emerson | Reed | Merritt | Davis | Total |
|---|---|---|---|---|---|---|
| 4/13/88 | | | | | | |
| Initial investment | $ 10,000 | $ 10,000 | | | | $ 20,000 |
| 12/31/88 | | | | | | |
| Income (equal) | 7,500 | 7,500 | | | | 15,000 |
| Withdrawals | (4,000) | (7,000) | | | | (11,000) |
| Ending balance | $ 13,500 | $ 10,500 | | | | $ 24,000 |
| 1/1/89 | | | | | | |
| New investment | | | $ 12,000 | | | 12,000 |
| 12/31/89 | | | | | | |
| 10% interest | 1,350 | 1,050 | 1,200 | | | 3,600 |
| Salaries | | 5,000 | 5,000 | | | 10,000 |
| Remainder (equal) | 8,800 | 8,800 | 8,800 | | | 26,400 |
| Withdrawals | (5,000) | (12,500) | (11,000) | | | (28,500) |
| Ending balance | $ 18,650 | $ 12,850 | $ 16,000 | | | $ 47,500 |
| 1/1/90 | | | | | | |
| Transfer interest | (18,650) | | | $ 18,650 | | –0– |
| 12/31/90 | | | | | | |
| Salaries | | 25,000 | 25,000 | | | 50,000 |
| Remainder (equal) | | (5,000) | (5,000) | (5,000) | | (15,000) |
| Withdrawals | | (2,500) | (2,000) | | | (4,500) |
| Ending balance | $ –0– | $ 30,350 | $ 34,000 | $ 13,650 | | $ 78,000 |
| 1/1/91 | | | | | | |
| New investment | | | | | $ 60,000 | 60,000 |
| Bonuses to Davis | | (3,000) | (3,000) | (3,000) | 9,000 | –0– |
| Adjusted balance | | $ 27,350 | $ 31,000 | $ 10,650 | $ 69,000 | $ 138,000 |

| Event | Kelly | Emerson | Reed | Merritt | Davis | Total |
|---|---|---|---|---|---|---|
| 12/31/91 | | | | | | |
| 20% interest | | 5,470 | 6,200 | 2,130 | 13,800 | 27,600 |
| Remainder (1:1:1:2) | | 20,000 | 20,000 | 20,000 | 40,000 | 100,000 |
| Withdrawals | | (25,000) | (27,000) | (15,000) | (40,000) | (107,000) |
| Ending balance | | $ 27,820 | $ 30,200 | $ 17,780 | $ 82,800 | $ 158,600 |
| Gain (1:1:1:2) | | 10,000 | 10,000 | 10,000 | 20,000 | 50,000 |
| Adjusted balance | | $ 37,820 | $ 40,200 | $ 27,780 | $ 102,800 | $ 208,600 |
| Transfer interests | | (37,820) | (40,200) | | 78,020 | -0- |
| Adjusted balance | | $ -0- | $ -0- | $ 27,780 | $ 180,820 | $ 208,600 |
| 2/29/92 | | | | | | |
| Income (1:9) | | | | 1,000 | 9,000 | 10,000 |
| Adjusted balance | | | | $ 28,780 | $ 189,820 | $ 218,600 |
| Settlements | | | | (28,780) | (189,820) | (218,600) |
| Final balance | | | | $ -0- | $ -0- | $ -0- |

## Glossary

Define or explain the words and phrases listed in the chapter Glossary. (L. O. 5)

**Deficit** a negative balance in an account. p. 596

**General partner(s)** a partner who assumes unlimited liability for the debts of the partnership. p. 578

**General partnership** a partnership in which all partners have unlimited liability for partnership debts. p. 579

**Limited partners** partners who have no personal liability for debts of the limited partnership beyond the amounts they have invested in the partnership. p. 578

**Limited partnership** a partnership that has two classes of partners, limited partners and one or more general partners. p. 578

**Mutual agency** a characteristic of the relationship between the partners in a partnership whereby each partner is able to bind the partnership to contracts within the apparent scope of the partnership business. pp. 577–578

**Partnership** an association by contract of two or more persons to carry on a business as co-owners for profit. p. 577

**Partnership contract** the agreement between partners that sets forth the terms under which the affairs of a partnership will be conducted. p. 577

**Partnership liquidations** the winding up of a partnership business by converting its assets to cash and distributing the cash to the proper parties. p. 592

**Statement of Changes in Partners' Equity** a financial statement that shows the total capital balances at the beginning of the period, any additional investments by the partners, the net income or loss of the period, the partners' withdrawals during the period, and the ending capital balances. p. 583

**Unlimited liability of partners** the legal characteristic of a partnership that makes each general partner responsible for paying all the debts of the partnership if the other partners are unable to pay their shares. p. 578

## Objective Review

Answers to the following questions are listed in Appendix I at the end of the book. Be sure that you decide which is the one best answer to each question *before* you check the answers in the appendix.

1. Which of the following is a characteristic of a partnership?
   *a.* A partnership is a voluntary association between two or more persons.
   *b.* A partnership is organized by means of a partnership contract.
   *c.* The life of a partnership is always limited.
   *d.* Unless the partnership contract specifies otherwise, each partner can act on behalf of the other partners and commit the partnership to any contract within the scope of its business.
   *e.* All of the above are characteristics of a partnership.
2. Jekyll and Hyde form a partnership with initial investments of $50,000 and $25,000, respectively. The partners agree to annual salary allowances of $30,000 to Jekyll and $20,000 to Hyde. Also, they agree to an

interest allowance equal to 10% of each partner's beginning-of-year capital balance. The remaining balance of income or loss is to be shared equally. How would a first year net income of $15,000 be shared between Jekyll and Hyde?
*a.* Jekyll, $ 8,750; Hyde, $6,250.
*b.* Jekyll, $ 7,500; Hyde, $7,500.
*c.* Jekyll, $ 9,500; Hyde, $5,500.
*d.* Jekyll, $13,750; Hyde, $1,250.
*e.* Jekyll, $ 9,000; Hyde, $6,000.

3. Crosby and Stills operate a partnership and share earnings equally. Crosby's recorded equity is $80,000, and Still's recorded equity is $70,000. Crosby and Stills agree to accept Nash's $60,000 investment in the business in return for a one quarter share of the partnership's earnings and a one quarter equity in net assets. The entry to record Nash's investment in the partnership would include:
*a.* A credit to Crosby, Capital for $13,750.
*b.* A credit to Stills, Capital for $7,500.
*c.* A credit to Nash, Capital for $60,000.
*d.* A debit to Stills, Capital for $11,250.
*e.* Both (*a*) and (*c*) are correct.

4. The balance sheet for the partnership of Miller, Perry, and Thornton before liquidation is as follows:

| Assets | | Liabilities and Owners' Equity | |
|---|---|---|---|
| Cash | $ 6,000 | Accounts payable | $15,000 |
| Merchandise inventory | 42,000 | Miller, capital | 30,000 |
| Other assets | 27,000 | Perry, capital | 10,000 |
| | | Thornton, capital | 20,000 |
| Total assets | $75,000 | Total liabilities and owners' equity | $75,000 |

The merchandise inventory and other assets are sold for a total of $60,000. If incomes and losses are shared on a 3:2:1 ratio, what amount of cash should Perry receive upon distribution of the remaining cash?
*a.* $20,000.
*b.* $10,000.
*c.* $ 7,000.
*d.* $17,000.
*e.* $ 8,500.

## Questions for Class Discussion

1. Groan and Moan are partners. Groan dies, and his son claims the right to take his father's place in the partnership. Does he have this right? Why?
2. If Sue Wiles cannot legally enter into a contract, can she become a partner?
3. If a partnership contract does not state the period of time the partnership is to exist, when does the partnership end?
4. What does the term *mutual agency* mean as applied to a partnership?

5. Kurt and Ellen are partners in the operation of a store. Without consulting Kurt, Ellen enters into a contract for the purchase of merchandise for resale by the store. Kurt contends that he did not authorize the order and refuses to take delivery. The vendor sues the partners for the contract price of the merchandise. Will the partnership have to pay? Why?
6. Would your answer to Question 5 differ if Kurt and Ellen were partners in a public accounting firm?
7. May partners limit the right of a member of their firm to bind their partnership to contracts? Is such an agreement binding (*a*) on the partners and (*b*) on outsiders?
8. What does the term *unlimited liability* mean when it is applied to members of a general partnership?
9. South organized a limited partnership and is the only general partner. North invested $20,000 in the partnership and was admitted as a limited partner with the understanding that he would receive 10% of the profits. After two unprofitable years, the partnership ceased doing business. At that point, partnership liabilities were $85,000 larger than partnership assets. How much money can the creditors of the partnership obtain from North in satisfaction of the unpaid partnership debts?
10. How does a general partnership differ from a limited partnership?
11. George, Burton, and Dillman have been partners for three years. The partnership is dissolving. George is leaving the firm while Burton and Dillman plan to carry on the business. In the final settlement, George places a $75,000 salary claim against the partnership. His contention is that since he devoted all of his time for three years to the affairs of the partnership, he has a claim for a salary of $25,000 for each year. Is his claim valid? Why?
12. The partnership agreement of Barnes and Ardmore provides for a two-thirds, one-third sharing of income but says nothing about losses. The first year of partnership operations resulted in a loss, and Barnes argues that the loss should be shared equally since the partnership agreement said nothing about sharing losses. Do you agree?
13. A and B are partners who agree that A will receive a $50,000 salary allowance after which remaining incomes or losses will be shared equally. If B's capital account is credited $1,000 as his share of the net income in a given period, how much net income did the partnership earn?
14. W, X, and Y are partners with capital account balances of $7,000 each. Z pays W $8,000 for his one-third interest and is admitted to the partnership. The bookkeeper debits W, Capital and credits Z, Capital for $7,000. Z objects; he wants his capital account to show an $8,000 balance, the amount he paid for his interest. Explain why Z's capital account is credited for $7,000.
15. If the partners in Blatt Partnership want the financial statements to show the procedures used to allocate the partnership income among the partners, on what financial statement should the allocation appear?

16. After all partnership assets are converted to cash and all liabilities have been paid, the remaining cash should equal the sum of the balances of the partners' capital accounts. Why?
17. Fern, Vern, and Hern are partners. In a liquidation, Fern's share of partnership losses exceeds her capital account balance. She is unable to meet the deficit from her personal assets, and the excess losses are shared by her partners. Does this relieve Fern of liability?
18. A partner withdraws from a partnership and receives assets of greater value than the book value of his equity. Should the remaining partners share the resulting reduction in their equities in the ratio of their relative capital balances or in their income-and-loss-sharing ratio?

## Exercises

**Exercise 14–1**
**Journalizing partnership entries**
(L. O. 2)

On February 1, 1990, Young and Olde formed a partnership in which Young contributed $70,000 and Olde contributed land valued at $80,000 and a building valued at $90,000. The partnership also is to assume responsibility for Olde's $30,000 long-term note payable. The partners agreed to share profits as follows: Young is to receive an annual salary allowance of $35,000, each partner is to receive 10% of his or her original capital investment, and any remaining profit or loss is to be shared equally. On November 20, 1990, Young withdrew cash of $40,000 and Olde withdrew $30,000. Present general journal entries to record the initial capital investments of the partners, the cash withdrawals of the partners, the December 31 closing of the withdrawals accounts and the Income Summary account, which had a credit balance of $68,000.

**Exercise 14–2**
**Income allocation in a partnership**
(L. O. 2)

Newberg and Scampi began a partnership by investing $52,000 and $78,000, respectively. During its first year, the partnership earned $180,000. Prepare calculations that show how the income should be allocated to the partners under each of the following plans for sharing net incomes and losses:

*a.* The partners failed to agree on a method of sharing income.
*b.* The partners agreed to share incomes and losses in their investment ratio.
*c.* The partners agreed to share income by allowing an $85,000 per year salary allowance to Newberg, a $65,000 per year salary allowance to Scampi, 10% interest on beginning capital balances, and the remainder equally.

**Exercise 14–3**
**Income allocation in a partnership**
(L. O. 2)

Assume the partners to Exercise 14–2 agreed to share net incomes and losses by allowing yearly salary allowances of $85,000 to Newberg and $65,000 to Scampi, 10% interest allowances on their investments, and the balance equally. (*a*) Determine the shares of Newberg and Scampi in a first-year net income of $145,300. (*b*) Determine the partners' shares in a first-year net loss of $30,200.

**Exercise 14–4**
**Sale of a partnership interest**
(L. O. 3)

The partners in the Duprix Partnership have agreed that partner Dupont may sell his $70,000 equity in the partnership to Queen, for which Queen will pay Dupont $55,000. Present the partnership's journal entry to record the sale on April 30.

**Exercise 14–5**
**Admission of a new partner**
(L. O. 3)

The Hagen-Baden Partnership has total partners' equity of $380,000, which is made up of Hagen, Capital, $300,000, and Baden, Capital, $80,000. The partners share net incomes and losses in a ratio of 75% to Hagen and 25% to Baden. On July 1, Megan is admitted to the partnership and given a 20% interest in equity and in gains and losses. Prepare the journal entry to record the entry of Megan under each of the following unrelated assumptions: Megan invests cash of (*a*) $95,000; (*b*) $115,000; and (*c*) $55,000.

**Exercise 14–6**
**Retirement of a partner**
(L. O. 3)

Hollis, Evans, and Bowen have been partners sharing net incomes and losses in a 3:5:2 ratio. On October 31, the date Bowen retires from the partnership, the equities of the partners are Hollis, $130,000; Evans, $200,000; and Bowen, $50,000. Present general journal entries to record Bowen's retirement under each of the following unrelated assumptions:

*a.* Bowen is paid $50,000 in partnership cash for his equity.
*b.* Bowen is paid $60,000 in partnership cash for his equity.
*c.* Bowen is paid $45,000 in partnership cash for his equity.

**Exercise 14–7**
**Liquidation of a partnership**
(L. O. 4)

The Whiz-Bam-Boom partnership was begun with investments by the partners as follows: Whiz, $115,600; Bam, $88,600; and Boom, $95,800. The first year of operations did not go well, and the partners finally decided to liquidate the partnership, sharing all losses equally. On December 31, after all assets were converted to cash and all creditors were paid, only $30,000 in partnership cash remained.

*Required*

1. Calculate the capital account balances of the partners after the liquidation of assets and payment of creditors.
2. Assume that any partner with a deficit pays cash to the partnership to cover the deficit. Then, present the general journal entries on December 31 to record the cash receipt from the deficient partner(s) and the final disbursement of cash to the partners.
3. Now make the contrary assumption that any partner with a deficit is not able to reimburse the partnership. Present journal entries (*a*) to transfer the deficit of any deficient partners to the other partners and (*b*) to record the final disbursement of cash to the partners.

**Exercise 14–8**
**Liquidation of a partnership**
(L. O. 4)

Prince, Count, and Earl are partners who share incomes and losses in a 1:3:4 ratio. After lengthy disagreements among the partners and several unprofitable periods, the partners decided to liquidate the partnership. Before the liquidation, the partnership balance sheet showed total assets, $238,000; liabilities, $200,000; Prince, Capital, $8,000; Count, Capital, $10,000; and Earl, Capital, $20,000. The cash proceeds from selling the assets were sufficient to repay all but $45,000 to the creditors. Calculate the loss from selling the assets, allocate the loss to the partners, and determine how much of the remaining liability should be paid by each partner.

**Exercise 14–9**
**Liquidation of a limited partnership**
(L. O. 4)

Assume that the Prince, Count, and Earl partnership of Exercise 14–8 is a limited partnership. Prince and Count are general partners, and Earl is a limited partner. How much of the remaining $45,000 liability should be paid by each partner?

## Problems

**Problem 14–1**
**Methods of allocating partnership income**
(L. O. 2)

Dell Willis, Lara Hart, and Susan Butler invested $66,400, $58,100, and $41,500, respectively, in a partnership. During its first year, the firm earned $175,500.

*Required*

Prepare entries to close the firm's Income Summary account as of December 31 and to allocate the net income to the partners under each of the assumptions below. (Round your answers to the nearest whole dollar.)

*a.* The partners could not agree as to the method of sharing incomes.
*b.* The partners agreed to share net incomes and losses in the ratio of their beginning investments.
*c.* The partners agreed to share income by allowing annual salary allowances of $52,000 to Willis, $58,000 to Hart, and $45,000 to Butler; allowing 10% interest on the partners' investments; and sharing the remainder equally.

**Problem 14–2**
**Allocating partnership incomes and losses; sequential years**
(L. O. 2)

Linda Meade and Richard Munez are in the process of forming a partnership to which Meade will devote one-third time and Munez will devote full time. They have discussed the following plans for sharing net incomes and losses:

*a.* In the ratio of their investments which they have agreed to maintain at $33,000 for Meade and $49,500 for Munez.
*b.* In proportion to the time devoted to the business.
*c.* A salary allowance of $3,500 per month to Munez and the balance in their investment ratio.

*d.* A $3,500 per month salary allowance to Munez, 10% interest on their investments, and the balance equally.

The partners expect the business to generate income as follows: year 1, $20,000 net loss; year 2, $60,000 net income; and year 3, $95,000 net income.

*Required*

1. Prepare three schedules with the following columnar headings:

| Income/ Loss Sharing Plan | Year ______ | | |
|---|---|---|---|
| | Calculations | Meade | Munez |
| | | | |

2. Complete a schedule for each of the first three years by showing how the partnership net income or loss for each year should be allocated to the partners under each of the four plans being considered. Round your answers to the nearest whole dollar.

**Problem 14–3**
**Partnership income allocation, statement of changes in partners' equity, and closing entries**
(L. O. 2)

Lou Cass, Red Sanders, and Barbara Archer formed the CSA Partnership by making capital contributions of $116,640, $129,600, and $142,560, respectively. They anticipate annual net incomes of $195,000 and are considering the following alternative plans of sharing net incomes and losses: *(a)* equally; *(b)* in the ratio of their initial investments; or *(c)* salary allowances of $35,000 to Cass, $20,000 to Sanders, and $45,000 to Archer, interest allowances of 10% on initial investments, with any remaining balance shared equally.

*Required*

1. Prepare a schedule with the following column headings:

| Income/Loss Sharing Plan | Calculations | Share to Cass | Share to Sanders | Share to Archer | Totals |
|---|---|---|---|---|---|
| | | | | | |

   Use the schedule to show how a net income of $195,000 would be distributed under each of the alternative plans being considered. Round your answers to the nearest whole dollar.

2. Prepare a statement of changes in partners' equity showing the allocation of income to the partners, assuming they agree to use alternative *(c)* and the net income earned is $85,000. During the year, Cass, Sanders, and Archer withdrew $15,000, $20,000, and $23,000, respectively.
3. Prepare the December 31 journal entry to close Income Summary assuming they agree to use alternative *(c)* and the net income is $85,000. Also close the withdrawals accounts.

**Problem 14–4**
**Withdrawal of a partner**
(L. O. 3)

**Part 1.** Pushkin, Tolstoy, and Chekhov are partners with capital balances as follows: Pushkin, $183,750; Tolstoy, $131,250; and Chekhov, $315,000. The partners share incomes and losses in a 1:2:3 ratio. Prepare general journal entries to record the August 1 withdrawal of Tolstoy from the partnership under each of the following unrelated assumptions:

*a.* Tolstoy sells his interest to Gogol for $168,000 after Pushkin and Chekhov approve the entry of Gogol as a partner.
*b.* Tolstoy gives his interest to a son-in-law, Lermontov. Pushkin and Chekhov accept Lermontov as a partner.
*c.* Tolstoy is paid $131,250 in partnership cash for his equity.
*d.* Tolstoy is paid $194,250 in partnership cash for his equity.
*e.* Tolstoy is paid $27,250 in partnership cash plus delivery equipment recorded on the partnership books at $115,000 less accumulated depreciation of $63,000.

**Part 2.** Assume that Tolstoy does not retire from the partnership described in Part 1. Instead, Nabokov is admitted to the partnership on August 1 with a 25% equity. Prepare general journal entries to record the entry of Nabokov into the partnership under each of the following unrelated assumptions:

*a.* Nabokov invests $210,000.
*b.* Nabokov invests $157,500.
*c.* Nabokov invests $262,500.

**Problem 14–5**
**Liquidation of a partnership**
(L. O. 4)

Maxwell, Adams, and Nelson plan to liquidate their partnership. They have always shared losses and gains in a 1:4:5 ratio, and on the day of the liquidation their balance sheet appeared as follows:

**MAXWELL, ADAMS AND NELSON**
**Balance Sheet**
**June 30, 19—**

| Assets | | Liabilities and Owners' Equity | |
|---|---|---|---|
| Cash | $ 27,500 | Accounts payable | $ 52,150 |
| Other assets | 180,500 | Pam Maxwell, capital | 30,500 |
| | | Greg Adams, capital | 80,350 |
| | | Linda Nelson, capital | 45,000 |
| Total assets | $208,000 | Total liabilities and owners' equity | $208,000 |

*Required*

Prepare general journal entries to record the sale of the other assets and the distribution of the cash to the proper parties under each of the following unrelated assumptions:

*a.* The other assets are sold for $195,250.
*b.* The other assets are sold for $150,000.

*c.* The other assets are sold for $85,000, and any partners with resulting deficits can and do pay in the amount of their deficits.

*d.* The other assets are sold for $75,000, and the partners have no assets other than those invested in the business.

**Problem 14–6**
**Withdrawal of a partner**
(L. O. 3)

Until May 28, 1990, Block, Sun, and Steen were partners that shared incomes and losses in the ratio of their beginning-of-year capital account balances. On May 28, Sun suffered a heart attack and died. Block and Steen immediately ended the business operations and prepared the following adjusted trial balance:

**BLOCK, SUN, AND STEEN**
**Adjusted Trial Balance**
**May 28, 1990**

| | | |
|---|---|---|
| Cash | $ 23,625 | |
| Accounts receivable | 55,125 | |
| Allowance for doubtful accounts | | $ 2,625 |
| Supplies inventory | 111,750 | |
| Equipment | 70,875 | |
| Accumulated depreciation, equipment | | 18,375 |
| Land | 23,625 | |
| Building | 262,500 | |
| Accumulated depreciation, building | | 49,875 |
| Accounts payable | | 15,750 |
| Note payable (secured by mortgage) | | 52,500 |
| Bob Block, capital | | 157,500 |
| Joan Sun, capital | | 157,500 |
| Tim Steen, capital | | 78,750 |
| Bob Block, withdrawals | 8,250 | |
| Joan Sun, withdrawals | 8,250 | |
| Tim Steen, withdrawals | 8,250 | |
| Revenues | | 204,750 |
| Expenses | 165,375 | |
| Totals | $737,625 | $737,625 |

*Required*

1. Prepare May 28 entries to close the revenue, expense, income summary, and withdrawals accounts of the partnership.
2. Assume the estate of Sun agreed to accept the land and building and to assume the mortgage note thereon in settlement of its claim against the partnership assets, and that Block and Steen planned to continue the business and rent the building from the estate. Give the partnership's June 15 entry to transfer the land, building, and mortgage note in settlement with the estate.
3. Assume that in place of the foregoing, the estate of Sun demanded a cash settlement, and the business had to be sold to a competitor who gave $355,000 for the noncash assets and assumed the mortgage note but not the accounts payable. Give the June 15 entry to transfer the noncash assets and mortgage note to the competitor, and give the entries to allocate the loss to the partners and to distribute the partnership cash to the proper parties.

## Alternate Problems

**Problem 14–1A**
**Methods of allocating partnership income**
(L. O. 2)

Rhonda Zeller, Brian Jackson, and Debby Rogers invested $92,400, $74,800, and $52,800, respectively, in a partnership. During its first year, the firm earned $198,000.

*Required*

Prepare entries to close the firm's Income Summary account as of December 31 and to allocate the net income to the partners under each of the assumptions below. (Round your answers to the nearest whole dollar.)

*a.* The partners could not agree as to the method of sharing incomes.
*b.* The partners had agreed to share net incomes and losses in the ratio of their beginning investments.
*c.* The partners had agreed to share income by allowing annual salary allowances of $75,000 to Zeller, $40,500 to Jackson, and $45,500 to Rogers; allowing a share of the income equal to 10% interest on the partners' investments; and sharing the remainder equally.

**Problem 14–2A**
**Allocating partnership incomes and losses; sequential years**
(L. O. 2)

Harriet Monroe and Ozzie Young are in the process of forming a partnership to which Monroe will devote one-fourth time and Young will devote full time. They have discussed the following plans for sharing net incomes and losses:

*a.* In the ratio of their investments which they have agreed to maintain at $49,800 for Monroe and $74,700 for Young.
*b.* In proportion to the time devoted to the business.
*c.* A salary allowance of $5,250 per month to Young and the balance in their investment ratio.
*d.* A $5,250 per month salary allowance to Young, 10% interest on their investments, and the balance equally.

The partners expect the business to generate income as follows: year 1, $30,500 net loss; year 2, $82,500 net income; and year 3, $215,000 net income.

*Required*

1. Prepare three schedules with the following columnar headings:

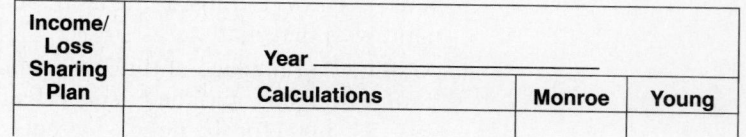

| Income/ Loss Sharing Plan | Year ______ | | |
|---|---|---|---|
| | Calculations | Monroe | Young |
| | | | |

2. Complete a schedule for each of the first three years by showing how the partnership income for each year would be allocated to the partners under each of the four plans being considered. Round your answers to the nearest whole dollar.

**Problem 14–3A**
**Partnership income allocation, statement of changes in partners' equity, and closing entries**
(L. O. 2)

Betty Iris, Jim Dolan, and Bob Carrow formed the IDC Partnership by making capital contributions of $245,000, $280,000, and $175,000, respectively. They anticipate annual net incomes of $390,000 and are considering the following alternative plans of sharing net incomes and losses: (*a*) equally; (*b*) in the ratio of their initial investments; or (*c*) interest allowances of 12% on initial investments, salary allowances of $95,000 to Iris, $46,000 to Dolan, and $60,000 to Carrow, with any remaining balance shared equally.

*Required*

1. Prepare a schedule with the following column headings:

| Income/Loss Sharing Plan | Calculations | Share to Iris | Share to Dolan | Share to Carrow | Totals |
|---|---|---|---|---|---|
| | | | | | |

   Use the schedule to show how a net income of $390,000 would be distributed under each of the alternative plans being considered. Round your answers to the nearest whole dollar.

2. Prepare a statement of changes in partners' equity showing the allocation of income to the partners, assuming they agree to use alternative (*c*) and the net income actually earned is $135,000. During the year, Iris, Dolan, and Carrow withdrew $40,000, $30,000, and $20,000, respectively.
3. Prepare the December 31 journal entry to close Income Summary assuming they agree to use alternative (*c*) and the net income is $135,000. Also close the withdrawals accounts.

**Problem 14–4A**
**Withdrawal of a partner**
(L. O. 3)

**Part 1.** Gagin, Fagin, and Onegin are partners with capital balances as follows: Gagin, $153,000; Fagin, $51,000; and Onegin, $102,000. The partners share incomes and losses in a 2:4:2 ratio. Prepare general journal entries to record the November 30 withdrawal of Onegin from the partnership under each of the following unrelated assumptions:

*a.* Onegin sells his interest to Sagin for $42,800 after Gagin and Fagin approve the entry of Sagin as a partner.
*b.* Onegin gives his interest to a son-in-law, Narwood. Gagin and Fagin accept Narwood as a partner.
*c.* Onegin is paid $102,000 in partnership cash for his equity.
*d.* Onegin is paid $75,000 in partnership cash for his equity.
*e.* Onegin is paid $36,000 in partnership cash plus delivery equipment recorded on the partnership books at $78,000 less accumulated depreciation of $45,000.

**Part 2.** Assume that Onegin does not retire from the partnership described in Part 1. Instead, Smitz is admitted to the partnership on November 30 with a 20% equity. Prepare general journal entries to record the entry of Smitz under each of the following unrelated assumptions:

*a.* Smitz invests $76,500.
*b.* Smitz invests $54,000.
*c.* Smitz invests $123,000.

**Problem 14–5A**
**Liquidation of a partnership**
(L. O. 4)

Poppy, Sweetbean, and Olive, who have always shared incomes and losses in a 3:1:1 ratio, plan to liquidate their partnership. Just prior to the liquidation their balance sheet appeared as follows:

**POPPY, SWEETBEAN, AND OLIVE**
**Balance Sheet**
**October 15, 19—**

| Assets | | Liabilities and Owners' Equity | |
|---|---|---|---|
| Cash | $ 13,500 | Accounts payable | $ 56,700 |
| Other assets | 237,600 | E. Poppy, capital | 91,200 |
| | | L. Sweetbean, capital | 60,000 |
| | | N. Olive, capital | 43,200 |
| Total assets | $251,100 | Total liabilities and owners' equity | $251,100 |

*Required*

Under the assumption the other assets are sold and the cash is distributed to the proper parties on October 15, give the entries for the sales, the loss or gain allocations, and the distributions if—

*a.* The other assets are sold for $270,000.
*b.* The other assets are sold for $170,100.
*c.* The other assets are sold for $72,600, and any partners with resulting deficits can and do pay in the amount of their deficits.
*d.* The other assets are sold for $55,200, and the partners have no assets other than those invested in the business.

**Problem 14–6A**
**Withdrawal of a partner**
(L. O. 3)

Rayburn, Myers, and Newton are partners. Rayburn devotes full time to partnership affairs; Myers and Newton devote very little time; and as a result, they share incomes and losses in a 4:1:1 ratio. Of late, the business has not been too profitable, and the partners have decided to liquidate. Just prior to the first realization sale, a partnership balance sheet appeared as follows:

**RAYBURN, MYERS, AND NEWTON**
**Balance Sheet**
**July 10, 1990**

| Assets | | | Liabilities and Owners' Equity | |
|---|---|---|---|---|
| Cash | | $ 4,500 | Accounts payable | $12,600 |
| Accounts receivable | | 17,100 | Rayburn, capital | 10,800 |
| Merchandise inventory | | 28,800 | Myers, capital | 21,600 |
| Equipment | $21,600 | | Newton, capital | 21,600 |
| Less accum. depr. | 5,400 | 16,200 | | |
| Total assets | | $66,600 | Total liabilities and owners' equity | $66,600 |

The assets were sold, the creditors were paid, and the remaining cash was distributed to the partners on the following dates:

July 11 The accounts receivable were sold for $11,300.
12 The merchandise inventory was sold for $19,800.
14 The equipment was sold for $8,800.
15 The creditors were paid.
17 The remaining cash was distributed to the partners.

*Required*

1. Prepare general journal entries to record the asset sales, the allocation of the realization loss, and the payment of the creditors.
2. Under the assumption that any partners with capital deficits can and do pay in the amount of their deficits on July 17, give the entry to record the receipt of the cash and the distribution of partnership cash to the remaining partners.
3. Under the assumption that any partners with capital deficits cannot pay, give the entry to allocate the deficits to the remaining partners. Then give the entry to distribute the partnership cash to the remaining partners.

## Provocative Problems

**Provocative Problem 14–1**
**White and Black Partnership**
(L. O. 2)

Karen White and Joe Black agreed to share the annual net incomes or losses of their partnership as follows. If the partnership earns a net income, the first $50,000 is allocated 25% to White and 75% to Black so as to reflect the time devoted to the business by each partner. Income in excess of $50,000 is shared equally. However, if business operations result in a loss for the year, the partners have agreed to share the loss equally.

*Required*

1. Prepare a schedule showing how the 1990 net income of $59,000 should be allocated to the partners.
2. Immediately after the closing entries for 1990 were posted on December 31, 1990, the partners discover $70,000 of unrecorded accounts payable. These accounts payable relate to expenses incurred by the business. Black suggests that the $70,000 should be allocated equally between the partners as a loss. White disagrees and argues that an entry should be made to record the accounts payable and correct the capital accounts to reflect an $11,000 net loss for 1990. (*a*) Present the January 1, 1991, journal entry to record the accounts payable and allocate the loss to the partners according to Black's suggestion. (*b*) Now give the January 1, 1991, journal entry to record the accounts payable and correct the capital accounts according to White's argument. Show how you calculated the amounts in the entry.
3. Which partner do you think is right? Why?

**Provocative Problem 14–2**
**The Fitness Place**
(L. O. 3)

Maddie Hall and Amanda Miller are partners that own and operate The Fitness Place, an exercise and casual wear shop. Hall has a $75,000 equity in the business, and Miller has a $60,000 equity. They share incomes and losses by allowing annual salary allowances of $33,750 to Hall and $27,000 to Miller, with any remaining balance being shared 60% to Hall and 40% to Miller.

Susie Hall, Maddie Hall's daughter, has been working in the store on a salary basis. In addition to working in the store, Susie is a popular aerobics teacher and is well known among other aerobics teachers and a number of students. As a result, Susie attracts a great deal of business to the store. The partners believe that at least one third of the past three years' sales can be traced directly to Susie's association with the store, and it is reasonable to assume she was instrumental in attracting even more.

Susie is paid $1,800 per month, but feels this is not sufficient to induce her to remain with the firm as an employee. However, she likes her work and would like to remain in the fitness-wear business. What she really wants is to become a partner in the business.

Her mother is anxious for her to remain in the business and proposes the following:

*a.* That Susie be admitted to the partnership with a 20% equity in the partnership assets.

*b.* That she, Maddie Hall, transfer from her capital account to that of Susie's one half the 20% interest; that Susie contribute to the firm's assets a noninterest-bearing note for the other half; and that she, Maddie Hall, will guarantee payment of the note.

*c.* That incomes and losses be shared by continuing the $33,750 and $27,000 salary allowances of the original partners and that Susie be given a $21,600 annual salary allowance, after which any remaining income or loss would be shared 40% to Maddie Hall, 40% to Amanda Miller, and 20% to Susie Hall.

Prepare a report to Ms. Miller on the advisability of accepting Maddie Hall's proposal. Under the assumption that net incomes for the past three years have been $65,400, $68,500, and $70,500, respectively, prepare schedules showing (*a*) how net income was allocated during the past three years and (*b*) how it would have been allocated had the proposed new agreement been in effect. Also, (*c*) prepare a schedule showing the partners' capital interests as they would be immediately after the admission of Susie.

**Provocative Problem 14–3**
**Venerable Partnership**
(L. O. 3)

The balance sheet of the Venerable Partnership on December 31, 1990, is as follows:

| Assets | | Liabilities and Owners' Equity | |
|---|---|---|---|
| Cash | $ 45,250 | Hamilton, capital | $ 22,750 |
| Other assets | 56,250 | Adams, capital | 33,750 |
| Land | 33,750 | Hay, capital | 78,750 |
| Total assets | $135,250 | Total liabilities and owners' equity | $135,250 |

The income-and-loss-sharing percentages are: Hamilton, 20%; Adams, 30%; and Hay, 50%. Hamilton wishes to withdraw from the partnership, and the partners finally agree that the land owned by the partnership should be transferred to Hamilton in full payment for his equity. In reaching this decision, they recognize that the land has appreciated since it was purchased and is now worth $60,000. If Hamilton retires on January 1, 1991, what journal entries should be made on that date?

# E Accounting Principles and the FASB's Conceptual Framework

Accounting concepts and principles are not laws of nature. They are broad ideas that are developed as a way of describing current accounting practices and prescribing new and improved practices. In studying this appendix, you will learn about some new accounting concepts that the FASB has developed in an effort to guide future changes and improvements in accounting.

**Learning Objectives**

*After studying Appendix E, you should be able to:*

1. Explain the difference between descriptive concepts and prescriptive concepts.
2. Explain the difference between ''bottom up'' and ''top down'' approaches to the development of accounting concepts.
3. Describe the major components in the FASB's conceptual framework.

## Descriptive and Prescriptive Accounting Concepts

Explain the difference between descriptive concepts and prescriptive concepts.
(L. O. 1)

To fully understand the importance of financial accounting concepts and principles, you must realize that they serve two purposes. First, they provide general descriptions of existing accounting practices. In doing this, concepts and principles serve as guidelines that help you learn about accounting. Thus, after learning how the concepts and principles are applied in a few situations, you develop the ability to apply them in different situations. This is easier and more effective than memorizing a very long list of specific practices.

Second, accounting concepts and principles help accountants analyze unfamiliar situations and develop procedures to account for those situations. This purpose is especially important for the Financial Accounting Standards Board (FASB), which is charged with developing uniform practices for financial reporting in the United States and with improving the quality of financial reporting.

In prior chapters, we defined and illustrated several important accounting concepts and principles. These concepts and principles, which are listed below, describe in general terms the practices currently used by accountants.

| | |
|---|---|
| **Generally accepted concepts:** | |
| Business entity concept | Stable-dollar concept |
| Continuing-concern concept | Time-period concept |
| **Generally accepted principles:** | |
| Cost principle | Materiality principle |
| Objectivity principle | Full-disclosure principle |
| Realization principle | Consistency principle |
| Matching principle | Conservatism principle |

To help you learn accounting, we first listed these concepts and principles in Chapter 1 (p. 16) and have referred to them frequently in later chapters. Although some of these ideas are labeled *concepts* and some are labeled *principles,* in this appendix we will use the term *concepts* to include both concepts and principles as well as other general rules that have been developed by the FASB. The FASB also uses the word *concepts* in this general manner.

The concepts listed above are useful for teaching and learning about accounting practice and are helpful for dealing with some unfamiliar transactions. However, as business practices have evolved in recent years, these concepts have become less useful as guides for accountants to follow in dealing with new and different types of transactions. This problem has occurred because the concepts are intended to provide general descriptions of current accounting practices. In other words, they describe what accountants currently do; they do not necessarily describe what accountants should do. Also, since these concepts do not identify weaknesses in accounting practices, they do not lead to major changes or improvements in accounting practices.

Because the FASB is charged with improving financial reporting, its first members decided that a new set of concepts should be developed. They also decided that the new set of concepts should not merely *describe* what was being done under current practice. Instead, the new concepts should *prescribe* what ought to be done to make things better. The project to develop a new set of prescriptive concepts was initiated in 1973, and quickly became known as the FASB's *conceptual framework project*.

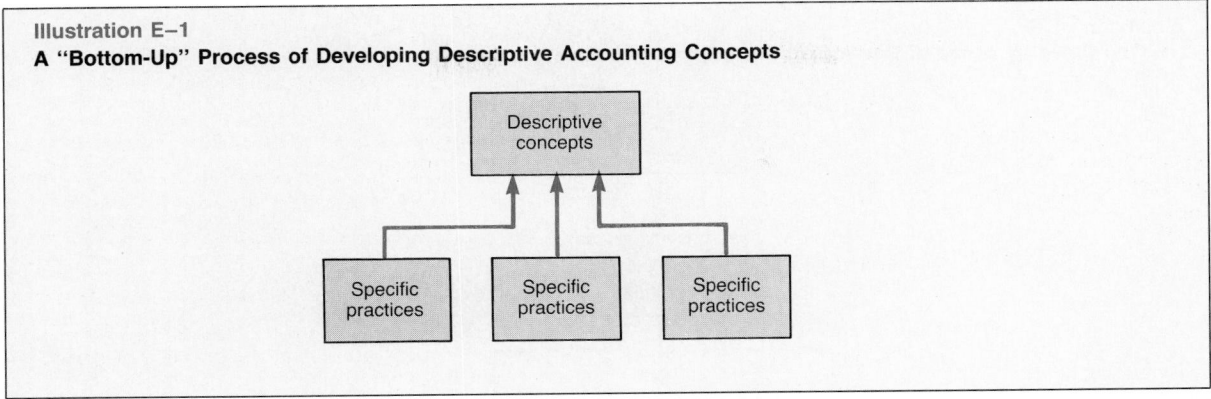

**Illustration E–1**
**A "Bottom-Up" Process of Developing Descriptive Accounting Concepts**

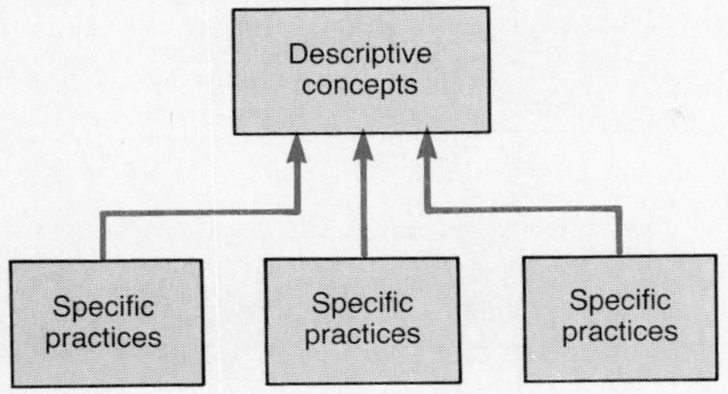


However, before we examine the concepts developed by the FASB, we need to look more closely at the differences between descriptive and prescriptive uses of accounting concepts.

## The Processes of Developing Descriptive and Prescriptive Accounting Concepts

Explain the difference between "bottom up" and "top down" approaches to the development of accounting concepts. (L. O. 2)

Sets of concepts differ in how they are developed and used. In general, when concepts are intended to describe current practice, they are developed by looking at accepted specific practices, and then making some general rules to encompass them. This "bottom-up" approach is diagrammed in Illustration E–1, which shows the arrows going from the practices to the concepts. The outcome of the process is a set of general rules that summarize practice and that can be used for education and for solving some new problems. For example, this approach leads to the concept that asset purchases are recorded at cost. However, these kinds of concepts often fail to show how many new problems should be solved. For example, the concept that assets are recorded at cost does not provide much direct guidance for situations in which assets have no cost because they are donated to a company by a local government. Further, because these concepts are based on the presumption that current practices are adequate, they do not lead to the development of new and improved accounting methods. To continue the example, the concept that assets are initially recorded at cost does not encourage asking the question of whether they should always be carried at that amount.

In contrast, if concepts are intended to *prescribe* improvements in accounting practices, they are likely to be designed by a "top-down" approach such as is shown in Illustration E–2. Note that the "top-down" approach starts with the objectives of accounting. From these broad objectives, the process then generates broad concepts about the types of information that should be reported. Finally, these broad concepts should lead to specific practices that ought to be used. The advantage of this approach is that the concepts are good for solving new problems and for evaluating old answers; its disadvantage is that the concepts may not be very descriptive of current practice. In fact, the practices suggested by this approach may not be in current use.

Since the FASB uses accounting concepts to prescribe accounting practices, the Board used a "top-down" approach to develop its conceptual framework. The Board's concepts are not necessarily more correct than the

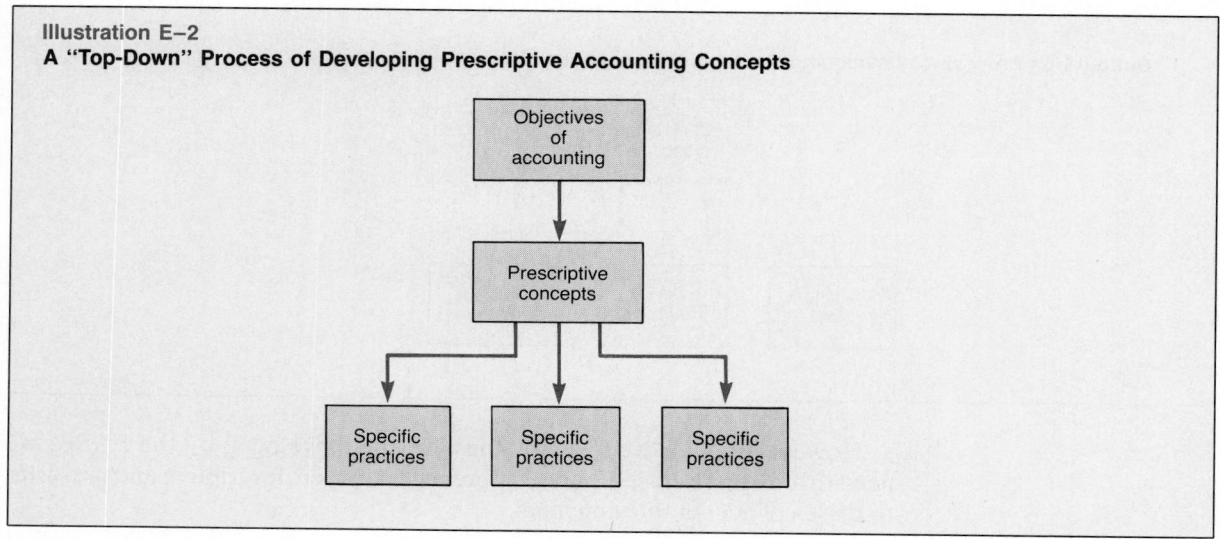

**Illustration E–2**
**A "Top-Down" Process of Developing Prescriptive Accounting Concepts**

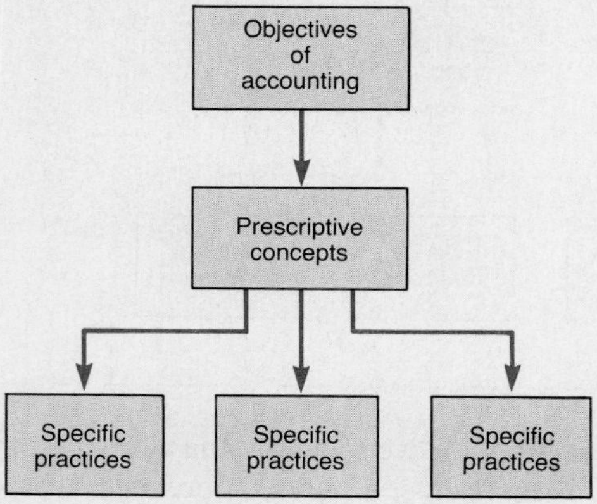


previously developed concepts. However, the new concepts are intended to provide better guidelines for developing new and improved accounting practices. The Board has stated that it will use them as a major basis for its future actions, and already has used them to justify important changes in financial reporting.

## The FASB's Conceptual Framework

Describe the major components in the FASB's conceptual framework. (L. O. 3)

The FASB's approach to developing its conceptual framework is diagrammed in Illustration E–3. Between 1978 and 1985, the Board issued six *Statements of Financial Accounting Concepts* (abbreviated *SFAC*). These concepts statements are not the same as its *Statements of Financial Accounting Standards* (abbreviated *SFAS*). The latter (*SFAS*'s) are authoritative statements of generally accepted accounting principles which must be followed. The former (*SFAC*'s) are guidelines the Board uses in developing new standards. But, accountants are not required to follow the *SFAC*'s in current practice.

### The Objectives of Financial Reporting

As shown in Illustration E–3, the FASB's first *Statement of Financial Accounting Concepts* (*SFAC 1*) identified the broad objectives of financial reporting. The first and most general objective stated in *SFAC 1* is to "provide information that is useful to present and potential investors and creditors and other users in making rational investment, credit, and similar decisions."[1] From this beginning point in *SFAC 1,* the Board expressed other more specific objectives. These objectives recognize that (1) financial reporting should help

[1] FASB, *Statement of Financial Accounting Concepts No. 1,* "Objectives of Financial Reporting by Business Enterprises" (Norwalk, Conn., 1988), par. 34. Copyright © by the Financial Accounting Standards Board, Norwalk, Conn. 06856, U.S.A. Quoted (or excerpted) with permission. Copies of the complete document are available from the FASB.

**Illustration E–3**
**The FASB's Conceptual Framework**

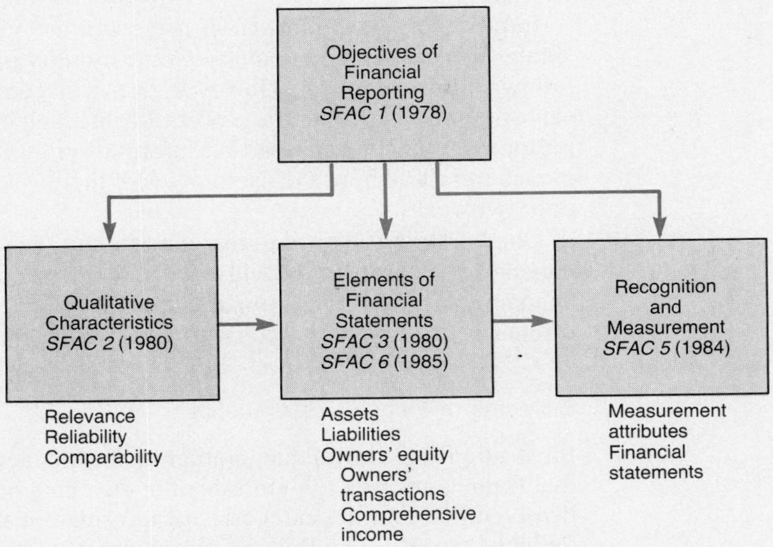


users predict future cash flows, and (2) in making such predictions, information about a company's resources and obligations is useful. All of the concepts in the conceptual framework are intended to be consistent with these general objectives. Of course, present accounting practice already provides information about a company's resources and obligations. Thus, although the conceptual framework is intended to be prescriptive of new and improved practices, the concepts in the framework are also descriptive of many current practices.

### The Qualities of Useful Information

Illustration E–3 shows that the next step in the conceptual framework project was to identify the qualities (or "qualitative characteristics") financial information should have if it is to be useful in decision making. The Board discussed the fact that information can be useful only if it is "understandable" to users. However, the users are assumed to have the training, experience, and motivation to analyze financial reports. With this decision, the Board indicated that financial reporting should not try to meet the needs of unsophisticated or other casual report users.

In *SFAC 2,* the FASB said that information is useful if it is (1) relevant, (2) reliable, and (3) comparable. Information is *relevant* if it can make a difference in a decision. Information has this quality when it helps users either predict the future or evaluate the past, as long as it is received in time to affect their decisions.

Information is *reliable* if users can depend on it to be free from bias and error. Reliable information is verifiable and faithfully represents what is supposed to be described. In addition, users can depend on information only if it is neutral. This means that the rules used to produce information should not be designed so that they lead users to accept or reject any specific decision alternative.

Information is *comparable* if users can use it to identify differences and similarities between companies. Comparability is possible only if companies follow uniform practices. However, even if all companies uniformly follow the same practices, comparable reports do not result if the practices are not appropriate. For example, comparable information would not be provided if all companies were to ignore the useful lives of their assets and depreciate all assets over two years.

Comparability also requires consistency (see Chapter 9, p. 400), which means that a company should not change its accounting practices unless the change is justified as a reporting improvement. Another important concept discussed in *SFAC 2* is materiality (see Chapter 8, p. 362).

### Elements of Financial Statements

Illustration E–3 shows that another important step in developing the conceptual framework was to determine the elements of financial statements. This involved defining the categories of information that should be contained in financial reports. The Board's discussion of financial statement elements includes definitions of important elements such as assets, liabilities, equity, revenues, expenses, gains, and losses. In earlier chapters, we referred to many of these definitions when we explained various accounting procedures. The Board's pronouncement on financial statement elements was first published in 1980 as *SFAC 3*. In 1985, *SFAC 3* was replaced by *SFAC 6*, which modified the discussion of financial statement elements to include several elements for not-for-profit accounting entities.[2]

### Recognition and Measurement

In its pronouncement titled "Recognition and Measurement in Financial Statements of Business Enterprises" (*SFAC 5*), the FASB established concepts for deciding (1) when items should be presented (or "recognized") in the financial statements and (2) how to assign numbers to (or "measure") those items. In general, the Board concluded that items should be recognized in the financial statements if they meet the following criteria:

*a.* Definitions. The item meets the definition of an element of financial statements.
*b.* Measurability. It has a relevant attribute measurable with sufficient reliability.
*c.* Relevance. The information about it is capable of making a difference in user decisions.
*d.* Reliability. The information is representationally faithful, verifiable, and neutral.

---

[2] Among the six *Statements of Financial Accounting Concepts* issued by the FASB, one (*SFAC 4*) is directed toward accounting by not-for-profit organizations. Although important, *SFAC 4* is beyond the scope of this course.

The question of how items should be measured raises the fundamental question of whether financial statements should be based on cost or on value. Since this question is quite controversial, the Board's discussion of this issue is perhaps more descriptive of current practice than it is prescriptive of new measurement methods.

In *SFAC 5*, the Board stated that a full set of financial statements should show:

*a.* Financial position at the end of the period.
*b.* Earnings for the period. [This concept is very similar to the concept of net income that is used in current practice.]
*c.* Comprehensive income for the period. [This new concept is broader than earnings and includes all changes in owner's equity other than those that resulted from transactions with the owners. Some changes in asset values are included in this concept whereas they are excluded from earnings.]
*d.* Cash flows during the period.
*e.* Investments by and distributions to owners during the period.

We should note that *SFAC 5* was the first official pronouncement to call for the presentation of a statement of cash flows. As you will learn from studying Chapter 18, the statement of cash flows is now required under *SFAS 95*, which was issued two years after *SFAC 5*.

## Summary of the Appendix in Terms of Learning Objectives

**1.** Some accounting concepts provide general descriptions of the accounting practices currently in use. These descriptive concepts are most useful in learning about accounting. Other accounting concepts prescribe the practices accountants should follow. These prescriptive concepts are most useful in developing accounting procedures for new types of transactions and making improvements in accounting practice.

**2.** A "bottom-up" approach to developing concepts begins by examining the practices currently in use. From this examination, concepts are developed that provide general descriptions of those practices. In contrast, a "top down" approach begins by stating the objectives of accounting. From these objectives, concepts are developed which prescribe the types of accounting practices accountants should follow to accomplish the objectives.

**3.** The FASB's conceptual framework begins (*SFAC 1*) by stating the broad objectives of financial reporting. Then, (in *SFAC 2*) the qualitative characteristics accounting information should possess are identified. Thereafter (in *SFAC 6*), the elements contained in the financial reports are defined and the recognition and measurement criteria to be used are identified (in *SFAC 5*).

## Questions for Class Discussion

1. Why are concepts developed with a "bottom-up" approach less useful in leading to accounting improvements than are concepts developed with a "top-down" approach?

2. Can a concept be used descriptively and prescriptively?
3. What is the starting point in a "top-down" approach to developing accounting concepts?
4. What is the starting point in a "bottom-up" approach to developing accounting concepts?
5. Explain the difference between the FASB's Statements of Financial Accounting Concepts and the Statements of Financial Accounting Standards.
6. What three qualitative characteristics of accounting information did the FASB identify as being necessary if the information is to be useful?
7. What is implied by saying that financial information should have the qualitative characteristics of relevance?
8. What are the characteristics of accounting information that makes it reliable?
9. What is the meaning of the phrase "elements of financial statements"?
10. What are the four criteria an item should satisfy to be recognized in the financial statements?

Part Five

# Accounting for Corporations, Long-Term Installment Notes, and Bonds

Most students of business will at some time work for a corporation. Perhaps all students will own (either directly or indirectly through a retirement fund) some debt or stock securities issued by corporations. For these reasons, you should have a basic understanding of corporations and the methods used to account for corporations and for stocks and bonds. These topics are discussed in Part Five, which consists of the following chapters:

15. Organization and Operation of Corporations
16. Additional Corporate Transactions; Reporting Income and Retained Earnings; Earnings per Share
17. Installment Notes Payable and Bonds

# 15 Organization and Operation of Corporations

Of the three common types of business organizations (proprietorships, partnerships and corporations), corporations are fewest in number. However, they transact more business than do the other two combined. In the United States, the dollar sales volume of corporations is approximately nine times the combined sales of unincorporated businesses. Thus, from an overall economic point of view, corporations are clearly the most important form of business organization. As you study this chapter, you will learn how corporations are organized and operated and some of the procedures used to account for corporations.

## Learning Objectives

*After studying Chapter 15, you should be able to:*

1. Explain the advantages, disadvantages, and organization of corporations, the differences in accounting for partnerships and corporations, and the concept of minimum legal capital.
2. Record the issuance of par value stock and the issuance of no-par stock with or without a stated value.
3. Record transactions involving stock subscriptions and explain the effects of subscribed stock on corporation assets and stockholders' equity.
4. Explain the differences between common and preferred stocks and allocate dividends between common and preferred stocks.
5. Describe convertible preferred stock and explain the meaning of par, redemption, book, and market values of stock.
6. Define or explain the words and phrases listed in the chapter Glossary.

## Advantages of the Corporate Form

Explain the advantages, disadvantages, and organization of corporations, the differences in accounting for partnerships and corporations, and the concept of minimum legal capital.
(L. O. 1)

Corporations have become the dominant type of business in our country because of the advantages offered by this form of business organization. Among the advantages are the following:

### Corporations Are Separate Legal Entities

Unlike a proprietorship or partnership, a corporation is a separate legal entity; it is separate and distinct from its owners. Because it is a separate legal entity, a corporation, through its agents, may conduct its affairs with the same rights, duties, and responsibilities as a person.

### Stockholders Are Not Liable for a Corporation's Debts

As a separate legal entity a corporation is responsible for its own acts and its own debts. Its shareholders are not liable for either. From the viewpoint of an investor, this lack of stockholders' liability is perhaps the most important advantage of the corporate form of business.

### Ownership Rights of Corporations Are Easily Transferred

The ownership of a corporation is represented by shares of stock that generally can be transferred and disposed of any time the owners wish. Also, the transfer of shares from one stockholder to another has no effect on the corporation or its operations.

### Corporations Have Continuity of Life

A corporation's life may continue for the time stated in its charter. This may be of any length permitted by the laws of the state of its incorporation. Also, if the stated time expires, the corporation's charter may be renewed and the period extended. Thus, a corporation that continues to be successful may have a perpetual life.

### Stockholders Do Not Have a Mutual Agency Relationship

The stockholders of a corporation do not have the mutual agency relationship that is typical of partnerships. Therefore, a stockholder, acting as a stockholder, does not have the power to bind the corporation to contracts. The participation of stockholders in the affairs of the corporation is limited to the right to vote in the stockholders' meetings. As a result, if you become a stockholder in a corporation, you do not have to worry about the character of the other stockholders to the same extent that you would if the business were a partnership.

### Ease of Capital Assembly

Buying stock in a corporation often is more attractive to investors than is investing in a partnership. This is because: (1) stockholders are not liable for the corporation's actions and debts, (2) stockholders do not have a relationship of mutual agency regarding the corporation, and (3) stock often is easily transferred or sold. These advantages make it possible for some corporations to assemble large amounts of capital from the combined investments of many stockholders. Actually, a corporation's ability to raise capital is limited only by its ability to convince investors that it can use their funds profitably. This is very different from most partnerships where mutual agency and unlimited liability limit the number of investors who are willing to become partners.

## Disadvantages of the Corporate Form

### Governmental Regulation

Corporations are created by fulfilling the requirements of a state's corporation laws. These laws subject a corporation to considerable state regulation and control. Single proprietorships and partnerships escape this regulation as well as the filing of many governmental reports required of corporations.

### Taxation

As business units, corporations are subject to the same taxes as single proprietorships and partnerships. In addition, corporations are subject to taxes that are not levied on either of the other two. The most burdensome of these taxes are state and federal income taxes, which may amount to as much as 50% of a corporation's pretax income. However, for the stockholders of a corporation, the tax burden does not end there. The income of a corporation is taxed twice, first as income of the corporation and again as personal income when it is distributed to the stockholders as dividends. This differs from single proprietorships and partnerships, which as business units are not subject to income taxes. Normally, their income is taxed only as the personal income of their owners.[1]

The tax characteristics of a corporation are generally viewed as a disadvantage. In some cases, however, they work to the advantage of stockholders. Corporation and individual tax rates are progressive. In other words, high levels of income are taxed at higher rates and lower levels of income are taxed at lower rates. Therefore, taxes may be saved or at least delayed if a large amount of income is divided between two or more tax-paying entities. So, if an individual has a large personal income and pays taxes at a high rate, the individual may benefit if some of the income is earned by a corporation owned by the individual. Then, if the corporation avoids paying dividends, the income of the corporation is, at least temporarily, taxed only once at the lower corporate rate.

## Organizing a Corporation

A corporation is created by securing a charter from a state government. The requirements that must be met to secure a charter vary among the states. Usually, a charter application must be signed by three or more subscribers to the prospective corporation's stock. Then, the charter application is filed with the proper state official. If the application complies with the law and all fees are

[1] Some corporations that have a limited number of shareholders can elect to be treated like a partnership for tax purposes. These are called *Sub-Chapter S Corporations*.

paid, the charter is issued and the corporation is formed. The subscribers then purchase the corporation's stock, after which the stockholders meet and elect a board of directors who are responsible for directing the corporation's affairs.

## Organization Costs

The costs of organizing a corporation, such as legal fees, promoters' fees, and amounts paid to secure a charter, are called **organization costs.** In the corporation's books, these costs are debited to an asset account called *Organization Costs*. This is an intangible asset that benefits the corporation throughout its life. Theoretically, the asset should be amortized over the estimated life of the corporation. However, generally accepted accounting principles preclude amortizing any intangible asset over a period in excess of 40 years.[2]

Although not necessarily related to the benefit period, income tax rules permit a corporation to write off organization costs as a tax-deductible expense over a period of not less than five years. And since the expected life of a corporation is indefinite, many corporations adopt five years as the period over which to write off such costs. There is no theoretical justification for this, but it is generally accepted in practice. Also, organization costs often are not material in amount, in which case a write-off over five years is justified under the *materiality principle*.

## Management of a Corporation

The organizational structure by which stockholders govern the activities of a corporation is not the same in all corporations. However, Illustration 15–1 shows two alternative structures that are widely used. Notice that ultimate control of a corporation rests with its stockholders. However, this control is exercised indirectly through the election of the board of directors. The individual stockholders' right to participate in management begins and ends with a vote in the stockholders' meeting, where each stockholder usually has one vote for each share of stock owned.

Normally, a corporation's stockholders meet once each year to elect directors and vote on any other business matters which, according to the corporation's bylaws, must be approved by the stockholders. If a group of stockholders own or control the votes of 50% plus one share of a corporation's stock, they can elect the board and control the corporation. However, in many companies, a large number of stockholders do not attend the annual meeting or get involved in the voting process. As a result, a much smaller percentage is frequently able to dominate the election of board members.

Stockholders who do not attend stockholders' meetings usually can delegate their voting rights to an agent. This is done by signing a legal document called a **proxy,** which gives the agent the right to vote the stock.

A corporation's board of directors is responsible and has final authority for the direction of corporate affairs. However, it may act only as a collective body. An individual director, as a director, has no power to transact corporate business. Although the board has final authority, it usually limits its actions to

---

[2] FASB, *Accounting Standards—Current Text* (Norwalk, Conn., 1988), sec. I60.110. First published in *APB Opinion No. 17*, par. 29.

**Illustration 15–1**
**Alternative structures of authority in a corporation**

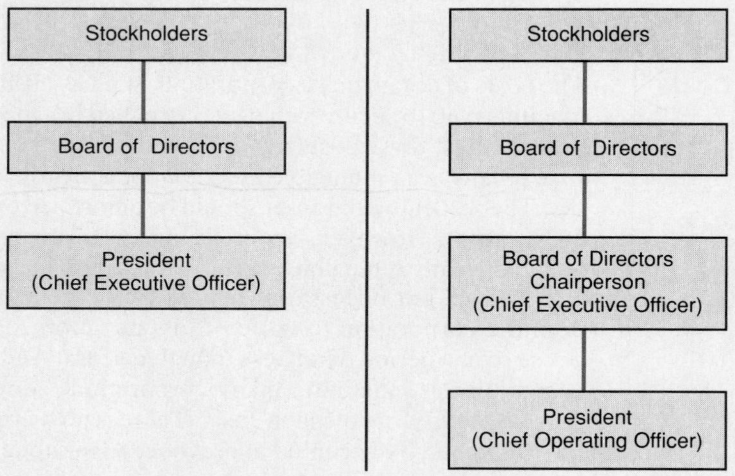


establishing policy. Day-by-day direction of corporate business is delegated to executive officers who are appointed by the board to manage the business.

Traditionally, the chief executive officer (CEO) of the corporation is the president. Under the president, there may be several vice presidents who are assigned specific areas of management responsibility such as finance, production, and marketing. In addition, the corporation secretary keeps the minutes of the meetings of the stockholders and directors. In a small corporation, the secretary also may be responsible for keeping a record of the stockholders and the transfer of shares between stockholders.

In recent years, many corporations have a slightly different structure in which the board of directors chairperson assumes the position of chief executive officer. When this is done, the president usually is designated the chief operating officer (COO).

## Stock Certificates and the Transfer of Stock

When a person invests in a corporation by buying its stock, the person receives a stock certificate as proof of the shares purchased. Usually, in a small corporation, only one certificate is issued for each block of stock purchased. This certificate may be for any number of shares. For example, the certificate of Illustration 15–2 is for 50 shares. Large corporations commonly use preprinted certificates, each of which represents 100 shares, plus blank certificates that may be made out for any number of shares.

When a stockholder sells shares of a corporation, the seller completes and signs the transfer endorsement on the back of the certificate and sends it to the corporation's secretary (or transfer agent). The old certificate is canceled and retained, and a new certificate is issued to the new stockholder. If the old certificate represents more shares than were sold, the corporation issues two certificates. One goes to the new stockholder for the shares sold, and another

## AS A MATTER OF ETHICS

The Board of Directors and the officers of Skyline Corporation are meeting to discuss and plan the agenda for the corporation's 1991 annual stockholders' meeting. The first item considered by the directors and officers was whether to report a large government contract that Skyline has just obtained. Although this contract will significantly increase income and cash flows in 1991 and beyond, the management felt that there is no need to reveal the news at the stockholders' meeting. After all, the meeting is intended to be the forum for describing the past year's activities, not the plans for the next year.

After concluding that the contract will not be mentioned, the group has moved on to the next topic for the stockholders' meeting. This topic is a motion for the stockholders to approve a compensation plan that will award the managers the rights to acquire large quantities of shares over the next several years. According to the plan, the managers will have a three-year option to buy shares at a fixed price that equals the market value of the stock as measured 30 days after the upcoming stockholders' meeting. In other words, the managers will be able to buy stock in 1992, 1993, or 1994 by paying the 1991 market value. Obviously, if the stock increases in value over the next several years, the managers will realize large profits without having to invest any cash. The financial vice president asks the group whether they should reconsider the decision about the government contract in light of its possible relevance to the vote on the stock option plan.

certificate is issued to the original stockholder for the remaining shares that were not sold.

### Transfer Agent and Registrar

If a corporation's stock is traded on a major stock exchange, the corporation must have a registrar and a transfer agent. The registrar keeps the stockholder records and prepares official lists of stockholders for stockholders' meetings and for payment of dividends. Usually, registrars and transfer agents are large banks or trust companies.

When a stockholder wants to sell some shares of stock, the owner usually requests a stockbroker to act on the owner's behalf and sell the shares. Then, the owner completes the transfer endorsement on the back of the stock certificate and gives the certificate to the stockbroker who sends it to the corporation's transfer agent. The transfer agent cancels the old certificate and issues one or more new certificates and sends them to the registrar. The registrar enters the transfer in the stockholder records and sends the new certificate or certificates to the proper owners.

## Corporation Accounting

Corporation accounting was initially discussed in Chapter 4. In that discussion, we explained the entries to record several basic transactions of corporations. The entries included recording an issue of common stock for cash and closing a net income or a net loss from Income Summary to Retained Earnings. Also, the declaration and later payment of cash dividends were recorded. *At this point, you should review the Chapter 4 discussion of these entries, which was presented on pages 165 through 168.* After completing that review, keep in mind that the stockholders' equity accounts of a corporation are divided into (1) contributed capital accounts and (2) retained earnings accounts. Also, remember that when a corporation's board of directors declares a cash divi-

**Illustration 15–2**
**A stock certificate**

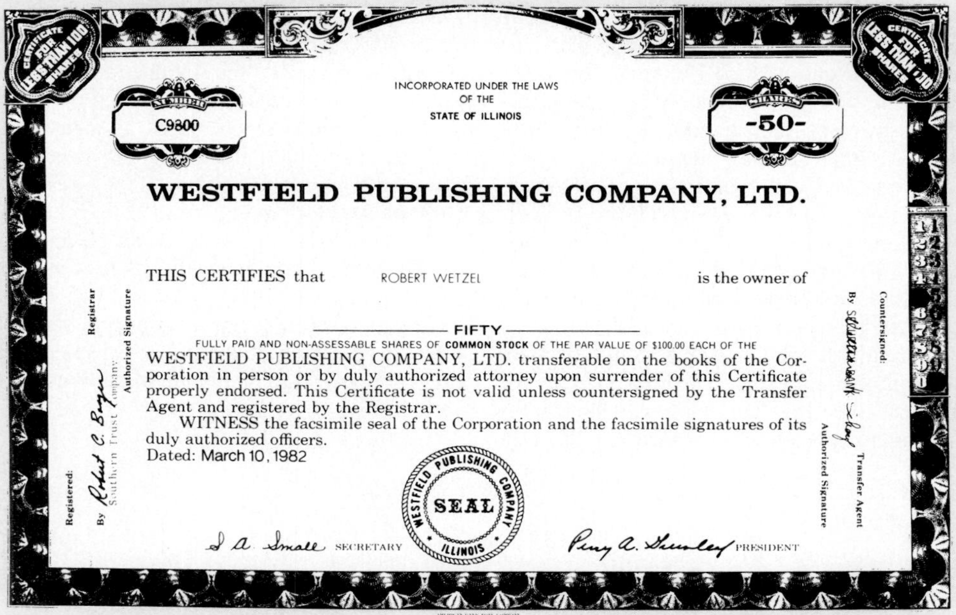
CERTIFICATE FOR LESS THAN 100 SHARES

INCORPORATED UNDER THE LAWS OF THE STATE OF ILLINOIS

C9800 -50-

WESTFIELD PUBLISHING COMPANY, LTD.

THIS CERTIFIES that ROBERT WETZEL is the owner of

FIFTY

FULLY PAID AND NON-ASSESSABLE SHARES OF COMMON STOCK OF THE PAR VALUE OF $100.00 EACH OF THE WESTFIELD PUBLISHING COMPANY, LTD. transferable on the books of the Corporation in person or by duly authorized attorney upon surrender of this Certificate properly endorsed. This Certificate is not valid unless countersigned by the Transfer Agent and registered by the Registrar.

WITNESS the facsimile seal of the Corporation and the facsimile signatures of its duly authorized officers.

Dated: March 10, 1982

SEAL — WESTFIELD PUBLISHING COMPANY — ILLINOIS

SECRETARY PRESIDENT

Registered: Southern Trust Company Registrar By Authorized Signature

Countersigned: Transfer Agent By Authorized Signature

dend on the *date of declaration*, a legal liability of the corporation is incurred. The board of directors declares that on a specific future date, the *date of record*, the stockholders according to the corporation's records will be designated as those to receive the dividend. Finally, on the *date of payment*, the liability for the declared cash dividend is paid by the corporation.

The financial statements of a corporation were first illustrated in Chapter 5. The income statement was shown in Illustration 5–1 on page 210; the retained earnings statement was shown in Illustration 5–3 on page 215; and the balance sheet was shown in Illustration 5–4 on page 216. When you review these illustrations, you should note that income taxes were deducted on the income statement as an expense. Recall that a business organized as a corporation must pay income taxes, while a proprietorship or partnership does not pay income taxes. Also, cash dividends to stockholders are not an expense of the corporation; they are not deducted on the income statement. Instead, dividends are a *distribution* of net income and are subtracted on the retained earnings statement. Finally, notice that the stockholders' equity in Illustration 5–4 is divided into common stock and retained earnings.

## Stockholders' Equity Accounts Compared to Partnership Accounts

To demonstrate the use of separate accounts for contributed capital and retained earnings as found in corporation accounting and to contrast their use with the accounts used in partnership accounting, assume the following. On January 5, 1990, a partnership involving two partners and a corporation having five stockholders were formed. Also assume that $25,000 was invested in each. In the partnership, J. Olm invested $10,000 and A. Baker invested $15,000. In the corporation, each of the five stockholders bought 500 shares of its $10 par value common stock at $10 per share. Without dates and explanations, general journal entries to record the investments are:

| Partnership | | | Corporation | | |
|---|---|---|---|---|---|
| Cash . . . . . . . . . . . . | 10,000 | | Cash . . . . . . . . . . . . | 25,000 | |
| J. Olm, Capital . . . . | | 10,000 | Common Stock . . . . | | 25,000 |
| Cash . . . . . . . . . . . . | 15,000 | | | | |
| A. Baker, Capital. . . . | | 15,000 | | | |

After the entries are posted, the owners' equity accounts of the two companies appear as follows:

**Partnership**

**J. Olm, Capital**

| Date | Dr. | Cr. | Bal. |
|---|---|---|---|
| Jan. 5, 1990 | | 10,000 | 10,000 |

**A. Baker, Capital**

| Date | Dr. | Cr. | Bal. |
|---|---|---|---|
| Jan. 5, 1990 | | 15,000 | 15,000 |

**Corporation**

**Common Stock**

| Date | Dr. | Cr. | Bal. |
|---|---|---|---|
| Jan. 5, 1990 | | 25,000 | 25,000 |

To continue the illustration, assume that during 1990, each company earned a net income of $8,000 and also distributed $5,000 to its owners. According to the partnership agreement, incomes are allocated 40% to Olm and 60% to Baker. The cash distribution to the partners was divided equally. The corporation declared the dividends on December 20, 1990, and both companies made the cash payments to owners on December 25, 1990. The entries to record the distribution of cash to partners and the declaration and payments of dividends to stockholders are as follows:

| Partnership | | | Corporation | | |
|---|---|---|---|---|---|
| J. Olm, Withdrawals. . . . . . | 2,500 | | Dividends Declared . . . . . . | 5,000 | |
| A. Baker, Withdrawals . . . . | 2,500 | | Dividends Payable . . . . | | 5,000 |
| Cash . . . . . . . . . . . | | 5,000 | | | |
| | | | Dividends Payable . . . . . . | 5,000 | |
| | | | Cash . . . . . . . . . . . | | 5,000 |

At the end of the year, the entries to close the Income Summary accounts are as follows:

| Partnership | | | Corporation | | |
|---|---|---|---|---|---|
| Income Summary . . . . . . . | 8,000 | | Income Summary . . . . . . | 8,000 | |
| J. Olm, Capital . . . . . | | 3,200 | Retained Earnings . . . . | | 8,000 |
| A. Baker, Capital . . . . . | | 4,800 | | | |

Finally, the entries to close the withdrawals accounts and the Dividends Declared account are:

| Partnership | | | Corporation | | |
|---|---|---|---|---|---|
| J. Olm, Capital . . . . . . . . | 2,500 | | Retained Earnings . . . . . . | 5,000 | |
| A. Baker, Capital . . . . . . . | 2,500 | | Dividends Declared . . . | | 5,000 |
| J. Olm, Withdrawals . . . | | 2,500 | | | |
| A. Baker, Withdrawals . . | | 2,500 | | | |

After posting the above entries, the owners' equity accounts of the two companies are as follows:

**Partnership**

**J. Olm, Capital**

| Date | Dr. | Cr. | Bal. |
|---|---|---|---|
| Jan. 5, 1990 | | 10,000 | 10,000 |
| Dec. 31, 1990 | | 3,200 | 13,200 |
| Dec. 31, 1990 | 2,500 | | 10,700 |

**A. Baker, Capital**

| Date | Dr. | Cr. | Bal. |
|---|---|---|---|
| Jan. 5, 1990 | | 15,000 | 15,000 |
| Dec. 31, 1990 | | 4,800 | 19,800 |
| Dec. 31, 1990 | 2,500 | | 17,300 |

**J. Olm, Withdrawals**

| Date | Dr. | Cr. | Bal. |
|---|---|---|---|
| Dec. 25, 1990 | 2,500 | | 2,500 |
| Dec. 31, 1990 | | 2,500 | –0– |

**A. Baker, Withdrawals**

| Date | Dr. | Cr. | Bal. |
|---|---|---|---|
| Dec. 25, 1990 | 2,500 | | 2,500 |
| Dec. 31, 1990 | | 2,500 | –0– |

**Corporation**

**Common Stock**

| Date | Dr. | Cr. | Bal. |
|---|---|---|---|
| Jan. 5, 1990 | | 25,000 | 25,000 |

**Retained Earnings**

| Date | Dr. | Cr. | Bal. |
|---|---|---|---|
| Dec. 20, 1990 | 5,000 | | (5,000) |
| Dec. 31, 1990 | | 8,000 | 3,000 |

**Dividends Declared**

| Date | Dr. | Cr. | Bal. |
|---|---|---|---|
| Dec. 20, 1990 | 5,000 | | 5,000 |
| Dec. 31, 1990 | | 5,000 | –0– |

Observe that in the partnership, after all entries have been posted, the $28,000 equity of the owners appears in the capital accounts of the partners:

| | |
|---|---|
| J. Olm, Capital . . . . . . . | $10,700 |
| A. Baker, capital . . . . . . | 17,300 |
| Total owners' equity . . . . | $28,000 |

By comparison, the stockholders' equity of the corporation is divided between contributed capital and the Retained Earnings account, as follows:

| | |
|---|---|
| Common stock . . . . . . . . . | $25,000 |
| Retained earnings . . . . . . . . | 3,000 |
| Total stockholders' equity . . . . | $28,000 |

## Authorization and Issuance of Stock

When a corporation is organized, it is authorized in its charter to issue a certain amount of stock. If all of the authorized shares have the same rights and characteristics, the stock is called **common stock**. However, a corporation may be authorized to issue both common and preferred stock. (Preferred stock is discussed later in this chapter.) Whether the corporation is authorized to issue one or more classes of stock, it may issue no more of each than the authorized amounts stated in its charter.

Usually, a corporation will secure an authorization to issue more stock than it plans to sell at the time of its organization. By so doing, the corporation avoids having to obtain the state's approval to sell more shares when additional capital is needed to finance future expansion of the business. When a balance sheet is prepared, both the amount of stock authorized and the amount issued are commonly disclosed as shown on page 636.

### Sale of Stock for Cash

When stock is sold for cash and immediately issued, an entry in general journal form like the following may be used to record the sale and issuance:

| | | | | |
|---|---|---|---|---|
| June | 5 | Cash . . . . . . . . . . . . . . . . . . . . . . . . . . . . | 300,000.00 | |
| | | Common Stock . . . . . . . . . . . . . . . . . . . . . | | 300,000.00 |
| | | Sold at par and issued 30,000 shares of $10 par value common stock. | | |

### Exchanging Stock for Noncash Assets

A corporation may accept assets other than cash in exchange for its stock. In the process, the corporation also may assume some liabilities. Transactions such as these are recorded as follows:

| | | | | |
|---|---|---|---|---|
| Apr. | 3 | Machinery | 10,000.00 | |
| | | Buildings | 65,000.00 | |
| | | Land | 15,000.00 | |
| | | Long-Term Notes Payable | | 50,000.00 |
| | | Common Stock | | 40,000.00 |
| | | Exchanged 4,000 shares of $10 par value common stock for machinery, buildings, land, and assumption of note payable. | | |

A corporation also may issue shares of its stock to its promoters in exchange for their services in organizing the corporation. In this case, the corporation receives the intangible asset of being organized in exchange for its stock. The transaction is recorded as follows:

| | | | | |
|---|---|---|---|---|
| Apr. | 5 | Organization Costs | 5,000.00 | |
| | | Common Stock | | 5,000.00 |
| | | Gave promoters 500 shares of $10 par value common stock in exchange for services in organizing the corporation. | | |

## Par Value and Minimum Legal Capital

Many stocks have a **par value**. In the nineteenth century, the par value was always an initial market value for the shares. However, in modern times, the par value of a stock is nothing more than an arbitrary amount that is assigned to the stock when it is authorized. A corporation may choose any par value, and a variety of numbers such as $100, $25, $10, $5, $1, $0.05, or even $0.01 are commonly used.

When a corporation issues par value stock, the par value is printed on each certificate and is used in accounting for the stock. Also, in many states, the par value of a corporation's stock establishes a **minimum legal capital** for the corporation. The minimum legal capital equals the par value of the issued stock. For example, if a corporation issues 1,000 shares of $100 par value stock, the minimum legal capital of the corporation is $100,000.

Laws that establish minimum legal capital normally require stockholders to invest in a corporation assets equal in value to the minimum legal capital. Otherwise, the stockholders may become liable to the corporation's creditors for the deficiency. In other words, persons who buy stock from a corporation must give the corporation par value for its stock or be liable for the difference. Minimum legal capital requirements also make illegal any dividend payments to stockholders when these payments reduce the stockholders' equity below minimum legal capital.

The concept of a minimum legal capital is intended to protect the creditors of a corporation. In general, a corporation's creditors may look only to the assets of the corporation to satisfy their claims. As a result, creditors are only willing to make loans to a corporation if the corporation has enough assets to ensure that the creditors will be repaid. Some of these assets are represented by the minimum legal capital. If corporations were allowed to sell stock, then borrow money, and then pay the minimum legal capital to the stockholders as dividends, the creditors would lose the security they had relied on when making the loans. Therefore, when stock is issued by a corporation, the stockholders must provide it with a fund of assets equal to its minimum legal capital. Thereafter, this fund of assets should remain with the corporation and should not be returned to the stockholders in any form until all creditor claims are paid.

Par value helps establish minimum legal capital and is used in accounting for par value stock. However, it does not establish a stock's worth or the price at which a corporation must issue the stock. If purchasers are willing to pay more than par, a corporation may sell and issue its stock at a price above par. Most often, the par value of a stock is set at a nominal amount that is substantially less than the price at which the stock is offered to investors.

## Stock Premiums and Discounts

Record the issuance of par value stock and the issuance of no-par stock with or without a stated value.
(L. O. 2)

### Premiums on Stock

When a corporation sells and issues stock at a price above the stock's par value, the difference between the issue price and the par value is called a **premium on stock**. For example, if a corporation sells and issues its $10 par value common stock at $40 per share, the stock is sold at a $30 per share premium. Although a premium is an amount in excess of par paid by purchasers of newly issued stock, it is not a revenue and does not appear on the income statement. Rather, a premium is part of the investment of stockholders who pay more than par for their stock.

In accounting for stock sold at a premium, the premium is recorded separately from the par value and is called contributed capital in excess of par value. For example, if a corporation sells and issues 10,000 shares of its $10 par value common stock for cash at $25 per share, you record the stock issue as follows:

| | | | | |
|---|---|---|---|---|
| Dec. | 1 | Cash | 250,000.00 | |
| | | Common Stock | | 100,000.00 |
| | | Contributed Capital in Excess of Par Value, Common Stock | | 150,000.00 |
| | | Issued 10,000 shares of $10 par value common stock at $25 per share. | | |

When stock is issued in exchange for assets other than cash and the fair value of the assets exceeds the par value of the stock, a premium is recorded as contributed capital in excess of par value. If fair value for the assets cannot be determined within reasonable limits, a price established by recent sales of the stock may be used to record the exchange. This too may require that you record a premium.

When a balance sheet is prepared, any contributed capital in excess of par value is added in the equity section to the par value of the stock, as follows:

**Stockholders' Equity**

| | |
|---|---|
| Common stock, $10 par value, 25,000 shares authorized, 20,000 shares issued | $200,000 |
| Contributed capital in excess of par value, common stock | 450,000 |
| Total contributed capital | $650,000 |
| Retained earnings | 282,400 |
| Total stockholders' equity | $932,400 |

### Discounts on Stock

If stock is issued at a price below par value, the difference between par and the issue price is called a **discount on stock**. Most states prohibit issuing stock at a discount because the stockholders would be investing less than minimum legal capital. Where stock can be issued at a discount, purchasers of the stock usually become contingently liable to the issuing corporation's creditors for the amount of the discount. As a result, corporations usually set the par value of their stock at a low or nominal amount so that a discussion of stock discounts has little practical importance. However, if stock is issued at less than par, you should understand that the discount is not an expense and does not appear on the income statement. Rather, the discount is debited to a discount account and subtracted on the balance sheet from the par value of the stock.

## No-Par Stock

At one time, all stocks were required to have a par value. Today, nearly all states permit the issuance of stocks that do not have a par value, and the trend is toward issuing stocks without a par value. The primary advantage of issuing **no-par stock** is that it may be issued at any price without having a discount liability attached. Also, printing a par value on a stock certificate may cause an uninformed person to think that the share must be worth par value, when it actually may be worthless.

In some states, the entire proceeds from the sale of no-par stock become minimum legal capital. In this case, the entire proceeds are credited to a no-par stock account. For example, if a corporation issues 1,000 shares of no-par stock at $42 per share, the transaction is recorded as follows:

| | | | | |
|---|---|---|---|---|
| Oct. | 20 | Cash | 42,000.00 | |
| | | No-Par Common Stock | | 42,000.00 |
| | | Sold and issued 1,000 shares of no-par common stock at $42 per share. | | |

In other states, a corporation may place a **stated value** on its no-par stock. The stated value then becomes minimum legal capital and is credited to the no-par stock account. If the stock is issued at an amount in excess of stated value, the excess is credited to Contributed Capital in Excess of Stated Value, No-Par Common Stock. For example, a corporation issues 1,000 shares of no-par common stock that has a stated value of $25 per share. If the stock is issued for $42 per share, the transaction is recorded as follows:

| | | | | |
|---|---|---|---|---|
| Oct. | 20 | Cash . . . . . . . . . . . . . . . . . . . . . . . . . . . . | 42,000.00 | |
| | | No-Par Common Stock . . . . . . . . . . . . . . . . . | | 25,000.00 |
| | | Contributed Capital in Excess of Stated Value, No-Par Common Stock . . . . . . . . | | 17,000.00 |
| | | Issued 1,000 shares of no-par stock, $25 stated value, at $42 per share. | | |

## Sale of Stock through Subscriptions

Record transactions involving stock subscriptions and explain the effects of subscribed stock on corporation assets and stockholders' equity.
(L. O. 3)

Usually, stock is sold for cash and immediately issued. However, corporations sometimes sell stock by means of **stock subscriptions**. For example, when a new corporation is formed, the organizers may realize that the new business has limited immediate needs for cash but will need additional capital in the future. To get the corporation started on a sound footing, the organizers may sell stock to investors who agree to contribute some cash now and also agree to make additional contributions in the future.

When stock is sold through subscriptions, the investor signs a subscription blank or a subscription list and agrees to buy a certain number of the shares at a specified price. The agreement also states when payments are to be made. When the subscription is accepted by the corporation, it becomes a contract and the corporation acquires an asset. The asset is the right to receive payment from the subscriber. At the same time, the subscriber obtains an equity in the corporation.

To illustrate the sale of stock through subscriptions, assume that on May 6, Northgate Corporation accepted subscriptions to 5,000 shares of its $10 par value common stock at $12 per share. The subscription contracts called for a 10% down payment to accompany the subscriptions and the balance in two equal installments due in three months and six months. You record the subscriptions as follows:

| | | | | |
|---|---|---|---|---|
| May | 6 | Subscriptions Receivable, Common Stock . . . . . . . . . | 60,000.00 | |
| | | Contributed Capital in Excess of Par Value, Common Stock . . . . . . . . . . . . . . . . | | 10,000.00 |
| | | Common Stock Subscribed. . . . . . . . . . . . . . . . | | 50,000.00 |
| | | Accepted subscriptions to 5,000 shares of $10 par value common stock at $12 per share. | | |

Notice that at the time the subscriptions are accepted, the subscriptions receivable account is debited for the sum of the stock's par value and premium. This is the amount the subscribers agree to pay. Also notice that the **Common Stock Subscribed** account is credited for par value and that the premium is credited to Contributed Capital in Excess of Par Value. Later, the subscriptions receivable will be converted into cash when the subscribers pay for their stock. And when payment is completed, the subscribed stock will be issued and will become outstanding stock.

Receipt of the down payments and the two installment payments are recorded with these entries:

| | | | | |
|---|---|---|---|---|
| May | 6 | Cash | 6,000.00 | |
| | | Subscriptions Receivable, Common Stock | | 6,000.00 |
| | | Collected 10% down payments on the common stock subscribed. | | |
| Aug. | 6 | Cash | 27,000.00 | |
| | | Subscriptions Receivable, Common Stock | | 27,000.00 |
| | | Collected the first installment payments on the common stock subscribed. | | |
| Nov. | 6 | Cash | 27,000.00 | |
| | | Subscriptions Receivable, Common Stock | | 27,000.00 |
| | | Collected the second installment payments on the common stock subscribed. | | |

In this case, the down payments accompanied the subscriptions. Therefore, the May 6 entries to record the receipt of the subscriptions and to record the down payments could have been combined.

When stock is sold through subscriptions, the stock usually is not issued until the subscriptions are paid in full. Also, if dividends are declared before subscribed stock has been issued, the dividends go only to outstanding shares, not to the subscribed shares. However, as soon as the subscriptions are paid, the stock is issued. The entry to record the issuance of the Northgate common stock appears as follows:

| | | | | |
|---|---|---|---|---|
| Aug. | 5 | Common Stock Subscribed | 50,000.00 | |
| | | Common Stock | | 50,000.00 |
| | | Issued 5,000 shares of common stock sold through subscriptions. | | |

Most subscriptions are collected in full, but not always. Sometimes a subscriber fails to pay. If this happens, the subscription contract must be canceled. In such a case, if the subscriber has made a partial payment on the contract, the amount paid may be returned. Or, an amount of stock equal to the partial payment may be issued. Or, in some states, the subscriber's partial payment may be kept by the corporation to compensate for any damages suffered.

#### Subscriptions Receivable and Stock Subscribed on the Balance Sheet

Subscriptions receivable are reported on the balance sheet as a current asset or as a long-term asset, depending on when collection is expected. If a corporation prepares a balance sheet after accepting subscriptions to its stock but before the stock is issued, both the issued stock and the subscribed stock should be reported on the balance sheet, as follows:

| | | |
|---|---|---|
| Common stock, $10 par value, 25,000 shares authorized, 20,000 shares issued | $200,000 | |
| Common stock subscribed, 5,000 shares | 50,000 | |
| Total common stock issued and subscribed | $250,000 | |
| Contributed capital in excess of par value, common stock | 40,000 | |
| Total contributed capital | | $290,000 |

## Rights of Common Stockholders

When investors buy a corporation's common stock, they acquire all the *specific* rights granted by the corporation's charter to its common stockholders. They also acquire the *general* rights granted stockholders by the laws of the state in which the company is incorporated. The laws vary, but common stockholders generally have the following rights:

1. The right to vote at the stockholders' meetings.
2. The right to sell or otherwise dispose of their stock.
3. The right of first opportunity to purchase any additional shares of common stock issued by the corporation. (This is called the common stockholders' **preemptive right**. It gives common stockholders the opportunity to protect their proportionate interest in the corporation. For example, a stockholder who owns one fourth of a corporation's common stock has the first opportunity to buy one fourth of any new common stock issued. This enables the stockholder to maintain a one-fourth interest.)
4. The right to share with other common stockholders in any dividends distributed to common stockholders, so that each common share receives the same amount.
5. The right to share in any assets that remain after creditors are paid if the corporation is liquidated.

## Preferred Stock

Explain the differences between common and preferred stocks and allocate dividends between common and preferred stocks.
(L. O. 4)

A corporation may issue more than one kind or class of stock. If two classes are issued, one is usually called **preferred stock** and the other is common stock. Preferred stock generally has a par value and, like common stock, may be sold at a price that is greater than par (or perhaps less than par). Separate contributed capital accounts are used to record the issuance of preferred stock. For example, if 1,000 shares of $100 par, preferred stock are issued for $120,000 cash, the entry to record the issue is:

| | | | | |
|---|---|---|---|---|
| June | 1 | Cash . . . . . . . . . . . . . . . . . . . . . . . . . . . . | 120,000.00 | |
| | | Preferred Stock . . . . . . . . . . . . . . . . . . . | | 100,000.00 |
| | | Contributed Capital in Excess of Par Value, Preferred Stock . . . . . . . . . . . . . . . | | 20,000.00 |
| | | Issued preferred stock for cash. | | |

The name *preferred* comes from the fact that preferred shares have a higher priority or senior status relative to common shares in one or more ways. These commonly include a preference as to payment of dividends and may include a preference in the distribution of assets if the corporation is liquidated.

In addition to the preferences it receives, preferred stock carries all the rights of common stock, unless such rights are specifically denied in the corporation's charter. Preferred stock often is denied the right to vote in the stockholders' meetings.

### Preferred Dividends

A preference as to dividends gives the preferred stockholders the right to receive their preferred dividends before the common stockholders receive a dividend. In other words, dividends cannot be paid to common stockholders unless preferred stockholders also receive a dividend. The amount of dividends that the preferred stockholders must receive usually is expressed as a dollar amount per share or as a percentage that is applied to the par value. For example, 9%, $100 par value, preferred stock must be paid $9 per share before the common shares can receive any dividend. However, a preference as to dividends does not grant an absolute right to dividends. If the board of directors does not declare a dividend, then neither the preferred nor the common stockholders receive a dividend.

### Cumulative and Noncumulative Preferred Stock

Preferred stock is either **cumulative** or **noncumulative**. If it is cumulative, any undeclared dividends accumulate each year until paid. If it is noncumulative, the right to receive dividends is forfeited in any year that dividends are not declared.

If preferred stock is cumulative and the corporation fails to declare a dividend to the preferred stockholders as called for in the corporate charter, the unpaid dividend is called a **dividend in arrears**. The accumulation of dividends in arrears on cumulative preferred stocks does not guarantee payment. However, with cumulative preferred stock, the preferred stockholders must be paid both the current dividend and any dividends in arrears before any dividend is paid to common stockholders.

To show the difference between cumulative and noncumulative preferred stock, assume that a corporation has outstanding 1,000 shares of $100 par, 9%, preferred stock and 4,000 shares of $50 par, common stock. During the first two years of the corporation's operations, the board of directors declared cash dividends of: year 1, $5,000; and year 2, $42,000. The allocations are:

| | To Preferred | To Common |
|---|---|---|
| Assuming noncumulative preferred: | | |
| Year 1 | $ 5,000 | $ -0- |
| Year 2: | | |
| First: Current preferred dividend | $ 9,000 | |
| Remainder to common | | $33,000 |
| Assuming cumulative preferred: | | |
| Year 1 | $ 5,000 | $ -0- |
| Year 2: | | |
| First: Dividends in arrears | $ 4,000 | |
| Next: Current preferred dividend | 9,000 | |
| Remainder to common | | $29,000 |
| Totals | $13,000 | $29,000 |

Notice that the year 2 allocation of dividends depends on whether the preferred stock is noncumulative or cumulative. With noncumulative preferred stock, the preferred stockholders never receive the $4,000 that was unpaid in year 1. However, when the preferred stock is cumulative, the $4,000 must be paid before the common stockholders receive a dividend.

### Disclosure of Dividends in Arrears in the Financial Statements

Unlike interest expense, which is incurred as time passes and therefore must be accrued, dividends do not accrue. A liability for a dividend does not come into existence until the dividend is declared by the board of directors. Therefore, if a preferred dividend date passes and the corporation's board fails to declare the dividend on its cumulative preferred stock, the dividend in arrears is not a liability. It does not appear on the balance sheet as a liability. However, when you prepare the financial statements, the *full-disclosure principle* requires that you report the amount that preferred dividends are in arrears on the balance sheet date. Normally, this information is given in a footnote to the financial statements. If there is no such disclosure, readers of the financial statements have the right to assume that preferred dividends are not in arrears.

### Participating and Nonparticipating Preferred Stock

Dividends to preferred stock are generally limited each year to an amount that is determined by applying the preferred percentage to the par value. When preferred stock is so limited, it is called *nonparticipating preferred stock*. Most preferred stock is nonparticipating. However, some preferred stock may be paid additional dividends in excess of the stated percentage or amount that is preferred. Such preferred stock is called **participating preferred stock.**

Large corporations with publicly traded stock rarely issue participating preferred stock. However, this kind of stock sometimes is issued by smaller corporations that need to raise more capital than the organizers can provide. If the organizers are not willing to share control but are willing to share profits with other investors, the corporation may issue participating preferred stock that has limited voting rights.

To illustrate participating preferred stock, assume that the 1,000 shares of $100 par, 9%, preferred stock in the above example are participating. Also, assume that cash dividends of $48,000 are declared in year 3. The allocation between preferred and common shares is as follows:

| | To Preferred | To Common |
|---|---|---|
| First, to preferred [9% × (1,000 × $100)] . . . . | $ 9,000 | |
| Next, to common [9% × (4,000 × $50)] . . . . . | | $18,000 |
| Remainder maintains equal percentage to preferred and common: | | |
| ($48,000 − $9,000 − $18,000 = $21,000) | | |
| $21,000 × ($100,000 ÷ $300,000) . . . . . . | 7,000 | |
| $21,000 × ($200,000 ÷ $300,000) . . . . . . | | 14,000 |
| Totals . . . . . . . . . . . . . . . . . . . . . . | $16,000 | $32,000 |

Observe that the first step satisfies the preferred stock's right to 9% before any dividends are paid to common. Next, the common shares receive 9%. Finally, any additional dividends are allocated on the basis of the relative par value amounts outstanding. As a result, both preferred and common shares are paid the same percentage (16% in this case). This is confirmed by the following calculation:

| | Par Value | Total Dividend | Percent of Par |
|---|---|---|---|
| Preferred (1,000 × $100) . . . . | $100,000 | $16,000 | 16 |
| Common (4,000 × $50) . . . . . | 200,000 | 32,000 | 16 |
| Totals . . . . . . . . . . . . . . | $300,000 | $48,000 | 16 |

In this example, no matter how much larger the dividend declaration might be, the preferred stock has the right to participate with common on an equal percentage basis. Thus, the preferred stock in this example is called *fully participating preferred stock*. In other cases, the right to receive additional dividends beyond the basic preferred percentage is limited to a stated amount or percentage. For example, a 9%, $100 par value, preferred stock might have the right to participate in dividend declarations, up to an additional 3%. This type of stock is called *partially participating preferred stock*.

## Why Preferred Stock Is Issued

Two common reasons why preferred stock is issued are best shown with an example. Suppose that the organizers of a business have $100,000 to invest but wish to organize a corporation that requires $200,000 capital. If they sell and issue $200,000 of common stock, they will have to share control with other stockholders. However, if they issue $100,000 of common stock to themselves and can sell to outsiders $100,000 of 8%, cumulative preferred stock that has no voting rights, they will retain control of the corporation.

Also, suppose the organizers expect their new corporation to earn an annual after-tax return of $24,000. If they sell and issue $200,000 of common stock, this will mean a 12% return. However, if they sell and issue $100,000 of each kind of stock, retaining the common for themselves, they can increase their own return to 16%, as follows:

| | |
|---|---|
| Net after-tax income . . . . . . . . . . . . . . . . . . . | $24,000 |
| Less preferred dividends at 8% . . . . . . . . . . . | (8,000) |
| Balance to common stockholders (equal to 16% on their $100,000 investment) . . . . . . . . . . . . . | $16,000 |

In this case, the common stockholders earn 16% because the dividends on the preferred stock are less than the amount that can be earned on the preferred stockholders' investment. This issuance of preferred stock is an example of **financial leverage**. Whenever the dividend rate on preferred stock is less than the rate the corporation earns on its operations, the effect is to increase or *lever* the rate earned by common stockholders. Financial leverage also occurs if money is borrowed and the creditors are paid an interest rate less than the rate earned from using the borrowed money.

There are other reasons why corporations issue preferred stock. For example, a corporation's preferred stock may appeal to some investors who believe that its common stock is too risky. Also, if a corporation's management wants to issue common stock but believes the current market price for the common stock is too low, the corporation may issue preferred stock that is convertible into common stock. Later, if the price of the common stock recovers, the preferred stockholders may be asked to convert their shares into common shares.

## Convertible Preferred Stock

Describe convertible preferred stock and explain the meaning of par, redemption, book, and market values of stock.
(L. O. 5)

To make an issue of preferred stock more attractive, investors may be given the right to exchange their preferred shares for a fixed number of shares of the issuing company's common stock. **Convertible preferred stocks** offer investors more security than would common stock. Also, if the issuing company prospers and its common stock increases in price, the investors have the opportunity to share in the prosperity by converting their preferred stock into the more valuable common stock. Conversion is always at the option of the investors and therefore does not occur unless it is to their advantage.

To see how the conversion of preferred stock is recorded, assume that a corporation has outstanding 1,000 shares of 10%, $100 par value, convertible preferred stock. The stock was originally issued for $103 per share. Each preferred share is convertible into four shares of $10 par value, common stock. If all of the preferred shares are converted on May 1, the entry to record the conversion is:

| | | | | |
|---|---|---|---|---|
| May | 1 | Preferred Stock . . . . . . . . . . . . . . . . . . . . . | 100,000.00 | |
| | | Contributed Capital in Excess of Par Value, Preferred Stock . . . . . . . . . . . . . . . . . . . . | 3,000.00 | |
| | | Common Stock . . . . . . . . . . . . . . . . . | | 40,000.00 |
| | | Contributed Capital in Excess of Par Value, Common Stock . . . . . . . . . . . . . | | 63,000.00 |
| | | To record the conversion of preferred stock. | | |

Note that when the preferred stock is converted into common stock, the balances in the preferred stock accounts are removed and replaced with account balances related to common stock. No gain or loss is recorded.

## Stock Values

In addition to a par value, stocks may have a redemption value, a market value, and a book value.

### Redemption Value of Callable Preferred Stock

Some issues of preferred stock are callable. This means that the issuing corporation has the right to retire the **callable preferred stock** by paying a specified amount to the preferred stockholders. The amount that must be paid to call and retire a callable preferred share is its **redemption value** or **call price**. This amount is set at the time the stock is issued. Normally, the redemption value includes the par value of the stock plus a premium. To retire a callable preferred stock, the issuing corporation must pay any dividends in arrears in addition to the redemption value of the stock.

### Market Value

The market value of a share of stock is the price at which a share can be bought or sold. Market values are influenced by earnings, dividends, future prospects, and general market conditions.

### Book Value

The **book value of a share of stock** is one share's equity in the corporation's net assets as recorded in the corporation's accounts. To determine the book value per share when the only outstanding stock is common stock, you divide total stockholders' equity by the number of shares outstanding. For example, if total stockholders' equity is $285,000 and there are 10,000 shares outstanding, the book value per share is $28.50 ($285,000 ÷ 10,000 = $28.50).

To compute book values when both common and preferred stock are outstanding, you must allocate the total stockholders' equity between the preferred and common shares. The preferred stock's portion is its redemption value (or par value if there is no redemption value) plus any cumulative dividends in arrears. The remaining stockholders' equity is then assigned to the common shares outstanding. To determine the book value of each class, you divide the portion of stockholders' equity assigned to a class by the number of shares of that class outstanding. For instance, assume a corporation has the stockholders' equity as shown in Illustration 15–3.

If the preferred stock is redeemable at $103 per share and two years of cumulative preferred dividends are in arrears, the book values of the corporation's shares are calculated as follows:

| | | | |
|---|---|---|---|
| Total stockholders' equity | | $ 447,000 | |
| Less equity applicable to preferred shares: | | | |
| Redemption value | $103,000 | | |
| Cumulative dividends in arrears | 14,000 | (117,000) | |
| Equity applicable to common shares | | | $330,000 |
| Book value of preferred shares ($117,000 ÷ 1,000) | | $117 | |
| Book value of common shares ($330,000 ÷ 10,000) | | 33 | |

In their annual reports to shareholders, corporations sometimes report the increase in the book value of the corporation's shares that has occurred during a year. Also, book value may have significance in a contract. For example, a stockholder may enter into a contract to sell shares at their book value on some future date. However, book value should not be confused with *liquidation value*. If a corporation is liquidated, its assets will probably sell at prices quite different from the amounts at which they are carried on the books. Also, book

**Illustration 15–3**
**Stockholders' equity with preferred and common stock**

| Stockholders' Equity | | | |
|---|---|---|---|
| Preferred stock, $100 par value, 7%, cumulative and nonparticipating, 2,000 shares authorized, 1,000 shares issued and outstanding | $100,000 | | |
| Contributed capital in excess of par value, preferred stock | 5,000 | | |
| Total capital contributed by preferred stockholders | | $105,000 | |
| Common stock, $25 par value, 12,000 shares authorized, 10,000 shares issued and outstanding | $250,000 | | |
| Contributed capital in excess of par value, common stock | 10,000 | | |
| Total capital contributed by common stockholders | | 260,000 | |
| Total contributed capital | | $365,000 | |
| Retained earnings | | 82,000 | |
| Total stockholders' equity | | | $447,000 |

value generally has little bearing on the market value of stock. Dividends, earning capacity, and future prospects are usually of much more importance.

## Summary of the Chapter in Terms of Learning Objectives

**1.** Advantages of the corporate form of business include the following: (*a*) corporations are separate legal entities, (*b*) lack of stockholder liability for the corporate debts, (*c*) a corporation's continuity of life, and (*d*) stockholders are not agents of the corporation. A disadvantage is that corporations are closely regulated by government. Also, corporations must pay various taxes, especially income taxes, which is often a disadvantage.

A corporation is governed by its board of directors, which is elected by its stockholders. Officers that manage the corporation include a president, perhaps one or more vice presidents, and a secretary. The chief executive officer may be the president or the board of directors chairperson.

Stockholders must contribute assets equal to the legal minimum capital of a corporation or be liable for the deficiency. In an effort to protect creditors, this amount cannot be paid to stockholders as dividends if liabilities remain unpaid.

**2.** When stock is issued, the par or stated value is credited to the stock account, and any excess is credited to a separate contributed capital account. If the stock has no par or stated value, the entire proceeds are credited to the stock account.

**3.** If a corporation sells stock through subscriptions, the right to receive payment is an asset of the corporation, and the subscriber's equity is recorded in contributed capital accounts. The Common Stock Subscribed account is transferred to Common Stock when the shares are issued, which normally occurs after all payments are received.

**4.** Preferred stock has a priority or senior status relative to common stock in one or more ways. Usually, this means that common stockholders cannot be paid dividends unless a specified amount of dividends is also paid to preferred shares. Also, preferred stock may have a priority status if the corporation is liquidated. The dividend preference for many preferred stocks is cumulative, and a few preferred stocks also participate in dividends beyond the preferred amount.

**5.** Upon the conversion of convertible preferred stock into common stock, the carrying value of the preferred stock or bonds is transferred to contributed capital accounts that relate to common stock. No gain or loss is recorded.

Par value is an arbitrary amount assigned to a share of stock when the class of stock is authorized. If preferred stock is callable, the amount that must be paid to retire the stock is its redemption value plus any dividends in arrears. The book value of preferred stock is any dividends arrearage plus its par value or, if it is callable, its redemption value. The remaining stockholders' equity is divided by the number of outstanding common shares to determine the book value per share of the common stock. Market value is the price a stock commands if bought or sold.

## Demonstration Problem

Barton Corporation was created on January 1, 1990. Listed below are the transactions relating to stockholders' equity, which occurred during the first two years of the company's operations. Prepare the journal entries to record these transactions. Also prepare the balance sheet presentation of the organization costs, liabilities, and stockholders' equity as of December 31, 1990, and December 31, 1991. Include appropriate footnotes.

1990

Jan. 1 Authorized the issuance of 2,000,000 shares of $5 par value common stock and 100,000 shares of $100 par value preferred stock. The preferred stock pays a 10% annual dividend and is cumulative.

1 Issued 200,000 shares of common stock at $12 per share.

1 Issued 100,000 shares of common stock in exchange for a building valued at $820,000 and merchandise inventory valued at $380,000.

1 Accepted subscriptions for 150,000 shares of common stock at $12 per share. The subscribers made no down payments, and the full purchase price was due on April 1, 1990.

1 Reimbursed the company's founders for $100,000 of organization costs which are to be amortized over 10 years.

1 Issued 12,000 shares of preferred stock for $110 per share.

Apr. 1 Collected the full subscription price for the January 1 common stock and issued the stock.

Dec. 31 The Income Summary account for 1990 had a $125,000 credit balance before being closed to Retained Earnings: no dividends were declared on either the common or preferred stocks.

1991

June 4 Issued 100,000 shares of common stock for $15 per share.

Dec. 10 Declared dividends payable on January 10, 1992, as follows:

| | |
|---|---|
| To preferred stockholders for 1990 . . | $120,000 |
| To preferred stockholders for 1991 . . | 120,000 |
| To common stockholders for 1991 . . | 300,000 |

31 The Income Summary account for 1991 had a $1,000,000 credit balance before being closed to Retained Earnings.

## Solution to Demonstration Problem

| | | | | |
|---|---|---|---|---|
| 1990 | | | | |
| Jan | 1 | Cash | 2,400,000.00 | |
| | | Common Stock | | 1,000,000.00 |
| | | Contributed Capital in Excess of Par Value, Common Stock | | 1,400,000.00 |
| | | Issued 200,000 shares of common stock. | | |
| | 1 | Building | 820,000.00 | |
| | | Merchandise Inventory | 380,000.00 | |
| | | Common Stock | | 500,000.00 |
| | | Contributed Capital in Excess of Par Value, Common Stock | | 700,000.00 |
| | | Issued 100,000 shares of common stock. | | |
| | 1 | Subscriptions Receivable | 1,800,000.00 | |
| | | Common Stock Subscribed | | 750,000.00 |
| | | Contributed Capital in Excess of Par Value, Common Stock | | 1,050,000.00 |
| | | Accepted subscriptions for 150,000 shares of common stock. | | |
| | 1 | Organization Costs | 100,000.00 | |
| | | Cash | | 100,000.00 |
| | | Reimbursed the founders for organization costs. | | |
| | 1 | Cash | 1,320,000.00 | |
| | | Preferred Stock | | 1,200,000.00 |
| | | Contributed Capital in Excess of Par Value, Preferred Stock | | 120,000.00 |
| | | Issued 12,000 shares of preferred stock. | | |
| Apr. | 1 | Cash | 1,800,000.00 | |
| | | Subscriptions Receivable | | 1,800,000.00 |
| | | Collected balance due on subscribed common stock. | | |
| | 1 | Common Stock Subscribed | 750,000.00 | |
| | | Common Stock | | 750,000.00 |
| | | Issued 150,000 shares of subscribed common stock. | | |
| Dec. | 31 | Income Summary | 125,000.00 | |
| | | Retained Earnings | | 125,000.00 |
| | | To close the Income Summary account and update Retained Earnings. | | |

| Date | | Account Titles and Explanation | Debit | Credit |
|---|---|---|---|---|
| 1991 June | 4 | Cash | 1,500,000.00 | |
| | | Common Stock | | 500,000.00 |
| | | Contributed Capital in Excess of Par Value, Common Stock | | 1,000,000.00 |
| | | Issued 100,000 shares of common stock. | | |
| Dec. | 10 | Retained Earnings | 540,000.00 | |
| | | Dividends Payable, Common Stock | | 300,000.00 |
| | | Dividends Payable, Preferred Stock | | 240,000.00 |
| | | Declared current dividends and dividends in arrears to common and preferred stockholders, payable on January 10, 1992. | | |
| | 31 | Income Summary | 1,000,000.00 | |
| | | Retained Earnings | | 1,000,000.00 |
| | | To close the Income Summary account and update Retained Earnings. | | |

**Balance Sheet Presentations**

| | As of 12/31/90 | As of 12/31/91 |
|---|---|---|
| Assets: | | |
| Organization costs | $ 90,000 | $ 80,000 |
| Liabilities: | | |
| Dividends payable, common stock | | $ 300,000 |
| Dividends payable, preferred stock | | 240,000 |
| Total liabilities | | $ 540,000 |
| Stockholders' equity: | | |
| Contributed capital: | | |
| Preferred stock, $100 par value, 10%, cumulative dividends, 100,000 shares authorized, 12,000 shares issued | $1,200,000 | $1,200,000 |
| Contributed capital in excess of par, preferred stock | 120,000 | 120,000 |
| Total capital contributed by preferred stockholders | $1,320,000 | $1,320,000 |
| Common stock, $5 par value, 2,000,000 shares authorized, 450,000 shares issued in 1990, and 550,000 shares in 1991 | $2,250,000 | $2,750,000 |
| Contributed capital in excess of par, common stock | 3,150,000 | 4,150,000 |
| Total capital contributed by common stockholders | $5,400,000 | $6,900,000 |
| Total contributed capital | $6,720,000 | $8,220,000 |
| Retained earnings (see Note 1) | 125,000 | 585,000 |
| Total stockholders' equity | $6,845,000 | $8,805,000 |

Note 1: As of December 31, 1990, there were $120,000 of dividends in arrears on the cumulative preferred stock.

## Glossary

Define or explain the words and phrases listed in the chapter Glossary. (L. O. 6)

**Book value of a share of stock** the equity of one share of outstanding stock in the issuing corporation's net assets as recorded in the corporation's accounts. p. 644

**Callable preferred stock** preferred stock that the issuing corporation, at its option, may retire by paying to the stockholders the redemption value of the stock plus any dividends in arrears. pp. 643–44

**Call price of preferred stock** another name for *redemption value*. p. 643

**Common stock** stock of a corporation that has only one class of stock, or if there is more than one class, the class that has no preferences relative to the corporation's other classes of stock. p. 633

**Common Stock Subscribed** a stockholders' equity account in which a corporation records the par or stated value of unissued common stock that investors have contracted to purchase. pp. 637–38

**Convertible preferred stock** preferred stock that, at the option of the stockholder, may be exchanged for a fixed number of the issuing corporation's common shares. p. 643

**Cumulative preferred stock** preferred stock that has the right to receive all preferred dividends including undeclared dividends from past years before outstanding common shares can receive any dividend. p. 640

**Discount on stock** the difference between the par value of stock and the amount contributed by stockholders when the amount contributed is less than par. p. 636

**Dividend in arrears** a dividend to cumulative preferred stock which remains unpaid after the date for payment called for in the corporate charter. p. 640

**Financial leverage** increasing the return to common stock as a result of paying preferred stock or creditors a given dividend or interest rate that is less than the rate earned from using the assets received by the corporation from the preferred stockholders or creditors. p. 642

**Minimum legal capital** an amount, as defined by state law, that stockholders must invest in a corporation or be contingently liable to its creditors. p. 634

**Noncumulative preferred stock** a preferred stock for which the right to receive dividends is forfeited in any year in which dividends are not declared. p. 640

**No-par stock** a class of stock that does not have an arbitrary (par) value placed on the stock at the time the stock is first authorized. p. 636

**Organization costs** costs of bringing a corporation into existence, such as legal fees, promoters' fees, and amounts paid the state to secure a charter. p. 627

**Participating preferred stock** preferred stock that has the right to share in dividends above the fixed amount or percentage that is preferred. p. 641

**Par value** an arbitrary value placed on a share of stock at the time the stock is authorized. p. 634

**Preemptive right** the right of common stockholders to protect their proportionate interests in a corporation by having the first opportunity to purchase additional shares of common stock issued by the corporation. p. 639

**Preferred stock** stock the owners of which are granted a priority status over common stockholders in one or more ways such as in the payment of dividends or in the distribution of assets upon liquidation. p. 639

**Premium on stock** the difference between the par value of stock and the amount contributed by stockholders when the amount contributed is more than par value. p. 635

**Proxy** a legal document that gives an agent of a stockholder the right to vote the stockholder's shares. p. 627

**Redemption value of preferred stock** the amount a corporation must pay in addition to dividends in arrears if and when it exercises its right to retire a share of callable preferred stock. pp. 643–44

**Stated value of no-par stock** an amount, established by a corporation's board of directors, that is credited to the no-par stock account at the time the stock is issued. pp. 636–37

**Stock subscription** a contractual commitment by an investor to purchase unissued shares of stock and become a stockholder. pp. 637–38

## Objective Review

Answers to the following questions are listed in Appendix I at the end of the book. Be sure that you decide which is the one best answer to each question *before* you check the answers in the appendix.

1. An advantage of the corporate form of organization is:
   *a.* The ease of organization.
   *b.* That stockholders have a mutual agency relationship with the corporation.
   *c.* The ease of capital assembly.
   *d.* The lack of governmental regulation compared to single proprietorships and partnerships.
   *e.* The method of taxation.
2. Viva Corporation has no-par common stock with a stated value of $10 per share. The company issued 3,000 shares of its stock in exchange for some equipment valued at $45,000. The entry to record the transaction would include:
   *a.* A debit to Equipment for $30,000.
   *b.* A credit to No-Par Common Stock for $45,000.
   *c.* A credit to Contributed Capital in Excess of Stated Value, No-Par Common Stock for $15,000.
   *d.* A credit to Contributed Capital in Excess of Stated Value, No-Par Common Stock for $30,000.
   *e.* A credit to Retained Earnings for $15,000.
3. Iota Corporation accepted subscriptions to 5,000 shares of $10 par value common stock at $84 per share. A 10% down payment was made at the

time of the subscription contract, and the balance was to be paid in full six months later. The entries to record receipt of the final balance and the issuance of the stock would include:

*a.* A debit to Subscriptions Receivable, Common Stock for $378,000.
*b.* A credit to Subscriptions Receivable, Common Stock for $420,000.
*c.* A debit to Common Stock Subscribed for $420,000.
*d.* A credit to Contributed Capital in Excess of Par Value, Common Stock for $333,000.
*e.* A credit to Common Stock for $50,000.

4. Jinn Corporation has stockholders' equity as follows:

| | | |
|---|---|---|
| Preferred stock, $50 par value, 10%, cumulative and nonparticipating, 10,000 shares authorized, 5,000 shares issued and outstanding | $250,000 | |
| Contributed capital in excess of par value, preferred stock | 750,000 | |
| Total capital contributed by preferred stockholders | | $1,000,000 |
| Common stock, $10 par value, 100,000 shares authorized, 15,000 shares issued and outstanding | $150,000 | |
| Contributed capital in excess of par value, common stock | 300,000 | |
| Total capital contributed by common stockholders | | 450,000 |
| Total contributed capital | | $1,450,000 |
| Retained earnings | | 700,000 |
| Total stockholders equity | | $2,150,000 |

Dividends have not been declared for the past two years, but in the third year, Jinn Corporation declared $160,000 of dividends distributable to both preferred and common stockholders. Determine the amount of dividends to be paid the common stockholders.

*a.* $ 50,000.
*b.* $160,000.
*c.* $ 75,000.
*d.* $ 85,000.
*e.* $135,000.

5. Raysome, Inc.'s callable preferred stock has a redemption value of $90 plus any dividends in arrears. The stockholders' equity of the company is as follows:

| | | |
|---|---|---|
| Preferred stock, $75 par value, 10%, cumulative and nonparticipating, 5,000 shares authorized, 1,000 issued and outstanding (dividends are in arrears for two years) | $ 75,000 | |
| Contributed capital in excess of par value, preferred stock | 5,000 | |
| Total capital contributed by preferred stockholders | | $ 80,000 |
| Common stock, $20 par value, 50,000 shares authorized, 12,000 shares issued and outstanding | $240,000 | |
| Contributed capital in excess of par value, common stock | 60,000 | |
| Total capital contributed by common stockholders | | 300,000 |
| Total contributed capital | | $380,000 |
| Retained earnings | | 145,000 |
| Total stockholders' equity | | $525,000 |

The book values per share of the preferred and common shares are:

*a.* Preferred shares, $105.00; common shares, $35.00.
*b.* Preferred shares, $ 75.00; common shares, $37.50.
*c.* Preferred shares, $ 90.00; common shares, $36.25.
*d.* Preferred shares, $ 80.00; common shares, $27.08.
*e.* Preferred shares, $ 95.00; common shares, $25.83.

## Questions for Class Discussion

1. What are the advantages and disadvantages of the corporate form of business organization?
2. Why is the income of a corporation said to be taxed twice?
3. Who is responsible for directing the affairs of a corporation?
4. Who serves as the chief executive officer of a corporation?
5. What is a proxy?
6. What are organization costs? List several.
7. How are organization costs classified on the balance sheet?
8. What are the duties and responsibilities of a corporation's registrar and transfer agent?
9. List the general rights of common stockholders.
10. What is the preemptive right of common stockholders?
11. Laws place no limit on the amounts partners may withdraw from a partnership. On the other hand, laws regulating corporations place definite limits on the amount of dividends stockholders may withdraw from a corporation. Why is there a difference?
12. What is a stock premium? What is a stock discount?
13. In what account would you record a premium on common stock?
14. Does a corporation earn a profit by selling its stock at a premium? Does it incur a loss by selling its stock at a discount?
15. Why do corporation laws make purchasers of stock at a discount contingently liable for the discount? To whom are such purchasers contingently liable?
16. What is the main advantage of no-par stock?
17. What distinguishes preferred stock from common stock?
18. What is the difference between cumulative and noncumulative preferred stock?
19. What is the difference between participating and nonparticipating preferred stock?
20. What are the balance sheet classifications of the accounts: (*a*) Subscriptions Receivable, Common Stock and (*b*) Common Stock Subscribed?
21. What is the difference between the par value and redemption value of callable preferred stock?
22. What is the difference between the market value and book value of a stock?

## Exercises

**Exercise 15–1**
**Recording issuances of stock**
(L. O. 2)

Prepare general journal entries on November 12 to record the following issuances of stock by various corporations:

1. One hundred shares of $5 par value common stock are issued for $30,000 cash.
2. Fifty shares of no-par common stock are issued to promoters in exchange for their efforts in organizing the corporation. The promoters' efforts are estimated to be worth $9,500, and the stock has no stated value.
3. Assume the same facts as in (2) above, except that the stock has a $10 stated value.

**Exercise 15–2**
**Comparative entries for partnership and corporation**
(L. O. 1, 2)

Jack Hunt and Dana Blake begin a new business on January 7 by investing $85,000 each in the company. Assume that on December 24, it is decided that $22,000 of the company's cash will be distributed equally between the owners. Checks for $11,000 are prepared and given to the owners on December 29. On December 31, the company reports a $30,000 net income. Prepare journal entries to record the investments by the owners, the distribution of cash to the owners, and the closing of the Income Summary account assuming: (*a*) the business is a partnership between equal partners; and (*b*) the business is a corporation that issued 1,500 shares of $10 par value, common stock to each owner.

**Exercise 15–3**
**Accounting for par and no-par stock**
(L. O. 2)

On June 8, Daily Corporation sold and issued 10,000 shares of its common stock for $315,000. Give the entry to record the sale under each of the following independent assumptions: (*a*) the stock is no-par stock, and the board of directors did not place a stated value on the stock; (*b*) the stock is no-par stock on which the board had placed a $5 per share stated value; and (*c*) the stock has a $10 par value.

**Exercise 15–4**
**Stock subscriptions**
(L. O. 3)

On May 13, Keefert Corporation accepted subscriptions to 30,000 shares of its $10 par value common stock at $15 per share. The subscription contracts called for one fourth of the subscription price to accompany each contract as a down payment and the balance to be paid on July 15. Give the entries to record: (*a*) the subscriptions, (*b*) the down payments, (*c*) receipt of the remaining amounts due on the subscriptions, and (*d*) issuance of the stock.

**Exercise 15–5**
**Allocating dividends between common and cumulative preferred stock**
(L. O. 4)

Farley Corporation has outstanding 15,000 shares of $50 par value, 9%, cumulative and nonparticipating preferred stock and 35,000 shares of $20 par value common stock. During the first four years in its life, the corporation declared and paid the following amounts in dividends: first year, $-0-; second year, $85,000; third year, $150,000; and fourth year, $75,000. Determine the total dividends paid to each class of stockholders each year.

**Exercise 15–6**
**Allocating dividends between common and noncumulative preferred stock**
(L. O. 4)

Refer to the facts presented in Exercise 15–5 and determine the total dividends paid to each class of stockholders assuming the preferred stock is noncumulative.

**Exercise 15–7**
**Allocating dividends between common and participating preferred stock**
(L. O. 4)

Ewing Corporation has outstanding 15,000 shares of $50 par value, 8%, cumulative and fully participating preferred stock and 50,000 shares of $10 par value common stock. It has regularly paid all dividends on the preferred stock. This year the board of directors declared and paid a total of $150,000 in dividends to the two classes of stockholders. Determine the percentage of par value each class of stockholders received this year and the dividend per share paid to each class.

**Exercise 15–8**
**Effect of preferred stock on rates of return**
(L. O. 4)

Four individuals have agreed to begin a new business that will require a total investment of $2 million. Each of the four will contribute $300,000, and the remaining $800,000 will be raised from other investors. Two alternative plans for raising the money are being considered: (1) issue $100 par value common stock to all investors, or (2) issue $100 par value common stock to the four founders and $100 par value, 9%, preferred stock to the remaining investors. In either case, all of the shares will be issued at par. If the business is expected to earn an after-tax net income of $250,000, which of the two plans will provide the highest return to the four founders? What rate of return will the founders earn under each alternative?

**Exercise 15–9**
**Effect of preferred stock on rates of return**
(L. O. 4)

What would be your answer to Exercise 15–8 if the business is expected to earn an annual, after-tax net income of only $150,000?

**Exercise 15–10**
**Book value per share of stock**
(L. O. 5)

The stockholders' equity section from Tingle Corporation's balance sheet is as follows:

**Stockholders' Equity**

| | |
|---|---|
| Preferred stock, 10%, cumulative and nonparticipating, $100 par value, $105 redemption value, 5,000 shares issued and outstanding | $ 500,000 |
| Common stock, $10 par value, 90,000 shares issued and outstanding | 900,000 |
| Retained earnings | 400,000 |
| Total stockholders' equity | $1,800,000 |

*Required*

1. Determine the book value per share of the preferred stock and of the common stock under the assumption there are no dividends in arrears on the preferred stock.
2. Determine the book value per share for each kind of stock under the assumption that two years' dividends are in arrears on the preferred stock.

## Problems

**Problem 15–1**
**Stock subscriptions**
(L. O. 2, 3)

Leotine Corporation is authorized to issue 20,000 shares of $100 par value, 10%, cumulative and nonparticipating preferred stock and 500,000 shares of no-par value common stock. The board of directors established a $10 stated value for the no-par common stock. Leotine Corporation then completed these transactions:

Aug. 6 Accepted subscriptions to 150,000 shares of common stock at $20 per share. Down payments equal to 20% of the subscription price accompanied each subscription.

15 Gave the corporation's promoters 4,000 shares of common stock for their services in getting the corporation organized. The board valued the services at $75,000.

Sept. 4 Accepted subscriptions to 10,000 shares of preferred stock at $130 per share. The subscriptions were accompanied by 40% down payments.

10 Collected the balance due on the August 6 common stock subscriptions and issued the stock.

30 Accepted subscriptions to 5,000 shares of preferred stock at $120 per share. The subscriptions were accompanied by 40% down payments.

Oct. 9 Collected the balance due on the September 4 preferred stock subscriptions and issued the stock.

*Required*

1. Prepare general journal entries to record the transactions.
2. Prepare the contributed capital section of the corporation's balance sheet as of the close of business on October 9.

**Problem 15–2**
**Stockholders' equity transactions**
(L. O. 2, 3, 4)

Settliff Company is authorized by its charter to issue 700,000 shares of $10 par value common stock and 35,000 shares of 11%, cumulative and nonparticipating, $100 par value preferred stock. The company completed the following transactions:

1989

June 6 Issued 35,000 shares of common stock at par for cash.

29 Gave the corporation's promoters 4,500 shares of common stock for their services in getting the corporation organized. The directors valued the services at $50,000.

July 2 Exchanged 90,000 shares of common stock for the following assets at fair market values: land, $200,000; buildings, $420,000; and machinery, $300,000.

Dec. 31 Closed the Income Summary account. A $50,000 loss was incurred.

1990

Jan. 24 Issued 2,500 shares of preferred stock at par.

Feb. 20 Accepted subscriptions to 7,000 shares of common stock at $15.20 per share. Down payments of 30% accompanied the subscription contracts.

Dec. 31 Closed the Income Summary account. A $175,000 net income was earned.

1991

Jan. 3 The board of directors declared an 11% dividend to preferred shares and $0.70 per share to outstanding common shares, payable on February 3 to the January 24 stockholders of record.

Feb. 3 Paid the previously declared dividends.

May 20 Settliff Company's $100,000 note payable (plus interest of $7,500) was due and payable on this date. The interest had already been credited to Interest Payable. The lender accepted 10,500 shares of Settliff's common stock in payment of this note and accrued interest.

Dec. 31 Closed the Dividends Declared and Income Summary accounts. A $275,000 net income was earned.

*Required*

1. Prepare general journal entries to record the transactions.
2. Prepare the stockholders' equity section of a balance sheet as of the close of business on December 31, 1991.

**Problem 15–3**
**Calculating book values; allocating dividends between preferred and common stock**
(L. O. 4, 5)

**Part 1.** The balance sheet of Romero Services Corporation includes the following information:

**Stockholders' Equity**

| | |
|---|---|
| Preferred stock, 10%, cumulative and nonparticipating, $100 par value, 2,000 shares authorized and issued . . . | $200,000 |
| Common stock, no-par value, 50,000 shares authorized and issued . . . . . . . . . . . . . . . . . . . . . . . . . | 500,000 |
| Retained earnings . . . . . . . . . . . . . . . . . . . . . . | 150,000 |
| Total stockholders' equity . . . . . . . . . . . . . . . . . . | $850,000 |

*Required*

Assume that the preferred stock has a redemption value of $106 plus any dividends in arrears. Calculate the book value per share of the preferred and common stocks under each of the following assumptions:

*a.* There are no dividends in arrears on the preferred stock.

*b.* One year's dividends are in arrears on the preferred stock.

*c.* Three years' dividends are in arrears on the preferred stock.

**Part 2.** Since its organization, Transom Corporation has had outstanding 5,000 shares of $100 par value, 12%, preferred stock and 75,000 shares of $10 par value common stock. No dividends have been paid this year, and none were paid during either of the past two years. However, the company has recently prospered, and the board of directors wants to know how much cash will be required for dividends if a $2.30 per share dividend is paid on the common stock.

*Required*

Prepare a schedule that shows the amounts of cash required for dividends to each class of stockholders under each of the following assumptions:

*a.* The preferred stock is noncumulative and nonparticipating.
*b.* The preferred stock is cumulative and nonparticipating.
*c.* The preferred stock is cumulative and fully participating.
*d.* The preferred stock is cumulative and participating to 14%.

**Problem 15–4**
**Allocating dividends in sequential years between preferred and common stock**
(L. O. 4)

Cummings Credit Company has outstanding 3,000 shares of $100 par value, 11%, preferred stock and 70,000 shares of $10 par value common stock. During a seven-year period, the company paid out the following amounts in dividends: 1987, $–0–; 1988, $50,000; 1989, $–0–; 1990, $55,000; 1991, $67,000; 1992, $70,000; and 1993, $150,000.

*Required*

1. Prepare three schedules with columnar headings as follows:

| Year | Calculations | Preferred Dividend per Share | Common Dividend per Share |
|---|---|---|---|
| | | | |

2. Complete a schedule under each of the following assumptions. There were no dividends in arrears for the years prior to 1987. (Round your answers to the nearest penny.)
   *a.* The preferred stock is noncumulative and nonparticipating.
   *b.* The preferred stock is cumulative and nonparticipating.
   *c.* The preferred stock is cumulative and fully participating.

**Problem 15–5**
**Calculation of book values**
(L. O. 5)

Fredrick Corporation's common stock is selling on a stock exchange today at $28.75 per share, and a just-published balance sheet shows the stockholders' equity of the corporation as follows:

**Stockholders' Equity**

| | |
|---|---|
| Preferred stock, 8.5%, cumulative and nonparticipating, $100 par value, 4,000 shares authorized and outstanding . . . | $ 400,000 |
| Common stock, $100 par value, 10,000 shares authorized and outstanding . . . | 1,000,000 |
| Retained earnings . . . | 476,000 |
| Total stockholders' equity . . . | $1,876,000 |

*Required*

Answer these questions: (1) What is the market value of the corporation's common stock? (2) What are the par values of its (*a*) preferred stock and (*b*) common stock? (3) If there are no dividends in arrears, what are the book values of the (*a*) preferred stock and (*b*) common stock? (4) If two years' dividends are in arrears on the preferred stock, what are the book values of the (*a*) preferred stock and (*b*) common stock? (Assume the preferred stock is not callable.)

## Alternate Problems

**Problem 15–1A**
**Stock subscriptions**
(L. O. 2, 3)

Zanobia Corporation is authorized to issue 15,000 shares of $100 par value, 10%, cumulative and nonparticipating preferred stock and 200,000 shares of no-par value common stock. The board of directors established a $10 stated value for the no-par common stock. Zanobia Corporation then completed these transactions:

May 6 Accepted subscriptions to 95,000 shares of common stock at $15 per share. Down payments equal to 30% of the subscription price accompanied each subscription.

10 Gave the corporation's promoters 2,500 shares of common stock for their services in getting the corporation organized. The board valued the services at $45,000.

June 5 Accepted subscriptions to 6,000 shares of preferred stock at $110 per share. The subscriptions were accompanied by 50% down payments.

8 Collected the balance due on the May 6 common stock subscriptions and issued the stock.

29 Accepted subscriptions to 3,000 shares of preferred stock at $105 per share. The subscriptions were accompanied by 50% down payments.

July 12 Collected the balance due on the June 5 preferred stock subscriptions and issued the stock.

*Required*

1. Prepare general journal entries to record the transactions.
2. Prepare the contributed capital section of the corporation's balance sheet as of the close of business on July 12.

**Problem 15–2A**
**Stockholders' equity transactions**
(L. O. 2, 3, 4)

Hernandez Company is authorized by its charter to issue 800,000 shares of $1 par value common stock and 45,000 shares of 12%, cumulative and nonparticipating, $100 par value preferred stock. The company completed the following transactions:

1989

Apr. 5 Issued 125,000 shares of common stock at par for cash.

28 Gave the corporation's promoters 80,000 shares of common stock for their services in getting the corporation organized. The directors valued the services at $175,000.

May 7 Exchanged 200,000 shares of common stock for the following assets at fair market values: land, $85,000; buildings, $200,000; and machinery, $325,000.

Dec. 31 Closed the Income Summary account. A $90,000 loss was incurred.

1990

Jan. 15 Issued 4,000 shares of preferred stock at par.

Mar. 20 Accepted subscriptions to 40,000 shares of common stock at $1.90 per share. Down payments of 25% accompanied the subscription contracts.

Dec. 31 Closed the Income Summary account. A $250,000 net income was earned.

1991

Jan. 9 The board of directors declared a 12% dividend to preferred shares and $0.20 per share to outstanding common shares, payable on January 22 to the January 15 stockholders of record.

22 Paid the previously declared dividends.

Mar. 13 Hernandez Company's $40,000 note payable (plus interest of $2,500) was due and payable on this date. The interest had already been credited to Interest Payable. The lender accepted 25,000 shares of Hernandez's common stock in payment of this note and accrued interest.

Dec. 31 Closed the Dividends Declared and Income Summary accounts. A $250,000 net income was earned.

*Required*

1. Prepare general journal entries to record the transactions.
2. Prepare the stockholders' equity section of a balance sheet as of the close of business on December 31, 1991.

**Problem 15–3A**
**Calculating book values; allocating dividends between preferred and common stock**
(L. O. 4, 5)

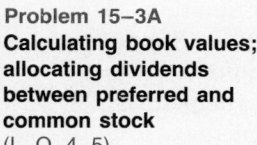

**Part 1.** The balance sheet of World Boat Charters Corporation includes the following information:

**Stockholders' Equity**

| | |
|---|---|
| Preferred stock, 9%, cumulative and nonparticipating, $100 par value, 3500 shares, authorized and issued . . . | $ 350,000 |
| Common stock, no-par value, 70,000 shares authorized and issued . . . | 700,000 |
| Retained earnings . . . | 80,000 |
| Total stockholders' equity . . . | $1,130,000 |

*Required*

Assume that the preferred stock has a redemption value of $105 plus any dividends in arrears. Calculate the book value per share of the preferred and common stocks under each of the following assumptions:

*a.* There are no dividends in arrears on the preferred stock.
*b.* One year's dividends are in arrears on the preferred stock.
*c.* Three years' dividends are in arrears on the preferred stock.

**Part 2.** Since its organization, Medley Corporation has had outstanding 4,800 shares of $100 par value, 11%, preferred stock and 72,000 shares of $10 par value common stock. No dividends have been paid this year, and none were paid during either of the past two years. However, the company has recently prospered and the board of directors wants to know how much cash will be required for dividends if a $1.85 per share dividend is paid on the common stock.

*Required*

Prepare a schedule showing the amounts of cash required for dividends to each class of stockholders under each of the following assumptions:

*a.* The preferred stock is noncumulative and nonparticipating.
*b.* The preferred stock is cumulative and nonparticipating.
*c.* The preferred stock is cumulative and fully participating.
*d.* The preferred stock is cumulative and participating to 14%.

**Problem 15–4A**
**Allocating dividends in sequential years between preferred and common stock**
(L. O. 4)

Kato Ranch Company has outstanding 1,500 shares of $100 par value, 10%, preferred stock and 30,000 shares of $10 par value common stock. During a seven-year period, the company paid out the following amounts in dividends: 1987, $–0–; 1988, $40,000; 1989, $–0–; 1990, $25,000; 1991, $30,000; 1992, $42,000; and 1993, $85,000.

*Required*

1. Prepare three schedules with columnar headings as follows:

| Year | Calculations | Preferred Dividend per Share | Common Dividend per Share |
|---|---|---|---|
| | | | |

2. Complete a schedule under each of the following assumptions. There were no dividends in arrears for the years prior to 1987. (Round your calculations of dividends per share to the nearest penny.)
   *a.* The preferred stock is noncumulative and nonparticipating.
   *b.* The preferred stock is cumulative and nonparticipating.
   *c.* The preferred stock is cumulative and fully participating.

**Problem 15–5A**
**Calculation of book values**
(L. O. 5)

Lanno Corporation's common stock is selling on a stock exchange today at $20.25 per share, and a just-published balance sheet shows the stockholders' equity in the corporation as follows:

**Stockholders' Equity**

| | |
|---|---|
| Preferred stock, 9.8%, cumulative and nonparticipating, $100 par value, 3,200 shares authorized and outstanding | $ 320,000 |
| Common stock, $10 par value, 85,000 shares authorized and outstanding | 850,000 |
| Retained earnings | 275,000 |
| Total stockholders' equity | $1,445,000 |

*Required*

Answer these questions: (1) What is the market value of the corporation's common stock? (2) What are the par values of its (*a*) preferred stock and (*b*) common stock? (3) If there are no dividends in arrears, what are the book values of the (*a*) preferred stock and (*b*) common stock? (4) If two years' dividends are in arrears on the preferred stock, what are the book values of the (*a*) preferred stock and (*b*) common stock? (Assume the preferred stock is not callable.)

## Provocative Problems

**Provocative Problem 15–1**
**X-L Sports, Inc.**
(L. O. 1, 2)

Jae Xu and Bob Lyle have operated a sports equipment company, X-L Sports, for a number of years as partners sharing net incomes and gains in a 3 to 2 ratio. Because the business is growing, the two partners entered into an agreement with Tom Celic to reorganize their firm into a corporation. The charter of the new corporation, X-L Sports, Inc., authorizes the corporation to issue 75,000 shares of $10 par value common stock. On the date of the reorganization, August 15, 1990, a trial balance of the partnership ledger appears as follows:

**X-L SPORTS**
**Trial Balance**
**August 15, 1990**

| | | |
|---|---|---|
| Cash | $ 38,255 | |
| Accounts receivable | 69,750 | |
| Allowance for doubtful accounts | | $ 2,625 |
| Merchandise inventory | 316,875 | |
| Store equipment | 73,500 | |
| Accumulated depreciation, store equipment | | 15,750 |
| Buildings | 375,000 | |
| Accumulated depreciation, buildings | | 75,000 |
| Land | 93,750 | |
| Accounts payable | | 41,625 |
| Notes payable | | 262,500 |
| Jae Xu, capital | | 339,380 |
| Bob Lyle, capital | | 230,250 |
| Totals | $967,130 | $967,130 |

The agreement between the partners and Celic carries these provisions:

1. The partnership assets are to be revalued as follows:
   *a.* The $2,250 account receivable of Blue Tigers is known to be uncollectible and is to be written off as a bad debt.
   *b.* After writing off the Blue Tigers account, the allowance for doubtful accounts is to be increased to 4% of the remaining accounts receivable.
   *c.* The merchandise inventory is to be written down to $285,000 to allow for damaged and shopworn goods.
   *d.* Insufficient depreciation has been taken on the store equipment. Therefore, its book value is to be decreased to $48,750 by increasing the balance of the accumulated depreciation account.
   *e.* The building is to be written up to its replacement cost, $487,500, and the balance of the accumulated depreciation account is to be increased to show the building to be one fifth depreciated.
2. After the partnership assets are revalued, the assets and liabilities are to be transferred to the corporation in exchange for its stock, with each partner accepting stock at par value for his equity in the partnership.
3. Tom Celic is to buy any remaining authorized stock for cash at par value.

After reaching the agreement outlined, the three principals hired you as accountant for the new corporation. Your first task is to determine the amount of stock each person should receive, and to prepare entries on the corporation's books to record the issuance of stock in exchange for the partnership's assets and liabilities and the issuance of stock to Celic for cash. In addition, prepare a balance sheet for the corporation as it should appear after all its stock is issued.

**Provocative Problem 15–2**
**Andrews Corporation**
(L. O. 4)

The management of Andrews Corporation is considering the expansion of its business operations to a new and exciting line of business in which newly invested assets can be expected to earn 20% per year. At present, Andrews Corporation has only 18,000 shares of $50 par value, common stock outstanding, no other contributed capital accounts, and retained earnings of $270,000. Existing operations consistently earn approximately $175,000 each year. To finance the new expansion, management is considering three alternatives: (*a*) Issue 5,000 shares of $100 par, 13%, cumulative, nonparticipating, nonvoting, preferred stock. Investment advisors of the company conclude that these shares could be issued at par. (*b*) Issue 2,000 shares of $100 par, 13%, cumulative, fully participating, nonvoting, preferred stock. The investment advisors conclude that these shares could be sold for $250 per share. (*c*) Issue 6,250 shares of common stock at $80 per share.

In evaluating these three alternatives, Andrews Company management asked you to calculate the dividends that would be distributed to each class of stockholder based on the assumption that each year the board of directors will declare dividends equal to the total net income earned by the corporation. Your calculations should show the distribution of dividends to preferred and common stockholders under each of the three alternative financing plans. You should also calculate dividends per share of preferred and dividends per share of common.

As a second part of your analysis, assume that you own 1,000 of the common shares outstanding prior to the expansion and that you will not acquire or purchase any of the newly issued shares. Based on your whole analysis, would you prefer that the proposed expansion in operations be rejected? If not, comment on the relative merits of each alternative from your point of view as a common stockholder.

**Provocative Problem 15–3**
**Reinhold Corporation and Rollins Company**
(L. O. 4, 5)

Having recently inherited $75,000, Brian Parker is thinking about investing the money in one of two securities. They are: Reinhold Corporation common stock or the preferred stock issued by Rollins Company. The companies manufacture and sell competing products, and both have been in business about the same length of time—four years in the case of Reinhold Corporation and five years for Rollins Company. Also, the two companies have about the same amounts of stockholders' equity, as the following equity sections from their latest balance sheets show:

**REINHOLD CORPORATION**

| | |
|---|---|
| Common stock, $1 par value, 10,000,000 shares authorized, 5,000,000 shares issued | $5,000,000 |
| Retained earnings | 2,000,000 |
| Total stockholders' equity | $7,000,000 |

**ROLLINS COMPANY**

| | |
|---|---|
| Preferred stock, $100 par value, 8%, cumulative and nonparticipating, 20,000 shares authorized and issued | $2,000,000* |
| Common stock, $10 par value, 400,000 shares authorized and issued | 4,000,000 |
| Retained earnings | 200,000 |
| Total stockholders' equity | $6,200,000 |

*The current and one prior year's dividends are in arrears on the preferred stock.

Reinhold Corporation did not pay a dividend on its common stock during its first year's operations; however, since then, for the past three years, it has paid a $0.20 per share annual dividend on the stock. The stock is currently selling for $1.50 per share. The preferred stock of Rollins Company, on the other hand, is selling for $95 per share. Mr. Parker favors this stock as an investment. He feels the stock is a real bargain since it is not only selling below its par value but also $21 below book value, and as he says, "Since it is a preferred stock, the dividends are guaranteed." Too, he feels the common stock of Reinhold Corporation, selling at 7% above book value and 50% above par value, while paying only a $0.20 per share dividend, is overpriced.

*Required*

*a.* Is the preferred stock of Rollins Company selling at a price $21 below its book value, and is the common stock of Reinhold Corporation selling at a price 7% above book value and 50% above par value?

*b.* From an analysis of the stockholders' equity sections, express your opinion of the two stocks as investments and describe some of the factors Mr. Parker should consider in choosing between the two securities.

# 16 Additional Corporate Transactions; Reporting Income and Retained Earnings; Earnings per Share

This chapter begins with a discussion of dividends and other transactions between a corporation and its stockholders. In this section of the chapter, you will learn about stock dividends, stock splits, and repurchases of stock by the issuing corporation. The second section of the chapter explains how income and retained earnings information is classified and reported. The third section explains how accountants report the earnings per share of a corporation. Your understanding of these topics will help you be able to interpret and evaluate corporate financial statements.

**Learning Objectives**

*After studying Chapter 16, you should be able to:*

1. Record cash dividends, stock dividends, and stock splits and explain their effects on the assets and stockholders' equity of a corporation.
2. Record purchases and sales of treasury stock and retirements of stock and describe their effects on stockholders' equity.
3. Describe restrictions and appropriations of retained earnings and the disclosure of such items in the financial statements.
4. Explain how the income effects of discontinued operations, extraordinary items, changes in accounting principles, and prior period adjustments are reported.
5. Calculate earnings per share for companies with simple capital structures and explain the difference between primary and fully diluted earnings per share.
6. Define or explain the words and phrases listed in the chapter Glossary.

## CORPORATE DIVIDENDS AND OTHER STOCK TRANSACTIONS

In Chapter 3, we first described a corporation's retained earnings as the total amount of its net incomes less its net losses and dividends declared since it began operations. Years ago, retained earnings were commonly called **earned surplus.** However, the term is rarely used anymore except in state laws that regulate corporations.

### Retained Earnings and Dividends

Record cash dividends, stock dividends, and stock splits and explain their effects on the assets and stockholders' equity of a corporation.
(L. O. 1)

Most state laws say that a corporation cannot pay cash dividends unless retained earnings are available. However, the payment of a cash dividend reduces both cash and stockholders' equity. Therefore, a corporation cannot pay a cash dividend simply because it has a credit balance in Retained Earnings; it also must have enough cash on hand to pay the dividend. If cash or assets that will shortly become cash are not available, a board of directors may choose to avoid a dividend declaration even though the Retained Earnings balance is adequate. Even if a corporation has a large Retained Earnings balance, the board of directors may refuse to declare a dividend because the available cash is needed in the operations of the business.

In deciding whether to declare dividends, a board of directors must recognize that operating activities are a source of cash. Perhaps some cash from operating activities should be paid out in dividends and some should be retained for emergencies. In addition, some cash may be retained to pay dividends in years when current operating activities do not generate enough cash to pay normal dividends. Furthermore, management may want to retain some cash from operating activities to finance expanded operations.

Entries for the declaration and distribution of a cash dividend were discussed on pages 166–67 and are not repeated here.

### Distributions from Contributed Capital

Generally, the Dividends Declared account may not be closed to any of the contributed capital accounts. However, in some states, dividends may be debited or charged to certain contributed capital accounts. Since contributed capital account balances result from stockholder contributions, dividends charged to contributed capital accounts are called **liquidating dividends.** Usually, the accounts that reflect the par or stated value of the outstanding stock cannot be used as a source of liquidating dividends. Whether or not other contributed capital accounts may be used depends on state law. For this reason, a board of directors should seek legal advice before voting to charge dividends to any contributed capital account.

### Stock Dividends

Sometimes, a corporation will distribute additional shares of its own stock to its stockholders without receiving any consideration from the stockholders. This type of distribution is called a **stock dividend.** You should understand that a stock dividend and a cash dividend are very different. A cash dividend transfers assets from the corporation to the stockholders. As a result, a cash dividend reduces the corporation's assets and its stockholders' equity. On the other hand, a stock dividend does not transfer assets from the corporation to the stockholders; it has no effect on assets and no effect on *total* stockholders' equity.

However, a stock dividend does have an effect on the *components* of stockholders' equity. To record a stock dividend, you must transfer some of the Retained Earnings balance to contributed capital accounts. For example, assume that Northwest Corporation's stockholders' equity is as follows:

**Stockholder's Equity**

| | | |
|---|---|---|
| Common stock, $10 par value, 15,000 shares authorized, 10,000 shares issued and outstanding . . | $100,000 | |
| Contributed capital in excess of par value, common stock . . . . . . . . . . . . . . . . . . . . . . . . . . | 8,000 | |
| Total contributed capital . . . . . . . . . . . . . . . . . . . | $108,000 | |
| Retained earnings . . . . . . . . . . . . . . . . . . . . . . | 35,000 | |
| Total stockholders' equity . . . . . . . . . . . . . . . . . | | $143,000 |

On December 31, the directors of Northwest Corporation declared a 10% or 1,000-share stock dividend distributable on January 20 to the stockholders of record on January 15.

If the market value of Northwest Corporation's stock on December 31 is $15 per share, the dividend declaration is recorded as follows:

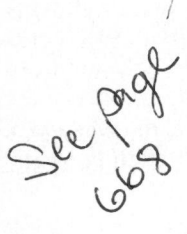

| | | | | |
|---|---|---|---|---|
| Dec. | 31 | Stock Dividends Declared . . . . . . . . . . . . . . . . . . | 15,000.00 | |
| | | Common Stock Dividend Distributable . . . . . . . . . | | 10,000.00 |
| | | Contributed Capital in Excess of Par Value, Common Stock . . . . . . . . . . . . . . . . . | | 5,000.00 |
| | | To record the declaration of a 1,000-share common stock dividend. | | |

Note that the debit is to Stock Dividends Declared. In previous chapters, when we discussed cash dividends, they were debited to Dividends Declared. However, since a corporation may declare stock dividends as well as cash dividends, a convenient system of accounts would include separate Cash Dividends Declared and Stock Dividends Declared accounts.

In the year-end closing process, the Stock Dividends Declared account is closed to Retained Earnings, as follows:

| | | | | |
|---|---|---|---|---|
| Dec. | 31 | Retained Earnings . . . . . . . . . . . . . . . . . . . . . . | 15,000.00 | |
| | | Stock Dividends Declared . . . . . . . . . . . . . . . . | | 15,000.00 |

The distribution of the stock on January 20 is recorded as follows:

**Illustration 16–1**
**The effect of Northwest Corporation's stock dividend on stockholders**

| | |
|---|---|
| **Before the 10% stock dividend:** | |
| Common stock (10,000 shares) | $100,000 |
| Contributed capital in excess of par value, common stock | 8,000 |
| Retained earnings | 35,000 |
| Total contributed and retained capital | $143,000 |

$143,000 ÷ 10,000 shares outstanding = $14.30 per share book value.
$14.30 × 100 = $1,430 the book value of Johnson's 100 shares.

| | |
|---|---|
| **After the 10% stock dividend is distributed:** | |
| Common stock (11,000 shares) | $110,000 |
| Contributed capital in excess of par value, common stock | 13,000 |
| Retained earnings | 20,000 |
| Total contributed and retained capital | $143,000 |

$143,000 ÷ 11,000 shares outstanding = $13 per share book value.
$13 × 110 = $1,430, the book value of Johnson's 110 shares.

| | | | | |
|---|---|---|---|---|
| Jan. | 20 | Common Stock Dividend Distributable | 10,000.00 | |
| | | Common Stock | | 10,000.00 |
| | | To record the distribution of a 1,000-share common stock dividend. | | |

Note that these entries shift $15,000 of the stockholders' equity from retained earnings to contributed capital or, in other words, $15,000 of retained earnings is *capitalized*. Note also that the amount of retained earnings capitalized is equal to the market value of the 1,000 shares issued ($15 × 1,000 shares = $15,000).

As you already learned, a stock dividend does not distribute assets to the stockholders; it has no effect on the corporation's assets. Also, it has no effect on total stockholders' equity and no effect on the percentage of the company owned by each individual stockholder. To illustrate these last points, assume that Johnson owned 100 shares of Northwest Corporation's stock prior to the stock dividend. Then, the 10% stock dividend gave each stockholder 1 new share for each 10 shares previously held. Therefore, Johnson received 10 new shares.

Illustration 16–1 shows Northwest Corporation's total contributed and retained capital and the book value of Johnson's 100 shares before the dividend and after the dividend.

Illustration 16–1 shows that before the stock dividend, Johnson owned 100/10,000 or 1/100 of the Northwest Corporation stock, and his holdings had a $1,430 book value. After the dividend, he owns 110/11,000 or 1/100 of the corporation, and his holdings still have a $1,430 book value. In other words, there was no effect on Johnson's investment except that it was repackaged from 100 units into 110. Also, the only effect on the corporation's capital was a transfer of $15,000 from retained earnings to contributed capital. To summarize, there was no change in the corporation's total assets, no change in its total capital or equity, and no change in percentage of that equity owned by Johnson.

### Why Stock Dividends Are Distributed

If stock dividends have no effect on corporation assets and stockholders' equities other than to repackage the equities into more units, why are such dividends declared and distributed? The primary reason for stock dividends is related to the market price of a corporation's common stock. For example, if a profitable corporation grows by retaining earnings, the price of its common stock also tends to grow. Eventually, the price of a share may become high enough to discourage some investors from buying the stock. Thus, the corporation may declare stock dividends to keep the price of its shares from increasing too much. For this reason, some corporations declare small stock dividends each year.

Some stockholders may like stock dividends for another reason. Often, corporations that declare stock dividends continue to pay the same cash dividend per share after a stock dividend as before. The result is that stockholders receive more cash each time dividends are declared.

See pg 666

### Amount of Retained Earnings Capitalized

If a corporation declares a **small stock dividend,** accounting principles require that the corporation capitalize an amount of retained earnings that equals the market value of the shares to be distributed. This rule is based on the idea that a small stock dividend is likely to have only a small impact on the price of the stock. In applying this rule, a small stock dividend is defined as one that amounts to 25% or less of the previously outstanding shares. The rule makers concluded that some stockholders may incorrectly believe that earnings are distributed in a small stock dividend. Thus, the amount of retained earnings capitalized and made unavailable for future dividends should equal the market value of the shares to be distributed.[1]

On the other hand, a stock dividend that exceeds 25% of the outstanding shares normally has a pronounced impact on the stock's market price and is not apt to be perceived as a distribution of earnings. Therefore, in recording a stock dividend that is over 25%, it is necessary to capitalize retained earnings only to the extent required by law. In most states, this means that you ignore the market value of the shares. Instead, you debit Retained Earnings and credit the stock account for the par value or stated value of the shares issued.[2]

---

[1] FASB, *Accounting Standards—Current Text* (Norwalk, Conn., 1988), sec. C20.103, 106. Previously published in *Accounting Research Bulletin No. 43,* ch. 7, sec B, pars. 10, 13.

[2] Ibid., sec. C20.104.

### Stock Dividends on the Balance Sheet

Since a stock dividend is "payable" in stock rather than in assets, it is not a liability of its issuing corporation. Therefore, if a balance sheet is prepared between the declaration and distribution dates of a stock dividend, the amount of the dividend distributable should appear on the balance sheet in the stockholders' equity section, as follows:

| | |
|---|---|
| Common stock, $10 par value, 15,000 shares authorized, 10,000 shares issued and outstanding | $100,000 |
| **Common stock dividend distributable, 1,000 shares** | **10,000** |
| Total common stock issued and to be issued | $110,000 |
| Contributed capital in excess of par value, common stock | 13,000 |
| Total capital contributed and subscribed by common stockholders | $123,000 |
| Retained earnings | 20,000 |
| Total stockholders' equity | $143,000 |

## Stock Splits

Sometimes, when a corporation's stock is selling at a high price, the corporation will call it in and issue two, three, or more new shares in the place of each previously outstanding share. For example, a corporation that has outstanding $100 par value stock selling for $375 a share may call in the old shares and issue to the stockholders 4 shares of $25 par, or 10 shares of $10 par, or any number of shares of no-par stock in exchange for each $100 share formerly held. This is known as a **stock split.** The usual purpose of a stock split is to reduce the market price of the stock and thereby facilitate trading in the stock.

A stock split has no effect on total stockholders' equity, and no effect on the equities of the individual stockholders. Also, the balances of the contributed capital and retained earnings accounts are not changed. Thus, a stock split does not require a journal entry. All that is required is a memorandum entry in the stock account reciting the facts of the split. For example, such a memorandum might read, "Called in the outstanding $100 par value common stock and issued 10 shares of $10 par value common stock for each old share previously outstanding." And when you prepare the balance sheet, the new par value and number of shares outstanding must be used in describing the stock.

## Treasury Stock

Record purchases and sales of treasury stock and retirements of stock and describe their effects on stockholders' equity. (L. O. 2)

Corporations often reacquire shares of their own stock. This is done for a variety of reasons. Some shares may be given to employees as a bonus. Others may be used to pay for the acquisition of another corporation. Sometimes, shares are repurchased to avoid a "hostile takeover" by an investor who seeks control of the company. Occasionally, shares are bought in order to maintain a favorable market for the stock. For example, in the 1986 annual report of W. R. Grace & Co., the chief executive officer described the reason for the company's repurchases of its stock as follows:

> The year began with the unexpected need to repurchase 13.6 million Grace common shares plus some preferred shares for nearly $600 million. This was an unplanned action made necessary when Grace's largest shareholder divested its entire holdings. And, it was done to avoid a potentially dangerous downturn in the market value of your Grace shares.

## AS A MATTER OF FACT

New York—Morgan Stanley Group Inc. said net income soared in the fourth quarter, split its stock 3-for-2, and boosted the quarterly dividend 35%.

The securities firm said net income rose to $108.3 million, or $4.25 a share, from $31.4 million, or $1.16 a share. Revenue climbed 62% to $1.16 billion from $718.3 million.

Morgan Stanley had particularly strong gains in its investment banking business, where fourth-quarter revenue soared to $276.2 million from $60.6 million, and from sale of investments. Revenue from principal transactions rose 9.6% to $160.3 million from $146.2 million; revenue from investments totaled $27.7 million in the quarter; there was no comparable item a year earlier. Commissions declined 28% to $56.9 million from $79.5 million.

Directors approved the 3-for-2 stock split, payable Feb. 27 to shares of record Feb. 8, and an increase in the quarterly cash dividend on presplit shares to 33.75 cents from 25 cents, payable Feb. 22 to shares of record Feb. 8. The company expects to pay 22.5 cents a share quarterly after the split.

The announcement boosted Morgan Stanley's shares, which rose $1.125 and closed at $89.625 in composite trading on the New York Stock Exchange, after trading as high as $90.75.

* * * * *

Morgan Stanley boosted its total capital by 41% in the year, to $2.4 billion, including $1.6 billion of stockholder equity, and book value at year end was $53.13.

Source: James C. Hyatt, "Morgan Stanley Earnings Soar: Stock is Split," *The Wall Street Journal*, January 25, 1989, p. C5. Reprinted by permission of *The Wall Street Journal*, © Dow Jones & Company, Inc. 1989. ALL RIGHTS RESERVED.

Whatever the reason, if a corporation reacquires shares of its own stock, the reacquired shares are called **treasury stock.** Treasury stock is a corporation's stock that was issued and then reacquired by the issuing corporation. Notice that the acquired stock must be the issuing corporation's own stock. The acquisition of another corporation's stock does not create treasury stock. Also, treasury stock must have been issued and then reacquired. This distinguishes treasury stock from unissued stock. The distinction is important because stock once issued at par or above may be reacquired and then reissued at a discount without burdening the new stockholders with discount liability.

Although treasury stock differs from unissued stock in that it may be sold at a discount without discount liability, in other respects it has the same status as unissued stock. Neither is an asset. Both are subtracted from authorized stock to determine outstanding stock when such things as book values are calculated. Neither receives cash dividends nor has a vote in the stockholders' meetings.

## Purchase of Treasury Stock[3]

When a corporation purchases its own stock, it reduces in equal amounts both its assets and its stockholders' equity. To illustrate, assume that on May 1 of the current year, the condensed balance sheet of Curry Corporation appears as in Illustration 16–2.

On May 1, Curry Corporation purchases 1,000 shares of its outstanding stock at $11.50 per share, and the transaction is recorded as follows:

[3]This text discusses the *cost method* of accounting for treasury stock, which is the most widely used. Other methods are discussed in more advanced courses.

**Illustration 16–2**
**Curry Corporation's balance sheet prior to the purchase of treasury stock**

CURRY CORPORATION
Balance Sheet
May 1, 1990

| Assets | | Stockholders' Equity | |
|---|---|---|---|
| Cash | $ 30,000 | Common stock, $10 par value, authorized and issued 10,000 shares | $100,000 |
| Other assets | 95,000 | Retained earnings | 25,000 |
| Total assets | $125,000 | Total stockholders' equity | $125,000 |

**Illustration 16–3**
**Curry Corporation's balance sheet immediately after the purchase of treasury stock**

CURRY CORPORATION
Balance Sheet
May 1, 1990

| Assets | | Stockholders' Equity | |
|---|---|---|---|
| Cash | $ 18,500 | Common stock, $10 par value, authorized and issued 10,000 shares of which 1,000 are in the treasury | $100,000 |
| Other assets | 95,000 | Retained earnings of which $11,500 is restricted by the purchase of treasury stock | 25,000 |
| | | Total | $125,000 |
| | | Less cost of treasury stock | 11,500 |
| Total assets | $113,500 | Total stockholders' equity | $113,500 |

| | | | | |
|---|---|---|---|---|
| May | 1 | Treasury Stock, Common | 11,500.00 | |
| | | Cash | | 11,500.00 |
| | | Purchased 1,000 shares of treasury stock at $11.50 per share. | | |

The debit of the entry records a reduction in the equity of the stockholders. The credit records a reduction in assets. Both are equal to the cost of the treasury stock. After the entry is posted, a new balance sheet shows the reductions as in Illustration 16–3.

In Illustration 16–3, notice that the cost of the treasury stock appears in the stockholders' equity section as a deduction from common stock and retained earnings. In comparing the two balance sheets (Illustration 16–2 and 16–3), you can see that the treasury stock purchase reduced both assets and stockholders' equity by the $11,500 cost of the stock. Also, the amount of *issued stock* is not changed by the purchase of treasury stock. The dollar amount of issued stock remains at $100,000 and is unchanged from the first balance sheet. However, the purchase does reduce the amount of *outstanding stock*. Curry Corporation's outstanding stock was reduced from 10,000 to 9,000 shares.

There is a distinction between issued stock and outstanding stock. Issued stock may or may not be outstanding. Outstanding stock was issued and remains currently in the hands of stockholders. Only outstanding stock receives cash dividends and has a vote in the meetings of stockholders.

### Restricting Retained Earnings by the Purchase of Treasury Stock

Describe restrictions and appropriations of retained earnings and the disclosure of such items in the financial statements. (L. O. 3)

The purchase of treasury stock by a corporation has the same effect on its assets and stockholders' equity as the payment of a cash dividend. Both transfer corporate assets to stockholders and thereby reduce assets and stockholders' equity. Therefore, in most states, a corporation may purchase treasury stock or it may pay cash dividends, but the sum of both cannot exceed the amount of its retained earnings available for dividends.

Unlike the payment of a cash dividend, the purchase of treasury stock does not reduce the balance of the Retained Earnings account. Instead, the purchase places a restriction on the amount of retained earnings available for dividends. Note how **restricted retained earnings** are shown in Illustration 16–3. Usually, the restriction also is described in a footnote to the financial statements.

The restriction of retained earnings because of treasury stock purchases is a matter of state law. Other types of legal restrictions on retained earnings may be imposed by law or by contract.

## Reissuing Treasury Stock

Treasury stock may be reissued at cost, above cost, or below cost. If reissued at cost, the entry to record the transaction is the reverse of the entry used to record the purchase.

If treasury stock is sold at a price that is above cost, the amount received in excess of cost is credited to a contributed capital account called Contributed Capital, Treasury Stock Transactions. For example, if Curry Corporation sells for $12 per share 500 of the treasury shares purchased at $11.50 per share, the entry to record the transaction is as follows:

| | | | | |
|---|---|---|---|---|
| June | 3 | Cash . . . . . . . . . . . . . . . . . . . . . . . . . . . . . . | 6,000.00 | |
| | | Treasury Stock, Common . . . . . . . . . . . . . . . . | | 5,750.00 |
| | | Contributed Capital, Treasury Stock Transactions . . . | | 250.00 |
| | | Sold at $12 per share 500 treasury shares that cost $11.50 per share. | | |

When treasury stock is reissued at a price below cost, the entry to record the sale depends on whether there is a preexisting credit balance in the Contributed Capital, Treasury Stock Transactions account. If none exists, the amount by which sales price is less than cost is debited to Retained Earnings. However, if the contributed capital account has a credit balance, the difference between sales price and cost is charged to the contributed capital account to the extent possible. After the credit balance in the contributed capital account is eliminated, any remaining difference between sales price and cost is debited to Retained Earnings. For example, if Curry Corporation sells its remaining 500 shares of treasury stock at $10 per share, the entry to record the sale is:

| | | | | |
|---|---|---|---|---|
| July | 10 | Cash | 5,000.00 | |
| | | Contributed Capital, Treasury Stock Transactions | 250.00 | |
| | | Retained Earnings | 500.00 | |
| | | Treasury Stock, Common | | 5,750.00 |
| | | Sold at $10 per share 500 treasury shares that cost $11.50 per share. | | |

## Retirement of Stock

A corporation may purchase shares of its own stock in order to retire the stock rather than holding it as treasury stock. If so, such shares are permanently canceled upon receipt. Like the purchase of treasury stock, the purchase and retirement of the stock is permissible only if the interests of creditors and other stockholders are not jeopardized.

When stock is purchased for retirement, all contributed capital amounts that relate to the retired shares are removed from the accounts. If the cash paid to purchase the shares exceeds the net amount removed from the contributed capital accounts, the difference is debited to Retained Earnings. And if the cash paid is less than the net amount removed from the contributed capital accounts, the difference is credited to a contributed capital account.

For example, assume a corporation originally issued its $10 par value common stock at $12 per share so that the $2 premium was credited to Contributed Capital in Excess of Par Value, Common Stock. If the corporation later purchased and retired 1,000 shares of this stock at the price for which it was issued, the entry to record the retirement is:

| | | | | |
|---|---|---|---|---|
| Apr. | 12 | Common Stock | 10,000.00 | |
| | | Contributed Capital in Excess of Par Value, Common Stock | 2,000.00 | |
| | | Cash | | 12,000.00 |
| | | Purchased and retired 1,000 shares of common stock at $12 per share. | | |

If on the other hand the corporation paid $11 per share instead of $12, the entry for the retirement is:

| | | | | |
|---|---|---|---|---|
| Apr. | 12 | Common Stock | 10,000.00 | |
| | | Contributed Capital in Excess of Par Value, Common Stock | 2,000.00 | |
| | | Cash | | 11,000.00 |
| | | Contributed Capital from the Retirement of Common Stock | | 1,000.00 |
| | | Purchased and retired 1,000 shares of common stock at $11 per share. | | |

Or, if the corporation paid $15 per share, the entry for the purchase and retirement is:

| | | | | |
|---|---|---|---|---|
| Apr. | 12 | Common Stock | 10,000.00 | |
| | | Contributed Capital in Excess of Par Value, Common Stock | 2,000.00 | |
| | | Retained Earnings | 3,000.00 | |
| | | Cash | | 15,000.00 |
| | | Purchased and retired 1,000 shares of common stock at $15 per share. | | |

### Appropriations of Retained Earnings

A corporation may voluntarily **appropriate retained earnings** for some special purpose as a means of explaining to stockholders why the retained earnings are not being declared as dividends. In contrast to retained earnings restrictions, which are binding by law or by contract, appropriations of retained earnings are voluntarily made by the board of directors. In earlier years, such appropriations were recorded by transferring portions of retained earnings from the Retained Earnings account to another stockholders' equity account such as Retained Earnings Appropriated for Contingencies or Retained Earnings Appropriated for Plant Expansion. When the contingency or other reason for an appropriation was passed, the appropriation account was eliminated by returning its balance to the Retained Earnings account.

Today, appropriations of retained earnings are seldom seen on balance sheets. Instead, management's reasons for not declaring dividends usually are conveyed in a letter to the stockholders that is published with the financial statements.

## REPORTING INCOME AND RETAINED EARNINGS INFORMATION

### Income Statement Items Not Related to Continuing Operations

When the revenue and expense transactions of a company consist of routine, continuing operations, the company's single-step income statement will show revenues followed by a list of operating expenses and finally by net income. Often, however, the activities of a business include items that are not closely related to its continuing operations. In these cases, the income effects of such items should be separated from the revenues and expenses of continuing operations. Otherwise, the income statement will fail to provide readers with clear information about the results of business activities.

To see how various income statement items should be classified, look at Illustration 16–4. Observe that the income statement is separated into five sections labeled 1 through 5. The first portion of the income statement (the portion labeled as 1) shows the revenues, expenses, and income generated by the company's continuing operations. This portion looks just like the single-step income statement we first discussed in Chapter 5. The next income statement section, labeled 2, relates to discontinued operations.

**Illustration 16–4**
**Income statement for a corporation**

CONNELLY CORPORATION
Income Statement
For Year Ended December 31, 1990

| | | | |
|---|---|---|---|
| 1 | Net sales | | $ 8,443,000 |
| | Gain on sale of old equipment | | 30,000 |
| | Total | | $ 8,473,000 |
| | Costs and expenses: | | |
| | Cost of goods sold | $5,950,000 | |
| | Depreciation expense | 35,000 | |
| | Other selling, general, and administrative expenses | 515,000 | |
| | Interest expense | 20,000 | |
| | Income taxes | 792,000 | (7,312,000) |
| | Unusual loss on sale of surplus land | | (45,000) |
| | Infrequent gain on relocation of a plant | | 72,000 |
| | Income from continuing operations | | $ 1,188,000 |
| 2 | **Discontinued operations:** | | |
| | Income from operation of discontinued Division A (net of $166,000 income taxes) | $ 400,000 | |
| | Loss on disposal of Division A (net of $60,000 tax benefit) | (150,000) | 250,000 |
| | Income before extraordinary items and cumulative effect of a change in accounting principle | | $ 1,438,000 |
| 3 | **Extraordinary items:** | | |
| | Gain on sale of unused land expropriated by the state for a highway interchange (net of $35,000 income taxes) | $ 142,500 | |
| | Loss from earthquake damage (net of $310,000 income taxes) | (670,000) | |
| 4 | **Cumulative effect of a change in accounting principle:** | | |
| | Effect on prior years' income (to December 31, 1990) of changing to a different depreciation method (net of $18,000 income taxes) | 27,000 | (500,500) |
| | Net income | | $ 937,500 |
| 5 | **Earnings per common share** (250,000 shares outstanding): | | |
| | Income from continuing operations | | $ 4.75 |
| | Discontinued operations | | 1.00 |
| | Extraordinary items | | (2.11) |
| | Cumulative effect of a change in accounting principle | | .11 |
| | Net income | | $ 3.75 |

## Discontinued Operations

Explain how the income effects of discontinued operations, extraordinary items, changes in accounting principles, and prior period adjustments are reported.
(L. O. 4)

Large companies often have several different lines of business operations or have several different classes of customers. A company's operations that involve a particular line of business or class of customers may qualify as a **segment of the business.** To qualify as a segment of a business, the assets, activities, and financial results of operations involving a particular line of business or class of customers must be distinguished from other parts of the business.

### Separating Discontinued Operations on the Income Statement

Normally, the revenues and expenses of all business segments are added together and reported as the continuing operations of the business (as in section 1 of Illustration 16–4). However, when a business sells or disposes of a business segment, the results of that segment's operations must be separated and reported as you see in section 2 of Illustration 16–4.[4] In the illustration, the results of the discontinued operations are completely separated from the results of other activities. This separation makes it easier for financial statement readers to evaluate the continuing operations of the business.

### Separating the Results of Operating a Segment that Is Being Discontinued from the Gain or Loss on Disposal

Within section 2 of Illustration 16–4, note that the income from *operating* Division A (the operation that is being discontinued) during the period is reported separately from the loss on the final *disposal* of Division A. Also, the income tax effects of the discontinued operations are separated from the income tax expense shown in section 1 of Illustration 16–4. Thus, the results of the discontinued operations are reported net of tax. Also, the amount of tax related to each item is disclosed.

The above discussion summarizes the method of *reporting* the results of discontinued operations on the income statement. The detailed requirements for *measuring* the income or losses of discontinued operations are discussed in a more advanced accounting course.

## Extraordinary Items

Section 3 of the income statement in Illustration 16–4 discloses gains and losses that are defined as extraordinary. To qualify as an **extraordinary gain or loss,** an item must be both unusual and infrequent. An **unusual gain or loss** is abnormal and unrelated or only incidentally related to the ordinary activities and environment of the business. An **infrequent gain or loss** is not expected to occur again, given the operating environment of the business.[5]

Given these definitions of *unusual* and *infrequent*, very few items meet both criteria; in other words, very few items qualify as extraordinary gains or losses. For example, none of the following generally qualify as extraordinary:

*a.* Write-down or write-off of assets unless caused by major casualty, an expropriation, or prohibition under a newly enacted law.
*b.* Gains or losses from exchange or translation of foreign currencies.
*c.* Gains and losses on disposal of a segment of a business.
*d.* Other gains and losses from sale or abandonment of property, plant, or equipment unless caused by a major casualty, an expropriation, or prohibition under a newly enacted law.
*e.* Effects of a strike, including those against competitors and major suppliers.
*f.* Adjustment of accruals on long-term contracts.[6]

Some gains or losses are *neither* unusual *nor* infrequent. They are reported among the revenues or costs and expenses of continuing operations. Other

---

[4] FASB, *Accounting Standards—Current Text* (Norwalk, Conn., 1988), sec. I13.105. Originally published as *APB Opinion No. 30,* par. 8.

[5] Ibid., sec. I17.107. Originally published as *APB Opinion No. 30,* par. 20.

[6] Ibid., sec. I17.110. Originally published as *APB Opinion No. 30,* par. 23.

**Illustration 16–5**
**Calculating the cumulative effect of a change in an accounting principle**

| Year | | Sum-of-the-Years'-Digits Depreciation | Straight-Line Depreciation | After-Tax Difference in Methods | |
|---|---|---|---|---|---|
| | | *a* | *b* | *(a − b)* × 60% | |
| Prior years: | | | | | |
| 1 . . . . . . | (6/21) | $ 60,000 | $ 35,000 | $ 25,000 × 60% = | $ 15,000 |
| 2 . . . . . . | (5/21) | 50,000 | 35,000 | 15,000 × 60% = | 9,000 |
| 3 . . . . . . | (4/21) | 40,000 | 35,000 | 5,000 × 60% = | 3,000 |
| Totals . . . . . | | | | $ 45,000 | **$ 27,000*** |
| Year of change: | | | | | |
| 4 . . . . . . | (3/21) | 30,000 | **35,000*** | (5,000) × 60% = | (3,000) |
| Future years: | | | | | |
| 5 . . . . . . | (2/21) | 20,000 | 35,000 | (15,000) × 60% = | (9,000) |
| 6 . . . . . . | (1/21) | 10,000 | 35,000 | (25,000) × 60% = | (15,000) |
| Totals . . . . . | | $210,000 | $210,000 | | $ -0- |

*These two numbers are reported on the income statement in Illustration 16–4.

gains or losses may be unusual *or* infrequent but not both. Such gains or losses are *not* extraordinary items. On the income statement, items that are unusual or infrequent but not both are listed below the costs and expenses of continuing operations. Section 1 of Illustration 16–4 displays a ''Gain on sale of old equipment'' that is neither unusual nor infrequent. The illustration also shows an unusual loss and an infrequent gain. Note that the correct classification of these items is not obvious from their descriptions. Instead, you need to examine carefully the circumstances surrounding each gain or loss to determine the correct classification.

## Changes in Accounting Principles

### The Consistency Principle Does Not Preclude Changes in Accounting Principles

After a company chooses to use a particular accounting method or principle, it must continue to use the same principle each period. This is required by the *consistency principle*. (In this discussion, methods such as FIFO and straight-line depreciation are called accounting principles.) Nevertheless, the *consistency principle* does not mean that a company may never make changes. A company may change from one accounting principle to another as long as it justifies the change as an improvement in financial reporting.

When a company changes from one accounting principle to another, the change often affects the amount of income that will be reported. For example, assume a company has only one asset that cost $210,000, has no salvage value, and is being depreciated on a sum-of-the-years'-digits basis over six years. Also, assume a 40% income tax rate. Early in year 4, the company decides to switch to straight-line depreciation and justifies the change as an improvement in financial reporting. A comparison of the two depreciation methods during the six-year life of the asset is shown in Illustration 16–5.

### Reporting Requirements for Changes in Accounting Principles

How should the change in depreciation methods be reported on the income statement? Illustration 16–4 shows the correct method of disclosure. In section 1 of Illustration 16–4, note that depreciation expense for the current year is $35,000. This is the straight-line amount in the year of change as calculated in Illustration 16–5. In section 4 of Illustration 16–4, the effect of the change on prior years' income is reported as $27,000 (net of $18,000 income taxes). Compare this with the calculations in Illustration 16–5, which show that the after-tax difference between the two depreciation methods in prior years is $27,000.

To summarize, a company that wants to make a change in accounting principles must report several items of information, including the following:[7]

*a.* The nature of and justification for the change should be described in the footnotes to the financial statements.
*b.* The cumulative effect of the change on prior periods should be shown on the income statement below extraordinary items. Also, the effect on earnings per share must be shown separately. (See section 5 of Illustration 16–4.)
*c.* In the year of the change, the footnotes also should state the effect of the change on income before extraordinary items and on net income.

## Earnings per Share on the Income Statement

Observe in section 5 of Illustration 16–4 that earnings per share information is presented on the face of the income statement. Also note that separate earnings per share numbers are presented for each of the income statement categories. Later in the chapter, we will explain the procedures you must use to calculate earnings per share.

## Prior Period Adjustments and the Statement of Retained Earnings

In the annual financial statements of a corporation, the income effect of one type of item is excluded entirely from the current income statement. This type of item is called a **prior period adjustment.** Very few items qualify as prior period adjustments. They are limited primarily to corrections of errors made in past years. The errors may have involved mathematical mistakes, or mistakes in applying accounting principles, or a failure to take known facts into consideration.[8] For example, the accountant may have forgotten to take depreciation on a plant asset, or calculated the depreciation incorrectly.

Prior period adjustments are reported in the statement of retained earnings as corrections to the beginning retained earnings balance. They are reported net of any related tax effect. For example, a statement of retained earnings with a prior period adjustment might appear as follows:

---

[7] Ibid., sec. A06.113–116. Originally published as *APB Opinion No. 20,* pars. 17–20.

[8] Ibid, sec. A35.104. Originally published as *APB Opinion No. 20,* par. 13.

**CONNELLY CORPORATION**
**Statement of Retained Earnings**
**For Year Ended December 31, 1990**

| | |
|---|---|
| Retained earnings, December 31, 1989 | $4,745,000 |
| Prior period adjustment: | |
| Cost of land that was incorrectly charged to expense (net of $60,000 income taxes) | 130,000 |
| Retained earnings, December 31, 1989, as adjusted | $4,875,000 |
| Plus net income | 937,500 |
| Less cash dividends declared | (240,000) |
| Retained earnings, December 31, 1990 | $5,572,500 |

### Changes in Accounting Estimates

Errors of past periods that qualify as prior period adjustments must be distinguished from revisions or **changes in accounting estimates**. Errors include mathematical mistakes or failure to consider known facts. On the other hand, the preparation of financial statements requires many estimates about the future. For example, depreciation is based on estimates of useful life and estimates of salvage value. As new information becomes available, it may become necessary to change such estimates. Changes of this sort are not errors and do not qualify as prior period adjustments. Changes in accounting estimates are not allowed to affect the income of prior periods. Instead, the revised estimate is applied in calculating the appropriate revenue or expense of the current and future periods. One example of a change in an accounting estimate, the revision of depreciation rates, was discussed on page 473 in Chapter 11.

### Statement of Changes in Stockholders' Equity

In Chapter 5, we explained that some corporations do not present a separate statement of retained earnings. Instead, they present a combined statement of income and retained earnings, an example of which was shown in Illustration 5–7, on page 220. Other corporations show the statement of retained earnings information in an expanded statement called a **statement of changes in stockholders' equity**. In that statement, the beginning and ending balances of each stockholders' equity account are reconciled by listing all changes that occurred during the year. For example, the 1986 annual report of Dycom Industries, Inc., included the financial statement shown in Illustration 16–6.

## EARNINGS PER SHARE

Among the most commonly quoted statistics on the financial pages of daily newspapers is **earnings per share** of common stock. Investors use earnings per share data when they evaluate the past performance of a corporation, project its future earnings, and weigh investment opportunities.

### Companies with Simple Capital Structures

Earnings per share calculations may be simple or complex. The calculations are not as difficult for companies that have simple capital structures. A company has a **simple capital structure** if it has only common stock and perhaps nonconvertible preferred stock outstanding. In other words, to have a simple capital structure, the company cannot have outstanding any options or rights

Illustration 16–6

**DYCOM INDUSTRIES, INC., AND SUBSIDIARIES**
**CONSOLIDATED STATEMENTS OF STOCKHOLDERS' EQUITY**
**FOR THE YEARS ENDED JULY 31, 1986, 1985, AND 1984**

| | Notes | Common Stock | Additional Paid-in Capital | Retained Earnings | Total |
|---|---|---|---|---|---|
| BALANCE JULY 31, 1983 | | $ 534,942 | $2,103,423 | $1,594,181 | $4,232,546 |
| Adjustment for change in fiscal year of pooled businesses | | | | (87,607) | (87,607) |
| Net income | | | | 492,740 | 492,740 |
| BALANCE JULY 31, 1984 | | 534,942 | 2,103,423 | 1,999,314 | 4,637,679 |
| Net income | | | | 1,106,471 | 1,106,471 |
| BALANCE JULY 31, 1985 | | 534,942 | 2,103,423 | 3,105,785 | 5,744,150 |
| 5% stock dividend including payment for fractional shares | 11 | 26,796 | 704,982 | (732,289) | (511) |
| Exercise of stock options | 12 | 492 | 12,481 | | 12,973 |
| Shares issued for acquisitions | 2 | 45,629 | 1,385,865 | | 1,431,494 |
| Two-for-one stock split | 11 | 566,543 | (566,543) | | — |
| Net income | | | | 1,926,961 | 1,926,961 |
| BALANCE JULY 31, 1986 | | $1,174,402 | $3,640,208 | $4,300,457 | $9,115,067 |

*Courtesy of Dycom Industries, Inc.*

Calculate earnings per share for companies with simple capital structures and explain the difference between primary and fully diluted earnings per share. (L. O. 5)

to purchase common stock at a specified price or any securities that are convertible into common stock.

### Calculating Earnings per Share When the Number of Common Shares Outstanding Does Not Change

Consider a company that has only common stock and nonconvertible preferred stock outstanding. If the number of common shares outstanding does not change during the period, earnings per share is calculated as follows:

$$\text{Earnings per share} = \frac{\text{Net income} - \text{Preferred dividends}}{\text{Common shares outstanding}}$$

For example, assume that in 1989, Blackwell Company earned a $40,000 net income and paid its preferred dividends of $7,500. On January 1, 1989, the company had 5,000 common shares outstanding and this number did not change during the year. Earnings per share for 1989 is:

$$\text{Earnings per share} = \frac{\$40,000 - \$7,500}{5,000} = \$6.50$$

However, the calculation becomes more complex if the number of common shares outstanding changes during the period. The number of common shares outstanding may change (1) because the company sells additional shares or buys treasury shares or (2) because of stock dividends and stock splits.

### Adjusting the Denominator for Sales or Purchases of Common Shares

If additional shares are sold or treasury shares are purchased during the year, earnings per share is based on the weighted-average number of shares outstanding during the year. For example, suppose that in 1990, Blackwell Company again earned $40,000 and preferred dividends were $7,500. However, on July 1, 1990, Blackwell sold 4,000 additional common shares. Also, on November 1, 1990, Blackwell purchased 3,000 treasury shares. In other words, 5,000 shares were outstanding for six months; then 9,000 shares were outstanding for four months; then 6,000 shares were outstanding for two months. If these changes occurred, you calculate the weighted-average number of shares outstanding during 1990 as follows:

| Time Period | Shares Outstanding | Weighted by Portion of Year Outstanding |
|---|---|---|
| January–June . . . . . . . . | 5,000 | (6/12) = 2,500 |
| July–October . . . . . . . . | (5,000 + 4,000) | (4/12) = 3,000 |
| November–December . . . . | (9,000 − 3,000) | (2/12) = 1,000 |
| Weighted-average common shares outstanding . . . . . . | | 6,500 |

The calculation of earnings per share for 1990 is:

$$\text{Earnings per share} = \frac{\$40{,}000 - \$7{,}500}{6{,}500} = \$5$$

### Adjusting the Denominator for Stock Splits and Stock Dividends

A stock split or stock dividend is different from a stock sale. When stock is sold, the company receives new assets that it uses to generate additional earnings. On the other hand, stock splits and stock dividends do not provide additional assets for the company. Instead, a stock split or stock dividend simply means that the company's earnings must be allocated to a larger number of outstanding shares.

Because of the nature of stock splits and stock dividends, you must treat them differently from stock sales when you calculate the weighted-average number of shares outstanding. When a stock split or stock dividend occurs, the number of shares outstanding during previous portions of the year must be retroactively restated to reflect the stock split or dividend. For example, consider the above example of Blackwell Company. However, assume that the stock transactions in 1990 included a stock split, as follows:

| | |
|---|---|
| Jan. 1: | 5,000 common shares were outstanding. |
| July 1: | Blackwell sold 4,000 additional shares of common stock. |
| Nov. 1: | Blackwell purchased 3,000 common shares as treasury stock. |
| **Dec. 1:** | **Outstanding common shares were split 2 for 1.** |

Given these changes in the number of shares outstanding during 1990, you calculate the weighted-average number of shares outstanding as follows:

| Time Period | Shares Outstanding | Restated for Stock Split | Weighted by Portion of Year Outstanding |
|---|---|---|---|
| January–June . . . . | 5,000 | 2 | (6/12) = 5,000 |
| July–October . . . . | (5,000 + 4,000) | 2 | (4/12) = 6,000 |
| November . . . . . . | (9,000 − 3,000) | 2 | (1/12) = 1,000 |
| December . . . . . . | 12,000 | — | (1/12) = 1,000 |
| Weighted-average common shares outstanding . . . . . . . . . . . | | | 13,000 |

Note that every time stock was sold or purchased, the resulting number of outstanding shares was restated for the subsequent stock split. The same type of restatement is required for stock dividends. If, for example, the 2 for 1 stock split on December 1 had been a 10% stock dividend, the previous amounts of outstanding shares would have been adjusted by a multiplier of 1.10 instead of 2.

The calculation of Blackwell Company's earnings per share for 1990 is:

$$\text{Earnings per share} = \frac{\$40{,}000 - \$7{,}500}{13{,}000} = \$2.50$$

## Companies with Complex Capital Structures

Companies with **complex capital structures** have outstanding securities such as bonds or preferred stock that are convertible into common stock. Earnings per share calculations for companies with complex capital structures are more complicated. Often, such companies must present two types of earnings per share calculations. One is called **primary earnings per share**, and the other is called **fully diluted earnings per share**.

Suppose that a corporation has convertible preferred stock outstanding throughout the current year. However, consider what the effects would have been if the preferred shares had been converted at the beginning of the year. The result of this assumed conversion would have been to increase the number of common shares outstanding and to reduce preferred dividends. The net result may have been to reduce earnings per share, or to increase earnings per share. When the assumed conversion of a security reduces earnings per share, the security is said to be **dilutive**; those that increase earnings per share are **antidilutive**.

### Primary Earnings per Share

Based on detailed rules, convertible securities are evaluated at the time they are issued.[9] If eventual conversion appears highly probable, the convertible security is called a **common stock equivalent**. Primary earnings per share is calculated *as if* dilutive, common stock equivalents had already been converted at the beginning of the period.

[9] FASB, *Accounting Standards—Current Text* (Norwalk, Conn., 1988), sec. E09.122–127. First published as *APB Opinion No. 15*, par. 31, 33, 35–37. Also see *FASB, Statement of Financial Accounting Standards No. 85* (March 1985), par. 2.

Illustration 16–7
**Reporting earnings per share on the income statement**

**Textron, Inc.**
**Consolidated Statement of Income**

| For each of the three years in the period ended January 3, 1987<br>In millions, except per share amounts | **1986** | 1985 | 1984 |
|---|---|---|---|
| **Net Income** | **$239.2** | $251.8 | $113.5 |
| **Income Per Common Share** | | | |
| **Income from continuing operations before extraordinary item and cumulative effect of a change in accounting principle** | **$ 5.85** | 4.83 | 2.12 |
| Discontinued operations | **.10** | 1.16 | .99 |
| Extraordinary item | **(.16)** | .44 | — |
| Cumulative effect of a change in accounting principle | — | .32 | — |
| **Net Income** | $ 5.79 | $ 6.75 | $ 3.11 |

*See notes to consolidated financial statements.*
*Courtesy of Textron, Inc.*

### Fully Diluted Earnings per Share

Common stock equivalents have terms that make their eventual conversion very probable. Other convertible securities are less apt to be converted. Nevertheless, if we assume those securities were converted at the beginning of the period, the effect may be to reduce earnings per share; in other words, the assumed conversion will have a dilutive effect. Fully diluted earnings per share is calculated as if *all* dilutive securities had already been converted.

## Presentations of Earnings per Share on the Income Statement

Because of the importance attached to earnings per share data, generally accepted accounting principles require that you show this information on the face of published income statements. Separate earnings per share calculations must be presented for (1) income from continuing operations, (2) gains or losses from discontinued operations, (3) extraordinary items, (4) the cumulative effect of changes in accounting principles, and (5) net income. Good examples of these presentations are provided by the 1986 financial statements of Textron, Inc., and American Can Company. The bottom portions of Textron's and American Can Company's comparative income statements for 1986, 1985, and 1984, are shown in Illustration 16–7 and Illustration 16–8.

In Illustration 16–7, notice that the activities of Textron, Inc., required earnings per share data on each of the income statement categories discussed earlier in the chapter. Textron, Inc., has a simple capital structure and did not have to report both primary and fully diluted statistics. On the other hand, American Can Company's report (Illustration 16–8) includes both earnings per share of common stock (primary earnings per share) and fully diluted earnings per share.

Illustration 16–8
**Reporting primary and fully diluted earnings per share**

**Statement of Income** American Can Company and Consolidated Subsidiaries

| For each of the three years in the period ended January 3, 1987 (In millions of dollars except per share amounts) | Years ended December 31, 1986 | 1985 | 1984 |
|---|---|---|---|
| Net Income | $ 196.3 | $ 149.1 | $ 136.0 |
| **Earnings per share of common stock** | | | |
| Income from continuing operations | $ 3.04 | $ 1.57 | $ 1.35 |
| Discontinued operations | .60 | .96 | 1.02 |
| Extraordinary items | (.43) | | .08 |
| Net Income | $ 3.21 | $ 2.53 | $ 2.45 |
| **Earnings per share assuming full dilution** | | | |
| Income from continuing operations | $ 2.89 | $ 1.54 | $ 1.35 |
| Discontinued operations | .55 | .86 | .90 |
| Extraordinary items | (.39) | | .07 |
| Net Income | $ 3.05 | $ 2.40 | $ 2.32 |

*See notes to consolidated financial statements.*
*Courtesy of American Can Company.*

## Summary of Chapter in Terms of Learning Objectives

**1.** Whereas cash dividends transfer corporate assets to the stockholders, stock dividends do not. Stock dividends and stock splits have no effect on assets, no effect on total stockholders' equity, and no effect on the equity of each stockholder. Small stock dividends are recorded by capitalizing retained earnings equal to the market value of the distributed shares. But if the stock dividend is over 25% of the outstanding shares, only the par value of the distributed shares is capitalized.

**2.** When outstanding shares are repurchased by the issuing corporation and held as treasury stock, the cost of the shares is debited to Treasury Stock, which is subtracted in the stockholders' equity section of the balance sheet. If treasury stock is reissued, proceeds in excess of cost are credited to Contributed Capital, Treasury Stock Transactions. If the proceeds are less than cost, the difference is debited to Contributed Capital, Treasury Stock Transactions to the extent a credit balance exists in that account. Any remaining amount is debited to Retained Earnings.

**3.** In most states, retained earnings is legally restricted by an amount equal to the cost of treasury stock. Retained earnings also may be restricted by contract. Corporations may voluntarily appropriate retained earnings to inform stockholders why dividends are not larger in amount. More often, however, this information is expressed in a letter to the stockholders.

**4.** If management implemented a plan to discontinue a business segment, the net income or loss from operating the segment and the gain or loss on disposal are separately reported on the income statement below income from continuing operations. Next, extraordinary gains or losses, which are both unusual and infrequent, are listed and followed by the cumulative effect on past years' incomes of changes in accounting principles.

Prior period adjustments, which include the income effects of accounting errors made in prior periods, are reported on the statement of retained earnings. However, many companies omit the statement of retained earnings and report the changes in each stockholders' equity account on a statement of changes in stockholders' equity.

Changes in accounting estimates are made because new information shows the old estimates to be invalid. When an accounting estimate is changed, the new estimate is used to calculate revenue or expense in the current and future periods.

**5.** Companies with simple capital structures do not have outstanding securities that are convertible into common stock. For such companies, earnings per share is calculated by dividing net income less dividends to preferred stock by the weighted-average number of outstanding common shares. In calculating the weighted-average number of shares outstanding, the number of shares outstanding prior to a stock dividend or stock split must be restated to reflect the effect of the stock dividend or stock split.

Companies with complex capital structures have outstanding securities that are convertible into common stock. These companies may have to report both primary earnings per share and fully diluted earnings per share. In calculating primary earnings per share, the denominator is the weighted-average number of common shares outstanding plus dilutive common stock equivalents. Fully diluted earnings per share assumes the conversion of all dilutive securities.

## Demonstration Problem

The Precision Company began 1990 with the following balances in its stockholders' equity accounts:

| | |
|---|---|
| Common stock, $10 par, 500,000 shares authorized, 200,000 shares issued and outstanding | $2,000,000 |
| Contributed capital in excess of par | 1,000,000 |
| Retained earnings | 5,000,000 |
| Total | $8,000,000 |

All of the stock was issued for $15 when the company was created.

**Part 1.** Prepare journal entries to account for the following transactions:

1990

Mar. 31 Declared a 20% stock dividend. The market value of the stock was $18 per share.

Apr. 15 Issued the common shares declared as stock dividend on March 31.
June 30 Purchased 30,000 shares of treasury stock at $20 per share.
Aug. 31 Sold 20,000 of the treasury shares at $26 per share.
Nov. 30 Purchased and retired 50,000 shares at $24 per share.

**Part 2.** Use the following information to prepare an income statement for 1990, including earnings per share amounts for each category of income:

| | |
|---|---|
| Cumulative effect on prior years' net incomes of a change in depreciation methods (net of income tax) | $ (136,500) |
| Expenses of continuing operations | (2,072,500) |
| Extraordinary gain on legal settlement (net of income tax) | 182,000 |
| Gain on disposal of discontinued division (net of income tax) | 29,000 |
| Gain on sale of stock investment | 400,000 |
| Income from operation of discontinued division (net of income tax) | (120,000) |
| Income taxes on income from continuing operations | (225,000) |
| Prior period adjustment for error (net of income tax) | (75,000) |
| Sales | 4,140,000 |
| Infrequent loss on purchase commitment | (650,000) |

**Part 3.** Based on all of the above information, prepare a statement of changes in stockholders' equity for 1990.

## Solution to Demonstration Problem

**Part 1**

| | | | | |
|---|---|---|---|---|
| 1990 | | | | |
| Mar. | 31 | Stock Dividends Declared | 720,000.00 | |
| | | Common Stock Dividends Distributable | | 400,000.00 |
| | | Contributed Capital in Excess of Par Value, Common Stock | | 320,000.00 |
| | | Declared a stock dividend of 20% or 40,000 shares; market value is $18 per share. | | |
| Apr. | 15 | Common Stock Dividends Distributable | 400,000.00 | |
| | | Common Stock | | 400,000.00 |
| | | Distributed 40,000 shares common stock. | | |
| June | 30 | Treasury Stock, Common | 600,000.00 | |
| | | Cash | | 600,000.00 |
| | | Purchased 30,000 shares of common stock at $20 per share. | | |
| Aug. | 31 | Cash | 520,000.00 | |
| | | Treasury Stock | | 400,000.00 |
| | | Contributed Capital, Treasury Stock Transactions | | 120,000.00 |
| | | Sold 20,000 shares of treasury stock at $26 per share. | | |
| Nov. | 30 | Common Stock | 500,000.00 | |
| | | Contributed Capital in Excess of Par Value, Common Stock | 250,000.00 | |
| | | Retained Earnings | 450,000.00 | |
| | | Cash | | 1,200,000.00 |

## Part 2

**PRECISION COMPANY**
**Income Statement**
**For Year Ended December 31, 1990**

| | | |
|---|---|---|
| Sales | | $ 4,140,000 |
| Expenses of continuing operations | | (2,072,500) |
| Income taxes | | (225,000) |
| Gain on sale of stock investment | | 400,000 |
| Infrequent loss on purchase commitment | | (650,000) |
| Income from continuing operations | | $ 1,592,500 |
| **Discontinued operations:** | | |
| Loss from operation of discontinued division (net of income tax) | $(120,000) | |
| Gain on disposal of discontinued division's assets (net of income tax) | 29,000 | |
| Loss from discontinued division | | $ (91,000) |
| Income before extraordinary items and cumulative effect of a change in accounting principle | | $ 1,501,500 |
| **Extraordinary items:** | | |
| Extraordinary gain on legal settlement (net of income tax) | | 182,000 |
| **Cumulative effect of a change in accounting principle:** | | |
| Change in depreciation methods (net of income tax) | | (136,500) |
| Net income | | $ 1,547,000 |
| **Earning per share** (227,500 average shares outstanding): | | |
| Income from continuing operations | | $ 7.00 |
| Loss from discontinued operations | | (.40) |
| Extraordinary gain | | .80 |
| Cumulative effect of change in accounting principle | | (.60) |
| Net income | | $ 6.80 |

(Note that the prior period adjustment for the error is not an income statement item.)

Calculation of the weighted average of outstanding shares:

| Time Period | Shares Outstanding | Portion of Year Outstanding | Weighted by Portion of Year Outstanding |
|---|---|---|---|
| January–June | (200,000 × 1.2) | 6/12 | 120,000 |
| July–August | (240,000 − 30,000) | 2/12 | 35,000 |
| September–November | (210,000 + 20,000) | 3/12 | 57,500 |
| December | (230,000 − 50,000) | 1/12 | 15,000 |
| | | | 227,500 |

## Part 3

**PRECISION COMPANY**
**Statement of Changes in Stockholders' Equity**
**For Year Ended December 31, 1990**

| | Common Stock | Additional Paid-in Capital | Retained Earnings | Treasury Stock | Total |
|---|---|---|---|---|---|
| Balance, January 1, 1990 | $2,000,000 | $1,000,000 | $5,000,000 | | $ 8,000,000 |
| Prior-period adjustment | | | (75,000) | | (75,000) |
| Common stock dividend | 400,000 | 320,000 | (720,000) | | |
| Treasury stock purchase | | | | $(600,000) | |
| Treasury stock sale | | 120,000 | | 400,000 | 520,000 |
| Retirement | (500,000) | (250,000) | (450,000) | | (1,200,000) |
| Net income | | | 1,547,000 | | 1,547,000 |
| Balance, December 31, 1990 | $1,900,000 | $1,190,000 | $5,302,000 | $(200,000) | $ 8,192,000 |

## Glossary

Define or explain the words and phrases in the chapter Glossary. (L. O. 6)

**Antidilutive securities** convertible securities the assumed conversion of which would have the effect of increasing earnings per share. p. 682

**Appropriated retained earnings** retained earnings voluntarily earmarked for a special use as a way of informing stockholders that assets from earnings equal to the appropriations are not available for dividends. p. 674

**Changes in accounting estimates** adjustments to previously made assumptions about the future such as salvage values and the length of useful lives of buildings and equipment. p. 679

**Common stock equivalent** a security that is convertible into common stock and for which, according to detailed rules applied at the time of issuance, eventual conversion appears very probable. p. 682

**Complex capital structure** a capital structure that includes outstanding rights or options to purchase common stock or securities that are convertible into common stock. pp. 682–83

**Dilutive securities** convertible securities the assumed conversion of which would have the effect of decreasing earnings per share. p. 682

**Earned surplus** a synonym for retained earnings; no longer in general use. p. 665

**Earnings per share** the amount of net income (or components of income) that accrues to common shares divided by the weighted-average number of common shares outstanding. pp. 679–84

**Extraordinary gain or loss** a gain or loss that is both unusual and infrequent. p. 676

**Fully diluted earnings per share** earnings per share statistics that are calculated as if all dilutive securities had already been converted. p. 683

**Infrequent gain or loss** a gain or loss that is not expected to occur again, given the operating environment of the business. p. 676

**Liquidating dividends** distributions of corporate assets to stockholders, which are charged to contributed capital accounts and which therefore represent amounts that had been originally contributed by the stockholders. p. 665

**Primary earnings per share** earnings per share statistics that are calculated as if those outstanding common stock equivalents which are dilutive had already been converted. p. 682

**Prior period adjustment** items that are reported in the current statement of retained earnings as corrections to the beginning retained earnings balance; limited primarily to corrections of errors that were made in past years. pp. 678–79

**Restricted retained earnings** retained earnings that are not available for dividends because of law or binding contract. p. 672

**Segment of a business** operations of a company that involve a particular line of business or class of customer, providing the assets, activities, and financial results of the operations can be distinguished from other parts of the business. p. 675

**Simple capital structure** a capital structure that does not include any rights or options to purchase common shares or any securities that are convertible into common stock. pp. 679–80

**Small stock dividend** a stock dividend that amounts to 25% or less of the issuing corporation's previously outstanding shares. p. 668

**Statement of changes in stockholders' equity** a financial statement that reconciles the beginning and ending balances of each stockholders' equity account by listing all changes that occurred during the year. pp. 679–80

**Stock dividend** a distribution by a corporation of shares of its own stock to its stockholders without any consideration being received in return. pp. 665–68

**Stock split** the act of a corporation to call in its stock and issue more than one new share in the place of each share previously outstanding. p. 669

**Treasury stock** issued stock that was reacquired and is currently held by the issuing corporation. pp. 669–73

**Unusual gain or loss** a gain or loss that is abnormal and unrelated or only incidentally related to the ordinary activities and environment of the business. p. 676

## Objective Review

Answers to the following questions are listed in Appendix I at the end of the book. Be sure that you decide which is the one best answer to each question *before* you check the answers in the appendix.

1. Which of the following statements is true with regard to stock dividends and stock splits?
   *a.* The distribution of stock dividends reduces both cash and stockholders' equity while a stock split reduces neither one.
   *b.* Stock dividends and stock splits have the same effect on total assets and total retained earnings of the issuing corporation.
   *c.* A stock dividend does not transfer assets from a corporation to the stockholders but requires that an amount of retained earnings be capitalized.
   *d.* A corporation should capitalize an amount of retained earnings equal to the market value of the shares to be distributed if the stock dividend exceeds 25% of its outstanding shares.
   *e.* In a stock split, Retained Earnings is debited and the stock account is credited for the par value or stated value of the shares issued.
2. The purchase of treasury stock by a corporation:
   *a.* Requires a debit to Retained Earnings.
   *b.* Reduces in equal amounts both its total assets and its total stockholders' equity.
   *c.* Is recorded with an increase to assets and a decrease to assets.
   *d.* Decreases the amount of issued stock.
   *e.* Does not change the amount of outstanding stock.
3. When a corporation appropriates retained earnings:

*a.* The board of directors becomes permanently committed not to pay dividends from those appropriated amounts.
*b.* The appropriation is recorded by transferring the appropriated amount from Retained Earnings to a contributed capital account.
*c.* The amount of the appropriation must be matched by available cash.
*d.* The board of directors voluntarily allocates a portion of retained earnings for some special purpose, thereby indicating why those retained earnings are not being declared as dividends.
*e.* None of the above.

4. Which of the following qualifies as an extraordinary gain or loss?
   *a.* A manufacturer of three-wheeled recreational vehicles incurred a loss as a result of a customer's lawsuit over injuries the customer suffered from using the product.
   *b.* A loss due to compensating a worker for injuries the worker suffered while working at the company's plant.
   *c.* A gain from the exchange of British pounds for dollars which resulted from credit sales of goods to British customers.
   *d.* A loss of plant and equipment damaged as a result of a meteorite shower.
   *e.* None of the above are extraordinary items.
5. Tupelo Corporation earned $120,000 in 1990, and preferred dividends were $30,000. On January 1, 1990, the company had 12,000 common shares outstanding. However, on May 1, 1990, Tupelo Corporation purchased 3,000 treasury shares. Earnings per share for 1990 is:
   *a.* $13.33.
   *b.* $12.00.
   *c.* $10.00.
   *d.* $ 9.00.
   *e.* $ 7.50.

## Questions for Class Discussion

1. What effect does the declaration of a cash dividend have on the assets, liabilities, and stockholders' equity of the corporation that declares the dividend? What is the effect of the subsequent payment of the cash dividend?
2. Why are cash dividends charged against contributed capital accounts called liquidating dividends?
3. What effect does the declaration of a stock dividend have on the assets, liabilities, and total stockholders' equity of the corporation that declares the dividend? What is the effect of the subsequent distribution of the stock dividend?
4. In accounting for a stock dividend, what criterion distinguishes a small stock dividend?
5. What amount of retained earnings should be capitalized in accounting for a small stock dividend?
6. What is the difference between a stock dividend and a stock split?

7. Courts have held that a stock dividend is not taxable income to its recipients. Why?
8. If a balance sheet is prepared between the date of declaration and the date of payment or distribution of a dividend, how should the dividend be shown if it is (*a*) a cash dividend, or (*b*) a stock dividend?
9. What is treasury stock? How is it like unissued stock? How does it differ from unissued stock? What is the legal significance of this difference?
10. Southern Products Corporation bought 15,000 shares of Regional Steel Corporation stock and turned it over to the treasurer of Southern Products for safekeeping. Is this treasury stock? Why or why not?
11. What effect does the purchase of treasury stock have on assets and total stockholders' equity?
12. Distinguish between issued stock and outstanding stock.
13. Why do state laws place limitations on the purchase of treasury stock?
14. In the annual income statement of a corporation, what are four major sections of the statement that might appear below "Income from continuing operations"?
15. If a company has business operations in several different lines of business, what criteria must be met if the operations in a particular line of business are to qualify as a business segment?
16. If a company operates one of its business segments at a loss during much of 1990 and then finds a buyer and disposes of that segment during November of that year, what two items concerning that segment should appear on the company's 1990 income statement?
17. Where on the income statement should a company disclose a gain that is abnormal and unrelated to the ordinary activities of the business and that is expected to recur no more often than once every other year?
18. Which of the following items would qualify as an extraordinary gain or loss: (*a*) operating losses resulting from a strike against a major supplier, (*b*) a gain from the sale of surplus equipment, or (*c*) a loss from damage to a building caused by a tornado (a type of storm that rarely occurs in the geographical region of the company's operations).
19. In past years, Daley Company paid its sales personnel annual salaries without additional incentive payments. This year, a new policy is being instituted whereby they will receive sales commissions rather than annual salaries. Does this new policy require a prior period adjustment? Explain why or why not.
20. After taking five years' straight-line depreciation on an asset that was expected to have an eight-year life, a company concluded that the asset would last another six years. Does this decision involve a change in accounting principles? If not, how would you describe this change?
21. How are earnings per share calculated for a corporation with a simple capital structure?
22. In calculating the weighted-average number of common shares outstanding, how are stock splits and stock dividends treated?

23. Why are not all convertible securities considered to be common stock equivalents?
24. What is the difference between primary earnings per share and fully diluted earnings per share?
25. What is the difference between simple capital structures and complex capital structures?

## Exercises

**Exercise 16–1**
**Stock dividends**
(L. O. 1)

Brazos Corporation's stockholders' equity appeared as follows on March 15:

| | |
|---|---|
| Common stock, $10 par value, 100,000 shares authorized, 25,000 shares issued | $250,000 |
| Contributed capital in excess of par value, common stock | 18,750 |
| Total contributed capital | $268,750 |
| Retained earnings | 30,000 |
| Total stockholders' equity | $298,750 |

On March 15, when the stock was selling at $13.50 per share, the corporation's directors voted a 5% stock dividend distributable on April 11 to the March 25 stockholders of record. The stock was selling at $13 per share at the close of business on April 12.

*Required*

1. Prepare general journal entries to record the declaration and distribution of the dividend.
2. Under the assumption that Rebecca Brady owned 800 of the shares on March 15 and received her dividend shares on April 11, prepare a schedule showing the number of shares she held on March 25 and on April 12, with their total book values and total market values. Assume no change in total stockholders' equity from March 15 to April 12.

**Exercise 16–2**
**Stock dividends and stock splits**
(L. O. 1)

On July 31, 1990, Fairey Corporation's common stock was selling for $50 per share, and the stockholders' equity section of the corporation's balance sheet appeared as follows:

| | |
|---|---|
| Common stock, $10 par value, 500,000 shares authorized, 10,000 shares issued | $100,000 |
| Contributed capital in excess of par value, common stock | 20,000 |
| Total contributed capital | $120,000 |
| Retained earnings | 200,000 |
| Total stockholders' equity | $320,000 |

*Required*

1. Assume the corporation declares and immediately issues a 100% stock dividend and capitalizes the minimum required amount of retained earnings. Answer the following questions about the stockholders' equity of the corporation after the new shares are issued:
   *a.* What is the retained earnings balance?
   *b.* What is the total amount of stockholders' equity?
   *c.* How many shares are outstanding?

2. Assume that instead of declaring a 100% stock dividend, the corporation changes the par value of the stock to $5 and immediately effects a 2 for 1 stock split. Answer the following questions about the stockholders' equity of the corporation after the stock split takes place:
   *a.* What is the retained earnings balance?
   *b.* What is the total amount of stockholders' equity?
   *c.* How many shares are outstanding?

Exercise 16–3
**Treasury stock purchases**
(L. O. 2, 3)

On May 31, Narco, Inc.'s stockholders' equity section appeared as follows:

**Stockholders' Equity**

| | |
|---|---|
| Common stock, $50 par value, 15,000 shares authorized and issued . . | $750,000 |
| Retained earnings . . . . . . . . . . . . . . . . . . . . . . . . . . . . . . | 150,250 |
| Total stockholders' equity . . . . . . . . . . . . . . . . . . . . . . . . . | $900,250 |

On May 31, the corporation purchased 500 shares of treasury stock at $75 per share. Give the entry to record the purchase and prepare a stockholders' equity section as it would appear immediately after the purchase.

Exercise 16–4
**Sales of treasury stock**
(L. O. 2)

On June 30, Narco, Inc., of Exercise 16–3 sold at $80 per share 300 of the treasury shares purchased on May 31, and on September 15, it sold the remaining treasury shares at $65 per share. Prepare general journal entries to record the sales.

Exercise 16–5
**Retirement of stock**
(L. O. 2)

The stockholders' equity section of Hackbart Company's December 31, 1990, balance sheet is as follows:

| | |
|---|---|
| Common stock, $1 par value, 250,000 shares authorized, 80,000 shares issued . . . . . . . . . . . . . . . . . . . . | $ 80,000 |
| Contributed capital in excess of par value, common stock . . | 480,000 |
| Total contributed capital . . . . . . . . . . . . . . . . . . . . | $560,000 |
| Retained earnings . . . . . . . . . . . . . . . . . . . . . . . | 250,000 |
| Total stockholders' equity . . . . . . . . . . . . . . . . . . . | $810,000 |

On the date of the balance sheet, the company purchased and retired 1,000 shares of its common stock. Prepare general journal entries to record the purchase and retirement under each of the following independent assumptions: (*a*) the stock was purchased for $5 per share, (*b*) the stock was purchased for $7 per share, and (*c*) the stock was purchased for $14 per share.

Exercise 16–6
**Income statement categories**
(L. O. 4)

The following list of items was extracted from the December 31, 1990, trial balance of Yellow Company. Using the information contained in this listing, prepare Yellow Company's income statement for 1990. You need not complete the earnings per share calculations.

| | Debit | Credit |
|---|---|---|
| Salaries expense | $21,000 | |
| Income tax expense (continuing operations) | 22,500 | |
| Loss from operating segment G (net of $27,000 tax) | 63,000 | |
| Sales | | $140,250 |
| Cumulative effect on prior years' income of change from declining-balance to straight-line depreciation (net of $4,500 tax) | | 10,800 |
| Extraordinary gain on state's condemnation of land owned by Yellow Company (net of $15,000 tax) | | 39,000 |
| Depreciation expense | 19,800 | |
| Gain on sale of segment G (net of $12,000 tax) | | 30,000 |
| Cost of goods sold | 43,500 | |

**Exercise 16–7**
**Change in accounting principles**
(L. O. 4)

Davis Company has one depreciable asset that cost $450,000 and has decided to switch from straight line depreciation to sum-of-the-years'-digits depreciation. In prior years, the company depreciated the asset for two years based on straight-line deprecaition, no salvage value, and a nine-year life. The company is subject to a 40% income tax rate. Calculate the amount of depreciation expense to be reported in the current year and the cumulative effect of the change on prior years' incomes. Indicate whether the cumulative effect of the change on prior years' incomes should be added or subtracted when calculating the current year's net income.

**Exercise 16–8**
**Classifying income it not related to contin operations**
(L. O. 4)

In preparing the annual financial statements for Terry Corporation, the correct manner of reporting the following items was not clear to the company's employees. Explain where each of the following items should appear in the financial statements:

*a.* The company keeps its delivery equipment for several years before disposing of the old equipment and buying new equipment. This year, for the first time in eight years, the company sold old equipment for a gain of $7,500 and then purchased new equipment.

*b.* After amortizing a trademark for five years based on an expected life of seven years, the company decided this year that the value of the trademark would last four more years. As a result, the amortization for the current year is $5,000 instead of $10,000.

*c.* This year the accounting department of the company discovered that two years ago, a cost had been charged to maintenance expense when it should have been charged to land. The after-tax effect of the charge to maintenance expense was $35,000.

**Exercise 16–9**
**Weighted-average shares outstanding and earnings per share**
(L. O. 5)

Janes Corporation reported $249,500 net income in 1990 and declared preferred dividends of $22,000. The following changes in common shares outstanding occurred during the year:

| | |
|---|---|
| Jan. 1: | 30,000 common shares were outstanding. |
| Mar. 1: | Sold 20,000 common shares for par. |
| July 1: | Declared and issued a 50% common stock dividend, or (50,000 × 50%) = 25,000 additional shares. |

Calculate the weighted-average number of common shares outstanding during the year and earnings per share.

**Exercise 16–10**
**Weighted-average shares outstanding and earnings per share**
(L. O. 5)

Stahl Incorporated reported $605,625 net income in 1990 and declared preferred dividends of $37,500. The following changes in common shares outstanding occurred during the year:

Jan. 1: 45,000 common shares were outstanding.
Apr. 1: Sold 55,000 common shares for par plus a $10 premium.
Aug. 1: Purchased 5,000 shares to be held as treasury stock.
Nov. 1: Declared and issued a 3 for 1 stock split.

Calculate the weighted-average number of common shares outstanding during the year and earnings per share.

**Exercise 16–11**
**Reporting earnings per share**
(L. O. 5)

Rachet Corporation's 1990 income statement, excluding the earnings per share portion of the statement, was as follows:

| | | |
|---|---|---|
| Sales | | $225,000 |
| Costs and expenses: | | |
| Depreciation | $ 12,000 | |
| Income taxes | 18,000 | |
| Other expenses | 132,000 | 162,000 |
| Income from continuing operations | | $ 63,000 |
| Loss from operating discontinued business segment (net of $11,400 taxes) | $ 30,000 | |
| Loss on sale of business segment (net of $13,500 tax) | 39,000 | (69,000) |
| Loss before extraordinary items and change in accounting principle | | $ (6,000) |
| Extraordinary gain (net of $24,000 taxes) | $ 81,000 | |
| Cumulative effect of a change in accounting principle (net of $13,100 taxes) | 49,500 | 130,500 |
| Net income | | $124,500 |

Assuming that dilutive, common stock equivalents were converted at the beginning of the year, the weighted-average number of common shares outstanding during the year was 90,000. Assuming that all dilutive securities had been converted at the beginning of the year, the weighted-average number of common shares outstanding during the year was 112,000.

*Required*

Present the earnings per share portion of the 1990 income statement.

## Problems

**Problem 16–1**
**Treasury stock transactions and stock dividends**
(L. O. 1, 2, 3)

Davenport Corporation's stockholders' equity on December 31, 1989, consisted of the following:

| | |
|---|---|
| Common stock, $1 par value, 500,000 shares authorized, 205,000 shares issued | $205,000 |
| Contributed capital in excess of par value, common stock | 52,300 |
| Retained earnings | 145,200 |
| Total stockholders' equity | $402,500 |

During 1990, the company completed these transactions:

Feb. 10 Purchased 15,000 shares of treasury stock at $1.25 per share.
Mar. 25 The directors voted a $0.05 per share cash dividend payable on April 20 to the April 10 stockholders of record.
Apr. 20 Paid the dividend declared on March 25.
June 8 Sold 5,000 of the treasury shares at $1.30 per share.
Nov. 9 Sold 10,000 of the treasury shares at $0.80 per share.
Dec. 21 The directors voted a $0.10 per share cash dividend payable on January 20 to the January 5 stockholders of record, and they voted a 3% stock dividend distributable on February 2 to the January 21 stockholders of record. The market value of the stock was $1.15 per share.
31 Closed the Income Summary account and carried the company's $50,500 net income to Retained Earnings.
31 Closed the Cash Dividends Declared and Stock Dividends Declared accounts.

*Required*

1. Prepare general journal entries to record the transactions.
2. Prepare a retained earnings statement for the year and the stockholders' equity section of the company's year-end balance sheet.

**Problem 16–2**
**Cash dividend, stock dividend, and stock split**
(L. O. 1)

Last May 31, Rubinett Corporation had a $2.1 million credit balance in its Retained Earnings account. On that date, the corporation's contributed capital consisted of 300,000 authorized shares of $10 par, common stock, of which 105,000 shares had been issued at $15 and were outstanding. It then completed the following transactions:

June 1 The board of directors declared a $5 per share dividend on the common stock, payable on July 5 to the June 15 stockholders of record.
July 5 Paid the dividend declared on June 1.
12 The board declared a 25% stock dividend, distributable on August 10 to the July 28 stockholders of record. The stock was selling at $50 per share.
Aug. 10 Distributed the stock dividend declared on July 12.
31 Since August 31 is the end of the company's fiscal year, closed the Income Summary account, which had a credit balance of $656,250. Also closed the Cash Dividends Declared and Stock Dividends Declared accounts.
Sept. 8 The board of directors voted to split the corporation's stock 5 for 1 by calling in the old stock and issuing five $2 par value shares for each $10 share held. The stockholders voted approval of the split and authorization of 1,000,000 new $2 par value shares to replace the $10 shares; all legal requirements were met; and the split was completed on October 5.

*Required*

1. Prepare general journal entries to record these transactions.
2. Under the assumption Jill Owens owned 1,500 of the $10 par value shares on May 31 and neither bought nor sold any shares during the period of the transactions, prepare a schedule with columns for the date, supporting calculations, book value per share, and book value of Owens' shares. Then complete the schedule by calculating the book value per share of the corporation's stock and the book value of Owens' shares at the close of business on May 31, June 1, July 5, August 10, August 31, and September 8. Assume that the only income earned by the company during these periods was the $656,250 earned and closed on August 31.
3. Prepare three stockholders' equity sections for the corporation, the first showing the stockholders' equity on May 31, the second on August 31, and the third on September 8.

**Problem 16–3**
**Calculating net income from balance sheet comparison**
(L. O. 1, 2, 3)

The equity sections from the 1989 and 1990 balance sheets of Teller Industries, Inc., appeared as follows:

**Stockholders' Equity**
**(As of December 31, 1989)**

| | |
|---|---|
| Common stock, $10 par value, 600,000 shares authorized, 80,000 shares issued | $ 800,000 |
| Contributed capital in excess of par value, common stock | 180,000 |
| Total contributed capital | $ 980,000 |
| Retained earnings | 750,250 |
| Total stockholders' equity | $1,730,250 |

**Stockholders' Equity**
**(As of December 31, 1990)**

| | |
|---|---|
| Common stock, $10 par value, 600,000 shares authorized, 87,920 shares issued of which 800 are in the treasury | $ 879,200 |
| Contributed capital in excess of par value, common stock | 298,800 |
| Total contributed capital | $1,178,000 |
| Retained earnings, of which $17,600 is restricted | 675,120 |
| Total | $1,853,120 |
| Less cost of treasury stock | 17,600 |
| Total stockholders' equity | $1,835,520 |

On April 8, July 5, September 20, and again on December 15, 1990, the board of directors declared $0.40 per share dividends on the outstanding stock. The treasury stock was purchased on July 25. On September 20, while the stock was selling for $25 per share, the corporation declared a 10% stock dividend on the outstanding shares. The new shares were issued on October 19.

*Required*

Under the assumption that there were no transactions affecting retained earnings other than the ones given, determine the 1990 net income of Teller Industries, Inc. Show your calculations.

**Problem 16–4**
**Classifying income items in a published income statement**
(L. O. 4)

Fremont Corporation had several unusual transactions during 1990 and has prepared the following list of trial balance items from which the appropriate items should be selected and used in constructing the 1990 income statement for the company.

| | Debit | Credit |
|---|---|---|
| Loss on sale of antique automobile displayed in company showroom (an unusual transaction for the company that occurs about once every four years when a new customer attraction is obtained) | $ 27,900 | |
| Cost of goods sold | 170,400 | |
| Gain on settlement with supplier to compensate for negative customer reaction to receipt of products with faulty materials Fremont had purchased from the supplier. (In this industry, attempts to obtain such settlements with suppliers are not unusual but occur very infrequently.) | | $ 46,800 |
| Income tax expense | 71,250 | |
| Loss from operating Preuss Division (net of $11,700 income tax benefit) | 29,250 | |
| Revenue received in advance late last year and incorrectly credited to a revenue account instead of a liability account (net of $9,750 income taxes) | 23,500 | |
| Depreciation expense | 28,350 | |
| Gain on sale of investment in stock (Fremont regularly maintains a large portfolio of stock investments as part of its business activities, expecting to enhance the earnings of the company through purchases and sales of such securities.) | | 85,350 |
| Accumulated depreciation, buildings | | 76,500 |
| Effect on prior years' income of switching from straight-line depreciation to declining-balance depreciation, justified in this case as an improvement in financial reporting (net of $32,000 income taxes) | 91,650 | |
| Other operating expenses | 140,850 | |
| Loss on sale of Preuss Division (net of $17,100 income taxes) | 40,950 | |
| Interest earned | | 10,800 |
| Gain on condemnation of land by city. (This is probably the only time in the company's past or future that it will have land condemned by a government. The event is highly unusual.) (net of $39,000 income taxes) | | 136,500 |
| Sales | | 569,400 |
| Accrued liabilities | | 48,000 |

*Required*

Prepare Fremont Corporation's income statement for 1990, excluding the earnings per share statistics.

**Problem 16–5**
**Changes in accounting principles**
(L. O. 4)

On January 1, 1985, Russell Corporation purchased a large item of machinery for use in its manufacturing operations. The machine cost $1,000,000 and was expected to have a salvage value of $65,000. Depreciation was taken through 1989 on a sum-of-the-years'-digits method assuming a 10-year life. Early in 1990, the company concluded that given the economic conditions in the industry, a straight-line method would result in more meaningful financial statements. They argue that straight-line depreciation would allow better comparisons with the financial results of other firms in the industry.

*Required*

1. Is Russell Corporation allowed to change depreciation methods in 1990?
2. Prepare a table that shows the depreciation expense to be reported each year of the asset's life under both depreciation methods and the cumulative effect of the change on prior years' incomes. Assume an income tax rate of 30%, and round your answers to the nearest whole dollar.
3. State the amount of depreciation expense to be reported in 1990 and the cumulative effect of the change on prior years' incomes. How should the cumulative effect be reported? Does the cumulative effect increase or decrease net income?
4. Now assume that Russell Corporation had used straight-line depreciation through 1989 and justified a change to sum-of-the-years'-digits depreciation in 1990. What amount of depreciation expense should be reported in 1990? How does the reporting of the cumulative effect of the change differ from your answer to Requirement 3?

**Problem 16–6**
**Earnings per share calculations and presentation**
(L. O. 5)

Except for the earnings per share statistics, the 1990, 1989, and 1988 income statements of Glowworm Corporation were originally presented as follows:

| | 1990 | 1989 | 1988 |
|---|---|---|---|
| Sales | $918,000 | $692,400 | $774,000 |
| Costs and expenses | 796,800 | 537,600 | 562,800 |
| Income from continuing operations | $121,200 | $154,800 | $211,200 |
| Loss on discontinued operations | — | (99,600) | (66,000) |
| Income (loss) before extraordinary items and changes in accounting principles | $121,200 | $ 55,200 | $145,200 |
| Extraordinary gains (losses) | | (81,600) | (45,600) |
| Cumulative effect of change in accounting principle | 35,400 | — | — |
| Net income (loss) | $156,600 | $(26,400) | $ 99,600 |

Information on common stock:

| | |
|---|---|
| Shares outstanding on January 1, 1988 | 28,800 |
| Sale of shares on June 1, 1988 | +3,600 |
| Purchase of treasury shares on October 1, 1988 | −1,800 |
| Shares outstanding on December 31, 1988 | 30,600 |
| Sale of shares on March 1, 1989 | +6,120 |
| Sale of shares on April 1, 1989 | +9,720 |
| Stock split of 2 for 1 on September 1, 1989 | +46,440 |
| Shares outstanding on December 31, 1989 | +92,880 |
| Purchase of treasury shares on March 1, 1990 | −3,600 |
| Sale of shares on June 1, 1990 | +16,920 |
| Stock dividend of 20% on November 1, 1990 | +21,240 |
| Shares outstanding on December 31, 1990 | 127,440 |

*Required*

1. Calculate the weighted-average number of common shares outstanding during (*a*) 1988, (*b*) 1989, and (*c*) 1990.

2. Present the earnings per share portions of: (*a*) the 1988 income statement, (*b*) the 1989 income statement, and (*c*) the 1990 income statement.

## Alternate Problems

**Problem 16–1A**
**Treasury stock transactions and stock dividends**
(L. O. 1, 2, 3)

Brevet Corporation's stockholders' equity on December 31, 1989, consisted of the following:

| | |
|---|---|
| Common stock, $25 par value, 30,000 shares authorized, 10,500 shares issued | $262,500 |
| Contributed capital in excess of par value, common stock | 42,000 |
| Retained earnings | 95,000 |
| Total stockholders' equity | $399,500 |

During 1990, the company completed these transactions:

Apr. 8 Purchased 900 shares of treasury stock at $40 per share.
27 The directors voted a $0.45 per share cash dividend payable on May 26 to the May 15 stockholders of record.
May 26 Paid the dividend declared on April 27.
July 19 Sold 500 of the treasury shares at $45 per share.
Oct. 10 Sold 400 of the treasury shares at $35 per share.
Dec. 22 The directors voted a $0.45 per share cash dividend payable on January 25 to the January 10 stockholders of record, and they voted a 2% stock dividend distributable on February 15 to the February 1 stockholders of record. The market value of the stock was $42 per share.
31 Closed the Income Summary account and carried the company's $25,000 net income to Retained Earnings.
31 Closed the Cash Dividends Declared and Stock Dividends Declared accounts.

*Required*

1. Prepare general journal entries to record the transactions.
2. Prepare a retained earnings statement for the year and the stockholders' equity section of the company's year-end balance sheet.

**Problem 16–2A**
**Cash dividend, stock dividend, and stock split**
(L. O. 1)

Last August 31, Redondo Corporation had a $650,000 credit balance in its Retained Earnings account. On that date, the corporation's contributed capital consisted of 60,000 authorized shares of $100 par, common stock of which 5,000 shares had been issued at $115 and were outstanding. It then completed the following transactions:

Sept. 1 The board of directors declared a $7 per share dividend on the common stock, payable on October 4 to the September 15 stockholders of record.
Oct. 4 Paid the dividend declared on September 1.
Nov. 11 The board declared a 10% stock dividend, distributable on December 8 to the November 20 stockholders of record. The stock was selling at $125 per share.
Dec. 8 Distributed the stock dividend declared on November 11.
31 Since December 31 is the end of the accounting year, closed the

Income Summary account, which had a credit balance of $192,500. Also closed the Cash Dividends Declared and Stock Dividends Declared accounts.

Jan. 10 The board of directors voted to split the corporation's stock 5 for 1 by calling in the old stock and issuing five $20 par value shares for each $100 share held. The stockholders voted approval of the split and authorization of 100,000 new $20 par value shares to replace the $100 shares; all legal requirements were met; and the split was completed on February 5.

*Required*

1. Prepare general journal entries to record these transactions and to close the Income Summary account at year-end. (No entry is required for the split; however, a memorandum reciting the facts would be entered in the Common Stock account.)
2. Under the assumption Chris Reed owned 500 of the $100 par value shares on August 31 and neither bought nor sold any shares during the period of the transactions, prepare a schedule with columns for the date, supporting calculations, book value per share, and book value of Reed's shares. Then complete the schedule by calculating the book value per share of the corporation's stock and the book value of Reed's shares at the close of business on August 31, September 1, October 4, December 8, December 31, and February 5. Assume that the only income earned by the company during these periods was the $192,500, which was earned and closed on December 31.
3. Prepare three stockholders' equity sections for the corporation, the first showing the stockholders' equity on August 31, the second on December 31, and the third on February 5.

**Problem 16–3A**
**Calculating net income from balance sheet comparison**
(L. O. 1, 2, 3)

The equity sections from the 1989 and 1990 balance sheets of St. James Corporation appeared as follows:

**Stockholders' Equity**
**(As of December 31, 1989)**

| | |
|---|---|
| Common stock, no-par, $10 stated value, 500,000 shares authorized, 60,000 shares issued | $ 600,000 |
| Contributed capital in excess of stated value | 130,000 |
| Total contributed capital | $ 730,000 |
| Retained earnings | 595,250 |
| Total stockholders' equity | $1,325,250 |

**Stockholders' Equity**
**(As of December 31, 1990)**

| | |
|---|---|
| Common stock, no-par, $10 stated value, 500,000 shares authorized, 62,965 shares issued of which 700 are in the treasury | $ 629,650 |
| Contributed capital in excess of stated value | 189,300 |
| Total contributed capital | $ 818,950 |
| Retained earnings | 475,250 |
| Total | $1,294,200 |
| Less cost of treasury stock | 14,500 |
| Total stockholders' equity | $1,279,700 |

On April 2, June 8, September 25, and again on December 18, 1990, the board of directors declared $0.20 per share dividends on the outstanding stock. The treasury stock was purchased on June 25. On October 25, while the stock was selling for $30 per share, the corporation declared a 5% stock dividend on the outstanding shares. The new shares were issued on October 21.

*Required*

Under the assumption that there were no transactions affecting retained earnings other than the ones given, determine the 1990 net income of St. James Corporation. Show your calculations.

**Problem 16–4A**
**Classifying income items in a published income statement**
(L. O. 4)

Milano Company had several unusual transactions during 1990 and has prepared the following list of trial balance items from which the appropriate items should be selected and used in constructing the 1990 income statement for the company.

| | Debit | Credit |
|---|---|---|
| Depreciation expense | $ 21,900 | |
| Income from operations of Maz Division (net of $9,000 income taxes) | | $ 22,500 |
| Sales | | 438,000 |
| Cost of goods sold | 131,100 | |
| Gain on sale of artwork in company offices (an unusual transaction for the company that occurs only when major redecorations are required and expensive new artwork is purchased, which happens about every five to seven years) | | 48,750 |
| Loss on a patent infringement suit. (This patent is essential to the operations of the business and it is not unusual for companies in this industry to be involved in patent infringement suits. However, the lawsuit appears to have settled the matter in this case and the problem is not expected to arise in the foreseeable future.) | 210,000 | |
| Income tax expense | 54,900 | |
| Gain on payment from supplier to compensate for loss of customers who had been sold products containing inferior materials purchased from the supplier. (In this industry, such settlements with suppliers occur quite frequently.) | | 36,000 |
| Maintenance expense costs (net of $7,500 income taxes) incurred in late December of last year and incorrectly charged to building | 18,150 | |
| Gain on sale of investment in stock (The stock was originally donated to Milano by an elderly stockholder and was held out of courtesy until that stockholder's death. Milano has never held stock investments before and has no intention of doing so in the future.) (net of $10,500 income taxes) | | 65,700 |
| Accumulated depreciation, buildings | | 54,000 |
| Loss on sale of Maz Division (net of $13,200 income taxes) | 31,500 | |
| Interest earned | | 5,250 |
| Other operating expenses | 108,450 | |
| Effect on prior years' income of switching from accelerated depreciation to straight-line depreciation (net of $28,000 income taxes) | | 70,500 |
| Estimated product warranty liability | | 34,500 |

*Required*

Prepare Milano Company's income statement for 1990, excluding the earnings per share statistics.

**Problem 16–5A**
**Changes in accounting principles**
(L. O. 4)

On January 1, 1986, the Jett Company purchased a major item of machinery for use in its operations. The machine cost $650,000 and was expected to have a salvage value of $50,000. Depreciation was taken through 1989 on a declining-balance method at twice the straight-line rate assuming an eight-year life. Early in 1990, the company concluded that given the economic conditions in the industry, a straight-line method would result in more meaningful financial statements. They argue that straight-line depreciation would allow better comparisons with the financial results of other firms in the industry.

*Required*

1. Is Jett Company allowed to change depreciation methods in 1990?
2. Prepare a table that shows the depreciation expense to be reported each year of the asset's life under both depreciation methods and the cumulative effect of the change on prior years' incomes. Assume an income tax rate of 40%, and round your answers to the nearest whole dollar.
3. State the amount of depreciation expense to be reported in 1990 and the cumulative effect of the change on prior years' incomes. How should the cumulative effect be reported? Does the cumulative effect increase or decrease net income?
4. Now assume that Jett Company had used straight-line depreciation through 1989 and justified a change to declining-balance depreciation in 1990. What amount of depreciation expense should be reported in 1990? How does the reporting of the cumulative effect of the change differ from your answer to Requirement 3?

**Problem 16–6A**
**Earnings per share calculations and presentation**
(L. O. 5)

Except for the earnings per share statistics, the 1990, 1989, and 1988 income statements of Berber Company were originally presented as follows:

| | 1990 | 1989 | 1988 |
|---|---|---|---|
| Sales | $720,000 | $ 652,500 | $597,000 |
| Costs and expenses | 622,500 | 585,000 | 480,000 |
| Income from continuing operations | $ 97,500 | $ 67,500 | $117,000 |
| Loss on discontinued operations | — | (180,000) | — |
| Income (loss) before extraordinary items and changes in accounting principles | $ 97,500 | $(112,500) | $117,000 |
| Extraordinary gains (losses) | 168,000 | — | (40,500) |
| Cumulative effect of change in accounting principle | — | — | 49,500 |
| Net income (loss) | $265,500 | $(112,500) | $126,000 |

Information on common stock:

| | |
|---|---|
| Shares outstanding on January 1, 1988 | 30,000 |
| Sale of shares on April 1, 1988 | +12,000 |
| Purchase of treasury shares on May 1, 1988 | −6,000 |
| Stock dividend of 10% on September 1, 1988 | +3,600 |
| Shares outstanding on December 31, 1988 | 39,600 |
| Sale of shares on April 1, 1989 | +9,000 |
| Sale of shares on July 1, 1989 | +13,500 |
| Shares outstanding on December 31, 1989 | 62,100 |
| Purchase of treasury shares on April 1, 1990 | −4,500 |
| Sale of shares on June 1, 1990 | +22,500 |
| Stock split of 2 for 1 on November 1, 1990 | +80,100 |
| Shares outstanding on December 31, 1990 | 160,200 |

*Required*

1. Calculate the weighted-average number of common shares outstanding during (*a*) 1988, (*b*) 1989, and (*c*) 1990.
2. Present the earnings per share portions of (*a*) the 1988 income statement, (*b*) the 1989 income statement, and (*c*) the 1990 income statement.

## Provocative Problems

**Provocative Problem 16–1**
**Cornfield Corporation**
(L. O. 1, 2, 3)

On January 1, 1988, Hal Peeks purchased 800 shares of Cornfield Corporation stock at $45.50 per share. On that date, the corporation had the following stockholders' equity:

| | |
|---|---|
| Common stock, $25 par value, 500,000 shares authorized, 250,000 shares issued and outstanding | $6,250,000 |
| Contributed capital in excess of par value, common stock | 750,000 |
| Retained earnings | 2,500,000 |
| Total stockholders' equity | $9,500,000 |

Since purchasing the 800 shares, Mr. Peeks has neither purchased nor sold any additional shares of the company's stock. On December 31 of each year, he has received dividends on the shares held as follows: 1988, $1,408; 1989, $1,672; and 1990, $2,200.

On June 15, 1988, at a time when its stock was selling for $51.25 per share, Cornfield Corporation declared a 10% stock dividend that was distributed one month later. On October 25, 1989, the corporation doubled the number of its authorized shares and split its stock 2 for 1. On May 10, 1990, it purchased 10,000 shares of treasury stock at $35.50 per share. The shares were still in its treasury at year-end.

*Required*

Assume that Cornfield Corporation's outstanding stock had a book value of $35.75 per share on December 31, 1988, a book value of $20 per share on December 31, 1989, and a book value of $22.25 on December 31, 1990. Do the following:

1. Prepare statements that show the nature of the stockholders' equity in the corporation at the end of 1988, 1989, and 1990.
2. Prepare a schedule that shows the amount of the corporation's net income each year for 1988, 1989, and 1990. Assume that the changes in the company's retained earnings during the three-year period resulted from earnings and dividends.

**Provocative Problem 16–2**
**BiState Company**
(L. O. 1)

BiState Company's stockholders' equity on September 15 consisted of the following amounts:

| | |
|---|---|
| Common stock, $50 par value, 500,000 shares authorized, 50,000 shares issued and outstanding | $2,500,000 |
| Contributed capital in excess of par value, common stock | 375,000 |
| Retained earnings | 1,286,000 |
| Total stockholders' equity | $4,161,000 |

On September 15, when the stock was selling at $100 per share, the corporation's directors voted a 20% stock dividend, distributable on October 5 to the September 25 stockholders of record. The directors also voted a $3.45 per share annual cash dividend, payable on November 23 to the November 15 stockholders of record. The amount of the latter dividend was a disappointment to some stockholders, since the company had for a number of years paid a $4 per share annual cash dividend.

Nancy Cooper owned 1,000 shares of BiState Company stock on September 25, received her stock dividend shares, and continued to hold all of her shares until after the November 23 cash dividend. She also observed that her stock had a $100 per share market value on September 15, a market value it held until the close of business on September 25, when the market value declined to $90.50 per share.

*Required*

Give the entries to record the declaration and distribution or payment of the dividends involved here, and answer these questions:

*a.* What was the book value of Cooper's total shares on September 15 (after taking into consideration the cash dividend declared on that day)? What was the book value on October 5, after she received the dividend shares?

*b.* What fraction of the corporation did Cooper own on September 15? What fraction did she own on October 5?

*c.* What was the market value of Cooper's total shares on September 15? What was the market value at the close of business on September 25?

*d.* What did Cooper gain from the stock dividend?

**Provocative Problem 16–3**
**Rutland Corporation**
(L. O. 4)

Rutland Corporation had several rather special transactions and events in 1990 which are described below:

*a.* Rutland Corporation's continuing operations involve a high technology production process. Technical developments in this area occur regularly, and the production machinery becomes obsolete surprisingly often. Because such developments occurred recently, Rutland decided that it was forced to sell certain items of machinery at a loss and replace those items with a different type of machinery. The problem is how to report the loss.

*b.* Early last year, Rutland purchased a new type of equipment for use in its production process. Although much of the production equipment is depreciated over 5 years, a careful analysis of the situation led the company to decide that the new equipment should be depreciated over 10 years. Nevertheless, in the rush of year-end activities, the new equipment was included with the older equipment and depreciated on a five-year basis. In preparing adjustments at the end of 1990, the accountant discovered that $90,000 depreciation was taken on the new equipment last year, when only $45,000 should have been taken. The company is subject to a 30% income tax rate.

*c.* Rutland has a mining operation in several foreign countries, one of which has been subject to political unrest. After a sudden change in governments, the new ruling body resolved that the amount of foreign investment in the country was excessive. As a result, Rutland was forced to transfer ownership in its mines in that country to the new government. Rutland was able to continue its mining operation in a neighboring country and was allowed to transfer much of its mining equipment to the neighboring country. Nevertheless, the price paid to Rutland for its mines resulted in a significant loss.

*d.* Two years earlier, Rutland Corporation purchased some highly specialized equipment that was to be used in the operations of a new division that Rutland intended to acquire. The new division was in a separate line of business and would have been a separate segment of the business. After lengthy negotiations, the acquisition of the division was not accomplished and the company abandoned any hope of entering that line of business. Although the equipment had never been used, it was sold in 1990 at a loss. Rutland Corporation does not have a history of expanding into new lines of business and has no plans of doing so in the future.

*Required*

Examine Rutland Corporation's special transactions and events and describe how each one should be reported on the income statement or statement of retained earnings. Also state the specific characteristics of the item that support your decision.

# 17 Installment Notes Payable and Bonds

In Chapter 12, you learned to account for notes payable that require a single payment on the date the note matures. In such cases, the single payment includes the entire amount borrowed plus interest. However, many notes require a series of payments that consist of interest plus a part of the amount borrowed. We begin this chapter with a discussion of these installment notes. Then, we turn to a discussion of bonds, which are liabilities issued by corporations as well as a variety of governmental bodies. The chapter concludes with a brief introduction to bond investments.

**Learning Objectives**

*After studying Chapter 17, you should be able to:*

1. Calculate and record the payments on an installment note payable.
2. Describe the various characteristics of differing bond issues and prepare entries to record bonds that are issued between interest dates.
3. Calculate the price of a bond issue that sells at a discount and prepare entries to account for bonds issued at a discount.
4. Prepare entries to account for bonds issued at a premium.
5. Explain the purpose and operation of a bond sinking fund and prepare entries for sinking fund operations, for the retirement of bonds, and for the conversion of bonds into stock.
6. Describe the procedures used to account for investments in bonds.
7. Define or explain the words and phrases listed in the chapter Glossary.

Although some promissory notes require a single lump-sum payment of the amount borrowed plus interest, most long-term notes require a series of payments and are called **installment notes.** Each payment on an installment note includes interest and usually includes a partial repayment of the amount originally borrowed.

## Installment Notes Payable

Calculate and record the payments on an installment note payable. (L. O. 1)

When an installment note is used to borrow money, the borrower records the note just like a single-payment note. For example, suppose a company borrows $60,000 by signing a 12% installment note that requires six annual payments. The borrower records the note as follows:

| | | | | |
|---|---|---|---|---|
| 1990 | | | | |
| Dec. | 31 | Cash | 60,000.00 | |
| | | Notes Payable | | 60,000.00 |
| | | Borrowed by signing a 12% note. | | |

An installment note payable requires the borrower to pay back the debt in a series of periodic payments. Usually, each payment includes all of the interest accrued to the date of the payment plus some portion of the original amount borrowed (the principal amount). The terms of installment notes commonly call for one of two alternative payment patterns.

### Installment Payments of Accrued Interest plus Equal Amounts of Principal

Some installment notes require payments that consist of accrued interest to date plus equal amounts of principal. Since each periodic payment reduces the amount borrowed, the next period's interest is reduced and the total amount of the payment is smaller than the previous payment. For example, suppose that the $60,000, 12% note recorded above requires that $10,000 of principal plus accrued interest be paid at the end of each year. The entries to record the first and the second annual payments are as follows:

| | | | | |
|---|---|---|---|---|
| 1991 | | | | |
| Dec. | 31 | Notes Payable ($60,000 ÷ 6) | 10,000.00 | |
| | | Interest Expense ($60,000 × .12) | 7,200.00 | |
| | | Cash | | 17,200.00 |
| | | To record first installment payment. | | |
| 1992 | | | | |
| Dec. | 31 | Notes Payable ($60,000 ÷ 6) | 10,000.00 | |
| | | Interest Expense ($50,000 × .12) | 6,000.00 | |
| | | Cash | | 16,000.00 |
| | | To record second installment payment. | | |

Note that the balance of the debt at the beginning of each interest period is used to calculate the interest expense for the period. As a result, each payment is smaller than the previous payment.

**Illustration 17–1**
**Interest and principal included in installment note payments**

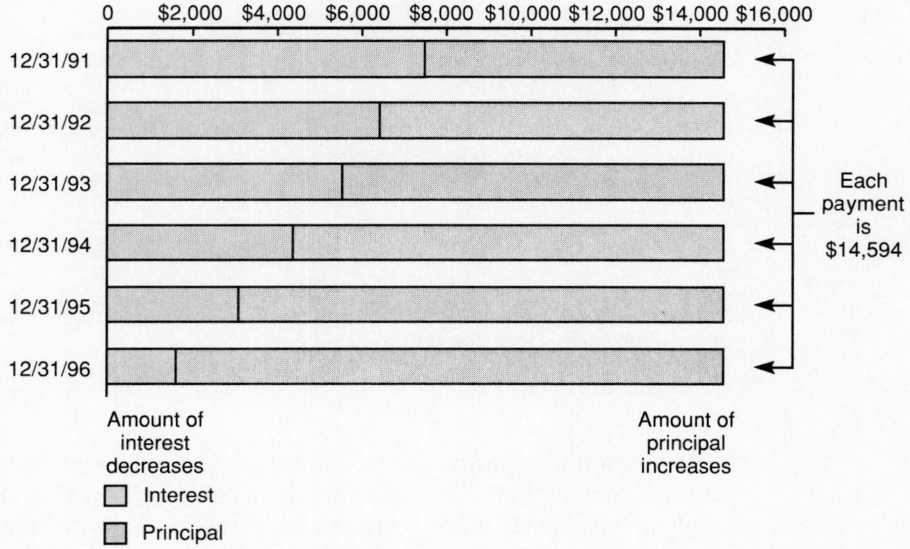


### Installment Payments that Are Equal in Total Amount

*At this point, if you are not sure of your understanding of the concept of present value, you should turn back to Chapter 12 and review this concept. Also, for additional study of discounting, Appendix G (at the end of the book) contains an expanded analysis of present and future values.*

Many installment notes require a series of payments where the total amount of each payment is equal to each of the other payments. Since the payments are equal in amount, they consist of changing amounts of interest and principal. For example, assume that the $60,000, 12% note does not require six principal payments of $10,000 each plus accrued interest. Instead, assume that the note requires a series of six equal payments to be made at the end of each year. Each payment is to be $14,594. The amount of each payment is $14,594 because $60,000 is the present value of $14,594 to be paid annually for six years, discounted at 12%. (In this chapter, all dollar amounts are rounded to the nearest whole dollar.)

**Allocating Each Payment between Interest and Principal.** Each payment of $14,594 includes both interest and principal. The allocation of each payment between interest and principal is shown graphically in Illustration 17–1. Notice that the interest included in each payment is less than the interest in the previous payment. Therefore, since each payment consists of interest and principal, the declining amount of interest is matched by an increasing amount of principal.

**Illustration 17–2**
**Installment note amortization schedule**

| Period Ending | (a) Beginning-of-Period Principal Balance | (b) Periodic Payment | (c) Interest Expense for the Period (a) × 12% | (d) Portion of Payment that Is Principal (b) − (c) | (e) End-of-Period Principal Balance (a) − (d) |
|---|---|---|---|---|---|
| 12/31/91 . . . . | $60,000 | $14,594 | $7,200 | $ 7,394 | $52,606 |
| 12/31/92 . . . . | 52,606 | 14,594 | 6,313 | 8,281 | 44,325 |
| 12/31/93 . . . . | 44,325 | 14,594 | 5,319 | 9,275 | 35,050 |
| 12/31/94 . . . . | 35,050 | 14,594 | 4,206 | 10,388 | 24,662 |
| 12/31/95 . . . . | 24,662 | 14,594 | 2,959 | 11,635 | 13,027 |
| 12/31/96 . . . . | 13,027 | 14,590* | 1,563 | 13,027 | –0– |

*Note that the final payment is $4 smaller than the first five payments due to rounding. Although the note called for equal payments, a minor adjustment to the final payment is commonly necessary to repay the exact amount of debt.

Illustration 17–2 shows you how to calculate the changing amounts of interest and principal. Because the presentation in Illustration 17–2 shows how the principal balance is reduced through the periodic payments, the presentation is sometimes called an *installment note amortization schedule*.

In Illustration 17–2, observe that interest expense is calculated each period as 12% multiplied by the beginning-of-period principal balance. Then, the interest expense is subtracted from the periodic payment to determine the portion of the payment that is a repayment of principal. Each number in the table is rounded to the nearest whole dollar.

The journal entry to record the first periodic payment is:

| | | | | |
|---|---|---|---|---|
| 1991 | | | | |
| Dec. | 31 | Notes Payable . . . . . . . . . . . . . . . . . . . . . . | 7,394.00 | |
| | | Interest Expense . . . . . . . . . . . . . . . . . . . . | 7,200.00 | |
| | | Cash . . . . . . . . . . . . . . . . . . . . . . . . | | 14,594.00 |
| | | To record first installment payment. | | |

Similar entries are used to record each of the remaining payments.

**How to Calculate the Periodic Payments.** In the example, the $60,000, 12% loan required six annual payments of $14,594. Illustration 17–2 proves that these payments are precisely the amounts needed to repay the loan. But, how do you calculate the $14,594?

The correct amount of the periodic payments may be calculated by using a table for the present value of $1 received (or paid) periodically for a number of periods. (See Table 12–2 on page 514.) In Table 12–2, the present value of $1 paid at the end of each year for six years, discounted at 12%, is $4.1114. This relationship between the periodic payments of $1 and the present value of $4.1114 may be expressed as a ratio, as follows:

$$\frac{\text{Periodic payment}}{\text{Present value}} = \frac{1}{4.1114}$$

This ratio of periodic payments to present value is the same for all situations in which six payments ($n = 6$) are discounted at an interest rate of 12% ($i =$ 12%). In other words, when the present value is \$60,000, the periodic payments can be calculated as follows:

$$\frac{\text{Periodic payment}}{\$60{,}000} = \frac{1}{4.1114}$$

$$\text{Periodic payment} = \frac{\$60{,}000 \times 1}{4.1114} = \$14{,}593.57\text{, or } \$14{,}594$$

## Borrowing by Issuing Bonds

Corporations often borrow money by issuing **bonds.**[1] Like notes payable, bonds involve a written promise to pay interest and principal or **par value.** The par value, also called the **face amount,** is printed on the bond. The interest rate stated on the bond is applied to the par value to determine the annual interest to be paid. Also, the par value is the amount that is repaid when the bond matures. Most bonds require that the borrower pay interest semiannually and repay the par value at a fixed future date (the maturity date).

### Difference between Notes Payable and Bonds

When a business (or an individual) borrows money by signing a note payable, the money is generally borrowed from a single creditor such as a bank. In contrast to a note payable, a bond issue typically includes a large number of bonds, usually in denominations of \$1,000, that are sold to many different lenders. After they are originally issued, bonds are frequently bought and sold by investors and may be owned by a number of people before they mature.

### Difference between Stocks and Bonds

The phrase *stocks and bonds* commonly appears on the financial pages of newspapers and is often a topic of conversation. However, the difference between stocks and bonds should be clearly understood. A share of stock represents an equity or ownership right in a corporation. For example, if a person owns 1,000 of the 10,000 shares a corporation has outstanding, the person has an equity in the corporation measured at 1/10 of the corporation's total stockholders' equity. Also, the person has an equity in 1/10 of the corporation's earnings. On the other hand, if a person owns a \$1,000, 11%, 20-year bond issued by a corporation, the bond represents a debt or a liability of the corporation. The owner of the bond has two rights: (1) the right to receive 11% or \$110 interest each year the bond is outstanding and (2) the right to be paid \$1,000 when the bond matures 20 years after its date of issue.

[1] The federal government and other governmental units, such as cities, states, and school districts, also issue bonds. Although the examples in this chapter are of bonds issued by business corporations, the methods used to account for bonds are the same for all organizations.

**Illustration 17–3**
**Financing with stock or with bonds**

| | Plan A | Plan B |
|---|---|---|
| Earnings before bond interest and income taxes | $ 900,000 | $ 900,000 |
| Deduct interest expense | | (100,000) |
| Income before corporation income taxes | $ 900,000 | $ 800,000 |
| Deduct income taxes (assumed 40% rate) | (360,000) | (320,000) |
| Net income | $ 540,000 | $ 480,000 |
| Plan A income per share (300,000 shares) | $1.80 | |
| Plan B income per share (200,000 shares) | | $2.40 |

## Why Issue Bonds Instead of Stock

A corporation that needs long-term funds may consider issuing additional shares of stock or issuing bonds. Each has its advantages and disadvantages. Present stockholders may see the issuance of additional shares as a disadvantage if the shares are issued to new stockholders. Since the new stockholders are owners, the additional stock spreads ownership, control of management, and earnings over more shares. Bondholders, on the other hand, are creditors and do not share in either management or earnings. However, a disadvantage of issuing bonds is that the interest on the bonds must be paid whether or not there are any earnings.

A potential advantage of issuing bonds instead of stock is that if bonds are issued, the result may be increased earnings for the common stockholders. For example, assume a corporation that has 200,000 shares of common stock outstanding needs $1 million to expand its operations. Management estimates that after the expansion, the company can earn $900,000 annually before bond interest, if any, and before corporation income taxes. Two plans for securing the needed funds are proposed. Plan A calls for issuing 100,000 additional shares of the corporation's common stock at $10 per share. This will increase the total outstanding shares to 300,000. Plan B calls for the sale at par of $1 million of 10% bonds. Illustration 17–3 shows how the plans will affect the corporation's earnings.

Corporations must pay federal income taxes and in some states also must pay state income taxes. These federal and state taxes may amount to as much as 40% or more of the corporation's before-tax income. However, interest expense is a deductible expense in arriving at income subject to taxes. Therefore, when the combined state and federal tax rate is 40%, as in Illustration 17–3, the tax reduction from issuing bonds equals 40% of the annual interest on the bonds. In other words, the tax saving in effect pays 40% of the interest cost.

## Characteristics of Bonds

Over the years, corporation lawyers and financiers have created a wide variety of bonds, each with different combinations of characteristics. We describe some of the more common characteristics of different bond issues in the following paragraphs.

## AS A MATTER OF FACT

Washington—Congressional tax writers, who appear increasingly eager to curb leveraged buy-outs, are moving toward a two-pronged plan that would curtail tax benefits for corporate debt while creating a new tax break for dividends.

* * * * *

"There's the understanding that something is going to be done," Chairman Dan Rostenkowski (D., Ill.) of the House Ways and Means Committee said in an interview. And of the plan to touch both debt and equity, he added, "You have some heavy horses pulling that cart."

Still, the tax writers said caution would be their watchword. No one has yet devised a widely accepted way to trim the deduction for corporate interest payments. How much to provide in tax relief for dividend payments—and how to structure the change—also remains unresolved. "It's a long, long bumpy road," to enactment of legislation, said a senior Democratic aide in the Senate.

* * * * *

At the Senate Finance Committee hearing, David Ruder, chairman of the Securities and Exchange Commission, argued that leveraged buy-outs have helped the economy overall, but he expressed concern about increasing levels of corporate debt. He endorsed the concept of treating equity and debt equally under the tax code.

In a leveraged buy-out, a group of investors takes a company private largely with borrowed money. The borrowings are later repaid with profits from the company's operations or sales of its assets. In the past few years such transactions have proliferated, and lawmakers have grown increasingly restive about them.

* * * * *

Congressional leaders say they worry that corporations taken private in leveraged buy-outs could be vulnerable to calamity should the economy turn sour. They also question whether executives are unduly profiting from the transactions at the expense of the shareholders.

Lawmakers will be wrestling with how to curtail these types of takeovers over the next several months. Wall Street firms have expressed worry that legislators would change the tax treatment of equity and debt.

* * * * *

SEC Chairman Ruder said in an interview after the hearing that modifying the tax treatment of debt and equity might not significantly rein in leveraged buy-outs. He said SEC economists have tentatively concluded that the acquiring parties in most buy-outs are more concerned with the target company's cash flow than in adding debt in order to escape taxes related to equity.

Source: Jeffrey H. Birnbaum and Paul Duke, Jr., "Tax Writers Move on Plan to Curb LBOs," *The Wall Street Journal,* January 26, 1989, p. A2. Reprinted by permission of *The Wall Street Journal,* 

### Serial Bonds

Describe the various characteristics of differing bond issues and prepare entries to record bonds that are issued between interest dates. (L. O. 2)

Some bond issues include bonds that mature at different points in time so that the entire bond issue is repaid gradually over a period of years. Bonds of this type are called **serial bonds.** For example, a $1 million issue of serial bonds may include $100,000 of bonds that mature each year from year 6 through year 15.

### Sinking Fund Bonds

In contrast to serial bonds, **sinking fund bonds** all mature on the same date. However, sinking fund bonds require that a separate pool of assets (a sinking fund) be established specifically for the purpose of providing the cash necessary to retire the bonds at maturity. We will discuss bond sinking funds later in this chapter.

### Coupon Bonds

Interest payments on registered bonds are usually made by checks mailed to the registered owners. If interest is not paid in this manner, the bonds are called **coupon bonds**. Coupon bonds obtain their name from the interest coupons attached to each bond. Each coupon calls for payment on the interest payment date of the interest due on the bond. The coupons are detached as they become due and are deposited with a bank for collection.

### Registered Bonds and Bearer Bonds

Most bonds are registered, which means that the name and address of the owner of a **registered bond** are recorded with the issuing corporation. This offers some protection from loss or theft. If bonds are not registered, they are made payable to bearer and are called **bearer bonds**. Whoever holds bearer bonds is presumed to be the rightful owner of the bonds. Generally, bearer bonds are also coupon bonds so that the holder of the bonds receives interest payments by clipping the coupons and depositing them with a bank for collection. At maturity, the holder or bearer usually follows the same process and deposits the bond certificates with a bank for collection.

### Secured Bonds and Debentures

When bonds are secured, specific assets of the issuing corporation are pledged or mortgaged to be sold, if necessary, to repay the bonds. Mortgages are discussed later in this chapter. Unsecured bonds that depend on the general credit standing of the issuing corporation for security are called **debentures**. A company generally must be financially strong if it is to successfully issue unsecured bonds.

## The Process of Issuing Bonds

When a corporation issues bonds, it normally sells the bonds to an investment firm called the *underwriter*. The underwriter in turn resells the bonds to the public. The legal document that states the rights and obligations of the company and the bondholders is called the **bond indenture**. In other words, the bond indenture is the written, legal contract between the issuing company and the bondholders. Each bondholder receives a *bond certificate* which is evidence of the corporation's debt to the bondholder.

When bonds are going to be issued to a large number of bondholders, they are represented by a *trustee*. The trustee monitors the corporation's actions so that the corporation fulfills its obligations as stated in the bond indenture. In most cases, the trustee is a large bank or trust company that is selected by the issuing company.

### Accounting for the Issuance of Bonds

When a corporation issues bonds, the bond certificates are printed and the indenture is drawn and deposited with the trustee of the bondholders. At that point, a memorandum describing the bond issue is commonly entered in the Bonds Payable account. Such a memorandum might read, "Authorized to issue $8 million of 9%, 20-year bonds dated January 1, 19—, and with interest payable semiannually on each July 1 and January 1.'' Note that the bonds in this example are typical of most bonds in that interest is payable semiannually.

After the bond indenture is deposited with the trustee of the bondholders, all or a portion of the bonds may be sold. If all are sold at their par value, an entry like the following is made to record the sale:

| | | | | |
|---|---|---|---|---|
| Jan. | 1 | Cash | 8,000,000.00 | |
| | | Bonds Payable | | 8,000,000.00 |
| | | Sold 9%, 20-year bonds at par on their interest date. | | |

When the semiannual interest is paid on these bonds, the transaction is recorded as follows:

| | | | | |
|---|---|---|---|---|
| July | 1 | Interest Expense | 360,000.00 | |
| | | Cash | | 360,000.00 |
| | | Paid the semiannual interest on the bonds. | | |

And when the bonds are paid at maturity, an entry like the following is made:

| | | | | |
|---|---|---|---|---|
| Jan. | 1 | Bonds Payable | 8,000,000.00 | |
| | | Cash | | 8,000,000.00 |
| | | Paid bonds at maturity. | | |

## Bonds Sold between Interest Dates

Sometimes bonds are sold on their date of issue, which is also their interest date, as in the previous illustration. More often they are sold after their date of issue and between interest dates. In such cases, it is customary to charge and collect from the purchasers the interest that has accrued on the bonds since the last interest payment date and to return this accrued interest to the purchasers on the next interest date. For example, assume that on March 1, a corporation sold at par $100,000 of 9% bonds on which interest is payable semiannually on each January 1 and July 1. The entry to record the sale between interest dates is:

| | | | | |
|---|---|---|---|---|
| Mar. | 1 | Cash | 101,500.00 | |
| | | Interest Payable | | 1,500.00 |
| | | Bonds Payable | | 100,000.00 |
| | | Sold $100,000 of 9%, 20-year bonds on which two months' interest has accrued | | |

At the end of four months, on the July 1 semiannual interest date, the purchasers of these bonds are paid a full six months' interest. This payment includes four months' interest earned by the bondholders after March 1 and the two months' accrued interest collected from them at the time the bonds were sold. The entry to record the payment is:

| | | | | |
|---|---|---|---|---|
| July | 1 | Interest Payable | 1,500.00 | |
| | | Interest Expense | 3,000.00 | |
| | | Cash | | 4,500.00 |
| | | Paid the semiannual interest on the bonds. | | |

It may seem strange to charge bond purchasers for accrued interest and then to return this accrued interest in the next interest payment. However, bond transactions are made on a "plus accrued interest" basis because it is easier for the bond issuer. For instance, if a corporation sold bonds on a variety of dates during an interest period and did not collect accrued interest, it would have to keep records of the purchasers and the dates on which they bought their bonds. Otherwise, it could not pay the correct amount of interest to each bondholder. However, if each buyer is charged for accrued interest at the time of purchase, the corporation does not have to keep records of the purchasers and their purchase dates. It can pay a full period's interest to all purchasers for the period in which they bought their bonds; each receives the interest earned and gets back the accrued interest paid at the time of the purchase.

## Bond Interest Rates

A corporation issuing bonds specifies in the bond indenture and on each bond certificate the interest rate to be paid. This rate is called the **contract rate.** Even though bond interest normally is paid semiannually, the contract rate usually is stated on an annual basis. The contract rate of interest is applied to the par value of the bonds to determine the amount of interest to be paid each year. For example, if a corporation issues a $1,000, 8% bond on which interest is paid semiannually, $80 will be paid each year in two semiannual installments of $40 each.

Although the contract rate establishes the interest a corporation will pay, it is not necessarily the interest the corporation will incur in issuing bonds. The interest it will incur depends on what lenders consider their risks will be in lending to the corporation and on the current **market rate for bond interest** available to the corporation. The market rate for bond interest is the rate borrowers are willing to pay and lenders are willing to take for the use of money at the level of risk involved. It fluctuates daily as the supply and demand for loanable funds fluctuate. It goes up when the demand for bond money increases and the supply decreases, and it goes down when the supply increases and the demand decreases.

Also, note that on any single day, the market rate for bond interest is not the same for all corporations. The rate for a specific corporation's bonds depends on the level of risk investors attach to those bonds. As the level of risk increases, the rate increases.

In many cases, the corporation issuing bonds offers a contract rate of interest equal to what it estimates the market will demand on the day the bonds are to be issued. If its estimate is correct and the contract rate and market rate coincide on the day the bonds are issued, the bonds will sell at par, their face amount. However, when bonds are sold, their contract rate may not coincide with the market rate. As a result, bonds often sell at a discount or at a premium. Sometimes, the issuing corporation offers a contract rate that results in very large discounts.

## Bonds Sold at a Discount

Calculate the price of a bond issue that sells at a discount and prepare entries to account for bonds issued at a discount. (L. O. 3)

A **discount on bonds payable** results when a corporation issues and sells bonds that have a contract rate below the prevailing market rate. Given the level of risk, investors can get the market rate of interest elsewhere for the use of their money. So they will buy the bonds only at a price that will yield the prevailing market rate on the investment. In other words, to determine the price of the bonds, you discount the cash flows from the bond investment at the current market rate for bond interest. The price of the bonds is the *present value* of the expected cash flows.

To illustrate how bond prices are determined, assume that on a day when the market rate for bond interest is 9%, a corporation offers to sell and issue bonds that have a $100,000 par value, a 10-year life, and on which interest will be paid semiannually at an 8% annual rate.[2] In exchange for current dollars, the buyers of these bonds obtain the right to receive two different future cash inflows. They are:

1. The right to receive $100,000 at the end of the bond issue's 10-year life.
2. The right to receive $4,000 in interest at the end of each 6-month interest period throughout the 10-year life of the bonds.

To determine the price of the bonds, you must calculate the present value of the future cash flows by discounting the amounts to be received at the market rate of interest. If the market rate is 9% annually, it is 4½% semiannually; and in 10 years, there are 20 semiannual periods. Therefore, you use the last number in the 4½% column of Table 12–1, page 512, to discount the $100,000 receipt; and you use the last number in the 4½% column of Table 12–2, page 514, to discount the series of $4,000 amounts. The present value of these cash flows and the price informed buyers will offer for the bonds is:

| | |
|---|---|
| Present value of $100,000 to be received 20 periods hence, discounted at 4½% per period ($100,000 × 0.4146) . . . | $41,460 |
| Present value of $4,000 to be received periodically for 20 periods, discounted at 4½% ($4,000 × 13.0079) . . . . . | 52,032 |
| Present value of the bonds . . . . . . . . . . . . . . . . . . | $93,492 |

If the corporation accepts the $93,492 offered for its bonds and sells them on their date of issue, the sale will be recorded with an entry like this:

[2] The spread between the contract rate and the market rate of interest on a new bond issue is seldom more than a fraction of a percent. However, a spread of a full percent is used here to simplify the illustrations.

| | | | | |
|---|---|---|---|---|
| Jan. | 1 | Cash | 93,492.00 | |
| | | Discount on Bonds Payable | 6,508.00 | |
| | | Bonds Payable | | 100,000.00 |
| | | Sold 8%, 10-year bonds at a discount on their date of issue. | | |

If the corporation prepares financial statements on the day the bonds are sold, the bonds will appear in the long-term liability section of the balance sheet as follows:

| | | |
|---|---|---|
| Long-term liabilities: | | |
| First-mortgage, 8% bonds payable, due January 1, 2001 | $100,000 | |
| Less unamortized discount based on the 9% market rate for bond interest prevailing on the date of issue | 6,508 | $93,492 |

On a balance sheet, any unamortized discount on bonds payable is deducted from the par value of the bonds to show the **carrying amount of the bonds payable**, which is the amount at which the bonds are recorded in the books.

### Amortizing the Discount

In the discussion above, the corporation received $93,492 for its bonds, but in 10 years it must pay the bondholders $100,000. The difference, the $6,508 discount, is a cost of using the $93,492. This cost is incurred because the contract rate of interest on the bonds was below the prevailing market rate. It is a cost that must be paid when the bonds mature. However, each semiannual interest period in the life of the bond issue benefits from the use of the $93,492. Therefore, each period should bear a fair share of this cost.

**Straight-Line Method.** The process of allocating a discount among the periods in the life of the bond issue is called *amortizing* the discount. A simple amortization method is the **straight-line method of amortizing bond discount or premium.** This method allocates an equal portion of the discount to each interest period. To apply the straight-line method in the present example, you divide the $6,508 discount by 20, the number of interest periods in the life of the bond issue. The $325 answer ($6,508 ÷ 20 = $325.40, or $325)[3] is the amount of discount to be amortized at the end of each interest period. The periodic amortization of discount is recorded with the semiannual cash payment of interest, as follows:

| | | | | |
|---|---|---|---|---|
| July | 1 | Interest Expense | 4,325.00 | |
| | | Discount on Bonds Payable | | 325.00 |
| | | Cash | | 4,000.00 |
| | | To record payment of six months' interest and amortization of the discount. | | |

[3] In this chapter and in the problems at the end of the chapter, all calculations involving bonds have been rounded to the nearest whole dollar.

**Illustration 17–4**
**Calculation of interest expense and bond discount amortization: straight-line method**

| Period | Beginning-of-Period Carrying Amount | Interest Expense to Be Recorded | Interest to Be Paid the Bondholders | Discount to Be Amortized | Unamortized Discount at End of Period | End-of-Period Carrying Amount |
|---|---|---|---|---|---|---|
| 1 . . . . | $93,492 | $4,325 | $4,000 | $325 | $6,183 | $ 93,817 |
| 2 . . . . | 93,817 | 4,325 | 4,000 | 325 | 5,858 | 94,142 |
| 3 . . . . | 94,142 | 4,325 | 4,000 | 325 | 5,533 | 94,467 |
| 4 . . . . | 94,467 | 4,325 | 4,000 | 325 | 5,208 | 94,792 |
| 5 . . . . | 94,792 | 4,325 | 4,000 | 325 | 4,883 | 95,117 |
| 6 . . . . | 95,117 | 4,325 | 4,000 | 325 | 4,558 | 95,442 |
| 7 . . . . | 95,442 | 4,325 | 4,000 | 325 | 4,233 | 95,767 |
| 8 . . . . | 95,767 | 4,325 | 4,000 | 325 | 3,908 | 96,092 |
| 9 . . . . | 96,092 | 4,325 | 4,000 | 325 | 3,583 | 96,417 |
| 10 . . . . | 96,417 | 4,325 | 4,000 | 325 | 3,258 | 96,742 |
| 11 . . . . | 96,742 | 4,325 | 4,000 | 325 | 2,933 | 97,067 |
| 12 . . . . | 97,067 | 4,325 | 4,000 | 325 | 2,608 | 97,392 |
| 13 . . . . | 97,392 | 4,325 | 4,000 | 325 | 2,283 | 97,717 |
| 14 . . . . | 97,717 | 4,325 | 4,000 | 325 | 1,958 | 98,042 |
| 15 . . . . | 98,042 | 4,325 | 4,000 | 325 | 1,633 | 98,367 |
| 16 . . . . | 98,367 | 4,325 | 4,000 | 325 | 1,308 | 98,692 |
| 17 . . . . | 98,692 | 4,325 | 4,000 | 325 | 983 | 99,017 |
| 18 . . . . | 99,017 | 4,325 | 4,000 | 325 | 658 | 99,342 |
| 19 . . . . | 99,342 | 4,325 | 4,000 | 325 | 333 | 99,667 |
| 20 . . . . | 99,667 | 4,333* | 4,000 | 333* | –0– | 100,000 |

*Adjusted to compensate for accumulated rounding of amounts.

Illustration 17–4 shows the interest expense to be recorded, the discount to be amortized, and so forth, when the straight-line method is applied to the present example. In Illustration 17–4, notice the following points:

1. The bonds were sold at a $6,508 discount, which when subtracted from their face amount gives a beginning-of-period-1 carrying amount of $93,492.
2. The semiannual $4,325 interest expense amounts equal $4,000 paid to bondholders plus $325 amortization of discount.
3. Interest paid to bondholders each period is determined by multiplying the par value of the bonds by the contract rate of interest ($100,000 × 4% = $4,000).
4. The discount amortized each period is $6,508 ÷ 20 = $325.40, or $325.
5. The unamortized discount at the end of each period is determined by subtracting the discount amortized that period from the unamortized discount at the beginning of the period.
6. The end-of-period carrying amount of the bonds is determined by subtracting the end-of-period amount of unamortized discount from the face amount of the bonds. For example, at the end of period 1: $100,000 – $6,183 = $93,817.

Straight-line amortization once was generally accepted. However, generally accepted accounting principles now allow the straight-line method only

**Illustration 17–5**
**Calculation of interest expense and bond discount amortization: interest method**

| Period | Beginning-of-Period Carrying Amount | Interest Expense to Be Recorded | Interest to Be Paid the Bondholders | Discount to Be Amortized | Unamortized Discount at End of Period | End-of-Period Carrying Amount |
|---|---|---|---|---|---|---|
| 1 . . . . | $93,492 | $4,207 | $4,000 | $207 | $6,301 | $ 93,699 |
| 2 . . . . | 93,699 | 4,216 | 4,000 | 216 | 6,085 | 93,915 |
| 3 . . . . | 93,915 | 4,226 | 4,000 | 226 | 5,859 | 94,141 |
| 4 . . . . | 94,141 | 4,236 | 4,000 | 236 | 5,623 | 94,377 |
| 5 . . . . | 94,377 | 4,247 | 4,000 | 247 | 5,376 | 94,624 |
| 6 . . . . | 94,624 | 4,258 | 4,000 | 258 | 5,118 | 94,882 |
| 7 . . . . | 94,882 | 4,270 | 4,000 | 270 | 4,848 | 95,152 |
| 8 . . . . | 95,152 | 4,282 | 4,000 | 282 | 4,566 | 95,434 |
| 9 . . . . | 95,434 | 4,295 | 4,000 | 295 | 4,271 | 95,729 |
| 10 . . . . | 95,729 | 4,308 | 4,000 | 308 | 3,963 | 96,037 |
| 11 . . . . | 96,037 | 4,322 | 4,000 | 322 | 3,641 | 96,359 |
| 12 . . . . | 96,359 | 4,336 | 4,000 | 336 | 3,305 | 96,695 |
| 13 . . . . | 96,695 | 4,351 | 4,000 | 351 | 2,954 | 97,046 |
| 14 . . . . | 97,046 | 4,367 | 4,000 | 367 | 2,587 | 97,413 |
| 15 . . . . | 97,413 | 4,384 | 4,000 | 384 | 2,203 | 97,797 |
| 16 . . . . | 97,797 | 4,401 | 4,000 | 401 | 1,802 | 98,198 |
| 17 . . . . | 98,198 | 4,419 | 4,000 | 419 | 1,383 | 98,617 |
| 18 . . . . | 98,617 | 4,438 | 4,000 | 438 | 945 | 99,055 |
| 19 . . . . | 99,055 | 4,457 | 4,000 | 457 | 488 | 99,512 |
| 20 . . . . | 99,512 | 4,488* | 4,000 | 488 | –0– | 100,000 |

*Adjusted to compensate for accumulated rounding of amounts.

when the results do not materially differ from those obtained through use of the **interest method of amortizing bond discount or premium.**[4]

**Interest Method.** When the interest method is used, the amount of recorded interest expense changes each period. To calculate the amount of interest expense each period, you must multiply the beginning-of-period carrying amount of the bonds by a constant rate of interest. The constant interest rate is the market rate for the bonds at the time the bonds were issued.

After interest expense for a period is calculated, you can determine the amount of discount to be amortized. This is calculated by subtracting the cash payment of interest from the interest expense. Illustration 17–5 shows the interest expense to be recorded, the cash payment of interest, the discount to be amortized, and the remaining balance sheet amounts when the interest method is applied to the bonds in this discussion.

Compare Illustration 17–5 with 17–4 and note these unique aspects of the interest method as shown in Illustration 17–5.

1. The interest expense amounts result from multiplying each beginning-of-period carrying amount by the 4½% semiannual market rate that prevailed when the bonds were issued. For example, $93,492 × 4½% = $4,207 and $93,699 × 4½% = $4,216.

[4] FASB, *Accounting Standards—Current Text* (Norwalk, Conn., 1988), sec. I69.108. First published in *APB Opinion No. 21*, par. 15.

2. The discount to be amortized each period is determined by subtracting the amount of interest to be paid the bondholders from the amount of interest expense.

When the interest method is used to amortize a discount, the periodic amortizing entries are like the entries used with the straight-line method; only the dollar amounts are different. For example, the entry to pay the bondholders and amortize a portion of the discount at the end of the first semiannual interest period of the bond issue in Illustration 17–5 is:

| | | | | |
|---|---|---|---|---|
| July | 1 | Interest Expense . . . . . . . . . . . . . . . . . . . . . . | 4,207.00 | |
| | | Discount on Bonds Payable . . . . . . . . . . . . | | 207.00 |
| | | Cash . . . . . . . . . . . . . . . . . . . . . . . . . | | 4,000.00 |
| | | To record payment to the bondholders and amortization of a portion of the discount. | | |

Similar entries, differing only in the amount of interest expense recorded and discount amortized, are made at the end of each semiannual interest period in the life of the bond issue.

Consider the differences between the interest method of amortizing a discount and the straight-line method (previously discussed). The following table shows these financial statement differences:

| | Interest-Method Amortization | | | Straight-Line Amortization | | |
|---|---|---|---|---|---|---|
| Period | Beginning-of-Period Carrying Amount | Interest Expense to Be Recorded | Interest Expense as a Percentage of Carrying Amount | Beginning-of-Period Carrying Amount | Interest Expense to Be Recorded | Interest Expense as a Percentage of Carrying Amount |
| 1 . . | $93,492 | $4,207 | 4.5 | $93,492 | $4,325 | 4.63 |
| 11 . . | 96,037 | 4,322 | 4.5 | 96,742 | 4,325 | 4.47 |
| 19 . . | 99,055 | 4,457 | 4.5 | 99,342 | 4,325 | 4.35 |

The table shows the beginning-of-period carrying amount of the bond liability and the interest expense for each of three six-month periods during the life of the bonds. The first three columns of the table show that in every six-month period, the interest method provides an interest expense amount that is 4.5% of the beginning-of-period carrying amount. The last three columns show the amounts that you get if you use the straight-line method. Observe that when the straight-line method is used, the percentage changes each period. Recall that the bonds were issued at a price that reflected a discounting of cash flows at 4.5% per six-month period. The interest method is most consistent with this fact; and it is the preferred method.

Because the above example involves a bond discount, the straight-line method causes a declining percentage. When a premium is amortized, the straight-line method results in an increasing percentage. In either case, however, the straight-line method can be used only where the results do not differ materially from those obtained through use of the interest method.

## Bonds Sold at a Premium

Prepare entries to account for bonds issued at a premium.
(L. O. 4)

When a corporation offers to sell bonds that carry a contract rate of interest above the prevailing market rate for the risks involved, the bonds will sell at a **premium.** Buyers will bid up the price of the bonds, going as high, but no higher, than a price that will return the current market rate of interest on the investment. What price will they pay? They will pay the present value of the expected cash flows from the investment, determined by discounting these cash flows at the market rate of interest for the bonds. For example, assume that on a given day a corporation offers to sell bonds that have a $100,000 par value and a 10-year life. The interest is to be paid semiannually at an 11% annual rate. On the day of issue, the market rate of interest for the corporation's bonds is 10%. Buyers of these bonds will discount the expected receipt of $100,000, 20 six-month periods hence, and the expected receipt of $5,500 semiannually for 20 periods at the current market rate of 5% per six-month period, as follows:

| | |
|---|---|
| Present value of $100,000 to be received 20 periods hence, discounted at 5% per period ($100,000 × 0.3769) . . . . | $ 37,690 |
| Present value of $5,500 to be received periodically for 20 periods, discounted at 5% ($5,500 × 12.4622) . . . . | 68,542 |
| Present value of the bonds . . . . . . . . . . . . . . . . . | $106,232 |

Investors will offer the corporation a total of $106,232 for its bonds. If the corporation accepts and sells the bonds on their date of issue, say, May 1, 1990, it will record the sale as follows:

| | | | | |
|---|---|---|---|---|
| 1990 | | | | |
| May | 1 | Cash . . . . . . . . . . . . . . . . . . . . . . . . . . . . | 106,232.00 | |
| | | Premium on Bonds Payable . . . . . . . . . . . . | | 6,232.00 |
| | | Bonds Payable . . . . . . . . . . . . . . . . . . . . | | 100,000.00 |
| | | Sold bonds at a premium on their date of issue. | | |

It may then show the bonds on a balance sheet prepared on the day of the sale as follows:

| | | |
|---|---|---|
| Long-term liabilities: | | |
| First-mortgage, 11% bonds payable, due May 1, 2000 . . | $100,000 | |
| Add unamortized premium based on the 10% market rate for bond interest prevailing on the date of issue . . . . . . . . . . . . . . . . . . . . . . . . . | 6,323 | $106,232 |

On a balance sheet, any unamortized premium on bonds payable is added to the par value of the bonds to show the carrying amount of the bonds, as illustrated.

### Amortizing the Premium

In the present example, the corporation received $106,232 for its bonds. However, when the bonds mature, the corporation will have to repay only $100,000. The difference, the $6,232 premium, represents a reduction in the cost of using the $106,232. It should be amortized over the life of the bond issue

**Illustration 17–6**
**Calculation of interest expense and bond premium amortization: interest method**

| Period | Beginning-of-Period Carrying Amount | Interest Expense to Be Recorded | Interest to Be Paid the Bondholders | Premium to Be Amortized | Unamortized Premium at End of Period | End-of-Period Carrying Amount |
|---|---|---|---|---|---|---|
| 1 . . . . | $106,232 | $5,312 | $5,500 | $188 | $6,044 | $106,044 |
| 2 . . . . | 106,044 | 5,302 | 5,500 | 198 | 5,846 | 105,846 |
| 3 . . . . | 105,846 | 5,292 | 5,500 | 208 | 5,638 | 105,638 |
| 4 . . . . | 105,638 | 5,282 | 5,500 | 218 | 5,420 | 105,420 |
| 5 . . . . | 105,420 | 5,271 | 5,500 | 229 | 5,191 | 105,191 |
| 6 . . . . | 105,191 | 5,260 | 5,500 | 240 | 4,951 | 104,951 |
| 7 . . . . | 104,951 | 5,248 | 5,500 | 252 | 4,699 | 104,699 |
| 8 . . . . | 104,699 | 5,235 | 5,500 | 265 | 4,434 | 104,434 |
| 9 . . . . | 104,434 | 5,222 | 5,500 | 278 | 4,156 | 104,156 |
| 10 . . . . | 104,156 | 5,208 | 5,500 | 292 | 3,864 | 103,864 |
| 11 . . . . | 103,864 | 5,193 | 5,500 | 307 | 3,557 | 103,557 |
| 12 . . . . | 103,557 | 5,178 | 5,500 | 322 | 3,235 | 103,235 |
| 13 . . . . | 103,235 | 5,162 | 5,500 | 338 | 2,897 | 102,897 |
| 14 . . . . | 102,897 | 5,145 | 5,500 | 355 | 2,542 | 102,542 |
| 15 . . . . | 102,542 | 5,127 | 5,500 | 373 | 2,169 | 102,169 |
| 16 . . . . | 102,169 | 5,108 | 5,500 | 392 | 1,777 | 101,777 |
| 17 . . . . | 101,777 | 5,089 | 5,500 | 411 | 1,366 | 101,366 |
| 18 . . . . | 101,366 | 5,068 | 5,500 | 432 | 934 | 100,934 |
| 19 . . . . | 100,934 | 5,047 | 5,500 | 453 | 481 | 100,481 |
| 20 . . . . | 100,481 | 5,019* | 5,500 | 481 | –0– | 100,000 |

*Adjusted to compensate for accumulated rounding of amounts.

and have the effect of reducing the recorded interest expense. Illustration 17–6 shows the interest expense and the premium amortization each period when the $6,232 is amortized by the interest method.

Observe in Illustration 17–6 that the premium to be amortized each period is determined by subtracting the interest to be recorded from the interest to be paid the bondholders.

Based on Illustration 17–6, the entry to record the first semiannual interest payment and premium amortization is:

| | | | | |
|---|---|---|---|---|
| 1990 | | | | |
| Nov. | 1 | Interest Expense . . . . . . . . . . . . . . . . . . . . | 5,312.00 | |
| | | Premium on Bonds Payable . . . . . . . . . . . . . . . | 188.00 | |
| | | Cash . . . . . . . . . . . . . . . . . . . . . . . . . | | 5,500.00 |
| | | To record payment of the bondholders and amortization of a portion of the premium. | | |

Note that the amortization of the premium has the effect of reducing interest expense. Similar entries, with decreasing amounts of interest expense and increasing amounts of premium amortized, are made at the end of the remaining periods in the life of the bond issue.

## Accrued Interest Expense

When bonds are sold, the bond interest periods often do not coincide with the issuing company's accounting periods. In these cases, you must make an adjustment for accrued interest at the end of each accounting period. For example, we previously assumed that the bonds of Illustration 17–6 were issued on

May 1, 1990, and interest was first recorded and paid on November 1 of that year. By December 31, 1990, two months' interest has accrued on these bonds. If the accounting period ends on that date, the following adjusting entry is required:

| | | | | |
|---|---|---|---|---|
| 1990 | | | | |
| Dec. | 31 | Interest Expense ($5,302 × 2/6) . . . . . . . . . . . . . | 1,767.00 | |
| | | Premium on Bonds Payable ($198 × 2/6) . . . . . . . . | 66.00 | |
| | | Interest Payable ($5,500 × 2/6) . . . . . . . . . . . | | 1,833.00 |
| | | To record two months' accrued interest and amortize one third of the premium applicable to the interest period. | | |

Two months are one third of a semiannual interest period. Therefore, the amounts in the entry are one third of the amounts applicable to the second interest period in the life of the bond issue. Similar entries will be made on each December 31 throughout the life of the issue. However, the amounts will differ, since in each case they will apply to a different interest period.

On May 1, 1991, the entry to record the semiannual payment of interest is:

| | | | | |
|---|---|---|---|---|
| 1991 | | | | |
| May | 1 | Interest Payable . . . . . . . . . . . . . . . . . . . . . | 1,833.00 | |
| | | Interest Expense ($5,302 × 4/6) . . . . . . . . . . . . . | 3,535.00 | |
| | | Premium on Bonds Payable ($198 × 4/6) . . . . . . . . | 132.00 | |
| | | Cash . . . . . . . . . . . . . . . . . . . . . . . . | | 5,500.00 |
| | | Paid the interest on the bonds, a portion of which was previously accrued, and amortized four months' premium. | | |

## Redemption of Bonds

Bond indentures commonly include a provision that give the issuing corporation the option of redeeming the bonds prior to their maturity date. Often, the provision states that if the corporation calls and redeems the bonds before they mature, the corporation must pay the par value plus a redemption premium. Bonds that can be redeemed at the option of the issuing corporation are known as **callable bonds.** One reason corporations insert redemption clauses in the bond indenture is that if interest rates decline sharply, the corporations can redeem and replace the outstanding bonds with new bonds that pay a lower interest rate.

Not all bonds are callable. However, even though the right is not provided, the issuing corporation often can retire its bonds by purchasing them on the open market. When bonds are redeemed or purchased in the open market by the issuing corporation, the price paid usually is not equal to the carrying value of the bonds. Since the market rate of interest changes as economic conditions change, the present value of a bond's remaining cash flows to the bondholder also changes. Therefore, the price paid to purchase and retire bonds may result in a gain or loss. For example, assume that a company has outstanding $1 million of bonds. After interest is recorded on a given interest date, there remains a $12,000 unamortized premium. The bonds are selling at 98½ (98½% of par value). If the company buys and retires 1/10 of the issue, the entry to record the purchase and retirement is:

| | | | | |
|---|---|---|---|---|
| Apr. | 1 | Bonds Payable | 100,000.00 | |
| | | Premium on Bonds Payable | 1,200.00 | |
| | | Gain on the Retirement of Bonds | | 2,700.00 |
| | | Cash | | 98,500.00 |
| | | To record the retirement of bonds. | | |

In this case, the retirement resulted in a $2,700 gain because the bonds were purchased at a price $2,700 below their carrying value.

In the last paragraph, we stated that the bonds were selling at 98½. Bond quotations are commonly made in this manner. For example, a bond may be quoted for sale at 101¼. This means the bond is for sale at 101¼% of its par value, plus accrued interest, if applicable.

## Bond Sinking Fund

Explain the purpose and operation of a bond sinking fund and prepare entries for sinking fund operations, for the retirement of bonds, and for the conversion of bonds into stock. (L. O. 5)

One reason investors may buy bonds instead of stocks is that bonds usually provide greater security than stocks. Often, a corporation will give additional security to the bondholders by agreeing in the bond indenture to create a **bond sinking fund.** This fund consists of assets that are committed to be used to repay the bondholders at maturity.

When a bond indenture specifies that a bond sinking fund is to be created, the issuing corporation normally is required to make periodic cash deposits with a sinking fund trustee. The trustee's duties are to safeguard the cash, to invest it in securities of reasonably low risk, and to add the interest or dividends earned to the sinking fund. Generally, when the bonds become due, it is also the duty of the sinking fund trustee to sell the sinking fund securities and use the proceeds to pay the bondholders.

When a sinking fund is created, the amount that must be deposited periodically to provide enough money to retire a bond issue at maturity will depend on the net rate of interest that can be earned on the invested funds. It is a net rate because the fee for the trustee's services commonly is deducted from the earnings.

To illustrate the operation of a sinking fund, assume a corporation issues $1 million par value, 10-year bonds. The bond indenture requires that the corporation make annual deposits with a sinking fund trustee at the end of each year in the bond issue's life. Based on the assumption that the trustee will be able to earn an annual return of 8% on the invested assets, net of expenses, the corporation must deposit $69,029 each year.[5] Illustration 17–7 shows that these deposits will generate an amount that is sufficient to retire the bonds at maturity.

When a sinking fund is created by periodic deposits, the entry to record the amount deposited each year appears as follows:

[5] To understand how the periodic deposits to a sinking fund are calculated, you should study Appendix G at the end of the book. Using the "future value of an annuity of 1 per period" table in Appendix G, the payment of $69,029 is calculated as $1,000,000 ÷ 14.486 = $69,029.

**Illustration 17–7**
**Expected asset accumulation of a bond sinking fund that earns 8%**

| End of Year | Beginning-of-Period Sinking Fund Balance | 8% Interest Earned on Fund Balance | Amount Deposited | Total Increase in Sinking Fund | End-of-Period Sinking Fund Balance |
|---|---|---|---|---|---|
| 1 . . . . | $ -0- | $ -0- | $69,029 | $ 69,029 | $ 69,029 |
| 2 . . . . | 69,029 | 5,522 | 69,029 | 74,551 | 143,580 |
| 3 . . . . | 143,580 | 11,486 | 69,029 | 80,515 | 224,095 |
| 4 . . . . | 224,095 | 17,928 | 69,029 | 86,957 | 311,052 |
| 5 . . . . | 311,052 | 24,884 | 69,029 | 93,913 | 404,965 |
| 6 . . . . | 404,965 | 32,397 | 69,029 | 101,426 | 506,391 |
| 7 . . . . | 506,391 | 40,511 | 69,029 | 109,540 | 615,931 |
| 8 . . . . | 615,931 | 49,274 | 69,029 | 118,303 | 734,234 |
| 9 . . . . | 734,234 | 58,739 | 69,029 | 127,768 | 862,002 |
| 10 . . . . | 862,002 | 68,969* | 69,029 | 137,998 | 1,000,000 |

*Adjusted to compensate for accumulated rounding of amounts.

| | | | | |
|---|---|---|---|---|
| Dec. | 31 | Bond Sinking Fund . . . . . . . . . . . . . . . . . . . . | 69,029.00 | |
| | | Cash . . . . . . . . . . . . . . . . . . . . . . . . . . | | 69,029.00 |
| | | To record the annual sinking fund deposit. | | |

The sinking fund trustee invests the amount deposited, and each year the trustee sends to the issuing corporation a report of the earnings on the investments. The corporation then records the sinking fund earnings in its accounts and reports them on its income statement. For example, if $69,029 is deposited at the end of the first year in the sinking fund and 8% is earned, the corporation that issued the bonds records the second year's sinking fund earnings as follows:

| | | | | |
|---|---|---|---|---|
| Year | 2 | | | |
| Dec. | 31 | Bond Sinking Fund . . . . . . . . . . . . . . . . . . . . | 5,522.00 | |
| | | Sinking Fund Earnings . . . . . . . . . . . . . . . | | 5,522.00 |
| | | To record the sinking fund earnings. | | |

A sinking fund is the property of the company that created the fund and should appear on its balance sheet in the long-term investments section.

When bonds mature, it is usually the duty of the sinking fund trustee to convert the fund's investments into cash and pay the bondholders. Normally, the sinking fund securities, when sold, produce either a little more or a little less cash than is needed to pay the bondholders. If more cash than needed is produced, the extra cash is returned to the corporation; and if less cash is produced than needed, the corporation must make up the deficiency. For example, if the securities in the sinking fund of a $1 million bond issue produce $1,001,325 when converted to cash, the trustee will use $1 million to pay the bondholders and will return the extra $1,325 to the corporation. The corporation will then record the payment of its bonds and the return of the extra cash with an entry like the following:

| | | | | |
|---|---|---|---|---|
| Jan. | 3 | Cash | 1,325.00 | |
| | | Bonds Payable | 1,000,000.00 | |
| | | Bond Sinking Fund | | 1,001,325.00 |
| | | To record payment of our bonds and the return of extra cash from the sinking fund. | | |

## Restriction on Dividends Due to Outstanding Bonds

To protect a corporation's financial position and the interests of its bondholders, a bond indenture may restrict the dividends the corporation may pay while its bonds are outstanding. Commonly, the restriction provides that the corporation may pay dividends in any year only to the extent that the year's earnings exceed sinking fund requirements.

## Converting Bonds to Stock

To make a bond issue more attractive, bondholders may be given the right to exchange their bonds for a fixed number of shares of the issuing company's common stock. Such **convertible bonds** offer investors initial investment security, and if the issuing company prospers and its stock increases in price, an opportunity to share in the prosperity by converting their bonds to the more valuable stock. Conversion is always at the bondholders' option and therefore does not take place unless it is to their advantage.

When bonds are converted into stock, the conversion changes a liability into owners' equity. The generally accepted rule for measuring the contribution for the issued shares is that the carrying amount of the converted bonds becomes the book value of the capital contributed for the new shares. For example, assume the following: (1) A company has outstanding $1 million of bonds on which there is $8,000 unamortized discount. (2) The bonds are convertible at the rate of a $1,000 bond for 90 shares of the company's $10 par value common stock. And (3) $100,000 in bonds have been presented on their interest date for conversion. The entry to record the conversion is:

| | | | | |
|---|---|---|---|---|
| May | 1 | Bonds Payable | 100,000.00 | |
| | | Discount on Bonds Payable | | 800.00 |
| | | Common Stock | | 90,000.00 |
| | | Contributed Capital in Excess of Par Value, Common Stock | | 9,200.00 |
| | | To record the conversion of bonds. | | |

Note in this entry that the bonds' $99,200 carrying amount sets the accounting value for the capital contributed. Usually, when bonds have a conversion privilege, it is not exercised until the stock's market value and normal dividend payments are sufficiently high to make the conversion profitable to the bondholders.

## Investments in Bonds

Describe the procedures used to account for investments in bonds. (L. O. 6)

So far, the discussion of bonds has focused on the issuing corporation. We now shift our attention to the purchasers of bonds. When bonds are purchased as an investment, they are recorded at cost, including any brokerage fees. If interest has accrued at the date of purchase, the purchaser also pays for the accrued interest and records it with a debit to Interest Receivable. The entry to record a bond purchase is as follows:

| | | | | |
|---|---|---|---|---|
| May | 1 | Investment in X Corporation Bonds . . . . . . . . . . . | 46,400.00 | |
| | | Interest Receivable . . . . . . . . . . . . . . . . . . . . | 1,500.00 | |
| | | Cash . . . . . . . . . . . . . . . . . . . . . . . . . . | | 47,900.00 |
| | | Purchased 50 $1,000, 9%, 10-year bonds dated December 31, 1990, at a price of 92 plus a $400 brokerage fee and accrued interest. | | |

Note that the $46,400 cost of the bonds was 92% × $50,000 par value plus the $400 brokerage fee, which leaves a discount of $3,600. Most companies do not record the discount (or premium) in a separate account. The investment account is simply debited for the net cost. The accrued interest on May 1 was 4/12 × 9% × $50,000, or $1,500.

### Short-Term Investments in Bonds

Assuming interest is paid semiannually on June 30 and December 31, the entry to record the receipt of interest on June 30 is as follows:

| | | | | |
|---|---|---|---|---|
| June | 30 | Cash . . . . . . . . . . . . . . . . . . . . . . . . . . . | 2,250.00 | |
| | | Interest Receivable . . . . . . . . . . . . . . . . . | | 1,500.00 |
| | | Interest Earned . . . . . . . . . . . . . . . . . . . | | 750.00 |
| | | To record the first semiannual receipt of interest. | | |

This entry correctly reflects the fact that the purchaser owned the bonds for two months during which time interest amounted to 2/12 × 9% × $50,000, or $750. However, recall that the bonds were purchased at a discount and observe that the June 30 entry does not include any amortization of the discount. This is acceptable only if the bonds are held as a short-term, temporary investment. Under these conditions, the bond investment is reported at cost in the current asset section of the balance sheet. The market value of the bonds on the date of the balance sheet should also be disclosed, as follows:

| | |
|---|---|
| Current assets: | |
| Investment in X Corporation bonds (market value is $xx,xxx) . . | $46,400 |

When the bonds are sold, the gain or loss on the sale is calculated as the difference between the sale proceeds and cost.

### Long-Term Investments in Bonds

What if the bonds are held as a long-term investment? In this case, you should expect the market value of the bonds to move generally toward par value as the maturity date approaches. In a similar fashion, any discount (or premium) should be amortized so that each interest period includes some amortization in the calculation of interest earned. The procedures for amortizing discount or premium on bond investments parallel those that were discussed and applied previously to bonds payable. The only difference is that the amount of discount (or premium) to be amortized is debited (or credited) directly to the investment account. As a consequence, on the maturity date, the investment account balance will equal the par value on the bonds.

### Sale of Bonds by Investors

An investor who buys a bond may not hold it to maturity but may sell it after a period of months or years. When this occurs, the price at which the bond is sold is determined by the market rate for bond interest on the day of the sale. The market rate for bond interest on the day of the sale determines the price because the new investor could get this current rate elsewhere. Therefore, the new investor will discount the right to receive the bond's face amount at maturity and the right to receive its interest for the remaining periods of life at the current market rate to determine the price to pay for the bond. As a result, since bond interest rates vary over time, a bond that originally sold at a premium may later sell at a discount, and vice versa.

## Mortgages as Security for Notes Payable and Bonds

Earlier in this chapter, we said that some bonds are secured and some are unsecured. This is also true of notes payable. When bonds or notes are unsecured, the obligation to pay interest and par or principal is equal in standing with other unsecured liabilities of the issuing company. If the company becomes financially troubled and is unable to pay, none of the unsecured creditors has preference over any other.

The ability of a company to borrow money by signing an unsecured note or issuing unsecured bonds depends on the company's general credit standing. In many cases, a company cannot obtain debt financing without providing security to the creditors. In other cases, the rate of interest that creditors would charge to provide unsecured debt is very high. As a result, many notes payable and bond issues are secured by a mortgage.

A **mortgage** is a legal agreement that helps protect a lender if a borrower fails to make the payments required by a note payable or bond indenture. A mortgage gives the lender the right to be paid from the cash proceeds from the sale of the borrower's mortgaged assets.

The terms of a mortgage are written in a separate legal document, the **mortgage contract**. The mortgage contract is given to the trustee of the bond issue or to the lender along with the note payable. A mortgage contract commonly requires the borrower to pay all property taxes on the mortgaged property, to keep the mortgaged property repaired, and to keep it adequately insured. In addition, it normally grants the mortgage holder (the lender) the right to foreclose if the borrower fails to pay. In a foreclosure, a court either sells the property or grants possession of the mortgaged property to the lender who sells it. When the property is sold, the proceeds go first to pay court costs and the claims of the mortgage holder. Any money remaining is then paid to the former owner of the property.

## Summary of the Chapter in Terms of Learning Objectives

**1.** Installment notes typically require either of two alternative methods of payment: (1) payments that include accrued interest plus a principal amount equal to the total principal divided by the number of payments, or (2) payments that are equal in amount and that consist of a declining amount of interest and an increasing amount of principal. If the second payment pattern is used, the payments are determined by expressing the amount borrowed as the present value of the payments, discounted at the rate of interest specified in the note.

**2.** An installment note usually is given when a company borrows money from a single creditor. A bond issue, on the other hand, usually is divided into bonds that have a par value of $1,000 each so that many investors can participate in the issue. A share of stock represents an equity interest in a corporation while bonds and installment notes are liabilities. A bond issue may be of serial bonds, which mature at different points in time, or of bonds that all mature on the same date. Some of the latter are sinking fund bonds, for which a fund of assets is established to retire the bonds. If bonds are registered, the name and address of each bondholder is recorded with the issuing corporation. In contrast, bearer bonds are payable to whomever holds or "bears" the bonds. Interest on coupon bonds is paid when the coupons are detached and presented for payment. Mortgages are used to secure some bonds, and other bonds, called debentures, are unsecured.

When bonds are sold between interest dates, the accrued interest is charged to the purchaser, who then is repaid that interest on the next interest payment date.

**3.** The contract rate of interest is applied to the par value of bonds to determine the annual cash payment of interest, which usually is paid in two installments. The present value of a bond is determined by discounting the series of interest payments, discounting the repayment of the par value, and adding the two present values.

When issued at a discount, the Bonds Payable account is credited for the par value of the bonds and the difference between the cash proceeds and the par value is debited to Discount on Bonds Payable. Each time interest is paid, the discount is amortized, the effect being to increase interest expense. The interest method of amortization is required by generally accepted accounting principles, but the straight-line method may be used if the results are not materially different from the interest method.

**4.** When the market rate for a corporation's bonds is less than the contract rate, the bonds will sell at a premium. The premium is recorded by the issuer in a separate account and is amortized over the life of the bonds in a manner that is similar to the amortization of bond discount.

**5.** A corporation that issues sinking fund bonds makes periodic deposits of cash with a sinking fund trustee. The trustee invests the assets, reports the earnings to the issuing corporation, and uses the accumulated sinking fund assets to repay the bondholders on the maturity date of the bonds.

When convertible preferred stock is converted into common stock, the carrying value of the preferred stock is transferred to contributed capital accounts that relate to common stock. No gain or loss is recorded.

**6.** The cost of a bond investment (including brokerage fees) usually is debited to an Investment in Bonds account without separately identifying any premium or discount on the investment. If held as a short-term investment, cash receipts of interest are recorded as interest earned, and no attempt is made to amortize the premium or discount on bond investment. However, if bonds are held as a long-term investment, the difference between the cost and par value of the investment must be amortized. The methods used to amortize premium or discount on bond investments parallel the amortization of premium or discount on bonds payable.

## Demonstration Problem

The Moore Company patented and successfully test-marketed a new product. However, to expand its ability to produce and market the product, the company needed $2.5 million of additional financing. On January 1, 1990, the company borrowed the money in the following ways:

1. Moore signed a $500,000, 10% installment note that is to be repaid in five annual payments. Each payment is to include principal of $100,000 plus accrued interest. The payments will be made on December 31, 1990–94.
2. Moore also signed a second $500,000, 10% installment note that calls for five annual installment payments that are equal in amount. The payments will be made on December 31, 1990–94.
3. Moore also issued three separate groups of five-year bonds, each of which has a face amount of $500,000. On January 1, 1990, the market interest rate for all three groups of bonds was 10% per year.
   *a.* Group A will pay 10% annual interest on June 30 and December 31, 1990–94.
   *b.* Group B will pay 12% annual interest on June 30 and December 31, 1990–94.
   *c.* Group C will pay 8% annual interest on June 30 and December 31, 1990–94.

*Required*

1. For the first installment note, (*a*) prepare an amortization schedule and (*b*) present the entry for the first installment payment on December 31, 1990.

2. For the second installment note, (*a*) calculate the amount of each installment payment, (*b*) prepare an amortization schedule, and (*c*) present the entry for the first installment payment on December 31, 1990.
3. For the 10% (Group A) bonds, present (*a*) the January 1, 1990, entry to record the issuance of the bonds; and (*b*) the June 30, 1990, entry to record the first payment of interest.
4. For the 12% (Group B) bonds, (*a*) calculate the issuance price of the bonds; (*b*) present the January 1, 1990, entry to record the issuance of the bonds; (*c*) prepare a schedule that shows periodic interest expense and premium amortization, using the interest method; (*d*) present the June 30, 1990, entry to record the first payment of interest; and (*e*) present a January 1, 1992, entry to record the retirement of the bonds at the contractual call price of $505,000.
5. For the 8% (Group C) bonds, (*a*) calculate the issuance price of the bonds; (*b*) present the January 1, 1990, entry to record the issuance of the bonds; (*c*) prepare a schedule that shows periodic interest expense and discount amortization, using the interest method; and (*d*) present the June 30, 1990, entry to record the first payment of interest.

## Solution to Demonstration Problem

1. *a*. The amortization schedule for the first installment note:

| Period Ending | Beginning-of-Period Principal Balance | Interest Expense for the Period | Portion of Payment that Is Principal | Periodic Payment | End-of-Period Principal Balance |
|---|---|---|---|---|---|
| 12/31/90 . . | $500,000 | $50,000 | $100,000 | $150,000 | $400,000 |
| 12/31/91 . . | 400,000 | 40,000 | 100,000 | 140,000 | 300,000 |
| 12/31/92 . . | 300,000 | 30,000 | 100,000 | 130,000 | 200,000 |
| 12/31/93 . . | 200,000 | 20,000 | 100,000 | 120,000 | 100,000 |
| 12/31/94 . . | 100,000 | 10,000 | 100,000 | 110,000 | –0– |

*b*. The entry for the first payment on this note on December 31, 1990:

| | | | | |
|---|---|---|---|---|
| 1990 | | | | |
| Dec. | 31 | Interest Expense . . . . . . . . . . . . . . . . . . . . . | 50,000.00 | |
| | | Notes Payable . . . . . . . . . . . . . . . . . . . . . | 100,000.00 | |
| | | Cash . . . . . . . . . . . . . . . . . . . . . . . | | 150,000.00 |
| | | Made first payment on installment note. | | |

2. *a*. Calculating the dollar amount of the five equal payments for the second installment note:

From Table 12–2, the present value of $1 to be paid annually for five years, discounted at 10%, is $3.7908.

Periodic payment = $500,000 ÷ 3.7908 = $131,898.

*b*. The amortization schedule for the second installment note:

| Period Ending | Beginning-of-Period Principal Balance | Periodic Payment | Interest Expense for the Period | Portion of Payment that Is Principal | End-of-Period Principal Balance |
|---|---|---|---|---|---|
| 12/31/90 . . | $500,000 | $131,898 | $50,000 | $ 81,898 | $418,102 |
| 12/31/91 . . | 418,102 | 131,898 | 41,810 | 90,088 | 328,014 |
| 12/31/92 . . | 328,014 | 131,898 | 32,801 | 99,097 | 228,917 |
| 12/31/93 . . | 228,917 | 131,898 | 22,892 | 109,006 | 119,911 |
| 12/31/94 . . | 119,911 | 131,902* | 11,991 | 119,911 | –0– |

*Payment increased by $4 because of rounding.

*c.* The entry for the first payment on this note on December 31, 1990:

| | | | | |
|---|---|---|---|---|
| 1990 | | | | |
| Dec. | 31 | Interest Expense . . . . . . . . . . . . . . . . . . . . | 50,000.00 | |
| | | Notes Payable . . . . . . . . . . . . . . . . . . . . | 81,898.00 | |
| | | Cash . . . . . . . . . . . . . . . . . . . . . . . . | | 131,898.00 |
| | | Made first payment on installment note. | | |

3. *a.* The entry for issuance of the 10% bonds on January 1, 1990:

| | | | | |
|---|---|---|---|---|
| 1990 | | | | |
| Jan. | 1 | Cash . . . . . . . . . . . . . . . . . . . . . . . . . . | 500,000.00 | |
| | | Bonds Payable, Group A . . . . . . . . . . . . . . | | 500,000.00 |
| | | Issued 10% bonds at face value. | | |

*b.* The entry for the first payment of interest on the bonds on June 30, 1990:

| | | | | |
|---|---|---|---|---|
| 1990 | | | | |
| June | 30 | Interest Expense . . . . . . . . . . . . . . . . . . . . | 25,000.00 | |
| | | Cash . . . . . . . . . . . . . . . . . . . . . . . . | | 25,000.00 |
| | | Paid interest on 10% bonds. | | |

4. *a.* Calculating the issue price of the 12% bonds:

| | |
|---|---|
| Present value of $500,000 to be paid 10 periods hence, discounted at 5% ($500,000 × 0.6139) . . . . . . | $306,950 |
| Present value of $30,000 to be paid periodically for 10 periods, discounted at 5% ($30,000 × 7.7217) . . | 231,651 |
| Present value of the bonds . . . . . . . . . . . . . . . . . . | $538,601 |

*b.* The entry for issuance of the 12% bonds on January 1, 1990:

| | | | | |
|---|---|---|---|---|
| 1990 | | | | |
| Jan. | 1 | Cash . . . . . . . . . . . . . . . . . . . . . . . . . . | 538,601.00 | |
| | | Bonds Payable, Group B . . . . . . . . . . . . . . | | 500,000.00 |
| | | Premium on Bonds Payable, Group B . . . . . . | | 38,601.00 |
| | | Issued 12% bonds at a premium. | | |

*c.* The premium amortization table for the 12% bonds (interest method):

| Period Ending | Beginning-of-Period Carrying Balance | Interest Expense to Be Recorded | Interest to Be Paid the Bondholders | Premium to Be Amortized | Unamortized Premium at End of Period | End-of-Period Carrying Amount |
|---|---|---|---|---|---|---|
| 6/30/90 . . | $538,601 | $26,930 | $30,000 | $3,070 | $35,531 | $535,531 |
| 12/31/90 . . | 535,531 | 26,777 | 30,000 | 3,223 | 32,308 | 532,308 |
| 6/30/91 . . | 532,308 | 26,615 | 30,000 | 3,385 | 28,923 | 528,923 |
| 12/31/91 . . | 528,923 | 26,446 | 30,000 | 3,554 | 25,369 | 525,369 |
| 6/30/92 . . | 525,369 | 26,268 | 30,000 | 3,732 | 21,637 | 521,637 |
| 12/31/92 . . | 521,637 | 26,082 | 30,000 | 3,918 | 17,719 | 517,719 |
| 6/30/93 . . | 517,719 | 25,886 | 30,000 | 4,114 | 13,605 | 513,605 |
| 12/31/93 . . | 513,605 | 25,680 | 30,000 | 4,320 | 9,285 | 509,285 |
| 6/30/94 . . | 509,285 | 25,464 | 30,000 | 4,536 | 4,749 | 504,749 |
| 12/31/94 . . | 504,749 | 25,251* | 30,000 | 4,749 | –0– | 500,000 |

*Adjusted to compensate for accumulated rounding of amounts.

*d.* The entry for the first payment of interest on bonds on June 30, 1990:

| | | | | |
|---|---|---|---|---|
| 1990 | | | | |
| June | 30 | Interest Expense . . . . . . . . . . . . . . . . . . . . . | 26,930.00 | |
| | | Premium on Bonds Payable, Group B . . . . . . . . . | 3,070.00 | |
| | | Cash . . . . . . . . . . . . . . . . . . . . . . . . | | 30,000.00 |
| | | Paid interest on 12% bonds. | | |

*e.* The entry that would be made on January 1, 1992, for the retirement of the 12% bonds at the contractual call price of $505,000:

| | | | | |
|---|---|---|---|---|
| 1992 | | | | |
| Jan. | 1 | Bonds Payable, Group B . . . . . . . . . . . . . . . . | 500,000.00 | |
| | | Premium on Bonds Payable, Group B . . . . . . . . . | 25,369.00 | |
| | | Gain on the Retirement of Bonds . . . . . . . . . | | 20,369.00 |
| | | Cash . . . . . . . . . . . . . . . . . . . . . . . . | | 505,000.00 |
| | | Retired 12% bonds at contractual call price of $505,000. | | |

5. *a.* Calculating the issue price of the 8% bonds:

| | |
|---|---|
| Present value of $500,000 to be paid 10 periods hence, discounted at 5% ($500,000 × 0.6139). . . . . . | $306,950 |
| Present value of $20,000 to be paid periodically for 10 periods, discounted at 5% ($20,000 × 7.7217) . . | 154,434 |
| Present value of the bonds. . . . . . . . . . . . . . . . . | $461,384 |

*b.* The entry for issuance of the 8% bonds on January 1, 1990:

| | | | | |
|---|---|---|---|---|
| 1990 | | | | |
| Jan. | 1 | Cash . . . . . . . . . . . . . . . . . . . . . . . . . . | 461,384.00 | |
| | | Discount on Bonds Payable, Group C . . . . . . . . . | 38,616.00 | |
| | | Bonds Payable, Group C . . . . . . . . . . . . . . | | 500,000.00 |
| | | Issued 8% bonds at a discount. | | |

*c.* The discount amortization table for the 8% bonds (interest method):

| Period Ending | Beginning-of-Period Carrying Balance | Interest Expense to Be Recorded | Interest to Be Paid the Bondholders | Discount to Be Amortized | Unamortized Discount at End of Period | End-of-Period Carrying Amount |
|---|---|---|---|---|---|---|
| 6/30/90 . . | $461,384 | $23,069 | $20,000 | $3,069 | $35,547 | $464,453 |
| 12/31/90 . . | 464,453 | 23,223 | 20,000 | 3,223 | 32,324 | 467,676 |
| 6/30/91 . . | 467,676 | 23,384 | 20,000 | 3,384 | 28,940 | 471,060 |
| 12/31/91 . . | 471,060 | 23,553 | 20,000 | 3,553 | 25,387 | 474,613 |
| 6/30/92 . . | 474,613 | 23,731 | 20,000 | 3,731 | 21,656 | 478,344 |
| 12/31/92 . . | 478,344 | 23,917 | 20,000 | 3,917 | 17,739 | 482,261 |
| 6/30/93 . . | 482,261 | 24,113 | 20,000 | 4,113 | 13,626 | 486,374 |
| 12/31/93 . . | 486,374 | 24,319 | 20,000 | 4,319 | 9,307 | 490,693 |
| 6/30/94 . . | 490,693 | 24,535 | 20,000 | 4,535 | 4,772 | 495,228 |
| 12/31/94 . . | 495,228 | 24,772* | 20,000 | 4,772 | –0– | 500,000 |

*Adjusted to compensate for accumulated rounding of amounts.

*d.* The entry for the first payment of interest on the bonds on June 30, 1990:

| | | | | |
|---|---|---|---|---|
| 1990 | | | | |
| June | 30 | Interest Expense . . . . . . . . . . . . . . . . . . . . . | 23,069.00 | |
| | | Discount on Bonds Payable, Group C . . . . . . | | 3,069.00 |
| | | Cash . . . . . . . . . . . . . . . . . . . . . . . . . . | | 20,000.00 |
| | | Paid interest on 8% bonds. | | |

## Glossary

Define or explain the words or phrases listed in the chapter Glossary. (L. O. 7)

**Bearer bond** a bond that is not registered and is made payable to whomever holds the bond (the bearer). p. 714

**Bond** a long-term liability of a corporation or governmental unit, usually issued in denominations of $1,000, that requires periodic payments of interest and final payment of par value when it matures. p. 711

**Bond indenture** the contract between the issuing corporation and the bondholders that states the rights and obligations of both parties. p. 714

**Bond sinking fund** a separate pool of assets that is established by deposits from the issuing corporation of a bond issue and from earnings on investments of the assets, and which is established for the purpose of providing the cash to repay the bondholders when the bonds mature. pp. 725–27

**Callable bond** a bond that may be redeemed or repaid before its maturity date at the option of the issuing corporation. p. 724

**Carrying amount of bonds payable** the par value of bonds payable less any unamortized discount or plus any unamortized premium. p. 718

**Contract rate of bond interest** a rate of interest specified in the bond indenture as the rate that is applied to the par value of the bonds to determine the annual amount of cash payments to the bondholders. p. 716

**Convertible bond** a bond that may be exchanged for shares of its issuing corporation's stock at the option of the bondholder. p. 727

**Coupon bond** a bond that is issued with interest coupons attached to the bond certificate so that as each interest payment date approaches, the bondholder detaches a coupon and submits it to the issuing corporation as a demand for payment. p. 714

**Debenture** an unsecured bond. p. 714

**Discount on bonds payable** the difference between the par value of a bond and the price at which it is issued when the issue price is below par. p. 717

**Face amount of a bond** the bond's par value. p. 711

**Installment notes** promissory notes that require a series of payments which consist of interest plus a portion of the original amount borrowed. p. 708

**Interest method of amortizing bond discount or premium** a method that calculates interest expense by multiplying the beginning-of-period carrying value of the bonds by the market rate of interest at the date of issuance and then subtracts the cash payment of interest from interest expense to determine the periodic amortization of discount or premium. pp. 720–23

**Market rate for bond interest** the interest rate that a corporation is willing to pay and investors are willing to take for the use of their money to buy that corporation's bonds. p. 716

**Mortgage** a legal agreement that helps protect a lender by giving the lender the right to be paid from the cash proceeds from the sale of specified assets that belong to the borrower. p. 729

**Mortgage contract** a legal document that states the rights of the lender and the obligations of the borrower with respect to assets that are pledged as security for a bond or note payable. pp. 729–30

**Par value of a bond** the face amount of the bond, which is the amount the borrower agrees to repay at maturity and the amount on which interest payments are based. p. 711

**Premium on bonds payable** the difference between the par value of a bond and the price at which it is issued when issued at a price above par. p. 722

**Registered bond** a bond for which the name and address of the owner are recorded with the issuing corporation. p. 714

**Serial bonds** an issue of bonds that mature at different points in time so that the entire bond issue is repaid gradually over a period of years. p. 713

**Sinking fund bonds** bonds that require the issuing corporation to make deposits to a separate fund of assets during the life of the bonds for the purpose of repaying the bondholders at maturity. p. 713

**Straight-line method of amortizing bond discount or premium** a method that allocates to each accounting period an equal amount of discount or premium. pp. 718–20

## Objective Review

Answers to the following questions are listed in Appendix I at the end of the book. Be sure that you decide which is the one best answer to each question *before* you check the answers in the appendix.

1. When an installment note requires a series of payments that are equal in amount:
   *a.* The payments consist of changing amounts of interest, but the principal amount remains constant.
   *b.* The payments consist of changing amounts of the principal portion of the payment, but the interest portion of the payment remains constant.
   *c.* The interest expense for a given period is calculated by multiplying the face amount of the note by the interest rate.
   *d.* The portion of the payment that is a repayment of principal is determined by multiplying the beginning-of-period principal balance by the interest rate and deducting that amount of interest expense from the periodic payment.
   *e.* The payments consist of an increasing amount of interest and a decreasing amount of principal.
2. On May 1, a corporation sold $200,000 of 9% bonds on which interest is payable semiannually on each January 1 and July 1. If the bonds were sold at par value plus accrued interest, the entry to record the first semiannual interest payment on July 1 would include:
   *a.* A debit to Bonds Payable for $9,000.
   *b.* A credit to Cash for $18,000.
   *c.* A debit to Interest Payable for $3,000.
   *d.* A credit to Interest Payable for $6,000 and a debit to Interest Expense for $9,000.
   *e.* A debit to Interest Payable for $6,000.

3. What would be the selling price of 10% bonds that have a $100,000 par value and an eight-year life if interest is to be paid semiannually? Assume the market rate of interest is 12% and the bonds were sold six months before the first interest payment.
   *a.* $115,644.
   *b.* $110,836.
   *c.* $100,000.
   *d.* $ 89,900.
   *e.* $ 86,050.
4. On December 31, 1990, Cetto Corporation received $109,444 from the sale of 16% bonds payable, $100,000 par value, interest payable June 30 and December 31. The bonds were sold to yield a 14% market rate of interest, which resulted in $109,444 cash proceeds from the sale. The entry to record the second payment of interest on December 31, 1991, would include a debit to Premium on Bonds Payable in the amount of:
   *a.* $ 339.
   *b.* $ 363.
   *c.* $ 678.
   *d.* $7,637.
   *e.* $7,661.
5. When the bond indenture requires the issuing corporation to establish a bond sinking fund:
   *a.* The issuing corporation usually is required to make periodic cash deposits with a sinking fund trustee.
   *b.* Interest and dividends earned from investing the assets in the sinking fund are credited to Sinking Fund Earnings and reported on the income statement of the issuing corporation.
   *c.* The issuing corporation reports the accumulated amount of assets in the fund on its balance sheet as a long-term investment.
   *d.* The final entry to retire the bonds with sinking fund assets may include a debit or credit to Cash if the total amount of sinking fund assets differs from the par value of the bonds.
   *e.* All of the above.
6. When an investor purchases corporate bonds:
   *a.* And the bonds are held as a long-term investment, any premium or discount on the investment must be amortized in the process of recording interest income.
   *b.* And the bonds are held as a short-term investment, any premium or discount on the investment must be amortized in the process of recording interest income.
   *c.* The investment should be recorded at cost, excluding any brokerage fees.
   *d.* Accrued interest on the date of purchase should be included in the amount of interest earned that is recognized when the first cash interest payment is received.
   *e.* And the purchase price includes a premium, the amount of interest earned recorded in later periods will exceed the amount of cash received each period.

## Questions for Class Discussion

1. What are two commonly used payment patterns on installment notes?
2. How is the interest portion of an installment note payment calculated?
3. What is the difference between a note payable and a bond issue?
4. What is the primary difference between a share of stock and a bond?
5. Why may bonds be preferred to stock as a means of long-term financing?
6. What is a bond indenture? What are some of the provisions commonly contained in an indenture?
7. What role is played by the underwriter when bonds are issued?
8. What is the function of the trustee on a bond issue?
9. Define or describe: (*a*) registered bonds, (*b*) coupon bonds, (*c*) serial bonds, (*d*) sinking fund bonds, (*e*) callable bonds, (*f*) convertible bonds, and (*g*) debenture bonds.
10. Why does a corporation that issues bonds between interest dates collect accrued interest from the purchasers of the bonds?
11. As it relates to a bond issue, what is the meaning of "contract rate of interest"? What is the meaning of "market rate for bond interest"?
12. What determines bond interest rates?
13. When the straight-line method is used to amortize bond discount, how is the interest expense for each period calculated?
14. When the interest method is used to amortize bond discount or premium, how is the interest expense for each period calculated?
15. If a $1,000 bond is sold at 98¼, at what price is it sold? If a $1,000 bond is sold at 101½, at what price is it sold?
16. If the quoted price for a bond is 97¾, does this include accrued interest?
17. What purpose is served by creating a bond sinking fund?
18. How are bond sinking funds classified for balance sheet purposes?
19. If when a bond issue matures the sinking fund has insufficient assets to repay the bondholders, who pays the bondholders the deficiency? If the sinking fund has more than enough cash to repay the bondholders, what happens to the extra cash?
20. Why might a corporation issue convertible preferred stock or convertible bonds?
21. What two legal documents are involved when a company signs a note payable that is secured by a mortgage? What is the purpose of each?

## Exercises

*In solving the exercises at the end of this chapter, round all dollar amounts to the nearest whole dollar.*

**Exercise 17–1**
**Installment note with payments of accrued interest plus equal amounts of principal**
(L. O. 1)

On December 31, 1990, Cutter Company borrowed $95,000 by signing a five-year, 12% installment note. The note requires annual payments on December 31 of accrued interest plus equal amounts of principal. Prepare journal entries to record the first payment on December 31, 1991, and the last payment on December 31, 1995.

**Exercise 17–2**
**Installment note with equal payments**
(L. O. 1)

On December 31, 1990, Butter Company borrowed $95,000 by signing a five-year, 12% installment note. The note requires annual payments of $26,354 to be made on December 31. Prepare journal entries to record the first payment on December 31, 1991, and the second payment on December 31, 1992.

**Exercise 17–3**
**Calculating installment note payments**
(L. O. 1)

Flag Company borrowed $100,000 by signing a six-year, 14% installment note. The terms of the note require six annual payments of an equal amount, the first of which is due one year after the date of the note. Calculate the amount of the installment payments, based on the present values contained in Table 12–2.

**Exercise 17–4**
**Bonds sold between interest dates**
(L. O. 2)

On March 31 of the current year, Ester Corporation sold at par plus accrued interest $2 million of its 9.8% bonds. The bonds were dated January 1 of the current year, with interest payable on each July 1 and January 1. (*a*) Give the entry to record the sale. (*b*) Give the entry to record the first interest payment. Answer these questions: (*c*) How many months' interest were accrued on these bonds when they were sold? (*d*) How many months' interest were paid on July 1? (*e*) How many months' interest did the bondholders earn during the first interest period?

**Exercise 17–5**
**Straight-line amortization of bond discount**
(L. O. 3)

On May 1 of the current year, Beasley Corporation sold $1 million of its 10.2%, 20-year bonds. The bonds were dated May 1 of the current year, with interest payable on each November 1 and May 1. Give the entries to record the sale at 95½ and the first semiannual interest payment under the assumption that the straight-line method is used to amortize the discount.

**Exercise 17–6**
**Calculating sales price of bonds sold at discount**
(L. O. 3)

On November 1 of the current year, Henrett Corporation sold $3 million of its 10.8%, 10-year bonds at a price that reflected a 14% market rate for bond interest. Interest is payable each May 1 and November 1. Calculate the sales price of the bonds and prepare a general journal entry to record the sale of the bonds. (Use the present value tables, Tables 12–1 and 12–2, pages 512 and 514.)

**Exercise 17–7**
**Interest method of amortizing bond discount**
(L. O. 3)

Henrett Corporation of Exercise 17–6 uses the interest method of amortizing bond discount or premium. Under the assumption the Henrett Corporation sold its bonds for $2,491,428, prepare a schedule with the columnar headings of Illustration 17–5 and present the amounts in the schedule for the first two interest periods. Also, prepare general journal entries to record the first and second payments of interest to bondholders.

**Exercise 17–8**
**Calculating sales price of bonds sold at premium**
(L. O. 4)

Frissel Corporation sold $900,000 of its own 13%, 9-year bonds on November 1, 1990, at a price that reflected a 12% market rate of bond interest. The bonds pay interest each May 1 and November 1. (*a*) Calculate the price at which the bonds sold, and (*b*) prepare a general journal entry to record the sale. (Use the present value tables, Tables 12–1 and 12–2, pages 512 and 514.)

**Exercise 17–9**
**Interest method of amortizing bond premium**
(L. O. 4)

Assume the bonds of Exercise 17–8 sold for $948,685 and that Frissel Corporation uses the interest method to amortize bond discount or premium. Prepare general journal entries to accrue interest on December 31, 1990, and to record the first payment of interest on May 1, 1991.

**Exercise 17–10**
**Retirement of bonds**
(L. O. 5)

Golfer Corporation sold $800,000 of its 10.2%, 20-year bonds at 98¾ on their date of issue, January 1, 1990. Five years later, on January 1, after the bond interest for the period had been paid and 25% of the total discount on the issue had been amortized, the corporation purchased $200,000 par value of the bonds on the open market at 102¼ and retired them. Give the entry to record the retirement.

**Exercise 17–11**
**Bond sinking fund**
(L. O. 5)

On January 1, 1989, Daisy Corporation sold $2.5 million of 10-year sinking fund bonds. The corporation expects to earn 10% on assets deposited with the sinking fund trustee and is required to deposit $156,864 with the trustee at the end of each year in the life of the bonds. (*a*) Prepare a general journal entry to record the first deposit of $156,864 with the trustee on January 1, 1990. (*b*) Prepare a general journal entry on December 31, 1990, to record the $15,686 earnings for 1990 reported to the corporation by the trustee. (*c*) After the final payment to the trustee, the sinking fund had an accumulated balance of $2,503,765. Prepare the general journal entry to record the payment to the bondholders on January 1, 1999.

**Exercise 17–12**
**Convertible preferred stock and convertible bonds**
(L. O. 5)

Naft Corporation has outstanding 4,000 shares of 7%, $100 par value, preferred stock that is convertible into the corporation's no-par common stock at the rate of one share of preferred for six shares of common. The preferred stock was issued at a premium of $10 per share. All shares are presented for conversion.

Piper Corporation has outstanding $20,000,000 of 9%, 20-year bonds on which there is $350,000 of unamortized bond premium. The bonds are convertible into the corporation's $1 par value common stock at the rate of one $1,000 bond for 200 shares of the stock, and $1 million of the bonds are presented for conversion.

Present entries dated June 10 to record the conversions on the books of the two corporations.

**Exercise 17–13**
**Bonds as temporary investments**
(L. O. 6)

On November 1, 1990, Rennco Company purchased 50 $1,000 par value, 11%, 10-year Quatrain Corporation bonds dated December 31, 1989. The bonds pay interest semiannually on June 30 and December 31. Rennco Company bought the bonds at 98 plus accrued interest and an $800 brokerage fee. Rennco intends to hold the bonds as a temporary investment. Prepare journal entries for Rennco Company to record the purchase and to record the receipt of interest on December 31, 1990.

## Problems

*In solving the problems at the end of this chapter, round all dollar amounts to the nearest whole dollar.*

**Problem 17–1**
**Installment notes**
(L. O. 1)

On June 30, 1990, Potter Company borrowed $450,000 at the bank by signing a five-year, 12% installment note. The terms of the note require equal semiannual payments beginning December 31, 1990.

*Required*

1. Calculate the amount of the installment payments. (Use Table 12–2 on page 514.)
2. Prepare a table with column headings like the table in Illustration 17–2. Complete the table for the Potter Company note.
3. Prepare general journal entries to record the first and the last payments on the note.
4. Assume that the note does not require equal payments. Instead, assume the note requires payments of accrued interest plus equal amounts of principal. Prepare general journal entries to record the first and the last payments on the note.

**Problem 17–2**
**Straight-line method of amortizing bond discount**
(L. O. 3)

Baxter Corporation sold $750,000 of its own 8.5%, 10-year bonds on their date of issue, December 31, 1989. Interest was payable on the bonds on each June 30 and December 31, and they were sold at a price to yield the buyers a 9% annual return. The corporation uses the straight-line method of amortizing discount or premium.

*Required*

1. Prepare a calculation to show the price at which the bonds were sold. (Use the present value tables, Tables 12–1 and 12–2, pages 512 and 514.)
2. Prepare a form with the columnar headings of Illustration 17–4 and fill in the amounts for the first two interest periods of the bond issue. Round all amounts to the nearest whole dollar.
3. Prepare entries in general journal form to record the sale of the bonds and the first two payments of interest.

**Problem 17–3**
**Interest method of amortizing bond premium**
(L. O. 4)

Redman Corporation sold $1 million of its own 11%, 10-year bonds on December 31, 1989. The bonds were dated December 31, 1989, with interest payable on each June 30 and December 31, and were sold to yield the buyers a 10% annual return. The corporation uses the interest method of amortizing premium or discount.

*Required*

1. Prepare a calculation to show the price at which the bonds were sold. (Use the present value tables, Tables 12–1 and 12–2, pages 512 and 514.)
2. Prepare a form with the columnar headings of Illustration 17–6 and fill in the amounts for the first two interest periods of the bond issue. Round all amounts to the nearest whole dollar.
3. Prepare entries in general journal form to record the sale of the bonds and the first two payments of interest.

**Problem 17–4**
**Interest method of amortizing bond discount; bond sinking fund**
(L. O. 3, 5)

Prepare general journal entries to record the following transactions of Warren Corporation. Use the present value tables, Tables 12–1 and 12–2, pages 512 and 514, as necessary, to calculate the amounts in your entries. Remember to round all amounts to the nearest whole dollar.

1989

Dec. 31 Sold $1.2 million of its own 11.2%, 10-year bonds dated December 31, 1989, with interest payable on each June 30 and December 31. The bonds sold for a price that reflected a 14% market rate of bond interest.

1990

June 30 Paid the semiannual interest on the bonds and amortized a portion of the discount calculated by the interest method.

Dec. 31 Paid the semiannual interest on the bonds and amortized a portion of the discount calculated by the interest method.

Dec. 31 Deposited $68,381 with the sinking fund trustee to establish the sinking fund to repay the bonds.

1991

Dec. 30 Received the report of the sinking fund trustee that the sinking fund had earned $8,260.

1999

Dec. 31 Received a report from the sinking fund trustee which noted that the bondholders had been paid $1.2 million on that day. Included was a $3,420 check for the extra cash accumulated in the sinking fund.

**Problem 17–5**
**Straight-line method of amortizing bond premium; retirement of bonds**
(L. O. 4, 5)

Prepare general journal entries to record the following bond transactions of Cradle Corporation:

1989

Nov. 1 Sold $2.5 million par value of its own 9.5%, 10-year bonds at a price to yield the buyers a 9% annual return. The bonds were dated November 1, 1989, with interest payable on each May 1 and November 1.

Dec. 31 Made an adjusting entry to record the accrued interest on the bonds and to amortize the premium applicable to 1989. The straight-line method was used to calculate the premium amortized.

1990

May 1 Paid the semiannual interest on the bonds and amortized the remainder of the premium applicable to the first interest period.

Nov. 1 Paid the semiannual interest on the bonds and amortized the premium applicable to the second interest period of the issue.

1991

Nov. 1 After recording the entry paying the semiannual interest on the bonds on this date and amortizing a portion of the premium, Cradle Corporation purchased 1/10 of the bonds at 100¾ and retired them. Present only the entry to record the purchase and retirement of the bonds.

**Problem 17–6**
**Comparison of straight-line and interest methods**
(L. O. 3, 4)

On December 31, 1989, Nelsbore Corporation sold $3 million of 10-year, 9.5% bonds payable at a price that reflected a 10% market rate of bond interest. The bonds pay interest on June 30 and December 31. Use the present value tables, Tables 12–1 and 12–2, pages 512 and 514, as necessary, in calculating the amounts in your answers.

*Required*

1. Present a general journal entry to record the sale of the bonds.
2. Present general journal entries to record the first and second payments of interest on June 30, 1990, and on December 31, 1990, assuming straight-line amortization of premium or discount.
3. Present general journal entries to record the first and second payments

of interest on June 30, 1990, and on December 31, 1990, assuming the use of the interest method to amortize premium or discount.

4. Prepare a schedule like the one on page 721 that has columns for the beginning-of-period carrying amount, interest expense to be recorded, and interest expense as a percentage of carrying amount, assuming use of the (1) interest method and (2) straight-line method. In completing the schedule, present the amounts for period 1 and period 2.

## Alternate Problems

*In solving the following alternate and provocative problems, round all dollar amounts to the nearest whole dollar.*

**Problem 17–1A**
**Installment notes**
(L. O. 1)

Schaefer Company financed a major expansion of its production capacity by borrowing money and signing an installment note at the bank. The four-year, 14%, $200,000 note is dated June 30, 1990, and requires equal semiannual payments beginning December 31, 1990.

*Required*

1. Calculate the amount of the installment payments. (Use Table 12–2 on page 514.)
2. Prepare a table with column headings like the table in Illustration 17–2. Complete the table for the Schaefer Company note.
3. Prepare general journal entries to record the first and the last payments on the note.
4. Assume that the note does not require equal payments. Instead, assume the note requires payments of accrued interest plus equal amounts of principal. Prepare general journal entries to record the first and the last payments on the note.

**Problem 17–2A**
**Interest method of amortizing bond discount**
(L. O. 3)

Nunley Corporation sold $1.5 million of its own 9.2%, 10-year bonds on their date of issue, December 31, 1989. Interest was payable on the bonds on each June 30 and December 31, and they were sold at a price to yield the buyers a 10% annual return. The corporation uses the interest method of amortizing discount or premium.

*Required*

1. Prepare a calculation to show the price at which the bonds were sold. (Use the present value tables, Tables 12–1 and 12–2, pages 512 and 514.)
2. Prepare a form with the columnar headings of Illustration 17–4 and fill in the amounts for the first two interest periods of the bond issue. Round all amounts to the nearest whole dollar.
3. Prepare entries in general journal form to record the sale of the bonds and the first two payments of interest.

**Problem 17–3A**
**Straight-line method of amortizing bond premium**
(L. O. 4)

On December 31, 1989, Molly Corporation sold $2.4 million of its own 13.5%, 10-year bonds. The bonds were dated December 31, 1989, with interest payable on each June 30 and December 31, and were sold to yield the buyers a 12% annual return. The corporation uses the straight-line method of amortizing premium or discount.

*Required*

1. Prepare a calculation to show the price at which the bonds were sold. (Use the present value tables, Tables 12–1 and 12–2, pages 512 and 514.)
2. Prepare a form with the columnar headings of Illustration 17–6 and fill in the amounts for the first two interest periods of the bond issue. Round all amounts to the nearest whole dollar.
3. Prepare entries in general journal form to record the sale of the bonds and the first two payments of interest.

**Problem 17–4A**
**Straight-line method of amortizing bond discount; bond sinking fund**
(L. O. 3, 5)

Prepare general journal entries to record the following transactions of Transcon Corporation. Use the present value tables, Tables 12–1 and 12–2, pages 512 and 514, as necessary, to calculate the amounts in your entries. Remember to round all amounts to the nearest whole dollar.

1989
Dec. 31 Sold $900,000 of its own 13.3%, 10-year bonds dated December 31, 1989, with interest payable on each June 30 and December 31. The bonds sold for a price that reflected a 14% market rate of bond interest.

1990
June 30 Paid the semiannual interest on the bonds and amortized a portion of the discount calculated by the straight-line method.
Dec. 31 Paid the semiannual interest on the bonds and amortized a portion of the discount calculated by the straight-line method.
31 Deposited $46,542 with the sinking fund trustee to establish the sinking fund to repay the bonds.

1991
Dec. 30 Received the report of the sinking fund trustee that the sinking fund had earned $6,516.

1999
Dec. 31 Received a report from the sinking fund trustee which noted that the bondholders had been paid $900,000 on that day. Included was a $2,840 check for the extra cash accumulated in the sinking fund.

**Problem 17–5A**
**Interest method of amortizing bond premium; retirement of bonds**
(L. O. 4, 5)

Prepare general journal entries to record the following bond transactions of Bennett Corporation:

1989
Oct. 1 Sold $3.5 million par value of its own 9.7%, 10-year bonds at a price to yield the buyers a 9% annual return. The bonds were dated October 1, 1989, with interest payable on each April 1 and October 1.
Dec. 31 Made an adjusting entry to record the accrued interest on the bonds

and to amortize the premium applicable to 1989. The interest method was used in calculating the premium amortized.

1990

Apr. 1 Paid the semiannual interest on the bonds and amortized the remainder of the premium applicable to the first interest period.

Oct. 1 Paid the semiannual interest on the bonds and amortized the premium applicable to the second interest period of the issue.

1991

Oct. 1 After recording the entry paying the semiannual interest on the bonds on this date and amortizing a portion of the premium, Bennett Corporation purchased 1/10 of the bonds at 101¼ and retired them. Present only the entry to record the purchase and retirement of the bonds.

**Problem 17–6A**
**Comparison of straight-line and interest methods**
(L. O. 3, 4)

On December 31, 1989, Frankens Corporation sold $5 million of 10-year, 11.5% bonds payable at a price that reflected a 10% market rate of bond interest. The bonds pay interest on June 30 and December 31, Use the present value tables, Tables 12–1 and 12–2, pages 512 and 514, as necessary, to calculate the amounts in your answers.

*Required*

1. Present a general journal entry to record the sale of the bonds.
2. Present general journal entries to record the first and second payments of interest on June 30, 1990, and on December 31, 1990, assuming straight-line amortization of premium or discount.
3. Present general journal entries to record the first and second payments of interest on June 30, 1990, and on December 31, 1990, assuming the use of the interest method to amortize premium or discount.
4. Prepare a schedule like the one on page 721 that has columns for the beginning-of-period carrying amount, interest expense to be recorded, and interest expense as a percentage of carrying amount, assuming use of the (1) interest method and (2) straight-line method. In completing the schedule, present the amounts for period 1 and period 2.

## Provocative Problems

**Provocative Problem 17–1**
**Transfer Sales Company**
(L. O. 2)

Transfer Sales Company is planning a major expansion of its operations and needs $2.5 million to finance the expansion. The company has been presented with three alternative financing proposals. Each involves issuing bonds that pay interest semiannually. The alternatives are:

Plan A: Issue at par $2.5 million of 10-year, 12% bonds.

Plan B: Issue $2,830,000 of 10-year, 10% bonds.

Plan C: Issue $2,250,000 of 10-year, 14% bonds.

Regardless of which plan is followed, the market rate of interest for the bonds is expected to be 12%.

For each bond issue, calculate the cash proceeds of the issue, the interest expense for the first six-month period, and the expected cash outflow each six-month period for interest. Use the interest method to amortize bond premium or discount. Which plan has the smallest cash demands on the company prior to the final payment at maturity? Which requires the largest payment upon maturity?

**Provocative Problem 17–2**
**Hardin Corporation**
(L. O. 2)

The stockholders' equity of Hardin Corporation consists of 250,000 shares of outstanding common stock on which the corporation has earned an average of $0.50 per share during each of the last three years. In an effort to increase earnings, management is planning an expansion that will require the investment of an additional $1.5 million in the business. The $1.5 million is to be acquired either by selling an additional 150,000 shares of the company's common stock at $10 per share or selling at par $1.5 million of 8%, 20-year bonds. Management estimates that the expansion will double the company's before-tax earnings the first year after it is completed and will increase before-tax earnings an additional 25% over that level in the years that follow.

Hardin Corporation's management wants to finance the expansion in the manner that will serve the best interests of present stockholders and has asked you to evaluate the two alternatives from this perspective. In your report, express an opinion as to the relative merits and disadvantages of each of the proposed ways of securing the funds needed for the expansion. Attach to your report a schedule that shows expected earnings per share of the common stockholders under each method of financing. In preparing your schedule, assume the company presently pays out in state and federal income taxes 50% of its before-tax earnings and that it will continue to pay out the same share after the expansion.

Part Six

# Financial Statements: Interpretation and Modifications

Your study of Part Six will contribute a great deal to your ability to understand and use financial statements. You will learn about the statement of cash flows, which has only recently become a required disclosure in public financial reports. Also, you will learn how businesses account for and report their investments in other companies and their operations in foreign countries. Finally, you will learn some important techniques to use in analyzing financial statements.

Part Six consists of the following chapters:

# 18 Statement of Cash Flows

Cash is the lifeblood of a business enterprise. It is the fuel that keeps a business alive. Without cash, employees and suppliers are not paid, loans are not repaid, and owners do not receive dividends. In other words, a business must have an adequate amount of cash to operate. For these reasons, decision makers pay close attention to a company's cash position and the events and transactions that cause that position to change. Information about the events and transactions that affect the cash position of a company is reported in a financial statement called the **statement of cash flows.** By studying this chapter, you will learn how to prepare and interpret a statement of cash flows.

**Learning Objectives**

*After studying Chapter 18, you should be able to:*

1. Describe the information contained in a statement of cash flows and classify the cash flows of a company as operating, investing, or financing activities.
2. Prepare a statement of cash flows in which cash flows from operating activities are reported according to the direct method and prepare a schedule of noncash investing and financing activities.
3. Calculate cash inflows and outflows by inspecting the noncash account balances of a company and related information about its transactions.
4. Prepare a working paper for a statement of cash flows so that cash flows from operating activities are reported according to the direct method.
5. Define or explain the words or phrases listed in the chapter Glossary.

*After studying the appendix at the end of this chapter (Appendix F), you should be able to:*

6. Calculate the net cash provided or used by operating activities according to the indirect method and prepare the statement of cash flows.
7. Prepare a working paper for a statement of cash flows so that the net cash flows from operating activities are calculated by the indirect method.

## Why Cash Information Is Important

Information about cash flows can influence decision makers in many ways. For example, if a company's regular operations bring in more cash than it uses, investors will value the company higher than if property and equipment must be sold to finance operations. Information about cash flows can help creditors decide whether a company will have enough cash to pay its debts as they mature. Management and investors use cash flow information to evaluate a company's ability to meet unexpected obligations. Cash flow information is also used to evaluate a company's ability to take advantage of new business opportunities that may arise. These are just a few of the many ways that different people use cash flow information.

The importance of cash flow information to decision makers has directly influenced the thinking of accounting authorities. For example, the FASB's stated objectives of financial reporting clearly reflect the importance of cash flow information. The FASB stated that financial statements should include information:

About how a business obtains and spends cash,

About its borrowing and repayment activities,

About the sale and repurchase of its ownership securities,

About dividend payments and other distributions to its owners, and

About other factors that affect a company's liquidity or solvency.[1]

To accomplish these objectives, a financial statement is needed to summarize, classify, and report the periodic cash inflows and outflows of a business. This information is contained in a statement of cash flows.

## Statement of Cash Flows

Describe the information contained in a statement of cash flows and classify the cash flows of a company as operating, investing, or financing activities. (L. O. 1)

In November 1987, the FASB issued *Statement of Financial Accounting Standards No. 95*, "Statement of Cash Flows." This standard requires businesses to include a **statement of cash flows** in all financial reports that contain both a balance sheet and an income statement. The primary purpose of this statement is to present information about a company's cash receipts and disbursements during the reporting period.

Illustration 18–1 shows the content of the statement of cash flows. In the Illustration, note that cash flows are grouped in three categories: cash flows from operating activities, cash flows from investing activities, and cash flows from financing activities. Within each category, there may be both inflows and outflows. Because all cash inflows and outflows are reported, the statement reconciles the beginning-of-period and end-of-period balances of cash plus cash equivalents.

### Direct Method of Presenting Cash Flows from Operating Activities

When you prepare a statement of cash flows, the net cash provided (or used) by operating activities can be calculated two different ways. One is called the **direct method of calculating net cash provided (or used) by operating activities.**

---

[1] FASB, *Statement of Financial Accounting Concepts No. 1*, "Objectives of Financial Reporting by Business Enterprises" (Norwalk, Conn., 1978), par. 49. Copyright © by the Financial Accounting Standards Board, Norwalk, Conn. 06856, U.S.A. Quoted (or excerpted) with permission. Copies of the complete document are available from the FASB.

## AS A MATTER OF FACT

That the present U.S. corporate income tax introduces distortions into decisions about investment, corporate finance and saving is well known. Now fears are expressed in and out of Washington that it is spurring takeovers accompanied by "excessive leverage" that mitigates the tax burden (and causes a loss of government revenue). Also, Treasury officials have restated the longstanding concern that dividend payments are discriminated against.

Elimination of the separate corporate layer of taxation poses important practical problems. First, revenue considerations are important in the current budget environment. It may be difficult to tax by any other means capital income received by some shareholders—in particular foreign corporations. In addition, absent other provisions, eliminating the corporate tax would confer windfall gains on owners of existing corporate capital—at best, a very roundabout way of encouraging new investment.

An alternative system is a cash-flow corporate tax. The guiding principle is that the base for taxation should be the net cash flow received from business activities. No attempt is made to measure firms' economic income. In that sense, the economic rationale behind the tax is akin to that favoring a consumption tax over the income tax at the personal level.

* * * * *

A cash-flow tax has the advantage over a corporate income tax in that it avoids the important distortions of investment and financing decisions inherent in the current system, arguably without sacrificing revenue. At the root of this advantage is the fact that the cash-flow tax does not try to measure "profits" or the "cost of capital employed," the source of most complications in the current system. The tax can be calculated from the sources and uses of funds by firms, without attempting to infer economic profits from accounting data.

Recent developments in financial markets suggest the importance of giving the cash-flow tax proposal a fresh look. For example, the idea that corporate managers should focus their attention on the "long run" has been the centerpiece of recent policy discussions about corporate tax issues. There is a concern that the existing corporate income tax encourages leverage, diminishing firms' flexibility in the future. Furthermore, the substitution of debt for equity—a shuffling of financial claims—will affect significantly the level of corporate tax revenues from the same stream of corporate profits. Finally, the repeal of the investment tax credit is argued by many to damp incentives for new investment.

The cash-flow tax addresses directly the issue of incentives for new investment. While the tax would raise revenue from existing investments, new investment would be expensed—a feature that would benefit in particular many growing enterprises that face high capital costs and credit constraints. Because the difference between net revenue and investment would be taxed, such companies would defer taxation, paying taxes later as they mature.

* * * * *

Given the generous investment incentives embodied in the cash-flow tax, there is an obvious concern over its ability to raise revenue. Recall, though, that the tax base would eliminate depreciation deductions and interest deductions. Studies for the U.S. and Britain over the past decade suggest that a revenue-neutral switch to a cash-flow tax could be accomplished with a lower rate of taxation than under the existing income-tax system.

* * * * *

Source: Glenn Hubbard, "Tax Corporate Cash-Flow, Not Income," *The Wall Street Journal*, February 16, 1989, p. A14. Reprinted by permission of *The Wall Street Journal*, © Dow Jones & Company, Inc. 1989. ALL RIGHTS RESERVED.

The other is the indirect method. When the direct method is used, you separately list each major class of operating cash receipts (for example, cash received from customers) and each major class of cash payments (such as payments for merchandise). Then, the payments are subtracted from the receipts to determine the net cash provided (or used) by operating activities. The FASB encourages companies to use the direct method.

**Illustration 18–1**
**Categories of information in the statement of cash flows**

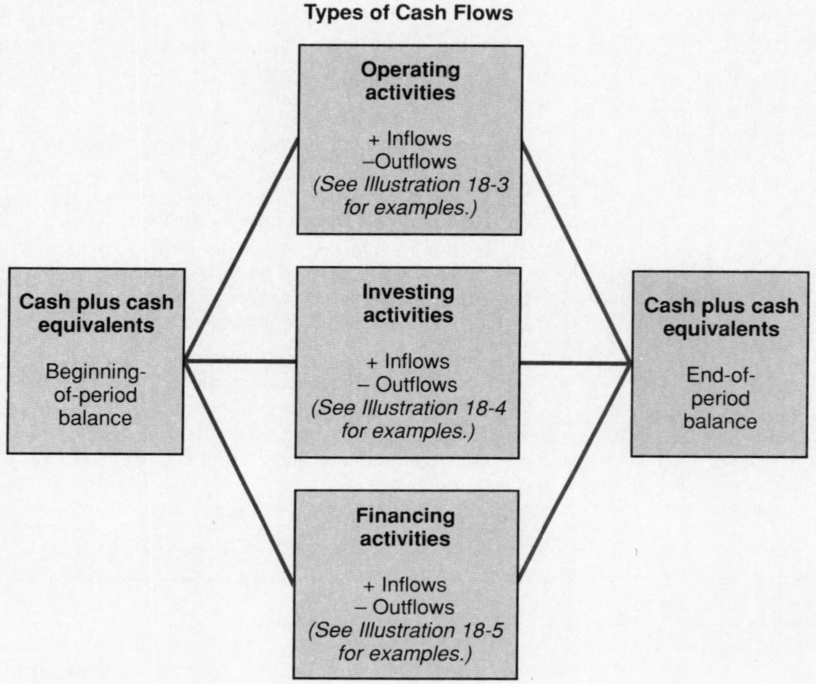


### Indirect Method of Presenting Cash Flows from Operating Activities

The **indirect method of calculating net cash provided (or used) by operating activities** is not as informative as the direct method. The indirect method is not as informative because it does not disclose the individual cash inflows and outflows from operating activities. Instead, the indirect method discloses only the *net* cash provided (or used) by operating activities.

When the indirect method is used, net income is listed first. Then, it is adjusted for items that are necessary to reconcile net income to the net cash provided (or used) by operating activities. For example, you know that depreciation expense is subtracted in the calculation of net income. But, depreciation expense does not involve a current cash payment. Therefore, depreciation expense is added back to net income in the process of reconciling net income to the net cash provided (or used) by operating activities.

Since the direct method is most informative and is the method the FASB recommends, the remainder of this chapter will focus on that approach. However, the indirect method is allowed, and some companies will use that method in spite of the FASB's recommendation. Therefore, we will explain and illustrate the indirect method in the appendix at the end of this chapter.

Illustration 18–2

**GROVER COMPANY**
**Statement of Cash Flows**
**For Year Ended December 31, 1990**

| | | |
|---|---|---|
| Cash flows from operating activities: | | |
| Cash received from customers | $ 570,000 | |
| Cash payments for merchandise | (319,000) | |
| Payments for wages and other operating expenses | (218,000) | |
| Payments for interest | (8,000) | |
| Payments for taxes | (5,000) | |
| Net cash provided by operating activities | | $ 20,000 |
| Cash flows from investing activities: | | |
| Cash paid for purchase of plant assets | $ (10,000) | |
| Cash received from sale of plant assets | 12,000 | |
| Net cash provided by investing activities | | 2,000 |
| Cash flows from financing activities: | | |
| Cash received from issuance of stock | $ 15,000 | |
| Cash paid to retire bonds | (18,000) | |
| Cash paid for dividends | (14,000) | |
| Net cash used in financing activities | | (17,000) |
| Net increase in cash | | $ 5,000 |
| Cash balance at beginning of 1990 | | 12,000 |
| Cash balance at end of 1990 | | $ 17,000 |

### Designing the Statement of Cash Flows (Direct Method)

Illustration 18–2 contains the statement of cash flows for Grover Company. Notice that in the operating activities section of the statement, major classes of cash inflows and cash outflows are listed separately. This is the direct method. Within the operating activities category, the cash outflows are subtracted from the cash inflows to determine the net cash provided (or used) by operating activities. Also, in each of the other two categories, the cash outflows are subtracted from the cash inflows to determine the cash provided (or used) by those categories of transactions.

Compare Illustration 18–2 with Illustration 18–1. Notice that in Illustration 18–1, the beginning and ending balances are called *cash plus cash equivalents*. However, in Illustration 18–2, the beginning and ending balances refer only to cash. The balances in Illustration 18–2 are called *cash* because Grover Company does not own any **cash equivalents**. However, this difference between the two illustrations raises the question: What are cash equivalents?

### Cash and Cash Equivalents

In *Statement of Financial Accounting Standards No. 95*, the FASB concluded that a statement of cash flows should explain the differences between the beginning and ending balances of cash and cash equivalents. Prior to this new standard, cash equivalents were generally understood to be short-term, temporary investments of cash. However, not all short-term investments meet the FASB's definition of cash equivalents. To qualify as a cash equivalent, an investment must satisfy two criteria. They are:

1. The investment must be readily convertible to a *known* amount of cash.
2. The investment must be sufficiently close to its maturity date so that its market value is relatively insensitive to interest rate changes.

In general, only investments that are purchased within three months of their maturity dates satisfy these criteria.[2] Examples of cash equivalents include short-term investments in U.S. treasury bills, commercial paper (short-term corporate notes payable), and money market funds.

The idea of classifying short-term, highly liquid investments as cash equivalents is based on the assumption that companies make these investments to earn a return on idle cash balances. However, some companies have other reasons for investing in items that meet the criteria of cash equivalents. For example, an investment company that specializes in the purchase and sale of securities may buy such items as part of its investing activities.

Sometimes, items that meet the criteria of cash equivalents are not held as temporary investments of idle cash balances. Companies that have such investments are allowed to exclude them from the cash equivalents classification. However, the companies must develop a clear policy for determining which items are included and which are excluded. These policies must be disclosed in the footnotes to the financial statements and must be followed consistently from period to period.

## Classifying Cash Transactions

A statement of cash flows describes the change in cash plus cash equivalents. Therefore, cash payments to purchase cash equivalents and cash receipts from selling cash equivalents are not reported on the statement. All other cash receipts and payments are classified as operating, investing, or financing activities. Within each category, individual cash receipts and payments are summarized and described in a manner that clearly presents the general nature of the company's cash transactions. Then, the summarized cash receipts and payments within each category are netted against each other. A category provides a net cash flow if the receipts in the category exceed the payments. And if the payments in a category exceed the receipts, the category is a net user of cash during the period.

### Operating Activities

In Illustration 18–2, look at the types of cash flows that are reported as flows that result from **operating activities.** You should recognize that operating activities generally include only transactions that relate to the calculation of net income. However, some income statement items are not related to operating activities. These items will be discussed later.

As disclosed in a statement of cash flows, operating activities involve the production or purchase of merchandise and the sale of goods and services to

[2] FASB, *Statement of Financial Accounting Standards No. 95,* "Statement of Cash Flows" (Norwalk, Conn., 1987), par. 8. Copyright © by the Financial Accounting Standards Board, Norwalk, Conn. 06856, U.S.A. Quoted (or excerpted) with permission. Copies of the complete document are available from the FASB.

**Illustration 18–3**
**Cash flows from operating activities**

| Cash Inflows | Cash Outflows |
|---|---|
| Cash sales to customers. | Payments to employees for salaries and wages. |
| Cash collections from credit customers. | Payments to suppliers of goods and services. |
| Receipts of cash dividends from stock investments in other entities. | Payments to government agencies for taxes, fines, and penalties. |
| Receipts of interest payments. | Interest payments, net of amounts capitalized. |
| Refunds from suppliers. | Contributions to charities. |
| Cash collected from a lawsuit. | Cash refunds to customers. |

customers. Operating activities also include the expenditures related to administering the business. In fact, cash flows from operating activities include all cash flows from transactions that are not defined as investing or financing activities. Illustration 18–3 shows typical cash inflows and outflows from operating activities.

### Investing Activities

Transactions that involve making and collecting loans or that involve purchasing and selling plant assets, other productive assets, and investments (other than cash equivalents) are called **investing activities.** Usually, investing activities involve the purchase or sale of assets that are classified on the balance sheet as plant and equipment, intangible assets, or long-term investments. However, the purchase and sale of short-term investments other than cash equivalents are also investing activities. Illustration 18–4 shows examples of cash flows from investing activities.

The second type of receipt listed in Illustration 18–4 involves proceeds from collecting the principal amount of loans. Regarding this item, you must examine carefully any cash receipts that relate to notes receivable. If the notes resulted from sales to customers, the cash receipts are classified as operating activities. This is true even if the notes are long-term notes. But, if a company loans money to other parties, the cash receipts from collecting the loans are classified as investing activities. Nevertheless, the FASB concluded that collections of *interest* are not investing activities; they are reported as operating activities.

### Financing Activities

A company's transactions with its owners and long-term creditors are typically called **financing activities.** Also, financing activities include borrowing cash on a short-term basis. However, cash payments to settle credit purchases of merchandise, whether on account or by note, are operating activities. Payments of interest expense are also operating activities. Examples of cash flows from financing activities are shown in Illustration 18–5.

**Illustration 18–4**
**Cash flows from investing activities**

| Cash Inflows | Cash Outflows |
|---|---|
| Proceeds from selling productive assets (e.g., land, buildings, equipment, natural resources, and intangible assets). | Payments to purchase property, plant, and equipment or other productive assets (excluding merchandise inventory). |
| Proceeds from collecting the principal amount of loans. | Payments to acquire equity securities of other companies. |
| Proceeds from selling investments in the equity securities of other companies. | Payments to acquire debt securities of other entities, except cash equivalents. |
| Proceeds from selling investments in the debt securities of other entities, except cash equivalents. | Payments in the form of loans made to other parties. |
| Proceeds from the sale (discounting) of loans made by the enterprise. | |

**Illustration 18–5**
**Cash flows from financing activities**

| Cash Inflows | Cash Outflows |
|---|---|
| Proceeds from the issuance of equity securities (e.g., common and preferred stock). | Payments of dividends and other distributions to owners. |
| Proceeds from the issuance of bonds and notes payable. | Payments to purchase treasury stock. |
| Proceeds from other short- or long-term borrowing transactions. | Repayments of cash loans. |
| | Payments of the principal amounts involved in long-term credit arrangements. |

## Noncash Investing and Financing Activities

Some important investing and financing activities do not involve cash receipts or payments during the current period. For example, a company might purchase land and buildings and finance 100% of the purchase by giving a long-term note payable. Although this transaction clearly involves both investing and financing activities, it is not reported in the current period's statement of cash flows because no cash was received or paid.

Other investing and financing activities may involve some cash receipt or payment but also involve giving or receiving other types of consideration. An example is if you purchase machinery valued at $12,000 by paying cash of $5,000 and trading in old machinery that has a market value of $7,000. In this case, the statement of cash flows reports only the $5,000 cash outflow for the purchase of machinery. As a result, this $12,000 investing transaction is only partially described in the statement of cash flows.

In its 1987 pronouncement, the FASB concluded that the noncash portions of investing and financing activities should *not* be reported in the statement of cash flows. However, the Board recognized that noncash investing and financing activities are important events that should be disclosed. To accomplish this, you must prepare a separate schedule of noncash investing and

**Illustration 18–6**
**Decco Company—schedule of noncash investing and financing activities**

The company issued 1,000 shares of common stock for the purchase of land and buildings with fair values of $5,000 and $15,000, respectively.

The company entered into a capital lease obligation of $12,000 for new computer equipment.

The company exchanged old machinery with a fair value of $7,000 and a book value of $8,000 for new machinery valued at $12,000. The balance of $5,000 was paid in cash.

financing activities. Or, you must provide a narrative description of these activities. Illustration 18–6 shows an example of how a company might disclose its noncash investing and financing activities.

In Illustration 18–6, notice the last item which describes an exchange of machinery. Following the requirements of the FASB, the schedule describes *both* the cash and noncash aspects of this transaction. The $5,000 cash payment is reported in Decco Company's statement of cash flows as an investing activity. Nevertheless, the schedule of noncash investing and financing activities includes both the cash and noncash aspects of the transaction.

Examples of transactions that must be disclosed as noncash investing and financing activities include the following:

The conversion of debt securities to equity securities.

The conversion of preferred stock into common stock.

The leasing of assets in a transaction that qualifies as a capital lease.

The purchase of long-term assets financed by a note payable to the seller.

The exchange of a noncash asset for other noncash assets.

The purchase of noncash assets in exchange for equity or debt securities.

## Preparing a Statement of Cash Flows

Prepare a statement of cash flows in which cash flows from operating activities are reported according to the direct method, and prepare a schedule of noncash investing and financing activities.
(L. O. 2)

The information you need to prepare a statement of cash flows comes from a variety of sources. These include comparative balance sheets at the beginning and the end of the accounting period, an income statement for the period, and a careful analysis of each noncash balance sheet account. However, since our goal is to report cash inflows and cash outflows, we might begin our investigation by looking at the transactions recorded in the Cash account.

### Analyzing the Cash Account

All of a company's cash receipts and cash payments are recorded in the Cash account in the general ledger. Therefore, the Cash account would seem to be the logical place to look for information about cash flows from operating, investing, and financing activities. To demonstrate, review the summarized Cash account of Grover Company presented below.

**Summarized Cash Account, Grover Company**

| | | | |
|---|---|---|---|
| Balance, 12/31/89 | 12,000 | | |
| Receipts from customers | 570,000 | Payments for merchandise | 319,000 |
| Proceeds from sale of plant assets | 12,000 | Payments for wages and other operating expenses | 218,000 |
| Proceeds from stock issuance | 15,000 | Interest payments | 8,000 |
| | | Tax payments | 5,000 |
| | | Payments for purchase of plant assets | 10,000 |
| | | Payments to retire bonds | 18,000 |
| | | Dividend payments | 14,000 |
| Balance, 12/31/90 | 17,000 | | |

In this account, the individual cash transactions are already summarized in terms of major types of receipts and payments. For example, individual receipts from customers were totaled and are listed in the account as a single debit. All that remains is to determine whether each type of cash inflow or outflow is an operating, investing, or financing activity and to place it in its proper category on the statement of cash flows. The completed statement of cash flows appears in Illustration 18–2.

While an analysis of the Cash account may appear to be an easy way to prepare a statement of cash flows, it has two serious drawbacks. First, most companies have so many individual cash receipts and disbursements that it is not practical to review them all. Imagine what a problem this would be for IBM, General Motors, Kodak, or Exxon, or even for a relatively small business. Second, the Cash account usually does not contain a description of each cash transaction. Therefore, even though the Cash account shows the amount of each debit and credit, you generally cannot determine the type of transaction by looking at the Cash account. Thus, the Cash account does not provide the information that you need to prepare a statement of cash flows. To obtain the necessary information, you must analyze the changes in the noncash accounts.

### Analyzing Noncash Accounts to Determine Cash Flows

Calculate cash inflows and outflows by inspecting the noncash account balances of a company and related information about its transactions. (L. O. 3)

When a company records cash inflows and outflows with debits and credits to the Cash account, it also records credits and debits in other accounts. Some of these accounts are balance sheet accounts. Others are revenue and expense accounts that are closed to Retained Earnings, a balance sheet account. As a result, all cash transactions eventually affect the noncash balance sheet accounts. Therefore, the nature of the cash inflows and outflows can be determined by examining the changes in the noncash balance sheet accounts. Illustration 18–7 shows this important relationship between the Cash account and the noncash balance sheet accounts.

In Illustration 18–7, notice that the balance sheet equation labeled (1) is expanded in (2) so that cash is separated from the other assets. Then, the equation is rearranged in (3) so that cash is set equal to the sum of the liability and equity accounts less the noncash asset accounts. The illustration then points out in (4) that changes in one side of the equation (cash) must be equal to

**Illustration 18–7**
**Why an analysis of the noncash accounts explains the change in cash**

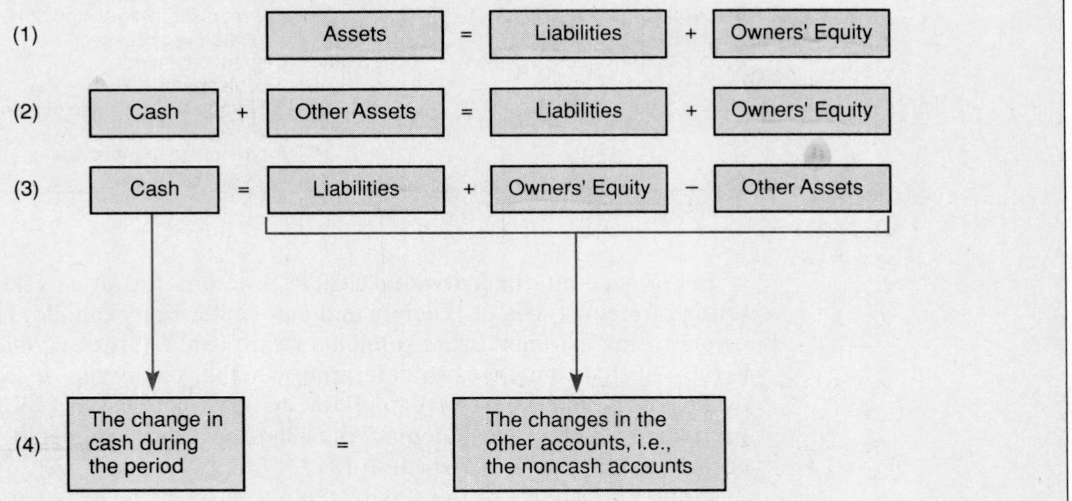


the changes in the other side (noncash accounts). Part (4) shows that if you discover the changes in liabilities, owners' equity, and noncash assets, it is possible to fully explain the changes in cash. This information is all that you need to prepare a statement of cash flows.

This overall process has one added advantage. The examination of each noncash account also identifies any noncash investing and financing activities that occurred during the period. As you learned earlier, these noncash items must also be disclosed, but not on the statement of cash flows.

When you begin to analyze the changes in the noncash balance sheet accounts, recall that Retained Earnings is affected by revenues, expenses, and dividend declarations. Therefore, you need to look at the income statement accounts to help explain the change in Retained Earnings. In fact, the income statement accounts provide important information that relates to the changes in several balance sheet accounts.

Some of these relationships between income statement accounts, balance sheet accounts, and possible cash flows are summarized in Illustration 18–8. For example, to determine the cash receipts from customers during a period, you must adjust the amount of sales revenue for the increase or decrease in Accounts Receivable.[3] If the Accounts Receivable balance did not change, you may infer that the cash collected from customers is equal to sales revenue. On the other hand, if the Accounts Receivable balance decreased, cash collec-

[3] This introductory explanation assumes that there is no bad debts expense. However, if bad debts occur and are written off directly to Accounts Receivable, the change in the Accounts Receivable balance will be due in part to the write-off. The remaining change results from credit sales and from cash receipts. This chapter does not discuss the allowance method of accounting for bad debts since it would make the analysis unnecessarily complex at this time.

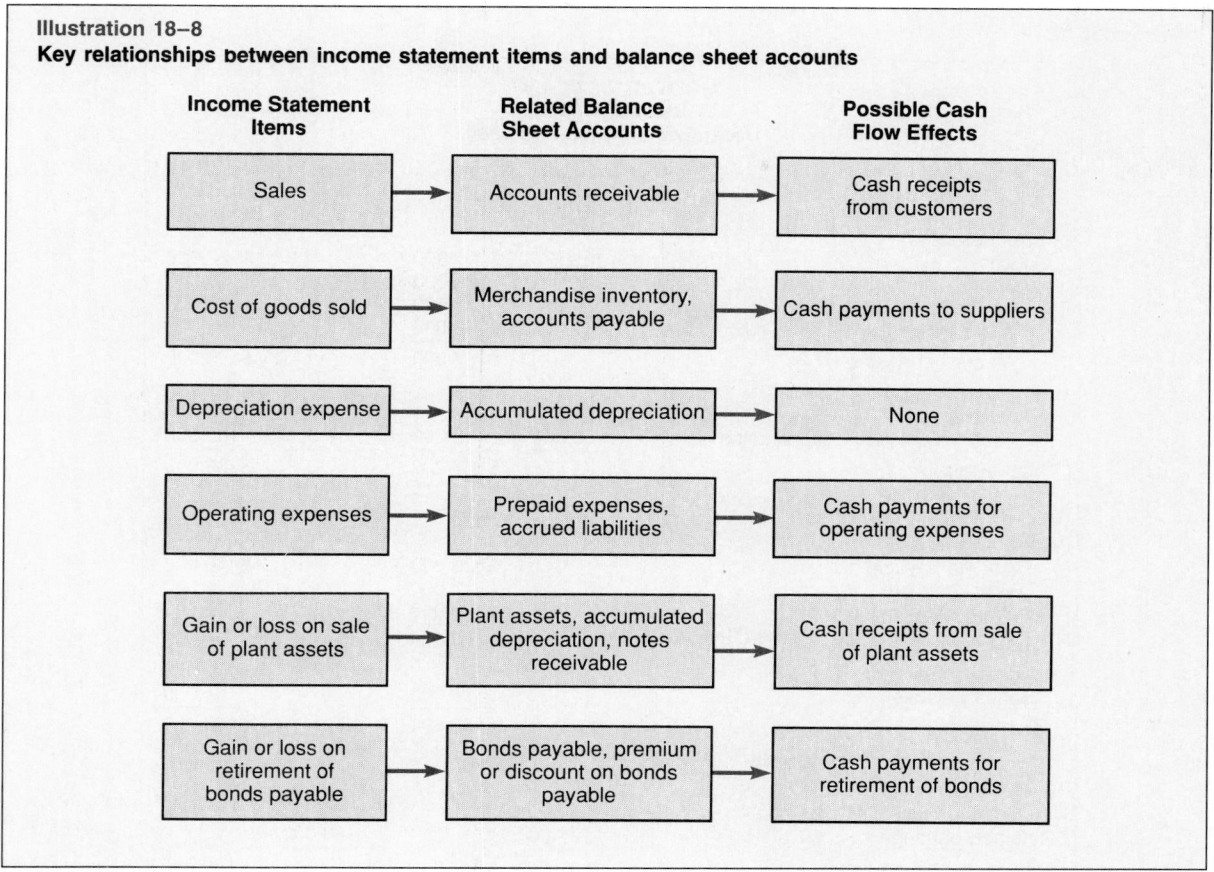

**Illustration 18–8**
**Key relationships between income statement items and balance sheet accounts**

| Income Statement Items | Related Balance Sheet Accounts | Possible Cash Flow Effects |
|---|---|---|
| Sales → | Accounts receivable → | Cash receipts from customers |
| Cost of goods sold → | Merchandise inventory, accounts payable → | Cash payments to suppliers |
| Depreciation expense → | Accumulated depreciation → | None |
| Operating expenses → | Prepaid expenses, accrued liabilities → | Cash payments for operating expenses |
| Gain or loss on sale of plant assets → | Plant assets, accumulated depreciation, notes receivable → | Cash receipts from sale of plant assets |
| Gain or loss on retirement of bonds payable → | Bonds payable, premium or discount on bonds payable → | Cash payments for retirement of bonds |

tions must have been equal to sales revenue plus the reduction in Accounts Receivable. And if the Accounts Receivable balance increased, the cash collected from customers must have been equal to Sales less the increase in Accounts Receivable.

If you analyze all of the noncash balance sheet accounts and the related income statement accounts in this fashion, you will obtain the information you need for a statement of cash flows. So that you will clearly understand this process, we will illustrate this process by examining the accounts of Grover Company.

## Grover Company—A Comprehensive Example

Grover Company's December 31, 1989 and 1990 balance sheets and its 1990 income statement are presented in Illustration 18–9. The objective is to prepare a statement of cash flows that explains the $5,000 increase in Cash, based on these financial statements and the additional information about 1990 transactions that follows:

*a*. All Accounts Payable balances resulted from merchandise purchases.
*b*. Plant assets that cost $70,000 were purchased by paying $10,000 cash and issuing $60,000 of bonds payable to the seller.

**Illustration 18–9**

**GROVER COMPANY**
**Balance Sheet**
**December 31, 1990 and 1989**

| | 1990 | | 1989 | |
|---|---|---|---|---|
| **Assets** | | | | |
| Current assets: | | | | |
| Cash | | $ 17,000 | | $ 12,000 |
| Accounts receivable | | 60,000 | | 40,000 |
| Merchandise inventory | | 84,000 | | 70,000 |
| Prepaid expenses | | 6,000 | | 4,000 |
| Total current assets | | $167,000 | | $126,000 |
| Long-term assets: | | | | |
| Plant assets | $250,000 | | $ 210,000 | |
| Less accumulated depreciation | 60,000 | 190,000 | 48,000 | 162,000 |
| Total assets | | $357,000 | | $288,000 |
| **Liabilities** | | | | |
| Current liabilities: | | | | |
| Accounts payable | | $ 35,000 | | $ 40,000 |
| Interest payable | | 3,000 | | 4,000 |
| Income taxes payable | | 22,000 | | 12,000 |
| Total current liabilities | | $ 60,000 | | $ 56,000 |
| Long-term liabilities: | | | | |
| Bonds payable | | 90,000 | | 64,000 |
| Total liabilities | | $150,000 | | $120,000 |
| **Stockholders' Equity** | | | | |
| Contributed capital: | | | | |
| Common stock, $10 par value | $ 95,000 | | $ 80,000 | |
| Retained earnings | 112,000 | | 88,000 | |
| Total stockholders' equity | | 207,000 | | 168,000 |
| Total liabilities and stockholders' equity | | $357,000 | | $288,000 |

**Income Statement**
**For Year Ended December 31, 1990**

| | | |
|---|---|---|
| Sales | | $ 590,000 |
| Cost of goods sold | $300,000 | |
| Wages and other operating expenses | 216,000 | |
| Interest expense | 7,000 | |
| Income taxes expense | 15,000 | |
| Depreciation expense | 24,000 | (562,000) |
| Loss on sale of plant assets | | (6,000) |
| Gain on retirement of debt | | 16,000 |
| Net income | | $ 38,000 |

*c.* Plant assets with an original cost of $30,000 and accumulated depreciation of $12,000 were sold for $12,000 cash. The result was a $6,000 loss.

*d.* The proceeds from issuing 3,000 shares of common stock was $15,000.

*e.* The $16,000 gain on retirement of bonds resulted from paying $18,000 to retire bonds with a book value of $34,000.

*f.* Cash dividends of $14,000 were declared and paid.

### Operating Activities

We begin the analysis by calculating the cash flows from operating activities. In general, this involves adjusting the income statement items that relate to operating activities for changes in their related balance sheet accounts.

**Cash Received from Customers.** The calculation of cash receipts from customers begins with sales revenue. If all sales are for cash, the amount of cash received from customers is equal to sales. However, when sales are on account, you must adjust the amount of sales revenue for the change in Accounts Receivable to determine the cash received.

In Illustration 18–9, look at the Accounts Receivable balances on December 31, 1989 and 1990. The beginning balance was $40,000, and the ending balance was $60,000. And the income statement shows that sales revenue was $590,000. With this information, you can reconstruct the Accounts Receivable account and determine the amount of cash received from customers, as follows:

**Accounts Receivable**

| | | | |
|---|---|---|---|
| Balance, 12/31/89 | 40,000 | | |
| Sales, 1990 | 590,000 | Collections = | 570,000 |
| Balance, 12/31/90 | 60,000 | | |

This account shows that since the balance of Accounts Receivable increased from $40,000 to $60,000, cash receipts from customers are equal to sales of $590,000 plus the $40,000 beginning balance less the $60,000 ending balance, or $570,000. To state the calculation in more general terms:

Cash received from customers = Sales − Increase in accounts receivable

And if the balance of Accounts Receivable decreases, the calculation is:

Cash received from customers = Sales + Decrease in accounts receivable

Now turn back to Illustration 18–2. Note that the $570,000 of cash Grover Company received from customers is shown on the statement of cash flows as a cash inflow from operating activities.

**Cash Payments for Merchandise.** The calculation of cash payments for merchandise begins with cost of goods sold and merchandise inventory. For a moment, suppose that all merchandise purchases are for cash and that the ending balance of Merchandise Inventory is unchanged from the beginning balance. In this case, the total cash payments for merchandise is equal to cost of goods sold. However, this case is not typical. Usually, you expect some change in a company's Merchandise Inventory balance during a period. Also, purchases of merchandise usually are made on account, and you expect some change in the Accounts Payable balance.

When the balances of Merchandise Inventory and Accounts Payable change, you must adjust cost of goods sold for the changes in these accounts to determine the cash payments for merchandise. This adjustment has two steps. First, you combine the change in the balance of Merchandise Inventory with cost of goods sold to determine the cost of purchases during the period. Second, combine the change in the balance of Accounts Payable with the cost of purchases to determine the total cash payments to suppliers of merchandise.

Consider the example of Grover Company. First, the reported amount of cost of goods sold ($300,000) is combined with the Merchandise Inventory beginning balance ($70,000) and with the ending balance ($84,000) to determine the amount that was purchased during the period. You can accomplish this by reconstructing the Merchandise Inventory account, as follows:

**Merchandise Inventory**

| | | | |
|---|---|---|---|
| Balance, 12/31/89 | 70,000 | | |
| **Purchases =** | **314,000** | Cost of goods sold | 300,000 |
| Balance, 12/31/90 | 84,000 | | |

This account shows that the $14,000 increase in merchandise inventory is added to cost of goods sold of $300,000 to get purchases of $314,000.

To determine the cash paid for merchandise, you adjust purchases for the change in accounts payable. This can be done by reconstructing the Accounts Payable account, as follows:

**Accounts Payable**

| | | | |
|---|---|---|---|
| | | Balance, 12/31/89 | 40,000 |
| **Payments =** | **319,000** | Purchases | 314,000 |
| | | Balance, 12/31/90 | 35,000 |

In this account, you can see that purchases of $314,000 plus a beginning balance of $40,000, less the ending balance of $35,000, equals cash payments of $319,000. In other words, purchases of $314,000 plus the $5,000 decrease in accounts payable equals cash payments of $319,000.

To summarize the adjustments to cost of goods sold that are necessary to calculate cash payments for merchandise:

$$\text{Purchases} = \text{Cost of goods sold} \begin{bmatrix} + \text{ Increase in merchandise inventory} \\ \textit{or} \\ - \text{ Decrease in merchandise inventory} \end{bmatrix}$$

And,

$$\text{Cash payments for merchandise} = \text{Purchases} \begin{bmatrix} + \text{ Decrease in accounts payable} \\ \textit{or} \\ - \text{ Increase in accounts payable} \end{bmatrix}$$

Now look at Illustration 18–2. Notice that Grover Company's payments of $319,000 for merchandise are reported on the statement of cash flows as a cash outflow from operating activities.

**Cash Payments for Wages and Other Operating Expenses.** Grover Company's income statement shows wages and other operating expenses of $216,000 (see Illustration 18–9). To determine the amount of cash paid during the period for wages and other operating expenses, you must combine this amount with the changes in any related balance sheet accounts. In Grover Company's beginning and ending balance sheets (Illustration 18–9), you must look for prepaid expenses and any accrued liabilities that relate to wages and other operating expenses. In this example, the balance sheets show that Grover Company has prepaid expenses but does not have any accrued liabilities. Thus, the adjustment to the expense item is limited to the change in prepaid expenses. The amount of the adjustment can be determined by assuming that all cash payments of wages and other operating expenses were originally debited to Prepaid Expenses. With this assumption, we can reconstruct the Prepaid Expenses account as follows:

**Prepaid Expenses**

| | | | |
|---|---|---|---|
| Balance, 12/31/89 | 4,000 | | |
| **Payments** | **218,000** | Wages and other operating expenses | 216,000 |
| Balance, 12/31/90 | 6,000 | | |

This account shows that because prepaid expenses increased by $2,000 during the period, the cash payments for wages and other operating expenses were $2,000 more than the reported expense. Thus, the amount paid for wages and other operating expenses is $216,000 plus $2,000, or $218,000.

In reconstructing the Prepaid Expenses account, we assumed that all cash payments for wages and operating expenses were debited to Prepaid Expenses. However, this assumption does not have to be true. If cash payments were debited directly to the expense account, the total amount of cash payments would be the same. In other words, the cash paid for operating expenses still equals the $216,000 expense plus the $2,000 increase in prepaid expenses.

If Grover Company's balance sheets had shown accrued liabilities, you would also have to adjust the expense for the change in accrued liabilities. In general terms, the calculation is as follows:

$$\text{Cash paid for wages and other operating expenses} = \text{Wages and other operating expenses} \begin{bmatrix} + \text{ Increase in prepaid expenses} \\ or \\ - \text{ Decrease in prepaid expenses} \end{bmatrix} \begin{bmatrix} + \text{ Decrease in accrued liabilities} \\ or \\ - \text{ Increase in accrued liabilities} \end{bmatrix}$$

**Payments for Interest and Taxes.** Grover Company's remaining operating cash flows involve cash payments for interest and for taxes. The analysis of these items is similar because both require adjustments for changes in related liability accounts. Grover Company's income statement shows interest expense of $7,000 and income taxes expense of $15,000. To calculate the related cash payments, interest expense must be adjusted for the change in interest payable and income taxes expense must be adjusted for the change in income taxes payable. These calculations are accomplished by reconstructing the liability accounts, as follows:

**Interest Payable**

| | | | |
|---|---|---|---|
| | | Balance, 12/31/89 | 4,000 |
| **Interest paid =** | **8,000** | Interest expense | 7,000 |
| | | Balance, 12/31/90 | 3,000 |

**Income Taxes Payable**

| | | | |
|---|---|---|---|
| | | Balance, 12/31/89 | 12,000 |
| **Income taxes paid =** | **5,000** | Income tax expense | 15,000 |
| | | Balance, 12/31/90 | 22,000 |

These reconstructed accounts show that interest payments were \$8,000 and income tax payments were \$5,000. The general form of each calculation is:

$$\text{Cash payment} = \text{Expense} \begin{bmatrix} + \text{ Decrease in related payable} \\ \textit{or} \\ - \text{ Increase in related payable} \end{bmatrix}$$

Both of these cash payments appear as operating items on Grover Company's statement of cash flows in Illustration 18–2.

### Investing Activities

Investing activities usually refer to transactions that affect long-term assets. Recall from the information that was provided about Grover Company's transactions that the company purchased plant assets and also sold plant assets. Both of these transactions are investing activities.

**Purchase of Plant Assets.** Grover Company purchased plant assets that cost \$70,000 by issuing \$60,000 of bonds payable to the seller and paying the \$10,000 balance in cash. The \$10,000 payment is reported as a cash outflow on the statement of cash flows (see Illustration 18–2). Also, since \$60,000 of the purchase was financed by issuing bonds payable, this transaction involves noncash investing and financing activities. Therefore, it must be described in a schedule of noncash investing and financing activities or described narratively in the financial statement footnotes. This description might appear as follows:

| **Schedule of noncash investing and financing activities:** | |
|---|---|
| Purchased plant assets | \$70,000 |
| Issued bonds payable to finance purchase | 60,000 |
| Balance paid in cash | \$10,000 |

**Sale of Plant Assets.** Grover Company sold plant assets that cost \$30,000 and were depreciated \$12,000. The result of the sale was a loss of \$6,000 and a cash receipt of \$12,000. This cash receipt is reported in the statement of cash flows as a cash inflow from investing activities (see Illustration 18–2).

Recall from Grover Company's income statement that depreciation expense was \$24,000. Depreciation does not use or provide cash. However, we should notice the effects of depreciation expense, the plant asset purchase, and the plant asset sale on the Plant Assets and Accumulated Depreciation accounts. These accounts are reconstructed, as follows:

**Plant Assets**

| | | | |
|---|---|---|---|
| Balance, 12/31/89 | 210,000 | | |
| Purchase | 70,000 | Sale | 30,000 |
| Balance, 12/31/90 | 250,000 | | |

**Accumulated Depreciation**

| | | | |
|---|---|---|---|
| | | Balance, 12/31/89 | 48,000 |
| Sale | 12,000 | Depreciation expense | 24,000 |
| | | Balance, 12/31/90 | 60,000 |

The beginning and ending balances of these accounts were taken from Grover Company's balance sheets (Illustration 18–9). Reconstructing the accounts shows that the beginning and ending balances of both accounts are completely reconciled by the purchase, the sale, and the depreciation expense. As a result, you can conclude that you did not omit any of the investing activities that relate to plant assets.

### Financing Activities

Financing activities usually relate to a company's long-term debt and stockholders' equity accounts. In the information about Grover Company, there were four transactions that involved financing activities. One of these, the $60,000 issuance of bonds payable to purchase plant assets, was discussed above as a noncash investing and financing activity. The remaining three transactions were the retirement of bonds, the issuance of common stock, and the payment of cash dividends.

**Payment to Retire Bonds Payable.** Grover Company's December 31, 1990, balance sheet showed bonds payable of $90,000. These were retired for $18,000 cash in 1990. The income statement reports the $16,000 difference as a gain. The statement of cash flows shows the $18,000 payment as a cash outflow from financing activities (see Illustration 18–2).

Notice that the beginning and ending balances of Bonds Payable are reconciled by the $60,000 issuance of new bonds and the retirement of $34,000 of old bonds. This is shown in the reconstructed Bonds Payable account that follows:

**Bonds Payable**

| | | | |
|---|---|---|---|
| | | Balance, 12/31/89 | 64,000 |
| Retired bonds | 34,000 | Issued bonds | 60,000 |
| | | Balance, 12/31/90 | 90,000 |

**Receipt from Common Stock Issuance.** During 1990, Grover Company issued 3,000 shares of common stock for $5 per share. This $15,000 cash receipt is reported on the statement of cash flows as a financing activity. Look at the December 31, 1989, and 1990 balance sheets in Illustration 18–9. Notice that the Common Stock account balance increased from $80,000 at the beginning of 1990 to $95,000 at the end of 1990. Thus, the $15,000 stock issue reconciles the change in the Common Stock account.

**Payment of Cash Dividends.** According to the facts provided about Grover Company's transactions, cash dividends of $14,000 were paid during 1990. This payment is reported as a cash outflow from financing activities. Also, note that the effects of this $14,000 payment and the reported net income of $38,000 fully reconcile the beginning and ending balances of Retained Earnings. This is shown in the reconstructed Retained Earnings account that follows:

**Retained Earnings**

| | | | |
|---|---|---|---|
| | | Balance, 12/31/89 | 88,000 |
| Cash dividend | 14,000 | Net income | 38,000 |
| | | Balance, 12/31/90 | 112,000 |

All of Grover Company's cash inflows and outflows were described in the previous paragraphs. We also described one noncash investing and financing transaction. In the process of making these analyses, we reconciled the changes in all of the noncash balance sheet accounts. The change in the Cash account is reconciled by the statement of cash flows, as shown in Illustration 18–2.

## Preparing a Working Paper for a Statement of Cash Flows (Direct Method)

When a company has a large number of accounts and many operating, investing, and financing transactions, the analysis of noncash accounts can be difficult and confusing. In these situations, a working paper can help you organize the information you need to prepare a statement of cash flows. A working paper also makes it easier for you to check the accuracy of your work.

### Designing the Working Paper

Prepare a working paper for a statement of cash flows so that cash flows from operating activities are reported according to the direct method. (L. O. 4)

Examine the working paper for Grover Company shown in Illustration 18–10. Observe that the balance sheet account balances at the beginning and end of the period are entered in the first and fourth money columns, respectively. The middle two columns are for reconciling the differences in these balances and for the development of the statement of cash flows.

The process of reconciling the changes in the balance sheet accounts begins with the income statement. The income statement is recorded below the balance sheet in the Analysis of Changes columns. The statement of cash flows is developed below the income statement. And, as noncash investing and financing activities are identified during the analysis, they are recorded at the bottom of the working paper.

In Illustration 18–10, note that the beginning and ending balances of each noncash balance sheet account are reconciled by the amounts shown in the Analysis of Changes columns. Look at the Cash account and note that the Analysis of Changes columns are empty. The reconciliation of the Cash account is not done on the Cash account row. Instead, the Cash account is reconciled by all of the items shown in the statement of cash flows section of the working paper.

**Illustration 18–10**

**GROVER COMPANY**
**Working Paper for Statement of Cash Flows (Direct Method)**
**For Year Ended December 31, 1990**

| | December 31, 1989 | Analysis of Changes: Debit | Analysis of Changes: Credit | December 31, 1990 |
|---|---|---|---|---|
| **Balance sheet—debits:** | | | | |
| Cash | 12,000 | | | 17,000 |
| Accounts receivable | 40,000 | (*a1*) 590,000 | (*a2*) 570,000 | 60,000 |
| Merchandise inventory | 70,000 | (*b2*) 314,000 | (*b1*) 300,000 | 84,000 |
| Prepaid expenses | 4,000 | (*c2*) 2,000 | | 6,000 |
| Plant assets | 210,000 | (*j1*) 70,000 | (*g*) 30,000 | 250,000 |
| | 336,000 | | | 417,000 |
| **Balance sheet—credits:** | | | | |
| Accumulated depreciation | 48,000 | (*g*) 12,000 | (*f*) 24,000 | 60,000 |
| Accounts payable | 40,000 | (*b3*) 319,000 | (*b2*) 314,000 | 35,000 |
| Interest payable | 4,000 | (*d2*) 8,000 | (*d1*) 7,000 | 3,000 |
| Income taxes payable | 12,000 | (*e2*) 5,000 | (*e1*) 15,000 | 22,000 |
| Bonds payable | 64,000 | (*h*) 34,000 | (*j2*) 60,000 | 90,000 |
| Common stock, $5 par value | 80,000 | | (*k*) 15,000 | 95,000 |
| Retained earnings | 88,000 | (*l*) 14,000 | (*i*) 38,000 | 112,000 |
| | 336,000 | | | 417,000 |
| **Income statement:** | | | | |
| Sales | | | (*a1*) 590,000 | |
| Cost of goods sold | | (*b1*) 300,000 | | |
| Wages and other operating expenses | | (*c1*) 216,000 | | |
| Interest expense | | (*d1*) 7,000 | | |
| Income taxes expense | | (*e1*) 15,000 | | |
| Depreciation expense | | (*f*) 24,000 | | |
| Loss on sale of plant assets | | (*g*) 6,000 | | |
| Gain on retirement of bonds | | | (*h*) 16,000 | |
| Net income | | (*i*) 38,000 | | |
| **Statement of cash flows:** | | | | |
| **Operating activities:** | | | | |
| Receipts from customers | | (*a2*) 570,000 | | |
| Payments for merchandise | | | (*b3*) 319,000 | |
| Payments for wages and other operating expenses | | | (*c1*) 216,000<br>(*c2*) 2,000 | |
| Payments for interest | | | (*d2*) 8,000 | |
| Payments for taxes | | | (*e2*) 5,000 | |
| **Investing activities:** | | | | |
| Receipt from sale of plant assets | | (*g*) 12,000 | | |
| Payment to purchase plant assets | | | (*j1*) 10,000 | |
| **Financing activities:** | | | | |
| Payment to retire bonds | | | (*h*) 18,000 | |
| Receipts from issuance of stock | | (*k*) 15,000 | | |
| Payments of dividends | | | (*l*) 14,000 | |
| **Noncash investing and financing activities:** | | | | |
| Purchase of plant assets financed by bonds | | (*j2*) 60,000 | (*j1*) 60,000 | |
| | | 2,631,000 | 2,631,000 | |

Three characteristics of the working paper in Illustration 18–10 are particularly important. First, it is designed to provide the information you need to report cash flows from operating activities by the direct method. Second, it provides all the information necessary to prepare the statement of cash flows. You can see this if you compare the statement of cash flows section of the working paper with the formal statement of cash flows shown in Illustration 18–2. Third, the working paper also provides the information you need to disclose the noncash investing and operating activities.

### Basic Steps to Prepare a Working Paper (Direct Method)

The information you need to prepare the working paper includes an income statement, the beginning and ending balance sheets, and other information about the activities of the period. There are six basic steps to prepare a working paper that includes enough information to report cash flows from operating activities by the direct method. They are:

1. List the beginning balance sheet in the first column and the ending balance sheet in the fourth column. Debit balance accounts are listed first and credit balance accounts second. Total and prove the equality of the debits and credits in each balance sheet.
2. List each income statement item below the balance sheets and enter its amount in the Analysis of Changes column (debit for expense, credit for revenue). As you record each income statement credit, also record the corresponding debit next to the appropriate noncash balance sheet account. And as you record each income statement debit, record the corresponding credit next to the related noncash balance sheet account.

   After an income statement item is entered, analyze the changes in the noncash balance sheet accounts related to that income statement item. Illustration 18–8 lists examples of these relationships. In the process of entering these changes, any cash flow effect is entered in the statement of cash flows section of the working paper.

   If an expense (or revenue) was paid (or received) in cash, it had no effect on any of the noncash balance sheet accounts. Therefore, when you record the expense (or revenue) in the income statement section of the working paper, the corresponding credit (or debit) should be entered as a cash outflow (inflow) in the statement of cash flows section of the working paper.
3. As you enter income statement gains and losses, reconstruct the entries that created the gains or losses. These entries help reconcile the balance sheet accounts. The cash effects of gain and loss transactions are recorded as inflows or outflows in the investing or financing categories of the statement of cash flows.
4. Cross-reference the debits and credits of each entry by assigning them a letter (and number if more than one entry is needed to determine a specific cash flow). As your analyses of changes begin to fill out the income statement and statement of cash flows sections of the

working paper, leave some blank lines in each category to allow space for the rest of your analyses.

5. Review each balance sheet account to determine whether any differences between beginning and ending balances remain unreconciled. If any remain, examine the additional information about the activities of the company and enter the necessary reconciling amounts in the Analysis of Changes columns.
6. To prove the arithmetic accuracy of your work, total the two middle columns and note that they are equal.

### Entering the Analysis of Changes on the Working Paper

To help you understand the relationship between the items entered in the Analysis of Changes columns of the working paper and the facts of the Grover Company example, the information about the income statement and other transactions is restated below. Each item of information is identified with a letter (and sometimes a number) that corresponds to the entries on the working paper.

As you study the information below and the working paper in Illustration 18–10, you can clarify any items that appear confusing by reviewing the previous section of the chapter. Recall that each cash flow was calculated and explained by reconstructing the related noncash accounts.

Items (*a1*) and (*a2*) provide the facts and the analysis of changes that relate to *receipts from customers:*

*a1*. Sales revenue was $590,000. On the working paper, the analysis of change labeled (*a1*) enters the sales revenue as a credit in the income statement section and as a debit to Accounts Receivable. This starts the reconciliation of the change in Accounts Receivable.

*a2*. Receipts from customers were the only source of decreases in Accounts Receivable. On the working paper, the analysis of change labeled (*a2*) enters the receipts from customers as an operating activity and as a decrease in Accounts Receivable. This completes the reconciliation of the change in Accounts Receivable.

Notice that the analysis of (*a1*) and (*a2*) assumes that all sales were on account. However, even if some sales were for cash, the analysis would correctly determine cash receipts from customers. Whether sales are for cash or on account, total cash receipts from customers equals sales revenue minus the increase (or plus the decrease) in Accounts Receivable.

Items (*b1*), (*b2*), and (*b3*) give the facts and the analysis of changes that relate to *cash payments for merchandise:*

*b1*. Cost of goods sold was $300,000. On the working paper, the analysis of change entry enters cost of goods sold in the income statement section and reduces Merchandise Inventory.

*b2*. Purchases of merchandise were on credit. On the working paper, this entry increases Merchandise Inventory and increases Accounts Payable. Note that Merchandise Inventory is now reconciled.

*b3*. The only decreases in Accounts Payable were payments to creditors. The entry labeled (*b3*) reconciles the Accounts Payable account and records the cash payment for merchandise as an operating activity.

Items (*c1*) and (*c2*) provide the facts and the analysis of changes related to *cash payments for wages and other operating expenses:*

*c1*. Wages and other operating expenses were $216,000 and were paid in cash. On the working paper, entry (*c1*) records these expenses and shows them as a cash outflow from operating activities.

*c2*. Prepaid expenses increased. Entry (*c2*) reconciles the Prepaid Expense account. It also increases the amount of cash paid for wages and other operating expenses.

Items (*d1*) and (*d2*) provide the facts and the analysis of changes related to *payments for interest:*

*d1*. Interest expense was $7,000. Entry (*d1*), which assumes that all interest was accrued before being paid, records interest expense and credits Interest Payable.

*d2*. Decreases in Interest Payable involved payments of interest. Entry (*d2*) reconciles the Interest Payable account and classifies the cash payment of interest as an operating activity.

Items (*e1*) and (*e2*) provide the facts and the analysis of changes related to *payments for taxes:*

*e1*. Income taxes expense was $15,000. Entry (*e1*), which assumes that taxes were accrued before being paid, records the expense and credits Income Taxes Payable.

*e2*. Payments of taxes were debited to Income Taxes Payable. Entry (*e2*) reconciles the Income Taxes Payable account and classifies the cash payments of taxes as an operating activity.

*f*. Depreciation expense was $24,000. Entry (*f*) records the expense and credits the Accumulated Depreciation account. This begins the reconciliation of Accumulated Depreciation.

*g*. Plant assets with an original cost of $30,000 and accumulated depreciation of $12,000 were sold for $12,000 cash. The result was a $6,000 loss. Entry (*g*) decreases Plant Assets, completes the reconciliation of Accumulated Depreciation, enters the loss in the income statement section, and classifies the cash *receipt from sale of plant assets* as an investing activity.

*h*. A $16,000 gain on retirement of bonds resulted from paying $18,000 to retire bonds with a book value of $34,000. Entry (*h*) decreases bonds payable, enters the gain in the income statement section, and classifies the cash *payment to retire bonds* as a financing activity.

*i*. Net income was $38,000. Entry (*i*) completes the income statement section and helps start the reconciliation of Retained Earnings.

Items (*j1*) and (*j2*) provide the facts and the analysis of changes related to the purchase of plant assets, the issuance of bonds payable to finance part of the purchase, and the remaining cash *payment to purchase plant assets:*

*j1*. Plant assets that cost $70,000 were purchased by paying $10,000 cash and issuing $60,000 of bonds payable. Entry (*j1*) completes the reconciliation of Plant Assets, classifies the cash payment as an investing activity, and classifies the bond issue as part of a noncash investing and financing transaction.

*j2*. The issuance of bonds to purchase plant assets was recorded by increasing Bonds Payable. Entry (*j2*) completes the reconciliation of Bonds Payable and classifies this portion of the purchase as part of a noncash investing and financing transaction.

*k*. The proceeds from issuing 3,000 shares of common stock were $15,000. Entry (*k*) reconciles the Common Stock account and classifies the *receipt from issuing stock* as a financing activity.

*l*. Cash dividends of $14,000 were declared and paid. Entry (*l*) completes the reconciliation of Retained Earnings and classifies the *payment of dividends* as a financing activity.

After all the above analyses are performed, note that the balances of each noncash balance sheet account are completely reconciled. The Analysis of Changes columns are now totaled to show that they are equal.

### Reconciling Net Income to Net Cash Provided (or Used) by Operating Activities

As you learned earlier, the FASB recommends that the statement of cash flows be prepared according to the direct method. This means that the statement will disclose each major class of cash inflows and outflows from operating activities. However, when the direct method is used, the FASB also requires that companies disclose a reconciliation of net income to the net cash provided (or used) by operating activities. This reconciliation is precisely what is meant by the indirect method of calculating the net cash provided (or used) by operating activities. The indirect method is explained in Appendix F that follows this chapter.

## Summary of Chapter in Terms of Learning Objectives

**1.** The statement of cash flows reports cash receipts and disbursements as operating, investing, or financing activities. Operating activities include transactions that relate to production or purchase of merchandise, sale of goods and service to customers, and administrative functions. Investing activities include purchases and sales of noncurrent assets and short-term investments that are not cash equivalents. Transactions with long-term creditors, owners, and that involve short-term sources of cash and cash equivalents are financing activities.

**2.** Using the direct method to report the net cash provided (or used) by operating activities, you subtract individual classes of operating cash payments from operating cash receipts. This is the method encouraged by the FASB.

A company must supplement its statement of cash flows with a schedule or narrative description of its noncash investing and financing activities. Examples are the conversion of debt obligations to equity securities or exchanging a note payable for plant assets.

**3.** Cash receipts and payments are recorded in the Cash account and in offsetting balance sheet accounts or temporary accounts such as revenues and expenses. The temporary accounts are closed to Retained Earnings. Therefore, you can analyze the changes in the noncash balance sheet accounts brought about by income statement transactions and other events to determine cash receipts and cash payments. For example, cash collected from customers is calculated by adjusting sales revenues for the change in accounts receivable. Also, cash paid for interest is calculated by adjusting interest expense for the change in interest payable.

**4.** On the working paper, you enter the beginning and ending balances of each balance sheet account in columns 1 and 4. Then, income statement items are entered in the Analysis of Changes columns. As each income statement item is entered, the corresponding debit or credit is entered in the related noncash balance sheet accounts or in the statement of cash flows section. If a noncash current asset or current liability related to operations is involved, another entry is made to completely reconcile its change and to record its related cash inflow or outflow. In this manner, the working paper identifies individual classes of cash receipts and payments, such as cash received from customers.

## Demonstration Problem

Presented below are summarized journal entries that show the total debits and credits to the Pinnacle Corporation's Cash account that occurred during 1990. Use the information to prepare a statement of cash flows for 1990. The cash provided (or used) by operating activities should be presented according to the direct method. In the statement, identify the entry that records each item of cash flow. Assume that the beginning balance of cash was $111,000.

| | | | |
|---|---|---|---|
| *a.* | Cash | 1,200,000.00 | |
| | Common Stock | | 300,000.00 |
| | Contributed Capital in Excess of Par Value | | 900,000.00 |
| | Issued common stock for cash. | | |
| *b.* | Cash | 2,000,000.00 | |
| | Notes Payable | | 2,000,000.00 |
| | Borrowed cash with a note payable. | | |
| *c.* | Purchases | 400,000.00 | |
| | Cash | | 400,000.00 |
| | Purchased merchandise for cash. | | |
| *d.* | Accounts Payable | 1,000,000.00 | |
| | Cash | | 1,000,000.00 |
| | Paid for credit purchases of merchandise. | | |

| | | | |
|---|---|---|---|
| *e.* | Wages Expense | 500,000.00 | |
| | Cash | | 500,000.00 |
| | Paid wages to employees. | | |
| *f.* | Rent Expense | 350,000.00 | |
| | Cash | | 350,000.00 |
| | Paid rent for buildings. | | |
| *g.* | Cash | 2,500,000.00 | |
| | Sales | | 2,500,000.00 |
| | Made cash sales to customers. | | |
| *h.* | Cash | 1,500,000.00 | |
| | Accounts Receivable | | 1,500,000.00 |
| | Collected accounts from credit customers. | | |
| *i.* | Property, Plant, and Equipment | 1,780,000.00 | |
| | Cash | | 1,780,000.00 |
| | Purchased assets for cash. | | |
| *j.* | Investments | 1,800,000.00 | |
| | Cash | | 1,800,000.00 |
| | Purchased investments for cash. | | |
| *k.* | Interest Expense | 180,000.00 | |
| | Notes Payable | 320,000.00 | |
| | Cash | | 500,000.00 |
| | Paid notes and accrued interest. | | |
| *l.* | Cash | 172,000.00 | |
| | Dividend Income | | 172,000.00 |
| | Collected dividends from investments. | | |
| *m.* | Cash | 175,000.00 | |
| | Loss on Sale of Investment | 25,000.00 | |
| | Investment | | 200,000.00 |
| | Sold investments for cash. | | |
| *n.* | Cash | 600,000.00 | |
| | Accumulated Depreciation | 350,000.00 | |
| | Property, Plant, and Equipment | | 800,000.00 |
| | Gain on disposal | | 150,000.00 |
| | Sold plant assets for cash. | | |
| *o.* | Dividends Payable | 425,000.00 | |
| | Cash | | 425,000.00 |
| | Paid cash dividends to stockholders. | | |
| *p.* | Income Taxes Payable | 400,000.00 | |
| | Cash | | 400,000.00 |
| | Paid income taxes owed for the year. | | |
| *q.* | Treasury Stock | 190,000.00 | |
| | Cash | | 190,000.00 |
| | Acquired treasury stock for cash. | | |

## Solution to Demonstration Problem

**PINNACLE CORPORATION**
**Statement of Cash Flows**
**For Year Ended December 31, 1990**

| | | | |
|---|---|---|---|
| | Cash flows from operating activities: | | |
| *g, h.* | Cash received from customers | $ 4,000,000 | |
| *l.* | Cash received as dividends | 172,000 | |
| *c, d.* | Cash payments for merchandise | (1,400,000) | |
| *e.* | Payments for wages | (500,000) | |
| *f.* | Payments for rent | (350,000) | |
| *k.* | Payments for interest | (180,000) | |
| *p.* | Payments for taxes | (400,000) | |
| | Net cash provided by operating activities | | $ 1,342,000 |
| | Cash flows from investing activities: | | |
| *i.* | Cash paid for purchases of plant assets | $(1,780,000) | |
| *j.* | Cash paid for purchases of investments | (1,800,000) | |
| *m.* | Cash received from sale of investments | 175,000 | |
| *n.* | Cash received from sale of plant assets | 600,000 | |
| | Net cash used in investing activities | | (2,805,000) |
| | Cash flows from financing activities: | | |
| *a.* | Cash received from issuing stock | $ 1,200,000 | |
| *b.* | Cash received from borrowing | 2,000,000 | |
| *k.* | Cash paid for repayment of note payable | (320,000) | |
| *o.* | Cash paid for dividends | (425,000) | |
| *q.* | Cash paid for purchases of treasury stock | (190,000) | |
| | Net cash provided by financing activities | | 2,265,000 |
| | Net increase in cash | | $ 802,000 |
| | Beginning balance of cash | | 111,000 |
| | Ending balance of cash | | $ 913,000 |

**Appendix F**

## THE INDIRECT METHOD OF CALCULATING NET CASH PROVIDED (OR USED) BY OPERATING ACTIVITIES

Calculate the net cash provided or used by operating activities according to the indirect method and prepare the statement of cash flows. (L. O. 6)

When the indirect method is used, net income is listed first. Then, it is adjusted for items that are necessary to reconcile the net income amount to the net cash provided (or used) by operating activities. To see the results of the indirect method, look at Illustration F–1. This illustration shows the reconciliation of Grover Company's net income to the net cash provided by operating activities.

In Illustration F–1, notice that the net cash provided by operating activities is $20,000. This is the same amount that was reported on the statement of cash flows (direct method) in Illustration 18–2. However, these illustrations show entirely different ways to calculate the $20,000 net cash inflow. In Illustration 18–2 (the direct method), major classes of operating cash outflows were subtracted from major classes of cash inflows. By comparison, none of the individual cash inflows or cash outflows are reported in Illustration F–1 (the indirect method). Instead, net income is adjusted to exclude amounts that were included in the determination of net income but that did not provide operating cash inflows or outflows during the period.

**Illustration F–1**
**Grover Company—reconciliation of net income to net cash provided by operating activities**

| | | | |
|---|---|---|---|
| | Net income | | $ 38,000 |
| | Adjustments to reconcile net income to net cash provided by operating activities: | | |
| 1 | Increase in accounts receivable | $(20,000) | |
| | Increase in merchandise inventory | (14,000) | |
| | Increase in prepaid expenses | (2,000) | |
| | Decrease in accounts payable | (5,000) | |
| | Decrease in interest payable | (1,000) | |
| | Increase in income taxes payable | 10,000 | |
| 2 | Depreciation expense | 24,000 | |
| 3 | Loss on sale of plant assets | 6,000 | |
| | Gain on retirement of bonds | (16,000) | |
| | Total adjustments | | (18,000) |
| | Net cash provided by operating activities | | $ 20,000 |

There are three types of adjustments shown in Illustration F–1. The adjustments grouped under (1) are for changes in noncash current assets and current liabilities that relate to operating activities. The adjustment identified as (2) is for an item that relates to operating activities but which did not provide cash inflows or cash outflows during the period. The adjustments grouped under (3) eliminate gains and losses that do not relate to operating activities. These gains and losses resulted from investing and financing activities.

## Adjustments for Changes in Current Assets and Current Liabilities

To help you understand why adjustments for changes in noncash current assets and current liabilities are necessary, we will use the transactions of a very simple company as an example. Assume that Simple Company's income statement shows only two items, as follows:

| | |
|---|---|
| Sales | $20,000 |
| Operating expenses | 12,000 |
| Net income | $ 8,000 |

For a moment, assume that all of Simple Company's sales and operating expenses are for cash. The company has no current assets other than cash and has no current liabilities. Given these assumptions, the net cash provided by operating activities during the period is $8,000, which is the cash received from customers less the cash paid for operating expenses. The net cash provided by operating activities also equals net income.

### Adjustments for Changes in Noncash Current Assets

Now assume that Simple Company's sales are on account. Also assume that its Accounts Receivable balance was $2,000 at the beginning of the year and $2,500 at the end of the year. Under these assumptions, cash receipts from customers equal sales of $20,000 minus the $500 increase in Accounts Receivable, or \$19,500. Therefore, using the direct method, the net cash provided by operating activities is \$19,500 − \$12,000 = \$7,500.

When the indirect method is used to calculate the net cash flow, net income of \$8,000 is adjusted for the \$500 increase in accounts receivable to get a net cash provided by operating activities of \$7,500. Both calculations are as follows:

| | |
|---|---|
| **Direct method:** | |
| Receipts from customers (\$20,000 − \$500) . . . . | \$19,500 |
| Payments for operating expenses . . . . . . . . . | −12,000 |
| Cash provided (or used) by operating activities . . | \$ 7,500 |
| **Indirect method:** | |
| Net income . . . . . . . . . . . . . . . . . . . . . | \$8,000 |
| Less the increase in Accounts Receivable . . . | −500 |
| Cash provided (or used) by operating activities . . | \$7,500 |

Notice that in the indirect method calculation the increase in Accounts Receivable is *subtracted* from net income.

As an another example, assume that the Accounts Receivable balance decreased from \$2,000 to \$1,200. Under this assumption, cash receipts from customers equal sales of \$20,000 plus the \$800 decrease in Accounts Receivable, or \$20,800. By the direct method, the net cash provided by operating activities is \$20,800 − \$12,000 = \$8,800. And when the indirect method is used, the \$800 decrease in Accounts Receivable is *added* to the \$8,000 net income to get \$8,800 net cash provided by operating activities.

When the indirect method is used, adjustments like those for Accounts Receivable are required for all noncash current assets related to operating activities. When a noncash current asset increases, part of the assets derived from operating activities are allocated to the increase. This leaves a smaller amount as a net cash inflow. Therefore, when you calculate the net cash inflow using the indirect method, the noncash current asset increase must be *subtracted* from net income. But when a noncash current asset decreases, the opposite adjustment is necessary. These adjustments for changes in current assets related to operating activities are as follows:

| |
|---|
| Net income |
| Add: Decreases in current assets |
| Subtract: Increases in current assets |
| Net cash provided (or used) by operating activities |

### Adjustments for Changes in Current Liabilities

To illustrate the adjustments for changes in current liabilities, return to the original assumptions about Simple Company. Sales of \$20,000 are for cash, and operating expenses are \$12,000. However, assume now that Simple Company has one current liability, Interest Payable, that relates to operating expenses. Also assume that the beginning-of-year balance in Interest Payable was \$500 and the end-of-year balance was \$900. This increase means that the operating expenses of \$12,000 include \$400 of interest that was not paid in cash during the period. Therefore, the cash payments for operating expenses were \$11,600, or \$12,000 – \$400. Under these assumptions, the direct method calculation of net cash provided by operating activities is \$8,400, or \$20,000 receipts from customers less \$11,600 payments for expenses. The indirect method calculation of \$8,400 is net income of \$8,000 plus the \$400 increase in Interest Payable.

Alternatively, if the Interest Payable balance decreased by \$600, the cash outflow for operating expenses would have been the \$12,000 expense plus the \$600 liability decrease, or \$12,600. Then, the direct calculation of net cash flow is \$20,000 – \$12,600 = \$7,400. The indirect calculation is \$8,000 – \$600 = \$7,400. In other words, when the indirect method is used, a *decrease* in Interest Payable is *subtracted* from net income.

When the indirect method is used, adjustments like those for Interest Payable are required for all current liabilities related to operating activities. When a current liability decreases, part of the assets derived from operating activities are allocated to pay for the decrease. Therefore, the decrease is subtracted from net income to determine the remaining net cash inflow. And when a current liability increases, the opposite adjustment is necessary. These adjustments for changes in current liabilities related to operating activities are:

| |
|---|
| Net income |
| Add: Increases in current liabilities |
| Subtract: Decreases in current liabilities |
| Net cash provided (or used) by operating activities |

### Adjustments for Other Operating Items that Do Not Provide or Use Cash

Some operating items that appear on an income statement do not provide or use cash during the current period. One example is depreciation. Other examples are amortization of intangible assets, depletion of natural resources, and bad debts expense.

These expenses are recorded with debits to expense accounts and credits to noncash accounts. They reduce net income but do not require cash outflows during the period. Therefore, when adjustments to net income are made according to the indirect method, these noncash expenses must be added back to net income.

In addition to noncash expenses such as depreciation, net income may include some revenues that do not provide cash inflows during the current period. An example is equity method earnings from a stock investment in another entity. If net income includes revenues that do not provide cash inflows, the revenues must be subtracted from net income in the process of reconciling net income to the net cash provided by operating activities.

The (indirect method) adjustments for expenses and revenues that do not provide or use cash during the current period are:

| |
|---|
| Net income |
| Add: Expenses that do not use cash |
| Subtract: Revenues that do not provide cash |
| Net cash provided (or used) by operating activities |

### Adjustments for Nonoperating Items

Some income statement items are not related to the operating activities of the company. These are gains and losses that result from investing and financing activities. Examples are gains or losses on the sale of plant assets and gains or losses on the retirement of bonds payable.

Remember that the indirect method reconciles net income to the net cash provided (or used) by *operating* activities. Therefore, net income must be adjusted to exclude gains and losses from investing and financing activities. In making the adjustments under the indirect method, gains from financing and investing activities are subtracted from net income and losses are added back to net income.

| |
|---|
| Net income |
| Add: Losses from investing or financing activities |
| Subtract: Gains from investing or financing activities |
| Net cash provided (or used) by operating activities |

## Applying the Indirect Method to Grover Company

To determine the net cash flows provided (or used) by operating activities according to the indirect method, you need balance sheets at the beginning and end of the period, the current period's income statement, and other information about selected transactions. Illustration 18–9 shows the income statement and balance sheet information for Grover Company. Based on this information, Illustration F–1 presents the indirect method reconciliation of net income to net cash provided by operating activities.

### Preparing the Indirect Method Working Paper

Prepare a working paper for a statement of cash flows so that the net cash flows from operating activities are calculated by the indirect method. (L. O. 7)

In addition to Grover Company's comparative balance sheets and income statement presented in Illustration 18–9, the information that is needed to prepare the working paper is restated below. The letter that identifies each item of information is also used in the working paper to cross-reference related debits and credits.

*a.* Net income was $38,000.

*b.* Accounts receivable increased by $20,000.

*c.* Merchandise inventory increased by $14,000.

*d.* Prepaid expenses increased by $2,000.

*e.* Accounts payable decreased by $5,000.

*f.* Interest payable decreased by $1,000.

*g*. Income taxes payable increased by $10,000.

*h*. Depreciation expense was $24,000.

*i*. Loss on sale of plant assets was $6,000; assets that cost $30,000 with accumulated depreciation of $12,000 were sold for $12,000 cash.

*j*. Gain on retirement of bonds was $16,000; bonds with a book value of $34,000 were retired with a cash payment of $18,000.

*k*. Plant assets that cost $70,000 were purchased; the payment consisted of $10,000 cash and the issuance of a $60,000 note payable.

*l*. Sold 3,000 shares of common stock for $15,000.

*m*. Paid cash dividends of $14,000.

Illustration F–2 shows the indirect method working paper for Grover Company. Notice that the beginning and ending balance sheets are recorded on the working paper the same as when the direct method is used. Following the balance sheets, information is entered in the Analysis of Changes columns about cash flows from operating, investing, and financing activities and about noncash investing and financing activities. Note that the working paper does not include a reconstruction of the income statement. Instead, net income is entered as the first source of cash flows from operating activities.

### Entering the Analysis of Changes on the Working Paper

After the balance sheets are entered, we recommend that you use the following sequence of procedures to complete the working paper:

1. Enter net income as an operating cash inflow (a debit) and as a credit to Retained Earnings.
2. In the statement of cash flows section, adjustments to net income are entered as debits if they increase cash inflows and as credits if they decrease cash inflows. Following this rule, adjust net income for the change in each noncash current asset and current liability related to operating activities. For each adjustment to net income, the offsetting debit or credit should reconcile the beginning and ending balances of a current asset or current liability.
3. Enter the adjustments to net income for income statement items, such as depreciation, that did not provide or use cash during the period. For each adjustment, the offsetting debit or credit should help reconcile a noncash balance sheet account.
4. Adjust net income to eliminate any gains or losses from investing and financing activities. Since the cash inflow of a gain is excluded from operating activities, it is entered as a credit. On the other hand, losses are entered with debits. For each of these adjustments, the related debits and/or credits help reconcile balance sheet accounts and also involve entries to show the cash flow from investing or financing activities.
5. After reviewing any unreconciled balance sheet accounts and related information, enter the reconciling entries for all remaining investing and financing activities. These include items such as purchases of

**Illustration F–2**

**GROVER COMPANY**
**Working Paper for Statement of Cash Flows (Indirect Method)**
**For Year Ended December 31, 1990**

| | December 31, 1989 | Analysis of Changes | | December 31, 1990 |
|---|---|---|---|---|
| | | Debit | Credit | |
| **Balance sheet—debits:** | | | | |
| Cash | 12,000 | | | 17,000 |
| Accounts receivable | 40,000 | (*b*) 20,000 | | 60,000 |
| Merchandise inventory | 70,000 | (*c*) 14,000 | | 84,000 |
| Prepaid expenses | 4,000 | (*d*) 2,000 | | 6,000 |
| Plant assets | 210,000 | (*k1*) 70,000 | (*i*) 30,000 | 250,000 |
| | 336,000 | | | 417,000 |
| **Balance sheet—credits:** | | | | |
| Accumulated depreciation | 48,000 | (*i*) 12,000 | (*h*) 24,000 | 60,000 |
| Accounts payable | 40,000 | (*e*) 5,000 | | 35,000 |
| Interest payable | 4,000 | (*f*) 1,000 | | 3,000 |
| Income taxes payable | 12,000 | | (*g*) 10,000 | 22,000 |
| Bonds payable | 64,000 | (*j*) 34,000 | (*k2*) 60,000 | 90,000 |
| Common stock, $5 par value | 80,000 | | (*l*) 15,000 | 95,000 |
| Retained earnings | 88,000 | (*m*) 14,000 | (*a*) 38,000 | 112,000 |
| | 336,000 | | | 417,000 |
| **Statement or cash flows:** | | | | |
| **Operating activities:** | | | | |
| Net income | | (*a*) 38,000 | | |
| Increase in accounts receivable | | | (*b*) 20,000 | |
| Increase in merchandise inventory | | | (*c*) 14,000 | |
| Increase in prepaid expenses | | | (*d*) 2,000 | |
| Decrease in accounts payable | | | (*e*) 5,000 | |
| Decrease in interest payable | | | (*f*) 1,000 | |
| Increase in income taxes payable | | (*g*) 10,000 | | |
| Depreciation expense | | (*h*) 24,000 | | |
| Loss on sale of plant assets | | (*i*) 6,000 | | |
| Gain on retirement of bonds | | | (*j*) 16,000 | |
| **Investing activities:** | | | | |
| Receipts from sale of plant assets | | (*i*) 12,000 | | |
| Payment for purchase of plant assets | | | (*k1*) 10,000 | |
| **Financing activities:** | | | | |
| Payments to retire bonds | | | (*j*) 18,000 | |
| Receipts from issuance of stock | | (*l*) 15,000 | | |
| Payments of dividends | | | (*m*) 14,000 | |
| **Noncash investing and financing activities:** | | | | |
| Purchase of plant assets financed by bonds | | (*k2*) 60,000 | (*k1*) 60,000 | |
| | | 337,000 | 337,000 | |

plant assets, issuance of long-term debt, sale of capital stock, and dividend payments. Some of these may require entries in the noncash investing and financing activities section of the working paper.

6. Confirm the accuracy of your work by totaling the Analysis of Changes columns and by determining that the change in each balance sheet account has been explained.

For Grover Company, these steps were performed in Illustration F–2. Step 1 is reflected in entry (*a*); step 2 in entries (*b*) through (*g*); step 3 in entry (*h*); step 4 in entries (*i*) through (*j*); and step 5 in entries (*k*) through (*m*). These adjustments correspond with the individual items of information presented earlier in the appendix. Because adjustments (*i*), (*j*), and (*k*) are more complex, they are shown below in debit and credit form.

| | | | |
|---|---|---|---|
| *i.* | Loss from Sale of Plant Assets | 6,000.00 | |
| | Accumulated Depreciation | 12,000.00 | |
| | Receipt from Sale of Plant Assets | 12,000.00 | |
| | Plant Assets | | 30,000.00 |
| | To reconstruct the sale of plant assets. | | |
| *j.* | Bonds Payable | 34,000.00 | |
| | Payments to Retire Bonds | | 18,000.00 |
| | Gain on Retirement of Bonds | | 16,000.00 |
| | To reconstruct the retirement of bonds. | | |
| *k1.* | Plant Assets | 70,000.00 | |
| | Payment to Purchase Plant Assets | | 10,000.00 |
| | Purchase of Plant Assets Financed by Bonds | | 60,000.00 |
| | To show purchase of plant assets, the cash payment and the use of noncash financing. | | |
| *k2.* | Purchase of Plant Assets Financed by Bonds | 60,000.00 | |
| | Bonds Payable | | 60,000.00 |
| | To show the issuance of bonds payable to finance purchase of plant assets. | | |

## Summary of Appendix F in Terms of Learning Objectives

**6.** Using the indirect method to calculate the net cash provided (or used) by operating activities, you first list the net income and then adjust it for three types of events. They are: (*a*) changes in noncash current assets and current liabilities related to operating activities, (*b*) revenues and expenses that did not provide or use cash, and (*c*) gains and losses from investing and financing activities. If the direct method is used, the reconciliation between net income and net cash provided (or used) by operating activities is reported on a separate schedule.

**7.** To prepare an indirect method working paper, you first enter the beginning and ending balances of the balance sheet accounts in columns 1 and 4. Then, the three sections of the statement of cash flows are established. Net income is entered as the first item in the operating activities section. Then, you adjust the net income for events (*a*) through (*c*) identified in the paragraph labeled (6) above. This reconciles the changes in the noncash current assets and current liabilities related to operations. Any remaining balance sheet account changes are reconciled and their cash effects are reported in the appropriate sections. Noncash investing and financing activities are entered at the bottom of the working paper.

## Glossary

Define or explain the words or phrases listed in the chapter Glossary. (L. O. 5)

**Cash equivalent** an investment that is readily convertible to a known amount of cash and that is sufficiently close to its maturity date so that its market value is relatively insensitive to interest rate changes. p. 754

**Direct method of calculating net cash provided or used by operating activities** a calculation of the net cash provided or used by operating activities that lists the major classes of operating cash receipts, such as receipts from customers, and subtracts the major classes of operating cash disbursements, such as cash paid for merchandise. pp. 751–52

**Financing activities** transactions with the owners or long-term creditors of the business or that involve borrowing cash on a short-term basis. p. 756

**Indirect method of calculating net cash provided or used by operating activities** a calculation that begins with net income and then adjusts the net income amount by adding and subtracting items that are necessary to reconcile net income to the net cash provided or used by operating activities. p. 753

**Investing activities** transactions that involve making and collecting loans or that involve purchasing and selling plant assets, other productive assets, or investments (other than cash equivalents). p. 756

**Operating activities** activities that involve the production or purchase of merchandise and the sale of goods and services to customers, including expenditures to administer the business. pp. 755–56

**Statement of cash flows** a financial statement that reports the cash inflows and outflows for an accounting period, and that classifies those cash flows as operating activities, investing activities, and financing activities. p. 751

## Objective Review

Answers to the following questions are listed in Appendix I at the end of the book. Be sure that you decide which is the one best answer to each question *before* you check the answers in the appendix.

1. Repayment of a cash loan is an example of a:
   *a.* Cash flow from operating activities.
   *b.* Cash flow from investing activities.
   *c.* Cash flow from financing activities.
   *d.* Noncash investing and financing activity.
   *e.* Cash payment to purchase a cash equivalent.
2. The following T-account is a summary of the Cash account of Evans Company.

**Summarized Cash Account, Evans Company**

| | | | |
|---|---|---|---|
| Balance, 12/31/90 | 4,000 | | |
| Receipts from customers | 182,000 | Payments for merchandise | 100,000 |
| Proceeds from dividends from stock investments | 3,000 | Payments for other operating expenses | 70,000 |
| Proceeds from issuance of bonds payable | 50,000 | Interest payments | 5,000 |
| | | Tax payments | 4,000 |
| Proceeds from sale of stock investment | 18,000 | Payments to purchase treasury stock | 50,000 |
| | | Dividend payments | 15,000 |
| Balance, 12/31/91 | 11,000 | | |

A statement of cash flows prepared according to the direct method would state:

*a.* Net cash provided (or used) by operating activities, $ 7,000.
*b.* Net cash provided (or used) by investing activities, $ 21,000.
*c.* Net cash provided (or used) by financing activities, $(15,000).
*d.* Net cash provided (or used) by operating activities, $ 11,000.
*e.* Net cash provided (or used) by investing activities, $(32,000).

3. Banghart Company's Merchandise Inventory account balance decreased during a period from a beginning balance of $40,000 to an ending balance of $35,000. Cost of goods sold for that same period was $210,000. If the Accounts Payable balance increased $3,000 during the period, what was the amount of cash paid for merchandise?
   *a.* $202,000.
   *b.* $208,000.
   *c.* $210,000.
   *d.* $212,000.
   *e.* $218,000.
4. In preparing a working paper for a statement of cash flows so that cash flows from operating activities are reported according to the direct method:
   *a.* Sales revenue is entered as a credit in the income statement section and as a debit to Accounts Receivable.
   *b.* The amount of net income is credited to retained earnings.
   *c.* The net effect on cash of entries under the noncash investing and financing activities for the purchase of plant assets financed by bonds is $–0– (the debits equal the credits).
   *d.* Expenses paid in cash have no effect on the noncash balance sheet accounts and are recorded as debits in the income statement section and credits in the statement of cash flows section.
   *e.* All of the above.

## Questions for Class Discussion

*An asterisk (*) identifies the questions, exercises, and problems that are based on Appendix F at the end of the chapter.*

1. What information is shown on a statement of cash flows?
2. What are the three categories of cash flows shown on a statement of cash flows?
3. What are some examples of items that are reported on a statement of cash flows as investing activities?
4. What are some examples of items that are reported on a statement of cash flows as financing activities?
5. When a statement of cash flows is prepared by the direct method, what are some examples of items that are reported as cash flows from operating activities?
6. A machine that was held as a long-term asset for use in business operations is sold for cash. Where should this cash flow appear on the statement of cash flows?

7. A business purchases merchandise inventory for cash. Where should this cash flow appear on the statement of cash flows?
8. If a corporation pays cash dividends, where on the corporation's statement of cash flows should the payment be reported?
9. A company purchases land for $200,000 and finances 100% of the purchase with a long-term note payable. Should this transaction be reported on a statement of cash flows? If so, where on the statement should it be reported?
10. A company purchases land for $100,000, paying $20,000 cash and borrowing the remainder on a long-term note payable. How should this transaction be reported on a statement of cash flows?
11. What is meant by the direct method of reporting cash flows from operating activities?
12. What is meant by the indirect method of reporting cash flows from operating activities?
13. Do the direct and indirect methods of calculating cash flows from operating activities lead to the same net amount?
14. Is depreciation a source of cash?
15. On June 3, a company borrowed $50,000 by giving its bank a 60-day, interest-bearing note. On the statement of cash flows, where should this item be reported?
16. A company borrowed $50,000 by giving its bank a 60-day, 12% interest-bearing note. When the note was repaid, the company also paid interest of $1,000. On the statement of cash flows, where should the $1,000 interest payment be reported?
17. When a working paper for the preparation of a statement of cash flows is prepared, all changes in noncash balance sheet accounts are accounted for on the working paper. Why?
18. A company retired a long-term note payable by issuing, at par, shares of common stock. How is this event analyzed on the statement of cash flows working paper?

*19. If a company reports a net income for the year, is it possible for the company to show a net cash outflow from operating activities? Explain your answer.

*20. Why are expenses such as depreciation and amortization of goodwill added to net income when cash flow from operations is calculated by the indirect method?

*21. A company had $70,000 of merchandise inventory at the beginning of a period and $40,000 of merchandise inventory at the end of the same period. If the net cash flow from operating activities is calculated by the indirect method, how should this decrease in inventory be treated in the calculation?

*22. A company reports a net income of $15,000 that includes a $3,000 gain on sale of plant assets. Why is this gain subtracted from net income in the process of reconciling net income to the net cash provided or used by operating activities?

## Exercises

**Exercise 18–1**
**Classifying transactions on statement of cash flows**
(L. O. 1)

HW due 10-12

Examine each of the following items to determine (*a*) where on the statement of cash flows the item should be included, (*b*) if it should be included in the schedule of noncash investing and financing activities, or (*c*) if it should not be included in either the statement of cash flows or the schedule of noncash investing and financing activities. Prepare a table for your answers and record your answers by placing check marks in the appropriate columns.

| | Statement of Cash Flows | | | Schedule of Noncash Investing and Financing Activities | Not Reported on Statement or Schedule |
|---|---|---|---|---|---|
| | Operating Activities | Investing Activities | Financing Activities | | |
| *a.* A six-month note receivable was accepted in exchange for a building that had been used in operations. | ____ | ____ | ____ | ____ | ____ |
| *b.* A cash dividend that was declared in a previous period was paid in the current period. | ____ | ____ | ____ | ____ | ____ |
| *c.* Surplus merchandise inventory was sold for cash. | ____ | ____ | ____ | ____ | ____ |
| *d.* Paid cash to purchase a trademark. | ____ | ____ | ____ | ____ | ____ |
| *e.* Long-term bonds payable were retired by issuing common stock. | ____ | ____ | ____ | ____ | ____ |
| *f.* Borrowed cash from the bank by signing a six-month note payable. | ____ | ____ | ____ | ____ | ____ |

**Exercise 18–2**
**Organizing the statement of cash flows and supporting schedule**
(L. O. 1, 2)

Use the following information about the 1990 cash flows of Techniboard Company to prepare a statement of cash flows and a schedule of noncash investing and financing activities:

| | |
|---|---|
| Cash and cash equivalents balance, December 31, 1989 . . | $ 24,000 |
| Cash and cash equivalents balance, December 31, 1990 . . | 17,000 |
| Cash paid to retire long-term notes payable . . . . . . . . . | 150,000 |
| Cash received from sale of building . . . . . . . . . . . . . | 85,000 |
| Cash payments for merchandise . . . . . . . . . . . . . . . | 72,000 |
| Cash paid for store equipment . . . . . . . . . . . . . . . | 15,000 |
| Cash borrowed on six-month note payable . . . . . . . . . | 22,000 |
| Cash dividends paid . . . . . . . . . . . . . . . . . . . . . | 12,000 |
| Bonds payable retired by issuing common stock . . . . . . | 100,000 |
| Cash paid for salaries . . . . . . . . . . . . . . . . . . . . | 37,000 |
| Cash payments for other expenses . . . . . . . . . . . . . | 46,000 |
| Land purchased and financed by long-term note payable . . | 60,000 |
| Cash received from customers . . . . . . . . . . . . . . . | 210,000 |
| Cash received as interest . . . . . . . . . . . . . . . . . . | 8,000 |

**Exercise 18–3**
**Calculating cash flows**
(L. O. 3)

In each of the following cases, use the information provided about the 1990 operations of Barney Company to calculate the indicated cash flow:

Case A: Calculate cash paid for rent:

| | |
|---|---|
| Rent expense . . . . . . . . . . . . . . . . | $19,000 |
| Prepaid rent, January 1 . . . . . . . . . . . . | 4,500 |
| Prepaid rent, December 31 . . . . . . . . . . | 3,000 |

| | | |
|---|---|---|
| Case B: | Calculate cash paid to employees: | |
| | Salaries expense . . . . . . . . . . . . . . . | $14,000 |
| | Salaries payable, January 1 . . . . . . . . . | 5,000 |
| | Salaries payable, December 31 . . . . . . . | 8,000 |
| Case C: | Calculate cash received from customers: | |
| | Sales revenue . . . . . . . . . . . . . . . . . . | $60,000 |
| | Accounts receivable, January 1 . . . . . . . | 12,000 |
| | Accounts receivable, December 31 . . . . . | 9,000 |

**Exercise 18–4**
**Calculating cash flows**
(L. O. 3)

In each of the following cases, use the information provided about the 1990 operations of Lehman Company to calculate the indicated cash flow:

| | | |
|---|---|---|
| Case A: | Calculate cash received from interest: | |
| | Interest revenue . . . . . . . . . . . . . . . . | $34,000 |
| | Interest receivable, January 1 . . . . . . . . | 2,500 |
| | Interest receivable, December 31 . . . . . . | 1,800 |
| Case B: | Calculate cash paid for utilities: | |
| | Utilities expense . . . . . . . . . . . . . . . | $16,800 |
| | Utilities payable, January 1 . . . . . . . . . . | 7,500 |
| | Utilities payable, December 31 . . . . . . . . | 4,700 |
| Case C: | Calculate cash paid for merchandise: | |
| | Cost of goods sold . . . . . . . . . . . . . . | $59,000 |
| | Merchandise inventory, January 1 . . . . . . | 18,600 |
| | Accounts payable, January 1 . . . . . . . . . | 14,300 |
| | Merchandise inventory, December 31 . . . . | 19,200 |
| | Accounts Payable, December 31 . . . . . . | 11,700 |

**Exercise 18–5**
**Cash flows from operating activities (direct method)**
(L. O. 2, 3)

Use the following income statement and information about changes in noncash current assets and current liabilities to present the cash flows from operating activities using the direct method:

**ECOSYSTEMS COMPANY**
**Income Statement**
**For Year Ended December 31, 1990**

| | | |
|---|---|---|
| Sales . . . . . . . . . . . . . . | | $225,000 |
| Cost of goods sold . . . . . . . . | | 130,000 |
| Gross profit from sales . . . . . | | $ 95,000 |
| Operating expenses: | | |
| Salaries and wages . . . . . . | $31,250 | |
| Depreciation expense . . . . . | 3,750 | |
| Rent expense . . . . . . . . . . | 9,000 | |
| Amortization of goodwill . . . . | 1,750 | |
| Interest expense . . . . . . . . | 2,375 | 48,125 |
| Total . . . . . . . . . . . . . . | | $ 46,875 |
| Gain on sale of machinery . . . . | | 1,000 |
| Net income . . . . . . . . . . . . | | $ 47,875 |

Changes in current asset and current liability accounts during the year, all of which related to operating activities, were as follows:

| | |
|---|---|
| Accounts receivable . . . . . . . . | $4,000 decrease |
| Merchandise inventory . . . . . . . | 5,000 increase |
| Accounts payable . . . . . . . . . . | 7,000 increase |
| Salaries and wages payable . . . . | 3,000 decrease |

***Exercise 18–6**
**Cash flows from operating activities (indirect method)**
(L. O. 3, 6)

Refer to the information about Ecosystems Company presented in Exercise 18–5. Use the indirect method and calculate the cash provided (or used) by operating activities.

***Exercise 18–7**
**Cash flows from operating activities (indirect method)**
(L. O. 6)

Megan Corporation's 1990 income statement showed the following: net income, $42,000; depreciation expense, $7,000; amortization expense, $3,500; and loss on sale of plant assets, $4,000. An examination of the company's current assets and current liabilities showed that the following changes occurred because of operating activities: accounts receivable increased $5,600; merchandise inventory decreased $7,000; prepaid expenses increased $2,800; accounts payable decreased $4,200; other payables increased $1,900. Use the indirect method to calculate the cash flow from operating activities.

**Exercise 18–8**
**Noncash investing and financing activities**
(L. O. 2)

Use the following information to prepare a schedule of noncash investing and financing activities for Digit Corp.

*a.* The income statement shows a $5,000 loss on exchange of machinery. The loss relates to an old machine that had a book value of $25,000 when it was exchanged for a new machine that had a cash price of $20,000.

*b.* Outstanding bonds payable carried on the books at $100,000 were retired by issuing 800 shares of $100 par, common stock.

*c.* Land valued at $250,000 was purchased by paying cash of $50,000 and signing a long-term note payable for the balance.

*d.* The income statement shows a $30,000 gain on the sale of a building. The building had a book value of $90,000 and was sold for $120,000. Digit Corp. received $50,000 cash and accepted a long-term promissory note for the balance of the sales price.

**Exercise 18–9**
**Statement of cash flows (direct method)**
(L. O. 2, 3)

Gail Company's 1990 and 1989 balance sheets showed the following items:

| | December 31 | |
|---|---|---|
| | **1990** | **1989** |
| **Debits** | | |
| Cash | $ 15,000 | $ 12,000 |
| Accounts receivable | 24,000 | 27,000 |
| Merchandise inventory | 63,000 | 54,000 |
| Equipment | 53,000 | 45,000 |
| Totals | $155,000 | $138,000 |
| **Credits** | | |
| Accumulated depreciation, equipment | $ 14,000 | $ 9,000 |
| Common stock, $10 par value | 75,000 | 75,000 |
| Retained earnings | 66,000 | 54,000 |
| Totals | $155,000 | $138,000 |

An examination of the company's activities during 1990, including the income statement, reveals the following:

| | | | |
|---|---|---|---|
| *a.* | Sales (all on credit) | | $190,000 |
| *b.* | The only decreases in Accounts Receivable were receipts from customers. | | |
| *c.* | Cost of goods sold | $103,000 | |
| *d.* | All merchandise purchases were for cash. | | |
| *e.* | Depreciation expense | 5,000 | |
| *f.* | Other operating expenses | 60,000 | 168,000 |
| | Net income | | $ 22,000 |
| *g.* | Equipment was purchased for $8,000 cash. | | |
| *h.* | The company declared and paid $10,000 of cash dividends during the year. | | |

*Required*

Prepare a statement of cash flows that follows the direct method to calculate the net cash provided (or used) by operating activities. Do not prepare a working paper but show any supporting calculations.

***Exercise 18–10**
**Statement of cash flows (indirect method)**
(L. O. 3, 6)

Refer to the facts about Gail Company presented in Exercise 18–9. Prepare a statement of cash flows that follows the indirect method of calculating the net cash provided (or used) by operating activities. Do not prepare a working paper but show any supporting calculations.

## Problems

**Problem 18–1**
**Statement of cash flows (direct method)**
(L. O. 1, 2, 3)

Mason Corporation's 1990 and 1989 balance sheets carried the following items:

| | December 31 | |
|---|---|---|
| | **1990** | **1989** |
| **Debits** | | |
| Cash | $ 63,000 | $ 24,000 |
| Accounts receivable | 48,000 | 54,000 |
| Merchandise inventory | 126,000 | 108,000 |
| Equipment | 111,000 | 90,000 |
| Totals | $348,000 | $276,000 |
| **Credits** | | |
| Accumulated depreciation, equipment | $ 27,000 | $ 18,000 |
| Accounts payable | 51,000 | 30,000 |
| Income taxes payable | 6,000 | 12,000 |
| Common stock, $10 par value | 165,000 | 150,000 |
| Contributed capital in excess of par value, common stock | 33,000 | 30,000 |
| Retained earnings | 66,000 | 36,000 |
| Totals | $348,000 | $276,000 |

An examination of the company's activities during 1990, including the income statement, shows the following:

| | | | |
|---|---|---|---|
| *a1.* | Sales (all on credit) . . . . . . . . . . . . . . | | $750,000 |
| *a2.* | Credits to Accounts Receivable during the period were receipts from customers. | | |
| *b1.* | Cost of goods sold . . . . . . . . . . . . . . | $400,000 | |
| *b2.* | Purchases of merchandise were on credit. | | |
| *b3.* | Debits to Accounts Payable during the period resulted from payments for merchandise. | | |
| *c.* | Depreciation expense . . . . . . . . . . . . | 9,000 | |
| *d.* | Other operating expenses . . . . . . . . . . . | 241,000 | |
| *e1.* | Income taxes expense . . . . . . . . . . . . | 40,000 | 690,000 |
| *e2.* | The only decreases in Income Taxes Payable were payments of taxes. | | |
| *f.* | Net income . . . . . . . . . . . . . . . . . . | | $ 60,000 |

*g.* Equipment was purchased for $21,000 cash.
*h.* Fifteen hundred shares of stock were issued for cash at $12 per share.
*i.* The company declared and paid $30,000 of cash dividends during the year.

*Required*

Prepare a statement of cash flows that reports the cash inflows and outflows from operating activities according to the direct method. Do not prepare a working paper. Instead, prepare the statement directly from your examination of the balance sheets and the additional information provided about the income statement and other transactions of the company. Show your supporting calculations.

**Problem 18–2**
**Cash flows working paper (direct method)**
(L. O. 1, 4)

Refer to the information about Mason Corporation presented in Problem 18–1. Prepare a working paper for a statement of cash flows according to the direct method.

***Problem 18–3**
**Reconciling net income to cash flows from operating activities**
(L. O. 6)

Refer to Mason Corporation's balance sheets presented in Problem 18–1. The additional information about the company's activities during 1990 is restated as follows:

*a.* Net income was $60,000.
*b.* Accounts receivable decreased.
*c.* Merchandise inventory increased.
*d.* Accounts payable increased.
*e.* Income taxes payable decreased.
*f.* Depreciation expense was $9,000.
*g.* Equipment was purchased for $21,000 cash.
*h.* Fifteen hundred shares of stock were issued for cash at $12 per share.
*i.* The company declared and paid $30,000 of cash dividends during the year.

*Required*

Prepare a schedule that reconciles net income to the net cash provided or used by operating activities.

***Problem 18–4**
**Cash flows working paper (indirect method)**
(L. O. 1, 7)

Refer to the facts about Mason Corporation presented in Problem 18–1 and Problem 18–3. Prepare a statement of cash flows working paper that follows the indirect method of calculating cash flows from operating activities. Identify the debits and credits in the Analysis of Changes columns with letters that correspond to the list of information about the company presented in Problem 18–3.

**Problem 18–5**
**Statement of cash flows (direct method)**
(L. O. 1, 2, 3)

Skipper Corporation's 1990 and 1989 balance sheets included the following items:

| | December 31 | |
|---|---|---|
| | 1990 | 1989 |
| **Debits** | | |
| Cash | $ 97,800 | $ 25,800 |
| Accounts receivable | 48,000 | 60,000 |
| Merchandise inventory | 189,000 | 192,000 |
| Prepaid expenses | 6,000 | 7,200 |
| Equipment | 220,600 | 154,000 |
| Totals | $561,400 | $439,000 |
| **Credits** | | |
| Accumulated depreciation, equipment | $ 36,600 | $ 32,800 |
| Accounts payable | 129,000 | 107,400 |
| Short-term notes payable | 15,000 | 9,000 |
| Long-term notes payable | 76,000 | 60,000 |
| Common stock, $10 par value | 155,000 | 150,000 |
| Contributed capital in excess of par value, common stock | 40,000 | |
| Retained earnings | 109,800 | 79,800 |
| Totals | $561,400 | $439,000 |

Additional information about the 1990 activities of the company is as follows:

| | | | |
|---|---|---|---|
| *a1.* | Sales revenue, all on credit | | $425,000 |
| *a2.* | Credits to Accounts Receivable during the period were receipts from customers. | | |
| *b1.* | Cost of goods sold | $260,000 | |
| *b2.* | All merchandise purchases were on credit. | | |
| *b3.* | Debits to Accounts Payable during the period resulted from payments to creditors. | | |
| *c.* | Depreciation expense | 12,600 | |
| *d1.* | Other expenses | 90,150 | |
| *d2.* | The decrease in prepaid expenses was charged to Other Expenses. | | |
| *e.* | Income taxes expense | 12,450 | |
| *f.* | Loss on sale of equipment | 1,800 | 377,000 |
| | The equipment cost $14,800, was depreciated $8,800, and was sold for $4,200. | | |
| *g.* | Net income | | $ 48,000 |

*h1.* Equipment that cost $81,400 was purchased by paying cash of $41,400 and (*h2*) by signing a long-term note payable for the balance.
*i.* Borrowed $6,000 by signing a short-term note payable.
*j.* Paid $24,000 to reduce a long-term note payable.
*k.* Issued 500 shares of common stock for cash at $90 per share.
*l.* Declared and paid cash dividends of $18,000.

*Required*

Prepare a statement of cash flows that reports the cash inflows and outflows from operating activities according to the direct method. Do not prepare a working paper. Instead, prepare the statement directly from your examination of the balance sheets and the additional information provided about the income statement and other transactions of the company. Show your supporting calculations.

Also prepare a schedule of noncash investing and financing activities.

**Problem 18–6**
**Cash flows working paper (direct method)**
(L. O. 1, 4)

Refer to the information about Skipper Corporation presented in Problem 18–5. Prepare a working paper for a statement of cash flows according to the direct method.

***Problem 18–7**
**Reconciling net income to cash flows from operating activities**
(L. O. 6)

Refer to Skipper Corporation's balance sheets presented in Problem 18–5. The additional information about the company's activities during 1990 is restated as follows:

*a.* Net income was $48,000.
*b.* Accounts receivable decreased.
*c.* Merchandise inventory decreased.
*d.* Prepaid expenses decreased.
*e.* Accounts payable increased.
*f.* Depreciation expense was $12,600.
*g.* Equipment that cost $14,800 and was depreciated $8,800 was sold for $4,200 cash, which caused a loss of $1,800.
*h.* Equipment that cost $81,400 was purchased by paying cash of $41,400 and (*i*) by signing a long-term note payable for the balance.
*j.* Borrowed $6,000 by signing a short-term note payable.
*k.* Paid $24,000 to reduce a long-term note payable.
*l.* Issued 500 shares of common stock for cash at $90 per share.
*m.* Declared and paid cash dividends of $18,000.

*Required*

Prepare a schedule that reconciles net income to the net cash provided or used by operating activities.

***Problem 18–8**
**Cash flows working paper (indirect method)**
(L. O. 1, 7)

Refer to the facts about Skipper Corporation presented in Problem 18–5 and Problem 18–7. Prepare a statement of cash flows working paper that follows the indirect method of calculating cash flows from operating activities. Identify the debits and credits in the Analysis of Changes columns with letters that correspond to the list of information about the company presented in Problem 18–7.

## Alternate Problems

**Problem 18–1A**
**Statement of cash flows (direct method)**
(L. O. 1, 2, 3)

Cemco Corporation's 1990 and 1989 balance sheets carried the following items:

| | December 31 1990 | December 31 1989 |
|---|---|---|
| **Debits** | | |
| Cash | $ 50,400 | $ 19,200 |
| Accounts receivable | 38,400 | 43,200 |
| Merchandise inventory | 100,800 | 86,400 |
| Equipment | 88,800 | 72,000 |
| Totals | $278,400 | $220,800 |
| **Credits** | | |
| Accumulated depreciation, equipment | $ 21,600 | $ 14,400 |
| Accounts payable | 40,800 | 24,000 |
| Income taxes payable | 4,800 | 9,600 |
| Common stock, $10 par value | 132,000 | 120,000 |
| Contributed capital in excess of par value, common stock | 26,400 | 24,000 |
| Retained earnings | 52,800 | 28,800 |
| Totals | $278,400 | $220,800 |

An examination of the company's activities during 1990, including the income statement, shows the following:

| | | | |
|---|---|---|---|
| *a1.* | Sales (all on credit) | | $600,000 |
| *a2.* | The only decreases in Accounts Receivable were receipts from customers. | | |
| *b1.* | Cost of goods sold | $320,000 | |
| *b2.* | Purchases of merchandise were on credit. | | |
| *b3.* | Debits to Accounts Payable during the period resulted from payments for merchandise. | | |
| *c.* | Depreciation expense | 7,200 | |
| *d.* | Other operating expenses | 192,800 | |
| *e1.* | Income taxes expense | 32,000 | 552,000 |
| *e2.* | The only decreases in Income Taxes Payable were payments of taxes. | | |
| *f.* | Net income | | $ 48,000 |

*g.* Equipment was purchased for $16,800 cash.
*h.* Twelve hundred shares of stock were issued for cash at $12 per share.
*i.* The company declared and paid $24,000 of cash dividends during the year.

*Required*

Prepare a statement of cash flows that reports the cash inflows and outflows from operating activities according to the direct method. Do not prepare a working paper. Instead, prepare the statement directly from your examination of the balance sheets and the additional information provided about the income statement and other transactions of the company. Show your supporting calculations.

**Problem 18–2A**
**Cash flows working paper (direct method)**
(L. O. 1, 4)

Refer to the information about Cemco Corporation presented in Problem 18–1A. Prepare a working paper for a statement of cash flows according to the direct method.

***Problem 18–3A**
**Reconciling net income to cash flows from operating activities**
(L. O. 6)

Refer to Cemco Corporation's balance sheets presented in Problem 18–1A. The additional information about the company's activities during 1990 is identified as follows:

*a.* Net income was $48,000.
*b.* Accounts receivable decreased.
*c.* Merchandise inventory increased.
*d.* Accounts payable increased.
*e.* Income taxes payable decreased.
*f.* Depreciation expense was $7,200.
*g.* Equipment was purchased for $16,800 cash.
*h.* Twelve hundred shares of stock were issued for cash at $12 per share.
*i.* The company declared and paid $24,000 of cash dividends during the year.

*Required*

Prepare a schedule that reconciles net income to the net cash provided or used by operating activities.

***Problem 18–4A**
**Cash flows working paper (indirect method)**
(L. O. 1, 7)

Refer to the facts about Cemco Corporation presented in Problem 18–1A and Problem 18–3A. Prepare a statement of cash flows working paper that follows the indirect method of calculating cash flows from operating activities. Identify the debits and credits in the Analysis of Changes columns with letters that correspond to the list of information about the company presented in Problem 18–3A.

**Problem 18–5A**
**Statement of cash flows (direct method)**
(L. O. 1, 2, 3)

Columbus Corporation's 1990 and 1989 balance sheets included the following items:

| | December 31 | |
|---|---|---|
| | 1990 | 1989 |
| **Debits** | | |
| Cash | $146,700 | $ 38,700 |
| Accounts receivable | 72,000 | 90,000 |
| Merchandise inventory | 283,500 | 288,000 |
| Prepaid expenses | 9,000 | 10,800 |
| Equipment | 330,900 | 231,000 |
| Totals | $842,100 | $658,500 |

| | December 31 | |
|---|---|---|
| | 1990 | 1989 |
| **Credits** | | |
| Accumulated depreciation, equipment | $ 54,900 | $ 49,200 |
| Accounts payable | 193,500 | 161,100 |
| Short-term notes payable | 22,500 | 13,500 |
| Long-term notes payable | 114,000 | 90,000 |
| Common stock, $15 par value | 232,500 | 225,000 |
| Contributed capital in excess of par value, common stock | 60,000 | |
| Retained earnings | 164,700 | 119,700 |
| Totals | $842,100 | $658,500 |

Additional information about the 1990 activities of the company is as follows:

| | | | |
|---|---|---|---|
| *a1.* | Sales revenue, all on credit | | $637,500 |
| *a2.* | Decreases in Accounts Receivable were only from receipts from customers. | | |
| *b1.* | Cost of goods sold | $390,000 | |
| *b2.* | All merchandise purchases were on credit. | | |
| *b3.* | Debits to Accounts Payable during the period were from payments for merchandise. | | |
| *c.* | Depreciation expense | 18,900 | |
| *d1.* | Other expenses | 135,225 | |
| *d2.* | The decrease in prepaid expenses was charged to Other Expenses. | | |
| *e.* | Income taxes expense | 18,675 | |
| *f.* | Loss on sale of equipment | 2,700 | 565,500 |
| | The equipment cost $22,200, was depreciated $13,200, and was sold for $6,300. | | |
| *g.* | Net income | | $ 72,000 |

*h1.* Equipment that cost $122,100 was purchased by paying cash of $62,100 and (*h2*) by signing a long-term note payable for the balance.
*i.* Borrowed $9,000 by signing a short-term note payable.
*j.* Paid $36,000 to reduce a long-term note payable.
*k.* Issued 500 shares of common stock for cash at $135 per share.
*l.* Declared and paid cash dividends of $27,000.

*Required*

Prepare a statement of cash flows that reports the cash inflows and outflows from operating activities according to the direct method. Do not prepare a working paper. Instead, prepare the statement directly from your examination of the balance sheets and the additional information provided about the income statement and other transactions of the company. Show your supporting calculations.

Also prepare a schedule of noncash investing and financing activities.

**Problem 18–6A**
**Cash flows working paper (direct method)**
(L. O. 1, 4)

Refer to the information about Columbus Corporation presented in Problem 18–5A. Prepare a working paper for a statement of cash flows according to the direct method.

***Problem 18–7A**
**Reconciling net income to cash flows from operating activities**
(L. O. 6)

Refer to Columbus Corporation's balance sheets presented in Problem 18–5A. The additional information about the company's activities during 1990 is restated as follows:

*a.* Net income was $72,000.
*b.* Accounts receivable decreased.
*c.* Merchandise inventory decreased.
*d.* Prepaid expenses decreased.
*e.* Accounts payable increased.
*f.* Depreciation expense was $18,900.
*g.* Equipment that cost $22,200 and was depreciated $13,200 was sold for $6,300 cash, which caused a loss of $2,700.
*h.* Equipment that cost $122,100 was purchased by paying cash of $62,100 and by signing a long-term note payable for the balance.
*i.* Borrowed $9,000 by signing a short-term note payable.
*j.* Paid $36,000 to reduce a long-term note payable.
*k.* Issued 500 shares of common stock for cash at $135 per share.
*l.* Declared and paid cash dividends of $27,000.

*Required*

Prepare a schedule that reconciles net income to the net cash provided or used by operating activities.

***Problem 18–8A**
**Cash flows working paper (indirect method)**
(L. O. 1, 7)

Refer to the facts about Columbus Corporation presented in Problem 18–5A and Problem 18–7A. Prepare a statement of cash flows working paper that follows the indirect method of calculating cash flows from operating activities. Identify the debits and credits in the Analysis of Changes columns with letters that correspond to the list of information about the company presented in Problem 18–7A.

## Provocative Problems

**Provocative Problem 18–1**
**Yaupon, Inc.**
(L. O. 3)

Yaupon, Inc.'s 1990 statement of cash flows appeared as follows:

| | | |
|---|---|---|
| Cash flows from operating activities: | | |
| Cash receipts from customers | $ 772,800 | |
| Cash payments for merchandise | (425,400) | |
| Payments for other operating expenses | (169,800) | |
| Payments of income taxes | (32,400) | |
| Net cash provided by operating activities | | $145,200 |
| Cash flows from investing activities: | | |
| Receipt from sale of office equipment | $ 5,100 | |
| Purchase of store equipment | (33,000) | |
| Net cash used by investing activities | | (27,900) |
| Cash flows from financing activities: | | |
| Payment to retire bonds payable | $ (42,300) | |
| Payment of dividends | (30,000) | |
| Net cash used by financing activities | | (72,300) |
| Net increase in cash | | $ 45,000 |
| Cash balance at beginning of year | | 45,400 |
| Cash balance at end of year | | $ 90,400 |

Yaupon, Inc.'s beginning and ending balance sheets were as follows:

| | December 31 1990 | December 31 1989 |
|---|---|---|
| **Debits** | | |
| Cash | $ 90,400 | $ 45,400 |
| Accounts receivable | 114,900 | 100,200 |
| Merchandise inventory | 212,700 | 260,300 |
| Prepaid expenses | 9,000 | 4,400 |
| Equipment | 99,100 | 108,600 |
| Totals | $526,100 | $518,900 |
| **Credits** | | |
| Accumulated depreciation, equipment | $ 18,200 | $ 30,200 |
| Accounts payable | 58,500 | 74,800 |
| Income taxes payable | 10,900 | 6,500 |
| Dividends payable | –0– | 7,500 |
| Bonds payable | –0– | 50,000 |
| Common stock, $5 par value | 300,000 | 300,000 |
| Retained earnings | 138,500 | 49,900 |
| Totals | $526,100 | $518,900 |

An examination of the company's statements and accounts showed:

*a.* All sales were made on credit.
*b.* All merchandise purchases were on credit.
*c.* Accounts Payable balances resulted from merchandise purchases.
*d.* Prepaid expenses relate to other operating expenses.
*e.* Equipment that cost $42,500 and was depreciated $24,000 was sold for cash.
*f.* Equipment was purchased for cash.
*g.* The change in the balance of Accumulated Depreciation resulted from depreciation expense and from the sale of equipment.
*h.* The change in the balance of Retained Earnings resulted from dividend declarations and net income.

*Required*

Present Yaupon, Inc.'s income statement for 1990. Show your supporting calculations.

**Provocative Problem 18–2**
**James Company**
(L. O. 1, 2, 4, 6)

The following items include the 1990 and 1989 balance sheets and the 1990 income statement of the James Company. Additional information about the company's 1990 transactions is presented after the financial statements.

JAMES COMPANY
Balance Sheet
December 31, 1990 and 1989

| | 1990 | | 1989 | |
|---|---|---|---|---|
| **Assets** | | | | |
| Current assets: | | | | |
| Cash and cash equivalents | $ 1,000 | | $ 800 | |
| Accounts receivable | 4,500 | | 3,100 | |
| Merchandise inventory | 19,000 | | 16,000 | |
| Prepaid expenses | 700 | | 600 | |
| Total current assets | | $25,200 | | $20,500 |
| Long-term investments: | | | | |
| Icahn Corporation common stock | | 10,000 | | 12,000 |
| Plant assets: | | | | |
| Land | | 9,000 | | 4,000 |
| Buildings | $60,000 | | $60,000 | |
| Less accumulated depreciation | 38,000 | 22,000 | 36,000 | 24,000 |
| Equipment | $21,000 | | $16,000 | |
| Less accumulated depreciation | 6,000 | 15,000 | 4,000 | 12,000 |
| Total assets | | $81,200 | | $72,500 |
| **Liabilities** | | | | |
| Current liabilities: | | | | |
| Notes payable | $ 5,000 | | $ 3,500 | |
| Accounts payable | 9,000 | | 10,000 | |
| Other accrued liabilities | 5,300 | | 4,200 | |
| Interest payable | 400 | | 300 | |
| Taxes payable | 300 | | 500 | |
| Total current liabilities | | $20,000 | | $18,500 |
| Long-term liabilities: | | | | |
| Bonds payable, due in 1999 | | 25,000 | | 22,000 |
| Total liabilities | | $45,000 | | $40,500 |
| **Stockholders' Equity** | | | | |
| Contributed capital: | | | | |
| Common stock, $1 par value | $11,000 | | $10,000 | |
| Contributed capital in excess of par value | 5,000 | | 4,000 | |
| Retained earnings | 22,000 | | 18,000 | |
| Total | $38,000 | | $32,000 | |
| Less cost of treasury stock | 1,800 | | -0- | |
| Total stockholders' equity | | 36,200 | | 32,000 |
| Total liabilities and stockholders' equity | | $81,200 | | $72,500 |

**JAMES COMPANY**
**Income Statement**
**For Year Ended December 31, 1990**

| | | |
|---|---|---|
| Revenues: | | |
| Sales | $120,000 | |
| Gain on sale of stock investment | 3,000 | |
| Dividend income | 500 | |
| Interest income | 400 | $123,900 |
| Expenses and losses: | | |
| Cost of goods sold | $ 50,000 | |
| Other expenses | 54,800 | |
| Interest expense | 2,000 | |
| Income tax expense | 2,500 | |
| Depreciation expense, buildings | 2,000 | |
| Depreciation expense, equipment | 4,000 | |
| Loss on sale of equipment | 600 | |
| Total expenses and losses | | 115,900 |
| Net income | | $ 8,000 |

*Additional Information:*

1. Received $5,000 from the sale of Icahn Corporation common stock that originally cost $2,000.
2. Received a cash dividend of $500 from the Icahn Corporation.
3. Received $400 cash from the First National Bank on December 31, 1990, as interest income.
4. Sold old equipment for $1,400. The old equipment originally cost $4,000 and had accumulated depreciation of $2,000.
5. Purchased land costing $5,000 on December 31, 1990, in exchange for a note payable. Both principal and interest are due on June 30, 1991.
6. Purchased new equipment for $9,000 cash.
7. Purchased treasury stock for $1,800.
8. Paid $3,500 of notes payable.
9. Sold additional bonds payable at par of $3,000 on January 1, 1990.
10. Issued 1,000 shares of common stock for cash at $2 per share.
11. Declared and paid a $4,000 cash dividend on October 1, 1990.

*(The working papers that accompany the text include forms for this problem.)*

*Required*

*a.* Prepare a direct method working paper for James Company's 1990 statement of cash flows.

*b.* Prepare the statement of cash flows for 1990.

*c.* Prepare a schedule that reconciles net income to the company's net cash provided (or used) by operating activities for 1990.

# 19 Stock Investments, Consolidations, and International Operations

Most large corporations invest in the stock of other corporations, and many have operations in foreign countries. The financial statement effects of such investments and foreign operations often are very important. As a result, your study of these topics in this chapter will enrich your ability to understand and interpret the financial reports of most large businesses.

**Learning Objectives**

*After studying Chapter 19, you should be able to:*

1. State the criteria for classifying stock investments as current assets or as long-term investments.
2. Describe the circumstances under which the cost method, the equity method, and consolidated financial statements are used to account for long-term stock investments.
3. Prepare entries to account for long-term stock investments according to the cost method and the equity method and to reflect lower of cost or market.
4. Prepare consolidated balance sheets and explain how to report any excess of investment cost over book value or minority interests.
5. Describe the primary problems of accounting for international operations and prepare entries to account for sales to foreign customers.
6. Define or explain the words and phrases listed in the chapter Glossary.

## Stocks as Investments

In Chapters 15 and 16, we discussed stock transactions in which the issuing corporation sold or repurchased its own stock. The focus of our discussion was the stockholders' equity accounts of the issuing corporation. However, such transactions represent only a small portion of the stock transactions that take place each day. Most stock transactions are between stockholders and do not involve the issuing corporation. These purchase/sales transactions between investors usually are arranged through brokers who charge a commission for their services.

Brokers who act as agents for their customers buy and sell stocks and bonds on exchanges such as the New York Stock Exchange. Some securities are not listed or traded on an organized stock exchange. Instead, they are bought and sold in the "over-the-counter" market. Each security in this market is handled by one or more brokers who receive from other brokers offers to buy or sell the security at specific "bid" or "asked" prices.

Recall that stock prices are quoted on the basis of dollars and ⅛ dollars per share; that is, a stock quoted at 29¼ means $29.25 per share, and a stock quoted at 28⅞ means $28.875 per share. For example, the purchases and sales of American Telephone & Telegraph's common stock and Ford Motor Company's common stock on Monday, January 30, 1989, were reported in many newspapers as follows:

| Stock | High | Low | Close | Net Change |
|---|---|---|---|---|
| AT&T . . . . | 31⅝ | 30½ | 30½ | −1 |
| FordM . . . . | 53⅞ | 52⅝ | 53⅝ | +1⅛ |

These reported prices are the highest and lowest prices at which the stock traded during the day and the price of the last transaction that occurred before the stock exchange closed at the end of the day. The net change is the difference between the closing price that day and the closing price for the previous day.

## Classifying Investments

State the criteria for classifying stock investments as current assets or as long-term investments.
(L. O. 1)

Equity securities include common and preferred stocks. **Marketable equity securities** are identified by the FASB as those that have "sales prices or bid and ask prices . . . currently available on a national securities exchange or in the over-the-counter market."[1] In order to have this price information available, these securities must be actively traded.

If an investment in marketable equity securities is held as "an investment of cash available for current operations," it is classified as a current asset.[2] You already learned how to account for short-term investments in marketable equity securities when you studied Chapter 8.

[1] FASB, *Accounting Standards—Current Text* (Norwalk, Conn., 1988), sec. I89.404. First published in *Statement of Financial Accounting Standards No. 12,* par. 7.

[2] Ibid., sec. B05.105. Previously published in *Accounting Research Bulletin No. 43,* ch. 3, sec. A, par. 4.

Investments that are not held as a ready source of cash are called **long-term investments.** They include funds earmarked for a special purpose, such as bond sinking funds, as well as land or other assets that are owned but not used in the regular operations of the business. Long-term investments also include investments in bonds and stocks that are not marketable or that, although marketable, are not intended to serve as a ready source of cash. These assets are reported on the balance sheet in a separate category titled *Long-term investments*.

## Accounting for Long-Term Investments in Stock

Describe the circumstances under which the cost method, the equity method, and consolidated financial statements are used to account for long-term stock investments. (L. O. 2)

The method used to account for a long-term stock investment depends on the relationship between the investor and the investee. In deciding what type of relationship exists between the investor and the investee, three alternatives are considered:

1. The investor is not able to significantly influence the operations of the investee.
2. The investor has a significant influence but does not control the investee.
3. The investor controls the investee.

When a company invests in another company's stock, the shares owned by the investor often represent a small percentage of the total amount of stock outstanding. As a result, the investor does not have the ability to influence the operations of the investee corporation. According to generally accepted accounting principles, if an investor owns less than 20% of a corporation's voting stock, you usually should presume that the investor does not have a significant influence over the investee.[3]

Sometimes, an investor buys a large block of a corporation's voting stock and is able to exercise a significant influence over the investee corporation. An investor that owns 20% or more of a corporation's voting stock normally is presumed to have a significant influence over the investee. There may be cases, however, where the accountant concludes that the 20% test of significant influence should be overruled by other, more persuasive, evidence.[4]

If an investor owns more than 50% of a corporation's voting stock, the investor can dominate all of the other stockholders in electing the corporation's board of directors. Thus, the investor has control over the investee corporation's management.

As we stated earlier, the method of accounting for a stock investment depends on the relationship between the investor and the investee. Illustration 19–1 shows each type of investor/investee relationship and the corresponding accounting methods used. In Illustration 19–1, note that if the investor does not have a significant influence, the accounting method used is the **cost method.** However, when the cost method is used, lower of cost or market is also applied. If the investor has a significant influence, the accounting method

[3] Ibid., sec. I82.104. First published in *APB Opinion No. 18,* par. 17.

[4] Ibid., sec. I82.107–108. First published in *FASB Interpretation No. 35,* pars. 3–4.

**Illustration 19–1**
**Accounting for long-term stock investments**

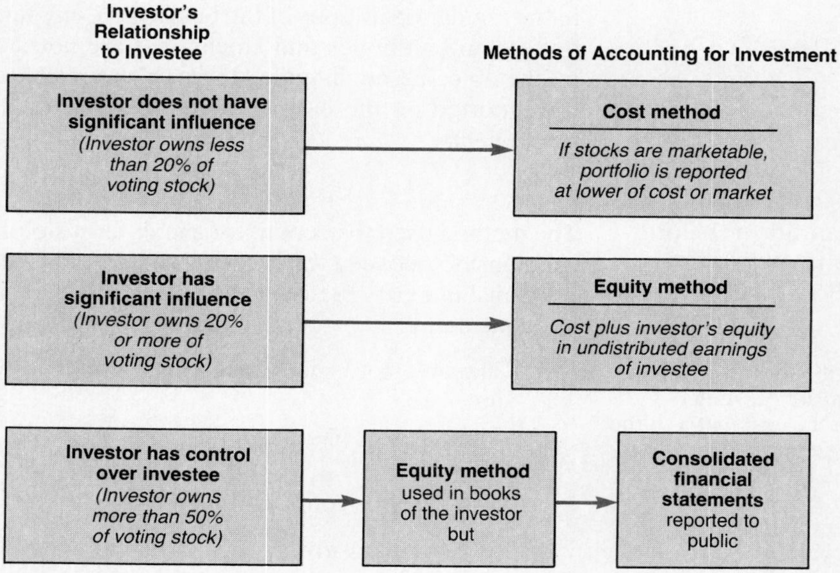


used is the **equity method.** Finally, if the investor controls the investee, the investor reports **consolidated financial statements** to the public. Each of these accounting methods is explained in the following sections.

### The Cost Method of Accounting for Stock Investments

Prepare entries to account for long-term stock investments according to the cost method and the equity method and to reflect lower of cost or market.
(L. O. 3)

When stock is purchased, the purchase is recorded at total cost, which includes any commission paid to the broker. For example, 1,000 (10%) of Dot Corporation's 10,000 outstanding common shares were purchased as an investment at 23¼ plus a $300 broker's commission. The entry to record the transaction is:

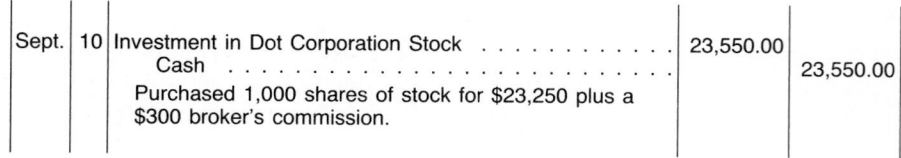

| | | | | |
|---|---|---|---|---|
| Sept. | 10 | Investment in Dot Corporation Stock . . . . . . . . . . . . | 23,550.00 | |
| | | Cash . . . . . . . . . . . . . . . . . . . . . . . . . . . . | | 23,550.00 |
| | | Purchased 1,000 shares of stock for $23,250 plus a $300 broker's commission. | | |

Observe that nothing is said about a premium or a discount on the Dot Corporation stock. Premiums and discounts normally are recorded only by the corporation that issues the stock. An investor records the entire cost as a debit to the investment account, even though the cost may be above or below par value.

When the cost method is used and a cash dividend is received on the stock, the dividend is recorded as follows:

| | | | | |
|---|---|---|---|---|
| Oct. | 5 | Cash . . . . . . . . . . . . . . . . . . . . . . . . . . . . . | 1,000.00 | |
| | | Dividends Earned . . . . . . . . . . . . . . . . . . . . . . | | 1,000.00 |
| | | Received a $1 per share dividend on the stock. | | |

Dividends do not accrue as time passes; therefore, you never make an end-of-period entry to record accrued dividends. However, if a balance sheet is prepared after a cash dividend is declared but before it is paid, you should record the declaration with a debit to Dividends Receivable and a credit to Dividends Earned.

When a stock dividend is declared, the shares distributed to the stockholders are not revenue or income. Therefore, an investor does not make a journal entry to record a stock dividend. However, a memorandum entry or a notation about the additional shares should be made in the investment account. Also, receipt of a stock dividend does affect the per share cost of the old shares. For example, if a 20-share dividend is received on 100 shares originally purchased for $15 per share (100 × $15 = $1,500), the cost of all 120 shares is $1,500, and the cost per share is $12.50 ($1,500 ÷ 120 shares = $12.50 per share).

Under the cost method, when an investment in stock is sold and the proceeds net of any sales commission differ from cost, a gain or loss must be recorded. For example, consider the 1,000 shares of Dot Corporation common stock that were purchased at a cost of $23,550. If these shares are sold at 25¾ less a sales commission of $315, there is a $1,885 gain, and the transaction is recorded as follows:

| | | | | |
|---|---|---|---|---|
| Jan. | 7 | Cash . . . . . . . . . . . . . . . . . . . . . . . . . . . . . | 25,435.00 | |
| | | Investment in Dot Corporation Stock . . . . . . . . . . | | 23,550.00 |
| | | Gain on Sale of Investments . . . . . . . . . . . . . . | | 1,885.00 |
| | | Sold 1,000 shares of stock for $25,750 less a $315 commission. | | |

If the net amount received for these shares had been less than their $23,550 cost, there would have been a loss on the transaction.

### Lower of Cost or Market

If the cost method is used to account for a stock investment that is not marketable, the asset is reported on the balance sheet at cost. However, as you learned in Chapter 8, investments in marketable equity securities are divided into two portfolios: (1) those that are current assets and (2) those that are long-term investments. Then, the total current market value of each portfolio is calculated and compared to the total cost of each portfolio. Each portfolio is reported at the lower of cost or market.[5]

Recall from Chapter 8 that if the total market value of the current asset portfolio declines below cost, the decline is reported in the income statement

---

[5] Ibid., sec. I89.102–3. First published in *Statement of Financial Accounting Standards No. 12*, pars. 8–9.

as a loss. Later recoveries of market value are reported in the income statement as gains, but market value increases above original cost are not recorded.[6]

In the case of a long-term investment portfolio of marketable equity securities, market value declines are reported on the balance sheet but are reported in the income statement *only* if they appear to be permanent. Usually, they are not assumed to be permanent, in which case the market value decline is called an *unrealized loss* and is reported as a separate stockholders' equity item in the balance sheet.[7]

For example, assume that a company purchased a portfolio of long-term investments in marketable equity securities at a cost of $67,000. On December 31, the end of the accounting period, the market value of the portfolio had declined to $58,000. However, the decline was believed to be temporary. The entry to record the market decline is:

| | | | | |
|---|---|---|---|---|
| Dec. | 31 | Unrealized Loss on Market Decline of Long-Term Investments | 9,000.00 | |
| | | Allowance to Reduce Long-Term Investments to Market | | 9,000.00 |
| | | To record market decline of long-term investments in marketable stocks. | | |

In the long-term investments section of the balance sheet, the investments will be reported at a cost of $67,000 less the $9,000 allowance, or $58,000. The stockholders' equity section might appear as follows:

| | | |
|---|---|---|
| Common stock | $100,000 | |
| Retained earnings | 80,000 | |
| Less unrealized loss on market decline of long-term investments | (9,000) | |
| Total stockholders' equity | | $171,000 |

### The Equity Method of Accounting for Common Stock Investments

If a common stock investor has significant influence over the investee, the equity method of accounting for the investment must be used. When the stock is acquired, the purchase is recorded at cost just as it is under the cost method. For example, on January 1, 1990, James, Inc., purchased 3,000 shares (30%) of RMS, Inc., common stock for a total cost of $70,650. The entry to record the purchase on the books of James, Inc., is as follows:

---

[6] Ibid., I89.105.

[7] Ibid., I89.105, 115.

| | | | | |
|---|---|---|---|---|
| Jan. | 1 | Investment in RMS, Inc. . . . . . . . . . . . . . . . . . . .<br>Cash . . . . . . . . . . . . . . . . . . . . . . . . . . .<br>Purchased 3,000 shares of common stock. | 70,650.00 | <br>70,650.00 |

Under the equity method, the earnings of the investee corporation not only increase the net assets of the investee corporation but also increase the investor's equity in the assets. Therefore, when the investee closes its books and reports the amount of its earnings, the investor takes up its share of those earnings in its investment account. For example, RMS, Inc., reported net income of $20,000. James, Inc.'s entry to record its share of these earnings is:

| | | | | |
|---|---|---|---|---|
| Dec. | 31 | Investment in RMS, Inc. . . . . . . . . . . . . . . . . . . .<br>Earnings from Investment in RMS, Inc. . . . . . . . .<br>To record 30% equity in investee's earnings of $20,000. | 6,000.00 | <br>6,000.00 |

The debit records the increase in James, Inc.'s equity in RMS, Inc. The credit causes 30% of RMS, Inc.'s net income to appear on James, Inc.'s income statement as earnings from the investment. Then, James, Inc., closes the earnings to its Income Summary account and on to its Retained Earnings account just as it would close earnings from any investment.

If, instead of a net income, the investee corporation incurs a net loss, the investor debits the loss to an account called Loss from Investment and credits (reduces) its Investment in Stock account. It then transfers the loss to its Income Summary account and on to its Retained Earnings account.

Dividends paid by an investee corporation decrease the investee's assets and retained earnings, and also decrease the investor's equity in the investee. Since, under the equity method, the investor records its equity in the full amount of earnings reported by an investee, the receipt of cash dividends is not income. Instead, dividend receipts from the investee represent a change in the form of the investor's assets; part of the investment is converted into cash. For example, RMS, Inc., declared and paid $10,000 in dividends on its common stock. The entry to record James, Inc.'s share of these dividends, which it received on January 9, 1991, is:

| | | | | |
|---|---|---|---|---|
| Jan. | 9 | Cash . . . . . . . . . . . . . . . . . . . . . . . . . . . . .<br>Investment in RMS, Inc. . . . . . . . . . . . . . . . . . .<br>To record receipt of 30% of the $10,000 dividend paid by RMS, Inc. | 3,000.00 | <br>3,000.00 |

Notice that when the equity method is used, the carrying value of a common stock investment equals the cost of the investment plus the investor's equity in the undistributed earnings of the investee. For example, after the above transactions are recorded on the books of James, Inc., the investment account appears as follows:

**Investment in RMS, Inc.**

| Date | | Explanation | Debit | Credit | Balance |
|---|---|---|---|---|---|
| 1990 | | | | | |
| Jan. | 1 | Investment | 70,650 | | 70,650 |
| Dec. | 31 | Share of earnings | 6,000 | | 76,650 |
| 1991 | | | | | |
| Jan. | 9 | Share of dividend | | 3,000 | 73,650 |

When an equity method stock investment is sold, the gain or loss on the sale is determined by comparing the proceeds from the sale with the carrying value of the stock on the date of sale. For example, on January 10, 1991, James, Inc., sold its RMS, Inc., stock for $80,000. The entry to record the sale is as follows:

| | | | | |
|---|---|---|---|---|
| Jan. | 10 | Cash | 80,000.00 | |
| | | Investment in RMS, Inc. | | 73,650.00 |
| | | Gain on Sale of Investments | | 6,350.00 |
| | | Sold 3,000 shares of stock for $80,000. | | |

## Parent and Subsidiary Corporations

Corporations commonly own stock in and may even control other corporations. For example, if Par Company owns more than 50% of the voting stock of Sub Company, Par company can elect Sub Company's board of directors and thus control its activities and resources. In this case, the controlling corporation, Par Company, is known as the **parent company,** and Sub Company is called a **subsidiary.**

When a corporation owns all the outstanding stock of a subsidiary, it can take over the subsidiary's assets, cancel its stock, and merge the subsidiary into the parent company. However, instead of operating the business as a single corporation, there often are financial, legal, and tax advantages if a large business is operated as a parent corporation that controls one or more subsidiary corporations. Actually, most large companies are parent corporations that own one or more subsidiaries.

When a business is operated as a parent company with subsidiaries, separate accounting records are kept for each corporation. Also, from a legal viewpoint, the parent and each subsidiary are separate entities with all the rights, duties, and responsibilities of a separate corporation. However, investors in the parent company depend on the parent to present consolidated financial statements. Consolidated statements show the financial position and results of all operations under the parent's control, including those of any subsidiaries. These statements are prepared as if the business is organized as a single company. In other words, the assets and liabilities of all affiliated companies are

**Illustration 19–2**

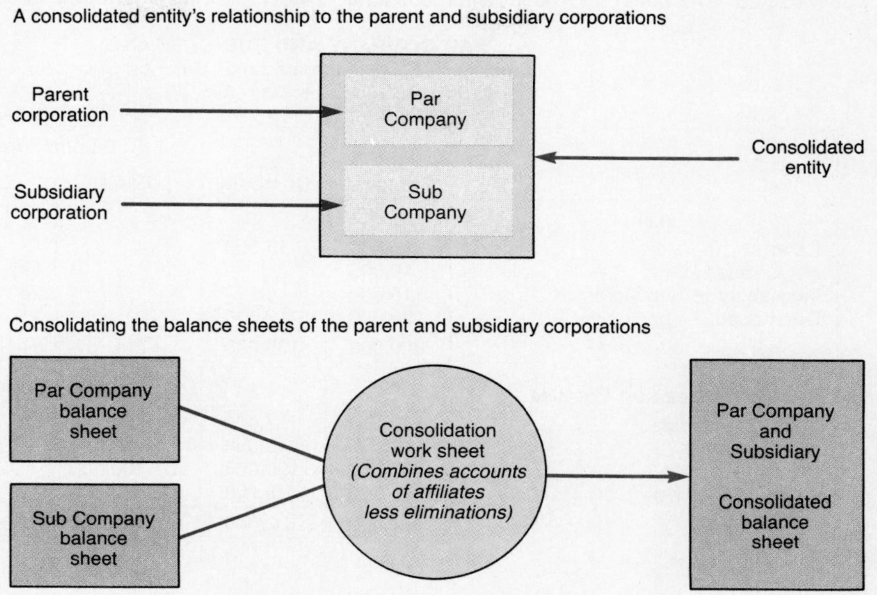


combined on a single balance sheet. Also, their revenues and expenses are combined on a single income statement and their cash flows are combined on a single statement of cash flows. The relationship between the consolidated entity and the separate parent and subsidiary corporations is shown in the top portion of Illustration 19–2.

## Consolidated Balance Sheets

Prepare consolidated balance sheets and explain how to report any excess of investment cost over book value or minority interests.
(L. O. 4)

The bottom portion of Illustration 19–2 shows the process of preparing a consolidated balance sheet from the separate balance sheets of the parent and the subsidiary. When parent and subsidiary balance sheets are consolidated, duplications in items are eliminated so that the combined figures do not show more assets and equities than actually exist. For example, a parent's investment in a subsidiary is evidence by shares of stock that are carried as an asset in the parent company's records. However, these shares actually represent an equity in the subsidiary's assets. Therefore, if the parent's investment in a subsidiary and the subsidiary's assets were both shown on the consolidated balance sheet, the same resources would be counted twice. To prevent this, the parent's investment and the subsidiary's capital accounts are offset and eliminated in preparing a consolidated balance sheet.

Likewise, a single enterprise cannot owe a debt to itself. This would be like a student who ''borrows'' $20 for a date from funds saved for next semester's expenses and who then prepares a balance sheet that shows the $20 as both a receivable from himself and a payable to himself. To prevent such double counting, intercompany debts and receivables are also eliminated in preparing a consolidated balance sheet.

Illustration 19–3
**Consolidated work sheet for 100% owned subsidiary; stock purchased at book value**

PAR COMPANY AND SUB COMPANY
Work Sheet for a Consolidated Balance Sheet
December 31, 1989

| | Par Company | Sub Company | Eliminations Debit | Eliminations Credit | Consolidated Amounts |
|---|---|---|---|---|---|
| **Assets** | | | | | |
| Cash | 5,000 | 15,000 | | | 20,000 |
| Notes receivable | 10,000 | | | (*a*) 10,000 | |
| Investment in Sub Company | 115,000 | | | (*b*) 115,000 | |
| Other assets | 190,000 | 117,000 | | | 307,000 |
| | 320,000 | 132,000 | | | 327,000 |
| **Liabilities and Equities** | | | | | |
| Accounts payable | 15,000 | 7,000 | | | 22,000 |
| Notes payable | | 10,000 | (*a*) 10,000 | | |
| Common stock | 250,000 | 100,000 | (*b*) 100,000 | | 250,000 |
| Retained earnings | 55,000 | 15,000 | (*b*) 15,000 | | 55,000 |
| | 320,000 | 132,000 | 125,000 | 125,000 | 327,000 |

### Balance Sheets Consolidated at Time of Acquisition

When a parent's and a subsidiary's assets are combined in the preparation of a consolidated balance sheet, a work sheet normally is used to organize the data. For example, Illustration 19–3 shows a work sheet to consolidate the accounts of Par Company and its subsidiary called Sub Company. In the work sheet, the account balances are on December 31, 1989, which was the day Par Company acquired Sub Company. On that day, Par Company paid cash to purchase all of Sub Company's outstanding $10 par value common stock. The stock had a book value of $115,000, or $11.50 per share, on the books of Sub Company. In this first illustration, we assume that Par Company paid $115,000, or book value, for the outstanding shares.

In Illustration 19–3, notice that the eliminations columns include two sets of debits and credits. One set is identified by the letter (*a*), and the other set is identified by the letter (*b*).

**Elimination (*a*).** On the day it acquired Sub Company, Par Company loaned Sub Company $10,000 to use in the subsidiary's operations. In exchange for the cash, Sub Company signed a promissory note to Par Company. This intercompany debt was in reality a transfer of funds within the consolidated entity. Therefore, since it did not increase the total assets and total liabilities of the affiliated companies, elimination (*a*) prevents these balances from appearing on the consolidated balance sheet. To understand this elimination, recall that the subsidiary's promissory note appears as a $10,000 debit in Par Company's Notes Receivable account. Then, observe that the first credit in the Eliminations column exactly offsets or eliminates this item. Next, recall that the subsidiary's note appears as a credit in its Notes Payable account. In the Eliminations columns, the $10,000 debit completes the elimination of this intercompany debt.

**Elimination (*b*).** When a parent company buys a subsidiary's stock, the investment is recorded in the accounts of the parent as an asset. This investment represents an equity in the subsidiary's net assets. However, you must not show both the subsidiary's (net) assets and the parent company's investment in the subsidiary on a consolidated balance sheet. To do so would be to double count those resources. On the work sheet, the credit portion of elimination (*b*) prevents double counting of Sub company's net assets.

Also, stockholders' equity accounts represent the equity of outside parties that own the company's stock. But, from a consolidated point of view, there are no outside parties that own the subsidiary's stock. Therefore, the stockholders' equity account balances of Sub Company should not appear on a consolidated balance sheet. On the work sheet, the debits of elimination (*b*) prevent Sub Company's stockholders' equity balances from appearing on the consolidated balance sheet.

After the intercompany items are eliminated on a work sheet as in Illustration 19–3, the assets of the parent and the subsidiary and the remaining equities in these assets are combined and carried into the work sheet's last column. The combined amounts are then used to prepare a consolidated balance sheet that shows all the assets and equities of the parent and its subsidiary.

### Parent Company Does Not Buy All of Subsidiary's Stock and Pays More than Book Value

In the above example, Par Company purchased all of its subsidiary's stock and paid book value for it. However, a parent company often purchases less than 100% of a subsidiary's stock and commonly pays a price that is either more or less than book value. To illustrate, assume Par Company purchased only 80% of Sub Company's outstanding stock. Also assume that Par company paid $13 per share, a price that was $1.50 more than the stock's book value.

These new assumptions result in a more complicated work sheet entry to eliminate the parent's investment and the subsidiary's stockholders' equity accounts. The entry is complicated by (1) the minority interest in the subsidiary and (2) the excess over book value paid by the parent company for the subsidiary's stock.

**Minority Interest.** When a parent buys a controlling interest in a subsidiary, the parent company is the subsidiary's majority stockholder. However, when the parent owns less than 100% of the subsidiary's stock, the subsidiary has other stockholders who own a **minority interest** in its assets and share its earnings.

When you prepare a consolidated work sheet for a parent and a subsidiary that has a minority interest, the equity of the minority interest must be recognized. This is done in the process of eliminating the stockholders' equity balances of the subsidiary, as shown in Illustration 19–4. In this case, the

Illustration 19–4

**Consolidated work sheet; 80% of subsidiary stock purchased at more than book value**

PAR COMPANY AND SUB COMPANY
Work Sheet for a Consolidated Balance Sheet
December 31, 1989

| | Par Company | Sub Company | Eliminations Debit | Eliminations Credit | Consolidated Amounts |
|---|---|---|---|---|---|
| **Assets** | | | | | |
| Cash | 16,000 | 15,000 | | | 31,000 |
| Notes receivable | 10,000 | | | (*a*) 10,000 | |
| Investment in Sub Company | 104,000 | | | (*b*) 104,000 | |
| Other assets | 190,000 | 117,000 | | | 307,000 |
| Excess of cost over book value | | | (*b*) 12,000 | | 12,000 |
| | 320,000 | 132,000 | | | 350,000 |
| **Liabilities and Equities** | | | | | |
| Accounts payable | 15,000 | 7,000 | | | 22,000 |
| Notes payable | | 10,000 | (*a*) 10,000 | | |
| Common stock | 250,000 | 100,000 | (*b*) 100,000 | | 250,000 |
| Retained earnings | 55,000 | 15,000 | (*b*) 15,000 | | 55,000 |
| Minority interest | | | | (*b*) 23,000 | 23,000 |
| | 320,000 | 132,000 | 137,000 | 137,000 | 350,000 |

minority stockholders have a 20% interest in the subsidiary. Therefore, on the work sheet, 20% of the subsidiary's stockholders' equity amounts [($100,000 + $15,000) × 20% = $23,000] is reclassified as the minority interest.

**Excess of Investment Cost over Book Value.** In Illustration 19–4, we assume that Par Company paid $13 per share for its 8,000 shares of Sub Company's stock. Therefore, the cost of these shares exceeded their book value by $12,000, calculated as follows:

| | |
|---|---|
| Cost of stock (8,000 shares at $13 per share) | $104,000 |
| Book value (8,000 shares at $11.50 per share) | 92,000 |
| Excess of cost over book value | $ 12,000 |

Now observe how in the process of eliminating the parent's investment in the subsidiary, this excess of cost over book value is set out on the work sheet. Then, it is carried into the Consolidated Amounts column as an asset.

After the work sheet of Illustration 19–4 was completed, the consolidated amounts in the last column were used to prepare the consolidated balance sheet of Illustration 19–5. Note the treatment of the minority interest in the balance sheet. The minority stockholders have a $23,000 equity in the consoli-

**Illustration 19–5**

**PAR COMPANY AND SUBSIDIARY**
**Consolidated Balance Sheet**
**December 31, 1989**

| | | |
|---|---|---|
| **Assets** | | |
| Cash | | $ 31,000 |
| Other assets | | 307,000 |
| Goodwill from consolidation | | 12,000 |
| Total assets | | $350,000 |
| **Liabilities and Stockholders' Equity** | | |
| Liabilities: | | |
| Accounts payable | | $ 22,000 |
| Minority interest | | 23,000 |
| Stockholders' equity: | | |
| Common stock | $250,000 | |
| Retained earnings | 55,000 | |
| Total stockholders' equity | | 305,000 |
| Total liabilities and stockholders' equity | | $350,000 |

dated assets of the affiliated companies. Some accountants argue that this item should be disclosed in the stockholders' equity section. Others believe it should be shown in the long-term liabilities section. However, the minority interest usually is shown as a separate item between the liabilities and stockholders' equity sections, as you see in Illustration 19–5.

Next, observe that the $12,000 excess over book value that Par Company paid for Sub Company's stock appears on the consolidated balance sheet as an asset called "Goodwill from consolidation." There are several reasons why a parent might pay more than book value for its equity in a subsidiary. (1) One reason may be that certain of the subsidiary's assets are carried on the subsidiary's books at less than fair value. (2) Another reason may be that certain of the subsidiary's liabilities are carried at book values that are greater than fair values. (3) Also, the subsidiary's earnings prospects may be good enough to justify paying more than the net fair (market) value of its assets and liabilities. In this illustration, we assume that the book values of Sub Company's assets and liabilities are equal to their fair values. However, Sub Company's expected earnings justified paying $104,000 for an 80% equity in the subsidiary's net assets (assets less liabilities).

When a company pays more than book value because the subsidiary's assets are undervalued or its liabilities are overvalued, the cost in excess of book value must be allocated to those assets and liabilities so that they are restated at fair values. After the subsidiary's assets and liabilities have been restated to reflect fair values, any remaining cost in excess of book value is reported on the consolidated balance sheet as "Goodwill from consolidation."[8]

---

[8] Ibid., sec. B50.403. First published in *APB Opinion No. 16*, par. 87.

## AS A MATTER OF FACT

In 1987 Ford Motor Co. reported $45 billion in assets and $27 billion in liabilities. Yet when investors get their 1988 annual reports from the company this spring, they'll very likely see $140 billion in assets and $125 billion in liabilities—increasing Ford's debt ratio from just 25% to an estimated 61%. General Electric, Chrysler, General Motors and other large companies will show similarly huge balance sheet increases.

Why? All these companies have enormous "off balance sheet" financial subsidiaries. Because of a new accounting rule, they're now going to have to fold the numbers of those subsidiaries into the consolidated financials of the parent corporations in any case where the parent owns more than 50% of its stock.

The new rule is but the first step in a Financial Accounting Standards Board project that could potentially alter balance sheet accounting for many companies. The change traces to a 1984 enforcement action by the Securities & Exchange Commission, which ordered a fast-growing microcomputer company, Digilog Inc., to restate and consolidate its financials after it had buried operating losses in the income statement of a minority-owned marketing subsidiary.

Are Ford, GM and GE that leveraged? Not really, because the financial subsidiaries' assets are self-liquidating and quite marketable. So, in illuminating, the new rule also distorts.

Now FASB is working to create more comprehensive accounting rules for consolidation. On the table are plans that eventually could require corporations to consolidate in cases where they own less than 50% of another company but exert effective control over the organization anyway.

* * * * *

Critics argue that it will be very difficult to create a comprehensive—and consistently accurate—definition for what constitutes control. The issue of corporate control is a knotty one, and no one test is likely ever to be completely accurate. The authorities are to be commended for trying to make financial reporting more concise, but they may, in the effort, simply end up confusing people.

Source: Penelope Wang, "What's off, what's on?" Excerpted by permission of *Forbes* magazine, February 20, 1989, p. 110, © Forbes Inc., 1989.

Occasionally, a parent company pays less than book value for its interest in a subsidiary. The probable reason for a price below book value is that some of the subsidiary's assets are carried on its books at amounts in excess of fair value. Therefore, the APB ruled that the excess of book value over cost should be allocated to reduce the balance sheet valuations of the overvalued assets.[9]

### Earnings and Dividends of a Subsidiary

As you already learned, a parent uses the equity method in its books to account for its investment in a subsidiary. As a result, the parent's recorded net income and Retained Earnings account include the parent's equity in the net income earned by the subsidiary since the date of acquisition. Also, the balance of the parent's Investment in Subsidiary account increases (or decreases) each year by an amount equal to the parent's equity in the subsidiary's earnings (or loss) less the parent's share of any dividends paid by the subsidiary.

For example, assume that Sub Company earned $12,500 during 1990, its first year as a subsidiary, and at year-end paid out $7,500 in dividends. Par Company records its 80% equity in these earnings and dividends as follows:

[9] Ibid., B50.160.

**Illustration 19–6**
**Work sheet for a consolidated balance sheet, one year after acquisition**

PAR COMPANY AND SUB COMPANY
Work Sheet for a Consolidated Balance Sheet
December 31, 1990

| | Par Company | Sub Company | Eliminations Debit | Eliminations Credit | Consolidated Amounts |
|---|---|---|---|---|---|
| **Assets** | | | | | |
| Cash | 22,000 | 20,000 | | | 42,000 |
| Notes receivable | 10,000 | | | (*a*) 10,000 | |
| Investment in Sub Company | 108,000 | | | (*b*) 108,000 | |
| Other assets | 190,000 | 117,000 | | | 307,000 |
| Excess of cost over book value | | | (*b*) 12,000 | | 12,000 |
| | 330,000 | 137,000 | | | 361,000 |
| **Liabilities and Equities** | | | | | |
| Accounts payable | 15,000 | 7,000 | | | 22,000 |
| Notes payable | | 10,000 | (*a*) 10,000 | | |
| Common stock | 250,000 | 100,000 | (*b*) 100,000 | | 250,000 |
| Retained earnings | 65,000 | 20,000 | (*b*) 20,000 | | 65,000 |
| Minority interest | | | | (*b*) 24,000 | 24,000 |
| | 330,000 | 137,000 | 142,000 | 142,000 | 361,000 |

| | | | | |
|---|---|---|---|---|
| Dec. | 31 | Investment in Sub Company | 10,000.00 | |
| | | Earnings from Investment in Subsidiary | | 10,000.00 |
| | | To record 80% of the net income reported by Sub Company. | | |
| | 31 | Cash | 6,000.00 | |
| | | Investment in Sub Company | | 6,000.00 |
| | | To record the receipt of 80% of the $7,500 dividend paid by Sub Company. | | |

## Consolidated Balance Sheets at a Date after Acquisition

Illustration 19–6 shows the December 31, 1990, work sheet to consolidate the balance sheets of Par Company and Sub Company. To simplify the illustration, it is assumed that Par Company had no transactions during the year other than to record its equity in Sub Company's earnings and dividends. Also, the other assets and liabilities of Sub Company did not change, and the subsidiary has not paid its note to Par Company.

Compare Illustration 19–6 with 19–4 to see the changes in Par Company's balance sheet (the first column). Par Company's cash increased from $16,000 to $22,000 because of the dividends received from Sub Company. The Investment in Sub Company account increased from $104,000 to $108,000 as a result of the equity method entries during the year. Finally, Par Company's Retained Earnings increased by $10,000, which was the parent's equity in the subsidiary's earnings.

In the second column of Illustration 19–6, note only two changes: (1) Sub Company's cash balance increased by $5,000, which is the difference between its $12,500 net income and $7,500 payment of dividends; and (2) retained earnings also increased from $15,000 to $20,000, which is explained by the $12,500 net income less $7,500 dividends. Note that the $20,000 balance is eliminated on the work sheet.

Two additional items need explanation. First, the minority interest set out on the December 31, 1990, work sheet (Illustration 19–6), is greater than on the December 31, 1989, work sheet (Illustration 19–4). The minority stockholders have a 20% equity in Sub Company. So, the $24,000 shown on the December 31, 1990, work sheet is 20% of Sub Company's Common Stock and Retained Earnings balances on December 31, 1990. This $24,000 is $1,000 greater than the beginning-of-year minority interest because the subsidiary's retained earnings increased $5,000 during the year; the minority stockholder's share of this increase is 20%, or $1,000.

Second, the $12,000 excess cost over book value shown in Illustration 19–6 is unchanged from a year earlier. However, generally accepted accounting principles require that this cost be amortized.[10] The procedures of amortizing this cost are explained in a more advanced course.

## Other Consolidated Statements

In addition to the balance sheet, the consolidated financial statements include a consolidated income statement, consolidated retained earnings statement, and consolidated statement of cash flows. However, you can have a general understanding of these statements without further discussion of the procedures to prepare them. At this point, you need only recognize that all duplications in items are eliminated. Also, when one affiliate records profit on sales to the other affiliate, the profit is eliminated in the consolidated statements. Finally, the amounts of net income and retained earnings that are reported in consolidated statements are equal to the amounts recorded by the parent under the equity method.

## The Corporation Balance Sheet

A number of balance sheet sections have been illustrated in this and previous chapters. To bring together the information from all these sections, the balance sheet of Betco Corporation is shown in Illustration 19–7. Three items of information in this balance sheet tell you that it is a consolidated balance sheet. They are the title and the two items "Goodwill from consolidation" and "Minority interest."

In Illustration 19–7, notice the asset called "Investment in Toledo Corporation common stock." You should understand that Toledo Corporation is not the subsidiary. When the balance sheet was prepared, Betco Corporation's investment in its subsidiary was eliminated. Therefore, the Toledo Corporation stock is an investment in an unconsolidated company.

---

[10] Ibid., sec. I60.108–12. First published in *APB Opinion No. 17*, pars. 27–31.

**Illustration 19–7**

**BETCO CORPORATION**
**Consolidated Balance Sheet**
**December 31, 1990**

**Assets**

| | | | |
|---|---|---|---|
| Current assets: | | | |
| Cash | | $ 15,000 | |
| Marketable securities | | 5,000 | |
| Accounts receivable | $ 50,000 | | |
| Less allowance for doubtful accounts | 1,000 | 49,000 | |
| Merchandise inventory | | 115,000 | |
| Subscriptions receivable, common stock | | 15,000 | |
| Prepaid expenses | | 1,000 | |
| Total current assets | | | $200,000 |
| Long-term investments: | | | |
| Bond sinking fund | | $ 15,000 | |
| Toledo Corporation common stock (cost approximates market) | | 5,000 | |
| Total long-term investments | | | 20,000 |
| Plant assets: | | | |
| Land | | $ 50,000 | |
| Buildings | $285,000 | | |
| Less accumulated depreciation | 30,000 | 255,000 | |
| Store equipment | $ 85,000 | | |
| Less accumulated depreciation | 20,000 | 65,000 | |
| Total plant assets | | | 370,000 |
| Intangible assets: | | | |
| Goodwill from consolidation | | | 10,000 |
| Total assets | | | $600,000 |

**Liabilities**

| | | | |
|---|---|---|---|
| Current liabilities: | | | |
| Notes payable | $ 10,000 | | |
| Accounts payable | 14,000 | | |
| State and federal income taxes payable | 16,000 | | |
| Total current liabilities | | $ 40,000 | |
| Long-term liabilities: | | | |
| Bonds payable, 8%, secured by mortgage, due in 1997 | $100,000 | | |
| Less unamortized discount based on the 8¼% market rate for bond interest prevailing on the date of issue | 2,000 | 98,000 | |
| Total liabilities | | | $138,000 |
| Minority interest | | | 15,000 |

**Stockholders' Equity**

| | | | |
|---|---|---|---|
| Contributed capital: | | | |
| Common stock, $10 par value, authorized 50,000 shares, issued 30,000 shares of which 1,000 are in the treasury | $300,000 | | |
| Unissued common stock subscribed, 2,500 shares | 25,000 | | |
| Contributed capital in excess of par value, common stock | 33,000 | | |
| Total contributed capital | | $358,000 | |
| Retained earnings (Note 1) | | 105,000 | |
| Total contributed and retained capital | | $463,000 | |
| Less cost of treasury stock | | 16,000 | |
| Total stockholders' equity | | | 447,000 |
| Total liabilities and stockholders' equity | | | $600,000 |

Note 1: Retained earnings in the amount of $31,000 is restricted under an agreement with the corporation's bondholders and because of the purchase of treasury stock, leaving $74,000 of retained earnings not so restricted.

## Accounting for International Operations

Describe the primary problems of accounting for international operations and prepare entries to account for sales to foreign customers.
(L. O. 5)

Many companies have business activities in more than one country. In fact, the operations of some large corporations involve so many different countries that they are called **multinational businesses**. The problems of managing and accounting for a company that has international operations can be very complex; and detailed study of these issues should be reserved for advanced courses in business.

However, you should know about two accounting problems that relate to international operations. Both of these problems occur because businesses with transactions in more than one country have to deal with more than one currency. To make the analysis clearer, we will discuss these problems from the perspective of companies that have a base of operations in the United States. Therefore, we will assume that the companies in our examples prepare their financial statements in terms of the U.S. dollar. Hence, the **reporting currency** of such firms is the U.S. dollar.

## Exchange Rates between Currencies

You should understand that there is an active market for the purchase and sale of foreign currencies. U.S. dollars may be exchanged for Canadian dollars, British pounds, French francs, or other currencies. The price of one currency is stated in terms of another currency and is called a **foreign exchange rate**. For example, on January 31, 1989, the current exchange rate for British pounds and U.S. dollars was $1.7515, which means that one pound could have been exchanged for $1.7515. On the same day, the exchange rate between West German marks and U.S. dollars was $0.5321. These foreign exchange rates fluctuate daily based on the changing supply and demand for each currency.

## Sales (or Purchases) Denominated in a Foreign Currency

When a U.S. company makes a sale to a foreign customer, a special problem may arise in accounting for the sale and account receivable. If the sales terms require the foreign customer's payment to be in U.S. dollars, no special problem arises. But if the terms of the sale state that payment is to be in a foreign currency, the U.S. company must go through special steps to account for the sale and account receivable.

For example, suppose a U.S. company, the Boston Company, makes a credit sale to London Outfitters, a British company. The sale occurs on December 12, 1990, and the price is 10,000 pounds due February 10, 1991. Boston Company keeps its accounting records in terms of U.S. dollars. Therefore, to record the sale, Boston Company must translate the sales price from pounds to dollars. This is done using the current exchange rate available on the date of the sale. Assuming the current exchange rate on December 12 is $1.80, the sale is recorded as follows:

| | | | | |
|---|---|---|---|---|
| Dec. | 12 | Accounts Receivable—London Outfitters . . . . . . . . . . | 18,000.00 | |
| | | Sales. . . . . . . . . . . . . . . . . . . . . . . . . . . . . | | 18,000.00 |
| | | 10,000 × $1.80 = $18,000. | | |

Now assume that Boston Company prepares annual financial statements on December 31. On that date, the current exchange rate is $1.84. Therefore, the current dollar value of Boston Company's receivable is $18,400, or 10,000 × $1.84. This is $400 higher than the amount originally recorded on December 12. According to generally accepted accounting principles, the receivable must be reported in the balance sheet at its current dollar value. Hence, Boston Company must make the following entry to record the increase in the dollar value of the receivable:

| | | | | |
|---|---|---|---|---|
| Dec. | 31 | Accounts Receivable—London Outfitters . . . . . . . . . . | 400.00 | |
| | | Exchange Gain or Loss . . . . . . . . . . . . . . . . . | | 400.00 |
| | | 10,000 × $1.84 = $18,400 | | |
| | | 10,000 × $1.80 = 18,000 | | |
| | | $ 400 | | |

The Exchange Gain or Loss is closed to Income Summary and included on the income statement.[11]

Assume that on February 10, Boston Company receives London Outfitters' payment of 10,000 pounds and immediately exchanges the pounds for U.S. dollars. On this date, the foreign exchange rate is $1.78. Therefore, Boston Company receives $17,800, or 10,000 × $1.78. The receipt and the loss associated with the decline in the exchange rate are recorded as follows:

| | | | | |
|---|---|---|---|---|
| Feb. | 10 | Cash (10,000 × $1.78) . . . . . . . . . . . . . . . . . . . | 17,800.00 | |
| | | Exchange Gain or Loss . . . . . . . . . . . . . . . . . . . | 600.00 | |
| | | Accounts Receivable—London Outfitters . . . . . . . . | | 18,400.00 |
| | | Received foreign currency payment of account and converted into dollars. | | |

Accounting for credit purchases from a foreign supplier are similar to the above example of a credit sale to a foreign customer. If the U.S. company is required to make payment in a foreign currency, the account payable must be translated into dollars before it can be recorded by the U.S. company. Then, if the exchange rate changes before payment is made, an exchange gain or loss must be recognized by the U.S. company.

## Consolidated Statements with Foreign Subsidiaries

A second problem of accounting for international operations involves the preparation of consolidated financial statements when the parent company has a foreign subsidiary. For example, suppose a U.S. company owns a controlling interest in a French subsidiary. The reporting currency of the U.S. parent is the dollar. However, the French subsidiary maintains its financial records in francs. Before a consolidated working paper can be prepared, the financial statements of the French company must be translated into U.S. dollars. After the translation is completed, the preparation of consolidated statements is not any different than for any other subsidiary.

[11] FASB, *Accounting Standards—Current Text* (Norwalk, Conn., 1988), sec. F60.122. First published as FASB, *Statement of Financial Accounting Standards No. 52*, par. 15.

The procedures for translating a foreign subsidiary's account balances depend on the nature of the subsidiary's operations. However, the general process is one of selecting appropriate foreign exchange rates and applying those rates to the account balances of the foreign subsidiary. Business students do not need any more detailed discussion of these procedures. For those who will major in accounting, a thorough analysis of these procedures is included in a senior level course in advanced accounting.

## Summary of the Chapter in Terms of Learning Objectives

**1.** Stock investments are classified as current assets if they are marketable and are held as a source of cash to be used in current operations. All other stock investments are classified as long-term investments.

**2.** The cost method is used if the investor does not have a significant influence over the investee corporation. Usually, this means the investor owns less than 20% of the investee's voting stock. Also, when the cost or equity method is used, lower of cost or market is applied to the portfolio of marketable stock investments. The equity method is used if the investor has a significant influence over the investee which usually means the investor owns 20% or more of the investee's voting stock.

Consolidated financial statements are used by an investor if the investor controls another corporation. If an investor corporation controls another corporation because the investor owns more than 50% of the investee's voting stock, the investor's financial reports are prepared on a consolidated basis.

**3.** With the cost method, the investment account is maintained at cost and dividends received are credited to a revenue account. With the equity method, the investor records its share of the investee's earnings with a debit to the investment account and a credit to a revenue account. Then, dividend receipts change the form of the investor's assets from investment to cash.

**4.** To prepare a consolidated balance sheet, all items that are duplicated on the books of the subsidiary and the parent are eliminated. These eliminations always include offsetting the parent's investment account against the stockholders' equity accounts of the subsidiary. If subsidiary stock is held by outside parties, that portion of the subsidiary's stockholders' equity is reclassified as minority interest. Also, if the cost of the parent's investment differs from the book value of the investment, the difference is recognized. The remaining account balances of the affiliates are added to get the consolidated amounts.

**5.** If a U.S. company makes a credit sale to a foreign customer and the sales terms call for payment in a foreign currency, the company must translate the foreign currency into dollars in order to record the receivable. Then, if the current exchange rate changes before payment is received, an exchange gain or loss must be recognized. The same problem arises if a U.S. company makes a credit purchase from a foreign supplier and is required to make payment in a foreign currency. Also, if a U.S. company has a foreign subsidiary that maintains its accounts in a foreign currency, the account balances must be translated into dollars before they can be consolidated with the parent's accounts.

## Demonstration Problem

Presented below are a series of events and facts related to Brown Company's investment activities during 1990 and 1991. Show the appropriate journal entries and the portions of each year's balance sheet and income statement that result from these events and facts:

1990

Sept. 9 Purchased as a long-term investment 1,000 shares of Packard, Inc., common stock for $80,000 cash. These shares represent less than 3% of the outstanding shares and are not marketable.

Oct. 2 Purchased as a long-term investment 2,000 shares of AT&T common stock for $60,000 cash. The stock is actively traded on the New York Stock Exchange.

17 Purchased as a long-term investment 1,000 shares of Apple Computers common stock for $40,000 cash. The stock is actively traded in the over-the-counter market.

Nov. 1 Received $5,000 cash dividends from Packard.

30 Received $3,000 cash dividends from AT&T.

Dec. 15 Received $1,400 cash dividends from Apple Computers.

31 Market values for the investments in marketable equity securities are: AT&T, $48,000; and Apple Computers, $45,000.

31 After closing the accounts, selected account balances are:

| | |
|---|---|
| Common stock | $1,000,000 |
| Contributed capital in excess of par value | 2,000,000 |
| Retained earnings | 750,000 |

1991

Jan. 5 Purchased 120,000 shares (a 30% interest) of Hanson Company common stock, a corporation that was just created by two former employees. Brown paid $600,000 cash, will have influence over the management of the company, and plans to hold the stock as a long-term investment.

Feb. 15 Packard, Inc., was taken over by other investors, and Brown sold its shares for $125,000 cash.

May 30 Received $3,100 cash dividends from AT&T.

June 15 Received $1,600 cash dividends from Apple Computers.

Aug. 17 Sold the AT&T stock for $52,000 cash.

19 Bought as a long-term investment 2,000 shares of Coca Cola common stock for $50,000. The stock is actively traded on the New York Stock Exchange.

Dec. 15 Received $1,800 cash dividends from Apple Computers.

19 Received $13,000 cash dividends from Hanson Company.

31 Total profits for Hanson Company for 1991 are determined to be $140,000.

Dec. 31 Market values of the investments in marketable equity securities are: Apple Computers, $39,000; and Coca Cola, $48,000.

31 After closing the accounts, selected account balances are:

| | |
|---|---|
| Common stock | $1,100,000 |
| Contributed capital in excess of par value | 2,300,000 |
| Retained earnings | 970,000 |

## Solution to Demonstration Problem

**Journal entries during 1990:**

| | | | | |
|---|---|---|---|---|
| Sept. | 9 | Investment in Packard, Inc., Common Stock | 80,000.00 | |
| | | Cash | | 80,000.00 |
| | | Acquired 1,000 shares as long-term investment. | | |
| Oct. | 2 | Investment in AT&T Common Stock | 60,000.00 | |
| | | Cash | | 60,000.00 |
| | | Acquired 2,000 shares as long-term investment. | | |
| | 17 | Investment in Apple Computers Common Stock | 40,000.00 | |
| | | Cash | | 40,000.00 |
| | | Acquired 1,000 shares as long-term investment. | | |
| Nov. | 1 | Cash | 5,000.00 | |
| | | Dividends Earned | | 5,000.00 |
| | | Received dividend from Packard, Inc. | | |
| | 30 | Cash | 3,000.00 | |
| | | Dividends Earned | | 3,000.00 |
| | | Received dividend from AT&T. | | |
| Dec. | 15 | Cash | 1,400.00 | |
| | | Dividends Earned | | 1,400.00 |
| | | Received dividend from Apple Computers. | | |
| | 31 | Unrealized Loss on Market Decline of Long-Term Investments | 7,000.00 | |
| | | Allowance to Reduce Long-Term Investments to Market | | 7,000.00 |
| | | To record market decline of long-term marketable equity securities portfolio. | | |

| | Cost | Market |
|---|---|---|
| AT&T | $ 60,000 | $48,000 |
| Apple Computers | 40,000 | 45,000 |
| Total | $100,000 | $93,000 |

$100,000 − $93,000 = $7,000

**December 31, 1990, balance sheet items:**

| | | |
|---|---|---|
| Long-term investments in equity securities: | | |
| Nonmarketable, at cost | | $ 80,000 |
| Marketable: | | |
| Cost | $100,000 | |
| Less: Allowance to reduce to market | (7,000) | 93,000 |
| Total | | $ 173,000 |

**Stockholders' Equity**

| | |
|---|---|
| Common stock | $1,000,000 |
| Contributed capital in excess of par value | 2,000,000 |
| Total contributed capital | $3,000,000 |
| Retained earnings | 750,000 |
| Less: Unrealized loss on market decline of long-term investments | (7,000) |
| Total | $3,743,000 |

**Income statement items for the year ended December 31, 1990:**

| | |
|---|---|
| Dividends earned | $ 9,400 |

## Journal entries during 1991:

| | | | | |
|---|---|---|---|---|
| Jan. | 5 | Investment in Hanson Company Common Stock | 600,000.00 | |
| | | Cash | | 600,000.00 |
| | | Acquired 120,000 shares as long-term investment. Equity method to be used. | | |
| Feb. | 15 | Cash | 125,000.00 | |
| | | Investment in Packard, Inc., Common Stock | | 80,000.00 |
| | | Gain on Sale of Investments | | 45,000.00 |
| | | Sold 1,000 shares for cash. | | |
| May | 30 | Cash | 3,100.00 | |
| | | Dividends Earned | | 3,100.00 |
| | | Received dividend from AT&T. | | |
| June | 15 | Cash | 1,600.00 | |
| | | Dividends Earned | | 1,600.00 |
| | | Received dividend from Apple Computers. | | |
| Aug. | 17 | Cash | 52,000.00 | |
| | | Loss on Sale of Investments | 8,000.00 | |
| | | Investment in AT&T Common Stock | | 60,000.00 |
| | | Sold 2,000 shares for cash. | | |
| | 19 | Investment in Coca Cola Common Stock | 50,000.00 | |
| | | Cash | | 50,000.00 |
| | | Acquired 2,000 shares as long-term investment. | | |
| Dec. | 15 | Cash | 1,800.00 | |
| | | Dividends Earned | | 1,800.00 |
| | | Received dividend from Apple Computers. | | |
| | 19 | Cash | 13,000.00 | |
| | | Investment in Hanson Company Common Stock | | 13,000.00 |
| | | Received dividend from Hanson Company, deducted from investment account under the equity method. | | |
| | 31 | Investment in Hanson Company Common Stock | 42,000.00 | |
| | | Earnings from Investment in Hanson Company | | 42,000.00 |
| | | $140,000 × 30% = $42,000. | | |
| | 31 | Allowance to Reduce Long-Term Investments to Market | 4,000.00 | |
| | | Unrealized Loss on Market Decline of Long-Term Investments | | 4,000.00 |
| | | To record the market value recovery of marketable equity securities long-term investments. | | |

| | Cost | Market |
|---|---|---|
| Apple Computers | $40,000 | $39,000 |
| Coca Cola | 50,000 | 48,000 |
| Total | $90,000 | $87,000 |
| Required allowance balance | | $ 3,000 |
| Existing balance | | 7,000 |
| Necessary decrease | | $ 4,000 |

**December 31, 1991, balance sheet items:**

| | | |
|---|---|---|
| Long-term investments in equity securities: | | |
| Nonmarketable, under equity method | | $ 629,000 |
| Marketable: | | |
| Cost | $90,000 | |
| Less: Allowance to reduce to market | (3,000) | 87,000 |
| Total | | $ 716,000 |

**Stockholders' Equity**

| | |
|---|---|
| Common stock | $1,100,000 |
| Contributed capital in excess of par value | 2,300,000 |
| Total contributed capital | $3,400,000 |
| Retained earnings | 970,000 |
| Less: Unrealized loss on market decline of long-term investments | (3,000) |
| Total | $4,367,000 |

**Income statement items for the year ended December 31, 1991:**

| | |
|---|---|
| Dividends earned | $ 6,500 |
| Earnings from equity method investment | 42,000 |
| Gain on sale of investments | 45,000 |
| Loss on sale of investments | (8,000) |
| Total | $85,500 |

## Glossary

Define or explain the words and phrases listed in the chapter Glossary. (L. O. 6)

**Consolidated financial statements** financial statements that show the results of all operations under the parent's control, including those of any subsidiaries. Assets and liabilities of all affiliated companies are combined on a single balance sheet, revenues and expenses are combined on a single income statement, and cash flows are combined on a single statement of cash flows as though the business were in fact a single company. p. 804

**Cost method of accounting for stock investments** an accounting method whereby the investment is recorded at total cost and maintained at that amount; subsequent investee earnings and dividends do not affect the investment account. pp. 803–05

**Equity method of accounting for stock investments** an accounting method whereby the investment is recorded at total cost, and the investment account balance is subsequently increased to reflect the investor's equity in earnings of the investee, and decreased to reflect the investor's equity in dividends of the investee. pp. 804, 806–8

**Foreign exchange rate** the price of one currency stated in terms of another currency. p. 818

**Long-term investments** investments not intended as a ready source of cash in case of need, such as bond sinking funds, land, bonds, and stocks that are not marketable or, if marketable, are not held as a temporary investment of cash available for current operations. p. 803

**Marketable equity securities** common and preferred stocks that are actively traded so that sales prices or bid and ask prices are currently available on a national securities exchange or in the over-the-counter market. p. 802

**Minority interest** the portion of a subsidiary company's stockholders' equity that is not owned by the parent corporation. pp. 811–12

**Multinational business** a company that operates in a large number of different countries. p. 818

**Parent company** a corporation that owns a controlling interest (more than 50% of the voting stock is required) in another corporation. p. 808

**Reporting currency** the currency in which a company presents its financial statements. p. 818

**Subsidiary** a corporation that is controlled by another (parent) corporation because the parent owns more than 50% of the subsidiary's voting stock. p. 808

## Objective Review

Answers to the following questions are listed in Appendix I at the end of the book. Be sure that you decide which is the one best answer to each question *before* you check the answers in the appendix.

1. Which of the following criteria must be satisfied in order for a stock investment to be classified as long term?
   *a.* The stock must be a marketable security.

*b*. The stock must not be a marketable security that is held as a ready source of cash.
*c*. The stock must not be a marketable security.
*d*. The stock must not be held longer than one year.
*e*. The stock must be common shares.

2. Under which of the following circumstances would a company account for its investment in another company's stock according to the equity method?
   *a*. The investor company owns 18% of the investee company's common stock and exercises a significant influence over the operations of the investee company.
   *b*. The investment represents 40% of the investee's outstanding preferred (nonvoting) stock.
   *c*. The investor owns 21% of the investee company's voting stock, but other facts disclose that the investor does not have a significant influence over the investee.
   *d*. The investment represents 30% of the investee's outstanding bonds payable.
   *e*. The investment represents 2% of the investee's outstanding common shares.
3. On January 1, 1990, Abbott Labs purchased 4,000 shares (40%) of Costello Company's common stock at a total cost of $103,000. Costello Company's net income over the next two years totaled $35,000, and the company declared and paid $25,000 in dividends on its outstanding common shares. Abbott Labs sold its Costello Company shares on January 14, 1993, for $27.75 per share. The entry to record the sale is as follows:

| | | | |
|---|---|---|---|
| a. | Cash | 111,000.00 | |
| | Investment in Costello Company | | 107,000.00 |
| | Gain on Sale of Investments | | 4,000.00 |
| b. | Cash | 111,000.00 | |
| | Investment in Costello Company | | 103,000.00 |
| | Gain on Sale of Investments | | 8,000.00 |
| c. | Cash | 111,000.00 | |
| | Loss on Sale of Investments | 2,000.00 | |
| | Investment in Costello Company | | 113,000.00 |
| d. | Cash | 111,000.00 | |
| | Loss on Sale of Investments | 6,000.00 | |
| | Investment in Costello Company | | 117,000.00 |
| e. | Cash | 111,000.00 | |
| | Investment in Costello Company | | 111,000.00 |

4. Lewis Company purchased 90% of Martin Company's stock at a total cost of $135,000, which amounted to $15 per share. The book value of the stock was $12.50 per share. Calculate the following amounts to report in Lewis Company's consolidated balance sheet on the date of ac-

quisition: *(1)* investment in Martin Company, *(2)* excess of cost over book value, and *(3)* minority interest.

*a.* *(1)* $135,000; *(2)* $ –0– ; *(3)* $15,000.
*b.* *(1)* $135,000; *(2)* $25,000; *(3)* $15,000.
*c.* *(1)* $112,500; *(2)* $22,500; *(3)* $12,500.
*d.* *(1)* $ –0– ; *(2)* $22,500; *(3)* $12,500.
*e.* Cannot be determined from information given.

5. If a U.S. company makes a credit sale of merchandise to a British customer and the sales terms require the customer's payment to be in British pounds:
   *a.* The U.S. company may be required to record an exchange gain or loss on the date of the sale.
   *b.* The British company may eventually have to record an exchange gain or loss.
   *c.* The U.S. company will incur an exchange loss if the foreign exchange rate between pounds and dollars increases from $1.70 at the date of sale to $1.80 at the date the account is settled.
   *d.* The British company will incur an exchange loss if the foreign exchange rate between pounds and dollars decreases from $1.70 at the date of sale to $1.623 at the date the account is settled.
   *e.* None of the above is correct.

## Questions for Class Discussion

1. What is meant by the term *marketable securities*?
2. Under what conditions should a stock investment be classified on the balance sheet as a long-term investment?
3. What types of assets are classified as long-term investments?
4. In accounting for common stock investments, when should the cost method be used? When should the equity method be used?
5. Under what circumstances would a company prepare consolidated financial statements?
6. When the cost method is used to account for a long-term stock investment, what events cause the investor to record revenue from the investment?
7. If a company prepares consolidated financial statements, what method would the company normally use on its books to account for its investment in the subsidiary?
8. When a parent corporation uses the equity method to account for its investment in a subsidiary, what recognition is given by the parent corporation to the income or loss reported by the subsidiary? What recognition is given to dividends declared by the subsidiary?
9. Under what circumstances is lower of cost or market applied to long-term investments in stock?
10. When a long-term portfolio of investments in marketable equity securities is written down to a market value that is less than cost, how is the loss reported on the financial statements?

11. What are consolidated financial statements?
12. What account balances must be eliminated in preparing a consolidated balance sheet?
13. Why are the stockholders' equity accounts of a subsidiary eliminated in the process of preparing a consolidated balance sheet?
14. What is meant by *minority interest*? Where is this item disclosed on a consolidated balance sheet?
15. Why would a parent corporation pay more than book value for the stock of a subsidiary?
16. When a parent pays more than book value for the stock of a subsidiary, how should this additional cost be reported on the consolidated balance sheet?
17. What are two basic problems of accounting for international operations?
18. If a U.S. company makes a credit sale to a foreign customer and the customer is required to make payment in U.S. dollars, might the U.S. company have an exchange gain or loss as a result of the sale?
19. A U.S. company makes a credit sale to a foreign customer, and the customer is required to make payment in a foreign currency. The foreign exchange rate was $1.40 on the date of the sale and is $1.30 on the date the customer pays the receivable. Will the U.S. company record an exchange gain or an exchange loss?
20. On December 31, 1990, a U.S. company has an account receivable from a British customer which requires the customer to pay 6,000 pounds to the U.S. company. How do you determine the amount to be reported on the U.S. company's December 31 balance sheet?
21. In preparing its December 31, 1990, financial statements, a U.S. company had to report an account receivable that was denominated in a foreign currency. The receivable stemmed from a sale made on November 14, 1989. In translating the receivable into dollars, should the accountant use the foreign exchange rate on November 14 or on December 31?

## Exercises

**Exercise 19–1**
**Classifying stock investments; lower of cost or market**
(L. O. 1, 3)

During 1990, Kest Corporation made five investments in equity securities. These securities, with their December 31, 1990, market values, are as follows:

*a.* Manor Corporation common stock: 3,000 shares, $36,000 cost, $32,000 market value. Purpose of investment is to develop a supplier relationship with Manor Corporation.

*b.* Blalock Company preferred stock: 1,000 shares, $22,000 cost, $23,500 market value. Purpose of investment is to earn dividends while holding as a source of cash for operations.

*c.* Cedar Company common stock: 1,500 shares, $37,000 cost, $39,000 market value. Purpose of investment is to hold for expected increase in value over the next few years.

*d.* Dipprey Corp. common stock: 1,200 shares, $44,000 cost, $41,000 market value. Purpose of investment is expected gains from increases in market value during next two years.

*e.* Neeley Company preferred stock: 800 shares, $25,000 cost, $26,000 market value. Purpose of the investment is to earn a return on surplus cash balances.

Calculate the lower-of-cost-or-market amount of the long-term portfolio of stock investments as of December 31, 1990. If necessary, prepare a journal entry dated December 31, 1990, to record any decline in market value. If a loss is recorded, explain how it should be reported by Kest Corporation.

**Exercise 19–2**
**Stock investment transactions**
(L. O. 2, 3)

Prepare general journal entries to record the following events on the books of K-Stop Company:

| | | |
|---|---|---|
| 1990 | | |
| Jan. | 5 | Purchased 10,000 shares of Mert Company common stock for $125,000 plus broker's fee of $2,150. Mert Company has 200,000 shares of common stock outstanding, and K-Stop Company does not have a significant influence on Mert Company policies. |
| May | 12 | Mert Company declared and paid a cash dividend of $0.90 per share. |
| Dec. | 31 | Mert Company announced that net income for the year amounted to $86,000. |
| 1991 | | |
| May | 25 | Mert Company declared and paid a cash dividend of $0.45 per share. |
| Aug. | 20 | Mert Company declared and issued a stock dividend of one additional share for each 10 shares already outstanding. |
| Dec. | 30 | K-Stop Company sold 5,500 shares of Mert Company for $73,200. |
| | 31 | Mert Company announced that net income for the year amounted to $80,000. |

**Exercise 19–3**
**Stock investment transactions**
(L. O. 2, 3)

Prepare general journal entries to record the following events on the books of Akvar Company:

| | | |
|---|---|---|
| 1990 | | |
| Jan. | 3 | Purchased 10,000 shares of Betel Company for $133,000 plus broker's fee of $1,890. Betel Company has 50,000 shares of common stock outstanding and has acknowledged the fact that its policies will be significantly influenced by Akvar Company. |
| Oct. | 15 | Betel Company declared and paid a cash dividend of $0.70 per share. |
| Dec. | 31 | Betel Company announced that net income for the year amounted to $77,600. |
| 1991 | | |
| May | 29 | Betel Company declared and paid a cash dividend of $1.80 per share. |

| | |
|---|---|
| Aug. 24 | Betel Company declared and issued a stock dividend of one additional share for each 10 shares already outstanding. |
| Dec. 31 | Betel Company announced that net income for the year amounted to $65,000. |
| 31 | Akvar Company sold 5,500 shares of Betel Company for $63,000. |

**Exercise 19–4**
**Comparison of cost and equity methods**
(L. O. 2, 3)

On December 31, 1989, Able Company and Baker Company each purchased 6,000 shares of Charlie Company stock at a cost of $30 per share. On that date, the stockholders' equity of Charlie Company appeared as follows:

| | |
|---|---|
| Common stock ($20 par) . . . . | $600,000 |
| Retained earnings . . . . . . . . | 300,000 |
| Total . . . . . . . . . . . . . . | $900,000 |

Because of certain legal agreements, Baker Company does not have a significant influence over Charlie Company. However, Able Company is presumed to have a significant influence over Charlie Company.

During 1990 and 1991, Charlie Company earned an annual net income of $90,000 and paid cash dividends of $30,000 each year. On December 31, 1991, calculate the carrying value of (*a*) Able Company's investment in Charlie Company and (*b*) Baker Company's investment in Charlie Company.

**Exercise 19–5**
**Consolidated statement elimination entry at acquisition**
(L. O. 4)

On December 31, Small Company had the following stockholders' equity:

| | |
|---|---|
| Common stock, $10 par value, 9,500 shares issued and outstanding . . | $ 95,000 |
| Retained earnings . . . . . . . . . . . . . . . . . . . . . . . . . . . . | 65,000 |
| Total stockholders' equity . . . . . . . . . . . . . . . . . . . . . . . . | $160,000 |

On the same day (December 31), Puff Company purchased 6,650 of Small Company's outstanding shares, paying $20 per share, and a work sheet to consolidate the balance sheets of the two companies was prepared. In general journal form, give the entry made on this work sheet to eliminate Puff Company's investment and the related stockholders' equity accounts of Small Company.

**Exercise 19–6**
**Consolidated statement elimination entry after acquisition**
(L. O. 4)

During the year following its acquisition by Puff Company (see Exercise 19–5), Small Company earned $25,000, paid out $12,000 in dividends, and retained the balance for use in its operations. In general journal form, give the entry under these assumptions to eliminate Puff Company's investment and Small Company's stockholders' equity account balances as of the end of the year.

**Exercise 19–7**
**Consolidated balance sheet**
(L. O. 4)

On December 31, 1990, Holter Company purchased 70% of Cats Corporation's outstanding stock. The balance sheets of the two companies on that date were as follows:

| | Holter Company | Cats Corporation |
|---|---|---|
| **Assets** | | |
| Investment in Cats Corporation | $ 98,000 | |
| Other assets | 402,000 | $160,000 |
| Total assets | $500,000 | $160,000 |
| **Liabilities and Stockholders' Equity** | | |
| Liabilities | $100,000 | $ 20,000 |
| Common stock, $10 par value | 250,000 | 100,000 |
| Retained earnings | 150,000 | 40,000 |
| Total liabilities and stockholders' equity | $500,000 | $160,000 |

Present the consolidated balance sheet for Holter Company and its subsidiary on December 31, 1990. (Do not prepare a consolidated work sheet.)

**Exercise 19–8**
**Calculating consolidated net income**
(L. O. 3, 4)

On January 1, 1990, Rayer Corporation purchased 80% of Safte Corporation's outstanding stock. During the year ended December 31, 1990, Rayer earned a net income (excluding its equity in the earnings of Safte Corporation) of $75,000. Safte Corporation earned a net income of $40,000 and paid cash dividends of $15,000 during 1990. Calculate the net income to be reported on Rayer Corporation's consolidated income statement for 1990.

**Exercise 19–9**
**Receivables denominated in a foreign currency**
(L. O. 5)

On June 15, 1990, Wilder Company made a credit sale to a Swedish company. The terms of the sale required the Swedish company to pay 46,000 kronor (Swedish) on January 15, 1991. Wilder prepares quarterly financial statements on March 31, June 30, September 30, and December 31. The current foreign exchange rates for kronor during the time the receivable was outstanding were:

| | |
|---|---|
| June 15, 1990 | $0.1680 |
| June 30, 1990 | 0.1825 |
| September 30, 1990 | 0.1960 |
| December 31, 1990 | 0.1800 |
| January 15, 1991 | 0.1700 |

Calculate the exchange gain or loss that Wilder Company should report on each of its quarterly income statements during the last three quarters of 1990 and the first quarter of 1991. Also calculate the amount that should be reported on Wilder Company's balance sheets at the end of each of those quarters.

**Exercise 19–10**
**Foreign currency transactions**
(L. O. 5)

Rhonder Company of Duluth, Minnesota, sells its products to customers in the United States and in Norway. On October 15, 1990, Rhonder Company sold merchandise on credit to the Norway Products Company at a price of 40,000 kroner. The exchange rate on that day was 1 krone equals $0.1572. On December 31, 1990, when Rhonder Company prepared its financial statements, the exchange rate was 1 krone for $0.1690. Norway Products paid its bill in full on January 12, 1991, at which time the exchange rate was 1 krone for $0.1625. Rhonder Company immediately exchanged the 40,000 kroner for U.S. dollars. Prepare journal entries on October 15, December 31, and January 12, to account for the sale and account receivable on the books of Rhonder Company.

## Problems

**Problem 19–1**
**Stock investments—cost and equity methods**
(L. O. 2, 3)

Ranger Company was organized on January 2, 1989, for the purpose of investing in the shares of other companies. Ranger Company immediately issued 50,000 shares of $5 par, common stock for which it received $250,000 cash. On January 9, 1989, Ranger Company purchased 10,000 shares (20%) of Trumpe Company's outstanding stock at a cost of $250,000. The following transactions and events subsequently occurred:

1989
Apr. 30 Trumpe Company declared and paid a cash dividend of $1 per share.
Dec. 31 Trumpe Company announced that its net income for the year was $125,000.

1990
June 12 Trumpe Company declared and issued a stock dividend of one share for each two shares already outstanding.
Aug. 10 Trumpe Company declared and paid a cash dividend of $0.80 per share.
Dec. 31 Trumpe Company announced that its net income for the year was $95,000.

1991
Jan. 4 Ranger Company sold all of its investment in Trumpe Company for $275,000 cash.

**Part 1.** Because Ranger Company owns 20% of Trumpe Company's outstanding stock, Ranger Company is presumed to have a significant influence over Trumpe Company.

*Required*

1. Give the entries on the books of Ranger Company to record the above events regarding its investment in Trumpe Company.
2. Calculate the cost per share of Ranger Company's investment as reflected in the investment account on January 1, 1991.
3. Calculate Ranger Company's retained earnings balance on January 5, 1991, after a closing of the books.

**Part 2.** Although Ranger Company owns 20% of Trumpe Company's outstanding stock, a thorough investigation of the surrounding circumstances indicates that Ranger Company does not have a significant influence over Trumpe Company, and the cost method is the appropriate method of accounting for the investment.

*Required*

1. Give the entries on the books of Ranger Company to record the above events regarding its investment in Trumpe Company.
2. Calculate the cost per share of Ranger Company's investment as reflected in the investment account on January 1, 1991.
3. Calculate Ranger Company's retained earnings balance on January 5, 1991, after a closing of the books.

**Problem 19–2**
**Consolidated statements, at acquisition and one year later**
(L. O. 4)

On January 1, 1990, Northwood Company purchased 80% of Souther Company's outstanding stock at $48 per share. On that date, Northwood Company had retained earnings of $517,500. Souther Company had retained earnings of $135,000 and had outstanding 15,000 shares of $15 par, common stock, originally issued at par.

**Part 1.**

*Required*

1. Give the elimination entry to be used on a work sheet for a consolidated balance sheet dated January 1, 1990.
2. Determine the amount of consolidated retained earnings that should be shown on a consolidated balance sheet dated January 1, 1990.

**Part 2.** During the year ended December 31, 1990, Northwood Company paid cash dividends of $67,500 and earned net income of $127,500 excluding earnings from its investment in Souther Company. Souther Company earned net income of $63,000 and paid dividends of $30,000. Except for Northwood Company's Retained Earnings account and the Investment in Souther Company account, the balance sheet accounts for the two companies on December 31, 1990, are as follows:

| | Northwood Company | Souther Company |
|---|---|---|
| **Assets** | | |
| Cash | $157,800 | $124,200 |
| Notes receivable | 54,000 | |
| Merchandise | 367,200 | 178,200 |
| Building, net | 348,000 | 216,000 |
| Land | 210,000 | 189,000 |
| Investment in Souther Company | ? | |
| Total assets | $ ? | $707,400 |
| **Liabilities and Stockholders' Equity** | | |
| Accounts payable | $439,500 | $260,400 |
| Note payable | | 54,000 |
| Common stock | 672,000 | 225,000 |
| Retained earnings | ? | 168,000 |
| Total liabilities and stockholders' equity | $ ? | $707,400 |

Northwood Company loaned $54,000 to Souther Company during 1990, for which Souther Company signed a note. On December 31, 1990, the note had not been repaid.

*Required*

1. Calculate the December 31, 1990, balances in Northwood Company's Investment in Souther Company account and Retained Earnings account.
2. Complete a work sheet to consolidate the balance sheets of the two companies.

**Problem 19–3**
**Consolidated work sheet and balance sheet**
(L. O. 4)

The following items appeared in the first two columns of a work sheet prepared to consolidate the balance sheets of Upper Company and Lower Company on the day Upper Company gained control of Lower Company by purchasing 6,375 shares of its $50 par value common stock at $65 per share.

| | Upper Company | Lower Company |
|---|---|---|
| **Assets** | | |
| Cash | $ 28,125 | $ 41,250 |
| Note receivable, Lower Company | 37,500 | |
| Accounts receivable, net | 105,000 | 90,000 |
| Inventories | 157,500 | 131,250 |
| Investment in Lower Company | 414,375 | |
| Equipment, net | 300,000 | 262,500 |
| Buildings, net | 318,750 | |
| Land | 75,000 | |
| Total assets | $1,436,250 | $525,000 |
| **Liabilities and Stockholders' Equity** | | |
| Accounts payable | $ 78,750 | $ 37,500 |
| Note payable, Upper Company | | 37,500 |
| Common stock | 937,500 | 375,000 |
| Retained earnings | 420,000 | 75,000 |
| Total liabilities and stockholders' equity | $1,436,250 | $525,000 |

At the time Upper Company acquired control of Lower Company, it took Lower Company's note in exchange for $37,500 in cash, and it sold and delivered $7,500 of equipment at cost to Lower Company on open account (account receivable). Both transactions are reflected in the foregoing accounts.

*Required*

1. Prepare a work sheet to consolidate the balance sheets of the two companies and prepare a consolidated balance sheet.
2. Under the assumption that Lower Company earned $37,500 during the first year after it was acquired by Upper Company, paid out $22,500 in dividends, and retained the balance of its earnings in its operations, give the entry to eliminate Upper Company's investment in the subsidiary and Lower Company's stockholders' equity accounts at the year's end.

**Problem 19–4**
**Foreign currency transactions**
(L. O. 5)

Paramount Sales Corporation, a United States company that has customers in several foreign countries, had the following transactions in 1990 and 1991:

1990

June 6 Sold merchandise for 125,000 francs to Poirot Co. of Brussels, payment in full to be received in 60 days. On this day, the foreign exchange rate for francs into dollars was $0.02822.

July 17 Sold merchandise to Nordhoff Distributors of West Germany for $8,880 cash. The exchange rate for marks into dollars was $0.5920.

Aug. 1 Received Poirot Co.'s payment for its purchase of June 6 and exchanged the francs for dollars. The current foreign exchange rate for francs into dollars was $0.02840.

Oct. 25 Sold merchandise on credit to British Imports, Ltd., a company located in London, England. The price of 3,000 pounds was to be paid 90 days from the date of sale. On October 25, the exchange rate for pounds into dollars was $1.7730.

Nov. 30 Sold merchandise for 350,000 yen to Yamoto Company of Japan; payment in full to be in 60 days. The exchange rate for yen into dollars was $0.007710.

Dec. 31 Prepared adjusting entries to recognize exchange gains or losses on the annual financial statements. Rates for exchanging foreign currencies into dollars on this day included the following:

| | |
|---|---|
| Francs (Belgium) . . . . . | $0.02833 |
| Marks (W. German) . . . . | 0.5944 |
| Pounds (England) . . . . . | 1.7125 |
| Yen (Japan) . . . . . . . . | 0.007897 |

1991

Jan. 23 Received British Imports, Ltd.'s full payment for the sale of October 25 and immediately exchanged the pounds for dollars. The exchange rate for pounds into dollars was $1.7628.

29 Received full payment from Yamoto Company for the sale of November 30 and immediately exchanged the yen for dollars. The exchange rate for yen into dollars was $0.007779.

*Required*

1. Prepare general journal entries to account for these transactions of Paramount Sales Corporation.
2. Calculate the exchange gain or loss to be reported on Paramount Sales Corporation's 1990 income statement.

## Alternate Problems

**Problem 19–1A**
**Stock investments—cost and equity methods**
(L. O. 2)

Universal Company was organized on January 1, 1989, for the purpose of investing in the shares of other companies. Universal Company immediately issued 46,000 shares of $5 par, common stock for which it received $230,000 cash. On January 7, 1989, Universal Company purchased 20,000 shares (20%) of Suburban Company's outstanding stock at a cost of $230,000. The following transactions and events subsequently occurred:

1989

May 20 Suburban Company declared and paid a cash dividend of $0.90 per share.

Dec. 31 Suburban Company announced that its net income for the year was $150,000.

1990

July 8 Suburban Company declared and issued a stock dividend of one share for each four shares already outstanding.

Nov. 15 Suburban Company declared and paid a cash dividend of $0.70 per share.

Dec. 31 Suburban Company announced that its net income for the year was $160,000.

1991

Jan. 4 Universal Company sold all of its investment in Suburban Company for $240,000 cash.

**Part 1.** Because Universal Company owns 20% of Suburban Company's outstanding stock, Universal Company is presumed to have a significant influence over Suburban Company.

*Required*

1. Give the entries on the books of Universal Company to record the above events regarding its investment in Suburban Company.
2. Calculate the cost per share of Universal Company's investment as reflected in the investment account on January 3, 1991.
3. Calculate Universal Company's retained earnings balance on January 5, 1991, after a closing of the books.

**Part 2.** Although Universal Company owns 20% of Suburban Company's outstanding stock, a thorough investigation of the surrounding circumstances indicates that Universal Company does not have a significant influence over Suburban Company, and the cost method is the appropriate method of accounting for the investment.

*Required*

1. Give the entries on the books of Universal Company to record the above events regarding its investment in Suburban Company.
2. Calculate the cost per share of Universal Company's investment as reflected in the investment account on January 3, 1991.
3. Calculate Universal Company's retained earnings balance on January 5, 1991, after a closing of the books.

**Problem 19–2A**
**Consolidated statements, at acquisition and one year later**
(L. O. 4)

On January 1, 1990, Larger Company purchased 90% of Smaller Company's outstanding stock at $24 per share. On that date, Larger Company had retained earnings of $350,500. Smaller Company had retained earnings of $225,000 and had outstanding 20,000 shares of $10 par, common stock, originally issued at par.

**Part 1.**

*Required*

1. Give the elimination entry to be used on a work sheet for a consolidated balance sheet dated January 1, 1990.
2. Determine the amount of consolidated retained earnings that should be shown on a consolidated balance sheet dated January 1, 1990.

**Part 2.** During the year ended December 31, 1990, Larger Company paid cash dividends of $45,000 and earned net income of $90,000 excluding earnings from its investment in Smaller Company. Smaller Company earned net income of $45,000 and paid dividends of $25,000. Except for Larger Company's Retained Earnings account and the Investment in Smaller Company account, the balance sheet accounts for the two companies on December 31, 1990, are as follows:

| | Larger Company | Smaller Company |
|---|---|---|
| **Assets** | | |
| Cash | $140,200 | $106,800 |
| Notes receivable | 45,000 | |
| Merchandise | 220,800 | 175,300 |
| Building, net | 284,250 | 240,000 |
| Land | 186,000 | 183,500 |
| Investment in Smaller Company | ? | |
| Total assets | $ ? | $705,600 |
| **Liabilities and Stockholders' Equity** | | |
| Accounts payable | $215,250 | $215,600 |
| Note payable | | 45,000 |
| Common stock | 675,000 | 200,000 |
| Retained earnings | ? | 245,000 |
| Total liabilities and stockholders' equity | $ ? | $705,600 |

Larger Company loaned $45,000 to Smaller Company during 1990, for which Smaller Company signed a note. On December 31, 1990, the note had not been repaid.

*Required*

1. Calculate the December 31, 1990, balances in Larger Company's Investment in Smaller Company account and Retained Earnings account.
2. Complete a work sheet to consolidate the balance sheets of the two companies.

**Problem 19–3A**
**Consolidated work sheet and balance sheet**
(L. O. 4)

The following items appeared in the first two columns of a work sheet prepared to consolidate the balance sheets of Parent Company and Subsidiary Company on the day Parent Company gained control of Subsidiary Company by purchasing 29,750 shares of its $10 par value common stock at $13 per share.

| | Parent Company | Subsidiary Company |
|---|---|---|
| **Assets** | | |
| Cash | $ 37,250 | $ 72,500 |
| Note receivable, Subsidiary Company | 54,000 | |
| Accounts receivable, net | 110,000 | 80,000 |
| Inventories | 215,000 | 162,500 |
| Investment in Subsidiary Company | 386,750 | |
| Equipment, net | 461,250 | 257,500 |
| Buildings, net | 337,500 | |
| Land | 150,000 | |
| Total assets | $1,751,750 | $572,500 |
| **Liabilities and Stockholders' Equity** | | |
| Accounts payable | $ 257,500 | $ 98,500 |
| Note payable, Parent Company | | 54,000 |
| Common stock | 875,000 | 350,000 |
| Retained earnings | 619,250 | 70,000 |
| Total liabilities and stockholders' equity | $1,751,750 | $572,500 |

At the time Parent Company acquired control of Subsidiary Company, it took Subsidiary Company's note in exchange for $54,000 in cash, and it sold and delivered $3,000 of equipment at cost to Subsidiary Company on open account (account receivable). Both transactions are reflected in the foregoing accounts.

*Required*

1. Prepare a work sheet to consolidate the balance sheets of the two companies and prepare a consolidated balance sheet.
2. Under the assumption that Subsidiary Company earned $50,000 during the first year after it was acquired by Parent Company, paid out $32,500 in dividends, and retained the balance of its earnings in its operations, give the entry to eliminate Parent Company's investment in the subsidiary and Subsidiary Company's stockholders' equity accounts at the year's end.

**Problem 19–4A**
**Foreign currency transactions**
(L. O. 5)

Global Sales Company, a United States corporation that has customers in several foreign countries, had the following transactions in 1990 and 1991:

1990

July 16 Sold merchandise for 950,000 yen to Shisedu Company of Japan, payment in full to be received in 60 days. On this day, the current foreign exchange rate for yen into dollars was $0.007897.

Aug. 21 Sold merchandise to Klaus Retailers of West Germany for $9,500 cash. The foreign exchange rate for marks into dollars was $0.6027.

Sept. 14 Received Shisedu Company's payment for its purchase of July 16 and exchanged the yen for dollars. The exchange rate for yen into dollars was $0.007779.

Oct. 6 Sold merchandise on credit to Trafalgar Distributors, Inc., a company located in London, England. The price of 5,000 pounds was to be paid 90 days from the date of sale. On October 6, the foreign exchange rate for pounds into dollars was $1.7644.

Nov. 18 Sold merchandise for 30,000 francs to Belgique Suppliers of Brussels' payment in full to be in 60 days. The exchange rate for Belgian francs into dollars was $0.2818.

Dec. 31 Prepared adjusting entries to recognize exchange gains or losses on the annual financial statements. Rates of exchanging foreign currencies into dollars on this day included the following:

| | |
|---|---|
| Francs (Belgium) . . . . . . . | $0.2850 |
| Marks (West Germany) . . . . | 0.5903 |
| Pounds (England) . . . . . . . | 1.7420 |
| Yen (Japan) . . . . . . . . . | 0.007791 |

1991

Jan. 4 Received Trafalgar Distributors, Inc.'s full payment for the sale of October 6 and immediately exchanged the pounds for dollars. The exchange rate for pounds into dollars was $1.7695.

Jan. 17 Received full payment from Belgique Suppliers for the sale of November 18 and immediately exchanged the francs for dollars. The exchange rate for francs into dollars was $0.2822.

*Required*

1. Prepare general journal entries to account for these transactions of Global Sales Company.
2. Calculate the exchange gain or loss to be reported on Global Sales Company's 1990 income statement.

## Provocative Problems

**Provocative Problem 19–1**
**Tamerack, Inc.**
(L. O. 2, 3)

When corporations have their annual meetings with stockholders, the managements often have to deal with difficult questions from stockholders. For example, at a recent stockholders' meeting of Tamerack, Inc., one of the stockholders made the following statements. "I have owned shares of Tamerack for several years but am now questioning whether management is telling the truth in the annual financial statements. At the end of 1989, you announced that Tamerack had just acquired a 30% interest in the outstanding stock of Franklin Corporation. You also stated that the 105,000 shares had cost Tamerack about $10.5 million. In the financial statements for 1990, you told us that the investments of Tamerack were proving to be very profitable and reported that earnings from all investments had amounted to more than $5.25 million. In the financial statements for 1991, you explained that Tamerack had sold the Franklin shares during the first week of the year, receiving $11,750,000 cash proceeds from the sale. Nevertheless, the income statement for 1991 reports only a $260,000 gain on the sale (before taxes). I realize that Franklin did not pay any dividends during 1990, but it was very profitable. As I recall, it reported net income of $3.3 million for 1990. Personally, I do not think you should have sold the shares. But, much more importantly, you reported to us that our company gained only $260,000 from the sale. How can that be true if the shares were purchased for $10,500,000 and were sold for $11,750,000?"

Explain to this stockholder why the $260,000 gain is correctly reported.

**Provocative Problem 19–2**
**American Motor Inns, Incorporated**
(L. O. 4)

American Motor Inns (AMI) is engaged in the business of operating hotels and restaurants. A recent annual report of AMI included the following footnote to its financial statements:

> (7) MINORITY INTEREST IN SUBSIDIARY
> In December, . . . the Company's previously wholly owned subsidiary, Universal Communication Systems, Inc. sold 750,000 shares of its common stock to the public resulting in net proceeds of $8,725,000. This reduced the Company's holding in that subsidiary to approximately 84% of the outstanding common stock.

Given this information, would you expect the future consolidated financial statements of American Motor Inns to report its investment in Universal Communication Systems according to the equity method? Why or why not? Also, assume that American Motor Inns prepared a consolidated balance sheet immediately after the subsidiary's sale of stock to the public. Did the sale of stock have any effects on that balance sheet? If so, explain the effects.

# 20 Analyzing Financial Statements

As a result of studying the previous chapters, you have learned the fundamental methods and principles that are used to generate financial statements. The focus of this chapter is on the analysis of financial statements. In studying this chapter, you will expand your understanding of how the information in financial statements can be used to evaluate the activities and financial status of a business.

**Learning Objectives**

*After studying Chapter 20, you should be able to:*

1. List the three broad objectives of financial reporting by business enterprises.
2. Describe, prepare, and interpret comparative financial statements and common-size comparative statements.
3. Calculate and explain the interpretation of the ratios, turnovers, and rates of return used to evaluate (*a*) short-term liquidity, (*b*) long-term risk and capital structure, and (*c*) operating efficiency and profitability.
4. State the limitations associated with using financial statement ratios and the sources from which standards for comparison may be obtained.
5. Define or explain the words and phrases listed in the chapter Glossary.

## Financial Reporting

Many different people receive and analyze financial information about business firms. These people range from managers, employees, directors, customers, suppliers, owners, lenders, and potential investors to brokers, regulatory authorities, lawyers, economists, labor unions, financial advisors, and the financial press. Some of these groups, such as managers and some regulatory agencies, are able to require a company to prepare specialized financial reports that meet their specific interests. Many other groups must rely on the **general purpose financial statements** that companies publish periodically. General purpose financial statements usually include (1) an income statement, (2) a balance sheet, (3) a statement of retained earnings or statement of changes in stockholders' equity, and (4) a statement of cash flows. A variety of additional financial information such as the financial statement footnotes typically is published with the statements. See, for example, the financial statements and related information from the annual report of Tyler Corporation in Appendix J at the end of the book. Also, news announcements by company managers often are a timely source of financial information.

**Financial reporting** is the process of preparing and issuing financial information about a company. While financial reporting includes more than general purpose financial statements, the same broad objectives apply to both.

## Objectives of Financial Reporting

List the three broad objectives of financial reporting by business enterprises.
(L. O. 1)

The great variety of persons who use financial information about a business have differing reasons for analyzing that information. However, the FASB suggests that such users are "generally interested in [the business's] ability to generate favorable cash flows because their decisions relate to amounts, timing, and uncertainties of expected cash flows."[1] Based on this general assumption about the interests of financial information users, the FASB stated three broad objectives of financial reporting. The three objectives, which flow from the more general to the more specific, are:

1. Financial reporting should provide information that is useful to present and potential investors and creditors and other users in making rational investment, credit, and similar decisions. The information should be comprehensible to those who have a reasonable understanding of business and economic activities and are willing to study the information with reasonable diligence.
2. Financial reporting should provide information to help present and potential investors and creditors and other users in assessing the amounts, timing, and uncertainty of prospective cash receipts from dividends or interest and the proceeds from the sale, redemption, or maturity of securities or loans. Since investors' cash flows are related to enterprise cash flows, financial reporting should provide information to help investors, creditors, and others assess the amounts, tim-

[1] FASB, *Statement of Financial Accounting Concepts No. 1,* "Objectives of Financial Reporting by Business Enterprises" (Norwalk, Conn., 1978), par. 25. Copyright © by the Financial Accounting Standards Board, Norwalk, Conn. 06856, U.S.A. Quoted (or excerpted) with permission. Copies of the complete document are available from the FASB.

ing, and uncertainty of prospective net cash inflows to the related enterprise.

3. Financial reporting should provide information about the economic resources of an enterprise, the claims to those resources (obligations of the enterprise to transfer resources to other entities and owners' equity), and the effects of transactions, events, and circumstances that change its resources and claims to those resources.[2]

These three objectives of financial reporting were published by the FASB as the first part of its conceptual framework for financial accounting.[3] The conceptual framework is intended to help accountants decide how accounting problems should be solved. In addition, the objectives provide important background information for the person who is learning how to understand and analyze financial statements.

Some users of financial information may analyze financial statements for reasons that are not covered by the FASB's stated objectives. Even so, they should understand that the authoritative body for establishing accounting principles (the FASB) intends for financial reporting (and financial statements) to reflect these basic objectives. The primary idea is that financial reporting should help readers predict the amounts, timing, and uncertainty of future net cash inflows to the business. The methods of analysis and techniques explained in this chapter contribute to this process.

When the financial statements of a business are analyzed, individual statement items usually are not too significant. However, relationships between items and groups of items plus changes that occurred are significant. As a result, financial statement analysis involves describing relationships between items and groups of items and changes in items.

## Comparative Statements

Describe, prepare, and interpret comparative financial statements and common-size comparative statements. (L. O. 2)

You can see changes in financial statement items most clearly when item amounts for two or more successive accounting periods are placed side by side in columns on a single statement. Statements prepared in this manner are called **comparative statements.** Each financial statement can be presented in the form of a comparative statement.

In its most simple form, a comparative balance sheet consists of the item amounts from two or more successive balance sheets arranged side by side so that you can see the changes in the amounts. However, the statement can be improved by also showing the changes in dollar amounts and in percentages.

---

[2] Ibid., p. viii.

[3] Other major sections of the FASB's conceptual framework project include *Statement of Financial Accounting Concepts No. 2,* "Qualitative Characteristics of Accounting Information" (May 1980); *Statement of Financial Accounting Concepts No. 4.* "Objectives of Financial Reporting by Nonbusiness Organizations" (December 1980); *Statement of Financial Accounting Concepts No. 5,* "Recognition and Measurement in Financial Statements of Business Enterprises" (December 1984); and *Statement of Financial Accounting Concepts No. 6,* "Elements of Financial Statements" (December 1985). *Statement No. 6* replaced an earlier version *(Statement No. 3)* that was also titled "Elements of Financial Statements."

**Illustration 20–1**

**RANGER WHOLESALE COMPANY**
**Comparative Balance Sheet**
**December 31, 1990, and December 31, 1989**

| | Years Ended December 31 | | Amount of Increase or (Decrease) during 1990 | Percent of Increase or (Decrease) during 1990 |
|---|---|---|---|---|
| | 1990 | 1989 | | |
| **Assets** | | | | |
| Current assets: | | | | |
| Cash | $ 15,000 | $ 20,500 | $ (5,500) | (26.8) |
| Short-term investments | 3,000 | 70,000 | (67,000) | (95.7) |
| Accounts receivable, net | 68,000 | 64,000 | 4,000 | 6.3 |
| Merchandise inventory | 90,000 | 84,000 | 6,000 | 7.1 |
| Prepaid expenses | 5,800 | 6,000 | (200) | (3.3) |
| Total current assets | $181,800 | $244,500 | $ (62,700) | (25.6) |
| Long-term investments: | | | | |
| Real estate | $ –0– | $ 30,000 | $ (30,000) | (100.0) |
| Apex Company common stock | –0– | 50,000 | (50,000) | (100.0) |
| Total long-term investments | $ –0– | $ 80,000 | $ (80,000) | (100.0) |
| Plant and equipment | | | | |
| Office equipment, net | $ 3,500 | $ 3,700 | $ (200) | (5.4) |
| Store equipment, net | 17,900 | 6,800 | 11,100 | 163.2 |
| Buildings, net | 176,800 | 28,000 | 148,800 | 531.4 |
| Land | 50,000 | 20,000 | 30,000 | 150.0 |
| Total plant and equipment | $248,200 | $ 58,500 | $189,700 | 324.3 |
| Total assets | $430,000 | $383,000 | $ 47,000 | 12.3 |
| **Liabilities** | | | | |
| Current liabilities: | | | | |
| Notes payable | $ 5,000 | $ –0– | $ 5,000 | |
| Accounts payable | 43,600 | 55,000 | (11,400) | (20.7) |
| Taxes payable | 4,800 | 5,000 | (200) | (4.0) |
| Wages payable | 800 | 1,200 | (400) | (33.3) |
| Total current liabilities | $ 54,200 | $ 61,200 | $ (7,000) | (11.4) |
| Long-term liabilities: | | | | |
| Notes payable (secured by mortgage) | $ 60,000 | $ 10,000 | $ 50,000 | 500.0 |
| Total liabilities | $114,200 | $ 71,200 | $ 43,000 | (60.4) |
| **Stockholders' Equity** | | | | |
| Common stock, $10 par value | $250,000 | $250,000 | –0– | –0– |
| Retained earnings | 65,800 | 61,800 | 4,000 | 6.5 |
| Total stockholder's equity | $315,800 | $311,800 | $ 4,000 | 1.3 |
| Total liabilities and equity | $430,000 | $383,000 | $ 47,000 | 12.3 |

When this is done, as in Illustration 20–1, large dollar and large percentage changes are readily apparent.

A comparative income statement is prepared in the same way as a comparative balance sheet. Income statement amounts for two or more successive periods are placed side by side, with dollar and percentage changes in additional columns. Illustration 20–2 shows such a statement.

**Illustration 20–2**

**RANGER WHOLESALE COMPANY**
**Comparative Income Statement**
**For Years Ended December 31, 1990, and 1989**

| | Years Ended December 31 | | Amount of Increase or (Decrease) during 1990 | Percent of Increase or (Decrease) during 1990 |
|---|---|---|---|---|
| | 1990 | 1989 | | |
| Gross sales | $973,500 | $853,000 | $120,500 | 14.1 |
| Sales returns and allowances | 13,500 | 10,200 | 3,300 | 32.4 |
| Net sales | $960,000 | $842,800 | $117,200 | 13.9 |
| Cost of goods sold | 715,000 | 622,500 | 92,500 | 14.9 |
| Gross profit from sales | $245,000 | $220,300 | $ 24,700 | 11.2 |
| Operating expenses: | | | | |
| Selling expenses: | | | | |
| Advertising expense | $ 7,500 | $ 5,000 | $ 2,500 | 50.0 |
| Sales salaries expense | 109,500 | 97,500 | 12,000 | 12.3 |
| Store supplies expense | 3,200 | 2,800 | 400 | 14.3 |
| Depreciation expense, store equipment | 2,400 | 1,700 | 700 | 41.2 |
| Delivery expense | 14,800 | 14,000 | 800 | 5.7 |
| Total selling expenses | $137,400 | $121,000 | $ 16,400 | 13.6 |
| General and administrative expenses: | | | | |
| Office salaries expenses | $ 41,000 | $ 40,050 | $ 950 | 2.4 |
| Office supplies expenses | 1,300 | 1,250 | 50 | 4.0 |
| Insurance expense | 1,600 | 1,200 | 400 | 33.3 |
| Depreciation expense, office equipment | 300 | 300 | –0– | –0– |
| Depreciation expense, buildings | 2,850 | 1,500 | 1,350 | 90.0 |
| Bad debts expense | 2,250 | 2,200 | 50 | 2.3 |
| Total general and admin. expenses | $ 49,300 | $ 46,500 | $ 2,800 | 6.0 |
| Total operating expenses | $186,700 | $167,500 | $ 19,200 | 11.5 |
| Operating income | $ 58,300 | $ 52,800 | $ 5,500 | 10.4 |
| Less interest expense | 6,300 | 1,500 | 4,800 | 320.0 |
| Income before taxes | $ 52,000 | $ 51,300 | $ 700 | 1.4 |
| Income taxes | 19,000 | 18,700 | 300 | 1.6 |
| Net income | $ 33,000 | $ 32,600 | $ 400 | 1.2 |
| Earnings per share | $1.32 | $1.30 | $0.02 | 1.5 |

### Analyzing and Interpreting Comparative Statements

In analyzing and interpreting comparative data, you should select for study any items that show significant dollar or percentage changes. Then, you try to determine the reasons for each change and if possible whether they are favorable or unfavorable. For example, in Illustration 20–1, the first item, "Cash," shows a decrease of $5,500. The next item, "Short-term investments," shows an extremely large decrease. Also, the "Long-term investments" were completely eliminated during the year. At first glance these changes appear unfavorable. However, these decreases must be evaluated in light of other changes that occurred. The increases in "Store equipment," "Buildings," and "Land," show that the company materially increased its plant assets between the two balance sheet dates. Further study suggests that the company has apparently constructed a new building on land that was held as an investment until needed in this expansion. Also, the company apparently paid for the new plant assets by reducing cash, selling the Apex Company common stock, and issuing a $50,000 note payable.

To help control operations, a comparative income statement is usually more valuable than a comparative balance sheet. For example, in Illustration 20–2, ''Gross sales'' increased 14.1% and ''Net sales'' increased 13.9%. At the same time, ''Sales returns'' increase 32.4%, or at a rate more than twice that of gross sales. Usually, returned sales represent wasted sales effort and dissatisfied customers. Therefore, the increased rate of ''Sales returns'' should be investigated, and the reason for the increase determined if possible.

In addition to the large increase in the ''Sales returns,'' it is significant that the rate of increase in ''Cost of goods sold'' is greater than that of ''Net sales.'' This unfavorable trend should be corrected if possible.

In attempting to find reasons for Ranger Wholesale Company's increase in sales, the increases in advertising and in plant assets must be considered. You might expect an increase in advertising to increase sales. Also, the increase in plant assets may have been necessary to support a larger sales volume.

### Calculating Percentage Increases and Decreases

To calculate the percentage increases and decreases shown on comparative statements, you divide the dollar increase or decrease in an item by the amount shown for the item in the base year. If no amount is shown in the base year, or if the base year amount is negative (such as a net loss), a percentage increase or decrease cannot be calculated. For example, in Illustration 20–1, there were no notes payable at the end of 1989, and a percentage change for this item cannot be calculated.

In this text, percentages and ratios typically are rounded to one or two decimal places. However, there is no uniform agreement on this matter. In general, percentages should be carried out far enough to assure that meaningful information is conveyed. However, they should not be carried so far that the significance of relationships tends to become ''lost'' in the length of the numbers.

### Trend Percentages

Trend percentages or index numbers emphasize changes that have occurred from period to period and are used to compare data that covers a number of years. You calculate trend percentages as follows:

1. Select a base year and assign each item amount on the base year statement a weight of 100%.
2. Then, express each item from the statements for the years after the base year as a percentage of its base year amount. To determine these percentages, divide the item amounts in the years after the base year by the amount of the item in the base year.

For example, if 1985 is selected as the base year for the following data, you divide the ''Sales'' amount in each year by $210,000 to get the trend percentages for sales. To get the trend percentages for cost of goods sold, you divide the "Cost of goods sold" amount in each year by $145,000. And the gross profit trend percentages equal the "Gross profit" amount in each year divided by $65,000.

| | 1990 | 1989 | 1988 | 1987 | 1986 | 1985 |
|---|---|---|---|---|---|---|
| Sales | $324,000 | $310,000 | $284,000 | $292,000 | $204,000 | $210,000 |
| Cost of goods sold | 229,000 | 218,000 | 198,000 | 204,000 | 139,000 | 145,000 |
| Gross profit | $ 95,000 | $ 92,000 | $ 86,000 | $ 88,000 | $ 65,000 | $ 65,000 |

When these divisions are made, the trends for these three items appear as follows:

| | 1990 | 1989 | 1988 | 1987 | 1986 | 1985 |
|---|---|---|---|---|---|---|
| Sales | 154% | 148% | 135% | 139% | 97% | 100% |
| Cost of goods sold | 158 | 150 | 137 | 141 | 96 | 100 |
| Gross profit | 146 | 142 | 132 | 135 | 100 | 100 |

Note that the sales trend is upward after the second year. However, cost of goods sold increases at a slightly more rapid rate. This indicates a contracting gross profit rate and should receive attention.

You should understand that the trend for a single balance sheet or income statement item is seldom very informative. However, you may learn a great deal from comparing the trends of related items. For example, a downward sales trend with an upward trend for merchandise inventory, accounts receivable, and bad debts expense indicates an unfavorable situation. On the other hand, an upward sales trend with a downward trend or a slower upward trend for accounts receivable, merchandise inventory, and selling expenses suggests an increase in operating efficiency.

### Common-Size Comparative Statements

Although the comparative statements illustrated so far show how each item has changed over time, they do not emphasize the relative importance of each item. Changes in the relative importance of each financial statement item are shown more clearly by **common-size comparative statements.**

In common-size statements, each item is expressed as a percentage of a base amount; that is, the items are shown in common-size figures—figures that are fractions of 100%. For example, on a common-size balance sheet (1) the amount of total assets is assigned a value of 100%. (2) This means that the total amount of liabilities plus owners' equity also equals 100%. Then (3), each asset, liability, and owners' equity item is shown as a percentage of total assets (or total liabilities plus owners' equity). If you show a company's successive balance sheets in this way (see Illustration 20–3), proportional changes are emphasized.

On a common-size income statement, the amount of net sales is assigned a value of 100%. Then, each statement item appears as a percentage of net sales. Such a statement is an informative and useful tool. If you think of the 100%

**Illustration 20–3**

**RANGER WHOLESALE COMPANY**
**Common-Size Comparative Balance Sheet**
**December 31, 1990, and December 31, 1989**

| | Years Ended December 31 | | Common-Size Percentages | |
|---|---|---|---|---|
| | **1990** | **1989** | **1990** | **1989** |
| **Assets** | | | | |
| Current assets: | | | | |
| Cash | $ 15,000 | $ 20,500 | 3.49 | 5.35 |
| Short-term investments | 3,000 | 70,000 | 0.70 | 18.28 |
| Accounts receivable, net | 68,000 | 64,000 | 15.81 | 16.71 |
| Merchandise inventory | 90,000 | 84,000 | 20.93 | 21.93 |
| Prepaid expenses | 5,800 | 6,000 | 1.35 | 1.57 |
| Total current assets | $181,800 | $244,500 | 42.28 | 63.84 |
| Long-term investments: | | | | |
| Real estate | –0– | $ 30,000 | | 7.83 |
| Apex Company common stock | –0– | 50,000 | | 13.05 |
| Total long-term investments | –0– | $ 80,000 | | 20.88 |
| Plant and equipment: | | | | |
| Office equipment, net | $ 3,500 | $ 3,700 | 0.81 | 0.97 |
| Store equipment, net | 17,900 | 6,800 | 4.16 | 1.78 |
| Buildings, net | 176,800 | 28,000 | 41.12 | 7.31 |
| Land | 50,000 | 20,000 | 11.63 | 5.22 |
| Total plant and equipment | $248,200 | $ 58,500 | 57.72 | 15.28 |
| Total assets | $430,000 | $383,000 | 100.00 | 100.00 |
| **Liabilities** | | | | |
| Current liabilities: | | | | |
| Notes payable | $ 5,000 | –0– | 1.16 | |
| Accounts payable | 43,600 | $ 55,000 | 10.14 | 14.36 |
| Taxes payable | 4,800 | 5,000 | 1.12 | 1.31 |
| Wages payable | 800 | 1,200 | 0.19 | 0.31 |
| Total current liabilities | $ 54,200 | $ 61,200 | 12.61 | 15.98 |
| Long-term liabilities: | | | | |
| Notes payable (secured by mortgage) | $ 60,000 | $ 10,000 | 13.95 | 2.61 |
| Total liabilities | $114,200 | $ 71,200 | 26.56 | 18.59 |
| **Stockholders' Equity** | | | | |
| Common stock, $10 par value | $250,000 | $250,000 | 58.14 | 65.27 |
| Retained earnings | 65,800 | 61,800 | 15.30 | 16.14 |
| Total stockholders' equity | $315,800 | $311,800 | 73.44 | 81.41 |
| Total liabilities and equity | $430,000 | $383,000 | 100.00 | 100.00 |

sales amount as representing one sales dollar, then the remaining items show how each sales dollar was distributed to costs, expenses, and profit. For example, on the comparative income statement in Illustration 20–4, the 1989 cost of goods sold consumed 73.86 cents of each sales dollar. In 1990, cost of goods sold consumed 74.48 cents of each sales dollar. While this increase is small, if the cost of goods sold percentage in 1990 had remained at the 1989 level, almost $6,000 of additional gross profit would have been earned.

Illustration 20–4

**RANGER WHOLESALE COMPANY**
**Common-Size Comparative Income Statement**
**For Year Ended December 31, 1990 and 1989**

| | Years Ended December 31 | | Common-Size Percentages | |
|---|---|---|---|---|
| | 1990 | 1989 | 1990 | 1989 |
| Gross sales | $973,500 | $853,000 | 101.41 | 101.21 |
| Sales returns and allowances | 13,500 | 10,200 | 1.41 | 1.21 |
| Net sales | $960,000 | $842,800 | 100.00 | 100.00 |
| Cost of goods sold | 715,000 | 622,500 | 74.48 | 73.86 |
| Gross profit from sales | $245,000 | $220,300 | 25.52 | 26.14 |
| Operating expenses: | | | | |
| Selling expenses: | | | | |
| Advertising expense | $ 7,500 | $ 5,000 | 0.78 | 0.59 |
| Sales salaries expense | 109,500 | 97,500 | 11.41 | 11.57 |
| Store supplies expense | 3,200 | 2,800 | 0.33 | 0.33 |
| Depreciation expense, store equipment | 2,400 | 1,700 | 0.25 | 0.20 |
| Delivery expense | 14,800 | 14,000 | 1.54 | 1.66 |
| Total selling expenses | $137,400 | $121,000 | 14.31 | 14.36 |
| General and administrative expenses: | | | | |
| Office salaries expense | $ 41,000 | $ 40,050 | 4.27 | 4.75 |
| Office supplies expense | 1,300 | 1,250 | 0.14 | 0.15 |
| Insurance expense | 1,600 | 1,200 | 0.17 | 0.14 |
| Depreciation expense, office equipment | 300 | 300 | 0.03 | 0.04 |
| Depreciation expense, buildings | 2,850 | 1,500 | 0.30 | 0.18 |
| Bad debts expense | 2,250 | 2,200 | 0.23 | 0.26 |
| Total general and administrative expenses | $ 49,300 | $ 46,500 | 5.14 | 5.52 |
| Total operating expenses | $186,700 | $167,500 | 19.45 | 19.87 |
| Operating income | $ 58,300 | $ 52,800 | 6.07 | 6.26 |
| Less interest expense | 6,300 | 1,500 | 0.66 | 0.18 |
| Income before taxes | $ 52,000 | $ 51,300 | 5.42 | 6.09 |
| Income taxes | 19,000 | 18,700 | 1.98 | 2.22 |
| Net income | $ 33,000 | $ 32,600 | 3.44 | 3.87 |
| Earnings per share | $1.32 | $1.30 | — | — |

Common-size percentages point out efficiencies and inefficiencies that are otherwise difficult to see. For this reason, they are a valuable management tool. To illustrate, sales salaries of Ranger Wholesale Company took a higher percentage of each sales dollar in 1990 than in 1989. On the other hand, office salaries took a smaller percentage. Although the amount of bad debts expense in 1990 was more than in 1989, bad debts expense took a smaller portion of each sales dollar in 1990 than in 1989.

## Analysis of Short-Term Liquidity

The amount of a business's current assets less its current liabilities is called the **working capital** or **net working capital** of the business. A business must maintain an adequate amount of working capital to meet current debts, carry sufficient inventories, and take advantage of cash discounts. Indeed, a business

Calculate and explain the interpretation of the ratios, turnovers, and rates of return used to evaluate (*a*) short-term liquidity, (*b*) long-term risk and capital structure, and (*c*) operating efficiency and profitability. (L. O. 3)

that runs out of working capital cannot continue its operations. Because current assets and current liabilities are so necessary to current operations, an important part of evaluating the financial position of a business involves the analysis of working capital.

When you evaluate the working capital of a business, you must look beyond the dollar amount by which current assets exceed current liabilities. To see why this is true, consider the following example of Ace Company and Box Company:

| | Ace Company | Box Company |
|---|---|---|
| Current assets . . . . | $100,000 | $20,000 |
| Current liabilities . . . . | 90,000 | 10,000 |
| Working capital . . . . | $ 10,000 | $10,000 |

Ace Company and Box Company have the same amount of working capital. However, Ace Company's current liabilities are nine times greater than its working capital, while Box Company's current liabilities and working capital are equal. As a result, to pay its liabilities on time, Ace Company must experience much less shrinkage and delay in converting its current assets to cash than Box Company. Thus, the dollar amount of a company's working capital does not adequately measure its working capital position. The ratio of its current assets to its current liabilities is a much better measure.

### Current Ratio

The relation of a company's current assets to its current liabilities is called the **current ratio**. To calculate the current ratio, you simply divide total current assets by total current liabilities. For example, the current ratio of Box Company is:

$$\frac{\text{Current assets, \$20,000}}{\text{Current liabilities, \$10,000}} = 2.0$$

In other words, Box Company's current assets are two times its current liabilities, or the current ratio is 2 to 1.

The current ratio expresses the relation of current assets and current liabilities mathematically. A high current ratio indicates a strong current position; that is, a higher ratio generally means the company is more capable of meeting its current obligations.

On the other hand, a company might have a current ratio that is too high. This would mean that the company has overinvested in current assets relative to its needs. Normally, surplus current assets do not generate very much additional revenue. Therefore, if a company invests too much of its capital in current assets, the investment is not used efficiently.

Years ago, bankers and other creditors often used a current ratio of 2 to 1 as a rule of thumb in evaluating the debt-paying ability of a credit-seeking company. A company with a 2 to 1 current ratio was generally thought to be a good credit risk in the short run. However, most credit grantors realize that the 2 to

1 rule of thumb is not an adequate test of debt-paying ability. They realize that whether or not a company's current ratio is good or bad depends upon at least three factors:

1. The nature of the company's business.
2. The composition of its current assets.
3. The turnover of certain of its current assets.

Whether or not a company's current ratio is adequate depends on the nature of its business. A public utility that has no inventories other than supplies and grants little or no credit can operate on a current ratio of less than 1 to 1. On the other hand, a company that sells high fashion clothing may occasionally misjudge future styles. If this happens, the company's inventory may be of little sales value. Such a company may need a current ratio of much more than 2 to 1.

Therefore, when the adequacy of working capital is studied, consideration must be given to the type of business under review. Before you decide whether a company's current ratio is too low (or too high), you should compare the company's current ratio with those of other companies in the same industry. Another important source of insight is to observe how the ratio compares to past periods.

The composition of a company's current assets also should be considered when you evaluate the company's working capital. Cash and short-term investments are more liquid than are accounts and notes receivable. And short-term receivables normally are more liquid than is merchandise inventory. Cash can be used to pay current debts at once. But accounts receivable and merchandise must be converted into cash before payments can be made.

### Acid-Test Ratio

An easily calculated check on current asset composition is the **acid-test ratio**, also called the **quick ratio** because it is the ratio of "quick assets" to current liabilities. Quick assets are cash, short-term investments, accounts receivable, and notes receivable. They are the current assets that can quickly be turned into cash. The traditional rule of thumb for an acceptable acid-test ratio is 1 to 1. However, as is true for all financial ratios, you should be skeptical about rules of thumb. The acid-test ratio of Ranger Wholesale Company as of the end of 1990 is calculated as follows:

| | | | |
|---|---|---|---|
| Quick assets: | | Current liabilities: | |
| Cash | $15,000 | Notes payable | $ 5,000 |
| Short-term investments | 3,000 | Accounts payable | 43,600 |
| Accounts receivable | 68,000 | Taxes payable | 4,800 |
| Total | $86,000 | Wages payable | 800 |
| | | Total | $54,200 |

$$\frac{\text{Quick assets, \$86,000}}{\text{Current liabilities, \$54,200}} = 1.59\text{, or 1.6 to 1}$$

The working capital requirements of a company are affected by how fast the company converts and replaces some of its current assets. For example, assume that Dot Company and Fox Company sell the same amounts of merchandise on credit each month. However, Dot Company grants 30-day terms to its customers, while Fox Company grants 60 days. Both collect their accounts at the end of these credit periods. As a result of the difference in terms, Dot Company turns over or collects its accounts twice as fast as Fox Company. Also, as a result of the more rapid turnover, Dot Company requires only one half the investment in accounts receivable that is required of Fox Company and can operate with a smaller current ratio.

### Accounts Receivable Turnover

One way to measure how fast a company converts its accounts receivable into cash is to calculate the **accounts receivable turnover.** To calculate the accounts receivable turnover, you divide credit sales (or net sales) for a year by the average accounts receivable balance during the year. If the company has short-term notes receivable, those balances should be included with the accounts receivable. The average balance usually is estimated by averaging the beginning and ending balances. For example, Ranger Wholesale Company's accounts receivable turnover for 1990 is calculated as follows:

| | | |
|---|---|---|
| *a.* | December 31, 1989, accounts receivable . . | $ 64,000 |
| *b.* | December 31, 1990, accounts receivable . . | 68,000 |
| *c.* | Average balance (*a* + *b*) ÷ 2 . . . . . . . . . | 66,000 |
| *d.* | Net sales for year . . . . . . . . . . . . . . . | 960,000 |

$$\frac{\text{Net sales, \$960,000}}{\text{Average accounts receivable, \$66,000}} = 14.5$$

If accounts receivable are collected quickly, the accounts receivable turnover will be high. In general, this is favorable because it means that the company does not have to invest large amounts of capital in accounts receivable. However, an accounts receivable turnover may be too high, if it means that credit terms are so limited that they have a negative effect on sales volume.

Sometimes the ending accounts receivable balance is used as a substitute for the average balance in calculating accounts receivable turnover. This is acceptable if the effect is not material. If possible, credit sales should be used rather than the sum of cash and credit sales. Also, accounts receivable before subtracting the allowance for doubtful accounts should be used. However, information as to credit sales is seldom available in published financial statements. Likewise, many published balance sheets report accounts receivable at their net amount. Therefore, you may be forced to use total sales and net accounts receivable.

### Days' Sales Uncollected

Accounts receivable turnover is one way to measure how fast a company collects its accounts. Another way is to calculate the **days' sales uncollected.** To illustrate the calculation of days' sales uncollected, assume a company had charge sales of $250,000 during a year and $25,000 of accounts and short-term notes receivable at the year's end. That means 1⁄10 of its charge sales are uncollected. In other words, the charge sales made during 1/10 of a year, or the charge sales of 36.5 days (1/10 × 365 days in a year = 36.5 days) are uncollected. This calculation of days' sales uncollected in equation form is as follows:

$$\frac{\text{Accounts receivable, \$25,000}}{\text{Charge sales, \$250,000}} \times 365 = 36.5 \text{ days' sales uncollected}$$

Days' sales uncollected has more meaning if you know the credit terms. According to a rule of thumb, a company's days' sales uncollected should not exceed one and one third times the days in its credit period when it does not offer discounts and one and one third times the days in its discount period when it does. If the company, whose days' sales uncollected is calculated in the illustration just given, offers 30-day terms, then 36.5 days is within the rule-of-thumb amount. However, if its terms are 2/10, n/30, its days' sales uncollected seem excessive.

### Turnover of Merchandise Inventory

Working capital requirements also are affected by how long a company holds merchandise inventory before selling it. This can be measured by calculating the **merchandise turnover**, which is the number of times the average inventory is sold during an accounting period. A high turnover generally indicates good merchandising. Also, from a working capital point of view, a company with a high turnover requires a smaller investment in inventory than one producing the same sales with a low turnover. On the other hand, the merchandise turnover may be too high if a company keeps such a small inventory that sales volume is restricted.

To calculate merchandise turnover, you divide cost of goods sold by average inventory. Cost of goods sold is the amount of merchandise at cost that was sold during an accounting period. Average inventory is the average amount of merchandise at cost on hand during the period. The 1990 merchandise turnover of Ranger Wholesale Company is calculated as follows:

$$\frac{\text{Cost of goods sold, \$715,000}}{\text{Average merchandise inventory, \$87,000}} = \begin{matrix}\text{Merchandise turnover} \\ \text{of 8.2 times}\end{matrix}$$

In the above calculation, the cost of goods sold is taken from the company's 1990 income statement. The average inventory is estimated by averaging the beginning inventory ($84,000) and the ending inventory ($90,000), or ($84,000 + $90,000) ÷ 2 = $87,000. In cases where the beginning and ending inventories do not represent the inventory normally on hand, a more accurate turnover may be secured by using the average of all the 12 month-end inventories.

## Standards of Comparison

After you compute ratios and turnovers in the process of analyzing financial statements, you then have to decide whether the calculated amounts suggest good, bad, or just average performance by the company. To make these judgments, you must have some basis for comparison. The following are possibilities:

State the limitations associated with using financial statement ratios and the sources from which standards for comparison may be obtained.
(L. O. 4)

1. An experienced analyst may compare the ratios and turnovers of the company under review with mental standards acquired from past experiences.
2. For purposes of comparison, an analyst may calculate the ratios and turnovers of a selected group of competitive companies in the same industry as the one whose statements are under review.
3. Ratios and turnovers such as those published by Dun & Bradstreet may be used for comparison.
4. Some local and national trade associations gather data from their members and publish standard or average ratios for their trade or industry. When available, these give the analyst a very good basis of comparison.
5. Rule-of-thumb standards may be used as a basis for comparison.

Of these five standards, the ratios and turnovers of a selected group of competitive companies normally are the best bases for comparison. Rule-of-thumb standards should be applied with great care and then only if they seem reasonable in light of past experience.

## Analysis of Long-Term Risk and Capital Structure

The analysis of working capital generally is intended to evaluate the short-term liquidity of the company. However, analysts are also interested in the long-run ability of the company to meet its obligations and provide security to its creditors. Indicators of this ability include debt and equity ratios, the relation of pledged plant assets to secured liabilities, and the company's capacity to earn enough to pay fixed interest charges.

### Debt and Equity Ratios

Financial statement analysts are always interested in the portion of a company's assets contributed by its owners and the portion contributed by creditors. These are measured by ratios that express total liabilities as a percentage of total assets and total stockholders' equity as a percentage of total assets. The debt and equity ratios of Ranger Wholesale Company are calculated as follows:

| | | 1990 | 1989 |
|---|---|---|---|
| *a.* | Total liabilities | $114,200 | $ 71,200 |
| *b.* | Total owners' equity | 315,800 | 311,800 |
| *c.* | Total liabilities and owners' equity | $430,000 | $383,000 |
| | Percentages provided by creditors ($a \div c$) × 100 | 26.6% | 18.6% |
| | Percentages provided by stockholders ($b \div c$) × 100 | 73.4 | 81.4 |

Creditors like to see a high proportion of owners' equity because owners' equity acts as a cushion that absorbs losses. The greater the equity of the

## AS A MATTER OF FACT

Washington—One big reason that U.S. companies are borrowing more heavily than they once did is that executives who lived through the Depression are gone, Federal Reserve Board Chairman Alan Greenspan said.

Offering a fresh explanation of the build-up of corporate debt, Mr. Greenspan recalled that in the 1950s and 1960s academic economists criticized business for not borrowing more.

"Most corporate executives basically remained extraordinarily conservative because back in their history was an awareness of what the risk of excessive debt was," he said.

As those executives "have retired and faded from the scene," they have been replaced by managers who grew up after World War II and who don't have that same lingering fear of debt, Mr. Greenspan said.

"That is a major factor in why we've had such a dramatic increase in the ratio of debt to equity in the post-World War II period," he said.

Source: "Fed Chief Ties Debt Surge to New Breed of Managers," *The Wall Street Journal*, January 27, 1989, p. A3. Reprinted by permission of *The Wall Street Journal*, © Dow Jones & Company, Inc. 1989. ALL RIGHTS RESERVED.

owners in relation to liabilities, the greater are the losses that can be absorbed by the owners before the creditors begin to lose.

From the creditors' standpoint, a high percentage of owners' equity is desirable. However, if a business can earn a return on borrowed capital that is higher than the cost of borrowing, the return to stockholders is increased.

### Pledged Plant Assets to Secured Liabilities

Companies commonly borrow by issuing a note or bonds secured by a mortgage on certain of their plant assets. The ratio of pledged plant assets to secured liabilities is often calculated to measure the protection provided to the secured creditors by the pledge of assets. To calculate this ratio, you divide the pledged assets' book value by the liabilities for which the assets are pledged. It is calculated for Ranger Wholesale Company as of the end of 1990 and 1989 as follows:

| | | 1990 | 1989 |
|---|---|---|---|
| | Buildings, net | $176,800 | $28,000 |
| | Land | 50,000 | 20,000 |
| *a.* | Book value of pledged plant assets | $226,800 | $48,000 |
| *b.* | Notes payable (secured by mortgage) | $ 60,000 | $10,000 |
| | Ratio of pledged assets to secured liabilities ($a \div b$) | 3.8 to 1 | 4.8 to 1 |

The usual rule-of-thumb minimum for this ratio is 2 to 1. However, the ratio needs careful interpretation because it is based on the *book value* of the pledged assets. Book values often bear little relation to the amount that would be received for the assets in a foreclosure or a liquidation. As a result, estimated liquidation values or foreclosure values are a better measure of the protection provided by pledged assets. Also, the long-term earning ability of the company with pledged assets is equally important to secured creditors as is the pledged assets' book value.

### Times Fixed Interest Charges Earned

The number of **times fixed interest charges were earned** often is calculated to measure the security of the return offered to creditors. The amount of income before the deduction of fixed interest charges and income taxes is the amount available to pay the fixed interest charges. Therefore, to calculate the number of times fixed interest charges were earned, you divide income before fixed interest charges and income taxes by fixed interest charges. The result is the number of times fixed interest charges were earned. Often, fixed interest charges are considered reasonably safe if the company earns its fixed interest charges two or more times each year.

The number of times fixed interest charges were earned by Ranger Wholesale Company are calculated as follows:

| | 1990 | 1989 |
|---|---|---|
| *a.* Income before interest and taxes | $58,300 | $52,800 |
| *b.* Interest expense | 6,300 | 1,500 |
| Times fixed interest charges earned (*a* ÷ *b*) | 9.3 | 35.2 |

## Analysis of Operating Efficiency and Profitability

Financial statement analysts are especially interested in the ability of a company to use its assets efficiently to produce profits for its owners. Several ratios are available to help you evaluate operating efficiency and profitability.

### Profit Margin

The operating efficiency of a company can be expressed in terms of two components. The first is the company's **profit margin**, which is the ability to earn a net income from sales. This is measured by expressing net income as a percentage of sales. For example, the profit margin of Ranger Wholesale Company in 1990 is calculated as follows:

$$\frac{\$33{,}000,\ \text{net income}}{\$960{,}000,\ \text{net sales}} \times 100 = 3.4\%$$

To evaluate the profit margin of a company, you must consider the nature of the industry in which the company operates. For example, a publishing company might be expected to have a profit margin between 10 and 15%, while a retail supermarket might have a normal profit margin of 1 or 2%.

### Total Asset Turnover

The second component of operating efficiency is **total asset turnover,** which is the ability of the company to use its assets to generate sales. To calculate this statistic, you divide net sales by the average total assets employed in the business. For Ranger Wholesale Company, the total asset turnover is:

$$\frac{\$960{,}000\text{, net sales}}{(\$430{,}000 + \$383{,}000) \div 2} = 2.4$$

Note that average total assets is estimated by averaging the total assets at the beginning and end of the period.

In general, the higher the total asset turnover, the more efficient the company is in using its assets. However, as in the case of profit margin, your evaluation of total asset turnover depends on the nature of the industry in which the company operates.

Profit margin and total asset turnover measure the two basic components of operating efficiency. However, they also are used to evaluate management performance since the management of a company is responsible for its operating efficiency.

### Return on Total Assets Employed

Although operating efficiency has two basic components that are measured by profit margin and total asset turnover, analysts also calculate a summary measure of these components. The summary measure is **return on total assets employed.** To calculate this measure you divide net income by the average total assets employed during the year and multiply the answer by 100. For example, the return on the total assets employed by Ranger Wholesale Company during 1990 is as follows:

| | | |
|---|---|---|
| *a.* | Net income | $ 33,000 |
| *b.* | Average total assets employed ($430,000 + $383,000) ÷ 2 | 406,500 |
| | Return on total assets employed (*a* ÷ *b*) × 100 | 8.1% |

Note that the beginning and ending amounts of total assets are divided by 2 to estimate the average total assets employed during the year.

The above calculation shows that Ranger Wholesale Company earned 8.1% return on its average total assets employed in the business during 1990. However, you cannot tell whether this return is good or bad without some basis of comparison. An important basis of comparison is the returns earned by similar-size companies engaged in the same kind of business. Also, you should evaluate the trend in the return earned by the company in recent years.

Earlier, we said that the return on total assets employed summarizes the two components of operating efficiency—profit margin and total asset turnover. Illustration 20–5 shows the relationship between these three measures. Notice that both profit margin and total asset turnover contribute to overall operating efficiency, as measured by return on total assets employed.

**Illustration 20–5**
**Profit margin, total asset turnover, and return on total assets employed**

| Profit margin | × | Total asset turnover | = | Return on total assets employed |
|---|---|---|---|---|
| $\frac{\text{Net income}}{\text{Net sales}}$ | × | $\frac{\text{Net sales}}{\text{Average total assets}}$ | = | $\frac{\text{Net income}}{\text{Average total assets}}$ |
| **For Ranger Wholesale Company:** | | | | |
| 3.4% | × | 2.4 | = | 8.1% |

### Return on Common Stockholders' Equity

A primary reason for the operation of a business is to earn a net income for its owners. The **return on the common stockholders' equity** measures the success achieved in this area. Usually an average of the beginning-of-year and end-of-year equities is used in calculating the return. For Ranger Wholesale Company, the 1990 calculation is as follows:

| | | 1990 |
|---|---|---|
| *a.* | Net income after taxes | $ 33,000 |
| *b.* | Average stockholders' equity | 313,800 |
| | Rate of return on stockholders' equity ($a \div b$) × 100 | 10.5% |

When there is preferred stock outstanding, the preferred dividend requirements must be subtracted from net income to arrive at the common stockholders' share of income to be used in this calculation.

Compare Ranger Wholesale Company's return on stockholders' equity (10.5%) with its return on total assets employed (8.1%) and note that the return on the stockholders' equity is greater. This occurred because Ranger Wholesale Company successfully employs **financial leverage** in its capital structure. This means that the company borrows assets from creditors and employs those assets to earn a return that is higher than the rate of interest the company has to pay the creditors.

### Price Earnings Ratio

A commonly used statistic in comparing investment opportunities is **price earnings ratio.** To calculate a price earnings ratio, you divide market price per share by earnings per share. For example, if Ranger Wholesale Company's common stock sold at $15 per share at the end of 1990, the stock's end-of-year price earnings ratio is calculated as:

$$\frac{\text{Market price per share, \$15}}{\text{Earnings per share, \$1.32}} = 11.4$$

See 849

Net Income / Common stock Shares outstanding = Earning per share

In comparing price earnings ratio, you must remember that such ratios vary from industry to industry. For example, in the steel industry, a price earnings

AS A MATTER OF FACT

**Investment Insight**

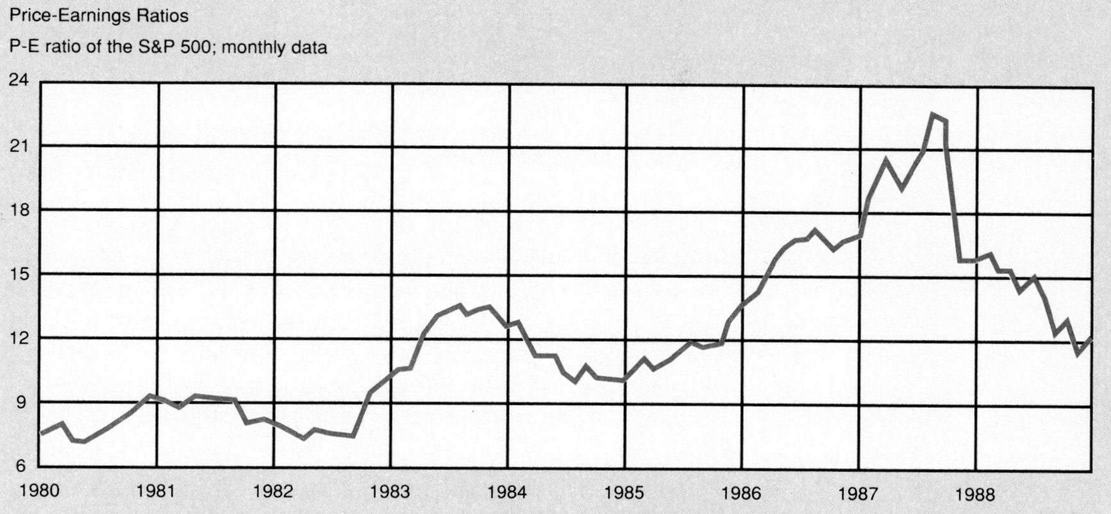

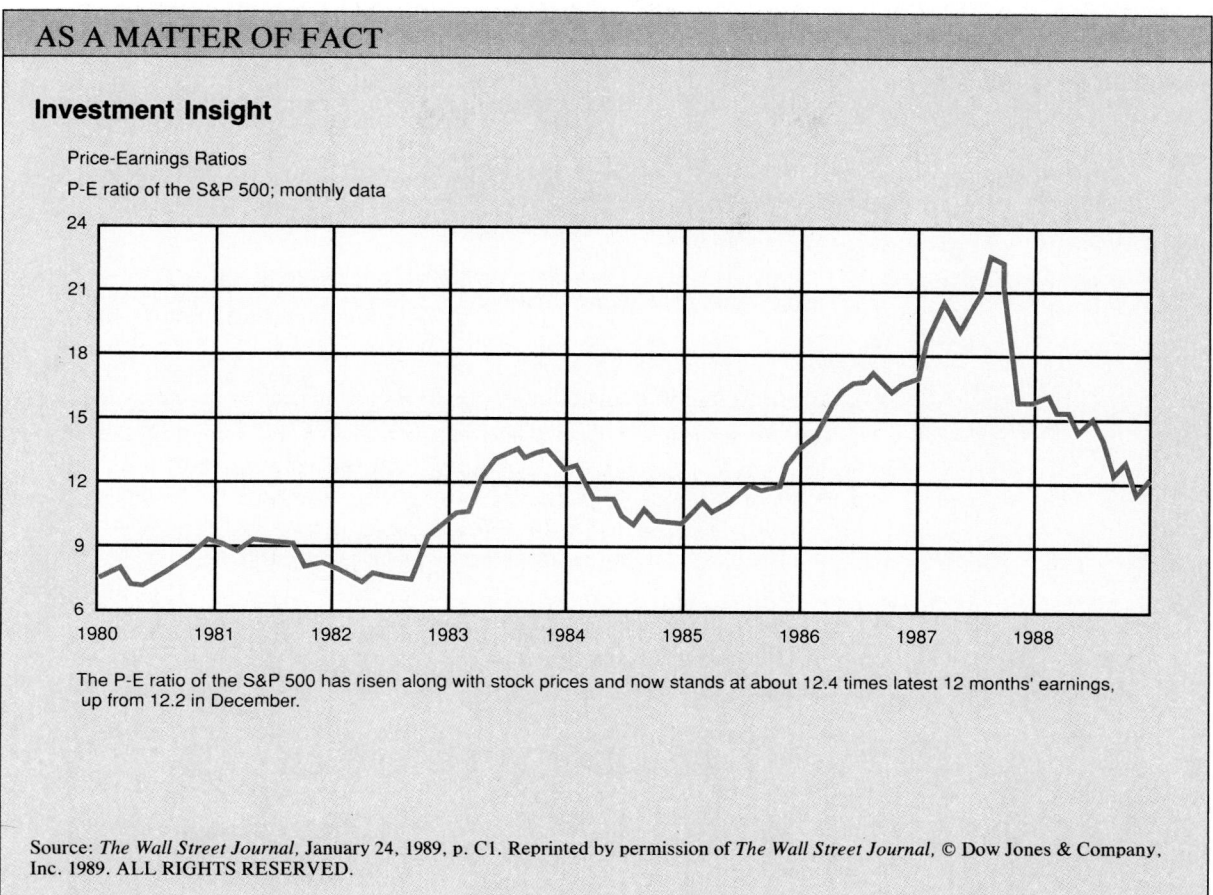

The P-E ratio of the S&P 500 has risen along with stock prices and now stands at about 12.4 times latest 12 months' earnings, up from 12.2 in December.



ratio of 8 to 10 is normal, while in a growth industry, such as high-technology electronics, a price earnings ratio of 20 might be expected.

### Dividend Yield

When investors evaluate whether to buy a stock at a given price per share, they often consider how much return they expect to receive in the form of cash dividends. A statistic that is used to compare the dividend-paying performance of different investment alternatives is **dividend yield**. To calculate the dividend yield of a stock you divide the annual amount of dividends paid by the market price per share and multiply the answer by 100. For example, Ranger Wholesale Company paid cash dividends in 1990 of $29,000, which amounted to $1.16 per share. If the market price per share is $15, the dividend yield is:

$$\frac{\$1.16}{\$15} \times 100 = 7.7\%$$

## Review of Financial Statement Ratios and Statistics for Analysis

**To evaluate short-term liquidity:**

$$\text{Current ratio} = \frac{\text{Current assets}}{\text{Current liabilities}}$$

$$\text{Acid-test ratio} = \frac{\text{Cash + Short-term investments + Current receivables}}{\text{Current liabilities}}$$

$$\text{Accounts receivable turnover} = \frac{\text{Credit sales}}{\text{Average accounts receivable}}$$

$$\text{Merchandise turnover} = \frac{\text{Cost of goods sold}}{\text{Average merchandise inventory}}$$

**To evaluate long-term risk and capital structure:**

$$\text{Debt ratio} = \frac{\text{Total liabilities}}{\text{Total assets}} \times 100$$

$$\text{Equity ratio} = \frac{\text{Total stockholders' equity}}{\text{Total assets}} \times 100$$

$$\begin{array}{l}\text{Pledged plant assets}\\ \text{to secured liabilities}\end{array} = \frac{\text{Book value of pledged plant assets}}{\text{Total secured liabilities}}$$

$$\text{Times fixed interest charges earned} = \frac{\text{Income before interest and taxes}}{\text{Interest expense}}$$

**To evaluate operating efficiency and profitability:**

$$\text{Profit margin} = \frac{\text{Net income}}{\text{Net sales}} \times 100$$

$$\text{Total asset turnover} = \frac{\text{Net sales}}{\text{Average total assets}}$$

$$\text{Return on total assets employed} = \frac{\text{Net income}}{\text{Average total assets}} \times 100$$

$$\begin{array}{l}\text{Return on common}\\ \text{stockholders' equity}\end{array} = \frac{\text{Net income} - \text{Preferred dividends}}{\text{Average common stockholders' equity}} \times 100$$

$$\text{Price earnings ratio} = \frac{\text{Market price per common share}}{\text{Earnings per share}}$$

$$\text{Dividend yield} = \frac{\text{Annual dividends declared}}{\text{Market price per share}} \times 100$$

## Summary of the Chapter in Terms of Learning Objectives

**1.** Financial reporting is intended to provide information that is useful to investors, creditors, and others in making investment, credit, and similar decisions. The information should help the users assess the amounts, timing, and uncertainty of prospective cash flows. Information should be provided about an enterprise's economic resources, claims against those resources, and the events that change its resources and the claims to those resources.

**2.** Comparative financial statements show amounts for two or more successive periods, sometimes with the changes in the items disclosed in absolute and of a base amount such as total assets or net sales.

**3.** In evaluating the short-term liquidity of a company, you might calculate a current ratio, an acid-test ratio, the accounts receivable turnover, the days' sales uncollected, and the merchandise turnover.

In evaluating the long-term risk and capital structure of a company, you might calculate debt and equity ratios, pledged plant assets to secured liabilities, and the number of times fixed interest charges were earned.

In evaluating operating efficiency and profitability, you might calculate profit margin, total asset turnover, return on total assets employed, and return on common stockholders' equity. Other statistics used to evaluate the profitability of alternative investments include price-earnings ratios, and dividend yield.

**4.** To decide whether financial statement ratios are desirable, too high, or too low, you must have some bases for comparison. These may come from past experience and personal judgment, from ratios of similar companies, or from ratios published by trade associations or other public sources. Traditional rules-of-thumb should be applied with great care and only if they seem reasonable in light of past experience.

## Demonstration Problem

Use the financial statements of Precision Company to satisfy the following requirements:

1. Prepare a comparative income statement showing the percentage increase or decrease for 1991 over 1990.
2. Prepare common-size, comparative balance sheets for 1991 and 1990.
3. Compute the following ratios for the year ended December 31, 1991:
   - *a.* Current ratio.
   - *b.* Acid-test ratio.
   - *c.* Accounts receivable turnover.
   - *d.* Days' sales uncollected.
   - *e.* Turnover of merchandise inventory.
   - *f.* Total liabilities as a percentage of total assets.
   - *g.* Pledged plant assets to secured liabilities.
   - *h.* Times fixed interest charges earned.
   - *i.* Profit margin.
   - *j.* Total asset turnover.
   - *k.* Return of total assets employed.
   - *l.* Return on common stockholders' equity.

**PRECISION COMPANY**
**Comparative Income Statement**
**For Years Ended December 31, 1991, and December 31, 1990**

| | 1991 | 1990 |
|---|---|---|
| Sales | $2,486,000 | $2,075,000 |
| Cost of goods sold | 1,523,000 | 1,222,000 |
| Gross profit from sales | $ 963,000 | $ 853,000 |
| Operating expenses: | | |
| Advertising expense | $ 145,000 | $ 100,000 |
| Sales salaries expense | 240,000 | 280,000 |
| Office salaries expense | 165,000 | 200,000 |
| Insurance expense | 100,000 | 45,000 |
| Supplies expense | 26,000 | 35,000 |
| Depreciation expense | 85,000 | 75,000 |
| Miscellaneous expense | 17,000 | 15,000 |
| Total operating expenses | $ 778,000 | $ 750,000 |
| Operating income | $ 185,000 | $ 103,000 |
| Less interest expense | 44,000 | 46,000 |
| Income before taxes | $ 141,000 | $ 57,000 |
| Income taxes | 47,000 | 19,000 |
| Net income | $ 94,000 | $ 38,000 |
| Earnings per share | $0.99 | $0.40 |

**PRECISION COMPANY**
**Comparative Balance Sheet**
**December 31, 1991, and December 31, 1990**

| **Assets** | 1991 | 1990 |
|---|---|---|
| Current assets: | | |
| Cash | $ 79,000 | $ 42,000 |
| Short-term investments | 65,000 | 96,000 |
| Accounts receivable, net | 120,000 | 100,000 |
| Merchandise inventory | 250,000 | 265,000 |
| Total current assets | $ 514,000 | $ 503,000 |
| Plant and equipment: | | |
| Store equipment, net | $ 400,000 | $ 350,000 |
| Office equipment, net | 45,000 | 50,000 |
| Buildings, net | 625,000 | 675,000 |
| Land | 100,000 | 100,000 |
| Total plant and equipment | $1,170,000 | $1,175,000 |
| Total assets | $1,684,000 | $1,678,000 |
| **Liabilities** | | |
| Current liabilities: | | |
| Accounts payable | $ 164,000 | $ 190,000 |
| Short-term notes payable | 75,000 | 90,000 |
| Taxes payable | 26,000 | 12,000 |
| Total current liabilities | $ 265,000 | $ 292,000 |
| Long-term liabilities: | | |
| Notes payable (secured by mortgage on building and land) | $ 400,000 | $ 420,000 |
| Total liabilities | $ 665,000 | $ 712,000 |
| **Stockholders' Equity** | | |
| Common stock, $5 par value | $ 475,000 | $ 475,000 |
| Retained earnings | 544,000 | 491,000 |
| Total stockholders' equity | $1,019,000 | $ 966,000 |
| Total liabilities and equity | $1,684,000 | $1,678,000 |

## Solution to Demonstration Problem

1.

**PRECISION COMPANY**
**Comparative Income Statement**
**For Years Ended December 31, 1991, and December 31, 1990**

| | 1991 | 1990 | Increase (Decrease) in 1991 Amount | Percent |
|---|---|---|---|---|
| Sales | $2,486,000 | $2,075,000 | $411,000 | 19.8 |
| Cost of goods sold | 1,523,000 | 1,222,000 | 301,000 | 24.6 |
| Gross profit from sales | $ 963,000 | $ 853,000 | $110,000 | 12.9 |
| Operating expenses: | | | | |
| Advertising expense | $ 145,000 | $ 100,000 | $ 45,000 | 45.0 |
| Sales salaries expense | 240,000 | 280,000 | (40,000) | (14.3) |
| Office salaries expense | 165,000 | 200,000 | (35,000) | (17.5) |
| Insurance expense | 100,000 | 45,000 | 55,000 | 122.2 |
| Supplies expense | 26,000 | 35,000 | (9,000) | (25.7) |
| Depreciation expense | 85,000 | 75,000 | 10,000 | 13.3 |
| Miscellaneous expense | 17,000 | 15,000 | 2,000 | 13.3 |
| Total operating expenses | $ 778,000 | $ 750,000 | $ 28,000 | 3.7 |
| Operating income | $ 185,000 | $ 103,000 | $ 82,000 | 79.6 |
| Less interest expense | 44,000 | 46,000 | (2,000) | (4.3) |
| Income before taxes | $ 141,000 | $ 57,000 | $ 84,000 | 147.4 |
| Income taxes | 47,000 | 19,000 | 28,000 | 147.4 |
| Net income | $ 94,000 | $ 38,000 | $ 56,000 | 147.4 |
| Earnings per share | $0.99 | $0.40 | $0.59 | 147.5 |

2.

**PRECISION COMPANY**
**Common-Size, Comparative Balance Sheet**
**December 31, 1991, and December 31, 1990**

| | Years Ended December 31 | | Common-Size Percentages | |
|---|---|---|---|---|
| | 1991 | 1990 | 1991 | 1990 |
| **Assets** | | | | |
| Current assets: | | | | |
| Cash | $ 79,000 | $ 42,000 | 4.69 | 2.50 |
| Short-term investments | 65,000 | 96,000 | 3.86 | 5.72 |
| Accounts receivable, net | 120,000 | 100,000 | 7.13 | 5.96 |
| Merchandise inventory | 250,000 | 265,000 | 14.85 | 15.79 |
| Total current assets | $ 514,000 | $ 503,000 | 30.52 | 29.98 |
| Plant and equipment: | | | | |
| Store equipment, net | $ 400,000 | $ 350,000 | 23.75 | 20.86 |
| Office equipment, net | 45,000 | 50,000 | 2.67 | 2.98 |
| Buildings, net | 625,000 | 675,000 | 37.11 | 40.23 |
| Land | 100,000 | 100,000 | 5.94 | 5.96 |
| Total plant and equipment | $1,170,000 | $1,175,000 | 69.48 | 70.02 |
| Total assets | $1,684,000 | $1,678,000 | 100.00 | 100.00 |
| **Liabilities** | | | | |
| Current liabilities: | | | | |
| Accounts payable | $ 164,000 | $ 190,000 | 9.74 | 11.32 |
| Short-term notes payable | 75,000 | 90,000 | 4.45 | 5.36 |
| Taxes payable | 26,000 | 12,000 | 1.54 | 0.72 |
| Total current liabilities | $ 265,000 | $ 292,000 | 15.74 | 17.40 |
| Long-term liabilities: | | | | |
| Notes payable (secured by mortgage on building and land) | $ 400,000 | $ 420,000 | 23.75 | 25.03 |
| Total liabilities | $ 665,000 | $ 712,000 | 39.49 | 42.43 |

**PRECISION COMPANY**
**Common-Size, Comparative Balance Sheet**
**December 31, 1991, and December 31, 1990**

| | Years Ended December 31 | | Common-Size Percentages | |
|---|---|---|---|---|
| | 1991 | 1990 | 1991 | 1990 |
| **Stockholders' Equity** | | | | |
| Common stock, $5 par value | $ 475,000 | $ 475,000 | 28.21 | 28.31 |
| Retained earnings | 544,000 | 491,000 | 32.30 | 29.26 |
| Total stockholders' equity | $1,019,000 | $ 966,000 | 60.51 | 57.57 |
| Total liabilities and equity | $1,684,000 | $1,678,000 | 100.00 | 100.00 |

3. Ratios for 1991:
   *a.* Current ratio: $514,000 ÷ $265,000 = 1.9.
   *b.* Acid-test ratio: $79,000 + $65,000 + $120,000 = $264,000
   $264,000 ÷ $265,000 = 1.0.
   *c.* Accounts receivable turnover:
   ($120,000 + $100,000) ÷ 2 = $110,000
   $2,486,000 ÷ $110,000 = 22.6.
   *d.* Days' sales uncollected: ($120,000/$2,486,000) × 365 = 17.6 days.
   *e.* Turnover of merchandise inventory:
   ($250,000 + $265,000) ÷ 2 = $257,500
   $1,523,000 ÷ $257,500 = 5.9 times.
   *f.* Total liabilities as a percentage of total assets:
   ($665,000/$1,684,000) × 100 = 39.5%.
   *g.* Pledged assets to secured liabilities:
   ($625,000 + $100,000) ÷ $400,000 = 1.8.
   *h.* Times fixed interest charges earned:
   $185,000 ÷ $44,000 = 4.2 times.
   *i.* Profit margin: ($94,000/$2,486,000) × 100 = 3.8%.
   *j.* Total asset turnover: ($1,684,000 + $1,678,000) ÷ 2 = $1,681,000
   $2,486,000 ÷ $1,681,000 = 1.48.
   *k.* Return on total assets employed: $94,000 ÷ $1,681,000 = 5.6%
   or 3.8% × 1.48 = 5.6%.
   *l.* Return on common stockholders' equity:
   ($1,019,000 + $966,000) ÷ 2 = $992,500
   ($94,000/$992,500) × 100 = 9.5%.

## Glossary

Define or explain the words and phrases listed in the chapter Glossary. (L. O. 5)

**Accounts receivable turnover** an indication of how long it takes a company to collect its accounts; calculated by dividing credit sales (or net sales) by the average accounts receivable balance. p. 852

**Acid-test ratio** the relation of quick assets, such as cash, short-term investments, accounts receivable, and notes receivable, to current liabilities; calculated as quick assets divided by current liabilities. pp. 851–52

**Common-size comparative statements** comparative financial statements in which each amount is expressed as a percentage of a base amount. In the balance sheet, the amount of total assets is usually selected as the base amount and is expressed as 100%. In the income statement, net sales is usually selected as the base amount. pp. 847–49

**Comparative statement** a financial statement with data for two or more successive accounting periods placed in columns side by side, sometimes with changes shown in dollar amounts and percentages. pp. 843–46

**Current ratio** the relation of a company's current assets to its current liabilities; that is, current assets divided by current liabilities. pp. 850–51

**Days' sales uncollected** the number of days of average credit sales volume that, if totaled, would equal the accounts receivable balance; calculated as the product of 365 times the accounts receivable balance divided by charge sales. pp. 852–53

**Dividend yield** the annual amount of cash dividends paid per share of stock expressed as a percentage of the market price per share; used to compare the dividend paying performance of different investment alternatives. p. 859

**Financial leverage** the use of debt as a source of assets in the hope of earning a return on those assets that is higher than the rate of interest paid to creditors, thereby increasing the return to stockholders. p. 858

**Financial reporting** the process of preparing and issuing financial information about a company. p. 842

**General purpose financial statements** statements that are published periodically for use by a wide variety of interested parties and that include the income statement, balance sheet, statement of retained earnings or statement of changes in stockholders' equity, and statement of cash flows. p. 842

**Merchandise turnover** the number of times a company's average inventory is sold during an accounting period; calculated by dividing cost of goods sold by the average merchandise inventory balance. p. 853

**Net working capital** a synonym for working capital. pp. 849–50

**Price-earnings ratio** a measure used to evaluate the profitability of alternative common stock investments; calculated as market price per share of common stock divided by earnings per share. pp. 858–59

**Profit margin** a component of operating efficiency and profitability; calculated by expressing net income as a percentage of net sales. p. 856

**Quick ratio** a synonym for acid-test ratio. pp. 851–52

**Return on common stockholders' equity** a measure of profitability in the use of assets provided by common stockholders; measured by expressing net income less preferred dividends as a percentage of average common stockholders' equity. p. 858

**Return on total assets employed** a summary measure of operating efficiency and management performance; calculated by expressing net income as a percentage of average total assets. p. 857

**Times fixed interest charges earned** a measure of a company's ability to satisfy fixed interest charges; calculated as income before interest and income taxes divided by fixed interest charges. p. 856

**Total asset turnover** a component of operating efficiency and profitability; calculated by dividing net sales by average total assets. p. 857

**Working capital** current assets minus current liabilities. pp. 849–50

## Objective Review

Answers to the following questions are listed in Appendix I at the end of the book. Be sure that you decide which is the one best answer to each question *before* you check the answers in the appendix.

1. Which of the following is not one of the broad objectives of financial reporting by business enterprises as identified by the FASB?
   *a.* Financial reporting should provide information that is useful to present and potential investors and creditors and other users in making rational investment, credit, and similar decisions.
   *b.* Financial reporting should provide information to help present and potential investors and creditors and other users in assessing the amounts, timing, and uncertainty of prospective cash receipts from dividends or interest and the proceeds from the sale, redemption, or maturity of securities or loans.
   *c.* Financial reporting should provide comparative data for two or more successive accounting periods so that users may analyze items that show significant changes as favorable or unfavorable.
   *d.* Financial reporting should provide information about the economic resources of an enterprise, the claims to those resources, and the effects of transactions, events, and circumstances that change its resources and claims to those resources.
   *e.* All of the above are identified by the FASB as broad objectives of financial reporting.
2. Given the following information for Pittard Corporation, determine the common-size percentages for gross profit from sales.

| | 1991 | 1990 |
|---|---|---|
| Net sales . . . . . . . . . | $96,000 | $82,000 |
| Cost of goods sold . . . . | 52,000 | 43,000 |

   *a.* 113% in 1991; 100% in 1990.
   *b.* 12.8% increase during 1991.
   *c.* 45.8% in 1991; 47.6% in 1990.
   *d.* 54.2% in 1991; 52.4% in 1990.
   *e.* 100% in 1991; 88.8% in 1990.

3. Times fixed interest charges earned is a measure of:
   *a.* The protection provided to the secured creditors by the pledge of assets.
   *b.* Short-term liquidity.
   *c.* Operating efficiency and profitability.
   *d.* The security of the return offered to creditors.
   *e.* How fast a company collects its accounts.
4. Which of the following may be a source for standards of comparing ratios and turnovers computed in the process of analyzing financial statements?
   *a.* Data gathered from members of some local and national trade associations which are published as standard or average ratios for their trade or industry.
   *b.* Ratios and turnovers of a selected group of competitive companies in the same industry as the one whose statements are under review.
   *c.* Past experience of the analyst with the company under review as well as other companies.
   *d.* Rule-of-thumb standards.
   *e.* All of the above.

## Questions for Class Discussion

1. Who are the intended readers of general purpose financial statements?
2. What statements are usually included in the general purpose financial statements published by corporations?
3. Explain the difference between financial reporting and financial statements.
4. General purpose financial statements should help readers make what kind of predictions?
5. What are the three broad objectives of financial reporting prescribed by the FASB?
6. Why are some comparative balance sheets prepared with columns that show increases and decreases in both dollar amounts and percentages?
7. Under what circumstances is it impossible to calculate a percentage increase or decrease in a comparative financial statement item?
8. When trends are calculated and compared, it is often informative to compare the trend of sales with the trends of several other financial statement items. What are some of the items that should be compared to sales in this fashion?
9. What is meant by *common-size* financial statements?
10. What items usually are assigned a value of 100% (*a*) on a common-size balance sheet and (*b*) on a common-size income statement?
11. Why is working capital given special attention in the process of analyzing balance sheets?
12. Which ratios provides the best indication of a company's ability to meet its debt obligations in the very near future, current ratio or acid-test ratio?

13. Indicate which of the following transactions increase working capital, which decrease working capital, and which have no effect on working capital:
    *a.* Collected accounts receivable.
    *b.* Borrowed money by giving a 90-day, interest-bearing note.
    *c.* Declared a cash dividend.
    *d.* Paid a cash dividend previously declared.
    *e.* Sold plant assets at their book value.
    *f.* Sold merchandise at a profit.
14. List several factors that have an effect on working capital requirements.
15. What are several reasons why a 2 to 1 current ratio may not be adequate for a particular company?
16. Why does turnover of accounts receivable provide information about a company's short-term liquidity?
17. What is the significance of the number of days' sales uncollected?
18. Why does turnover of merchandise inventory provide information about a company's short-term liquidity?
19. Why do creditors like to see a high proportion of total assets being financed by owners' equity?
20. Why is the capital structure of a company, as measured by debt and equity ratios, of importance to financial statement analysts?
21. Why must the ratio of pledged plant assets to secured liabilities be interpreted with care?
22. What is the relationship between profit margin, total asset turnover, and return on total assets employed?
23. Why might a company's return on total assets employed be different from its return on common stockholders' equity?
24. What ratios might you calculate for the purpose of evaluating management performance?
25. How might you use the information provided by price-earnings ratio and dividend yield?

## Exercises

**Exercise 20–1**
**Calculating trend percentages**
(L. O. 2)

Calculate trend percentages for the following items using 1987 as the base year. Then state whether the situation shown by the trends appears to be favorable or unfavorable:

| | 1991 | 1990 | 1989 | 1988 | 1987 |
|---|---|---|---|---|---|
| Sales . . . . . . . . . . . . | $595,000 | $561,000 | $527,000 | $497,250 | $425,000 |
| Cost of goods sold . . . . . | 374,170 | 350,455 | 329,375 | 313,565 | 263,500 |
| Accounts receivable . . . . | 59,640 | 56,700 | 54,600 | 52,500 | 42,000 |

**Exercise 20–2**
**Reporting percentage changes**
(L. O. 2)

Where possible, calculate percentages of increase and decrease for the following unrelated items. The parentheses indicate deficit items.

| | 1991 | 1990 |
|---|---|---|
| Equipment, net . . . . . | $114,750 | $85,000 |
| Notes receivable . . . . . | –0– | 15,000 |
| Notes payable . . . . . . | 30,000 | –0– |
| Retained earnings . . . . | (2,000) | 20,000 |
| Cash . . . . . . . . . . . | 7,500 | (500) |

**Exercise 20–3**
**Calculating common-size percentages**
(L. O. 2)

Express the following income statement information in common-size percentages and evaluate the situation shown as favorable or unfavorable:

**PADREN CORPORATION**
**Comparative Income Statement**
**For Years Ended December 31, 1990, and 1989**

| | 1990 | 1989 |
|---|---|---|
| Sales . . . . . . . . . . . . . | $250,000 | $235,000 |
| Cost of goods sold . . . . . . | 165,000 | 151,575 |
| Gross profit from sales . . . . | $ 85,000 | $ 83,425 |
| Operating expenses . . . . . | 63,500 | 42,770 |
| Net income . . . . . . . . . . | $ 21,500 | $ 40,655 |

**Exercise 20–4**
**Evaluating short-term liquidity**
(L. O. 3)

Rawhide Company's December 31 balance sheets included the following data:

| | 1990 | 1989 | 1988 |
|---|---|---|---|
| **Assets** | | | |
| Cash . . . . . . . . . . . . . . . . . . . . | $ 8,800 | $ 16,700 | $ 25,900 |
| Accounts receivable, net . . . . . . . . . | 63,000 | 51,000 | 47,500 |
| Merchandise inventory . . . . . . . . . . | 85,000 | 44,000 | 20,000 |
| Prepaid expenses . . . . . . . . . . . . . | 10,800 | 7,500 | 3,500 |
| Plant assets, net . . . . . . . . . . . . . | 195,000 | 201,000 | 180,000 |
| Total assets . . . . . . . . . . . . . . . | $362,600 | $320,200 | $276,900 |
| **Liabilities and Stockholders' Equity** | | | |
| Accounts payable . . . . . . . . . . . . . | $ 82,600 | $ 53,000 | $ 39,400 |
| Long-term notes payable secured by mortgage on plant assets . . . . . . . . | 105,000 | 105,000 | 80,000 |
| Common stock, $10 par value . . . . . . | 100,000 | 100,000 | 100,000 |
| Retained earnings . . . . . . . . . . . . | 75,000 | 62,200 | 57,500 |
| Total liabilities and stockholders' equity . . | $362,600 | $320,200 | $276,900 |

*Required*

Compare the short-term liquidity positions of the company at the end of 1990, 1989, and 1988 by calculating the following ratios: (*a*) current ratio and (*b*) acid-test ratio. Comment on any changes that occurred.

**Exercise 20–5**
**Evaluating short-term liquidity**
(L. O. 3)

Refer to the information in Exercise 20–4 about Rawhide Company. The company's income statement for years ended December 31, 1990, and 1989, included the following data:

| | 1990 | 1989 |
|---|---|---|
| Sales . . . . . . . . . . . . . . . . | $530,000 | $475,000 |
| Cost of goods sold . . . . . . . . | $314,000 | $290,000 |
| Other operating expenses . . . . | 173,000 | 152,000 |
| Interest expense . . . . . . . . . | 12,000 | 11,500 |
| Income taxes . . . . . . . . . . . | 8,200 | 6,800 |
| Total costs and expenses . . . . | $507,200 | $460,300 |
| Net income . . . . . . . . . . . . | $ 22,800 | $ 14,700 |
| Earnings per share . . . . . . . | $2.28 | $1.47 |

*Required*

For the years ended December 31, 1990, and 1989, calculate the following: (*a*) days' sales uncollected, (*b*) accounts receivable turnover, and (*c*) merchandise turnover. Comment on any changes that occurred from 1989 to 1990.

**Exercise 20–6**
**Evaluating long-term risk and capital structure**
(L. O. 3)

Refer to the information in Exercises 20–4 and 20–5 about Rawhide Company. Compare the long-term risk and capital structure positions of the company at the end of 1990 and 1989 by calculating the following ratios: (*a*) debt and equity ratios, (*b*) pledged plant assets to secured liabilities, and (*c*) times fixed interest charges earned. (Assume all sales were on credit.) Comment on any changes that occurred.

**Exercise 20–7**
**Evaluating operating efficiency and profitability**
(L. O. 3)

Refer to the financial statements of Rawhide Company presented in Exercises 20–4 and 20–5. To evaluate the operating efficiency and profitability of the company, calculate the following: (*a*) profit margin, (*b*) total asset turnover, and (*c*) return on total assets employed.

**Exercise 20–8**
**Evaluating profitability**
(L. O. 3)

Refer to the financial statements of Rawhide Company presented in Exercises 20–4 and 20–5. Additional information about the company is as follows:

| | |
|---|---|
| Common stock market price, December 31, 1990 . . . | $32.00 |
| Common stock market price, December 31, 1989 . . . | 15.00 |
| Annual cash dividends per share in 1990 and 1989 . . | 1.00 |

*Required*

To evaluate the profitability of the company, calculate the following for 1990 and 1989: (*a*) return on common stockholders' equity, (*b*) price-earnings ratio on December 31, and (*c*) dividend yield.

**Exercise 20–9**
**Determining income effects from common-size and trend percentages**
(L. O. 3)

Common-size and trend percentages for a company's sales, cost of goods sold, and expenses follow:

| Common-Size Percentages | 1991 | 1990 | 1989 |
|---|---|---|---|
| Sales | 100.0 | 100.0 | 100.0 |
| Cost of goods sold | 56.2 | 60.4 | 60.8 |
| Expenses | 28.8 | 27.1 | 28.2 |

| Trend Percentages | 1991 | 1990 | 1989 |
|---|---|---|---|
| Sales | 95.3 | 97.4 | 100.0 |
| Cost of goods sold | 87.3 | 95.2 | 100.0 |
| Expenses | 95.2 | 97.0 | 100.0 |

*Required*

Present statistics to show whether the company's net income increased, decreased, or remained unchanged during the three-year period represented above.

## Problems

**Problem 20–1**
**Calculating ratios and percentages**
(L. O. 2, 3)

The condensed statements of Falcon Hill Company follow:

**FALCON HILL COMPANY**
**Comparative Income Statement**
**For Years Ended December 31, 1991, 1990, and 1989**
**($000)**

| | 1991 | 1990 | 1989 |
|---|---|---|---|
| Sales | $62,000 | $57,000 | $47,000 |
| Cost of goods sold | 43,883 | 39,330 | 31,654 |
| Gross profit from sales | $18,117 | $17,670 | $15,346 |
| Selling expenses | $ 8,915 | $ 8,392 | $ 7,280 |
| Administrative expenses | 6,510 | 6,247 | 5,310 |
| Total expenses | $15,425 | $14,639 | $12,590 |
| Income before taxes | $ 2,692 | $ 3,031 | $ 2,756 |
| State and federal income taxes | 700 | 788 | 715 |
| Net income | $ 1,992 | $ 2,243 | $ 2,041 |

**FALCON HILL COMPANY**
**Comparative Balance Sheet**
**December 31, 1991, 1990, and 1989**
**($000)**

| | 1991 | 1990 | 1989 |
|---|---|---|---|
| **Assets** | | | |
| Current assets | $10,340 | $ 9,660 | $11,440 |
| Long-term investments | –0– | 75 | 700 |
| Plant and equipment | 17,760 | 18,540 | 15,060 |
| Total assets | $28,100 | $28,275 | $27,200 |
| **Liabilities and Capital** | | | |
| Current liabilities | $ 4,700 | $ 4,600 | $ 4,400 |
| Common stock | 12,000 | 12,000 | 11,900 |
| Other contributed capital | 1,300 | 1,325 | 1,050 |
| Retained earnings | 10,100 | 10,350 | 9,850 |
| Total liabilities and capital | $28,100 | $28,275 | $27,200 |

*Required*

1. Calculate each year's current ratio.
2. Express the income statement data in common-size percentages.
3. Express the balance sheet data in trend percentages with 1989 as the base year.
4. Comment on any significant relationships revealed by the ratios and percentages.

**Problem 20–2**
**Calculation and analysis of trend percentages**
(L. O. 2)

The condensed comparative statements of Rydmore Range Corporation follow:

**RYDMORE RANGE CORPORATION**
**Comparative Income Statement**
**For Years Ended December 31, 1992–1986**
**($000)**

| | 1992 | 1991 | 1990 | 1989 | 1988 | 1987 | 1986 |
|---|---|---|---|---|---|---|---|
| Sales | $792 | $740 | $660 | $592 | $540 | $480 | $400 |
| Cost of goods sold | 437 | 399 | 342 | 304 | 257 | 235 | 190 |
| Gross profit from sales | $355 | $341 | $318 | $288 | $283 | $245 | $210 |
| Operating expenses | 297 | 264 | 218 | 167 | 165 | 138 | 110 |
| Income before taxes | $ 58 | $ 77 | $100 | $121 | $118 | $107 | $100 |

**RYDMORE RANGE CORPORATION**
**Comparative Balance Sheet**
**December 31, 1992–1986**
**($000)**

| | 1992 | 1991 | 1990 | 1989 | 1988 | 1987 | 1986 |
|---|---|---|---|---|---|---|---|
| **Assets** | | | | | | | |
| Cash | $ 8 | $ 12 | $ 14 | $ 17 | $ 18 | $ 15 | $ 20 |
| Accounts receivable, net | 92 | 90 | 88 | 66 | 57 | 54 | 44 |
| Merchandise inventory | 232 | 225 | 212 | 176 | 156 | 130 | 112 |
| Other current assets | 5 | 7 | 4 | 8 | 7 | 7 | 4 |
| Long-term investments | –0– | –0– | –0– | 39 | 39 | 39 | 39 |
| Plant and equipment, net | 372 | 382 | 358 | 180 | 182 | 176 | 178 |
| Total assets | $709 | $716 | $676 | $486 | $459 | $421 | $397 |
| **Liabilities and Capital** | | | | | | | |
| Current liabilities | $135 | $140 | $125 | $100 | $ 85 | $ 70 | $ 60 |
| Long-term liabilities | 165 | 189 | 201 | 84 | 87 | 90 | 85 |
| Common stock | 165 | 165 | 165 | 135 | 135 | 125 | 125 |
| Other contributed capital | 65 | 65 | 65 | 50 | 50 | 50 | 50 |
| Retained earnings | 179 | 157 | 120 | 117 | 102 | 86 | 77 |
| Total liabilities and capital | $709 | $716 | $676 | $486 | $459 | $421 | $397 |

*Required*

1. Calculate trend percentages for the items of the statements using 1986 as the base year.
2. Analyze and comment on the situation shown in the statements.

**Problem 20–3**
**Calculation of financial statement relations**
(L. O. 3)

The year-end statements of Riverbank Corporation follow:

**RIVERBANK CORPORATION**
**Income Statement**
**For Year Ended December 31, 1991**

| | | |
|---|---|---|
| Sales | | $676,500 |
| Cost of goods sold: | | |
| Merchandise inventory, December 31, 1990 | $ 49,800 | |
| Purchases | 385,900 | |
| Goods available for sale | $435,700 | |
| Merchandise inventory, December 31, 1991 | 33,600 | |
| Cost of goods sold | | 402,100 |
| Gross profit from sales | | $274,400 |
| Operating expenses | | 195,900 |
| Operating income | | $ 78,500 |
| Interest expense | | 10,800 |
| Income before taxes | | $ 67,700 |
| Income taxes | | 23,700 |
| Net income | | $ 44,000 |

**RIVERBANK CORPORATION**
**Balance Sheet**
**December 31, 1991**

| Assets | | Liabilities and Stockholders' Equity | |
|---|---|---|---|
| Cash | $ 25,700 | Accounts payable | $ 48,700 |
| Short-term investments | 27,600 | Accrued wages payable | 5,800 |
| Accounts receivable, net | 45,200 | Income taxes payable | 6,900 |
| Notes receivable | 5,300 | Long-term note payable, secured by mortgage on plant assets | 105,000 |
| Merchandise inventory | 53,600 | | |
| Prepaid expenses | 2,100 | | |
| Plant assets, net | 352,700 | Common stock, $5 par value | 225,000 |
| | | Retained earnings | 120,800 |
| Total assets | $512,200 | Total liabilities and stockholders' equity | $512,200 |

Assume all sales were on credit. On the December 31, 1990, balance sheet, the assets totaled $350,300, common stock was $225,000, and retained earnings was $100,200.

*Required*

Calculate the following: (*a*) current ratio, (*b*) acid-test ratio, (*c*) days' sales uncollected, (*d*) merchandise turnover, (*e*) ratio of pledged plant assets to secured liabilities, (*f*) times fixed interest charges earned, (*g*) profit margin, (*h*) total asset turnover, (*i*) return on total assets employed, and (*j*) return on common stockholders' equity.

**Problem 20–4**
**Comparative analysis of financial statement ratios**
(L. O. 3)

Two companies that operate in the same industry as competitors are being evaluated by a bank that may lend money to each one. Summary information from the financial statements of the two companies is provided below:

**Data from the Current Year-End Balance Sheets**

| | Quaser Company | Pulser Company |
|---|---|---|
| **Assets** | | |
| Cash | $ 20,200 | $ 27,600 |
| Accounts receivable | 54,900 | 87,100 |
| Notes receivable | 9,000 | 7,700 |
| Merchandise inventory | 67,200 | 102,000 |
| Prepaid expenses | 7,500 | 9,700 |
| Plant and equipment, net | 300,700 | 308,600 |
| Total assets | $459,500 | $542,700 |
| **Liabilities and Capital** | | |
| Current liabilities | $ 80,800 | $110,100 |
| Long-term notes payable | 88,000 | 102,000 |
| Common stock, $10 par value | 160,000 | 190,000 |
| Retained earnings | 130,700 | 140,600 |
| Total liabilities and capital | $459,500 | $542,700 |
| **Data from the Current Year's Income Statements** | | |
| Sales | $745,000 | $969,000 |
| Cost of goods sold | 550,000 | 718,000 |
| Interest expense | 8,600 | 14,900 |
| Income tax expense | 11,200 | 15,300 |
| Net income | 35,300 | 44,200 |
| **Beginning-of-Year Data** | | |
| Accounts receivable, net | $ 38,200 | $ 70,000 |
| Notes receivable | –0– | –0– |
| Merchandise inventory | 55,200 | 88,400 |
| Total assets | 392,000 | 468,500 |
| Common stock, $10 par value | 160,000 | 190,000 |
| Retained earnings | 108,200 | 111,600 |

*Required*

1. Calculate current ratios, acid-test ratios, accounts (and notes) receivable turnovers, merchandise turnovers, and days' sales uncollected for the two companies. Then state which company you think is the better short-term credit risk and why.
2. Calculate profit margins, total asset turnovers, returns on total assets employed, and returns on common stockholders' equity. Assuming that each company paid cash dividends of $0.80 per share and each company's stock can be purchased at $18 per share, calculate price earnings ratio and dividend yield. Also state which company's stock you would recommend as the better investment and why.

**Problem 20–5**
**Analysis of working capital**
(L. O. 3)

City Sales Corporation began the month of August with $420,000 of current assets, a current ratio of 2.5 to 1, and an acid-test ratio of 1.5 to 1. During the month, it completed the following transactions:

Aug. 3 Bought $60,000 of merchandise on account. (The company uses a perpetual inventory system.)
6 Sold for $70,000 merchandise that cost $38,000.
9 Collected a $20,000 account receivable.
12 Paid a $25,000 account payable.

Aug. 17 Wrote off an $8,500 bad debt against the Allowance for Doubtful Accounts account.
21 Declared a $1 per share cash dividend on the 20,000 shares of outstanding common stock.
25 Paid the dividend declared on August 21.
27 Borrowed $80,000 by giving the bank a 60-day, 12% note.
29 Borrowed $90,000 by signing a long-term secured note.
31 Used the $170,000 proceeds of the notes to buy additional machinery.

*Required*

Prepare a schedule showing the company's current ratio, acid-test ratio, and working capital after each of the foregoing transactions. Round to two decimal places.

## Alternate Problems

**Problem 20–1A**
**Calculating ratios and percentages**
(L. O. 2, 3)

The condensed statements of Tradent Corporation follow:

**TRADENT CORPORATION**
**Comparative Income Statement**
**For Years Ended December 31, 1991, 1990, and 1989**
**($000)**

| | 1991 | 1990 | 1989 |
|---|---|---|---|
| Sales | $98,000 | $82,400 | $71,000 |
| Cost of goods sold | 54,500 | 43,300 | 33,800 |
| Gross profit from sales | $43,500 | $39,100 | $37,200 |
| Selling expenses | $13,100 | $10,350 | $10,900 |
| Administrative expenses | 9,800 | 10,450 | 9,500 |
| Total expenses | $22,900 | $20,800 | $20,400 |
| Income before taxes | $20,600 | $18,300 | $16,800 |
| State and federal income taxes | 7,210 | 6,405 | 5,880 |
| Net income | $13,390 | $11,895 | $10,920 |

**TRADENT CORPORATION**
**Comparative Balance Sheet**
**December 31, 1991, 1990, and 1989**
**($000)**

| | 1991 | 1990 | 1989 |
|---|---|---|---|
| **Assets** | | | |
| Current assets | $22,600 | $12,500 | $14,900 |
| Long-term investments | –0– | 700 | 5,700 |
| Plant and equipment | 51,000 | 53,000 | 39,200 |
| Total assets | $73,600 | $66,200 | $59,800 |
| **Liabilities and Capital** | | | |
| Current liabilities | $11,000 | $ 9,200 | $ 7,700 |
| Common stock | 15,000 | 15,000 | 12,000 |
| Other contributed capital | 4,600 | 4,600 | 4,000 |
| Retained earnings | 43,000 | 37,400 | 36,100 |
| Total liabilities and capital | $73,600 | $66,200 | $59,800 |

*Required*

1. Calculate each year's current ratio.

2. Express the income statement data in common-size percentages.
3. Express the balance sheet data in trend percentages with 1989 as the base year.
4. Comment on any significant relationships revealed by the ratios and percentages.

**Problem 20–2A**
**Calculation and analysis of trend percentages**
(L. O. 2)

The condensed comparative statements of Clear River Company follow:

**CLEAR RIVER COMPANY**
**Comparative Income Statement**
**For Years Ended December 31, 1992–1986**
**($000)**

| | 1992 | 1991 | 1990 | 1989 | 1988 | 1987 | 1986 |
|---|---|---|---|---|---|---|---|
| Sales | $450 | $470 | $460 | $490 | $530 | $520 | $560 |
| Cost of goods sold | 190 | 197 | 194 | 208 | 219 | 212 | 214 |
| Gross profit from sales | $260 | $273 | $266 | $282 | $311 | $308 | $346 |
| Operating expenses | 200 | 207 | 205 | 224 | 231 | 235 | 255 |
| Income before taxes | $ 60 | $ 66 | $ 61 | $ 58 | $ 80 | $ 73 | $ 91 |

**CLEAR RIVER COMPANY**
**Comparative Balance Sheet**
**December 31, 1992–1986**
**($000)**

| | 1992 | 1991 | 1990 | 1989 | 1988 | 1987 | 1986 |
|---|---|---|---|---|---|---|---|
| **Assets** | | | | | | | |
| Cash | $ 30 | $ 33 | $ 32 | $ 36 | $ 45 | $ 42 | $ 46 |
| Accounts receivable, net | 92 | 103 | 99 | 101 | 112 | 110 | 118 |
| Merchandise inventory | 143 | 149 | 147 | 156 | 159 | 169 | 162 |
| Other current assets | 20 | 21 | 22 | 24 | 23 | 26 | 28 |
| Long-term investments | 80 | 60 | 40 | 87 | 87 | 87 | 90 |
| Plant and equipment, net | 362 | 368 | 372 | 287 | 292 | 297 | 302 |
| Total assets | $727 | $734 | $712 | $691 | $718 | $731 | $746 |
| **Liabilities and Capital** | | | | | | | |
| Current liabilities | $162 | $169 | $152 | $121 | $143 | $171 | $216 |
| Long-term liabilities | 130 | 145 | 160 | 175 | 190 | 205 | 220 |
| Common stock | 145 | 145 | 145 | 145 | 145 | 145 | 145 |
| Other contributed capital | 60 | 60 | 60 | 60 | 60 | 60 | 60 |
| Retained earnings | 230 | 215 | 195 | 190 | 180 | 150 | 105 |
| Total liabilities and capital | $727 | $734 | $712 | $691 | $718 | $731 | $746 |

*Required*

1. Calculate trend percentages for the items of the statements using 1986 as the base year.
2. Analyze and comment on the situation shown in the statements.

**Problem 20–3A**
**Financial statement ratios**
(L. O. 3)

The year-end statements of Tooner Corporation follow:

**TOONER CORPORATION**
**Income Statement**
**For Year Ended December 31, 1991**

| | | |
|---|---|---|
| Sales | | $805,000 |
| Cost of goods sold: | | |
| Merchandise inventory, December 31, 1990 | $ 62,800 | |
| Purchases | 501,700 | |
| Goods available for sale | $564,500 | |
| Merchandise inventory, December 31, 1991 | 49,200 | |
| Cost of goods sold | | 515,300 |
| Gross profit from sales | | $289,700 |
| Operating expenses | | 227,800 |
| Operating income | | $ 61,900 |
| Interest expense | | 9,500 |
| Income before taxes | | $ 52,400 |
| Income taxes | | 15,720 |
| Net income | | $ 36,680 |

**TOONER CORPORATION**
**Balance Sheet**
**December 31, 1991**

| Assets | | Liabilities and Stockholders' Equity | |
|---|---|---|---|
| Cash | $ 18,500 | Accounts payable | $ 40,700 |
| Short-term investments | 20,400 | Accrued wages payable | 5,200 |
| Accounts receivable, net | 43,400 | Income taxes payable | 5,800 |
| Notes receivable | 8,800 | Long-term note payable, secured by mortgage on plant assets | 95,000 |
| Merchandise inventory | 49,200 | Common stock, $5 par value | 160,000 |
| Prepaid expenses | 4,800 | Retained earnings | 110,500 |
| Plant assets, net | 272,100 | | |
| Total assets | $417,200 | Total liabilities and stockholders' equity | $417,200 |

Assume all sales were on credit. On the December 31, 1990, balance sheet, the assets totaled $360,600, common stock was $160,000, and retained earnings was $89,700.

*Required*

Calculate the following: (*a*) current ratio, (*b*) acid-test ratio, (*c*) days' sales uncollected, (*d*) merchandise turnover, (*e*) ratio of pledged plant assets to secured liabilities, (*f*) times fixed interest charges earned, (*g*) profit margin, (*h*) total asset turnover, (*i*) return on total assets employed, and (*j*) return on common stockholders' equity.

**Problem 20–4A**
**Comparative analysis of financial statement ratios**
(L. O. 3)

Two companies that operate in the same industry as competitors are being evaluated by a bank that may lend money to each one. Summary information from the financial statements of the two companies is provided below:

**Data from the Current Year-End Balance Sheets**

| | Zesta Company | Festa Company |
|---|---|---|
| **Assets** | | |
| Cash | $ 30,200 | $ 57,100 |
| Accounts receivable | 105,500 | 118,500 |
| Notes receivable | 18,000 | 16,500 |
| Merchandise inventory | 98,700 | 133,300 |
| Prepaid expenses | 15,700 | 17,900 |
| Plant and equipment, net | 332,900 | 340,100 |
| Total assets | $601,000 | $683,400 |
| **Liabilities and Capital** | | |
| Current liabilities | $113,400 | $141,800 |
| Long-term notes payable | 120,000 | 135,000 |
| Common stock, $20 par value | 182,000 | 212,000 |
| Retained earnings | 185,600 | 194,600 |
| Total liabilities and capital | $601,000 | $683,400 |
| **Data from the Current Year's Income Statements** | | |
| Sales | $703,500 | $992,100 |
| Cost of goods sold | 518,000 | 708,200 |
| Interest expense | 14,100 | 17,800 |
| Income tax expense | 22,500 | 42,700 |
| Net income | 54,200 | 74,700 |
| **Beginning-of-Year Data** | | |
| Accounts receivable, net | $ 98,000 | $100,500 |
| Notes receivable | –0– | –0– |
| Merchandise inventory | 118,200 | 93,900 |
| Total assets | 514,300 | 600,000 |
| Common stock, $20 par value | 182,000 | 212,000 |
| Retained earnings | 158,700 | 151,700 |

*Required*

1. Calculate current ratios, acid-test ratios, accounts (and notes) receivable turnovers, merchandise turnovers, and days' sales uncollected for the two companies. Then state which company you think is the better short-term credit risk and why.
2. Calculate profit margins, total asset turnovers, returns on total assets employed, and returns on common stockholders' equity. Assuming that each company paid cash dividends of $3 per share and each company's stock can be purchased at $45 per share, calculate price earnings ratio and dividend yield. Also state which company's stock you would recommend as the better investment and why.

**Problem 20–5A**
**Analysis of working capital**
(L. O. 3)

Ft. Mason Corporation began the month of March with $286,000 of current assets, a current ratio of 2.2 to 1, and an acid-test ratio of 0.9 to 1. During the month, it completed the following transactions:

Mar. 3 Sold for $55,000 merchandise that cost $36,000.
5 Collected a $35,000 account receivable.
10 Bought $56,000 of merchandise on account. (The company uses a perpetual inventory system.)
12 Borrowed $60,000 by giving the bank a 60-day, 12% note.
15 Borrowed $90,000 by signing a long-term secured note.
22 Used the $150,000 proceeds of the notes to buy additional machinery.

Mar. 24 Declared a $1.75 per share cash dividend on the 40,000 shares of outstanding common stock.
26 Wrote off a $14,000 bad debt against Allowance for Doubtful Accounts.
28 Paid a $45,000 account payable.
30 Paid the dividend declared on March 24.

*Required*

Prepare a schedule showing the company's current ratio, acid-test ratio, and working capital after each of the foregoing transactions. Round to two decimal places.

## Provocative Problems

**Provocative Problem 20–1**
**The Clorox Company**
(L. O. 2, 3)

The Clorox Company is a diversified firm that develops, manufactures, and markets premium quality household products, architectural coatings, and food service products. In addition to the liquid bleach product from which it takes its name, the company markets the leading line of dry salad mixes. Founded in 1913, The Clorox Company has become an international company with sales in excess of $1 billion. Their 1986 annual report included a 10-year financial summary, from which the following information has been extracted:

| (In thousands, except per-share data) | **1986** | 1985 | 1984 | 1983 |
|---|---|---|---|---|
| **Operations** | | | | |
| Net sales | **$1,089,070** | $1,054,847 | $974,566 | $913,807 |
| Percent change | **+3.2** | +8.2 | +6.6 | +5.4 |
| Net earnings | **95,610** | 86,124 | 79,709 | 65,507 |
| Percent change | **+11.0** | +8.0 | +21.7 | +45.2 |
| **Common Stock** | | | | |
| Per share: | | | | |
| Earnings from continuing operations | **$3.60** | $3.27 | $3.09 | $2.72 |
| Earnings from discontinued operations | — | — | — | — |
| Net earnings | | | | |
| Assuming no dilution | **$3.60** | $3.27 | $3.09 | $2.72 |
| Assuming full dilution | **$3.50** | $3.17 | $3.01 | $2.64 |
| Dividends | **$1.40** | $1.24 | $1.08 | $ .95 |
| Shareholders' equity at end of year | **20.61** | 18.37 | 16.40 | 13.48 |
| **Other Data** | | | | |
| Working capital | **$240,180** | $203,011 | $144,424 | $117,333 |
| Total assets | **849,225** | 778,062 | 701,396 | 603,875 |
| Long-term debt | **38,151** | 38,945 | 43,174 | 72,597 |
| Shareholders' equity | **549,793** | 485,856 | 431,313 | 325,998 |
| Current ratio | **2.4** | 2.0 | 1.8 | 1.7 |
| Percent return on net sales—continuing operations | **8.8** | 8.2 | 8.2 | 7.2 |
| Percent return on average shareholders' equity | **18.5** | 18.8 | 20.2 | 21.6 |

*Courtesy of The Clorox Company*

Discuss the format of The Clorox Company's presentation relative to the illustrations in the chapter. Then evaluate the company's performance over the four-year period as it is disclosed by the above data.

**Provocative Problem 20–2**
**Tropical Trade Company**
(L. O. 2, 3)

In your position as controller of Tropical Trade Company, you have the responsibility of keeping the board of directors informed about the financial activities and status of the company. In preparation for the next meeting of the board, you have calculated the following ratios, turnovers, and percentages to enable you to answer questions:

| | 1991 | 1990 | 1989 |
|---|---|---|---|
| Current ratio | 2.5 to 1 | 2.4 to 1 | 1.9 to 1 |
| Acid-test ratio | 0.9 to 1 | 1.2 to 1 | 1.3 to 1 |
| Merchandise turnover | 8.3 times | 9.5 times | 10.4 times |
| Accounts receivable turnover | 7.5 times | 8.1 times | 8.9 times |
| Return on stockholders' equity | 10.50% | 12.25% | 12.75% |
| Profit margin | 3.4% | 3.6% | 3.8% |
| Total asset turnover | 2.9 times | 3.0 times | 3.1 times |
| Return on total assets | 9.9% | 10.8% | 11.8% |
| Sales to plant assets | 4.1 to 1 | 3.8 to 1 | 3.5 to 1 |
| Sales trend | 136.00 | 124.00 | 100.00 |
| Selling expenses to net sales | 10.2% | 15.4% | 16.8% |

*Required*

Using the statistics given, answer each of the following questions and explain how you arrived at your answer.

1. Is it becoming easier for the company to meet its current debts on time and to take advantage of cash discounts?
2. Is the company collecting its accounts receivable more rapidly?
3. Is the company's investment in accounts receivable decreasing?
4. Are dollars invested in inventory increasing?
5. Is the company's investment in plant assets increasing?
6. Is the stockholders' investment becoming more profitable?
7. Is the company using its assets efficiently?
8. Did the dollar amount of selling expenses decrease during the three-year period?

**Provocative Problem 20–3**
**Lodestar and Cosmos**
(L. O. 3)

Lodestar, Inc., and Cosmos, Inc., are competing companies with similar backgrounds. The stock of both companies is traded locally, and each stock can be purchased at its book value. Mary Link has an opportunity to invest in either company but is undecided as to which is the better managed company and which is the better investment. Prepare a report to Ms. Link stating which company you think is the better managed and which company's stock you think may be the better investment. Back your report with any ratios, turnovers, and other analyses you think pertinent.

**Balance Sheets**
**December 31, 1990**

| | Lodestar, Inc. | Cosmos, Inc. |
|---|---|---|
| **Assets** | | |
| Cash | $ 40,200 | $ 41,100 |
| Accounts receivable, net | 101,600 | 108,300 |
| Merchandise inventory | 140,700 | 148,500 |
| Prepaid expenses | 4,200 | 5,300 |
| Plant and equipment, net | 462,200 | 443,100 |
| Total assets | $ 748,900 | $ 746,300 |

| Liabilities and Capital | Lodestar, Inc. | Cosmos, Inc. |
|---|---|---|
| Current liabilities | $ 130,200 | $ 146,400 |
| Long-term notes payable | 150,800 | 137,600 |
| Common stock, $10 par value | 272,500 | 239,500 |
| Retained earnings | 195,400 | 222,800 |
| Total liabilities and capital | $ 748,900 | $ 746,300 |

**Income Statements**
**For Year Ended December 31, 1990**

| | | |
|---|---|---|
| Sales | $1,950,000 | $2,056,000 |
| Cost of goods sold | 1,350,400 | 1,453,400 |
| Gross profit on sales | $ 599,600 | $ 602,600 |
| Operating expenses | 516,600 | 552,400 |
| Operating income | $ 83,000 | 50,200 |
| Interest expense | 12,300 | 11,900 |
| Income before taxes | $ 70,700 | $ 38,300 |
| Income taxes | 24,200 | 13,100 |
| Net income | $ 46,500 | $ 25,200 |

**December 31, 1989, Data**

| | | |
|---|---|---|
| Accounts receivable | $ 125,400 | $ 170,400 |
| Merchandise inventory | 119,000 | 137,200 |
| Total assets | 700,600 | 662,400 |
| Common stock | 272,000 | 239,000 |
| Retained earnings | 177,300 | 190,600 |

**Provocative Problem 20–4**
**Tyler Corporation**
(L. O. 2, 3)

Use the financial statements and related footnotes of Tyler Corporation shown in Appendix J at the end of the book to complete the following requirements:

*Required*

1. Calculate the following ratios and turnovers for 1988 and 1987: (*a*) current ratio; (*b*) days' sales uncollected; (*c*) profit margin using net income as the numerator; (*d*) profit margin using income from continuing operations as the numerator; (*e*) debt ratio at the end of the year; (*f*) return on total assets employed using net income as the numerator; (*g*) return on total assets employed, using income from continuing operations as the numerator; (*h*) return on stockholders' equity using net income as the numerator; and (*i*) return on stockholders' equity using income from continuing operations as the numerator.
2. Prepare common-size statements for the 1988 and 1987 income statements.
3. After reviewing your answers to Requirements 1 and 2 and reviewing the financial statements and related disclosures of Tyler Corporation, write a brief summary and evaluation of the results of 1988 compared to 1987.

Part Seven

# Managerial Accounting for Costs

In this part of *Fundamental Accounting Principles*, we focus on the development of information about the costs of manufacturing operations and the costs of various subunits of a business. This information is used by the managers of a business and also is used to prepare financial statements for outside parties. Since manufacturing companies face unique problems in accounting for their production activities, your study of this part will begin with Chapter 21, which explains the manufacturing accounting systems used by many companies. These systems are based on periodic inventories. Then, in Chapter 22, you will learn about more sophisticated manufacturing accounting systems that are based on perpetual inventories. In Chapter 23, you will learn how accountants develop information that is used to evaluate various subunits of a business and to evaluate managerial performance.

Part Seven consists of the following chapters:

# 21 Accounting for Manufacturing Companies

Manufacturing and merchandising companies are alike because both depend on the sale of one or more commodities or products for revenue. However, they differ in one important way. A merchandising company sells goods in essentially the same condition as they were in when they were purchased. A manufacturing company, on the other hand, buys raw materials that it manufactures into the finished products it sells. For example, a shoe store buys shoes and sells them in the same form they were in when they were purchased; but a manufacturer of shoes buys leather, cloth, glue, nails, and dye and turns these items into salable shoes.

Most of the topics you learned about in previous chapters apply equally well to service companies, merchandising companies, and manufacturing companies. However, whenever inventories and cost of goods sold were discussed, the examples and illustrations were limited to merchandising companies. In this chapter (and in Chapter 22), you will learn about the unique problems of accounting for manufacturing companies.

**Learning Objectives**

*After studying Chapter 21, you should be able to:*

1. Describe the basic differences in the financial statements of manufacturing companies and merchandising companies and the procedures used in a general accounting system for a manufacturing company.
2. Describe the unique accounts that manufacturing companies use, prepare a manufacturing statement, and explain its purpose and relationship to the primary financial statements.
3. Prepare a work sheet and the financial statements for a manufacturing company.
4. Prepare the adjusting and closing entries for a manufacturing company.
5. Explain the procedures for assigning costs to the different manufacturing inventories.
6. Define or explain the words and phrases listed in the chapter Glossary.

## Alternative Systems of Accounting for Manufacturing Companies

Some manufacturing companies use accounting systems that are based on periodic inventories. In keeping records on raw materials to be used in production, goods that are in the production process, and finished goods that are ready for sale, each type of inventory is periodically counted to determine the ending inventory and the amount used or sold during the period. When a manufacturing company uses periodic inventories to determine the total cost of all goods manufactured during each accounting period, the accounting system is called a **general accounting system.**

General accounting systems are explained in the rest of this chapter. However, many manufacturing companies use accounting systems that are based on perpetual inventories. Systems of accounting for manufacturing operations that incorporate perpetual inventories are called **cost accounting systems.** These systems provide information about the unit cost of manufacturing a product and are more effective in assisting management's efforts to control costs. Cost accounting systems are explained in Chapter 22.

## What Is the Basic Difference between Accounting for Merchandisers and Manufacturers?

Describe the basic differences in the financial statements of manufacturing companies and merchandising companies and the procedures used in a general accounting system for a manufacturing company.
(L. O. 1)

The basic difference in accounting for manufacturing and merchandising companies stems from the fact that a merchandising company buys the goods it sells in their ready-for-sale state. As a result, the merchandising company can easily determine the cost of the goods it has bought for sale by examining the debit balance of its Purchases account. In contrast, a manufacturer uses the raw materials it buys to create the products it sells. Therefore, the manufacturer must combine the balances of a number of material, labor, and overhead accounts to determine the cost of the goods it manufactured for sale.

To emphasize this difference, the cost of goods sold section from a merchandising company's income statement is condensed and presented below next to the cost of goods sold section of a manufacturing company.

| **Merchandising Company** | | **Manufacturing Company** | |
|---|---|---|---|
| Cost of goods sold: | | Cost of goods sold: | |
| Beginning merchandise inventory . . . . . . . . . . | $14,200 | Beginning finished goods inventory . . . . . . . . . | $ 11,200 |
| Cost of goods purchased . . . | 34,150 | Cost of goods manufactured (see manufacturing statement) . . . . . . . . . | 170,500 |
| Goods available for sale . . . . | $48,350 | Goods available for sale . . . | $181,700 |
| Ending merchandise inventory . . . . . . . . . . . | 12,100 | Ending finished goods inventory . . . . . . . . . . | 10,300 |
| Cost of goods sold . . . . . . . | $36,250 | Cost of goods sold . . . . . . | $171,400 |

In the manufacturing company's cost of goods sold section, notice that the inventory of goods for sale is called *finished goods inventory* rather than merchandise inventory. Also note that the *Cost of goods purchased* element of the merchandising company becomes *Cost of goods manufactured (see manufacturing statement)* on the manufacturer's income statement. These differences exist because the merchandising company buys its goods ready for sale, while the manufacturer creates its salable products from raw materials.

The words *see manufacturing statement* refer the income statement reader to a separate schedule. A **manufacturing statement** (see page 893) shows the costs of manufacturing the products produced by a manufacturing company. The records and techniques used in accounting for these costs are the distinguishing characteristics of manufacturing accounting.

## Elements of Manufacturing Costs

In the process of manufacturing its products, a manufacturing company usually incurs a large variety of costs. There are, however, only three different types or classes of manufacturing costs. They are: direct materials, direct labor, and factory overhead.

### Direct Materials

The physical items that enter into and become a part of a finished product are called **direct materials**. For example, the direct materials of a shoe manufacturer might include leather, dye, cloth, nails, and glue. Since direct materials physically become part of the finished product, the cost of direct materials is easily traced to units of product or batches of production. As a result, the direct materials cost of production can be charged directly to units of product or batches of production without using arbitrary or highly judgmental cost allocation procedures.

Direct materials must be distinguished from **indirect materials**, which include factory supplies such as grease and oil for machinery, cleaning fluids, and so on. Indirect materials are used in the manufacturing process but do not enter into or become a part of the finished product. As a result, the cost of indirect materials is not easily traced to specific units or batches of production. Therefore, in accounting for production costs, the cost of indirect materials is treated as factory overhead.

The commodities that a company buys for use in the manufacturing process are called **raw materials**. Usually, raw materials are used in the production process as *direct* materials. When they are purchased, they are debited to an account called Raw Material Purchases. In contrast, when materials are intended for use as *indirect* materials, they are debited to a Factory Supplies account. Occasionally, however, some raw material purchases may be used as factory supplies (indirect materials). When this is done, a special adjusting entry is required to transfer the cost of those materials from Raw Material Purchases to an account called Factory Supplies Used.

### Direct Labor

The labor of those people who work specifically on the materials being converted into finished products is called **direct labor**. The cost of direct labor can be easily associated with and charged to the units or batches of production to which the labor was applied.

In accounting for manufacturing operations, direct labor must be distinguished from indirect labor. **Indirect labor** is used in the manufacturing process but is not applied specifically to the finished product. Therefore, indirect labor is not easily associated with or charged to units or batches of production.

**Illustration 21–1**
**Examples of factory overhead**

Indirect labor
Indirect materials:
- Cleaning supplies
- Machinery oil

Repairs to factory buildings and equipment
Insurance on factory equipment
Taxes on factory equipment
Taxes on raw materials and work in process
Factory utilities:
- Electricity
- Natural gas

Depreciation of plant and equipment
Amortization of patents
Small tools written off
Factory worker's compensation insurance
Payroll taxes on the wages of factory workers

Examples of indirect labor include the labor of supervisors, engineers, and janitors. These people do not work specifically on the manufactured products but do aid in production. The labor provided by these workers makes production possible but is not applied specifically to the finished product. Indirect labor is accounted for as a factory overhead cost.

In a general accounting system, an account called Direct Labor is debited for the wages of those workers who work directly on the product. Likewise, the wages of indirect workers are debited to one or more indirect labor accounts. Also, at the end of each period, the amounts of accrued direct and indirect labor are recorded in the direct and indirect labor accounts by means of adjusting entries. You can see that a manufacturing company's payroll accounting is similar to that of a merchandising company. No new techniques are required. Only the new direct and indirect labor accounts distinguish the payroll accounting of a manufacturer from that of a merchant.

### Factory Overhead

All manufacturing costs other than direct materials and direct labor costs are called **factory overhead**. Factory overhead is also called **manufacturing overhead** or **factory burden**. Examples of factory overhead are shown in Illustration 21–1.

Factory overhead does not include selling and administrative expenses. Selling and administrative expenses are not factory overhead because they are not incurred in the manufacturing process. These costs might be called selling and administrative overhead, but not factory overhead.

All factory overhead costs are accumulated in overhead cost accounts that vary in number and description from company to company. The exact accounts used in each case depend on the nature of the company and the information each company wants. For example, one account called Expired Insurance on Plant Equipment may be maintained, or separate expired insurance accounts may be used for buildings and the different kinds of equipment. Factory overhead costs, such as factory utilities and indirect labor, are recorded and posted to the accounts as they are paid. In addition, items such as depreciation of machinery and expired insurance are recorded in the process of making adjusting entries.

## AS A MATTER OF ETHICS

Three former college classmates got together to have dinner at an expensive restaurant to talk over the past and to share recent news about what they and their companies were doing. The evening was a long one but was entertaining and even fruitful with respect to business ideas.

When the check arrived, it was grabbed by one of the three. Because he was a self-employed entrepreneur, he said, "Here, let me pay it—I'll deduct it as a business expense on my tax return, and it won't cost me as much."

One of the others was the vice president of a medium-size corporation. She snatched the check out of his hand and said, "I'll put this on a company credit card, and it won't cost us anything."

The third, who was a factory manager for a company that sold products to the government, smiled and folded his hands. When his silence got the attention of the other two, he said, "Neither of you understand the system yet. I'll put this on my credit card and call it overhead on a cost-plus contract my company is doing for the government. That way, my company will not only pay for our dinner but we'll make a profit on it."

### Product Costs and Period Costs

A manufacturing company incurs both **period costs** and **product costs.** Product costs are incurred for the purpose of acquiring merchandise or manufacturing finished goods. Since product costs result in the acquisition of assets, they make up the cost of the assets. As Illustration 21–2 shows, product costs are not recorded in expense accounts. Instead, product costs are assigned to units of product and are reported in the balance sheet as inventories. They do not show up in the income statement until the units of product are sold; then product costs appear as cost of goods sold. Product costs include all manufacturing costs—direct materials, direct labor, and factory overhead.

Period costs are closely related to the periods of time in which they are incurred; they are not closely related to the manufacture of products. Thus, period costs are charged to expense in the period they are incurred. Period costs include all selling expenses and general administrative expenses.

### Comparing the Flow of Product Costs for Merchandising and Manufacturing Companies

Illustration 21–3 shows the flow of product costs for a manufacturing company that uses a periodic inventory (general accounting) system. Notice that the costs of raw materials, direct labor, and overhead are recorded as they are incurred throughout the period. Also, some manufacturing costs such as depreciation and accrued wages are recorded with adjusting entries at the end of the period. Then, in the end-of-period closing process, the inventory accounts are brought up-to-date, and the cost of goods sold is established in the Income Summary account. In the rest of this chapter, you will learn more about the accounts shown in Illustration 21–3 and the procedures that are necessary to account for and report these cost flows.

### Accounts Unique to a Manufacturing Company

Because of the nature of its operations, a manufacturing company's ledger normally contains more accounts than does a merchandising company's ledger. However, some of the same accounts are found in the ledgers of both; for example, Cash, Accounts Receivable, Sales, and many selling and administrative expenses. Nevertheless, many accounts are unique to a manufactur-

**Illustration 21–2**
**Product costs and period expenses in the financial statements**

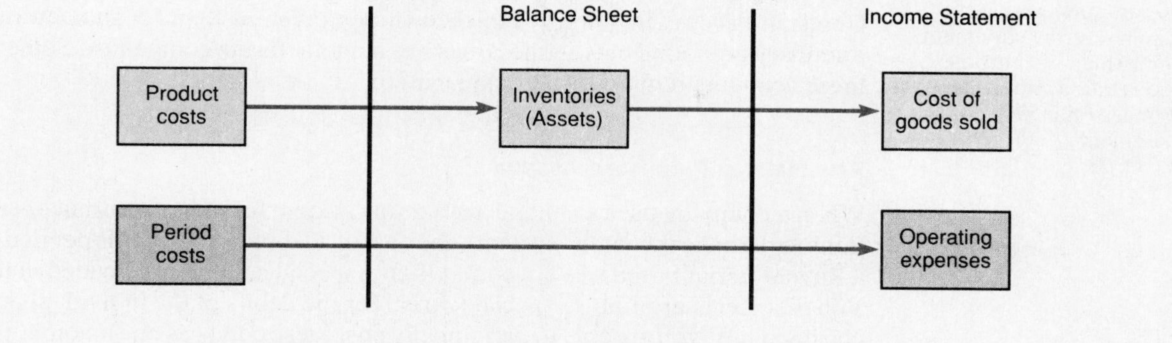


**Illustration 21–3**
**Flow of product costs for a manufacturer that uses a periodic inventory system (assumes no beginning inventories)**

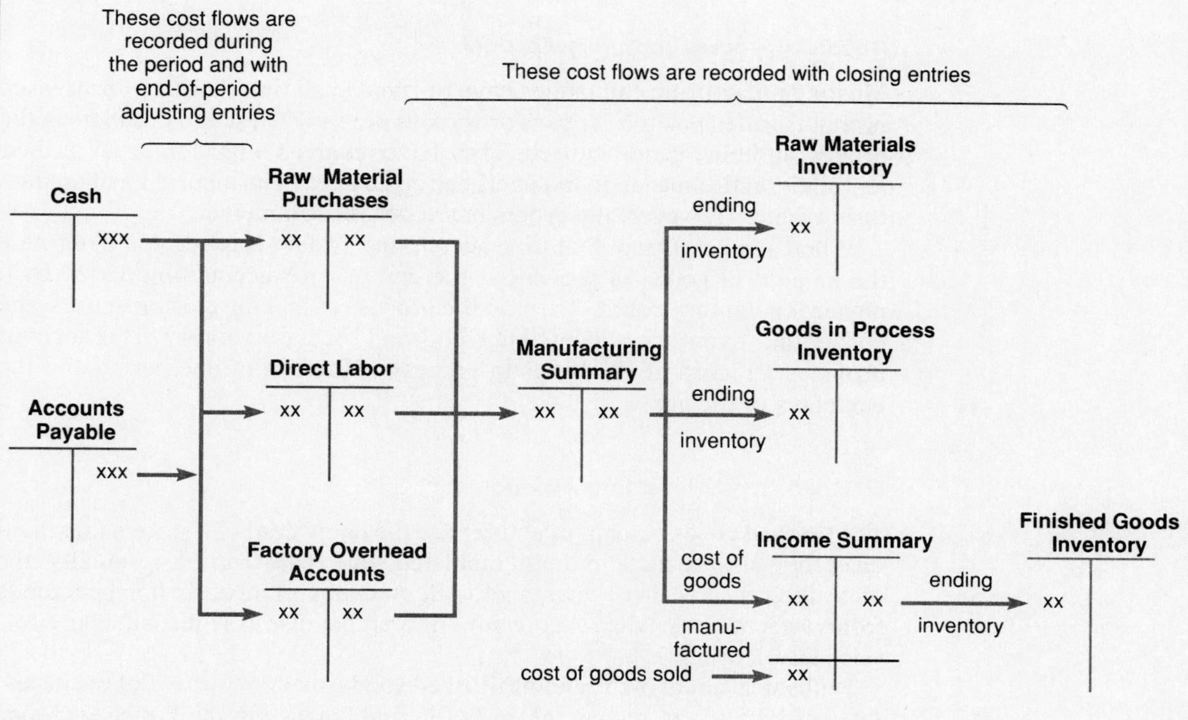

Describe the unique accounts that manufacturing companies use, prepare a manufacturing statement, and explain its purpose and relationship to the primary financial statements.
(L. O. 2)

ing company. For instance, accounts such as Machinery and Equipment, Accumulated Depreciation of Machinery and Equipment, Factory Supplies, Factory Supplies Used, Raw Materials Inventory, Raw Material Purchases, Goods in Process Inventory, Finished Goods Inventory, and Manufacturing Summary are found only in the ledgers of manufacturing companies. Some of these accounts require further explanation.

### Raw Material Purchases Account

When a company uses a general accounting system for manufacturing operations (a periodic inventory system), the cost of all direct materials is debited to a Raw Material Purchases account. Often a special column is provided in the Voucher Register or other special journal for the debits of the individual purchases. Thus, you are able to periodically post these debits as one amount, the column total.

### Raw Materials Inventory Account

When a general accounting system is used, the raw materials on hand at the end of each accounting period are determined by a physical inventory count. Then, when you make closing entries, the cost of this inventory is debited to Raw Materials Inventory. That account is a record of the materials on hand at the end of one period and the beginning of the next.

### Goods in Process Inventory Account

Most manufacturing companies have on hand at all times partially processed products called **goods in process** or **work in process**. These are products in the process of being manufactured. They have received a portion or all of their materials, and some labor and overhead costs have been incurred in manufacturing them. However, the products are not yet completed.

When a general manufacturing accounting system is used, you determine the amount of goods in process at the end of each accounting period by a physical inventory count. Then, in the process of making closing entries, the cost of this inventory is debited to Goods in Process Inventory. This account provides a record of the goods in process at the end of one period and the beginning of the next.

### Finished Goods Inventory Account

The **finished goods** of a manufacturer are the equivalent of a store's merchandise; they are products in their completed state ready for sale. Actually, the only difference is that a manufacturing company creates its finished goods from raw materials, while a store buys its merchandise in a finished, ready-for-sale state.

A physical count of the ending finished goods inventory provides the necessary information to record the end-of-period balance in the Finished Goods Inventory account. This is done in the closing entry process. Like the other

Illustration 21–4

**EXCEL MANUFACTURING COMPANY**
**Income Statement**
**For Year Ended December 31, 1990**

| | | | |
|---|---|---|---|
| Revenue: | | | |
| Sales | | | $310,000 |
| Cost of goods sold: | | | |
| Finished goods inventory, December 31, 1989 | | $ 11,200 | |
| Cost of goods manufactured (see manufacturing statement) | | 170,500 | |
| Goods available for sale | | $181,700 | |
| Finished goods inventory, December 31, 1990 | | 10,300 | |
| Cost of goods sold | | | 171,400 |
| Gross profit | | | $138,600 |
| Operating expenses: | | | |
| Selling expenses: | | | |
| Sales salaries expense | $18,000 | | |
| Advertising expense | 5,500 | | |
| Delivery wages expense | 12,000 | | |
| Shipping supplies expense | 250 | | |
| Delivery equipment insurance expense | 300 | | |
| Depreciation expense, delivery equipment | 2,100 | | |
| Total selling expenses | | $ 38,150 | |
| General and administrative expenses: | | | |
| Office salaries expense | $15,700 | | |
| Miscellaneous general expense | 200 | | |
| Bad debts expense | 1,550 | | |
| Office supplies expense | 100 | | |
| Depreciation expense, office equipment | 200 | | |
| Interest expense | 4,000 | | |
| Total general and administrative expenses | | 21,750 | |
| Total operating expenses | | | 59,900 |
| Income before state and federal income taxes | | | $ 78,700 |
| Less state and federal income taxes | | | 32,600 |
| Net income | | | $ 46,100 |
| Net income per common share (20,000 shares outstanding) | | | $2.31 |

inventory accounts, Finished Goods Inventory provides a record of the finished goods at the end of one period and the beginning of the next.

The three inventories—raw materials, goods in process, and finished goods—are classified as current assets on the balance sheet. Factory supplies is also a current asset.

## Income Statement of a Manufacturing Company

The income statement of a manufacturing company is similar to that of a merchandising company. To see this, compare the income statement of Iowa Sales Incorporated, Illustration 5–1 on page 210, with that of Excel Manufacturing Company, Illustration 21–4. Notice that both types of businesses show similar revenue, selling, and general and administrative expense sections. However, you can see that the cost of goods sold sections are slightly different. In this

Illustration 21–5
**Relationships between overhead items, the manufacturing statement, and the income statement**

| Factory Overhead Items | |
|---|---|
| Indirect labor. | $ x,xxx |
| Factory rent . | x,xxx |
| Other items . | x,xxx |
| Total . . . . . | $30,000 |

→

| Manufacturing Statement | |
|---|---|
| Direct materials . . . . . . . | $ xx,xxx |
| Direct labor . . . . . . . . . | xx,xxx |
| **Overhead** . . . . . . . . . . | **30,000** |
| Total . . . . . . . . . . . . . | $ xx,xxx |
| Beg. goods in process . . . | x,xxx |
| End. goods in process . . . | (x,xxx) |
| **Cost of goods manuf.** . . | **$170,500** |

→

| Income Statement | |
|---|---|
| Sales. . . . . . . . . . . . | $xxx,xxx |
| Beg. finished goods. . . . | $ xx,xxx |
| **Cost of goods manuf.** . | **170,500** |
| End. finished goods. . . . | (xx,xxx) |
| Cost of goods sold . . . . | $xxx,xxx |
| Gross profit . . . . . . . . | $ xx,xxx |
| Expenses . . . . . . . . . | xx,xxx |
| Net income . . . . . . . . | $ xx,xxx |

section, the ''Cost of goods manufactured'' item replaces ''Purchases,'' and finished goods inventories replace merchandise inventories.

Observe the cost of goods sold section of Excel Manufacturing Company's income statement. Only the *total* cost of goods manufactured is shown. You could expand this section to show the detailed costs of the materials, direct labor, and factory overhead entering into the cost of goods manufactured. However, this would make the income statement long and unwieldy. Therefore, the common practice is to show only the total cost of goods manufactured on the income statement and to show the details in a supporting schedule. This schedule is called a **schedule of the cost of goods manufactured** or a **manufacturing statement.** To show how manufacturing costs enter the financial statements, Illustration 21–5 shows the relationship between overhead cost items, the manufacturing statement, and the income statement.

## Manufacturing Statement

The cost elements of manufacturing are direct materials, direct labor, and factory overhead; and a manufacturing statement is normally designed to emphasize these elements. In Illustration 21–6, notice that section 1 of the statement shows the cost of direct materials used. Also observe that the format of the presentation in section 1 is the same as is used on the income statement of a merchandising company to show cost of goods purchased and sold.

Section 2 shows the cost of direct labor used in production, and section 3 shows factory overhead costs. If there are not too many overhead accounts, the balance of each may be listed in this third section, as in Illustration 21–6. However, if overhead accounts are numerous, only the total amount of overhead may be shown. In such cases, the total is supported by a separate schedule of overhead costs.

In section 4, the calculation of costs of goods manufactured is completed. Here the cost of the beginning goods in process inventory is added to the sum

**Illustration 21–6**

**EXCEL MANUFACTURING COMPANY**
**Manufacturing Statement**
**For Year Ended December 31, 1990**

| | | | | |
|---|---|---|---|---|
| 1 | Direct materials: | | | |
| | Raw materials inventory, December 31, 1989 | | $ 8,000 | |
| | Raw material purchases | $85,000 | | |
| | Freight on raw materials purchased | 1,500 | | |
| | Delivered cost of raw materials purchased | | 86,500 | |
| | Raw materials available for use | | $94,500 | |
| | Raw materials inventory, December 31, 1990 | | 9,000 | |
| | Direct materials used | | | $ 85,500 |
| 2 | Direct labor | | | 60,000 |
| 3 | Factory overhead costs: | | | |
| | Indirect labor | | $ 9,000 | |
| | Supervision | | 6,000 | |
| | Factory utilities | | 2,600 | |
| | Repairs and maintenance of machinery | | 2,500 | |
| | Factory taxes | | 1,900 | |
| | Factory supplies used | | 600 | |
| | Factory insurance expired | | 1,100 | |
| | Small tools written off | | 200 | |
| | Depreciation of machinery and equipment | | 3,500 | |
| | Depreciation of factory building | | 1,800 | |
| | Amortization of patents | | 800 | |
| | Total factory overhead costs | | | 30,000 |
| 4 | Total manufacturing costs | | | $175,500 |
| | Add goods in process inventory, December 31, 1989 | | | 2,500 |
| | Total goods in process during the year | | | $178,000 |
| | Deduct goods in process inventory, December 31, 1990 | | | 7,500 |
| | Cost of goods manufactured | | | $170,500 |

of the manufacturing costs to show the total cost of all goods in process during the period. From this total, you subtract the cost of the goods still in process at the end of the period to determine the cost of goods manufactured.

The manufacturing statement is prepared from the Manufacturing Statement columns of a work sheet. The items that appear on the statement are summarized in these columns, and all that is required in setting up the statement is to rearrange the items in the proper statement order. Illustration 21–7 shows the manufacturing work sheet.

## Work Sheet for a Manufacturing Company

Examine Illustration 21–7 and note that there are no Adjusted Trial Balance columns. As we explained in Chapter 5, these columns may be omitted to save time and effort. To understand the work sheet in Illustration 21–7, recall that a work sheet is a tool the accountant uses to—

1. Achieve the effect of adjusting the accounts before entering the adjustments in a journal and posting them to the accounts.

Illustration 21–7

**EXCEL MANUFACTURING COMPANY**
**Manufacturing Work Sheet for Year Ended December 31, 1990**

| Account Titles | Unadjusted Trial Balance Dr. | Unadjusted Trial Balance Cr. | Adjustments Dr. | Adjustments Cr. | Manufacturing Statement Dr. | Manufacturing Statement Cr. | Income Statement Dr. | Income Statement Cr. | Statement of Retained Earnings or Balance Sheet Dr. | Statement of Retained Earnings or Balance Sheet Cr. |
|---|---|---|---|---|---|---|---|---|---|---|
| Cash | 11,000 | | | | | | | | 11,000 | |
| Accounts receivable | 32,000 | | | | | | | | 32,000 | |
| Allowance for doubtful accounts | | 300 | | (*a*) 1,550 | | | | | | 1,850 |
| Raw materials inventory | 8,000 | | | | 8,000 | 9,000 | | | 9,000 | |
| Goods in process inventory | 2,500 | | | | 2,500 | 7,500 | | | 7,500 | |
| Finished goods inventory | 11,200 | | | | | | 11,200 | 10,300 | 10,300 | |
| Office supplies | 150 | | | (*b*) 100 | | | | | 50 | |
| Shipping supplies | 300 | | | (*c*) 250 | | | | | 50 | |
| Factory supplies | 750 | | | (*d*) 500 | | | | | 250 | |
| Prepaid insurance | 1,700 | | | (*e*) 1,400 | | | | | 300 | |
| Small tools | 1,300 | | | (*f*) 200 | | | | | 1,100 | |
| Delivery equipment | 9,000 | | | | | | | | 9,000 | |
| Accumulated depreciation of delivery equipment | | 1,900 | | (*g*) 2,100 | | | | | | 4,000 |
| Office equipment | 1,700 | | | | | | | | 1,700 | |
| Accumulated depreciation of office equipment | | 200 | | (*h*) 200 | | | | | | 400 |
| Machinery | 72,000 | | | | | | | | 72,000 | |
| Accumulated depreciation of machinery | | 3,000 | | (*i*) 3,500 | | | | | | 6,500 |
| Factory building | 90,000 | | | | | | | | 90,000 | |
| Accumulated depreciation of factory building | | 1,500 | | (*j*) 1,800 | | | | | | 3,300 |
| Land | 9,500 | | | | | | | | 9,500 | |
| Patents | 12,000 | | | (*k*) 800 | | | | | 11,200 | |
| Accounts payable | | 14,000 | | | | | | | | 14,000 |
| Long-term notes payable | | 50,000 | | | | | | | | 50,000 |
| Common stock, $5 par value | | 100,000 | | | | | | | | 100,000 |
| Retained earnings | | 3,660 | | | | | | | | 3,660 |
| Sales | | 310,000 | | | | | | 310,000 | | |
| Raw material purchases | 85,100 | | | (*d*) 100 | 85,000 | | | | | |
| Freight on raw materials | 1,500 | | | | 1,500 | | | | | |
| Direct labor | 59,600 | | (*l*) 400 | | 60,000 | | | | | |
| Indirect labor | 8,940 | | (*l*) 60 | | 9,000 | | | | | |

| | | | | | | | | | | |
|---|---|---|---|---|---|---|---|---|---|---|
| Supervision | 6,000 | | | | 6,000 | | | | | |
| Factory utilities | 2,600 | | | | 2,600 | | | | | |
| Repairs and maintenance of machinery | 2,500 | | | | 2,500 | | | | | |
| Factory taxes | 1,900 | | | | 1,900 | | | | | |
| Sales salaries expense | 18,000 | | | | | | 18,000 | | | |
| Advertising expense | 5,500 | | | | | | 5,500 | | | |
| Delivery wages expense | 11,920 | | (*l*) 80 | | | | 12,000 | | | |
| Office salaries expense | 15,700 | | | | | | 15,700 | | | |
| Miscellaneous general expense | 200 | | | | | | 200 | | | |
| Interest expense | 2,000 | | (*m*) 2,000 | | | | 4,000 | | | |
| | 484,560 | 484,560 | | | | | | | | |
| Bad debts expense | | | (*a*) 1,550 | | | | 1,550 | | | |
| Office supplies expense | | | (*b*) 100 | | | | 100 | | | |
| Shipping supplies expense | | | (*c*) 250 | | | | 250 | | | |
| Factory supplies used | | | (*d*) 600 | | 600 | | | | | |
| Factory insurance expired | | | (*e*) 1,100 | | 1,100 | | | | | |
| Delivery equipment insurance expense | | | (*e*) 300 | | | | 300 | | | |
| Small tools written off | | | (*f*) 200 | | 200 | | | | | |
| Depreciation expense, delivery equipment | | | (*g*) 2,100 | | | | 2,100 | | | |
| Depreciation expense, office equipment | | | (*h*) 200 | | | | 200 | | | |
| Depreciation of machinery | | | (*i*) 3,500 | | 3,500 | | | | | |
| Depreciation of factory building | | | (*j*) 1,800 | | 1,800 | | | | | |
| Amortization of patents | | | (*k*) 800 | | 800 | | | | | |
| Accrued wages payable | | | | (*l*) 540 | | | | | | 540 |
| Interest payable | | | | (*m*) 2,000 | | | | | | 2,000 |
| State and federal income taxes expense | | | (*n*) 32,600 | | | | 32,600 | | | |
| State and federal income taxes payable | | | | (*n*) 32,600 | | | | | | 32,600 |
| | | | 47,640 | 47,640 | 187,000 | 16,500 | | | | |
| Cost of goods manufactured to Income Statement columns | | | | | | 170,500 | 170,500 | | | |
| | | | | | 187,000 | 187,000 | 274,200 | 320,300 | 264,950 | 218,850 |
| Net income | | | | | | | 46,100 | | | 46,100 |
| | | | | | | | 320,300 | 320,300 | 264,950 | 264,950 |

Prepare a work sheet and the financial statements for a manufacturing company. (L. O. 3)

2. Sort the adjusted account balances into columns according to the financial statement on which they appear.
3. Calculate and confirm the mathematical accuracy of the net income.

### Comparing the Work Sheets of Manufacturing and Merchandising Companies

A primary difference between the work sheet of a manufacturing company and that of a merchandising company is an additional set of columns. The adjustments are made in the same way on both kinds of work sheets. Also, the mathematical accuracy of the net income is confirmed in the same way. However, remember that a manufacturing company prepares an additional schedule or statement (the manufacturing statement). Therefore, a manufacturing company's work sheet has two additional columns into which you must sort the items that appear on the manufacturing statement.

### Preparing a Manufacturing Company's Work Sheet

To prepare a work sheet for a manufacturing company, you first enter the unadjusted account balances in the Trial Balance columns. Next, you enter the appropriate adjustments in the Adjustments columns.

**Adjustments Information for Excel Manufacturing Company.** The adjustments information for the work sheet shown in Illustration 21–7 is as follows:

*a.* Bad debts expense is estimated to be 0.5% of sales, or $1,550.
*b.* Office supplies used was $100.
*c.* Shipping supplies used was $250.
*d.* Factory supplies used was $500. In addition, raw materials that cost $100 were used as factory supplies.
*e.* Expired insurance on factory was $1,100; and expired insurance on the delivery equipment was $300.
*f.* The small tools inventory shows $1,100 of usable small tools on hand. As is often done, Excel Company accounts for small hand tools in the same manner as supplies.
*g.* Depreciation of delivery equipment was $2,100.
*h.* Depreciation of office equipment was $200.
*i.* Depreciation of factory machinery was $3,500.
*j.* Depreciation of factory building was $1,800.
*k.* Yearly amortization of 1/17 of the cost of patents was $800.
*l.* At year-end, accrued wages were: direct labor, $400; indirect labor, $60; and delivery wages $80. All other employees are paid monthly on the last day of each month.
*m.* Interest expense results from the long-term note payable and $2,000, which is one-half year's interest, has accrued on the notes.
*n.* State and federal income taxes expense amounted to $32,600.

**Sorting Adjusted Amounts to the Proper Financial Statement Columns.** After the adjustments are completed, you must combine the amounts in the Unadjusted Trial Balance columns with the amounts in the Adjustments columns and sort the resulting amounts to the proper statement columns. Items that go in the Manufacturing Statement columns include raw materials, goods in process, direct labor, and all factory overhead items. Items that go in the Income Statement columns include the beginning finished goods inventory plus the revenue, selling, general and administrative, and financial expense items. Remember that items which appear in either the statement of retained earnings or the balance sheet go in the final two columns.

**Entering the Ending Inventory Amounts.** After the trial balance items with their adjustments are sorted to the proper statement columns, the ending inventory amounts are entered on the work sheet. Since the ending raw materials and goods in process inventories are subtracted on the manufacturing statement, they are entered in the Manufacturing Statement Credit column. And since these ending inventory balances are assets, they also must be entered in the final Debit column as balance sheet items.

Note in Illustration 21–7 that the ending raw materials inventory is assumed to be $9,000, and the ending work in process inventory is assumed to be $7,500. These amounts were determined on the basis of a physical inventory taken at the end of the year.

The ending finished goods inventory is also determined on the basis of a physical inventory taken at the end of the year. In Illustration 21–7, Excel Manufacturing Company's ending finished goods inventory of $10,300 is entered in the Income Statement Credit column and in the final Debit column as an asset to be reported on the balance sheet. You will note that this treatment of the finished goods inventory on the work sheet is exactly the same as is done for the ending merchandise inventory of a merchandising company.

After the ending inventories are entered on the work sheet, you total and balance the Manufacturing Statement columns. The amount necessary to balance these columns is the cost of the goods manufactured; it must be entered in the Manufacturing Statement Credit column to make the two columns equal. Also, it is entered in the Income Statement Debit column, the same column in which the balance of the Purchases account of a merchant is entered. After this, you complete the work sheet in the usual manner.

## Preparing the Financial Statements

After it is completed, the manufacturing work sheet is used to prepare the statements and to make adjusting and closing entries. The manufacturing statement is prepared from the information in the work sheet's Manufacturing Statement columns, the income statement from the information in the Income Statement columns, and the statement of retained earnings and balance sheet from information in the final two columns. After this, the adjusting and closing entries are entered in the journal and posted.

## Adjusting Entries

Prepare the adjusting and closing entries for a manufacturing company. (L. O. 4)

The adjusting entries of a manufacturing company are prepared in the same way as those of a merchandising company. For each adjustment that appears in the work sheet Adjustments columns, you must record an adjusting entry in the General Journal.

In the case of Excel Manufacturing Company, the only adjustment that may require further attention is adjustment (*d*) as described on page 896 (see also Illustration 21–7). At the time they were purchased, most of the factory supplies were debited to a Factory Supplies account. The information for adjustment (*d*) states that $500 of these supplies were used. However, the factory also used $100 of its raw materials as factory supplies. Therefore, the adjusting entry to record all of the factory supplies used is:

| | | | | |
|---|---|---|---|---|
| Dec. | 31 | Factory Supplies Used | 600.00 | |
| | | Factory Supplies | | 500.00 |
| | | Raw Material Purchases | | 100.00 |
| | | To record factory supplies used. | | |

After Raw Material Purchases is credited for $100, the remaining $85,000 is correctly shown on the manufacturing statement as part of the direct materials cost calculation. (See Illustration 21–6.)

## Closing Entries

The account balances that are used to calculate cost of goods manufactured reflect the manufacturing costs for the accounting period and must be closed at the end of the period. Normally, they are closed to a Manufacturing Summary account, which is in turn closed to the Income Summary account.

The entries to close the manufacturing accounts of Excel Manufacturing Company are as follows:

| | | | | |
|---|---|---|---|---|
| Dec. | 31 | Manufacturing Summary | 187,000.00 | |
| | | Raw Materials Inventory | | 8,000.00 |
| | | Goods in Process Inventory | | 2,500.00 |
| | | Raw Material Purchases | | 85,000.00 |
| | | Freight on Raw Materials | | 1,500.00 |
| | | Direct Labor | | 60,000.00 |
| | | Indirect Labor | | 9,000.00 |
| | | Supervision | | 6,000.00 |
| | | Factory Utilities | | 2,600.00 |
| | | Repairs and Maintenance of Machinery | | 2,500.00 |
| | | Factory Taxes | | 1,900.00 |
| | | Factory Supplies Used | | 600.00 |
| | | Factory Insurance Expired | | 1,100.00 |
| | | Small Tools Written Off | | 200.00 |
| | | Depreciation of Machinery | | 3,500.00 |
| | | Depreciation of Building | | 1,800.00 |
| | | Amortization of Patents | | 800.00 |
| | | To close those manufacturing accounts having debit balances. | | |
| | 31 | Raw Materials Inventory | 9,000.00 | |
| | | Goods in Process Inventory | 7,500.00 | |
| | | Manufacturing Summary | | 16,500.00 |
| | | To record the ending raw materials and goods in process inventories and to remove their balances from the Manufacturing Summary account. | | |

The above entries are taken from the information in the Manufacturing Statement columns of the Illustration 21–7 work sheet. Compare the first entry with the information shown in the Manufacturing Statement Debit column. Note how the debit to the Manufacturing Summary account is taken from the column total, and how each account with a balance in the column is credited to close it. Also observe that the second entry has the effect of subtracting the ending raw materials and goods in process inventories from the manufacturing costs shown in the work sheet's Debit column.

The effect of the two entries is to cause the Manufacturing Summary account to have a debit balance equal to the $170,500 cost of goods manufactured.

The $170,500 balance in Manufacturing Summary is closed to Income Summary along with the other cost and expense accounts that have balances in the Income Statement Debit column. This closing entry for Excel Manufacturing Company is shown below. Especially note the last account credited in the entry.

| | | | | |
|---|---|---|---|---|
| Dec. | 31 | Income Summary | 274,200.00 | |
| | | Finished Goods Inventory | | 11,200.00 |
| | | Sales Salaries Expense | | 18,000.00 |
| | | Advertising Expense | | 5,500.00 |
| | | Delivery Wages Expense | | 12,000.00 |
| | | Office Salaries Expense | | 15,700.00 |
| | | Miscellaneous General Expense | | 200.00 |
| | | Interest Expense | | 4,000.00 |
| | | Bad Debts Expense | | 1,550.00 |
| | | Office Supplies Expense | | 100.00 |
| | | Shipping Supplies Expense | | 250.00 |
| | | Delivery Equipment Insurance Expense | | 300.00 |
| | | Depreciation Expense, Delivery Equipment | | 2,100.00 |
| | | Depreciation Expense, Office Equipment | | 200.00 |
| | | State and Federal Income Taxes Expense | | 32,600.00 |
| | | Manufacturing Summary | | 170,500.00 |
| | | To close the income statement accounts having debit balances. | | |

After the foregoing entry, the remainder of the income statement accounts of Illustration 21–7 are closed as follows:

| | | | | |
|---|---|---|---|---|
| Dec. | 31 | Finished Goods Inventory | 10,300.00 | |
| | | Sales | 310,000.00 | |
| | | Income Summary | | 320,300.00 |
| | | To close the Sales account and to record the ending finished goods inventory. | | |
| | 31 | Income Summary | 46,100.00 | |
| | | Retained Earnings | | 46,100.00 |
| | | To close the Income Summary account. | | |

## Inventory Valuation Problems of a Manufacturer

With a general accounting system for manufacturing operations, the physical count of inventories must result in separate valuations for the end-of-period amounts of raw materials, goods in process, and finished goods. There are no particular problems in obtaining a valuation for raw materials because these items are in the same form they were in when they were purchased. However,

Explain the procedures for assigning costs to the different manufacturing inventories.
(L. O. 5)

placing valuations on goods in process and finished goods is not as easy. These goods consist of direct materials to which certain amounts of labor and overhead have been added. They are not in the same form in which they were purchased. Therefore, the inventory values of these items are not simply the amounts that were paid to a supplier. Instead, their inventory values must be calculated by adding together estimates of the direct materials, direct labor, and factory overhead costs that were applied to each item.

### Estimating Direct Material Costs in the Ending Inventories

Estimating the cost of direct materials that were applied to a goods in process or finished goods item is usually not too difficult. After the partially finished units of product in the work in process inventory are counted, a responsible plant official normally can estimate how much direct materials have been used in each unit and then calculate the cost of direct materials in the inventory. The same process is used to calculate the cost of direct materials in the finished goods inventory.

### Estimating Direct Labor Costs in the Ending Inventories

The process of estimating the direct labor costs in the ending goods in process and finished goods inventories is essentially the same as for direct materials. A responsible plant official must estimate the percentage of completion of the units in the goods in process inventory and then calculate the direct labor cost that was applied to those units. A similar estimate must be made of the direct labor cost that was applied to the units in the finished goods inventory.

### Estimating Factory Overhead Costs in the Ending Inventories

Factory overhead consists of many items, none of which is directly associated with specific units or batches of production. As a result, estimating factory overhead costs in the ending inventories presents a difficult problem. This problem is often solved by assuming that factory overhead costs are closely related to direct labor costs. Usually, this is a reasonable approach. There is often a close relation between direct labor costs and such indirect costs as supervision, factory utilities, repairs, and so forth. When this relation is used to apply overhead costs, you assume that the relation of overhead costs to the direct labor costs in each unit of goods in process and finished goods is the same as the relation between total factory overhead costs and total direct labor costs for the accounting period.

### Estimating the Ending Inventory Costs of Excel Manufacturing Company

For example, examine the manufacturing statement in Illustration 21–6 and you will see that Excel Manufacturing Company's total direct labor costs were \$60,000 and its overhead costs were \$30,000. In other words, during the year the company incurred in the production of all its products \$2 of direct labor for each \$1 of factory overhead costs; overhead costs were 50% of direct labor cost.

$$\frac{\text{Overhead costs, \$30,000}}{\text{Direct labor, \$60,000}} \times 100 = 50\%$$

Therefore, in estimating the overhead applicable to a goods in process or finished goods item, Excel Manufacturing Company may assume that this 50% overhead rate applies. Since total overhead costs were 50% of total labor costs, it would appear reasonable to assume that this relationship applies to each goods in process and finished goods item.

Recall from Illustration 21–7 that the ending goods in process inventory was $7,500, and the ending finished goods inventory was $10,300. To see how these amounts might have been determined, assume that a physical count of the ending inventories showed that there were 1,000 partially finished units in the goods in process inventory and 800 units in the finished goods inventory. The costs of the ending inventories were determined as follows:

| | Goods in Process | | | Finished Goods | | |
|---|---|---|---|---|---|---|
| | Cost per Unit | Units of Product | Total Cost | Cost per Unit | Units of Product | Total Cost |
| Direct materials | $3.75 | 1,000 | $3,750 | $5.00 | 800 | $ 4,000 |
| Direct labor | 2.50 | 1,000 | 2,500 | 5.25 | 800 | 4,200 |
| Factory overhead—50% of direct labor | 1.25 | 1,000 | 1,250 | 2.625 | 800 | 2,100 |
| | | | $7,500 | | | $10,300 |

To summarize, the per unit costs for direct materials and direct labor were estimated by appropriate plant officials. The factory overhead cost per unit was calculated as 50% of the direct labor cost. And the number of units of product in each inventory was determined by physically counting the units on hand.

## Summary of the Chapter in Terms of Learning Objectives

**1.** The only difference in the financial statements of manufacturers and merchandisers is in the descriptions of inventories and cost of goods sold. The manufacturer shows cost of goods manufactured instead of the cost of goods purchased and may describe its inventory as finished goods instead of as merchandise. A general accounting system for manufacturing operations is a periodic inventory system. Physical counts of the ending raw materials, goods in process, and finished goods are required. The costs of direct materials, direct labor, and factory overhead are combined to determine the financial statement valuations of goods in process, finished goods, and cost of goods sold.

**2.** Unique accounts of manufacturers include Raw Materials Purchases, Raw Materials Inventory, Goods in Process Inventory, Finished Goods Inventory, Manufacturing Summary, and several different accounts in which are recorded the costs of factory overhead. The manufacturing statement is a supporting schedule that shows the costs of direct materials, direct labor, and factory overhead that were incurred during the period. On the statement, these costs are adjusted for changes in the inventories to determine the cost of goods manufactured during the period.

**3.** The work sheet for a manufacturer includes two additional columns into which you sort the items that appear on the manufacturing statement. The cost of goods manufactured is determined in these columns and is extended to the Income Statement Debit column. Then, the financial statement information in the remaining columns is generated in the same manner as you would complete a merchandising company's work sheet.

**4.** Adjusting entries for a manufacturer include adjustments related to manufacturing costs as well as the typical revenue and expense adjustments for prepaid and accrued items. In the closing entry process, all items related to manufacturing costs are closed to a Manufacturing Summary account. This account is then closed with the expense accounts to Income Summary.

**5.** When a manufacturer determines the costs of its ending inventories, the raw materials and direct labor costs allocated to goods in process and finished goods are estimated by a responsible plant official. To determine the overhead cost allocated to goods in process and finished goods, the total overhead cost is first expressed as a percentage of total direct labor cost. Then, the overhead cost in each inventory is determined by multiplying this percentage by the direct labor cost allocated to each inventory.

## Demonstration Problem

The following information for the year ended December 31, 1990, was taken from the accounting records of Froh Corporation. Use the information to prepare a schedule of factory overhead costs, a manufacturing statement (in which overhead is shown in total), and an income statement.

| | |
|---|---|
| Advertising expense | $ 85,000 |
| Amortization of patents | 16,000 |
| Bad debts expense | 28,000 |
| Depreciation of production machinery | 78,000 |
| Depreciation of factory building | 133,000 |
| Depreciation of office equipment | 37,000 |
| Direct labor | 250,000 |
| Factory insurance | 62,000 |
| Factory utilities | 115,000 |
| Repairs and maintenance of machinery | 31,000 |
| Factory supervision | 74,000 |
| Factory supplies used | 21,000 |
| Taxes on production machinery | 14,000 |
| Finished goods inventory, December 31, 1990 | 12,500 |
| Finished goods inventory, December 31, 1989 | 15,000 |
| Goods in process inventory, December 31, 1990 | 9,000 |
| Goods in process inventory, December 31, 1989 | 8,000 |
| Income tax expense | 53,400 |
| Indirect labor | 26,000 |
| Insurance expense | 55,000 |
| Interest expense | 25,000 |
| Raw materials inventory, December 31, 1990 | 78,000 |
| Raw materials inventory, December 31, 1989 | 60,000 |
| Raw materials purchases | 313,000 |
| Salaries expense | 150,000 |
| Sales | 1,630,000 |

## Solution to Demonstration Problem

**FROH CORPORATION**
**Schedule of Factory Overhead Costs**
**For Year Ended December 31, 1990**

| | |
|---|---|
| Amortization of patents | $ 16,000 |
| Depreciation of production machinery | 78,000 |
| Depreciation of factory building | 133,000 |
| Factory insurance | 62,000 |
| Factory utilities | 115,000 |
| Repairs and maintenance of machinery | 31,000 |
| Factory supervision | 74,000 |
| Factory supplies used | 21,000 |
| Taxes on production machinery | 14,000 |
| Indirect labor | 26,000 |
| Total factory overhead | $570,000 |

**FROH CORPORATION**
**Manufacturing Statement**
**For Year Ended December 31, 1990**

| | | |
|---|---|---|
| Direct materials: | | |
| Raw materials inventory, December 31, 1989 | $ 60,000 | |
| Raw materials purchases | 313,000 | |
| Raw materials available for use | $ 373,000 | |
| Raw materials inventory, December 31, 1990 | 78,000 | |
| Direct materials used | | $ 295,000 |
| Direct labor | | 250,000 |
| Factory overhead costs | | 570,000 |
| Total manufacturing costs | | $1,115,000 |
| Goods in process inventory, December 31, 1989 | | 8,000 |
| Total goods in process | | $1,123,000 |
| Goods in process inventory, December 31, 1990 | | 9,000 |
| Cost of goods manufactured | | $1,114,000 |

**FROH CORPORATION**
**Income Statement**
**For Year Ended December 31, 1990**

| | | |
|---|---|---|
| Sales | | $1,630,000 |
| Cost of goods sold: | | |
| Finished goods inventory, December 31, 1989 | $ 15,000 | |
| Cost of goods manufactured | 1,114,000 | |
| Goods available for sale | $1,129,000 | |
| Finished goods inventory, December 31, 1990 | 12,500 | |
| Cost of goods sold | | 1,116,500 |
| Gross profit | | $ 513,500 |
| Operating expenses: | | |
| Advertising expense | $ 85,000 | |
| Bad debts expense | 28,000 | |
| Depreciation of office equipment | 37,000 | |
| Insurance expense | 55,000 | |
| Interest expense | 25,000 | |
| Salaries expense | 150,000 | |
| Total operating expenses | | 380,000 |
| Income before income taxes | | $ 133,500 |
| Income tax expense | | 53,400 |
| Net income | | $ 80,100 |

## Glossary

Define or explain the words and phrases listed in the chapter Glossary. (L. O. 6)

**Cost accounting system** an accounting system that uses perpetual inventories in accounting for manufacturing operations and that is designed to assist management's efforts to control costs. p. 885

**Direct labor** labor the cost of which can be easily associated with and charged to units or batches of production because the labor is of those employees who work specifically on the conversion of raw materials into finished products. pp. 886–87

**Direct materials** physical items the cost of which is easily traced to units of product or batches of production because the items enter into and become a part of a finished product. p. 886

**Factory burden** a synonym for *factory overhead* or *manufacturing overhead*. p. 887

**Factory overhead** all manufacturing costs other than for direct materials and direct labor. p. 887

**Finished goods** products that a company manufactures for sale and which have completed the manufacturing process and are ready for sale. p. 890

**General accounting system for manufacturers** an accounting system that uses periodic inventories to determine the total cost of all goods manufactured during each accounting period. p. 885

**Goods in process** products in the process of being manufactured that have received a portion or all of their materials and have had some labor and overhead applied but that are not completed. p. 890

**Indirect labor** labor the cost of which cannot be easily associated with specific units of product because the labor is by employees who, although contributing to production, do not work specifically on the manufactured products. pp. 886–87

**Indirect materials** commodities used in production and accounted for as factory overhead because they do not enter into or become a part of the finished product and, therefore, are not easily traced to specific units or batches of production. p. 886

**Manufacturing overhead** a synonym for *factory overhead* or *factory burden*. p. 887

**Manufacturing statement** a schedule that shows the costs incurred to manufacture a product or products during a period. pp. 886, 892–93

**Period costs** costs such as selling and general administrative expenses that are charged to expense in the period incurred because they are not related to the purchase of merchandise or the manufacture of finished goods. p. 888

**Product costs** costs incurred to acquire merchandise or manufacture finished goods and that, therefore, are charged to inventory accounts until the goods are sold, at which time they are reported as cost of goods sold. p. 888

**Raw materials** commodities that are purchased for use in the manufacturing process as direct materials but that are sometimes used as indirect materials. p. 886

**Schedule of the cost of goods manufactured** a synonym for *manufacturing statement*. pp. 892–93

**Work in process** a synonym for *goods in process*. p. 890

## Objective Review

Answers to the following questions are listed in Appendix I at the end of the book. Be sure that you decide which is the one best answer to each question *before* you check the answers in the appendix.

1. Which of the following statements is true with regard to the procedures used in a general accounting system for a manufacturing company?
   *a.* Perpetual inventory records are maintained for raw materials and goods in process but not for finished goods.
   *b.* Labor that contributes to production but that is not easily identified with units of product is accounted for as factory overhead.
   *c.* Examples of direct labor include the labor of supervisors and engineers.
   *d.* All manufacturing costs other than direct materials are called factory overhead.
   *e.* Product costs are recorded in expense accounts.
2. A manufacturing statement:
   *a.* Shows the elements of manufacturing costs incurred during the period and calculates the cost of goods sold during the period.
   *b.* Shows the changes that occurred during the period in raw materials inventory, goods in process inventory, and finished goods inventory.
   *c.* Shows the elements of manufacturing costs incurred during the period and calculates the cost of goods manufactured during the period.
   *d.* Shows all of the cost items that make up the operating expenses incurred during the period.
   *e.* None of the above is correct.
3. On a work sheet for a manufacturing company:
   *a.* Raw material purchases appear in the Income Statement Debit column.
   *b.* The cost of goods manufactured appears in the Manufacturing Statement Credit column and the Income Statement Debit column.
   *c.* All of the factory overhead costs appear in the Manufacturing Statement Credit column.
   *d.* Ending finished goods inventory appears in the Manufacturing Statement Credit column.
   *e.* Raw material purchases appear in the Statement of Retained Earnings or Balance Sheet Debit column.
4. In preparing the closing entries for a manufacturing company that uses a periodic inventory system:
   *a.* The beginning balance of Finished Goods Inventory is credited to Finished Goods Inventory and closed to Income Summary.

*b.* The beginning balance of Finished Goods Inventory plus the cost of goods completed during the period is debited to Finished Goods Inventory and credited to Income Summary.
*c.* The beginning balances of Raw Materials Inventory, Goods in Process Inventory, and Finished Goods Inventory are credited and closed to Manufacturing Summary.
*d.* All manufacturing overhead accounts are credited and closed to Manufacturing Summary.
*e.* Both (*a*) and (*d*) are correct.

5. During the annual accounting period, total manufacturing overhead was $70,000, and total direct labor was $175,000. If the ending balance of Finished Goods Inventory was $38,000, which included $10,000 of direct materials, the amount of direct labor included in the ending finished goods inventory was:
*a.* $ 8,000.
*b.* $10,000.
*c.* $20,000.
*d.* $28,000.
*e.* Cannot be determined from information given.

## Questions for Class Discussion

1. What is the difference between a general accounting system for manufacturers and a cost accounting system?
2. What is the basic difference between a manufacturing company and a merchandising company?
3. Manufacturing cost consist of three elements. What are they?
4. How does the income statement of a manufacturing company differ from the income statement of a merchandising company?
5. What is the difference between direct materials and indirect materials?
6. What is the difference between raw materials and direct materials?
7. What is the difference between direct labor and indirect labor?
8. How is the cost of indirect labor charged to production?
9. Factory overhead costs include a variety of items. List several examples of factory overhead costs.
10. What is the difference between factory overhead and selling or administrative expenses?
11. If a general accounting system is used, when in the accounting cycle are the costs of raw material purchases, direct labor, and factory overhead allocated to cost of goods sold and to the ending raw materials, goods in process, and finished goods inventories?
12. Name several accounts that are often found in the ledgers of both manufacturing and merchandising companies. Name several accounts that are found only in the ledgers of manufacturing companies.
13. What are three inventory accounts that appear in the ledger of a manufacturing company?

14. How are the beginning and ending inventories of raw materials, goods in process, and finished goods extended to or entered in the financial statement columns of a work sheet?
15. Which inventories of a manufacturing company receive the same work sheet treatment as the merchandise inventories of a merchandising company?
16. Which inventories of a manufacturing company appear on its manufacturing statement? Which appear on the income statement?
17. What accounts are summarized in the Manufacturing Summary account? What accounts are summarized in the Income Summary account?
18. What are the three manufacturing cost elements emphasized on the manufacturing statement?
19. What account balances are carried into the Manufacturing Statement columns of the manufacturing work sheet? What account balances are carried into the Income Statement columns? What account balances are carried into the Statement of Retained Earnings or Balance Sheet columns?
20. Why is the cost of goods manufactured entered in the Manufacturing Statement Credit column of a work sheet and again in the Income Statement Debit columns?
21. May prices paid to a supplier for items of raw materials be used to determine the balance sheet valuation of the items in the raw materials inventory? Why? Do such prices also determine the balance sheet valuations of the goods in process and finished goods inventories? Why?
22. Republic Company used an overhead rate of 60% of direct labor cost to apply overhead to the items of its goods in process inventory. If the manufacturing statement of the company showed total overhead costs of $156,000, how much direct labor did it show?

## Exercises

**Exercise 21–1**
**Raw materials used as indirect materials**
(L. O. 1)

This year Horizon Corporation began manufacturing operations and purchased on account $35,000 of raw materials. These materials included paint that is applied to the units being produced as they are finished. During the year, $205 of the paint was used to repaint some of the tools used in the factory. Prepare general journal entries to record the purchase of raw materials and the use of paint to repaint tools.

**Exercise 21–2**
**Classifying product costs and period costs**
(L. O. 1)

The costs listed below and on the next page were incurred by a manufacturing company. Indicate which of these costs should be classified as product costs and which should be classified as period costs.

| | |
|---|---|
| Advertising | Depreciation of factory building |
| Amortization of patents | Direct materials used |
| Bad debts expense | Insurance on factory workers |

Interest on long-term debt
Office salaries
Repairs to machinery
Sales salaries
Small tools written off
State and federal income taxes

**Exercise 21–3**
**Preparing a manufacturing statement**
(L. O. 2)

After Florian Corporation posted its adjusting entries on December 31, 1990, the general ledger included the following account balances. (Some accounts in the general ledger have not been listed.)

| | |
|---|---|
| Sales | $950,000 |
| Raw materials inventory, January 1, 1990 | 52,000 |
| Goods in process inventory, January 1, 1990 | 60,700 |
| Finished goods inventory, January 1, 1990 | 76,500 |
| Raw material purchases | 153,100 |
| Direct labor | 182,200 |
| Factory supplies used | 18,400 |
| Indirect labor | 44,800 |
| Machinery repairs | 8,000 |
| Rent on factory building | 66,000 |
| Selling expenses, controlling | 115,200 |
| Administrative expenses, controlling | 134,600 |

On December 31, 1990, the inventories of Florian Corporation were determined to be:

| | |
|---|---|
| Raw materials inventory | $47,500 |
| Goods in process inventory | 42,200 |
| Finished goods inventory | 71,300 |

Given the above information, prepare a manufacturing statement for Florian Corporation.

**Exercise 21–4**
**Preparing a manufacturing company's income statement**
(L. O. 3)

Use the information provided in Exercise 21–3 and prepare an income statement for Florian Corporation.

**Exercise 21–5**
**Closing entries for a manufacturing company**
(L. O. 4)

Use the information provided in Exercise 21–3 and prepare closing entries for Florian Corporation.

**Exercise 21–6**
**Calculating the cost of goods manufactured**
(L. O. 2)

The following information was taken from the accounting records of Dunlop Company and Elmore Company:

| | Dunlop Company | Elmore Company |
|---|---|---|
| Ending finished goods inventory . . . . | $ 360 | $1,140 |
| Direct labor . . . . . . . . . . . . . . . | 1,800 | 2,890 |
| Factory electricity . . . . . . . . . . . | 240 | 480 |
| Ending raw materials inventory . . . . . . | 420 | 540 |
| Machinery repairs . . . . . . . . . . . . | 240 | 480 |
| Raw material purchases . . . . . . . . . | 2,040 | 2,640 |
| Beginning goods in process inventory . . | 600 | 1,020 |
| Sales salaries . . . . . . . . . . . . . . | 720 | 1,080 |
| Beginning finished goods inventory . . . | 600 | 840 |
| Indirect labor . . . . . . . . . . . . . | 480 | 960 |
| Depreciation of factory . . . . . . . . . | 540 | 900 |
| Beginning raw materials inventory . . . | 780 | 600 |
| General and administrative expenses . . | 2,100 | 2,280 |
| Factory supplies used . . . . . . . . . . | 180 | 240 |
| Ending goods in process inventory . . . . | 660 | 780 |

Calculate the cost of goods manufactured and the cost of goods sold for each company.

**Exercise 21–7**
**Allocating costs to ending inventories**
(L. O. 5)

Hopper Company's ending goods in process inventory included 800 units of product; its finished goods inventory included 1,600 units of product. Factory officials determined that goods in process included direct materials cost of $6.30 per unit and direct labor cost of $8.60. Finished goods units were estimated to have $6.45 of direct materials and $10.60 of direct labor. During the period, the company incurred $94,100 of direct labor and $70,600 of factory overhead. Factory overhead is assumed to be closely related to direct labor. Calculate the total cost of each ending inventory. Also calculate how much direct labor and how much factory overhead will be included in cost of goods sold.

**Exercise 21–8**
**Closing entries for a manufacturing company**
(L. O. 4)

Guzman Corporation's accounting system uses highly summarized controlling accounts. The following account balances and ending inventories on December 31, 1990, were taken from the company's accounting records:

| | |
|---|---|
| Sales . . . . . . . . . . . . . . . . . . . . . . . | $176,000 |
| Raw material purchases . . . . . . . . . . . . . | 28,000 |
| Direct labor . . . . . . . . . . . . . . . . . . . | 41,300 |
| Factory overhead . . . . . . . . . . . . . . . . | 34,000 |
| Selling expenses, controlling . . . . . . . . . . | 19,100 |
| General and administrative expenses, controlling . . | 17,400 |
| State and federal income taxes . . . . . . . . . | 19,800 |
| Raw materials inventory . . . . . . . . . . . . | 5,200 |
| Goods in process inventory . . . . . . . . . . . | 7,100 |
| Finished goods inventory . . . . . . . . . . . . | 4,300 |
| Ending inventories: | |
| Raw materials . . . . . . . . . . . . . . . . . | 8,100 |
| Goods in process . . . . . . . . . . . . . . . | 10,500 |
| Finished goods . . . . . . . . . . . . . . . . | 6,600 |

Prepare closing entries for the company.

**Exercise 21–9**
**Overhead rate calculation and analysis**
(L. O. 5)

Ehler Company uses the relation between factory overhead and direct labor costs to apply factory overhead to its goods in process and finished goods inventories. The company incurred the following costs during a year: direct materials, $348,600; direct labor, $300,000; and factory overhead costs, $600,000. (*a*) Determine the company's overhead rate. (*b*) Under the assumption the company's $42,360 goods in process inventory had $8,600 of direct labor costs, determine the inventory's direct material costs. (*c*) Under the assumption the company's $53,600 finished goods inventory had $14,600 of direct material costs, determine the inventory's direct labor cost and factory overhead costs.

**Exercise 21–10**
**Work sheet for a manufacturing firm**
(L. O. 3)

The December 31 trial balance of Deitz Diesel Company follows:

**DEITZ DIESEL COMPANY**
**Unadjusted Trial Balance**
**December 31, 1990**

| | | |
|---|---|---|
| Cash | $ 1,350 | |
| Accounts receivable | 1,530 | |
| Allowance for doubtful accounts | | $ 480 |
| Raw materials inventory | 570 | |
| Goods in process inventory | 1,230 | |
| Finished goods inventory | 750 | |
| Factory supplies | 990 | |
| Prepaid factory insurance | 1,050 | |
| Factory machinery | 6,480 | |
| Accumulated depreciation, factory machinery | | 1,200 |
| Common stock | | 4,500 |
| Retained earnings | | 1,800 |
| Sales | | 24,300 |
| Raw material purchases | 5,100 | |
| Freight on raw materials | 300 | |
| Direct labor | 3,300 | |
| Indirect labor | 1,020 | |
| Factory utilities | 1,740 | |
| Machinery repairs | 450 | |
| Factory rent | 1,800 | |
| Selling expenses, controlling | 2,610 | |
| Administrative expenses, controlling | 2,010 | |
| Totals | $32,280 | $32,280 |

Additional information to be used in preparing a work sheet for 1990 financial statements is as follows:

*a.* Ending inventories:
  Raw materials, $960.
  Goods in process, $1,590.
  Finished goods, $540.
  Factory supplies, $210.

*b.* Allowance for doubtful accounts should be increased by $660.

*c.* Expired factory insurance for the year is $750.

*d.* Depreciation of factory machinery amounted to $840.

*e.* Accrued payroll on December 31:
Direct labor, $1,320.
Indirect labor, $480.
Office salaries, $330. (Debit Administrative Expenses, controlling account.)

*Required*
Prepare a work sheet for the year ended December 31, 1990.

## Problems

**Problem 21–1**
**Allocating costs to work in process; preparing the manufacturing statement**
(L. O. 2, 4, 5)

Doppler Company's December 31, 1990, work sheet had the following items in its manufacturing statement columns:

| | Manufacturing Statement | |
|---|---|---|
| | Debit | Credit |
| Raw materials inventory | 47,000 | 50,600 |
| Goods in process inventory | 55,200 | ? |
| Raw material purchases | 173,000 | |
| Direct labor | 280,000 | |
| Indirect labor | 107,900 | |
| Factory utilities | 60,800 | |
| Machinery repairs | 16,700 | |
| Factory rent | 47,000 | |
| Property taxes, machinery | 10,700 | |
| Expired factory insurance | 8,900 | |
| Factory supplies used | 19,400 | |
| Depreciation of machinery | 46,000 | |
| Amortization of patents | 7,400 | |
| | 880,000 | ? |
| Cost of goods manufactured | | ? |
| | 880,000 | 880,000 |

Doppler Company's work sheet does not show the amount of the ending goods in process inventory or the cost of goods manufactured. However, the company makes a single product, and on December 31, 1990, there were 2,600 units of goods in process. Each unit contained an estimated $7.40 of direct materials and had an estimated $10.00 of direct labor applied.

*Required*

1. Calculate the relation between direct labor and factory overhead costs and use this relation to place an accounting value on the ending goods in process inventory.
2. Prepare a 1990 manufacturing statement for the company.
3. Prepare entries to close the manufacturing accounts to Manufacturing Summary and to close the Manufacturing Summary account.

**Problem 21–2**
**Preparing manufacturing and income statements; closing entries**
(L. O. 2, 3, 4)

The following items appeared in the Manufacturing Statement and Income Statement columns of a work sheet prepared for Goodman Corporation on December 31, 1990:

| | Manufacturing Statement | | Income Statement | |
|---|---|---|---|---|
| | Debit | Credit | Debit | Credit |
| Raw materials inventory | 34,020 | 32,670 | | |
| Goods in process inventory | 39,960 | 34,830 | | |
| Finished goods inventory | | | 43,470 | 50,760 |
| Sales | | | | 976,050 |
| Raw material purchases | 159,300 | | | |
| Discounts on raw material purchases | | 2,160 | | |
| Direct labor | 243,000 | | | |
| Indirect labor | 37,260 | | | |
| Factory supervision | 32,400 | | | |
| Factory utilities | 49,680 | | | |
| Machinery repairs | 12,150 | | | |
| Factory rent | 19,440 | | | |
| Property taxes, machinery | 4,590 | | | |
| Selling expenses, controlling | | | 83,160 | |
| Administrative expenses, controlling | | | 78,030 | |
| Expired factory insurance | 6,480 | | | |
| Factory supplies used | 16,470 | | | |
| Depreciation of machinery | 28,350 | | | |
| Small tools written off | 1,080 | | | |
| Amortization of patents | 6,750 | | | |
| State and federal income taxes expense | | | 79,650 | |
| | 690,930 | 69,660 | | |
| Cost of goods manufactured | | 621,270 | 621,270 | |
| | 690,930 | 690,930 | 905,580 | 1,026,810 |
| Net income | | | 121,230 | |
| | | | 1,026,810 | 1,026,810 |

*Required*

1. Prepare a manufacturing statement and an income statement for the company.
2. Journalize closing entries for the company.

**Problem 21–3**
**Calculating cost components and preparing the manufacturing statement**
(L. O. 3, 5)

Calderon Company began this year with the following inventories: raw materials, $41,400; goods in process, $46,350; and finished goods, $56,250. The company uses the relation between its factory overhead and direct labor costs to apply overhead to its inventories of goods in process and finished goods; and at the end of this year its inventories were assigned these costs:

| | Raw Materials | Goods in Process | Finished Goods |
|---|---|---|---|
| Material costs | $38,700 | $12,600 | $20,250 |
| Direct labor costs | –0– | 16,200 | 25,200 |
| Overhead costs | –0– | ? | 31,500 |
| Totals | $38,700 | ? | $76,950 |

And this additional information was available from the company's records:

| | |
|---|---|
| Total factory overhead costs incurred during the year | $371,200 |
| Cost of all goods manufactured during the year | 892,800 |

*Required*

On the basis of the information given plus data you derive from it, prepare a manufacturing statement for Calderon Company.

**Problem 21–4**
**Preparing the work sheet, manufacturing statement, and income statement**
(L. O. 2, 3, 4, 5)

The December 31, 1990, unadjusted trial balance of Norwich Manufacturing Company is as follows:

**NORWICH MANUFACTURING COMPANY**
**Unadjusted Trial Balance**
**December 31, 1990**

| | | |
|---|---|---|
| Cash | $ 24,225 | |
| Accounts receivable | 27,150 | |
| Allowance for doubtful accounts | | $ 150 |
| Raw materials inventory | 27,825 | |
| Goods in process inventory | 25,800 | |
| Finished goods inventory | 36,525 | |
| Prepaid factory insurance | 3,075 | |
| Factory supplies | 9,825 | |
| Machinery | 170,625 | |
| Accumulated depreciation, machinery | | 58,800 |
| Accounts payable | | 18,975 |
| Common stock | | 75,000 |
| Retained earnings | | 71,175 |
| Sales | | 519,375 |
| Raw material purchases | 138,825 | |
| Direct labor | 119,625 | |
| Indirect labor | 27,450 | |
| Factory utilities | 10,200 | |
| Machinery repairs | 7,050 | |
| Selling expenses, controlling | 60,900 | |
| Administrative expenses, controlling | 54,375 | |
| Totals | $743,475 | $743,475 |

The following adjustments and inventory information was available at year-end:

*a.* Allowance for doubtful accounts should be increased to $1,275. (Debit Administrative Expenses, controlling account.)

*b.* An examination of policies shows $2,325 of factory insurance expired.

*c.* An inventory of factory supplies shows $7,275 of factory supplies used.

*d.* Depreciation of factory machinery was $23,475.

*e.* Accrued direct labor is $375; and accrued indirect labor is $225.

*f.* Accrued state and federal income taxes payable amount to $28,125.

*g.* Year-end inventories:

(1) Raw materials, $27,525.

(2) Goods in process consists of 1,200 units of product. Each unit is estimated to contain $8.40 of direct materials and $9.00 of direct labor.

(3) Finished goods inventory consists of 1,120 units of product. Each unit is estimated to contain $16 of direct materials and $13 of direct labor.

*Required*

1. Enter the unadjusted trial balance on a work sheet form and make the

adjustments from the information given. Then sort the items to the proper financial statement columns.

2. After the Direct Labor and factory overhead accounts have been adjusted and extended to the Manufacturing Statement columns, determine the relation between direct labor and overhead costs and use this relation to determine the overhead applicable to each unit of goods in process and finished goods. Next, calculate the balance sheet values for these inventories, enter the inventory amounts on the work sheet, and complete the work sheet.
3. From the work sheet prepare a manufacturing statement and an income statement.
4. Journalize the closing entries.

**Problem 21–5**
**Preparing the work sheet and financial statements for a manufacturing firm**
(L. O. 2, 3, 4, 5)

Enoch Company's unadjusted trial balance on December 31, 1990, the end of an annual accounting period, appears as follows:

**ENOCH COMPANY**
**Unadjusted Trial Balance**
**December 31, 1990**

| | | |
|---|---|---|
| Cash | $ 11,100 | |
| Raw materials inventory | 10,275 | |
| Goods in process inventory | 9,375 | |
| Finished goods inventory | 11,325 | |
| Prepaid factory insurance | 2,700 | |
| Factory supplies | 5,100 | |
| Factory machinery | 126,150 | |
| Accumulated depreciation, factory machinery | | $ 23,475 |
| Small tools | 3,075 | |
| Patents | 5,025 | |
| Common stock | | 75,000 |
| Retained earnings | | 12,525 |
| Sales | | 277,500 |
| Raw material purchases | 46,500 | |
| Discounts on raw material purchases | | 900 |
| Direct labor | 73,800 | |
| Indirect labor | 9,075 | |
| Factory supervision | 8,775 | |
| Factory utilities | 13,425 | |
| Machinery repairs | 3,150 | |
| Factory rent | 4,500 | |
| Property taxes, machinery | 1,275 | |
| Selling expenses, controlling | 23,550 | |
| Administrative expenses, controlling | 21,225 | |
| Totals | $389,400 | $389,400 |

*Additional Information*

*a.* Expired factory insurance, $1,800.
*b.* Factory supplies used, $4,425.
*c.* Depreciation of factory machinery, $7,650.
*d.* Small tools written off, $375.
*e.* Amortization of patents, $1,050.
*f.* Accrued wages payable:
   (1) Direct labor, $1,200.
   (2) Indirect labor, $525.
   (3) Factory supervision, $225.

*g.* Estimated state and federal income taxes payable, $22,500.

*h.* Ending inventories:

(1) Raw materials, $9,900.

(2) Goods in process consists of 750 units of product. Each unit is estimated to contain $4.50 of direct materials and $6.00 of direct labor.

(3) Finished goods consists of 600 units of product. Each unit is estimated to contain $8.75 of direct materials and $12.00 of direct labor.

*Required*

1. Enter the unadjusted trial balance on a work sheet form. Make the adjustments from the information given and sort the items to the proper financial statement columns.
2. Determine the relation between factory overhead costs and direct labor cost and use the relation to calculate the overhead that should be charged to the ending goods in process and finished goods inventories. Then, complete the work sheet.
3. From the work sheet prepare a manufacturing statement and an income statement.
4. Journalize the closing entries.

## Alternate Problems

**Problem 21–1A**
**Allocating costs to work in process; preparing the manufacturing statement**
(L. O. 2, 4, 5)

In Ingram Corporation's December 31, 1990, work sheet, the Manufacturing Statement columns appeared as shown below. The illustrated columns show the items as they appeared after all adjustments were completed but before the ending work in process inventory was calculated and entered and before the cost of goods manufactured was calculated.

Ingram Corporation makes a single product called Cifones. On December 31, 1990, the goods in process inventory consisted of 1,500 units of Cifones. Each unit was estimated to contain $13.80 of direct materials and $34.40 of direct labor.

| | Manufacturing Statement | |
|---|---|---|
| | **Debit** | **Credit** |
| Raw materials inventory | 91,580 | 83,370 |
| Goods in process inventory | 76,890 | ? |
| Raw material purchases | 351,640 | |
| Direct labor | 432,000 | |
| Indirect labor | 70,000 | |
| Factory supervision | 52,840 | |
| Factory utilities | 38,150 | |
| Machinery repairs | 27,220 | |
| Factory rent | 32,100 | |
| Property taxes, machinery | 8,200 | |
| Factory insurance expired | 14,250 | |
| Factory supplies used | 31,960 | |
| Depreciation of machinery | 73,000 | |
| Small tools written off | 2,200 | |
| | 1,302,030 | ? |
| Cost of goods manufactured | | ? |
| | 1,302,030 | 1,302,030 |

*Required*

1. Calculate the relation between direct labor and factory overhead costs and determine an accounting valuation of the ending goods in process inventory.
2. After placing a value on the ending goods in process inventory, prepare a manufacturing statement for Ingram Corporation.
3. Prepare entries to close the manufacturing accounts to Manufacturing Summary and to close the Manufacturing Summary account.

**Problem 21–2A**
**Preparing manufacturing and income statements; closing entries**
(L. O. 2, 3, 4)

The following alphabetically arranged items were taken from the Manufacturing Statement and Income Statement columns of Juvenal Manufacturing Company's year-end work sheet:

| | | | |
|---|---|---|---|
| Advertising | $ 8,100 | Goods in process, December 31 | $ 50,625 |
| Depreciation of machinery | 14,175 | Finished goods, January 1 | 70,875 |
| Depreciation of office equipment | 3,375 | Finished goods, December 31 | 56,700 |
| Depreciation of selling equipment | 4,050 | Miscellaneous production costs | 3,375 |
| Direct labor | 261,900 | Office salaries | 28,350 |
| Factory supplies used | 7,425 | Raw material purchases | 347,625 |
| Factory utilities | 13,500 | Rent on factory building | 32,400 |
| Federal income taxes expense | 54,675 | Rent expense, office space | 9,450 |
| Freight on raw materials | 10,125 | Rent expense, selling space | 10,800 |
| Indirect labor | 23,625 | Repairs to machinery | 12,150 |
| Inventories: | | Sales | 1,215,675 |
| Raw materials, January 1 | 66,150 | Sales discounts | 22,950 |
| Raw materials, December 31 | 68,175 | Sales salaries | 118,125 |
| Goods in process, January 1 | 55,350 | Factory supervision | 48,600 |

*Required*

Prepare a manufacturing statement and an income statement for the company.

**Problem 21–3A**
**Calculating cost components and preparing the manufacturing statement**
(L. O. 3, 5)

Mega Products Company incurred a total of $781,920 of direct material, direct labor, and factory overhead costs in manufacturing its product last year. Of this amount, $336,960 represented factory overhead costs. The company began last year with the following inventories: raw materials, $30,240; goods in process, $52,200; and finished goods, $63,000. It applies overhead to its goods in process and finished goods inventories on the basis of the relation of overhead to direct labor costs; and at the end of last year, it assigned the following costs to its inventories:

| | Raw Materials | Goods in Process | Finished Goods |
|---|---|---|---|
| Material costs | $33,120 | $16,920 | $20,700 |
| Direct labor costs | –0– | 17,280 | 20,880 |
| Overhead costs | –0– | ? | 31,320 |
| Totals | $33,120 | $ ? | $72,900 |

*Required*

Prepare a manufacturing statement for Mega Products Company using the above information and any other necessary data that can be derived from it.

**Problem 21–4A**
**Preparing the work sheet, manufacturing statement, and income statement**
(L. O. 2, 3, 4, 5)

Jakel Corporation's December 31, 1990, unadjusted trial balance included the following items:

JAKEL CORPORATION
Trial Balance
December 31, 1990

| | | |
|---|---|---|
| Cash | $ 45,900 | |
| Accounts receivable | 56,850 | |
| Allowance for doubtful accounts | | $ 1,350 |
| Raw materials inventory | 71,250 | |
| Goods in process inventory | 31,800 | |
| Finished goods inventory | 38,100 | |
| Prepaid factory insurance | 11,400 | |
| Factory supplies | 17,400 | |
| Machinery | 333,000 | |
| Accumulated depreciation, machinery | | 133,500 |
| Accounts payable | | 62,250 |
| Common stock | | 90,000 |
| Retained earnings | | 102,300 |
| Sales | | 1,018,050 |
| Raw material purchases | 262,500 | |
| Direct labor | 177,900 | |
| Indirect labor | 40,500 | |
| Factory utilities | 34,650 | |
| Machinery repairs | 10,950 | |
| Selling expenses, controlling | 131,100 | |
| Administrative expenses, controlling | 144,150 | |
| Totals | $1,407,450 | $1,407,450 |

The following adjustments and inventory information was available at year-end:

*a.* Allowance for doubtful accounts should be increased to $2,700. (Debit Administrative Expenses, controlling account.)
*b.* An examination of policies showed $7,500 of factory insurance expired.
*c.* An inventory of factory supplies showed $11,100 of factory supplies used.
*d.* Estimated depreciation of factory machinery was $47,400.
*e.* Accrued direct labor is $2,100; and accrued indirect labor is $900.
*f.* Accrued state and federal income taxes payable amount to $59,100.
*g.* Year-end inventories:
   (1) Raw materials, $55,050.
   (2) Goods in process consists of 1,700 units of product. Each unit is estimated to contain $12 of direct materials and $10 of direct labor.
   (3) Finished goods inventory consists of 2,200 units of product. Each unit is estimated to contain $18 of materials and $15 of direct labor.

*Required*

1. Enter the unadjusted trial balance on a work sheet form and make the adjustments from the information given. Then sort the items to the proper financial statement columns.
2. After the Direct Labor and factory overhead accounts have been adjusted and carried into the Manufacturing Statement columns, determine the relation between direct labor and overhead costs and use this

relation to determine the overhead applicable to each unit of goods in process and finished goods. Next, calculate the balance sheet values for these inventories (rounded to the nearest whole dollar), enter the inventory amounts on the work sheet, and complete the work sheet.

3. From the work sheet prepare a manufacturing statement and an income statement.
4. Prepare closing journal entries.

**Problem 21–5A**
**Preparing the work sheet and financial statements for a manufacturing company**
(L. O. 2, 3, 4, 5)

Overton Manufacturing Company's unadjusted trial balance on December 31, 1990, the end of its annual accounting period, appears as follows:

**OVERTON MANUFACTURING COMPANY**
**Unadjusted Trial Balance**
**December 31, 1990**

| | | |
|---|---|---|
| Cash | $ 31,500 | |
| Raw materials inventory | 23,940 | |
| Goods in process inventory | 27,540 | |
| Finished goods inventory | 29,880 | |
| Prepaid factory insurance | 7,560 | |
| Factory supplies | 11,520 | |
| Factory machinery | 315,900 | |
| Accumulated depreciation, factory machinery | | $ 51,840 |
| Small tools | 6,660 | |
| Patents | 8,100 | |
| Common stock | | 180,000 |
| Retained earnings | | 61,920 |
| Sales | | 647,460 |
| Raw material purchases | 111,240 | |
| Discounts on raw material purchases | | 1,800 |
| Direct labor | 160,380 | |
| Indirect labor | 23,940 | |
| Factory supervision | 21,240 | |
| Factory utilities | 32,220 | |
| Machinery repairs | 7,920 | |
| Factory rent | 12,960 | |
| Property taxes, machinery | 1,440 | |
| Selling expenses, controlling | 56,520 | |
| Administrative expenses, controlling | 52,560 | |
| Totals | $943,020 | $943,020 |

*Additional Information*

*a.* Expired factory insurance, $3,960.
*b.* Factory supplies used, $11,340.
*c.* Depreciation of machinery, $17,820.
*d.* Small tools written off, $1,260.
*e.* Amortization of patents, $2,340.
*f.* Accrued wages payable:
   (1) Direct labor, $1,620.
   (2) Indirect labor, $900.
   (3) Factory supervision, $360.
*g.* Estimated state and federal income taxes expense, $51,200.
*h.* Ending inventories:
   (1) Raw materials, $23,040.

(2) Goods in process consists of 2,200 units of product. Each unit is estimated to contain $5 of direct materials and $3 of direct labor.
(3) Finished goods consists of 1,700 units of product. Each unit is estimated to contain $7 of direct materials and $8 of direct labor.

*Required*

1. Enter the trial balance on a work sheet form. Make the adjustments from the information given and sort the items to the proper financial statement columns.
2. Determine the relation between direct labor and factory overhead costs and use this relation to calculate the overhead that should be charged to the ending goods in process and finished goods inventories. Then, complete the work sheet.
3. From the work sheet prepare a manufacturing statement and an income statement.
4. Journalize closing entries.

## Provocative Problems

**Provocative Problem 21–1**
**Universal Mechanism Company**
(L. O. 1, 3, 5)

Universal Mechanism Company has been in operation for three years, manufacturing and selling a single product. Although sales have increased materially, profits have increased only slightly. The company president, Clark Kentz, has asked you to analyze the situation and tell him why. Mr. Kentz is primarily a production man and knows little about accounting. The company bookkeeper knows a debit from a credit and is an excellent clerk, but has limited knowledge of accounting.

The company's condensed income statements for the past three years show:

| | 1989 | 1990 | 1991 |
|---|---|---|---|
| Sales | $270,000 | $378,000 | $432,000 |
| Cost of goods sold: | | | |
| Finished goods inventory, beginning | $ –0– | $ 19,800 | $ 59,400 |
| Cost of goods manufactured | 178,200 | 276,480 | 302,940 |
| Goods available for sale | $178,200 | $296,280 | $362,340 |
| Finished goods inventory, ending | 19,800 | 59,400 | 79,200 |
| Cost of goods sold | $158,400 | $236,880 | $283,140 |
| Gross profit from sales | $111,600 | $141,120 | $148,860 |
| Selling and administrative expenses | 81,000 | 105,840 | 116,640 |
| Net income | $ 30,600 | $ 35,280 | $ 32,220 |

Further investigation yields the following additional information:

*a.* The company sold 3,000 units of its product during the first year in business, 4,200 during the second year, and 4,800 during the third. All sales were priced at $110 per unit, and no discounts were granted.

*b.* There were 300 units in the finished goods inventory at the end of the first year, 900 at the end of the second, and 1,200 at the end of the third.

*c.* The units in the finished goods inventory were valued each year at 60% of their selling price, or at $66 per unit.

*Required*

Prepare a report for Mr. Kentz that shows (*a*) the number of units of product manufactured each year, (*b*) the cost each year to manufacture a unit of product, and (*c*) the selling and administrative expenses per unit of product sold each year. Also, (*d*) prepare an income statement that shows the correct net income each year, using a FIFO basis for pricing the finished goods inventory. And finally, (*e*) express an opinion as to why net income has not kept pace with the rising sales volume.

**Provocative Problem 21–2**
**Pacific Bass Boats**
(L. O. 5)

Several years ago Laura Unger took over the operation of her family's bass boat manufacturing company. The company previously specialized in manufacturing standard boats. However, it recently has turned more and more to building boats to the specifications of its customers. The seasonality of this business means that shop activity is rather slow during October, November, and December.

Laura has tried to increase business during the slow months. However, most prospective customers who come to the business during these months are shoppers; when Laura quotes a price for a boat, they commonly decide the price is too high and walk out. Laura thinks the trouble arises from her application of a rule established by her father when he ran the business. The rule is that in pricing a job to a customer, "always set the price so as to make a 10% profit over and above all costs, and be sure that all costs are included."

Laura says that in pricing a job, the direct material and direct labor costs are easy to figure but that overhead is another thing. Her overhead consists of depreciation of the factory building and machinery, manufacturing utilities, taxes, and so on. In total, these amount to $11,250 per month whether she builds any boats or not. Also, when she follows her father's rule, she has to charge more for a boat built during the slow months because the overhead is spread over fewer jobs. She readily admits that this seems to drive away business during the months she needs business most. Nevertheless, she finds it difficult to break her father's rule, for as she says, "Dad did all right in this business for many years."

*Required*

Explain why Laura charges more for a boat made in December than for one built in May, a very busy month. Use assumed figures to illustrate your point. Suggest how Laura might solve this pricing problem and still follow her father's rule.

**Provocative Problem 21–3**
**Geronimo Production Company**
(L. O. 3)

On January 1, 1990, Geronimo Production Company had outstanding 81,000 shares of $10 par value common stock. The stock was issued at par. The assets and liabilities of the company on that date were as follows:

| | |
|---|---|
| Cash | $180,000 |
| Accounts receivable | 90,000 |
| Raw materials inventory | 112,500 |
| Goods in process inventory | 135,000 |
| Finished goods inventory | 157,500 |
| Plant and equipment, net | 382,500 |
| Accounts payable | 90,000 |

During 1990, the company paid no dividends, although it earned a 1990 net income (ignore income taxes) of $84,375. At year-end, the amounts of the company's accounts receivable, accounts payable, and common stock outstanding were the same as at the beginning of the year. However, its cash decreased by $16,875, its raw materials inventory increased by 40%, its goods in process inventory increased by 25%, and its finished goods inventory increased by one half during the year. The net amount of its plant and equipment decreased by $56,250 due to depreciation, chargeable four fifths to factory overhead costs and one fifth to general and administrative expenses. The year's direct labor costs were $225,000, and factory overhead costs excluding depreciation were 60% of that amount. Cost of goods sold was $562,500, and all sales were made at prices 50% above cost. Selling expenses were 14%, and general and administrative expenses excluding depreciation were 8% of sales.

*Required*

Based on the information given and on amounts you can derive therefrom, prepare a manufacturing work sheet for the company.

# 22 Job Order and Process Cost Accounting Systems

In Chapter 21, you learned about manufacturing accounting systems that require physical counts of inventories at the end of each period to determine cost of goods manufactured. Those systems determine the total cost of all goods manufactured during the period; usually, no effort is made to determine unit costs.

In this chapter, you will learn about **cost accounting systems** that are designed to help managers control manufacturing costs. Cost accounting systems are based on perpetual inventories and are intended to emphasize unit costs. There are two basic types of cost accounting systems: (1) job order cost systems and (2) process cost systems. You will learn about both of these systems in this chapter.

### Learning Objectives

*After studying Chapter 22, you should be able to:*

1. Explain the conditions under which job order cost accounting systems are used and prepare entries to account for the flow of costs in a job order cost system.
2. Explain how costs for individual jobs are accumulated on job cost sheets and how controlling accounts are used in job order cost systems.
3. Allocate overhead to jobs and distribute any over- or underapplied overhead.
4. Explain the conditions under which process cost systems are used, prepare entries to account for the flow of costs in such a system, and prepare a process cost summary.
5. Calculate the equivalent finished units produced during a period and explain how the concept of equivalent finished units is used in process cost accounting systems.
6. Define or explain the words and phrases listed in the chapter Glossary.

## JOB ORDER COST ACCOUNTING

Explain the conditions under which job order cost accounting systems are used and prepare entries to account for the flow of costs in a job order cost system.
(L. O. 1)

The type of cost accounting system a manufacturing company uses depends on the nature of its products and the manufacturing process necessary to produce the products. In some cases, each unit of product has a unique design that requires the manufacturing process to focus on the production of that specific unit. Such products usually are large, high-cost items. They often are manufactured especially for and to the specifications of each customer. When a unique product of this sort is ordered to be produced, it is called a **job.** Examples of such products may include a custom-designed yacht, a special purpose machine, or a real estate construction project. Some jobs consist of a quantity of identical items, in which case they are called **job lots.** Illustration 22–1 shows the flow of materials that are converted into finished products when the manufacturing process is a typical job order process.

When a manufacturing process is designed to produce jobs or job lots like the one in Illustration 22–1, manufacturing costs must be assembled in terms of jobs or job lots. Accounting systems that assemble costs in this fashion are called **job order cost systems.**

### The Purpose and General Design of a Job Order Cost System

The primary purpose of a job order cost system is to determine the cost of producing each job or job lot. This differs from a general manufacturing accounting system (see Chapter 21) which determines the total cost of all goods manufactured during the period. Also, in a job cost system, all inventory accounts are maintained on a perpetual basis and are controlling accounts that control subsidiary ledgers. For example, in a job cost system, the purchase and use of all materials are recorded in a perpetual inventory account called Raw Materials. The Raw Materials account controls a subsidiary ledger that contains a separate record or ledger card (Illustration 22–2) for each different kind of material used. Likewise, in a job cost system, the Goods in Process and Finished Goods accounts are perpetual inventory accounts that control subsidiary ledgers.

### The Flow of Costs in a Job Order Cost System

In addition to perpetual inventory controlling accounts, job cost accounting is also distinguished by the flow of manufacturing costs through the accounts. Costs flow from the Raw Materials, Factory Payroll, and Factory Overhead accounts into and through the Goods in Process and Finished Goods accounts and on to the Cost of Goods Sold account. Illustration 22–3 diagrams this flow of costs. Examine the general ledger portion of Illustration 22–3. Notice that as manufacturing operations take place, the costs of direct materials, direct labor, and overhead flow into the Goods in Process account. Then, when a job is completed, the cost of the job is transferred from Goods in Process to Finished Goods. Finally, when the product is sold, the cost is transferred from Finished Goods to Cost of Goods Sold.

Illustration 22–3 also shows the relationships between the controlling accounts and the subsidiary ledgers in a job cost system. To better understand the role played by each component of the system, you should refer back to Illustration 22–3 as you study the discussion of each component.

**Illustration 22–1**
**The flow of materials in a job order manufacturing process**

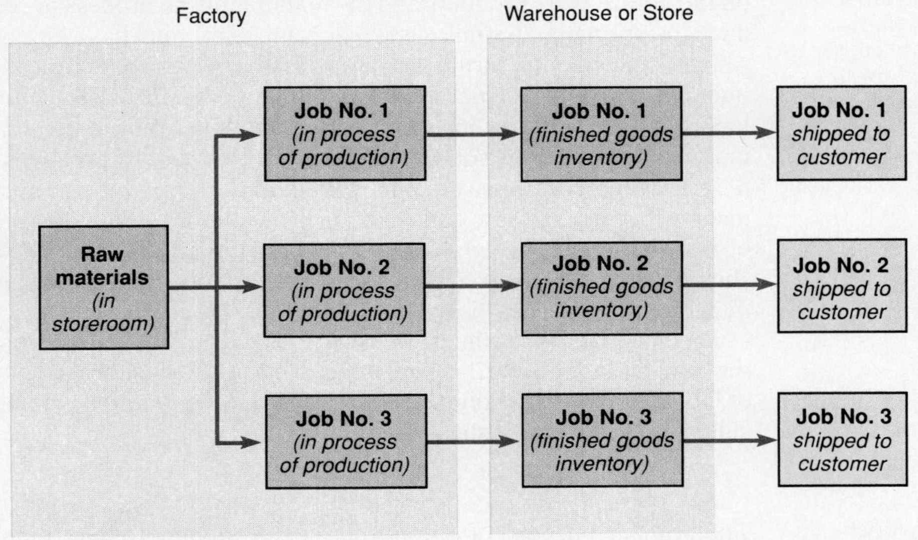


**Illustration 22–2**
**A raw materials ledger card**

Item *Whatsit clip* Stock No. *C-347* Location in Storeroom *Bin 137*

Maximum *400* Minimum *150* Number to Reorder *200*

| Received | | | | | Issued | | | | Balance | | |
|---|---|---|---|---|---|---|---|---|---|---|---|
| Date | Receiving Report No. | Units | Unit Price | Total Price | Requisition No. | Units | Unit Price | Total Price | Units | Unit Price | Total Price |
| 3/1 | | | | | | | | | 180 | 1.00 | 180.00 |
| 3/5 | | | | | 4345 | 20 | 1.00 | 20.00 | 160 | 1.00 | 160.00 |
| 3/11 | | | | | 4416 | 10 | 1.00 | 10.00 | 150 | 1.00 | 150.00 |
| 3/12 | C-114 | 200 | 1.00 | 200.00 | | | | | 350 | 1.00 | 350.00 |
| 3/25 | | | | | 4713 | 21 | 1.00 | 21.00 | 329 | 1.00 | 329.00 |

## Job Cost Sheets

The heart of a job cost system is a subsidiary ledger that is controlled by the Goods in Process account. This subsidiary ledger is called a **Job Cost Ledger.** It contains a separate record or **job cost sheet** for each job in the process of being manufactured. As the manufacture of a job progresses, the costs incurred to manufacture the job are accumulated on a job cost sheet. Illustration 22–4 shows an example of a job cost sheet.

Illustration 22–3

**Cost flows and subsidiary ledgers for a job cost system**

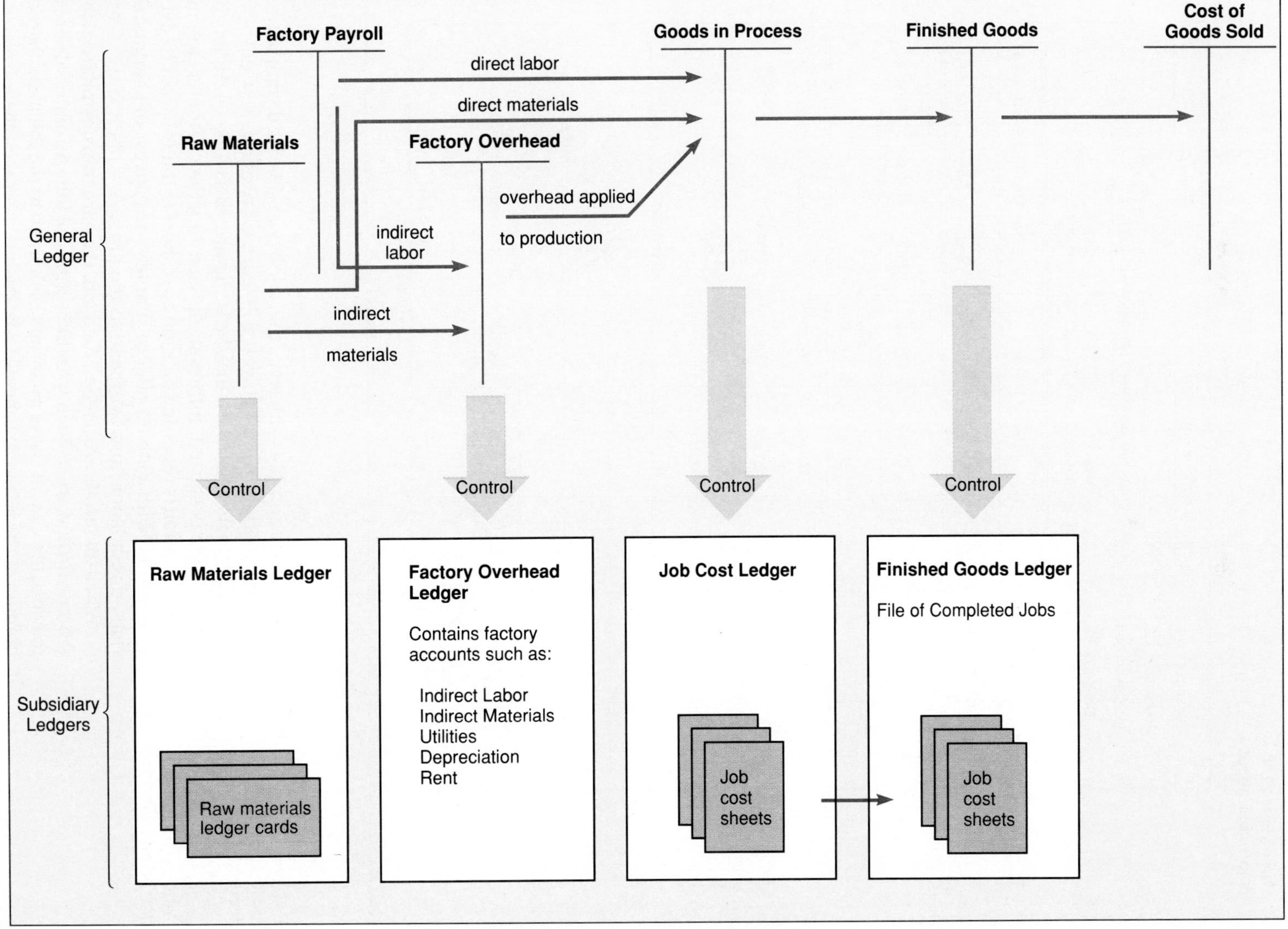

**Illustration 22–4**
**A job cost sheet**

Customer's Name *Cone Lumber Company* Job No. *7452*

Address *Eugene, Oregon*

Job Description *10 H.P. electric motor to customer's specifications*

Date Promised *4/1* Date Started *3/23* Date Completed *3/29*

| | Direct Materials | | Direct Labor | | Overhead Costs Applied | | |
|---|---|---|---|---|---|---|---|
| Date | Requisition No. | Amount | Time Ticket No. | Amount | Date | Rate | Amount |
| *19 --* Mar. 23 | *4698* | *53.00* | *C-3422* | *12.00* | *3/29* | *130 percent of the direct labor* | *$104.00* |
| *24* | | | *C-3478* <br> *C-3479* | *14.00* <br> *6.00* | | | |
| *25* | *4713* | *21.00* | *C-4002* | *16.00* | | | |
| *26* | | | *C-4015* | *10.00* | | | |
| *27* | | | *C-4032* | *12.00* | | | |
| *28* | | | *C-4044* | *10.00* | | | |
| | Total | *74.00* | Total | *80.00* | | | |

Summary of Costs

| | |
|---|---|
| Materials | *$ 74.00* |
| Labor | *80.00* |
| Overhead | *104.00* |
| Total Cost of the Job | *258.00* |

Remarks:
Completed and shipped 3/29

Explain how costs for individual jobs are accumulated on job cost sheets and how controlling accounts are used in job order cost systems. (L. O. 2)

In Illustration 22–4, observe that a job cost sheet is designed to accumulate cost information. Although you will learn more about how costs are accumulated later in the chapter, it may be summarized as follows. When the manufacture of a job is started, information regarding the customer, job number, and job description is recorded on a job cost sheet in the Job Cost Ledger. Each job is identified with a job number to simplify the process of charging direct materials, direct labor, and overhead to the job.

When materials are needed for a job, they are transferred from the materials storeroom and are used in manufacturing the job. As materials are transferred to a job, the cost of those materials is charged to the job in the Direct Materials column of the job's cost sheet. Labor used directly on the job also is charged to the job in the Direct Labor column. Overhead costs usually are charged to a job when the job is finished. On the job cost sheet, the overhead cost is entered in the Overhead Costs Applied column. After this, the total amount of each cost and the total manufacturing cost of the job are calculated. Also, at the end of each accounting period, overhead is charged to any jobs that remain unfinished.

## The Goods in Process Account

The job cost sheets in the Job Cost Ledger are controlled by Goods in Process, which is a General Ledger account. And, the Goods in Process account and its subsidiary ledger of cost sheets operate in the usual manner of controlling accounts and subsidiary ledgers. The direct materials, direct labor, and overhead costs debited to each individual job on its cost sheet also must be debited to Goods in Process. Similarly, all credits to jobs on their cost sheets must be credited to Goods in Process.

Besides being a controlling account, Goods in Process is a perpetual inventory account. This means that the account balance is updated from time to time without having to physically count the inventory. At the beginning of a period, the cost of unfinished jobs in process appears in the Goods in Process account as a debit balance. Every time a job is finished, the total cost of the completed job (the sum of the job's direct materials, direct labor, and overhead costs) is credited to the account.

Throughout the period, direct materials, direct labor, and overhead costs are charged to the job cost sheets in the subsidiary ledger. Usually, records of these costs are collected in the accounting department but are not entered in the Goods in Process account until the end of the period. (Note the last three debits in the Goods in Process account that follows.) As a result, after all entries are posted at the end of the period, the account balance is up-to-date. The debit balance represents the cost of the unfinished jobs still in process. For example, the following Goods in Process account shows a $10,786 March 31 ending inventory of unfinished jobs in process.

**Goods in Process**

| Date | | Explanation | Debit | Credit | Balance |
|---|---|---|---|---|---|
| Mar. | 1 | Balance, beginning inventory | | | 2,850 |
| | 10 | Job No. 7449 completed | | 7,920 | (5,070) |
| | 18 | Job No. 7448 completed | | 9,655 | (14,725) |
| | 24 | Job No. 7450 completed | | 8,316 | (23,041) |
| | 29 | Job No. 7452 completed | | 258 | (23,299) |
| | 29 | Job No. 7451 completed | | 6,295 | (29,594) |
| | 31 | Direct materials used | 17,150 | | (12,444) |
| | 31 | Direct labor applied | 10,100 | | (2,344) |
| | 31 | Overhead applied | 13,130 | | 10,786 |

This current balance is obtained without taking a physical count of inventory. Thus, Goods in Process is a perpetual inventory account. Physical counts of inventory are taken only as necessary to audit or confirm the fact that the account balance is correct.

Illustration 22–5
**A materials requisition**

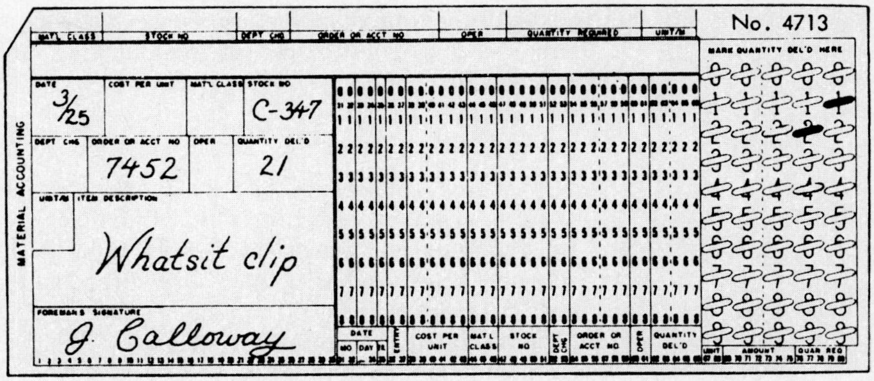
No. 4713

MATERIAL ACCOUNTING

| Date | Cost per unit | Mat'l class | Stock no |
|---|---|---|---|
| 3/25 | | | C-347 |

| Dept chg | Order or acct no | Oper | Quantity del'd |
|---|---|---|---|
| | 7452 | | 21 |

Item description: Whatsit clip

Foreman's signature: G. Calloway

## Accounting for Materials under a Job Cost System

In most manufacturing operations, raw materials are kept in a materials storeroom under the control of a storeroom keeper. Materials are issued for use in production only in exchange for properly prepared **materials requisitions** (see Illustration 22–5). The requisitions enhance control over materials and also provide a means of charging material costs to jobs. When materials are issued for use as indirect materials such as factory supplies, they are charged to factory overhead.

### Using Materials Requisitions

When a raw material is needed in the factory, a materials requisition is prepared and signed by a superintendent or other responsible person. The requisition identifies the material and shows the job number or overhead account to which it will be charged and is given to the storeroom keeper in exchange for the material. The storeroom keeper collects the requisitions and forwards them to the accounting department.

When a materials requisition reaches the accounting department, it is first recorded in the Issued column of the appropriate raw materials ledger card. This reduces the number of units of that material shown to be on hand. Note the last entry in Illustration 22–2, which records the requisition of Illustration 22–5.

### Charging the Cost of Materials to Jobs and to Overhead

Materials issued to the factory may be used on jobs or for some overhead task, such as machinery repairs. Therefore, after issued materials are entered in the Issued columns of the proper raw materials ledger card, a batch of requisitions is sorted by jobs and overhead accounts and charged to the proper jobs and overhead accounts. Direct materials used on jobs are charged to the jobs in the Direct Materials columns of the job cost sheets. (Note the last entry in the

Direct Materials column of the cost sheet in Illustration 22–4 where the requisition of Illustration 22–5 is recorded.)

In a job cost system, the Factory Overhead account in the General Ledger usually is a controlling account that controls a subsidiary Factory Overhead Ledger. The subsidiary ledger contains separate accounts for each type of overhead cost. Raw materials used for overhead tasks are charged to the proper overhead accounts in the Factory Overhead Ledger. For example, a requisition for light bulbs would be charged to the Factory Utilities account in the subsidiary Factory Overhead Ledger.

Raw materials ledger cards, job cost sheets, and overhead cost accounts are all subsidiary ledger accounts controlled by accounts in the General Ledger. Therefore, in addition to the entries made in these subsidiary ledgers, entries must also be made in the controlling accounts. To do this, the requisitions charged to jobs and the requisitions charged to overhead accounts usually are accumulated until the end of a month or other cost period when they are separately totaled. If, for example, the requisitions charged to jobs during the month total $17,150 and those charged to overhead accounts total $320, an entry like the following is made:

| | | | | |
|---|---|---|---|---|
| Mar. | 31 | Goods in Process | 17,150.00 | |
| | | Factory Overhead | 320.00 | |
| | | Raw Materials | | 17,470.00 |
| | | To record the materials used during March. | | |

The debit to Goods in Process in the illustrated entry is equal to the sum of the materials requisitions charged to jobs as detailed on the job cost sheets during March. The debit to Factory Overhead is equal to the sum of the requisitions charged to overhead accounts. The credit to Raw Materials is equal to the sum of all requisitions entered in the Issued columns of the raw materials ledger cards during the month.

## Accounting for Labor in a Job Cost System

Time clocks, clock cards, and a Payroll Register are commonly used in factories to record the hours and cost of the direct and indirect labor provided by employees. Without the complications of payroll taxes, income taxes, and other deductions, the entry to pay the employees is as follows:

| | | | | |
|---|---|---|---|---|
| Mar. | 7 | Factory Payroll | 2,900.00 | |
| | | Cash | | 2,900.00 |
| | | To record the factory payroll and pay the employees. | | |

This entry is repeated at the end of each pay period. Thus, at the end of a month or other cost period, the Factory Payroll account has a series of debits (see Illustration 22–7) like the debit of this entry. The sum of these debits is the total amount paid to employees during the month for direct and indirect labor.

**Illustration 22–6**
**A labor time ticket**

**TIME TICKET** C-3422

EMPLOYEE
name George Jones
clock number 342

JOB
number 7452
description Armature winding

OVERHEAD ACCOUNT NUMBER
TIME/RATE

| started | stopped | elapsed | rate | pay |
|---|---|---|---|---|
| 8:00 | 10:00 | 2 | 6.00 | 12.00 |

Date: 3/23

George Jones
employee

J. Calloway
foreman

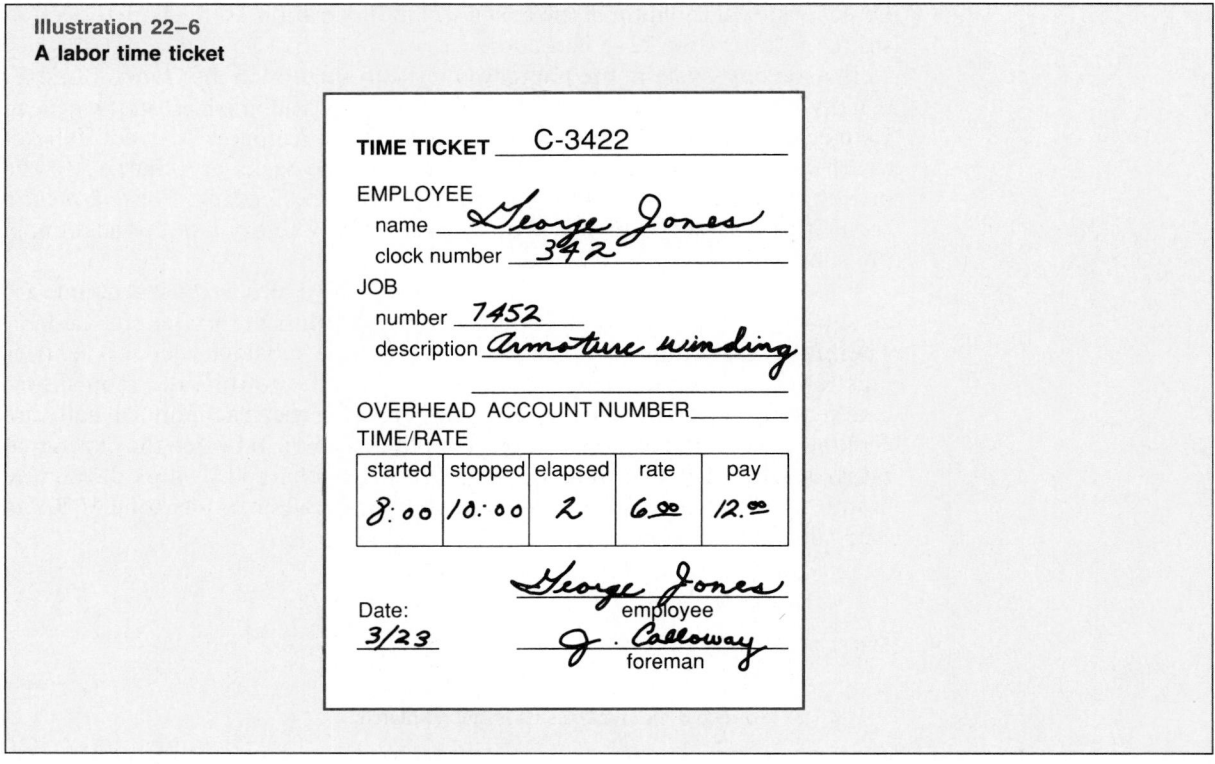

### Gathering Information about Factory Labor Costs

Employee clock cards provide a record of the hours worked each day by each employee. However, the clock cards do not show how the employees spent their time or the specific jobs and overhead tasks on which they worked. Therefore, if the hours worked by each employee are to be charged to specific jobs and overhead accounts, another record called a **labor time ticket** must be prepared. Labor time tickets like the one shown in Illustration 22–6 describe how each employee's work time was used.

Time tickets like the one shown in Illustration 22–6 are not directly readable by computer input devices. As a result, time tickets of this sort are not efficient in a large plant that employs a large number of workers. In large plants with many workers, time tickets that are easily made machine readable often are used. These may be similar to the materials requisition in Illustration 22–5.

Labor time tickets serve as a basis for charging jobs and overhead accounts for an employee's wages. Each time an employee moves from one job or overhead task to another during the day, a labor time ticket is prepared. The tickets may be prepared by the worker, the worker's supervisor, or a clerk called a timekeeper. If the employee works on only one job all day, only one ticket is prepared. If work is done on more than one job, a separate ticket is made for each job. At the end of the day all the tickets prepared that day are sent to the accounting department.

**Illustration 22–7**

**Factory Payroll**

| Date | | Explanation | Debit | Credit | Balance |
|---|---|---|---|---|---|
| Mar. | 7 | Weekly payroll payment | 2,900 | | 2,900 |
| | 14 | Weekly payroll payment | 2,950 | | 5,850 |
| | 21 | Weekly payroll payment | 3,105 | | 8,955 |
| | 28 | Weekly payroll payment | 3,040 | | 11,995 |
| | 31 | Labor cost summary | | 12,600 | (605) |

### Charging Labor Costs to Jobs and to Overhead

In the accounting department, the direct labor time tickets are charged to jobs on the job cost sheets. (See the first entry in the Labor column of Illustration 22–3 where the ticket of Illustration 22–5 is recorded.) The indirect labor tickets are charged to overhead accounts in the Factory Overhead Ledger. Then, at the end of the period, the accumulated direct labor tickets and the indirect labor tickets are totaled and recorded in the general ledger accounts. For example, if the direct labor tickets total $10,100 and the indirect labor tickets total $2,500, the following entry is made:

| | | | | |
|---|---|---|---|---|
| Mar. | 31 | Goods in Process . . . . . . . . . . . . . . . . . . . . . . | 10,100.00 | |
| | | Factory Overhead . . . . . . . . . . . . . . . . . . . . . . | 2,500.00 | |
| | | Factory Payroll . . . . . . . . . . . . . . . . . . . . . . | | 12,600.00 |
| | | To record the March time tickets. | | |

The first debit in the above entry is the sum of all direct labor time tickets charged to jobs on the job cost sheets, and the second debit is the sum of all tickets charged to overhead accounts. The credit is the total of the month's labor time tickets, both direct and indirect. In Illustration 22–7, notice that after this credit is posted, the Factory Payroll account has a $605 credit balance. This $605 is the accrued factory payroll payable at the month's end. It is the dollar amount of time tickets prepared and recorded during the last three days of March.

## Accounting for Overhead in a Job Cost System

Allocate overhead to jobs and distribute any over- or underapplied overhead. (L. O. 3)

In a job cost system, the total cost to manufacture a job must be determined at the time the job is finished. This includes overhead cost as well as direct materials and direct labor. The costs of direct materials and direct labor are determined based on materials requisitions and time tickets. However, overhead costs are incurred for the benefit of all jobs and cannot be related directly to any one job. Therefore, to associate overhead with jobs you must relate overhead to another variable such as direct labor costs or hours of factory machine use. Then, you apply overhead to jobs by means of a **predetermined overhead application rate.**

A predetermined overhead application rate is established before a cost period begins. If the rate is based on direct labor cost, you must (1) estimate the total overhead that will be incurred during the period and (2) estimate the cost of the direct labor that will be incurred during the period. Then (3), you express the estimated overhead as a percentage of the estimated direct labor cost. For example, if you estimate that a factory will incur $156,000 of overhead during the next year and that $120,000 of direct labor will be applied to production during the year, these estimates are used to establish an overhead application rate of 130%, as follows:

$$\frac{\text{Next year's estimated overhead costs, \$156,000}}{\text{Next year's estimated direct labor costs, \$120,000}} \times 100 = 130\%$$

### Charging Overhead to Jobs as They Are Finished

After a predetermined overhead application rate is established, it is used throughout the year to apply overhead to jobs as they are finished. To do this, you first determine the total direct labor cost of a job. This is done by adding the amounts of direct labor that have been posted in the Direct Labor column of the job cost sheet. Then, you multiply the job's total direct labor cost by the predetermined overhead application rate to determine the overhead to be applied to the job. This amount is entered in the Overhead Costs Applied column.

After overhead is applied to a finished job, the total cost of the job is determined by adding the total costs of direct materials, direct labor, and overhead that appear on the job cost sheet.

### Charging Overhead to Ending Goods in Process

The predetermined overhead application rate is also used to assign overhead to any jobs still in process at the end of the accounting period. Then, the total overhead assigned to all jobs during the period is recorded in the general ledger accounts as follows:

| | | | | |
|---|---|---|---|---|
| Mar. | 31 | Goods in Process | 13,130.00 | |
| | | Factory Overhead | | 13,130.00 |
| | | To record the overhead applied to jobs during March. | | |

The above entry assumes that the overhead applied to all jobs during March totaled $13,130. This is 130% of the $10,100 direct labor applied to jobs as shown in the Goods in Process account on page 927. After you post this entry, the Factory Overhead account appears as in Illustration 22–8.

In the Factory Overhead account of Illustration 22–8, the four debits represent the actual overhead costs incurred during March. The third debit in the account represents payments for various overhead items such as water, telephone, and factory rent. The fourth debit represents end-of-period adjustments for overhead items such as depreciation of machinery, expired insurance on factory assets, and accrued taxes on factory assets.

An important assumption underlies the use of a predetermined overhead rate to apply overhead to jobs. The assumption is that the relation between

Illustration 22–8

**Factory Overhead**

| Date | | Explanation | Debit | Credit | Balance |
|---|---|---|---|---|---|
| Mar. | 31 | Indirect materials | 320 | | 320 |
| | 31 | Indirect labor | 2,500 | | 2,820 |
| | 31 | Miscellaneous payments | 3,306 | | 6,126 |
| | 31 | Accrued and prepaid items | 9,054 | | 15,180 |
| | 31 | Applied | | 13,130 | 2,050 |

*total* overhead and *total* direct labor or perhaps *total* machine-hours for the period is appropriate for *each* job manufactured during the period. Whether direct labor or direct machine-hours provides the more dependable basis depends on the nature of the manufacturing operations.

## Overapplied and Underapplied Overhead

Since a predetermined overhead application rate is based on estimates at the beginning of the period, the amount of overhead applied to jobs during the period will not be equal to the amount incurred. Sometimes actual overhead incurred exceeds overhead applied, and at other times overhead applied exceeds actual overhead incurred. This means that at the end of the period, the Factory Overhead account will not have a zero balance. As shown below, if the account has a debit balance (overhead incurred in excess of overhead applied), the balance is known as **underapplied overhead.** If the account has a credit balance (overhead applied in excess of overhead incurred), the balance is called **overapplied overhead.**

**Factory Overhead**

| | | | |
|---|---|---|---|
| Overhead incurred | X,XXX | Overhead applied | X,XXX |
| A debit balance means overhead was underapplied | | A credit balance means overhead was overapplied | |

In the example of Illustration 22–8, the final $2,050 debit balance represents underapplied overhead. It is manufacturing cost that was incurred during the period but which was not applied to jobs.

Regardless of whether the ending balance in the Factory Overhead account is a debit or credit, any remaining balance must be disposed of before a new accounting period begins. Assuming the balance is material in amount, it should be allocated to all of the jobs that were worked on during the period. Those jobs remain unfinished or are in the finished goods inventory or have been sold to customers. Therefore, the Factory Overhead balance should be allocated among goods in process, finished goods, and cost of goods sold. This has the effect of restating the inventories and goods sold at "actual" cost.

For example, consider the $2,050 debit balance in Illustration 22–8. Also, assume that the company of Illustration 22–8 had charged overhead to jobs during the period as follows:

| | | |
|---|---|---|
| Jobs still in process | $ 1,313 | 10% |
| Jobs finished but unsold | 2,626 | 20 |
| Jobs finished and sold | 9,191 | 70 |
| Total overhead applied to jobs during the period | $13,130 | 100% |

The following entry allocates the underapplied overhead to the jobs worked on during the period:

| | | | | |
|---|---|---|---|---|
| Dec. | 31 | Goods in Process | 205.00 | |
| | | Finished Goods | 410.00 | |
| | | Cost of Goods Sold | 1,435.00 | |
| | | Factory Overhead | | 2,050.00 |
| | | To clear the Factory Overhead account and charge the underapplied overhead to the work of the accounting period. | | |

If the amount of over- or underapplied overhead is not material, all of it may be closed to Cost of Goods Sold. Over a year, most of the overhead cost is charged to this account anyway, and any extra exactness gained from prorating may not be worth the extra effort.

### Recording the Completion of a Job

When a job is completed, its cost is transferred from the Goods in Process account to the Finished Goods account. For example, the job cost sheet in Illustration 22–4 showed that the total cost to manufacture Job No. 7452 was $258. The following entry transfers the cost of this job from goods in process to finished goods:

| | | | | |
|---|---|---|---|---|
| Mar. | 29 | Finished Goods | 258.00 | |
| | | Goods in Process | | 258.00 |
| | | To transfer the cost of Job No. 7452 to Finished Goods. | | |

At the same time this entry is made, the completed job's cost sheet is removed from the Job Cost Ledger, marked "completed," and filed. As a result, the total cost of the remaining job cost sheets in the subsidiary Job Cost Ledger continues to equal the debit balance in the Goods in Process controlling account.

### Recording Cost of Goods Sold

When a job order cost system is used, the cost to manufacture a job or job lot of product is known as soon as the goods are finished. Therefore, cost of goods sold can be recorded at the time of sale. For example, if goods that cost $258 are sold for $450, the cost of goods sold may be recorded at the time of sale as follows:

| | | | | |
|---|---|---|---|---|
| Mar. | 29 | Accounts Receivable—Cone Lumber Company | 450.00 | |
| | | Cost of Goods Sold | 258.00 | |
| | | Sales | | 450.00 |
| | | Finished Goods | | 258.00 |
| | | Sold for $450 goods costing $258. | | |

When cost of goods sold is recorded at the time of each sale, the Cost of Goods Sold account balance at the end of an accounting period shows the total cost of goods sold during the period.

## PROCESS COST ACCOUNTING

Explain the conditions under which process cost systems are used, prepare entries to account for the flow of costs in such a system, and prepare a process cost summary. (L. O. 4)

At the beginning of this chapter, you learned that the type of cost accounting system a manufacturing company uses depends on the nature of its products and its manufacturing process. When companies produce a large volume of standardized units, the units under production generally pass from one *manufacturing process* or step in the production of a product to another. Each process or step usually is organized as a separate manufacturing department, and the focus of the manufacturing activity is on the series of processes through which units pass. For example, assume a company makes a product from metal pieces that are cut to size and bent into shape in a cutting department. Then, the pieces are sent to an assembly department in which the pieces are bolted together to form the finished product. Illustration 22–9 shows the flow of materials in a process manufacturing operation such as this.

Companies that use a series of manufacturing processes to produce standardized products use a **process cost system** in which costs are assembled in terms of processes or manufacturing steps. Process cost systems are found in companies that produce products such as cement, flour, automobiles, or television sets. In such companies, manufacturing costs are assembled by and assigned to each processing department. A record is kept of the number of units that pass through each department. Periodically, the costs assigned to each department are divided by the number of units produced to determine the average cost per unit. The efficiency of each department is measured by comparing planned and actual processing costs incurred in processing the units of product that flow through the department.

### Cost Flows in a Process Cost System

When costs are assembled by departments in a process cost system, a separate goods in process account is used for the costs of each department. For example, the manufacturing company illustrated in Illustration 22–9 would collect costs in two goods in process accounts, one for each department. Illustration 22–10 shows how costs would flow through the accounts.

Observe in Illustration 22–10 that direct materials, direct labor, and factory overhead costs are charged to each department's goods in process account. Direct materials charged to the cutting department relate to metal used in that department. Direct materials charged to the assembly department consist of bolts, washers, and nuts.

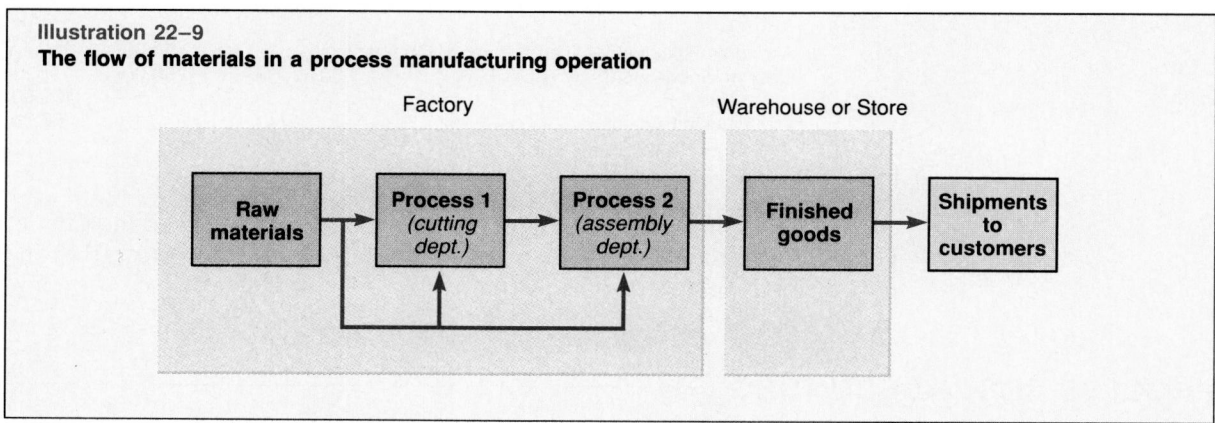

Illustration 22–9
**The flow of materials in a process manufacturing operation**

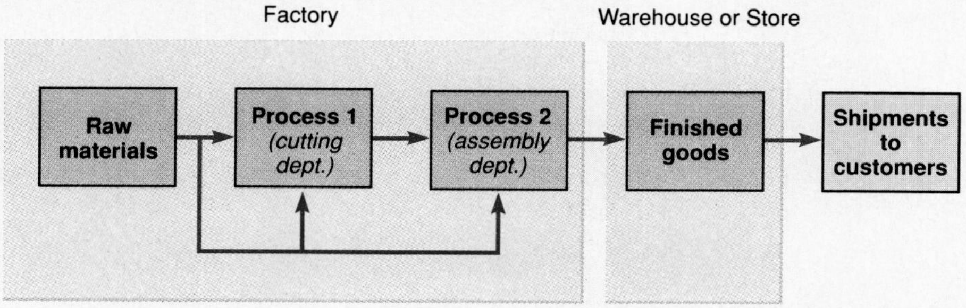


In Illustration 22–10, observe how costs are transferred from the cutting department to the assembly department and then to finished goods, just as the product physically moves in the manufacturing procedure. The costs transferred from the cutting department to the assembly department include all of the direct materials, direct labor, and factory overhead costs that were charged to the cutting department and assigned to units that completed that process. The costs transferred from the assembly department to finished goods include the costs that were first transferred out of the cutting department plus the additional direct materials, direct labor, and factory overhead that were charged to the assembly department and assigned to finished units.

## Charging Costs to Departments

### Materials Costs

Companies with process cost systems often use materials requisitions like those used in a job order cost system. However, some companies substitute a **materials consumption report** prepared by the materials storeroom keeper. This report shows the materials issued to each department during a cost period. It provides the necessary information to prepare journal entries charging the cost of direct materials to the appropriate departments. If materials are used for maintenance or other types of factorywide activities, the materials consumption report shows that they should be charged to factory overhead.

### Direct Labor Costs

In a process cost system, costs are assembled in terms of manufacturing processes. This differs from a job order cost system in which costs are assembled in terms of jobs or job lots. There is a related difference between the concepts of direct and indirect labor. In a process cost system, all costs that are easily identified with a particular department are direct costs of that department. For example, suppose a person works full time doing maintenance on the production machinery in the cutting department. In a process cost system, the cost of that person's labor is a direct cost of the cutting department; it would be treated as direct labor. But, if a job order cost system were used, the cost of the

Illustration 22–10
**Cost flows for a process cost system**

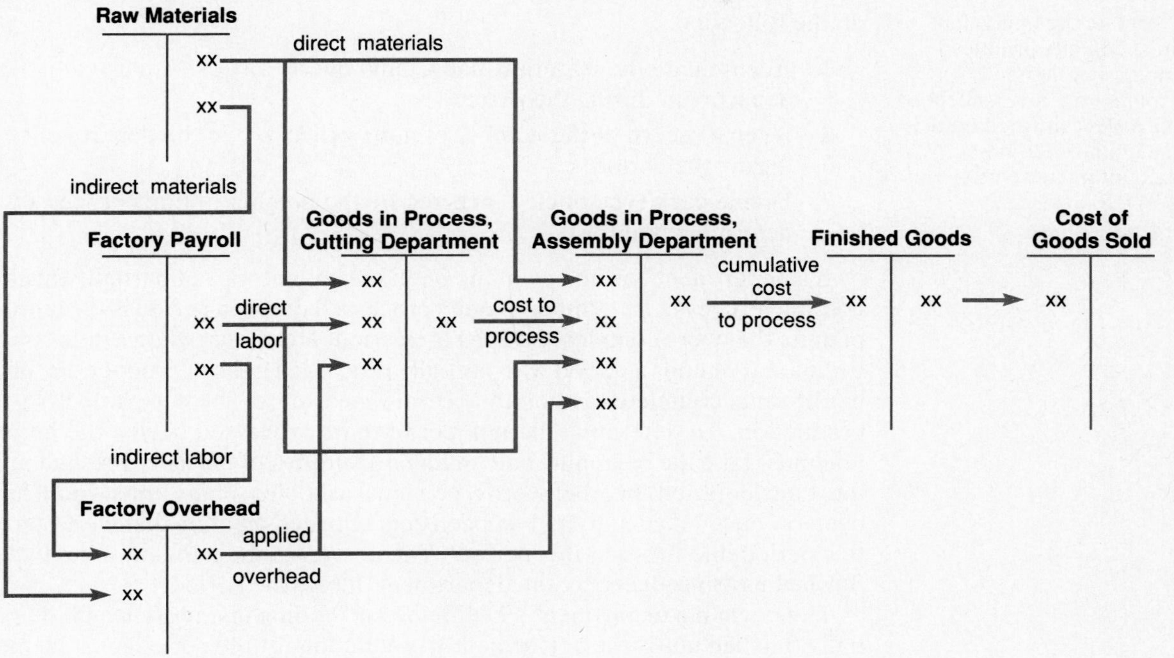


maintenance person's labor would be indirect labor, since maintenance on production machinery is not easily associated with specific jobs.

### Indirect Labor Costs

In a process cost system, not all labor is classified as direct labor. Indirect labor relates to persons whose work contributes to more than one department. Examples may include the labor of some maintenance workers, quality control inspectors, and overall plant supervisors.

### Factory Overhead

In a process cost system, factory overhead includes all those manufacturing costs that are not easily traced to a specific department. These costs are incurred for the benefit of more than one manufacturing department and must be allocated to the departments on some reasonable basis. The procedure you follow to allocate overhead costs in a process cost system is similar to the one used in a job order cost system. Factory overhead costs are estimated before the accounting period begins and are expressed as a percentage of another variable such as estimated total direct labor costs. Then, to assign factory overhead to the departments, you apply this predetermined overhead application rate to the actual direct labor cost incurred by each department.

## Equivalent Finished Units

Calculate the equivalent finished units produced during a period and explain how the concept of equivalent finished units is used in process cost accounting systems. (L. O. 5)

A basic objective of a process cost system is to determine each processing department's unit processing costs for direct materials, direct labor, and overhead. To calculate a department's unit processing costs for a period, you must do the following:

1. Accumulate the materials, labor, and overhead costs incurred by the department during the period.
2. Keep a record of the number of units processed in the department during the period.
3. Divide each type of cost incurred by the number of units processed to determine unit costs.

If a department has no beginning or ending inventories of partially finished goods in process, the number of units processed during a period is the number of units that were completed during the period. However, when a department begins and/or ends a period with partially processed units of product, the number of units completed is not an accurate measure of the department's total production. To determine the number of units processed during the period, you must take the beginning and ending inventories of partially finished units into consideration. In other words, you must ask: How many units would have been produced if all activity had been concentrated on units that were started this period and finished this period? The answer is the number of **equivalent finished units produced** by the department during the period.

Thus, when a department's beginning and ending inventories include partially finished units, the department's production for the period must be measured in terms of *equivalent finished units produced.* Then, to determine unit costs, you divide total costs by the number of equivalent finished units produced.

The equivalent finished units concept is based on the idea that it takes the same amount of direct labor, for instance, to one-half finish each of two units of product as it takes to fully complete one. Or, it takes the same amount of labor to one-third finish each of three units as to complete one.

Also, since a department may add direct materials to production at a different rate than it adds labor and overhead, separate measures of production are often required for direct materials and for direct labor and overhead. For example, during a period, a department may add enough materials to produce 1,000 equivalent finished units. However, during the same period, the department may have added enough labor and overhead to produce 900 equivalent finished units. You will learn more about the concept of equivalent finished units produced and the related calculations in the Delta Processing Company illustration that follows.

## Process Cost Accounting Illustrated

Delta Processing Company manufactures a nonprescription medicine called Noxall. Since Noxall is produced by moving a raw material through a series of two manufacturing processes, the company uses a process cost accounting system.

The procedure for manufacturing Noxall is as follows: Material A is finely ground in Delta Processing Company's grinding department. Then, it is transferred to the mixing department where Material B is added and the two materials are thoroughly mixed. The mixing process results in the finished product, Noxall, which is transferred to finished goods inventory.

In the grinding department, all the Material A to be processed is entered into production at the beginning of the grinding process. However, in the mixing department, Material B is added gradually throughout the mixing process. In other words, if the mixing process for a batch of product is one-third complete at the end of a period, that batch of product has received one third of its Material B. In both departments, direct labor and overhead are applied evenly throughout the production processes.

At the end of the April cost period, entries were made to charge direct materials, direct labor, and factory overhead to the departments. After posting those entries, the company's two goods in process accounts appeared as follows:

**Goods in Process, Grinding Department**

| Date | | Explanation | Debit | Credit | Balance |
|---|---|---|---|---|---|
| Apr. | 1 | Beginning inventory | | | 4,250 |
| | 30 | Direct materials | 9,900 | | 14,150 |
| | 30 | Direct labor | 5,700 | | 19,850 |
| | 30 | Overhead | 4,275 | | 24,125 |

**Goods in Process, Mixing Department**

| Date | | Explanation | Debit | Credit | Balance |
|---|---|---|---|---|---|
| Apr. | 1 | Beginning inventory | | | 3,785 |
| | 30 | Direct materials | 2,040 | | 5,825 |
| | 30 | Direct labor | 4,080 | | 9,905 |
| | 30 | Overhead | 1,020 | | 10,925 |

The production reports prepared by the company's two department managers give the following information about inventories and goods started and finished in each department during the month:

| | Grinding Department | Mixing Department |
|---|---|---|
| Units in the beginning goods in process inventories | 30,000 | 16,000 |
| April 1 stage of completion of the beginning inventories of goods in process | 1/3 | 1/4 |
| Units started in process and finished during period | 70,000 | 85,000 |
| Total units finished and transferred to next department or to finished goods | 100,000 | 101,000 |
| Units in the ending goods in process inventories | 20,000 | 15,000 |
| Stage of completion of ending goods in process inventories | 1/4 | 1/3 |

### Process Cost Summary

Based on the above production report information, you should prepare a process cost summary for each department. A process cost summary shows (1) the costs charged to the department, (2) the department's equivalent unit processing costs, and (3) the assignment of costs to the department's goods in process inventories and to the goods that were started and finished. Illustration 22–11 shows the process cost summary for the grinding department.

**Costs Charged to the Department.** Observe in Illustration 22–11 that a process cost summary has three sections. Section 1 is titled Costs Charged to the Department. In this section, the total cost to be accounted for is determined by adding the direct materials, direct labor, and overhead costs charged to the department to the beginning goods in process. Information for this section comes from the department's Goods in Process account. Compare the first section of Illustration 22–11 with the Goods in Process account of the grinding department shown on page 939.

**Equivalent Unit Processing Costs.** The second section of a process cost summary shows the calculation of equivalent unit processing costs. In this section, information about the units involved and fractional units applicable to the inventories comes from the production report prepared by the department manager. Information about the total costs of direct materials, direct labor, and overhead comes from the first section of the summary.

In section 2 of Illustration 22–11, *note that there are two separate calculations of equivalent units produced.* Two calculations are required because direct labor and overhead are not applied to production at the same rate as direct materials are entered into production. Remember that all direct materials are added at the beginning of this department's process, and direct labor is applied evenly throughout the process. Since Delta Processing Company applies overhead as a percentage of direct labor, overhead also is applied evenly throughout the process. Therefore, the number of equivalent units produced for direct materials is not the same as the number of equivalent units produced for direct labor and overhead.

In the calculation of equivalent finished units produced for direct materials, note that the beginning-of-month inventory was not assigned any additional direct materials. This is because all materials are entered into production at the beginning of the grinding process. The 30,000 beginning inventory units were entered in production during March and were one-third complete at the beginning of April. Therefore, these units received all their direct materials during March when their processing first began.

Note also that the $9,900 cost of the materials charged to the department in April is divided by 90,000 equivalent units produced to arrive at an $0.11 per equivalent unit cost for direct materials used in this department.

Now move on to the calculation of equivalent finished units for direct labor and overhead. Notice that the beginning inventory units were each assigned two thirds of a unit of direct labor and overhead. If these units were one-third completed on April 1, then two thirds of the work done on these units was done in April. Study this carefully. Do not make the common mistake of assigning only an additional one-third unit of direct labor and overhead when two thirds is required.

Before going further, be sure you understand the meaning of the equivalent units calculation for direct labor and overhead. In this example, the grinding department did two thirds of the work on 30,000 units, all the work on 70,000 units, and one fourth the work on 20,000 units. That was the equivalent of

**Illustration 22–11**

**DELTA PROCESSING COMPANY**
**Process Cost Summary, Grinding Department**
**For Month Ended April 30, 1990**

1

| | |
|---|---|
| COSTS CHARGED TO THE DEPARTMENT: | |
| Direct materials requisitioned | $ 9,900 |
| Direct labor charged | 5,700 |
| Overhead costs incurred (predetermined overhead rate is 75% of direct labor) | 4,275 |
| Total processing costs | $19,875 |
| Goods in process at the beginning of the month | 4,250 |
| Total costs to be accounted for | $24,125 |

2

EQUIVALENT UNIT PROCESSING COSTS:

| | Units Involved | Fraction of a Unit Added | Equivalent Units Added |
|---|---|---|---|
| Direct materials: | | | |
| Beginning inventory | 30,000 | –0– | –0– |
| Units started and finished | 70,000 | One | 70,000 |
| Ending inventory | 20,000 | One | 20,000 |
| Total equivalent units | | | 90,000 |

Equivalent unit processing cost for direct materials: $9,900 ÷ 90,000 = $0.11

| | Units Involved | Fraction of a Unit Added | Equivalent Units Added |
|---|---|---|---|
| Direct labor and overhead: | | | |
| Beginning inventory | 30,000 | ⅔ | 20,000 |
| Units started and finished | 70,000 | One | 70,000 |
| Ending inventory | 20,000 | ¼ | 5,000 |
| Total equivalent units | | | 95,000 |

Equivalent unit processing cost for direct labor: $5,700 ÷ 95,000 = $0.06
Equivalent unit processing cost for overhead: $4,275 ÷ 95,000 = $0.045

3

| | | |
|---|---|---|
| ASSIGNMENT OF COSTS TO THE WORK OF THE DEPARTMENT: | | |
| Goods in process, one-third processed at the beginning of April: | | |
| Costs charged to the beginning inventory of goods in process during previous month | $4,250 | |
| Direct materials added (all added during March) | –0– | |
| Direct labor applied (20,000 × $0.06) | 1,200 | |
| Overhead applied (20,000 × $0.045) | 900 | |
| Cost to process | | $ 6,350 |
| Goods started and finished in the department during April: | | |
| Direct materials added (70,000 × $0.11) | $7,700 | |
| Direct labor applied (70,000 × $0.06) | 4,200 | |
| Overhead applied (70,000 × $0.045) | 3,150 | |
| Cost to process | | 15,050 |
| Total cost of the goods processed in the department and transferred to the mixing department (100,000 units at $0.214 each) | | $21,400 |
| Goods in process, one-fourth processed at the end of April: | | |
| Direct materials added (20,000 × $0.11) | $2,200 | |
| Direct labor applied (5,000 × $0.06) | 300 | |
| Overhead applied (5,000 × $0.045) | 225 | |
| Cost to one-fourth process | | 2,725 |
| Total costs accounted for | | $24,125 |

completing all the work on 95,000 units. Therefore, the $5,700 of direct labor cost and $4,275 of overhead cost charged to the department are each divided by 95,000 to determine equivalent unit costs for direct labor and overhead.

**Assignment of Costs to the Work of the Department.** When a department begins and ends a period with partially processed units of product, you must allocate the department's costs among the units that were in process in the department at the beginning of the period, the units started and finished during the period, and the ending inventory units. This division is necessary to determine the cost of the units completed in the department during the period. Section 3 of the process cost summary shows this allocation of costs.

Notice in section 3 of Illustration 22–11 how costs are assigned to the beginning inventory. The first amount assigned is the $4,250 beginning inventory costs. This represents the direct materials, direct labor, and overhead costs used to partially complete the inventory during March, the previous period. In many departments, the second charge to a beginning inventory is for additional direct materials assigned to it. However, in the grinding department, the beginning inventory units received all of their materials when their processing first began during March. Thus, no additional materials costs are assigned during April.

The second charge to the beginning inventory is for direct labor. This $1,200 cost is the number of equivalent finished units for labor used to complete the beginning inventory multiplied by the cost of an equivalent finished unit for labor (20,000 equivalent finished units at $0.06 each). The third charge to the beginning inventory is for overhead. This $900 is the equivalent finished units for labor or overhead used to complete the beginning inventory multiplied by the cost of an equivalent finished unit for overhead (20,000 × $0.045).

The procedures for assigning costs to the beginning inventory are also used to determine the cost of the units started and finished by the department during the period. Then, the cost of the units completed and transferred to finished goods is determined by adding the costs of the completed beginning inventory units and the units started and completed during the period. In this example, the units completed were 30,000 from the beginning inventory and 70,000 started and completed during April. The total cost of these 100,000 units was $21,400 or $0.214 per unit ($21,400 ÷ 100,000 units = $0.214 per unit).

In section 2 of Illustration 22–11, notice that the equivalent finished unit cost for direct materials is $0.11, for direct labor is $0.06, and for overhead is $0.045. These total $0.215 ($0.11 + $0.06 + $0.045). However, in section 3 of the process cost summary, the unit cost of the 100,000 units finished and transferred is $0.214, which is less than $0.215. It is less because costs were less in the department during the previous month and the 30,000 beginning units were one-third processed at these lower costs.

### Transferring Costs from One Department to the Next

A process cost summary is completed by assigning costs to the ending inventory. Then, you must prepare an entry to transfer the cost of completed units out of the department. For the grinding department, this entry transfers the

**Illustration 22–12**

**Goods in Process, Grinding Department**

| Date | | Explanation | Debit | Credit | Balance |
|---|---|---|---|---|---|
| Apr. | 1 | Beginning inventory | | | 4,250 |
| | 30 | Direct materials | 9,900 | | 14,150 |
| | 30 | Direct labor | 5,700 | | 19,850 |
| | 30 | Overhead | 4,275 | | 24,125 |
| | 30 | Units to mixing department | | 21,400 | 2,725 |

**Goods in Process, Mixing Department**

| Date | | Explanation | Debit | Credit | Balance |
|---|---|---|---|---|---|
| Apr. | 1 | Beginning inventory | | | 3,785 |
| | 30 | Direct materials | 2,040 | | 5,825 |
| | 30 | Direct labor | 4,080 | | 9,905 |
| | 30 | Overhead | 1,020 | | 10,925 |
| | 30 | Units from grinding department | 21,400 | | 32,325 |

cost of the 100,000 units processed in the department and transferred out during April. Information for the entry was taken from section 3 of Illustration 22–11.

| | | | | |
|---|---|---|---|---|
| Apr. | 30 | Goods in Process, Mixing Department . . . . . . . . . . . | 21,400.00 | |
| | | Goods in Process, Grinding Department . . . . . . . | | 21,400.00 |
| | | To transfer the cost of 100,000 units from the grinding to the mixing department. | | |

Posting this entry has the effect on the accounts shown in Illustration 22–12. Observe that the effect is to transfer or advance costs from one department to the next just as the product is physically transferred or advanced in the manufacturing operation.

### Process Cost Summary—Mixing Department

After posting the entry to transfer the cost of units sent from the grinding department to the mixing department, a process cost summary should be prepared for the mixing department. The information for this summary is taken from the mixing department's goods in process account and production report. Illustration 22–13 shows the mixing department's process cost summary.

Two points in Illustration 22–13 require special attention. The first is the calculation of equivalent finished units produced. Since the direct materials and direct labor (and therefore overhead) are added evenly throughout the mixing process, you need only one equivalent finished units calculation. This differs from the grinding department, where two equivalent unit calculations were required. Two were required because all direct materials are added when

**Illustration 22–13**

**DELTA PROCESSING COMPANY**
**Process Cost Summary, Mixing Department**
**For Month Ended April 30, 1990**

| | | |
|---|---|---|
| | COSTS CHARGED TO THE DEPARTMENT: | |
| | Direct materials requisitioned | $ 2,040 |
| | Direct labor charged | 4,080 |
| 1 | Overhead costs incurred (predetermined overhead rate is 25% of direct labor) | 1,020 |
| | Total processing costs | $ 7,140 |
| | Goods in process at the beginning of the month | 3,785 |
| | Cost transferred from the grinding department (100,000 units at $0.214 each) | 21,400 |
| | Total costs to be accounted for | $32,325 |

| | EQUIVALENT UNIT PROCESSING COSTS: | Units Involved | Fraction of a Unit Added | Equivalent Units Added |
|---|---|---|---|---|
| | Direct materials, direct labor, and overhead: | | | |
| | Beginning inventory | 16,000 | ¾ | 12,000 |
| | Units started and finished | 85,000 | One | 85,000 |
| 2 | Ending inventory | 15,000 | ⅓ | 5,000 |
| | Total equivalent units | | | 102,000 |

Equivalent unit processing cost for direct materials: $2,040 ÷ 102,000 = $0.02
Equivalent unit processing cost for direct labor: $4,080 ÷ 102,000 = $0.04
Equivalent unit processing cost for overhead: $1,020 ÷ 102,000 = $0.01

| | | | |
|---|---|---|---|
| | ASSIGNMENT OF COSTS TO THE WORK OF THE DEPARTMENT: | | |
| | Goods in process, one-fourth completed at the beginning of April: | | |
| | Costs charged to the beginning inventory of goods in process during previous month | $ 3,785 | |
| | Direct materials added (12,000 × $0.02) | 240 | |
| | Direct labor applied (12,000 × $0.04) | 480 | |
| | Overhead applied (12,000 × $0.01) | 120 | |
| | Cost to process | | $ 4,625 |
| | Goods started and finished in the department during April: | | |
| | Costs in the grinding department (85,000 × $0.214) | $18,190 | |
| | Direct materials added (85,000 × $0.02) | $1,700 | |
| | Direct labor applied (85,000 × $0.04) | 3,400 | |
| 3 | Overhead applied (85,000 × $0.01) | 850 | |
| | Cost to process | | 24,140 |
| | Total accumulated costs of goods transferred to finished goods (101,000 units at $0.2848) | | $28,765 |
| | Goods in process, one-third processed at the end of April: | | |
| | Costs from the grinding department (15,000 × $0.214) | $ 3,210 | |
| | Direct materials added (5,000 × $0.02) | 100 | |
| | Direct labor applied (5,000 × $0.04) | 200 | |
| | Overhead applied (5,000 × $0.01) | 50 | |
| | Cost to one-third process | | 3,560 |
| | Total costs accounted for | | $32,325 |

the grinding process begins while direct labor (and therefore overhead) are applied evenly throughout the process.

The second point to notice in the mixing department cost summary is the method of handling the grinding department costs transferred to this department. During April, 100,000 units of product, with accumulated grinding department costs of $21,400, were transferred to the mixing department. Of these 100,000 units, 85,000 were started in process in the department, finished, and transferred to finished goods. The remaining 15,000 were still in process in the department at the end of the cost period.

Notice in section 1 of Illustration 22–13 that the $21,400 cost transferred from the grinding department is added to the other costs charged to the mixing department. Compare the information in this first section with the mixing department's Goods in Process account as it is shown on page 939 and again in Illustration 22–12.

In section 3 of Illustration 22–13, note how the $21,400 of grinding department costs are allocated between the 85,000 units started and finished and the 15,000 units that remain in process at the end of the period. The 16,000 beginning goods in process units received none of this $21,400 charge because they were transferred from the grinding department during the previous month. The grinding department costs of the beginning inventory are included in the $3,785 beginning inventory costs.

Section 3 of the mixing department's process cost summary shows that 101,000 units of product were completed during April and transferred to finished goods. The 101,000 units is the total of the 16,000 beginning inventory units plus the 85,000 units that were started and finished during April. The total manufacturing cost of the units finished during April was $28,765, and the following entry transfers this cost from the mixing department to finished goods:

| | | | | |
|---|---|---|---|---|
| Apr. | 30 | Finished Goods . . . . . . . . . . . . . . . . . . . . . . . . | 28,765.00 | |
| | | Goods in Process, Mixing Department . . . . . . . . . | | 28,765.00 |
| | | To transfer the accumulated grinding department and mixing department costs of the 101,000 units transferred to Finished Goods. | | |

Illustration 22–14 shows the effects of posting the above entry.

## Summary of the Chapter in Terms of Learning Objectives

**1.** Job order cost accounting systems are used when each product or job has a unique design so that the manufacturing process focuses on the production of that specific job. In the General Ledger, raw materials purchases are recorded in a Raw Materials account. The cost of production labor is debited to Factory Payroll, and overhead costs are debited to Factory Overhead. When a job is completed, the cost of the job is transferred from Goods in Process to Finished Goods. (Until costs are charged to Goods in

**Illustration 22–14**

**Goods in Process, Mixing Department**

| Date | | Explanation | Debit | Credit | Balance |
|---|---|---|---|---|---|
| Apr. | 1 | Beginning inventory | | | 3,785 |
| | 30 | Direct materials | 2,040 | | 5,825 |
| | 30 | Direct labor | 4,080 | | 9,905 |
| | 30 | Overhead | 1,020 | | 10,925 |
| | 30 | Units from grinding department | 21,400 | | 32,325 |
| | 30 | Units to finished goods | | 28,765 | 3,560 |

**Finished Goods**

| Date | | Explanation | Debit | Credit | Balance |
|---|---|---|---|---|---|
| Apr. | 30 | Units from mixing department | 28,765 | | 28,765 |

Process at the end of the period, the entries that transfer completed jobs to Finished Goods usually result in a credit balance in the Goods in Process account.) Then, at the end of each period, the cost of raw materials used, direct labor, and overhead are transferred from Raw Materials, Factory Payroll, and Factory Overhead to the Goods in Process account.

**2.** As production of a job progresses, the cost of raw materials used and direct labor applied to the job are entered on the job cost sheet in the subsidiary ledger. When the job is completed, overhead is entered on the job cost sheet based on a predetermined overhead application rate.

**3.** At the beginning of the period, the total amount of overhead cost for the period is estimated and then expressed as a percentage of a related variable such as estimated total direct labor. This predetermined overhead application rate is used throughout the period to apply overhead to specific jobs. At the end of the period, any overapplied or underapplied overhead is allocated to cost of goods sold and the ending inventories of finished goods and goods in process. This allocation is based on the relative amounts of applied overhead in those accounts at the end of the period. If immaterial in amount, overapplied or underapplied overhead may be charged to cost of goods sold.

**4.** A process cost accounting system is used when manufacturing operations produce a large volume of standardized units that generally pass from one manufacturing process to another. Based on accumulated materials requisitions and labor time tickets, end-of-period entries transfer the costs of raw materials and direct labor from Raw Materials and Factory Payroll to the appropriate Goods in Process accounts of the manufacturing departments. Based on a predetermined overhead application rate, overhead costs are transferred from Factory Overhead to the Goods in Process accounts of the departments. Also, the information developed on each department's processing cost summary is the basis for entries to transfer the cost of goods from one processing department to another and from the final production department to Finished Goods.

**5.** The manufacturing costs charged to a processing department during a period are allocated to ending goods in process and to goods transferred out of the department based on the equivalent finished units produced by the department. If materials are added to a process at a different rate than labor and overhead are applied, separate equivalent finished units produced calculations are required for materials and for labor and overhead. When there are partially completed units in the beginning inventory, the percentage of the manufacturing process added during the current period is multiplied by the number of units in the beginning inventory to determine an equivalent number of totally processed units. The same calculation is done for units partially manufactured during the current period and which remain unfinished in the ending goods in process inventory. These equivalent numbers of totally processed units are added to the units started and completed during the current period to determine the total number of equivalent units finished during the period.

## Demonstration Problem

From the information about Range Mfg. Company presented below:

1. Determine the total cost of:
   *a.* Each job from No. 401 through No. 405.
   *b.* May 31 inventory of jobs in process.
   *c.* May 31 inventory of finished jobs.
   *d.* The jobs sold in May.
   *e.* Materials used during May.
   *f.* Factory labor incurred during May.
   *g.* Factory overhead incurred and applied during May.

   Overhead costs incurred during the month of May were:

| | |
|---|---|
| Indirect labor | $3,500 |
| Indirect materials | 5,000 |
| Factory rent | 1,450 |
| Factory utilities | 2,650 |
| Depreciation of machinery | 5,400 |

   The predetermined overhead application rate was 150% of the direct labor cost.

| | Job No. 401 | Job No. 402 | Job No. 403 | Job No. 404 | Job No. 405 |
|---|---|---|---|---|---|
| Balances at April 30: | | | | | |
| Direct labor | $1,000 | $ 700 | | | |
| Direct materials | 1,700 | 1,900 | | | |
| Applied overhead | 1,500 | 1,050 | | | |
| Costs during May: | | | | | |
| Direct labor | 1,100 | 4,000 | $3,200 | $2,800 | $ 800 |
| Direct materials | 50 | 3,500 | 2,200 | 1,300 | 1,400 |
| Status at May 31 | Sold | Sold | Finished | Finished | In process |

2. Present journal entries dated May 31 to:
   *a.* Record each element of overhead cost in the Factory Overhead account.

*b.* Assign the elements of manufacturing cost incurred during May to Goods in Process, with a separate debit to Goods in Process for the cost assigned to each job.
*c.* Transfer the cost of each completed job to Finished Goods.
*d.* Record cost of goods sold.
*e.* Assign any under- or overapplied overhead to cost of goods sold (based on the assumption that the amount is not material).

3. Prepare a manufacturing statement for the month of May.

## Solution to Demonstration Problem

**Total cost of jobs:**

| | No. 401 | No. 402 | No. 403 | No. 404 | No. 405 |
|---|---|---|---|---|---|
| From April: | | | | | |
| Direct labor . . . . . . . | $1,000 | $ 700 | | | |
| Direct materials . . . . | 1,700 | 1,900 | | | |
| *Applied overhead . . . . | 1,500 | 1,050 | | | |
| From May: | | | | | |
| Direct labor . . . . . . . | 1,100 | 4,000 | $ 3,200 | $2,800 | $ 800 |
| Direct materials . . . . | 50 | 3,500 | 2,200 | 1,300 | 1,400 |
| *Applied overhead . . . . | 1,650 | 6,000 | 4,800 | 4,200 | 1,200 |
| Total costs . . . . . . . | $7,000 | $17,150 | $10,200 | $8,300 | $3,400 |

*Equals 150% of the direct labor cost.

**Ending inventory of jobs in process:**

| | |
|---|---|
| Job No. 405 . . . . . . . . . . . . . | $ 3,400 |

**Ending inventory of finished jobs:**

| | |
|---|---|
| Job No. 403 . . . . . . . . . . . . . | $10,200 |
| Job No. 404 . . . . . . . . . . . . . | 8,300 |
| | $18,500 |

**Total cost of jobs sold during May:**

| | |
|---|---|
| Job No. 401 . . . . . . . . . . . . . | $ 7,000 |
| Job No. 402 . . . . . . . . . . . . . | 17,150 |
| | $24,150 |

**Total cost of materials used during May:**

| | |
|---|---|
| Indirect materials . . . . . . . . . . | $ 5,000 |
| Direct materials: | |
| No. 401 . . . . . . . . . . . . . . | 50 |
| No. 402 . . . . . . . . . . . . . . | 3,500 |
| No. 403 . . . . . . . . . . . . . . | 2,200 |
| No. 404 . . . . . . . . . . . . . . | 1,300 |
| No. 405 . . . . . . . . . . . . . . | 1,400 |
| | $13,450 |

**Total cost of factory labor for May:**

| | |
|---|---|
| Indirect labor | $ 3,500 |
| Direct labor: | |
| No. 401 | 1,100 |
| No. 402 | 4,000 |
| No. 403 | 3,200 |
| No. 404 | 2,800 |
| No. 405 | 800 |
| | $15,400 |

**Total cost of overhead for May (actual and applied):**

| | | |
|---|---|---|
| Actual: | | |
| Indirect labor | $ 3,500 | |
| Indirect material | 5,000 | |
| Factory rent | 1,450 | |
| Factory utilities | 2,650 | |
| Depreciation of machinery | 5,400 | |
| | $18,000 | |
| Applied: | | |
| No. 401 | $ 1,650 | |
| No. 402 | 6,000 | |
| No. 403 | 4,800 | |
| No. 404 | 4,200 | |
| No. 405 | 1,200 | |
| | $17,850 | |
| Underapplied overhead | $ 150 | (to be added to Cost of Goods Sold) |

**Summarized journal entries:**

| | | | |
|---|---|---|---|
| *a.* | Factory Overhead (indirect labor) | 3,500.00 | |
| | Factory Payroll | | 3,500.00 |
| | Factory Overhead (indirect materials) | 5,000.00 | |
| | Raw Materials | | 5,000.00 |
| | Factory Overhead (factory rent) | 1,450.00 | |
| | Rent Payable | | 1,450.00 |
| | Factory Overhead (factory utilities) | 2,650.00 | |
| | Utilities Payable | | 2,650.00 |
| | Factory Overhead (depreciation of machinery) | 5,400.00 | |
| | Accumulated Depreciation, Machinery | | 5,400.00 |
| *b.* | Goods in Process (No. 401) | 50.00 | |
| | Goods in Process (No. 402) | 3,500.00 | |
| | Goods in Process (No. 403) | 2,200.00 | |
| | Goods in Process (No. 404) | 1,300.00 | |
| | Goods in Process (No. 405) | 1,400.00 | |
| | Raw Materials | | 8,450.00 |
| | To allocate direct material costs to jobs. | | |

| | | | |
|---|---|---|---|
| | Goods in Process (No. 401) | 1,100.00 | |
| | Goods in process (No. 402) | 4,000.00 | |
| | Goods in Process (No. 403) | 3,200.00 | |
| | Goods in Process (No. 404) | 2,800.00 | |
| | Goods in Process (No. 405) | 800.00 | |
| | Factory Payroll | | 11,900.00 |
| | To allocate direct labor cost to jobs. | | |
| | Goods in Process (No. 401) | 1,650.00 | |
| | Goods in Process (No. 402) | 6,000.00 | |
| | Goods in Process (No. 403) | 4,800.00 | |
| | Goods in Process (No. 404) | 4,200.00 | |
| | Goods in Process (No. 405) | 1,200.00 | |
| | Factory Overhead | | 17,850.00 |
| | To allocate factory overhead cost to jobs. | | |
| *c.* | Finished Goods | 42,650.00 | |
| | Goods in Process (No. 401) | | 7,000.00 |
| | Goods in Process (No. 402) | | 17,150.00 |
| | Goods in Process (No. 403) | | 10,200.00 |
| | Goods in Process (No. 404) | | 8,300.00 |
| | To allocate cost of completed jobs to finished goods. | | |
| *d.* | Cost of Goods Sold | 24,150.00 | |
| | Finished Goods | | 24,150.00 |
| | To allocate cost of jobs No. 401 and No. 402 to cost of goods sold. | | |
| *e.* | Cost of Goods Sold | 150.00 | |
| | Factory Overhead | | 150.00 |
| | To assign underapplied overhead. | | |

**RANGE MFG. COMPANY**
**Manufacturing Statement**
**For the Month Ended May 31**

| | | |
|---|---|---|
| Direct materials used | | $ 8,450 |
| Direct labor used | | 11,900 |
| Factory overhead: | | |
| Indirect labor | $3,500 | |
| Indirect material | 5,000 | |
| Factory rent | 1,450 | |
| Factory utilities | 2,650 | |
| Depreciation of machinery | 5,400 | 18,000 |
| Total manufacturing costs | | $38,350 |
| Add: Goods in process, April 30 (No. 401 and No. 402) | | 7,850 |
| Total goods in process during the month | | $46,200 |
| Deduct goods in process, May 31 (No 405) | | 3,400 |
| Cost of goods manufactured (No. 401, No. 402, No. 403, and No. 404, and underapplied overhead) | | $42,800 |

## Glossary

Define or explain the words and phrases listed in the chapter Glossary. (L. O. 6)

**Cost accounting system** an accounting system based on perpetual inventory records that is designed to emphasize the determination of unit costs and the control of costs. p. 922

**Equivalent finished units produced** a measure of production with respect to direct materials or direct labor (and overhead), expressed as the number of units that could have been manufactured from start to finish during a period given the amount of direct materials or direct labor (and overhead) used during the period. p. 938

**Job** a special production order of a unique product, often manufactured especially for and to the specifications of a customer. p. 923

**Job Cost Ledger** a subsidiary ledger that contains the job cost sheets of unfinished jobs and that is controlled by the Goods in Process account. p. 924

**Job cost sheet** a record of the costs incurred on a single job. pp. 924, 926

**Job lot** a job that consists of a quantity of identical items. p. 923

**Job order cost system** a system of accounting for manufacturing costs in which costs are assembled in terms of jobs or job lots. p. 923

**Labor time ticket** a record of how an employee's time at work was used; the record serves as the basis for charging jobs and overhead accounts for the employee's wages. p. 930

**Materials consumption report** a document which is prepared by the materials storeroom keeper as a substitute for materials requisitions and that shows the raw materials issued to each department during a cost period; provides the information necessary for journal entries that charge materials costs to the appropriate accounts. p. 936

**Materials requisition** a document that is given to the materials storeroom keeper in exchange for raw materials and that improves control over materials and provides a basis for charging the cost of raw materials to jobs, or processing departments, or factory overhead; the document identifies the materials needed for a specific job, processing department, or purpose, and the account to which the materials cost should be charged. p. 928

**Overapplied overhead** the amount by which overhead applied on the basis of a predetermined overhead application rate exceeds overhead actually incurred during the period. p. 933

**Predetermined overhead application rate** a rate that is used to charge overhead cost to production; calculated by relating estimated overhead cost for a period to another variable such as estimated direct labor cost. pp. 931–32

**Process cost system** a system of accounting for manufacturing costs in which costs are assembled in terms of processes or steps in manufacturing a product. p. 935

**Underapplied overhead** the amount by which actual overhead incurred during a period exceeds the overhead applied to production based on a predetermined application rate. pp. 933–34

## Objective Review

Answers to the following questions are listed in Appendix I at the end of the book. Be sure that you decide which is the one best answer to each question *before* you check the answers in the appendix.

1. In a job cost accounting system:
   *a.* Each job or product has a similar design so that the manufacturing process focuses on the sequence of processes necessary to produce the jobs.
   *b.* Purchases of raw materials are recorded in the Raw Materials account in the Raw Materials Ledger, the cost of production labor is debited to Factory Payroll in the Job Cost Ledger, and overhead costs are debited to Factory Overhead in the Factory Overhead Ledger.
   *c.* Costs flow from the Raw Materials, Factory Payroll, and Factory Overhead accounts into and through the Goods in Process and Finished Goods accounts and on to the Cost of Goods Sold account.
   *d.* When a job is sold, the cost of the job is transferred from Goods in Process to Cost of Goods Sold.
   *e.* All of the above are correct.
2. The job cost sheets in the Job Cost Ledger are controlled by:
   *a.* The Factory Payroll account.
   *b.* The Goods in Process account.
   *c.* Factory Payroll and/or Factory Overhead depending on whether the costs are allocated to direct or indirect labor.
   *d.* The Finished Goods account.
   *e.* The Job Cost Ledger.
3. A company used a predetermined overhead application rate of 150% to apply overhead during a period in which actual direct labor costs totaled $14,700. Actual overhead costs incurred during the period were $21,550. An analysis at the end of the period shows that the total overhead applied during the period was distributed as follows:

| | |
|---|---|
| Jobs still in process . . . . . . . | 20% |
| Jobs finished but unsold . . . . | 15 |
| Jobs finished and sold . . . . . | 65 |

   The entry to allocate the overapplied or underapplied overhead to the jobs worked on during the period would include:
   *a.* A debit to Goods in Process for $500.
   *b.* A credit to Finished Goods for $75.
   *c.* A debit to Factory Overhead for $500.
   *d.* A debit to Cost of Goods Sold for $325.
   *e.* No entry is required.
4. A process cost accounting system:
   *a.* Is another name for a job order cost accounting system.
   *b.* Is used when each product or job has a unique design so that the manufacturing process focuses on the production of each specific job.

*c.* Is a system in which the cost of raw materials is recorded in a Goods in Process account at the time the materials are purchased.
*d.* Is a system in which direct labor is transferred from Factory Payroll to Goods in Process based on a predetermined application rate.
*e.* Is an accounting system which has a separate Goods in Process account for the costs of each manufacturing department.

5. The following information for a company's assembly department relates to the manufacturing operations of one month:

| | |
|---|---|
| Costs charged to the department: | |
| Direct materials requisitioned | $ 60,000 |
| Direct labor charged | 30,000 |
| Overhead costs (predetermined overhead rate is 50% of direct labor) | 15,000 |
| Total processing costs | $105,000 |
| Goods in process at the beginning of the month | 10,000 |
| Cost transferred from prior department (26,000 units at $3.25 each) | 84,500 |
| Total costs to be accounted for | $199,500 |

Equivalent unit processing costs:

| | Units Involved | Fraction of a Unit Added |
|---|---|---|
| Direct materials, direct labor, and overhead: | | |
| Beginning inventory | 6,000 | 2/3 |
| Units started and finished | 24,000 | one |
| Ending inventory | 8,000 | 1/4 |

What are the total accumulated costs of goods transferred to finished goods from this department during the month?
*a.* $186,000.
*b.* $162,000.
*c.* $ 98,500.
*d.* $192,500.
*e.* $176,000.

## Questions for Class Discussion

1. What are the two primary types of cost accounting systems? Indicate which of the two would best fit the needs of a manufacturer who (*a*) produces customized motor homes designed to the specifications of each customer; (*b*) produces in lots of three to five, a variety of large industrial-use, electric generators; and (*c*) manufactures copper tubing.
2. What is the difference between a job and a job lot?
3. What accounts do raw materials costs flow through in a job order cost system?
4. Why are materials requisitions used?
5. A manufacturing company produces a single product by processing it first through a mixing department and next through a cutting department. What accounts do direct labor costs flow through in this company's process cost system?

6. What purpose is served by a job cost sheet?
7. What use is made of labor time tickets?
8. In a job order cost system, the Raw Materials account and the Goods in Process account each serve as a controlling account for a subsidiary ledger. What subsidiary ledgers do these accounts control?
9. How is the ending inventory of goods in process determined in a general accounting system like that described in Chapter 21? How may this inventory be determined in a job cost system?
10. What is a job cost sheet?
11. What is the name of the ledger that contains the job cost sheets of the unfinished jobs in process? What account controls this ledger?
12. What business papers provide the information that is used to make the job cost sheet entries for (*a*) direct materials and (*b*) direct labor?
13. Refer to the job cost sheet of Illustration 22–4. How was the amount of overhead costs charged to this job determined?
14. How is a predetermined overhead application rate established? Why is such a predetermined rate used to charge overhead to jobs?
15. Why does a company that uses a job cost system normally have either overapplied or underapplied overhead at the end of each accounting period?
16. At the end of a period, the Factory Overhead controlling account has a debit balance. Does this represent overapplied or underapplied overhead?
17. What are the basic differences in the products and in the manufacturing procedures of a job order manufacturer and a process manufacturer?
18. What is meant by the equivalent finished units produced with respect to direct labor?
19. What is the basic idea that underlies the concept of equivalent finished units produced?
20. What is the production of a department measured in equivalent finished units if it began an accounting period with 8,000 units of product that were one-fourth completed, started and finished 50,000 units during the period, and ended the period with 6,000 units that were one-third processed?
21. The process cost summary of a department commonly has three sections. What is shown in each section?

## Exercises

**Exercise 22–1**
**Recording costs in a job order cost system**
(L. O. 1)

During the month of November, a company that uses a job cost system purchased raw materials for $18,000 cash, used $450 of raw materials as factory supplies, and entered $15,600 of raw materials into production as direct materials. Factory payroll incurred for the month (paid in cash) amounted to $22,500, of which $2,100 was classified as indirect labor. Prepare general journal entries to record these activities.

**Exercise 22–2**
**Diagramming cost flows in a job cost system**
(L. O. 1)

A company that uses a job cost system provides the following information:

| | March 31 | April 30 | During April |
|---|---|---|---|
| Raw materials inventory | $ 3,000 | $12,000 | |
| Goods in process | 6,000 | 7,500 | |
| Finished goods | 12,000 | 10,500 | |
| Raw materials purchased | | | $24,000 |
| Factory payroll costs incurred | | | 22,050 |
| Overhead incurred (includes $750 of raw materials used as supplies and $1,050 of indirect labor) | | | 13,050 |
| Cost of goods sold | | | ? |

The company's predetermined overhead application rate is 60% of direct labor. Set up T-accounts like those in Illustration 22–3. Show the April flows of manufacturing costs in the company by entering the above information in the T-accounts and drawing arrows similar to those in Illustration 22–3. Leave any underapplied or overapplied overhead in the Factory Overhead account.

**Exercise 22–3**
**Calculating overhead application rate; assigning costs to jobs**
(L. O. 2, 3)

**Part 1.** During December 1990, Walker Corporation's cost accountant established the company's 1991 overhead application rate based on direct labor cost. In setting the rate, the cost accountant estimated the company would incur $675,000 of overhead costs during 1991 and would apply $843,750 of direct labor to the products that would be manufactured during 1991. Determine the rate.

**Part 2.** During April 1991, Walker Corporation of Part 1 began and completed Job No. 310. Determine the job's cost under the assumption that when it was completed the job's cost sheet showed the following materials and labor charged to it:

**Job Cost Sheet**

Customer's Name Carney Corp. Job No. 310
Job Description 2.5 Watt Power Supply

| | Direct Materials | | Direct Labor | | Overhead Costs Applied | | |
|---|---|---|---|---|---|---|---|
| Date | Requisition No. | Amount | Time-Ticket No. | Amount | Date | Rate | Amount |
| Apr. 4 | 2450 | 1,335.00 | 3227 | 975.00 | | | |
| 5 | 2478 | 2,820.00 | 3228 | 1,350.00 | 4-11 | 80% | 3660 |
| 10 | 2490 | 1,110.00 | 3233 | 2,250.00 | | | |
| | | 5265 | | 4575.00 | | | |

13500

**Exercise 22–4**
**Analysis of cost flows**
(L. O. 2, 3)

At the end of April, the job cost sheets of a company had been assigned the following costs:

| | Job 4 | Job 5 | Job 6 |
|---|---|---|---|
| Direct materials . . . . | $3,900 | $13,800 | $8,250 |
| Direct labor . . . . . . | 5,100 | 11,700 | 9,000 |
| Overhead . . . . . . . | 5,610 | 12,870 | 9,900 |

Job 4 was started in production during March and had direct materials of $1,800, direct labor of $750, and overhead of $825 assigned to the job at the end of March. Jobs 5 and 6 were started during April, Jobs 4 and 5 were finished during April, and Job 6 will be finished during May. Answer the following questions: (*a*) Assuming no raw materials costs were assigned to overhead during April, what amount of raw materials were requisitioned during April? (*b*) How much direct labor was incurred during April? (*c*) What is the predetermined overhead application rate? (*d*) What amount of cost was transferred to finished goods during April?

Exercise 22–5
**Eliminating the end-of-period balance in Factory Overhead**
(L. O. 3)

In December 1990, Parker Company established the following overhead application rate for applying overhead to the jobs during 1991:

$$\frac{\text{Estimated overhead costs, \$598,500}}{\text{Estimated direct labor costs, \$855,000}} \times 100 = 70\%$$

At the end of 1991, the company's accounting records showed that $612,000 of overhead costs had been incurred during 1991 and $900,000 of direct labor, distributed as follows, had been applied to jobs during the year.

| | |
|---|---|
| Direct labor on jobs completed and sold . . . | $765,000 |
| Direct labor on jobs completed and in the finished goods inventory . . . . . . . . . | 90,000 |
| Direct labor on jobs still in process . . . . . . | 45,000 |
| | $900,000 |

*Required*

1. Set up a T-account for Factory Overhead and enter in the account the amounts of overhead costs incurred and applied. State whether overhead was overapplied or underapplied during the year.
2. Give the entry to close the Factory Overhead account and allocate its balance between jobs sold, jobs finished but unsold, and jobs in process.

Exercise 22–6
**Analysis of costs assigned to Goods in Process**
(L. O. 2, 3)

Grange Company uses a job cost system in which overhead is charged to jobs on the basis of direct labor cost. At the end of a year, the company's Goods in Process account showed the following:

**Goods in Process**

| | | | |
|---|---|---|---|
| Direct materials | 408,000 | To finished goods | 984,000 |
| Direct labor | 288,000 | | |
| Overhead | 360,000 | | |

*Required*

1. Determine the overhead application rate used by the company under the assumption that the direct labor and overhead costs actually incurred were the same as the amounts estimated.

2. Determine the cost of direct labor and the cost of overhead charged to the one job in process at year-end under the assumption it had $26,550 of materials charged to it.

**Exercise 22–7**
**Recording cost flows in a process cost system**
(L. O. 4)

Blalock Company's product is manufactured by processing it first through Department X and then through Department Y. Information about manufacturing operations during February is as follows:

| | Department X | Department Y |
|---|---|---|
| Direct materials requisitioned by . . . . . . . . . . . | $27,000 | $ 6,000 |
| Direct labor charged to . . . . . . . . . . . . . . | 22,500 | 33,000 |
| Predetermined overhead application rate . . . . . | 80% | 80% |
| Cost of goods transferred from Department X to . . | | 51,000 |
| Cost of goods transferred out of Department Y . . | | 78,000 |
| Cost of goods sold . . . . . . . . . . . . . . . . . | | 73,500 |

Based on the cost flows diagramed in Illustration 22–10, prepare general journal entries to record the February cost flows shown above.

**Exercise 22–8**
**Calculating equivalent finished units produced**
(L. O. 5)

During an accounting period, a department finished and transferred 79,800 units of product to finished goods, of which 36,800 were in process in the department at the beginning of the cost period and 43,000 were begun and completed during the period. The 36,800 beginning inventory units were three-fourths completed when the period began. In addition to the 79,800 units completed, 15,600 more units were in process in the department, one-half completed when the period ended.

*Required*

Calculate the equivalent finished units produced in the department during the period.

**Exercise 22–9**
**Assigning costs to inventories in a process cost system**
(L. O. 4, 5)

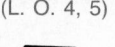

Assume the department of Exercise 22–8 had $42,000 of direct labor charged to it during the cost period of the exercise and that direct labor is applied in the process of the department evenly through the process.

*Required*

Calculate the cost of an equivalent unit of labor in the department and the portion of the department's $42,000 labor cost that should be assigned to each of its inventories and to the units started and finished.

**Exercise 22–10**
**Calculating equivalent finished units produced**
(L. O. 5)

A department completed and transferred to finished goods 86,400 units of product during a cost period. Of these units, 21,600 were in process one-third complete at the beginning of the period, and 64,800 units were started and completed during the period. In addition to the 86,400 units completed, 18,000 more units were in process at the end of the period, three-fifths processed.

*Required*

Calculate the equivalent units for direct materials added to the product processed in the department during the period under each of the following unrelated assumptions: (*a*) All direct materials added to the product of the department are added when processing begins. (*b*) The direct materials added to the product of the department are added evenly throughout the department's process. (*c*) One half the direct materials added in the department is added when the department's process first begins, and the other half is added when the process is three-fourths completed.

## Problems

**Problem 22–1**
**Allocating overhead based on predetermined overhead application rate**
(L. O. 2, 3)

In December 1990, Oprah Company's accountant estimated that during the next year, the company would incur the direct labor cost of 32 persons working 2,000 hours each at an average rate of $9 per hour. The accountant also estimated that the following manufacturing overhead costs would be incurred during the year:

| | |
|---|---|
| Indirect labor | $ 75,600 |
| Superintendence | 57,600 |
| Rent of factory building | 34,560 |
| Factory utilities | 23,040 |
| Insurance expense | 16,320 |
| Depreciation of machinery | 116,160 |
| Machinery repairs | 14,400 |
| Supplies expense | 7,200 |
| Miscellaneous factory expenses | 6,480 |
| Total | $351,360 |

At the end of 1991, the cost records showed the company had actually incurred $349,440 of overhead costs and had completed and sold five jobs that had direct labor costs as follows: Job 604, $121,950; Job 605, $111,300; Job 606, $104,250; Job 607, $109,350; and Job 608, $119,550. In addition, Job 609 was in process at the end of the year and had been charged $12,000 of direct labor plus its share of overhead costs.

*Required*

If the company used a predetermined overhead application rate based on the above overhead and direct labor estimates, determine: (*a*) the predetermined overhead application rate used, (*b*) the total overhead applied to jobs during the year, and (*c*) the over- or underapplied overhead at year-end. (*d*) Assuming the amount of over- or underapplied overhead is not material, give the entry to close the Factory Overhead account.

**Problem 22–2**
**Recording and posting manufacturing costs—job order system**
(L. O. 1, 2, 3)

Ehlers Incorporated's transactions and activities during June included the following:

*a*. Purchased raw materials on account, $60,000.
*b*. Paid factory wages, $46,500.
*c*. Paid miscellaneous factory overhead costs, $3,000.
*d*. Material requisitions are used to charge direct materials to jobs. The requisitions are then accumulated until the end of the month at which time they are totaled and recorded with a general journal entry. A sum-

mary of the requisitions shows the following materials were used on jobs and used as indirect materials:

| | |
|---|---|
| Job 21 | $ 9,750 |
| Job 22 | 4,875 |
| Job 23 | 10,500 |
| Job 24 | 11,250 |
| Job 25 | 2,250 |
| Total direct materials | $38,625 |
| Indirect materials | 7,500 |
| Total materials used | $46,125 |

Charge the direct materials to the jobs by making entries directly in the job T-accounts in the subsidiary Job Cost Ledger. In the General Journal, prepare an entry to record the materials used.

*e.* Labor time tickets are used to charge jobs with direct labor. The tickets are then accumulated until the end of the month at which time they are totaled and recorded with a general journal entry. A summary of the tickets shows factory labor was applied to jobs and used as indirect labor, as follows:

| | |
|---|---|
| Job 21 | $ 9,000 |
| Job 22 | 5,250 |
| Job 23 | 9,750 |
| Job 24 | 10,500 |
| Job 25 | 1,500 |
| Total direct labor | $36,000 |
| Indirect labor | 11,625 |
| Total | $47,625 |

Charge the direct labor to the jobs by making entries directly in the T-accounts in the Job Cost Ledger. In the General Journal, prepare an entry to record the total labor charged to jobs and the portion used as indirect labor.

*f.* Jobs 21, 23, and 24 were completed and transferred to finished goods. A predetermined overhead application rate, 150% of direct labor cost, is used to apply overhead to each job upon its completion. (Enter the overhead in the job T-accounts; mark the jobs "completed"; and make a general entry to transfer their costs to the Finished Goods account.)

*g.* Jobs 21 and 23 were sold on account for a total of $90,000.

*h.* At the end of June, overhead should be charged to the jobs in process at the rate of 150% of direct labor cost. (Enter the overhead in the job T-accounts.)

*i.* Prepare a general journal entry dated June 30 to record: depreciation of factory building, $8,625; depreciation of machinery, $15,375; expired factory insurance, $2,250; and accrued factory taxes payable, $4,500.

*j.* Determine the total overhead assigned to all jobs and make a general journal entry to record the assignment.

*Required*

1. Open the following general ledger T-accounts: Raw Materials, Goods in Process, Finished Goods, Factory Payroll, Factory Overhead, and Cost of Goods Sold.

2. Open an additional T-account for each of the five jobs. Assume that each job's T-account is a job cost sheet in a subsidiary Job Cost Ledger.
3. Prepare general journal entries to record the items listed above. Post the portions of the entries that affect the general ledger accounts listed in Requirement 1.
4. Enter the applicable information of items (*d*), (*e*), (*f*), and (*h*) directly in the T-accounts that represent job cost sheets.
5. Present statistics to prove the balances of the Goods in Process and Finished Goods accounts.
6. List the general ledger accounts and describe what is represented by the balance of each.

**Problem 22–3**
**Recording manufacturing transactions and preparing financial statements**
(L. O. 1, 2, 3)

*If the working papers that accompany this text are not being used, omit this problem.*

The Thompson Company manufactures to the special order of its customers a machine called a pictocomp. On October 1, the company had a raw materials inventory of $13,380 but no inventories of goods in process and finished goods. However, on that date it began Job 25, a pictocomp for Mountain Company, and Job 26, for Nature Company. During the October cost period, the company completed the following activities and transactions:

*a.* Recorded invoices for the purchase of raw materials on credit. The invoices and receiving reports carried this information:
   Receiving Report No. 10, Material Y, 60 units at $220 each.
   Receiving Report No. 11, Material Z, 70 units at $120 each.
   *(Record the invoices with a single general journal entry and post to the general ledger T-accounts, using the transaction letter to identify the amounts in the accounts. Enter the receiving report information on the proper raw materials ledger cards.)*

*b.* Raw materials were requisitioned as follows:
   Requisition No. 11, for Job 25, 30 units of Material Y.
   Requisition No. 12, for Job 25, 28 units of Material Z.
   Requisition No. 13, for Job 26, 25 units of Material Y.
   Requisition No. 14, for Job 26, 25 units of Material Z.
   Requisition No. 15, for 3 units of machinery lubricant.
   *(Enter the requisition amounts for direct materials on the raw materials ledger cards and on the job cost sheets. Enter the indirect material amount on the proper raw materials ledger card and debit it to the Indirect Materials account in the subsidiary Factory Overhead Ledger. Assume the requisitions are accumulated until the end of the month and will be recorded with a general journal entry. Instructions for this entry follow in the problem.)*

*c.* Received the following labor time tickets from the timekeeping department:
   Time tickets Nos. 1 through 60 for direct labor on Job 25, $6,000.
   Time tickets Nos. 61 through 100 for direct labor on Job 26, $4,800.
   Time tickets Nos. 101 through 120 for machinery repairs, $2,250.
   *(Charge the direct labor time tickets to the proper jobs and charge the*

*indirect labor time tickets to the Indirect Labor account in the subsidiary Factory Overhead Ledger. Assume the time tickets are accumulated until the end of the month for recording with a general journal entry.)*

*d.* Made the following cash disbursements during the month:
Paid the month's factory payroll, $12,600.
Paid for miscellaneous overhead items totaling $6,000.
*(Record the payments with general journal entries and post to the general ledger accounts. Enter the charge for miscellaneous overhead items in the subsidiary Factory Overhead Ledger.)*

*e.* Finished Job 25 and transferred it to the finished goods warehouse. *(The company charges overhead to each job by means of a predetermined overhead application rate based on direct labor costs. The rate is 80%. (1) Enter the overhead charge on the cost sheet of Job 25. (2) Complete the cost summary section of the cost sheet and mark the cost sheet as "Finished." (3) Prepare and post a general journal entry to record the job's completion and transfer to finished goods.)*

*f.* The sale price of Job 25 was $30,000. *(Prepare and post a general journal entry to record both the cost of goods sold and the sale of Job 25 to Mountain Company.)*

*g.* At the end of the cost period, charged overhead to Job 26 based on the amount of direct labor applied to the job thus far. *(Enter the applicable amount of overhead on the job's cost sheet.)*

*h.* Totaled the requisitions for direct materials and for indirect materials. *(Prepare and post a general journal entry to record them.)*

*i.* Totaled the direct labor time tickets and the indirect labor time tickets. *(Prepare and post a general journal entry to record them.)*

*j.* Determined the total amount of overhead applied to jobs. *(Prepare and post a general journal entry to record it.)*

*Required*

1. Record the transactions as instructed in the narrative.
2. Complete the statements in the book of working papers by filling in the blanks.

**Problem 22–4**
**Calculating costs per equivalent unit of product finished**
(L. O. 5)

In the mixing department of Dox Manufacturing Company, direct labor is added to the department's product evenly throughout its processing. During the month of May, 168,725 units of product were finished in this department and transferred to finished goods. Of these 168,725 units, 50,625 were in process at the beginning of the period and 118,100 were begun and completed during the period. The 50,625 beginning goods in process units were one-fifth completed when the period began. In addition to the foregoing units, 30,375 additional units were in process and were two-thirds completed at the end of May.

*Required*

Under the assumption that $153,811 of direct labor was charged to the mixing department during May, determine (*a*) the equivalent finished units produced with respect to direct labor applied to the department's product; (*b*) the cost of an equivalent finished unit for labor; and (*c*) the portion of the $153,811 that should be charged to the beginning inventory, to the units started and finished, and to the ending inventory.

**Problem 22–5**
**Preparing a process cost summary**
(L. O. 4, 5)

The product of Untermyer Manufacturing Company is produced on a continuous basis in a single processing department. Direct materials, direct labor, and overhead are added to the product evenly throughout the manufacturing process.

At the end of the June 1991 cost period, after the direct materials, direct labor, and overhead costs were charged to the Goods in Process account of the department, the account appeared as follows:

**Goods in Process**

| | | | | |
|---|---|---|---|---|
| June | 1 | Balance | 20,430 | |
| | 30 | Direct materials | 79,875 | |
| | 30 | Direct labor | 178,920 | |
| | 30 | Overhead | 134,190 | |
| | | | 413,415 | |

During June, the company finished and transferred to finished goods 81,000 units of the product, of which 10,125 were in process at the beginning of the period and 70,875 were started and finished during the period. The 10,125 units that were in process were one-third processed when the period began. In addition, 9,000 units were in process and were one-fourth completed at the end of the period.

*Required*

1. Prepare a process cost summary for the department.
2. Draft the general journal entry to transfer to Finished Goods the cost of the product finished in the department during the month.

**Problem 22–6**
**Preparing a process cost summary**
(L. O. 4, 5)

Midtown Production Company manufactures a single product on a continuous basis in one department. All direct materials are added at the beginning of the manufacturing process. Direct labor and overhead are added evenly throughout the process.

During the current July cost period, the company completed and transferred to finished goods 96,750 units of the product. These consisted of 11,250 units that were in process at the beginning of the period and 85,500 units started and finished during the period. The 11,250 beginning goods in process units were complete as to direct materials and four-fifths complete as to direct labor and overhead when the period began. In addition to these units, 13,500 additional units were in process at the end of the period, complete as to direct materials and one-half complete as to direct labor and overhead.

Since the company has only one processing department, it has only one Goods in Process account. At the end of the period, after entries recording direct materials, direct labor, and overhead had been posted, the account appeared as follows:

**Goods in Process**

| | | | | |
|---|---|---|---|---|
| July | 1 | Balance | 18,300 | |
| | 31 | Direct materials | 94,050 | |
| | 31 | Direct labor | 98,280 | |
| | 31 | Overhead | 122,850 | |
| | | | 333,480 | |

*Required*

Prepare a process cost summary and the entry to transfer to Finished Goods the cost of the product completed in the department during July.

## Alternate Problems

**Problem 22–1A**
**Allocating overhead based on predetermined overhead application rate**
(L. O. 2, 3)

Late in 1990, the cost accountant for Frankeny Company established the 1991 overhead application rate by estimating that the company would assign 20 persons to direct labor tasks during 1991 and that each person would work 2,000 hours at $10 per hour during the year. At the same time the accountant estimated that the company would incur the following amounts of overhead costs during 1991:

| | |
|---|---|
| Indirect labor | $135,000 |
| Factory building rent | 81,000 |
| Depreciation expense, machinery | 98,500 |
| Machinery repairs expense | 20,250 |
| Factory utilities | 38,500 |
| Factory supplies expense | 6,750 |
| Total | $380,000 |

At the end of 1991, the accounting records showed the company had actually incurred $395,280 of overhead costs during the year while completing four jobs and beginning the fifth. The completed jobs were assigned overhead on completion, and the in-process job was assigned overhead at year-end. The jobs had the following direct labor costs:

| | |
|---|---|
| Job 17 (sold and delivered) | $ 86,550 |
| Job 18 (sold and delivered) | 87,750 |
| Job 19 (sold and delivered) | 95,800 |
| Job 20 (in finished goods inventory) | 94,500 |
| Job 21 (in process, unfinished) | 47,100 |
| Total | $411,700 |

*Required*

1. Determine the overhead application rate established by the cost accountant under the assumption it was based on direct labor cost.
2. Determine the total overhead applied to jobs during the year and the amount of over- or underapplied overhead at year-end.
3. Give the entry to dispose of the over- or underapplied overhead by prorating it between goods in process, finished goods inventory, and cost of goods sold.

**Problem 22–2A**
**Recording and posting manufacturing costs—job order system**
(L. O. 1, 2, 3)

During its first cost period, Luong Company completed the following activities and transactions:

*a.* Purchased raw materials on account, $49,500.

*b.* Paid factory wages, $42,300.

*c.* Paid miscellaneous factory overhead costs, $6,750.

*d.* Material requisitions are used during the period to charge direct materials to jobs. The requisitions are accumulated until the end of the period and then are totaled and recorded with a general journal entry. A summary of the requisitions shows the following direct materials charged to jobs and used as indirect materials:

| | |
|---|---|
| Job 35 | $ 9,000 |
| Job 36 | 4,725 |
| Job 37 | 8,775 |
| Job 38 | 9,675 |
| Job 39 | 1,800 |
| Total direct materials | $33,975 |
| Indirect materials | 9,000 |
| Total materials used | $42,975 |

Charge the materials to the jobs by making entries directly in the job T-accounts in the subsidiary Job Cost Ledger. In the General Journal, prepare an entry to record the materials used.

*e.* Labor time tickets are used to charge jobs with direct labor. The tickets are accumulated until the end of the cost period and then are totaled and recorded with a general journal entry. A summary of the tickets shows that factory labor was applied to jobs and used as indirect labor, as follows:

| | |
|---|---|
| Job 35 | $ 8,550 |
| Job 36 | 4,950 |
| Job 37 | 9,000 |
| Job 38 | 8,100 |
| Job 39 | 900 |
| Total direct labor | $31,500 |
| Indirect labor | 11,250 |
| Total factory labor | $42,750 |

Charge the direct labor to the jobs by making entries directly in the job T-accounts in the Job Cost Ledger. In the General Journal, prepare an entry to record the total labor charged to jobs and the portion used as indirect labor.

*f.* Jobs 35, 37, and 38 were completed and transferred to finished goods. A predetermined overhead application rate, 200% of direct labor cost, is used to apply overhead to each job upon its completion. (Enter the overhead in the job T-accounts; mark the jobs "completed"; and make a general journal entry to transfer their costs to the Finished Goods account.)

*g*. Jobs 35 and 38 were sold on account for a total of $93,600.

*h*. At the end of the period, overhead should be charged to the jobs in process, using the 200% of direct labor cost application rate. (Enter the overhead in the job T-accounts.)

*i*. Prepare a general journal entry at the end of the period to record depreciation on the factory building, $13,500; machinery depreciation, $15,075; expired factory insurance, $2,700; and accrued factory taxes payable, $4,200.

*j*. Determine the total overhead assigned to all jobs and make a general journal entry to record it.

*Required*

1. Open the following general ledger T-accounts: Raw Materials, Goods in Process, Finished Goods, Factory Payroll, Factory Overhead, and Cost of Goods Sold.
2. Open an additional T-account for each of the five jobs. Assume that each job's T-account is a job cost sheet in a subsidiary Job Cost Ledger.
3. Prepare general journal entries to record the items listed above. Post the portions of the entries that affect the general ledger accounts listed in Requirement 1.
4. Enter the applicable information of items (*d*), (*e*), (*f*), and (*h*) directly in the T-accounts that represent job cost sheets.
5. Present statistics to prove the balances of the Goods in Process and Finished Goods accounts.
6. List the general ledger accounts and describe what is represented by the balance of each.

**Problem 22–3A**
**Recording manufacturing transactions and preparing financial statements**
(L. O. 1, 2, 3)

*If the working papers that accompany this text are not being used, omit this problem.*

The Durango Company manufactures to the special order of its customers a machine called a loader-lift. On October 1, the company had a $13,380 raw materials inventory but no inventories of goods in process and finished goods. However, on that date it began Job 25, a loader-lift for Mountain Company, and Job 26, for Nature Company. During the October cost period, it completed the following activities and transactions:

*a*. Recorded invoices for the purchase of raw materials on credit. The invoices and receiving reports carried this information:

Receiving Report No. 15, Material Y, 40 units at $220 each.
Receiving Report No. 16, Material Z, 46 units at $120 each.
*(Record the invoices with a single general journal entry and post to the general ledger T-accounts, using the transaction letter to identify the amounts in the accounts. Enter the receiving report information on the proper raw materials ledger cards.)*

*b*. Raw materials were requisitioned as follows:

Requisition No. 21, for Job 25, 20 units of Material Y.

Requisition No. 22, for Job 25, 18 units of Material Z.
Requisition No. 23, for Job 26, 17 units of Material Y.
Requisition No. 24, for Job 26, 15 units of Material Z.
Requisition No. 25, for 5 units of machinery lubricant.
*(Enter the requisition amounts for direct materials on the raw materials ledger cards and on the job cost sheets. Enter the indirect material amount on the proper raw materials ledger card and debit it to the Indirect Materials account in the subsidiary Factory Overhead Ledger. Assume the requisitions are accumulated until the end of the month and will be recorded with a general journal entry. Instructions for this entry follow in the problem.)*

*c.* Received the following labor time tickets from the timekeeping department:
Time tickets Nos. 50 through 75 for direct labor on Job 25, $8,250.
Time tickets Nos. 76 through 105 for direct labor on Job 26, $10,800.
Time tickets Nos. 106 through 118 for machinery repairs, $1,800.
*(Charge the direct labor time tickets to the proper jobs and charge the indirect labor time tickets to the Indirect Labor account in the subsidiary Factory Overhead Ledger. Assume the time tickets are accumulated until the end of the month for recording with a general journal entry.)*

*d.* Made the following cash disbursements during the month:
Paid the month's factory payroll, $17,850.
Paid for miscellaneous overhead items totaling $9,300.
*(Record the payments with general journal entries and post to the general ledger accounts. Enter the charge for miscellaneous overhead items in the subsidiary Factory Overhead Ledger.)*

*e.* Finished Job 25 and transferred it to the finished goods warehouse. *(The company charges overhead to each job by means of a predetermined overhead application rate based on direct labor costs. The rate is 70%. (1) Enter the overhead charge on the cost sheet of Job 25. (2) Complete the cost summary section of the cost sheet. (3) Mark "Finished" on the cost sheet. (4) Prepare and post a general journal entry to record the job's completion and transfer to finished goods.)*

*f.* The sale price of Job 25 was $48,000. *(Prepare and post a general journal entry to record both the cost of goods sold and the sale of Job 25 to Mountain Company.)*

*g.* At the end of the cost period, charge overhead to Job 26 based on the amount of direct labor applied to the job thus far. *(Enter the applicable amount of overhead on the job's cost sheet.)*

*h.* Totaled the requisitions for direct materials and for indirect materials. *(Prepare and post a general journal entry to record them.)*

*i.* Totaled the direct labor time tickets and the indirect labor time tickets. *(Prepare and post a general journal entry to record them.)*

*j.* Determined the amount of overhead applied to jobs. *(Prepare and post a general journal entry to record it.)*

*Required*

1. Record the transactions as instructed in the narrative.
2. Complete the statements in the book of working papers by filling in the blanks.

**Problem 22–4A**
**Calculating costs per equivalent unit of product finished**
(L. O. 5)

The NVK Company is a one-department operation in which direct labor and overhead are added to the department's product evenly throughout the production process. In August, 78,750 units of product were transferred from the shop to finished goods inventory. Included in these 78,750 units were 30,000 units from the July 31 work in process inventory, at which time those units were one-fourth finished. In addition to the beginning inventory, 101,250 units were placed in process during August. On August 31, the units that remained in process were one-half complete. Total overhead costs incurred during August were $1,396,200.

*Required*

Determine *(a)* the equivalent finished units produced in August to be used in applying overhead costs to the product of the shop; *(b)* the overhead cost of an equivalent finished unit produced; and *(c)* the portion of August overhead cost that should be charged to completing the units in beginning inventory, to units started and finished during August, and to the ending inventory.

**Problem 22–5A**
**Preparing a process cost summary**
(L. O. 4, 5)

Two operations, mixing and molding, are used in the manufacturing procedure of the Maine Manufacturing Company. The procedure begins in the mixing department and is finished in the molding department.

At the beginning of the November cost period there were 7,500 units of product in the mixing department that were three-fifths processed. These units were completed during the period and transferred to the molding department. Also, the processing of 46,500 additional units was started in the mixing department during the period. Of these 46,500 units, 34,500 were finished and transferred to the molding department. The remaining 12,000 units were in the mixing department in a one-half processed state at the end of the period.

In the mixing department, direct materials, direct labor, and overhead are applied evenly throughout the mixing process.

At the end of the cost period, after posting entries to record direct materials, direct labor, and overhead, the company's Goods in Process, Mixing Department account appeared as follows:

**Goods in Process, Mixing Department**

| | | | | |
|---|---|---|---|---|
| Nov. | 1 | Balance | 69,600 | |
| | 30 | Direct materials | 222,720 | |
| | 30 | Direct labor | 295,800 | |
| | 30 | Overhead | 147,900 | |
| | | | 736,020 | |

*Required*

1. Prepare a process cost summary for the mixing department.
2. Prepare the journal entry to transfer to the molding department the cost of the goods completed in the mixing department and transferred.

**Problem 22–6A**
**Preparing a process cost summary**
(L. O. 4, 5)

The product of Biloxi Company is manufactured in one continuous process in which all direct materials are entered into production at the beginning of the process. Direct labor and overhead are applied evenly throughout the process.

Biloxi Company's Goods in Process account reflects the following charges during the month of September:

| | |
|---|---|
| Beginning balance . . . . . . . . . . . . | $ 57,600 |
| Direct materials added to production . . | 274,815 |
| Direct labor charged to production . . . | 206,340 |
| Overhead charged to production . . . . | 165,072 |

During September, the company completed the manufacture of 52,350 units of product. These included 8,550 units that had entered production the previous month, and on September 1 were complete as to direct materials and two-thirds complete as to direct labor and overhead. At the end of September, 15,300 units remained in process, completed as to direct materials and one-half complete as to direct labor and overhead.

*Required*

Prepare a process cost summary and the entry to transfer to Finished Goods the cost of the product completed during September.

## Provocative Problems

**Provocative Problem 22–1**
**The Crowell Corporation**
(L. O. 1, 2)

The Crowell Corporation uses a job order cost system to account for manufacturing costs, and a number of its general ledger accounts with the January 1 balances and some January postings are shown below. The postings are incomplete. Often, only the debit or credit of a journal entry appears in the accounts, with the offsetting debits and credits being omitted. Also, the amounts shown represent total postings for the month, and no date appears. However, this additional information is available: (*a*) The company charges jobs with overhead on the basis of direct labor cost, using an overhead application rate of 150%. (*b*) The $76,500 debit in the Factory Overhead account represents the sum of all overhead costs for January other than indirect materials and indirect labor. (*c*) The accrued factory payroll on January 31 is $13,500.

**Raw Materials**

| | | | |
|---|---|---|---|
| Bal., Jan. 1 | 49,500 | | 54,000 |
| | 67,500 | | |

**Factory Payroll**

| | | | |
|---|---|---|---|
| | 85,500 | Bal., Jan. 1 | 9,000 |

**Goods in Process**

| | | | |
|---|---|---|---|
| Bal., Jan. 1 | 27,000 | | 216,000 |
| Dir. mat. | 45,000 | | |
| Dir. labor | 72,000 | | |

**Cost of Goods Sold**

| | |
|---|---|
| | |

| Finished Goods | | | | Factory Overhead | |
|---|---|---|---|---|---|
| Bal., Jan. 1 | 54,000 | | 225,000 | 76,500 | |

*Required*

Copy the accounts on a sheet of paper, supply the missing debits and credits, and tie together the debits and credits of an entry with key letters. Answer these questions: (*a*) What is the January 31 balance of the Finished Goods account? (*b*) How many dollars of factory labor cost (direct plus indirect) were incurred during January? (*c*) What was the cost of the goods sold during January? (*d*) How much overhead was actually incurred during the month? (*e*) How much overhead was charged to jobs during the month? (*f*) Was overhead overapplied or underapplied during the month? By what amount?

**Provocative Problem 22–2**
**Quirk Company**
(L. O. 2)

The production facility of Quirk Company was nearly destroyed on April 6, 1991, as a consequence of an explosion and fire in the plant. Assets lost in the blaze included all of the inventories. In addition, many of the accounting records were destroyed. In preparation for settlement with the insurance company, you are requested to estimate the amounts of raw materials, goods in process, and finished goods destroyed. Through your investigation, you determined that the company used a job order cost system, and you also obtained the following additional information:

*a.* The company's December 31, 1990, balance sheet showed the following inventory amounts: raw materials, $45,000; goods in process, $63,000; and finished goods, $72,000. The balance sheet also showed a $9,000 liability for accrued factory wages payable.

*b.* The overhead application rate used by the company was 70% of direct labor cost.

*c.* Goods costing $243,000 were sold and delivered to customers between January 1 and April 6, 1991.

*d.* Raw materials purchased between January 1 and April 6 amounted to $93,000, and $81,000 of direct and indirect materials were issued to the factory during the same period.

*e.* Factory wages totaling $105,000 were paid between January 1 and April 6, and there were $3,000 of accrued factory wages payable on the latter date.

*f.* The debits to the Factory Overhead account during the period before the fire totaled $63,000 of which $9,000 was for indirect materials and $15,000 was for indirect labor.

*g.* The cost of goods finished and transferred to finished goods inventory during the January 1 to April 6 period amounted to $228,000.

*h.* It was decided that the April 6 balance of the Factory Overhead account should be apportioned between goods in process, finished goods, and cost of goods sold. Between January 1 and April 6, the company had charged the following amounts of overhead to jobs: to jobs sold, $38,220; to jobs finished but unsold, $11,760; and to jobs still in process on April 6, $8,820.

Determine the April 6 inventories of raw materials, goods in process, and finished goods. (T-accounts may be helpful in organizing the data.)

**Provocative Problem 22–3**
**Goetz Company**
(L. O. 5)

The processing department of Goetz Company began January 1991 with 19,200 units in the goods in process inventory, each of which was 60% complete. During January, an additional 230,400 units were entered into the production process.

A total of 201,600 units were completed and transferred to finished goods. If January's equivalent finished units produced amounted to 203,520 units, how many units remained in process at the end of the month and what was their average stage of completion?

## COMPREHENSIVE PROBLEM

**Riley Company**
(Review of Chapters 2, 5, 9, 21, 22)

The Riley Company produces a product by sending it through two processes, one of which takes place in Department A and the other in Department B. All of A's output is transferred to B. In addition to the goods in process inventories in Departments A and B, Riley maintains inventories of raw materials and finished goods. Riley uses its raw materials as direct materials in Departments A and B, and as indirect materials. Its factory payroll costs also include direct labor in each department and indirect labor.

In this problem, you are to maintain certain records and produce various measures of the inventories to reflect the events of August 1991. Round all calculations of unit costs to the nearest penny and all other dollar amounts to the nearest whole dollar. To begin, set up the following general ledger accounts and enter their July 31 balances:

| | |
|---|---|
| Raw Materials | $15,000 |
| Factory Payroll | –0– |
| Factory Overhead | –0– |
| Goods in Process—Department A | 25,000 |
| Goods in Process—Department B | 65,000 |
| Finished Goods | 85,000 |
| Cost of Goods Sold | –0– |
| Sales | –0– |

1. Prepare summary general journal entries to record the following events during August:
   *a.* Purchased raw materials for $65,000 cash (use a perpetual inventory system).
   *b.* Used raw materials as follows:

| | |
|---|---|
| Department A | $21,760 |
| Department B | 46,760 |
| Indirect materials | 5,000 |

   *c.* Paid factory payroll cost of $125,000 cash (ignore income and other taxes).
   *d.* Assigned factory payroll costs as follows:

| | |
|---|---|
| Department A | $25,420 |
| Department B | 60,900 |
| Indirect labor | 38,680 |

   *e.* Incurred additional factory overhead costs of $54,725, paid in cash.
   *f.* Factory overhead is allocated to Departments A and B as a percentage of the direct labor costs. (Note: You will have to compute the overhead application rate using direct labor and overhead costs incurred during August.)
2. The following information was known about the units of product on hand or worked on during August:

| | Department A | Department B |
|---|---|---|
| Units in beginning inventory | 200 | 300 |
| Percent completed with respect to: | | |
| Materials | 90% | 30% |
| Labor and overhead | 80 | 10 |

| | Department A | Department B |
|---|---|---|
| Units started and finished in August . . | 500 | 450 |
| Percent completed with respect to: | | |
| Materials . . . . . . . . . . . . . . | 100% | 100% |
| Labor and overhead . . . . . . . . . | 100 | 100 |
| Ending inventory . . . . . . . . . . . . . | 400 | 250 |
| Percent completed with respect to: | | |
| Materials . . . . . . . . . . . . . . | 40% | 70% |
| Labor and overhead . . . . . . . . . | 20 | 60 |

Use this information and the facts from part (1) to make the following calculations:

Equivalent units of production in Department A and the per unit cost for labor, materials, and overhead.

Equivalent units of production in Department B and the per unit cost for labor, materials, and overhead.

3. Using the results from part (2) and previously given information, make the following calculations and prepare general journal entries to record:
   *g*. Total cost of units transferred from Department A to Department B during August.
   *h*. Total cost of units transferred from Department B to finished goods during August.
   *i*. Sale of finished goods that cost $279,000 for $500,000 cash.
4. As of August 31, 1990, determine the cost of the:

   Raw materials inventory
   Goods in process inventory for Department A
   Goods in process inventory for Department B
   Finished goods inventory
5. Post the journal entries from parts (1) and (3) to the ledger accounts that you set up at the beginning of the problem. (Note: The ending balances of the inventory accounts should equal the amounts determined in part (4).)
6. Compute the amount of gross profit from the sales in August 1990.
7. Complete this table by filling in the lettered blanks. The letters in parentheses should contain negative numbers.

| | Raw Materials | Factory Payroll | Factory Overhead | Goods in Process Dept. A | Goods in Process Dept. B | Finished Goods |
|---|---|---|---|---|---|---|
| Beginning inventories . . | $ 15,000 | | | $25,000 | $65,000 | $ 85,000 |
| Costs incurred . . . . . . | 65,000 | $125,000 | $54,725 | | | |
| Materials used: | | | | | | |
| In Department A . . . | (21,760) | | | *e* | | |
| In Department B . . . | (46,760) | | | | *j* | |
| Overhead . . . . . . . | ( 5,000) | | *b* | | | |
| Labor used: | | | | | | |
| In Department A . . . | | (25,420) | | *f* | | |
| In Department B . . . | | (60,900) | | | *k* | |
| Overhead . . . . . . . | | (38,680) | *c* | | | |
| Overhead applied . . . . | | | *(d)* | *g* | *l* | |
| Transfer from A to B . . . | | | | *(h)* | *m* | |
| Transfer from B . . . . . | | | | | *(n)* | *p* |
| Cost of goods sold . . . | | | | | | (279,000) |
| Ending inventories . . . | *a* | $ -0- | $ -0- | *i* | *o* | *q* |

# 23 Accounting for the Segments and Departments of a Business; Responsibility Accounting

In previous chapters, your attention was focused on understanding financial statements and related accounting information for a *whole* business. This chapter shifts your attention to accounting for the *parts* or subunits of a business. This aspect of accounting is called **segmental reporting** or **departmental accounting.** Information on the subunits of a business is useful to (1) outsiders who are interested in an overall evaluation of the business and (2) internal managers who are responsible for planning and controlling the operations of the business.

### Learning Objectives

*After studying Chapter 23, you should be able to:*

1. Describe the segmental information disclosed in the financial reports of large companies that have operations in several lines of business and list the four basic issues faced by accountants in developing segmental information.
2. Explain why businesses are divided into subunits or departments and explain the difference between cost centers and profit centers.
3. Describe the difference between direct and indirect expenses of departments, the bases used to allocate indirect expenses, and the procedures involved in the allocation process.
4. Prepare reports that are designed to measure the performance of a profit center and describe the factors to be considered in eliminating an unprofitable department.
5. Explain the concept of controllable costs and prepare reports to be used in evaluating the performance of a department manager.
6. Describe the problems associated with the allocation of joint costs between departments.
7. Define or explain the words and phrases listed in the chapter Glossary.

The term *segmental reporting* is used most often in reference to published information for the use of outsiders; this information generally relates to a company's operations in different industries or geographical areas. Usually, the term *departmental accounting* relates to information on the subunits of a business that is prepared for the use of internal managers.

## Reporting on Broad Business Segments

When a company is large and has operations in more than one type of business, outsiders can better understand the overall business if they examine information on each segment. For example, Illustration 23–1 shows segmental information provided in the annual report of Anheuser-Busch Companies, Inc.

### Segmental Information to Be Disclosed

Describe the segmental information disclosed in the financial reports of large companies that have operations in several lines of business and list the four basic issues faced by accountants in developing segmental information. (L. O. 1)

In Illustration 23–1, observe that the activities of the business are grouped into three segments: Beer and Beer-Related, Food Products, and Diversified Operations. The diversified operations category includes a variety of activities that individually do not constitute a significant segment. Note that five different items of information are presented for each segment. They are:

1. Revenues or net sales.
2. Operating profits (before interest and taxes).
3. Depreciation and amortization expense.
4. Capital expenditures.
5. Identifiable assets.

Large firms that operate in more than one industry are required to disclose these items of information on each industrial segment of the business. In addition, they may be required to report (1) a geographical distribution of sales and (2) sales to major customers.

### Four Basic Issues in Segmental Reporting

Companies face four basic problems in developing segmental information. Detailed guidelines for dealing with these problems are provided by the FASB. While the study of these guidelines is too detailed for inclusion at this introductory level, you should be aware of each basic issue.

**Identifying Significant Segments.** The operations of a business may not be neatly organized in terms of segments that are important to financial statement readers. For purposes of segmental reporting, the business must be divided into enough segments to show the basic industries in which the business operates. On the other hand, it should not be divided into so many segments that the information becomes confusing.

**Transfer Pricing between Segments.** Sometimes one or more segments of a business make sales of products or services to the other segments. These sales are eliminated when the overall statements for the business are prepared. However, sales between segments should not be eliminated when evaluating

**Illustration 23–1**
**Anheuser-Busch Companies, Inc., segmental information in the 1987 annual report**

**11 *Business Segments***

The company has identified its principal business segments as beer and beer-related, food products and diversified operations. The beer and beer-related segment produces and sells the company's beer products. Included in this segment are the company's raw material acquisition, malting, can manufacturing and recycling operations.

The food products segment consists of the company's food and food-related operations which include the company's baking, yeast and snack food subsidiaries and certain rice operations.

Diversified operations consist of the company's entertainment, communications, transportation and real estate operations.

Sales between segments, export sales and non-United States sales are not material. The company's equity in earnings of unconsolidated subsidiaries has been included in other income and expense. No single customer accounted for more than 10% of sales.

Summarized below is the company's business segment information for 1987, 1986 and 1985 (in millions). Intra-segment sales have been eliminated from each segment's reported net sales.

| *1987:* | *Beer and Beer-Related* | *Food Products* | *Diversified Operations* | *Eliminations* | *Consolidated* |
|---|---|---|---|---|---|
| Net sales | $6,375.8 | $1,627.2 | $263.8 | $ (8.4) | $8,258.4 |
| Operating income/(loss)* | 1,090.2 | 54.3 | (15.4)** | | 1,129.1 |
| Depreciation and amortization expense*** | 215.4 | 70.4 | 29.7 | | 315.5 |
| Capital expenditures | 630.4 | 149.1 | 43.4 | | 822.9 |
| Identifiable assets | 4,580.5 | 1,230.1 | 189.0 | | 5,999.6 |
| Corporate assets**** | | | | | 492.0 |
| Total assets | | | | | 6,491.6 |

| *1986:* | *Beer and Beer-Related* | *Food Products* | *Diversified Operations* | *Eliminations* | *Consolidated* |
|---|---|---|---|---|---|
| Net sales | $5,898.2 | $1,552.7 | $247.3 | $(21.0) | $7,677.2 |
| Operating income* | 945.8 | 56.6 | 2.7 | | 1,005.1 |
| Depreciation and amortization expense*** | 192.3 | 60.5 | 24.7 | | 277.5 |
| Capital expenditures | 544.8 | 164.3 | 68.2 | | 777.3 |
| Identifiable assets | 4,083.8 | 1,114.1 | 178.0 | | 5,375.9 |
| Corporate assets**** | | | | | 457.9 |
| Total assets | | | | | 5,833.8 |

| *1985:* | *Beer and Beer-Related* | *Food Products* | *Diversified Operations* | *Eliminations* | *Consolidated* |
|---|---|---|---|---|---|
| Net sales | $5,412.6 | $1,416.4 | $189.6 | $(18.3) | $7,000.3 |
| Operating income* | 797.0 | 28.5 | 6.8 | | 832.3 |
| Depreciation and amortization expense*** | 161.7 | 53.2 | 21.2 | | 236.1 |
| Capital expenditures | 461.2 | 103.7 | 36.1 | | 601.0 |
| Identifiable assets | 3,515.6 | 935.9 | 174.6 | | 4,626.1 |
| Corporate assets**** | | | | | 495.3 |
| Total assets | | | | | 5,121.4 |

*Operating income excludes other expense, net, which is not allocated among segments. For 1987, 1986 and 1985 other expense, net of $73.0, $63.9 and $51.8 million, respectively, includes net interest expense, other income and expense, and equity in earnings of unconsolidated subsidiaries.

**Primarily related to the planned disposition of Exploration Cruise Lines.

***Consolidated depreciation and amortization expenses include $11.8, $9.2 and $7.6 million of depreciation expense related to corporate assets for 1987, 1986 and 1985, respectively.

****Corporate assets principally include cash, marketable securities, investment in equity subsidiaries, excess of cost over net assets of acquired businesses and certain fixed assets.

the performance of each segment. Sales between segments result in revenues to the selling segment and costs to the purchasing segment. The problem is to determine a fair price at which to report such sales so that the profitability of both the selling segment and the purchasing segment are fairly measured.

## AS A MATTER OF ETHICS

You are the manager of Division A of a large company and a good friend of yours is the manager of Division B. Your product is not sold to the public but is transferred to Division B, where it is added to other components to produce the finished product. You and the manager of Division B are each compensated in proportion to the "profit" that you earn for the company. Your division's profit is affected by the transfer price assigned to the products you forward to Division B. The manager of Division B is also affected by this price, but in the opposite direction. You know that B could buy comparable components in the outside market for $5 million next year, but you can produce them at a cost of only $2 million.

In considering this issue, you wonder what price you should charge. Since you know that top management will not really let Division B buy from outsiders, you may be able to charge more than $5 million. You are also concerned with top management's reaction to your decision.

**Measuring Segmental Profitability.** Even if each segment operates as a highly independent unit, some expenses of the business will benefit more than one segment. Some of these **common expenses** can be allocated to the segments on a reasonable basis. Others may defy meaningful allocation. When you prepare information on the profitability of each business segment, you first must decide which expenses are to be allocated and which are to be left unallocated. Then, for those expenses to be allocated, you must determine the most reasonable basis for allocation.

**Identifying Segmental Assets.** Many assets are easily identified with specific segments because they are used solely by one segment or another. Other assets are shared by more than one segment. To report the investment of assets in each segment, you must determine reasonable bases for allocating shared assets to the segments that benefit from the assets.

## Departmental Accounting

Explain why businesses are divided into subunits or departments, and explain the difference between cost centers and profit centers.
(L. O. 2)

The previous discussion of segmental reporting related external financial statements about large businesses that have operations in more than one industry. However, you should not assume that accounting for the subunits of a business is limited to large companies with diverse operations. Businesses are divided into subunits or departments whenever they become too large to be effectively managed as a single unit.

Accounting for the departments of a business is characterized by two primary goals. One goal is to provide information that management can use in evaluating the profitability or cost effectiveness of each department. The second goal is to assign costs and expenses to the particular managers who are responsible for controlling those costs and expenses. In this way, the performance of managers can be evaluated in terms of their responsibilities. Thus, *departmental accounting* is closely related to what is called **responsibility accounting.**

### Departmentalizing a Business

Most businesses are large and complex enough to require that they be divided into subunits or departments. When a business is departmentalized, a manager usually is placed in charge of each department. If the business grows even larger, each department may be further divided into smaller segments. Thus, a particular manager can be assigned responsibilities over the activities of a unit that is not too large for the manager to effectively oversee and control. Also, departments can be organized so that the specialized skills of each manager can be used most effectively.

### Basis for Departmentalization

In a departmentalized business, there are two basic kinds of departments, **production departments** and **service departments.** In a factory, the production departments are those engaged directly in manufacturing operations. In a store, they are the departments making sales. Departmental divisions in a factory are commonly based on manufacturing processes employed or products or components manufactured. The divisions in a store are usually based on kinds of goods sold; each selling or production department is assigned the sale of one or more lines of merchandise. In either type of business, the service departments include functions such as advertising, purchasing, payroll, personnel, and corporate executive offices. These service departments assist or perform services for the production departments but do not themselves manufacture products or produce revenues.

### Information to Evaluate Departments

When a business is divided into departments, management must be able to find out how well each department is performing. Therefore, the accounting system must supply information about the resources expended and outputs achieved by each department. This requires that revenue and expense information be measured and accumulated by departments. However, you should understand that this type of information usually is not distributed publicly because it might be of considerable benefit to competitors. Rather, information about departmental operating performance is prepared for the use of internal management. Managers use this information in controlling operations, appraising performances, allocating resources, and in taking corrective actions. For example, if one of several departments is particularly profitable, management may decide to expand its operations. Or, if a department is showing poor results, information about its revenues, costs, and expenses may suggest proper corrective actions.

The information used to evaluate a department depends on whether the department is a **cost center** or a **profit center.** A cost center is a unit of the business that incurs costs (or expenses) but does not directly generate revenues. The manufacturing departments of a factory and such service departments as the accounting, advertising, and purchasing departments are cost centers. A profit center differs from a cost center in that it not only incurs costs but also generates revenues. The selling departments of a business are profit centers.

Evaluating the efficiency of a department depends on whether the department is a cost center or a profit center. Managers of cost centers are judged on their ability to control costs and keep costs within a satisfactory range. Managers of profit centers, on the other hand, are judged on their ability to generate earnings, which are the excess of revenues over departmental expenses.

## Securing Departmental Information

The methods used to gather information about the departments of a business vary from business to business. They often depend on the extent to which a company uses computers and modern cash registers.

**Methods Used with Computerized Systems.** Modern cash registers enable a merchandising company to accumulate information as to sales and sales returns by departments. Often, the registers transfer the information directly into the store's computer. This kind of system is capable of much more than accumulating sales information by departments. The cash registers will print all pertinent information on the sales ticket given to the customer, total the ticket, and initiate entries to record credit sales in the customer's account. Also, if the required information as to type of goods sold is keyed into the registers by means of code numbers, the computer can save and print out detailed daily departmental summaries of goods sold and remaining inventories of unsold goods.

**Using Separate Accounts for Each Department.** Cash registers also enable a business to determine daily totals for sales and sales returns by departments. However, if the registers are not connected to a computer, the totals must be accumulated by some other method. Two methods may be used. First, a business may provide separate Sales and Sales Returns accounts in its ledger for each of its departments. Second, the business may keep a supplementary spreadsheet analysis of departmental sales and sales returns. Either method may also be used to accumulate information as to purchases and purchases returns by departments.

If a business chooses to provide separate Sales, Sales Returns, Purchases, and Purchases Returns accounts in its ledger for each of its sales departments, it may also provide columns in its journals to record transactions by departments. Illustration 23–2 shows such a journal for recording sales by departments. The amounts to be debited to the customers' accounts are entered in the Accounts Receivable Debit column and are posted to these accounts each day. At the end of the month, the column's total is debited to the Accounts Receivable controlling account. The departmental sales are entered in the last three columns and are posted as column totals at the end of the month.

**Illustration 23–2**
**A departmentalized sales journal**

**Sales Journal**

| Date | | Account Debited | Invoice No. | PR | Accounts Receivable Debit | Departmental Sales | | |
|---|---|---|---|---|---|---|---|---|
| | | | | | | Dept. 1 Credit | Dept. 2 Credit | Dept. 3 Credit |
| Oct. | 1 | Walter Marshfield . . . | 737 | | 145.00 | 90.00 | 55.00 | |
| | 1 | Thomas Higgins . . . . | 738 | | 85.00 | | 40.00 | 45.00 |

**Illustration 23–3**
**Departmental sales spreadsheet**

| Date | | Men's Wear Dept. | Boys' Wear Dept. | Shoe Dept. | Leather Goods Dept. | Women's Wear Dept. | Total Sales |
|---|---|---|---|---|---|---|---|
| May | 1 | $957.15 | $775.06 | $615.00 | $575.25 | $927.18 | $3,849.64 |
| | 2 | 898.55 | 736.27 | 545.80 | 410.20 | 887.27 | 3,478.09 |

**Departmental Sales Spreadsheet Analyses.** If separate departmental accounts are not maintained in the general ledger, a business can develop departmental information by using a supplementary spreadsheet analysis. If this approach is followed, only one undepartmentalized general ledger account is used for sales, another account for sales returns, another for purchases, and another for purchases returns. Transactions are then recorded in these accounts as though the business were not departmentalized. In addition to this, each day it also summarizes its transactions by departments and enters the summarized amounts on a spreadsheet.

For example, in addition to recording sales in its usual manner, a company may total each day's sales by departments and enter the daily totals on a sales spreadsheet like Illustration 23–3. As a result, at the end of a month or other period, the column totals of the spreadsheet show sales by departments, and the grand total of all the columns should equal the balance of the Sales account.

When a store uses a spreadsheet analysis of department sales, it may use one spreadsheet to accumulate sales figures, another for sales returns, another for purchases, and still another for purchases returns. At the end of the period, the several spreadsheets show the store's sales, sales returns, purchases, and purchases returns by departments. If the store then takes inventories by departments, it can calculate gross profits by departments.

Accumulating information and arriving at a gross profit figure for each selling department in a departmentalized business is not too difficult, as you have learned. However, to go beyond this and arrive at useful departmental net income figures is not so easy. As a result, many companies make no effort to calculate more than gross profits by departments.

## Allocating Expenses

Describe the difference between direct and indirect expenses of departments, the bases used to allocate indirect expenses, and the procedures involved in the allocation process. (L. O. 3)

If a business attempts to measure not only departmental gross profit but also departmental net income, special problems are confronted. They involve dividing the expenses of the business among the selling departments of the business.

**Direct Expenses Do Not Require Allocation.** Some expenses, called **direct expenses**, are easily traced to specific departments because they are incurred for the sole benefit of one department. For example, the salary of an employee who works in only one department is a direct expense of that department.

Note that the concept of direct expense is just like the concept of direct cost that was first introduced in Chapter 21. The term *direct cost* was used in reference to a manufacturing operation; all manufacturing costs are treated as product costs rather than as expenses. In departments that are not related to manufacturing, costs are charged to expense as they are incurred; hence the term *direct expense* is used.

**Allocating Indirect Expenses.** The expenses of a business include both direct expenses and **indirect expenses**. Indirect expenses (like indirect costs) are incurred for the joint benefit of more than one department. For example, where two or more departments share a single building, the expenses of renting, heating, and lighting the building jointly benefit all of the departments in the building. Such indirect expenses cannot be easily traced to a specific department. However, if management wants information on the incomes produced by each department, the indirect expenses must be allocated among the departments that benefited from the expenses. Each indirect expense should be allocated on a basis that fairly approximates the relative benefit received by each department. However, measuring the benefit each department receives from an indirect expense is often difficult. Even after a reasonable allocation basis is chosen, considerable doubt often exists regarding the proper share to be charged to each department.

To illustrate the allocation of an indirect expense, assume that a jewelry store purchases janitorial services from an outside firm. The jewelry store then allocates the cost among its three departments according to the floor space occupied. The cost of janitorial services for a short period is $280, and the amounts of floor space occupied are:

| | |
|---|---|
| Jewelry department . . . . . . . . . | 250 sq. ft. |
| Watch repair department . . . . . . | 125 |
| China and silver department . . . . | 500 |
| Total . . . . . . . . . . . . . . . . . | 875 sq. ft. |

The calculations to allocate janitorial expense to the departments are:

Jewelry department: $\frac{250}{875} \times \$280 = \$80$

$$\text{Watch repair department: } \frac{125}{875} \times \$280 = \$40$$

$$\text{China and silver department: } \frac{500}{875} \times \$280 = \$160$$

Remember that you can apply the concepts of **direct costs or expenses** and **indirect costs or expenses** in a variety of situations. In general, direct costs or expenses are easily traced to or associated with a "cost object." In this chapter, the cost object of significance is the department. However, other cost objects may also be of interest. When we discussed general accounting systems for manufacturing operations (Chapter 21) and job order cost systems (Chapter 22), the cost object was a unit or batch of product. When we discussed process cost systems (Chapter 22), the cost object was a process or processing department.

### Bases for Allocating Indirect Expenses

In the following paragraphs, we discuss some bases that are often used to allocate some common indirect expenses. You will discover that we do not give hard-and-fast rules about which basis is best for a given expense. Such rules are not appropriate because several factors are often involved in an expense allocation, and the relative importance of the factors varies from situation to situation. As we have said, indirect expenses are, by definition, subject to doubt as to how they should be allocated between departments. Judgment rather than hard-and-fast rules is required, and different accountants sometimes do not agree on the proper basis for allocating an indirect expense.

**Wages and Salaries.** An employee's wages may be either a direct or an indirect expense. If an employee's time is spent entirely in one department, the employee's wages are a direct expense of that department. But if an employee works in more than one department, the wages are an indirect expense to be allocated between or among the benefited departments. In general, a worker's contribution to the activities of a department depends on the amount of time spent working in the department. Thus, a reasonable basis for allocating the wages of a worker is the relative amount of time spent in each department.

A supervisory employee may supervise more than one department. In such cases, the time spent in each department usually is a fair basis for allocating the supervisor's salary. However, since a supervisory employee is frequently on the move from department to department, the time spent in each may be difficult to measure. Therefore, some companies allocate the salary of such an employee to the benefited departments on the basis of the number of employees in each department. Others make the allocation on the basis of the supervised departments' sales. If you allocate a supervisor's salary based on the number of employees in each department, you are assuming that the supervisor's primary task is to supervise people. Hence, the supervisor's relative contribution to the departments is reflected by the relative number of employees in each. If you allocate the supervisor's salary based on the sales of each department, you are assuming that the supervisor's relative contribution to the departments is best reflected by the overall productivity of the departments.

**Rent or Depreciation and Related Expenses of Buildings.** Rent expense may be allocated to departments on the basis of the amount of the floor space occupied by each department. However, some space may be more valuable than other space, and this should be taken into consideration. For example, all customers who enter a store must pass the departments by the entrance and only a fraction of these people go beyond the first floor. Thus, ground floor space usually is more valuable for retail purposes than is basement or upper floor space. And space near the entrance is more valuable than is space in an out-of-the-way corner. Yet, since there is no exact measure of the floor space values, all such values and the allocations of rent based on such values must depend on judgment. To support your judgment, you may obtain statistics as to customer traffic patterns and also get opinions from real estate leasing agents who are familiar with current rental values. When a building is owned instead of being rented, expenses such as depreciation, taxes, and insurance on the building should be allocated like rent expense.

**Advertising.** When a store advertises a department's products and the advertising is effective, people come into the store to buy the advertised products. However, at the same time they may also buy other products that were not advertised. Thus, for many businesses, advertising the products of some departments results in benefit to all departments, even those whose products are not advertised. As a result, many stores treat advertising as an indirect expense and allocate it on the basis of sales. When advertising costs are allocated on a sales basis, a department that produces $\frac{1}{10}$ of the total sales is charged with $\frac{1}{10}$ of the advertising cost.

Although many stores allocate advertising costs to departments on the basis of sales, in other stores each advertisement is analyzed and the cost of the column inches of newspaper space or minutes of TV or radio time devoted to the products of a department is charged to the department.

**Depreciation of Equipment.** To account for depreciation, you should maintain plant asset records that are detailed enough to show which departments use the plant assets. Depreciation on equipment used solely in one department is a direct expense of that department. When assets are used by more than one department, depreciation must be treated as an indirect expense. In many cases, the relative number of hours equipment is used by the departments is a reasonable basis for allocating depreciation to the departments.

**Utilities Expenses.** Utilities expenses such as for heating and lighting are usually allocated on the basis of floor space occupied under the assumption that the amount of heat and the number of lights, their wattage, and the extent of their use are uniform throughout the store. Should there be a material variation in lighting, however, further analysis and a separate allocation may be advisable.

**Service Departments.** In order to manufacture products and make sales, the production departments must have the services supplied by service departments such as the general office, personnel, payroll, advertising, and purchasing departments. Since service departments do not produce revenues, managers evaluate the effectiveness of service departments as cost centers. To do this, the costs incurred directly by a service department and the indirect costs that benefit that department must be accumulated and reported to the appropriate managers.

Remember that a service department contributes to the activities of other departments. Therefore, when the effectiveness of a department is evaluated, the cost of any benefits it receives from a service department should be considered. This means that the costs of operating a service department should be allocated to the departments it services. In other words, the costs of service departments are, in effect, indirect expenses of the production or selling departments. If management wants to evaluate selling departments as profit centers, the costs of operating the service department must be allocated to the selling departments. The following list shows commonly used bases for allocating service department costs:

| Departments | Commonly Used Expense Allocation Bases |
|---|---|
| General office department . . . . | Number of employees in each department or sales. |
| Personnel department . . . . . . | Number of employees in each department. |
| Payroll department . . . . . . . . | Number of employees in each department. |
| Advertising department . . . . . . | Sales or amounts of advertising charged directly to each department. |
| Purchasing department . . . . . . | Dollar amounts of purchases or number of purchase invoices processed. |
| Cleaning and maintenance department . . . . . . . . . . . | Square feet of floor space occupied. |

## Mechanics of Allocating Expenses

At the time many indirect expenses are first recorded, the information that is needed to allocate them to departments often is not yet available. Therefore, expense amounts paid or incurred, both direct and indirect, are commonly accumulated in undepartmentalized expense accounts until the end of a period. Then, a *departmental expense allocation spreadsheet* (see Illustration 23–4) is used to allocate and charge each expense to the benefited departments.

In Illustration 23–4, notice that the indirect expense items are listed in the first column, followed by the names of the service departments whose costs are to be allocated. Next, the bases of allocation to be used are entered in the second column, and the expense amounts are entered in the third. Each expense is allocated according to the basis shown, and the allocated portions

Illustration 23–4

**A departmental expense allocation spreadsheet**

**ALPHAMAX HARDWARE STORE**
**Departmental Expense Allocations**
**For Year Ended December 31, 1991**

| | | Allocation of Expenses to Departments | | | | | |
|---|---|---|---|---|---|---|---|
| **Undepartmentalized Expense Accounts and Services Departments** | **Bases of Allocation** | **Expense Accounts Balance** | **General Office Dept.** | **Purchasing Dept.** | **Hardware Dept.** | **Housewares Dept.** | **Appliances Dept.** |
| Salaries expense | Direct, payroll records | 51,900 | 13,300 | 8,200 | 15,600 | 7,000 | 7,800 |
| Rent expense | Amount and value of space | 12,000 | 500 | 500 | 6,000 | 1,400 | 3,600 |
| Utilities expense | Floor space | 2,000 | 100 | 100 | 1,000 | 200 | 600 |
| Advertising expense | Sales | 1,000 | — | — | 500 | 300 | 200 |
| Depreciation, equipment | Direct, depreciation records | 1,500 | 500 | 300 | 400 | 100 | 200 |
| Supplies expense | Direct, requisitions | 900 | 200 | 100 | 300 | 200 | 100 |
| Insurance expense | Value of assets insured | 2,500 | 400 | 200 | 900 | 600 | 400 |
| Total expenses by departments | | 71,800 | 15,000 | 9,400 | 24,700 | 9,800 | 12,900 |
| Allocation of service department expenses: | | | | | | | |
| General office department | Sales | | 15,000 | | 7,500 | 4,500 | 3,000 |
| Purchasing department | Purchase requisitions | | | 9,400 | 3,900 | 3,400 | 2,100 |
| Total expenses applicable to selling departments | | 71,800 | | | 36,100 | 17,700 | 18,000 |

Illustration 23–5

ALPHAMAX HARDWARE STORE
Departmental Income Statement
For Year Ended December 31, 1991

| | Hardware Dept. | Housewares Dept. | Appliances Dept. | Combined |
|---|---|---|---|---|
| Sales | $119,500 | $71,700 | $47,800 | $239,000 |
| Cost of goods sold | 73,800 | 43,800 | 30,200 | 147,800 |
| Gross profit on sales | $ 45,700 | $27,900 | $17,600 | $ 91,200 |
| Gross profit percentages | 38.2% | 38.9% | 36.8% | 38.2% |
| Operating expenses: | | | | |
| Salaries expense | $ 15,600 | $ 7,000 | $ 7,800 | $ 30,400 |
| Rent expense | 6,000 | 1,400 | 3,600 | 11,000 |
| Utilities expense | 1,000 | 200 | 600 | 1,800 |
| Advertising expense | 500 | 300 | 200 | 1,000 |
| Depreciation expense, equipment | 400 | 100 | 200 | 700 |
| Supplies expense | 300 | 200 | 100 | 600 |
| Insurance expense | 900 | 600 | 400 | 1,900 |
| Share of general office department expenses | 7,500 | 4,500 | 3,000 | 15,000 |
| Share of purchasing department expenses | 3,900 | 3,400 | 2,100 | 9,400 |
| Total operating expenses | $ 36,100 | $17,700 | $18,000 | $ 71,800 |
| Net income (loss) | $ 9,600 | $10,200 | $ (400) | $ 19,400 |

appear in the departmental columns. Then, the departmental columns are totaled, and the service department column totals are allocated to the departments that benefit from their services. When the spreadsheet is completed, the amounts in the departmental columns can be used to prepare income statements that show net income by departments, as in Illustration 23–5.

## Departmental Contributions to Overhead

Prepare reports that are designed to measure the performance of a profit center and describe the factors to be considered in eliminating an unprofitable department.
(L. O. 4)

In some cases, departmental net incomes may not provide a fair basis for evaluating departmental performance. This might be true if the indirect expenses represent a large portion of total expenses. Remember that the net income numbers are affected by the assumptions and somewhat arbitrary decisions involved in allocating the indirect expenses. No doubt the criticism of departmental net incomes is most likely heard in companies where indirect expenses represent a large portion of total expenses. Those who criticize departmental net income numbers usually suggest that departments be evaluated based on their **departmental contributions to overhead.** A department's contribution to overhead is the amount by which its revenues exceed its direct costs and expenses. Illustration 23–6 shows the departmental contributions to overhead for Alphamax Company.

Compare the performance of the appliance department as it is shown in Illustrations 23–5 and 23–6. Illustration 23–5 shows an absolute loss of $400 resulting from the department's operations. On the other hand, Illustration 23–6 shows a positive contribution to overhead of $9,500, which is 19.9% of

Illustration 23–6

**ALPHAMAX HARDWARE STORE**
**Income Statement Showing Departmental Contributions to Overhead**
**For Year Ended December 31, 1991**

| | Hardware Dept. | Housewares Dept. | Appliances Dept. | Combined |
|---|---|---|---|---|
| Sales | $119,500 | $71,400 | $47,800 | $239,000 |
| Cost of goods sold | 73,800 | 43,800 | 30,200 | 147,800 |
| Gross profit on sales | $ 45,700 | $27,900 | $17,600 | $ 91,200 |
| Direct expenses: | | | | |
| Salaries expense | $ 15,600 | $ 7,000 | $ 7,800 | $ 30,400 |
| Depreciation expense, equipment | 400 | 100 | 200 | 700 |
| Supplies expense | 300 | 200 | 100 | 600 |
| Total direct expenses | $ 16,300 | $ 7,300 | $ 8,100 | $ 31,700 |
| Departmental contributions to overhead | $ 29,400 | $20,600 | $ 9,500 | $ 59,500 |
| Contribution percentages | 24.6% | 28.9% | 19.9% | 24.9% |
| Indirect expenses: | | | | |
| Rent expense | | | | $ 11,000 |
| Utilities expense | | | | 1,800 |
| Advertising expense | | | | 1,000 |
| Insurance expense | | | | 1,900 |
| General office department expense | | | | 15,000 |
| Purchasing department expense | | | | 9,400 |
| Total indirect expenses | | | | $ 40,100 |
| Net income | | | | $ 19,400 |

sales. While the appliance department's contribution is not as good as is the other departments, a $9,500 contribution to overhead appears much better than a $400 loss. Which is the better basis of evaluation? To resolve the matter, you must critically review the bases used for allocating the indirect expenses to departments. In the final analysis, answering the question is a matter of judgment.

## Eliminating the Unprofitable Department

When a department's net income shows a loss or when its contribution to overhead appears very poor, management may consider the extreme action of eliminating the department. However, in considering this extreme action, neither the net income figure nor the contribution to overhead provides the best information on which to base a decision. Instead, consideration should be given to the department's **escapable expenses** and **inescapable expenses.** Escapable expenses are those that would not be incurred if the department were eliminated; inescapable expenses are those that would continue even though the department were eliminated. For example, the management of Alphamax Company is considering whether to eliminate its appliances department. An evaluation of the inescapable expenses and escapable expenses of the appliances department reveals the following:

| | Escapable Expenses | Inescapable Expenses |
|---|---|---|
| Salaries expense | $ 7,800 | |
| Rent expense | | $3,600 |
| Utilities expense | | 600 |
| Advertising expense | 200 | |
| Depreciation expense, equipment | | 200 |
| Supplies expense | 100 | |
| Insurance expense (merchandise and equipment) | 300 | 100 |
| Share of office department expenses | 2,200 | 800 |
| Share of purchasing department expenses | 1,000 | 1,100 |
| Totals | $11,600 | $6,400 |

If the appliances department is discontinued, $6,400 of inescapable expenses will have to be borne by the remaining departments. Thus, as long as the appliances department's revenues cover all escapable expenses and also make a contribution toward covering some of the department's inescapable expenses, Alphamax is better off continuing the unprofitable department. Stated another way, if the department's net loss is less than $6,400, the department should be continued.

When the elimination of an unprofitable department is under discussion, you should also consider whether the revenues of other departments are affected by the existence of the unprofitable department. The existence of a department, even though unprofitable, may contribute to the sales and profits of the other departments. In such a case, a department might be continued even when the department's losses shown on the departmental income statement exceed its inescapable expenses.

## Controllable Costs and Expenses

Explain the concept of controllable costs, and prepare reports to be used in evaluating the performance of a department manager. (L. O. 5)

Net income figures and contributions to overhead are used in judging departmental efficiency. However, is either a good index of how well a department manager has performed? The answer is that neither may be a good index. Many expenses that enter into the calculation of a department's net income or into its contribution to overhead may be beyond the control of the department's manager. As a result, neither net income nor contribution to overhead is the best means of judging how well the manager has performed. Instead, the performance of a manager should be evaluated in terms of **controllable costs.**

### Controllable Costs Are Different than Direct Costs

What is the distinguishing characteristic of controllable costs? The critical factor is that the manager must have the power to determine or at least strongly influence the amounts to be expended. Controllable costs are not the same thing as direct costs. Direct costs are easily traced and therefore chargeable to a specific department, but the amounts expended may or may not be under the control of the department's manager. For example, a department manager often has little or no control over the amount of equipment assigned to the department and the resulting depreciation expense. Also, the manager has no control over his or her own salary. On the other hand, a department manager usually has control over the supplies used in the department.

When controllable costs are used to judge a manager's efficiency, statistics are prepared that show the department's output and its controllable costs and expenses. The manager's performance is judged in terms of the current period's statistics compared with planned levels and with the results of prior periods.

### Why a Cost Is Controllable or Uncontrollable

The concepts of controllable costs and **uncontrollable costs** must be defined with reference to a particular manager and within a definite time period. Without these two reference points, all costs are controllable; that is, *all costs are controllable at some level of management if the time period is long enough.* For example, a cost such as property insurance may not be controllable at the level of a department manager, but it is subject to control by the executive who is responsible for obtaining insurance coverage for the company. Likewise, the executive responsible for obtaining insurance coverage may not have any control over insurance expense resulting from insurance contracts presently in force. But when a contract expires, the executive is free to renegotiate and thus has control over the long run. Thus, it is recognized that all costs are subject to the control of some manager at some point in time. Revenues are likewise subject to the control of some manager.

## Responsibility Accounting

The concept of controllable costs and expenses provides the basis for a system of responsibility accounting. In responsibility accounting, each manager is held responsible for the costs and expenses that fall under the manager's control. Prior to each period of activity, plans are developed that specify the expected costs or expenses under the control of each manager. Those plans are called **responsibility accounting budgets.** To secure the cooperation of each manager and to be sure that the budgets represent reasonable goals, each manager should be closely involved in the preparation of his or her budget.

The accounting system is then designed to accumulate costs and expenses so that timely reports can be made to each manager of the costs for which the manager is responsible. These reports (called **performance reports**) compare actual costs and expenses to the budgeted amounts. Managers use these reports to focus their attention on the specific areas in which actual costs exceed budgeted amounts. With this information in hand, they can proceed to take corrective action.

Performance reports are also used to evaluate the effectiveness of each manager. The reports allow managers to be evaluated in terms of their ability to control costs and keep them within budgeted amounts. Importantly, managers should not be held responsible for costs over which they have no control. Further consideration is given to performance reports in Chapter 26.

A responsibility accounting system must reflect the fact that control over costs and expenses applies to several levels of management. For example, consider the organization chart shown in Illustration 23–7. In Illustration

**Illustration 23–7**
**Levels of organizational responsibility**

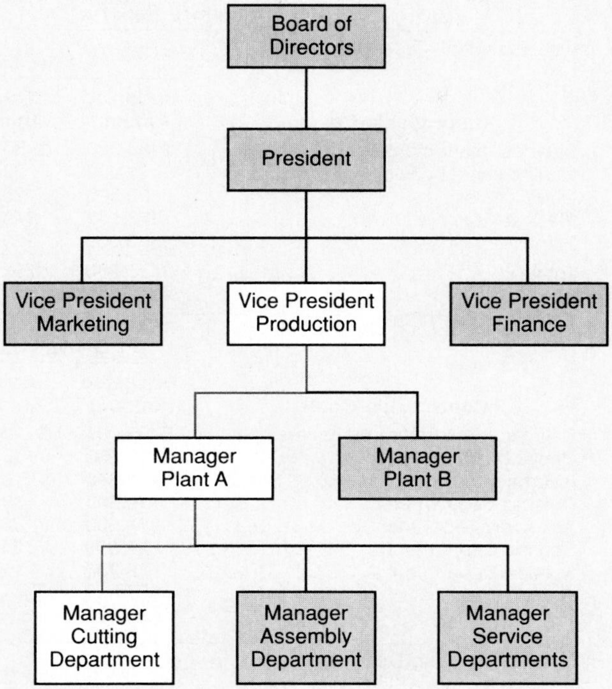


23–7, the lines connecting the various managerial positions represent lines of authority. Thus, while each department manager is responsible for the controllable costs and expenses incurred in his or her department, those same costs are subject to the general control of the plant manager. More generally, those costs are also subject to the control of the vice president of production, and of the president, and finally of the board of directors.

At the lowest levels of management, responsibilities and costs over which control is exercised are limited. Therefore, performance reports for this management level should cover only those costs over which the department managers exercise control. Moving up the management hierarchy, responsibilities and control broaden. Reports to higher level managers are therefore broader and cover a wider range of costs. However, reports to higher level managers normally do not contain the details reported to their subordinates. Rather, the details reported to lower level managers are normally summarized on the reports to their superiors. The details are summarized for two reasons: (1) lower level managers are primarily responsible, and (2) a report with too many details can fail to highlight important points. If reports to higher level managers contain too much detail, the reports may draw attention away from the broad, more important issues confronting the company.

**Illustration 23–8**
**Responsibility accounting performance reports**

**Performance Reports**

Vice President, Production

| | For the Month of July | | |
|---|---|---|---|
| **Controllable Costs** | **Budgeted Amount** | **Actual Amount** | **Over (under) Budget** |
| Salaries, plant managers | $ 80,000 | $ 80,000 | $ –0– |
| Quality control costs | 21,000 | 22,400 | 1,400 |
| Office costs | 29,500 | 28,800 | (700) |
| **Plant A** | **276,700** | **279,500** | **2,800** |
| Plant B | 390,000 | 380,600 | (9,400) |
| Totals | $797,200 | $791,300 | $(5,900) |

Manager, Plant A

| | For the Month of July | | |
|---|---|---|---|
| **Controllable Costs** | **Budgeted Amount** | **Actual Amount** | **Over (under) Budget** |
| Salaries, department managers | $ 75,000 | $ 78,000 | $ 3,000 |
| Depreciation | 10,600 | 10,600 | –0– |
| Insurance | 6,800 | 6,300 | (500) |
| **Cutting department** | **79,600** | **79,900** | **300** |
| Assembly department | 61,500 | 60,200 | (1,300) |
| Service Department 1 | 24,300 | 24,700 | 400 |
| Service Department 2 | 18,900 | 19,800 | 900 |
| Totals | $276,700 | $279,500 | $ 2,800 |

Manager, Cutting Department

| | For the Month of July | | |
|---|---|---|---|
| **Controllable Costs** | **Budgeted Amount** | **Actual Amount** | **Over (under) Budget** |
| Raw materials | $ 26,500 | $ 25,900 | $ (600) |
| Direct labor | 32,000 | 33,500 | 1,500 |
| Indirect labor | 7,200 | 7,000 | (200) |
| Supplies | 4,000 | 3,900 | (100) |
| Other controllable costs | 9,900 | 9,600 | (300) |
| Totals | $ 79,600 | $ 79,900 | $ 300 |

Illustration 23–8 shows summarized performance reports for three of the management levels depicted in Illustration 23–7. Observe in Illustration 23–8 how the costs under the control of the cutting department manager are totaled and included among the controllable costs of the plant manager. Also, the costs under the control of the plant manager are totaled and included among the controllable costs of the vice president of production. In this manner, a responsibility accounting system provides information that is relevant to the control responsibilities of each management level.

In conclusion, we should recognize that the ability to produce vast amounts of raw data mechanically and electronically has far outstripped our ability to use the data. What is needed is the ability to select the data that are meaningful for planning and control. This is recognized in responsibility accounting, and every effort is made to get the right information to the right person at the right time. The right person is the person who can control the cost or revenue.

**Illustration 23–9**
**Allocating a joint cost based on relative market values**

| Grade of Lumber | Production in Board Feet | Market Price per 1,000 Board Feet | Market Value of Production of Each Grade | Ratio of Market Value of Each Grade to Total |
|---|---|---|---|---|
| Structural . . . . . . . | 100,000 | $120 | $12,000 | 12/50 |
| No. 1 Common . . . . | 300,000 | 60 | 18,000 | 18/50 |
| No. 2 Common . . . . | 400,000 | 40 | 16,000 | 16/50 |
| No. 3 Common . . . . | 200,000 | 20 | 4,000 | 4/50 |
| | 1,000,000 | | $50,000 | |

## Joint Costs

Describe the problems associated with the allocation of joint costs between departments. (L. O. 6)

Some manufacturing processes involve **joint costs,** which are somewhat similar to indirect expenses. A joint cost is a cost that is incurred to produce or obtain two or more essentially different products. For example, a meat-packing company incurs a joint cost when it buys a pig from which it will get bacon, hams, shoulders, liver, pig feet, and a variety of other products. Likewise, a sawmill incurs joint costs when it buys a log and saws it into portions of Clears, Select Structurals, No. 1 Common, No. 2 Common, and other grades of lumber.

When a joint cost is incurred in producing two or more products, a question arises as to how the cost should be allocated to the different products. Because the allocation of a joint cost always is arbitrary, the best answer is to avoid allocating the cost to the products whenever possible. Many managerial decisions such as whether or not to continue buying logs should be based on unallocated cost information.

However, when financial statements are prepared, the accountant is faced with the problem of allocating the joint cost between the products that result from incurring the cost. For example, if some of the products are sold and others remain in inventory, the joint cost must be allocated to determine the cost of the inventory and the cost of goods sold.

A joint cost may be allocated on some physical basis, such as the ratio of pounds, square feet, or gallons of each joint product to total pounds, square feet, or gallons of all joint products flowing from the cost. Usually, however, this method should not be used because the resulting cost allocations may not be consistent with the market values of the joint products. If a physical basis is used, the sale of some joint products may appear more profitable than does the sale of others. Some products may even be reported as selling at a loss while others show a profit.

For example, a sawmill bought a number of logs for $30,000. When sawed, the logs produced a million board feet of lumber in the grades and amounts shown in Illustration 23–9.

Observe in Illustration 23–9 that the logs produced 200,000 board feet of No. 3 Common lumber and that this is 2/10 of the total lumber produced from the logs. If the No. 3 lumber were assigned 2/10 of the $30,000 cost of the logs, it would be assigned $6,000 of the cost ($30,000 × 2/10 = $6,000); and since this lumber can be sold for only $4,000, the assignment would cause this grade to show a loss. Yet, since the logs were purchased for $30,000 and the total market value of the lumber is $50,000, some grades of lumber would show a profit. *To avoid showing different profit rates on products that flow from a joint cost, such costs should be allocated to the joint products in the ratio of the market values of the joint products at the point of separation.*

The ratios of the market values of the joint products flowing from the $30,000 of log cost are shown in the last column of Illustration 23–9. When these ratios are used to allocate the $30,000 cost, the cost is allocated to the grades as follows:

| | | Allocated Cost | Market Value | Profit from Sales at Point of Separation | Profit Rate |
|---|---|---|---|---|---|
| Structural: | $30,000 × 12/50 = | $ 7,200 | $12,000 | $ 4,800 | 40% |
| No. 1 Common: | $30,000 × 18/50 = | 10,800 | 18,000 | 7,200 | 40 |
| No. 2 Common: | $30,000 × 16/50 = | 9,600 | 16,000 | 6,400 | 40 |
| No. 3 Common: | $30,000 × 4/50 = | 2,400 | 4,000 | 1,600 | 40 |
| | | $30,000 | $50,000 | $20,000 | 40 |

Observe that when the joint lumber products are allocated a share of the $30,000 joint cost based on relative market values, each grade reflects the same 40% profit rate if sold at the point they become separate products.

## Summary of the Chapter in Terms of Learning Objectives

**1.** Large companies that operate in more than one industry disclose the following information on each industrial segment: revenues, operating profits (before interest and taxes), depreciation and amortization expense, capital expenditures, and identifiable assets. They also report a geographical distribution of sales and sales to major customers. The four problems accountants face in preparing segmental information include: identifying significant segments, transfer pricing between segments, measuring segmental profitability, and identifying segmental assets.

**2.** Businesses are divided into subunits whenever they become too large to be effectively managed as a single unit. Subunits are evaluated as cost centers if the units incur costs but do not generate revenues. They are evaluated as profit centers if they generate revenues so that the performance of the units can be measured in terms of contribution to overhead or net income.

**3.** Direct expenses are easily traced to a specific department because they are incurred for the sole benefit of one department. Indirect expenses, on the other hand, benefit more than one department. If departmental net incomes are to be measured, indirect expenses must be allocated to the departments on some reasonable basis. The basis selected for allocating an indirect expense is a matter of judgment but should attempt to reflect the relative benefit the departments receive as a result of the expense. The allocation process may be done by using separate departmental expense accounts but often is accomplished with a spreadsheet analysis.

**4.** Departmental income statements may be used to evaluate the profitability of the departments. Or, if indirect expenses are large and especially difficult to allocate, the departments may be evaluated in terms of their contributions to overhead. In general, an unprofitable department should be eliminated if its net losses exceed the inescapable expenses that continue if the department is eliminated. However, the decision to eliminate a department should also consider the effect of the department's existence on the performance of the other departments.

**5.** The concept of a controllable cost must be defined in terms of a specific level of management and a specific time period. The expenses of operating a department often include items that are not controllable by the department manager. Therefore, performance reports used to evaluate departmental managers should include only the expenses (and revenues) that are controllable by the managers.

**6.** A joint cost is a single cost that results in the production of two or more essentially different products. When income statements are prepared, joint costs must be allocated to the resulting joint products based on the relative market value of the joint products at the point they become separate products.

## Demonstration Problem

From the information presented below, develop departmental income statements for Hacker's Haven, a computer store. The store has five departments: three are production departments (hardware, software, and customer service), and two are service departments (general office and purchasing).

Information about the five departments' activities for 1991 is as follows:

| | Hardware | Software | Customer Service | General Office | Purchasing |
|---|---|---|---|---|---|
| Sales | $960,000 | $600,000 | $840,000 | — | — |
| Cost of goods sold | 500,000 | 300,000 | 200,000 | — | — |
| Payroll costs | 80,000 | 25,000 | 325,000 | $60,000 | $45,000 |
| Depreciation | 33,000 | 4,200 | 9,600 | 6,000 | 7,200 |
| Supplies | 10,000 | 2,000 | 25,000 | 15,000 | 10,000 |

In addition to the above, several costs must be allocated first among the five departments, and then the costs of the two service departments must be allocated to the three production departments. The total amounts and the allocation bases of each cost are shown below:

| Type of Cost | Total Cost | Allocation Basis |
|---|---|---|
| Rent expense | $150,000 | Square footage occupied |
| Utilities | 50,000 | Square footage occupied |
| Advertising | 125,000 | Dollars of sales |
| Insurance | 30,000 | Value of assets insured |
| Service departments: | | |
| General office | ? | Number of employees |
| Purchasing | ? | Dollars of cost of goods sold |

Necessary information to apply the allocation bases:

| Type of Cost | Total | General Office | Purchasing | Hardware | Software | Customer Service |
|---|---|---|---|---|---|---|
| Rent expense . . . | 10,000 sq. ft. | 500 sq. ft. | 500 sq. ft. | 4,000 sq. ft. | 3,000 sq. ft. | 2,000 sq. ft. |
| Utilities . . . . . . . . | 10,000 sq. ft. | 500 sq. ft. | 500 sq. ft. | 4,000 sq. ft. | 3,000 sq. ft. | 2,000 sq. ft. |
| Advertising . . . . . | $2,400,000 | — | — | $960,000 | $600,000 | $840,000 |
| Insurance . . . . . . | $ 600,000 | $60,000 | $72,000 | $330,000 | $42,000 | $96,000 |
| General office . . . . | 20 employees | — | 2 employees | 4 employees | 4 employees | 10 employees |
| Purchasing . . . . . | $1,000,000 | — | — | $500,000 | $300,000 | $200,000 |

## Solution to Demonstration Problem

Percentages to be used in the allocations (department portion/total allocation basis):

| | Total | General Office | Purchasing | Hardware | Software | Customer Service |
|---|---|---|---|---|---|---|
| Rent expense . . . | 100% | 5% | 5% | 40% | 30% | 20% |
| Utilities . . . . . . . . | 100 | 5 | 5 | 40 | 30 | 20 |
| Advertising . . . . . | 100 | — | — | 40 | 25 | 35 |
| Insurance . . . . . . | 100 | 10 | 12 | 55 | 7 | 16 |
| General office . . . . | 100 | — | 10 | 20 | 20 | 50 |
| Purchasing . . . . . | 100 | — | — | 50 | 30 | 20 |

**Departmental Expense Allocation Spreadsheet**
**For Year Ended December 31, 1991**

| | Total | General Office | Purchasing | Hardware | Software | Customer Service |
|---|---|---|---|---|---|---|
| Allocated costs: | | | | | | |
| Rent expense . . . . | $150,000 | $ 7,500 | $ 7,500 | $ 60,000 | $ 45,000 | $30,000 |
| Utilities . . . . . . . | 50,000 | 2,500 | 2,500 | 20,000 | 15,000 | 10,000 |
| Advertising . . . . . | 125,000 | -0- | -0- | 50,000 | 31,250 | 43,750 |
| Insurance . . . . . . | 30,000 | 3,000 | 3,600 | 16,500 | 2,100 | 4,800 |
| Total . . . . . . . . . | $355,000 | $13,000 | $13,600 | $146,500 | $ 93,350 | $88,550 |
| General office . . . . . | | $13,000 | 1,300 | 2,600 | 2,600 | 6,500 |
| | | | $14,900 | $149,100 | $ 95,950 | $95,050 |
| Purchasing . . . . . . . | | | 14,900 | 7,450 | 4,470 | 2,980 |
| Total expenses applicable to production departments . . . . . . | | | | $156,550 | $100,420 | $98,030 |

**HACKER'S HAVEN COMPUTER STORE**
**Departmental Income Statement**
**For Year Ended December 31, 1991**

| | Hardware | Software | Customer Service | Combined |
|---|---|---|---|---|
| Sales . . . . . . . . . . . . . . . . | $960,000 | $600,000 | $840,000 | $2,400,000 |
| Cost of goods sold . . . . . . . . . | 500,000 | 300,000 | 200,000 | 1,000,000 |
| Gross profit . . . . . . . . . . . . | $460,000 | $300,000 | $640,000 | $1,400,000 |
| Operating expenses: | | | | |
| Payroll costs . . . . . . . . . . . | $ 80,000 | $ 25,000 | $325,000 | $ 430,000 |
| Depreciation . . . . . . . . . . . | 33,000 | 4,200 | 9,600 | 46,800 |
| Supplies . . . . . . . . . . . . . | 10,000 | 2,000 | 25,000 | 37,000 |
| Rent expense . . . . . . . . . . | 60,000 | 45,000 | 30,000 | 135,000 |
| Utilities . . . . . . . . . . . . . . | 20,000 | 15,000 | 10,000 | 45,000 |
| Advertising . . . . . . . . . . . | 50,000 | 31,250 | 43,750 | 125,000 |
| Insurance . . . . . . . . . . . . | 16,500 | 2,100 | 4,800 | 23,400 |
| General office . . . . . . . . . . | 2,600 | 2,600 | 6,500 | 11,700 |
| Purchasing . . . . . . . . . . . | 7,450 | 4,470 | 2,980 | 14,900 |
| Total operating expenses . . . . | $279,550 | $131,620 | $457,630 | $ 868,800 |
| Net income (loss) . . . . . . . . . | $180,450 | $168,380 | $182,370 | $ 531,200 |

## Glossary

Define or explain the words and phrases listed in the chapter Glossary. (L. O. 7)

**Common expenses** those expenses of a business that benefit more than one segment of the business. p. 976

**Controllable costs** costs over which the manager has the power to determine or strongly influence amounts to be expended. pp. 987–88

**Cost center** a unit of business that incurs costs (or expenses) but does not directly generate revenues; as a result, a unit the efficiency of which cannot be judged in terms of its ability to generate earnings. pp. 977–78

**Departmental accounting** accounting for the ''parts'' or subunits of a business, especially developing subunit information for internal use by management, pp. 973, 976–88

**Departmental contribution to overhead** the amount by which a department's revenues exceed its direct costs and expenses. pp. 985–86

**Direct costs or expenses** costs or expenses that are easily traced to or associated with a cost object; for example, the cost of materials that become part of a manufactured product, or the cost of labor that is used solely in one processing department of a manufacturer, or wages expense incurred solely for the benefit of a specific department of a merchandising company. p. 981

**Direct expenses** expenses that are easily associated with and assigned to specific departments because they are incurred for the sole benefit of one department. p. 980

**Escapable expenses** expenses that will no longer be incurred if a department is eliminated. pp. 986–87

**Indirect costs or expenses** costs or expenses that are not easily traced to a cost object such as a department; for example, costs incurred for the joint benefit of more than one department. p. 981

**Indirect expenses** expenses that are not easily associated with a specific department. p. 980

**Inescapable expenses** expenses that will continue even if the department is eliminated. pp. 986–87

**Joint cost** a cost incurred to produce or obtain two or more essentially different products. pp. 991–92

**Performance report** a financial report that compares actual costs and expenses to the budgeted amounts. pp. 988–90

**Production departments** subunits of a business, the operations of which involve manufacturing or selling the goods or services of the business. p. 977

**Profit center** a unit of business that incurs costs and generates revenues, the efficiency of which therefore can be judged in terms of its ability to generate earnings. pp. 977–78

**Responsibility accounting** accounting systems that are designed to accumulate controllable costs in timely reports to be given to each manager who is responsible for the costs, and also to be used in judging the performance of each manager. pp. 976, 988–91

**Responsibility accounting budget** a plan that specifies the expected costs and expenses falling under the control of a manager. p. 988

**Segmental reporting** providing information about the subunits of a business, especially published information about a company's operations in different industries or geographical areas. pp. 973–76

**Service departments** departments that do not manufacture products or produce revenue but that supply other departments with essential services. p. 977

**Uncontrollable cost** a cost the amount of which a specific manager cannot control within a given period of time. p. 988

## Objective Review

Answers to the following questions are listed in Appendix I at the end of the book. Be sure that you decide which is the one best answer to each question *before* you check the answers in the appendix.

1. Which of the following is not one of the items of segmental information that must be disclosed in the financial reports of large companies having operations in several lines of business?
   *a.* Depreciation and amortization expense.
   *b.* Extraordinary gains and losses.
   *c.* Operating profits (net of interest and taxes).
   *d.* Revenues.
   *e.* All of the above would be disclosed.
2. If a business is organizationally divided into departments:
   *a.* All of the departments will probably by evaluated as cost centers.
   *b.* Only the departments that produce revenues can be evaluated as cost centers.
   *c.* All of the departments will probably be evaluated as profit centers.
   *d.* Each department must represent a separable industrial segment of the businesses's operations.
   *e.* None of the above are correct.
3. If a company has two sales departments (A and B) and two service departments (payroll and advertising), which of the following is correct?
   *a.* Part of the wages incurred in the payroll department may end up being allocated to the sales departments as part of the advertising department expense.
   *b.* Wages incurred in the payroll department are defined as indirect expenses of all departments.
   *c.* Wages incurred in the payroll department are direct expenses of the payroll department and indirect expenses of the other departments.
   *d.* Advertising department expenses should be allocated to the other three departments.
   *e.* Both (*a*) and (*c*) are true.
4. Information on the fixtures department of The Decorator Store follows:

| | |
|---|---|
| Net loss . . . . . . . . . . . . . . . . . . . . . | $(600) |
| Departmental contribution to overhead . . | 5% of sales |
| Escapable expenses . . . . . . . . . . . . | $17,400 |
| Inescapable expenses . . . . . . . . . . . | $ 9,600 |

Which of the following is the best reason for eliminating or not eliminating the fixtures department.

*a.* Since the fixtures department has a net loss, it should be eliminated.
*b.* Because of the combination of the net loss and a poor contribution to overhead, the department should be eliminated.
*c.* The fixtures department should be eliminated based on the $17,400 of escapable expenses that could be avoided by eliminating the department.
*d.* Since the fixtures department's revenues cover all of the escapable expenses and some of the inescapable expenses, The Decorator Store is better off continuing the department.
*e.* None of the above is correct.

5. What provides the best index of how well a sales department manager has performed?
   *a.* Net income figures.
   *b.* Contributions to overhead.
   *c.* Escapable expenses.
   *d.* Controllable revenues and expenses.
   *e.* All of the above.
6. Kilian Company produces three products, T1, T2, and T3. The joint costs incurred for the current month on these products is $90,000. The following data relate to this month's production.

| Product | Units | Unit Sales Price at Separation | Additional Costs | Final Unit Sales Price |
|---|---|---|---|---|
| T1 . . . . | 48,000 | $3.00 | $1.00 | $ 5.00 |
| T2 . . . . | 32,000 | 6.00 | 1.20 | 9.00 |
| T3 . . . . | 16,000 | 9.00 | 0.80 | 12.00 |

The joint cost that should be allocated to T3 is:
*a.* $24,000.
*b.* $15,000.
*c.* $27,000.
*d.* $45,000.
*e.* $42,000.

## Questions for Class Discussion

1. What is the difference, if any, between segmental reporting and departmental accounting?
2. What are five items of segmental information about operations in different industries that may be required disclosures in the annual report of a company?
3. What are four basic issues confronted by the accountant in developing information on broad industrial segments?

4. Why does the existence of common expenses cause the accountant difficulty in preparing segmental reports?
5. Why are businesses divided into departments?
6. What are two primary goals of departmental accounting?
7. Is it possible to evaluate the profitability of a cost center? Why?
8. What is the difference between production departments and service departments?
9. Name several examples of service departments.
10. Are service departments analyzed as cost centers or as profit centers? Why?
11. If a company with a computerized accounting system uses modern cash registers that are directly connected to its computer, is the company likely to require the use of departmental sales analysis spreadsheets? Why?
12. How is a departmental sales analysis spreadsheet used in determining sales by departments?
13. What is the difference between direct and indirect expenses?
14. In a merchandising company, what are the typical cost objects that serve as the basis for classifying expenses as direct or indirect?
15. Suggest a reasonable basis for allocating each of the following indirect expenses to departments: (*a*) salary of a supervisory employee, (*b*) rent, (*c*) heat, (*d*) electricity used in lighting, (*e*) janitorial services, (*f*) advertising, (*g*) expired insurance, and (*h*) taxes on equipment.
16. How is a departmental expense allocation spreadsheet used in allocating indirect expenses to departments?
17. How reliable are the amounts shown as net incomes for the various departments of a store when indirect expenses are allocated to the departments?
18. How is a department's contribution to overhead measured?
19. As the terms are used in departmental accounting, what are (*a*) escapable expenses and (*b*) inescapable expenses?
20. What are controllable costs and expenses?
21. Why should a manager be closely involved in preparing his or her responsibility accounting budget?
22. In responsibility accounting, who is the right person to be given timely reports and statistics on a given cost?
23. What is a joint cost? How are joint costs normally allocated?

## Exercises

**Exercise 23–1**
**Segmental reporting with sales between segments**
(L. O. 1)

Twilite Corporation has two business segments for which the following operating information is available:

| | Segment A | Segment B |
|---|---|---|
| Sales to outside parties . . . . . . . . . . | $84,000 | $112,000 |
| Sales to segment B . . . . . . . . . . . . | ? | |
| Purchases from segment A . . . . . . . | | ? |
| Other expenses of each segment . . . . | 63,000 | 42,000 |

The items that segment A sold to segment B were resold by B to outside parties. In reporting the intersegment sales, the manager of segment A argues that the sales to segment B should be priced at $42,000, which is approximately the same price that would have been charged to outside parties. The segment B manager argues that segment B should be charged only $21,000, since segment B is a member of the Twilite Corporation family. A price of $21,000 more than covers segment A's cost according to the segment B manager.

*Required*

Prepare reports that show the sales, expenses, and income from operations of each segment assuming the intersegment sales are priced at (*a*) $42,000 and (*b*) $21,000. Then, express each segment's income from operations as a percent of sales. Comment on the importance of the intersegment pricing decision in evaluating the performance of each segment. Which price do you think provides the best basis for evaluating the performance of each segment?

**Exercise 23–2**
**Allocating rent expense to departments**
(L. O. 3)

A company pays $225,000 annually to rent all the space in a building, which is assigned to its departments as follows:

| | |
|---|---|
| Department 1: | 1,400 square feet of first-floor space |
| Department 2: | 2,200 square feet of first-floor space |
| Department 3: | 900 square feet of second-floor space |
| Department 4: | 1,100 square feet of second-floor space |
| Department 5: | 1,600 square feet of second-floor space |

The company allocates 60% of the total rent to the first floor and 40% to the second floor, and then allocates the rent of each floor to the departments on that floor on the basis of the space occupied. Determine the rent to be allocated to each department. (Round all amounts to the nearest whole dollar.)

**Exercise 23–3**
**Allocating rent expense to departments**
(L. O. 3)

A company pays $360,000 per year to rent all the space in a small building, and it occupies the space as follows:

| | |
|---|---|
| Department A: | 1,350 square feet of first-floor space |
| Department B: | 3,150 square feet of first-floor space |
| Department C: | 4,500 square feet of second-floor space |

Determine the rent expense to be allocated to each department under the assumption that first-floor space rents for twice as much as second-floor space in the city in which this company is located.

**Exercise 23–4**
**Allocating common wages expense to departments**
(L. O. 3)

Renee DeLoretto works part-time in the appliances department and in the hardware department of Macley's Department Store. Her work consists of waiting on customers who enter either department and also in straightening and rearranging merchandise in either department as needed. The store allocates her annual wages of $19,800 to the two departments in which she works. Last year the allocation was based on a sample of the time DeLoretto spent working in the two departments. To obtain the sample, observations were made on several days throughout the year of the manner in which DeLoretto spent her time while at work. Following are the results of the observations:

| | |
|---|---|
| Minutes spent on various activities: | |
| Selling in the appliances department . . . . . | 3,800 |
| Straightening and rearranging merchandise in the appliances department . . . . . . . . | 700 |
| Selling in the hardware department . . . . . . | 1,800 |
| Straightening and rearranging merchandise in the hardware department . . . . . . . . . | 900 |
| Idle time spent waiting for a customer to enter one of the selling departments . . . . | 500 |

*Required*

Prepare a calculation to show the shares of the employee's wages that should be allocated to the departments.

**Exercise 23–5**
**Departmental expense allocation spreadsheet**
(L. O. 3)

Edwards Company has two service departments, the purchasing department and the advertising department, and two sales departments, sails and spars. During 1990, the departments had the following direct expenses: purchasing department, $8,550; advertising department, $6,300; sails department, $22,500; and spars department, $15,750. The departments occupy the following amounts of floor space: purchasing, 600; advertising, 450; sails, 1,200; and spars, 750. The sails department had four times as many dollars of sales during the year as did the spars department, and during the year the purchasing department processed twice as many purchase orders for the sails department as it did for the spars department.

*Required*

Prepare an expense allocation sheet for Edwards Company on which the direct expenses are entered by departments, the year's $63,000 of rent expense is allocated to the departments on the basis of floor space occupied, advertising department expenses are allocated to the sales departments on the basis of sales, and purchasing department expenses are allocated on the basis of purchase orders processed.

**Exercise 23–6**
**Income effects of eliminating departments**
(L. O. 4)

A company has five departments that are expected to have the following results of operations next year:

| | Dept. 1 | Dept. 2 | Dept. 3 | Dept. 4 | Dept. 5 |
|---|---|---|---|---|---|
| Sales | $13,000 | $18,800 | $ 9,400 | $ 15,800 | $16,200 |
| Expenses: | | | | | |
| Escapable | $ 7,800 | $19,600 | $ 5,600 | $ 17,200 | $ 7,000 |
| Inescapable | 10,000 | 8,800 | 5,200 | 8,800 | 4,400 |
| Total expenses | $17,800 | $28,400 | $10,800 | $ 26,000 | $11,400 |
| Net income (loss) | $ (4,800) | $ (9,600) | $ (1,400) | $(10,200) | $ 4,800 |

*Required*

Prepare a combined income statement for the company under each of the following conditions: (*a*) none of the departments are eliminated, (*b*) all of the unprofitable departments are eliminated, and (*c*) departments are only eliminated if the effect is to increase the net income or reduce the net loss of the company.

**Exercise 23–7**
**Evaluating managerial performance**
(L. O. 5)

Robert Freeman is the manager of the automobile service department of a large department store. A 1991 income statement for the department included the following:

| | | |
|---|---|---|
| Revenues: | | |
| Sales of services | $343,000 | |
| Sales of parts | 238,000 | $581,000 |
| Costs and expenses: | | |
| Cost of parts sold | $109,200 | |
| Wages (hourly) | 203,000 | |
| Salary of manager | 39,200 | |
| Payroll taxes | 26,700 | |
| Supplies | 53,100 | |
| Depreciation of building | 30,800 | |
| Utilities | 47,600 | |
| Interest on long-term debt | 24,000 | |
| Income taxes allocated to department | 15,400 | |
| Total costs and expenses | | 549,000 |
| Department net income | | $ 32,000 |

*Required*

Which of the income statement items do you think should be excluded from a report to be used in evaluating Mr. Freeman's performance? State your reasons. If the exclusion of some items is questionable, list those items and explain why the exclusion is questionable.

**Exercise 23–8**
**Assigning joint real estate costs**
(L. O. 6)

Kiley Development Company has just completed a subdivision containing 40 building lots, of which 32 lots are for sale at $36,000 each and 8 are for sale at $72,000 each. The land for the subdivision cost $264,000, and the company spent $312,000 on street and utilities improvements. Assume that the land and improvement costs are to be assigned to the lots as joint costs and determine the share of the costs to assign to a lot in each price class. (Round all amounts to the nearest whole dollar.)

**Exercise 23–9**
**Assigning joint product costs**
(L. O. 6)

Abilene Packing Company purchases front quarters of beef and processes them into round steaks and hamburger. It then sells the round steaks for $3.25 per pound and sells the hamburger for $2.00 per pound. On average, 100 pounds of front quarter can be processed into 16 pounds of round steak and 74 pounds of hamburger.

Assume that 100 pounds of front quarter is purchased for $1 per pound. The 100 pounds is then processed into round steak and hamburger, which requires additional labor cost of $50. If 8 pounds of round steak are sold and 30 pounds of hamburger are sold, what cost of goods sold and ending inventory amounts should be reported?

## Problems

**Problem 23–1**
**Allocation of building occupancy costs**
(L. O. 3)

Prescott-Alpine, Inc., occupies all the space in a two-story building, and it has an account in its ledger called Building Occupancy to which it charged the following during the past year:

| | |
|---|---|
| Depreciation, building . . . . . . . | $ 36,000 |
| Interest, building mortgage . . . . | 29,700 |
| Taxes, building and land . . . . . | 11,100 |
| Heating expenses . . . . . . . . . | 5,000 |
| Lighting expense . . . . . . . . . | 6,400 |
| Cleaning and maintenance . . . . | 25,200 |
| Total . . . . . . . . . . . . . . . | $113,400 |

The building has 3,500 square feet of floor space on each of its two floors, a total of 7,000 square feet; and the bookkeeper divided the $113,400 by 7,000 and charged the selling departments on each floor with $16.20 of occupancy cost for each square foot of floor space occupied.

Danielle German, the manager of a second-floor department occupying 1,700 square feet of floor space, saw the $16.20 per square foot, or $27,540 of occupancy cost, charged to her department and complained. She cited a recent real estate board study that showed average rental charges for similar space, including heat but not including lights, cleaning, and maintenance, as follows:

| | |
|---|---|
| Ground-floor space . . . . | $19.50 per sq. ft. |
| Second-floor space . . . . | 13.00 per sq. ft. |

*Required*

Prepare a computation showing how much building occupancy cost you think should have been charged to Danielle German's department last year.

**Problem 23–2**
**Departmental income statement**
(L. O. 4)

Beckwith Corporation began its operations in early January 1991 with two selling departments and one office department. The 1991 operating results are:

**BECKWITH CORPORATION**
**Departmental Income Statement**
**For Year Ended December 31, 1991**

| | Dept. A | Dept. B | Combined |
|---|---|---|---|
| Revenue from sales | $180,000 | $112,500 | $292,500 |
| Cost of goods sold | 117,000 | 67,500 | 184,500 |
| Gross profit from sales | $ 63,000 | $ 45,000 | $108,000 |
| Direct expenses: | | | |
| Sales salaries | $ 23,700 | $ 13,500 | $ 37,200 |
| Advertising | 2,100 | 1,500 | 3,600 |
| Store supplies used | 900 | 450 | 1,350 |
| Depreciation of equipment | 2,400 | 1,350 | 3,750 |
| Total direct expense | $ 29,100 | $ 16,800 | $ 45,900 |
| Allocated expenses: | | | |
| Rent expense | $ 10,800 | $ 5,400 | $ 16,200 |
| Heating and lighting expense | 2,700 | 1,350 | 4,050 |
| Share of office department expenses | 10,800 | 6,750 | 17,550 |
| Total allocated expenses | $ 24,300 | $ 13,500 | $ 37,800 |
| Total expenses | $ 53,400 | $ 30,300 | $ 83,700 |
| Net income | $ 9,600 | $ 14,700 | $ 24,300 |

The company plans to open a third selling department that it estimates will produce $67,500 in sales with a 35% gross profit margin and will require the following direct expenses: sales salaries, $10,200; advertising, $1,050; store supplies, $390; and depreciation of equipment, $750.

A year ago, when operations began, it was necessary to rent store space in excess of requirements. This extra space was assigned to and used by Departments A and B during the year; but when the new Department C is opened, it will take one fourth of the space presently assigned to Department A and one sixth of the space assigned to Department B.

The company allocates its general office department expenses to its selling departments on the basis of sales. It expects the new department to cause a $1,182 increase in general office department expenses.

The company expects Department C to bring new customers into the store who, in addition to buying goods in the new department, will also buy sufficient merchandise in the two old departments to increase their sales by 5% each. However, the old departments' gross profit percentages are not expected to change. Likewise, their direct expenses, other than supplies, are not expected to change. The supplies used will increase in proportion to sales.

*Required*

Prepare a departmental income statement showing the company's expected operations with three selling departments. (Round all amounts to the nearest whole dollar.)

**Problem 23–3**
**Analysis of escapable and inescapable expenses**
(L. O. 4)

Emporium Company is considering the elimination of its unprofitable Department Q. The company's 1991 income statement appears as follows:

**EMPORIUM COMPANY**
**Income Statement**
**For Year Ended December 31, 1991**

| | Dept. P | Dept. Q | Combined |
|---|---|---|---|
| Sales | $324,000 | $154,800 | $478,800 |
| Cost of goods sold | 179,400 | 112,500 | 291,900 |
| Gross profit from sales | $144,600 | $ 42,300 | $186,900 |
| Operating expenses: | | | |
| Direct expenses: | | | |
| Advertising | $ 4,050 | $ 2,970 | $ 7,020 |
| Store supplies used | 3,780 | 2,430 | 6,210 |
| Depreciation of store equipment | 3,270 | 1,980 | 5,250 |
| Total direct expenses | $ 11,100 | $ 7,380 | $ 18,480 |
| Allocated expenses: | | | |
| Sales salaries | $ 68,250 | $ 40,950 | $109,200 |
| Rent expense | 11,400 | 5,400 | 16,800 |
| Bad debts expense | 1,230 | 1,020 | 2,250 |
| Office salaries | 20,475 | 12,285 | 32,760 |
| Insurance expense | 1,200 | 600 | 1,800 |
| Miscellaneous office expenses | 1,650 | 900 | 2,550 |
| Total allocated expenses | $104,205 | $ 61,155 | $165,360 |
| Total expenses | $115,305 | $ 68,535 | $183,840 |
| Net income (loss) | $ 29,295 | $ (26,235) | $ 3,060 |

If Department Q is eliminated:

*a.* The company has one office worker who earns $630 per week or $32,760 per year and four salesclerks each of whom earns $525 per week or $27,300 per year. At present the salaries of two and one-half salesclerks are charged to Department P and one and one-half salesclerks to Department Q. The sales salaries and office salaries presently assigned to Department Q can be avoided if the department is eliminated. However, management is considering another plan, as follows. It is the opinion of management that two salesclerks may be dismissed if Department Q is eliminated, leaving only two full-time salesclerks in Department P and making up the difference by assigning the office worker to part-time sales work in the department. It is felt that although the office worker has not devoted half of his time to the office work of Department Q, if he devotes the same amount of time to selling in Department P during rush hours as he has to the office work of Department Q, it will be sufficient to carry the load.

*b.* The lease on the store building is long term and cannot be changed; therefore, the space presently occupied by Department Q will have to be used by and charged to Department P. Likewise, Department P will have to make whatever use of Department Q's equipment it can, since the equipment has little or no sales value.

*c.* The elimination of Department Q will eliminate the Department Q advertising expense, losses from bad debts, and store supplies used. It will also eliminate 80% of the insurance expense allocated to the department (the portion on merchandise) and 25% of the miscellaneous office expenses presently allocated to Department Q.

*Required*

1. List in separate columns the amounts of Department Q's escapable and inescapable expenses.
2. Under the assumption that Department P's sales and gross profit will not be affected by the elimination of Department Q, prepare an income statement showing what the company can expect to earn from the operation of Department P after Department Q is eliminated. Assume that the plan of assigning part of the office worker's time to the sales force is used.

**Problem 23–4**
**Departmental contributions to overhead**
(L. O. 4)

Elwood and Darlene Snerd own a farm that produces potatoes. After preparing the following 1991 income statement, Elwood remarked to Darlene that they should have fed the No. 3 potatoes to the pigs and thus avoided the loss from the sale of this grade.

**ELWOOD AND DARLENE SNERD**
**Income from the Production and Sale of Potatotes**
**For Year Ended December 31, 1991**

| | Results by Grades | | | |
|---|---|---|---|---|
| | **No. 1** | **No. 2** | **No. 3** | **Combined** |
| Sales by grades: | | | | |
| No. 1, 202,500 lbs. @ $0.30 per lb. . . . . | $60,750 | | | |
| No. 2, 360,000 lbs. @ $0.25 per lb. . . . . | | $90,000 | | |
| No. 3, 135,000 lbs. @ $0.20 per lb. . . . . | | | $27,000 | |
| Combined . . . . . . . . . . . . . . . . . | | | | $177,750 |
| Costs: | | | | |
| Land preparation, seed, planting, and cultivating @ $0.0948 per lb. . . . . | $19,197 | $34,128 | $12,798 | $ 66,123 |
| Harvesting, sorting, and grading @ $0.079 per lb. . . . . . . . . . . . . | 15,998 | 28,440 | 10,665 | 55,103 |
| Marketing @ $0.0277 per lb. . . . . . . . . | 5,602 | 9,960 | 3,735 | 19,297 |
| Total costs . . . . . . . . . . . . . . . . | $40,797 | $72,528 | $27,198 | $140,523 |
| Net income (or loss) . . . . . . . . . . . . . | $19,953 | $17,472 | $ (198) | $ 37,227 |

On the foregoing statement, Elwood and Darlene divided their costs among the grades on a per pound basis. They did this because, with the exception of marketing costs, their records did not show costs per grade. As to marketing costs, the records did show that $18,000 of the $19,297 was the cost of placing the No. 1 and No. 2 potatoes in bags and hauling them to the warehouse of the produce buyer. Bagging and hauling costs per pound were the same for both grades. The remaining $1,297 of marketing costs was the cost of loading the No. 3 potatoes into trucks of a potato starch factory that bought these potatoes in bulk and picked them up at the farm.

*Required*

Prepare an income statement that will show better the results of producing and marketing the potatoes. (Round all amounts to the nearest whole dollar.)

**Problem 23–5**
**Departmental expense allocation spreadsheet**
(L. O. 3)

Albuquerque Company has three selling departments, E, F, and G, and two service departments, general office and purchasing. At the end of the year, its bookkeeper brought together the following information for use in preparing the year-end statements:

| | Dept. E | Dept. F | Dept. G |
|---|---|---|---|
| Sales | $286,200 | $153,600 | $220,200 |
| Purchases | 203,700 | 105,900 | 125,400 |
| January 1 (beginning) inventory | 36,900 | 25,500 | 30,600 |
| December 31 (ending) inventory | 43,500 | 28,200 | 21,900 |

Albuquerque Company treats salaries, supplies used, and depreciation as direct departmental expenses. The payroll, requisition, and plant asset records showed the following amounts of these expenses by departments:

| | Salaries Expense | Supplies Used | Depreciation of Equipment |
|---|---|---|---|
| General office | $ 28,035 | $ 705 | $1,875 |
| Purchasing department | 18,480 | 585 | 1,125 |
| Department E | 31,080 | 1,155 | 2,550 |
| Department F | 16,530 | 645 | 1,350 |
| Department G | 24,420 | 885 | 1,500 |
| | $118,545 | $3,975 | $8,400 |

The company incurred the following amounts of indirect expenses:

| | |
|---|---|
| Rent expense | $19,800 |
| Advertising expense | 16,500 |
| Expired insurance | 2,250 |
| Heating and lighting expense | 5,250 |
| Janitorial expense | 6,300 |

Albuquerque Company allocates the foregoing expenses to its departments as follows:

*a.* Rent expense on the basis of the amount and value of floor space occupied. The general office and purchasing departments occupy space in the rear of the store that is not as valuable as space in the front; consequently, $1,800 of the total rent is allocated to these two departments in proportion to the space occupied by each. The remainder of the rent is divided between the selling departments in proportion to the space occupied. The five departments occupy these amounts of space: general office, 720 square feet; purchasing department, 480 square feet; Department E, 3,600 square feet; Department F, 1,800 square feet; and Department G, 1,800 square feet.

*b.* Advertising expense on the basis of sales.

*c.* Expired insurance on the basis of equipment book values. The book values of the equipment in the departments are: general office, $10,500; purchasing department, $6,000; Department E, $27,000; Department F, $15,000; and Department G, $16,500.

*d.* Heating and lighting and janitorial expenses on the basis of floor space occupied.

Albuquerque Company allocates its general office department expenses to its selling departments on the basis of sales, and it allocates purchasing department expenses on the basis of purchases.

*Required*

1. Prepare a departmental expense allocation spreadsheet for the company. (Round all amounts to the nearest whole dollar.)
2. Prepare a departmental income statement showing sales, cost of goods sold, expenses, and net incomes by departments and for the entire store.
3. Prepare a second departmental income statement showing departmental contributions to overhead and overall net income.

**Problem 23–6**
**Responsibility accounting performance reports**
(L. O. 5)

L'Equipe Company's Denver plant is managed by Barbara Jenson, who is responsible for all costs of the Denver operation other than her own salary. The plant is divided into two production departments and an office department. The motor and the generator departments manufacture different products and have separate managers; the office department is managed by the plant manager. L'Equipe Company prepares a monthly budget for each of the production departments (motor and generator) and then accumulates costs in a manner that assigns all of the Denver plant costs to the departments.

The department budgets and cost accumulations for the month of March were as follows:

| | Budget | | Actual Costs | | |
|---|---|---|---|---|---|
| | Motor Dept. | Generator Dept. | Motor Dept. | Generator Dept. | Combined |
| Raw materials | $312,000 | $224,000 | $334,400 | $229,600 | $ 564,000 |
| Wages | 176,000 | 160,000 | 186,560 | 165,120 | 351,680 |
| Salary—department manager | 40,000 | 35,200 | 40,000 | 36,800 | 76,800 |
| Supplies used | 16,000 | 14,400 | 13,760 | 15,840 | 29,600 |
| Depreciation of equipment | 9,600 | 8,000 | 9,600 | 9,280 | 18,880 |
| Heating and lighting | 32,000 | 16,000 | 40,000 | 20,000 | 60,000 |
| Rent on building | 38,400 | 19,200 | 38,400 | 19,200 | 57,600 |
| Share of office department costs | 65,600 | 65,600 | 62,080 | 62,080 | 124,160 |
| | $689,600 | $542,400 | $724,800 | $557,920 | $1,282,720 |

Office department costs consisted of the following:

| | Budget | Actual |
|---|---|---|
| Salary—plant manager | $67,200 | $67,200 |
| Other salaries | 44,800 | 42,400 |
| Other costs | 19,200 | 14,560 |

Each department manager is responsible for the purchase and maintenance of equipment in the department. Heating and lighting cost and building rent are allocated to the production departments on the basis of relative space used by those departments.

*Required*

Prepare responsibility accounting performance reports on the managers of each production department and on the plant manager.

## Alternate Problems

**Problem 23–1A**
**Allocation of building occupancy costs**
(L. O. 3)

Talmart Budget Store has in its ledger an account called Building Occupancy Costs to which it charged the following last year:

| | |
|---|---|
| Building | $324,000 |
| Lighting expense | 12,000 |
| Cleaning and maintenance | 60,000 |
| Total | $396,000 |

The store occupies all the space in a building having selling space on three levels—basement level, street level, and second-floor level. Each level has 10,000 square feet of selling space, a total of 30,000 square feet. The bookkeeper divided the $396,000 of building occupancy cost by 30,000 and charged each selling department with $13.20 of building occupancy cost for each square foot of space occupied.

Lamar Crockett, the manager of a basement-level department having 3,000 square feet of floor space, has complained about the $13.20 per square foot of building occupancy cost charged to his department. He cites a recent local real estate study that shows average charges for like space, including heat but not including lights and janitorial service, as follows:

| | |
|---|---|
| Basement-level space | $10 per sq. ft. |
| Street-level space | 30 per sq. ft. |
| Second-floor-level space | 20 per sq. ft. |

*Required*

Prepare a computation that shows the amount of building occupancy cost you think should be charged to Lamar Crockett's department.

**Problem 23–2A**
**Departmental income statement**
(L. O. 4)

The Montana Company began business early in 1991 with two selling departments and a general office department. The company's operating results for 1991 are:

**MONTANA COMPANY**
**Departmental Income Statement**
**For Year Ended December 31, 1991**

| | Dept. 1 | Dept. 2 | Combined |
|---|---|---|---|
| Sales | $720,000 | $360,000 | $1,080,000 |
| Cost of goods sold | 504,000 | 216,000 | 720,000 |
| Gross profit from sales | $216,000 | $144,000 | $ 360,000 |
| Direct expenses: | | | |
| Sales salaries | $ 75,000 | $ 43,200 | $ 118,200 |
| Advertising expense | 6,750 | 4,500 | 11,250 |
| Store supplies used | 3,600 | 1,800 | 5,400 |
| Depreciation of equipment | 6,150 | 3,300 | 9,450 |
| Total direct expenses | $ 91,500 | $ 52,800 | $ 144,300 |
| Allocated expenses: | | | |
| Rent expense | $ 32,400 | $ 21,600 | $ 54,000 |
| Heating and lighting expense | 6,480 | 4,320 | 10,800 |
| Share of office expenses | 42,000 | 21,000 | 63,000 |
| Total allocated expenses | $ 80,880 | $ 46,920 | $ 127,800 |
| Total expenses | $172,380 | $ 99,720 | $ 272,100 |
| Net income | $ 43,620 | $ 44,280 | $ 87,900 |

The company plans to add a third selling department which it estimates will produce $240,000 in sales with a 35% gross profit margin. The new department will require the following estimated direct expenses: sales salaries, $27,000; advertising expense, $2,700; store supplies, $1,500; and depreciation on equipment, $3,150.

When the company began its operations, it was necessary to rent a store room having selling space in excess of requirements. This extra space was assigned to and used by Departments 1 and 2 during the year; but when Department 3 is opened, it will take over one third the space assigned to Department 2. The space reductions are not expected to affect the operations or sales of the old departments.

The company allocates its general office department expenses to its selling departments on the basis of sales. It expects the new department to cause a $5,700 increase in general office department expenses.

The company expects the addition of Department 3 to bring new customers to the store who, in addition to buying Department 3 merchandise, will also do sufficient buying in the old departments to increase their sales by 5% each. It is not expected that the increase in sales in the old departments will affect their gross profit percentages nor any of their direct expenses other than supplies. It is expected the supplies used will increase in proportion to sales.

*Required*

Prepare a departmental income statement showing the company's expected operations with three departments.

**Problem 23–3A**
**Analysis of escapable and inescapable expenses**
(L. O. 4)

Keroack Company is considering the elimination of its unprofitable Department L. The company's 1991 income statement appears as follows:

**KEROACK COMPANY**
**Income Statement**
**For Year Ended December 31, 1991**

| | Dept. K | Dept. L | Combined |
|---|---|---|---|
| Sales | $270,000 | $120,000 | $390,000 |
| Cost of goods sold | 132,000 | 93,000 | 225,000 |
| Gross profit from sales | $138,000 | $ 27,000 | $165,000 |
| Operating expenses: | | | |
| Direct expenses: | | | |
| Advertising | $ 6,000 | $ 2,700 | $ 8,700 |
| Store supplies used | 2,400 | 1,800 | 4,200 |
| Depreciation of store equipment | 4,500 | 2,250 | 6,750 |
| Total direct expenses | $ 12,900 | $ 6,750 | $ 19,650 |
| Allocated expenses: | | | |
| Sales salaries | $ 67,500 | $ 13,500 | $ 81,000 |
| Rent expense | 9,600 | 7,200 | 16,800 |
| Bad debts expense | 1,500 | 1,200 | 2,700 |
| Office salaries | 18,750 | 18,750 | 37,500 |
| Insurance expense | 2,250 | 800 | 3,050 |
| Miscellaneous office expenses | 1,650 | 600 | 2,250 |
| Total allocated expenses | $101,250 | $ 42,050 | $143,300 |
| Total expenses | $114,150 | $ 48,800 | $162,950 |
| Net income (loss) | $ 23,850 | $ (21,800) | $ 2,050 |

If Department L is eliminated:

*a.* The company has one office worker who earns $37,500 per year and three salesclerks each of whom earns $2,250 per month or $27,000 per year. At present the salaries of two and one-half salesclerks are charged to Department K and one-half salesclerk to Department L. The sales salaries presently assigned to Department L can be avoided if the department is eliminated and the office worker's salary could be reduced from full time to three-fourths time. However, management is considering another plan, as follows. It is the opinion of management that one salesclerk may be dismissed if Department L is eliminated, leaving only two full-time salesclerks in Department K and making up the difference by assigning the office worker to half-time sales work in the department. The office work could be squeezed into the remaining half-time.

*b.* The lease on the store building is long term and cannot be changed; therefore, the space presently occupied by Department L will have to be charged to Department K. Also, Department K will have to make whatever use of Department L's equipment it can, since the equipment has little or no sales value.

*c.* The elimination of Department L will eliminate the Department L advertising expense, losses from bad debts, and store supplies used. It will also eliminate 75% of the insurance expense allocated to the department (the portion on merchandise) and 50% of the miscellaneous office expenses presently allocated to Department L.

*Required*

1. List in separate columns the escapable and inescapable expenses associated with eliminating Department L.
2. Under the assumption that Department K's sales and gross profit will not be affected by the elimination of Department L, prepare an income statement showing what the company can expect to earn from the operation of Department K after Department L is eliminated. Assume that the plan of assigning part of the office worker's time to the sales force is used.

**Problem 23–4A**
**Departmental contributions to overhead**
(L. O. 4)

Luke Casey's business produced and sold a half million pounds of pears during 1991, and he prepared the following statement to show the results:

**LUKE CASEY**
**Income from the Sale of Pears**
**For Year Ended December 31, 1991**

| | Results by Grades | | | |
|---|---|---|---|---|
| | **No. 1** | **No. 2** | **No. 3** | **Combined** |
| Sales by grades: | | | | |
| No. 1, 120,000 lbs. @ $0.50 per lb. . . . . | $60,000 | | | |
| No. 2, 120,000 lbs. @ $0.35 per lb. . . . . | | $42,000 | | |
| No. 3, 60,000 lbs. @ $0.20 per lb. . . . . . | | | $12,000 | |
| Combined . . . . . . . . . . . . . . . . . . | | | | $114,000 |
| Costs: | | | | |
| Tree pruning and orchard care @ $0.10 per lb. . . . . . . . . . . . . . . . | $12,000 | $12,000 | $ 6,000 | $ 30,000 |
| Fruit picking, grading, and sorting @ $0.125 per lb. . . . . . . . . . . . . . | 15,000 | 15,000 | 7,500 | 37,500 |
| Marketing @ $0.038 per lb. . . . . . . . . . | 4,560 | 4,560 | 2,280 | 11,400 |
| Total costs . . . . . . . . . . . . . . . . . . | $31,560 | $31,560 | $15,780 | $ 78,900 |
| Net income (or loss) . . . . . . . . . . . . . | $28,440 | $10,440 | $ (3,780) | $ 35,100 |

Upon completing the statement, Mr. Casey thought a wise course of future action might be to leave the No. 3 pears on the trees to fall off and be plowed under when the ground is cultivated between the trees, and thus avoid the loss from their sale. However, before doing so he consulted you.

When you examined the statement, you recognized that Mr. Casey had divided all his costs by 300,000 and allocated them on a per pound basis. You asked him about the marketing costs and learned that $10,600 of the $11,400 was incurred in placing the No. 1 and No. 2 fruit in boxes and delivering them to the warehouse of the fruit buyer. The cost per pound of doing this was the same for both grades. You also learned that the remaining $800 was for loading the No. 3 fruit on the trucks of a fruit juice manufacturer who bought this grade of fruit in bulk at the orchard for use in making fruit juice.

*Required*

Prepare an income statement that will reflect better the results of producing and marketing the pears. (Round all amounts to the nearest whole dollar.)

**Problem 23–5A**
**Departmental expense allocation spreadsheet**
(L. O. 3)

Curie Company carries on its operations with two service departments, the general office department and the purchasing department, and with three selling departments, 1, 2, and 3. At the end of its annual accounting period the company's accountant prepared the following adjusted trial balance:

**CURIE COMPANY**
**Adjusted Trial Balance**
**December 31, 1991**

| | | |
|---|---|---|
| Cash | $ 31,500 | |
| Merchandise inventory, Department 1 (beginning) | 37,200 | |
| Merchandise inventory, Department 2 (beginning) | 72,800 | |
| Merchandise inventory, Department 3 (beginning) | 58,000 | |
| Supplies | 2,480 | |
| Equipment | 147,760 | |
| Accumulated depreciation, equipment | | $ 40,540 |
| Thomas Curie, capital | | 291,700 |
| Thomas Curie, withdrawals | 36,000 | |
| Sales, Department 1 | | 209,600 |
| Sales, Department 2 | | 416,800 |
| Sales, Department 3 | | 273,600 |
| Purchases, Department 1 | 137,600 | |
| Purchases, Department 2 | 317,200 | |
| Purchases, Department 3 | 166,800 | |
| Salaries expense | 147,420 | |
| Rent expense | 30,000 | |
| Advertising expense | 22,500 | |
| Expired insurance | 2,000 | |
| Heating and lighting expense | 4,800 | |
| Depreciation of equipment | 7,280 | |
| Supplies used | 4,500 | |
| Janitorial services | 6,400 | |
| Totals | $1,232,240 | $1,232,240 |

*Required*

1. Prepare a departmental expense allocation spreadsheet for Curie Company, using the following information:
   *a.* Curie Company treats salaries, supplies used, and depreciation of equipment as direct departmental expenses. The payroll, requisition, and plant asset records show the following amounts of these expenses by departments:

| | Salaries Expense | Supplies Used | Depreciation of Equipment |
|---|---|---|---|
| General office | $ 41,180 | $ 580 | $1,000 |
| Purchasing department | 28,160 | 520 | 880 |
| Department 1 | 18,640 | 1,100 | 1,700 |
| Department 2 | 33,280 | 1,260 | 2,460 |
| Department 3 | 26,160 | 1,040 | 1,240 |
| | $147,420 | $4,500 | $7,280 |

   *b.* The company treats the remainder of its expenses as indirect and allocates them as follows:
   (1) Rent expense on the basis of the amount and value of floor space occupied. The general office occupies 900 square feet and the purchasing department occupies 600 square feet on a balcony at the rear of the store. This space is not as valuable as space on the main floor; therefore, the store allocates $2,000 of its rent to these two departments on the basis of space occupied and allocates the remainder to the selling departments on the basis of the main-floor space they occupy. The selling departments occupy main-floor space as follows: Department 1, 3,000

square feet; Department 2, 5,250 square feet; and Department 3, 2,250 square feet.

(2) Advertising expense on the basis of sales.

(3) Insurance expense on the basis of the book values of the equipment in the departments, which are: general office, $10,000; purchasing, $8,000; Department 1, $26,000; Department 2, $38,000; and Department 3, $18,000.

(4) Heating and lighting and janitorial services on the basis of floor space occupied.

*c.* The company allocates general office department expenses to the selling departments on the basis of sales, and it allocates purchasing department expenses on the basis of purchases.

2. Prepare a departmental income statement for the company showing sales, cost of goods sold, expenses, and net incomes by departments and for the entire store. The year-end inventories were Department 1, $46,400; Department 2, $93,600; and Department 3, $53,600.
3. Prepare a second income statement for the company showing departmental contributions to overhead and overall net income.

**Problem 23–6A**
**Responsibility accounting performance reports**
(L. O. 5)

Interlace Company's Philadelphia plant is managed by Albert Rockford, who is responsible for all costs of the Philadelphia operation other than his own salary. The plant is divided into two production departments and an office department. The webbing and dalite departments manufacture different products and have separate managers; the office department is managed by the plant manager. Interlace prepares a monthly budget for each of the production departments (webbing and dalite) and then accumulates costs in a manner that assigns all of the Philadelphia plant costs to the departments.

The department budgets and cost accumulations for the month of May were as follows:

| | Budget | | Actual Costs | | |
|---|---|---|---|---|---|
| | Webbing Dept. | Dalite Dept. | Webbing Dept. | Dalite Dept. | Combined |
| Raw materials | $138,000 | $168,000 | $134,100 | $172,560 | $306,660 |
| Wages | 100,800 | 118,800 | 104,340 | 115,740 | 220,080 |
| Salary—department manager | 15,600 | 16,800 | 16,500 | 16,800 | 33,300 |
| Supplies used | 4,500 | 4,800 | 5,760 | 5,520 | 11,280 |
| Depreciation of equipment | 8,400 | 6,000 | 8,400 | 6,600 | 15,000 |
| Heating and lighting | 9,600 | 14,400 | 11,660 | 17,500 | 29,160 |
| Rent on building | 6,000 | 9,000 | 6,000 | 9,000 | 15,000 |
| Share of office department costs | 39,000 | 39,000 | 41,700 | 41,700 | 83,400 |
| | $321,900 | $376,800 | $328,460 | $385,420 | $713,880 |

Office department costs consisted of the following:

| | Budget | Actual |
|---|---|---|
| Salary—plant manager | $32,400 | $32,400 |
| Other salaries | 36,000 | 37,200 |
| Other costs | 9,600 | 13,800 |

Each department manager is responsible for the purchase and maintenance of equipment in the department. Heating and lighting cost and building rent are allocated to the production departments on the basis of relative space used by those departments.

*Required*

Prepare responsibility accounting performance reports on the managers of each production department and on the plant manager.

## Provocative Problems

**Provocative Problem 23–1**
**Bristol-Myers Company**
(L. O. 1)

Bristol-Myers Company is organized into 5 corporate groups and 20 divisions. Its operations cover much of the globe. In its 1987 annual report, the segmental information included the following:

Bristol-Myers Company

| Industry Segments (in millions of dollars) | Net Sales 1987 | Net Sales 1986 | Net Sales 1985 | Profit 1987 | Profit 1986 | Profit 1985 | Year-End Assets 1987 | Year-End Assets 1986 | Year-End Assets 1985 |
|---|---|---|---|---|---|---|---|---|---|
| Pharmaceutical and Medical Products | $2,217.1 | $1,961.7 | $1,754.0 | $ 484.2 | $396.5 | $333.4 | $1,654.7 | $1,574.2 | $1,284.0 |
| Non-Prescription Health Products | 1,504.1 | 1,377.3 | 1,231.4 | 404.5 | 346.5 | 304.6 | 553.8 | 550.0 | 508.9 |
| Toiletries and Beauty Aids | 1,188.9 | 1,057.5 | 1,019.9 | 199.4 | 181.0 | 166.4 | 489.2 | 484.2 | 507.7 |
| Household Products | 491.0 | 439.2 | 439.3 | 71.3 | 67.1 | 64.4 | 176.5 | 174.0 | 156.3 |
| Inter-segment and other sales | .1 | .2 | .2 | | | | | | |
| Net sales, operating profit and assets | $5,401.2 | $4,835.9 | $4,444.8 | $1,159.4 | $991.1 | $868.8 | $2,874.2 | $2,782.4 | $2,456.9 |

| Geographic Areas (in millions of dollars) | Net Sales 1987 | Net Sales 1986 | Net Sales 1985 | Profit 1987 | Profit 1986 | Profit 1985 | Year-End Assets 1987 | Year-End Assets 1986 | Year-End Assets 1985 |
|---|---|---|---|---|---|---|---|---|---|
| United States | $3,949.8 | $3,594.8 | $3,381.0 | $ 897.7 | $778.3 | $662.6 | $1,790.1 | $1,821.5 | $1,577.4 |
| Europe, Mid-East and Africa | 763.1 | 653.1 | 501.9 | 136.8 | 106.4 | 92.6 | 578.7 | 466.7 | 404.7 |
| Other Western Hemisphere | 485.5 | 432.1 | 436.2 | 97.2 | 85.0 | 91.7 | 273.4 | 279.1 | 285.1 |
| Pacific | 505.3 | 415.8 | 376.7 | 59.3 | 31.5 | 28.7 | 387.5 | 353.4 | 330.6 |
| Inter-area eliminations | (302.5) | (259.9) | (251.0) | (31.6) | (10.1) | (6.8) | (155.5) | (138.3) | (140.9) |
| Net sales, operating profit and assets | $5,401.2 | $4,835.9 | $4,444.8 | 1,159.4 | 991.1 | 868.8 | 2,874.2 | 2,782.4 | 2,456.9 |
| Unallocated expenses and other assets | | | | (41.9) | (60.7) | (22.5) | 1,857.8 | 1,400.6 | 1,313.5 |
| Earnings before income taxes and total assets | | | | $1,117.5 | $930.4 | $846.3 | $4,732.0 | $4,183.0 | $3,770.4 |

| Industry Segments (in millions of dollars) | Capital Expenditures 1987 | Capital Expenditures 1986 | Capital Expenditures 1985 | Depreciation 1987 | Depreciation 1986 | Depreciation 1985 |
|---|---|---|---|---|---|---|
| Pharmaceutical and Medical Products | $ 91.9 | $125.4 | $145.6 | $ 55.9 | $ 50.1 | $40.2 |
| Non-Prescription Health Products | 36.7 | 42.8 | 33.3 | 25.3 | 22.6 | 20.4 |
| Toiletries and Beauty Aids | 16.2 | 19.6 | 19.1 | 17.3 | 15.8 | 14.4 |
| Household Products | 10.6 | 14.6 | 12.5 | 7.0 | 6.2 | 5.1 |
| Identifiable industry totals | 155.4 | 202.4 | 210.5 | 105.5 | 94.7 | 80.1 |
| Other | 34.6 | 19.5 | 15.0 | 10.4 | 10.2 | 7.9 |
| Consolidated totals | $190.0 | $221.9 | $225.5 | $115.9 | $104.9 | $88.0 |

Unallocated expenses consist principally of general administrative expenses and net interest income. Other assets are principally cash, time deposits and marketable securities. Inter-area sales are usually billed at or above manufacturing costs. Inter-area sales principally include $115.1 million, $96.1 million and $95.6 million in 1987, 1986 and 1985, respectively, attributable to the United States and $150.9 million, $129.0 million and $111.9 million in 1987, 1986 and 1985, respectively, attributable to Europe, Mid-East and Africa.

Net assets relating to operations outside the United States amount to approximately $717 million, $614 million and $591 million at December 31, 1987, 1986 and 1985, respectively.

Answer the following questions about Bristol-Myers Company's segmental information.

1. What are the industrial segments into which the operations of Bristol-Myers Company are divided?

2. What was the 1987 net sales of the Toiletries and Beauty Aids segment?
3. Which segment earned the largest profit in 1987? Which had the smallest?
4. In which segment did Bristol-Myers Company have a declining asset investment over the three-year period?
5. What possible explanation might you give for the $302.5 million inter-area elimination of net sales?
6. What amount of total assets would you expect to have been presented on the company's 1987 balance sheet?
7. What possible explanation might you give for the $155.5 million inter-area elimination of identifiable assets at the end of 1987?

**Provocative Problem 23–2**
**B-O-P, a Real Estate Partnership**
(L. O. 6)

Jerry Bosley, Jane O'Shay, and Jack Parker entered into a partnership for the purpose of developing and selling a plot of land currently owned by Bosley. O'Shay invested $208,000 cash in the partnership, Bosley invested land at its $240,000 fair market value, and Parker invested $32,000. The partners agreed to share losses and gains equally. Parker was to provide the necessary real estate expertise to make the project a success. The partnership installed streets and water mains costing $240,000 and divided the land into 14 building lots. They priced Lots 1, 2, 3, and 4 for sale at $48,000 each; Lots 5, 6, 7, 8, 9, 10, 11, and 12 at $56,000 each; and Lots 13 and 14 at $64,000 each. The partners agreed that Parker could take Lot 13 at cost for his personal use. The remaining lots were sold, and the partnership dissolved. Determine the amount of partnership cash each partner should receive in the dissolution.

**Provocative Problem 23–3**
**Sunray Company**
(L. O. 3, 4)

The Sunray Company bookkeeper prepared the following income statement for April 1991:

**SUNRAY COMPANY**
**Income Statement for April 1991**

| | Patio Door Department | Skylight Department | Combined |
|---|---|---|---|
| Sales | $240,000 | $360,000 | $600,000 |
| Cost of goods sold | 171,600 | 257,400 | 429,000 |
| Gross profit on sales | $ 68,400 | $102,600 | $171,000 |
| Warehousing expenses | $ 17,700 | $ 17,700 | $ 35,400 |
| Selling expenses | 33,600 | 36,600 | 70,200 |
| General and administrative expenses | 9,150 | 9,150 | 18,300 |
| Total expenses | $ 60,450 | $ 63,450 | $123,900 |
| Net income | $ 7,950 | $ 39,150 | $ 47,100 |

The company is a wholesaler of patio doors and skylights and is organized on a departmental basis. However, the company manager does not feel that the bookkeeper's statement reflects the profit situation in the company's two selling departments, and he has asked you to redraft it with any supporting schedules or comments you think desirable. Your investigation reveals the following:

1. The company sold 1,200 patio doors and 960 skylights during April. The bookkeeper allocated cost of goods sold between the two departments

on an arbitrary basis. A skylight actually costs the company twice as much as a patio door.

2. A patio door and a skylight take approximately the same space for storage. However, because there are four styles of patio doors and six styles of skylights, the company must carry a 50% greater inventory of skylights than of patio doors.
3. The company occupies its building on the following bases:

| | Area of Space | Value of Space |
|---|---|---|
| Warehouse | 80% | 60% |
| Patio door sales office | 5 | 10 |
| Skylight sales office | 5 | 10 |
| General office | 10 | 20 |

4. Warehousing expenses for April consisted of the following:

| | |
|---|---|
| Wages expense | $18,000 |
| Depreciation of building | 12,000 |
| Heating and lighting expenses | 3,000 |
| Depreciation of warehouse equipment | 2,400 |
| Total | $35,400 |

The bookkeeper had charged all of the building's depreciation plus all of the heating and lighting expenses to warehousing expenses.

5. Selling expenses for April consisted of the following:

| | Patio Door Department | Skylight Department |
|---|---|---|
| Sales salaries | $24,000 | $27,000 |
| Advertising | 9,000 | 9,000 |
| Depreciation of office equipment | 600 | 600 |
| Totals | $33,600 | $36,600 |

Sales salaries and depreciation were charged to the two departments on the basis of actual amounts incurred. Advertising was allocated by the bookkeeper. The company has an established advertising budget based on dollars of sales which it followed rather closely in April.

6. General and administrative expenses for April consisted of the following:

| | |
|---|---|
| Salaries and wages | $16,800 |
| Depreciation of office equipment | 1,200 |
| Miscellaneous office expenses | 300 |
| Total | $18,300 |

**Provocative Problem 23–4**
**Slide View Corporation**
(L. O. 4)

Slide View Corporation wholesales high-quality slide projectors that are designed for professional usage. Operations of the company during the past year resulted in the following:

| | Standard | Deluxe |
|---|---|---|
| Units sold . . . . . . . . . . . . . | 300 | 100 |
| Selling price per unit . . . . . . . | $600 | $800 |
| Cost per unit . . . . . . . . . . . | 320 | 420 |
| Sales commission per unit . . . | 90 | 120 |
| Indirect selling and administrative expenses per unit . . . . . . . | 150 | 200 |

Indirect selling and administrative expenses totaled $65,000 and were allocated between the sales of Standard and Deluxe units on the basis of their relative sales volumes. The Standard model produced $180,000 of revenue, and the Deluxe model produced $80,000; thus, the Standard model was assigned 18/26 of the $65,000 of indirect expenses and the Deluxe model was assigned 8/26. After allocating the total indirect expenses to the two models, the indirect expenses per unit were determined by dividing the total by the number of units sold. Hence, the Standard model's cost per unit was $150, and the Deluxe model's cost per unit was $200.

Management of Slide View Corporation is attempting to decide between three courses of action and asks you to evaluate which of the three courses is most desirable. The three alternatives are: (1) through advertising push the sales of the Standard model; (2) through advertising push the sales of the Deluxe model; or (3) do no additional advertising, in which case sales of each model will continue at present levels. The demand for slide projectors is fairly stable, and an increase in the number of units of one model sold will cause an equally large decrease in unit sales of the other model. However, through the expenditure of $2,000 for advertising, the company can shift the sale of 50 units of the Standard model to the Deluxe model, or vice versa, depending upon which model receives the advertising attention. Should the company advertise; and if so, which model? Back your position with income statements.

Part Eight

# Planning and Controlling Business Operations

The process of managing a business can be summarized in two words: planning and control. In both of these two management functions, accounting information plays a critical role. As you study the remaining chapters of the book, you will learn how accounting information is developed and used in a variety of ways to accomplish the planning and control responsibilities of management.

Part Eight consists of the following chapters:

# 24 Cost-Volume-Profit Analysis

This chapter explains how changes in the operating volume of a business affect different kinds of costs. In studying the chapter, you will learn how to analyze the costs of a business in a way that allows you to describe the effect of sales volume changes on a business's profit or loss. Managers use this kind of analysis to evaluate what will happen if changes are made in sales volume, selling prices, costs, or product mix.

**Learning Objectives**

*After studying Chapter 24, you should be able to:*

1. Describe the different types of cost behavior experienced by a typical company.
2. State the assumptions that underlie cost-volume-profit analysis and explain how these assumptions restrict the usefulness of the information obtained from the analysis.
3. Prepare and interpret a scatter diagram of past costs and sales volume.
4. Calculate a break-even point for a single product company and graphically plot its costs and revenues.
5. Describe some extensions that may be added to the basic cost-volume-profit analysis of a business's break-even point.
6. Calculate a composite sales unit for a multiproduct company and a break-even point for such a company.
7. Define or explain the words and phrases listed in the chapter Glossary.

## Questions Answered by Cost-Volume-Profit Analysis

**Cost-volume-profit analysis** is a means of predicting the effects of changes in costs and sales levels on the income of a business. In its simplest form, it involves determining the sales level at which a company neither earns a profit nor incurs a loss or, in other words, the point at which it breaks even. For this reason, cost-volume-profit analysis is often called **break-even analysis.** However the technique can be expanded to answer additional questions, such as: What sales volume is necessary to earn a desired net income? What income will be earned if unit selling prices are reduced in order to increase sales volume? What income will be earned if a new machine that will reduce unit labor costs is installed? What income will be earned if we change the sales mix? When the technique is expanded to answer such additional questions, the descriptive phrase *cost-volume-profit analysis* is more appropriate than *break-even analysis*.

## Cost Behavior

Describe the different types of cost behavior experienced by a typical company. (L. O. 1)

Conventional cost-volume-profit analyses require that costs be classified as either fixed or variable. Some costs are definitely fixed in nature. Others are strictly variable. However, when you examine different costs, you will observe that some are neither completely fixed nor completely variable.

### Fixed Costs

The amount of a **fixed cost** that is incurred each period remains unchanged in total amount even though production volume may vary over a wide range from period to period. For example, if a factory building is rented for $5,000 per month, this cost remains the same whether the factory operates on a one-shift, two-shift, or an around-the-clock basis. Likewise, the cost is the same whether 100 units of product are produced in a month, 1,000 units are produced, or any other number up to the full production capacity of the plant. Note, however, that while the total amount of a fixed cost remains constant as the level of production changes, the fixed cost per unit of product decreases as volume increases. For example, if rent is $5,000 per month and 20 units of product are produced in a month, the rent cost per unit is $250; but if production is increased to 100 units per month, rent cost per unit decreases to $50. Likewise, it decreases to $10 per unit if production is increased to 500 units per month.

When production volume is plotted on a graph, units of product usually are shown on the horizontal axis, and dollars of cost are shown on the vertical axis. Fixed costs are then expressed as a horizontal line, since the total amount of fixed costs remains constant at all levels of production. This is shown in the graph of Illustration 24–1, where the fixed costs remain at $32,000 at all production levels up to 2,000 units of product.

### Variable Costs

The total amount of a **variable cost** changes in proportion to production volume changes. For example, the cost of the material that enters into a product is a variable cost. If material that costs $20 is required to produce one unit of product, total material costs are $200 if 10 units of product are manufactured, $400

Illustration 24–1
**The relationships between fixed costs, variable costs, and units produced**

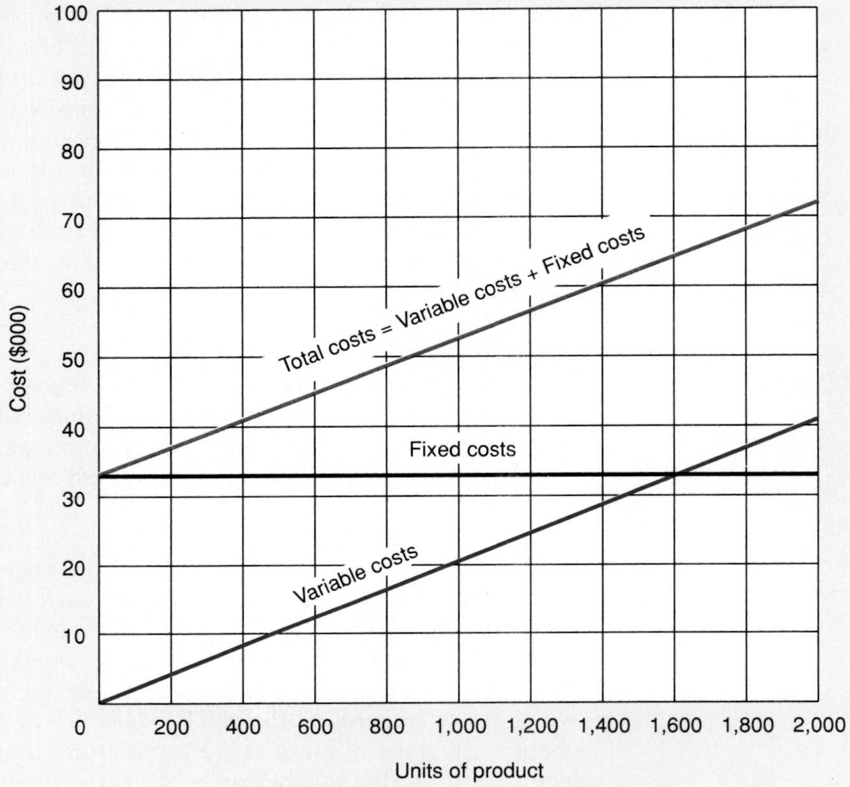


if 20 units are manufactured, $600 if 30 units are manufactured, and so on. In other words, the variable cost per unit produced remains constant while the total amount of variable cost changes in direct proportion to changes in the level of production. Variable costs appear on a graph as a straight line with a positive slope; the line rises as the production volume increases, as in Illustration 24–1.

### Stair-Step Costs and Semivariable Costs

All costs are not necessarily either fixed or variable. For example, some costs go up in steps. Consider the salaries of production supervisors. Supervisory salaries may be more or less fixed for any production volume from zero to the maximum that can be completed on a one-shift basis. Then, if an additional shift must be added to increase production, additional supervisors must be hired, and supervisory salaries go up by a lump-sum amount. Total supervisory costs then remain fixed at this level until a third shift is added when they increase by another lump sum. Costs such as these are called **stair-step costs** or **step-variable costs** and are shown graphically in Illustration 24–2.

**Illustration 24–2**
**Stair-step costs, fixed costs, semivariable costs, and the relevant range**

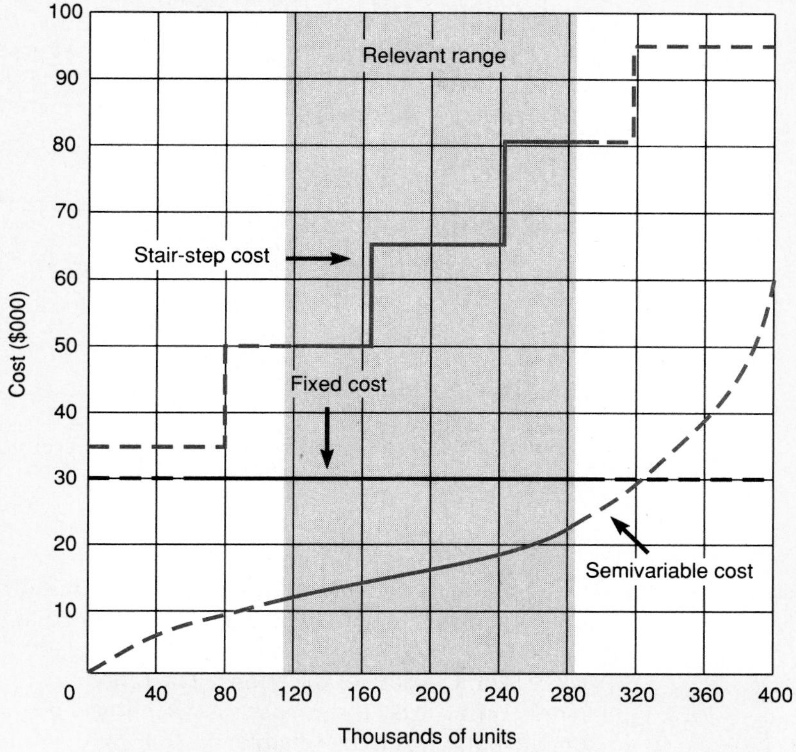


In addition to stair-step costs, some costs may be semivariable or curvilinear in nature. **Semivariable costs** go up with volume increases, but when plotted on a graph, they must be plotted as a curved line (see Illustration 24–2). These costs change with production-level changes, but not proportionately.

For example, at low levels of production, the addition of more laborers may allow each laborer to specialize so that the whole crew becomes more efficient. Each new laborer increases the total cost, but the increased production more than compensates for the increased cost so that the cost per unit is reduced. Eventually, however, the addition of more laborers in a given plant may cause inefficiencies. For example, laborers may have to spend more time communicating with each other. Thus, additional laborers may increase production, but the cost per unit also may increase.

**Mixed Costs.** Although some costs are easily classified as variable or fixed, the behavior of other costs may be less obvious. For example, compensation to sales personnel might include a constant monthly salary plus a commission based on sales. A cost of this type is called a **mixed cost** (see Illustration 24–3). Instead of classifying a mixed cost as variable or fixed, it should be

**Illustration 24–3**
**A mixed cost**

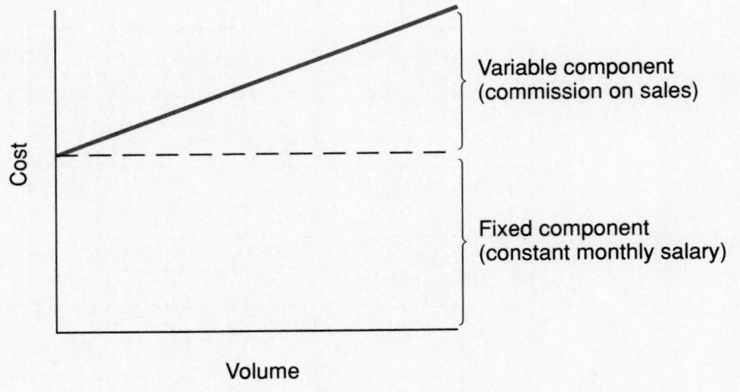


divided into its separate fixed and variable components so that each can be classified correctly.

### Cost Assumptions

State the assumptions that underlie cost-volume-profit analysis and explain how these assumptions restrict the usefulness of the information obtained from the analysis. (L. O. 2)

Conventional cost-volume-profit analysis is based on relationships that can be expressed as straight lines. Costs are assumed to be either fixed or variable. With the costs expressed as straight lines, the costs are then analyzed in order to answer a variety of questions. The reliability of the answers, however, depends on at least three basic assumptions. If a conventional cost-volume-profit analysis is to be reliable:

1. The per unit selling price must be constant. (The selling price per unit must remain the same regardless of production level.)
2. The costs classified as *variable* must, in fact, behave as variable costs; that is, the actual (variable) cost per unit of production must remain constant.
3. The costs classified as *fixed* must, in fact, remain constant over wide changes in the level of production.

In this discussion, we have defined variable costs and fixed costs in terms of levels of production activity. However, in cost-volume-profit analysis, the level of activity is usually measured in terms of sales volume, whether stated as sales dollars or number of units sold. Thus, an additional assumption is frequently made that the level of production will be the same as the level of sales, or if they are not the same, that the difference will not be enough to materially damage the reliability of the analysis.

When the above assumptions are valid, costs and revenues may be correctly represented by straight lines. However, the actual behavior of costs and revenues often is not completely consistent with these assumptions. If the assumptions are violated by significant amounts, the results of cost-volume-profit analysis will not be reliable. Yet, there are at least two reasons why these assumptions tend to provide reliable analyses.

**Aggregating Costs May Support Assumptions.** While individual variable costs may not act in a truly variable manner, the process of adding such costs together may offset such violations of the assumption. In other words, the assumption of variable behavior may be satisfied with respect to total variable costs even though it is violated by individual variable costs. Similarly, the assumption that fixed costs remain constant may be satisfied for total fixed costs even though individual fixed costs may violate the assumption.

**Relevant Range of Operations.** Another reason why the assumptions that revenues, variable costs, and fixed costs can be reasonably represented as straight lines is that the assumptions are only intended to apply over the **relevant range of operations.** The relevant range of operations, as plotted in Illustration 24–2, is the normal operating range for the business. It excludes extremely high and low levels of production that are not apt to be encountered. Thus, a specific fixed cost is expected to be truly fixed only within the relevant range. It may be that beyond the limits of the relevant range, the fixed cost would not remain constant.

**Cost-Volume-Profit Analysis Is Not Precise.** You must understand that cost-volume-profit analysis yields *approximate* answers to questions concerning the relationships between costs, volume, and profits. The answers are not precise because the analysis is used to make predictions about what will happen in the future. So long as managers understand that the answers provided are approximations, cost-volume-profit analysis can be a useful managerial tool.

### Estimating Cost Behavior

The process of estimating the behavior of a company's costs requires judgment and, to the extent past data is available, a careful examination of past experience. Initially, the individual costs should be reviewed and classified as fixed or variable based on your understanding of how each cost is likely to behave. Some costs may be classified quite easily. For example, raw material costs of a manufacturer or cost of goods sold of a merchandiser are undoubtedly variable costs. Similarly, a constant monthly rent expense or the monthly salaries of administrative personnel are clearly fixed costs.

Prepare and interpret a scatter diagram of past costs and sales volume. (L. O. 3)

**Scatter Diagrams.** The classification of costs as fixed or variable should be based, to the extent possible, on an analysis of past experience. One helpful technique of analyzing past experience is to display past data on a **scatter diagram** like the one in Illustration 24–4. In preparing a scatter diagram, volume in dollars or units is measured on the horizontal axis, and cost is measured on the vertical axis. The cost and volume of each period are entered as a single point on the diagram.

Illustration 24–4 shows a scatter diagram of a company's total costs and sales for each of 12 months. Each point shows the total costs incurred and the sales volume during a given month. For example, in one month, sales amounted to $30,000 and total costs were $26,000. These results were entered on the diagram as the point labeled "A."

**Illustration 24–4**
**A scatter diagram with an estimated line of cost behavior**

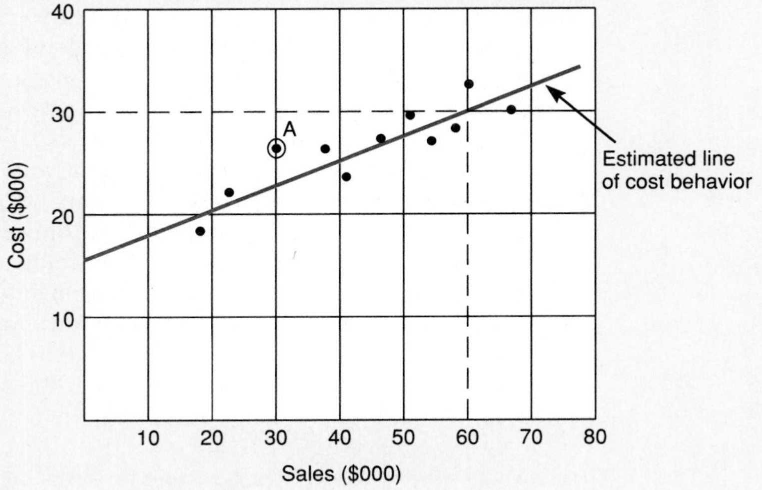


**Estimated Line of Cost Behavior.** In Illustration 24–4, observe the **estimated line of cost behavior.** This line attempts to reflect the average relationship between total costs and sales volume. Several alternative methods can be used to derive this line.

A crude means of deriving this line is called the **high-low method.** To use this method, all you must do is identify the two points in the diagram that represent the highest total cost and the lowest total cost. Then, draw a line between these two points. The most obvious deficiency in this approach is that it totally ignores all of the available cost and sales volume points except the highest and lowest. Also, the line is based on the most extreme points rather than what is more likely to be repeated in the future.

Another, somewhat better approach is to visually inspect the scatter of points and draw a line through the scatter that appears to provide an average reflection of the relationship between costs and volume. For quick and rough analyses, this approach is often satisfactory.

More sophisticated methods of approximating cost behavior are also available. Among these, perhaps the most often used is the statistical method of **least-squares regression.** This method requires fairly extensive calculations but results in an approximation that can be described as a line that best fits the actual cost and sales volume experience of the company. The calculations for least-squares regressions are typically covered in statistics courses and are applied to accounting data in more advanced cost accounting courses.

Return to Illustration 24–4 and observe that the monthly sales volume ranged from approximately $20,000 to $67,000. If the estimated line of cost behavior is extended too far beyond this range, it is not likely to be useful for predicting actual costs. Also, note that the line has been extended downward to the point at which it intersects the horizontal axis ($15,000). This should be interpreted as follows: Assuming sales volume in the range of past operations ($20,000 to $67,000), the company's total costs acted as if the fixed costs were approximately $15,000.

Variable costs per sales dollar are represented in Illustration 24–4 by the slope of the estimated line of cost behavior. The slope may be calculated by comparing any two points on the line. To estimate variable cost per sales dollar, the change in total cost between the two points is divided by the change in dollar sales volume between the two points.

For example, in Illustration 24–4, two points could be selected and the variable cost per sales dollar calculated as follows:

| | Sales | Cost |
|---|---|---|
| First point . . . . . | $60,000 | $30,000 |
| Second point . . . . | –0– | 15,000 |
| Changes . . . . . . | $60,000 | $15,000 |

$$\frac{\text{Change in cost}}{\text{Change in sales}} = \frac{\$15{,}000}{\$60{,}000} = \$0.25 \text{ of cost per sales dollar}$$

If you analyze past experience of a company's costs, you may be able to estimate total fixed costs and variable costs per unit of volume without making a detailed classification of each individual cost. However, you will have greater confidence in the analysis if you classify individual costs and then test the results against observations of past experience. In testing the classifications, scatter diagrams may be prepared for individual costs, total variable costs, total fixed costs, and total costs.

## Break-Even Point

Calculate a break-even point for a single product company and graphically plot its costs and revenues.
(L. O. 4)

A company's **break-even point** is the sales level at which it neither earns a profit nor incurs a loss. It may be expressed either in units of product or in dollars of sales. To illustrate, assume that Alpha Company sells a single product for $100 per unit and incurs $70 of variable costs per unit sold. If the fixed costs involved in selling the product are $24,000 per month, the company breaks even as soon as it sells 800 units or as soon as sales volume reaches $80,000. This break-even point may be determined as follows:

1. Each unit sold at $100 recovers its $70 variable costs and contributes $30 toward the fixed costs.
2. The fixed costs are $24,000 per month, and 800 units ($24,000 ÷ $30 = 800) must be sold each month to pay the fixed costs.
3. And if 800 units are sold at $100 each, the total sales volume is $800,000.

The $30 amount by which the sales price exceeds variable costs per unit is this product's **contribution margin per unit.** In other words, the contribution margin per unit is the amount that the sale of one unit contributes toward recovery of the fixed costs and then toward a profit.

**Illustration 24–5**
**Income statement at a break-even sales level**

ALPHA COMPANY
Income Statement for One Month

| | | |
|---|---|---|
| Sales (800 units @ $100 each) | | $80,000 |
| Costs: | | |
| Fixed costs | $24,000 | |
| Variable costs (800 units @ $70 each) | 56,000 | 80,000 |
| Net income | | $ -0- |

Also, the contribution margin of a product expressed as a percentage of its sales price is its **contribution rate.** For instance, the contribution rate of the $100 product of this illustration is 30%, that is ($30 ÷ $100) × 100 = 30%.

The concept of contribution margin can be used in a formula to calculate a break-even point that is expressed in units of product. Similarly, the concept of contribution rate can be used in a formula to calculate a break-even point in dollars. These formulas are:

$$\text{Break-even point in units} = \frac{\text{Fixed costs}}{\text{Contribution margin per unit}}$$

$$\text{Break-even point in dollars} = \frac{\text{Fixed costs}}{\text{Contribution rate}}$$

Inserting Alpha Company's fixed costs and contribution rate in the second formula gives this result:

$$\text{Break-even point in dollars} = \frac{\$24{,}000}{30\%} = \frac{\$24{,}000}{.30} = \$80{,}000$$

Although the solution in this example comes out evenly, a contribution rate should be carried out several decimal places to avoid minor rounding errors when calculating the break-even point in dollars. In solving the exercises and problems at the end of this chapter, for example, you should carry the calculations of contribution rates to six decimal places unless the requirements state otherwise.

Calculated either way, Alpha Company's break-even point may be verified with an income statement, as in Illustration 24–5. This income statement shows that revenue from sales exactly equals sum of the fixed and variable costs at the break-even point.

## Break-Even Graph

Illustration 24–6 shows graphically the cost-volume-profit relationships for Alpha Company. This type of graphical presentation is called a **break-even graph** or **break-even chart.** Note that the horizontal axis on the graph shows units sold, and the vertical axis shows both dollars of sales and dollars of costs. Costs and revenues appear on the graph as straight lines. To prepare a break-even graph, you do the following:

**Illustration 24–6**
**Break-even chart**

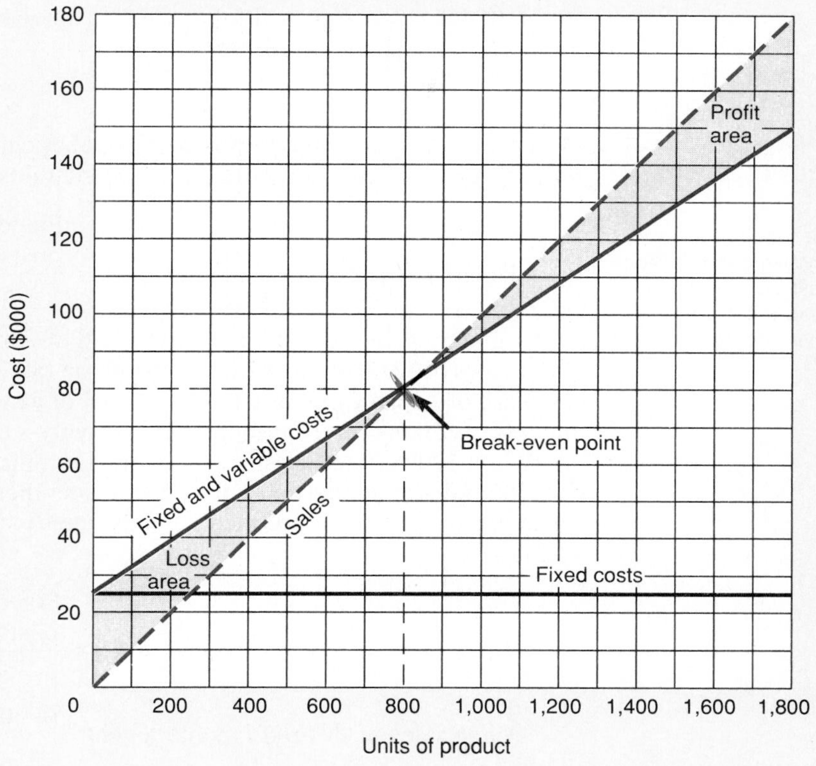


1. Mark a point on the vertical axis at a level that represents the amount of fixed costs. You may draw a horizontal line at this level to show on the graph that fixed costs remain unchanged regardless of sales volume. Illustration 24–6 shows this line. However, the fixed costs line is not essential to the analysis, and you may complete the break-even chart without showing the fixed costs line.
2. Next, draw a line to represent total variable costs plus fixed costs. This line must intersect the vertical axis at the fixed costs level since at the zero sales level there are no variable costs. For any specific sales level shown on the graph, the line shows the sum of the fixed costs plus the variable costs for that level.
3. Next, draw a sales line from the point of zero units and zero dollars of sales to the point of maximum sales shown on the graph. In choosing the maximum number of units to be shown, a better graph results if the relevant range of operations appears in the middle of the graph.

In Illustration 24–6, observe that the variable costs plus fixed costs line intersects the sales line at 800 units of product. At this break-even point, the total sales revenue of $80,000 equals the sum of the fixed and variable costs.

In reading a break-even chart, the vertical distance between the sales line and the total costs line at any given sales level represents the profit or loss. At volume levels to the left of the break-even point, this vertical distance is the amount of the loss. And at volume levels to the right of the break-even point, it represents the amount of profit.

## Sales Required for a Desired Net Income

Describe some extensions that may be added to the basic cost-volume-profit analysis of a business's break-even point.
(L. O. 5)

A slight extension of the break-even concept can be used to determine the sales level necessary to produce a desired net income. The formula is:

$$\text{Dollar sales at desired income level} = \frac{\text{Fixed costs} + \text{Net income} + \text{Income taxes}}{\text{Contribution rate}}$$

To illustrate the formula's use, recall that Alpha Company has monthly fixed costs of $24,000 and a 30% contribution rate. Now assume that the management of Alpha Company has set a goal of generating a monthly after-tax income of $20,000. Furthermore, the company's tax rate is such that in order to have a $20,000 net income, the company must earn a pre-tax income of $28,500 and pay income taxes of $8,500. Under these assumptions, $175,000 of sales are necessary to produce a $20,000 net income. This is calculated as follows:

$$\text{Dollar sales at desired income level} = \frac{\text{Fixed costs} + \text{Net income} + \text{Income taxes}}{\text{Contribution rate}}$$

$$\text{Dollar sales at desired income level} = \frac{\$24,000 + \$20,000 + \$8,500}{30\%}$$

$$\text{Dollar sales at desired income level} = \frac{\$52,500}{30\%} = \$175,000$$

In the above calculations, the contribution rate was used as the divisor, and the resulting answer was in dollars of sales. However, the contribution margin can also be used as the divisor, in which case the resulting answer is in units of products as shown below:

$$\text{Unit sales at desired income level} = \frac{\text{Fixed costs} + \text{Net income} + \text{Income taxes}}{\text{Contribution margin}}$$

$$\text{Unit sales at desired income level} = \frac{\$24,000 + \$20,000 + \$8,500}{\$30} = 1,750$$

## Margin of Safety

When the sales volume of a company exceeds its break-even point, the difference between the actual sales and sales at its break-even point is known as its **margin of safety.** The margin of safety is the amount sales may decrease before the company will incur a loss. It may be expressed in units of product, in dollars, or as a percentage of sales. For example, if current sales are $100,000 and the break-even point is $80,000, the margin of safety is $20,000, or 20% of sales, calculated as follows:

$$\frac{\text{Sales} - \text{Break-even sales}}{\text{Sales}} = \text{Margin of safety}$$

or

$$\frac{\$100{,}000 - \$80{,}000}{\$100{,}000} \times 100 = 20\% \text{ margin of safety}$$

## Income from a Given Sales Level

Cost-volume-profit analysis can be used to answer a variety of questions. For example, what income will result from a given sales level? To understand the analysis used in answering this question, recall the factors that enter into the calculation of income. When expressed in equation form, they are:

$$\text{Sales} - (\text{Fixed costs} + \text{Variable costs}) = \text{Income}$$

or

$$\text{Income} = \text{Sales} - (\text{Fixed costs} + \text{Variable costs})$$

This equation may be used to calculate the income that will result at a given sales level. For example, assume the management of Alpha Company wants to know what income will result if the monthly sales level is increased to $200,000. That would require sales of 2,000 units at $100 per unit. To determine the answer, recall that the variable costs per unit are $70, which is 70% or 0.7 of the product's selling price. Therefore, variable costs for 2,000 units of product are 0.7 of the selling price of these units, or $(.7 \times \$200{,}000) = \$140{,}000$. Alpha Company's fixed costs are $24,000 per month. Substituting these facts in the equation, the income is calculated as follows:

$$\text{Income} = \$200{,}000 - [\$24{,}000 + (.7 \times \$200{,}000)]$$

$$\text{Income} = \$200{,}000 - \$164{,}000$$

$$\text{Income} = \$36{,}000$$

The $36,000 is "before-tax" income. As a result, if Alpha Company wants to learn its after-tax income from the sale of 2,000 units of its product, it will have to apply the appropriate tax rates to the $36,000.

## Other Questions

In planning future business operations, managers often consider a variety of different ways that business operations might be changed. Many of these possible changes are likely to affect the costs and revenues of the business. Cost-volume-profit analysis is a useful method managers use to evaluate the likely effects of changing business operations. For example, managers may want to know what would happen to the company's break-even point if it reduced the selling price of its product in order to increase sales. Or, managers might want to know what would happen if they installed a new machine that would increase fixed costs but which would also reduce variable costs. Whenever managers can estimate the impact of a change on fixed costs, variable costs, and revenues, cost-volume-profit analysis can be used to predict the profit that will result from an expected sales volume.

At first glance, such changes may seem to violate the basic assumptions on which cost-volume-profit analysis is based. But this is not true. A constant selling price, truly variable costs, and truly fixed costs are assumed to hold for any analysis involving the assumed price and costs. However, when changes in price and costs are considered, the new price and new costs are assumed to remain constant for the analyses involving that price and those costs. The fact that such changes can be considered is why cost-volume-profit analysis is helpful for planning purposes.

To illustrate the effect of changes, assume that Alpha Company is considering the purchase of a new machine that will increase the fixed costs of producing and selling its product from \$24,000 to \$30,000 per month. However, the machine will reduce the variable costs from \$70 per unit of product to \$60. The selling price of the product will remain unchanged at \$100, and management wants to know what the break-even point will be if the machine is purchased. An examination of the costs shows that the purchase will not only increase the company's fixed costs but will also change the contribution margin and contribution rate of the company's product. The new contribution margin will be \$40, that is, (\$100 − \$60) = \$40, and the new contribution rate will be 40%, that is, \$40 ÷ \$100 = .4, or 40%. Therefore, if the machine is purchased, the company's new break-even point will be:

$$\text{Break-even point in dollars} = \frac{\$30{,}000}{.4} = \$75{,}000$$

In addition to their use in determining Alpha Company's break-even point, the new fixed costs and the new contribution rate may be used to determine the sales level needed to earn a desired net income. They may also be used to determine the expected income at a given sales level, or to answer other questions management may raise before purchasing the new machine.

## Multiproduct Break-Even Point

Calculate a composite sales unit for a multiproduct company and a break-even point for such a company. (L. O. 6)

The break-even point for a company that sells a number of products can be determined by using a composite unit made up of units of each of the company's products in their expected **sales mix**. Then, the composite unit is treated in all analyses as though it were a single product. To illustrate the use of a composite unit, assume that Beta Company sells three products, A, B, and C, and management wants to calculate the company's break-even point. Unit selling prices for the three products are Product A, \$5; Product B, \$8; and Product C, \$4. The sales mix or ratio in which the products are expected to be sold is 4:2:1, and the company's fixed costs are \$48,000 per month. Under these assumptions a composite unit selling price for the three products is calculated as follows:

| | |
|---|---|
| 4 units of Product A @ \$5 per unit = | \$20 |
| 2 units of Product B @ \$8 per unit = | 16 |
| 1 unit of Product C @ \$4 per unit = | 4 |
| Selling price of a composite unit . . | \$40 |

## AS A MATTER OF ETHICS

A small management group in a major corporation is discussing a proposal they are about to submit to the division manager for approval. If approved, several million dollars will be committed to new equipment and to new employees who will work for this group. The critical factor in the decision is the range of possible profits that will result from different sales volume projections. The data under consideration are the likely sales figures and operating costs of the project.

The sales figures are subjective because the proposed product has not been produced before. One team member suggests that they might as well pick some numbers that will produce a profit because any estimate is "as good as any other."

The cost predictions are based on experience with another manufacturing system that was quite similar to the proposed process. As a result, the management team has assumed that the fixed and variable costs of the proposed project would occur in the same relationship as they did in the comparable manufacturing system. The fixed and variable cost components for the proposal are being estimated from a scatter diagram of 20 months' production by the comparable manufacturing system. However, the results are not as supportive of an investment in the project as the group thinks may be necessary to get the proposal approved.

At this point, a team member asks whether some of the less favorable data points might be dropped from the analysis to see if the cost picture could be improved. He argues that the innovative nature of this venture makes one cost estimate "as good as any other." The accountant member of the team has been asked to produce a cost-volume-profit analysis that will reflect the proposed modifications but wonders whether it is the right thing to do.

Also, if the variable costs of selling the three products are Product A, \$3.25; Product B, \$4.50; and Product C, \$2, the variable costs of a composite unit of the products are:

| | |
|---|---|
| 4 units of Product A @ \$3.25 per unit = | \$13 |
| 2 units of Product B @ \$4.50 per unit = | 9 |
| 1 unit of Product C @ \$2.00 per unit = | 2 |
| Variable costs of a composite unit . . . | \$24 |

After the variable costs and selling price of a composite unit of the company's products are calculated, you can determine the contribution margin for a composite unit by subtracting the variable costs of a composite unit from the selling price of such a unit, as follows:

\$40 − \$24 = \$16 contribution margin per composite unit

The \$16 contribution margin may then be used to determine the company's break-even point in composite units. The break-even point is:

$$\text{Break-even point in composite units} = \frac{\text{Fixed costs}}{\text{Composite contribution margin per unit}}$$

$$\text{Break-even point in composite units} = \frac{\$48{,}000}{\$16}$$

$$\text{Break-even point} = 3{,}000 \text{ composite units}$$

Illustration 24–7

**BETA COMPANY**
**Income Statement at the Break-Even Point**

| | | | |
|---|---|---|---|
| Sales: | | | |
| Product A (12,000 units @ $5) . . . . | | | $ 60,000 |
| Product B (6,000 units @ $8) . . . . . . | | | 48,000 |
| Product C (3,000 units @ $4) . . . . . . | | | 12,000 |
| Total revenues . . . . . . . . . . . . . . | | | $120,000 |
| Costs: | | | |
| Fixed costs . . . . . . . . . . . . . . . . | | $48,000 | |
| Variable costs: | | | |
| Product A (12,000 units @ $3.25) . . | $39,000 | | |
| Product B (6,000 units @ $4.50) . . . | 27,000 | | |
| Product C (3,000 units @ $2.00) . . . | 6,000 | | |
| Total variable costs . . . . . . . . . . | | 72,000 | |
| Total costs . . . . . . . . . . . . . . . . | | | 120,000 |
| Net income . . . . . . . . . . . . . . . . . . | | | –0– |

The company breaks even when it sells 3,000 composite units of its products. However, to determine the number of units of each product it must sell to break even, the number of units of each product in the composite unit must be multiplied by the number of composite units needed to break even, as follows:

Product A: 4 × 3,000 = 12,000 units
Product B: 2 × 3,000 = 6,000 units
Product C: 1 × 3,000 = 3,000 units

These computations can be verified by preparing an income statement showing the company's revenues and costs at the break-even point. Illustration 24–7 shows such a statement.

A composite unit made up of units of each of a company's products in their expected sales mix may be used in answering a variety of cost-volume-profit questions. All such analyses are based on the assumption that the product mix remains constant at all sales levels, just as the other factors entering into an analysis are assumed to be constant. Nevertheless, this does not prevent changes in the assumed sales mix in order to predict what would happen if the mix were changed. However, if problems involve changes in the sales mix, you must recompute the composite unit selling price and composite unit variable costs for each change in the mix.

## Evaluating the Results of Cost-Volume-Profit Analyses

Cost-volume-profit analyses are useful whenever management wants to predict what will happen when changes are made in selling prices, product mix, and the various cost factors. However, in evaluating the results of such analyses, you should keep several points in mind. First, the analyses are used to predict future results. Therefore, the data used in the formulas and on the graphs are assumed or forecasted data, and the results of the analyses are no more reliable than the data used. Second, cost-volume-profit analyses as presented here are based on the assumptions that in any one analysis selling price will remain constant, fixed costs are truly fixed, and variable costs are truly variable. These assumptions do not always reflect reality. Therefore, at best the answers obtained through cost-volume-profit analyses are approximations. If you keep these assumptions in mind, cost-volume-profit analysis is a useful tool in making business decisions.

The cost-volume-profit analyses presented in this chapter are based on the assumption that revenues and costs may be expressed as straight lines. But as we have recognized, this assumption does not always hold. Therefore, it should be noted that cost-volume-profit analyses based on curvilinear relationships are also possible. However, the use of curvilinear relationships requires more sophisticated mathematics which are considered in more advanced courses.

## Summary of the Chapter in Terms of Learning Objectives

**1.** The behavior of a cost refers to how the amount of the cost changes in relation to production and sales volume changes. Total fixed costs remain unchanged while total variable costs change in proportion to volume changes. Stair-step costs remain constant over a short range of volume, then increase by a lump-sum, then remain constant over another volume range, and so on. Semivariable costs change in a curvilinear relation to volume changes, and mixed costs include fixed and variable components.

**2.** Conventional cost-volume-profit analysis is based on the assumptions that selling price remains constant and that costs classified as variable and costs classified as fixed actually behave in manners that are consistent with their classifications. These assumptions are not likely to hold at volume levels beyond the normal operating range of the business (the relevant range of operations). To the extent the assumptions are not valid descriptions of total variable costs and total fixed costs, the results of a cost-volume-profit analysis may be misleading.

**3.** A scatter diagram is a graph that has volume marked on one axis and dollar amounts on the other and on which each point represents the cost and sales volume of a given period. Using a method of approximating the cost behavior such as the high-low method, visual approximation, or least-squares regression, an estimated line of cost behavior is drawn through the points.

**4.** The break-even point of a company is the sales volume at which total revenues equal the sum of variable costs plus fixed costs. To calculate a break-even point in terms of units, divide total fixed costs by the contribution margin per unit. To calculate a break-even point in terms of sales dollars, divide total fixed costs by the contribution rate.

**5.** Cost-volume-profit analysis can be used to predict what will happen when changes are made in sales volume, selling prices, variable costs, or fixed costs. As a result, it is a useful tool for evaluating alternative ways of doing business.

**6.** Cost-volume-profit analysis can be applied to a multiproduct company if you measure the sales volume of the company in terms of composite units of product. When this is done, the analysis is based on the additional assumption that the sales mix remains constant as total sales volume changes.

## Demonstration Problem

The Tutt Manufacturing Company produces and sells a single product on a simple production line. The fixed costs of operating the business have averaged about $140,000 per month, and the variable costs have been about $5 per unit. All of the manufactured product can be sold at about $8 per unit, and the fixed costs provide a production capacity of up to 100,000 units per month. Use this information to answer Requirements 1, 2, and 3. Requirements 4 and 5 are based on additional facts provided below.

*Required*

1. Use formulas to calculate the following:
   *a.* Contribution margin per unit.
   *b.* Break-even point in terms of the number of units produced and sold.
   *c.* Amount of profit at 30,000 units per month (ignore income taxes).
   *d.* Amount of profit at 85,000 units per month (ignore income taxes).
   *e.* Quantity of units to be produced and sold to have $48,000 of after-tax profits, assuming an income tax rate of 25%.
2. Draw a break-even graph for the company, showing units of output on the horizontal axis. Identify the break-even point and the amount of profit when the level of production is 75,000 units.
3. Use formulas to calculate the following:
   *a.* Contribution rate.
   *b.* Break-even point in terms of sales dollars.
   *c.* Amount of profit at $200,000 of sales per month (ignoring income taxes).
   *d.* Amount of profit at $600,000 of sales per month (ignoring income taxes).
   *e.* Dollars of sales needed to have $48,000 of after-tax profits, assuming an income tax rate of 25%.

Mr. Tom Tutt, the president, is considering a new plan for operating the production line and marketing the product. If implemented, the plan would produce several changes. The fixed costs of operating the line for a month would increase to $300,000. The variable costs of producing a unit of product would decrease to $3.15 per unit. All of the manufactured product could be sold for $7 per unit. The increased fixed costs would allow Tutt to produce up to 200,000 units per month.

4. Calculate the following:
   *a.* The change in the contribution margin per unit.
   *b.* The change in the break-even point in units.
   *c.* The change in the amount of profit at 30,000 units per month (ignoring income taxes).

   *d.* The change in the amount of profit at 85,000 units per month (ignoring income taxes).
   *e.* The change in the necessary quantity of units produced and sold to have $48,000 of after-tax profits, assuming an income tax rate of 25%.

5. Draw a break-even graph for the company under the proposed operating plan, showing units of output on the horizontal axis. Identify the break-even point and the amount of profit when the level of production is 150,000 units.

## Solution to Demonstration Problem

1.

*a.* Contribution margin per unit = Selling price per unit − Variable cost per unit = $8 − $5 = $3.

*b.* $\text{Break-even point in units} = \dfrac{\text{Fixed costs}}{\text{Contribution margin per unit}} = \dfrac{\$140{,}000}{\$3} = 46{,}667 \text{ units.}$

*c.* Profit at 30,000 unit sales = (Units × Contribution margin per unit) − Fixed costs
= (30,000 × $3) − $140,000 = $−50,000 (a loss).

*d.* Profit at 85,000 unit sales = (Units × Contribution margin per unit) − Fixed costs
= (85,000 × $3) − $140,000 = $115,000 profit.

*e.* Pre-tax profit = $48,000 ÷ 75% = $64,000.
Income taxes = $64,000 × 25% = $16,000.

$$\text{Units needed for \$48,000 profit} = \frac{\text{Fixed costs + Net income + Income taxes}}{\text{Contribution margin per unit}}$$

$$= \frac{\$140{,}000 + \$48{,}000 + \$16{,}000}{\$3} = 68{,}000 \text{ units.}$$

2. Break-even graph:

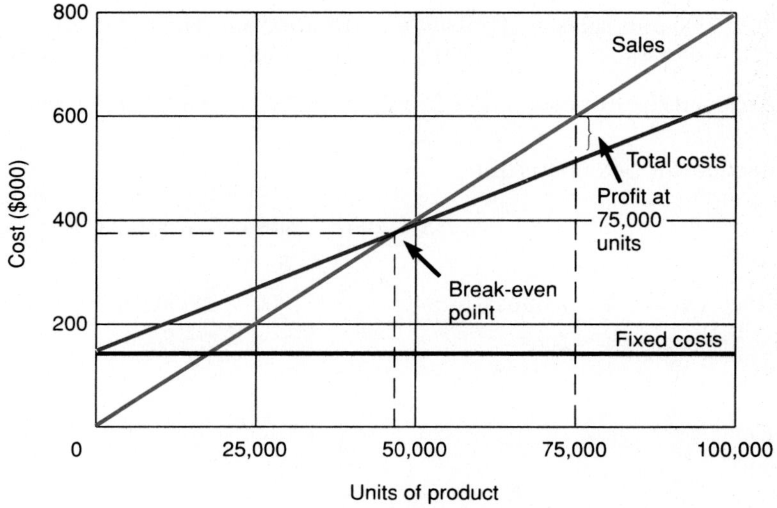

3.

*a.* Contribution rate $= \dfrac{\text{Contribution margin per unit}}{\text{Selling price per unit}} = \dfrac{\$3}{\$8} = .375$, or 37.5%.

*b.* Break-even point in dollars $= \dfrac{\text{Fixed costs}}{\text{Contribution rate}} = \dfrac{\$140{,}000}{37.5\%} = \$373{,}333$.

*c.* Profit at sales of \$200,000 = (Sales × Contribution rate) − Fixed costs
= (\$200,000 × 37.5%) − \$140,000 = \$−65,000 (a loss).

*d.* Profit at sales of \$600,000 = (Sales × Contribution rate) − Fixed costs
= (\$600,000 × 37.5%) − \$140,000 = \$85,000 profit.

*e.* Dollars of sales to have \$48,000 profits $= \dfrac{\text{Fixed costs + Net income + Income taxes}}{\text{Contribution rate}}$

$= \dfrac{\$140{,}000 + \$48{,}000 + \$16{,}000}{37.5\%} = \$544{,}000.$

4.

*a.* Contribution margin per unit = Selling price per unit − Variable cost per unit
= \$7.00 − \$3.15 = \$3.85.

Change caused by proposal = \$3.85 − \$3.00 = \$0.85 increase.

*b.* Break-even point in units $= \dfrac{\text{Fixed costs}}{\text{Contribution margin per unit}}$

$= \dfrac{\$300{,}000}{\$3.85} = 77{,}922$ units.

Change caused by proposal = 77,922 − 46,667 = 31,255 increase.

*c.* Profit at 30,000 unit sales = (Units × Contribution margin per unit) − Fixed costs
= (30,000 × \$3.85) − \$300,000 = \$−184,500 (a loss).

Change caused by proposal = \$(184,500) − \$(50,000) = \$−134,500 (increased loss).

*d.* Profit at 85,000 unit sales = (Units × Contribution margin per unit) − Fixed costs
= (85,000 × \$3.85) − \$300,000 = \$27,250 profit.

Change caused by proposal = \$27,250 − \$115,000 = \$−87,750 (decreased profit).

*e.* Units needed for \$48,000 profit $= \dfrac{\text{Fixed costs + Net income + Income taxes}}{\text{Contribution margin per unit}}$

$= \dfrac{\$300{,}000 + \$48{,}000 + \$16{,}000}{\$3.85} = 94{,}545$ units.

Change caused by proposal = 94,545 − 68,000 = 26,545 more units.

5. Break-even graph:

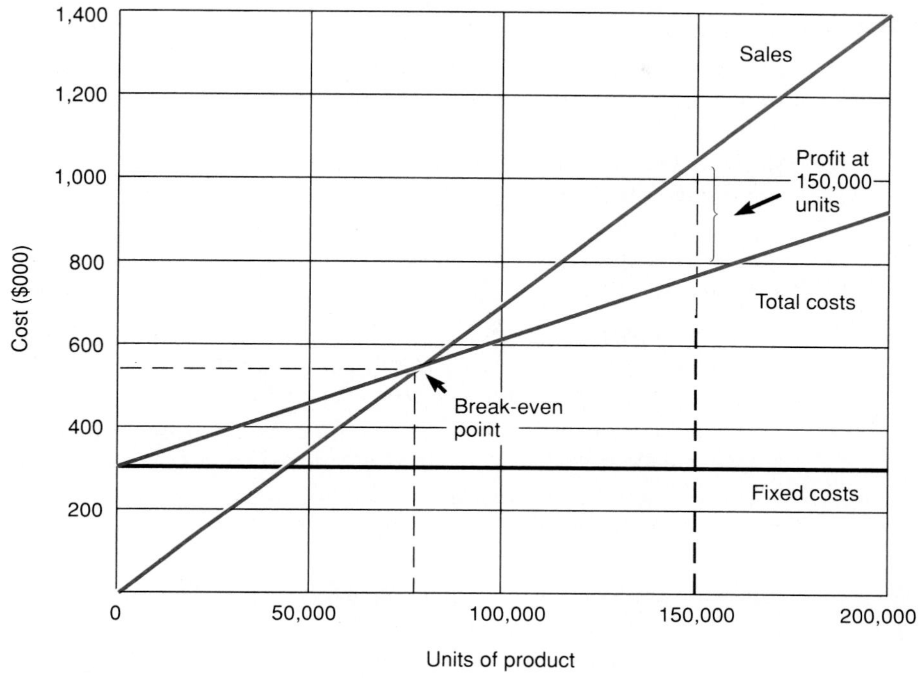

## Glossary

Define or explain the words and phrases listed in the chapter Glossary. (L. O. 7)

**Break-even analysis** a synonym for *cost-volume-profit analysis*. p. 1021

**Break-even chart** a synonym for *break-even graph*. pp. 1028–29

**Break-even graph** a graphical presentation of the revenues and total costs of a business that shows the sales volume at which the business neither earns a profit nor incurs a loss. pp. 1028–29

**Break-even point** the sales level at which a company neither earns a profit nor incurs a loss. p. 1027

**Contribution margin per unit** the dollar amount that the sale of one unit contributes toward the recovery of fixed costs and profits. p. 1027

**Contribution rate** the contribution margin per unit expressed as a percentage of sales price. p. 1028

**Cost-volume-profit analysis** a method of predicting the effects of changes in costs and sales level on the income of a business. p. 1021

**Estimated line of cost behavior** a line on a scatter diagram that is intended to reflect the average relationship between costs and volume. p. 1026

**Fixed cost** a cost that remains unchanged in total amount from period to period even though production volume may vary over a wide range. p. 1021

**High-low method** a crude technique for deriving an estimated line of cost behavior that connects the highest and lowest costs shown on a scatter diagram with a straight line. p. 1026

**Least-squares regression** a sophisticated method of deriving an estimated line of cost behavior, the result of which is a line that best fits the actual cost and sales volume experience of a company. p. 1026

**Margin of safety** the amount by which a company's current sales exceed the sales necessary to break even. pp. 1030–31

**Mixed cost** a cost that can be separated into two components, one of which is fixed and one of which is variable. pp. 1023–24

**Relevant range of operations** the normal operating range of a business, which excludes extremely high and low levels of production that are not apt to be encountered. p. 1025

**Sales mix** the ratio in which a company's different products are sold. p. 1032

**Scatter diagram** a graph used to display the relationship between costs and volume in which the cost and volume for each period is shown as a point on the diagram. pp. 1025–26

**Semivariable cost** a cost that changes with production volume, not in the same proportion but in a curvilinear manner. p. 1023

**Stair-step cost** a cost that remains constant over a range of production, then increases by a lump sum if production is expanded beyond this range, then remains constant over another range of production, and so forth. p. 1022

**Step-variable cost** a synonym for *stair-step cost*. p. 1022

**Variable cost** a cost the total amount of which changes proportionately with changes in production volume. pp. 1021–22

## Objective Review

Answers to the following questions are listed in Appendix I at the end of the book. Be sure that you decide which is the one best answer to each question *before* you check the answers in the appendix.

1. Which of the following statements is true with regard to the behavior of a typical company's costs?
   *a.* The amount of a fixed cost per unit of product decreases as volume increases.
   *b.* The amount of variable cost per unit of product increases as volume increases.
   *c.* A semivariable cost includes both fixed and variable elements and should be divided into its separate components for correct classification.
   *d.* Total costs decrease at the rate of variable costs per unit as the volume of the company decreases.
   *e.* Both (*a*) and (*d*) are correct.
2. In conventional cost-volume-profit analysis:
   *a.* Costs are assumed to be either fixed or variable.
   *b.* The relationships of costs to volume can be expressed as straight lines.
   *c.* The selling price per unit is assumed to remain constant regardless of the production level.
   *d.* The basic assumptions of linear representations are intended to apply only over the relevant range of operations.
   *e.* All of the above.
3. In a scatter diagram of a company's past cost experience:
   *a.* Cost per unit usually is measured on the vertical axis with volume in dollars or units measured on the horizontal axis.
   *b.* Each point shows the total cost for a given period and the sales price per unit during that period.
   *c.* The high-low method results in an estimated line of cost behavior that is described as being a "best fit" of the cost and volume data on the graph.
   *d.* The estimated line of cost behavior is intended to represent the average relationship between costs and sales volume.
   *e.* The cost and volume of each period are entered as two points on the diagram.
4. Global Company sells a single product for $80 per unit and incurs $55 of variable costs per unit sold. If the fixed costs involved in selling the product are $17,475 per month:
   *a.* The contribution margin per unit is $55.
   *b.* The break-even point is 318 units.
   *c.* The break-even point in dollars is $55,920.
   *d.* The contribution rate is 69.4375%.
   *e.* The break-even point is 219 units.

5. Assume the following data:

| | |
|---|---|
| Units sold | 9,000 |
| Revenue | $270,000 |
| Fixed costs | 108,000 |
| Variable costs | 108,000 |

The margin of safety is:

*a.* $18 per unit.
*b.* 6,000 units.
*c.* $90,000.
*d.* 60%.
*e.* $54,000.

6. The sales mix of Bell Corporation's three products (P1, P2, and P3) is 2:1:4. Fixed costs total $160,000, and unit price and variable cost data are:

| | P1 | P2 | P3 |
|---|---|---|---|
| Unit sales price | $5 | $4 | $4 |
| Unit variable cost | 2 | 2 | 3 |

Bell Corporation's break-even point is:
*a.* $355,555.
*b.* $400,000.
*c.* $266,667.
*d.* $320,000.
*e.* $480,000.

## Questions for Class Discussion

1. Why is cost-volume-profit analysis used?
2. What is a fixed cost? Name two fixed costs.
3. When there are fixed costs in manufacturing a product and the number of units manufactured is increased, do fixed costs per unit increase or decrease? Why?
4. What is a variable cost? Name two variable costs.
5. If production and sales are increased from period 1 to period 2, what effect will the increase have upon variable costs per unit?
6. What is a semivariable cost?
7. Are step-variable costs and semivariable costs different?
8. How should a mixed cost be treated in a cost-volume-profit analysis?
9. The reliability of cost-volume-profit analysis rests upon several basic assumptions. What are they?
10. What two factors tend to make it useful to classify costs as either fixed or variable even though individual costs may not behave in a manner that is consistent with their classification?
11. Why is the relevant range concept of significance in cost-volume-profit analysis?

12. Does cost-volume-profit analysis provide definite answers to questions about the effect of cost changes on profits?
13. How are scatter diagrams used in the process of estimating the behavior of a company's costs?
14. What is the primary weakness of the high-low method of deriving an estimated line of cost behavior?
15. What is meant by a company's break-even point?
16. A company sells a product for $90 per unit. The variable costs of producing and selling the product are $54 per unit. What is the product's contribution margin per unit? What is its contribution rate?
17. If a straight line on a break-even graph intersects the vertical axis at the level of fixed costs and has a positive slope, rising with each additional unit of production by the amount of the variable costs per unit, what does the line represent?
18. If a fixed costs line is drawn on a break-even graph, why is the line drawn as a horizontal line?
19. Two similar companies each have sales of $100 and total costs of $80. A Company's total costs include $20 variable costs and $60 fixed costs. If B Company's total costs include $60 variable costs and $20 fixed costs, which company will profit most by an increase in sales?
20. What is a company's margin of safety?
21. What is meant by the sales mix of a company?
22. If a company produces and sells more than one product, the reliability of cost-volume-profit analysis depends on an additional assumption in regard to sales mix. What is that assumption?

## Exercises

**Exercise 24–1**
**Scatter diagram and cost behavior—six data points**
(L. O. 3)

The past experience of a company discloses the following information about a particular cost and sales volume:

| Period | Sales | Cost |
|---|---|---|
| 1 . . . . | $44,000 | $18,000 |
| 2 . . . . | 22,000 | 12,600 |
| 3 . . . . | 42,000 | 19,000 |
| 4 . . . . | 28,000 | 14,600 |
| 5 . . . . | 36,000 | 16,200 |
| 6 . . . . | 30,000 | 14,400 |

Prepare a scatter diagram of the cost and volume data, estimate the line of cost behavior, and decide whether the cost is a variable, fixed, or mixed cost.

**Exercise 24–2**
**Scatter diagram and cost behavior—six data points**
(L. O. 3)

Given the following information about a particular cost and sales volume, prepare a scatter diagram of the cost and volume data; draw a line that appears to reflect the typical cost behavior; and decide whether the cost is a variable, semivariable, stair-step, fixed, or mixed cost.

| Period | Sales | Cost |
|---|---|---|
| 1 . . . . | $15,000 | $12,300 |
| 2 . . . . | 45,000 | 30,600 |
| 3 . . . . | 29,700 | 23,700 |
| 4 . . . . | 22,800 | 14,100 |
| 5 . . . . | 39,300 | 29,700 |
| 6 . . . . | 31,500 | 23,400 |

**Exercise 24–3**
**Scatter diagram and cost behavior—12 data points**
(L. O. 3)

Given the following information about a particular cost and sales volume, prepare a scatter diagram of the cost and volume data; draw a line that appears to reflect the typical cost behavior; and decide whether the cost is a variable, semivariable, stair-step, fixed, or mixed cost.

| Period | Sales | Cost | Period | Sales | Cost |
|---|---|---|---|---|---|
| 1 . . . . | $22,500 | $31,200 | 7 . . . . | $49,500 | $34,500 |
| 2 . . . . | 88,500 | 64,500 | 8 . . . . | 67,500 | 43,800 |
| 3 . . . . | 52,800 | 32,400 | 9 . . . . | 31,200 | 31,200 |
| 4 . . . . | 79,800 | 59,100 | 10 . . . . | 76,200 | 46,500 |
| 5 . . . . | 37,500 | 29,400 | 11 . . . . | 59,100 | 36,600 |
| 6 . . . . | 63,900 | 38,700 | 12 . . . . | 83,100 | 55,800 |

**Exercise 24–4**
**Scatter diagram and cost behavior—15 data points**
(L. O. 3)

Given the following information about a particular cost and sales volume, prepare a scatter diagram of the cost and volume data; draw a line that appears to reflect the typical cost behavior; and decide whether the cost is a variable, semivariable, stair-step, fixed, or mixed cost.

| Period | Sales | Cost | Period | Sales | Cost |
|---|---|---|---|---|---|
| 1 . . . . | $23,400 | $17,700 | 9 . . . . | $82,800 | $57,300 |
| 2 . . . . | 42,600 | 14,100 | 10 . . . . | 73,200 | 54,600 |
| 3 . . . . | 89,400 | 59,400 | 11 . . . . | 34,800 | 12,900 |
| 4 . . . . | 69,300 | 58,200 | 12 . . . . | 60,300 | 38,700 |
| 5 . . . . | 54,900 | 37,200 | 13 . . . . | 50,400 | 35,400 |
| 6 . . . . | 63,900 | 35,100 | 14 . . . . | 45,600 | 37,500 |
| 7 . . . . | 29,100 | 14,700 | 15 . . . . | 79,800 | 54,600 |
| 8 . . . . | 38,400 | 15,600 | | | |

**Exercise 24–5**
**Calculating contribution margin and rate**
(L. O. 4)

Laflor Corporation manufactures a single product that it sells for $53 per unit. The variable costs of manufacturing the product are $41 per unit, and the annual fixed costs incurred in manufacturing it are $59,580. Calculate the company's (*a*) contribution margin, (*b*) contribution rate, (*c*) break-even point for the product in units, and (*d*) break-even point in dollars of sales. The calculation of contribution rate should be carried to six decimal places.

**Exercise 24–6**
**Calculating additional sales necessary to break even**
(L. O. 5)

Prepare an income statement for Laflor Corporation's operations (Exercise 24–5) showing sales, fixed costs, and variable costs at the break-even point. Also, if Laflor Corporation's fixed costs increased by $4,740, calculate the sales (in dollars) that would be necessary to break even.

**Exercise 24–7**
**Calculating sales required to obtain desired income**
(L. O. 5)

Assume that Laflor Corporation of Exercise 24–5 wants to earn an $18,000 annual after-tax income from the sale of its product, and that it must pay 40% of its income in state and federal income taxes. Calculate (*a*) the number of units of its product it must sell to earn an $18,000 after-tax income from the sale of the product and (*b*) the number of dollars of sales that are needed to earn an $18,000 after-tax income.

**Exercise 24–8**
**Estimating the income result from increased volume**
(L. O. 5)

The sales manager of Laflor Corporation (Exercise 24–5) thinks that within two years the annual sales of the company's product will reach 9,600 units while the price per unit will go up to $60. Variable costs are expected to increase only $5 per unit, fixed costs are not expected to change, and the expected income tax rate is 40%. Calculate the company's (*a*) before-tax income from the sale of these units and (*b*) calculate its after-tax income from the sale of the units.

**Exercise 24–9**
**Calculating total variable and fixed costs**
(L. O. 5)

Axel Company sold 14,000 units of its product, producing $504,000 in sales. The before-tax income of the company was $67,500, and the contribution margin per unit was $7.50. Calculate (*a*) the total variable costs and (*b*) the total fixed costs of the company.

**Exercise 24–10**
**Calculating unit and dollar sales using contribution margin**
(L. O. 5)

In selling its product last period, Pasel Company incurred $195,000 of variable costs and $67,500 of fixed costs and earned a before-tax income of $30,000. Assuming the contribution margin per unit was $30, calculate (*a*) the number of units sold and (*b*) total dollar sales.

**Exercise 24–11**
**Calculating sales and variable costs using contribution rate**
(L. O. 5)

In selling its product last period, Jung Company incurred fixed costs of $72,000 and earned a before-tax income of $33,000. Assuming the company's contribution rate was 40%, calculate (*a*) total dollar sales and (*b*) total variable costs.

**Exercise 24–12**
**Composite unit analysis**
(L. O. 6)

Devito Company markets Products 1 and 2 which it sells in the ratio of three units of Product 1 at $15 per unit to four units of Product 2 at $60 per unit. The variable costs of marketing Product 1 are $9 per unit, and the variable costs for Product 2 are $39 per unit. The annual fixed costs for marketing both products are $249,900. Calculate (*a*) the selling price of a composite unit of these products, (*b*) the variable costs per composite unit, (*c*) the break-even point in composite units, and (*d*) the number of units of each product that will be sold at the break-even point.

## Problems

**Problem 24–1**
**Scatter diagram with estimated line of cost behavior**
(L. O. 3)

Jensen Company has collected the following monthly total cost and sales volume data related to its recent operations:

| Period | Costs | Sales |
|---|---|---|
| 1 . . . . | $127,500 | $168,000 |
| 2 . . . . | 135,000 | 180,000 |
| 3 . . . . | 75,000 | 60,000 |
| 4 . . . . | 108,000 | 168,000 |
| 5 . . . . | 112,500 | 108,000 |
| 6 . . . . | 127,500 | 180,000 |
| 7 . . . . | 82,500 | 96,000 |
| 8 . . . . | 120,000 | 144,000 |
| 9 . . . . | 105,000 | 132,000 |
| 10 . . . . | 112,500 | 120,000 |
| 11 . . . . | 90,000 | 72,000 |
| 12 . . . . | 127,500 | 204,000 |

*Required*

1. Design a diagram with sales volume marked off in $24,000 intervals on the horizontal axis and cost marked off in $15,000 intervals on the vertical axis. Record the cost and sales data of Jensen Company as a scatter of points on the diagram.
2. Based on your visual inspection of the scatter diagram, draw an estimated line of cost behavior that appears to show the average relationship between cost and sales.
3. Based on the estimated line of cost behavior, estimate the amount of Jensen Company's fixed costs.
4. Use the estimated line of cost behavior to approximate cost when sales volume is $48,000 and when sales volume is $192,000. Calculate an estimate of variable cost per sales dollar.

**Problem 24–2**
**Preparing and using a break-even graph**
(L. O. 4)

Sanders Company manufactures a number of products, one of which, Product Q, is produced and sold quite independently from the others and sells for $720 per unit. The fixed costs of manufacturing and selling Product Q are $126,000, and the variable costs are $495 per unit. In your answers to the following requirements, carry the calculation of contribution rate to four decimal places.

*Required*

1. Calculate the company's break-even point in the sale of Product Q (*a*) in units and (*b*) in dollars of sales.
2. Prepare a break-even graph for Product Q. Use 1,000 as the maximum number of units on your graph and $750,000 as the maximum number of dollars.
3. Prepare an income statement showing sales, fixed costs, and variable costs for Product Q at the break-even point.
4. Determine the sales volume in dollars that the company must achieve to earn a $32,400 after-tax (40% rate) income from the sale of Product Q.
5. Determine the after-tax income the company will earn from a $612,000 sales level for Product Q.

**Problem 24–3**
**Break-even graph and income statements to confirm projections**
(L. O. 4, 5)

Niagra Company sells one product. Last year the company sold 9,000 units and incurred an $11,000 loss, as shown in the following income statement:

**NIAGRA COMPANY**
**Last Year's Income Statement**

| | | |
|---|---|---|
| Sales . . . . . . . | | $225,000 |
| Costs: | | |
| Fixed . . . . . | $ 56,000 | |
| Variable . . . . | 180,000 | 236,000 |
| Net loss . . . . . | | $ (11,000) |

The production manager has pointed out that variable costs can be reduced 25% by installing a machine that performs operations presently done by hand. However, the new machine will increase fixed costs by $20,000 annually.

*Required*

1. Calculate last year's dollar break-even point.
2. Calculate the dollar break-even point under the assumption the new machine is installed.
3. Prepare a break-even chart under the assumption the new machine is installed. Use 12,000 as the maximum number of units on your chart.
4. Prepare an income statement showing expected annual results with the new machine installed. Assume no change in the selling price, no change in the number of units sold, and a 30% income tax rate.
5. Calculate the sales level required to earn a $70,000 per year after-tax income with the new machine installed and no change in the selling price. Prepare an income statement showing the results at this sales level.

**Problem 24–4**
**Analyzing the effects of price and volume changes on profits**
(L. O. 5)

Last year Goodman Company earned an unsatisfactory 4.9% after-tax return on sales from the sale of 55,000 packages of its product called Phaser II. The company buys Phaser II in bulk and packages it for resale, at a price of $5 each. Following are last year's costs for the product:

| | |
|---|---|
| Cost of bulk Phaser II (sufficient for 55,000 packages) . . . | $137,500 |
| Packaging materials and other variable packaging costs . . | 27,500 |
| Fixed costs . . . . . . . . . . . . . . . . . . . . . . | 87,500 |
| Income tax rate . . . . . . . . . . . . . . . . . . . . | 40% |

It has been suggested that if the selling price of the product is reduced 10% and a change is made in its packaging, the number of units sold can be increased by 50%. The packaging change will increase packaging costs 30% per unit, but the 50% increase in sales volume will allow the company to take advantage of a quantity discount of 9% on the product's bulk purchase price. The packaging and volume changes will not affect fixed costs.

*Required*

1. Calculate the dollar break-even points for Phaser II at (*a*) the $5 per unit sales price and (*b*) at $4.50 per unit assuming the packaging change is implemented.
2. Prepare a break-even chart for the sale of the product at each price. Use 100,000 units as the upper limit of your charts.

3. Prepare a condensed comparative income statement showing the anticipated results of selling the product at $5 per unit and the estimated results of selling it at $4.50 per unit.

**Problem 24–5**
**Break-even analysis comparing different cost structures**
(L. O. 5)

Brownfield Company sells two products, X and Y, which are produced and sold independently. Last year, the company sold 7,500 units of each of these products, earning $225,000 from the sale of each, as the following condensed income statement shows:

| | Product X | Product Y |
|---|---|---|
| Sales | $1,800,000 | $1,800,000 |
| Costs: | | |
| Fixed costs | $ 300,000 | $1,125,000 |
| Variable costs | 1,125,000 | 300,000 |
| Total costs | $1,425,000 | $1,425,000 |
| Income before taxes | $ 375,000 | $ 375,000 |
| Income taxes (40% rate) | 150,000 | 150,000 |
| Net income | $ 225,000 | $ 225,000 |

*Required*

1. Calculate the break-even point for each product in units.
2. Prepare a break-even graph for each product. Use 10,000 as the maximum number of units on each graph.
3. Prepare a condensed income statement showing in separate columns the net income the company will earn from the sale of each product under the assumption that without a change in selling prices, the number of units of each product sold declines to 5,625 units.
4. Prepare a second condensed income statement showing in separate columns the net income the company will earn if the number of units of each product increases 20% to 9,000 units.

**Problem 24–6**
**Break-even analysis with composite units**
(L. O. 6)

Milano Company manufactures and sells three products, A, B, and C. Product A sells for $63 per unit, Product B sells for $42 per unit, and Product C sells for $18 per unit. Their sales mix is in the ratio of 2:3:6, and the variable costs of manufacturing and selling the products have been: Product A, $36; Product B, $27; and Product C, $12. The fixed costs of manufacturing the three products are $324,000. A special material labeled XA2 has been used in manufacturing both Products A and B; however, a new material called XR4 has just become available, and if it is substituted for material XA2, it will reduce the variable cost of manufacturing Product A by $5.25 and Product B by $1.50. However, fixed costs will go up to $354,000 because of special equipment needed to process material XR4.

*Required*

1. Determine the company's break-even point in dollars and the number of units of each product sold at the break-even point under the assumption that material XA2 is used in manufacturing Products A and B. Show all pertinent calculations.

2. Determine the company's break-even point in dollars and the number of units of each product sold at the break-even point under the assumption that the new material XR4 is used in manufacturing Products A and B. Show all pertinent calculations.

## Alternate Problems

**Problem 24–1A**
**Preparing and using scatter diagram and estimated line of cost behavior**
(L. O. 3)

Legendary Company has collected the following monthly total cost and sales volume data related to its recent operations:

| Period | Costs | Sales |
|---|---|---|
| 1 . . . . | $117,000 | $201,000 |
| 2 . . . . | 81,000 | 72,000 |
| 3 . . . . | 138,000 | 216,000 |
| 4 . . . . | 114,000 | 156,000 |
| 5 . . . . | 138,000 | 243,000 |
| 6 . . . . | 90,000 | 114,000 |
| 7 . . . . | 123,000 | 144,000 |
| 8 . . . . | 123,000 | 129,000 |
| 9 . . . . | 138,000 | 201,000 |
| 10 . . . . | 132,000 | 171,000 |
| 11 . . . . | 99,000 | 84,000 |
| 12 . . . . | 147,000 | 216,000 |

*Required*

1. Design a diagram with sales volume marked off in $24,000 intervals on the horizontal axis and cost marked off in $15,000 intervals on the vertical axis. Record the cost and sales data of Legendary Company as a scatter of points on the diagram.
2. Based on your visual inspection of the scatter diagram, draw an estimated line of cost behavior that appears to show the average relationship between cost and sales.
3. Based on the estimated line of cost behavior, estimate the amount of Legendary Company's fixed costs.
4. Use the estimated line of cost behavior to approximate cost when sales volume is $120,000 and when sales volume is $216,000. Calculate an estimate of variable cost per sales dollar.

**Problem 24–2A**
**Preparing and using a break-even graph**
(L. O. 4)

Among the products sold by The Danube Company is Product X, which is produced and sold independently from the other products of the company, and which sells for $750 per unit. The fixed costs of manufacturing and selling Product X are $78,000, and the variable costs are $360 per unit.

*Required*

1. Calculate the company's break-even point in the sale of Product X (*a*) in units and (*b*) in dollars of sales.
2. Prepare a break-even graph for Product X, using 400 as the maximum number of units on the graph.
3. Prepare an income statement showing sales, fixed costs, and variable costs for Product X at the break-even point.

4. Determine the sales volume in dollars required to achieve a $27,300 after-tax (30% rate) income from the sale of Product X.
5. Determine the after-tax income the company will earn from a $259,500 sales level for Product X.

**Problem 24–3A**
**Break-even graph and income statements to confirm projections**
(L. O. 4, 5)

Brazos Company lost $3,000 last year in selling 1,800 units of its product as the following income statement shows:

**BRAZOS COMPANY**
**Income Statement for Last Year**

| | | |
|---|---|---|
| Sales . . . . . . . | | $180,000 |
| Costs: | | |
| Fixed . . . . . | $ 48,000 | |
| Variable . . . . | 135,000 | 183,000 |
| Net loss . . . . . | | $ (3,000) |

The company management is convinced that if a new machine is installed, enough piece-rate labor and spoiled materials can be saved to reduce variable costs by 20%. However, the new machine will increase fixed costs by $8,800 annually.

*Required*

1. Calculate last year's dollar break-even point.
2. Calculate the dollar break-even point assuming the new machine is installed.
3. Prepare a break-even chart under the assumption the new machine is installed. Use 3,000 as the maximum number of units on your chart.
4. Prepare an income statement showing expected annual results with the new machine installed, no change in the product's price, and sales at last year's level. Assume a 30% income tax rate.
5. Calculate the sales level required to earn a $14,000 per year after-tax income with the new machine installed and no change in the product's selling price. Prepare an income statement showing the results at this sales level.

**Problem 24–4A**
**Analyzing the effects of price and volume changes on profits**
(L. O. 5)

Last year Monaco Company sold 17,500 units of its product at $10 per unit. To manufacture and sell the product required $42,500 of fixed manufacturing costs and $17,500 of fixed selling and administrative expenses. Last year's variable costs and expenses per unit were:

| | |
|---|---|
| Material . . . . . . . . . . . . . . . . . . . . . . | $3.00 |
| Direct labor (paid on a piece-rate basis) . . . . . | 2.50 |
| Variable manufacturing overhead costs . . . . | 0.275 |
| Variable selling and administrative expenses . . | 0.225 |

A new material has just come on the market that is cheaper than the old material and also easier to work with. When the new material is substituted for the material presently being used, material costs will be decreased by 40%

($1.20) and direct labor costs will be decreased by 32% ($0.80). The substitution will have no effect on the product's quality, but it will give the company a choice in pricing the product. (1) The company can maintain the present per unit price, sell the same number of units, and make a larger profit as a result of the substitution. Or (2) it can reduce the product's price $2 per unit to an amount equal to the material and labor savings and, because of the reduction, increase the number of units sold by 80%. If the latter choice is made, the fixed manufacturing overhead and fixed selling and administrative expenses will not change, and the remaining variable costs per unit will not change.

*Required*

1. Calculate the break-even point in dollars for each alternative.
2. Prepare a break-even chart for each. The company's production capacity is 40,000 units, and this should be used as the upper limit of your charts.
3. Prepare a comparative income statement showing sales, total fixed costs, and total variable costs and expenses, operating income, income taxes (40% rate), and net income for each alternative.

**Problem 24–5A**
**Break-even analysis comparing different cost structures**
(L. O. 5)

Craftless Company has two essentially unrelated divisions, each of which produces a single product. The two products, L and M, are produced and sold independently. Coincidentally, each product sold last year at a price of $300 and 6,250 units of each product were sold.

Last year's income statements for the two products are as follows:

| | Product L | Product M |
|---|---|---|
| Sales | $1,875,000 | $1,875,000 |
| Costs: | | |
| Fixed costs | $1,000,000 | $ 375,000 |
| Variable costs | 375,000 | 1,000,000 |
| Total costs | $1,375,000 | $1,375,000 |
| Income before taxes | $ 500,000 | $ 500,000 |
| Income taxes (40% rate) | 200,000 | 200,000 |
| Net income | $ 300,000 | $ 300,000 |

*Required*

1. Calculate the break-even point for each product in units.
2. Prepare a break-even graph for each product. Use 10,000 as the maximum number of units on each graph.
3. Prepare a condensed income statement showing in separate columns the net income the company will earn from the sale of each product under the assumption that without a change in selling prices, the number of units of each product sold declines to 4,167 units.
4. Prepare a second condensed income statement showing in separate columns the net income the company will earn if sales of each product increase to 8,000 units.

**Problem 24–6A**
**Break-even analysis with composite units**
(L. O. 6)

Hudgens Company manufactures and sells three products, H, I, and J, which sell for $225 per unit, $150 per unit, and $120 per unit, respectively. Their sales mix is in the ratio of 2:5:8, and the variable costs of manufacturing and selling the products have been: Product H, $120; Product I, $102; and Product J, $75. Fixed manufacturing, selling, and administrative costs amount to $793,800.

The management of Hudgens Company is considering the purchase of a new machine that will be used in the manufacture of Products I and J. If the machine is purchased, fixed manufacturing costs will increase by $81,000. However, variable costs of Product I will decrease by $18 per unit, and variable costs of Product J will decrease by $9 per unit.

*Required*

1. Determine the company's break-even point in dollars and the number of units of each product sold at the break-even point assuming the new machine is not purchased. Show all necessary calculations.
2. Determine the company's break-even point in dollars and the number of units of each product sold at the break-even point assuming that the new machine is purchased. Show all pertinent calculations.

## Provocative Problems

**Provocative Problem 24–1**
**Mortar Makers Corporation**
(L. O. 4, 5)

Mortar Makers Corporation produces a mortar mix called Magic Mud for use in various types of construction. The company's plant produced at near capacity last year with the results shown in the following condensed income statement:

| | |
|---|---|
| Sales (720,000 lbs.) | $720,000 |
| Cost of goods manufactured and sold (fixed, $120,000; variable, $288,000) | 408,000 |
| Gross profit | $312,000 |
| Selling and administrative expenses (fixed, $96,000; variable, $72,000) | 168,000 |
| Income before taxes | $144,000 |

Builder's Supplies Company has offered Mortar Makers a two-year contract whereby Builder's Supplies will buy 480,000 pounds of Magic Mud annually at $0.80 per pound for export sales. Delivery on the contract would require a plant addition that would double fixed manufacturing costs. The contract would not affect present selling and administrative expenses. Variable manufacturing costs per unit would be the same in the new plant as they have been in the old plant.

*Required*

Management is not certain it should enter into the contract and has asked for your opinion and for the following information:

1. An estimated income statement for the first year following the plant addition, assuming no change in domestic sales.
2. A comparison of break-even sales levels before the plant addition and after the contract with Builder's Supplies expires. Assume after-

contract sales and expense levels, other than fixed manufacturing costs, will be at the same levels as last year.

3. A statement showing net income after the contract expiration but at sales and expense levels of last year, other than fixed manufacturing costs.

**Provocative Problem 24–2**
**RetroRocket Corporation**
(L. O. 4, 5, 6)

RetroRocket Corporation manufactures and sells three products called Spaceman, Propel, and Rocket. Last year's sales mix for the three products was in the ratio of 5:1:4, with combined sales of all products totaling 9,000 units. Spaceman sells for $120 per unit and has a 20% contribution rate. Propel sells for $100 per unit and has a 30% contribution rate, and Rocket sells for $90 per unit and has a 40% contribution rate. The fixed costs of manufacturing and selling the products amount to $145,200. The company estimates that combined sales of the three products will continue to be 9,000 total units next year. However, the sales manager is of the opinion that if the company's advertising and sales efforts are slanted further towards Propel and Rocket during the coming year, with no increases in the amounts of money expended, the sales mix of the three products can be changed to the ratio of 2:3:5.

*Required*

Should the company change its sales mix through advertising and sales efforts? What effect will the change have on the combined contribution rate of the three products? What effect will it have on the company's break-even point? Back your answers with figures. Calculations of contribution rate should be carried to seven decimal places.

**Provocative Problem 24–3**
**Garden Master Company**
(L. O. 5)

Garden Master Company operated at near capacity during 1991, and a 25% annual increase in the demand for its product is expected in 1992. As a result, the company's management is trying to decide how to meet this demand. Two alternatives are being considered. The first calls for changes that will increase variable costs to 57.5% of the selling price of the company's product but will not change fixed costs. The second calls for a capital investment that will increase fixed costs 15% but will not affect variable costs.

Garden Master Company's income statement for 1991 provided the following summarized information:

| | | |
|---|---|---|
| Sales | | $960,000 |
| Costs: | | |
| Variable costs | $480,000 | |
| Fixed costs | 360,000 | 840,000 |
| Income before taxes | | $120,000 |

*Required*

Which alternative do you recommend? Back your recommendation with income statement information and any other data you consider relevant.

# 25 The Master Budget: A Formal Plan for the Business

The management functions of planning and control are perhaps equally important to the long-run success of a business. Nevertheless, most business failures appear to result from inadequate planning. Countless pitfalls can be avoided if management carefully anticipates the future conditions within which the business will operate and prepares a detailed plan of the activities the business should pursue. In this chapter, you will learn how to design and prepare a formal plan for the future activities of a business. If you ever go into business for yourself, your ability to put this chapter into practice could very well make the difference between success and failure.

**Learning Objectives**

*After studying Chapter 25, you should be able to:*

1. Explain the importance of budgeting and describe the benefits that result from budgeting.
2. Describe the content of a master budget and list the sequence of steps required to prepare a master budget.
3. Prepare each budget in a master budget and explain the importance of each budget to the overall budgeting process.
4. Integrate the individual budgets into planned financial statements.
5. Define or explain the words and phrases listed in the chapter Glossary.

## The Importance of Budgeting

Explain the importance of budgeting and describe the benefits that result from budgeting.
(L. O. 1)

If a business is to accomplish the variety of objectives expected of it, management must first carefully plan the activities the business should engage in during future weeks, months, and years. Then, as the activities take place, they must be monitored and controlled so that actual events conform as closely as possible to the plan.

The process of planning future business actions and expressing those plans in a formal manner is called **budgeting.** Correspondingly, a **budget** is a formal statement of future plans. Since the economic or financial aspects of the business are primary matters of consideration, budgets are usually expressed in monetary terms.

## Benefits from Budgeting

All business managements engage in planning; some planning is absolutely necessary if business activities are to continue. However, a typical characteristic of poor management is sloppy or incomplete planning. If management plans carefully and formalizes its plans completely enough, that is, if management engages in a thorough budgeting process, it may expect to obtain the following benefits.

### Budgeting Promotes Study, Research, and a Focus on the Future

When a business plans with sufficient care and detail to prepare a budget, the planning process usually involves thorough study and research. Not only should this result in the best conceivable plans but it should also instill in executives the habit of doing a reasonable amount of research and study before decisions are made. In short, budgeting tends to promote good decision-making processes. In addition, the items of interest to a budgetary investigation lie in the future. Thus, the attention of management is focused on future events and the associated opportunities available to the business. The pressures of daily operating problems naturally tend to take precedence over planning, thereby leaving the business without carefully thought-out objectives. Budgeting counteracts this tendency by formalizing the planning process; it makes planning an explicit responsibility of management.

### Budgeting Provides a Basis for Evaluating Performance

The control function of management requires that business operations be evaluated in light of some norms or objectives. On the basis of this evaluation, appropriate corrective actions can be implemented. In evaluating current operations, there are two alternative norms or objectives against which actual results can be compared: (1) past performance or (2) expected (budgeted) performance.

Although past performance is sometimes used as the basis of comparison, budgeted performance is potentially superior for determining whether actual results are acceptable or in need of corrective action. Past performance fails to take into account all of the environmental changes that may be affecting current activities. For example, in evaluating sales performance, past sales occurred under economic conditions that may have been dramatically different from those that apply to the current sales effort. Economywide fluctuations, competitive shifts within the industry, new product line developments, increased or decreased advertising commitments, and so forth, all tend to invalidate comparisons between past results and present performance.

On the other hand, budgeted (anticipated) performance levels are developed after a research and study process that attempts to take such environmental factors into account. Thus, budgeting provides the benefit of a superior basis for evaluating performance and a more effective control mechanism.

### Budgeting Is a Source of Motivation

Because budgets provide the standards against which actual performance is evaluated, the budget and the manner in which it is used can significantly affect the attitudes of those who are to be evaluated. If management is not careful, the budgeting process may have a negative impact on the attitudes of employees. Budgeted levels of performance must be realistic. Also, the personnel who will be evaluated in terms of a budget should be consulted and involved in preparing the budget. Finally, the subsequent evaluations of performance must not be given critically without offering the affected employees an opportunity to explain the reasons for performance failures. These three guidelines are important:

1. The employees that will be affected by a budget should be consulted when the budget is prepared.
2. The objectives reflected in a budget should be obtainable.
3. The subsequent evaluations of performance should be made fairly with opportunities provided to explain performance deficiencies.

If these guidelines are followed, budgeting can be a strongly positive, motivating force in the organization. Budgeted performance levels can provide goals that individuals will attempt to attain or even exceed as they fulfill their responsibilities to the organization.

### Budgeting Is a Means of Coordinating Business Activities

When a business is large enough to be organized into several departments, an important management task is to be sure that the activities of the various departments contribute to the overall goals of the business. This usually requires careful coordination of the various departments' activities. Budgeting provides this coordination.

When a budget plan is prepared, each department's objectives are determined in advance. In doing this, the objectives of each department can be established in a way that contributes most effectively to the overall objectives of the business. For example, the production department can be budgeted to produce approximately the number of units the selling department is expected to sell. Then, the purchasing department can be budgeted to buy raw materials on the basis of budgeted production; also, the hiring activities of the personnel department can be budgeted to take into account budgeted production levels. In this way, the budgeting process provides the means by which the activities of the various departments are coordinated to meet companywide goals.

## AS A MATTER OF ETHICS

In the course of his work in the budget office of a large public corporation, an accounting clerk discovers that the actual earnings for the current quarter are going to be far below what was budgeted and even announced in the press as the expected amount. In light of this information, the clerk calls his stockbroker and gives an order to sell "short" 1,000 shares of the corporation's stock. (Under this arrangement, the broker borrows shares from another customer who owns them, sells the borrowed shares in the market, and then later buys the same number of shares to go back into the customer's account. If the value of the shares declines, the short-seller makes a profit.)

At about the same time, one of the company's top officers decides to take a higher position with a competitor in the same industry but in a different part of the country. Before his departure is announced to the public, he sells all the shares of the company that were granted to him or bought by him as part of his compensation plan. He intends to use the proceeds to acquire a new house and to buy shares issued by his new employer. At the time he sells, he knows about the coming earnings shortfall. He also knows that his leaving will significantly hamper the company's ability to improve earnings, and that his arrival at the new company will greatly enhance its ability to capture market share.

Do either or both of these actions seem unethical?

### Budgeting Is a Means of Communicating Plans and Instructions

In a very small business, adequate communication of business plans might be accomplished by the manager's direct contact with the employees. Frequent conversations might serve as the means by which the manager's plans for business operations are communicated to the employees. However, oral conversations often leave ambiguities and potential confusion if not backed up by documents that clearly state the content of the plans. Further, businesses need not be very large before such conversations become inadequate. When a budget is prepared, the budget becomes a means of informing the organization of the broad plans for the business that have been approved by management. The budget also can communicate management's directive of specific actions to be taken by responsible employees during the budget period.

## The Budget Committee

The task of preparing a budget should not be made the responsibility of any one department; and the budget generally should not be handed down from above as the "final word." Rather, budget figures and budget estimates are often more useful if they are developed from "the bottom up." For example, the sales department should have a hand in preparing sales estimates. Similarly, the production department should have initial responsibility for preparing its own expense budget. Otherwise, production and salespeople may say the budget figures are meaningless because they were prepared by front office personnel who know little if anything of sales and production problems.

Although budgets usually should be developed from "the bottom up," the preparation of a budget needs central guidance. This is commonly supplied by a budget committee of department heads or other high-level executives who are responsible for seeing that budgeted amounts are realistic and coordinated. If a department submits budget figures that do not reflect proper performance, the figures should be returned to the department with the budget committee's comments. The originating department then either adjusts its proposals or explains why they should be accepted. Communication between the originating department and the budget committee should continue as necessary to ensure that both parties accept the budget as reasonable and attainable.

## The Budget Period

Budget periods normally coincide with accounting periods. This means that most companies prepare an annual budget. However, in addition to their annual budgets, many companies prepare long-range budgets that set forth major objectives for periods of 3 to 5 or 10 years in advance. These long-range budgets are particularly important in planning for major expenditures of capital to buy plant and equipment. Additionally, the financing of major capital projects, for example, by issuing bonds, by issuing stock, by retaining earnings, and so forth, can be anticipated and planned as part of preparing long-range budgets.

Long-range budgets of 2, 3, 5, and 10 years should reflect the planned accomplishment of long-range objectives. Within this context, the annual master budget for a business reflects the objectives that have been adopted for the next year. Also, the annual budget is commonly broken down into quarterly or monthly budgets. Short-term budgets of a quarter or a month are useful yardsticks that allow management to evaluate actual performance and take corrective actions promptly. After the quarterly or monthly results are known, the actual performance is compared to the budgeted amounts in a report similar to the one presented in Illustration 25–1.

Many businesses follow the practice of **continuous budgeting** and are said to prepare **rolling budgets.** As each monthly or quarterly budget period goes by, these firms revise their entire set of budgets, adding new monthly or quarterly sales, production, expense, equipment, and cash budgets to replace the ones that have elapsed. Thus, at any point in time, monthly or quarterly budgets are available for the next 12 months or 4 quarters.

## The Master Budget

Describe the content of a master budget and list the sequence of steps required to prepare a master budget.
(L. O. 2)

When the plan to be formalized is a comprehensive or overall plan for the business, the resulting budget is called a **master budget.** As an overall plan, the master budget should include specific plans for expected sales, the units of product to be produced, the materials or merchandise to be purchased, the expense payments to be made, the long-term assets to be purchased, and the amounts of cash to be borrowed or loans to be repaid. The planned activities of each subunit of the business should be separately organized and presented within the master budget.

In order to include definite plans for all of the above functions, a master budget consists of several sub-budgets. All of the sub-budgets articulate or join with each other to form the overall, coordinated plan for the business. As finally presented, the master budget typically includes sales, expense, production, equipment, and cash budgets. Also, the expected financial results of the planned activities may be expressed in terms of a planned income statement for the budget period and a planned balance sheet for the end of the budget period.

**Illustration 25–1**
**Comparing actual performance with budgeted performance**

CONSOLIDATED STORES, INC.
Income Statement with Variations from Budget
For Month Ended April 30, 1991

| | Actual | Budget | Variance |
|---|---|---|---|
| Sales | $63,500 | $60,000 | $+3,500 |
| Less: Sales returns and allowances | 1,800 | 1,700 | +100 |
| Sales discounts | 1,200 | 1,150 | +50 |
| Net sales | $60,500 | $57,150 | $+3,350 |
| Cost of goods sold: | | | |
| Merchandise inventory, April 1, 1991 | $42,000 | $44,000 | $−2,000 |
| Purchases, net | 39,100 | 38,000 | +1,100 |
| Freight-in | 1,250 | 1,200 | +50 |
| Goods available for sale | $82,350 | $83,200 | $ −850 |
| Merchandise inventory, April 30, 1991 | 41,000 | 44,100 | −3,100 |
| Cost of goods sold | $41,350 | $39,100 | $+2,250 |
| Gross profit | $19,150 | $18,050 | $+1,100 |
| Operating expenses: | | | |
| Selling expenses: | | | |
| Sales salaries | $ 6,250 | $ 6,000 | $ +250 |
| Advertising expense | 900 | 800 | +100 |
| Store supplies used | 550 | 500 | +50 |
| Depreciation of store equipment | 1,600 | 1,600 | |
| Total selling expenses | $ 9,300 | $ 8,900 | $ +400 |
| General and administrative expenses: | | | |
| Office salaries | $ 2,000 | $ 2,000 | |
| Office supplies used | 165 | 150 | $ +15 |
| Rent | 1,100 | 1,100 | |
| Expired insurance | 200 | 200 | |
| Depreciation of office equipment | 100 | 100 | |
| Total general and administrative expenses | $ 3,565 | $ 3,550 | $ +15 |
| Total operating expenses | $12,865 | $12,450 | $ +415 |
| Income from operations | $ 6,285 | $ 5,600 | $ +685 |

## Preparing the Master Budget

As indicated in the previous discussion, the master budget consists of a number of budgets that collectively express the planned activities of the business. The number and arrangement of the budgets included in the master budget depend on the size and complexity of the business. However, a master budget typically includes the following items:

1. Operating budgets.
   *a.* Sales budget.
   *b.* For merchandising companies: merchandise purchases budget.
   *c.* For manufacturing companies:
      (1) Production budget (stating the number of units to be produced).
      (2) Manufacturing budget (stating planned manufacturing costs).

   *d*. Selling expense budget.
   *e*. General and administrative expense budget.
2. Capital expenditures budget, which includes the budgeted expenditures for new plant and equipment.
3. Financial budgets.
   *a*. Budgeted statement of cash receipts and disbursements; called the cash budget.
   *b*. Budgeted income statement.
   *c*. Budgeted balance sheet.

In addition to these budgets, numerous supporting calculations or schedules may be required.

Some of the budgets listed above cannot be prepared until other budgets on the list are first completed. For example, the merchandise purchases budget cannot be prepared until the sales budget is available, since the number of units to be purchased depends on how many units are to be sold. As a result, you must prepare the budgets within the master budget in a definite sequence, as follows:

**First:** The sales budget must be prepared first because the operating and financial budgets depend on information provided by the sales budget.

**Second:** The remaining operating budgets are prepared next. For manufacturing companies, the production budget must be prepared prior to the manufacturing budget, since the number of units to be manufactured obviously affects the amounts of materials, direct labor, and overhead to be budgeted. Other than this, the budgets for manufacturing costs or merchandise costs, general and administrative expenses, and selling expenses may be prepared in any sequence.

**Third:** If capital expenditures are anticipated during the budget period, the capital expenditures budget is prepared next. This budget usually depends on long-range sales forecasts more than it does on the sales budget for the next year.

**Fourth:** Based on the information provided in the above budgets, the budgeted statement of cash receipts and disbursements is prepared. If this budget discloses an imbalance between disbursements and planned receipts, the previous plans may have to be revised.

**Fifth:** The budgeted income statement is prepared next. If the plans contained in the master budget result in unsatisfactory profits, the entire master budget may be revised to incorporate any corrective measures available to the firm.

**Sixth:** The budgeted balance sheet for the end of the budget period is prepared last. An analysis of this statement may also lead to revisions in the previous budgets. For example, the budgeted balance sheet may disclose too much debt resulting from an overly ambitious capital expenditures budget, and revised plans may be necessary.

**Illustration 25–2**
**The balance sheet immediately prior to future (budgeted) periods**

**NORTHERN COMPANY**
**Balance Sheet**
**September 30, 1991**

| | | | |
|---|---|---|---|
| Cash | $ 20,000 | Accounts payable | $ 58,200 |
| Accounts receivable | 42,000 | Note payable to bank | 10,000 |
| Inventory (9,000 units @ $6) | 54,000 | Accrued income taxes payable | |
| Equipment* | 200,000 | (due October 15, 1991) | 20,000 |
| Less accumulated | | Common stock | 150,000 |
| depreciation | (36,000) | Retained earnings | 41,800 |
| Total | $280,000 | Total | $280,000 |

*The equipment is being depreciated on a straight-line basis over 10 years. Estimated salvage value is $20,000.

## Preparation of the Master Budget Illustrated

Prepare each budget in a master budget and explain the importance of each budget to the overall budgeting process. (L. O. 3)

The following sections explain the procedures involved in preparing the budgets that comprise the master budget. Northern Company, a wholesaler of a single product, provides an illustrative basis for the discussion. The September 30, 1991, balance sheet for Northern Company is presented in Illustration 25–2. The master budget for Northern Company is prepared on a monthly basis, with a budgeted balance sheet prepared for the end of each quarter. Also, a budgeted income statement is prepared for each quarter. In the following sections, Northern Company budgets are prepared for October, November, and December 1991.

### Preparing a Sales Budget

The **sales budget** provides an estimate of goods to be sold and revenue to be derived from sales. It is the starting point in the budgeting procedure, since the plans of most departments are related to sales and expected revenue. The sales budget commonly grows from a reconciliation of forecasted business conditions, plant capacity, proposed selling expenses such as advertising, and estimates of sales. Since people normally feel a greater responsibility for reaching goals they have had a hand in setting, the sales personnel of a company usually are asked to submit, through the sales manager, estimates of sales for each territory and department. The final sales budget is then based on these estimates as reconciled for the forecasted business conditions, selling expenses, and so forth.

During September 1991, Northern Company sold 7,000 units of product at a price of $10 per unit. After obtaining the estimates of sales personnel and considering the economic market conditions affecting Northern Company's product, the sales budget (Illustration 25–3) is established for October, November, and December 1991. Since the purchasing department must base December 1991 purchases on estimated sales for January 1992, the sales budget is expanded to include January 1992.

**Illustration 25–3**
**Sales budget showing planned unit sales and dollar sales**

NORTHERN COMPANY
Monthly Sales Budget
October 1991–January 1992

| | Budgeted Unit Sales | | Budgeted Unit Price | | Budgeted Total Sales |
|---|---|---|---|---|---|
| September 1991 (actual) . . . . | 7,000 | × | $10 | = | $ 70,000 |
| October 1991 . . . . . . . . . . | 10,000 | × | 10 | = | 100,000 |
| November 1991 . . . . . . . . . | 8,000 | × | 10 | = | 80,000 |
| December 1991 . . . . . . . . . | 14,000 | × | 10 | = | 140,000 |
| January 1992 . . . . . . . . . . | 9,000 | × | 10 | = | 90,000 |

Observe in Illustration 25–3 that the sales budget is more detailed than simple projections of total sales; both unit sales and unit prices are forecasted. Some companies prepare a less detailed sales budget that is expressed only in terms of total sales volume. However, many sales budgets are far more detailed than the one illustrated. More detailed sales budgets may show units and unit prices for each of many different products, classified by salesperson and by territory or by department.

### Preparing a Merchandise Purchases Budget

A variety of sophisticated techniques have been developed to assist management in making inventory purchase decisions. All of these techniques recognize that the number of units to be added to inventory depends on the budgeted sales volume. Whether a company manufactures or purchases the product it sells, budgeted future sales volume is the primary factor to be considered in most inventory management decisions.

**Just-in-Time Inventory Systems.** A relatively new technique for making inventory purchase (or production) decisions is called a **just-in-time inventory system.** With this approach, sales budgets for very short periods of time (perhaps one or two days) are used to order just enough merchandise to satisfy the immediate sales demand. As a result, the level of inventory on hand is held to a minimum or may even be held to zero in some situations. If a just-in-time inventory system can be used, the costs of maintaining an investment in inventory are minimized. However, just-in-time inventory systems are not practical unless sales demand can be determined with very little error. Also, you must have complete confidence in your supplier, who must be able and willing to ship small quantities regularly and without delay.

**Safety Stock Inventory Systems.** The market conditions and production problems for most products do not allow you to use a just-in-time inventory system. Instead, many companies maintain enough inventory to avoid or minimize the risk of running out of inventory. This requires that purchases be planned to satisfy the budgeted sales amounts and also that an additional

**Illustration 25–4**

**NORTHERN COMPANY**
**Merchandise Purchases Budget**
**October, November, and December 1991**

| | October | November | December |
|---|---|---|---|
| Next month's budgeted sales (in units) | 8,000 | 14,000 | 9,000 |
| Ratio of inventory to future sales | ×90% | ×90% | ×90% |
| Desired end-of-month inventory | 7,200 | 12,600 | 8,100 |
| Budgeted sales for the month (in units) | 10,000 | 8,000 | 14,000 |
| Required units of available merchandise | 17,200 | 20,600 | 22,100 |
| Deduct beginning-of-month inventory | (9,000) | (7,200) | (12,600) |
| Number of units to be purchased | 8,200 | 13,400 | 9,500 |
| Budgeted cost per unit | ×$6 | ×$6 | ×$6 |
| Budgeted cost of merchandise purchases | $49,200 | $80,400 | $57,000 |

quantity of inventory be maintained as a **safety stock.** The safety stock compensates for unexpected demand or delays in receipts from suppliers.

A **merchandise purchases budget** may be expressed in both units and dollars. A general format of such a budget is as follows:

| | Units |
|---|---|
| Budgeted sales for the month | 10,000 |
| Add the budgeted end-of-month inventory | 7,200 |
| Required amount of available merchandise | 17,200 |
| Deduct the beginning-of-month inventory | (9,000) |
| Inventory to be purchased | 8,200 |

If the calculation is in units and only one product is involved, the number of dollars of inventory to be purchased may be added to the budget simply by multiplying units to be purchased by the cost per unit.

After considering the cost of maintaining an investment in inventory and the potential cost associated with a temporary inventory shortage, Northern Company has decided that the number of units in its inventory at the end of each month should equal 90% of the next month's sales. In other words, the inventory at the end of October should equal 90% of the budgeted November sales, the November ending inventory should equal 90% of the expected December sales, and so on. Also, the company's suppliers have indicated that the September 1991 per unit cost of $6 can be expected to remain unchanged through January 1992. Based on these factors and on the fact that 9,000 units were on hand on September 30 (see Illustration 25–2), the company prepared the merchandise purchases budget of Illustration 25–4.

The calculations of Northern Company's merchandise purchases budget differ slightly from the general format previously given in that the first lines are devoted to determining the desired end-of-month inventory. Then, budgeted sales are added to the desired end-of-month inventory and the beginning inventory is subtracted to determine the budgeted number of units to be purchased. Also, on the last lines the budgeted cost of the purchases is calculated by multiplying units to be purchased by the expected cost per unit.

Recall from the previous discussion that some budgeting procedures are designed to provide only the total dollars of budgeted sales. Likewise, the merchandise purchases budget may not state the number of units to be purchased, and may be expressed only in terms of the total cost of merchandise to be purchased. When this is done, however, you must assume that there is a constant relationship between sales and cost of goods sold. For example, Northern Company expects that costs of goods sold will equal 60% of sales. (Note that the budgeted sales price is $10, and the budgeted unit cost is $6.) Thus, its cost of purchases could be budgeted in dollars on the basis of budgeted sales without requiring information on the number of units involved.

### Preparing Production Budgets and Manufacturing Budgets

Since Northern Company does not manufacture the product it sells, its budget for acquiring goods to be sold is a merchandise purchases budget (Illustration 25–4). If Northern Company had been a manufacturing company, a **production budget** rather than a merchandise purchases budget would be required. A production budget shows the number of units to be produced each month. For Northern Company, such a budget would be very similar to a merchandise purchases budget. It would differ in that the number of units to be purchased each month (see Illustration 25–4) would be described as the number of units to be manufactured each month. Also, it would not show costs, since a production budget is always expressed entirely in terms of units of product and does not include budgeted production costs. Such costs are shown in the **manufacturing budget**, which is based on the production volume shown in the production budget.

A manufacturing budget shows the budgeted costs for raw materials, direct labor, and manufacturing overhead. In many manufacturing companies, the manufacturing budget is actually prepared in the form of three sub-budgets: a raw materials purchases budget, a direct labor budget, and a manufacturing overhead budget. These budgets show the total budgeted cost of goods to be manufactured during the budget period.

### Preparing a Selling Expense Budget

The initial responsibility for preparing a budget of selling expenses typically falls on the vice president of marketing or the equivalent sales manager. Although budgeted selling expenses should affect the expected amount of sales, the typical procedure is to prepare a sales budget first and then to budget selling expenses. Estimates of selling expenses are based on the tentative sales budget and on the experience of previous periods adjusted for expected changes. After the entire master budget is prepared on a tentative basis, management may decide that the projected sales volume is inadequate. If so, subsequent adjustments in the sales budget may require corresponding adjustments in the selling expense budget.

Northern Company's selling expenses consist of commissions paid to sales personnel and a $24,000 per year salary, paid on a monthly basis to the sales

**Illustration 25–5**

**NORTHERN COMPANY**
**Selling Expense Budget**
**October, November, and December 1991**

| | October | November | December | Total |
|---|---|---|---|---|
| Budgeted sales | $100,000 | $80,000 | $140,000 | $320,000 |
| Sales commission percentage | ×10% | ×10% | ×10% | ×10% |
| Sales commissions | $ 10,000 | $ 8,000 | $ 14,000 | $ 32,000 |
| Salary for sales manager ($24,000 ÷ 12 = $2,000 per month) | 2,000 | 2,000 | 2,000 | 6,000 |
| Total selling expenses | $ 12,000 | $10,000 | $ 16,000 | $ 38,000 |

manager. Sales commissions amount to 10% of total sales and are paid during the month the sales are made. The selling expense budget for Northern Company is presented in Illustration 25–5.

### Preparing a General and Administrative Expense Budget

General and administrative expenses usually are the responsibility of the office manager, who should therefore be charged with the task of proposing a budget for these items. The amounts of some general and administrative expenses may depend on budgeted sales volume. However, most of these expenses depend more on other factors such as management policies, the effects of inflation, and so forth, than they do on monthly changes in sales volume. Although interest expense and income tax expense are often classified as general and administrative expenses, they generally cannot be budgeted at this point in the budgeting sequence. Interest expense must await preparation of the cash budget, which determines the need for loans, if any. Income tax expense must await preparation of the budgeted income statement, at which time taxable income and income tax expense can be estimated.

General and administrative expenses for Northern Company include administrative salaries of $54,000 per year and depreciation on equipment of $18,000 per year (see Illustration 25–2). The salaries are paid each month as they are earned. Illustration 25–6 shows the budget for these expenses.

### Preparing a Capital Expenditures Budget

The **capital expenditures budget** lists equipment to be scrapped and additional equipment to be purchased if the proposed production program is carried out. Since production capacity usually is limited by the investment in plant and equipment, the long-range plans for business expansion may affect this budget more than next year's sales budget. Nevertheless, the annual sales budget also may disclose production needs that require additional expenditures for equipment.

The process of evaluating and planning capital expenditures is called capital budgeting. Since capital expenditures often involve long-run commitments of large amounts, planning those expenditures is an important responsibility of

**Illustration 25–6**

NORTHERN COMPANY
General and Administrative Expense Budget
October, November, and December 1991

| | October | November | December | Total |
|---|---|---|---|---|
| Administrative salaries | | | | |
| ($54,000 ÷ 12 = $4,500) . . . . | $4,500 | $4,500 | $4,500 | $13,500 |
| Depreciation of equipment | | | | |
| ($18,000 ÷ 12 = $1,500) . . . . | 1,500 | 1,500 | 1,500 | 4,500 |
| | $6,000 | $6,000 | $6,000 | $18,000 |

management. Typically, capital expenditures involve large dollar amounts that have a major impact on the cash budget and perhaps on the company's need for debt financing. Accordingly, the capital expenditures budget may be closely tied to management's evaluation of the company's ability to service more debt. You will learn more about capital budgeting in Chapter 27.

Northern Company does not anticipate any sales or retirements of equipment through December 1991. However, management plans to acquire additional equipment for $25,000 cash near the end of December 1991.

### Preparing a Cash Budget

After tentative sales, merchandise purchases, expenses, and capital expenditures budgets have been developed, the **cash budget** is prepared. This budget is especially important since a company must maintain a cash balance that is adequate to meet its obligations. On the other hand, a cash balance can be too large. Too much cash is undesirable because it usually earns a low rate of interest, if any is earned at all. A cash budget requires management to forecast cash receipts and disbursements, and usually results in better cash management. Also, it enables management to arrange well in advance for loans to cover any anticipated cash shortages.

In preparing the cash budget, you add expected receipts to the beginning cash balance and deduct expected expenditures. If the resulting cash balance is inadequate, the required additional cash is shown in the budget as planned increases in loans.

Much of the information that is needed to prepare the cash budget can be obtained directly from the previously prepared operating and capital expenditures budgets. However, further investigation and additional calculations may be necessary to determine the amounts to be included.

Illustration 25–7 shows the cash budget for Northern Company. In the illustration, October's beginning cash balance was obtained from the September 30, 1991, balance sheet (Illustration 25–2).

Budgeted sales of Northern Company were shown in Illustration 25–3. An investigation of previous sales records indicates that 40% of Northern Company's sales are for cash. The remaining 60% are credit sales, and customers can be expected to pay for these sales in the month after the sales are made. Thus, the budgeted cash receipts from customers are calculated as follows:

**Illustration 25–7**

**NORTHERN COMPANY**
**Cash Budget**
**October, November, and December 1991**

| | October | November | December |
|---|---|---|---|
| Beginning cash balance | $ 20,000 | $ 20,000 | $ 22,272 |
| Cash receipts from customers | 82,000 | 92,000 | 104,000 |
| Totals | $102,000 | $112,000 | $126,272 |
| Cash disbursements: | | | |
| Payments for merchandise | $ 58,200 | $ 49,200 | $ 80,400 |
| Sales commissions (Illustration 25–5) | 10,000 | 8,000 | 14,000 |
| Salaries: Sales (Illustration 25–5) | 2,000 | 2,000 | 2,000 |
| Administrative (Illustration 25–6) | 4,500 | 4,500 | 4,500 |
| Accrued income taxes payable | 20,000 | | |
| Dividends ($150,000 × 0.02 = $3,000) | | 3,000 | |
| Interest on loan from bank | | | |
| $10,000 × 0.01 = $100 | 100 | | |
| $22,800 × 0.01 = $228 | | 228 | |
| Purchase of equipment | | | 25,000 |
| Total cash disbursements | $ 94,800 | $ 66,928 | $125,900 |
| Balance | $ 7,200 | $ 45,072 | $ 372 |
| Additional loan from bank | 12,800 | | 19,628 |
| Repayment of loan from bank | | (22,800) | |
| Ending cash balance | $ 20,000 | $ 22,272 | $ 20,000 |
| Loan balance, end of month | $ 22,800 | $ -0- | $ 19,628 |

| | September | October | November | December |
|---|---|---|---|---|
| Sales | $70,000 | $100,000 | $80,000 | $140,000 |
| Credit sales percentage | ×60% | ×60% | ×60% | ×60% |
| Accounts receivable, end of month | $42,000 | $ 60,000 | $48,000 | $ 84,000 |
| Cash sales percentage | | ×40% | ×40% | ×40% |
| Cash sales | | $ 40,000 | $32,000 | $ 56,000 |
| Collections of accounts receivable | | 42,000 | 60,000 | 48,000 |
| Total cash receipts | | $ 82,000 | $92,000 | $104,000 |

Observe in the calculation that the October cash receipts consist of $40,000 from cash sales (100,000 × 40%) plus the collection of $42,000 of accounts receivable as calculated in the September column. Also, note that each month's total cash receipts are listed on the second line of Illustration 25–7.

Northern Company's purchases of merchandise are entirely on account, and full payments are made regularly in the month following purchase. Thus, in Illustration 25–7, the cash disbursements for purchases are obtained from the September 30, 1991, balance sheet (Illustration 25–2) and from the merchandise purchases budget (Illustration 25–4) as follows:

| | |
|---|---|
| September 30, accounts payable equal October payments | $58,200 |
| October purchases equal November payments | 49,200 |
| November purchases equal December payments | 80,400 |

Sales commissions and all salaries are paid monthly, and the budgeted cash disbursements for these items are obtained from the selling expense budget (Illustration 25–5) and the general and administrative expense budget (Illustration 25–6).

As indicated in the September 30, 1991, balance sheet (Illustration 25–2), accrued income taxes are paid in October. Estimated income tax expense for the quarter ending December 31 is 40% of net income and is due in January 1992.

Northern Company pays 2% quarterly cash dividends, and the November payment of $3,000 is the planned disbursement for this item. Also, Northern Company has an agreement with the bank whereby additional loans are granted at the end of each month if they are necessary to maintain a minimum cash balance of $20,000 at the end of the month. Interest is paid at the end of each month at the rate of 1% per month. Finally, if the cash balance exceeds $20,000 at the end of a month, the excess is used to repay the loans to the bank.

Illustration 25–7 shows that the October 31 balance before any loan related activity falls below the $20,000 minimum. Thus, Northern Company will have to borrow $12,800 of additional cash through another short-term note to bring the balance up to the minimum. At the end of November, the budget shows a balance of $45,072 before any loan activity. As a result, the company will be able to repay the $22,800 previously borrowed. Note, however, that the equipment purchase budgeted for December will again draw the cash balance below the $20,000 minimum, so $19,628 will have to be borrowed in that month.

### Preparing a Budgeted Income Statement

Integrate the individual budgets into planned financial statements. (L. O. 4)

One of the final steps in preparing a master budget is to summarize the effects of the various budgetary plans on the **budgeted income statement.** The necessary information to prepare a budgeted income statement is drawn primarily from the previously prepared budgets or from the investigations that were made in the process of preparing those budgets.

For many companies, the volume of information that must be summarized in the budgeted income statement and the budgeted balance sheet is so large that a work sheet must be used to accumulate all of the budgeted transactions and to classify them in terms of their impact on the income statement and/or on the balance sheet. However, the transactions and account balances of Northern Company are few in number, and the budgeted income statement (and balance sheet) can be prepared simply by inspecting the previously discussed budgets and recalling the information that was provided in the related discussions. Northern Company's budgeted income statement is shown in Illustration 25–8.

### Preparing a Budgeted Balance Sheet

If a work sheet is used to prepare the budgeted income statement and **budgeted balance sheet,** the first two columns of the work sheet are used to list the estimated post-closing trial balance of the period prior to the budget period. Next, the budgeted transactions and adjustments are entered in the second pair of work sheet columns in the same manner as end-of-period adjustments are entered on an ordinary work sheet. For example, if the budget calls for sales on

**Illustration 25–8**

**NORTHERN COMPANY**
**Budgeted Income Statement**
**For Three Months Ended December 31, 1991**

| | | |
|---|---|---|
| Sales (Illustration 25–3, 32,000 units @ $10) | | $320,000 |
| Cost of goods sold (32,000 units @ $6) | | 192,000 |
| Gross profit | | $128,000 |
| Operating expenses: | | |
| Sales commissions (Illustration 25–5) | $32,000 | |
| Sales salaries (Illustration 25–5) | 6,000 | |
| Administrative salaries (Illustration 25–6) | 13,500 | |
| Depreciation on equipment (Illustration 25–6) | 4,500 | |
| Interest expense (Illustration 25–7) | 328 | (56,328) |
| Net income before income taxes | | $ 71,672 |
| Income tax expense ($71,672 × 40%) | | (28,669) |
| Net income | | $ 43,003 |

account of $250,000, the name of the Sales account is entered on the work sheet in the Account Titles column below the names of post-closing trial balance accounts; and then Sales is credited and Accounts Receivable is debited for $250,000 in the second pair of money columns. After all budgeted transactions and adjustments are entered on the work sheet, the estimated post-closing trial balance amounts in the first pair of money columns are combined with the budget amounts in the second pair of columns and are sorted to the proper Income Statement and Balance Sheet columns of the work sheet. Finally, the information in these columns is used to prepare the budgeted income statement and budgeted balance sheet.

As previously mentioned, the transactions and account balances of Northern Company are few in number, and its budgeted balance sheet, shown in Illustration 25–9, can be prepared simply by inspecting the previously prepared budgets and recalling the related discussions of those budgets.

Observe that the retained earnings balance in Illustration 25–9 is $81,803. This amount was determined as follows:

| | |
|---|---|
| Retained earnings, September 30, 1991 (Illustration 25–2) | $41,800 |
| Net income for three months ended December 31, 1991 (Illustration 25–8) | 43,003 |
| Total | $84,803 |
| Dividends declared in November 1991 (Illustration 25–7) | (3,000) |
| Retained earnings, December 31, 1991 | $81,803 |

## Summary of the Chapter in Terms of Learning Objectives

**1.** Planning is a management responsibility of critical importance to business success, and budgeting is the process by which management formalizes its plans. Budgeting promotes study and research by management and focuses its attention on the future. Budgeting also provides a basis for

**Illustration 25–9**

**NORTHERN COMPANY**
**Budgeted Balance Sheet**
**December 31, 1991**

| | | |
|---|---|---|
| **Assets** | | |
| Cash (Illustration 25–7) | | $ 20,000 |
| Accounts receivable (page 1067) | | 84,000 |
| Inventory (Illustration 25–4, 8,100 units @ $6) | | 48,600 |
| Equipment (Illustrations 25–2 and 25–7) | $225,000 | |
| Less accumulated depreciation (Illustrations 25–2 and 25–6) | 40,500 | 184,500 |
| Total assets | | $337,100 |
| **Liabilities and Stockholders' Equity** | | |
| Liabilities: | | |
| Accounts payable (Illustration 25–4) | $ 57,000 | |
| Accrued income taxes payable (Illustration 25–8) | 28,669 | |
| Bank loan payable (Illustration 25–7) | 19,628 | $105,297 |
| Stockholders' equity: | | |
| Common stock (Illustration 25–2) | $150,000 | |
| Retained earnings (see discussion) | 81,803 | 231,803 |
| Total liabilities and stockholders' equity | | $337,100 |

evaluating performance, serves as a source of motivation, is a means of coordinating business activities, and is a means of communicating managements plans and instructions to employees.

**2.** A master budget is a formalized, overall plan for a business that consists of specific plans for business operations, capital expenditures, and the financial results of those activities. The budgeting process begins with the preparation of a sales budget. Based on the expected sales volume, manufacturing companies can budget production quantities and costs, materials purchases, selling expenditures, and administrative expenditures. Next, the capital expenditures budget is prepared, followed by the financial budgets.

**3.** In the process of preparing a master budget, each budget is designed to provide guidance for the persons who are responsible for the activities covered by that budget. The budgets show how much money is to be received from or expended on each activity and when the receipts and expenditures are to occur. The budgets are designed so that the activities of one area (such as manufacturing) will support the activities of the others (such as sales). As a result, the various components of the business are directed to pursue activities that are consistent with and supportive of the overall objectives of the business.

**4.** The operating budgets and the capital expenditures budget, along with their supporting calculations and the balance sheet prior to the first budget period, contain all of the information that is needed to prepare a planned income statement for the budget period and a planned balance sheet at the end of the budget period. If a company is not too complex, these planned financial statements can be prepared simply by extracting the necessary information from the budgets, related calculations, and beginning-of-period financial statements. The statements show the financial consequences that will result if the planned activities, as disclosed in the budgets, actually take place.

## Demonstration Problem

The management of Daredevil Company has asked you to prepare a master budget for the company given the following information. The budget is to cover the period April, May, and June 1991.

**DAREDEVIL COMPANY**
**Balance Sheet**
**As of March 31, 1991**

| | | |
|---|---|---|
| **Assets** | | |
| Cash | $ 50,000 | |
| Accounts receivable | 175,000 | |
| Inventory | 126,000 | |
| Total current assets | | $351,000 |
| Fixed assets | $480,000 | |
| Accumulated depreciation | (90,000) | 390,000 |
| Total assets | | $741,000 |
| **Liabilities and Stockholders' Equity** | | |
| Accounts payable | $156,000 | |
| Short-term notes payable | 12,000 | |
| Total current liabilities | | $168,000 |
| Long-term note payable | | 200,000 |
| Total liabilities | | $368,000 |
| Common stock | $235,000 | |
| Retained earnings | 138,000 | |
| Total stockholders' equity | | 373,000 |
| Total liabilities and stockholders' equity | | $741,000 |

*Required*

1. Develop a monthly sales budget for the quarter. In doing so, first project the expected unit sales of the company's product for each month during the quarter and also for July. Each month's sales figure is expected to exceed the prior month's results by 5%. Actual unit sales for March were 10,000 units. Use these projected unit sales to prepare the sales budget for the three months and the quarter combined. Assume a selling price of $25 per unit.
2. Using the results of part 1 and the policy that the ending inventory in a given month should equal 80% of the succeeding month's expected unit sales, prepare a purchases budget. First project the units to be purchased in each month and then determine the dollar amount, assuming a cost of $15 per unit. The March 31 inventory was 8,400 units, which was according to plan. Also calculate the projected cost of goods sold and the June 30 ending inventory.
3. Using the results from above, prepare the selling expenses budget for the three months and the quarter. There are two expense items: sales representatives' commissions which are awarded at 12.5% of dollar

sales, and the manager's salary which will be $3,500 in April and $4,000 thereafter.

4. Next, prepare the general and administrative expenses budget. Three items are expected: administrative salaries of $8,000 per month; depreciation of $5,000 per month; and 0.9% interest on the long-term note will be paid each month.
5. Prepare estimates of cash sales and collections of accounts receivable. Sales are expected to be 30% for cash and 70% on credit. Receivables are collected in full in the month following the sale (none is collected in the month of the sale). The March 31 balance of receivables was $175,000, which was in accordance with expectations. Also determine the expected accounts receivable balance as of June 30.
6. Calculate expected cash payments of accounts payable. All purchases of merchandise are on credit, and no payables arise from any other transactions. The purchases of one month are paid in full during the succeeding month. The March 31 balance of accounts payable was $156,000, which was in accordance with expectations. Also determine the expected accounts payable balance as of June 30.
7. Prepare a monthly cash budget for the quarter, given the above information and the following additional information:
   *a.* A minimum cash balance at the end of each month of $50,000 must be maintained, if necessary by borrowing on a short-term note that requires an interest payment of 1% at the end of the next month. If the end-of-month balance exceeds the minimum, the excess will be applied to repaying the short-term notes payable.
   *b.* Sales commissions are paid in the month of the sale. Interest and all salaries are paid currently. Dividends of $100,000 are to be declared and paid in May. No income taxes are to be paid during the quarter. Fixed assets of $55,000 are to be acquired in June.
   *c.* The cash budgets should show the beginning and ending balances of cash, and the ending balance of the short-term notes payable.
8. Prepare the following budgeted financial statements for the quarter: income statement, statement of retained earnings, and balance sheet dated June 30. (The income tax rate is 35%.)

## Solution to Demonstration Problem

1. Projected units sales (10% growth):

| | April | May | June | July |
|---|---|---|---|---|
| Prior month's sales | 10,000 | 10,500 | 11,025 | 11,576 |
| Plus 5% | 500 | 525 | 551 | 579 |
| Projected unit sales | 10,500 | 11,025 | 11,576 | 12,155 |

| | | | | Quarter |
|---|---|---|---|---|
| Projected unit sales | 10,500 | 11,025 | 11,576 | |
| Selling price per unit | ×$25 | ×$25 | ×$25 | |
| Projected sales revenue | $262,500 | $275,625 | $289,400 | $827,525 |

2. Projected purchases:

| | April | May | June | Quarter |
|---|---|---|---|---|
| Next month's unit sales | 11,025 | 11,576 | 12,155 | |
| Ending inventory percentage | ×80% | ×80% | ×80% | |
| Desired ending inventory | 8,820 | 9,261 | 9,724 | |
| This month's unit sales | 10,500 | 11,025 | 11,576 | |
| Units to be available | 19,320 | 20,286 | 21,300 | |
| Beginning inventory | (8,400) | (8,820) | (9,261) | |
| Units to be purchased | 10,920 | 11,466 | 12,039 | |
| Budgeted cost per unit | ×$15 | ×$15 | ×$15 | |
| Projected purchases | $163,800 | $171,990 | $180,585 | $516,375 |

Projected cost of goods sold:

| | April | May | June | Quarter |
|---|---|---|---|---|
| This month's unit sales | 10,500 | 11,025 | 11,576 | |
| Budgeted cost per unit | ×$15 | ×$15 | ×$15 | |
| Projected cost of goods sold | $157,500 | $165,375 | $173,640 | $496,515 |
| Projected inventory for June 30: | | | | |
| Units | | | 9,724 | |
| Cost per unit | | | ×$15 | |
| Total | | | $145,860 | |

3. Selling expense budget:

| | April | May | June | Quarter |
|---|---|---|---|---|
| Budgeted sales | $262,500 | $275,625 | $289,400 | $827,525 |
| Commission percentage | ×12.5% | ×12.5% | ×12.5% | ×12.5% |
| Sales commissions | $ 32,813 | $ 34,453 | $ 36,175 | $103,441 |
| Manager's salary | 3,500 | 4,000 | 4,000 | 11,500 |
| Projected selling expenses | $ 36,313 | $ 38,453 | $ 40,175 | $114,941 |

4. General and administrative expense budget:

| | April | May | June | Quarter |
|---|---|---|---|---|
| Administrative salaries | $ 8,000 | $ 8,000 | $ 8,000 | $ 24,000 |
| Depreciation | 5,000 | 5,000 | 5,000 | 15,000 |
| Interest on mortgage payable | 1,800 | 1,800 | 1,800 | 5,400 |
| Projected expenses | $ 14,800 | $ 14,800 | $ 14,800 | $ 44,400 |

5. Projected cash receipts from customers:

| | April | May | June | Quarter |
|---|---|---|---|---|
| Budgeted sales in prior month | | $262,500 | $275,625 | |
| Credit sales percentage | | ×70% | ×70% | |
| Cash collections of receivables | $175,000 | $183,750 | $192,938 | $551,688 |
| Budgeted sales this month | $262,500 | $275,625 | $289,400 | |
| Cash sales percentage | ×30% | ×30% | ×30% | |
| Cash sales this month | $ 78,750 | $ 82,687 | $ 86,820 | 248,257 |
| Total cash to be collected | $253,750 | $266,437 | $279,758 | $799,945 |
| Budgeted sales for June | | | $289,400 | |
| Credit sales percentage | | | ×70% | |
| Expected June 30 balance of accounts receivable | | | $202,580 | |

6. Projected cash payments to suppliers of inventory:

| | April | May | June | Quarter |
|---|---|---|---|---|
| Cash payments (equal to prior month's purchases) | $156,000 | $163,800 | $171,990 | $491,790 |
| Expected June 30 balance of accounts payable (June purchases) | | | $180,585 | |

7. Cash budget:

| | April | May | June |
|---|---|---|---|
| Beginning cash balance | $ 50,000 | $ 89,517 | $ 50,000 |
| Cash received from customers | 253,750 | 266,437 | 279,758 |
| Total | $303,750 | $355,954 | $329,758 |
| Cash payments: | | | |
| Payments for merchandise | $156,000 | $163,800 | $171,990 |
| Sales commissions | 32,813 | 34,453 | 36,175 |
| Salaries: | | | |
| Sales | 3,500 | 4,000 | 4,000 |
| Administrative | 8,000 | 8,000 | 8,000 |
| Interest on long-term note | 1,800 | 1,800 | 1,800 |
| Dividends | | 100,000 | |
| Asset purchase | | | 55,000 |
| Interest on short-term notes: | | | |
| $12,000 × 1.0% | 120 | | |
| $ 0 × 1.0% | | –0– | |
| $ 6,099 × 1.0% | | | 61 |
| Total | $202,233 | $312,053 | $277,026 |
| Balance before loan activity | $101,517 | $ 43,901 | $ 52,732 |
| Additional loan | –0– | 6,099 | –0– |
| Loan repayment | (12,000) | –0– | (2,732) |
| Ending cash balance | $ 89,517 | $ 50,000 | $ 50,000 |
| Ending short-term notes | $ –0– | $ 6,099 | $ 3,367 |

8.

**DAREDEVIL COMPANY**
**Budgeted Income Statement**
**For the Quarter Ended June 30, 1991**

| | | | |
|---|---|---|---|
| Sales | | $827,525 | (part 1) |
| Cost of goods sold | | (496,515) | (part 2) |
| Gross profit | | $331,010 | |
| Operating expenses: | | | |
| Sales commissions | $103,441 | | (part 3) |
| Sales salaries | 11,500 | | (part 3) |
| Administrative salaries | 24,000 | | (part 4) |
| Depreciation | 15,000 | | (part 4) |
| Interest on long-term note | 5,400 | | (part 4) |
| Interest on short-term notes | 181 | | (part 7) |
| Total operating expenses | | (159,522) | |
| Income before income taxes | | $171,488 | |
| Income taxes (35%) | | (60,021) | |
| Net income | | $111,467 | |

**DAREDEVIL COMPANY**
**Budgeted Statement of Retained Earnings**
**For the Quarter Ended June 30, 1991**

| | | |
|---|---|---|
| Beginning retained earnings | $138,000 | (given) |
| Net income | 111,467 | (above) |
| Total | $249,467 | |
| Dividends | (100,000) | (given) |
| Ending retained earnings | $149,467 | |

**DAREDEVIL COMPANY**
**Budgeted Balance Sheet**
**June 30, 1991**

| | | | |
|---|---|---|---|
| Cash | $ 50,000 | | (part 7) |
| Accounts receivable | 202,580 | | (part 5) |
| Inventory | 145,860 | | (part 2) |
| Total current assets | | $398,440 | |
| Fixed assets | $535,000 | | (given plus purchase) |
| Accumulated depreciation | (105,000) | 430,000 | (given plus expense) |
| Total assets | | $828,440 | |
| Accounts payable | $180,585 | | (part 6) |
| Short-term notes payable | 3,367 | | (part 7) |
| Estimated income taxes payable | 60,021 | | (above) |
| Total current liabilities | | $243,973 | |
| Long-term note payable | | 200,000 | (given) |
| Total liabilities | | $443,973 | |
| Common stock | $235,000 | | (given) |
| Retained earnings | 149,467 | | (above) |
| Total stockholders' equity | | 384,467 | |
| Total liabilities and equity | | $828,440 | |

## Glossary

Define or explain the words and phrases listed in the chapter Glossary. (L. O. 5)

**Budget** a formal statement of future plans, usually expressed in monetary terms. p. 1055

**Budgeted balance sheet** a projected balance sheet estimated to result at the end of the budget period if the activities projected in each of the related budgets actually occur. pp. 1068–70

**Budgeted income statement** a projected income statement that draws on the estimates shown in all of the related revenue and expense budgets and shows the effects of the separate budgets on the income of the budget period. pp. 1068–69

**Budgeting** the process of planning future business actions and expressing those plans in a formal manner. p. 1055

**Capital expenditures budget** a plan that states the plant and equipment to be purchased during each period covered by the budget, based on the budgeted sales and manufacturing needs and the long-range plans for business expansion. pp. 1065–66

**Cash budget** a plan that states the expected cash receipts and disbursements during each of the periods covered by the budget, including receipts from loans necessary to maintain an adequate cash balance and repayments of such loans. pp. 1066–68

**Continuous budgeting** the practice of preparing budgets for each of several future periods and revising those budgets each period, adding a new budget each time so that budgets are always available for a given number of future periods. p. 1058

**Just-in-time inventory system** a method of keeping inventory levels at or near zero by ordering just enough merchandise (or materials) to satisfy the immediate sales demand. p. 1062

**Manufacturing budget** a statement of the estimated costs for raw materials, direct labor, and manufacturing overhead to be incurred in producing the number of units estimated in the production budget. p. 1064

**Master budget** a comprehensive or overall plan for the business that typically includes budgets for sales, expenses, production, capital expenditures, cash, and also a planned income statement and balance sheet. p. 1058

**Merchandise purchases budget** a plan that states the units and/or cost of merchandise to be purchased by a merchandising company during each future period covered by the budget. pp. 1063–64

**Production budget** a plan that states the number of units to be manufactured during each future period covered by the budget, based on the budgeted sales for the period and the levels of inventory necessary to support future sales. p. 1064

**Rolling budgets** a sequence of revised budgets that are prepared in the practice of continuous budgeting. p. 1058

**Safety stock** a quantity of merchandise or materials, in addition to the amount necessary to satisfy budgeted sales demand, that is held as inventory to compensate for unexpected demand or delays in receipts from suppliers. pp. 1062–63

**Sales budget** a plan that states the estimated amount of goods to be sold and revenue to be derived from sales during each of the future periods covered by the budget; serves as the usual starting point in the budgeting procedure. pp. 1061–62

## Objective Review

Answers to the following questions are listed in Appendix I at the end of the book. Be sure that you decide which is the one best answer to each question *before* you check the answers in the appendix.

1. Which of the following is a reason why budgeting is useful?
   *a.* Budgeting is a means of communicating management's plans and directives to employees.
   *b.* Budgeting promotes good decision-making processes by focusing management's attention on study, research, and planning the future.
   *c.* Budgeting can motivate employees to meet established goals.
   *d.* Budgeting provides a basis for evaluating performance.
   *e.* All of the above.
2. A master budget:
   *a.* Includes a manufacturing budget that specifies the number of units to be produced.
   *b.* Begins with the preparation of the operating budgets followed by the preparation of the capital expenditures budget and the financial budgets.
   *c.* Begins with the preparation of the budgeted income statement.
   *d.* Ends with the preparation of the budgeted income statement.
   *e.* Includes a sales budget that specifies the units of product to be purchased or manufactured.
3. In preparing budgets for the third quarter of 1991, Doorun, Inc., budgeted the following unit sales each month: July, 120; August, 140; September, 150; and October, 200. Although the June 30 finished goods inventory consists of 50 units, management expects the ending inventory each month to be 60% of the next month's sales. The production budget for the third quarter should call for monthly production as follows:

| | July | August | September |
|---|---|---|---|
| *a.* | 84 | 90 | 120 |
| *b.* | 132 | 146 | 180 |
| *c.* | 154 | 140 | 150 |
| *d.* | 154 | 146 | 180 |
| *e.* | 120 | 140 | 150 |

4. In preparing a budgeted balance sheet:
   *a.* The cost of plant and equipment can be determined by inspecting the capital expenditures budget and the balance sheet at the beginning of the budget period.
   *b.* The cash balance is determined by comparing the sales budget with the merchandise purchases budget.

*c.* Retained earnings is calculated from information contained in the cash budget and the prior balance sheet.
*d.* Liabilities are determined by inspecting the general and administrative expense budget.
*e.* All of the above are correct.

## Questions for Class Discussion

1. What are the two basic elements involved in managing a business?
2. What relationship does budgeting have to the managerial control function?
3. What is a budget? What is a master budget?
4. What are some of the benefits of budgeting?
5. How does the process of budgeting tend to promote good decision making?
6. What are the two alternative norms or objectives against which actual performance is sometimes compared and evaluated? Which of the two is generally superior?
7. What are three guidelines that should be followed if budgeting is to effectively motivate employees?
8. Why should each department be asked to participate in the preparation of its own budget estimates?
9. How does budgeting contribute to the coordination of business activities?
10. If the managers of a business are able to communicate business plans to their employees through direct conversations, in what sense are budgets still useful in facilitating that communication?
11. What are the duties of the budget committee?
12. What is the normal length of time covered by a master budget? How far in advance are long-range budgets generally prepared?
13. What is meant by the terms *continuous budgeting* and *rolling budgets?*
14. What are the three primary types of budgets that make up the master budget?
15. In comparing merchandising companies and manufacturing companies, what differences show up in the operating budgets?
16. What is the sequence that is followed in preparing the set of budgets that collectively make up the master budget?
17. What is a sales budget? A selling expense budget? A capital expenditures budget?
18. What is the difference between a production budget and a manufacturing budget?
19. How does a just-in-time inventory system differ from a safety stock system?
20. What is a cash budget? Why must the operating budgets and the capital expenditures budget be prepared before the cash budget?

## Exercises

**Exercise 25–1**
**Merchandise purchases budget**
(L. O. 3)

The sales budget of Sportsland's team sales department calls for sales of $85,500 during March. The department expects to begin March with a $41,400 inventory and end the month with a $46,800 inventory. Its cost of goods sold averages 60% of sales.

*Required*

Prepare a merchandise purchases budget for the team sales department showing the amount of goods to be purchased during March.

**Exercise 25–2**
**Production budget for two quarters**
(L. O. 3)

Truffle Company manufactures a product called Trux. The company's management estimates there will be 29,700 units of Trux in the March 31 finished goods inventory, that 66,150 units will be sold during the year's second quarter, that 78,750 units will be sold during the third quarter, and that 86,400 units will be sold during the fourth quarter. Management also believes the company should begin each quarter with units in the finished goods inventory equal to 30% of the next quarter's budgeted sales.

*Required*

Prepare a production budget showing the units of Trux to be manufactured during the year's second quarter and third quarter.

**Exercise 25–3**
**Cash budget for three months**
(L. O. 3)

Darter Company budgeted the following cash receipts and cash disbursements from operations for the third quarter of 1991:

| | Receipts | Disbursements |
|---|---|---|
| July . . . . . . . . | $322,500 | $271,500 |
| August . . . . . . | 153,000 | 329,825 |
| September . . . . | 279,000 | 201,000 |

According to a credit agreement with the bank, the company promises to maintain a minimum, end-of-month cash balance of $30,000. In return, the bank has agreed to provide the company the right to borrow up to $225,000 with interest of 14% per year, paid monthly on the last day of the month. If the loan must be increased during the last 10 days of a month to provide enough cash to pay bills, interest will not begin to accrue until the end of the month.

The company is expected to have a cash balance of $30,000 and a loan balance of $15,000 on June 30, 1991.

*Required*

Prepare a monthly cash budget for the third quarter of 1991.

**Exercise 25–4**
**Cash budget from transaction data**
(L. O. 3)

Use the following information to prepare a cash budget showing expected cash receipts and disbursements for the month of June and the balance expected on June 30, 1991:

*a.* Beginning cash balance on June 1: $94,500.

*b.* Budgeted sales for June: $630,000; 40% are collected in the month of sale, 50% in the next month, 5% in the following month, and 5% are uncollectible.

*c.* Sales for May: $720,000.
*d.* Sales for April: $540,000.
*e.* Budgeted merchandise purchases for June: $405,000; 50% are paid in month of purchase; 50% are paid in the month following purchase.
*f.* Merchandise purchased in May: $270,000.
*g.* Budgeted cash disbursements for salaries in June: $180,000.
*h.* Depreciation expense in June: $9,000.
*i.* Other cash expenses budgeted for June: $45,000.
*j.* Accrued income taxes due in June: $101,250.
*k.* Bank loan interest due in June: $6,750.

**Exercise 25–5**
**Budgeted income statement and balance sheet**
(L. O. 4)

Based on the information provided in Exercise 25–4 and the additional information that follows, prepare a budgeted income statement for the month of June and a budgeted balance sheet for June 30, 1991.

*a.* Cost of goods sold is 50% of sales.
*b.* The inventory at the end of May was $121,500.
*c.* Salaries payable on May 31 was $31,500 and is expected to be $18,000 on June 30.
*d.* The Equipment account shows a balance of $922,500. On May 31, accumulated depreciation amounted to $236,250.
*e.* The $6,750 cash payment of interest represents the 1% monthly expense on a bank loan of $675,000.
*f.* Income taxes payable on May 31 amounted to $101,250, and the income tax rate applicable to the company is 40%.
*g.* The 5% of sales that prove to be uncollectible are debited to Bad Debts Expense and credited to Allowance for Doubtful Accounts during the month of sale. However, specific accounts that prove to be uncollectible are not written off until the second month after the sale, at which time all such accounts not yet collected are written off.
*h.* The only balance sheet accounts other than those implied by the previous discussion are Common Stock, which shows a balance of $225,000, and Retained Earnings, which has a balance of $157,500 on May 31.

**Exercise 25–6**
**Merchandise purchases budget for three months**
(L. O. 3)

Daley Company prepared monthly budgets for the year 1991. The budgets called for a July 31 inventory of 22,500 units. The company follows a policy of ending each month with merchandise inventory on hand equal to a specific percentage of the budgeted sales for the next month. Budgeted unit sales and merchandise purchases for selected months were as follows:

| | Sales (in units) | Purchases (in units) |
|---|---|---|
| May . . . . | 60,000 | 65,625 |
| June . . . | 82,500 | 90,000 |
| July . . . . | 112,500 | 106,875 |

Based on the information above, reconstruct the merchandise purchases budget for May, June, and July. Also show your calculation of the budgeted relationship between ending inventory and next month's sales.

**Exercise 25–7**
**Calculations of budgeted cash payments**
(L. O. 3)

Ritter Company's cost of goods sold is consistently 60% of sales. The company plans to have a merchandise inventory at the start of each month that is 40% of the next month's cost of goods sold. All merchandise is purchased on credit, and 30% of the purchases during a month are paid for during the same month. Another 50% is paid for during the month after purchase, and the remaining 20% is paid for during the second month after purchase. Calculate the expected cash payments to be made during June, given the following sales budget: April, $30,000; May, $45,000; June, $37,500; and July, $60,000.

**Exercise 25–8**
**Budgeting monthly cost of goods sold**
(L. O. 3)

Shoup Company purchases its merchandise on credit and budgets its accounts payable balances and merchandise inventory balances to be as follows:

| | Accounts Payable | Merchandise Inventory |
|---|---|---|
| July 31 . . . . . . . . | $22,500 | $28,500 |
| August 31 . . . . . . | 30,000 | 19,500 |
| September 30 . . . . | 27,000 | 36,000 |
| October 31 . . . . . . | 37,500 | 31,500 |

Cash payments of accounts payable during each month are expected to be: July, $70,500; August, $85,500; September, $63,000; and October, $99,000. Calculate the budgeted amounts of cost of goods sold for August, September, and October.

**Exercise 25–9**
**Budgeting accounts payable balances**
(L. O. 3)

A merchandising company budgets cost of goods sold to be 55% of sales and plans to purchase enough merchandise each month to provide a beginning inventory each month that is 30% of budgeted cost of goods sold for the month. All purchases are on credit, and 10% of the purchases in any month are paid for during the same month. Another 50% is paid during the first month after purchase, and the remaining 40% is paid in the second month after purchase. Calculate the budgeted amounts of accounts payable at the end of May and June given the following sales budget:

| | |
|---|---|
| March . . . . | $ 84,000 |
| April . . . . . | 108,000 |
| May . . . . . | 72,000 |
| June . . . . | 96,000 |
| July . . . . . | 120,000 |

## Problems

**Problem 25–1**
**Production budget and merchandise purchases budget**
(L. O. 3)

Havdon Manufacturing Company manufactures a steel product called a Tolenger. Each Tolenger requires 10 pounds of steel and is produced in a single operation by a stamping process. The company's management estimates there will be 900 units of the product and 6 tons of steel on hand on March 31 of the current year, and that 5,100 units of the product will be sold during the year's second quarter. Management also believes that due to the possibility of a strike in the steel industry, the company should begin the third quarter with a 15-ton steel inventory and 2,000 finished Tolengers. Steel can be purchased for approximately $800 per ton ($0.40 per pound).

*Required*

Prepare a second-quarter production budget and a second-quarter steel purchases budget for the company.

**Problem 25–2**
**Sequential cash budgets for three months**
(L. O. 3)

During the latter part of March, the owner of Lynwood Store approached the bank for a $50,000 loan to be made on May 1 and repaid 60 days thereafter with interest at 12%. The owner planned to increase the store's inventory by $50,000 during April and needed the loan to pay for the merchandise during May. The bank's loan officer was interested in Lynwood Store's ability to repay the loan and asked the owner to forecast the store's June 30 cash position.

On April 1, Lynwood Store was expected to have a $25,000 cash balance, $135,000 of accounts receivable, and $75,500 of accounts payable. Its budgeted sales, purchases, and cash expenditures for the following three months are as follows:

| | April | May | June |
|---|---|---|---|
| Sales . . . . . . . . . . . . . . . | $115,000 | $125,000 | $110,000 |
| Merchandise purchases . . . . | 125,500 | 65,000 | 63,500 |
| Payroll . . . . . . . . . . . . . . | 12,000 | 12,000 | 12,000 |
| Rent . . . . . . . . . . . . . . | 3,750 | 3,750 | 3,750 |
| Other cash expenses . . . . . . | 6,000 | 6,500 | 6,750 |
| Repayment of bank loan . . . . | | | 51,000 |

The budgeted April purchases include the inventory increase. All sales are on account; and past experience indicates 80% is collected in the month following the sale, 15% in the next month, 4% in the next, and the remainder is not collected. Application of this experience to the April 1 accounts receivable balance indicates $108,000 of the $135,000 will be collected during April, $20,250 during May, and $5,400 during June. All merchandise is paid for in the month following its purchase.

*Required*

Prepare cash budgets for April, May, and June 1991 for Lynwood Store under the assumption the bank loan will be paid on June 30.

**Problem 25–3**
**Cash budgets with supporting schedules**
(L. O. 3)

Fasbinder Company has a cash balance of $34,560 on June 1, 1991. The product sold by the company sells for $32 per unit. Actual and projected sales are:

| | |
|---|---|
| April, actual . . . . . . . | $230,400 |
| May, actual . . . . . . . | 172,800 |
| June, estimated . . . . . | 288,000 |
| July, estimated . . . . . | 230,400 |
| August, estimated . . . . | 207,360 |

Experience has shown that 50% of the billings are collected in the month of sale, 30% in the second month, 15% in the third month, and 5% will prove to be uncollectible.

All purchases are payable within 15 days. Thus, approximately 50% of the purchases in a month are due and payable in the next month. The unit purchase cost is $25. Fasbinder Company's management had established a policy of maintaining an end-of-month inventory of 350 units plus 50% of the next month's unit sales, and the June 1 inventory is consistent with this policy.

Selling and general administrative expenses (excluding depreciation) for the year amount to $518,400 and are distributed evenly throughout the year.

*Required*

Prepare a monthly cash budget for June and July, with supporting schedules showing cash receipts from collections of receivables and cash payments for merchandise purchases.

**Problem 25–4**
**Preparation and evaluation of budgeted income statements**
(L. O. 4)

Dolington Company buys merchandise at $26.10 per unit and sells it at $45 per unit. Sales personnel are paid a commission of 10% of sales. The June 1991 income statement of Dolington Company is as follows:

**DOLINGTON COMPANY**
**Income Statement**
**For June 1991**

| | |
|---|---|
| Sales | $450,000 |
| Cost of goods sold | 261,000 |
| Gross profit | $189,000 |
| Expenses: | |
| Sales commissions | $ 45,000 |
| Advertising | 27,000 |
| Store rent | 9,000 |
| Administrative salaries | 18,000 |
| Depreciation expense | 4,500 |
| Other expenses | 13,500 |
| Total | $117,000 |
| Net income | $ 72,000 |

The management of Dolington Company expects the June results to be repeated during July, August, and September. However, certain changes are being considered. Management believes that if selling price is reduced to $40 and advertising expenses are increased by 50%, unit sales will increase at a rate of 10% each month during the third quarter of 1991. If these changes are made, merchandise will still be purchased at $26.10 per unit. Sales personnel will continue to earn a commission of 10%, and the remaining expenses will remain constant.

*Required*

Prepare a budgeted income statement that shows in three columns the planned results of operations for July, August, and September 1991, assuming the changes are implemented. Based on the budgeted income statement, decide whether management should make the changes.

**Problem 25–5**
**Preparing a complete master budget**
(L. O. 2, 3, 4)

Shortly before the end of 1990, the management of Quotz Corporation prepared a budgeted balance sheet for December 31, 1990, which is presented on the next page.

**QUOTZ CORPORATION**
**Budgeted Balance Sheet**
**For December 31, 1990**

| | | | |
|---|---|---|---|
| Cash | $ 36,000 | Accounts payable | $ 60,000 |
| Accounts receivable | 112,500 | Loan from bank | 36,000 |
| Inventory | 187,500 | Taxes payable (due March 15, 1991) | 90,000 |
| Equipment | 450,000 | Common stock | 375,000 |
| Accumulated depreciation | (45,000) | Retained earnings | 180,000 |
| Total | $741,000 | Total | $741,000 |

In the process of preparing a master budget for January, February, and March 1991, the following information has been obtained:

*a.* The product sold by Quotz Corporation is purchased for $10 per unit and resold for $15 per unit. Although the inventory level on December 31 (18,750 units) is smaller than desired, management has established a new inventory policy for 1991 whereby the end-of-month inventory should be 80% of the next month's expected sales (in units). Budgeted unit sales are: January, 75,000; February, 67,500; March, 90,000; and April, 90,000.

*b.* Total sales each month are 50% for cash and 50% on account. Of the credit sales, 80% are collected in the first month after the sale and 20% in the second month after the sale. Similarly, 80% of the Accounts Receivable balance on December 31, 1990, should be collected during January, and 20% should be collected in February.

*c.* Merchandise purchased by the company is paid for as follows: 70% in the month after purchase, and 30% in the second month after purchase. Similarly, 70% of the Accounts Payable balance on December 31, 1990, will be paid during January, and 30% will be paid during February.

*d.* Sales commissions amounting to 10% of sales are paid each month. Additionally, the salary of the sales manager is $90,000 per year.

*e.* Repair expenses amount to $3,750 per month and are paid in cash. General and administrative salaries amount to $810,000 per year.

*f.* The equipment shown in the December 31, 1990, balance sheet was purchased one year ago. It is being depreciated over 10 years according to the straight-line method. Regarding new purchases of equipment, management has decided to take a full month's depreciation during the month the equipment is purchased, and to use straight-line depreciation over 10 years, assuming no salvage value. The company plans to purchase additional equipment worth $82,800 in January, $43,200 in February, and $108,000 in March.

*g.* The company plans to acquire some land in March at a cost of $750,000. The land will not require a cash outlay until the last day of March. Thus, if a bank loan is necessary, the first payment of interest will be due at the end of April.

*h.* Quotz Corporation has an arrangement with the bank whereby additional loans are available as they are needed at a rate of 12% per year, paid monthly. If part or all of a loan is repaid during a month, the payment will be made on the last day of the month, along with any interest that is due. Quotz Corporation has agreed to maintain an end-of-month cash balance of at least $36,000.

*i.* The income tax rate applicable to the company is 40%. However, tax on the income for the first quarter of 1991 will not be paid until April.

*Required*

Prepare a master budget for the first quarter of 1991, with the operating budgets, capital expenditures budget, and the cash budget prepared on a monthly basis. The budgeted income statement should show operations for the first quarter, and the budgeted balance sheet should be prepared as of March 31, 1991. The operating budgets included in the master budget should include a sales budget (showing both budgeted unit sales and dollar sales), a merchandise purchases budget, a selling expense budget, and a general and administrative expense budget. (Round all amounts to the nearest dollar.)

## Alternate Problems

**Problem 25–1A**
**Production budget and merchandise purchases budget**
(L. O. 3)

Urtone Corporation sells three products that it purchases in their finished ready-for-sale state. The company's May 31 inventories are Product X, 23,400 units; Product Y, 22,550 units; and Product Z, 37,800 units. The company's management is disturbed because each product's May 31 inventory is excessive in relation to immediately expected sales. Consequently, management has set as a goal a month-end inventory for each product that is equal to one half the following month's expected sales. Expected sales in units for June, July, August, and September are as follows:

| | Expected Sales in Units | | | |
|---|---|---|---|---|
| | June | July | August | September |
| Product X . . . . | 30,000 | 27,600 | 30,000 | 22,800 |
| Product Y . . . . | 16,800 | 16,800 | 20,400 | 21,600 |
| Product Z . . . . | 36,000 | 32,400 | 31,200 | 34,800 |

*Required*

Prepare purchases budgets in units for the three products for June, July, and August 1991.

**Problem 25–2A**
**Sequential cash budgets for three months**
(L. O. 3)

Carlo Company expects to have a $26,100 cash balance on December 31, 1990. It also expects to have a $158,400 balance of accounts receivable and $94,050 of accounts payable. Its budgeted sales, purchases, and cash expenditures for the first three months of 1991 are:

| | January | February | March |
|---|---|---|---|
| Sales . . . . . . . . . . . . . . . . . | $108,000 | $81,000 | $121,500 |
| Purchases . . . . . . . . . . . . . . . | 63,000 | 77,850 | 81,000 |
| Payroll . . . . . . . . . . . . . . . . | 10,800 | 10,800 | 12,600 |
| Rent . . . . . . . . . . . . . . . . . | 4,500 | 4,500 | 4,500 |
| Other cash expenses . . . . . . . . . | 5,400 | 7,200 | 6,300 |
| Purchase of store equipment . . . . . | — | 22,500 | — |
| Payment of quarterly dividend . . . . | — | — | 18,000 |

All sales are on account; and past experience indicates that 85% will be collected in the month following the sale, 10% in the next month, and 4% in the third month. Notwithstanding these expectations for future sales, an analysis of the December 31 accounts receivable balance indicates that $126,000 of the $158,400 balance will be collected in January, $23,400 in February, and $7,200 in March.

Purchases of merchandise on account are paid in the month following each purchase; likewise, the store equipment will be paid for in the month following its purchase.

*Required*

Prepare cash budgets for the months of January, February, and March 1991.

**Problem 25–3A**
**Cash budgets with supporting schedules**
(L. O. 3)

The actual and projected monthly sales of Coster Company are as follows:

| | |
|---|---|
| September 1991, actual . . . . . . | $576,000 |
| October 1991, actual . . . . . . . | 384,000 |
| November 1991, estimated . . . . | 456,000 |
| December 1991, estimated . . . . | 552,000 |
| January 1992, estimated . . . . . | 504,000 |

Experience has shown that 40% of the sales are collected in the month of sale, 40% are collected in the first month after the sale, 18% in the second month after the sale, and 2% prove to be uncollectible.

Approximately one fourth of the merchandise purchased by Coster Company is paid for during the month of purchase. The remaining three fourths is paid in the following month. Coster Company pays $25 per unit of merchandise and subsequently sells the merchandise for $50 per unit. The company always plans to maintain an end-of-month inventory of 750 units plus 60% of the next month's unit sales, and the October 31, 1991, inventory is consistent with this policy.

In addition to cost of goods sold, Coster Company incurs other operating expenses (excluding depreciation) of $1,396,800 per year, and they are distributed evenly throughout the year. On October 31, 1991, the company has a cash balance of $96,000.

*Required*

Prepare a monthly cash budget for November and December, with supporting schedules showing cash receipts from collections of receivables and cash payments for merchandise purchases.

**Problem 25–4A**
**Preparation and evaluation of budgeted income statements**
(L. O. 4)

Exelle Company buys merchandise at $50 per unit and sells it at $90 per unit. Sales personnel are paid a commission of 8% of sales. The management of Exelle Company expects the September results to be repeated during October, November, and December. However, certain changes are being considered. Management believes that if selling price is reduced to $80 and advertising expenses are increased by 40%, unit sales will increase at a rate of 10% each month during the fourth quarter of 1991. If these changes are made, merchandise will still be purchased at $55 per unit. Sales personnel will continue to earn a commission of 8% (rounded to the nearest whole dollar), and the remaining expenses will remain constant.

The September 1991 income statement of Exelle Company is as follows:

**EXELLE COMPANY**
**Income Statement**
**For September 1991**

| | | |
|---|---|---|
| Sales | | $810,000 |
| Cost of goods sold | | 450,000 |
| Gross profit | | $360,000 |
| Expenses: | | |
| Sales commissions | $ 64,800 | |
| Advertising | 57,600 | |
| Store rent | 18,000 | |
| Administrative salaries | 21,600 | |
| Depreciation expense | 10,800 | |
| Other expenses | 27,000 | |
| Total | $199,800 | |
| Net income | $160,200 | |

*Required*

Prepare a budgeted income statement that shows in three columns the planned results of operations for October, November, and December 1991, assuming the changes are implemented. Based on the budgeted income statement, decide whether management should make the changes.

**Problem 25–5A**
**Preparing a complete master budget**
(L. O. 2, 3, 4)

During March 1991, Carlon Corporation's management prepared a budgeted balance sheet for March 31, 1991, as follows:

**CARLON CORPORATION**
**Budgeted Balance Sheet**
**For March 31, 1991**

| | | | |
|---|---|---|---|
| Cash | $ 18,000 | Accounts payable | $ 28,800 |
| Accounts receivable | 54,000 | Loan from bank | 18,000 |
| Inventory | 90,000 | Taxes payable (due June 15, 1991) | 43,200 |
| Equipment | 216,000 | Common stock | 180,000 |
| Accumulated depreciation | (21,600) | Retained earnings | 86,400 |
| Total | $356,400 | Total | $356,400 |

In the process of preparing a master budget for April, May, and June 1991, the following information has been obtained:

*a.* The product sold by Carlon Corporation is purchased for $10 per unit and resold for $15 per unit. Although the inventory level on March 31, 1991 (9,000 units), is smaller than desired, management has established a new inventory policy whereby the end-of-month inventory should be 80% of the next month's expected sales (in units). Budgeted unit sales are: April, 36,000; May, 32,400; June, 43,200; and July, 43,200.

*b.* Total sales each month are 50% for cash and 50% on account. Of the credit sales, 80% are collected in the first month after the sale, and 20% in the second month after the sale. Similarly, 80% of the Accounts Receivable balance on March 31 should be collected during April, and 20% should be collected in May.

*c.* Merchandise purchased by the company is paid for as follows: 70% in the month after purchase, and 30% in the second month after purchase. Similarly, 70% of the Accounts Payable balance on March 31 will be paid during April, and 30% will be paid during May.

*d.* Sales commissions amounting to 10% of sales are paid each month. Additionally, the salary of the sales manager is $43,200 per year.

*e.* Repair expenses amount to $1,800 per month and are paid in cash. General administrative salaries amount to $388,800 per year.

*f.* The equipment shown in the March 31, 1991, balance sheet was purchased one year ago. It is being depreciated over 10 years according to the straight-line method. Regarding new purchases of equipment, management has decided to take a full month's depreciation (rounded to the nearest dollar) during the month the equipment is purchased, and to use straight-line depreciation over 10 years, assuming no salvage value. The company plans to purchase additional equipment worth $36,000 in April, $18,000 in May, and $54,000 in June. Capital Exp

*g.* The company plans to acquire some land in June at a cost of $360,000. The land will not require a cash outlay until the last day of June. Thus, if a bank loan is necessary, the first payment of interest will be due at the end of July. Capital Budget

*h.* Carlon Corporation has an arrangement with the bank whereby additional loans are available as they are needed at a rate of 10% per year, paid monthly. If part or all of a loan is repaid during a month, the payment will be made on the last day of the month, along with any interest that is due. Carlon Corporation has agreed to maintain an end-of-month cash balance of at least $18,000. Cash Budget

*i.* The income tax rate applicable to the company is 40%. However, tax on the income for the second quarter of 1991 will not be paid until July.

*Required*

Prepare a master budget for the second quarter of 1991, with the operating budgets, capital expenditures budget, and the cash budget prepared on a monthly basis. The budgeted income statement should show operations for the second quarter, and the budgeted balance sheet should be prepared as of June 30, 1991. The operating budgets included in the master budget should include a sales budget (showing both budgeted unit sales and dollar sales), a merchandise purchases budget, a selling expense budget, and a general and administrative expense budget. (Round all amounts to the nearest dollar.)

## Provocative Problems

**Provocative Problem 25–1**
**Nanook Company**
(L. O. 3)

Nanook Company produces a Product N that requires 5 pounds of Enilate per unit of N. The owner of Nanook Company is in the process of negotiating with the bank for the approval to make loans as they are needed by the company. One of the important items in their discussion has been the question of how much cash will be needed to pay for purchases of Enilate. Nanook Company purchases Enilate on account, and the resulting payables are paid in cash as follows: 75% during the month after purchase, and 25% during the second month after purchase. The company plans to manufacture enough units of N to maintain an end-of-month inventory of finished units equal to 80% of the next month's sales, and enough Enilate is purchased each month to maintain an end-of-month inventory equal to 60% of the next month's production requirements. During 1991, budgeted sales (in units) are as follows: June, 9,000; July, 10,000; August, 11,000; and September, 14,000. On May 31, 1991, the following data are available: finished units of Product N on hand, 7,500; pounds of Enilate on hand, 35,400; and Accounts Payable, $220,000 due in June plus $50,000 due in July.

In recent months, the price of Enilate has varied substantially, and the owner estimates that during the next few months the price could range from $7 to $12 per pound. You are asked to assist the owner by estimating the cash payments to be made in June, in July, and in August. In preparing your answer, you should prepare separate estimates based on a $7 price and a $12 price.

**Provocative Problem 25–2**
**Inray Corporation**
(L. O. 3)

The Inray Corporation has budgeted the following monthly sales volumes: February, 21,000 units; March, 7,000 units; April, 10,000 units; and May, 16,000 units. The company policy is to maintain an end-of-month finished goods inventory equal to 3,000 units plus 25% of the next month's budgeted sales in units. However, the February 1 inventory was 8,000 units.

An analysis of Inray Corporation's manufacturing costs show the following:

| | |
|---|---|
| Material cost per unit | $25.50 |
| Direct labor cost per unit | $19.00 |
| Fixed manufacturing overhead costs | $40,000 per month |
| Variable manufacturing overhead costs | $9.50 per unit manufactured |

*Required*

Prepare production budgets and manufacturing budgets for the months of February, March, and April.

# 26 Flexible Budgets; Standard Costs

In the last chapter, you learned how budgeting serves to organize and formalize the planning function of management. You also learned that budgets can provide a basis for evaluating actual performance. In this chapter, we look more closely at the use of budgeted data in the process of evaluating performance. Evaluations of this nature are an important step in the process of controlling business operations. Thus, as you study this chapter, you will learn how accounting contributes to the fulfillment of management's control responsibility.

**Learning Objectives**

*After studying Chapter 26, you should be able to:*

1. Describe the differences between and relative advantages of fixed budgets and flexible budgets and be able to prepare a flexible budget.
2. State what standard costs represent, how they are determined, and how they are used by management to evaluate performance.
3. Calculate material, labor, and overhead variances, and state what each variance indicates about the performance of a company.
4. Explain the relevance of standard cost accounting to the management philosophy known as management by exception.
5. Prepare entries to record standard costs and to account for price and quantity variances.
6. Define or explain the words and phrases listed in the chapter Glossary.

## Fixed Budgets and Performance Reports

Describe the differences between and relative advantages of fixed budgets and flexible budgets and be able to prepare a flexible budget. (L. O. 1)

As explained in Chapter 25, the initial step in preparing a master budget is to determine the expected sales volume for the budget period. Then, all of the budgets in the master budget are based on this specific estimate of sales volume. In other words, the estimated amount of each cost is based on the assumption that a specific or fixed amount of sales will take place. When a budget is based on a single estimate of sales or production volume, the budget is called a **fixed** or **static budget.** In budgeting the total amount of each cost, a fixed budget gives no consideration to the possibility that the actual sales or production volume may be different from the fixed or budgeted amount.

You will recall from Chapter 25 that an advantage of a budget is that it provides a basis for comparing actual accomplishments with what was planned. This comparison is often presented in a **performance report** like the one in Illustration 26–1. This particular report is based on a fixed budget. Note that the performance report compares budgeted and actual performance and designates the differences as variances.

In Illustration 26–1, the budgeted sales volume of Tampa Manufacturing Company is 10,000 units. In this example, we also assume that production volume is equal to sales volume so that the amount of inventory maintained by the company does not change. In evaluating Tampa Manufacturing Company's operations, management is likely to ask a variety of questions such as the following:

Why is the actual income from operations $13,400 higher than the budgeted amount?

Are the prices being paid for each expense item too high?

Is the manufacturing department using too much direct material?

Is it using too much direct labor?

The performance report in Illustration 26–1 provides little help in answering questions such as these. Since the actual sales volume was 2,000 units higher than the budgeted amount, you might assume that this increase caused total dollar sales and many of the expenses to be higher. But other factors may also have influenced the amount of income. The problem with the fixed budget performance report is that it fails to show whether actual costs were out of line, given the fact that sales volume was 2,000 units higher than the budgeted amount. The report really does not provide management much information beyond the fact that the sales volume was higher than budgeted.

# FLEXIBLE BUDGETS

To help answer questions such as those mentioned above, many companies prepare **flexible** or **variable budgets.** In contrast to fixed budgets which are based on one expected amount of budgeted sales or production, flexible budgets recognize that different levels of activity should produce different amounts of cost. As a result, the comparisons of actual with planned performance direct management's attention toward the reasons why overall results differed from the plan.

**Illustration 26–1**
**A performance report based on a fixed budget**

TAMPA MANUFACTURING COMPANY
Performance Report
For Month Ended November 30, 1991

| | Fixed Budget | Actual Performance | Variances |
|---|---|---|---|
| Sales: In units | 10,000 | 12,000 | |
| In dollars | $100,000 | $125,000 | $25,000 F |
| Cost of goods sold: | | | |
| Direct materials | $ 10,000 | $ 13,000 | $ 3,000 U |
| Direct labor | 15,000 | 20,000 | 5,000 U |
| Overhead: | | | |
| Factory supplies | 2,000 | 2,100 | 100 U |
| Utilities | 3,000 | 4,000 | 1,000 U |
| Depreciation of machinery | 8,000 | 8,000 | |
| Supervisory salaries | 11,000 | 11,000 | |
| Selling expenses: | | | |
| Sales commissions | 9,000 | 10,800 | 1,800 U |
| Shipping expenses | 4,000 | 4,300 | 300 U |
| General and administrative expenses: | | | |
| Office supplies | 5,000 | 5,200 | 200 U |
| Insurance expense | 1,000 | 1,200 | 200 U |
| Depreciation of office equipment | 7,000 | 7,000 | |
| Administrative salaries | 13,000 | 13,000 | |
| Total expenses | $ 88,000 | $ 99,600 | $11,600 U |
| Income from operations | $ 12,000 | $ 25,400 | $13,400 F |

F = Favorable variance; that is, compared to the budget, the actual cost or revenue contributes to a higher income.
U = Unfavorable variance; that is, compared to the budget, the actual cost or revenue contributes to a lower income.

## Preparing a Flexible Budget

To prepare a flexible budget, you must examine each type of cost and determine whether it should be classified as a variable cost or as a fixed cost. Recall from Chapter 24 that the total amount of a variable cost changes in direct proportion to a change in the level of activity. Thus, variable cost per unit of activity remains constant. On the other hand, the total amount of a fixed cost remains unchanged regardless of changes in the level of activity (within the relevant or normal operating range of activity).[1]

After each cost item is classified as variable or fixed, each variable cost is expressed as a constant amount of cost per unit of sales (or per sales dollar). In contrast, the budgeted amount of each fixed cost is expressed as the total amount that is expected regardless of the sales volume that may occur within the relevant range.

Illustration 26–2 shows how the fixed budget of Tampa Manufacturing Company can be restated as a flexible budget. Compare the first column of

[1] In Chapter 24, we recognized that some costs are neither strictly variable nor strictly fixed. However, in the present discussion, we assume that all costs can be reasonably classified as being either variable or fixed.

**Illustration 26–2**
**Converting a fixed budget to a flexible budget**

TAMPA MANUFACTURING COMPANY
Fixed and Flexible Budgets
For Month Ended November 30, 1991

| | Reorganized Fixed Budget | Flexible Budget: Variable Cost per Unit | Flexible Budget: Total Fixed Cost | Flexible Budget for Unit Sales of 12,000 | Flexible Budget for Unit Sales of 14,000 |
|---|---|---|---|---|---|
| Sales: In units | 10,000 | | | 12,000 | 14,000 |
| In dollars | $100,000 | $10.00 | | $120,000 | $140,000 |
| Variable costs: | | | | | |
| Direct materials | $ 10,000 | $ 1.00 | | $ 12,000 | $ 14,000 |
| Direct labor | 15,000 | 1.50 | | 18,000 | 21,000 |
| Factory supplies | 2,000 | 0.20 | | 2,400 | 2,800 |
| Utilities | 3,000 | 0.30 | | 3,600 | 4,200 |
| Sales commissions | 9,000 | 0.90 | | 10,800 | 12,600 |
| Shipping expenses | 4,000 | 0.40 | | 4,800 | 5,600 |
| Office supplies | 5,000 | 0.50 | | 6,000 | 7,000 |
| Total variable costs | $ 48,000 | $ 4.80 | | $ 57,600 | $ 67,200 |
| Contribution margin | $ 52,000 | $ 5.20 | | $ 62,400 | $ 72,800 |
| Fixed costs: | | | | | |
| Depreciation of machinery | $ 8,000 | | $ 8,000 | $ 8,000 | $ 8,000 |
| Supervisory salaries | 11,000 | | 11,000 | 11,000 | 11,000 |
| Insurance expense | 1,000 | | 1,000 | 1,000 | 1,000 |
| Depreciation of office equipment | 7,000 | | 7,000 | 7,000 | 7,000 |
| Administrative salaries | 13,000 | | 13,000 | 13,000 | 13,000 |
| Total fixed costs | $ 40,000 | | $40,000 | $ 40,000 | $ 40,000 |
| Income from operations | $ 12,000 | | | $ 22,400 | $ 32,800 |

Illustration 26–2 with the first column of Illustration 26–1. Notice that seven of the expenses have been reclassified as variable costs. The remaining five expenses have been reclassified as fixed costs. This classification results from an investigation of each expense incurred by Tampa Manufacturing Company. However, do not misinterpret this classification. It does not mean that these particular expenses are always variable costs in every company. For example, depending on the nature of the company's operations, office supplies expense may be a fixed cost or a variable cost. Nevertheless, in the present example, we assume that Tampa Manufacturing Company's accountant investigated this item and concluded that the cost of office supplies behaves as a variable cost.

Notice that when a fixed budget is reorganized as in Illustration 26–2, the variable costs of Tampa Manufacturing Company are listed after sales, then totaled and subtracted from sales. As you learned in Chapter 24, the difference between sales and variable costs is identified as the contribution margin. The budgeted amounts of fixed costs are then listed and totaled.

In Illustration 26–2, the second and third columns of numbers show the flexible budget amounts that can be applied to any volume of sales within the relevant range. The other columns merely illustrate what form the flexible budget takes when the budget amounts are applied to particular sales volumes.

Recall from Illustration 26–1 that Tampa Manufacturing Company's actual sales volume for November was 12,000 units. This was 2,000 units more than the 10,000 units originally forecasted in the master budget. The effect of this sales increase on the income from operations can be determined by comparing the budget for 10,000 units with the budget for 12,000 units (see column 1 and column 4 of Illustration 26–2).

At a sales volume of 12,000 units, the budgeted income from operations is $22,400, whereas the budget for sales of 10,000 units shows income from operations of $12,000. Thus, if sales volume is 12,000 rather than 10,000 units, management should expect income from operations to be higher by $10,400 ($22,400 − $12,000). In other words, the difference between the $25,400 actual income from operations (see Illustration 26–1) and the $12,000 income from operations shown on the fixed master budget can be analyzed as follows:

| | | |
|---|---|---|
| Actual income from operations (12,000 units) | | $ 25,400 |
| Income from operations on master budget (10,000 units) | | 12,000 |
| Difference to be explained | | $ 13,400 |
| Income from operations: | | |
| On the flexible budget for 12,000 units | $22,400 | |
| On the budget for 10,000 units | 12,000 | |
| Additional income caused by increase in sales volume | | (10,400) |
| Unexplained difference | | $ 3,000 |

This $3,000 unexplained difference is the amount by which the actual income from operations exceeds budgeted income from operations as shown on the flexible budget for a sales volume of 12,000 units. As management seeks to determine what steps should be taken to control Tampa Manufacturing Company's operations, the next step is to determine what caused this $3,000 unexplained difference. Information to help answer this question is provided by a flexible budget performance report.

## Flexible Budget Performance Report

A **flexible budget performance report** is designed to analyze the difference between actual performance and budgeted performance, where the budgeted amounts are based on the actual sales volume or level of activity. The report should direct management's attention toward those particular costs or revenues where actual performance has differed substantially from the budgeted amount.

Illustration 26–3 shows the flexible budget performance report for Tampa Manufacturing Company. Observe in Illustration 26–3 the $5,000 favorable variance in total dollar sales. Since the actual number of units sold amounted to 12,000 and the budget was also based on unit sales of 12,000, the $5,000 variance must have resulted entirely from a difference between the average price per unit and the budgeted price per unit. Further analysis of the $5,000 variance is as follows:

**Illustration 26–3**

**TAMPA MANUFACTURING COMPANY**
**Flexible Budget Performance Report**
**For Month Ended November 30, 1991**

| | Flexible Budget | Actual Performance | Variances |
|---|---|---|---|
| Sales (12,000 units) | $120,000 | $125,000 | $5,000 F |
| Variable costs: | | | |
| Direct materials | $ 12,000 | $ 13,000 | $1,000 U |
| Direct labor | 18,000 | 20,000 | 2,000 U |
| Factory supplies | 2,400 | 2,100 | 300 F |
| Utilities | 3,600 | 4,000 | 400 U |
| Sales commissions | 10,800 | 10,800 | |
| Shipping expenses | 4,800 | 4,300 | 500 F |
| Office supplies | 6,000 | 5,200 | 800 F |
| Total variable costs | $ 57,600 | $ 59,400 | $1,800 U |
| Contribution margin | $ 62,400 | $ 65,600 | $3,200 F |
| Fixed costs: | | | |
| Depreciation of machinery | $ 8,000 | $ 8,000 | |
| Supervisory salaries | 11,000 | 11,000 | |
| Insurance expense | 1,000 | 1,200 | $ 200 U |
| Depreciation of office equipment | 7,000 | 7,000 | |
| Administrative salaries | 13,000 | 13,000 | |
| Total fixed costs | $ 40,000 | $ 40,200 | $ 200 U |
| Income from operations | $ 22,400 | $ 25,400 | $3,000 F |

F = Favorable variance; that is, compared to the budget, the actual cost or revenue contributes to a higher income.
U = Unfavorable variance; that is, compared to the budget, the actual cost or revenue contributes to a lower income.

| | |
|---|---|
| Average price per unit, actual | $125,000 ÷ 12,000 = $10.42 |
| Budgeted price per unit | $120,000 ÷ 12,000 = 10.00 |
| Favorable variance in price per unit | $ 5,000 ÷ 12,000 = $ 0.42 |

The variances in Illustration 26–3 direct management's attention toward the areas in which corrective action may be necessary to control Tampa Manufacturing Company's operations. In addition, you should recognize that each of the cost variances can be analyzed in a manner similar to the above discussion of sales. Each of the expenses can be thought of as involving the use of a given number of units of the expense item, and paying a specific price per unit. Following this approach, the cost variances shown in Illustration 26–3 might result in part from a difference between the actual price per unit and the budgeted price per unit (a **price variance**); and they may also result in part from a difference between the actual number of units used and the budgeted number of units to be used (a **quantity variance**). You will learn more about this type of analysis, which is called **variance analysis**, in the following section on standard costs.

## STANDARD COSTS

State what standard costs represent, how they are determined, and how they are used by management to evaluate performance. (L. O. 2)

In Chapter 22, you learned that there are two basic types of manufacturing cost systems, job order and process. You may recall, however, we recognized the fact that many different variations of these two basic types are used in the business world. One important variation that many companies use is a *standard cost system,* one based on *standard* or *budgeted costs*.

The costs that we discussed in Chapter 22 are **historical costs.** In other words, they are the dollar amounts of consideration that were given by the business in past transactions. Such historical (or actual) costs provide useful information for some purposes, but to judge whether or not they are reasonable or excessive, management needs a basis of comparison. **Standard costs** offer such a basis.

Standard costs are the costs that should be incurred under normal conditions to produce a given product or part or to perform a particular service. Standard costs are established by means of engineering and accounting studies based on past experience and other data. Then, after they are established, standard costs are used to judge the reasonableness of the actual (historical) costs incurred when the product or service is produced during the current period. When actual costs vary from standard, management can use that information to identify possible problems and take corrective actions.

Since standard costs are the amounts that should be incurred under normal conditions, they are the amounts that are used in preparing budgets. Thus, standard costs are budgeted costs, and terms such as *standard material cost, standard labor cost,* and *standard overhead cost* refer to the amounts budgeted for direct materials, direct labor, and overhead.

### Establishing Standard Costs

The combined efforts of people in accounting, engineering, personnel administration, and other management areas are required to establish standard costs. Time and motion studies are made of each labor operation in a product's production or in performing a service. From these studies, management learns the best way to perform the operation and the standard labor time required under normal conditions for performance. Exhaustive investigations are commonly made of the quantity, grade, and cost of each material required; and machines and other productive equipment are subject to detailed studies in an effort to achieve maximum efficiencies and to learn what costs should be.

Regardless of the care exercised in establishing standard costs and in revising them as conditions change, actual costs incurred in producing a given product or service commonly differ from standard costs. When this occurs, the difference may result from more than one factor. For example, the quantity of the material used may have differed from standard and the price paid per unit of material also may have differed from standard. Similar quantity and price differences from standard amounts might occur with respect to labor cost. Also, the labor time and/or the labor price may have varied. Later in the chapter, you will learn about factors that may cause actual overhead cost to differ from standard.

## Variances

Calculate material, labor, and overhead variances, and state what each variance indicates about the performance of a company.
(L. O. 3)

When actual costs vary from standard costs, the differences are called **cost variances.** Variances may be favorable or unfavorable. A variance is favorable if actual cost is below standard cost, and it is unfavorable if actual cost is above standard.

When a cost variance occurs, you should examine the variance to determine the factors that may have caused it. When this is done, management may be able to identify who has responsibility for the variance and take corrective actions. For example, assume the standard direct material cost for producing 2,000 units of Product A is $800, but material that cost $840 was used in producing the units. The $40 variance may have resulted from paying a price for the material that was higher than the standard price; or, a greater quantity of material than standard may have been used; or, there may have been some combination of these causes.

The price paid for a material usually is a responsibility of the purchasing department. Therefore, if the variance was caused by a price greater than standard, responsibility normally rests with the purchasing department. On the other hand, the production department is usually responsible for the amount of material used. Thus, if a quantity greater than standard was used, responsibility normally rests with the production department. However, more than a standard amount of material may have been used because the quality of the material purchased was below standard, causing more than a normal waste. In this case, responsibility is back on the purchasing department for buying material of substandard quality.

### Isolating Material and Labor Variances

When a cost variance occurs, you can break the variance into components that give more detailed information about the factors that caused the cost variance to occur. However, before doing so, you should understand that in the case of materials cost or labor cost, the actual cost incurred can be expressed as an equation, as follows:

$$\begin{array}{ccccc} \text{Actual Quantity} & \times & \text{Actual Price} & = & \text{Actual Cost} \\ \text{AQ} & \times & \text{AP} & = & \text{AC} \end{array}$$

Also, the standard cost that should have been incurred can be expressed as follows:

$$\begin{array}{ccccc} \text{Standard Quantity} & \times & \text{Standard Price} & = & \text{Standard Cost} \\ \text{SQ} & \times & \text{SP} & = & \text{SC} \end{array}$$

The difference between actual cost and standard cost is the cost variance, as follows:

$$\begin{array}{ccccc} \text{Actual Cost} & - & \text{Standard Cost} & = & \text{Cost Variance} \\ \text{AC} & - & \text{SC} & = & \text{CV} \end{array}$$

As we stated earlier, the cost variance may have been caused by two factors: (1) the actual price may have been different from the standard price and (2) the actual quantity may have been different from the standard quantity. To determine the effects of these two factors, the cost variance can be expressed as the sum of a *quantity variance* and a *price variance*. The quantity variance may be calculated as follows:

$$\text{(Actual Quantity} - \text{Standard Quantity)} \times \text{Standard Price} = \text{Quantity Variance}$$
$$(AQ - SQ) \times SP = QV$$

And the price variance may be calculated as follows:

$$\text{(Actual Price} - \text{Standard Price)} \times \text{Actual Quantity} = \text{Price Variance}$$
$$(AP - SP) \times AQ = PV$$

To illustrate how cost variances are analyzed, the following discussion is based on the example of XL Company. For this example, assume that XL Company has established the following standard costs per unit for its Product Z:

| | |
|---|---|
| Direct materials (1 lb. per unit at $1 per lb.) . . . | $1.00 |
| Direct labor (1 hr. per unit at $6 per hr.) . . . . . | 6.00 |
| Overhead ($2 per standard direct labor hour) . . | 2.00 |
| Total standard cost per unit . . . . . . . . . . . . | $9.00 |

### Material Variances

Assume further that during the month of May, XL Company completed 3,500 units of Product Z, using 3,600 pounds of direct materials that cost $1.05 per pound, a total cost of $3,780. Under these assumptions, the actual and standard direct material costs for the 3,500 units and the direct material cost variance are:

| | |
|---|---|
| Actual cost: 3,600 lbs. @ $1.05 per lb. . . . . . | $3,780 |
| Standard cost: 3,500 lbs. @ $1 per lb. . . . . . | 3,500 |
| Direct material cost variance—unfavorable . . | $ 280 |

This table shows the same information as the equations presented earlier. Thus, for actual cost:

$$AQ \times AP = AC$$
$$3{,}600 \times \$1.05 = \$3{,}780$$

For standard cost:

$$SQ \times SP = SC$$
$$3{,}500 \times \$1.00 = \$3{,}500$$

And the direct material cost variance is:

$$AC - SC = CV$$
$$\$3{,}780 - \$3{,}500 = \$280 \text{ an unfavorable variance}$$

Regardless of which way the information is presented, note that the actual direct material cost for these units is $280 above their standard cost. As indicated by the equations presented earlier, the factors that caused this unfavorable direct material cost variance may be measured by calculating a direct material quantity variance and a direct material price variance. These calculations are presented in tabular form as follows:

| | | |
|---|---|---|
| QUANTITY VARIANCE: | | |
| Actual units at the standard price . . . . . . | 3,600 lbs. @ $1.00 = $3,600 | |
| Standard units at the standard price . . . . . | 3,500 lbs. @ $1.00 = 3,500 | |
| Variance—unfavorable . . . . . . . . . . . . | 100 lbs. @ 1.00 = | $100 |
| PRICE VARIANCE: | | |
| Actual units at the actual price . . . . . . . . | 3,600 lbs. @ $1.05 = $3,780 | |
| Actual units at the standard price . . . . . . | 3,600 lbs. @ $1.00 = 3,600 | |
| Variance—unfavorable . . . . . . . . . . . . | 3,600 lbs. @ 0.05 = | 180 |
| Direct material cost variance—unfavorable . . | | $280 |

Note that the information in this table could be calculated using the equations presented earlier. Thus, for the quantity variance:

$$(AQ - SQ) \times SP = QV$$
$$(3{,}600 - 3{,}500) \times \$1.00 = \$100 \text{ an unfavorable variance}$$

And for the price variance:

$$(AP - SP) \times AQ = PV$$
$$(\$1.05 - \$1.00) \times 3{,}600 = \$180 \text{ an unfavorable variance}$$

Regardless of which way it is presented, the analysis shows that $100 of the excess direct material cost resulted from using 100 more pounds than standard, and $180 resulted from a unit purchase price that was $0.05 above standard. With this information management can go to the responsible individuals for explanations.

## Labor Variances

The labor cost to manufacture a given part or to perform a service depends on the number of hours worked (quantity) and the wage rate paid (price). Therefore, when the labor cost for a task differs from standard, the labor cost variance can be divided into a quantity variance and a price variance, just like we did in the case of a material cost variance.

For example, the direct labor standard for the 3,500 units of Product Z is one hour per unit, or 3,500 hours at $6 per hour. If 3,400 hours that cost $6.30 per hour were used to complete the units, the actual and standard labor costs for these units are:

| | |
|---|---|
| Actual cost: 3,400 hrs. @ $6.30 per hr. . . | $21,420 |
| Standard cost: 3,500 hrs. @ $6.00 per hr. . | 21,000 |
| Direct labor cost variance—unfavorable . . | $ 420 |

In this case, actual cost is only $420 over standard, but isolating the quantity and price variances reveals the following:

| | | |
|---|---|---|
| QUANTITY VARIANCE: | | |
| Actual hours at standard price | 3,400 hrs. @ $6.00=$20,400 | |
| Standard hours at standard price | 3,500 hrs. @ $6.00= 21,000 | |
| Variance—favorable | (100) hrs. @ $6.00= | $ (600) |
| PRICE VARIANCE: | | |
| Actual hours at actual price | 3,400 hrs. @ $6.30=$21,420 | |
| Actual hours at standard price | 3,400 hrs. @ $6.00= 20,400 | |
| Variance—unfavorable | 3,400 hrs. @ $0.30= | 1,020 |
| Direct labor cost variance—unfavorable | | $ 420 |

The information in this table also could be presented with equations. Thus, for the quantity variance:

$$(AQ - SQ) \times SP = QV$$
$$(3{,}400 - 3{,}500) \times \$6.00 = \$-600 \text{ a favorable variance}$$

And for the price variance:

$$(AP - SP) \times AQ = PV$$
$$(\$6.30 - \$6.00) \times 3{,}400 = \$1{,}020 \text{ an unfavorable variance}$$

In this case, the analysis shows a favorable quantity variance of $600, which resulted from using 100 fewer direct labor hours than standard for the units produced. However, this favorable variance was more than offset by a wage rate that was $0.30 above standard.

One possible explanation of these labor variances is the following. When a factory or department has workers of various skill levels, it is the responsibility of the foreman or other supervisor to assign to each task a worker or workers with the appropriate skill level to accomplish the task. In this case, an investigation might reveal that workers of a higher skill level were used to produce the 3,500 units of Product Z. Hence, fewer labor hours were required for the work. However, because the workers were of a higher skill level, the wage rate paid to them was higher than standard.

## Charging Overhead to Production

When standard costs are used, the predetermined overhead rate that is used to assign overhead cost to production is designed so that the standard overhead costs are assigned to production. The rate may be based on the relationship between standard overhead and standard labor cost, or standard labor hours, or standard machine-hours, or some other measure of production. For example, XL Company charges its Product Z with $2 of overhead per standard direct labor hour. Therefore, since the direct labor standard for Product Z is one hour per unit, the 3,500 units manufactured in May were charged with $7,000 of overhead.

Before going on, recall that only 3,400 actual direct labor hours were used in producing these units. Then, note again that overhead is charged to the units on the basis of standard labor hours, not on the basis of actual labor hours. Standard labor hours are used because the amount of overhead charged to these units should not be less than standard simply because less than the standard (normal) amount of labor was used in their production. In other words, overhead should not vary from normal simply because labor varied from normal.

Illustration 26–4

**XL COMPANY**
**Flexible Overhead Costs Budget**
**For Month Ended May 31, 1991**

| | Budget Amounts | Production Levels | | | |
|---|---|---|---|---|---|
| | | 70% | 80% | 90% | 100% |
| Production in units | 1 unit | 3,500 | 4,000 | 4,500 | 5,000 |
| Standard direct labor hours | | 3,500 | 4,000 | 4,500 | 5,000 |
| Budgeted factory overhead: | | | | | |
| Variable costs: | | | | | |
| Indirect labor | $ 0.40 | $ 1,400 | $ 1,600 | $ 1,800 | $ 2,000 |
| Indirect materials | 0.30 | 1,050 | 1,200 | 1,350 | 1,500 |
| Power lights | 0.20 | 700 | 800 | 900 | 1,000 |
| Maintenance | 0.10 | 350 | 400 | 450 | 500 |
| Totals | $ 1.00 | $ 3,500 | $ 4,000 | $ 4,500 | $ 5,000 |
| Fixed costs: | | | | | |
| Building rent | $1,000 | $ 1,000 | $ 1,000 | $ 1,000 | $ 1,000 |
| Depreciation, machinery | 1,200 | 1,200 | 1,200 | 1,200 | 1,200 |
| Supervisory salaries | 1,800 | 1,800 | 1,800 | 1,800 | 1,800 |
| Totals | $4,000 | $ 4,000 | $ 4,000 | $ 4,000 | $ 4,000 |
| Total factory overhead | | $ 7,500 | $ 8,000 | $ 8,500 | $ 9,000 |
| Overhead rate per direct labor hour | | $2.1429 | $2.0000 | $1.8889 | $1.8000 |

↑ Expected production level during May (80%)

### Establishing Overhead Standards

A variable or flexible factory overhead budget is the starting point in establishing reasonable standards for overhead costs. A flexible budget is necessary because the actual production level may vary from the expected level. When this happens, certain costs vary with production, but others remain fixed. You can see this by examining XL Company's flexible overhead costs budget shown in Illustration 26–4.

Observe in Illustration 26–4 that XL Company's flexible budget has been used to establish standard costs for four production levels ranging from 70% to 100% of capacity. When actual costs are known, they should be compared with the standards for the level actually achieved and not with the standards at some other level. For example, if the plant actually operated at 70% capacity during May, actual costs incurred should be compared with standard costs for the 70% level.

In setting overhead standards, after the flexible overhead budget is prepared, management must determine the expected operating level for the plant. This can be 100% of capacity, but more often is something less. Errors in scheduling work, breakdowns, and, perhaps, the inability of the sales force to sell all the product produced are factors that commonly reduce the operating level to some point below full capacity. Also, many companies maintain plant capacity in excess of current operating needs to allow for future growth.

After the flexible budget is set up and the expected operating level is determined, budgeted overhead costs at the expected level are related to, for example, labor hours at this level to establish the standard overhead rate. Thereafter, this predetermined rate is used to apply overhead to production. For example, assume XL Company decided that 80% of capacity is the expected operating level for its plant. With this expectation, the overhead application rate is $2 per direct labor hour. That is, $8,000 of budgeted overhead costs at the 80% level divided by the 4,000 standard direct labor hours required to produce the product manufactured at this level is $2.

## Overhead Variances

Remember that when standard costs are used, overhead is applied to production on the basis of a predetermined standard cost overhead rate. Then, at the end of a cost period the difference between overhead applied and overhead actually incurred is the **overhead cost variance.** This may be expressed as follows:

Actual Overhead Incurred − Standard Overhead Applied = Overhead Cost Variance
AOI − SOA = OCV

In order to help management determine the factors that caused the overhead cost variance, you can divide the overhead cost variance into two components. First, the actual production volume during the period may have been different from the production volume that was expected at the beginning of the period when the standard overhead application rate was established. Second, the overhead costs incurred may have differed from the budgeted overhead at the actual production volume. To determine the effects of these two factors, the overhead cost variance can be expressed as the sum of a **volume variance** and a **controllable variance.**

### Volume Variance

The volume variance is the difference between the amount of overhead budgeted at the actual operating level achieved during the period and the standard amount of overhead charged to production during the period. This may be expressed as follows:

Overhead Budgeted at the Actual Production Volume Achieved − Standard Overhead Applied = Volume Variance
OB − SOA = VV

For example, recall that during May, XL Company actually operated at 70% of capacity. Also, recall that when the predetermined overhead application rate was determined, production volume was expected to be 80% of capacity. The company produced 3,500 units of Product Z, which were charged with overhead at the standard rate. Under this assumption the company's volume variance for May is:

**Illustration 26–5**
**The volume variance**

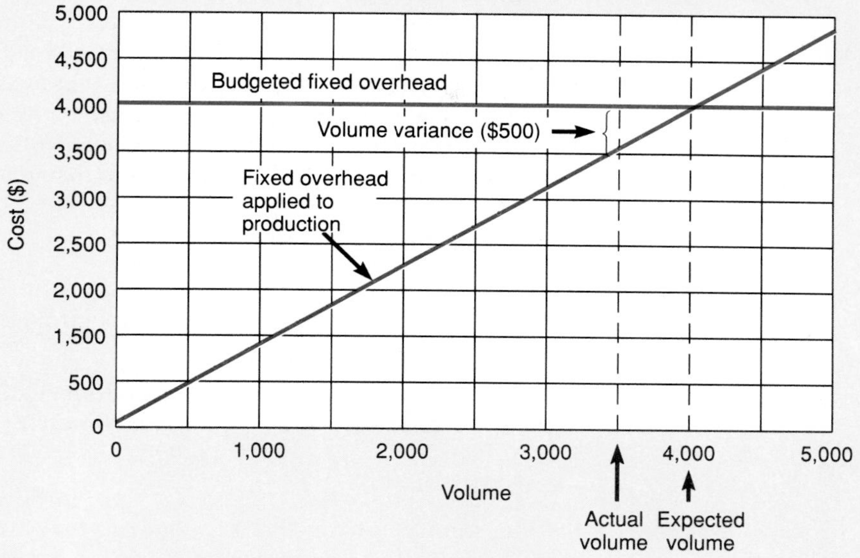


| | |
|---|---|
| VOLUME VARIANCE: | |
| Budgeted overhead at 70% of capacity . . . . . . . . . . . . | $7,500 |
| Standard overhead applied to production (3,500 standard labor hours at the $2 per hour standard rate) . . . . . . . . | 7,000 |
| Variance—unfavorable . . . . . . . . . . . . . . . . . . . . . | $ 500 |

The above table shows the same information as the equation above. That is,

$$OB - SOA = VV$$
$$\$7,500 - \$7,000 = \$500 \text{ an unfavorable variance}$$

To understand why this volume variance occurred, reexamine the flexible budget in Illustration 26–4. Observe that at the 80% level the $2 per hour overhead rate may be subdivided into $1 per hour for variable overhead and $1 per hour for fixed overhead. Furthermore, at the 80% (expected) level, the $1 fixed portion of the rate allocates to production the exact amount of fixed overhead that was budgeted. However, when the $2 overhead rate is applied to production at the 70% level, the $1 portion of the rate that relates to fixed overhead allocates less overhead to production than was budgeted. This is shown graphically in Illustration 26–5.

In Illustration 26–5, you can see that the volume variance resulted simply because the plant did not reach the expected operating level. Budgeted overhead of $500 was not applied to production because the application rate was applied to only 3,500 labor hours when 4,000 hours had been expected.

An unfavorable volume variance tells management that the plant did not reach its normal operating level. You should understand that the variance does not tell management why the production volume was below expectations; that is for management to determine. Machine breakdowns, failure to schedule an even flow of work, or a lack of sales orders are some possible reasons. In any case, the analysis of cost variances never tells management exactly why costs were out of line. It simply directs management's attention toward possible causes. In this case, it directs management in the direction of searching for reasons why production volume was less than expected.

### Controllable Variance

The controllable variance is the difference between overhead actually incurred and the overhead budgeted at the operating level achieved. This may be calculated as follows:

| | | | | |
|---|---|---|---|---|
| Actual Overhead Incurred | − | Overhead Budgeted at the Actual Production Volume Achieved | = | Controllable Variance |
| AOI | − | OB | = | CV |

For example, assume that XL Company incurred $7,650 of overhead during May. Since its plant operated at 70% of capacity during the month, its controllable overhead variance for May is:

| CONTROLLABLE VARIANCE: | |
|---|---|
| Actual overhead incurred . . . . . . . . . . . . . . | $7,650 |
| Overhead budgeted at operating level achieved . . | 7,500 |
| Variance—unfavorable . . . . . . . . . . . . . . . | $ 150 |

The calculation in this table is the same as in the equation above. Thus,

$$\text{AOI} - \text{OB} = \text{CV}$$
$$\$7{,}650 - \$7{,}500 = \$150 \quad \text{an unfavorable variance}$$

The controllable overhead variance measures management's effectiveness in adjusting controllable overhead costs (normally variable overhead) to the operating level achieved. In this case, management failed by $150 to maintain overhead costs at the amount budgeted for the 70% level.

The controllable overhead variance is an indicator of management's overall effectiveness in controlling overhead costs. However, an overhead variance report gives more detailed information about the specific overhead costs that differed from the budgeted amounts. Illustration 26–6 shows the May overhead variance report for XL Company.

### Combining the Volume and Controllable Variances

The volume and controllable variances may be combined to account for the difference between overhead actually incurred and overhead charged to production, as follows:

**Illustration 26–6**

**XL COMPANY**
**Factory Overhead Variance Report**
**For Month Ended May 31, 1991**

VOLUME VARIANCE:

| | |
|---|---|
| Normal production level | 80% of capacity. |
| Production level achieved | 70% of capacity. |
| Volume variance | $500 (unfavorable) |

CONTROLLABLE VARIANCE:

| | Budget | Actual | Favorable | Unfavorable |
|---|---|---|---|---|
| Fixed overhead costs: | | | | |
| Building rent | $1,000 | $1,000 | | |
| Depreciation, machinery | 1,200 | 1,200 | | |
| Supervisory salaries | 1,800 | 1,800 | | |
| Total fixed costs | $4,000 | $4,000 | | |
| Variable overhead costs: | | | | |
| Indirect labor | $1,400 | $1,525 | | $125 |
| Indirect materials | 1,050 | 1,025 | $ 25 | |
| Power and lights | 700 | 750 | | 50 |
| Maintenance | 350 | 350 | | |
| Total variable costs | $3,500 | $3,650 | | |
| Total controllable variances | | | $ 25 | $175 |
| Net controllable variance (unfavorable) | | | 150 | |
| | | | $175 | $175 |

$$\text{Volume Variance} + \text{Controllable Variance} = \text{Overhead Cost Variance}$$
$$VV + CV = OCV$$

For example, XL Company actually incurred $7,650 of overhead during May and charged $7,000 to production, so the overhead cost variance was $650. You can combine the volume variance and the controllable variance in a tabular format to explain this overhead cost variance, as follows:

| | | |
|---|---|---|
| VOLUME VARIANCE: | | |
| Overhead budgeted at operating level achieved | $7,500 | |
| Standard overhead applied to production (3,500 standard hours at $2 per hour) | 7,000 | |
| Variance—unfavorable | | $500 |
| CONTROLLABLE VARIANCE: | | |
| Actual overhead incurred | $7,650 | |
| Overhead budgeted at operating level achieved | 7,500 | |
| Variance—unfavorable | | 150 |
| OVERHEAD COST VARIANCE (Excess of overhead incurred over overhead charged to production)—unfavorable | | $650 |

## AS A MATTER OF ETHICS

You are an internal auditor looking into your company's procedures for comparing actual results with budgeted amounts. You notice that for several years running, one manager (who has managed several different departments over the years) always spends exactly what is budgeted for discretionary supplies and temporary labor.

Looking into the records further, you find that 25 to 35% of the annual budget for these items has been spent by this manager in November and December, right before the end of the budget year. An interview with the manager reveals that he always spends what is budgeted, whether or not the supplies and equipment are really needed. His justification is threefold. First, he doesn't want his budget to be cut back, and he thinks it will be if he doesn't spend all that he is allocated. Second, he says that the company's practice of following "management by exception" calls attention to big deviations from the budget, and he would just as soon avoid that kind of attention. Third, he feels that the practice doesn't hurt anyone because the money was budgeted to be spent anyway.

Although there is substantial logic in the manager's actions and explanation, you wonder whether you should comment on this matter in your report. You also wonder what recommendations, if any, you should offer.

## Using Standard Costs to Control a Business

Explain the relevance of standard cost accounting to the management philosophy known as management by exception. (L. O. 4)

Business operations are carried on by people, and if management is to control the operations of a business, it must control the actions of the people who are responsible for its revenues, costs, and expenses. After a budget is prepared and standard costs are established, management maintains control by taking appropriate action when actual costs differ from the standard or budgeted amounts.

Reports like the ones in this chapter are a means of calling management's attention to these variances from business plans. When managers use these reports to focus on problem areas, the budgeting process makes a contribution to the control function. However, in evaluating the budget performance reports, management should practice the control technique known as **management by exception.** Under this technique, management focuses its attention on the variances in which actual costs are significantly different from standard; it gives less attention to the cost situations in which performance is satisfactory. In other words, management concentrates its attention on the exceptional or irregular situations and pays less attention to areas where actual results are reasonably close to the plan.

## Using Standard Costs for Activities Other than Manufacturing

Many companies develop standard costs and apply variance analysis only when dealing with manufacturing costs. In these companies, the master budget includes selling, general, and administrative expenses, but the subsequent process of controlling these expenses is not based on established standard costs and variance analysis. However, other companies have recognized that standard costs and variance analysis may help control selling, general, and administrative expenses just as well as manufacturing costs. You should understand that the previous discussions of material and labor cost variances can easily be adapted to many selling, general, and administrative expenses.

### Standard Costs in the Accounts

Prepare entries to record standard costs and to account for price and quantity variances. (L. O. 5)

Standard costs can be used solely in the preparation of management reports and need not be recorded in the accounts. However, in most standard cost systems such costs are recorded in the accounts to facilitate both the record-keeping and the preparation of reports.

To gain a conceptual understanding of standard costs and how they are used, you do not have to go through the detailed procedures associated with keeping records in a standard cost system. Nevertheless, you should understand how standard costs and variances are recorded. To illustrate, the following entries record XL Company's standard manufacturing costs and related variances for the month of May. We discussed the calculation of these variances on pages 1098–1105.

The first entry records standard material cost in the Goods in Process account and also isolates the material variances in separate variance accounts. Note that since the material quantity variance and material price variance are both unfavorable, they are recorded as debits. Both variances represent cost incurred in addition to the standard amounts.

| | | | | |
|---|---|---|---|---|
| May | 31 | Goods in Process | 3,500.00 | |
| | | Direct Material Quantity Variance | 100.00 | |
| | | Direct Material Price Variance | 180.00 | |
| | | Raw Materials | | 3,780.00 |
| | | To charge production for the standard quantity of materials used (3,500 pounds) at the standard price ($1 per pound) and to record the direct material quantity and price variances. | | |

The next entry charges Goods in Process for the standard labor cost of the goods manufactured during May and also records the direct labor variances:

| | | | | |
|---|---|---|---|---|
| May | 31 | Goods in Process | 21,000.00 | |
| | | Direct Labor Price Variance | 1,020.00 | |
| | | Direct Labor Quantity Variance | | 600.00 |
| | | Factory Payroll | | 21,420.00 |
| | | To charge production with 3,500 standard hours of direct labor at the standard $6 per hour rate and to record the direct labor quantity and price variances. | | |

The next entry applies the standard overhead cost of the goods manufactured during the period to Goods in Process and also records the volume and controllable variances:

| | | | | |
|---|---|---|---|---|
| May | 31 | Goods in Process | 7,000.00 | |
| | | Volume Variance | 500.00 | |
| | | Controllable Variance | 150.00 | |
| | | Factory Overhead | | 7,650.00 |
| | | To apply overhead at the standard rate of $2 per standard direct labor hour (3,500 hours) and to record overhead variances. | | |

When variances are recorded in separate variance accounts, they are allowed to accumulate in those accounts until the end of an accounting period. Then, if the variance amounts are immaterial, they are closed directly to Cost of Goods Sold. However, if the amounts are material, they should be prorated between Goods in Process, Finished Goods, and Cost of Goods Sold.

## Summary of the Chapter in Terms of Learning Objectives

**1.** A fixed budget shows the expected revenues, costs, and expenses that will occur given one specific production and sales volume. Therefore, if the production and sales volume actually is at some other level, the amounts in the fixed budget do not provide a reasonable basis for evaluating actual performance. A flexible budget expresses variable costs in per unit terms so that it can be used to develop budgeted amounts for any production and sales volume within the relevant range. As a result, budgeted amounts can be calculated for the volume that actually occurs.

**2.** Standard costs are the normal costs that should be incurred to produce a product or perform a service. As such, they are the amounts that should be budgeted. Standard costs should be based on a careful examination of the production processes used to produce a product or perform a service and the quantities and prices that should be expected to carry out those production processes. On a performance report, these flexible budget amounts are compared to actual costs and the differences are presented as variances. The variances suggest areas for management investigation and possible corrective action.

**3.** Material and labor cost variances are the differences between actual cost incurred and budgeted costs. These total cost variances can be broken into quantity variances and price variances which direct management's attention to investigate the actions of those who are responsible for quantities used or prices paid. The overhead cost variance is the difference between actual overhead incurred and overhead applied to production. This can be broken into a volume variance and a controllable variance. The volume variance occurs because the standard overhead application rate is applied to a volume that differs from the expected or budgeted volume. The controllable variance is the difference between actual overhead incurred and the budgeted overhead at the actual volume achieved during the period.

**4.** Standard cost accounting provides management with information about costs that differ from budgeted amounts. Performance reports disclose the costs or areas of operations that have significant variances from normal or budgeted amounts. This disclosure of exceptions from the normal allows managers to devote their attention to the exceptions and pay less attention to areas in which operations are proceeding normally.

**5.** When a company records standard costs in its accounts, the standard costs of materials, labor, and overhead are debited to Goods in Process. Based on an analysis of the material, labor, and overhead cost variances, each quantity variance, price variance, volume variance, and controllable variance is recorded in a separate account. Then, at the end of the period, if the variances are material, they are allocated to Goods in Process, Finished Goods, and Cost of Goods Sold. If not material in amount, they may be charged to Cost of Goods Sold.

## Demonstration Problem

The Gregory Company provides the following information about its budgeted and actual results for April 1991. The expected (budgeted) volume for April was 25,000 units produced and sold, but the company actually produced and sold 27,000 units.

**Budget data—25,000 units (asterisks identify factory overhead items):**

| | | |
|---|---|---|
| Selling price | | $5.00 per unit |
| Variable costs (per unit of output): | | |
| Direct materials | | 1.24 per unit |
| Direct labor | | 1.50 per unit |
| *Factory supplies | | 0.25 per unit |
| *Utilities | | 0.50 per unit |
| Selling costs | | 0.40 per unit |
| Fixed costs (per month): | | |
| *Depreciation of machinery | $3,750 | |
| *Depreciation of building | 2,500 | |
| General liability insurance | 1,200 | |
| Property taxes on office equipment | 500 | |
| Other administrative expense | 750 | |

**Actual results during the month of April—27,000 units produced:**

| | | |
|---|---|---|
| Selling price (per unit of output) | | $5.23 per unit |
| Variable costs (per unit of output): | | |
| Direct materials | | 1.12 per unit |
| Direct labor | | 1.40 per unit |
| *Factory supplies | | 0.37 per unit |
| *Utilities | | 0.60 per unit |
| Selling costs | | 0.34 per unit |
| Fixed costs (per month): | | |
| *Depreciation of machinery | $3,710 | |
| *Depreciation of building | 2,500 | |
| General liability insurance | 1,250 | |
| Property taxes on office equipment | 485 | |
| Other administrative expense | 900 | |

*Required*

1. Prepare a set of flexible budgets for April that shows the expected revenues, costs, and income under assumptions of 20,000, 25,000, and 30,000 units of output made and sold.

2. Prepare a performance report that contrasts the actual performance with what would have been budgeted if the actual volume had been expected.
3. Develop variance analyses for direct materials, direct labor, and manufacturing overhead, given the following information:

Standard manufacturing costs based on expected output of 25,000 units:

| | Per Unit of Output | Quantity to Be Used | Total Cost |
|---|---|---|---|
| Direct materials, 4 oz. @ $0.31/oz. | $1.24/unit | 100,000 oz. | $31,000 |
| Direct labor, 0.25 hrs. @ $6.00/hr. | 1.50/unit | 6,250 hrs. | 37,500 |
| Overhead | 1.00/unit | | 25,000 |

Actual costs incurred to produce 27,000 units:

| | Per Unit of Output | Quantity to Be Used | Total Cost |
|---|---|---|---|
| Direct materials, 4 oz. @ $0.28/oz. | $1.12/unit | 108,000 oz. | $30,240 |
| Direct labor, 0.20 hrs. @ $7.00/hr. | 1.40/unit | 5,400 hrs. | 37,800 |
| Overhead | 1.20/unit | | 32,400 |

If standards had been based on an expected output of 27,000 units, standard manufacturing costs would have been:

| | Per Unit of Output | Quantity to Be Used | Total Cost |
|---|---|---|---|
| Direct materials, 4 oz. @ $0.31/oz. | $1.24/unit | 108,000 oz. | $33,480 |
| Direct labor, 0.25 hrs. @ $6.00/hr. | 1.50/unit | 6,750 hrs. | 40,500 |
| Overhead | | | 26,500 |

## Solution to Demonstration Problem

1. Flexible budgets:

| | 20,000 Units | 25,000 Units | 30,000 Units |
|---|---|---|---|
| Sales | $100,000 | $125,000 | $150,000 |
| Variable costs: | | | |
| Direct materials | $ 24,800 | $ 31,000 | $ 37,200 |
| Direct labor | 30,000 | 37,500 | 45,000 |
| Factory supplies | 5,000 | 6,250 | 7,500 |
| Utilities | 10,000 | 12,500 | 15,000 |
| Selling costs | 8,000 | 10,000 | 12,000 |
| Total variable costs | $ 77,800 | $ 97,250 | $116,700 |
| Contribution margin | $ 22,200 | $ 27,750 | $ 33,300 |
| Fixed costs: | | | |
| Depreciation of machinery | $ 3,750 | $ 3,750 | $ 3,750 |
| Depreciation of building | 2,500 | 2,500 | 2,500 |
| General liability insurance | 1,200 | 1,200 | 1,200 |
| Property taxes on office equipment | 500 | 500 | 500 |
| Other administrative expense | 750 | 750 | 750 |
| Total fixed costs | $ 8,700 | $ 8,700 | $ 8,700 |
| Income from operations | $ 13,500 | $ 19,050 | $ 24,600 |

2.

**THE GREGORY COMPANY**
**Flexible Budget Performance Report**
**For Month of April 1991**

| | Flexible Budget | Actual Performance | Variance |
|---|---|---|---|
| Sales (27,000 units) | $135,000 | $141,210 | $6,210 F |
| Variable costs: | | | |
| Direct materials | $ 33,480 | $ 30,240 | $3,240 F |
| Direct labor | 40,500 | 37,800 | 2,700 F |
| Factory supplies | 6,750 | 9,990 | 3,240 U |
| Utilities | 13,500 | 16,200 | 2,700 U |
| Selling costs | 10,800 | 9,180 | 1,620 F |
| Total variable costs | $105,030 | $103,410 | $1,620 F |
| Contribution margin | $ 29,970 | $ 37,800 | $7,830 F |
| Fixed costs: | | | |
| Depreciation of machinery | $ 3,750 | $ 3,710 | $ 40 F |
| Depreciation of building | 2,500 | 2,500 | |
| General liability insurance | 1,200 | 1,250 | 50 U |
| Property taxes on office equipment | 500 | 485 | 15 F |
| Other administrative expense | 750 | 900 | 150 U |
| Total fixed costs | $ 8,700 | $ 8,845 | $ 145 U |
| Income from operations | $ 21,270 | $ 28,955 | $7,685 F |

3. Variance analyses of manufacturing costs:

| | | | |
|---|---|---|---|
| Material variances: | | | |
| Actual cost | 108,000 oz. @ $0.28 | $30,240 | |
| Standard cost | 108,000 oz. @ $0.31 | 33,480 | |
| Direct material cost variance—favorable | | | $3,240 |
| Quantity variance: | | | |
| Actual units at standard price | 108,000 oz. @ $0.31 | $33,480 | |
| Standard units at standard price | 108,000 oz. @ $0.31 | 33,480 | |
| Variance | | | $-0- |
| Price variance: | | | |
| Actual units at actual price | 108,000 oz. @ $0.28 | $30,240 | |
| Actual units at standard price | 108,000 oz. @ $0.31 | 33,480 | |
| Variance—favorable | | | 3,240 |
| Direct material cost variance—favorable | | | $3,240 |
| Labor variances: | | | |
| Actual cost | 5,400 hrs. @ $7.00 | $37,800 | |
| Standard cost | 6,750 hrs. @ $6.00 | 40,500 | |
| Direct labor cost variance—favorable | | | $2,700 |
| Quantity variance: | | | |
| Actual hours at standard price | 5,400 hrs. @ $6.00 | $32,400 | |
| Standard hours at standard price | 6,750 hrs. @ $6.00 | 40,500 | |
| Variance—favorable | | | $8,100 |
| Price variance: | | | |
| Actual hours at actual price | 5,400 hrs. @ $7.00 | $37,800 | |
| Actual hours at standard price | 5,400 hrs. @ $6.00 | 32,400 | |
| Variance—unfavorable | | | 5,400 |
| Direct labor cost variance—favorable | | | $2,700 |

| | | | |
|---|---|---|---|
| Overhead variances: | | | |
| Total overhead cost incurred . . . . . . | 27,000 units @ $1.20 | $32,400 | |
| Total overhead applied . . . . . . . . . | 27,000 units @ $1.00 | 27,000 | |
| Overhead cost variance—unfavorable . . . . . . . . . . . . . | | | $5,400 |
| Volume variance: | | | |
| Budgeted overhead at 27,000 units . . . . . . . . . . . . . | | $26,500 | |
| Standard overhead applied to production (27,000 units @ $1 per unit rate) . . . . . . . . . . . . . . . . . . . . . | | 27,000 | |
| Variance—favorable . . . . . . . . . . . . . . . . . . . . . | | | $ 500 |
| Controllable variance: | | | |
| Actual overhead incurred . . . . . . . . . . . . . . . . . . | | $32,400 | |
| Overhead budgeted at operating level achieved . . . . . . . . | | 26,500 | |
| Variance—unfavorable . . . . . . . . . . . . . . . . . . . . . | | | 5,900 |
| Total overhead variance—unfavorable . . . . . . . . . . . . . | | | $5,400 |

## Glossary

Define or explain the words and phrases listed in the chapter Glossary. (L. O. 6)

**Controllable variance** the difference between the overhead actually incurred and the overhead budgeted at the operating level achieved. pp. 1102, 1104

**Cost variance** the difference between the actual or incurred amount of a cost and the standard amount or, in the case of overhead, the standard amount applied to production. p. 1097

**Fixed budget** a budget that is based on a single estimate of sales or production volume and that gives no consideration to the possibility that the actual sales or production volume may differ from the assumed amount. p. 1091

**Flexible budget** a budget that separates variable costs from fixed costs and presents variable costs on a per unit basis so that budgeted amounts can be calculated for all levels of production within the relevant range. pp. 1091–95

**Flexible budget performance report** a financial report that compares actual performance to budgeted amounts that are based on the actual sales volume or level of activity and presents the differences between actual and budgeted amounts as variances. pp. 1094–95

**Historical costs** dollar amounts of consideration given by the business in past transactions. p. 1096

**Management by exception** a technique whereby management focuses its attention on areas in which actual costs are significantly different from standard costs and pays less attention to the cost situations in which performance is satisfactory. p. 1106

**Overhead cost variance** the difference between the actual overhead incurred during a period and the standard overhead applied to production. p. 1102

**Performance report** a financial report that compares actual cost and/or revenue performance with budgeted amounts and designates the differences between them as favorable or unfavorable variances. p. 1091

**Price variance** a difference between actual and budgeted revenue or cost caused by the actual price per unit being different from the budgeted price per unit. p. 1095

**Quantity variance** the difference between actual cost and budgeted cost that was caused by a difference between the actual number of units used and the number of units budgeted. p. 1095

**Standard costs** the costs that should be incurred under normal conditions to produce a given product or part or to perform a particular service. p. 1096

**Static budget** a synonym for *fixed budget*. p. 1091

**Variable budget** a synonym for *flexible budget*. pp. 1091–95

**Variance analysis** a process of examining the differences between actual revenues or costs and budgeted revenues or costs and describing the differences in terms of the amounts that resulted from factors such as price and quantity differences. p. 1095

**Volume variance** the difference between the amount of overhead budgeted at the actual operating level achieved during the period and the standard amount of overhead charged to production during the period. pp. 1102–4

## Objective Review

Answers to the following questions are listed in Appendix I at the end of the book. Be sure that you decide which is the one best answer to each question *before* you check the answers in the appendix.

1. A flexible budget:
   *a.* Cannot be prepared without first classifying each cost as variable or fixed.
   *b.* Shows the budgeted amount of each fixed cost as the total amount that is expected regardless of the sales volume that may occur.
   *c.* Shows variable costs as constant amounts of cost per unit of activity.
   *d.* Items (*a*), (*b*), and (*c*) are correct statements about fixed budgets, but not correct statements about flexible budgets.
   *e.* Items (*a*), (*b*), and (*c*) are all correct.
2. Standard costs:
   *a.* Are costs that change in direct proportion to changes in the level of activity.
   *b.* Are the costs that should be incurred under normal conditions to produce a given product or part or to perform a particular service.
   *c.* Are the costs that were actually incurred at the level of production that actually occurred during the period.
   *d.* Are compared to the fixed budget costs for the purpose of presenting a flexible budget performance report.
   *e.* Are calculated as the average of the historical costs incurred during recent periods of production.
3. Given the following data:

| | |
|---|---|
| Actual hours worked per unit . . . . . . | 2.5 |
| Standard direct labor hours per unit . . | 2.0 |
| Actual units produced . . . . . . . . . | 2,500 |
| Budgeted production in units . . . . . | 3,000 |
| Actual price per hour . . . . . . . . . | $3.10 |
| Standard cost per hour . . . . . . . . . | $3.00 |

   What is the direct labor cost variance?
   *a.* $3,750 (U).
   *b.* $3,125 (F).
   *c.* $4,375 (F).
   *d.* $4,375 (U).
   *e.* $5,000 (U).
4. The use of standard cost accounting to implement the philosophy of management by exception:
   *a.* Requires that a company record standard costs in its accounts.
   *b.* Requires that fixed budget performance reports be presented to management on a timely basis.
   *c.* Involves the calculation of variances based on flexible budgets so that management can focus its attention on significant differences between actual and budgeted performance.

*d.* Is limited to the calculation of quantity and price variances for direct materials and direct labor.

*e.* None of the above is correct.

5. Jastrow Company uses a standard cost system. Based on the following information what would be the entry to record the company's material variances?

| | |
|---|---|
| Direct material cost actually incurred | $73,200 |
| Direct material quantity variance—favorable | 3,800 |
| Direct material price variance—unfavorable | 1,300 |

| | | | |
|---|---|---|---|
| *a.* | Goods in Process | 73,200.00 | |
| | Direct Material Price Variance | 1,300.00 | |
| | Direct Material Quantity Variance | | 3,800.00 |
| | Raw Materials | | 70,700.00 |
| *b.* | Goods in Process | 70,700.00 | |
| | Direct Material Quantity Variance | 3,800.00 | |
| | Direct Material Price Variance | | 1,300.00 |
| | Raw Materials | | 73,200.00 |
| *c.* | Goods in process | 73,200.00 | |
| | Direct Material Quantity Variance | 3,800.00 | |
| | Direct Material Price Variance | | 1,300.00 |
| | Raw Materials | | 75,700.00 |
| *d.* | Direct Material Quantity Variance | 3,800.00 | |
| | Direct Material Price Variance | | 1,300.00 |
| | Goods in Process | | 2,500.00 |
| *e.* | Goods in Process | 75,700.00 | |
| | Direct Material Price Variance | 1,300.00 | |
| | Direct Material Quantity Variance | | 3,800.00 |
| | Raw Materials | | 73,200.00 |

## Questions for Class Discussion

1. What is a *fixed* or *static* budget?
2. What limits the usefulness of fixed budget performance reports?
3. What is the essential difference between a fixed budget and a flexible budget?
4. What is the initial step in preparing a flexible budget?
5. Is there any sense in which a variable cost may be thought of as being constant in amount? Explain.
6. Might it be appropriate for a particular type of cost to be classified as variable by one company and fixed by another company?
7. What is meant by contribution margin?
8. What is a flexible budget performance report designed to analyze?
9. In cost accounting, what is meant by a cost variance?
10. A cost variance often consists of a price variance and a quantity variance. What is a price variance? What is a quantity variance?

11. If a material quantity variance is favorable and the material price variance is favorable, might the material cost variance be unfavorable?
12. What is the purpose of a standard cost?
13. What department usually is responsible for a direct material price variance? What department generally is responsible for a direct material quantity variance?
14. If a labor cost variance is favorable and the labor quantity variance is favorable, might the labor price variance be unfavorable?
15. What is a predetermined standard overhead rate?
16. In analyzing the overhead variance, what is meant by a volume variance?
17. Under what conditions is the overhead volume variance said to be favorable?
18. In analyzing the overhead variance, what is meant by a controllable variance?
19. If a company is budgeted to operate at 80% of capacity and actually operates at 84% of capacity, what effect will the 4% excess have on the controllable variance?
20. If a company's overhead costs were entirely variable costs and the actual sales volume was 5% lower than the budgeted sales volume, what kind of volume variance would the company experience?
21. If the standard overhead applied to production exceeds the budgeted overhead at the actual production and sales volume achieved, is the volume variance favorable or unfavorable?
22. What is the relationship between standard costs, variance analysis, and management by exception?
23. If standard costs of manufacturing are recorded in the accounts, how are the manufacturing cost variances disposed of at the end of each accounting period?

## Exercises

**Exercise 26–1**
**Classifying costs as fixed or variable**
(L. O. 1)

Flyer Company manufactures and sells racing bicycles and normally operates eight hours a day, five days per week. On the basis of this general information, classify the following costs as fixed or variable. In those instances where further investigation might reverse your classification, comment on the possible reasons for treating the item in the opposite manner.

*a.* Management salaries.
*b.* Direct labor.
*c.* Bolts and screws.
*d.* Electricity to run power tools.
*e.* Repair expense on power tools.
*f.* Paint.
*g.* Shipping expenses.
*h.* Utilities (gas and water).
*i.* Depreciation on power tools.
*j.* Fire insurance on property.
*k.* Alloy.
*l.* Brake assemblies.
*m.* Office supplies.
*n.* Sales commissions.
*o.* Wheels and tires.

**Exercise 26–2**
**Preparing a flexible budget**
(L. O. 1)

Sanford Company's fixed budget for the third quarter of 1991 is presented below. Recast the budget as a flexible budget and show the budgeted amounts for 19,200 units and 21,600 units of production.

| | | |
|---|---|---|
| Sales (20,400 units) | | $ 642,600 |
| Cost of goods sold: | | |
| Direct materials | $119,340 | |
| Direct labor | 133,008 | |
| Production supplies | 18,360 | |
| Depreciation | 13,500 | |
| Plant manager's salary | 19,800 | (304,008) |
| Gross profit | | $ 338,592 |
| Selling expenses: | | |
| Sales commissions | $ 53,244 | |
| Packaging expense | 13,872 | (67,116) |
| Administrative expenses: | | |
| Administrative salaries | $ 27,000 | |
| Insurance expense | 6,840 | |
| Office rent expense | 22,500 | |
| Executive salaries | 45,000 | (101,340) |
| Income from operations | | $ 170,136 |

**Exercise 26–3**
**Analysis of fixed budget performance report**
(L. O. 1)

Creosote Company's fixed budget performance report for last period appeared as follows:

| | Fixed Budget | Actual Performance | Variance |
|---|---|---|---|
| Sales: In units | 12,400 | 15,500 | |
| In dollars | $297,600 | $383,625 | $86,025 F |
| Expenses | 260,400 | 312,150 | 51,750 U |
| Income from operations | $ 37,200 | $ 71,475 | $34,275 F |

The budgeted expenses of $260,400 included $186,000 of variable expenses; the remainder were fixed. Prepare an analysis of the variance in the income from operations that shows (1) how much of the variance resulted from operating at a level that was higher than budgeted, and (2) how much of the variance remains to be explained by other factors.

**Exercise 26–4**
**Direct material variances**
(L. O. 2, 3)

Sante Fe Furniture Company has just completed 120 units of its finest couches using 18,200 board feet of lumber that cost $22,204. The company's direct material standards for one couch are 145 board feet of lumber at $1.24 per board foot.

*Required*

Isolate the direct material variances incurred in manufacturing these desks.

**Exercise 26–5**
**Direct labor variances**
(L. O. 2, 3)

After carefully evaluating Hing Company's production process, management decided to budget 0.8 hours of direct labor per unit of product, at an average cost of $10.60 per hour. During January, the company used 1,530 hours of direct labor at a total cost of $16,524 to produce 1,800 units of product. In February, the company used 1,570 hours of direct labor at a total cost of $16,171 to produce 2,050 units of product. Calculate the quantity variance, the price variance, and the direct labor cost variance for January and for February.

**Exercise 26–6**
**Calculation of quantity used based on variance information**
(L. O. 2, 3)

During a recent period's manufacturing operations, Garner Company's use of direct material resulted in a favorable price variance of $630. The actual price per pound of material was $9.30 while the standard price was $9.75. How many pounds of material were used during the period?

**Exercise 26–7**
**Calculations of costs based on variance information**
(L. O. 2, 3)

Calculate an answer for each of the following independent cases:

*a.* Parker Company's production for the period required standard direct material cost of $39,450. During the period, the direct material variances included a favorable price variance of $540 and an unfavorable quantity variance of $1,110. What was the total actual cost of direct materials incurred during the period?

*b.* During a period, Lakeridge Company had a favorable direct labor price variance of $485 and a favorable direct labor quantity variance of $1,335. Goods produced during the period required standard direct labor cost of $21,450. What was the total actual cost of direct labor incurred during the period?

*c.* During a period, Hecker Company reported an unfavorable overhead volume variance of $3,750 and a favorable overhead controllable variance of $900. Standard overhead charged to production during the period amounted to $14,550. What was the total actual overhead incurred during the period?

**Exercise 26–8**
**Calculating volume and controllable variances**
(L. O. 3)

Lockhart Company normally operates at 70% of capacity, which requires 3,500 standard direct labor hours to produce 3,500 units of product per period. At that level of production, its overhead budget includes $21,000 of fixed overhead plus $13,650 of variable overhead. Calculate the volume variance and the controllable variance if the company incurred $34,800 of overhead during a period in which it produced 3,000 units of product.

**Exercise 26–9**
**Overhead variances**
(L. O. 3)

A company has established the following standard costs for one unit of its product:

| | |
|---|---|
| Direct material (1.5 gals. @ $3.20 per unit) . . | $ 4.80 |
| Direct labor (2 hrs. @ $6.40 per hr.) . . . . . | 12.80 |
| Factory overhead (2 hrs. @ $5.60 per hr.) . . | 11.20 |
| Standard cost . . . . . . . . . . . . . . . . . | $28.80 |

The $5.60 per direct labor hour overhead rate is based on a normal 80% of capacity operating level and the following monthly flexible budget information:

| | Operating Levels | | |
|---|---|---|---|
| | 75% | 80% | 85% |
| Budgeted production in units | 11,250 | 12,000 | 12,750 |
| Budget production in standard labor hours | 22,500 | 24,000 | 25,500 |
| Budgeted overhead: | | | |
| Variable overhead | $63,000 | $67,200 | $71,400 |
| Fixed overhead | 67,200 | 67,200 | 67,200 |

During the past month, the company operated at 75% of capacity and incurred the following overhead costs:

| | |
|---|---|
| Variable overhead costs | $ 67,500 |
| Fixed overhead costs | 67,200 |
| Total overhead costs | $134,700 |

*Required*

Isolate the overhead variances into a volume variance and a controllable variance.

**Exercise 26–10**
**Recording material variances**
(L. O. 5)

Sante Fe Furniture Company records standard costs in its accounts. As a result, in charging material costs to Goods in Process, it also records any variances in separate accounts.

*Required*

1. Under the assumption that the direct materials used to manufacture the couches of Exercise 26–4 were charged to Goods in Process on November 30, give the entry to charge the direct materials and to record the variances in the accounts.
2. Under the further assumption that the direct material variances of Exercise 26–4 were the only variances of the accounting period and are not considered material, give the December 31 entry to close the variance accounts.

## Problems

**Problem 26–1**
**Preparing and using a flexible budget**
(L. O. 1)

Camellia Company's master (fixed) budget for 1991 was based on an expected production and sales volume of 6,900 units and included the operating items shown on the next page.

*Required*

1. Prepare a flexible budget for the company and show detailed budgets for sales and production volumes of 6,300 units and 7,500 units.
2. A consultant to the company has suggested that developing business conditions in the area are reaching a crossroads, and that the impact of these events on the company could result in a sales volume of approximately 8,500 units. The president of Camellia Company is confident that this is within the relevant range of existing production capacity but is hesitant to estimate the impact of such a change on operating income. What would be the expected increase in operating income?

3. In the consultant's report, the possibility of unfavorable business events was also mentioned, in which case production and sales volume for 1991 would likely fall to 6,000 units. What amount of income from operations should the president expect if these unfavorable events occur?

**CAMELLIA COMPANY**
**Fixed Budget**
**For Year Ended December 31, 1991**

| | | |
|---|---|---|
| Sales | | $ 828,000 |
| Cost of goods sold: | | |
| Direct materials | $207,000 | |
| Direct labor | 124,200 | |
| Machinery repairs (variable cost) | 6,210 | |
| Depreciation of plant | 22,500 | |
| Utilities (40% of which is a variable cost) | 41,400 | |
| Supervisory salaries | 54,000 | (455,310) |
| Gross profit | | $ 372,690 |
| Selling expenses: | | |
| Packaging | $ 20,700 | |
| Shipping | 31,050 | |
| Sales salary (an agreed-upon annual salary) | 63,000 | (114,750) |
| General and administrative expenses: | | |
| Insurance expense | $ 13,500 | |
| Salaries | 94,500 | |
| Rent expense | 72,000 | (180,000) |
| Income from operations | | $ 77,940 |

**Problem 26–2**
**Flexible budget performance report**
(L. O. 1)

Refer to the discussion of Camellia Company in Problem 26–1. Camellia Company's actual statement of income from 1991 operations is as follows:

**CAMELLIA COMPANY**
**Statement of Income from Operations**
**For Year Ended December 31, 1991**

| | | |
|---|---|---|
| Sales (7,500 units) | | $ 855,000 |
| Cost of goods sold: | | |
| Direct materials | $202,500 | |
| Direct labor | 139,500 | |
| Machinery repairs | 4,500 | |
| Depreciation of plant | 22,500 | |
| Utilities (50% of which is a variable cost) | 49,680 | |
| Supervisory salaries | 52,650 | (471,330) |
| Gross profit | | $ 383,670 |
| Selling expenses: | | |
| Packaging | $ 20,250 | |
| Shipping | 35,550 | |
| Sales salary | 63,000 | (118,800) |
| General and administrative expenses: | | |
| Insurance expense | $ 13,950 | |
| Salaries | 96,750 | |
| Rent expense | 72,000 | (182,700) |
| Income from operations | | $ 82,170 |

*Required*

1. Using the flexible budget you prepared for Problem 26–1, present a flexible budget performance report for 1991.
2. Explain the sales variance.

**Problem 26–3**
**Calculating material, labor, and overhead variances**
(L. O. 2, 3)

Henry Manufacturing Company makes a single product for which it has established the following standard costs per unit:

| | |
|---|---|
| Direct material (15 lbs. @ $2.10 per lb.) . . . | $ 31.50 |
| Direct labor (3 hrs. @ $18 per hr.) . . . . . . | 54.00 |
| Factory overhead (3 hrs. @ $5.10 per hr.) . . | 15.30 |
| Total standard cost . . . . . . . . . . . . . | $100.80 |

The $5.10 per direct labor hour overhead rate is based on a normal, 90% of capacity, operating level and the following flexible budget information:

| | Operating Levels | | |
|---|---|---|---|
| | 80% | 90% | 100% |
| Production in units . . . . . . . . . | 12,800 | 14,400 | 16,000 |
| Standard direct labor hours . . . . | 38,400 | 43,200 | 48,000 |
| Budgeted overhead: | | | |
| Fixed factory overhead . . . . . | $129,600 | $129,600 | $129,600 |
| Variable factory overhead . . . | 80,640 | 90,720 | 100,800 |

During March, the company operated at 80% of capacity, producing 12,800 units of product that were charged with the following standard costs:

| | |
|---|---|
| Direct material (192,000 lbs. @ $2.10 per lb.). . . . . . . | $ 403,200 |
| Direct labor (38,400 hrs. @ $18 per hr.) . . . . . . . . . | 691,200 |
| Factory overhead costs (38,400 hrs. @ $5.10 per hr.) . . | 195,840 |
| Total standard cost . . . . . . . . . . . . . . . . . . . | $1,290,240 |

Actual costs incurred during March were:

| | |
|---|---|
| Direct material (189,500 lbs.) . . . . . | $ 411,215 |
| Direct labor (39,200 hrs.) . . . . . . . . | 693,840 |
| Fixed factory overhead costs . . . . . . | 129,900 |
| Variable factory overhead costs . . . . | 78,336 |
| Total actual costs . . . . . . . . . . . | $1,313,291 |

*Required*

Divide the direct material and direct labor cost variances into price and quantity variances and divide the overhead cost variance into volume and controllable variances.

**Problem 26–4**
**Calculating and reporting material, labor, and overhead variances**
(L. O. 2, 3)

Tickler Company has established the following standard costs per unit for the product it manufactures:

| | |
|---|---|
| Direct material (6 lbs. @ $4 per lb.) . . . | $24.00 |
| Direct labor (2 hrs. @ $7.20 per hr.) . . | 14.40 |
| Overhead (2 hrs. @ $5 per hr.) . . . . . | 10.00 |
| Total standard cost . . . . . . . . . . . | $48.40 |

The $5 per direct labor hour overhead rate is based on a normal, 85% of capacity, operating level and the following flexible budget information for one month's operations:

| | Operating Levels | | |
|---|---|---|---|
| | 80% | 85% | 90% |
| Production in units | 2,720 | 2,890 | 3,060 |
| Standard direct labor hours | 5,440 | 5,780 | 6,120 |
| Budgeted factory overhead: | | | |
| Variable costs: | | | |
| Indirect materials | $ 6,528 | $ 6,936 | $ 7,344 |
| Indirect labor | 2,176 | 2,312 | 2,448 |
| Power | 870 | 925 | 979 |
| Maintenance | 3,482 | 3,699 | 3,917 |
| Total variable costs | $13,056 | $13,872 | $14,688 |
| Fixed costs: | | | |
| Rent of factory building | $ 5,600 | $ 5,600 | $ 5,600 |
| Depreciation, machinery | 3,880 | 3,880 | 3,880 |
| Taxes and insurance | 1,156 | 1,156 | 1,156 |
| Supervisory salaries | 4,392 | 4,392 | 4,392 |
| Total fixed costs | $15,028 | $15,028 | $15,028 |
| Total factory overhead costs | $28,084 | $28,900 | $29,716 |

During May 1991, the company operated at 90% of capacity, produced 3,060 units of product, and incurred the following actual costs:

| | | |
|---|---|---|
| Direct material (16,830 lbs. @ $3.90 per lb.) | | $ 65,637 |
| Direct labor (6,730 hrs. @ $7.20 per hr.) | | 48,456 |
| Overhead costs: | | |
| Indirect materials | $7,590 | |
| Indirect labor | 2,940 | |
| Power | 1,100 | |
| Maintenance | 3,670 | |
| Rent of factory building | 5,600 | |
| Depreciation, machinery | 3,880 | |
| Taxes and insurance | 1,280 | |
| Supervisory salaries | 4,800 | 30,860 |
| Total costs | | $144,953 |

*Required*

1. Isolate the direct material and direct labor variances into quantity and price variances and isolate the overhead variance into the volume variance and the controllable variance.
2. Prepare a factory overhead variance report showing the volume and controllable variances.

**Problem 26–5**
**Flexible budget, variance analysis, and report for overhead costs**
(L. O. 1, 2, 3, 4)

Blowfeld Company has established the following standard costs for one unit of its product:

| | |
|---|---|
| Direct material (6 lbs. @ $1.20 per lb.) | $ 7.20 |
| Direct labor (1 hr. @ $8 per hr.) | 8.00 |
| Overhead (1 hr. @ $7.68 per hr.) | 7.68 |
| Total standard cost | $22.88 |

The $7.68 per direct labor hour overhead rate is based on a normal, 80% of capacity, operating level; and at this level the company's monthly output is 9,600 units. Following are the company's budgeted overhead costs at the 80% level for one month:

**BLOWFELD COMPANY**
**Budgeted Monthly Factory Overhead at 80% Level**

| | | |
|---|---|---|
| Variable costs: | | |
| Indirect materials . . . . . . . . . | $ 8,448 | |
| Indirect labor . . . . . . . . . . . | 9,984 | |
| Power . . . . . . . . . . . . . . . | 6,144 | |
| Repairs and maintenance . . . . | 6,912 | |
| Total variable costs . . . . . . . . | | $31,488 |
| Fixed costs: | | |
| Depreciation, building . . . . . . | $ 9,216 | |
| Depreciation, machinery . . . . | 13,824 | |
| Taxes and insurance . . . . . . . | 3,840 | |
| Supervision . . . . . . . . . . . . | 15,360 | |
| Total fixed costs . . . . . . . . . | | 42,240 |
| Total overhead costs . . . . . . . . | | $73,728 |

During August 1991, the company operated at 70% of capacity and incurred the following actual costs:

| | |
|---|---|
| Direct material (50,000 lbs.) . . . . | $ 57,000 |
| Direct labor (8,550 hrs.) . . . . . . | 71,820 |
| Indirect materials . . . . . . . . . | 7,728 |
| Indirect labor . . . . . . . . . . . . | 10,080 |
| Power . . . . . . . . . . . . . . . . | 5,040 |
| Repairs and maintenance . . . . . | 5,960 |
| Depreciation, building . . . . . . . | 9,216 |
| Depreciation, machinery . . . . . | 13,824 |
| Taxes and insurance . . . . . . . | 4,080 |
| Supervision . . . . . . . . . . . . | 16,000 |
| Total costs . . . . . . . . . . . . . | $200,748 |

*Required*

1. Prepare a flexible overhead budget for the company showing the amount of each fixed and variable cost at the 70%, 80%, and 90% levels.
2. Isolate the material and labor variances into quantity and price variances and isolate the overhead variance into the volume variance and the controllable variance.
3. Prepare a factory overhead variance report showing the volume and controllable variances.

**Problem 26–6**
**Recording material, labor, and overhead variances**
(L. O. 4, 5)

Donley Company uses a standard cost system to account for its manufacturing operations and provides the following information concerning its operations during the month of July:

| | |
|---|---|
| Direct material cost actually incurred . . . . . . . . | $16,000 |
| Direct material quantity variance—unfavorable . . | 1,400 |
| Direct material price variance—favorable . . . . | 700 |
| Standard direct labor cost of goods produced . . . | 23,000 |
| Direct labor quantity variance—favorable . . . . | 1,000 |
| Direct labor price variance—unfavorable . . . . . | 1,600 |
| Actual overhead cost incurred . . . . . . . . . . . | 11,000 |
| Volume variance—favorable . . . . . . . . . . . . | 350 |
| Controllable variance—favorable . . . . . . . . . | 800 |

*Required*

1. Prepare journal entries dated July 31 to record the company's standard costs and the related variances.
2. List the areas that deserve special consideration if management follows the practice of management by exception.

## Alternate Problems

**Problem 26–1A**
**Preparing and using a flexible budget**
(L. O. 1)

In the process of preparing a master budget for 1991, Jennings Company assumed a sales volume of 6,750 units. The resulting budgeted income statement included the following items that comprise income from operations:

**JENNINGS COMPANY**
**Fixed Budget**
**For Year Ended December 31, 1991**

| | | |
|---|---|---|
| Sales | | $ 354,375 |
| Cost of goods sold: | | |
| Direct materials | $58,500 | |
| Direct labor | 46,800 | |
| Factory supplies | 4,650 | |
| Depreciation of plant | 8,700 | |
| Utilities (of which $6,750 is a fixed cost) | 13,200 | |
| Salary of plant manager | 42,750 | (174,600) |
| Gross profit | | $ 179,775 |
| Selling expenses: | | |
| Packaging | $26,250 | |
| Sales commissions | 27,750 | |
| Shipping | 15,900 | |
| Salary of vice president—marketing | 42,000 | |
| Promotion (variable) | 12,600 | (124,500) |
| General and administrative expenses: | | |
| Depreciation | $ 7,800 | |
| Consultant's fees (annual retainer) | 8,400 | |
| Administrative salaries | 38,250 | (54,450) |
| Income from operations | | $ 825 |

*Required*

1. Prepare a flexible budget for the company, showing specific budget columns for sales and production volumes of 7,500 units and 8,250 units. (Round unit costs to three decimal places and total dollar amounts to the nearest whole dollar.)
2. What would be the expected increase in income from operations if sales and production volume were 8,775 units rather than 6,750 units?
3. Although the management of Jennings Company believes that the master budget was a conservative estimate of sales and production volume, it is possible that the level of activity could fall to 5,670 units. What will be the effect on income from operations if this occurs?

**Problem 26–2A**
**Flexible budget performance report**
(L. O. 1)

Refer to the discussion of Jennings Company in Problem 26–1A. Jennings Company's actual statement of income from 1991 operations is as follows:

**JENNINGS COMPANY**
**Statement of Income from Operations**
**For Year Ended December 31, 1991**

| | | |
|---|---|---|
| Sales (7,500 units) | | $ 410,625 |
| Cost of goods sold: | | |
| Direct materials | $64,350 | |
| Direct labor | 55,125 | |
| Factory supplies | 5,513 | |
| Depreciation of plant | 8,775 | |
| Utilities (of which 50% is a fixed cost) | 13,950 | |
| Salary of plant manager | 42,750 | (190,463) |
| Gross profit | | $ 220,162 |
| Selling expenses: | | |
| Packaging | $28,875 | |
| Sales commissions | 35,100 | |
| Shipping | 16,818 | |
| Salary of vice president—marketing | 40,500 | |
| Promotion (variable) | 17,400 | (138,693) |
| General and administrative expenses: | | |
| Depreciation | $ 7,800 | |
| Consultant's fees | 8,940 | |
| Administrative salaries | 37,500 | (54,240) |
| Income from operations | | $ 27,229 |

*Required*

1. Using the flexible budget you prepared for Problem 26–1A, present a flexible budget performance report for 1991.
2. Explain the sales variance.

**Problem 26–3A**
**Calculating material, labor, and overhead variances**
(L. O. 3)

Wolfson Company has established the following standard costs for one unit of its product:

| | |
|---|---|
| Direct material (5 lbs. @ $1.80 per lb.) | $ 9.00 |
| Direct labor (1.5 hrs. @ $9.60 per hr.) | 14.40 |
| Overhead (1.5 hrs. @ $6 per hr.) | 9.00 |
| Total standard cost | $32.40 |

The overhead rate of $6 per direct labor hour is based on a normal, 90% of capacity, operating level for the company's plant and the following flexible budget information for April 1991:

| | Operating Levels | | |
|---|---|---|---|
| | 80% | 90% | 100% |
| Production in units | 1,200 | 1,350 | 1,500 |
| Direct labor hours | 1,800 | 2,025 | 2,250 |
| Budgeted overhead: | | | |
| Fixed factory overhead | $5,832 | $5,832 | $5,832 |
| Variable factory overhead | 5,616 | 6,318 | 7,020 |

During April, the company operated at 80% of capacity, producing 1,200 units of product and incurring actual costs as follows:

| | |
|---|---|
| Direct material (6,600 lbs. @ $1.92 per lb.) | $12,672 |
| Direct labor (1,720 hrs. @ $11.75 per hr.) | 20,210 |
| Fixed factory overhead costs | 5,832 |
| Variable factory overhead costs | 5,460 |

*Required*

Divide the direct material and direct labor cost variances into price and quantity variances, and divide the overhead cost variance into volume and controllable variances.

**Problem 26–4A**
**Calculating and reporting material, labor, and overhead variances**
(L. O. 2, 3)

Flagship Company has established the following standard costs per unit for the product it manufactures:

| | |
|---|---|
| Direct material (3 lbs. @ $3 per lb.) | $ 9.00 |
| Direct labor (1 hr. @ $13.50 per hr.) | 13.50 |
| Overhead (1 hr. @ $10.50 per hr.) | 10.50 |
| Total standard cost | $33.00 |

The $10.50 per direct labor hour overhead rate is based on a normal, 80% of capacity, operating level and the following flexible budget information for one month's operations:

| | Operating Levels | | |
|---|---|---|---|
| | 75% | 80% | 85% |
| Production in units | 3,000 | 3,200 | 3,400 |
| Standard direct labor hours | 3,000 | 3,200 | 3,400 |
| Budgeted factory overhead: | | | |
| Variable costs: | | | |
| Indirect materials | $ 4,500 | $ 4,800 | $ 5,100 |
| Indirect labor | 6,750 | 7,200 | 7,650 |
| Power | 2,025 | 2,160 | 2,295 |
| Maintenance | 900 | 960 | 1,020 |
| Total variable costs | $14,175 | $15,120 | $16,065 |
| Fixed costs: | | | |
| Depreciation, building | $ 6,750 | $ 6,750 | $ 6,750 |
| Depreciation, machinery | 5,400 | 5,400 | 5,400 |
| Taxes and insurance | 1,830 | 1,830 | 1,830 |
| Supervisory salaries | 4,500 | 4,500 | 4,500 |
| Total fixed costs | $18,480 | $18,480 | $18,480 |
| Total factory overhead costs | $32,655 | $33,600 | $34,545 |

During August 1991, the company operated at 75% of capacity, produced 3,000 units of product, and incurred the following actual costs:

| | | |
|---|---|---|
| Direct material (8,860 lbs. @ $3.15 per lb.) | | $ 27,909 |
| Direct labor (3,120 hrs. @ $13.10 per hr.) | | 40,872 |
| Overhead costs: | | |
| Indirect materials | $4,920 | |
| Indirect labor | 7,005 | |
| Power | 1,785 | |
| Maintenance | 540 | |
| Depreciation, building | 6,750 | |
| Depreciation, machinery | 5,400 | |
| Taxes and insurance | 2,175 | |
| Supervisory salaries | 4,500 | 33,075 |
| Total costs | | $101,856 |

*Required*

1. Isolate the direct material and direct labor variances into price and

quantity variances and isolate the overhead variance into the volume variance and the controllable variance.

2. Prepare a factory overhead variance report showing the volume and controllable variances.

**Problem 26–5A**
**Flexible budget, variance analysis, and report for overhead costs**
(L. O. 1, 2, 3, 4)

MacArthur Company has established the following standard costs for one unit of its product:

| | |
|---|---|
| Direct material (2 lbs. @ $1.20 per lb.) . . | $2.40 |
| Direct labor (1/2 hr. @ $8.80 per hr.) . . . | 4.40 |
| Overhead (1/2 hr. @ $4.80 per hr.) . . . . | 2.40 |
| Total standard cost . . . . . . . . . . . . | $9.20 |

The $4.80 per direct labor hour overhead rate is based on a normal, 95% of capacity, operating level. At this level, the company's monthly output is 3,800 units. Following are the company's budgeted overhead costs at the 95% level for one month:

**MACARTHUR COMPANY**
**Budgeted Monthly Factory Overhead at 95% Level**

| | | |
|---|---|---|
| Variable costs: | | |
| Indirect materials . . . . . . . . . | $1,064 | |
| Indirect labor . . . . . . . . . . . | 912 | |
| Power . . . . . . . . . . . . . . . | 608 | |
| Repairs and maintenance . . . . | 456 | |
| Total variable costs . . . . . . . . | | $3,040 |
| Fixed costs: | | |
| Depreciation, building . . . . . . | $1,920 | |
| Depreciation, machinery . . . . | 1,440 | |
| Taxes and insurance . . . . . . . | 960 | |
| Supervision . . . . . . . . . . . . | 1,760 | |
| Total fixed costs . . . . . . . . . | | 6,080 |
| Total overhead costs . . . . . . . . | | $9,120 |

During July of the current year, the company operated at 85% of capacity and incurred the following actual costs:

| | |
|---|---|
| Direct material (7,050 lbs.) . . . . | $ 9,024 |
| Direct labor (1,750 hrs.) . . . . . . | 14,700 |
| Indirect materials . . . . . . . . . | 960 |
| Indirect labor . . . . . . . . . . . | 800 |
| Power . . . . . . . . . . . . . . . | 600 |
| Repairs and maintenance . . . . | 320 |
| Depreciation, building . . . . . . . | 1,920 |
| Depreciation, machinery . . . . . | 1,440 |
| Taxes and insurance . . . . . . . | 920 |
| Supervision . . . . . . . . . . . . | 1,760 |
| Total costs . . . . . . . . . . . . . | $32,444 |

*Required*

1. Prepare a flexible overhead budget for the company showing the amount of each fixed and variable cost at the 75%, 85%, and 95% levels.
2. Isolate the material and labor variances into quantity and price vari-

ances and isolate the overhead variance into the volume variance and the controllable variance.

3. Prepare a factory overhead variance report showing the volume and controllable variances.

**Problem 26–6A**
**Recording material, labor, and overhead variances**
(L. O. 4, 5)

Bradshaw Company uses a standard cost system to account for its manufacturing operations and provides the following information concerning its operations during the month of March:

| | |
|---|---|
| Standard material cost of goods produced . . . | $24,000 |
| Direct material quantity variance—favorable . . | 2,000 |
| Direct material price variance—unfavorable . . | 2,700 |
| Direct labor cost actually incurred . . . . . . . . | 37,000 |
| Direct labor quantity variance—unfavorable . . | 4,500 |
| Direct labor price variance—favorable . . . . . | 2,600 |
| Actual overhead cost incurred . . . . . . . . . | 16,000 |
| Volume variance—unfavorable . . . . . . . . . | 500 |
| Controllable variance—favorable . . . . . . . . | 900 |

*Required*

1. Prepare journal entries dated March 31 to record the company's standard costs and the related variances.
2. List the areas that deserve special consideration if management follows the practice of management by exception.

## Provocative Problems

**Provocative Problem 26–1**
**Ambassador Company**
(L. O. 2, 3)

Ambassador Company's management plans to sell artistic, hand-blown glass vases for $42 each. Each vase should require 2.5 pounds of a specially processed glass that the company expects to purchase for $7.50 per pound. The vases ought to be produced at the rate of three vases per direct labor hour, and the company should be able to hire the needed laborers for $13.50 per hour. Each vase will be packaged in a cardboard container which weighs one pound, and the company will seek to buy cardboard for $0.75 per pound.

If actual sales and production volume range from 10,000 to 20,000 vases, the manager would expect the company to incur administrative and sales personnel salaries of $90,000, depreciation of $27,000, utilities expenses of $21,000, and insurance expense of $15,000.

In 1991, Ambassador Company actually produced and sold 15,000 vases at $39 each. It used 38,600 pounds of glass, purchased at $7.80 per pound. Laborers were paid $13.05 per hour and worked 4,800 hours to produce the vases. Cardboard was purchased for $0.81 per pound and 14,550 pounds were used. All other expenses occurred as planned.

Although the above facts are available to the company's managers, they have not yet been able to clearly evaluate the operating performance of the company. They recognize that the actual operating income was different from the expected amount but haven't sorted out which items caused the change. They also expressed interest in learning the magnitude of the impact of price changes in specific items purchased by the company as well as any other factors that might be of help in evaluating the company's performance. Can you help management?

**Provocative Problem 26–2**
**NDT Company**
(L. O. 2, 3)

Ansel Tudbury has been an employee of NDT Company for nine years, the last seven of which he has worked in the pipe threading department. Eight months ago he was made supervisor of the department, and since then has been able to end a long period of internal dissension, high employee turnover, and inefficient operation in the department. Under Ansel's supervision, the department's production has increased, employee morale has improved, and absenteeism has dropped. For the past two months, the department has regularly been beating its standard for the first time in years.

However, a few days ago Rita Hawthorne, an employee in the department, suggested to Ansel that the company install new controls on the department's machinery similar to those developed by a competitor. The controls would cost $32,000 installed and would have an eight-year life and no salvage value. They should increase production 10%, reduce maintenance costs $600 per year, and do away with the labor of one person.

Ansel's answer to Rita was: "Forget it. We are doing OK now; we don't need the extra production; and besides, jobs are hard to find and if we have to let someone go, who'll it be?"

Do you think standard costs have anything to do with Ansel's answer to Rita? Explain. Do you agree with Ansel's answer? Should Ansel be the person to make a decision such as this? How can a company be sure that suggestions such as Rita's are not lost in the chain of command?

**Provocative Problem 26–3**
**Borneo Company**
(L. O. 2)

Borneo Company manufactures a product that has a seasonal demand and that cannot be stored for long periods. As a result, the number of units manufactured varies with the season. In accounting for costs, the company charges actual costs incurred to a Goods in Process account maintained for the product, which it closes at the end of each quarter to Finished Goods. At the end of last year, which was an average year, the following cost report was prepared for the company manager:

**BORNEO COMPANY**
**Quarterly Report of Product Costs**
**Year Ended December 31, 1991**

| | First Quarter | Second Quarter | Third Quarter | Fourth Quarter |
|---|---|---|---|---|
| Direct materials | $ 23,400 | $ 29,175 | $11,775 | $ 5,925 |
| Direct labor | 70,050 | 87,000 | 35,250 | 17,700 |
| Fixed overhead costs | 31,500 | 31,500 | 31,500 | 31,500 |
| Variable overhead costs | 38,400 | 47,925 | 19,425 | 9,750 |
| Total manufacturing costs | $163,350 | $195,600 | $97,950 | $64,875 |
| Production in units | 10,000 | 12,500 | 5,000 | 2,500 |
| Cost per unit | $ 16.335 | $ 15.648 | $19.590 | $25.950 |

The manager has asked you to explain why unit costs for the product varied from a low of $15.648 in the second quarter to a high of $25.950 in the last quarter. Also, you are expected to offer suggested improvements in the methods used to accumulate or allocate costs. The manager feels that the quarterly reports are needed for purposes of control, so attach to your explanation a schedule that shows what last year's direct material, direct labor, and overhead costs per unit would have been had your suggestion or suggestions been followed for the year.

# 27 Capital Budgeting; Managerial Decisions

Business decisions involve choosing between two or more courses of action, and the typical objective is to gain the highest return on investment or the greatest cost savings. Some decisions must be based to a great extent on an intuitive understanding of the issues—perhaps the available information is too sketchy to allow a more systematic approach. In other situations, intangible factors such as convenience, prestige, and public opinion are more important than the factors that can be reduced to a quantitative basis. Nevertheless, in many situations you can reduce the anticipated consequences of alternative choices to a quantitative basis and measure them systematically. This chapter examines several areas of decision making in which more or less systematic methods of analysis are available.

### Learning Objectives

*After studying Chapter 27, you should be able to:*

1. Explain the importance of capital budgeting, calculate the expected payback period of an investment, and state the limitations of this method of evaluating capital investments.
2. Calculate the expected rate of return on an investment and state the assumptions on which this method of evaluating capital investments is based.
3. Describe the information obtained by using a net present value method, the procedures involved in using this method, and the problems associated with its use.
4. Explain the effects of incremental costs on decisions to accept or reject additional business and whether to make or buy a given product.
5. State the meaning of sunk costs, out-of-pocket costs, and opportunity costs, and describe the importance of each type of cost to decisions such as to scrap or rebuild defective units or to sell a product as is or process it further.
6. Define or explain the words and phrases listed in the chapter Glossary.

## Capital Budgeting

Explain the importance of capital budgeting, calculate the expected payback period of an investment, and state the limitations of this method of evaluating capital investments.
(L. O. 1)

Planning plant asset investments is called **capital budgeting.** The plans may involve new buildings, new machinery, or whole new projects. In all such cases, a fundamental objective of business firms is to earn a satisfactory return on the invested funds. Capital budgeting often requires some of the most risky and difficult decisions faced by management. The decisions are difficult because they are commonly based on estimates projected well into a future that is at best uncertain. Capital budgeting decisions are risky because (1) large sums of money are often involved; (2) funds are committed for long periods of time; and (3) once a decision is made and a project is begun, it may be difficult or impossible to reverse the effects of a poor decision.

Capital budgeting is a topic that covers a wide range of decisions and a variety of different decision-making techniques. Nevertheless, essentially all of these techniques involve estimating the cash inflows and outflows of each proposed project, examining the merits of each, and choosing those projects worthy of investment. In this chapter, we will consider three widely recognized methods that are used to compare investment alternatives. They are the **payback period**, the **rate of return on average investment**, and **net present value.**

### Payback Period

Generally, any investment project, whether it involves a machine or some other long-term commitment, produces periodic cash inflows and requires some periodic cash outflows. The difference between these inflows and outflows each period is the *net cash flow*. The *payback period* of an investment is the time required to recover the investment through this net cash flow. For example, assume that Murray Company is considering several capital investments. One investment involves the purchase of a machine to be used in manufacturing a new product. The machine will cost $16,000 and is expected to have an eight-year life with no salvage value. Management also estimates that the machine will produce 10,000 units of product each year and that the product will be sold for $3 per unit. Illustration 27–1 shows the expected annual revenues and expenses (including income taxes) and also the cash flows from the investment.

Illustration 27–1 shows that the cash flows from the project can be calculated directly by subtracting cash outflows from cash inflows. The final column simply excludes noncash items—in this case depreciation is the only noncash item. An alternative presentation is to adjust the projected net income for revenue and expense items that do not involve cash flows. For the example in Illustration 27–1, the net income of $2,100 plus the $2,000 depreciation equals the $4,100 annual net cash flow.

Based on an expected net cash flow of $4,100 each year, the payback period for the project is calculated as follows:

$$\frac{\text{Cost of new machine, \$16,000}}{\text{Annual net cash flow, \$4,100}} = 3.9 \text{ years to recover investment}$$

The answer of 3.9 years is rounded to one decimal place because carrying it any further would not be meaningful. Remember that the calculation is based on estimates of net cash flow. In this case, the estimates relate to cash flows

**Illustration 27–1**
**Expected revenues, expenses, and cash flows from an investment**

| | Expected Income | Cash Flows |
|---|---|---|
| Annual sales of new product | $ 30,000 | $ 30,000 |
| Deduct: | | |
| Cost of materials, labor, and overhead other than depreciation on the new machine | (15,500) | (15,500) |
| Depreciation on the new machine | (2,000) | |
| Additional selling and administrative expenses | (9,500) | (9,500) |
| Annual before-tax income | $ 3,000 | |
| Income tax (assumed rate, 30%) | (900) | (900) |
| Annual after-tax net income and net cash flow | $ 2,100 | $ 4,100 |

that will occur nearly four years in the future. Estimates of this sort are not dependable enough to justify a more precise calculation, and carrying the calculation further would suggest a degree of accuracy that is not appropriate. One might even argue that carrying the calculation to one decimal place is questionable. Perhaps the most meaningful interpretation of the statistic is to say that the payback appears to be approximately four years.

**Calculating Payback When Cash Flows Are Not Uniform.** The previous example assumed that net cash flows were $4,100 each and every year. However, the payback period can be calculated just as easily when cash flows vary from year to year. For example, assume an investment of $15,000 is expected to produce annual net cash flows as follows:

| | Annual Net Cash Flows | Total Net Cash Flows |
|---|---|---|
| Year 1 | $3,000 | $ 3,000 |
| Year 2 | 4,000 | 7,000 |
| Year 3 | 5,000 | 12,000 |
| Year 4 | 6,000 | 18,000 |

Total net cash flows are $12,000 at the end of year 3 and $18,000 at the end of year 4. Obviously, the expected payback period for the $15,000 investment is between three and four years. Of the $15,000 investment, $12,000 is paid back during the first three years. The remaining $3,000 that is paid back during year 4 amounts to one half or 0.5 of the $6,000 net cash flow for the entire year. Thus, the payback period is approximately 3.5 years.

**Evaluating Payback Period as a Method of Comparing Investments.** In choosing between investment opportunities, a short payback period is desirable because (1) the sooner cash is received, the sooner the funds are available for other uses; and (2) a short payback period also means the invested funds are at risk for a shorter period of time. In other words, a short "bail-out period" improves the company's ability to respond if conditions change.

The payback period should never be the only consideration in evaluating investments because it ignores at least two important factors. First, it fails to reflect differences in the timing of net cash flows. In the previous example, the net cash flows in years 1, 2, and 3 were \$3,000, \$4,000, and \$5,000. If they had been \$5,000, \$4,000, and \$3,000 in years 1, 2, and 3, the payback period would still be 3.5 years.

Second, payback period ignores the length of time cash will continue to be received after the end of the payback period. For example, one investment may pay back its cost in 3 years and cease to produce cash at that point, while a second investment may require 5 years to pay back its cost but will continue to produce net cash flows for another 15 years.

### Rate of Return on Average Investment

Calculate the expected rate of return on an investment and state the assumptions on which this method of evaluating capital investments is based. (L. O. 2)

The *rate of return on the average investment* in a project or asset is calculated by dividing the after-tax net income from the project by the average investment in the project.

**Rate of Return When Net Cash Flows Are Received Evenly throughout Year.** In calculating the average investment, an assumption must be made as to the timing of the cost recovery from depreciation. If the net cash flows are received evenly throughout the year, the reduction in the investment may be assumed to occur at the middle of the year. Under these conditions, the average investment each year may be calculated as the average of the beginning-of-year book value and the end-of-year book value. If Murray Company's \$16,000 machine is depreciated \$2,000 each year, the average investment each year and the average investment over the life of the machine may be calculated as shown in Illustration 27–2.

More simply, the average investment may be calculated as:

$$\$16,000 \div 2 = \$8,000$$

Note that the above example is simplified by the fact that the machine has no salvage value. If the machine had a salvage value, the average investment would be calculated as (Original cost + Salvage value) ÷ 2.

After average investment is determined, the rate of return on average investment is calculated. As previously stated, this involves dividing the estimated annual after-tax net income from the sale of the machine's product by average investment. Since Murray Company expects an after-tax net income of \$2,100, the expected rate of return, rounded to the nearest percentage point, is calculated as follows:

$$\$2,100 \div \$8,000 = 26\% \text{ return on average investment}$$

**Rate of Return When Net Cash Flows Are Received at Year-End.** In some investments, the revenue from the investment is not spread evenly over each year and may be received near the end of each year. If the net cash flow is expected to be received at the end of the year, the cost recovery from depreciation also occurs at the year's end. Thus, the average investment each year is the beginning-of-year book value. Referring back to Illustration 27–2, these assumptions result in the following calculation of average investment:

**Illustration 27–2**
**Calculating average investment when net cash flows are received evenly throughout each period**

| Year | Beginning-of-Year Book Value | Average Investment Each Year |
|---|---|---|
| 1 . . . . | $16,000 | $15,000 |
| 2 . . . . | 14,000 | 13,000 |
| 3 . . . . | 12,000 | 11,000 |
| 4 . . . . | 10,000 | 9,000 |
| 5 . . . . | 8,000 | 7,000 |
| 6 . . . . | 6,000 | 5,000 |
| 7 . . . . | 4,000 | 3,000 |
| 8 . . . . | 2,000 | 1,000 |
| Totals . . | $72,000 | $64,000 |

$\frac{\$64{,}000}{8} = \$8{,}000$ average investment over life of machine

$72,000 ÷ 8 = $9,000 average investment over life of investment

Instead of adding the beginning-of-year book values and averaging over eight years, a shorter way to the same answer is to average the book values of the machine's first and last years in this manner:

$16,000 book value at beginning of (and throughout) first year
2,000 book value at beginning of (and throughout) last year
$18,000

$18,000 ÷ 2 = $9,000 average investment over life of investment

Note that if the machine had a salvage value, the book value at the beginning of (and throughout) the last year would be the salvage value plus the depreciation expense of the last year.

**Evaluating the Return on Average Investment.** Given a $9,000 average investment, the return on investment (rounded to the nearest percentage point) is:

$2,100 ÷ $9,000 = 23% return on average investment

At this point the question naturally arises whether 23% or 26% are good rates of return. Obviously, 26% appears better than 23%. However, even this may not be true. A project that is expected to yield 26% may be much riskier than another project that has a 23% expected return. And, depending on other available investment alternatives, neither may be acceptable. In other words, a return is good or bad only when related to other returns and taking into consideration the differing riskiness of the alternatives. However, when average investment returns are used to compare and decide between capital investments, the one with the least risk, the shortest payback period, and the highest return for the longest time is usually the best.

Perhaps because rate of return on average investment is easy to calculate, it has long been used in selecting investment opportunities. However, its usefulness as a method of evaluating investments is limited when the net incomes are expected to vary from year to year. If the annual net income from an investment is expected to vary from year to year, the calculation of rate of return on average investment must be based on the average annual net income. Two investments with the same average annual net income may not be equally desirable because one is expected to have higher net incomes in the early years and lower net incomes in the later years. Rate of return on average investment fails to distinguish between these two investments. In such cases, a comparison of net present values generally offers a better means of selection.

*An understanding of net present values requires an understanding of the concept of discounting. This concept was explained in Chapter 12, beginning on page 511. That explanation should be reviewed at this point if you do not fully understand it. An expanded explanation of discounting is presented in Appendix G, beginning on page 1209. You can use the present value tables in Appendix G, on pages 1215 and 1217, to solve some of the problems at the end of this chapter.*

### Net Present Values

Describe the information obtained by using a net present value method, the procedures involved in using this method, and the problems associated with its use.
(L. O. 3)

When a business invests in a new plant asset, it expects the investment to produce a stream of future net cash flows. Normally, a business should not invest unless the expected cash flows are sufficient to return the amount of the investment plus a satisfactory return on the investment. For example, assume that the cash flows from Murray Company's investment will be received at the end of each year. Will the investment in the machine return the amount of the investment plus a satisfactory return? If Murray Company considers a 12% compound annual return a satisfactory return on its capital investments, it can answer this question with the calculations of Illustration 27–3.

To purchase the machine of Illustration 27–3, Murray Company must invest $16,000. However, from the sale of the machine's product the company expects to receive net cash flows of $4,100 each year for eight years. The first column of Illustration 27–3 indicates that the net cash flows of the first year are received one year hence, and so forth for the years thereafter. This means that the net cash flows are received at the end of the year. To simplify the discussion of net present values and the related problems at the end of the chapter, we will generally assume that net cash flows are received at year-end. More refined calculations are considered in advanced accounting and finance courses.

The annual net cash flows, shown in the second column of Illustration 27–3, are multiplied by the amounts in the third column to determine their present values, which are shown in the last column. Observe that the total of these present values exceeds the amount of the required investment by $4,367. Therefore, if Murray Company considers a 12% compounded return satisfactory, this machine will recover its required investment, plus a 12% compounded return, and $4,367 in addition.

Generally, when the cash flows from an investment are discounted at a satisfactory rate and have a positive *net present value,* the investment is worthy of acceptance. Also, when several investment opportunities are being compared and each requires the same investment and has the same risk, the one with the highest positive net present value is the best.

**Illustration 27–3**

| Years Hence | Net Cash Flows | Present Value of $1 at 12% | Present Value of Net Cash Flows |
|---|---|---|---|
| 1 . . . . | $4,100 | 0.8929 | $ 3,661 |
| 2 . . . . | 4,100 | 0.7972 | 3,269 |
| 3 . . . . | 4,100 | 0.7118 | 2,918 |
| 4 . . . . | 4,100 | 0.6355 | 2,606 |
| 5 . . . . | 4,100 | 0.5674 | 2,326 |
| 6 . . . . | 4,100 | 0.5066 | 2,077 |
| 7 . . . . | 4,100 | 0.4523 | 1,854 |
| 8 . . . . | 4,100 | 0.4039 | 1,656 |
| Total present value . . . . . . . . . . . . . . | | | $20,367 |
| Amount to be invested . . . . . . . . . . . . . | | | 16,000 |
| Positive net present value . . . . . . . . . . . | | | $ 4,367 |

### Shortening the Calculation

In Illustration 27–3, the present values of $1 at 12% for each of the eight years involved are shown. Each year's cash flow is multiplied by the present value of $1 at 12% for that year to determine its present value. Then, the present values of the eight cash flows are added to determine their total. This is one way to determine total present value. However, since in this case the cash flows are uniform, there are two shorter ways. One shorter way is to add the eight yearly present values of $1 at 12% and to multiply $4,100 by the total. Another even shorter way is based on Table G–3 on page 1217. Table G–3 shows the present value of $1 to be received periodically for a number of periods. In the case of the Murray Company machine, $4,100 is to be received annually for eight years. Consequently, to determine the present value of these annual receipts discounted at 12%, go down the 12% column of Table G–3 to the amount opposite eight periods. It is 4.9676. Therefore, the present value of the eight annual $4,100 receipts is $4,100 multiplied by 4.9676, or is $20,367.

### Cash Flows Not Uniform

Net present value analysis is especially useful when cash flows are not uniform. For example, assume a company can choose one capital investment from among Projects A, B, and C. Each requires a $12,000 investment and will produce cash flows as follows:

| Years Hence | Annual Cash Flows | | |
|---|---|---|---|
| | Project A | Project B | Project C |
| 1 . . | $ 5,000 | $ 8,000 | $ 1,000 |
| 2 . . | 5,000 | 5,000 | 5,000 |
| 3 . . | 5,000 | 2,000 | 9,000 |
| | $15,000 | $15,000 | $15,000 |

**Illustration 27–4**
**Comparing net present values of projects when the timing of cash flows differ**

| Years Hence | Present Values of Cash Flows Discounted at 10% | | |
|---|---|---|---|
| | Project A | Project B | Project C |
| 1 . . . . . . . . . . . . . | $ 4,546 | $ 7,273 | $ 909 |
| 2 . . . . . . . . . . . . . | 4,132 | 4,132 | 4,132 |
| 3 . . . . . . . . . . . . . | 3,756 | 1,503 | 6,762 |
| Total present values . . . . | $12,434 | $12,908 | $11,803 |
| Required investments . . . | 12,000 | 12,000 | 12,000 |
| Net present values . . . . | $ +434 | $ +908 | $ −197 |

Note that all three projects produce the same total cash flow. However, the flows of Project A are uniform, those of Project B are greater in the earlier years, while those of Project C are greater in the later years. Therefore, if the present values of the cash flows are discounted, say, at 10%, to determine the net present values, the statistics of Illustration 27–4 result.

Note that an investment in Project A has a $434 positive net present value; an investment in Project B has a $908 positive net present value; and an investment in Project C has a $197 negative net present value. Therefore, if a 10% return is required, an investment in Project C should be rejected, since the investment's net present value indicates it will not earn such a return. Furthermore, if only one project can be accepted, Project B appears to be the better investment since its cash flows have the higher net present value. Recognizing that present values are always approximations, the present value numbers in Illustration 27–4 are rounded to the nearest whole dollar.

### Salvage Value and Accelerated Depreciation

The $16,000 machine of the Murray Company example was assumed to have no salvage value at the end of its useful life. More often, a machine is expected to have a salvage value, and in such cases the expected salvage value is treated as an additional cash flow to be received in the last year of the machine's life.

Also, in the Murray Company example, depreciation was deducted on a straight-line basis. In actual practice, however, accelerated depreciation often is used for tax purposes. Accelerated depreciation results in larger depreciation deductions in the early years of an asset's life and smaller deductions in the later years. This results in smaller income tax payments in the early years and larger payments in later years. Nevertheless, this does not change the basic nature of a present value analysis. (Accelerated depreciation for tax purposes affects the outcome of the investment and the analysis because it results in larger net cash flows in the early years of the asset's life and smaller ones in later years.) Because early cash flows are more valuable than later ones, accelerated depreciation for tax purposes usually makes an investment more desirable.

## AS A MATTER OF ETHICS

Several months ago, Colfus Corporation's top management adopted new policies to control equipment purchases. According to the new policy, if a proposed equipment purchase will cost more than $5,000, the proposal must be submitted for a careful review and capital budgeting analysis. When a manager prepares a proposal, the manager must include predictions of future cash flows that will result from the equipment purchase. These predictions will be evaluated by a central financial analysis group and modified as necessary. Based on its analysis of the proposal, the financial analysis group has the authority to approve or disapprove the proposal.

Gary Waters, one of Colfus Corporation's middle-level managers, has very recently decided that his group can perform more efficiently and effectively with a major upgrade of its personal computer network. The upgrade will require several new computers, large capacity hard disks, additional internal memory, a new network controller, software, and various other items. All items can be delivered quickly, and the benefits are expected to be realizable within a short time.

Although the total cost of the items Mr. Waters wants to purchase is approximately $25,000, he is thinking about planning the purchase in a way that will avoid the hassle of preparing a lengthy proposal. No single component costs more than $5,000, and if he prepares six or seven purchase orders, all of the proposed items could be purchased without exceeding $5,000 on any one.

You are a trusted friend of Mr. Waters, and he asks your opinion. He says that the new equipment will definitely improve profits. But, it will take a lot of effort to develop suitable predictions of cash flows, and the financial analysis group's decision will probably take two months. By that time, Waters is confident that he could receive the equipment, add it to the network, and start getting the job done.

### Selecting the Earnings Rate

The selection of a satisfactory earnings rate for capital investments is always a matter for top-management decision. Although formulas have been designed to aid this selection, the choice of a satisfactory or required rate of return is largely subjective in many companies. Management simply decides that enough investment opportunities can be found that will earn, say, a 10% compounded return; and this becomes the minimum below which the company refuses to make an investment of average risk.

Whatever the required rate, it is always higher than the rate at which money can be borrowed, since the return on a capital investment must include not only interest but also an additional allowance for the risks involved. For example, when the rate at which money can be borrowed is around 10%, a required after-tax return of 15% may be acceptable in industrial companies, with a lower rate for public utilities and a higher rate for companies in which the risks are unusually high.

## Replacing Plant Assets

In a dynamic economy, new and better machines are constantly coming on the market. As a result, the decision to replace an existing machine with a new and better machine is common. Often, the existing machine is in good condition and will produce the required product; but the new machine will do the job with a large savings in operating costs. In such a situation, management must decide whether the after-tax savings in operating costs justifies the investment.

The amount of after-tax savings from the replacement of an existing machine with a new machine is complicated by the fact that depreciation on the new machine for tax purposes is based on the book value of the old machine plus the cash given in the exchange. There can be other complications as well. Therefore, a discussion of the replacement of plant assets is deferred to a more advanced course.

## Accepting Additional Business

Explain the effects of incremental costs on decisions to accept or reject additional business and whether to make or buy a given product. (L. O. 4)

Costs obtained from a cost accounting system are average costs and also historical costs. They are useful in product pricing and in controlling operations. But, in a decision to accept an additional volume of business, they are not necessarily the relevant costs. In such a decision, the relevant costs are the additional costs, commonly called the **incremental** or **differential costs.**

For example, assume that a company operates at its normal capacity, which is 80% of full capacity. The company produces and sells approximately 100,000 units of product annually, with the following results:

| | Per Unit | Total |
|---|---|---|
| Sales (100,000 units) | $10.00 | $1,000,000 |
| Direct materials | $ (3.50) | $ (350,000) |
| Direct labor | (2.20) | (220,000) |
| Factory overhead | (1.10) | (110,000) |
| Selling expenses | (1.40) | (140,000) |
| Administrative expenses | (0.80) | (80,000) |
| Total expenses | $ (9.00) | $ (900,000) |
| Operating income | $ 1.00 | $ 100,000 |

The company's sales department reports it has an exporter who has offered to buy 10,000 units of product at $8.50 per unit. The sale to the exporter is several times larger than any previous sale made by the company; and since the units are being exported, the new business will have no effect on present business. Therefore, in order to determine whether the order should be accepted or rejected, management of the company asks that statistics be prepared to show the estimated net income or loss that would result from accepting the offer. It received the following figures based on the average costs previously given:

| | Per Unit | Total |
|---|---|---|
| Sales (10,000 units) | $ 8.50 | $ 85,000 |
| Direct materials | $(3.50) | $(35,000) |
| Direct labor | (2.20) | (22,000) |
| Factory overhead | (1.10) | (11,000) |
| Selling expenses | (1.40) | (14,000) |
| Administrative expenses | (0.80) | (8,000) |
| Total expenses | $(9.00) | $(90,000) |
| Operating loss | $(0.50) | $ (5,000) |

If a decision were based on these average costs, the new business would likely be rejected. However, in this situation, average costs are not relevant.

**Illustration 27–5**
**The effects of accepting additional business**

| | Present Business | | Additional Business | | Present Plus the Additional Business | |
|---|---|---|---|---|---|---|
| Sales | | $1,000,000 | | $85,000 | | $1,085,000 |
| Direct materials | $350,000 | | $35,000 | | $385,000 | |
| Direct labor | 220,000 | | 22,000 | | 242,000 | |
| Factory overhead | 110,000 | | 5,000 | | 115,000 | |
| Selling expenses | 140,000 | | 2,000 | | 142,000 | |
| Administrative expense | 80,000 | | 1,000 | | 81,000 | |
| Total | | 900,000 | | 65,000 | | 965,000 |
| Operating income | | $ 100,000 | | $20,000 | | $ 120,000 |

The relevant costs are the added costs of accepting the new business. Therefore, before rejecting the order, the costs of the new business were examined more closely and the following additional information obtained: (1) Manufacturing 10,000 additional units of product would require direct materials and direct labor at $3.50 and $2.20 per unit just as with normal production. (2) However, the 10,000 units could be manufactured with factory overhead costs, in addition to those already incurred, of only $5,000 for power, packing, and handling labor. (3) Commissions and other selling expenses resulting from the sale would amount to $2,000 in addition to the selling expenses already incurred. And (4), $1,000 additional administrative expenses in the form of clerical work would be required if the order were accepted. Based on this added information, the statement of Illustration 27–5 showing the effect of the additional business on the company's normal business was prepared.

Illustration 27–5 shows that the additional business should be accepted. Present business should be charged with all present costs, and the additional business should be charged only with its incremental or differential costs. When this is done, accepting the additional business at $8.50 per unit will apparently result in additional income before taxes of $20,000.

Incremental or differential costs always apply to a particular situation at a particular time. For example, adding units to a given production volume may or may not increase depreciation expense. If the additional units require the purchase of more machines, depreciation expense is increased. Likewise, if present machines are used but the additional units shorten their useful lives, more depreciation expense results. However, if present machines are used and their depreciation depends on the passage of time or obsolescence more than on use, additional depreciation expense might not result from the added units of product.

## Make or Buy Decisions

Incremental or differential costs are often a factor in a decision as to whether a given part or product should be manufactured or purchased. For example, a manufacturer has idle machines that can be used to manufacture one of the components (Part 417) of the company's product. This part is presently purchased at a $1.20 delivered cost per unit. The manufacturer estimates that to make Part 417 would cost $0.45 for direct materials, $0.50 for direct labor, and an amount of factory overhead. At this point a question arises as to how much overhead should be charged. If the normal overhead rate of the department in which the part would be manufactured is 100% of direct labor cost, and this amount is charged against Part 417, then the unit costs of making Part 417 would be $0.45 for direct materials, $0.50 for direct labor, and $0.50 for factory overhead, a total of $1.45. At this cost, the manufacturer would be better off to buy the part at $1.20 each.

However, on a short-run basis the manufacturer might be justified in ignoring the normal overhead rate and charging Part 417 for only the additional overhead costs resulting from its manufacture. Among these additional overhead costs might be, for example, power to operate the machines that would otherwise be idle, depreciation on the machines if the part's manufacture resulted in additional depreciation, and any other overhead that would be added to that already incurred. If these added overhead items total less than $0.25 per unit, the manufacturer might be justified on a short-run basis in manufacturing the part. However, on a long-term basis, Part 417 should be charged a full share of all overhead.

Any amount of overhead less than $0.25 per unit results in a total cost for Part 417 that is less than the $1.20 per unit purchase price. Nevertheless, in making a final decision as to whether the part should be bought or made, the manufacturer should consider in addition to costs such things as quality, the reactions of customers and suppliers, and other intangible factors. When these additional factors are considered, small cost differences may become a minor factor.

## Other Cost Concepts

State the meaning of sunk costs, out-of-pocket costs, and opportunity costs, and describe the importance of each type of cost to decisions such as to scrap or rebuild defective units or to sell a product as is or process it further. (L. O. 5)

**Sunk costs**, **out-of-pocket costs**, and **opportunity costs** are additional concepts that may be encountered in managerial decisions.

A *sunk cost* is a cost that results from a past irrevocable decision. It is sunk in the sense that it cannot be avoided. As a result, sunk costs are irrelevant to decisions affecting the future.

An *out-of-pocket cost* is a cost that requires a current outlay of funds. Material costs, supplies, heat, and power are examples. Generally, out-of-pocket costs can be avoided; therefore, they are relevant in decisions affecting the future.

The costs discussed so far have been outlays or expenditures made to obtain some benefit, usually goods or services. However, the concept of cost can be expanded to include *opportunity costs*. These are potential benefits that are lost as a result of choosing an alternative course of action. For example, if a job that will pay a student $1,200 for working during the summer must be rejected in order to attend summer school, the $1,200 is an opportunity cost of attending summer school.

Opportunity costs are not entered in the accounting records; but they may be relevant to a decision that involves rejected opportunities. For example, decisions to scrap or rebuild defective units of product commonly involve situations that evidence both sunk costs and opportunity costs.

## Scrap or Rebuild Defective Units

Any costs incurred in manufacturing units of product that do not pass inspection are sunk costs and as such should not enter into a decision as to whether the units should be sold for scrap or be rebuilt to pass inspection. For example, a company has 10,000 defective units of product that cost $1 per unit to manufacture. The units can be sold as they are for $0.40 each, or they can be rebuilt for $0.80 per unit, after which they can be sold for their full price of $1.50 per unit. Should the company rebuild the units or should it sell them in their present form? The original manufacturing costs of $1 per unit are sunk costs and are irrelevant in the decision. Based on the information given, the comparative returns from scrapping or rebuilding the units are as follows:

| | As Scrap | Rebuilt |
|---|---|---|
| Sales of defective units | $4,000 | $15,000 |
| Less cost to rebuilt | | (8,000) |
| Net return | $4,000 | $ 7,000 |

Given this information, it appears that rebuilding is the better decision. This is true if the rebuilding does not interfere with normal operations. However, suppose that to rebuild the defective units the company must forgo manufacturing 10,000 new units that will cost $1 per unit to manufacture and can be sold for $1.50 per unit. In this situation the comparative returns may be analyzed as follows:

| | As Scrap | Rebuilt |
|---|---|---|
| Sales of defective units | $ 4,000 | $15,000 |
| Less cost to rebuild | | (8,000) |
| Sale of new units | 15,000 | |
| Less cost to manufacture the new units | (10,000) | |
| Net return | $ 9,000 | $ 7,000 |

If the defective units are sold without rebuilding, then the new units can also be manufactured and sold, with a $9,000 return from the sale of both the new and old units, as shown in the first column of the analysis. Obviously, this is better than forgoing the manufacture of the new units and rebuilding the defective units for a $7,000 net return.

This situation also may be analyzed on an opportunity cost basis as follows: If rebuilding the defective units requires that the company forgo manufacturing the new units, then the return on the sale of the new units is an opportunity cost of rebuilding the defective units. This opportunity cost is measured as $5,000 (revenue from sale of new units, $15,000, less their manufacturing costs, $10,000, equals the $5,000 benefit that will be sacrificed if the old units are rebuilt). An opportunity cost analysis of the situation is as follows:

| | As Scrap | Rebuilt |
|---|---|---|
| Sale of defective units | $4,000 | $15,000 |
| Less cost to rebuild the defective units | | (8,000) |
| Less opportunity cost (return sacrificed by not manufacturing the new units) | | (5,000) |
| Net return | $4,000 | $ 2,000 |

Observe that this and the previous analysis lead to the same conclusion. Either way there is a $2,000 difference in favor of scrapping the defective units.

**Process or Sell**

Sunk costs, out-of-pocket costs, and opportunity costs are also encountered in a decision to sell an intermediate product as it is or process the product further and sell the product or products that result from the additional processing. For example, a company has 40,000 units of Product A that cost $0.75 per unit, a total of $30,000, to manufacture. The 40,000 units can be sold as they are for $50,000 or they can be processed further into Products X, Y, and Z at a cost of $2 per original Product A unit. The additional processing will produce the following numbers of each product, which can be sold at the unit prices indicated:

| | |
|---|---|
| Product X | 10,000 units @ $3 |
| Product Y | 22,000 units @ $5 |
| Product Z | 6,000 units @ $1 |
| Lost through spoilage | 2,000 units (no salvage value) |
| Total | 40,000 units |

The net advantage of processing the product further is $16,000, as shown in Illustration 27–6.

Note that the revenue available through the sale of the Product A units is an opportunity cost of further processing these units. Also notice that the $30,000 cost of manufacturing the 40,000 units of Product A does not appear in the analysis of Illustration 27–6. This cost is present regardless of which alternative is chosen. Therefore, it is irrelevant to the decision. However, the $30,000 does enter into a calculation of the net income from the alternatives. For example, if the company chooses to further process the Product A units, the gross return from the sale of Products X, Y, and Z may be calculated as follows:

| | | |
|---|---|---|
| Revenue from the sale of Products X, Y, and Z | | $146,000 |
| Less: | | |
| Cost to manufacture the Product A units | $30,000 | |
| Cost to further process the Product A units | 80,000 | 110,000 |
| Gross return from the sale of Products X, Y, and Z | | $ 36,000 |

Illustration 27–6
**Analyzing the effect of selling a product as is or doing further processing**

| | | |
|---|---|---|
| Revenue from further processing: | | |
| Product X, 10,000 units @ $3 | $ 30,000 | |
| Product Y, 22,000 units @ $5 | 110,000 | |
| Product Z, 6,000 units @ $1 | 6,000 | |
| Total revenue | | $146,000 |
| Less: | | |
| Additional processing costs, 40,000 units @ $2 | $ 80,000 | |
| Opportunity cost (revenue sacrificed by not selling the Product A units) | 50,000 | |
| Total | | 130,000 |
| Net advantage of further processing | | $ 16,000 |

## Deciding the Sales Mix

When a company sells a combination of products, some of the products usually are more profitable than others. As a result, management usually should concentrate its sales efforts on the more profitable products. However, if production facilities or other factors are limited, an increase in the production and sale of one product may require a reduction in the production and sale of another. In such a situation, management's job is to determine the most profitable combination or sales mix for the products and concentrate on selling the products in this combination.

To determine the best sales mix for its products, management must have information as to the contribution margin of each product, the facilities required to produce and sell each product, and any limitations on these facilities. For example, assume that a company produces and sells two products, A and B. The same machines are used to produce both products, and the products have the following selling prices and variable costs per units:

| | Product A | Product B |
|---|---|---|
| Selling price | $5.00 | $7.50 |
| Variable costs | 3.50 | 5.50 |
| Contribution margin | $1.50 | $2.00 |

If the amount of production facilities required to produce each product is the same and there is an unlimited market for Product B, the company should devote all its facilities to Product B because of its larger contribution margin. However, suppose that the company's facilities are limited to, say, 100,000 machine-hours of production per month. Also, one machine-hour is required to produce each unit of Product A, but two machine-hours are required for each unit of Product B. Under these circumstances, if the market for Product A is unlimited, the company should devote all its production to this product because it produces $1.50 of contribution margin per machine-hour, while Product B produces only $1 per machine-hour.

Actually, when there are no market or other limitations, a company should devote all its efforts to its most profitable product. It is only when there is a market or other limitation on the sale of the most profitable product that a need for a sales mix arises. For example, in the above case, if one machine-hour of production facilities is needed to produce each unit of Product A and 100,000 machine-hours are available, 100,000 units of the product can be produced. However, if only 80,000 units can be sold, the company has 20,000 machine-hours that can be devoted to the production of Product B, and 20,000 machine-hours will produce 10,000 units of Product B. Therefore, the company's most profitable sales mix under these assumptions is 80,000 units of Product A and 10,000 units of Product B.

## Summary of the Chapter in Terms of Learning Objectives

**1.** Capital budgeting is a process of evaluating and selecting investments in plant assets. Generally, the process involves estimating the cash flows of alternative projects, evaluating the merits of each, and choosing those worthy of investment. One method of comparing investments is to calculate and compare the payback periods of the projects. This statistic is an estimate of the length of time that will pass before the total net cash flows from a project will equal the initial cost of the investment. It fails to reflect differences in the timing of cash flows within the payback period, the riskiness of the cash flows, and the length of time that cash flows will continue after the payback period.

**2.** A project's expected rate of return on the average investment is calculated by dividing the periodic after-tax net income by the average investment in the project. When the net cash flows are received evenly throughout each period, the average investment may be calculated as the average of the initial book value of the investment plus its salvage value. If the net cash flows are received at the end of each year, the average investment may be calculated as the average of the initial book value of the investment and the book value at the beginning of the last year in the investment's life. A major limitation of rate of return on investment is that the statistic fails to take into consideration any variation in the expected net incomes from year to year.

**3.** The net present value of an investment is determined by estimating the cash flows from the investment, discounting them at a rate that represents an acceptable return, and subtracting the initial cost of the investment from the sum of the present values. This technique takes into consideration any variations in the timing of expected cash flows but is limited by the inherent subjectivity in selecting a discount rate.

**4.** In deciding whether to accept an opportunity to produce and sell additional units of product, the relevant factors are the incremental costs and revenues that will result from producing the business. Costs that will not change as a result of the decision should not be considered. This reasoning also applies to a decision whether to make or buy a given product.

**5.** Sunk costs cannot be avoided because they result from past, irrevocable decisions. Out-of-pocket costs require current outlays of funds, and opportunity costs are potential benefits that are lost as a result of choosing a particular course of action. Because sunk costs cannot be avoided, they are not relevant to decisions such as to scrap or rebuild defective units or to sell a product or process it further. To the extent that out-of-pocket costs will change as a result of choosing one alternative or another, they should be considered in making a choice between alternatives. Also, when one course of action precludes taking an alternative action, the benefits of the alternative should be included among the costs of taking the first course of action.

## Demonstration Problem

**Part 1**

Darling Company is considering three investment opportunities, X, Y, and Z. Straight-line depreciation will be used in each case, and the salvage value will be received at the end of the life of the investment. In estimating the periodic net incomes of each project, the only noncash item is depreciation. The following information is available about these investments:

| Investment | X | Y | Z |
|---|---|---|---|
| Purchase price | $40,000 | $40,000 | $40,000 |
| Useful life | 6 years | 8 years | 8 years |
| Salvage value | $ 1,000 | $ –0– | $10,000 |
| Expected net incomes: | | | |
| Year 1 | $ 3,500 | $11,000 | $ (3,750) |
| Year 2 | 3,500 | 9,000 | 4,250 |
| Year 3 | 3,500 | 7,000 | 8,250 |
| Year 4 | 3,500 | 5,000 | 16,250 |
| Year 5 | 3,500 | 3,000 | (1,750) |
| Year 6 | 3,500 | 1,000 | (1,750) |
| Year 7 | –0– | (1,000) | (1,750) |
| Year 8 | –0– | (3,000) | 21,250 |
| Total income | $21,000 | $32,000 | $41,000 |

*Required*

Rank the three investments, first is best, third is worst, based on the following:

*a.* Payback periods, assuming the cash flows from each investment are spread evenly throughout each period.

*b.* Return on average investment, assuming the cash flows from each investment are spread evenly throughout each period.

*c.* Net present values, using 8% per year as the discount rate. For this purpose, assume that the cash flows each year are received at the end of the year.

**Part 2**

Determine the appropriate action in each of the following decision situations:

*a.* The Eagle View Company has been operating at 80% of its 100,000 unit per year capacity in manufacturing a product. It has been asked by a chain store to produce an additional 10,000 units, for which the chain store will pay $22 each. Consider the following facts:

| | Per Unit | Total |
|---|---|---|
| Costs at 80% usage of capacity: | | |
| Direct materials | $ 8.00 | $ 640,000 |
| Direct labor | 7.00 | 560,000 |
| Total (fixed and variable) overhead | 12.50 | 1,000,000 |
| Totals | $27.50 | $2,200,000 |

In producing the 10,000 additional units, fixed overhead costs would remain constant, but additional variable overhead costs of $3 per unit would be incurred. Should the company accept or reject this order?

*b.* The Foothills Company uses Part YX345 in manufacturing its products. In the past, it has always purchased this part from a supplier for $40 each. It recently upgraded its own manufacturing capabilities and has enough excess capacity (including trained workers) to begin manufacturing Part YX345 instead of buying it. The bookkeeper has prepared the following projection of the cost of making the part, assuming that overhead should be allocated to its cost at 200% of the direct labor cost.

| | |
|---|---|
| Direct materials | $11.00 |
| Direct labor | 15.00 |
| Total fixed and variable overhead (200% of direct labor cost) | 30.00 |
| Total | $56.00 |

However, the company's accountant examined these cost calculations and determined that the volume of output of the part will not require any additional fixed overhead cost. Additional variable overhead cost will be only $17 per unit. Should the part be made or bought?

*c.* Georgetown Company's manufacturing process causes a relatively large number of defective parts to be produced. The defective parts can be melted down to recover the metal for reuse, or sold for scrap, or retooled and otherwise repaired. However, if they are retooled, the production output of other good units is diminished because there is no excess capacity. In fact, each unit retooled means that one new unit cannot be produced.

The following information is available about 500 defective parts:

| | |
|---|---|
| Proceeds of selling as scrap | $2,500 |
| Additional cost of melting down | $ 400 |
| Cost of metal purchases that can be avoided by recycling melted metal | 4,800 |
| Cost to retool 500 defective parts: | |
| Direct materials | $-0- |
| Direct labor | 1,500 |
| Incremental overhead | 1,750 |
| Cost to produce 500 new parts: | |
| Direct materials | $6,000 |
| Direct labor | 5,000 |
| Incremental overhead | 3,200 |

Should the company melt down the parts, sell them as scrap, or retool them?

## Solution to Demonstration Problem

**Part 1**

*a.* **Payback period:**

Investment X:

Annual depreciation = ($40,000 − $1,000) ÷ 6 = $6,500

$$\frac{\text{Cost}}{\text{Annual cash flow}} = \frac{\$40{,}000}{\$3{,}500 + \$6{,}500} = 4.0 \text{ years}$$

Investment Y:

Annual depreciation = $40,000 ÷ 8 = $5,000

| | | Annual Cash Flow | Cumulative Cash Flow |
|---|---|---|---|
| Year 1 . . . . | $1,000 + $5,000 = | $16,000 | $16,000 |
| Year 2 . . . . | 9,000 + $5,000 = | 14,000 | 30,000 |
| Year 3 . . . . | 7,000 + $5,000 = | 12,000 | 42,000 |

Thus, the $40,000 cost is paid back in slightly less than three years.

Investment Z:

Annual depreciation = ($40,000 − $10,000) ÷ 8 = $3,750

| | | Annual Cash Flow | Cumulative Cash Flow |
|---|---|---|---|
| Year 1 . . . . | $−3,750 + $3,750 = | $ −0− | $ −0− |
| Year 2 . . . . | 4,250 + 3,750 = | 8,000 | 8,000 |
| Year 3 . . . . | 8,250 + 3,750 = | 12,000 | 20,000 |
| Year 4 . . . . | 16,250 + 3,750 = | 20,000 | 40,000 |

Thus, the $40,000 cost is paid back in four years.

Ranking:

Investment Y is ranked first because it will pay back the cost in less than three years. Investments X and Z are tied for second with four-year payback periods.

*b.* **Return on average investment:**

(Since cash flows are spread evenly throughout each period, the average investment is calculated as the average of the original cost and the salvage value.)

| | X | Y | Z |
|---|---|---|---|
| Average net income per year: | | | |
| Total income over life . . . . . . . . . . | $21,000 | $32,000 | $41,000 |
| Estimated useful life . . . . . . . . . . | 6 years | 8 years | 8 years |
| Annual net income . . . . . . . . . . . | $ 3,500 | $ 4,000 | $ 5,125 |
| Average investment: | | | |
| Purchase price . . . . . . . . . . . . . . | 40,000 | 40,000 | 40,000 |
| Salvage value . . . . . . . . . . . . . . . | 1,000 | −0− | 10,000 |
| Average (sum ÷ 2) . . . . . . . . . . . | 20,500 | 20,000 | 25,000 |
| Average return on average investment . . | 17.1% | 20.0% | 20.5% |
| Rank . . . . . . . . . . . . . . . . . . . . . | Third | Second | First |

*c.* **Net present value (using 8% per year as the discount rate):**

| | | Net Cash Flows | Present Value at 8% | Present Value of Cash Flows |
|---|---|---|---|---|
| Investment X: | | | | |
| Year 1 . . . . | $ 3,500 + $6,500 = | $10,000 | 0.9259 | $ 9,259 |
| Year 2 . . . . | 3,500 + 6,500 = | 10,000 | 0.8573 | 8,573 |
| Year 3 . . . . | 3,500 + 6,500 = | 10,000 | 0.7938 | 7,938 |
| Year 4 . . . . | 3,500 + 6,500 = | 10,000 | 0.7350 | 7,350 |
| Year 5 . . . . | 3,500 + 6,500 = | 10,000 | 0.6806 | 6,806 |
| Year 6 . . . . | 3,500 + 6,500 = | 10,000 | 0.6302 | 6,302 |
| Salvage value . . . . . . . . . . . . | | 1,000 | 0.6302 | 630 |
| Total present value of cash flows . . . . . | | | | $46,858 |
| Amount to be invested . . . . . | | | | 40,000 |
| Positive net present value . . . . . | | | | $ 6,858 |
| Investment Y: | | | | |
| Year 1 . . . . | $11,000 + $5,000 = | $16,000 | 0.9259 | $14,814 |
| Year 2 . . . . | 9,000 + 5,000 = | 14,000 | 0.8573 | 12,002 |
| Year 3 . . . . | 7,000 + 5,000 = | 12,000 | 0.7938 | 9,526 |
| Year 4 . . . . | 5,000 + 5,000 = | 10,000 | 0.7350 | 7,350 |
| Year 5 . . . . | 3,000 + 5,000 = | 8,000 | 0.6806 | 5,445 |
| Year 6 . . . . | 1,000 + 5,000 = | 6,000 | 0.6302 | 3,781 |
| Year 7 . . . . | −1,000 + 5,000 = | 4,000 | 0.5835 | 2,334 |
| Year 8 . . . . | −3,000 + 5,000 = | 2,000 | 0.5403 | 1,081 |
| Salvage value . . . . . . . . . . . . | | –0– | 0.5403 | –0– |
| Total present value of cash flows . . . . . | | | | $56,333 |
| Amount to be invested . . . . . | | | | 40,000 |
| Positive net present value . . . . . | | | | $16,333 |
| Investment Z: | | | | |
| Year 1 . . . . | $−3,750 + $3,750 = | $ –0– | 0.9259 | $ –0– |
| Year 2 . . . . | 4,250 + 3,750 = | 8,000 | 0.8473 | 6,858 |
| Year 3 . . . . | 8,250 + 3,750 = | 12,000 | 0.7938 | 9,526 |
| Year 4 . . . . | 16,250 + 3,750 = | 20,000 | 0.7350 | 14,700 |
| Year 5 . . . . | −1,750 + 3,750 = | 2,000 | 0.6806 | 1,361 |
| Year 6 . . . . | −1,750 + 3,750 = | 2,000 | 0.6302 | 1,260 |
| Year 7 . . . . | −1,750 + 3,750 = | 2,000 | 0.5835 | 1,167 |
| Year 8 . . . . | 21,250 + 3,750 = | 25,000 | 0.5403 | 13,508 |
| Salvage value . . . . . . . . . . . . | | 1,000 | 0.5403 | 5,403 |
| Total present value of cash flows . . . . . | | | | $53,783 |
| Amount to be invested . . . . . | | | | 40,000 |
| Positive net present value . . . . . | | | | $13,783 |

On the basis of the present values, the investments are rated as follows:

| | | |
|---|---|---|
| X . . . . | $ 6,858 | Third |
| Y . . . . | 16,333 | First |
| Z . . . . | 13,783 | Second |

**Part 2**

*a.* This is a decision about "accepting additional business." Because the unit costs have been $27.50, it may appear as though the offer for $22.00 should be rejected. However, the incremental cost per unit is only:

| | |
|---|---|
| Direct materials. . . . . . . . | $ 8.00 |
| Direct labor . . . . . . . . . | 7.00 |
| Variable overhead . . . . . . | 3.00 |
| Total incremental cost . . . . | $18.00 |

Therefore, the offer should be accepted because it will produce $4 of additional profit per unit, which is $40,000 profit for the 10,000 units.

*b.* This is a "buy or make" decision. The bookkeeper's analysis is faulty because it includes the nonincremental overhead of $13 per unit. When only the incremental overhead of $17 is included, the unit cost of manufacturing the part is:

| | |
|---|---|
| Direct materials. . . . . . . . | $11.00 |
| Direct labor . . . . . . . . . | 15.00 |
| Variable overhead . . . . . . | 17.00 |
| Total incremental cost . . . . | $43.00 |

Therefore, it appears to be better to continue to buy the part for $40 instead of making it for $43. (This analysis shows that it is possible to reach the right decision even though the information is incorrect.)

*c.* This is a "scrap or rebuild" decision. The goal is to identify the alternative that produces the greatest benefit to the company. To compare the alternatives on an equal basis, you should determine the net cost of obtaining 500 salable units. The comparison is as follows:

| | Sell as Is and Make 500 New Units | Melt Down and Reuse Metal in 500 New Units | Retool Old Units to Get 500 Salable Units |
|---|---|---|---|
| Incremental cost to produce 500 salable units: | | | |
| Direct material: | | | |
| Cost of new materials . . . | $ 6,000 | $ 6,000 | |
| Melting costs . . . . . . . . | | 400 | |
| Costs avoided by reusing melted metal . . | | (4,800) | |
| Total . . . . . . . . . . . . | $ 6,000 | $ 1,600 | |
| Direct labor . . . . . . . . . | 5,000 | 5,000 | $1,500 |
| Incremental overhead . . . . | 3,200 | 3,200 | 1,750 |
| Less proceeds of selling defective units as scrap . . | (2,500) | | |
| Total cost to obtain 500 salable units . . . . . . . . | $11,700 | $ 9,800 | $3,250 |

Clearly, the new cost of obtaining 500 salable parts is smallest if the defective parts are retooled.

## Glossary

Define or explain the words and phrases listed in the chapter Glossary. (L. O. 6)

**Capital budgeting** planning plant asset investments in a process that involves preparing cost and revenue estimates for all proposed projects, examining the merits of each, and choosing those worthy of investment. p. 1131

**Differential cost** a synonym for *incremental cost*. p. 1139

**Incremental cost** an additional cost that results from a particular course of action. p. 1139

**Net present value** the value of an investment calculated by discounting the future cash flows from the investment at an interest rate that gives a satisfactory return on investment and then subtracting the present cost of the investment. pp. 1131, 1135–38

**Opportunity cost** the benefit of one course of action that is lost or sacrificed as a result of choosing an alternative course of action. p. 1141

**Out-of-pocket cost** a cost that requires a current outlay of funds. p. 1141

**Payback period** the length of time necessary for the accumulated net cash flows from an investment to equal the original cost of the investment. pp. 1131–33

**Rate of return on average investment** the annual, after-tax income that results from using an asset divided by the average investment in the asset. pp. 1131, 1133–35

**Sunk cost** a cost incurred as a consequence of a past irrevocable decision and that, therefore, cannot be avoided; hence, irrelevant to decisions affecting the future. p. 1141

## Objective Review

Answers to the following questions are listed in Appendix I at the end of the book. Be sure that you decide which is the one best answer to each question *before* you check the answers in the appendix.

1. Collins Corporation is considering the purchase of a new piece of equipment that costs $75,000. Annual net cash flows to be produced by this investment are $30,000, $25,000, $15,000, $10,000, and $5,000. The payback period is:
   *a.* 4 years.
   *b.* 5 years.
   *c.* 3.5 years.
   *d.* 3.0 years.
   *e.* 2.5 years.
2. The following data relate to a proposed machinery purchase:

| | |
|---|---|
| Cost | $180,000 |
| Salvage value | 5,000 |
| Estimated useful life | 8 years |
| Annual income before depreciation | $39,450 |

Calculate the rate of return, assuming the net cash flows from the investment are received evenly throughout the year:

*a.* 38%.
*b.* 18%.
*c.* 20%.
*d.* 19%.
*e.* 43%.

3. Casior Company is considering investing capital in one of four projects. Each project requires a $20,000 investment and will produce end-of-period cash flows as follows:

| Years Hence | Annual Cash Flows Project 1 | Project 2 | Project 3 | Project 4 |
|---|---|---|---|---|
| 1 . . . . | $ 8,500 | $12,000 | $ 4,500 | $ –0– |
| 2 . . . . | 8,500 | 8,500 | 8,500 | 9,200 |
| 3 . . . . | 8,500 | 4,000 | 13,000 | 9,200 |
| 4 . . . . | –0– | –0– | –0– | 9,200 |
| Total . . | $25,500 | $24,500 | $26,000 | $27,600 |

Which of the projects has the greatest net present value, assuming a discount rate of 10%?

*a.* Project 1.
*b.* Project 2.
*c.* Project 3.
*d.* Project 4.
*e.* Cannot be determined from information given.

4. Brown Company has just received a special order for 200 units of product. The buyer wants his name stamped on each unit, which will cost an additional $400 above normal manufacturing costs. The company normally operates at 75% of capacity, producing 7,500 units of product and incurring the following costs:

| | |
|---|---|
| Direct materials . . . . . . . . . . . . . . . . . . | $37,500 |
| Direct labor . . . . . . . . . . . . . . . . . . . . | 60,000 |
| Factory overhead, of which 30% is variable . . . | 20,000 |
| Selling expenses, of which 60% are variable . . | 25,000 |

The special order will not affect Brown Company's normal unit sales and will not increase fixed costs. Also, variable selling expenses on the special order will be reduced 50% below the normal level. What price per unit will Brown Company need in order to earn $1,000 on the order?

*a.* $24.00.
*b.* $20.80.
*c.* $19.80.
*d.* $15.80.
*e.* $14.80.

5. Xeno, Inc., incurs a joint cost of $1,000 in producing its four products. Listed below are sales and additional cost data:

| Product | Sales Value at Split-Off | Additional Processing Costs | Final Sales Value |
|---|---|---|---|
| Alpha . . . . | $300 | $150 | $600 |
| Beta . . . . | 450 | 300 | 900 |
| Delta . . . . | 150 | 75 | 210 |
| Gamma . . | 30 | 15 | 60 |

Which of these products should not be processed further?

*a.* Alpha.
*b.* Beta.
*c.* Delta.
*d.* Gamma.
*e.* All of the above should be processed further.

## Questions for Class Discussion

1. What is capital budgeting? Why are capital budgeting decisions risky?
2. Why are capital budgeting decisions often difficult decisions?
3. What is the difference between comprehensive budgeting and capital budgeting?
4. The estimated net cash flows from an investment may be calculated and expressed two different ways, directly or indirectly. What is the difference between these two presentations?
5. If depreciation is an expense, why is it acceptable to calculate the net cash flows from a depreciable investment by adding depreciation to the net income from the investment?
6. Why is a short payback period on an investment desirable?
7. If two alternate investments have the same payback period, will the investments be equally desirable?
8. What is the average amount invested in a machine during its life if the machine costs $132,000 and has an estimated five-year life with an estimated $27,000 salvage value? Assume that annual revenues are received at the end of each year.
9. What is your answer to Question 8, assuming the annual revenues are received evenly throughout each year?
10. Is a 15% return on the average investment in a machine a good return?
11. Why is the present value of $100 that you expect to receive one year hence less than $100? What is the present value of $100 that you expect to receive one year hence, discounted at 12%?
12. Two investment alternatives are expected to generate annual cash flows for six years and, when discounted at 11%, have the same net present values. Based on this information, can you say with confidence that the two alternatives are equally desirable?
13. If the present value of the expected net cash flows from an investment in a machine, discounted at 12%, exceeds the amount of the investment, what can you say about the expected rate of return on the invest-

ment? What if the present value of the net cash flows, discounted at 12%, is less than the amount of the investment?

14. When two investment alternatives have the same total expected cash flows but differ in the timing of those flows, which method of evaluating those investments is superior: (*a*) rate of return on average investment, or (*b*) net present values?
15. Why might the selection of accelerated depreciation for tax purposes make an investment more attractive than it would be if straight-line depreciation were used?
16. What are the differential costs of accepting an additional volume of business?
17. A company manufactures and sells in this country 250,000 units of product at $5 per unit. The product costs $3 per unit to manufacture. Can you describe a situation under which the company may be willing to sell an additional 25,000 units of the product abroad at $2.75 per unit?
18. Under what conditions is a sunk cost relevant to decision making?
19. What is the difference between an out-of-pocket cost and an opportunity cost? Is an opportunity cost typically recorded in the accounting records?
20. Any costs that have been incurred in manufacturing a product are sunk costs. Why are such costs irrelevant in deciding whether to sell the product in its present condition or to make it into a new product through additional processing?

## Exercises

**Exercise 27–1**
**Payback period, uniform cash flows**
(L. O. 1)

Calculate the payback periods for each of the following independent investments:

*a.* A machine costs $33,000, has a $6,000 salvage value, is expected to last six years, and will generate net income of $7,500 per year after straight-line depreciation and after income taxes of 40%.

*b.* A product packaging system is expected to cost $210,000 and have a useful life of 10 years. The system should save $65,250 (after taxes) each year, after deducting straight-line depreciation on the system. Estimated salvage value of the system is $22,500.

**Exercise 27–2**
**Payback period, cash flows not uniform**
(L. O. 1)

A company is asked to advance $150,000 to an affiliate in return for which the company will receive cash payments as follows: during year 1, $45,000; during year 2, $37,500; during year 3, $52,500; during year 4, $60,000; during year 5, $75,000. The payments are spread evenly throughout each year. Calculate the payback period for the advance to the affiliate.

**Exercise 27–3**
**Payback period from income statement data**
(L. O. 1)

A limousine can be purchased for $70,500 and used for six years to generate net incomes as follows: year 1, $13,500; year 2, $12,000; year 3, $9,000; year 4, $6,000; year 5, $4,500; and year 6, $4,500. In calculating the net incomes, sum-of-the-years' digits depreciation on the limousine was deducted, based on a six-year life and a salvage value of $7,500. Present calculations to show the payback period for the limousine. Assume no income taxes.

**Exercise 27–4**
**Calculating average investment**
(L. O. 2)

Machine A costs $180,000 and has an estimated four-year life and no salvage value. Machine B costs $225,000 and has an estimated five-year life and a $37,500 salvage value. Calculate the average investment in each machine under the assumptions that the revenues from using the machine are to be received *(a)* uniformly throughout each year and *(b)* at the end of each year.

**Exercise 27–5**
**Payback and return on average investment**
(L. O. 1, 2)

Forest Company is planning to purchase a machine and add a new product to its line. The machine will cost $180,000, have a four-year life, no salvage value, and will be depreciated on a straight-line basis. The company expects to sell 24,000 units of the machine's product each year. However, the product is only marketable during the holiday season at the end of each year, and all sales will occur during the last 15 days of the year. Expected annual results are as follows:

| | | |
|---|---|---|
| Sales | | $450,000 |
| Costs: | | |
| Materials, labor, and overhead excluding depreciation on the new machine | $234,000 | |
| Depreciation on the new machine | 45,000 | |
| Selling and administrative expenses | 141,000 | 420,000 |
| Operating income | | $ 30,000 |
| Income taxes | | 12,000 |
| Net income | | $ 18,000 |

*Required*

Calculate *(a)* the payback period and *(b)* the return on the average investment in this machine.

**Exercise 27–6**
**Net present value of an investment**
(L. O. 3)

After evaluating the risk characteristics of the investment described in Exercise 27–5, the company concludes that it must earn at least a 12% compound return on the investment in the machine. Based on this decision, determine the net present value of the cash flows from the machine the company is planning to buy.

**Exercise 27–7**
**Net present values of investments**
(L. O. 3)

A company can invest in each of three projects, X, Y, and Z. Each project requires an initial investment of $105,000 and will produce cash flows as follows:

| Years Hence | Annual Cash Flows | | |
|---|---|---|---|
| | Project X | Project Y | Project Z |
| 1 . . . . | $ 25,200 | $ 42,000 | $ 58,800 |
| 2 . . . . | 42,000 | 42,000 | 42,000 |
| 3 . . . . | 58,800 | 42,000 | 25,200 |
| | $126,000 | $126,000 | $126,000 |

*Required*

Under the assumption the company requires a 10% compound return from its investments, determine which of the projects are worthy of investment based on net present values.

**Exercise 27–8**
**Analysis of selling added units at reduced price**
(L. O. 4)

Charter Company expects to sell 4,000 units of its product during the next period with the following results:

| | | |
|---|---|---|
| Sales . . . . . . . . . . . . . . . . | | $39,000 |
| Costs and expenses: | | |
| Direct materials . . . . . . . . . . | $7,200 | |
| Direct labor . . . . . . . . . . . | 8,400 | |
| Factory overhead . . . . . . . . | 4,200 | |
| Selling expenses . . . . . . . | 4,500 | |
| Administrative expenses . . . . | 7,500 | 31,800 |
| Net income . . . . . . . . . . . . | | $ 7,200 |

The company has an opportunity to sell 1,500 additional units at a price of $7.50. The additional sales will not affect the regular sales but will have the following effects on costs. Costs per unit for direct materials and direct labor will be the same for the additional sales as they are for regular sales. Factory overhead will increase by 10%, selling expenses will be unchanged, and administrative expenses will increase by $1,500. Present calculations to show whether the company should accept the offer to sell the additional units.

**Exercise 27–9**
**Analysis of whether to further process units of product**
(L. O. 5)

A company has 8,000 units of Product X that cost $13.20 per unit to manufacture. The 8,000 units can be sold for $198,000, or they can be further processed at a cost of $92,400 into Products Y and Z. The additional processing will produce 3,200 units of Product Y that can be sold for $26.40 each and 4,800 units of Product Z that can be sold for $29.70 each.

*Required*

Prepare an analysis to show whether the Product X units should be further processed.

**Exercise 27–10**
**Analysis of best sales mix**
(L. O. 5)

Daley Company has a machine that can produce Product A at the rate of 2 units per hour or produce Product B at the rate of 3 units per hour. The capacity of the machine is 3,800 hours per year. The products are sold to a single customer who has agreed to buy all of the company's production up to a maximum of 5,000 units of A and 7,000 units of B. Selling prices and variable costs per unit to produce the products are:

| | Product A | Product B |
|---|---|---|
| Selling price | $12.75 | $9.00 |
| Variable costs | 7.50 | 6.00 |
| Contribution margin | $ 5.25 | $3.00 |

*Required*

Determine the most profitable sales mix for the company and calculate the contribution to fixed costs plus profits that will result from that sales mix.

## Problems

**Problem 27–1**
**Payback, return on investment, and net present value; cash flows at year-end**
(L. O. 1, 2, 3)

Gatter Company is planning to add a new product to its line, the production of which will require new machinery that costs $126,000 and has a five-year life and no salvage value. This additional information is available:

| | |
|---|---|
| Estimated annual sales of new product | $420,000 |
| Estimated costs: | |
| Direct materials | 84,000 |
| Direct labor | 112,000 |
| Factory overhead excluding depreciation on new machinery | 106,400 |
| Selling and administrative expenses | 76,400 |
| State and federal income taxes | 30% |

*Required*

Using straight-line depreciation, calculate (*a*) the payback period on the investment in new machinery, (*b*) the rate of return on the average investment, and (*c*) the net present value of the net cash flows discounted at 14%. In calculating the rate of return and the net present value, assume that all cash flows occur at the end of each year.

**Problem 27–2**
**Payback and return on investment, cash flows received throughout year; net present value**
(L. O. 1, 2, 3)

Danforth Company has an opportunity to invest in either of two projects. Project 1 requires an investment of $162,000 for new machinery having a five-year life and an $18,000 salvage value. Project 2 requires an investment of $138,600 for new machinery having a seven-year life and a $12,600 salvage value. The products of the projects differ; however, each will produce for the life of the machinery an annual profit of $10,800 after subtracting straight-line depreciation and taxes of 30%.

*Required*

1. Assuming the revenues are earned uniformly throughout each year, calculate the payback period and return on average investment for each project.
2. Now assume that the machines related to both projects have zero salvage values and that the expected annual profits after deducting depreciation and taxes of 30% are $10,080. Assume also that the annual cash flows from each project occur at year-end. Calculate the return on average investment and the net present value of the cash flows from each project, discounted at 10%.

**Problem 27–3**
**Income results of added sales**
(L. O. 4)

Permalox Company manufactures an adhesive product that it sells to wholesalers at $6.40 per tube. The company manufactures and sells approximately 50,000 tubes of the product each year, and a normal year's costs for the production and sale of this quantity are as follows:

| | |
|---|---|
| Direct materials . . . . . . . . | $ 60,000 |
| Direct labor . . . . . . . . . . . | 50,000 |
| Manufacturing overhead . . . . | 75,000 |
| Selling expenses . . . . . . . . | 30,000 |
| Administrative expenses . . . . | 25,000 |
| | $240,000 |

A mail-order company has offered to buy 5,000 tubes of the adhesive at $4.40 each to be marketed under the mail-order company's trade name. If accepted, the order is not expected to affect sales through present channels.

A study of normal costs and their relation to the new business reveals the following: (*a*) Direct material costs are 100% variable. (*b*) The per unit direct labor costs for the additional units will be 50% greater than normal since their production will require overtime at time and one half. (*c*) Of a normal year's manufacturing overhead costs, two thirds will remain fixed at any production level from zero to 65,000 units and one third will vary with volume. (*d*) There will be no additional selling costs if the new business is accepted. (*e*) Acceptance of the new business will increase administrative costs by $3,200.

*Required*

Prepare a comparative income statement that shows (*a*) in one set of columns the operating results and operating income of a normal year, (*b*) in the second set of columns the operating results and income that may be expected from the new business, and (*c*) in the third set of columns the combined results from the normal and the expected new business.

**Problem 27–4**
**Calculating cash flows and net present values with alternative depreciation methods for tax purposes**
(L. O. 3)

Standish Corporation is considering a project that requires a $450,000 investment in machinery having a six-year life and no salvage value. The project will produce $157,500 at the end of each year for six years, before deducting depreciation on the new machinery and income taxes of 30%.

For tax purposes, the company may choose between two alternative depreciation schedules, as follows:

| Year | Straight-line Depreciation Schedule | MACRS Depreciation Schedule |
|---|---|---|
| 1 . . . . | $45,000 | $ 90,000 |
| 2 . . . . | 90,000 | 144,000 |
| 3 . . . . | 90,000 | 86,400 |
| 4 . . . . | 90,000 | 51,840 |
| 5 . . . . | 90,000 | 51,840 |
| 6 . . . . | 45,000 | 25,920 |

*Required*

1. Calculate the company's cash flow from the project for each of the six years with depreciation for tax purposes calculated according to (*a*) the straight-line depreciation schedule and (*b*) the MACRS depreciation schedule.

2. Calculate the net present value of the net cash flows discounted at 14% assuming the straight-line depreciation schedule is used.
3. Calculate the net present value of the net cash flows discounted at 14% assuming the MACRS depreciation schedule is used.
4. Explain why the MACRS depreciation method increases the net present value of this project.

**Problem 27–5**
**Income results of alternative sales mixes**
(L. O. 5)

Wedding Company's sales and costs for its two products last year were:

| | Product 1 | Product 2 |
|---|---|---|
| Unit selling price . . . . . . . | $ 180 | $ 135 |
| Variable costs per unit . . . . | $ 108 | $ 45 |
| Fixed costs . . . . . . . . . . | $540,000 | $630,000 |
| Units sold . . . . . . . . . . | 12,000 | 13,500 |

Through sales effort the company can change its sales mix. However, sales of the two products are so interrelated that a percentage increase in the sales of one product causes an equal percentage decrease in the sales of the other, and vice versa.

*Required*

1. State which of its products the company should push, and why.
2. Prepare a columnar statement showing last year's sales, fixed costs, variable costs, and income before taxes for Product 1 in the first pair of columns, the results for Product 2 in the second set of columns, and the combined results for both products in the third set of columns.
3. Prepare a like statement for the two products under the assumption that the sales of Product 1 are increased 25%, with a resulting 25% decrease in the sales of Product 2.
4. Prepare a third statement under the assumption that the sales of Product 1 are decreased 25%, with a resulting 25% increase in the sales of Product 2.

## Alternate Problems

**Problem 27–1A**
**Payback, return on investment, and net present value; cash flows at year-end**
(L. O. 1, 2, 3)

Ehlers Company is considering adding a new product to its line, of which it estimates it can sell 18,000 units annually at $34.50 per unit. To manufacture the product will require new machinery having an estimated five-year life, no salvage value, and costing $192,000. The new product will have a $14.40 per unit direct material cost and a $7.20 per unit direct labor cost. Manufacturing overhead chargeable to the new product, other than for depreciation on the new machinery, will be $89,100 annually. Also, $67,500 of additional selling and administrative expenses will be incurred annually in producing and selling the product, and state and federal income taxes will take 30% of the before-taxes profit.

*Required*

Using straight-line depreciation, calculate (*a*) the payback period on the investment in new machinery, (*b*) the rate of return on the average investment, and (*c*) the net present value of the net cash flows discounted at 12%. Assume that revenues are received at year-end.

**Problem 27–2A**
**Payback and return on investment, cash flows received throughout year; net present value**
(L. O. 1, 2, 3)

Storey Company has the opportunity to invest in either of two projects. Project 1 requires an investment of $56,000 for new machinery having a seven-year life and no salvage value. Project 2 requires an investment of $60,000 for new machinery having a five-year life and no salvage value. Sales of the two projects will produce the following estimated annual results:

| | Project 1 | | Project 2 | |
|---|---|---|---|---|
| Sales | | $128,000 | | $148,000 |
| Costs: | | | | |
| Direct materials | $30,000 | | $36,000 | |
| Direct labor | 27,000 | | 35,000 | |
| Manufacturing overhead including depreciation on new machinery | 38,000 | | 44,000 | |
| Selling and administrative expenses | 25,000 | 120,000 | 25,000 | 140,000 |
| Operating income | | $ 8,000 | | $ 8,000 |
| State and federal income taxes | | 2,000 | | 2,000 |
| Net income | | $ 6,000 | | $ 6,000 |

*Required*

Calculate the payback period, the return on average investment, and the net present value of the net cash flows from each project discounted at 12%. State which project you think the better investment and why. Assume that cash flows occur at year-end.

**Problem 27–3A**
**Income results of added sales**
(L. O. 4)

Plastomaster Company annually sells 30,000 units of its product at a price of $30 per unit. At the 30,000-unit production level the product costs $27 a unit to manufacture and sell, and at this level the company has the following costs and expenses:

| | |
|---|---|
| Fixed manufacturing overhead costs | $ 90,000 |
| Fixed selling expenses | 45,000 |
| Fixed administrative expenses | 54,000 |
| Variable costs and expenses: | |
| Direct materials ($6.00 per unit) | 180,000 |
| Direct labor ($7.50 per unit) | 225,000 |
| Manufacturing overhead ($4.50 per unit) | 135,000 |
| Selling expenses ($1.50 per unit) | 45,000 |
| Administrative expense ($1.20 per unit) | 36,000 |

All the units the company presently sells are sold in this country. However, an exporter recently offered to buy 3,000 units of the product for sale abroad. However, the exporter will pay only $20 per unit, which is below the company's present $27 per unit manufacturing and selling costs.

*Required*

Prepare an income statement that shows (*a*) in one set of columns the revenue, costs, expenses, and income from selling 30,000 units of the product in this country; (*b*) in a second set of columns the additional revenue, costs, expenses, and income from selling 3,000 units to the exporter; and (*c*) in a third set of columns the combined results from both sources. (Assume that acceptance of the new business will not increase any of the company's fixed costs and expenses nor change any of the variable per unit costs and expenses.) What unit sales price would give Plastomaster a $3 profit per unit?

**Problem 27–4A**
**Calculating cash flows and net present values with alternative depreciation methods for tax purposes**
(L. O. 3)

Meridian Company is considering a project that requires a $324,000 investment in machinery having a six-year life and no salvage value. The project will produce $113,400 at the end of each year for six years, before deducting depreciation on the new machinery and income taxes of 25%.

For tax purposes, the company may choose between two alternative depreciation schedules, as follows:

| Year | Straight-line Depreciation Schedule | MACRS Depreciation Schedule |
|---|---|---|
| 1 . . | $32,400 | $ 64,800 |
| 2 . . | 64,800 | 103,680 |
| 3 . . | 64,800 | 62,208 |
| 4 . . | 64,800 | 37,325 |
| 5 . . | 64,800 | 37,325 |
| 6 . . | 32,400 | 18,662 |

*Required*

1. Calculate the company's cash flow from the project for each of the six years with depreciation for tax purposes calculated according to (*a*) the straight-line depreciation schedule and (*b*) the MACRS depreciation schedule.
2. Calculate the net present value of the net cash flows discounted at 12% assuming the straight-line depreciation schedule is used.
3. Calculate the net present value of the net cash flows discounted at 12% assuming the MACRS depreciation schedule is used.
4. Explain why the MACRS depreciation method changes the net present value of this project.

**Problem 27–5A**
**Income results of alternative sales mixes**
(L. O. 5)

Robstown Corporation manufactures and sells a machine called a Loadown. Last year the company made and sold 350 machines, with the following results:

| | | |
|---|---|---|
| Sales (350 units @ $360) . . . . . . . . . . | | $126,000 |
| Costs and expenses: | | |
| Variable: | | |
| Direct materials . . . . . . . . . . . . . | $27,720 | |
| Direct labor . . . . . . . . . . . . . . . . | 22,680 | |
| Factory overhead . . . . . . . . . . . . | 18,900 | |
| Selling and administrative expenses . . | 12,600 | |
| Fixed: | | |
| Factory overhead . . . . . . . . . . . . | 19,000 | |
| Selling and administrative expenses . . | 12,000 | 112,900 |
| Income before taxes . . . . . . . . . . . . | | $ 13,100 |

The city street department has asked for bids on 50 Loadowns almost identical to Robstown Corporation's machine, the only difference being a weigh system not presently installed on the Robstown Corporation Loadown. To install the weigh system would require the purchase of a new machine that costs $600, plus $8 per Loadown for additional direct material and $5.20 per Loadown for additional direct labor. The new machine would have no further use after the completion of the street department contract, but it could be sold for $200. Sale of the additional units would not affect the company's fixed costs and expenses, but all variable costs and expenses, including variable selling and administrative expenses, would increase proportionately with the volume increase.

*Required*

1. Calculate the lowest unit price the company could bid on the special order without causing a reduction in income from normal business.
2. Under the assumption the company bid $320 per unit and was awarded the contract for the 50 special units, prepare an income statement showing (*a*) in one set of columns the revenues, costs, expenses, and income before taxes from present business; (*b*) in a second set of columns the revenue, costs, expenses, and income before taxes from the new business; and (*c*) in a third set of columns the combined results of both the old and new business.

## Provocative Problems

**Provocative Problem 27–1**
**Texstone Corporation**
(L. O. 1, 2, 3, 5)

Texstone Corporation operates native stone extracting plants, one of which is located at Newcastle. The Newcastle plant no longer produces a satisfactory profit due to its distance from raw material sources, relatively high electric power costs, and lack of modern machinery. As a result, construction of a new plant to replace the Newcastle plant is under consideration.

The new plant would be located close to a raw material source and near low-cost electric power, but its construction would necessitate abandonment of the Newcastle plant. The company president favors the move; but several members of the board are not convinced the Newcastle plant should be abandoned in view of the great loss that would result.

You have been asked to make recommendations concerning the proposed abandonment and construction of the new plant. Data developed during the course of your analysis include the following:

**Loss from abandoning the Newcastle plant.** The land, buildings, and machinery of the Newcastle plant have a $1,875,000 book value. Very little of the machinery can be sold; most will have to be scrapped. Therefore, if the plant is abandoned, it is estimated that only $250,000 of the remaining investment in the plant can be recovered through the sale of its land and buildings and machinery. The remaining $1,625,000 will be lost.

**Investment in the new plant.** The new plant will cost $3,000,000, and will have double the 12,500-ton capacity of the Newcastle plant. Management estimates the 25,000 tons of stone extracted annually can be sold without a price reduction.

**Comparative production costs.** A comparison of the production costs per ton at the old plant with the estimated costs at the new plant shows the following:

| | Old Plant | New Plant |
|---|---|---|
| Raw material, labor, and plant costs (other than depreciation and income taxes) | $225 | $204 |
| Depreciation | 15 | 12 |
| Total costs per ton | $240 | $216 |

The higher per ton depreciation charge of the old plant results primarily from depreciation being allocated to fewer units of product.

Prepare calculations to analyze the consequences of investing in the new plant and give your recommendation. To make the problem manageable, you should assume that both plants can operate for 10 years. Also, the company is subject to income taxes at a rate of 25%, and the loss from abandoning the old plant has no tax benefit. If the old plant is retained, it will operate at the break-even point. Furthermore, a shortage of skilled personnel would not allow the company to operate both the Newcastle plant and the new plant. Present any pertinent analyses based on the available data.

**Provocative Problem 27–2**
**Comcon Corporation**
(L. O. 5)

Comcon Corporation has operated at substantially less than its full plant capacity for several years, producing and selling an average of 16,250 units of its product annually and receiving a per unit price of $78. Its costs at this sales level are:

| | |
|---|---|
| Direct materials | $399,750 |
| Direct labor | 312,000 |
| Manufacturing overhead: | |
| Variable | 121,875 |
| Fixed | 60,000 |
| Selling and administrative expenses: | |
| Variable | 58,500 |
| Fixed | 120,000 |
| Income taxes | 30% |

After searching for ways to utilize the plant capacity of the company more fully, management has begun to consider the possibility of processing the product beyond the present point at which it is sold. If the product is further processed, it can be sold for $90 per unit. Further processing will increase fixed manufacturing overhead by $24,750 annually, and it will increase variable manufacturing costs per unit as follows:

| | |
|---|---|
| Direct materials | $1.26 |
| Direct labor | 1.14 |
| Variable manufacturing overhead | 0.90 |
| Total | $3.30 |

Selling the further processed product will not affect fixed selling and administrative expenses, but it will increase variable selling and administrative expenses by 25%. Further processing is not expected to either increase or decrease the number of units sold.

Should the company further process the product? Back your opinion with a simple calculation and also a comparative income statement showing present results and the estimated results with the product further processed.

**Provocative Problem 27–3**
**Ontario Corporation**
(L. O. 4)

Ontario Corporation manufactures and sells an engineering instrument, selling an average of 21,000 units of the device each year. The company generally earns an after-tax (30% rate) net income of $128 per unit sold. Ontario Corporation's production process involves assembling the several components of the instrument, some of which are manufactured by the company and others of which are purchased from a variety of suppliers.

One of the components that has been manufactured by the company is a level which is also available from other suppliers. Ontario Corporation uses special equipment to make the level, and the equipment has no alternative uses. The equipment has a $63,000 book value, a seven-year remaining life, and is depreciated at the rate of $9,000 per year. In addition to depreciation of the equipment, the costs to manufacture the level are: direct materials, $16.00; direct labor, $12.80; and variable overhead, $3.20.

One of Ontario's suppliers has recently offered the company a contract to purchase levels from the supplier at a delivered cost of $34.08 per unit. If the company decides to purchase the levels, the special equipment used to manufacture them can be sold for cash at its book value (no profit or loss) and the cash can be invested in other projects that will pay a 14% compound after-tax return, which is the return the company demands on all of its capital investments.

Should the company continue to manufacture the level, or should it sell the special equipment and buy the level? Back your answer with explanations and computations.

# 28 Tax Considerations in Business Decisions

Perhaps the most common topic of conversation in the United States is taxes, especially federal income taxes. A large variety of individual and business decisions are influenced by income tax considerations. In studying this chapter, you should expect to gain an introductory understanding of the rules that govern federal income taxes and some of the ways in which they can affect personal and business decisions.

## Learning Objectives

*After studying Chapter 28, you should be able to:*

1. Explain the meaning and importance of tax planning.
2. List the classes of federal income taxpayers and describe the steps an individual must go through to calculate his or her taxable income.
3. Calculate an individual's gross income tax liability and the net tax payable.
4. Define capital assets and describe the tax treatment for capital losses in comparison with ordinary (noncapital) losses.
5. Describe the differences between the calculations of taxable income and tax liability for corporations and for individuals.
6. Analyse the basic tax consequences of various business decisions to determine which alternative provides the most favorable tax treatment.
7. Explain why income tax expenses shown in financial statements may differ from taxes currently payable.
8. Define or explain the terms and phrases listed in the chapter Glossary.

## Tax Planning

Explain the meaning and importance of tax planning.
(L. O. 1)

When taxpayers plan their affairs in such a way as to incur the smallest possible tax liability that is consistent with their other goals, they engage in **tax planning.** Many business deals can be designed in more than one alternative way. For example, equipment might be purchased for cash, purchased with borrowed money, or perhaps even leased from the owner. Tax planning involves evaluating each alternative in terms of the resulting tax liability and selecting the one alternative that will be most profitable.

To be effective, tax planning must be done at the time important transactions are under consideration, not after they are completed. Although you sometimes can take advantage of a previously overlooked tax saving, the common result of waiting until transactions are completed is a lost tax-saving opportunity. Many transactions cannot be retracted, and the Internal Revenue Service usually looks at the original action in a situation to determine the tax consequences.

Since effective tax planning requires an extensive knowledge of both tax laws and business procedures, this chapter is not intended to make expert tax planners out of you. Rather, the purpose is to make you aware of the merits of effective tax planning, recognizing that for complete and effective planning, the average student, business executive, or citizen should seek the advice of a certified public accountant, tax attorney, or other person qualified in tax matters.

## Tax Evasion and Tax Avoidance

In any discussion of taxes, a clear distinction should be drawn between tax evasion and tax avoidance. **Tax evasion** is illegal and may result in heavy penalties, including prison sentences in some instances. **Tax avoidance,** on the other hand, is a perfectly legal and profitable activity.

Taxes are avoided by preventing a tax liability from coming into existence or by lessening a tax liability. This may be accomplished by any legal means; for example, by the way in which a transaction is completed, or the manner in which a business is organized, or by a wise selection from among the options provided in the tax laws.

In contrast, tax evasion involves the fraudulent denial and concealment of an existing tax liability. For example, taxes are evaded if a taxpayer consciously fails to report taxable income, such as interest, dividends, tips, fees, or profits from the sale of stocks, bonds, and other assets. Taxes are also evaded when items not legally deductible from income are deducted. For example, taxes are evaded when the costs of operating the family automobile are deducted as a business expense, or when a charitable contribution deduction is claimed but contributions were not made. Tax evasion is illegal and should be scrupulously avoided.

## State and Municipal Income Taxes

Most states and a number of cities levy income taxes, in most cases modeling their laws after the federal laws. However, other than noting the existence of such laws and that they increase the total tax burden and make tax planning even more important, the following discussion is limited to the federal income tax.

## History and Objectives of the Federal Income Tax

Although the federal government first used an income tax during the War between the States, the history of today's federal income tax dates from the 1913 ratification of the Sixteenth Amendment. That amendment cleared away all questions as to the constitutionality of an income tax. Since its ratification, Congress has passed numerous revenue acts and other laws implementing the tax, and has placed the responsibility for enforcing income tax laws in the hands of the Treasury Department acting through the Internal Revenue Service. Collectively, the statutes dealing with taxation that have been adopted by Congress are called the **Internal Revenue Code.**

The original purpose of the federal income tax was to raise revenue. But, over the years this original goal has been expanded to include a variety of nonrevenue objectives. Examples of such objectives are:

1. To assist small businesses.
2. To encourage foreign trade.
3. To encourage exploration for oil and minerals.
4. To redistribute the national income.
5. To control inflation and deflation.
6. To stimulate business.
7. To attain full employment.
8. To support other social objectives.

When federal income taxes were first imposed in the United States, the tax rates were very low; in 1913, the maximum was 7%. As years passed, the rates were increased. For awhile, the maximum rate was in excess of 90%, but later, tax rates began to decline. Tax rates were reduced further with the passage of the Tax Reform Act of 1986. At the time of this writing, the law provides a maximum rate for individuals of 28% (33% in some circumstances) and a maximum rate for corporations of 34% (39% in some circumstances).

The Tax Reform Act of 1986 represented a major change in the tax structure. Two major thrusts of the legislation were to broaden the tax base, through the repeal of or reduction in many tax deductions, and to reduce tax rates. A third apparent objective was to make the tax more *neutral*. In other words, a goal was to reduce the number of instances in which one type of income or expenditure receives more favorable tax treatment than does some other type of income or expenditure.

The 1986 legislation instituted dramatic changes in the rules that have had and likely will continue to have a significant effect on investment (and other) business decisions. In lowering the rates, Congress expected that tax consequences would be less apt to dominate other economic considerations in decisions to make certain expenditures or investments. Nevertheless, despite the reduction in the tax rates, tax consequences continue to be important factors in many decisions.

## Changes in the Tax Law

Extensive changes in the tax laws have been enacted more and more frequently in recent years. During the period 1976–88, major changes were enacted in 1976, 1978, 1981, 1982, 1984, 1987, 1988, and especially in 1986. Because of the changing nature of the tax laws, businesses find it difficult to plan, especially with respect to investments in long-term projects. A project that is expected to be very profitable, given present tax laws, may become less profitable or even unprofitable if Congress enacts tax changes that have an unfavorable effect on the project. And other investment opportunities that were rejected as unprofitable might prove to be very profitable if favorable changes in the tax laws are passed. In any event, businesses and individuals must recognize that many transactions entered into today have uncertain consequences because tax laws may be changed.

Despite the fact that tax laws change frequently, the basic concepts of taxation and the tax formula have remained fairly consistent over many decades. While the tax rates and the amount of certain deductions will likely differ in the future, the overall structure of the system is not likely to change greatly. Tax-free treatment for certain types of income and deductibility of certain expenditures will likely continue, although the items eligible for such treatment may vary to some extent over the years.

## Synopsis of the Federal Income Tax

The following brief synopsis of the federal income tax is given at this point because you need to know something about the federal income tax in order to appreciate its effect on business decisions.

### Classes of Taxpayers

List the classes of federal income taxpayers and describe the steps an individual must go through to calculate his or her taxable income. (L. O. 2)

Federal income tax law recognizes three classes of taxpayers: individuals, corporations, and estates and trusts. Members of each class must file returns and pay taxes on taxable income.

A business that is organized as a single proprietorship or partnership is not treated as a separate taxable entity under the law. Rather, single proprietors must include the income from their businesses on their individual tax returns. A partnership must file an information return that shows its net income and the distributive shares of the partners. Nevertheless, the partnership is not subject to tax. Instead, the partners are required to include their shares on their individual returns. In other words, the income of a single proprietorship or partnership, whether withdrawn from the business or not, is taxed as the individual income of the single proprietor or partners.

The treatment given to corporations under the law is different from that of proprietorships or partnerships. A business that is organized as a corporation must file a return and pay taxes on its taxable income. Also, if a corporation pays out in dividends some or all of its after-tax income, its stockholders must report these dividends as income on their individual returns. Furthermore, when a corporation calculates its taxable income, it cannot deduct dividends it has paid to its stockholders. Because of this, the income of a corporation is commonly said to be taxed twice, once as income of the corporation and again as dividend income of its stockholders.

The income tax laws of the federal government also apply to estates and trusts. However, you do not need further exposure to this somewhat specialized topic to gain a basic understanding of the role federal income taxes play in business decisions. Hence, we leave the taxation of estates and trusts to a more advanced course.

**Illustration 28–1**
**A general format for calculating an individual's federal income tax**

| | | |
|---|---|---|
| **Gross income** . . . . . . . . . . . . . . . . . . . | | $ xx,xxx |
| Less: Deductions to arrive at adjusted gross income . . . . . . . . . . . . . . . . . | | (xx,xxx) |
| **Adjusted gross income** . . . . . . . . . . . . . . | | $ xx,xxx |
| Less: | | |
| Total itemized deductions or the standard deduction, whichever is larger . . . . . . . | $x,xxx | |
| Deduction for exemptions . . . . . . . . . . . | x,xxx | (x,xxx) |
| **Taxable income** . . . . . . . . . . . . . . . . . . | | $ xx,xxx |
| **Gross tax liability from tax rate schedule** . . . | | $ xx,xxx |
| Less: Tax credits and prepayments . . . . . . . | | (xx,xxx) |
| **Net tax payable (or refund)** . . . . . . . . . . . | | $ xxx |

### The Individual Income Tax

Calculate an individual's gross income tax liability and the net tax payable. (L. O. 3)

The amount of federal income tax individuals must pay each year depends on their **gross incomes, tax deductions, exemptions,** and **tax credits.** The typical calculation of the tax liability involves the sequence shown in Illustration 28–1.

To determine the federal income tax liability of an individual, the amounts of gross income, deductions, exemptions, tax credits (if any), and prepayments are listed on forms supplied by the federal government. Then, the appropriate calculations (additions, subtractions, and so forth) are performed according to the instructions. The listing of the items on the forms is not precisely the same for all classes of taxpayers and does not always follow the general pattern shown in Illustration 28–1. However, the illustration shows the relationship of the items and the basic mathematics required in completing the tax forms.

The items that appear on a tax return as gross income, adjusted gross income, deductions, exemptions, tax credits, and prepayments require additional description and explanation.

**Gross Income.** The income tax law defines gross income as *all income from whatever source derived, unless expressly excluded from taxation by law.* Gross income, therefore, includes income from operating a business, gains from property sales, dividends, interest, rents, royalties, and compensation for services, such as salaries, wages, fees, commissions, bonuses, and tips. Actually, the answers to two questions are all that is required to determine whether an item should be included or excluded. The two questions are: (1) Is the item income? (2) Is it expressly excluded by law? If an item is income and not specifically excluded, it must be included.

Certain items are specifically excluded from gross income, for example, gifts, inheritances, scholarships up to the cost of tuition, fees, and course-related materials, social security benefits (unless the taxpayer has a relatively large amount of other income), veterans' benefits, workmen's compensation insurance, and in most cases the proceeds of life insurance policies paid upon the death of the insured. Because these items are excluded from gross income, they are not subject to income tax.

Another item that generally is excluded from gross income is interest on the obligations of the states and their subdivisions. Therefore, states and their subdivisions are able to borrow at a lower rate than they could if their bondholders were taxed on the interest they received.

**Deductions to Arrive at Adjusted Gross Income.** Certain items are deducted from gross income to get **adjusted gross income (AGI)**. These deductions are limited to specific items identified in the law. For example, *a self-employed person's ordinary and necessary expenses to carry on a business, trade, or profession are deductions to arrive at adjusted gross income*. To understand this, recognize that under income tax law, gross profit from sales (sales less cost of goods sold) is gross income to a merchant, and gross legal fees earned are gross income to a lawyer. Therefore, the merchant and the lawyer may deduct all ordinary and necessary expenses of carrying on the business or profession, such as salaries, wages, rent, depreciation, supplies used, repairs, maintenance, insurance, taxes, and interest.

*Expenses of producing rent or royalty income are another category of deductions to arrive at adjusted gross income*. Examples of such deductions include depreciation, repairs, real estate taxes, and insurance expense related to the rent property.

Other deductions to arrive at adjusted gross income include certain alimony payments and limited amounts of Individual Retirement Account (IRA) contributions. Also, self-employed persons may deduct limited amounts of contributions to retirement programs that are designed for self-employed individuals (Keogh plans).

**Deductions from Adjusted Gross Income.** By legislative grace an individual taxpayer is permitted certain deductions from adjusted gross income. These are of two kinds: (1) the greater of itemized personal expenses or the standard deduction, and (2) the deduction for exemptions.

***The Standard Deduction.*** The federal income tax laws grant all individual taxpayers an automatic deduction of a set amount regardless of how they spend their money, on tax deductible expenditures or not. This deduction is known as the **standard deduction**. Taxpayers should elect to deduct the standard deduction if its amount exceeds their itemized deductions (described below). The amounts of the standard deduction for 1989 are:

$5,200 on a joint return.

$2,600 on a return for married taxpayers filing separately.

$4,550 for taxpayers classified as heads of households.

$3,100 for other single taxpayers.

However, if the taxpayer can be claimed as a dependent on another person's tax return, the standard deduction is generally limited to the greater of $500 or the taxpayer's **earned income** up to a maximum of $3,100. Earned income includes wages, professional fees, and other forms of compensation for personal services.

In addition to the above amounts, taxpayers and their spouses (in the case of a joint return) are entitled to an additional standard deduction if they are age 65 or older or blind. On a joint return the additional deduction is $600 per taxpayer per item. Thus, if both spouses are 65 or older and blind, they would receive additional standard deductions of $2,400 (4 × $600) plus the regular standard deduction of $5,200. For single taxpayers, the additional standard deduction is $750 per item instead of $600.

Note that the standard deduction amounts listed above (including the additional $600 or $750 amounts) applied to 1989. These items are indexed annually for inflation. As a result, the amounts that can be deducted in years after 1989 are not known at the time of this writing (April 1989).

***Itemized Personal Expenses.*** Instead of choosing the standard deduction, taxpayers may itemize and deduct their actual allowable personal expenses. Obviously, taxpayers tend to elect whichever alternative results in the largest deduction. Itemized deductions commonly consist of certain nonbusiness interest expenses, state and local property and income taxes, charitable contributions, a casualty loss deduction, a medical expense deduction, a moving expense deduction, and miscellaneous itemized deductions.

The rules for *interest expense* deductions are somewhat detailed, and some interest expense is not fully deductible. Interest classified as *qualified residence interest* is, however, deductible in its entirety. For interest to meet the test of qualified residence interest, the loan must be secured by either the taxpayer's principal residence or a second residence owned by the taxpayer. On such a loan, interest is deductible on a loan of up to $1 million if the purpose of the loan was to acquire, construct, or substantially improve the residence. However, if the loan against the principal or second residence was used for other purposes, the deduction is limited to interest on a loan of $100,000 or less.

After 1990, interest on money borrowed for investment purposes is deductible only up to the amount of the taxpayer's net investment income. Also, consumer interest (for example, interest on car loans and credit cards) is not generally deductible after 1990. However, the limitations on both investment interest and consumer interest are subject to phase-in rules that allow some additional investment interest and some consumer interest to be deducted through 1990.

*Casualty losses* are deductible only to the extent that each loss exceeds $100; then the resulting amounts are aggregated and deducted only to the extent they exceed 10% of adjusted gross income. The *medical expense deduction* is limited to prescription drugs, doctor, dental, hospital, and medical insurance expenses in excess of 7.5% of the taxpayer's adjusted gross income.

*Employees may claim itemized deductions for certain unreimbursed expenses they incur in connection with their employment.* (The expenses must be paid by the employees and must not be reimbursed by the employer.) These expenses include certain transportation and travel expenses, expenses of an outside salesperson, and moving expenses. Employees who work in more than one place during a day may deduct transportation costs incurred in traveling from one place of employment to another during the day. However, as a general rule they may not deduct the cost of commuting from home to the first place of employment or from the last place of employment to home.

Travel expenses include, in addition to transportation expenses, the cost of lodging and 80% of the cost of meals while away from home overnight on employment-connected business.[1] Other employee business expenses include such things as long-distance telephone calls, stationery, postage, and moving expenses. Moving expenses are expenses incurred by employees (or self-employed individuals) in moving their place of residence upon being transferred by their employer or to take a job with a new employer. Certain minimum requirements as to the distance moved and the length of employment in the new location must be met.

Unreimbursed employee business expenses (other than moving expenses) plus deductions such as tax return preparation fees and safe-deposit box rent are referred to as *miscellaneous itemized deductions*. The total amount of miscellaneous itemized deductions is deductible only to the extent that it exceeds 2% of adjusted gross income. For example, if a taxpayer's adjusted gross income is $30,000 and the sum of the taxpayer's miscellaneous itemized deductions is $1,000, only $400, or $1,000 − $600, can be included in the calculation of total itemized deductions.

***Exemptions.*** In addition to itemized deductions or the standard deduction, a taxpayer is allowed a second kind of deduction called the deduction for exemptions. The amount of the exemption deduction is $2,000 for 1989. However, a person (such as a child) who is claimed as a dependent on another taxpayer's return may not claim an exemption deduction for himself or herself on his or her own return.[2]

For years after 1989, the $2,000 amount will be adjusted for inflation. High-income taxpayers lose the benefit of the exemption deduction by means of a surcharge that implements the phase-out of the deduction. (The 5% surcharge is explained in the discussion of the tax rates.) A taxpayer is allowed one personal exemption for himself or herself. If a husband and wife file a joint return, each is a taxpayer and each is allowed one exemption. Taxpayers are also granted one exemption for each dependent.

To qualify as a dependent for whom an exemption may be claimed, the person must meet these tests: (1) be closely related to the taxpayer or have been a member of the taxpayer's household for the entire year; (2) have received over half his or her support from the taxpayer during the year; (3) if married, has not and will not file a joint return with his or her spouse; and (4) had gross income during the year of less than the amount of the personal

---

[1] Self-employed taxpayers and corporations are also subject to the rule that limits the deduction for meals to only 80% of the cost.

[2] In general, the unearned income of children younger than age 14 is taxed at the higher of their tax rate or their parent's top tax rate. In certain circumstances, an election can be made to report the child's unearned income directly on the parent's return.

exemption ($2,000 for 1989). However, you can ignore the gross income test if the person claimed as a dependent is (1) a child of the taxpayer and (2) under 19 years of age at the end of the tax year or under 24 years of age and also a full-time student in an educational institution during each of five months of the year.

Recall from the previous discussion that there are deductions to arrive at adjusted gross income and also deductions from adjusted gross income. Each of these two types of deductions must be subtracted at the proper point in the tax calculation because the allowable amounts of some deductions from adjusted gross income are affected by the amount of adjusted gross income.

**Federal Income Tax Rates.** A person's tax liability is calculated by applying the appropriate tax rates to his or her taxable income. Illustration 28–2 shows the 1989 rates for an unmarried person who does not qualify as a head of household and for married persons who file a joint return or for qualifying widows or widowers. The Tax Rate Schedules in Illustration 28–2 are used by taxpayers who do not qualify to use simplified Tax Tables, which are discussed later in the chapter. To use the rate schedules of Illustration 28–2, a taxpayer reads down the left column of the appropriate schedule until arriving at the bracket of his or her taxable income. For example, if an unmarried taxpayer's 1989 taxable income is $28,550, the taxpayer reads down the column of Schedule X to the bracket "over $18,500." The right column explains that the tax on $18,550 is $2,782.50, and the excess over $18,550 is taxed at 28%. Thus, the tax on $28,550 is $2,782.50 + (28% × $10,000) = $5,582.50.

Observe in Illustration 28–2 that, in general, the federal income tax rates are progressive in nature. This means that each additional segment or bracket of taxable income is subject to a higher rate than the preceding segment or bracket. The rates have a regressive feature, however, for taxpayers with high amounts of taxable income. Such persons are subject to a 33% rate (28% regular rate plus a 5% additional rate) on a portion of their income. Eventually, if their income is high enough, the highest portion is taxed at the 28% rate.

The 5% additional tax applicable to high-income taxpayers serves two functions. The first is to convert the 15% tax on the lowest level of income to a 28% tax. To illustrate the first function of the 5% additional tax, consider a single taxpayer in 1989. The 5% tax on a single taxpayer's taxable income between $44,900 and $93,130 recovers the tax savings from having the first $18,550 of taxable income taxed at 15%. For example, a single taxpayer with exactly $93,130 of taxable income will pay a tax of $26,076.40 (or 15% of $18,550 + 28% of $74,580 + 5% of $48,230). As a result, this taxpayer's tax is exactly 28% of the $93,130 taxable income.

The second function of the 5% additional tax is to eliminate the tax savings that were generated by the deduction for personal exemptions. For single taxpayers, this is accomplished by the 5% tax on taxable income in excess of $93,130. Recall that in 1989, the amount of the personal exemption for a single taxpayer is $2,000. Also, 28% of $2,000 = $560. Since the additional tax liability is limited to $560 times the number of exemptions claimed, the effect of

**Illustration 28–2**
**Federal income tax rate schedules**

**For taxable years beginning in 1989—**
**Schedule X—Single Taxpayers**

| If taxable income is: | The tax is: |
|---|---|
| Not over $18,550 | 15% of taxable income |
| Over $18,550 | $2,782.50 plus 28% of the excess over $18,550 |
| (See note below) | |

**For taxable years beginning in 1989—**
**Schedule Y—Married Individuals Filing Joint Returns and Qualifying Widows and Widowers**

| If taxable income is: | The tax is: |
|---|---|
| Not over $30,950 | 15% of taxable income |
| Over $30,950 | $4,642.50 plus 28% of the excess over $30,950 |
| (See note below) | |

Note: In addition to the tax computed under the above rate schedules for taxable years beginning in 1989, higher income taxpayers incur additional taxes as follows:

1. Single taxpayers—a 5% tax on taxable income between $44,900 and $93,130. Married taxpayers filing joint returns—a 5% tax on taxable income between $74,850 and $155,320.

PLUS—

2. Single taxpayers—a 5% tax on taxable income in excess of $93,130. Married taxpayers filing joint returns—a 5% tax on taxable income in excess of $155,320. However, the tax liability under this computation may not exceed a specified amount. For 1989, the maximum is $560 times the number of exemptions claimed.

this additional tax is to phase out the exemption deduction for high-income taxpayers.

To clarify the use of the rate schedules, assume that a single taxpayer has $250,000 of taxable income in 1989. The taxpayer claims only one exemption deduction. The taxpayer's tax liability is calculated as follows:

| | |
|---|---|
| 15% × $18,550 | $ 2,782.50 |
| 28% × ($250,000 − $18,550) | 64,806.00 |
| 5% × ($93,130 − $44,900) | 2,411.50 |
| The lesser of: | |
| *a.* 5% × ($250,000 − $93,130), or | |
| *b.* $560 × 1 exemption | 560.00 |
| Tax liability | $70,560.00 |

Note that this taxpayer's **marginal tax rate** is 28%. The marginal tax rate is the rate that applies to the next dollar of income to be earned. By comparison, a single taxpayer with a taxable income between $44,900 and $93,129 has a marginal tax rate of 33%. Thus, at certain levels of taxable income the rate structure is said to have a regressive feature.

A husband and wife have a choice concerning rate schedules. They may combine their incomes and use the rate schedule shown for married individuals filing joint returns (Schedule Y), or they may each file a separate return using a rate schedule (not shown) that results in a tax for each somewhat in excess of that shown in Illustration 28–2 for single taxpayers. The phrase **qualifying widows and widowers** in the title of Schedule Y refers to surviving spouses who if they have not remarried and if they have a dependent child may continue to use Schedule Y for two tax years after the year of their spouse's death.

Also, a person who can qualify as a **head of household** may use a rate schedule (not shown) in which the rates fall between those for unmarried individuals and those for married couples filing jointly. Generally, a head of household is an unmarried or legally separated person who maintains a home in which his or her unmarried child or a qualifying dependent lives for over half the year.

The brackets in the rate schedules shown in Illustration 28–2 for 1989 are adjusted each year for changes in the Consumer Price Index. In other words, the brackets are indexed for inflation. As a result, if a person's taxable income increases from year to year but the rate of increase does not exceed the rate of increase in the Consumer Price Index, that person's taxable income increase will not be thrown into a higher tax bracket.

**Tax Credits and Prepayments.** After an individual's gross income tax liability is computed from the appropriate tax rate schedule, the individual's tax credits, if any, and prepayments are deducted to determine the net tax liability. *Tax credits* represent direct, dollar for dollar, reductions in the amount of tax liability; that is, a $100 tax credit reduces the tax liability by $100. By comparison, deductions (as discussed earlier) reduce the amount of taxable income against which are applied the appropriate tax rates to determine the gross tax liability. Thus, a tax credit of $100 is more valuable to the taxpayer than would be a tax deduction of $100. Assuming a marginal tax rate of 28%, an additional tax deduction of $100 effectively reduces the tax liability by $28 ($100 × 28%), whereas a tax credit of $100 reduces the tax liability by $100.

Examples of tax credits include the following. A retired taxpayer with retirement income may receive a *credit for the elderly*. A taxpayer who has paid income taxes to a foreign government may be eligible for a *foreign tax credit*. Also, taxpayers with lower incomes may qualify for an *earned income credit*. The earned income credit, unlike the other tax credits, can generate a tax refund. Thus, it is similar to a negative income tax.

In addition to tax credits, any prepayments of tax are also deducted in order to determine the net tax liability. Most taxpayers have income taxes withheld from their salaries and wages. Other taxpayers have income that is not subject to withholding and on which they are required to estimate the tax and pay the estimated amount in advance installments. Both the income tax withholdings and the estimated tax paid in advance are examples of tax prepayments that are deducted in determining a taxpayer's net tax liability.

**Special Tax Treatment of Capital Gains and Losses.** From a tax planning point of view, one of the most important features of our federal income tax laws in past years has been the special treatment given to **capital gains and losses.** The Tax Reform Act of 1986 repealed the favorable treatment for long-term capital gains but retained the special treatment for capital losses. The Inter-

Define capital assets and describe the tax treatment for capital losses in comparison with ordinary (noncapital) losses. (L. O. 4)

nal Revenue Code defines a **capital asset** as any item of property except (*a*) inventories; (*b*) trade notes and accounts receivable; (*c*) real property and depreciable property used in a trade or business; and (*d*) copyrights, letters, and similar property in the hands of the creator or his or her donee or certain other transferees. Common examples of capital assets held by individuals and subject to sale or exchange are stocks, bonds, and a personal residence.

A gain on the sale of a capital asset occurs when the proceeds of the sale exceed the **basis** of the asset sold, and a loss occurs when the asset's basis exceeds the proceeds. The basis of a purchased asset is generally its cost less any depreciation previously allowed or allowable for tax purposes.

Although capital gains are currently treated just like other types of income, the distinction between capital gains and losses and noncapital (or ordinary) gains and losses is still important because of limitations on deductions for capital losses. When an individual's capital losses exceed capital gains, the individual may deduct no more than $3,000 of the excess losses ($1,500 for a married taxpayer filing a separate return) from ordinary income in the year of the loss. A carryover provision is available to allow deduction in subsequent years of losses that were in excess of the $3,000 or $1,500 limitations.

Remember that the definition of capital assets does not include real property and depreciable property used in a taxpayer's trade or business. When such properties are sold or exchanged, the excess of losses over gains is fully deductible in arriving at taxable income.

As of this writing, recommendations have been made to reinstate some form of preferential tax treatment for long-term capital gains. Critics of preferential treatment have contended that such a provision would violate the theme of the Tax Reform Act of 1986, which was that taxes should be "neutral." In other words, one type of income should not receive preferential tax treatment compared to another. If more favorable tax treatment of long-term capital gains is enacted, the definition of capital assets may be narrowed somewhat.

**Tax Tables.** We previously mentioned that not all taxpayers are required to use the Tax Rate Schedules such as those shown in Illustration 28–2. Instead, most individual taxpayers use simplified Tax Tables. The Tax Tables are constructed from the Tax Rate Schedules. Individuals who use the Tax Tables have to calculate their taxable income according to the formula of Illustration 28–1 and then search through the appropriate Tax Table to determine their gross income tax liability.

### The Corporate Income Tax

Describe the differences between the calculations of taxable income and tax liability for corporations and for individuals. (L. O. 5)

For federal tax purposes, the taxable income of a corporation organized for profit is calculated in much the same way as the taxable income of an individual. However, there are important differences, four of which follow:

*a.* A corporation (but not an individual) may deduct from gross income the first 70% of dividends received from stock it owns in other domestic corporations. The deduction rises to 80% if the corporation owns at least 20% of the other corporation's stock. This, in effect, means that only 30% (or 20%) of such dividends are taxed. However, if two corporations qualify as affiliated corporations, which essentially means that one owns 80% or more of the other's stock, then 100% of the dividends received by the investor corporation from the investee corporation may be deducted. These rules provide relief from the triple taxation of dividends that would otherwise apply.

*b.* A corporation may only offset capital losses against capital gains; and if in any year the offset results in a net capital loss, the loss may not be deducted from other income. However, it may be carried back to the three preceding years and forward to the next five years and deducted from any capital gains of those years.

*c.* The standard deduction and the deduction for exemptions do not apply to a corporation. Also, a corporation does not have certain other deductions of an individual, such as that for personal medical expenses.

*d.* The tax liability of a corporation is calculated using a different rate schedule than those used by individuals. The corporate income tax rates are as follows:

| Amount of Taxable Income | Tax Rate |
|---|---|
| Portion from $0 to $50,000 . . . . . . | 15% |
| Portion over $50,000 to $75,000 . . . . | 25 |
| Portion in excess of $75,000 . . . . . | 34 |

In addition, if the corporation's taxable income exceeds $100,000, the corporation will incur an additional tax equal to the lesser of (*a*) 5% of its taxable income in excess of $100,000 or (*b*) $11,750. Imposition of this additional tax results in recovering some, or all, of the tentative tax savings from having income taxed under the rate schedule at rates below 34%.

To illustrate the use of the corporate rate schedule, assume a corporation has taxable income of $130,000. Its tax liability is calculated as follows:

| | |
|---|---|
| 15% × $50,000 . . . . . . . . . . . . . . . . | $ 7,500 |
| 25% × $25,000 . . . . . . . . . . . . . . . . | 6,250 |
| 34% × $55,000 . . . . . . . . . . . . . . . . | 18,700 |
| The lesser of: | |
| *a.* 5% × ($130,000 − $100,000), or | |
| *b.* $11,750 . . . . . . . . . . . . . . . . . | 1,500 |
| | $33,950 |

## Tax Effects of Business Alternatives

Alternative decisions commonly have different tax effects. This is illustrated in the following examples.

### Form of Business Organization

The difference between individual and corporate tax rates commonly affects one of the basic decisions a business executive must make, which is to select the legal form the business should take. Should it be a single proprietorship, partnership, or corporation? The following factors influence the decision:

Analyze the basic tax consequences of various business decisions to determine which alternative provides the most favorable tax treatment.
(L. O. 6)

*a.* A corporation is a taxable entity and its income is taxed at corporate rates. Also, any portion paid in dividends is taxed again as individual income to its stockholders. By comparison, the income of a single proprietorship or partnership, whether withdrawn or left in the business, is taxed as individual income of the proprietor or partners.

*b.* A corporation may pay reasonable amounts in salaries to stockholders who work for the corporation, and the sum of these salaries is a tax deductible expense in arriving at the corporation's taxable income. In a partnership or a single proprietorship, on the other hand, salaries of the partners or the proprietor are nothing more than allocations of income.

In deciding on the legal form a business should take, a business executive, with the foregoing points in mind, can estimate the tax consequences of each form and select the best. For example, assume that Ralph Jones is choosing between the single proprietorship and corporate forms, and that he estimates the business will have annual gross sales of $250,000, with cost of goods sold and operating expenses, other than his own salary as manager, of $185,000. Assume further that $45,000 per year is a fair salary for managing such a business and that Mr. Jones plans to withdraw all profits from the business. Under these assumptions, the 1989 tax consequences of each alternative business form are calculated in Illustration 28–3.

Under the assumptions of Illustration 28–3, the smaller tax and the larger after-tax income will result from using the single proprietorship form. However, this may not be true in every case. For instance, if Mr. Jones has large amounts of income from other sources, or if the corporation did not pay dividends, he may find that he would incur less tax if the business were organized as a corporation.

In the example of Illustration 28–3, we assumed that all profits are withdrawn and none are left in the business for growth. This may be realistic in some situations. However, growth is commonly financed through the retention of earnings. If earnings are retained, the relative desirability of the two forms may change. This is because income retained in a business organized as a corporation is not taxed as individual income to its stockholders, but the income of a single proprietorship or partnership is so taxed, whether retained in the business or withdrawn.

For instance, if the business of Illustration 28–3 is organized as a single proprietorship, the tax burden of the owner remains the same whether he withdraws any of his profits or not. But, if organized as a corporation and assuming all $17,000 of the earnings are retained in the business, the owner is required to pay individual income taxes on his $45,000 salary only. This would reduce his annual individual income tax from the $9,417 shown in Illustration 28–3 to $4,657 and would reduce the total tax burden with the corporation form to $7,657 ($3,000 + $4,657), which is $2,600 less than the tax burden under the single proprietorship form.

The foregoing is by no means all of the picture. Other tax factors may be involved. For example, a corporation may incur an extra tax if it accumulates more than $250,000 of retained earnings and such accumulations are beyond the reasonable needs of the business. Also, under present laws a corporation

**Illustration 28–3**
**Comparing the income tax effects of organizing a business as a proprietorship or as a corporation**

| | Proprietorship | | Corporation | |
|---|---|---|---|---|
| Operating results under each form: | | | | |
| Estimated sales | | $ 250,000 | | $ 250,000 |
| Cost of goods sold and operating expenses other than owner-manager's salary | $185,000 | | $185,000 | |
| Salary of owner-manager | –0– | (185,000) | 45,000 | (230,000) |
| Before-tax income | | $ 65,000 | | $ 20,000 |
| Corporation income tax at 15% | | (–0–) | | (3,000) |
| Net income | | $ 65,000 | | $ 17,000 |
| Owner's after-tax income under each form: | | | | |
| Single proprietorship net income | | $ 65,000 | | |
| Corporation salary | | | | $ 45,000 |
| Dividends | | | | 17,000 |
| Total individual income | | $ 65,000 | | $ 62,000 |
| Individual income tax (assuming a joint return with itemized deductions of $10,000 and a deduction for exemptions of $4,000 under both forms) | | (10,257) | | (9,417) |
| Owner's after-tax income | | $ 54,743 | | $ 52,583 |

may elect to be treated for tax purposes like a partnership, thus eliminating the corporate tax. Furthermore, in deciding the legal form a business should take, factors other than taxes often are important. For example, lack of stockholder liability often is a strong reason for choosing the corporate form.

### Method of Financing

When a business organized as a corporation is in need of additional financing, the owners may supply whatever funds the corporation needs by purchasing additional shares of stock from the corporation. However, an overall tax advantage may be available if they supply the funds through long-term loans instead of by purchasing stock.

Insofar as the owners are concerned, it makes no difference on their individual returns whether they report interest or dividends from the funds supplied. However, whether the corporation issues stock or floats a loan usually makes a big difference on its return. Interest on borrowed funds is a tax-deductible expense, but dividends are a distribution of earnings and have no effect on the corporation's taxes. Therefore, if owners lend the corporation funds rather than buy its stock, the total tax liability (their own plus their corporation's) will be reduced. In addition, the repayment of long-term debt always is considered to be a return of capital. The redemption of stock, however, may result in the proceeds being treated as dividend income to the stockholders.

In making financial arrangements such as these, owners must be careful not to overreach themselves in attempting to maximize the interest deduction of their corporation. If they do so and thereby create what is called a *thin corporation,* one in which the owners have supplied an unreasonably small portion

## AS A MATTER OF FACT

WASHINGTON—Federal Reserve Board Chairman Alan Greenspan urged Congress not to tamper with the tax deductibility of corporate interest payments but welcomed proposals to reduce the taxes shareholders pay on dividends.

The Fed chairman offered Congress no guidance on how to make up the revenue lost by such a tax break. He specifically opposed suggestions, made by Treasury Secretary Nicholas Brady among others, that Congress combine a cut in taxes on dividends with restrictions on corporate interest deductions. Tinkering with the interest deduction has too many potential adverse side effects, Mr. Greenspan said.

* * * * *

Mr. Greenspan said Congress shouldn't attempt to restrain the leveraged, or debt-financed, buy-out boom because it "has generally enhanced operational efficiency" and because it may have peaked.

* * * * *

Yet the Fed chairman endorsed efforts to remove tax incentives for companies to rely on debt rather than equity financing. The increasing reliance of U.S. corporations on debt is "worrisome," he said, "If it continues . . . we will leverage to the point of being on the edge of being dangerous."

Mr. Greenspan voiced philosophic objections to limiting corporate tax deductions for loans used for takeovers or restructurings. "We must resist the temptation to seek to allocate credit to specific uses through the tax system," he said. Besides, limits to deductions are unavoidably arbitrary and may give "an artificial edge" to companies in countries that do permit interest deductions. "In time," he added, "borrowers and lenders find ways around them."

The Fed chairman also rejected as unreasonable the notion of eliminating the corporate interest deduction entirely and compensating companies by sharply cutting the corporate income tax rate.

Instead, Mr. Greenspan supported proposals to give shareholders credit on their tax returns for taxes paid by companies. Such credits would reduce—or even eliminate—the tax bite on dividends received by shareholders. Presumably the price of dividend-paying stocks would rise, encouraging companies to raise capital by selling shares rather than by borrowing.

Currently, corporate profits are taxed at the corporate level and again at the shareholder level when they are paid as dividends.

The Fed chairman also said that lowering the tax rate on capital gains would help encourage equity financing, but he advised against reopening the delicate political compromise that produced the 1986 Tax Reform Act. That law reduced overall personal income tax rates and eliminated the favorable treatment of capital gains.

Mr. Greenspan acknowledged that cutting taxes on either dividends or capital gains would cost the Treasury "significant revenues," and added, "I don't know how to get around that."

* * * * *

Source: David Wessel, "Greenspan Wants to Keep Deductibility of Interest Payments by Corporations," *The Wall Street Journal*, January 27, 1989, p. A3. Reprinted by permission of *The Wall Street Journal*, 

of capital through stock purchases, the Internal Revenue Service may disallow the interest deductions and require that such deductions be treated as dividends. Furthermore, repayments of "principal" may also be held to be taxable dividends.

The "As a Matter of Fact" article above describes how the tax statutes treat interest expense more favorably than dividends paid. Such treatment, of course, provides an incentive for a heavy reliance on debt as a means of financing an acquisition. Recent leveraged buyouts are a case in point. As suggested by the article, Congress may revise the laws to make the tax treatment of dividends and interest expense more neutral.

### Timing Transactions

The timing of transactions can be of major importance in tax planning. For example, taxpayers using the cash method of tax accounting instead of the accrual method have considerable flexibility in timing their income and deductions. Thus, if they anticipate that their tax rates will be lower during the next taxable year, it may be to their advantage to accelerate the payment of deductible expenditures into the current year and to postpone the receipt of income until early the next year. This planning tip assumes that the taxpayer will not experience cash flow problems from such behavior.

Because of the flexibility the cash method affords with respect to timing, the 1986 law placed restrictions on the availability of the cash method. In general, corporations other than those that have elected to be treated much like partnerships cannot use the cash method. Exceptions apply, however, for farm businesses, personal service corporations (such as professional corporations), and corporations with average annual gross receipts of less than $5 million.

### Forms in which Related Transactions Are Completed

The tax consequences of related transactions are often dependent on the forms in which they are completed. For example, the sale of one property at a profit and the immediate purchase of another like property normally results in a taxable gain on the property sold, but a direct exchange of these properties may result in a tax-free exchange.

A tax-free exchange occurs when like kinds of property are exchanged for each other, or when one or more persons transfer property to a corporation and immediately thereafter are in control of the corporation. Control in such cases is interpreted as meaning that after the transfer, the transferring persons (or person) must own at least 80% of the corporation's voting stock plus at least 80% of the total number of shares of all other classes of stock.

At first glance it seems that it should be to anyone's advantage to take a tax-free exchange rather than to pay taxes, but this may not be so. For example, 10 years ago a corporation paid $50,000 for land located at the edge of the city. Today, due to booming growth, the land is well within the city and has a fair market value of $250,000. The land has been held as an investment and is without improvements. The corporation plans to move part of its operations to a suburb and has an opportunity to trade the city property for vacant suburban acreage on which it would build a factory. Should it make the trade? From a tax viewpoint the answer is probably yes, the company should make the tax-free exchange. That way, the company avoids having to pay a tax on the gain at the present time. From a present value standpoint, postponing the tax payment is important.

However, assume a different set of facts in which the suburban property to be acquired consists of land having a fair market value of $25,000 with a suitable factory building thereon valued at $225,000. Also assume that the corporation experienced a $200,000 capital loss from selling stock held as an investment. The corporation had no other capital gains this year or in the past three years, nor does it expect to have any in the next five years (against which the capital loss might be offset).

If the corporation exchanges the city land for the suburban land and factory, it will receive no current benefit from its capital loss. On the other hand, if it sells the land, the $200,000 gain on the land sale can be exactly offset by the $200,000 loss on the stock sale. Then, the $250,000 cash proceeds can be used to buy the suburban land and factory. By purchasing the new factory, the corporation gains the right to deduct the building's $225,000 cost on a straight-line basis over the next 31½ years. On this set of facts, the corporation would likely choose a sale over a tax-free exchange.

### Compensation of Employees

Businesses can compensate their employees in a variety of ways. One way is to compensate them solely with salary payments. However, many employees prefer to receive a smaller amount of salary and to receive their additional compensation in some form of noncash compensation on which they are not taxed. Congress frequently discusses narrowing the range of fringe benefits eligible for tax-free treatment. Yet, several types of fringe benefits received by employees continue to be tax-free. For example, employers may pay premiums on health insurance or limited amounts of group-term life insurance for employees. Employers also may make payments to qualified retirement plans for employees. In all of these instances, the employees do not pay taxes on the value of such benefits received.

To illustrate the value of these forms of compensation, consider an employee-taxpayer who is in the 33% marginal tax bracket. The employee would need to receive $100 of before-tax compensation to pay a $67 life insurance premium from his or her own after-tax funds. But the employee can obtain the same benefit if the $67 premium is paid by the employer, in which case the employee would not pay tax on this $67 of noncash compensation. At the same time, the employer's before-tax cost of additional compensation is reduced from $100 to $67.

### Accounting Basis and Procedures

With certain exceptions, the accounting basis and procedures used by taxpayers in keeping their records must also be used in computing taxable income. Generally, taxpayers keep their records on either a cash or an accrual basis (see page 112). However, regardless of which they use, the basis and any procedures used must clearly reflect income and be consistently followed.

When inventories are a material factor in calculating income, taxpayers are required to use the accrual basis to calculate gross profit from sales. Also, plant assets cannot be expensed in the year of purchase but must be depreciated over the time periods specified in the tax laws (see Chapter 10). However, other than for gross profit from sales and depreciation, many taxpayers may use the cash basis to account for income and expenses.

Using the cash basis is often an advantage to the taxpayer. Under the cash basis, taxpayers can often shift expense payments and the receipt of items of revenue (other than from the sale of merchandise) from one accounting period to the next and thus increase or decrease taxable income of a particular year.

The ability to shift income or deductions from one tax year to another is especially beneficial when tax rates change from one year to the next.

An accrual basis taxpayer cannot shift income from year to year by timing receipts and payments. However, somewhat of the same thing may be accomplished through a choice of accounting procedures. For example, the choice of inventory affects the timing of income recognition. Consider the choice of LIFO versus FIFO. During periods of rising prices, the LIFO inventory method results in charging higher costs for goods sold against current revenues, and thus reduces taxable income and taxes. It may be argued that this only postpones taxes since in periods of declining prices the use of LIFO results in lower costs and higher taxes. However, the history of recent years has been one of rising prices. Thus, it may be argued that LIFO will postpone taxes indefinitely.

The choice of depreciation method is another example. Compared to straight-line depreciation, the Modified Accelerated Cost Recovery System (MACRS) results in higher depreciation charges in an asset's early years and lower charges in later years. Thus, the effect of MACRS is to postpone taxes. MACRS is also favorable because it generally allows taxpayers to recover the cost of a property over a period that is shorter than the asset's useful life. And, while tax postponement is not as desirable as tax avoidance, postponement gives the taxpayer interest-free use of tax dollars until these dollars must be paid to the government.

Before turning to a new topic, we should note that the opportunities for tax planning described in these pages are only illustrative of those available. The wise business executive will seek help from a professional who specializes in tax consultation in order to take advantage of every tax-saving opportunity.

## Financial Reporting of Income Tax Liabilities and Expense

Explain why income tax expenses shown in financial statements may differ from taxes currently payable.
(L. O. 7)

Financial statements for a business should be prepared in accordance with generally accepted accounting principles. Tax accounting, on the other hand, must be done in accordance with tax laws. As a result, income (before taxes) measured in accordance with generally accepted accounting principles is not always the same as taxable income calculated on state or federal income tax returns. They may differ for two reasons.

### Permanent Income Differences between Financial Accounting and Tax Accounting

The first reason is that some items are included in the calculation of income according to generally accepted accounting principles but, according to the tax laws, are permanently excluded from the calculation of taxable income. Also, some items are included in the calculation of taxable income according to the tax laws but are permanently excluded from the calculation of income according to generally accepted accounting principles.

For example, interest received on state and municipal bonds must be recognized as revenue on the income statement of the company that owns the bonds. In contrast, such interest usually is not subject to federal income tax and therefore is not included in taxable income. Another example is percentage depletion, which is a deduction allowed for tax purposes but is not an expense. These items involve *permanent differences* between taxable income and income before taxes.

### Temporary Income Differences between Financial Accounting and Tax Accounting

The second reason why there may be a difference between taxable income and income before taxes on the financial statements involves *temporary differences* between tax accounting procedures and financial accounting procedures. In other words, a business may use one accounting procedure for tax purposes and another accounting procedure for financial statement purposes where the income effect of the difference between the procedures is temporary or a matter of timing. For example, unearned income such as rent collected in advance usually is taxable in the year of receipt. In financial statements, however, such items are recognized as income when they are earned, not when cash is received. As another example, a business may apply straight-line depreciation over the estimated useful life of an asset for accounting purposes. At the same time, it may use the Modified Accelerated Cost Recovery System of accelerated depreciation for tax purposes.

When a corporation uses different procedures for tax and financial statement purposes and the difference between the procedures is temporary, a problem arises in measuring net income. The problem involves deciding how much income tax expense should be shown on the income statement. If the actual tax to be paid currently is shown as an expense, the amount of tax will appear inconsistent with the known tax rate. Also, if the actual tax to be paid currently is the only amount of tax recorded, the liabilities reported on the balance sheet may fail to show taxes that will become due in future years as a result of transactions that have already taken place.

Therefore, generally accepted accounting principles have for many years included special procedures to account for income taxes in the financial statements. These rules were changed very significantly by the FASB in its *Statement of Financial Accounting Standards No. 96,* issued in December 1987. The new rules originally were to become mandatory for fiscal years beginning after December 15, 1988. However, in *Statement of Financial Accounting Standards No. 100,* the FASB deferred the effective date to give companies more time to prepare for the new requirements. Now, the rules are required for fiscal years beginning after December 15, 1989.

Portions of the new rules are very complex and are beyond the introductory scope of this text. However, the most basic concepts of accounting for income taxes are important to your understanding of financial statements and the following paragraphs will give you this basic understanding.

### Financial Accounting for Income Taxes—An Illustration

To illustrate accounting for income taxes, assume that prior to 1990, Lott Company had no temporary differences between taxable income and income before taxes. Then, during 1990, Lott Company sold a tract of land in a transaction that qualified for tax purposes as an installment sale. As a result, the gain on the sale is recognized for tax purposes as cash is received. For financial

**Illustration 28–4**

| | 1990 | 1991 |
|---|---|---|
| Tax returns (applying installment sales method to sale of land): | | |
| Service revenue | $2,000 | $ –0– |
| Gain on sale of land | | 1,000 |
| Deductions for expenses | (–0–) | (–0–) |
| **Taxable income** | $2,000 | $1,000 |
| Tax rate | ×15% | ×15% |
| Taxes payable | $ 300 | $ 150 |
| Income statements: | | |
| Service revenue | $2,000 | $ –0– |
| Gain on sale of land | 1,000 | –0– |
| Operating expenses | (–0–) | (–0–) |
| **Income before income taxes** | $3,000 | $ –0– |
| Income taxes expense | ? | ? |
| Net income | ? | ? |

Notice the differences

accounting purposes, the gain was realized in 1990 and should be reported on the 1990 income statement. To keep the example simple, assume that Lott Company's income transactions during 1990 and 1991 were limited to the following:

| | | 1990 | 1991 |
|---|---|---|---|
| Service revenue | | $2,000 | $ –0– |
| Sales price of land sold in 1990 (cash to be received in 1991) | $ 8,000 | | |
| Cost of land | (7,000) | | |
| Gain on sale of land | | 1,000 | |
| Operating expenses | | –0– | –0– |
| Cash received from previous year's land sale | | | 8,000 |

Assuming an income tax rate of 15%, Lott Company's tax returns for 1990 and 1991 would contain the calculations shown in the top half of Illustration 28–4. The company's income statements, except for income taxes expense, appear in the bottom half of the illustration.

In Illustration 28–4, notice that the difference between taxable income and income before income taxes in 1990 is a temporary difference. The difference is temporary because the income statement gain in 1990 shows up on the tax return in 1991. In other words, the temporary difference in 1990 reverses in 1991.

Underlying Illustration 28–4 is the assumption that the company had no revenues and no expenses during 1991. The only transaction during 1991 was the collection of the $8,000 receivable that resulted from the land sale during 1990.

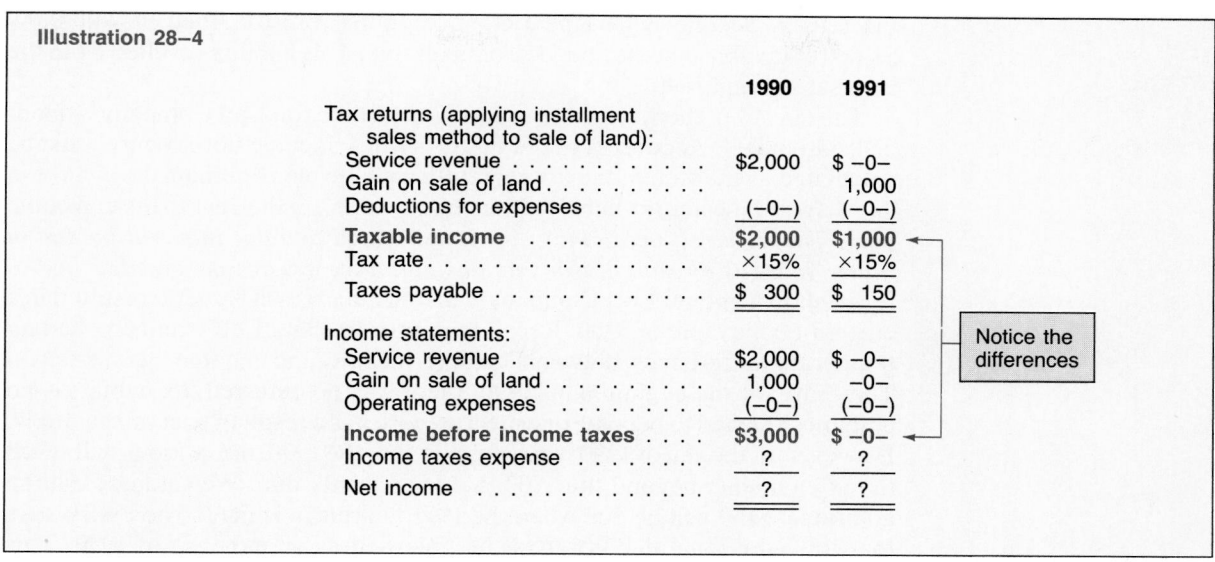

In Illustration 28–4, notice that the revenue and expense transactions of 1990 gave rise to two different income tax liabilities. First, the 1990 transactions resulted in a $300 liability that is due as a result of filing the 1990 income tax return. Second, when the 1991 income tax return is filed, it will show $1,000 of taxable income and $150 of taxes due. This liability resulted from the land sale during 1990.

The question, then, is how to report income taxes on Lott Company's financial statements. According to the FASB's rules, income tax expense must be calculated as the sum of the tax currently payable plus or minus the change in any **deferred income tax liability** from the beginning of the year to the end of the year. *The deferred tax liability is the estimated amount that will be due in future years as a result of transactions that have already occurred.*

As shown above, Lott Company's income tax return for 1990 resulted in a current tax payable of $300. Recall that prior to 1990, Lott Company had no temporary differences between taxable income and income before taxes. Therefore, at the beginning of 1990, there was no deferred tax liability—no amount expected to become due in future years as a result of past transactions. However, at the end of 1990, we recognize that the 1990 transactions will result in tax payments beyond the $300 that is currently due. We estimate that an additional $150 will be due when the 1991 tax return is filed. The FASB says that this additional liability must be recorded as an expense of 1990. This means that Lott Company's entry to record income taxes at the end of 1990 is as follows:

| | | | | |
|---|---|---|---|---|
| Dec. | 31 | Income Taxes Expense | 450.00 | |
| | | Income Taxes Payable | | 300.00 |
| | | Deferred Income Tax Liability | | 150.00 |

Based on the assumed facts, the only transaction that occurred during 1991 was the collection of the $8,000 receivable. However, even though there were no revenues or expenses during 1991, the tax return for that year reports a gain of $1,000 and $150 of taxes due. Also, remember that income tax expense for 1991 is calculated as the sum of the amount currently due plus or minus the change in the deferred tax liability during the year. On January 1, 1991, the Deferred Income Tax Liability account had a credit balance of $150. But, on December 31, 1991, there are no future tax liabilities expected as a result of past transactions. Thus, the deferred liability is analyzed as follows:

| | |
|---|---|
| Deferred income tax liability: | |
| Balance of account at beginning of 1991 | $150 credit |
| Correct balance at end of 1991 | –0– |
| Necessary change to obtain correct ending balance | $150 debit |

Thus, income tax expense for 1991 is calculated as the sum of the taxes currently payable minus the decrease in the deferred tax liability, or $150 – $150 = $–0–. As a result, the entry to record income taxes for 1991 is:

| | | | | |
|---|---|---|---|---|
| Dec. | 31 | Deferred Income Tax Liability | 150.00 | |
| | | Income Taxes Payable | | 150.00 |

As a result of the above entries, the Lott Company's financial statements show the following information concerning income taxes:

| | 1990 | 1991 |
|---|---|---|
| Income statements: | | |
| Service revenue | $2,000 | $ –0– |
| Gain on sale of land | 1,000 | –0– |
| Operating expenses | (–0–) | (–0–) |
| Income before income taxes | $3,000 | $ –0– |
| Income taxes expense | (450) | (–0–) |
| Net income | $2,550 | $ –0– |
| Balance sheets: | | |
| Income taxes payable (assumes no prepayments) | $ 300 | $ 150 |
| Deferred income tax liability | 150 | –0– |

Before concluding this chapter on income taxes, we should mention some additional features of the rules that govern accounting for income taxes.

1. In the Lott Company example, we assumed an income tax rate of 15% in both 1990 and 1991. However, at the end of 1990, if the existing laws stated that rates in 1991 were going to be different, for example, 20%, then the deferred income tax liability at the end of 1990 would be calculated using the 1991 tax rate of 20%.
2. In the Lott Company example, 1990 income before taxes was *more than* taxable income because of a temporary difference that was expected to reverse in 1991. As a result, we recognized a deferred tax liability on the December 31, 1990, balance sheet. In other situations, just the opposite kind of temporary difference may occur. In other words, a temporary difference that will reverse in the future may cause income before taxes to be *less than* taxable income. These later situations may, under certain conditions, result in the recognition of a deferred tax asset. However, in order to recognize a deferred tax asset, the future tax benefit or savings must be assured as a result of past transactions.
3. The Deferred Tax Liability account balance may be reported as a long-term liability or as a current liability, depending on how far in the future the liability will be satisfied.
4. Federal tax laws generally require corporations to estimate their current year's tax liability and make advance payments of the estimated amount before the final tax return is filed. As a result, the end-of-year entries to record income taxes, such as those shown above for Lott Company, often have to be altered to take into consideration any previously recorded prepayments.

## Summary of the Chapter in Terms of Learning Objectives

**1.** Many transactions can be structured in more than one way, and the choice of one alternative versus another often has an effect on current and/or future tax liabilities. With careful tax planning, a taxpayer can evaluate the tax effects of the available alternatives and oftentimes can legally avoid a tax liability or defer tax payments. This does not involve the illegal evasion of existing tax liabilities.

**2.** The federal income tax is levied on individuals, corporations, and estates and trusts. To calculate an individual's taxable income, you first decide whether their income received is excludable (tax-free) or includable in gross income. Next, you subtract deductions to arrive at adjusted gross income. These generally include expenses of a business nature such as the expenses of operating a business as a self-employed person and the expenses of producing rent income. From adjusted gross income you subtract (*a*) deductions for exemptions and (*b*) the greater of itemized deductions or the standard deduction to arrive at taxable income.

**3.** To calculate an individual's gross tax liability, you apply the appropriate tax rate schedule or tax table to taxable income. Thereafter, tax credits and prepayments are subtracted to determine the net tax payable. Unlike deductions, tax credits represent a dollar-for-dollar reduction in the amount of tax owed.

**4.** Capital assets include all property except (*a*) inventories; (*b*) trade notes and accounts receivable; (*c*) real and depreciable property used in a trade or business; and (*d*) copyrights, letters, and similar property in the hands of the creator, his or her donee, or certain other transferees. An unlimited amount of ordinary (noncapital) losses may be offset against income. However, the amount of net capital losses that can be used to reduce income in a given year is very limited in amount—$3,000 ($1,500 on a separate return) in the case of individuals and $0 for corporate taxpayers.

**5.** Corporations, but not individuals, are entitled to a dividends received deduction. Individuals can deduct up to $3,000 of net capital loss whereas corporations cannot deduct any. Individuals receive an exemption deduction and can take a standard deduction if it is greater than their itemized personal deductions; these are not available to corporations. Also, the rate schedules for individuals differ from the corporate rate schedule.

**6.** The effects of the income tax can influence a variety of business decisions. Examples are decisions about whether or not a business should be organized as a corporation, the methods used to finance business activities, the timing of transactions, the form in which related transactions are completed, the methods used to compensate employees, and the choice between alternative accounting methods.

**7.** Generally accepted accounting principles are not the same as income tax rules. This means that the amount of income before taxes reported on the income statement may differ from the taxable income on the tax return. When these differences are temporary or a matter of timing, the reported income tax expense may be different from the amount of tax currently payable. For example, some current income statement transactions result in tax liabilities that are deferred in the sense that they will be paid in the future but are not due as a result of filing the current tax return. These liabilities must be recorded and added to the taxes currently payable to determine income taxes expense.

## Demonstration Problem

Henry and Wanda White regularly file a joint individual income tax return. They provide all of the support for their two children, who are ages 8 and 5. Wanda is employed by a public relations firm and received salary income of $43,000 for 1989. FICA taxes of $3,229 and federal income taxes of $8,000 were withheld from her salary. Henry is the president of Henri, Inc., a firm in which he owns 100% of the stock. He received a salary of $30,000 from the firm in 1989. Taxes withheld from his salary included $5,000 for federal income taxes and $2,253 for FICA taxes. The couple received $8,000 interest income from City of New Orleans bonds.

Information that may affect the couple's itemized deductions follows. They spent $3,200 on property taxes, $4,100 on qualified residence interest, and $15,000 on medical expenses. They contributed $2,500 to various charitable organizations and experienced a casualty loss of $6,300.

Several years ago, Henry loaned $100,000 to Henri, Inc. During 1989, the firm paid Henry interest of $11,000 on this loan. Also during 1989, Henry received a dividend of $4,000 on his common stock in Henri, Inc. Henri, Inc., had sales of $400,000 for 1989, and its cost of goods sold was $190,000. Its expenses, exclusive of any payments to Henry, were $90,000. Henri, Inc., received dividend income of $10,000 from some shares it owns in a large corporation.

*Required*

*a.* Determine the corporation's taxable income and tax payable, assuming it paid estimated taxes of $15,000.

*b.* Also determine the taxable income and tax liability of Mr. and Mrs. White, assuming they file a joint return. Assume Mr. and Mrs. White made estimated tax payments totaling $2,000.

*c.* Indicate the marginal tax rate of Henri, Inc., and of the Whites.

*d.* Explain how the taxable income would differ if Mr. White, instead of the corporation, had received the dividends.

## Solution to Demonstration Problem

*a.* Henri, Inc.:

| | | |
|---|---|---|
| Sales | $ 400,000 | |
| Cost of goods sold | (190,000) | |
| Gross profit | | $ 210,000 |
| Dividend income | $ 10,000 | |
| Dividends received deduction | (7,000) | 3,000 |
| Expenses, exclusive of payments to Henry | $ 90,000 | |
| Salary expense—Henry | 30,000 | |
| Interest expense—Henry | 11,000 | (131,000) |
| Taxable income | | $ 82,000 |
| Gross tax liability | | $ 16,130 |
| Less estimated tax payments | | (15,000) |
| Net tax payable | | $ 1,130 |

*b.* Mr. and Mrs. White:

| | | | |
|---|---|---|---|
| Salary—Mr. White | | | $ 30,000 |
| Salary—Mrs. White | | | 43,000 |
| Interest income | | | 11,000 |
| Dividend income | | | 4,000 |
| Adjusted gross income | | | $ 88,000 |
| Less itemized deductions: | | | |
| Property taxes | | $ 3,200 | |
| Qualified residence interest | | 4,100 | |
| Charitable contributions | | 2,500 | |
| Medical expenses | $15,000 | | |
| Less 7½% of AGI | (6,600) | 8,400 | |
| Casualty loss | $ 6,300 | | |
| Less $100 and 10% of AGI | (8,900) | –0– | (18,200) |
| Less personal exemptions | | | (8,000) |
| Taxable income | | | $ 61,800 |
| Gross tax liability | | | $ 13,281 |
| Less withholding tax | | | (13,000) |
| Less estimated tax | | | (2,000) |
| Net tax payable (refund) | | | $ (1,719) |

*c.* Henri, Inc.'s marginal tax rate is 34%, and the marginal tax rate for Mr. and Mrs. White is 28%.

*d.* If Mr. White had received the dividend income, the corporation's taxable income would have been lower by $3,000. Mr. and Mrs. White's gross income and adjusted gross income would have been higher by $10,000, and their deductible medical expenses would have been lower by $750 (7.5% × $10,000). Thus, their taxable income would have been higher by $10,750.

## Glossary

Define or explain the terms and phrases listed in the chapter Glossary. (L. O. 8)

**Adjusted gross income (AGI)** gross income minus certain deductions such as business expenses of self-employed persons, expenses to produce rent or royalty income, alimony payments, and limited amounts of contributions to retirement programs for self-employed persons or to Individual Retirement Accounts. p. 1170

**Basis** in general, the cost of a purchased asset less any depreciation previously allowed or allowable for tax purposes. p. 1176

**Capital asset** any item of property except (1) inventories; (2) trade notes and accounts receivable; (3) real property and depreciable property used in a trade or business; and (4) copyrights, letters, or similar property. p. 1176

**Capital gain or loss** the difference between the proceeds from the sale of a capital asset and the basis of the asset. pp. 1175–76

**Deferred income tax liability** the estimated amount of income taxes that will be due in future years as a result of transactions that have already occurred. p. 1186

**Earned income** wages, professional fees, and other forms of compensation for personal services. pp. 1170–71

**Exemptions** a special deduction that each individual taxpayer is granted for himself or herself and for each dependent, the benefit of which high income taxpayers lose through a 5% surtax. pp. 1169, 1172–73

**Gross income** all income from whatever source derived, unless expressly excluded from taxation by law. pp. 1169–70

**Head of household** an unmarried or legally separated person who maintains for more than half the year a home in which lives his or her unmarried child or a qualifying dependent. p. 1175

**Internal Revenue Code** collectively, the statutes dealing with taxation that have been adopted by Congress. p. 1167

**Marginal tax rate** the rate that applies to the next dollar of income to be earned. p. 1174

**Qualifying widows and widowers** individuals whose spouses are deceased and who remain unmarried and have a dependent child and, therefore, who are allowed to use the income tax rate Schedule Y for two years after their spouses' death. p. 1175

**Standard deduction** a deduction from adjusted gross income that an individual may claim as an alternative to itemizing their personal deductions. p. 1170

**Tax avoidance** a legal course of action selected to prevent a tax liability from coming into existence or to reduce a tax liability. p. 1166

**Tax credit** an item, the dollar amount of which can be subtracted from the gross tax liability, thereby providing a dollar for dollar reduction in the liability. pp. 1169, 1175

**Tax deduction** an amount that can be legally subtracted from gross income or from adjusted gross income in the process of determining taxable income. pp. 1169–73

**Tax evasion** the fraudulent denial and concealment of an existing tax liability. p. 1166

**Tax planning** evaluating the alternative ways of conducting one's affairs in terms of their tax consequences and selecting the alternatives that incur the smallest tax liabilities and that are consistent with one's other goals. p. 1166

## Objective Review

Answers to the following questions are listed in Appendix I at the end of the book. Be sure that you decide which is the one best answer to each question *before* you check the answers in the appendix.

1. Tax planning can best be described as:
   *a.* Tax evasion.
   *b.* An opportunity to reduce tax liabilities that is only available to corporate taxpayers.
   *c.* An effort to minimize one's tax liabilities by considering alternative ways of doing business, evaluating each alternative in terms of its tax consequences, and choosing the one that is most profitable.
   *d.* Estimating future tax payments and setting aside cash in advance to make those payments.
   *e.* The legal requirement that taxpayers take advantage of all tax-saving opportunities.
2. In calculating the taxable income of an individual, which of the following statements is *not* correct?
   *a.* A taxpayer can choose to itemize deductions or claim the standard deduction.
   *b.* Items such as medical expenses and qualified residence interest are examples of itemized deductions.
   *c.* Trade or business expenses of a self-employed person are deductible in arriving at adjusted gross income.
   *d.* Taxpayers who itemize their personal expenses are not entitled to claim any deductions for exemptions.
   *e.* Tax credits are subtracted after taxable income has been determined (that is, they do not affect the amount of taxable income).
3. Which of the following statements concerning tax liabilities of individuals is *not* correct?
   *a.* The tax rate can go from 15%, to 28%, to 33%, and back to 28%.
   *b.* If married taxpayers filing a joint return have taxable income of $35,950 in 1989, they will have $5,000 of income subject to a 28% tax rate.
   *c.* If a taxpayer is in the 28% marginal tax bracket, a $100 tax deduction will reduce taxes by $28 and a $100 tax credit will reduce taxes by $100.
   *d.* Federal income tax withheld from the taxpayer's salary is an example of a prepayment.
   *e.* A single person with taxable income of $25,000 is taxed at a flat rate of 28%.

4. An individual taxpayer has taxable income, exclusive of capital gains and losses, of $50,000. In addition, the taxpayer sold a capital asset during the year. The taxpayer will report taxable income of:
   *a.* $50,000 if the taxpayer sold the capital asset for a $10,000 capital gain.
   *b.* $50,000 if the taxpayer sold the capital asset for a $10,000 capital loss.
   *c.* $53,000 if the taxpayer sold the capital asset for a $10,000 capital gain.
   *d.* $40,000 if the taxpayer sold the capital asset for a $10,000 capital loss.
   *e.* $47,000 if the taxpayer sold the capital asset for a $10,000 capital loss.
5. Which of the following statements is correct?
   *a.* Married individuals who file a joint return and corporations are subject to a 15% tax rate on the same dollar amount of income.
   *b.* Individuals are entitled to a standard deduction, but corporations are not.
   *c.* Both individuals and corporations are allowed to deduct a portion of any dividend income they receive.
   *d.* The tax rate schedules for individuals contain a regressive feature, but the rate schedule for corporations does not.
   *e.* The highest income tax rate applied to corporations is 28%.
6. Which of the following statements is correct?
   *a.* From a tax perspective, the partnership form of business organization always is preferred to the corporate form, since partnerships do not pay income taxes.
   *b.* A corporation's after-tax cost of paying $1 of dividends is the same as the after-tax cost of paying $1 of interest.
   *c.* An accrual basis taxpayer has more ability to defer taxes through timing of transactions than does a cash basis taxpayer.
   *d.* Some forms of noncash compensation, such as employer payments of employee health insurance premiums, are not treated as taxable income of the employee.
   *e.* None of the above is correct.
7. In following the FASB's rules of accounting for income taxes:
   *a.* Income tax expense is calculated as the sum of the income taxes currently payable plus the change in the deferred income tax liability that occurred during the year.
   *b.* Income taxes expense always is more than the amount of income taxes currently payable.
   *c.* A company may report a deferred income tax liability but never would report a deferred tax asset.
   *d.* Deferred tax liabilities are calculated as the amount shown to be due on the current year's tax return.
   *e.* All of the above are correct.

## Questions for Class Discussion

1. What event established the constitutionality of the federal income tax in the United States?
2. If an individual taxpayer expects to be in the 28% tax bracket, which should the taxpayer prefer: (*a*) a $150 expenditure that will provide a tax credit of $85 or (*b*) a $150 expenditure that will provide a business expense deduction of $150?
3. Why must effective tax planning be done before important transactions take place rather than after the transactions are completed?
4. What is the difference between tax avoidance and tax evasion?
5. What name identifies the collection of federal statutes that deal with taxation?
6. What are some of the nonrevenue objectives of various federal income tax laws?
7. What are the classes of taxpayers that are subject to the federal income tax?
8. What questions must be answered to determine whether an item should be included or excluded from gross income for tax purposes?
9. Name several items that are not included in gross income for tax purposes.
10. What justification might be given for permitting a corporation to claim a tax deduction for a portion of its dividend income?
11. For tax purposes, define a capital asset.
12. What is the significance of defining capital assets separately from other types of assets?
13. An individual had capital asset transactions that resulted in nothing but losses. What tax treatment is given to these losses?
14. What preferential tax treatment, if any, do long-term capital gains receive currently?
15. Why do tax planners try to have losses emerge as ordinary losses instead of as capital losses?
16. Why would an owner of an incorporated business prefer to be paid a salary by the corporation instead of having the money paid to him in the form of dividends?
17. Why might stockholders in a small corporation prefer to invest additional capital in the corporation through the purchase of long-term bonds from the corporation instead of through the purchase of additional shares of stock?
18. What are some ways that a corporation might provide tax-free compensation to its employees?
19. What does it mean when a corporation is said to be a "thin" corporation?
20. If a corporation is proven to be a thin corporation, what effect might this have on the Internal Revenue Service's treatment of the corpora-

tion's payment of interest and repayment of principal to the "creditors"?

21. Why does the taxable income of a business commonly differ from its net income?
22. For financial accounting purposes, what is the importance of the distinction between permanent differences and temporary differences in income before taxes and taxable income?

## Exercises

In some of the Exercises and Problems that follow, the taxpayers would qualify to use the simplified Tax Tables (not provided in the book) rather than the Tax Rate Schedules. However, to restrict the length of the chapter and to facilitate your understanding of the underlying concepts, you should base all calculations of individual tax liabilities on the Tax Rate Schedules in Illustration 28–2.

Exercise 28–1
**Including or excluding items in gross income**
(L. O. 2)

List the letters of the following items and write after each either the word *included* or *excluded* to tell whether the item should be included in or excluded from gross income for federal income tax purposes.

*a.* Gift of stock from wealthy uncle.
*b.* Scholarship received from a state university. The scholarship is for an amount substantially in excess of the cost of the tuition, fees, and course-related materials.
*c.* Tips received while working as a waiter.
*d.* Dividends from stock received by an individual.
*e.* Workmen's compensation insurance received as the result of an accident while working on a part-time job.
*f.* Interest income from state bonds.
*g.* Gain on the sale of a personal automobile bought and rebuilt.
*h.* Cash inherited from a deceased parent.

Exercise 28–2
**Calculating taxable incomes of single individuals**
(L. O. 2)

Sam Innis, Edna Lyle, and Nicolas Edwards are unmarried and have three income tax exemptions each. All are younger than age 65 and have good vision. In 1989, their adjusted gross incomes were: Innis, $35,000; Lyle, $56,000; and Edwards, $81,000. Their itemized deductions were: Innis, $2,500; Lyle, $10,600; and Edwards, $15,400. Prepare calculations to show the taxable income of each person.

**Exercise 28–3**
**Calculating taxable income on a joint return**
(L. O. 2)

Carl and Cathy Trenton had $47,000 of adjusted gross income in 1989. They are 35 and 38 years old, respectively, and have two children ages 10 and 15. Their automobile, which had a fair value of $8,500, was stolen during 1989 and their insurance did not cover the loss. They donated $500 to the college from which they had both graduated and incurred the following expenses during the year: local property taxes, $2,300; qualified residence interest on home mortgage, $2,500; hospital insurance, $2,100; and uninsured doctor and dentist bills, $2,100. Prepare a calculation to show their taxable income on a joint return.

**Exercise 28–4**
**Individual taxable income**
(L. O. 2)

In 1989, Anne Archer, who is single, had adjusted gross income of $50,000 and was entitled to only one personal exemption deduction. Her activities and expenditures during the year included the items listed below. Determine her taxable income.

| | |
|---|---|
| Charitable contributions | $3,000 |
| Qualified residence interest paid on mortgage on personal residence | 4,000 |
| Repairs to personal residence | 2,500 |
| State income taxes paid | 900 |
| Medical expenses paid | 4,300 |
| Fire loss to kitchen of her residence | 5,200 |
| Cost of vacation to Bermuda | 3,500 |

**Exercise 28–5**
**Standard deductions**
(L. O. 2)

Ray Longwood is single, age 69, and legally blind. What is the amount of the standard deduction he may claim on his 1989 return?

**Exercise 28–6**
**Calculating an individual's income tax payable**
(L. O. 2, 3)

Dawn Tiebol earned $53,000 during 1989 as an employee of a law firm. She is unmarried and furnishes more than half the support of her brother, a college student who lived in a dormitory and had no income. Dawn had $10,200 of federal income tax and $3,980 of FICA tax withheld from her paychecks. She received $400 interest on a savings account and $100 in dividends from a corporation in which she owned stock. During the year, she paid $2,260 state income tax, $1,150 qualified residence interest on the mortgage on her personal residence, and gave her church $3,500. Show the calculation of Dawn's taxable income in the manner outlined in Illustration 28–1. Then, using the rate schedule of Illustration 28–2, show the calculation of the net federal income tax payable or refund due Dawn.

**Exercise 28–7**
**Individual taxable income and tax liability**
(L. O. 2, 3)

In 1989, Dave had salary income of $45,000 and itemized deductions of $12,560. Dave's sister Debbi had the very same amounts of income and itemized deductions. Dave is married and filed a joint return with his wife Karen, who had no income. Debbi is single. Assume two personal exemption deductions are claimed on the joint return for Dave and Karen and one is claimed on Debbi's return. Calculate the taxable income and gross tax liability to be reported on each return.

**Exercise 28–8**
**Capital gains and losses**
(L. O. 4)

The following cases involve single individuals who sold some capital assets during 1989. In each case, the person's only other income was a $60,000 salary. Each case is independent from the others. For each case, indicate the dollar amount of capital losses that will provide a tax benefit to the individual in 1989.

*a.* One asset was sold for a $15,000 capital gain and another was sold for a $9,000 capital loss.

*b.* One asset was sold for a $15,000 capital gain and another was sold for a $17,000 capital loss.

*c.* One asset was sold for a $15,000 capital gain and another was sold for a $23,000 capital loss.

**Exercise 28–9**
**Calculating corporate tax liabilities**
(L. O. 4, 5)

Calculate the 1989 tax liability for each of the following corporations:

*a.* Nexxo Corporation sold two capital assets in 1989. Asset A was sold at a gain of $18,000. Asset B was sold at a loss of $20,000. Nexxo Corporation's taxable income exclusive of the above gains and losses was $150,000.

*b.* Delwood Corporation sold two capital assets in 1989. Asset A was sold at a gain of $20,000. Asset B was sold at a loss of $14,000. Delwood Corporation's taxable income exclusive of the above gains and losses was $310,000.

**Exercise 28–10**
**Analyzing corporate tax rates**
(L. O. 5)

Quitman Corporation reported taxable income for 1989 of $4 million. Determine its tax liability. Might it be argued that the corporation is paying tax at a flat rate? Explain.

**Exercise 28–11**
**Recording corporate income tax expense**
(L. O. 7)

Granger, Inc., began operations on January 1, 1989. During 1989, Granger, Inc.'s operations resulted in a current tax payable of $350,000. In addition, Granger sold land for $100,000 that had cost $20,000. The sale qualified as an installment sale for tax purposes so the gain was subject to tax as cash was received. The purchaser agreed to pay for the land on June 1, 1990. Present the December 31, 1989, entry to record Granger, Inc.'s income taxes.

## Problems

**Problem 28–1**
**Tax effects on partnership and corporate income**
(L. O. 2, 3, 5)

Jeff and Jennifer Moore are married and are also partners in Functional Furniture, a profitable business that averages $750,000 annually in sales, with a 50% gross profit and $168,750 of operating expenses. The Moores file a joint tax return, have no dependents, but each year have $7,500 of itemized deductions and two exemptions. In the past, the Moores have withdrawn $56,250 annually from the business for personal living expenses plus sufficient additional cash to pay the income tax on their joint return.

Jeff and Jennifer think they can save taxes by reorganizing their business into a corporation beginning with the 1989 tax year. If the corporation is organized, it will issued 1,000 shares of no-par stock, 500 to Jeff and 500 to Jennifer. Also, $56,250 per year is a fair salary for managing such a business, and the corporation will pay that amount to Jennifer.

*Required*

1. Prepare a comparative income statement for the business showing its net income as a partnership and as a corporation.
2. Use the rate schedule of Illustration 28–2 and determine the amount of federal income taxes the Moores will pay for themselves on a joint return and for the business under each of the following assumptions: (*a*) the business remains a partnership; (*b*) the business is incorporated, pays Jennifer a $56,250 salary, but pays no dividends; and (*c*) the business is incorporated, pays Jennifer a $56,250 salary, and pays $37,500 in dividends, $18,750 to Jennifer and $18,750 to Jeff.

**Problem 28–2**
**Tax consequences of financing by loan or stock**
(L. O. 5, 6)

Ralph and Laura Banes, husband and wife who file a joint return, own all the outstanding stock of Banes Corporation. The corporation, which currently has taxable income in excess of $600,000, has an opportunity to expand. To do so, however, it will need $375,000 of additional capital. The Banes's have the $375,000 and can either lend this amount to the corporation at 10% interest or they can invest the $375,000 in the corporation by purchasing additional shares of previously unissued stock from the corporation. They calculate that with the additional $375,000 the corporation will earn additional income of $60,000 annually before interest on the loan, if made, and before income taxes. If they invest the additional $375,000 in the corporation by purchasing stock, the corporation will pay the Banes's additional dividends of $45,000 per year. But, if they lend the corporation the $375,000, they will receive $37,500 interest on the loan, plus additional dividends of only $7,500 each year.

*Required*

Determine whether the loan to the corporation or an investment in its stock is in the best interest of the Banes's. Assume that the decision is being made in 1989.

**Problem 28–3**
**Comparing tax consequences of partnership versus corporation**
(L. O. 3, 5, 6)

Carol Reddy owns all the outstanding stock of Reddemade Company. The corporation is a small manufacturing company; however, over the years it has purchased stocks costing $187,500 (present market value is much higher) which it holds as long-term investments. Reddemade owns only a small interest in any one corporation. The corporation has seldom paid a dividend, but it does pay Ms. Reddy a $90,000 annual salary as president and manager. In 1989, the corporation earned $67,500, after its president's salary but before income taxes. The $67,500 consisted of $42,000 in manufacturing income and $25,500 in dividends on its long-term investments.

Ms. Reddy is unmarried and has no dependents. She had $17,175 of itemized deductions during 1989 plus a single exemption deduction. She had no income other than her corporation salary and $6,000 in interest from bank deposits:

*Required*

1. Prepare a comparative statement that shows for 1989 the operating income, investment income, total income, share of the dividend income deducted, taxable income, and income tax of the corporation under the (*a*) and (*b*) assumptions which follow. (*a*) The corporation owns the investment stocks and had the operating income just described. (*b*) The corporation had the operating income described; but instead of owning the investment stock, over the years it paid dividends (none in 1989), and Ms. Reddy used them to buy the stocks in her own name rather than in the name of the corporation.
2. Calculate the amounts of individual income tax and corporation income tax incurred by Ms. Reddy and the corporation under the (*a*) assumptions, and the amount that would have been incurred under the (*b*) assumptions. Also calculate the amount of individual income tax Ms. Reddy would have incurred with the business organized as a single proprietorship and the stocks registered in Ms. Reddy's name. Under this last assumption remember that the corporation's operating income plus its president's salary equal the operating income of the single proprietorship. Use the rate schedule of Illustration 28–2 in all individual income tax calculations.

**Problem 28–4**
**Reporting corporate tax expense with temporary differences between tax and financial accounting**
(L. O. 7)

In each of the cases described below, you should prepare a journal entry to record the income taxes on December 31, 1991. Each case involves a different company and is independent from the other cases.

**Case 1:**

| | |
|---|---|
| January 1, 1991, Deferred Tax Liability credit balance . . | $ 6,000 |
| Taxable income on tax return . . . . . . . . . . . . . . . | 180,000 |
| Tax rate in all years . . . . . . . . . . . . . . . . . . . . . | 15% |
| On December 31, 1991, an analysis of temporary differences shows that *as a result of past transactions,* future differences between taxable income and income before taxes will be: | |
| In 1992, additional taxable income that will not appear on the income statement as income before taxes . . . . . . . . . . . . . . . . . . . . | $ 40,000 |

**Case 2:**

| | |
|---|---|
| January 1, 1991, Deferred Tax Liability credit balance . . | $ 6,000 |
| Taxable income on tax return . . . . . . . . . . . . . . . | 120,000 |
| Tax rate in all years . . . . . . . . . . . . . . . . . . . . . | 15% |
| On December 31, 1991, an analysis of temporary differences shows that as a result of past transactions, future differences between taxable income and income before taxes will be . . . . . . . . . . . . . . | None |

**Case 3:**

| | |
|---|---|
| January 1, 1991, Deferred Tax Liability credit balance | $ 6,000 |
| Taxable income on tax return | 100,000 |
| Tax rate in all years | 15% |
| On December 31, 1991, an analysis of temporary differences shows that as a result of past transactions, future differences between taxable income and income before taxes will be: | |
| In 1992, additional taxable income that will not appear on the income statement as income before taxes | $ 30,000 |
| In 1993, additional taxable income that will not appear on the income statement as income before taxes | 60,000 |

**Case 4:**

| | |
|---|---|
| January 1, 1991, Deferred Tax Asset debit balance | $ 1,500 |
| Taxable income on tax return | 90,000 |
| Tax rate in all years | 15% |
| On December 31, 1991, an analysis of temporary differences shows that as a result of past transactions, future differences between taxable income and income before taxes will be | None |

**Case 5:**

| | |
|---|---|
| January 1, 1991, Deferred Tax Liability credit balance | $ 9,000 |
| Taxable income on tax return | 130,000 |
| Tax rate in 1991 | 15% |
| Law in 1991 says tax rate in 1992 will be | 20% |
| On December 31, 1991, an analysis of temporary differences shows that as a result of past transactions, future differences between taxable income and income before taxes will be: | |
| In 1992, additional taxable income that will not appear on the income statement as income before taxes | $ 60,000 |

**Problem 28–5**
**Calculation of individual income tax payable**
(L. O. 2, 3)

Mr. and Mrs. Don Galleher are both 51 years old and file a joint income tax return. They have two children, David and Susan. David is a student in high school, lives at home, and earned $1,395 from part-time jobs in 1989. Susan is 21 years old and a senior in college. She was a full-time student for two semesters in 1989; however, she did not go to summer school but drove a florist delivery truck during the summer and earned $3,900, which was less than half what her parents paid during the year for her tuition, books, and other items of support. David also received over half of his support from his parents.

Mr. and Mrs. Galleher had the following cash receipts and disbursements during 1989:

**Cash Receipts**

| | |
|---|---|
| **Mr. Galleher:** | |
| Salary as manager of Orange Grove Marina ($63,000 gross pay less $11,970 federal income taxes, $4,731 FICA taxes, and $2,100 hospital and medical insurance premiums withheld) | $44,199 |
| Dividends from stocks in domestic corporations | 1,095 |
| Interest on bonds of the City of Los Angeles | 2,790 |
| **Mrs. Galleher:** | |
| Rentals from a small house purchased in January 1987 (the house cost $157,500 and is depreciated on a straight-line basis over a period of 31.5 years) | 9,900 |
| Salary from part-time position ($18,000 gross pay less $1,875 federal income taxes and $1,352 FICA taxes) | 14,773 |
| Proceeds of insurance received on the death of an aunt | 18,000 |

**Cash Disbursements**

| | |
|---|---|
| Charitable contributions | 5,700 |
| Qualified residence interest on family residence mortgage | 7,425 |
| Property taxes on family residence | 3,300 |
| Property taxes on rental house | 1,320 |
| Interest on mortgage on rental house | 1,950 |
| Plumbing repairs at rental house | 270 |
| Insurance (one year) on rental house | 555 |
| Uninsured doctor and dental bills | 2,850 |
| Prescription drugs | 675 |
| Advance payments of estimated federal income tax on income not subject to withholding | 900 |

Also, Mr. Galleher had a $6,600 capital gain on shares of stock held five years.

*Required*

Follow the form of Illustration 28–1 and use the rate schedule of Illustration 28–2 to calculate the net federal income tax payable or refund for Mr. and Mrs. Galleher.

## Alternate Problems

**Problem 28–1A**
**Tax effects on partnership and corporate income**
(L. O. 2, 3, 5)

Kathy McIntyre has operated The Safari Store for a number of years with the following average annual results:

**THE SAFARI STORE**
**Income Statement for an Average Year**

| | | |
|---|---|---|
| Sales | | $450,000 |
| Cost of goods sold | $225,000 | |
| Operating expenses | 135,000 | 360,000 |
| Net income | | $ 90,000 |

Ms. McIntyre is unmarried and without dependents and has been operating The Safari Store as a single proprietorship. She has been withdrawing $60,000 each year to pay her personal living expenses, including $8,244 of charitable contributions, state and local income and property taxes, and other itemized deductions. She has no income other than from The Safari Store.

*Required*

1. Assume that Ms. McIntyre is considering the incorporation of her business beginning with the 1989 tax year and prepare a comparative income statement for the business showing its net income as a single proprietorship and as a corporation. Assume that if she incorporates, Ms. McIntyre will pay $60,000 per year to herself as a salary, which is a fair amount.
2. Use the rate schedule of Illustration 28–2 and determine the amount of federal income tax Ms. McIntyre will have to pay for herself and for her business under each of the following assumptions: (*a*) the business is not incorporated; (*b*) the business is incorporated, pays Ms. McIntyre a $60,000 annual salary as manager, and also pays her $9,600 per year in dividends; and (*c*) the business is incorporated, pays Ms. McIntyre a $60,000 salary, but does not pay any dividends.

**Problem 28–2A**
**Tax consequences of financing by loan or stock**
(L. O. 5, 6)

Exlane Corporation needs additional capital for a new investment that will cost $525,000 and will increase its earnings $140,000 annually before taxes and before interest on the money used in the expansion, if borrowed. The Lane family owns all the outstanding stock of Exlane Corporation and will supply the money to finance the investment, either investing an additional $525,000 in the corporation by purchasing its unissued stock or lending it $525,000 at 12% interest.

The corporation presently earns well in excess of $450,000 annually and pays $140,000 per year to the family in dividends. If the loan is made, the dividends will be reduced by an amount equal to the interest on the loan.

*Required*

Prepare an analysis showing whether it would be advantageous for the family to make the loan or to purchase the corporation's stock. Assume the decision is being made in 1989.

**Problem 28–3A**
**Comparing tax consequences of partnership versus corporation**
(L. O. 3, 5, 6)

Wayne Eanes, Jr., recently inherited the business of his father. The business, Sports, Inc., is a small manufacturing corporation; however, a share of its assets, $96,000 at cost, consists of blue-chip investment stocks purchased over the years by the corporation from earnings. Wayne's father was the sole owner of the corporation at his death, and before his death he had paid himself a $48,000 annual salary for a number of years as president and manager. Over the years, the corporation seldom paid a dividend but instead had invested any earnings not needed in the business in the blue-chip stocks previously mentioned. At the father's death the market value of these stocks far exceeded their cost. Wayne's father owned only a small interest in any one blue-chip firm.

Wayne's mother is deceased, and after Wayne graduated from college, the father had no dependents. The father's tax return for the 1989 year (the year before his death) showed $52,800 of gross income, consisting of his $48,000 corporation salary plus $4,800 interest from real estate loans. It also showed $6,000 of itemized deductions plus a single exemption deduction. During the year before the father's death, the corporation earned $72,000 from its manufacturing operations plus $18,000 in dividends from its investments, a total of $90,000 after the president's salary but before income taxes.

*Required*

1. Prepare a comparative statement showing for the year before the father's death the corporation's operating income, dividend income, total income, share of the dividend income deducted, taxable income, and income tax under the following (*a*) and (*b*) assumptions. (*a*) The corporation owns the investment stocks and had the operating income just described. (*b*) The corporation had the operating income described; but instead of owning the investment stocks, over the years it paid dividends (none last year), and Wayne Eanes, Sr., used the dividends to buy the stocks in his own name rather than in the corporation's name.
2. Calculate the amounts of individual income tax and corporation income tax incurred by Mr. Eanes, Sr., and the corporation for the year before

Mr. Eanes's death under the (*a*) assumptions, and the amount that would have been incurred under the (*b*) assumptions. Also calculate the amount of individual income tax Mr. Eanes would have incurred with the business organized as a single proprietorship and the stocks registered in his own name. Under this last assumption remember that the corporation's operating income plus the salary paid its president equal the operating income of the single proprietorship. Use the rate schedule of Illustration 28–2 in the individual income tax calculations.

**Problem 28–4A**
**Reporting corporate tax expense with temporary differences between tax and financial accounting**
(L. O. 7)

In each of the cases described below, you should prepare a journal entry to record the income taxes on December 31, 1991. Each case involves a different company and is independent from the other cases.

**Case 1:**

| | |
|---|---|
| January 1, 1991, Deferred Tax Liability credit balance . . | $ 2,400 |
| Taxable income on tax return . . . . . . . . . . . . . . . | 110,000 |
| Tax rate in all years . . . . . . . . . . . . . . . . . . . . . | 15% |
| On December 31, 1991, an analysis of temporary differences shows that *as a result of past transactions,* future differences between taxable income and income before taxes will be: | |
| In 1992 . . . . . . . . . . . . . . . . . . . . . . . . | None |
| In 1993, additional taxable income that will not appear on the income statement as income before taxes . . . . . . . . . . . . . . . . . . . | $ 16,000 |

**Case 2:**

| | |
|---|---|
| January 1, 1991, Deferred Tax Liability credit balance . . | $ 7,200 |
| Taxable income on tax return . . . . . . . . . . . . . . . | 190,000 |
| Tax rate in all years . . . . . . . . . . . . . . . . . . . . . | 15% |
| On December 31, 1991, an analysis of temporary differences shows that as a result of past transactions, future differences between taxable income and income before taxes will be . . . . . . . . . . . . . . | None |

**Case 3:**

| | |
|---|---|
| January 1, 1991, Deferred Tax Liability credit balance . . | $ 2,700 |
| Taxable income on tax return . . . . . . . . . . . . . . . | 160,000 |
| Tax rate in all years . . . . . . . . . . . . . . . . . . . . . | 15% |
| On December 31, 1991, an analysis of temporary differences shows that as a result of past transactions, future differences between taxable income and income before taxes will be: | |
| In 1992, additional taxable income that will not appear on the income statement as income before taxes . . . . . . . . . . . . . . . . . . . | $ 30,000 |
| In 1993, additional taxable income that will not appear on the income statement as income before taxes . . . . . . . . . . . . . . . . . . . | 24,000 |

**Case 4:**

| | |
|---|---|
| January 1, 1991, Deferred Tax Asset debit balance . . . | $ 8,400 |
| Taxable income on tax return . . . . . . . . . . . . . . . | 210,000 |
| Tax rate in all years . . . . . . . . . . . . . . . . . . . . . | 15% |
| On December 31, 1991, an analysis of temporary differences shows that as a result of past transactions, future differences between taxable income and income before taxes will be . . . . . . . . . . . . . . | None |

**Case 5:**

| | |
|---|---|
| January 1, 1991, Deferred Tax Liability credit balance | $ 9,600 |
| Taxable income on tax return | 150,000 |
| Tax rate in 1991 | 15% |
| Law in 1991 says tax rate in 1992 will be | 22 |
| On December 31, 1991, an analysis of temporary differences shows that as a result of past transactions, future differences between taxable income and income before taxes will be: | |
| In 1992, additional taxable income that will not appear on the income statement as income before taxes | $ 64,000 |

**Problem 28–5A**
**Calculation of individual income tax payable**
(L. O. 2, 3)

George and Martha Taylor are both 46 years old, have three sons, and file a joint tax return. Their oldest son, John, is a junior high school student and earned $825 in 1989 working at odd jobs. The other two sons earned nothing during the year. Mr. and Mrs. Taylor furnished over half of each son's support and had the following cash receipts and disbursements during 1989.

**Cash Receipts**

| | |
|---|---|
| Salary to George Taylor from his employer, a real estate developer, for which George is an outside salesman ($48,000 gross income less $4,800 federal income taxes withheld, $3,605 FICA taxes, and $1,350 hospital insurance premiums) | $38,245 |
| Dividends from AT&T common stock (jointly owned) | 2,850 |
| Interest from savings account owned by Martha Taylor | 3,450 |
| Interest from municipal bonds issued by El Paso, Texas | 5,100 |
| Proceeds from sale of Chrysler common stock that had been acquired 26 months ago at a cost of $18,000 (jointly owned) | 28,500 |

**Cash Disbursements**

| | |
|---|---|
| Cost of George driving from home to business office and back | $ 1,275 |
| Unreimbursed long-distance telephone calls to customers | 2,403 |
| Unreimbursed cost of meals incurred in connection with business travel | 2,250 |
| Contributions to church | 1,500 |
| Local property taxes on residence | 1,050 |
| Qualified residence interest on home mortgage | 4,875 |
| Uninsured doctor and dentist bills | 5,860 |
| Donation to college from which George and Martha graduated | 3,000 |
| Advance payments of estimated federal income tax | 450 |

*Required*

Follow the form of Illustration 28–1 and use the rate schedule of Illustration 28–2 to calculate for the Taylors the amount of federal income tax due or to be refunded.

## Provocative Problem

**Provocative Problem 28–1**
**Communication Services, Inc.**
(L. O. 7)

Samuel and Lois Ungerson own all the outstanding stock of Communication Services, Inc., a company they organized several years ago and which is growing rapidly and needs additional capital. At the request of the Ungersons, Lewis Trager examined the following comparative income statement, which shows the corporation's net income for the past two years and which was prepared by its bookkeeper. Lewis expressed a tentative willingness to invest the required capital by purchasing a portion of the corporation's unissued stock.

**COMMUNICATION SERVICES, INC.**
**Comparative Income Statement**
**For the Years 1990 and 1991**

| | 1990 | 1991 |
|---|---|---|
| Sales | $672,000 | $768,000 |
| Expenses other than income taxes | 518,400 | 556,800 |
| Income before income taxes | $153,600 | $211,200 |
| Federal income taxes | 53,760 | 72,960 |
| Net income | $ 99,840 | $138,240 |

Before making a final decision, Lewis asked permission for his own accountant to examine the accounting records of the corporation. Permission was granted, the examination was made, and the accountant prepared the following comparative income statement covering the same period of time.

**COMMUNICATION SERVICES, INC.**
**Comparative Income Statement**
**For the Years 1990 and 1991**

| | 1990 | 1991 |
|---|---|---|
| Sales | $672,000 | $768,000 |
| Expenses other than income taxes | 518,400 | 556,800 |
| Income before income taxes | $153,600 | $211,200 |
| Income taxes expense | 61,440 | 84,480 |
| Net income | $ 92,160 | $126,720 |

Attached to the accountant's statement was a note saying that the reason the income tax expense amounts are different from those reported by the bookkeeper is the fact that the bookkeeper did not consider the effects of temporary differences between financial and tax accounting procedures of accounting for expenses. No temporary differences existed prior to 1990 and those that occurred in 1990 and 1991 are expected to reverse in 1993.

The Ungersons were surprised at the difference in annual net incomes reported on the two statements and did not understand the accountant's note. You've been asked to explain more precisely why there is a difference between the net income figures on the two statements, and account for the difference in the net incomes. Prepare calculations that will explain the amounts shown on the corporation bookkeeper's statement. For simplicity, assume a 40% federal income tax rate on all taxable income.

Part Nine

# Appendixes

To supplement the topical coverage of *Fundamental Accounting Principles*, we have included 10 appendixes. Appendixes A through D and Appendix F are presented at the end of the chapters to which they relate. An appendix to the first half of the book (Appendix E) appears after Chapter 14. The remaining four appendixes make up the contents of Part Nine.

The appendixes to *Fundamental Accounting Principles* are:

# G Present and Future Values: An Expansion

The concept of present values was introduced in Chapter 12 and was applied to accounting problems in Chapters 12 and 17. This appendix is designed to supplement the treatment of present values with additional discussion, more complete tables, and additional homework exercises. In studying this appendix, you also will learn about the concept of future values.

**Learning Objectives**

*After studying Appendix G, you should be able to:*

1. Explain what is meant by the present value of a single amount and the present value of an annuity, and be able to use tables to solve problems that involve present values.
2. Explain what is meant by the future value of a single amount and the future value of an annuity, and be able to use tables to solve problems that involve future values.

## Present Value of a Single Amount

Explain what is meant by the present value of a single amount and the present value of an annuity, and be able to use tables to solve problems that involve present values.
(L. O. 1)

The present value of a single amount to be received or paid at some future date may be expressed as:

$$p = \frac{f}{(1 + i)^n} \quad (1)$$

where

$p$ = present value
$f$ = future value
$i$ = rate of interest per period
$n$ = number of periods

For example, assume $2.20 is to be received one period from now. This amount will be received because a smaller amount ($2.00) is invested now, for one period, at an interest rate of 10%. Using the formula:

$$p = \frac{f}{(1 + i)^n} = \frac{\$2.20}{(1 + .10)^1} = \$2.00$$

Alternatively, assume the present investment of $2.00 is to remain invested for two periods at 10% and the future amount to be received is $2.42. Using the formula:

$$p = \frac{f}{(1 + i)^n} = \frac{\$2.42}{(1 + .10)^2} = \$2.00$$

Note that $n$ (the number of periods) does not have to be expressed in years. Any period of time such as a day, a month, a quarter, or a year may be used. However, whatever period is used, $i$ (the interest rate) must be per the same period. Thus, if a problem requires that you express $n$ in months, then an $i$ of 1% means 1% per month. This means that each month, 1% of the invested amount at the beginning of the month is earned and added to the investment. Another way of expressing this is to say that interest is compounded monthly.

A present value table is designed to show present values for a variety of $i$'s (interest rates) and a variety of $n$'s (number of periods). Throughout the table, each present value is based on the assumption that $f$ (the future value) is 1.00. Since the future value is assumed to be 1 (in other words, $f = 1$), the formula to construct a table of present values of a single future amount is as follows:

Since $f = 1$,

$$p = \frac{f}{(1 + i)^n} = \frac{1}{(1 + i)^n}$$

A table of present values of a single future amount often is called a *present value of 1* table. Table G–1 on page 1215 is such a table.

## Future Value of a Single Amount

The formula for the present value of a single amount may be manipulated to solve for the future value of a single amount. Thus, the formula presented above as (1) may be manipulated as follows:

$$p = \frac{f}{(1 + i)^n} \quad (1)$$

Explain what is meant by the future value of a single amount and the future value of an annuity, and be able to use tables to solve problems that involve future values.
(L. O. 2)

multiply both sides of the equation by $(1 + i)^n$,

$$(1 + i)^n \times p = (1 + i)^n \times \frac{f}{(1 + i)^n}$$

cancel the common terms in the numerator and denominator,

$$(1 + i)^n \times p = \cancel{(1 + i)^n} \times \frac{f}{\cancel{(1 + i)^n}}$$

and the result is,

$$(1 + i)^n \times p = f$$

or

$$f = p \times (1 + i)^n \qquad (2)$$

For example, assume that $2.00 is invested for one period at an interest rate of 10%. The $2.00 amount will increase to a future value of $2.20. Using the formula:

$$f = p \times (1 + i)^n = \$2.00 \times (1 + .10)^1 = \$2.20$$

Alternatively, assume the present investment of $2.00 will remain invested for three periods at 10%. The amount that will be received three periods hence is $2.662, and is calculated with the formula as follows:

$$f = p \times (1 + i)^n = \$2.00 \times (1 + .10)^3 = \$2.662$$

A future value table is designed to show future values for a variety of $i$'s (interest rates) and a variety of $n$'s (number of periods). Throughout the table, each future value is based on the assumption that $p$ (the present value) is 1.00. Since the present value is assumed to be 1 (in other words, $p = 1$), the formula to construct a table of future values of a single amount is as follows:

Since $p = 1$,

$$f = p(1 + i)^n = (1 + i)^n$$

A table of future values of a single amount is often called a *future value of 1* table. Table G–2 on page 1216 is such a table.

In Table G–2, look at the row where $n = 0$ and observe that regardless of the interest rate, the future value is 1. When $n = 0$, the period of time over which interest is earned is zero. Hence, no interest is earned. The future value is calculated as of the date of the investment. Since the table assumes that the investment is 1, the ''future value'' on that date is also 1.

You should also observe that a table showing the present values of 1 and a table showing the future values of 1 contain exactly the same information. Both tables are based on the same equation. That is,

$$p = \frac{f}{(1 + i)^n}$$

is nothing more than a reformulation of

$$f = p(1 + i)^n$$

Both tables reflect the same four variables, $p$, $f$, $i$, and $n$. Therefore, any problem that can be solved using one of the two tables can also be solved using the other table.

For example, suppose a person invests $100 for five years and expects to earn 12% per year. How much should the person receive five years hence?

To solve the problem using Table G–2, look in the table to find the future value of 1, five periods hence, compounded at 12%. In the table, $f = 1.7623$. Thus,

$$\$100 \times 1.7623 = \$176.23$$

To solve the problem using Table G–1, look in the table to find the present value of 1, five periods hence, discounted at 12%. In the table, where $n = 5$, and $i = 12\%$, $p = 0.5674$. Recall that $f = 1$ in the table. This relationship between present value and future value may be expressed as:

$$\frac{p}{f} = \frac{0.5674}{1}$$

This relationship between $p$ and $f$ is the same as in the problem where $100 is invested for five years. Thus,

$$\frac{0.5674}{1}$$

is the same as

$$\frac{\$100}{f}$$

$$\frac{0.5674}{1} = \frac{\$100}{f}$$

$$0.5674 \times f = \$100 \times 1$$

$$f = \frac{\$100}{0.5674} = \$176.24$$

The $0.01 difference between the two answers ($176.23 and $176.24) occurs only because the numbers in the tables were rounded.

## Present Value of an Annuity

A series of equal payments is called an annuity. For example, if a person offers to make three annual payments of $100 each, the person is offering an annuity. The present value of an annuity is defined as the value of the payments one period prior to the first payment. Graphically, this may be presented as follows:

```
        $100    $100    $100
o--------o-------o-------o
p
```

To calculate the present value of this annuity, one might calculate the present value of each payment and add them together. For example, assuming an interest rate of 18%, the calculation is:

$$p = \frac{\$100}{(1 + .18)^1} + \frac{\$100}{(1 + .18)^2} + \frac{\$100}{(1 + .18)^3} = \$217.43$$

Another way to calculate the present value of the annuity is to use Table G–1. The calculation is as follows:

| | | |
|---|---|---|
| First payment: | $p = \$100 \times 0.8475 =$ | $ 84.75 |
| Second payment: | $p = \$100 \times 0.7182 =$ | 71.82 |
| Third payment: | $p = \$100 \times 0.6086 =$ | 60.86 |
| Total: | $p =$ | $217.43 |

Another way of using Table G–1 to solve the problem is to add the present values of three payments of 1 and multiply the answer times $100. Thus,

| | | |
|---|---|---|
| From Table G–1: | $i = 18\%, n = 1, p =$ | 0.8475 |
| | $i = 18\%, n = 2, p =$ | 0.7182 |
| | $i = 18\%, n = 3, p =$ | 0.6086 |
| | | 2.1743 |
| | $2.1743 \times \$100 =$ | $217.43 |

The easiest way to solve the problem is to use a table that shows the present values of a series of payments. That type of table often is called a *present value of an annuity of 1* table. Table G–3 on page 1217 is such a table. Look in Table G–3 on the row where $n = 3$ and $i = 18\%$ and observe that the present value is 2.1743. Stated in other words, an annuity of 1 for three periods, discounted at 18%, is 2.1743.

Although a formula is used to construct a table showing the present values of an annuity,[1] you should understand that the table can be constructed simply by adding together the amounts in a present value of 1 table (such as Table G–1). To check your understanding of this, examine Table G–1 and Table G–3 to confirm that the following numbers were drawn from those tables.

| From Table G–1 | | From Table G–3 | |
|---|---|---|---|
| $i = 8\%, n = 1$ . . . . . | 0.9259 | $i = 8\%, n = 1$ . . . . . . | 0.9259 |
| $i = 8\%, n = 2$ . . . . . | 0.8573 | | |
| $i = 8\%, n = 3$ . . . . . | 0.7938 | | |
| $i = 8\%, n = 4$ . . . . . | 0.7350 | | |
| Total . . . . . . . . . . | 3.3120 | $i = 8\%, n = 4$ . . . . . . | 3.3121 |

The minor difference in the results (3.3120 and 3.3121) occurs only because the numbers in the tables have been rounded.

[1] The formula for a table showing the present values of an annuity of 1 is:

$$p = \frac{1 - \dfrac{1}{(1 + i)^n}}{i}$$

## Future Value of an Annuity

Earlier, we defined an annuity as any series of equal payments. Just as you can calculate the present value of an annuity, you can also calculate the future value of an annuity. The future value of an annuity is defined as the value of the annuity on the date of the final payment. Consider the earlier example of a person who offers to make three annual payments of $100 each. Graphically, the points in time at which the present value and the future value are calculated may be shown as follows:

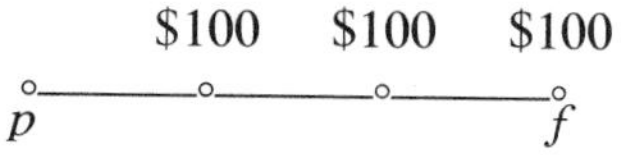


To calculate the future value of this annuity, you might calculate the future value of each payment and add them together. Assuming an interest rate of 18%, the calculation is:

$$f = \$100(1 + .18)^2 + \$100(1 + .18)^1 + \$100(1 + .18)^0 = \$357.24$$

Another way to calculate the future value of the annuity is to use Table G–2. The calculation is as follows:

| | | |
|---|---|---|
| First payment: | $f = \$100 \times 1.3924 =$ | $139.24 |
| Second payment: | $f = \$100 \times 1.1800 =$ | 118.00 |
| Third payment: | $f = \$100 \times 1.0000 =$ | 100.00 |
| Total: | $f =$ | $357.24 |

In the calculations and the graph above, note that the first payment is made two periods prior to the point at which future value is determined. Therefore, for the first payment, $n = 2$. For the second payment, $n = 1$. Since the third payment occurs on the future value date, $n = 0$.

Instead of adding the future value of each payment, another approach is to add the future values of three payments of 1 and multiply the answer by $100. This approach appears as follows:

| | | |
|---|---|---|
| From Table G–2: | $i = 18\%, n = 2, f =$ | 1.3924 |
| | $i = 18\%, n = 1, f =$ | 1.1800 |
| | $i = 18\%, n = 0, f =$ | 1.0000 |
| | | 3.5724 |
| | $3.5724 \times \$100 =$ | $357.24 |

The easiest way to solve the problem is to use a table that shows the future values of a series of payments. That type of table often is called a *future value of an annuity of 1* table. Table G–4 on page 1218 is such a table. Note in Table G–4 that when $n = 1$, the future values are equal to 1 ($f = 1$) for all rates of interest. When $n = 1$, the "annuity" consists of only one payment and the future value is determined on the date of the payment. Hence, the future value equals the payment.

Although a formula[2] is used to construct a table showing the future values of

[2] The formula for a table showing the future values of an annuity of 1 is:

$$f = \frac{(1 + i)^n - 1}{i}$$

an annuity of 1, you should understand that the table can be constructed simply by adding together the amount in a future value of 1 table (such as Table G–2). To check your understanding of this, examine Table G–2 and Table G–4 to confirm that the following numbers were drawn from those tables.

| From Table G–2 | | From Table G–4 | |
|---|---|---|---|
| $i = 8\%, n = 0$ . . . . . | 1.0000 | $i = 8\%, n = 1$ . . . . . . | 1.0000 |
| $i = 8\%, n = 1$ . . . . . | 1.0800 | | |
| $i = 8\%, n = 2$ . . . . . | 1.1664 | | |
| $i = 8\%, n = 3$ . . . . . | 1.2597 | | |
| Total . . . . . . . . . . | 4.5061 | $i = 8\%, n = 4$ . . . . . . | 4.5061 |

Minor differences in the results may sometimes occur but only because the numbers in the tables have been rounded.

Observe that in Table G–2, the future value is 1.0000 when $n = 0$. However, in Table G–4, the future value is 1.0000 when $n = 1$. Why is this true?

When $n = 0$ in Table G–2, the future value is determined on the same date as the single payment of 1 is made. The investment period over which interest is earned is zero ($n = 0$). However, Table G–4 is designed so that one payment is made each period. When $n = 2$, two payments are assumed, or when $n = 1$, one payment is assumed. And since future value is calculated as of the date of the last payment, future value = 1 when $n = 1$.

**Table G–1**
**Present value of 1 due in *n* periods**

| Periods | 1.0% | 1.5% | 3.0% | 4.0% | 8.0% | 10.0% | 12.0% | 14.0% | 16.0% | 18.0% | 20.0% |
|---|---|---|---|---|---|---|---|---|---|---|---|
| 1 | 0.9901 | 0.9852 | 0.9709 | 0.9615 | 0.9259 | 0.9091 | 0.8929 | 0.8772 | 0.8621 | 0.8475 | 0.8333 |
| 2 | 0.9803 | 0.9707 | 0.9426 | 0.9246 | 0.8573 | 0.8264 | 0.7972 | 0.7695 | 0.7432 | 0.7182 | 0.6944 |
| 3 | 0.9706 | 0.9563 | 0.9151 | 0.8890 | 0.7938 | 0.7513 | 0.7118 | 0.6750 | 0.6407 | 0.6086 | 0.5787 |
| 4 | 0.9610 | 0.9422 | 0.8885 | 0.8548 | 0.7350 | 0.6830 | 0.6355 | 0.5921 | 0.5523 | 0.5158 | 0.4823 |
| 5 | 0.9515 | 0.9283 | 0.8626 | 0.8219 | 0.6806 | 0.6209 | 0.5674 | 0.5194 | 0.4761 | 0.4371 | 0.4019 |
| 6 | 0.9420 | 0.9145 | 0.8375 | 0.7903 | 0.6302 | 0.5645 | 0.5066 | 0.4556 | 0.4104 | 0.3704 | 0.3349 |
| 7 | 0.9327 | 0.9010 | 0.8131 | 0.7599 | 0.5835 | 0.5132 | 0.4523 | 0.3996 | 0.3538 | 0.3139 | 0.2791 |
| 8 | 0.9235 | 0.8877 | 0.7894 | 0.7307 | 0.5403 | 0.4665 | 0.4039 | 0.3506 | 0.3050 | 0.2660 | 0.2326 |
| 9 | 0.9143 | 0.8746 | 0.7664 | 0.7026 | 0.5002 | 0.4241 | 0.3606 | 0.3075 | 0.2630 | 0.2255 | 0.1938 |
| 10 | 0.9053 | 0.8617 | 0.7441 | 0.6756 | 0.4632 | 0.3855 | 0.3220 | 0.2697 | 0.2267 | 0.1911 | 0.1615 |
| 11 | 0.8963 | 0.8489 | 0.7224 | 0.6496 | 0.4289 | 0.3505 | 0.2875 | 0.2366 | 0.1954 | 0.1619 | 0.1346 |
| 12 | 0.8874 | 0.8364 | 0.7014 | 0.6246 | 0.3971 | 0.3186 | 0.2567 | 0.2076 | 0.1685 | 0.1372 | 0.1122 |
| 13 | 0.8787 | 0.8240 | 0.6810 | 0.6006 | 0.3677 | 0.2897 | 0.2292 | 0.1821 | 0.1452 | 0.1163 | 0.0935 |
| 14 | 0.8700 | 0.8118 | 0.6611 | 0.5775 | 0.3405 | 0.2633 | 0.2046 | 0.1597 | 0.1252 | 0.0985 | 0.0779 |
| 15 | 0.8613 | 0.7999 | 0.6419 | 0.5553 | 0.3152 | 0.2394 | 0.1827 | 0.1401 | 0.1079 | 0.0835 | 0.0649 |
| 16 | 0.8528 | 0.7880 | 0.6232 | 0.5339 | 0.2919 | 0.2176 | 0.1631 | 0.1229 | 0.0930 | 0.0708 | 0.0541 |
| 17 | 0.8444 | 0.7764 | 0.6050 | 0.5134 | 0.2703 | 0.1978 | 0.1456 | 0.1078 | 0.0802 | 0.0600 | 0.0451 |
| 18 | 0.8360 | 0.7649 | 0.5874 | 0.4936 | 0.2502 | 0.1799 | 0.1300 | 0.0946 | 0.0691 | 0.0508 | 0.0376 |
| 19 | 0.8277 | 0.7536 | 0.5703 | 0.4746 | 0.2317 | 0.1635 | 0.1161 | 0.0829 | 0.0596 | 0.0431 | 0.0313 |
| 20 | 0.8195 | 0.7425 | 0.5537 | 0.4564 | 0.2145 | 0.1486 | 0.1037 | 0.0728 | 0.0514 | 0.0365 | 0.0261 |
| 21 | 0.8114 | 0.7315 | 0.5375 | 0.4388 | 0.1987 | 0.1351 | 0.0926 | 0.0638 | 0.0443 | 0.0309 | 0.0217 |
| 22 | 0.8034 | 0.7207 | 0.5219 | 0.4220 | 0.1839 | 0.1228 | 0.0826 | 0.0560 | 0.0382 | 0.0262 | 0.0181 |
| 23 | 0.7954 | 0.7100 | 0.5067 | 0.4057 | 0.1703 | 0.1117 | 0.0738 | 0.0491 | 0.0329 | 0.0222 | 0.0151 |
| 24 | 0.7876 | 0.6995 | 0.4919 | 0.3901 | 0.1577 | 0.1015 | 0.0659 | 0.0431 | 0.0284 | 0.0188 | 0.0126 |
| 25 | 0.7798 | 0.6892 | 0.4776 | 0.3751 | 0.1460 | 0.0923 | 0.0588 | 0.0378 | 0.0245 | 0.0160 | 0.0105 |
| 26 | 0.7720 | 0.6790 | 0.4637 | 0.3607 | 0.1352 | 0.0839 | 0.0525 | 0.0331 | 0.0211 | 0.0135 | 0.0087 |
| 27 | 0.7644 | 0.6690 | 0.4502 | 0.3468 | 0.1252 | 0.0763 | 0.0469 | 0.0291 | 0.0182 | 0.0115 | 0.0073 |
| 28 | 0.7568 | 0.6591 | 0.4371 | 0.3335 | 0.1159 | 0.0693 | 0.0419 | 0.0255 | 0.0157 | 0.0097 | 0.0061 |
| 29 | 0.7493 | 0.6494 | 0.4243 | 0.3207 | 0.1073 | 0.0630 | 0.0374 | 0.0224 | 0.0135 | 0.0082 | 0.0051 |
| 30 | 0.7419 | 0.6398 | 0.4120 | 0.3083 | 0.0994 | 0.0573 | 0.0334 | 0.0196 | 0.0116 | 0.0070 | 0.0042 |
| 31 | 0.7346 | 0.6303 | 0.4000 | 0.2965 | 0.0920 | 0.0521 | 0.0298 | 0.0172 | 0.0100 | 0.0059 | 0.0035 |
| 32 | 0.7273 | 0.6210 | 0.3883 | 0.2851 | 0.0852 | 0.0474 | 0.0266 | 0.0151 | 0.0087 | 0.0050 | 0.0029 |
| 33 | 0.7201 | 0.6118 | 0.3770 | 0.2741 | 0.0789 | 0.0431 | 0.0238 | 0.0132 | 0.0075 | 0.0042 | 0.0024 |
| 34 | 0.7130 | 0.6028 | 0.3660 | 0.2636 | 0.0730 | 0.0391 | 0.0212 | 0.0116 | 0.0064 | 0.0036 | 0.0020 |
| 35 | 0.7059 | 0.5939 | 0.3554 | 0.2534 | 0.0676 | 0.0356 | 0.0189 | 0.0102 | 0.0055 | 0.0030 | 0.0017 |
| 36 | 0.6989 | 0.5851 | 0.3450 | 0.2437 | 0.0626 | 0.0323 | 0.0169 | 0.0089 | 0.0048 | 0.0026 | 0.0014 |
| 37 | 0.6920 | 0.5764 | 0.3350 | 0.2343 | 0.0580 | 0.0294 | 0.0151 | 0.0078 | 0.0041 | 0.0022 | 0.0012 |
| 38 | 0.6852 | 0.5679 | 0.3252 | 0.2253 | 0.0537 | 0.0267 | 0.0135 | 0.0069 | 0.0036 | 0.0019 | 0.0010 |
| 39 | 0.6784 | 0.5595 | 0.3158 | 0.2166 | 0.0497 | 0.0243 | 0.0120 | 0.0060 | 0.0031 | 0.0016 | 0.0008 |
| 40 | 0.6717 | 0.5513 | 0.3066 | 0.2083 | 0.0460 | 0.0221 | 0.0107 | 0.0053 | 0.0026 | 0.0013 | 0.0007 |
| 41 | 0.6650 | 0.5431 | 0.2976 | 0.2003 | 0.0426 | 0.0201 | 0.0096 | 0.0046 | 0.0023 | 0.0011 | 0.0006 |
| 42 | 0.6584 | 0.5351 | 0.2890 | 0.1926 | 0.0395 | 0.0183 | 0.0086 | 0.0041 | 0.0020 | 0.0010 | 0.0005 |
| 43 | 0.6519 | 0.5272 | 0.2805 | 0.1852 | 0.0365 | 0.0166 | 0.0076 | 0.0036 | 0.0017 | 0.0008 | 0.0004 |
| 44 | 0.6454 | 0.5194 | 0.2724 | 0.1780 | 0.0338 | 0.0151 | 0.0068 | 0.0031 | 0.0015 | 0.0007 | 0.0003 |
| 45 | 0.6391 | 0.5117 | 0.2644 | 0.1712 | 0.0313 | 0.0137 | 0.0061 | 0.0027 | 0.0013 | 0.0006 | 0.0003 |
| 46 | 0.6327 | 0.5042 | 0.2567 | 0.1646 | 0.0290 | 0.0125 | 0.0054 | 0.0024 | 0.0011 | 0.0005 | 0.0002 |
| 47 | 0.6265 | 0.4967 | 0.2493 | 0.1583 | 0.0269 | 0.0113 | 0.0049 | 0.0021 | 0.0009 | 0.0004 | 0.0002 |
| 48 | 0.6203 | 0.4894 | 0.2420 | 0.1522 | 0.0249 | 0.0103 | 0.0043 | 0.0019 | 0.0008 | 0.0004 | 0.0002 |
| 49 | 0.6141 | 0.4821 | 0.2350 | 0.1463 | 0.0230 | 0.0094 | 0.0039 | 0.0016 | 0.0007 | 0.0003 | 0.0001 |
| 50 | 0.6080 | 0.4750 | 0.2281 | 0.1407 | 0.0213 | 0.0085 | 0.0035 | 0.0014 | 0.0006 | 0.0003 | 0.0001 |

**Table G–2**
**Future value of 1 due in *n* periods**

| Periods | 1.0% | 1.5% | 3.0% | 4.0% | 8.0% | 10.0% | 12.0% | 14.0% | 16.0% | 18.0% | 20.0% |
|---|---|---|---|---|---|---|---|---|---|---|---|
| 0 | 1.0000 | 1.0000 | 1.0000 | 1.0000 | 1.0000 | 1.0000 | 1.0000 | 1.0000 | 1.0000 | 1.0000 | 1.0000 |
| 1 | 1.0100 | 1.0150 | 1.0300 | 1.0400 | 1.0800 | 1.1000 | 1.1200 | 1.1400 | 1.1600 | 1.1800 | 1.2000 |
| 2 | 1.0201 | 1.0302 | 1.0609 | 1.0816 | 1.1664 | 1.2100 | 1.2544 | 1.2996 | 1.3456 | 1.3924 | 1.4400 |
| 3 | 1.0303 | 1.0457 | 1.0927 | 1.1249 | 1.2597 | 1.3310 | 1.4049 | 1.4815 | 1.5609 | 1.6430 | 1.7280 |
| 4 | 1.0406 | 1.0614 | 1.1255 | 1.1699 | 1.3605 | 1.4641 | 1.5735 | 1.6890 | 1.8106 | 1.9388 | 2.0736 |
| 5 | 1.0510 | 1.0773 | 1.1593 | 1.2167 | 1.4693 | 1.6105 | 1.7623 | 1.9254 | 2.1003 | 2.2878 | 2.4883 |
| 6 | 1.0615 | 1.0934 | 1.1941 | 1.2653 | 1.5869 | 1.7716 | 1.9738 | 2.1950 | 2.4364 | 2.6996 | 2.9860 |
| 7 | 1.0721 | 1.1098 | 1.2299 | 1.3159 | 1.7138 | 1.9487 | 2.2107 | 2.5023 | 2.8262 | 3.1855 | 3.5832 |
| 8 | 1.0829 | 1.1265 | 1.2668 | 1.3686 | 1.8509 | 2.1436 | 2.4760 | 2.8526 | 3.2784 | 3.7589 | 4.2998 |
| 9 | 1.0937 | 1.1434 | 1.3048 | 1.4233 | 1.9990 | 2.3579 | 2.7731 | 3.2519 | 3.8030 | 4.4355 | 5.1598 |
| 10 | 1.1046 | 1.1605 | 1.3439 | 1.4802 | 2.1589 | 2.5937 | 3.1058 | 3.7072 | 4.4114 | 5.2338 | 6.1917 |
| 11 | 1.1157 | 1.1779 | 1.3842 | 1.5395 | 2.3316 | 2.8531 | 3.4785 | 4.2262 | 5.1173 | 6.1759 | 7.4301 |
| 12 | 1.1264 | 1.1956 | 1.4258 | 1.6010 | 2.5182 | 3.1384 | 3.8960 | 4.8179 | 5.9360 | 7.2876 | 8.9161 |
| 13 | 1.1381 | 1.2136 | 1.4685 | 1.6651 | 2.7196 | 3.4523 | 4.3635 | 5.4924 | 6.8858 | 8.5994 | 10.6993 |
| 14 | 1.1495 | 1.2318 | 1.5126 | 1.7317 | 2.9372 | 3.7975 | 4.8871 | 6.2613 | 7.9875 | 10.1472 | 12.8392 |
| 15 | 1.1610 | 1.2502 | 1.5580 | 1.8009 | 3.1722 | 4.1772 | 5.4736 | 7.1379 | 9.2655 | 11.9737 | 15.4070 |
| 16 | 1.1726 | 1.2690 | 1.6047 | 1.8730 | 3.4259 | 4.5950 | 6.1304 | 8.1372 | 10.7480 | 14.1290 | 18.4884 |
| 17 | 1.1843 | 1.2880 | 1.6528 | 1.9479 | 3.7000 | 5.0545 | 6.8660 | 9.2765 | 12.4677 | 16.6722 | 22.1861 |
| 18 | 1.1961 | 1.3073 | 1.7024 | 2.0258 | 3.9960 | 5.5599 | 7.6900 | 10.5752 | 14.4625 | 19.6733 | 26.6233 |
| 19 | 1.2081 | 1.3270 | 1.7535 | 2.1068 | 4.3157 | 6.1159 | 8.6128 | 12.0557 | 16.7765 | 23.2144 | 31.9480 |
| 20 | 1.2202 | 1.3469 | 1.8061 | 2.1911 | 4.6610 | 6.7275 | 9.6463 | 13.7435 | 19.4608 | 27.3930 | 38.3376 |
| 21 | 1.2324 | 1.3671 | 1.8603 | 2.2788 | 5.0338 | 7.4002 | 10.8038 | 15.6676 | 22.5745 | 32.3238 | 46.0051 |
| 22 | 1.2447 | 1.3876 | 1.9161 | 2.3699 | 5.4365 | 8.1403 | 12.1003 | 17.8610 | 26.1864 | 38.1421 | 55.2061 |
| 23 | 1.2572 | 1.4084 | 1.9736 | 2.4647 | 5.8715 | 8.9543 | 13.5523 | 20.3616 | 30.3762 | 45.0076 | 66.2474 |
| 24 | 1.2697 | 1.4295 | 2.0328 | 2.5633 | 6.3412 | 9.8497 | 15.1786 | 23.2122 | 35.2364 | 53.1090 | 79.4968 |
| 25 | 1.2824 | 1.4509 | 2.0938 | 2.6658 | 6.8485 | 10.8347 | 17.0001 | 26.4619 | 40.8742 | 62.6686 | 95.3962 |
| 26 | 1.2953 | 1.4727 | 2.1566 | 2.7725 | 7.3964 | 11.9182 | 19.0401 | 30.1666 | 47.4141 | 73.9490 | 114.4755 |
| 27 | 1.3082 | 1.4948 | 2.2213 | 2.8834 | 7.9881 | 13.1100 | 21.3249 | 34.3899 | 55.0004 | 87.2598 | 137.3706 |
| 28 | 1.3213 | 1.5172 | 2.2879 | 2.9987 | 8.6271 | 14.4210 | 23.8839 | 39.2045 | 63.8004 | 102.9666 | 164.8447 |
| 29 | 1.3345 | 1.5400 | 2.3566 | 3.1187 | 9.3173 | 15.8631 | 26.7499 | 44.6931 | 74.0085 | 121.5005 | 197.8136 |
| 30 | 1.3478 | 1.5631 | 2.4273 | 3.2434 | 10.0627 | 17.4494 | 29.9599 | 50.9502 | 85.8499 | 143.3706 | 237.3763 |
| 31 | 1.3613 | 1.5865 | 2.5001 | 3.3731 | 10.8677 | 19.1943 | 33.5551 | 58.0832 | 99.5859 | 169.1774 | 284.8516 |
| 32 | 1.3749 | 1.6103 | 2.5751 | 3.5081 | 11.7371 | 21.1138 | 37.5817 | 66.2148 | 115.5196 | 199.6293 | 341.8219 |
| 33 | 1.3887 | 1.6345 | 2.6523 | 3.6484 | 12.6760 | 23.2252 | 42.0915 | 75.4849 | 134.0027 | 235.5625 | 410.1863 |
| 34 | 1.4026 | 1.6590 | 2.7319 | 3.7943 | 13.6901 | 25.5477 | 47.1425 | 86.0528 | 155.4432 | 277.9638 | 492.2235 |
| 35 | 1.4166 | 1.6839 | 2.8139 | 3.9461 | 14.7853 | 28.1024 | 52.7996 | 98.1002 | 180.3141 | 327.9973 | 590.6682 |
| 36 | 1.4308 | 1.7091 | 2.8983 | 4.1039 | 15.9682 | 30.9127 | 59.1356 | 111.8342 | 209.1643 | 387.0368 | 708.8019 |
| 37 | 1.4451 | 1.7348 | 2.9852 | 4.2681 | 17.2456 | 34.0039 | 66.2318 | 127.4910 | 242.6306 | 456.7034 | 850.5622 |
| 38 | 1.4595 | 1.7608 | 3.0748 | 4.4388 | 18.6253 | 37.4043 | 74.1797 | 145.3397 | 281.4515 | 528.9100 | 1020.6747 |
| 39 | 1.4741 | 1.7872 | 3.1670 | 4.6164 | 20.1153 | 41.1448 | 83.0812 | 165.6873 | 326.4838 | 635.9139 | 1224.8096 |
| 40 | 1.4889 | 1.8140 | 3.2620 | 4.8010 | 21.7245 | 45.2593 | 93.0510 | 188.8835 | 378.7212 | 750.3783 | 1469.7716 |
| 41 | 1.5083 | 1.8412 | 3.3599 | 4.9931 | 23.4625 | 49.7852 | 104.2171 | 215.3272 | 439.3165 | 885.4464 | 1763.7259 |
| 42 | 1.5188 | 1.8688 | 3.4607 | 5.1928 | 25.3395 | 54.7637 | 116.7231 | 245.4730 | 509.6072 | 1044.8268 | 2116.4711 |
| 43 | 1.5340 | 1.8969 | 3.5645 | 5.4005 | 27.3666 | 60.2401 | 130.7299 | 279.8392 | 591.1443 | 1232.8956 | 2539.7653 |
| 44 | 1.5493 | 1.9253 | 3.6715 | 5.6165 | 29.5560 | 66.2641 | 146.4175 | 319.0167 | 685.7274 | 1454.8168 | 3047.7183 |
| 45 | 1.5648 | 1.9542 | 3.7816 | 5.8412 | 31.9204 | 72.8905 | 163.9876 | 363.6791 | 795.4438 | 1716.6839 | 3657.2620 |
| 46 | 1.5805 | 1.9835 | 3.8950 | 6.0748 | 34.4741 | 80.1795 | 183.6661 | 414.5941 | 922.7148 | 2025.6870 | 4388.7144 |
| 47 | 1.5963 | 2.0133 | 4.0119 | 6.3178 | 37.2320 | 88.1975 | 205.7061 | 472.6373 | 1070.3492 | 2390.3106 | 5266.4573 |
| 48 | 1.6122 | 2.0435 | 4.1323 | 6.5705 | 40.2106 | 97.0172 | 230.3908 | 538.8065 | 1241.6051 | 2820.5665 | 6319.7487 |
| 49 | 1.6283 | 2.0741 | 4.2562 | 6.8333 | 43.4274 | 106.7190 | 258.0377 | 614.2395 | 1440.2619 | 3328.2685 | 7583.6985 |
| 50 | 1.6446 | 2.1052 | 4.3839 | 7.1067 | 46.9016 | 117.3909 | 289.0022 | 700.2330 | 1670.7038 | 3927.3569 | 9100.4382 |

**Table G–3**
**Present value of an annuity of 1 per period**

| Periods | 1.0% | 1.5% | 3.0% | 4.0% | 8.0% | 10.0% | 12.0% | 14.0% | 16.0% | 18.0% | 20.0% |
|---|---|---|---|---|---|---|---|---|---|---|---|
| 1 | 0.9901 | 0.9852 | 0.9709 | 0.9615 | 0.9259 | 0.9091 | 0.8929 | 0.8772 | 0.8621 | 0.8475 | 0.8333 |
| 2 | 1.9704 | 1.9559 | 1.9135 | 1.8861 | 1.7833 | 1.7355 | 1.6901 | 1.6467 | 1.6052 | 1.5656 | 1.5278 |
| 3 | 2.9410 | 2.9122 | 2.8286 | 2.7751 | 2.5771 | 2.4869 | 2.4018 | 2.3216 | 2.2459 | 2.1743 | 2.1065 |
| 4 | 3.9020 | 3.8544 | 3.7171 | 3.6299 | 3.3121 | 3.1699 | 3.0373 | 2.9137 | 2.7982 | 2.6901 | 2.5887 |
| 5 | 4.8534 | 4.7826 | 4.5797 | 4.4518 | 3.9927 | 3.7908 | 3.6048 | 3.4331 | 3.2743 | 3.1272 | 2.9906 |
| 6 | 5.7955 | 5.6972 | 5.4172 | 5.2421 | 4.6229 | 4.3553 | 4.1114 | 3.8887 | 3.6847 | 3.4976 | 3.3255 |
| 7 | 6.7282 | 6.5982 | 6.2303 | 6.0021 | 5.2064 | 4.8684 | 4.5638 | 4.2883 | 4.0386 | 3.8115 | 3.6046 |
| 8 | 7.6517 | 7.4859 | 7.0197 | 6.7327 | 5.7466 | 5.3349 | 4.9676 | 4.6389 | 4.3436 | 4.0776 | 3.8372 |
| 9 | 8.5660 | 8.3605 | 7.7861 | 7.4353 | 6.2469 | 5.7590 | 5.3282 | 4.9464 | 4.6065 | 4.3030 | 4.0310 |
| 10 | 9.4713 | 9.2222 | 8.5302 | 8.1109 | 6.7101 | 6.1446 | 5.6502 | 5.2161 | 4.8332 | 4.4941 | 4.1925 |
| 11 | 10.3676 | 10.0711 | 9.2526 | 8.7605 | 7.1390 | 6.4951 | 5.9377 | 5.4527 | 5.0286 | 4.6560 | 4.3271 |
| 12 | 11.2551 | 10.9075 | 9.9540 | 9.3851 | 7.5361 | 6.8137 | 6.1944 | 5.6603 | 5.1971 | 4.7932 | 4.4392 |
| 13 | 12.1337 | 11.7315 | 10.6350 | 9.9856 | 7.9038 | 7.1034 | 6.4235 | 5.8424 | 5.3423 | 4.9095 | 4.5327 |
| 14 | 13.0037 | 12.5434 | 11.2961 | 10.5631 | 8.2442 | 7.3667 | 6.6282 | 6.0021 | 5.4675 | 5.0081 | 4.6106 |
| 15 | 13.8651 | 13.3432 | 11.9379 | 11.1184 | 8.5595 | 7.6061 | 6.8109 | 6.1422 | 5.5755 | 5.0916 | 4.6755 |
| 16 | 14.7179 | 14.1313 | 12.5611 | 11.6523 | 8.8514 | 7.8237 | 6.9740 | 6.2651 | 5.6685 | 5.1624 | 4.7296 |
| 17 | 15.5623 | 14.9076 | 13.1661 | 12.1657 | 9.1216 | 8.0216 | 7.1196 | 6.3729 | 5.7487 | 5.2223 | 4.7746 |
| 18 | 16.3983 | 15.6726 | 13.7535 | 12.6593 | 9.3719 | 8.2014 | 7.2497 | 6.4674 | 5.8178 | 5.2732 | 4.8122 |
| 19 | 17.2260 | 16.4262 | 14.3238 | 13.1339 | 9.6036 | 8.3649 | 7.3658 | 6.5504 | 5.8775 | 5.3162 | 4.8435 |
| 20 | 18.0456 | 17.1686 | 14.8775 | 13.5903 | 9.8181 | 8.5136 | 7.4694 | 6.6231 | 5.9288 | 5.3527 | 4.8696 |
| 21 | 18.8570 | 17.9001 | 15.4150 | 14.0292 | 10.0168 | 8.6487 | 7.5620 | 6.6870 | 5.9731 | 5.3837 | 4.8913 |
| 22 | 19.6604 | 18.6208 | 15.9369 | 14.4511 | 10.2007 | 8.7715 | 7.6446 | 6.7429 | 6.0113 | 5.4099 | 4.9094 |
| 23 | 20.4558 | 19.3309 | 16.4436 | 14.8568 | 10.3711 | 8.8832 | 7.7184 | 6.7921 | 6.0442 | 5.4321 | 4.9245 |
| 24 | 21.2434 | 20.0304 | 16.9355 | 15.2470 | 10.5288 | 8.9847 | 7.7843 | 6.8351 | 6.0726 | 5.4509 | 4.9371 |
| 25 | 22.0232 | 20.7196 | 17.4131 | 15.6221 | 10.6748 | 9.0770 | 7.8431 | 6.8729 | 6.0971 | 5.4669 | 4.9476 |
| 26 | 22.7952 | 21.3986 | 17.8768 | 15.9828 | 10.8100 | 9.1609 | 7.8957 | 6.9061 | 6.1182 | 5.4804 | 4.9563 |
| 27 | 23.5596 | 22.0676 | 18.3270 | 16.3296 | 10.9352 | 9.2372 | 7.9426 | 6.9352 | 6.1364 | 5.4919 | 4.9636 |
| 28 | 24.3164 | 22.7267 | 18.7641 | 16.6631 | 11.0511 | 9.3066 | 7.9844 | 6.9607 | 6.1520 | 5.5016 | 4.9697 |
| 29 | 25.0658 | 23.3761 | 19.1885 | 16.9837 | 11.1584 | 9.3696 | 8.0218 | 6.9830 | 6.1656 | 5.5098 | 4.9747 |
| 30 | 25.8077 | 24.0158 | 19.6004 | 17.2920 | 11.2578 | 9.4269 | 8.0552 | 7.0027 | 6.1772 | 5.5168 | 4.9789 |
| 31 | 26.5423 | 24.6461 | 20.0004 | 17.5885 | 11.3498 | 9.4790 | 8.0850 | 7.0199 | 6.1872 | 5.5227 | 4.9824 |
| 32 | 27.2696 | 25.2671 | 20.3888 | 17.8736 | 11.4350 | 9.5264 | 8.1116 | 7.0350 | 6.1959 | 5.5277 | 4.9854 |
| 33 | 27.9897 | 25.8790 | 20.7658 | 18.1476 | 11.5139 | 9.5694 | 8.1354 | 7.0482 | 6.2034 | 5.5320 | 4.9878 |
| 34 | 28.7027 | 26.4817 | 21.1318 | 18.4112 | 11.5869 | 9.6086 | 8.1566 | 7.0599 | 6.2098 | 5.5356 | 4.9898 |
| 35 | 29.4086 | 27.0756 | 21.4872 | 18.6646 | 11.6546 | 9.6442 | 8.1755 | 7.0700 | 6.2153 | 5.5386 | 4.9915 |
| 36 | 30.1075 | 27.6607 | 21.8323 | 18.9083 | 11.7172 | 9.6765 | 8.1924 | 7.0790 | 6.2201 | 5.5412 | 4.9929 |
| 37 | 30.7995 | 28.2371 | 22.1672 | 19.1426 | 11.7752 | 9.7059 | 8.2075 | 7.0868 | 6.2242 | 5.5434 | 4.9941 |
| 38 | 31.4847 | 28.8051 | 22.4925 | 19.3679 | 11.8289 | 9.7327 | 8.2210 | 7.0937 | 6.2278 | 5.5452 | 4.9951 |
| 39 | 32.1630 | 29.3646 | 22.8082 | 19.5845 | 11.8786 | 9.7570 | 8.2330 | 7.0997 | 6.2309 | 5.5468 | 4.9959 |
| 40 | 32.8347 | 29.9158 | 23.1148 | 19.7928 | 11.9246 | 9.7791 | 8.2438 | 7.1050 | 6.2335 | 5.5482 | 4.9966 |
| 41 | 33.4997 | 30.4590 | 23.4124 | 19.9931 | 11.9672 | 9.7991 | 8.2534 | 7.1097 | 6.2358 | 5.5493 | 4.9972 |
| 42 | 34.1581 | 30.9941 | 23.7014 | 20.1856 | 12.0067 | 9.8174 | 8.2619 | 7.1138 | 6.2377 | 5.5502 | 4.9976 |
| 43 | 34.8100 | 31.5212 | 23.9819 | 20.3708 | 12.0432 | 9.8340 | 8.2696 | 7.1173 | 6.2394 | 5.5510 | 4.9980 |
| 44 | 35.4555 | 32.0406 | 24.2543 | 20.5488 | 12.0771 | 9.8491 | 8.2764 | 7.1205 | 6.2409 | 5.5517 | 4.9984 |
| 45 | 36.0945 | 32.5523 | 24.5187 | 20.7200 | 12.1084 | 9.8628 | 8.2825 | 7.1232 | 6.2421 | 5.5523 | 4.9986 |
| 46 | 36.7272 | 33.0565 | 24.7754 | 20.8847 | 12.1374 | 9.8753 | 8.2880 | 7.1256 | 6.2432 | 5.5528 | 4.9989 |
| 47 | 37.3537 | 33.5532 | 25.0247 | 21.0429 | 12.1643 | 9.8866 | 8.2928 | 7.1277 | 6.2442 | 5.5532 | 4.9991 |
| 48 | 37.9740 | 34.0426 | 25.2667 | 21.1951 | 12.1891 | 9.8969 | 8.2972 | 7.1296 | 6.2450 | 5.5536 | 4.9992 |
| 49 | 38.5881 | 34.5247 | 25.5017 | 21.3415 | 12.2122 | 9.9063 | 8.3010 | 7.1312 | 6.2457 | 5.5539 | 4.9993 |
| 50 | 39.1961 | 34.9997 | 25.7298 | 21.4822 | 12.2335 | 9.9148 | 8.3045 | 7.1327 | 6.2463 | 5.5541 | 4.9995 |

## Table G–4
**Future value of an annuity of 1 per period**

| Periods | 1.0% | 1.5% | 3.0% | 4.0% | 8.0% | 10.0% | 12.0% | 14.0% | 16.0% | 18.0% | 20.0% |
|---|---|---|---|---|---|---|---|---|---|---|---|
| 1 | 1.0000 | 1.0000 | 1.0000 | 1.0000 | 1.0000 | 1.0000 | 1.0000 | 1.0000 | 1.0000 | 1.0000 | 1.0000 |
| 2 | 2.0100 | 2.0150 | 2.0300 | 2.0400 | 2.0800 | 2.1000 | 2.1200 | 2.1400 | 2.1600 | 2.1800 | 2.2000 |
| 3 | 3.0301 | 3.0452 | 3.0909 | 3.1216 | 3.2464 | 3.3100 | 3.3744 | 3.4396 | 3.5056 | 3.5724 | 3.6400 |
| 4 | 4.0604 | 4.0909 | 4.1836 | 4.2465 | 4.5061 | 4.6410 | 4.7793 | 4.9211 | 5.0665 | 5.2154 | 5.3680 |
| 5 | 5.1010 | 5.1523 | 5.3091 | 5.4163 | 5.8666 | 6.1051 | 6.3528 | 6.6101 | 6.8771 | 7.1542 | 7.4416 |
| 6 | 6.1520 | 6.2296 | 6.4684 | 6.6330 | 7.3359 | 7.7156 | 8.1152 | 8.5355 | 8.9775 | 9.4420 | 9.9299 |
| 7 | 7.2135 | 7.3230 | 7.6625 | 7.8983 | 8.9228 | 9.4872 | 10.0890 | 10.7305 | 11.4139 | 12.1415 | 12.9159 |
| 8 | 8.2857 | 8.4328 | 8.8923 | 9.2142 | 10.6366 | 11.4359 | 12.2997 | 13.2328 | 14.2401 | 15.3270 | 16.4991 |
| 9 | 9.3685 | 9.5593 | 10.1591 | 10.5828 | 12.4876 | 13.5795 | 14.7757 | 16.0853 | 17.5185 | 19.0859 | 20.7989 |
| 10 | 10.4622 | 10.7027 | 11.4639 | 12.0061 | 14.4866 | 15.9374 | 17.5487 | 19.3373 | 21.3215 | 23.5213 | 25.9587 |
| 11 | 11.5668 | 11.8633 | 12.8078 | 13.4864 | 16.6455 | 18.5312 | 20.6546 | 23.0445 | 25.7329 | 28.7551 | 32.1504 |
| 12 | 12.6825 | 13.0412 | 14.1920 | 15.0258 | 18.9771 | 21.3843 | 24.1331 | 27.2707 | 30.8502 | 34.9311 | 39.5805 |
| 13 | 13.8093 | 14.2368 | 15.6178 | 16.6268 | 21.4953 | 24.5227 | 28.0291 | 32.0887 | 36.7862 | 42.2187 | 48.4966 |
| 14 | 14.9474 | 15.4504 | 17.0863 | 18.2919 | 24.2149 | 27.9750 | 32.3926 | 37.5811 | 43.6720 | 50.8180 | 59.1959 |
| 15 | 16.0969 | 16.6821 | 18.5989 | 20.0236 | 27.1521 | 31.7725 | 37.2797 | 43.8424 | 51.6595 | 60.9653 | 72.0351 |
| 16 | 17.2579 | 17.9324 | 20.1569 | 21.8245 | 30.3243 | 35.9497 | 42.7533 | 50.9804 | 60.9250 | 72.9390 | 87.4421 |
| 17 | 18.4304 | 19.2014 | 21.7616 | 23.6975 | 33.7502 | 40.5447 | 48.8837 | 59.1176 | 71.6730 | 87.0680 | 105.9306 |
| 18 | 19.6147 | 20.4894 | 23.4144 | 25.6454 | 37.4502 | 45.5992 | 55.7497 | 68.3941 | 84.1407 | 103.7403 | 128.1167 |
| 19 | 20.8109 | 21.7967 | 25.1169 | 27.6712 | 41.4463 | 51.1591 | 63.4397 | 78.9692 | 98.6032 | 123.4135 | 154.7400 |
| 20 | 22.0190 | 23.1237 | 26.8704 | 29.7781 | 45.7620 | 57.2750 | 72.0524 | 91.0249 | 115.3797 | 146.6280 | 186.6880 |
| 21 | 23.2392 | 24.4705 | 28.6765 | 31.9692 | 50.4229 | 64.0025 | 81.6987 | 104.7684 | 134.8405 | 174.0210 | 225.0256 |
| 22 | 24.4716 | 25.8376 | 30.5368 | 34.2480 | 55.4568 | 71.4027 | 92.5026 | 120.4360 | 157.4150 | 206.3448 | 271.0307 |
| 23 | 25.7163 | 27.2251 | 32.4529 | 36.6179 | 60.8933 | 79.5430 | 104.6029 | 138.2970 | 183.6014 | 244.4868 | 326.2369 |
| 24 | 26.9735 | 28.6335 | 34.4265 | 39.0826 | 66.7648 | 88.4973 | 118.1552 | 158.6586 | 213.9776 | 289.4945 | 392.4842 |
| 25 | 28.2432 | 30.0630 | 36.4593 | 41.6459 | 73.1059 | 98.3471 | 133.3339 | 181.8708 | 249.2140 | 342.6035 | 471.9811 |
| 26 | 29.5256 | 31.5140 | 38.5530 | 44.3117 | 79.9544 | 109.1818 | 150.3339 | 208.3327 | 290.0883 | 405.2721 | 567.3773 |
| 27 | 30.8209 | 32.9867 | 40.7096 | 47.0842 | 87.3508 | 121.0999 | 169.3740 | 238.4993 | 337.5024 | 479.2211 | 681.8528 |
| 28 | 32.1291 | 34.4815 | 42.9309 | 49.9676 | 95.3388 | 134.2099 | 190.6989 | 272.8892 | 392.5028 | 566.4809 | 819.2233 |
| 29 | 33.4504 | 35.9987 | 45.2189 | 52.9663 | 103.9659 | 148.6309 | 214.5828 | 312.0937 | 456.3032 | 669.4475 | 984.0680 |
| 30 | 34.7849 | 37.5387 | 47.5754 | 56.0849 | 113.2832 | 164.4940 | 241.3327 | 356.7868 | 530.3117 | 790.9480 | 1181.8816 |
| 31 | 36.1327 | 39.1018 | 50.0027 | 59.3283 | 123.3459 | 181.9434 | 271.2926 | 407.7370 | 616.1616 | 934.3186 | 1419.2579 |
| 32 | 37.4941 | 40.6883 | 52.5028 | 62.7015 | 134.2135 | 201.1378 | 304.8477 | 465.8202 | 715.7475 | 1103.4960 | 1704.1095 |
| 33 | 38.8690 | 42.2986 | 55.0778 | 66.2095 | 145.9506 | 222.2515 | 342.4294 | 532.0350 | 831.2671 | 1303.1253 | 2045.9314 |
| 34 | 40.2577 | 43.9331 | 57.7302 | 69.8579 | 158.6267 | 245.4767 | 384.5210 | 607.5199 | 965.2698 | 1538.6878 | 2456.1176 |
| 35 | 41.6603 | 45.5921 | 60.4621 | 73.6522 | 172.3168 | 271.0244 | 431.6635 | 693.5727 | 1120.7130 | 1816.6516 | 2948.3411 |
| 36 | 43.0769 | 47.2760 | 63.2759 | 77.5983 | 187.1021 | 299.1268 | 484.4631 | 791.6729 | 1301.0270 | 2144.6489 | 3539.0094 |
| 37 | 44.5076 | 48.9851 | 66.1742 | 81.7022 | 203.0703 | 330.0395 | 543.5987 | 903.5071 | 1510.1914 | 2531.6857 | 4247.8112 |
| 38 | 45.9527 | 50.7199 | 69.1594 | 85.9703 | 220.3159 | 364.0434 | 609.8305 | 1030.9981 | 1752.8220 | 2988.3891 | 5098.3735 |
| 39 | 47.4123 | 52.4807 | 72.2342 | 90.4091 | 238.9412 | 401.4478 | 684.0102 | 1176.3378 | 2034.2735 | 3527.2992 | 6119.0482 |
| 40 | 48.8864 | 54.2679 | 75.4013 | 95.0255 | 259.0565 | 442.5926 | 767.0914 | 1342.0251 | 2360.7572 | 4163.2130 | 7343.8578 |
| 41 | 50.3752 | 56.0819 | 78.6633 | 99.8265 | 280.7810 | 487.8518 | 860.1424 | 1530.9086 | 2739.4784 | 4913.5914 | 8813.6294 |
| 42 | 51.8790 | 57.9231 | 82.0232 | 104.8196 | 304.2435 | 537.6370 | 964.3595 | 1746.2358 | 3178.7949 | 5799.0378 | 10577.3553 |
| 43 | 53.3978 | 59.7920 | 85.4839 | 110.0124 | 329.5830 | 592.4007 | 1081.0826 | 1991.7088 | 3688.4021 | 6843.8646 | 12693.8263 |
| 44 | 54.9318 | 61.6889 | 89.0484 | 115.4129 | 356.9496 | 652.6408 | 1211.8125 | 2271.5481 | 4279.5465 | 8076.7603 | 15233.5916 |
| 45 | 56.4811 | 63.6142 | 92.7199 | 121.0294 | 386.5056 | 718.9048 | 1358.2300 | 2590.5648 | 4965.2739 | 9531.5771 | 18281.3099 |
| 46 | 58.0459 | 65.5684 | 96.5015 | 126.8706 | 418.4261 | 791.7953 | 1522.2176 | 2954.2439 | 5760.7177 | 11248.2610 | 21938.5719 |
| 47 | 59.6263 | 67.5519 | 100.3965 | 132.9454 | 452.9002 | 871.9749 | 1705.8838 | 3368.8380 | 6683.4326 | 13273.9480 | 26327.2863 |
| 48 | 61.2226 | 69.5652 | 104.4084 | 139.2632 | 490.1322 | 960.1723 | 1911.5898 | 3841.4753 | 7753.7818 | 15664.2586 | 31593.7436 |
| 49 | 62.8348 | 71.6087 | 108.5406 | 145.8337 | 530.3427 | 1057.1896 | 2141.9806 | 4380.2819 | 8995.3869 | 18484.8251 | 37913.4923 |
| 50 | 64.4632 | 73.6828 | 112.7969 | 152.6671 | 573.7702 | 1163.9085 | 2400.0182 | 4994.5213 | 10435.6488 | 21813.0937 | 45497.1908 |

## Exercises

**Exercise G–1**
**Present value of an amount**
(L. O. 1)

Ferrara Company is considering an investment which if paid for immediately is expected to return $750,000 six years hence. If Ferrara Company demands an 18% return, how much will Ferrara Company be willing to pay for this investment?

**Exercise G–2**
**Future value of an amount**
(L. O. 2)

Sandala Company invested $77,500 in a project that is expected to earn a 12% rate of return. The earnings will be reinvested in the project each year until the entire investment is liquidated 20 years hence. What will be the cash proceeds when the project is liquidated?

**Exercise G–3**
**Present value of an annuity**
(L. O. 1)

Zavala Company is considering a contract that will return $8,000 annually at the end of each year for 22 years. If Zavala Company demands an annual return of 18% and pays for the investment immediately, how much should it be willing to pay?

**Exercise G–4**
**Future value of an annuity**
(L. O. 2)

Carol Thornton is planning to begin an individual retirement program in which she will invest $1,200 annually at the end of each year. Ms. Thornton plans to retire after making 35 annual investments in a program that earns a return of 8%. What will be the value of the program on the date of the last investment?

**Exercise G–5**
**Interest rate on an investment**
(L. O. 1)

Mr. Lee has been offered the possibility of investing $0.0160 for 25 years, after which he will be paid $1. What annual rate of interest will Mr. Lee earn? (Use Table G–1 to find the answer.)

**Exercise G–6**
**Number of periods of an investment**
(L. O. 1)

Ms. Collins has been offered the possibility of investing $0.0779. The investment will earn 20% per year and will at the end of the investment return Ms. Collins $1. How many years must Ms. Collins wait to receive the $1? (Use Table G–1 to find the answer.)

**Exercise G–7**
**Number of periods of an investment**
(L. O. 2)

Mr. Farabee expects to invest $1 at 16% and at the end of the investment receive $55.0004. How many years will elapse before Mr. Farabee receives the payment? (Use Table G–2 to find the answer.)

**Exercise G–8**
**Interest rate on an investment**
(L. O. 2)

Ms. O'Connell expects to invest $1 for 12 years, after which she will receive $3.8960. What rate of interest will Ms. O'Connell earn? (Use Table G–2 to find the answer.)

**Exercise G–9**
**Interest rate on an investment**
(L. O. 1)

Mr. Wainwright expects an immediate investment of $18.7641 to return $1 annually for 28 years, the first payment to be received in 1 year. What rate of interest will Mr. Wainwright earn? (Use Table G–3 to find the answer.)

**Exercise G–10**
**Number of periods of an investment**
(L. O. 1)

Ms. Kubacek expects an investment of $6.0726 to return $1 annually for several years. If Ms. Kubacek is to earn a return of 16%, how many annual payments must she receive? (Use Table G–3 to find the answer.)

**Exercise G–11**
**Interest rate on an investment**
(L. O. 2)

Mr. Gibbs expects to invest $1 annually for 40 years and have an accumulated value of $1342.0251 on the date of the last investment. If this occurs, what rate of interest will Mr. Gibbs earn? (Use Table G–4 to find the answer.)

**Exercise G–12**
**Number of periods of an investment**
(L. O. 2)

Ms. Evans expects to invest $1 annually in a fund that will earn 10%. How many annual investments must Ms. Evans make to accumulate $201.1378 on the date of the last investment? (Use Table G–4 to find the answer.)

**Exercise G–13**
**Present value of an annuity**
(L. O. 1)

Jan Michaels financed a new automobile by paying $1,000 cash and agreeing to make 48 monthly payments of $350 each, the first payment to be made one month after the purchase. The loan was said to bear interest at an annual rate of 12%. What was the cost of the automobile?

**Exercise G–14**
**Future value of an amount**
(L. O. 2)

Edward Locker deposited $12,000 in a savings account that earns interest at an annual rate of 12%, compounded quarterly. The $12,000 plus earned interest must remain in the account three years before it can be withdrawn. How much money will be in the account at the end of three years?

**Exercise G–15**
**Future value of an annuity**
(L. O. 2)

Liz Storey plans to have $250 withdrawn from her monthly paycheck and deposited in a savings account that earns 12% annually, compounded monthly. If Liz continues with her plan for four years, how much will be accumulated in the account on the date of the last deposit?

**Exercise G–16**
**Present value of bonds**
(L. O. 1)

Cameron Company plans to issue 10%, 20-year, $750,000 par value, bonds payable that pay interest semiannually on June 30 and December 31. The bonds are dated December 31, 1990, and are to be issued on that date. If the market rate of interest for the bonds is 8% on the date of issue, what will be the cash proceeds from the bond issue?

**Exercise G–17**
**Future value of an amount plus an annuity**
(L. O. 2)

Pecan Street Company has decided to establish a fund that will be used seven years hence to replace an aging productive facility. The company makes an initial contribution of $120,000 to the fund and plans to make quarterly contributions of $30,000 beginning in three months. The fund is expected to earn

12%, compounded quarterly. What will be the value of the fund seven years hence?

**Exercise G–18**
**Present value of an amount**
(L. O. 1)

Jetson Company expects to earn 16% on an investment that will return $450,000, 10 years hence. Use Table G–2 to calculate the present value of the investment.

**Exercise G–19**
**Future value of an amount**
(L. O. 2)

J. B. Pharries Company invests $50,000 at 18% for five years. Use Table G–1 to calculate the future value of the investment, five years hence.

# H The Accounting Problem of Changing Prices

For many years, accountants have discussed the problem of how to account for changing prices. Sometimes, when prices are changing rapidly, the discussion is heated and attempts are made to improve accounting practices. Other times, when prices are changing at a slower rate, the problem of accounting for price changes gets less attention. In any case, the fact that the prices paid for economic goods and services change over time presents a major problem in accounting. In studying this appendix, you will learn why price changes are a problem in accounting. You will also gain an introductory understanding of proposed ways of dealing with this problem.

### Learning Objectives

*After studying Appendix H, you should be able to:*

1. Explain why conventional financial statements fail to adequately account for price changes.
2. Explain how price changes should be measured and how to construct a price index.
3. Restate historical cost/nominal dollar costs into constant purchasing power amounts and calculate purchasing power gains and losses.
4. Explain the difference between current costs and historical costs stated in constant purchasing power amounts.
5. Define or explain the words and phrases listed in the appendix Glossary.

## Conventional Financial Statements Fail to Account for Price Changes

Explain why conventional financial statements fail to adequately account for price changes.
(L. O. 1)

All accountants agree that conventional financial statements provide useful information for making economic decisions. However, many accountants also agree that conventional financial statements fail to adequately account for the impact of changing prices. Sometimes, this failure of conventional financial statements makes the statements misleading. That is, the statements may imply certain facts that are inconsistent with the real state of affairs. As a result, the information in the statements may lead decision makers to make decisions that are inconsistent with their objectives.

### Failure to Account for Price Changes on the Balance Sheet

In what ways do conventional financial statements fail to account for changing prices? The general problem is that transactions are recorded in terms of the historical number of dollars paid. These amounts are not adjusted even though subsequent price changes may dramatically change the value of the purchased items. For example, Old Company purchased 10 acres of land for $25,000. Then, at the end of each accounting period, Old Company presented a balance sheet showing "Land, $25,000." Six years later, after price increases of 97%, New Company purchased 10 acres of land that was next to and nearly identical to Old Company's land. New Company paid $49,250 for the land. In comparing the conventional balance sheets of the two companies, you would see the following balances:

**Balance Sheets**

| | Old Company | New Company |
|---|---|---|
| Land . . . . | $25,000 | $49,250 |

Without knowing the details that led to these balances, a statement reader is likely to conclude that New Company either has more land than does Old Company or that New Company's land is more valuable. But both companies own 10 acres that are of equal value. The entire difference between the prices paid by the two companies is explained by the 97% price increase between the two purchase dates. That is, $25,000 × 1.97 = $49,250.

### Failure to Account for Price Changes on the Income Statement

The failure of conventional financial statements to adequately account for changing prices also shows up in the income statement. For example, assume that in the above example, machines were purchased instead of land. Also, assume that the machines of Old Company and New Company are identical except for age; both are being depreciated on a straight-line basis over a 10-year period with no salvage value. As a result, the annual income statements of the two companies show the following:

**Income Statements**

| | Old Company | New Company |
|---|---|---|
| Depreciation expense, machinery . . . . | $2,500 | $4,925 |

Although assets of equal value are being depreciated, the income statements show depreciation expense for New Company that is 97% higher than Old Company's. This is inconsistent with the fact that both companies own the same machines that are affected by the same depreciation factors. Furthermore, although Old Company will appear more profitable, it must pay more income taxes due to the apparent extra profits. Also, Old Company may not recover the full replacement cost of its machinery through the sale of its product.

## Understanding Price-Level Changes

Explain how price changes should be measured and how to contruct a price index.
(L. O. 2)

In one way or another, all of us have experienced the effects of **inflation,** which is a general increase in the prices paid for goods and services. A general decrease in prices is called **deflation.** Of course, the prices of specific items do not all change at the same rate. Even when most prices are rising, the prices of some goods or services may be falling. For example, consider the following prices of four different items:

| Item | Price/Unit in 1990 | Price/Unit in 1989 | Percentage Change |
|---|---|---|---|
| A . . . . . . | $1.30 | $1.00 | +30 |
| B . . . . . . | 2.20 | 2.00 | +10 |
| C . . . . . . | 1.80 | 1.50 | +20 |
| D . . . . . . | 2.70 | 3.00 | −10 |
| Totals . . . . | $7.50 | $8.00 | |

**The Problem of Describing Price Changes.** How should you describe these price changes? One possibility is to state the percentage change in the price per unit of each item (see above). This information is useful for some purposes. But it does not show the average effect or impact of the price changes.

**The Average Change in Unit Prices.** A better indication of the average effect would be to determine the average increase in the per unit prices of the four items. Thus: $8.00 ÷ $7.50 − 1.00 = 6.7% average increase in per unit prices.[1] However, even this average probably fails to show the impact of the price changes on most individuals or businesses. It is a good indicator only if the typical buyer purchased an equal number of units of each item.

**The Weighted-Average Change in Prices.** What if the four items usually are purchased in unequal amounts? For example, assume that for each unit of A purchased, 2 units of B, 5 units of C, and 1 unit of D are purchased. When the items are purchased in unequal amounts, the impact of changing prices depends on the typical quantity of each item purchased. Hence, the average change in the price of the A, B, C, D "market basket" is calculated as follows:

[1] Throughout this appendix, only final answers are rounded. Percentages or index numbers are rounded to the nearest 1/10% and dollar amounts to the nearest whole dollar.

| Item | Units Purchased | 1989 Prices | | Units Purchased | 1990 Prices | |
|---|---|---|---|---|---|---|
| A . . . . . . . | 1 unit | $1.00 = | $ 1.00 | 1 unit | $1.30 = | $ 1.30 |
| B . . . . . . . | 2 units | $2.00 = | 4.00 | 2 units | $2.20 = | 4.40 |
| C . . . . . . . | 5 units | $1.50 = | 7.50 | 5 units | $1.80 = | 9.00 |
| D . . . . . . . | 1 unit | $3.00 = | 3.00 | 1 unit | $2.70 = | 2.70 |
| Totals . . . . | | | $15.50 | | | $17.40 |

Weighted-average price change = $17.40 ÷ $15.50 − 1.00 = 12.3%

Based on this calculation, you can say that the annual rate of inflation in the prices of these four items was 12.3%. However, not every individual and business will purchase these four items in exactly the same proportion of 1 unit of A, 2 units of B, 5 units of C, and 1 unit of D. As a result, the stated inflation rate only approximates the impact of price changes on each buyer. But if these proportions represent the typical buying pattern, the stated 12.3% inflation rate fairly reflects the inflationary impact on the average buyer.

## Construction of a Price Index

When the cost of purchasing a given market basket is determined for each of several periods, you can express the results as a **price index.** In constructing a price index, one year is arbitrarily selected as the "base" year. The cost of purchasing the market basket in that year is then assigned a value of 100. For example, suppose the cost of purchasing the A, B, C, D market basket in each year is:

| | |
|---|---|
| 1984 . . . . | $ 9.00 |
| 1985 . . . . | 11.00 |
| 1986 . . . . | 10.25 |
| 1987 . . . . | 12.00 |
| 1988 . . . . | 13.00 |
| 1989 . . . . | 15.50 |
| 1990 . . . . | 17.40 |

If you select 1987 as the base year, the $12 cost for 1987 is assigned a value of 100. Then, an index number for each of the other years is calculated and expressed as a percent of the base year's cost. For example, the index number for 1986 is 85.4 or ($10.25 ÷ $12.00 × 100 = 85.4). The index numbers for the remaining years are calculated in the same way. Illustration H–1 presents the entire price index for the years 1984 through 1990.

With this price index for the A, B, C, D market basket, you can make comparative statements about the cost of purchasing these items in various years. For example, you can say that the price level in 1990 was 45.0% (145 ÷ 100) higher than it was in 1987; the price level in 1990 was 33.9% (145 ÷ 108.3) higher than it was in 1988; and 12.2% (145 ÷ 129.2) higher than it was in 1989. Stated another way, $1 in 1990 would purchase the same amount of A, B, C, D as would $0.52 in 1984 (75 ÷ 145 = 0.51724).

**Illustration H–1**
**Constructing a price index**

| Year | Calculation of Price Level | | Price Index |
|---|---|---|---|
| 1984 . . | ($ 9.00 ÷ $12.00) × 100 | = | 75.0 |
| 1985 . . | ($11.00 ÷ $12.00) × 100 | = | 91.7 |
| 1986 . . | ($10.25 ÷ $12.00) × 100 | = | 85.4 |
| 1987 . . | ($12.00 ÷ $12.00) × 100 | = | 100.0 |
| 1988 . . | ($13.00 ÷ $12.00) × 100 | = | 108.3 |
| 1989 . . | ($15.50 ÷ $12.00) × 100 | = | 129.2 |
| 1990 . . | ($17.40 ÷ $12.00) × 100 | = | 145.0 |

## Specific versus General Price-Level Indexes

Price changes and price-level indexes can be calculated for narrow groups of commodities or services, such as housing construction material costs; or for broader groups of items, such as all construction costs; or for very broad groups of items, such as all items produced in the economy. A **specific price-level index**, such as for housing construction materials, indicates the changing purchasing power of a dollar spent for items in that specific category; that is, to pay for housing construction materials. A **general price-level index**, such as the Consumer Price Index for All Urban Consumers, indicates the changing purchasing power of a dollar spent for a very broad range of items.

## Using Price Index Numbers in Accounting

In accounting, one way general price indexes are used is to restate dollar amounts of cost that were paid in earlier years into the current price level. In other words, a specific dollar amount of cost in a previous year can be restated in terms of the comparable number of dollars that would have been incurred if the cost had been paid with dollars that have the current amount of purchasing power.

For example, suppose that in 1986, $1,000 was paid to purchase items A, B, C, D. Stated in terms of 1990 prices, that 1986 cost is $1,000 × (145 ÷ 85.4) = $1,698. Also, if $1,500 were paid for A, B, C, D in 1987, that 1987 cost restated in terms of 1990 prices, is $1,500 × (145 ÷ 100) = $2,175.

Note that the 1987 cost of $1,500 correctly states the number of monetary units (dollars) expended for items A, B, C, D in 1987. Also, the 1986 cost of $1,000 correctly states the units of money expended in 1986. However, in a very important way, the 1986 monetary units do not mean the same thing as the 1987 monetary units. A dollar (one monetary unit) in 1986 represented a different amount of purchasing power than a dollar in 1987. Both of these dollars represent different amounts of purchasing power than a dollar in 1990.

To communicate the amount of purchasing power expended or incurred, the historical number of monetary units must be restated in terms of dollars with the same amount of purchasing power. For example, the total amount of cost incurred during 1986 and 1987 could be stated in terms of the purchasing power of 1987 dollars, or stated in terms of the purchasing power of 1990 dollars. These calculations are presented in Illustration H–2.

**Illustration H–2**
**Expressing costs in constant dollars**

| Year Cost Was Incurred | Monetary Units Expended (*a*) | Price Index Factor for Adjustment to 1987 Dollars (*b*) | Historical Cost Stated in 1987 Dollars (*a* × *b* = *c*) | Price Index Factor for Adjustment to 1990 Dollars (*d*) | Historical Cost Stated in 1990 Dollars (*c* × *d*) |
|---|---|---|---|---|---|
| 1986 . . . . . . | $1,000 | 100 ÷ 85.4 = 1.17096 | $1,171 | 145 ÷ 100 = 1.45000 | $1,698* |
| 1987 . . . . . . | 1,500 | — | 1,500 | 145 ÷ 100 = 1.45000 | 2,175 |
| Total cost . . . | $2,500 | | $2,671 | | $3,873 |

*An alternative calculation is $1,000 × (145 ÷ 85.4) = $1,698.

## Accounting Systems that Make Adjustments for Price Changes

There are at least two important accounting systems that use price indexes to develop comprehensive financial statements. Both are alternatives to the conventional accounting system used in the United States. One alternative, called **current cost accounting**, is discussed later in the appendix. Current cost accounting uses specific price-level indexes (along with appraisals and other means) to develop statements that report assets and expenses in terms of the current costs to acquire those assets or services. The other alternative is called **historical cost/constant purchasing power accounting.**

## Historical Cost/ Constant Purchasing Power Accounting

Restate historical cost/ nominal dollar costs into constant purchasing power amounts and calculate purchasing power gains and losses.
(L. O. 3)

Conventional financial statements disclose revenues, expenses, assets, liabilities, and owners' equity in terms of the historical monetary units exchanged when the transactions occurred. As such, they are sometimes called **historical cost/nominal dollar financial statements.** This emphasizes the difference between conventional statements and historical cost/constant purchasing power statements. Historical cost/constant purchasing power accounting uses a general price index to restate the conventional financial statements into dollar amounts that represent current, general purchasing power.

You should understand that the same principles for determining depreciation expense, cost of goods sold, accruals of revenue, and so forth, apply to both historical cost/nominal dollar statements and historical cost/constant purchasing power statements. The same generally accepted accounting principles apply to both. The only difference between the two is that constant purchasing power statements reflect adjustments for general price-level changes; nominal dollar statements do not.

### The Impact of General Price Changes on Assets

**Monetary Assets.** The effect of general price-level changes on investments in assets depends on the nature of the assets. Some assets, called **monetary assets**, represent money or claims to receive a fixed amount of money. The number of dollars owned or to be received does not change even though the purchasing power of the dollar may change. Examples of monetary assets are cash, accounts receivable, notes receivable, and investments in bonds.

Because the amount of money that will be received from a monetary asset is fixed, a monetary asset is not adjusted for general price-level changes on a historical cost/constant purchasing power balance sheet. For example, assume that $800 in cash was owned at the end of 1990. Regardless of how the price level has changed since the cash was acquired, the amount to be reported on the December 31, 1990, historical cost/constant purchasing power balance sheet is $800.

**Purchasing Power Gains or Losses Result from Owning Monetary Assets.** Because the amount of money that will be received from monetary assets does not change with price-level changes, there is a special risk associated with owning these assets. An investment in monetary assets held during a period of inflation results in a loss of purchasing power. During a period of deflation, an investment in monetary assets results in a gain of purchasing power.

For example, assume that the $800 cash balance on December 31, 1990, resulted from the following:

| | |
|---|---|
| Cash balance, December 31, 1989 | $ 200 |
| Cash receipts, assumed to have been received uniformly throughout the year | 1,500 |
| Cash disbursements, assumed to have been made uniformly throughout the year | (900) |
| Cash balance, December 31, 1990 | $ 800 |

Also assume that the general price index was 150.0 at the end of 1989; that it averaged 160.0 throughout 1990; and was 168.0 at the end of that year. In this example, the beginning cash balance of $200 and the net receipts less disbursements of $600 lost purchasing power as the price level rose during 1990. This reduction in purchasing power is a loss. To calculate the loss during the year, the beginning cash balance and each receipt or disbursement is adjusted for price changes to the end of the year. Then, the adjusted balance is compared with the actual balance to determine the loss.

The amount of the loss is calculated as follows:

| | Nominal Dollar Amounts | Price Index Factor for Restatement to December 31, 1990 | Restated to December 31, 1990 | Gain or (Loss) |
|---|---|---|---|---|
| Beginning balance | $ 200 | 168.0 ÷ 150.0 = 1.12000 | $ 224 | |
| Receipts | 1,500 | 168.0 ÷ 160.0 = 1.05000 | 1,575 | |
| Disbursements | (900) | 168.0 ÷ 160.0 = 1.05000 | (945) | |
| Ending balance, adjusted | | | $ 854 | |
| Ending balance, actual | $ 800 | | (800) | |
| Purchasing power loss | | | | $(54) |

In the above calculation, note that the receipts and disbursements are adjusted from the *average* price level during the year (*160.0*) to the ending price level (168.0). Because the receipts and disbursements were assumed to have occurred uniformly throughout the year, the average price level is used to approximate the price level at the time each receipt and disbursement took place. If receipts and disbursements do not occur uniformly, then each receipt and each disbursement must be adjusted separately from the price index at the time of the receipt or disbursement to the price index at year-end.

**Nonmonetary Assets.** Assets that have fluctuating prices are called **nonmonetary assets.** In other words, nonmonetary assets include all assets other than monetary assets. The prices at which nonmonetary assets may be bought and sold tend to increase or decrease over time as the general price level increases or decreases. Therefore, as the general price level changes, investments in nonmonetary assets tend to retain the amounts of purchasing power originally invested. As a result, on historical cost/constant purchasing power balance sheets, nonmonetary assets are adjusted to reflect changes in the price level that occurred since the nonmonetary assets were acquired.

For example, assume that $500 was invested in land (a nonmonetary asset) at the end of 1982 and the investment was held throughout 1990. During this time, the general price index increased from 96.0 to 168.0. The historical cost/constant purchasing power balance sheets would disclose the following amounts:

| Asset | December 31, 1982 Historical Cost/Constant Purchasing Power Balance Sheet (*a*) | Price Index Factor for Adjustment to December 31, 1990 | December 31, 1990 Historical Cost/Constant Purchasing Power Balance Sheet (*a* × *b*) |
|---|---|---|---|
| Land . . . . | $500 | 168.0 ÷ 96.0 = 1.75000 | $875 |

The $875 shown as the investment in land at the end of 1990 has the same amount of general purchasing power as did $500 at the end of 1982. Thus, no change in general purchasing power is recognized from holding the land.

### The Impact of General Price Changes on Liabilities and Stockholders' Equity

The effect of general price-level changes on liabilities depends on the nature of the liability. Most liabilities are monetary items, but stockholders' equity and a few liabilities are nonmonetary items.[2]

**Monetary Liabilities.** Obligations that are fixed in terms of the amount owed are called **monetary liabilities.** The number of dollars to be paid does not change regardless of changes in the general price level. Since the amount of monetary liabilities owed does not change when price levels change, monetary liabilities are not adjusted for price-level changes.

[2] Depending on its nature, preferred stock may be treated as a monetary item. If so, it is an exception to the general rule that stockholders' equity items are nonmonetary items.

**Purchasing Power Gains and Losses Result from Owing Monetary Liabilities.** A company with monetary liabilities outstanding during a period of general price-level change experiences a **purchasing power gain or loss**. Assume, for example, that a note payable for $300 was outstanding on December 31, 1989, when the price index was 150.0. On April 5, 1990, when the price index was 157.0, a $700 increase in the note resulted in a $1,000 balance that remained outstanding throughout the rest of 1990. On December 31, 1990, the price index was 168.0. On the historical cost/constant purchasing power balance sheet for December 31, 1990, the note payable is reported at $1,000. The purchasing power gain or loss during 1990 is calculated as follows:

| | Nominal Dollar Amounts | Price Index Factor for Restatement to December 31, 1990 | Restated to December 31, 1990 | Gain or (Loss) |
|---|---|---|---|---|
| Beginning balance . . . . . . | $ 300 | 168.0 ÷ 150.0 = 1.12000 | $ 336 | |
| April 5 increase. . . . . . . . | 700 | 168.0 ÷ 157.0 = 1.07006 | 749 | |
| Ending balance, adjusted . . | | | $ 1,085 | |
| Ending balance, actual . . . | $1,000 | | (1,000) | |
| Purchasing power gain . . . | | | | $85 |

Stated in terms of general purchasing power at year-end, the amount borrowed was $1,085. Since the company can pay the note with $1,000, the $85 difference is a gain in general purchasing power earned by the firm. On the other hand, if the general price index had decreased during 1990, the monetary liability would have resulted in a general purchasing power loss.

To determine a company's total purchasing power gain or loss during a year, the accountant must analyze each monetary asset and each monetary liability. The final gain or loss is then described as *the purchasing power gain (or loss) on net monetary items owned or owed.*

**Nonmonetary Liabilities and Stockholders' Equity.** Obligations that are not fixed in amount are called **nonmonetary liabilities**. The amount needed to satisfy a nonmonetary liability tends to change with changes in the general price level. For example, product warranties may require that a manufacturer pay for repairs and replacements for a specified period of time after the product is sold. The amount of money required to make the repairs or replacements tends to change with changes in the general price level. As a result, there is no purchasing power gain or loss associated with such warranties. Further, the historical cost/constant purchasing power balance sheet amount of such a nonmonetary liability must be adjusted to reflect changes in the general price index that occur after the liability comes into existence. Stockholders' equity items, with the possible exception of preferred stock, are also nonmonetary items. Hence, they also must be adjusted for changes in the general price index.

Illustration H–3 summarizes the impact of general price-level changes on monetary and nonmonetary items. The illustration shows the adjustments made to prepare a historical cost/constant purchasing power balance sheet.

**Illustration H–3**
**The effect of price changes on monetary and nonmonetary items**

| Financial Statement Item | When the General Price Level Rises (inflation) Balance Sheet Adjustment Required | Income Statement Gain or Loss | When the General Price Level Falls (deflation) Balance Sheet Adjustment Required | Income Statement Gain or Loss |
|---|---|---|---|---|
| Monetary assets | No | Loss | No | Gain |
| Nonmonetary assets | Yes | None | Yes | None |
| Monetary liabilities | No | Gain | No | Loss |
| Nonmonetary equities and liabilities | Yes | None | Yes | None |

It also shows what purchasing power gains and losses are recognized on a constant purchasing power income statement.

### Historical Cost/Constant Purchasing Power Accounting Fails to Report Current Values

As we said before, prices do not all change at the same rate. In fact, when the general price level is rising, some specific prices may be falling. If this were not so, if prices all changed at the same rate, then historical cost/constant purchasing power accounting would report current values on the financial statements.

For example, suppose that a company purchased land for $50,000 on January 1, 1989, when the general price index was 130.0. Then the price level increased until December 1990, when the price index was 168.0. A historical cost/constant purchasing power balance sheet for this company on December 31, 1990, would report the land at $50,000 × 168.0/130.0 = $64,615. If all prices increased at the same rate during that period, the price of the land would have increased from $50,000 to $64,615, and the company's historical cost/constant purchasing power balance sheet would coincidentally disclose the land at its current value.

However, since all prices do not change at the same rate, the current value of the land may differ substantially from the historical cost/constant dollar amount of $64,615. For example, assume that the company had the land appraised and determined that its current value on December 31, 1990, was $80,000. The difference between the original purchase price of $50,000 and the current value of $80,000 is explained as follows:

| | | |
|---|---|---|
| Unrealized holding gain | $80,000 − $64,615 = | $15,385 |
| Adjustment for general price-level increase | $64,615 − $50,000 = | 14,615 |
| | | $30,000 |

In that case, the historical cost/constant purchasing power balance sheet would report land at $64,615, which is $15,385 ($80,000 − $64,615) less than its current value. This illustrates an important fact about historical cost/constant purchasing power accounting; it does not attempt to report current value.

Rather, historical cost/constant purchasing power accounting restates original transaction prices into equivalent amounts of current, *general* purchasing power. Only if current, *specific* purchasing power were the basis of valuation would the balance sheet display current values.

## Current Cost Accounting

Explain the difference between current costs and historical costs stated in constant purchasing power amounts.
(L. O. 4)

### Current Costs on the Income Statement

When the **current cost** approach to accounting is used, the reported amount of each expense is the number of dollars that would be required, at the time the expense was incurred, to acquire the resources consumed. For example, assume that the annual sales of a company included an item that was sold in May for $1,500. The item had been acquired on January 1 for $500. Also, suppose that in May, at the time of the sale, the cost to replace this item was $700. Then, the annual current cost income statement would show sales of $1,500 less cost of goods sold of $700. In other words, when an asset is acquired and then held for a time before it expires, the historical cost of the asset usually is different from its current cost at the time it expires. *Current cost accounting* measures the reported amount of expense at the time the asset expires.

The result of measuring expenses in terms of current costs is that revenue is matched with the current (at the time of the sale) cost of the resources that were used to earn the revenue. Thus, operating profit is not greater than zero unless revenues are large enough to replace all of the resources that were consumed in the process of producing those revenues. Therefore, the operating profit figure is an important (and improved) basis for evaluating the effectiveness of operating activities.

### Current Costs on the Balance Sheet

On the balance sheet, current cost accounting reports assets at the amounts that would have to be paid to purchase them as of the balance sheet date. Liabilities are reported at the amounts that would have to be paid to satisfy the liabilities as of the balance sheet date. Note that this valuation basis is similar to historical cost/constant purchasing power accounting in that a distinction exists between monetary and nonmonetary assets and liabilities. Monetary assets and liabilities are fixed in amount regardless of price changes. Therefore, monetary assets are not adjusted for price changes. But all of the nonmonetary items must be evaluated at each balance sheet date to determine the best estimate of current cost.

For a moment, think about the large variety of assets reported on balance sheets. Given that there are so many different kinds of assets, you should not be surprised that accountants have difficulty obtaining reliable estimates of current costs. In some cases, specific price indexes provide the most reliable source of current cost information. In other cases, where an asset is not new and has been partially depreciated, its current cost may be estimated by determining the cost to acquire a similar but new asset. Depreciation on the old asset is then based on the current cost of the new asset. Clearly, the accountant's professional judgment is an important factor in developing current cost data.

## Disclosing the Effects of Changing Prices

At the present time, the FASB encourages but does not require companies to disclose information about the effects of changing prices. The recommended disclosures include a five-year summary of financial statement items which has been adjusted for general changes in purchasing power. Some of the items recommended for disclosure include:

*a.* Net sales and other operating revenues.
*b.* Income from continuing operations on a current cost basis.
*c.* Purchasing power gain or loss on net monetary items.
*d.* Increase or decrease in the current cost or lower recoverable amount of inventory and property, plant, and equipment, net of inflation.
*e.* Net assets at year-end on a current cost basis.
*f.* Income per common share from continuing operations on a current cost basis.
*g.* Cash dividends declared per common share.
*h.* Market price per common share at year-end.[3]

## Summary of the Appendix in Terms of Learning Objectives

**1.** Conventional financial statements report transactions in terms of the historical number of dollars received or paid. Therefore, the statements are not adjusted to reflect general price-level changes or changes in the specific prices of the items reported.

**2.** To measure the effect of price changes for a group of items, you should estimate the relative quantities sold of the items in the market basket. Then, you calculate the total price of the entire market basket in each period. A price index expresses the market basket's price each period as a percentage of the price in a base period.

**3.** To restate a historical cost/nominal dollar cost in constant purchasing power terms, you multiply the nominal dollar cost by a factor that represents the change in the general price level since the cost was incurred. On the balance sheet, monetary assets and liabilities should not be adjusted for changes in prices. However, purchasing power gains or losses result from holding monetary assets and owing monetary liabilities during a period of general price changes.

**4.** Historical costs stated in constant purchasing power amounts are adjusted for changes in the general price level since the costs were incurred. By comparison, current costs on the balance sheet are the dollar amounts that would be required to purchase the assets at the balance sheet date. On the income statement, current costs are the dollar amounts that would be necessary to acquire the consumed assets on the date they were consumed.

---

[3] FASB, *Accounting Standards—Current Text* (Norwalk, Conn., 1988), sec. C28.103–104. Originally published as FASB, *Statement of Financial Accounting Standards No. 89,* December 1986. Copyright © by the Financial Accounting Standards Board, Norwalk, Conn., U.S.A. Quoted (or excerpted) with permission. Copies of the complete documents are available from the FASB.

## Glossary

Define or explain the words and phrases listed in the appendix Glossary. (L. O. 5)

**Current cost** in general, the cost that would be required to acquire (or replace) an asset or service at the present time. On the income statement, the numbers of dollars that would be required, at the time the expense is incurred, to acquire the resources consumed. On the balance sheet, the amounts that would have to be paid to replace the assets or satisfy the liabilities as of the balance sheet date. p. 1232

**Current cost accounting** an accounting system that uses specific price-level indexes (and other means) to develop financial statements that report items such as assets and expenses in terms of the costs to acquire or replace those assets or services at the present time. pp. 1227, 1232–33

**Deflation** a general decrease in the prices paid for goods and services. p. 1224

**General price-level index** a measure of the changing purchasing power of a dollar, spent for a very broad range of items; for example, the Consumer Price Index for All Urban Consumers. p. 1226

**Historical cost/constant purchasing power accounting** an accounting system that adjusts historical cost/nominal dollar financial statements for changes in the general purchasing power of the dollar. pp. 1227–31

**Historical cost/nominal dollar financial statements** conventional financial statements that disclose revenues, expenses, assets, liabilities, and owners' equity in terms of the historical monetary units exchanged at the time the transactions occurred. p. 1227

**Inflation** a general increase in the prices paid for goods and services. p. 1224

**Monetary assets** money or claims to receive a fixed amount of money; the number of dollars to be received does not change regardless of changes in the purchasing power of the dollar. pp. 1227–28

**Monetary liabilities** fixed amounts that are owed; the number of dollars to be paid does not change regardless of changes in the general price level. pp. 1229–30

**Nonmonetary assets** assets that are not claims to a fixed number of monetary units, the prices of which therefore tend to fluctuate with changes in the general price level. p. 1229

**Nonmonetary liabilities** obligations that are not fixed in terms of the number of monetary units needed to satisfy them, and that therefore tend to fluctuate in amount with changes in the general price level. pp. 1230–31

**Price index** a measure of the changes in prices of a particular market basket of goods and/or services. pp. 1225–26

**Purchasing power gain or loss** the gain or loss that results from holding monetary assets and/or owing monetary liabilities during a period in which the general price level changes. p. 1230

**Specific price-level index** an indicator of the changing purchasing power of a dollar spent for items in a category of items that includes a much narrower range of goods and services than does a general price index. p. 1226

## Questions for Class Discussion

1. Some people argue that conventional financial statements fail to adequately account for inflation. What is the general problem with conventional financial statements that generates this argument?
2. During a period of inflation, is it possible for the prices of specific items to fall? Why or why not?
3. Explain the difference between an *average* change in per unit prices and a *weighted-average* change in per unit prices.
4. What is the significance of the base year in constructing a price index? How is the base year chosen?
5. What is the difference between a specific price index and a general price index?
6. What is the fundamental difference in the price-level adjustments made under current cost accounting and under historical cost/constant purchasing power accounting?
7. What are historical cost/nominal dollar financial statements?
8. What is the difference between monetary assets and nonmonetary assets?
9. What is the difference between monetary liabilities and nonmonetary liabilities? Give examples of both.
10. If the monetary assets held by a firm exceed its monetary liabilities throughout a period in which prices are rising, which results: a purchasing power gain or loss? What if monetary liabilities exceed monetary assets during a period in which prices are falling?
11. If accountants preferred to display current values in the financial statements, would they use historical cost/constant purchasing power accounting or current cost accounting?
12. Describe the meaning of *operating profit* under a current cost accounting system.
13. "The distinction between monetary assets and nonmonetary assets is just as important for current cost accounting as it is for historical cost/constant purchasing power accounting." Is this statement true? Why?
14. What are some of the items the FASB recommends for disclosure concerning the effects of price changes?

## Exercises

**Exercise H–1**
**Calculating inflation rates**
(L. O. 2)

Market basket No. 1 consists of 2 units of A, 5 units of B, and 1 unit of D. Market basket No. 2 consists of 3 units of B, 4 units of C, and 2 units of D. The per unit prices of each item during 1990 and during 1991 were as follows:

| Item | 1990 Price per Unit | 1991 Price per Unit |
|---|---|---|
| A . . | $3.00 | $2.60 |
| B . . | 5.00 | 5.40 |
| C . . | 6.00 | 7.00 |
| D . . | 2.00 | 1.80 |

*Required*

Compute the annual rate of inflation for market basket No. 1 and for market basket No. 2. (Round your answers to the nearest 1/10%.)

**Exercise H–2**
**Constructing a price index**
(L. O. 2)

The following total prices of a specified market basket were calculated for each of the years 1987 through 1991:

| Year | Total Price |
|---|---|
| 1987 . . | $20,300 |
| 1988 . . | 30,400 |
| 1989 . . | 35,800 |
| 1990 . . | 40,500 |
| 1991 . . | 50,100 |

*Required*

1. Using 1989 as the base year, prepare a price index for the five-year period. (Round your answers to the nearest 1/10%.)
2. Convert the index from a 1989 base year to a 1991 base year.

**Exercise H–3**
**Adjusting costs for historical cost/constant purchasing power statements**
(L. O. 3)

A company's plant and equipment consisted of land purchased in late 1985 for $350,000, a building purchased in late 1987 for $470,000, and equipment purchased in late 1989 for $85,000. The general price index for December of the years 1985 through 1991 is as follows:

| | |
|---|---|
| 1985 . . . . | 100.0 |
| 1986 . . . . | 110.0 |
| 1987 . . . . | 120.0 |
| 1988 . . . . | 122.0 |
| 1989 . . . . | 125.0 |
| 1990 . . . . | 150.0 |
| 1991 . . . . | 160.5 |

*Required*

1. Assuming the above price index adequately represents end-of-year price levels, calculate the amount of each cost that would be shown on a historical cost/constant purchasing power balance sheet for (*a*) December 31, 1990, and (*b*) December 31, 1991. Ignore any accumulated depreciation.
2. Would the historical cost/constant purchasing power income statement for 1991 disclose any purchasing power gain or loss as a consequence of holding the above assets? If so, how much?

**Exercise H–4**
**Classifying monetary and nonmonetary items**
(L. O. 3)

Determine whether the following items are monetary or nonmonetary items.

1. Common stock.
2. Retained earnings.
3. Merchandise.
4. Prepaid rent.
5. Prepaid insurance.
6. Salaries payable.
7. Goodwill.
8. Furniture and fixtures.

9. Accounts payable.
10. Product warranties liability.
11. Trademarks.
12. Savings accounts.
13. Notes receivable.
14. Contributed capital in excess of par value, common stock.

**Exercise H–5**
**Calculating amounts for current cost statements**
(L. O. 4)

A company made the following purchases of land: in 1988 at a cost of $60,000, and in 1989 at a cost of $35,000. What is the current cost of the land purchases in *(a)* 1990 and *(b)* 1991, given the following specific price index for land costs? (Round your answers to the nearest whole dollar.)

| | |
|---|---|
| 1988 . . . . | 80.0 |
| 1989 . . . . | 100.0 |
| 1990 . . . . | 95.0 |
| 1991 . . . . | 110.0 |

**Exercise H–6**
**Calculating general purchasing power gain or loss**
(L. O. 3)

Calculate the general purchasing power gain or loss in 1991 given the following information:

| Time Period | Price Index |
|---|---|
| December 1990 . . . . . . . | 125.0 |
| Average during 1991 . . . . | 135.0 |
| December 1991 . . . . . . . | 162.0 |

*a.* The cash balance on December 31, 1990, was $2,500. During 1991, cash sales occurred uniformly throughout the year and amounted to $20,500. Payments of expenses also occurred evenly throughout the year and amounted to $15,500. Accounts payable of $5,200 were paid in December.

*b.* Accounts payable amounted to $3,000 on December 31, 1990. Additional accounts payable amounting to $4,600 were recorded evenly throughout 1991. The only payment of accounts during the year was $5,200 in late December.

## Problems

**Problem H–1**
**Constructing and using a price index**
(L. O. 2)

The costs of purchasing a common "market basket" in each of several years are as follows:

| Year | Cost of Market Basket |
|---|---|
| 1984 . . | $ 75,000 |
| 1985 . . | 82,500 |
| 1986 . . | 87,700 |
| 1987 . . | 96,400 |
| 1988 . . | 108,400 |
| 1989 . . | 105,700 |
| 1990 . . | 113,300 |
| 1991 . . | 127,100 |

*Required*

1. Construct a price index using 1987 as the base year. (Round each index number to 1/10%.)
2. Using the index constructed in Requirement 1, what was the percent increase in prices from 1984 to 1990?
3. Using the index constructed in Requirement 1, how many dollars in 1991 does it take to have the same purchasing power as $1 in 1986?
4. Using the index constructed in Requirement 1, if $90,000 were invested in land during 1985 and $60,000 were invested in land during 1987, what would be reported as the total land investment on a constant purchasing power balance sheet prepared in 1991? What would your answer be if the investments were in U.S. long-term bonds rather than in land?

**Problem H–2**
**Adjusting costs to historical cost/constant purchasing power amounts**
(L. O. 3)

Maxima Company purchased machinery for $675,000 on December 30, 1987. The equipment was expected to last eight years and have no salvage value; straight-line depreciation was to be used. The equipment was sold on December 31, 1991, for $525,000. End-of-year general price index numbers during this period of time were as follows:

| | |
|---|---|
| 1987 . . . . | 195.0 |
| 1988 . . . . | 252.8 |
| 1989 . . . . | 272.4 |
| 1990 . . . . | 310.5 |
| 1991 . . . . | 330.2 |

*Required*

(Round all answers to the nearest whole dollar.)

1. What should be presented for the equipment and accumulated depreciation on a historical cost/constant purchasing power balance sheet dated December 31, 1989? Hint: Depreciation is the total amount of cost that has been allocated to expense. Therefore, the price index numbers that are used to adjust the nominal dollar cost of the asset should also be used to adjust the nominal dollar amount of depreciation.
2. How much depreciation expense should be shown on the historical cost/constant purchasing power income statement for 1990?
3. How much depreciation expense should be shown on the historical cost/constant purchasing power income statement for 1991?
4. How much gain on the sale of equipment would be reported on the historical cost/nominal dollar income statement for 1991?
5. After adjusting the equipment's cost and accumulated depreciation to the end-of-1991 price level, how much gain in (loss of) purchasing power was realized by the sale of the equipment?

**Problem H–3**
**Calculating purchasing power gain or loss**
(L. O. 3)

Brookes Express had three monetary items during 1991: cash, accounts receivable, and accounts payable. The changes in these accounts during the year were as follows:

| | |
|---|---|
| Cash: | |
| Beginning balance | $ 10,000 |
| Cash proceeds from sale of surplus equipment (in mid-January 1991) | 15,700 |
| Cash receipts from customers (spread evenly throughout the year) | 95,300 |
| Payments of accounts payable (spread evenly throughout the year) | (51,200) |
| Payments of other cash expenses during March 1991 | (20,400) |
| Dividends declared and paid in mid-September 1991 | (18,000) |
| Ending balance | $ 31,400 |
| Accounts receivable: | |
| Beginning balance | $ 16,500 |
| Sales to customers (spread evenly throughout the year) | 105,200 |
| Cash receipts from customers (spread evenly throughout the year) | (95,300) |
| Ending balance | $ 26,400 |
| Accounts payable: | |
| Beginning balance | $ 18,800 |
| Merchandise purchases (spread evenly throughout the year) | 42,500 |
| Special purchase near end of December 1991 | 14,000 |
| Payments of accounts payable (spread evenly throughout the year) | (51,200) |
| Ending balance | $ 24,100 |

General price index numbers at the end of 1990 and during 1991 are as follows:

| | |
|---|---|
| December 1990 | 185.0 |
| January 1991 | 188.0 |
| March 1991 | 192.7 |
| September 1991 | 195.7 |
| December 1991 | 197.0 |
| Average for 1991 | 193.0 |

*Required*

Calculate the general purchasing power gain or loss experienced by Brookes Express in 1991. (Round all amounts to the nearest whole dollar.)

**Problem H–4**
**Historical cost/nominal dollars, historical cost/constant purchasing power, and current costs**
(L. O. 1, 4)

Krenidon, Incorporated, purchased a tract of land for $150,000 in 1984 when the general price index was 85.5. At the same time, a price index for land values in the area of Krenidon's tract was 81.5. In 1985, when the general price index was 90.2 and the specific price index for land was 95.2, Krenidon bought another tract of land for $210,000. In late 1991, the general price index is 175.3, and the price index for land values is 162.5.

*Required*

1. In preparing a balance sheet at the end of 1991, what amount should be shown for land on:
   *a.* A historical cost/nominal dollar balance sheet.
   *b.* A historical cost/constant purchasing power balance sheet.
   *c.* A current cost balance sheet.
   (Round all amounts to the nearest whole dollar.)
2. In Krenidon, Incorporated's December 1991 meeting of the board of directors, one director insists that Krenidon has earned a gain in purchasing power as a result of owning the land. A second director argues that there could not have been a purchasing power gain or loss since land is a nonmonetary asset. Which director do you think is correct? Explain your answer.

## Alternate Problems

**Problem H–1A**
**Constructing and using a price index**
(L. O. 2)

The costs of purchasing a common "market basket" in each of several years are as follows:

| Year | Cost of Market Basket |
|---|---|
| 1984 . . | $ 85,000 |
| 1985 . . | 89,850 |
| 1986 . . | 95,300 |
| 1987 . . | 94,750 |
| 1988 . . | 110,000 |
| 1989 . . | 115,400 |
| 1990 . . | 112,760 |
| 1991 . . | 125,300 |

*Required*

1. Construct a price index using 1985 as the base year. (Round each index number to 1/10%.)
2. Using the index constructed in Requirement 1, what was the percent increase in prices from 1987 to 1991?
3. Using the index constructed in Requirement 1, how many dollars in 1991 does it take to have the same purchasing power as $1 in 1984?
4. Using the index constructed in Requirement 1, if $85,000 were invested in land during 1986 and $95,000 were invested in land during 1989, what would be reported as the total land investment on a constant purchasing power balance sheet prepared in 1990? What would your answer be if the investments were in U.S. long-term bonds rather than in land?

**Problem H–2A**
**Adjusting costs to historical cost/constant purchasing power amounts**
(L. O. 3)

Bowldt Corporation purchased machinery for $585,000 on December 30, 1987. The equipment was expected to last nine years and have no salvage value; straight-line depreciation was to be used. The equipment was sold on December 31, 1991, for $435,000. End-of-year general price index numbers during this period of time were as follows:

| | |
|---|---|
| 1987 . . . . | 98.2 |
| 1988 . . . . | 125.5 |
| 1989 . . . . | 135.4 |
| 1990 . . . . | 155.6 |
| 1991 . . . . | 168.3 |

*Required*

(Round all answers to the nearest whole dollar.)

1. What should be presented for the equipment and accumulated depreciation on a historical cost/constant purchasing power balance sheet dated December 31, 1989? Hint: Depreciation is the total amount of cost that has been allocated to expense. Therefore, the price index numbers that are used to adjust the nominal dollar cost of the asset should also be used to adjust the nominal dollar amount of depreciation.
2. How much depreciation expense should be shown on the historical cost/constant purchasing power income statement for 1990?

3. How much depreciation expense should be shown on the historical cost/constant purchasing power income statement for 1991?
4. How much gain on the sale of equipment would be reported on the historical cost/nominal dollar income statement for 1991?
5. After adjusting the equipment's cost and accumulated depreciation to the end-of-1991 price level, how much gain in (loss of) general purchasing power was realized by the sale of the equipment?

**Problem H–3A**
**Calculating purchasing power gain or loss**
(L. O. 3)

Eastbend Drafters had three monetary items during 1991: cash, accounts receivable, and accounts payable. The changes in these accounts during the year were as follows:

| | |
|---|---|
| Cash: | |
| Beginning balance | $ 20,300 |
| Cash proceeds from sale of land (in mid-January 1991) | 32,450 |
| Cash receipts from customers (spread evenly throughout the year) | 215,620 |
| Payments of accounts payable (spread evenly throughout the year) | (120,050) |
| Dividends declared and paid during March 1991 | (50,090) |
| Payments of other cash expenses in mid-September 1991 | (41,000) |
| Ending balance | $ 57,230 |
| Accounts receivable: | |
| Beginning balance | $ 36,400 |
| Sales to customers (spread evenly throughout the year) | 240,020 |
| Cash receipts from customers (spread evenly throughout the year) | (215,620) |
| Ending balance | $ 60,800 |
| Accounts payable: | |
| Beginning balance | $ 42,750 |
| Merchandise purchases (spread evenly throughout the year) | 95,300 |
| Special purchase near end of December 1991 | 28,200 |
| Payments of accounts payable (spread evenly throughout the year) | (120,050) |
| Ending balance | $ 46,200 |

General price index numbers at the end of 1990 and during 1991 are as follows:

| | |
|---|---|
| December 1990 | 106.5 |
| January 1991 | 107.8 |
| March 1991 | 110.2 |
| September 1991 | 115.3 |
| December 1991 | 118.0 |
| Average for 1991 | 112.8 |

*Required*

Calculate the general purchasing power gain or loss experienced by Eastbend Drafters in 1991. (Round all amounts to the nearest whole dollar.)

**Problem H–4A**
**Historical cost/nominal dollars, historical cost/constant purchasing power, and current costs**
(L. O. 1, 4)

Olmos Company purchased a tract of land for $180,000 in 1983 when the general price index was 84.2. At the same time, a price index for land values in the area of Olmos's tract was 90.5. In 1984, when the general price index was 88.6 and the specific price index for land was 102.3, Olmos bought another tract of land for $240,000. In late 1991, the general price index is 160.2, and the price index for land values is 245.6.

*Required*

1. In preparing a balance sheet at the end of 1991, what amount should be shown for land on:
   *a.* A historical cost/nominal dollar balance sheet.
   *b.* A historical cost/constant purchasing power balance sheet.
   *c.* A current cost balance sheet.
   (Round all amounts to the nearest whole dollar.)
2. In Olmos Company's December 1991 meeting of the board of directors, one director insists that Olmos had incurred a loss of purchasing power as a result of owning the land. A second director argues that there could not have been a purchasing power gain or loss since land is a nonmonetary asset. Which director do you think is correct? Explain your answer.

## Provocative Problems

**Provocative Problem H–1**
**Laguna Corporation**
**Historical cost/constant dollar statements**
(L. O. 3)

Although Laguna Corporation is not required to present financial information adjusted for price changes, the company has often been willing to consider new, innovative ways of reporting to its stockholders. For example, it has presented supplemental historical cost/constant dollar financial statements in its annual reports. The constant dollar balance sheets of Laguna Corporation for December 31, 1990, and 1991, were as follows:

**LAGUNA CORPORATION**
**Historical Cost/Constant Dollar Balance Sheets**

| | As Presented on December 31, 1991 | As Presented on December 31, 1990 |
|---|---|---|
| **Assets** | | |
| Cash | $ 45,000 | $ 20,000 |
| Accounts receivable | 103,000 | 60,000 |
| Note receivable | 30,000 | — |
| Inventory | 35,672 | 22,690 |
| Equipment | 188,000 | 164,240 |
| Accumulated depreciation | (53,714) | (23,463) |
| Land | 166,930 | 117,314 |
| Total assets | $514,888 | $360,781 |
| **Liabilities and Stockholders' Equity** | | |
| Accounts payable | $ 72,000 | $ 21,000 |
| Notes payable | 55,000 | 24,000 |
| Common stock | 268,571 | 234,629 |
| Retained earnings | 119,317 | 81,152 |
| Total liabilities and stockholders' equity | $514,888 | $360,781 |

A new member of Laguna Corporation's board of directors has expressed interest in the relationship between historical cost/constant dollar statements and historical cost/nominal dollar statements. The board member understands that constant dollar statements are derived from nominal dollar statements, but wonders if the process can be reversed. Specifically, you are asked to show how the historical cost/constant dollar balance sheets for December 31, 1990, and 1991, could be restated back into nominal dollar statements.

*Additional Information*

1. The outstanding stock was issued in January 1990, and the company's equipment was purchased at that time. The equipment has no salvage value and is being depreciated over seven years.
2. The note receivable was acquired on June 30, 1991.
3. Notes payable consists of two notes, one for $24,000 which was issued on January 1, 1990, and the other for $31,000 which was issued on January 1, 1991.
4. The Land account includes two parcels, one of which was acquired for $100,000 on January 1, 1990. The remaining parcel was acquired in June 1991.
5. Selected numbers from a general price-level index are:

| | |
|---|---|
| January 1990 . . . . . . . . . . . . . . . | 175.0 |
| June 1990 (also average for 1990) . . . . | 195.0 |
| December 1990 . . . . . . . . . . . . . . | 205.3 |
| June 1991 (also average for 1991) . . . . | 220.0 |
| December 1991 . . . . . . . . . . . . . . | 235.0 |

6. The inventory at the end of each year was acquired evenly throughout that year.
7. Hint: If all other accounts are properly adjusted from constant dollars back to nominal dollars, the correct retained earnings balance can be determined simply by "plugging" the amount necessary to make the balance sheet balance.

# I Answers to Objective Review Questions

**Chapter 1**

1. *c*
2. *e*
3. *d*
4. *c*
5. *d*
6. *a*

**Chapter 2**

1. *a*
2. *e*
3. *c*
4. *c*
5. *a*

**Chapter 3**

1. *c*
2. *d*
3. *e*
4. *c*
5. *b*

**Chapter 4**

1. *d*
2. *b*
3. *c*
4. *d*
5. *d*
6. *c*

**Chapter 5**

1. *d*
2. *c*
3. *d*
4. *e*

**Chapter 6**

1. *c*
2. *e*
3. *a*
4. *e*

**Chapter 7**

1. *b*
2. *d*
3. *c*
4. *c*
5. *d*

**Chapter 8**

1. *b*
2. *b*
3. *a*
4. *c*
5. *d*

**Chapter 9**

1. *d*
2. *c*
3. *b*
4. *e*
5. *b*
6. *c*

**Chapter 10**

1. *d*
2. *d*
3. *e*
4. *e*
5. *c*

**Chapter 11**

1. *a*
2. *b*
3. *d*
4. *c*
5. *a*

**Chapter 12**

1. *e*
2. *c*
3. *c*
4. *e*
5. *b*
6. *b*

**Chapter 13**

1. *d*
2. *e*
3. *e*
4. *a*

**Chapter 14**

1. *e*
2. *d*
3. *a*
4. *c*

**Chapter 15**

1. *c*
2. *c*
3. *e*
4. *d*
5. *a*

**Chapter 16**

1. *c*
2. *b*
3. *d*
4. *d*
5. *d*

**Chapter 17**

1. *d*
2. *e*
3. *d*
4. *b*
5. *e*
6. *a*

**Chapter 18**

1. *c*
2. *c*
3. *a*
4. *e*

**Chapter 19**

1. *b*
2. *a*
3. *a*
4. *d*
5. *e*

**Chapter 20**

1. *c*
2. *c*
3. *d*
4. *e*

**Chapter 21**

1. *b*
2. *c*
3. *b*
4. *e*
5. *c*

**Chapter 22**

1. *c*
2. *b*
3. *b*
4. *e*
5. *a*

**Chapter 23**

1. *b*
2. *e*
3. *e*
4. *d*
5. *d*
6. *c*

**Chapter 24**

1. *e*
2. *e*
3. *d*
4. *c*
5. *c*
6. *b*

**Chapter 25**

1. *e*
2. *b*
3. *d*
4. *a*

**Chapter 26**

1. *e*
2. *b*
3. *d*
4. *c*
5. *e*

**Chapter 27**

1. *c*
2. *d*
3. *a*
4. *c*
5. *c*

**Chapter 28**

1. *c*
2. *d*
3. *e*
4. *e*
5. *b*
6. *d*
7. *a*

# J Financial Statements and Related Disclosures from Tyler Corporation 1988 Annual Report

# TYLER CORPORATION 1988 ANNUAL REPORT

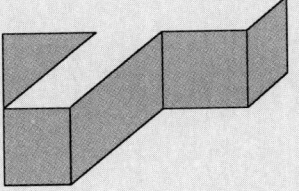

## CORPORATE PROFILE

Tyler Corporation, a multi-industry company headquartered in Dallas, was founded in 1966. The Company provides products and services to industrial customers through three major operating subsidiaries:

- Atlas Powder—The largest manufacturer of commercial and industrial explosives in the U.S.
- Reliance Universal—One of the nation's largest producers of specialty industrial coatings.
- Tyler Pipe—The nation's leading manufacturer of pipe and fittings for drain, waste and vent applications.

Tyler Corporation's primary purpose is to provide superior long-term rewards to shareholders. The statement of the Company's objective designed to achieve this purpose was first published in its 1969 annual report to shareholders and remains that of becoming a large, diversely based industrial enterprise selling products and services to professional buyers, these operations to be executed through a few operating companies carefully selected for two main characteristics: superior return on assets employed and growth probability.

Each operating company seeks to produce profits and to manage its assets to maximize the return on assets employed in its operations. Strong cash flow from operations and occasional divestitures, when considered timely, have allowed major and supplemental acquisitions for growth and diversification, debt repayment, funding of increases in working capital, repurchase of common stock, cash dividend increases and a special dividend in 1988.

In pursuing its diversified-company strategy, Tyler Corporation continues to evaluate different acquisition opportunities. Ideally, newly acquired companies would be approximately the same size as present companies but would operate on different economic cycles. Due to the Company's philosophy of autonomy, proven management is a necessity.

In addition to such major diversifying acquisitions, Tyler Corporation makes supplemental acquisitions designed to strengthen the operating companies. The high prices of major acquisitions in recent years have made this type of expansion more beneficial in the Company's opinion.

At December 31, 1988, Tyler had over 13,000 shareholders. Of the Company's 5,800 employees at year end, approximately 4,100 were shareholders in Tyler Corporation either directly or through participation in Company benefit plans. Directors, officers and other employees beneficially hold approximately 50% of the total shares outstanding.

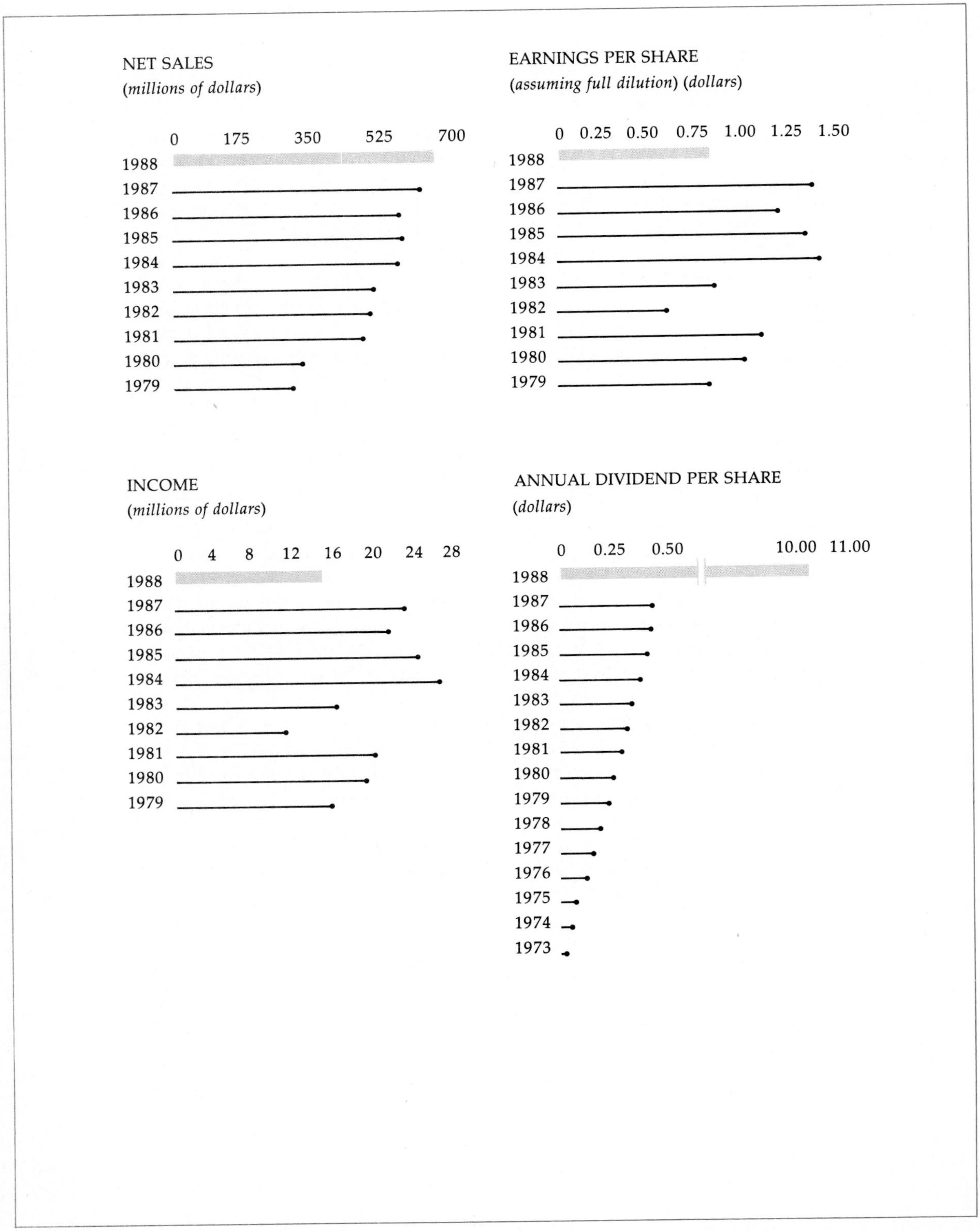
NET SALES
(millions of dollars)
0 175 350 525 700
1988
1987
1986
1985
1984
1983
1982
1981
1980
1979
EARNINGS PER SHARE
(assuming full dilution) (dollars)
0 0.25 0.50 0.75 1.00 1.25 1.50
1988
1987
1986
1985
1984
1983
1982
1981
1980
1979
INCOME
(millions of dollars)
0 4 8 12 16 20 24 28
1988
1987
1986
1985
1984
1983
1982
1981
1980
1979
ANNUAL DIVIDEND PER SHARE
(dollars)
0 0.25 0.50 10.00 11.00
1988
1987
1986
1985
1984
1983
1982
1981
1980
1979
1978
1977
1976
1975
1974
1973

FINANCIAL HIGHLIGHTS

| | 1988 | 1987 | 1988 vs 1987 | Five-Year Compound Growth Rate | Ten-Year Compound Growth Rate |
|---|---|---|---|---|---|
| Earnings per share | **$ .77** | $ 1.33 | −42% | −1% | — |
| Income | **14,575,000** | 23,508,000 | −38% | −2% | −1% |
| Net sales | **664,645,000** | 624,117,000 | + 6% | +5% | +9% |
| Dividend paid per share | **10.235** | .41 | | | |
| Return on average shareholders' equity before extraordinary charge | **16.1%** | 9.3% | | | |
| Return on average shareholders' equity after extraordinary charge | **16.1%** | 6.6% | | | |

*Throughout this report, net sales, income and earnings per share are from continuing operations before extraordinary items unless otherwise noted.*

TEN-YEAR PERFORMANCE SUMMARY
*(millions of dollars)*

| | 1988 | 1987 | 1986 | 1985 | 1984 | 1983 | 1982 | 1981 | 1980 | 1979 |
|---|---|---|---|---|---|---|---|---|---|---|
| Net sales | **$664.6** | 624.1 | 577.1 | 587.1 | 571.1 | 511.5 | 497.1 | 483.8 | 323.7 | 314.1 |
| Operating profits | **$ 47.8** | 58.7 | 52.0 | 58.2 | 65.5 | 48.1 | 39.0 | 54.7 | 41.9 | 39.4 |
| Operating profit margin | **7.2%** | 9.4% | 9.0% | 9.9% | 11.5% | 9.4% | 7.8% | 11.3% | 13.0% | 12.5% |

*In calculating operating profits, contributions to the employees' savings and investment plan, incremental depreciation on write-up of assets, and amortization of goodwill and other intangibles arising from acquisitions are excluded. While this treatment was developed for internal evaluation, management believes it has value for external reporting as well. However, in the Notes to Consolidated Financial Statements, segment operating profits are reduced by the costs mentioned above.*

## LETTER FROM THE CHIEF EXECUTIVE OFFICER

Dear Shareholder:

1988 was a year of dramatic change for Tyler. The Hall-Mark sale was the response to an opportunity to liquidate at a gain what had become a large investment whose continued ownership impeded our financial mobility. We consider Hall-Mark a fine company in an exciting industry, but the required capital dedication was not in our stockholders' best interests long term. The sale made possible the $10 per share dividend paid in August. We consider this a transfer of value, much of which was previously unrecognized in our stock price, from the corporation to its owners. What is left is a smaller, more leveraged company with sufficient cash flow to handle and reduce that immediate leverage and to rebuild our financial readiness to participate in expansion opportunities where reasonably priced.

Meanwhile, our operating picture is mixed. Reliance Universal's current performance is excellent, Atlas Powder's is good and Tyler Pipe's is poor. All of our companies are meeting their challenges with intelligence and hard work. As in the past, all of them will do well over the long haul.

Net sales from continuing operations rose 6% to $665 million from $624 million in the prior year as a result of higher volumes at Reliance Universal and Atlas Powder. Income from continuing operations was 38% lower than in 1987. This poor performance was primarily attributable to higher raw material costs and tough competitive markets which prohibited recovery of costs through higher prices. Per-share earnings fell from $1.33 in 1987 to $.77 in the year just ended.

Earnings comparisons for this year as well as next are made difficult because of the restatement of Hall-Mark's results into a discontinued operations category. This restatement eliminates from our historical picture all of Hall-Mark's results including the considerable interest expense associated with that company. Much of that interest expense continues since most of the sale proceeds were used to pay the special dividend instead of to retire debt.

Atlas Powder experienced a moderate sales gain for the year driven by strong advances in nonelectric blasting caps and distribution operations. Operating profit rose slightly, but operating margin was squeezed by rising raw material and production costs.

The specialty coatings division at Reliance Universal fueled a solid sales gain. Higher raw material costs, without corresponding price increases, restricted operating profit growth and resulted in a lower operating margin.

Lower volumes due to depressed nonresidential construction markets and higher raw material costs caused a substantial reduction in operating profit at Tyler Pipe. The company continued to battle these negative factors in its environment with cost-savings programs and strategies to enhance penetration in specific markets.

In November we hosted the sixteenth annual Tyler Cup Invitational, a two-mile run for senior corporate officers designed to promote physical fitness programs in the business community. The 1988 event attracted more than 150 participants from all over the country who ran to demonstrate their belief and interest in the benefits of aerobic exercise activities.

The company recently announced several management changes.

James E. Russell was promoted to president and chief executive officer of Tyler Pipe Industries, Inc. Mr. Russell joined Tyler Pipe in 1968 and advanced to vice president before moving to Tyler Corporation in 1979. He advanced from controller to senior vice president at Tyler Corporation and returned to Tyler Pipe in 1988 as president and chief operating officer.

Mr. Russell replaced John A. Warner who retired from Tyler Pipe at the end of the year. Mr. Warner was affiliated with Tyler Pipe for 39 years and had been chief executive officer since 1969. Under his guidance, the company established its industry-leadership position and its reputation as one of the most efficient foundries in the United States. Mr. Warner will remain on the Tyler Corporation board of directors.

Also retiring from Tyler Pipe is Glen Uzzel, executive vice president, who retired at the end of 42 years with the company. Mr. Uzzel was elected executive vice president in 1969 after serving as controller and treasurer. Mr. Uzzel's contributions in all areas of the business were invaluable. We are most appreciative of the contribution which both of these individuals made to the progress of Tyler Pipe and Tyler Corporation.

Richard W. Margerison was promoted to executive vice president of Tyler Corporation in January 1989. Associated with the Company from 1977 to 1980, Mr. Margerison rejoined Tyler Corporation in 1985 as vice president and was elected senior vice president in early 1988.

Linda K. Hill was elected controller of Tyler Corporation. Ms. Hill, a CPA, joined the Company in 1982 as a staff accountant and was promoted to assistant controller in 1986.

Following payment of the $10 dividend, the board of directors lowered the annual dividend rate from $.44 to $.06 per share. We hope to increase this modest rate regularly as was our history before the special dividend.

The sale of Hall-Mark Electronics was completed August 2. Proceeds from the sale received so far were approximately $220 million in cash before expenses. We will receive an additional cash payment in 1989.

As we have said elsewhere, the cash content of the profit dollars generated by Tyler Pipe, Reliance and Atlas made possible the buildup of our investment in Hall-Mark as that company expanded greatly during the seven years of our partnership. When we were able to liquidate this investment, the value passed on to our shareholders was in large part the product of our three ongoing companies' performance. It is all the more gratifying that many of the shareholder recipients are also fellow employees. As a result of the reinvestment of their dividends, employee ownership of the Company rose to approximately 50%.

As noted, our leverage increased after the special dividend with our debt/capitalization ratio jumping from 56% to 79%. The untrammeled cash-production capabilities of our ongoing companies will improve that ratio and provide for other opportunities.

The sale of Hall-Mark and the special dividend are now history. We now have a company that is smaller, simpler and, despite temporarily increased leverage, more agile. We think Tyler Corporation is more seaworthy if the economic weather worsens and is positioned to be more acquisitive when the climate justifies increased aggressiveness. Our job, meanwhile, is to improve operating results and to be alert for opportunity.

Because of the accounting presentation and the structural changes cited earlier, quarter-to-quarter earnings comparisons will be unattractive for a while. More important, seasonality and continued weakness in Tyler Pipe's markets will probably cause a loss in first-quarter 1989.

We thank our management teams who continue to demonstrate flexibility and sensitivity to challenging business environments and all of our employees for their industrious service and persevering loyalty.

Yours very truly,

JMcKinney

Joseph F. McKinney
February 7, 1989

ATLAS POWDER

Review of 1988 Operations

Atlas Powder attained a 9% sales gain despite an intensely price competitive market. Strong sales advances were accomplished in nonelectric blasting caps and distribution operations while more mature product areas remained flat.

Operating profit rose slightly, but strong competitive pressures inhibited any significant improvement in pricing. Higher raw material and production costs encountered during the year more than offset any price increases obtained causing operating margin to decline.

Distribution operations realized sales gains in all regions. The company-owned distributorship group was supplemented by one additional operation and contributions from a fledgling operation acquired in 1987. Independent and company-owned distributors combined to provide increased service to customers throughout the county.

The traditional role of the explosives manufacturer continued expanding to incorporate more value-added services. Greater use of bulk explosives during the last few years has created an opportunity for Atlas to provide not only more explosives products but additional services as well. Technical-service capabilities, such as cast blasting, high-speed photography and the Airdek pre-splitting system, have enabled Atlas to expand its role as a supplier and to maintain its premier position in the industry.

Coal producers are the major users of commercial explosives today. During 1988 coal production reached record levels due partially to greater usage by electric utilities because of unseasonably hot summer weather.

Expectations in 1989 for users of commercial explosives, including the coal, quarrying and construction industries, indicate little improvement over the previous year. In this environment Atlas will strive to increase its market penetration in both manufactured and distributed products and to improve profitability through better pricing.

SALES
(*millions of dollars*)

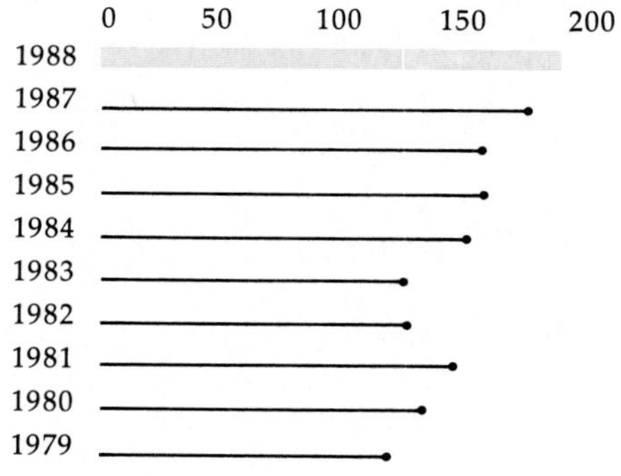


OPERATING PROFIT
(*millions of dollars*)

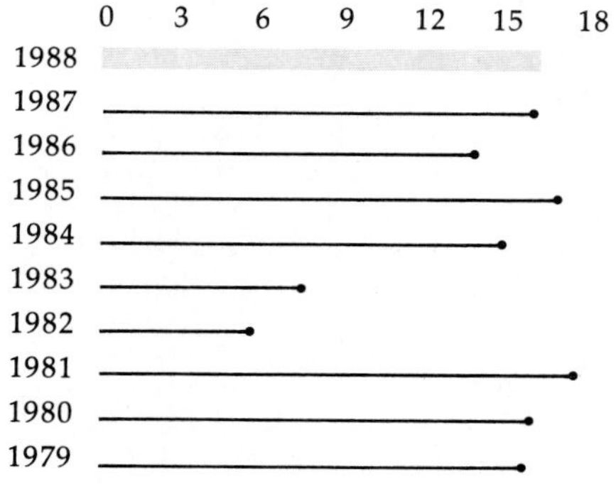

## RELIANCE UNIVERSAL

### Review of 1988 Operations

Reliance Universal achieved sales growth of 13% through expanded unit volume. Higher raw material costs and the inability to pass through these costs limited operating profit growth to 2% and resulted in a lower operating margin.

The specialty coatings division produced most of the sales growth in 1988. Coil coatings used on steel and aluminum for prepainted metal products and paper coatings grew vigorously during the year. Existing operations were aided by the acquisition early in the year of O'Brien Corporation's industrial coatings division. This acquisition provided entry into internal coatings for food containers, a previously untapped area.

The wood coatings division experienced a modest improvement in sales despite another year of declining housing starts. Although kitchen cabinetry and household furniture markets softened in the latter part of the year, the division continued to produce excellent sales results.

While expanding the company's product line, Reliance continued to emphasize improved technology in its existing markets. Special performance coatings that meet the needs of environmental improvement were the focus of its product development. Electron beam curable coatings for wood, ultraviolet light curable coatings for paper and high-speed flexible coil coatings for appliances are examples of such products. Not only are these coatings technologically advanced, but they also meet the well-defined needs of Reliance customers.

In 1989 operating management will seek expansion through increased market share and new product development programs. These programs target both wood and specialty areas as the company fills product needs and continues to broaden its customer base. Reliance's unique combination of practical experience and progressive technology enhances its leadership position in industrial coatings.

SALES
*(millions of dollars)*

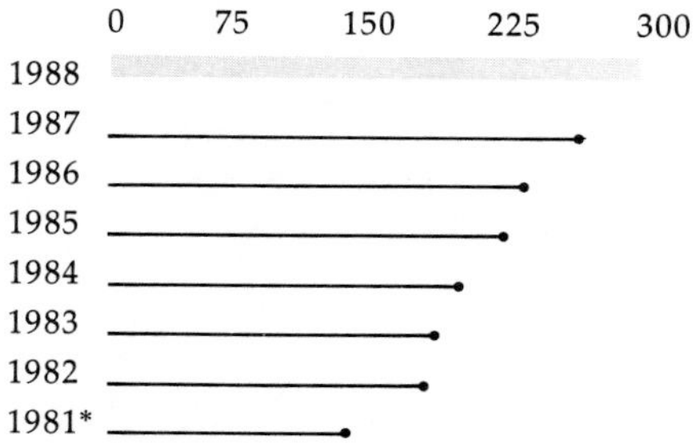


OPERATING PROFIT
*(millions of dollars)*

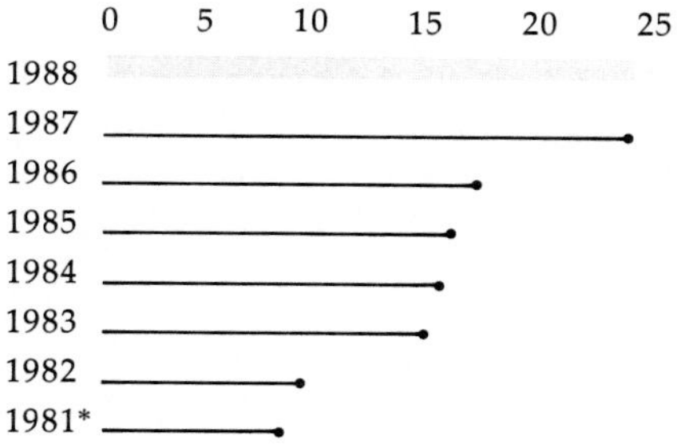


**Partial year; Reliance was acquired in May 1981.*

## TYLER PIPE

### Review of 1988 Operations

Tyler Pipe faced another difficult year in which the level, mix and location of construction spending were not conducive to satisfactory results for the company. In this environment sales declined 5% due to lower volumes across major product lines.

Volume sensitivity, coupled with higher raw material costs, severely depressed operating profit at Tyler Pipe. Both the drain, waste and vent and utilities divisions experienced a shrinkage in volume and a rise in scrap iron costs which resulted in significantly lower margins. Operating profit dropped 61% for the year.

Operating management worked hard to defray the effects of these volume declines. Cost-savings programs instituted during the year were effective and will also carry over into 1989. The company also hopes to benefit from strategies targeted to absorb excess plant capacity while strengthening its presence in specific geographic regions.

Tyler Pipe maintained industry leadership in both the drain, waste and vent and pressure fittings markets for its cast iron products. While certain markets experienced some shrinkage, Tyler Pipe retained its existing customer base and aggressively attempted to expand this base.

Presently, construction analysts do not predict any near-term improvement in commercial and industrial building sectors. If these forecasts are correct, and there is no visible reason to challenge them, 1989 will continue difficult for the company, particularly in the operating margin area.

SALES
(*millions of dollars*)

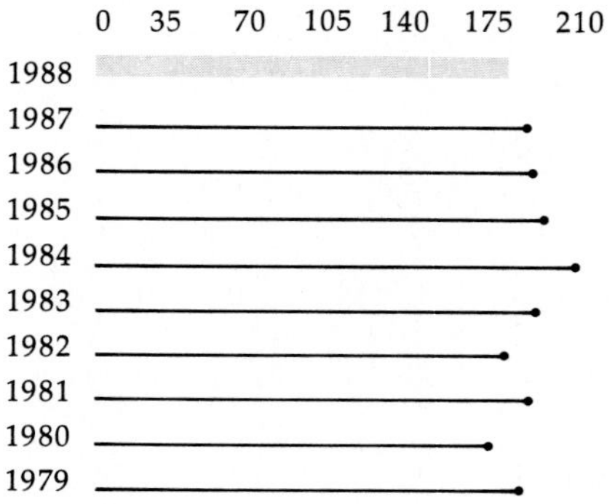


OPERATING PROFIT
(*millions of dollars*)

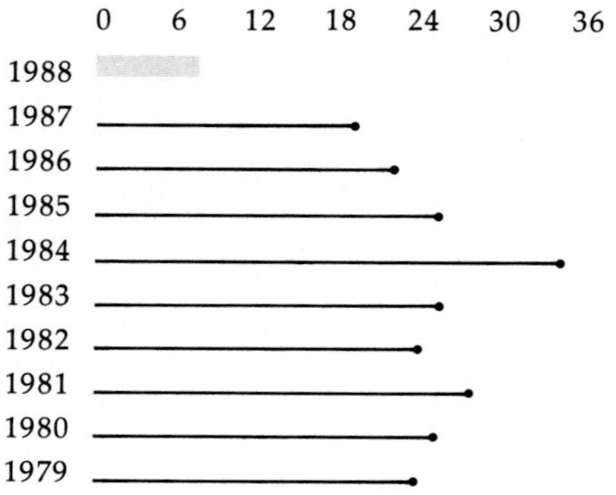

FINANCIAL COMMENT

## Cash Flow

Income from continuing operations of $14.6 million combined with depreciation and amortization charges of $19.0 million to produce total cash flow of $33.6 million.

Historically, the operating companies have generated more cash than was required to finance internal growth and expansion. This excess cash flow supported several achievements in the Company's financial history:

- A special dividend of $10 per share paid in August 1988; (The cash-generating characteristics of the continuing companies enabled Tyler to finance the rapid increase in its Hall-Mark investment. When that investment was liquidated, the proceeds became available for the special dividend.)
- Net capital spending of $17.9 million in 1988 well covered by cash flow of $33.6 million;
- An increase in cash dividends each year from $.025 per share in 1973 to an annual rate of $.44 per share during 1988 until payment of the special dividend;
- A share repurchase program implemented in 1972 which has reduced fully diluted shares outstanding from 29.7 million in late 1972 to 21.5 million at year end;
- The capacity to finance acquisition of major and supplemental operating units.

AVERAGE SHARES OUTSTANDING
(*assuming full dilution*) (*millions*)

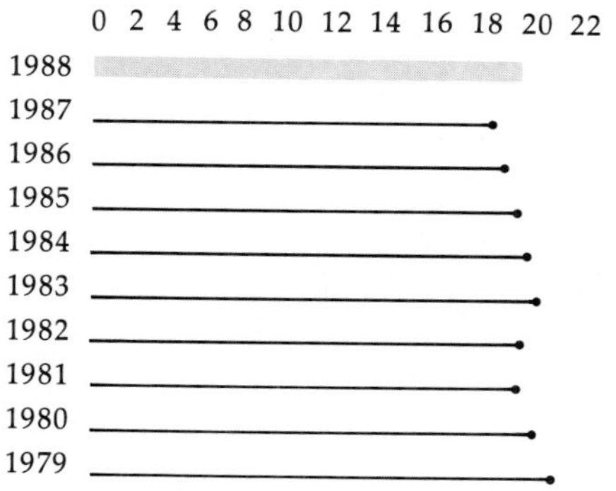


BOOK VALUE PER SHARE
(*dollars*)

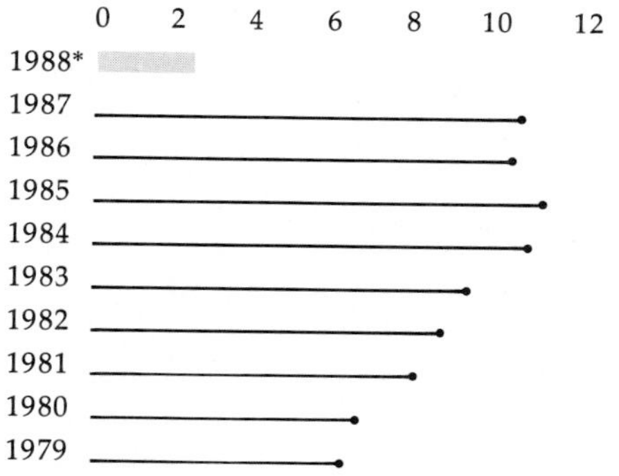


**After payment of $10 special dividend per share*

## RETURN ON EQUITY

Net income of $21.0 million in 1988 produced a 16.1% return on average shareholders' equity. This return was, of course, boosted by the gain on the sale of Hall-Mark and a decline in equity from $179.0 million at year-end 1987 to $51.6 million at year-end 1988 as a result of the $10 per share special dividend. The 1988 return on shareholders' equity was higher than the average return of 13.2% realized over the last ten years. Excluding income from discontinued operations, return on average shareholders' equity was 11.2% for 1988.

## TEN-YEAR TOTAL RETURN TO SHAREHOLDERS

For over a decade the Company has been included in *Fortune* magazine's list of the 500 largest U.S. industrial corporations. The Company's performance compared to the top 10% and the median of the *Fortune* 500 in ten-year total return to investors (stock appreciation plus dividends) is illustrated in the graph on page 13. For the ten-year period ending December 1987, the annual compound rate of return for Tyler shareholders was 8.1%. For the one-year period ending December 1988, the total return was 62.1%.

## CAPITALIZATION

Total capitalization of $240.4 million at the end of 1988 consisted of $51.6 million in shareholders' equity and $188.8 million in total debt.

Historically, Tyler's capital structure has varied depending on several factors. Common stock repurchases and acquisitions for cash generally increase debt as indicated in the graph on page 13. The cash-generating capabilities of our operating companies have provided the funds to reduce debt following major acquisitions.

RETURN ON AVERAGE EQUITY
*(millions of dollars)*

| | **1988** | 1987 | 1986 | 1985 | 1984 | 1983 | 1982 | 1981 | 1980 | 1979 |
|---|---|---|---|---|---|---|---|---|---|---|
| Net income | **$ 21.0**[(1)] | 12.0[(1)] | 11.9 | 15.4 | 37.6[(1)] | 18.4 | 10.2 | 32.0[(1)] | 13.6[(1)] | 23.5 |
| Average shareholders' equity | **$130.4** | 180.9 | 190.8 | 200.3 | 185.1 | 168.1 | 149.6 | 130.4 | 118.3 | 111.3 |
| Return on average equity[(2)] | **16.1%** | 6.6% | 6.3% | 7.7% | 20.3% | 11.0% | 6.8% | 24.5% | 11.5% | 21.1% |

*Net income is used in this table in order to follow the format used by Fortune magazine in compiling its comparative results and to be consistent with the graph on page 13. Tyler Corporation does not agree that Fortune's presentation is the most meaningful method of presenting return on equity in every case.*

*(1) Net income for these years is affected by special items described in footnotes to the Financial Summary Table on page 14.*

*(2) Equals net income divided by average quarterly shareholders' equity.*

When Hall-Mark Electronics was sold in 1988, approximately $174 million of the $220 million in proceeds was used to pay a special cash dividend. The dividend received by Tyler's Savings and Investment Plan was reinvested in Tyler stock which increased equity by $35 million. As a result of these actions, shareholders' equity declined from $179.0 million in 1987 to $51.6 million in 1988; and the debt-to-equity ratio rose from 56/44 at the end of 1987 to 79/21 at December 31, 1988.

Under the Company's bank lines of credit, outstanding balances were decreased from $96.0 million at December 31, 1987, to $65.0 million at December 31, 1988. The agreements are revolving lines of credit aggregating $125.0 million. During 1988 borrowings under these agreements were at an average rate of approximately 9%.

At December 31, 1988, subordinated debt totalled $117.2 million. During a temporarily higher leverage period beginning in August 1988, the Company has added 1% to the interest rate on its subordinated debt for a period of two and one-half years or five semiannual payments.

FINANCIAL SUMMARY TABLE

*(000 omitted from all dollar amounts, except per share data, and from average shares)*

| | 1988 vs 1987 | 1988 | 1987 | 1986 |
|---|---|---|---|---|
| Net sales | | | | |
| Atlas Powder | + 9% | **$196,273** | $180,824 | $161,997 |
| Reliance Universal | + 13 | **289,138** | 255,127 | 225,952 |
| Tyler Pipe | − 5 | **179,234** | 188,166 | 189,143 |
| Other | | — | — | — |
| Total | + 6 | **$664,645** | **$624,117** | **$577,092** |
| Operating profits | | | | |
| Atlas Powder | + 1 | **$ 16,305** | $ 16,128 | $ 13,636 |
| Reliance Universal | + 2 | **24,189** | 23,815 | 16,903 |
| Tyler Pipe | − 61 | **7,296** | 18,794 | 21,466 |
| Other | | — | — | — |
| Total | − 19 | **47,790** | **58,737** | **52,005** |
| Other expenses | | | | |
| Subsidiaries nonoperating expenses | | **(2,256)** | (2,256) | (2,256) |
| Interest expense | + 86 | **(11,973)** | (6,431) | (2,310) |
| Corporate expense | | **(9,780)** | (9,734) | (8,561) |
| Income from continuing operations before income tax | − 41 | **23,781** | 40,316 | 38,878 |
| Income tax | − 45 | **9,206** | 16,808 | 17,791 |
| Income from continuing operations | − 38 | **14,575** | 23,508 | 21,087 |
| Income from discontinued operations | | **6,413** [1] | (6,659) | (9,142) |
| Income before extraordinary items | + 25 | **$ 20,988** [1] | **$ 16,849** [4] | **$ 11,945** |
| Income from continuing operations to net sales | | **2.19%** | 3.77% | 3.65% |
| Tax rate—continuing operations | | **38.7%** | 41.7% | 45.8% |
| Earnings per common share from continuing operations—assuming full dilution | − 42 | **$ .77** | **$ 1.33** | **$ 1.16** |
| Earnings per common share—assuming full dilution | + 16 | **$ 1.11** [1] | $ .96 [4] | $ .66 |
| Average shares | + 8 | **19,009** | 17,642 | 18,208 |
| Total assets | − 32 | **$348,498** | $513,691 | $478,485 |
| Shareholders' equity | − 71 | **51,562** | 179,001 | 181,989 |
| Long-term debt, including current maturities | − 17 | **188,849** | 227,216 | 196,059 |
| Debt/equity ratio | | **79/21** | 56/44 | 52/48 |
| Capital expenditures (net) | | **$ 17,944** | $ 17,911 | $ 18,837 |
| Depreciation and amortization | + 2 | **18,971** | 18,647 | 18,892 |
| Dividend per share | | **$ 10.235** | $ .41 | $ .40 |
| Stock trading price range | | **18-5⅝** | 15¾-9¼ | 17¾-11¼ |
| Price/earnings ratio range | | **23-7** [2] | 16-10 [4] | 27-17 |
| Book value per share | − 77 | **$ 2.40** [3] | $ 10.34 | $ 10.15 |

*(1) Includes gain of $6,334, or $.33 per share, on sale of electronic components distribution operation in 1988 and $9,359, or $.48 per share, on sale of trucking operations in 1984*
*(2) Excludes gain on sale of discontinued operations*
*(3) After $10 per share special dividend paid in August 1988*
*(4) Before extraordinary charge from early extinguishment of the 12⅞% subordinated notes of $4,831, or $.28 per share*
*(5) Before extraordinary credit related to a tax benefit resulting from extraordinary write-off in 1980 (see Footnote 6) of $4,688, or $.25 per share*
*(6) Before extraordinary charge related to the write-off of the entire cost of route permits associated with trucking operations of $10,192, or $.53 per share*

| | 1985 | 1984 | 1983 | 1982 | 1981 | 1980 | 1979 |
|---|---|---|---|---|---|---|---|
| | $161,998 | $156,291 | $127,383 | $131,025 | $149,246 | $138,323 | $121,775 |
| | 213,122 | 189,255 | 176,680 | 170,552 | 127,363 | — | — |
| | 196,909 | 209,389 | 191,993 | 179,878 | 188,304 | 171,861 | 185,132 |
| | 15,078 | 16,178 | 15,457 | 15,659 | 18,895 | 13,502 | 7,154 |
| | **$587,107** | **$571,113** | **$511,513** | **$497,114** | **$483,808** | **$323,686** | **$314,061** |
| | $ 17,016 | $ 14,780 | $ 7,490 | $ 5,529 | $ 17,658 | $ 15,941 | $ 15,739 |
| | 15,936 | 15,382 | 14,533 | 9,007 | 8,079 | — | — |
| | 25,090 | 34,083 | 25,249 | 23,817 | 27,271 | 24,921 | 23,158 |
| | 140 | 1,252 | 840 | 648 | 1,677 | 1,080 | 497 |
| | **58,182** | **65,497** | **48,112** | **39,001** | **54,685** | **41,942** | **39,394** |
| | (2,202) | (1,944) | (1,944) | (2,234) | (1,665) | — | — |
| | (3,869) | (7,211) | (10,895) | (13,713) | (11,049) | (4,362) | (6,252) |
| | (8,531) | (8,964) | (5,149) | (5,880) | (6,227) | (5,294) | (5,072) |
| | 43,580 | 47,378 | 30,124 | 17,174 | 35,744 | 32,286 | 28,070 |
| | 19,358 | 21,192 | 13,981 | 6,175 | 15,723 | 13,367 | 12,467 |
| | 24,222 | 26,186 | 16,143 | 10,999 | 20,021 | 18,919 | 15,603 |
| | (8,859) | 11,373 [1] | 2,306 | (804) | 7,336 [5] | 4,917 [6] | 7,854 |
| | **$ 15,363** | **$ 37,559 [1]** | **$ 18,449** | **$ 10,195** | **$ 27,357 [5]** | **$ 23,836 [6]** | **$ 23,457** |
| | 4.13% | 4.59% | 3.16% | 2.21% | 4.14% | 5.84% | 4.97% |
| | 44.4% | 44.7% | 46.4% | 36.0% | 44.0% | 41.4% | 44.4% |
| | **$ 1.29** | **$ 1.36** | **$ .82** | **$ .58** | **$ 1.06** | **$ .98** | **$ .78** |
| | $ .82 | $ 1.95 [1] | $ .94 | $ .54 | $ 1.46 [5] | $ 1.23 [6] | $ 1.17 |
| | 18,810 | 19,222 | 19,624 | 18,928 | 18,802 | 19,396 | 20,080 |
| | $448,725 | $456,213 | $449,501 | $421,639 | $417,958 | $245,052 | $251,168 |
| | 200,135 | 197,991 | 175,189 | 162,906 | 143,464 | 120,490 | 115,535 |
| | 171,139 | 180,501 | 206,409 | 199,353 | 209,957 | 80,055 | 103,478 |
| | 46/54 | 48/52 | 54/46 | 55/45 | 59/41 | 40/60 | 47/53 |
| | $ 29,204 | $ 17,998 | $ 12,859 | $ 13,912 | $ 18,056 | $ 12,514 | $ 9,704 |
| | 18,343 | 17,075 | 16,963 | 16,389 | 13,051 | 9,348 | 8,611 |
| | $ .394 | $ .35 | $ .313 | $ .30 | $ .275 | $ .25 | $ .225 |
| | 17¾-12⅝ | 15½-11½ | 15¾-9⅛ | 11¾-6 | 14⅝-8 | 8¾-5¼ | 9⅛-7 |
| | 22-15 | 11-8 [2] | 17-10 | 22-11 | 10-6 [5] | 7-4 [6] | 8-6 |
| | $ 10.89 | $ 10.57 | $ 9.08 | $ 8.46 | $ 7.80 | $ 6.47 | $ 6.08 |

## DEBT/EQUITY RELATION AT YEAR END

(% of capitalization)

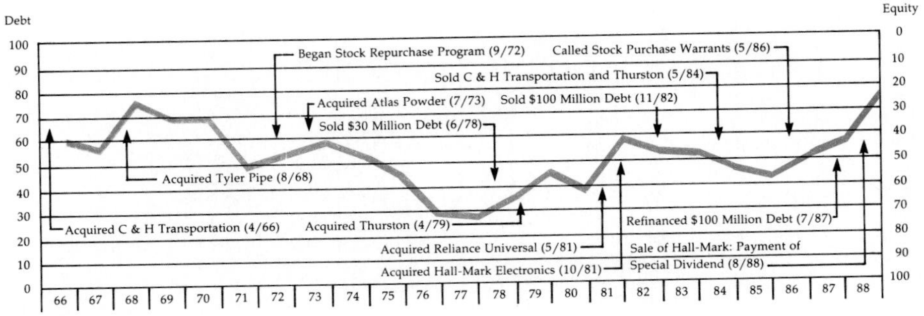


## RETURN ON YEAR-END EQUITY

- Tyler Corporation
- Top 10% (50th Company) of *Fortune* 500
- Median of *Fortune* 500

*According to Fortune magazine's formula, return on equity equals net income divided by ending shareholders' equity.*

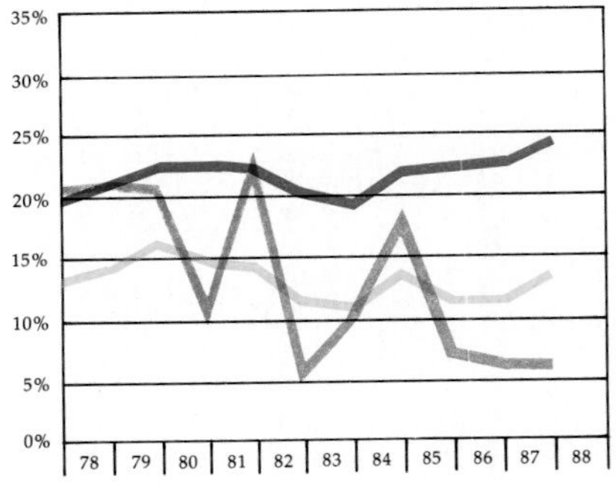


## TEN-YEAR TOTAL RETURN TO INVESTORS

(stock appreciation plus dividends)
(compound annual rate)

- Tyler Corporation
- Top 10% (50th Company) of *Fortune* 500
- Median of *Fortune* 500

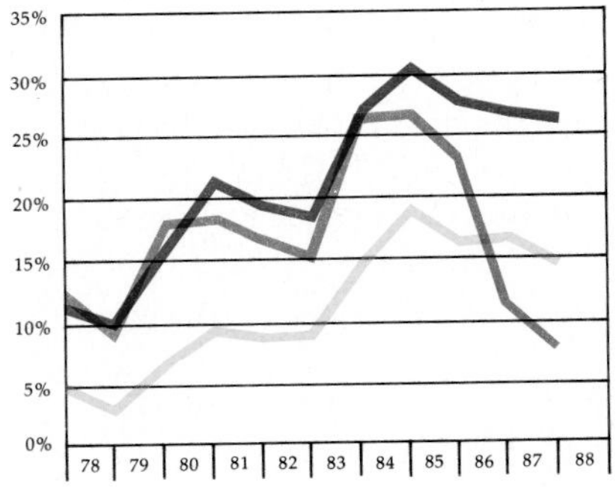


*Fortune 500 data for 1988 were not available at the time this report was published. This information is usually included in a May issue.*

## ACQUISITIONS/DIVESTITURES

### Divestitures

| | |
|---|---|
| 1988 | *Sold Hall-Mark Electronics Corp.* |
| 1984 | *Sold C & H Transportation Co., Inc. and Thurston Motor Lines, Inc.* |
| 1977 | *Spun off Southwestern Engineering Company (Cronus Industries)* |
| 1970 | *Sold Harbor Boat Building Co. and Crescent Precision Products, Inc.* |
| 1969 | *Sold L. T. Industries, Inc., Saturn Electronics Corporation and Mitchell Industries, Inc.* |

Tyler Corporation's primary purpose is to provide superior long-term rewards to shareholders through a large, diversely based industrial enterprise. Diversification produces the best chances for consistency of return but involves, from time to time, readjustment of our portfolio of operating companies. These readjustments present opportunities for increasing overall return to shareholders or for directing distributions to shareholders in a timely and economical manner. Locating appropriate opportunities is a constant objective of Tyler's management team.

Since inception, Tyler Corporation has distributed to shareholders $253 million in dividends, including the value of the spinoff of Southwestern Engineering in 1977.

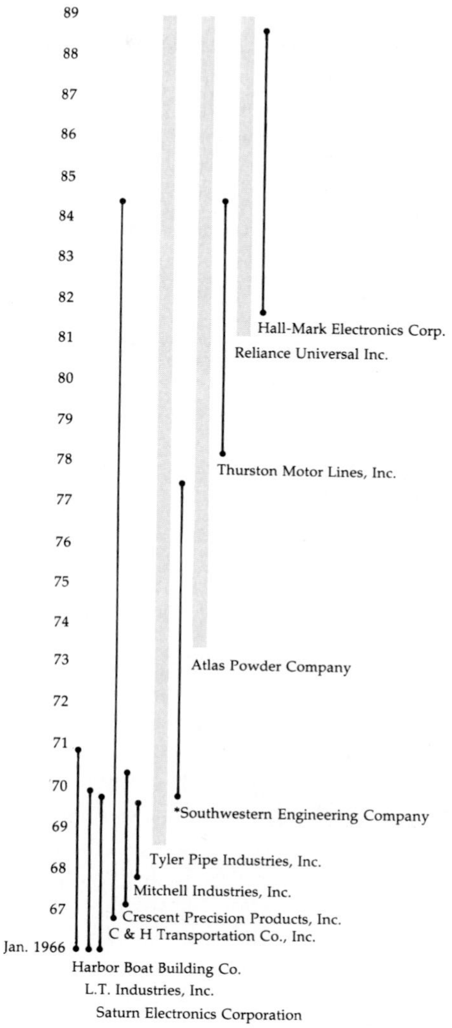


**Spinoff*

## MANAGEMENT'S DISCUSSION AND ANALYSIS OF OPERATIONS

### 1988 Compared with 1987

Operating results for 1988 fell below those posted for the prior year. Net sales rose 6% in 1988 while income and earnings per share from continuing operations dropped 38% and 42%, respectively.

The decline in earnings per share from continuing operations to $.77 in 1988 from $1.33 in 1987 reflected lower operating profit margin and increased shares outstanding. These figures exclude the gain on the sale and results of operations of Hall-Mark which are classified as discontinued operations as is the considerable interest expense associated with Hall-Mark. Much of that interest expense continues since most of the sale proceeds were used to pay the special dividend instead of to retire debt.

Consolidated operating profit margin from continuing operations decreased to 7.2% in 1988 from 9.4% in 1987. All three operating companies experienced higher raw material costs and competitive markets which prohibited significant price increases.

For the ten-year period ending in 1988, sales and operating profits grew at compound rates of 9% and 2%, respectively. A summary of the Company's ten-year operating performance is shown in the table on page 1.

In 1988 Atlas Powder's sales rose 9% due primarily to strength in distribution operations and nonelectric blasting caps. Operating profit increased slightly, but higher raw material and production costs prevented profit improvement in line with sales, causing a decline in operating margin.

Sales at Reliance Universal increased 13% through expanded unit volume which was aided by the acquisition of the industrial coatings division of O'Brien Corporation. Higher raw material costs and the inability to pass through these costs limited operating profit growth to 2% and resulted in a decrease in operating margin.

Tyler Pipe had another year of dismal construction markets which depressed sales and operating profit. Higher raw material costs and lower volumes due to declining nonresidential construction markets caused operating profit to fall 61% for the year.

Analysis of cash flow, return on equity and capitalization is presented in the Financial Comment section on page 10.

1987 Compared with 1986

The comparison of 1987 with 1986 excludes results of operations of Hall-Mark Electronics Corp. which was sold in August 1988.

Operating results for 1987 were moderately better than 1986. Net sales advanced 8% in 1987 while income and earnings per share from continuing operations rose 11% and 15%, respectively.

The boost in earnings per share from continuing operations to $1.33 in 1987 from $1.16 in 1986 reflected higher sales, a higher operating margin and a lower tax rate. These positive factors were partially negated by higher interest expense due primarily to higher debt levels.

Consolidated operating profit margin rose from 9.0% in 1986 to 9.4% in 1987. Operating efficiencies and lower selling, administrative and general expenses more than offset higher production costs during 1987. Operating margin gains at Reliance Universal and Atlas Powder contributed to this improvement, but Tyler Pipe suffered a decline due to poor industry conditions.

Inflation did not have a material impact on the Company in 1987.

Atlas Powder's sales rose 12% in 1987 due to better prices and market share gains. A more favorable product mix and cost efficiencies combined to produce substantially increased operating profit after excluding nonrecurring items in 1986.

Reliance Universal posted records in sales and operating profit. Volume gains in all divisions produced a 13% advance in sales while operating profit was up 41% due to effective cost-control measures. This excellent performance led the company to a second consecutive year as the highest return-on-assets producer of all the operating companies.

Tyler Pipe experienced a slight sales decline due to continued weakness in nonresidential construction markets. Competitive price reductions and higher costs contributed to a 12% decline in operating profit. Nonetheless, operating margin at Tyler Pipe was still the highest in the Company at 10%.

CONSOLIDATED STATEMENTS OF INCOME
*Years ended December 31*

| | 1988 | 1987 | 1986 |
|---|---|---|---|
| Net sales | **$664,645,000** | $624,117,000 | $577,092,000 |
| Costs and expenses | | | |
| Cost of sales | **522,638,000** | 475,610,000 | 438,988,000 |
| Selling, administrative and general expenses | **106,253,000** | 101,760,000 | 96,916,000 |
| Interest expense | **11,973,000** | 6,431,000 | 2,310,000 |
| | **640,864,000** | 583,801,000 | 538,214,000 |
| Income from continuing operations before income tax | **23,781,000** | 40,316,000 | 38,878,000 |
| Income tax (benefit) | | | |
| Current | **9,816,000** | 12,674,000 | 12,805,000 |
| Deferred | **(610,000)** | 4,134,000 | 4,986,000 |
| | **9,206,000** | 16,808,000 | 17,791,000 |
| Income from continuing operations | **14,575,000** | 23,508,000 | 21,087,000 |
| Discontinued operations | | | |
| Income (loss) from discontinued operations, after income tax (benefit) | **79,000** | (6,659,000) | (9,142,000) |
| Gain on disposal of discontinued operations, after income tax | **6,334,000** | — | — |
| Income (loss) from discontinued operations | **6,413,000** | (6,659,000) | (9,142,000) |
| Income before extraordinary charge | **20,988,000** | 16,849,000 | 11,945,000 |
| Extraordinary charge, after income tax benefit | **—** | (4,831,000) | — |
| Net income | **$ 20,988,000** | $ 12,018,000 | $ 11,945,000 |
| Earnings per common share | | | |
| Continuing operations | **$ .77** | $ 1.33 | $ 1.16 |
| Discontinued operations | **.34** | (.37) | (.50) |
| Income before extraordinary charge | **1.11** | .96 | .66 |
| Extraordinary charge | **—** | (.28) | — |
| Net earnings | **$ 1.11** | $ .68 | $ .66 |
| Average shares | **19,009,000** | 17,642,000 | 18,208,000 |

See accompanying notes.

CONSOLIDATED BALANCE SHEETS
*December 31*

| | 1988 | 1987 |
|---|---|---|
| **ASSETS** | | |
| Current assets | | |
| Cash and cash equivalents | **$ 3,403,000** | $ 3,629,000 |
| Accounts receivable (less allowance for losses of $3,163,000 in 1988 and $3,630,000 in 1987) | **94,115,000** | 75,336,000 |
| Inventories | **68,073,000** | 68,091,000 |
| Prepaid expense | **5,443,000** | 4,356,000 |
| Total current assets | **171,034,000** | 151,412,000 |
| Net assets of discontinued electronic components distribution segment | — | 187,920,000 |
| Property, plant and equipment, at cost | **262,837,000** | 249,451,000 |
| Less allowance for depreciation | **142,422,000** | 128,414,000 |
| | **120,415,000** | 121,037,000 |
| Other assets | | |
| Cost in excess of net assets of businesses acquired | **41,617,000** | 41,961,000 |
| Sundry | **15,432,000** | 11,361,000 |
| | **57,049,000** | 53,322,000 |
| | **$348,498,000** | $513,691,000 |
| **LIABILITIES AND SHAREHOLDERS' EQUITY** | | |
| Current liabilities | | |
| Accounts payable | **$ 36,576,000** | $ 36,141,000 |
| Accrued liabilities | **41,657,000** | 37,387,000 |
| Accrued interest | **6,410,000** | 6,686,000 |
| Income tax | **2,286,000** | 3,806,000 |
| Current maturities of long-term debt | **6,544,000** | 6,563,000 |
| Total current liabilities | **93,473,000** | 90,583,000 |
| Deferred income tax | **21,158,000** | 23,454,000 |
| Long-term debt, less current maturities | **65,091,000** | 103,305,000 |
| Subordinated debt | **117,214,000** | 117,348,000 |
| Shareholders' equity | | |
| Common stock, $.10 par value, 50,000,000 shares authorized, 25,914,188 shares issued | **2,591,000** | 2,591,000 |
| Capital surplus | **9,470,000** | 15,859,000 |
| Retained earnings | **67,170,000** | 224,408,000 |
| | **79,231,000** | 242,858,000 |
| Less 4,447,917 treasury shares in 1988 and 8,602,937 treasury shares in 1987, at cost | **27,669,000** | 63,857,000 |
| Total shareholders' equity | **51,562,000** | 179,001,000 |
| | **$348,498,000** | $513,691,000 |

See accompanying notes.

CONSOLIDATED STATEMENTS OF SHAREHOLDERS' EQUITY
*Years ended December 31, 1988, 1987 and 1986*

| | Common Stock $.10 Par Value | Capital Surplus | Retained Earnings | Treasury Stock |
|---|---|---|---|---|
| Balance at December 31, 1985 | $2,591,000 | $31,668,000 | $214,991,000 | $(49,115,000) |
| Issuance of treasury shares upon exercise of stock options | — | (459,000) | — | 827,000 |
| Sale of treasury shares to employee benefit plans | — | 14,000 | — | 2,600,000 |
| Purchase of common stock | — | — | — | (10,784,000) |
| Federal income tax benefit from exercise of nonqualified stock options | — | 8,000 | — | — |
| Redemption of detachable common stock purchase warrants | — | (14,999,000) | — | — |
| Net income | — | — | 11,945,000 | — |
| Dividend ($.40 per share) | — | — | (7,298,000) | — |
| Balance at December 31, 1986 | 2,591,000 | 16,232,000 | 219,638,000 | (56,472,000) |
| Issuance of treasury shares upon exercise of stock options | — | (60,000) | — | 132,000 |
| Sale of treasury shares to employee benefit plans | — | (313,000) | — | 3,077,000 |
| Purchase of common stock | — | — | — | (10,594,000) |
| Net income | — | — | 12,018,000 | — |
| Dividend ($.41 per share) | — | — | (7,248,000) | — |
| Balance at December 31, 1987 | 2,591,000 | 15,859,000 | 224,408,000 | (63,857,000) |
| Issuance of treasury shares upon exercise of stock options | — | **(351,000)** | — | **2,099,000** |
| Sale of treasury shares to employee benefit plans | — | **(6,241,000)** | — | **41,209,000** |
| Purchase of common stock | — | — | — | **(7,120,000)** |
| Federal income tax benefit from exercise of nonqualified stock options | — | **203,000** | — | — |
| Net income | — | — | **20,988,000** | — |
| Dividend ($10.235 per share) | — | — | **(178,226,000)** | — |
| Balance at December 31, 1988 | **$2,591,000** | **$ 9,470,000** | **$ 67,170,000** | **$(27,669,000)** |

See accompanying notes.

CONSOLIDATED STATEMENTS OF CASH FLOWS
*Years ended December 31*

| | 1988 | 1987 | 1986 |
|---|---|---|---|
| Cash flows from operating activities | | | |
| Income from continuing operations | **$ 14,575,000** | $ 23,508,000 | $21,087,000 |
| Adjustments to reconcile income from continuing operations to net cash provided by continuing operations: | | | |
| Depreciation and amortization | **18,971,000** | 18,647,000 | 18,892,000 |
| Provision for losses on accounts receivable | **2,205,000** | 2,660,000 | 2,955,000 |
| Deferred income tax | **(2,296,000)** | 4,233,000 | 1,292,000 |
| Increase in accounts receivable | **(20,984,000)** | (10,914,000) | (4,369,000) |
| (Increase) decrease in inventories | **18,000** | (6,335,000) | 1,052,000 |
| (Increase) decrease in prepaid expense | **(1,087,000)** | 555,000 | (415,000) |
| Increase (decrease) in accounts payable | **435,000** | (3,349,000) | 16,996,000 |
| Increase in accrued liabilities | **3,994,000** | 3,707,000 | 1,120,000 |
| Increase (decrease) in income tax | **(1,520,000)** | 2,446,000 | 3,578,000 |
| Net cash provided by continuing operations | **14,311,000** | 35,158,000 | 62,188,000 |
| Income (loss) from discontinued operations | **6,413,000** | (6,659,000) | (9,142,000) |
| Adjustments to reconcile income (loss) from discontinued operations to net cash used by discontinued operations: | | | |
| Gain on sale of electronic components distribution segment before income tax | **(9,222,000)** | — | — |
| Increase in net assets of electronic components distribution segment | **(17,534,000)** | (23,989,000) | (32,081,000) |
| Depreciation and amortization | **3,190,000** | 5,053,000 | 4,253,000 |
| Net cash used by discontinued operations | **(17,153,000)** | (25,595,000) | (36,970,000) |
| Tax benefit of early extinguishment of 12⅞% subordinated notes | — | 3,221,000 | — |
| Net cash provided (used) by operating activities | **(2,842,000)** | 12,784,000 | 25,218,000 |
| Cash flows from investing activities | | | |
| Proceeds from sale of electronic components distribution segment, after expenses | **211,486,000** | — | — |
| Additions to property, plant and equipment | **(21,625,000)** | (20,986,000) | (24,625,000) |
| Undepreciated value of asset disposals | **3,681,000** | 3,075,000 | 5,788,000 |
| Reduction of investment in tax benefit transfer lease | — | — | 2,579,000 |
| Other | **(4,147,000)** | (1,887,000) | (677,000) |
| Net cash provided (used) in investing activities | **189,395,000** | (19,798,000) | (16,935,000) |
| Cash flows from financing activities | | | |
| Long-term borrowings | — | 39,671,000 | 40,500,000 |
| Reduction of long-term debt | **(38,352,000)** | (10,258,000) | (13,130,000) |
| Issuance of 11% senior subordinated debentures | — | 96,629,000 | — |
| Early extinguishment of 12⅞% subordinated notes | — | (100,000,000) | — |
| Retirement of 10½% subordinated debentures | — | (3,750,000) | (3,265,000) |
| Issuance of common stock | **1,951,000** | 72,000 | 376,000 |
| Purchase of treasury shares | **(7,120,000)** | (10,594,000) | (10,784,000) |
| Sale of treasury shares to employee benefit plans | **34,968,000** | 2,764,000 | 2,614,000 |
| Redemption of detachable common stock purchase warrants | — | — | (14,999,000) |
| Cash dividends | **(178,226,000)** | (7,248,000) | (7,298,000) |
| Net cash provided (used) by financing activities | **(186,779,000)** | 7,286,000 | (5,986,000) |
| Net increase (decrease) in cash and cash equivalents | **(226,000)** | 272,000 | 2,297,000 |
| Cash and cash equivalents at beginning of year | **3,629,000** | 3,357,000 | 1,060,000 |
| Cash and cash equivalents at end of year | **$ 3,403,000** | $ 3,629,000 | $ 3,357,000 |

See accompanying notes.

## NOTES TO CONSOLIDATED FINANCIAL STATEMENTS

### Summary of Significant Accounting Policies

The consolidated financial statements include the accounts of the Company and its subsidiaries, all of which are wholly owned.

Cost in excess of net assets of businesses acquired after October 1970 is amortized over 40 years. Cost in excess of net assets of businesses acquired before October 31, 1970, of $30,374,000 is not amortized. Accumulated amortization at December 31, 1988 and 1987, was $2,492,000 and $2,148,000, respectively.

Inventories are valued at the lower of cost or market. Costs for inventories are determined principally by the last-in, first-out (LIFO) method.

Depreciation, for financial statement purposes, is provided principally by the straight-line method over the estimated useful lives of the various assets. For income tax purposes, accelerated depreciation is used with recognition of deferred income tax for the resulting timing differences.

Pension plans are in effect which provide income and death benefits for substantially all employees of the Company. The benefits are generally based on final average salary and years of service. The Company's policy is to fund net pension cost accrued. However, the Company will not contribute an amount less than the minimum funding requirements of the Employee Retirement Income Security Act of 1974 or more than the maximum tax deductible amount.

The Company's investment in a tax benefit transfer lease is included in sundry assets and is amortized over the period the tax benefit is utilized by the Company. The tax benefit purchased had no material effect on net income in 1988, 1987, and 1986.

For purposes of the statements of cash flows, the Company considers all highly liquid debt instruments purchased with a maturity of three months or less to be cash equivalents. The Company paid interest of $24,900,000 in 1988, $27,180,000 in 1987 and $23,708,000 in 1986 which includes interest charged to the results of discontinued operations.

In December 1987 the Financial Accounting Standards Board issued Statement of Financial Accounting Standards No. 96—Accounting for Income Taxes (FAS No. 96) which is effective January 1, 1990. FAS No. 96 requires a change from the deferred to the liability method of computing income tax. Deferred tax is adjusted for changes in tax rates and laws under the liability method. In addition, deferred tax is recorded for the tax effects of book and tax differences in the net assets of companies acquired in transactions accounted for as a purchase. The Company expects the cumulative effect of applying FAS No. 96 will not be material to results of operations in the period in which FAS No. 96 is first adopted.

### Inventories

| | **1988** | 1987 |
|---|---|---|
| Finished goods | **$59,790,000** | $59,775,000 |
| Work in process | **4,608,000** | 4,397,000 |
| Raw materials and supplies | **33,574,000** | 30,497,000 |
| | **97,972,000** | 94,669,000 |
| Less allowance to state inventories at LIFO cost | **29,899,000** | 26,578,000 |
| | **$68,073,000** | $68,091,000 |

Current replacement cost approximates the amounts shown above before the allowance to state inventories at LIFO cost.

### Property, Plant and Equipment

| | Depreciation Lives (in years) | **1988** | 1987 |
|---|---|---|---|
| Land | | **$ 9,734,000** | $ 10,177,000 |
| Buildings and leasehold improvements | 10 to 40 | **59,073,000** | 56,217,000 |
| Machinery and equipment | 5 to 20 | **175,293,000** | 164,090,000 |
| Transportation equipment | 3 to 10 | **18,737,000** | 18,967,000 |
| | | **$262,837,000** | $249,451,000 |

## Long-Term Debt

| | 1988 | 1987 |
|---|---|---|
| 8¼% unsecured note due in annual installments of $3,000,000 | **$ 3,000,000** | $ 6,000,000 |
| Revolving bank lines of credit | **65,000,000** | 96,000,000 |
| 10% installment notes due in annual installments of $3,452,000 | **3,452,000** | 6,785,000 |
| Other notes at varying rates | **183,000** | 1,083,000 |
| | **71,635,000** | 109,868,000 |
| Less current maturities | **6,544,000** | 6,563,000 |
| | **$65,091,000** | $103,305,000 |

The Company has agreements with certain banks for revolving lines of credit totalling $125,000,000. The Company has the option to fix interest rates at 1% over the London Interbank Offered Rate (LIBOR) or the certificate of deposit rate, or such other rate agreed to by the Company and any of its banks, or to allow it to fluctuate at the prime rate. Borrowings under the revolving lines of credit are secured by the outstanding common stock of the Company's subsidiaries. Unless extended by the Company with the consent of the banks, the outstanding borrowings are to be reduced at a rate of 5% per quarter commencing on June 30, 1990. During 1988 borrowings under these agreements were at an average rate of approximately 9%.

Scheduled repayments of long-term debt during the five years following December 31, 1988, are as follows: 1989—$6,544,000; 1990—$9,838,000; 1991—$13,003,000; 1992—$13,000,000; 1993—$13,000,000.

The Company's loan agreements limit retained earnings currently available for dividends to $14,639,000.

## Subordinated Debt

| | 1988 | 1987 |
|---|---|---|
| 11% senior subordinated debentures due July 15, 1997, net of debt discount and issuance costs of $3,353,000 in 1988 and $3,286,000 in 1987 | **$ 96,647,000** | $ 96,714,000 |
| 10½% subordinated debentures due June 1, 1998 | **20,567,000** | 20,634,000 |
| | **$117,214,000** | $117,348,000 |

During a period of temporarily higher leverage beginning in August 1988, the Company has added 1% to the interest rate on its subordinated debt for a period of two and one-half years or five semiannual payments. The additional interest is being charged to expense using the effective interest method over the term of the subordinated debt.

The 11% senior subordinated debentures may be redeemed at 107.33% on July 15, 1990, and at declining premiums thereafter to 1996, at which time they may be redeemed at par. No redemption may occur prior to 1992 out of the proceeds from a borrowing having an annual interest rate less than 11%.

The proceeds of the 11% senior subordinated debentures were used to redeem $100,000,000 of 12⅞% subordinated notes. The subordinated notes were issued with six million detachable common stock purchase warrants which were called in 1986 at the call price of $2.50 per warrant. The notes were called on November 2, 1987, by the Company at par. Since the notes were issued at a discount with warrants attached, their call resulted in an extraordinary charge to earnings of $4,831,000, after tax benefit of $3,221,000.

Sinking fund payments on the 10½% subordinated debentures beginning in 1992 are calculated to retire 75% of the issue prior to maturity. The debentures may be redeemed at par.

## Discontinued Operations

On August 2, 1988, the Company completed the sale of Hall-Mark Electronics to a new corporation controlled by Riordan Freeman & Spogli, a Los Angeles based merchant banking firm. The net assets of the discontinued electronic components distribution segment at December 31, 1987, consisted principally of working capital (including accounts receivable, inventories, accounts payable and accrued liabilities), property, plant and equipment, and intangibles and other assets.

Net cash proceeds from the sale, after deducting related expenses, were approximately $211,486,000. The cash proceeds included $18,750,000 received by the Company from the sale of $30,000,000 principal amount of 11-year 13% junior subordinated notes with warrants received from the purchaser at closing.

Operating results of the discontinued electronic components distribution segment for the seven months ended July 31, 1988, and for 1987 and 1986 were as follows:

| | 1988 | 1987 | 1986 |
|---|---|---|---|
| Net sales | $331,091,000 | $475,390,000 | $384,319,000 |
| Income (loss) before income tax | $ 513,000 | $(10,229,000) | $(16,341,000) |
| Income tax (benefit) | 434,000 | (3,570,000) | (7,199,000) |
| Income (loss) from operations | $ 79,000 | $ (6,659,000) | $ (9,142,000) |

Interest has been charged to discontinued operations based on average intercompany balances of the electronic components distribution segment owed to the Company at its average effective borrowing rate during each period.

Income tax has been charged (credited) to discontinued operations based on the income tax (benefit) resulting from inclusion of the discontinued segment in the Company's consolidated federal income tax return.

The income tax (benefit) differs from the amount which would be provided by applying the statutory income tax rate to income (loss) before income tax for 1988, 1987 and 1986 due primarily to permanent differences resulting from excess book over tax amortization and differences in book and tax bases of certain assets.

The income tax of $2,888,000 on the gain on disposal of discontinued operations differs from the amount which would be provided by applying the statutory incometax rate to the pretax gain primarily as a result of differences in book and tax bases of the related assets, and settlements of an employment agreement and amounts due upon termination of a nonqualified retirement plan not deductible for tax purposes.

Income Tax

As a result of the application of Accounting Principles Board Opinion No. 16 in accounting for the acquisition of industrial explosives and specialty industrial coatings businesses, the book basis of inventories exceeded the tax basis by $5,768,000 at December 31, 1988, and $6,007,000 at December 31, 1987. Taxable income for federal income tax purposes was higher than income for financial statement purposes as a result of the difference in bases by $239,000 in 1988, $4,000 in 1987 and $92,000 in 1986.

Income tax expense differs from the amount which would be provided by applying the statutory income tax rate to income from continuing operations before income tax for 1988, 1987 and 1986 primarily as a result of permanent differences including excess book over tax amortization and differences in book and tax bases of certain assets and state income taxes. State income tax expense was $1,729,000 in 1988, $1,531,000 in 1987 and $1,066,000 in 1986.

The tax effects of timing differences that exceeded 5% of the amount resulting from multiplying consolidated income from continuing operations before income tax by the statutory income tax rate were (1) excess tax over book depreciation and amortization of $637,000 in 1988 and $1,038,000 in 1986; (2) utilization of tax benefit from the tax benefit transfer lease of $2,802,000 in 1987 and $3,251,000 in 1986; (3) deductions for book in excess of tax of $500,000 in 1988 and $864,000 in 1987 related to different bases of inventories; and (4) settlements currently deductible but previously accrued for book purposes of $1,944,000 in 1987.

The Company paid income tax of $17,144,000 in 1988, $5,503,000 in 1987 and $6,618,000 in 1986. In addition, the Company received refunds of prior years' income tax of $814,000 in 1987 and $6,600,000 in 1986.

Leases

The Company leases certain facilities and transportation, computer and other equipment used in its operations under noncancellable operating lease agreements having an initial term of more than one year and expiring at various dates through 2005. Most leases contain renewal options and some contain purchase options. The leases generally provide that the Company pay taxes, maintenance, insurance and certain other operating expenses.

Rent expense was approximately $15,303,000 in 1988, $14,003,000 in 1987 and $12,568,000 in 1986.

Minimum rental payments under the leases described above are as follows:

| | |
|---|---|
| 1989 | **$11,490,000** |
| 1990 | **9,567,000** |
| 1991 | **5,650,000** |
| 1992 | **3,471,000** |
| 1993 | **1,723,000** |
| Later years | **1,366,000** |
| | **$33,267,000** |

Employee Benefit Plans

Substantially all employees are participants in non-contributory pension plans.

The components of net pension cost for 1988 and 1987 as determined under FAS No. 87 were:

| | **1988** | 1987 |
|---|---|---|
| Service cost | **$ 3,976,000** | $3,946,000 |
| Interest cost | **7,368,000** | 7,025,000 |
| Actual return on plan assets | **(15,687,000)** | (6,725,000) |
| Net amortization and deferral | **7,558,000** | (898,000) |
| Net pension cost | **$ 3,215,000** | $3,348,000 |

Pension expense of $3,632,000 in 1986 was determined in accordance with Accounting Principles Board Opinion No. 8.

The following table sets forth the funded status of the plans and amounts recognized in the Company's balance sheet.

| | **December 31, 1988** | January 1, 1988 |
|---|---|---|
| Actuarial present value of benefit obligation | | |
| Vested benefits | **$ 74,825,000** | $ 67,428,000 |
| Nonvested benefits | **6,158,000** | 5,971,000 |
| Accumulated benefit obligation | **80,983,000** | 73,399,000 |
| Effect of projected future compensation increases | **17,587,000** | 21,546,000 |
| Projected benefit obligation | **98,570,000** | 94,945,000 |
| Plan assets at fair value, primarily listed stocks and bonds and group annuity contracts | **114,232,000** | 102,656,000 |
| Plan assets in excess of projected benefit obligation | **15,662,000** | 7,711,000 |
| Unrecognized net (gain) loss from past experience different from that assumed and effect of change in assumptions | **(8,230,000)** | 82,000 |
| Prior service cost not yet recognized in net pension cost | **1,157,000** | — |
| Unrecognized net asset at date of initial application of FAS No. 87 | **(10,216,000)** | (10,383,000) |
| Accrued pension cost | **$ (1,627,000)** | $ (2,590,000) |

The pension plans held 251,200 shares of the Company's stock at December 31, 1988.

The weighted average discount rate and rate of increase in compensation used in determining the actuarial present value of the projected benefit obligation were approximately 8% and 6%, respectively. The expected long-term rate of return on assets was approximately 7%.

Cost related to the Company's savings and investment plan was $2,387,000 in 1988, $2,058,000 in 1987 and $2,086,000 in 1986. The plan provides that the Company will contribute not less than 50% of the eligible amount of employee contributions. Additional discretionary contributions may be made provided the Company or its subsidiaries has profits from which to pay its contributions.

Shareholders' Equity

On August 3, 1988, the Company declared a special $10 per share dividend which was paid to shareholders of record on August 15, 1988.

The Company has authorized 990,022 shares of $10 par value voting preferred stock. The board of directors designated 260,000 shares as Series B Junior Participating Preferred Stock (Series B Preferred Stock) which are reserved for issuance upon exercise of the Company's stock purchase rights. One stock purchase right accompanies each outstanding share of common stock. Each right may be exercised to purchase 1/100 of a share of Series B Preferred Stock for $50. Each share of Series B Preferred Stock will have a minimum preferential quarterly dividend of 100 times the dividend declared on common stock and a minimum liquidation preference of $100 per share. Upon liquidation or any merger or other business combination in which common stock is exchanged, the holders of the Series B Preferred Stock will be entitled to receive 100 times the amount received per share of common stock.

The stock purchase rights may be exercised only after public announcement that a person or group acquired 20% or more of the Company's common stock or public announcement of an offer for 30% or more of the Company's common stock. The rights, which do not have voting rights, will expire on December 4, 1990, unless activated prior to that date, in which case the rights will expire on December 4, 1997. The rights may be redeemed by the Company at a price of $.01 per right at any time prior to 15 days (or such longer period as the board of directors may determine) after the acquisition of 20% of the Company's common stock. If the Company is acquired in a merger or other business combination after the rights become activated, each right will entitle its holder to purchase, at the exercise price of $50, shares of common stock in the acquiring company having a market value of $100. If the Company is the surviving corporation, each right will entitle the holder to purchase, at the exercise price of $50, shares of common stock of the Company having a market value of $100.

The Tyler Corporation Stock Option Plan provides for the granting of nonqualified and incentive stock options, as defined by the Internal Revenue Code, to key employees of the Company and its susidiaries at prices which represent fair market value at dates of grant. In August 1988 the stock option prices and, in some instances, the number of shares subject to stock options were adjusted by the special dividend of $10 per share to reflect the decline in market value of the Company's stock. Following is a summary of option transactions during 1988 and 1987 after adjustment of the stock option price and the number of shares subject to stock options as described above:

| | **1988** | | 1987 | |
|---|---|---|---|---|
| | **Shares** | **Option Price** | Shares | Option Price |
| Outstanding at beginning of year | **539,592** | **$.10 to $6.75** | 531,602 | $.10 to $6.75 |
| Granted | **313,500** | **.87 to 6.37** | 58,000 | 2.50 to 3.87 |
| Cancelled | **(62,388)** | **.10 to 6.75** | (40,010) | .10 to 6.75 |
| Exercised | **(216,404)** | **.10 to 6.75** | (10,000) | .10 |
| Outstanding at end of year and reserved for issuance | **574,300** | **$.10 to $6.75** | 539,592 | $.10 to $6.75 |
| Exercisable at end of year | **283,800** | | 455,217 | |
| Reserved for future options | **93,162** | | 344,274 | |

## Industry Segments

The Company sells products and services to industrial customers through its three principal operating units. Selected financial information is presented below for 1988, 1987 and 1986 (000 omitted).

| | Segment Net Sales | | | Segment Operating Profits | | |
|---|---|---|---|---|---|---|
| | **1988** | 1987 | 1986 | **1988** | 1987 | 1986 |
| Industrial explosives | **$196,273** | $180,824 | $161,997 | **$15,745** | $15,613 | $13,089 |
| Specialty industrial coatings | **289,138** | 255,127 | 225,952 | **21,259** | 20,926 | 13,993 |
| Pipe and fittings | **179,234** | 188,166 | 189,143 | **6,551** | 17,919 | 20,625 |
| Segment totals | **$664,645** | $624,117 | $577,092 | **43,555** | 54,458 | 47,707 |
| Interest expense | | | | **(11,973)** | (6,431) | (2,310) |
| Unallocated corporate expense | | | | **(7,801)** | (7,711) | (6,519) |
| Income from continuing operations before income tax | | | | **$23,781** | $40,316 | $38,878 |

| | Capital Expenditures (Net) | | | Depreciation and Amortization | | |
|---|---|---|---|---|---|---|
| | **1988** | 1987 | 1986 | **1988** | 1987 | 1986 |
| Industrial explosives | **$ 6,344** | $ 5,402 | $ 8,640 | **$ 4,904** | $ 4,767 | $ 4,265 |
| Specialty industrial coatings | **2,457** | 4,419 | 4,473 | **5,375** | 4,477 | 4,847 |
| Pipe and fittings | **9,011** | 7,782 | 8,687 | **8,189** | 7,961 | 8,501 |
| Other | **132** | 308 | (2,963) | **503** | 1,442 | 1,279 |
| Total continuing operations | **17,944** | 17,911 | 18,837 | **18,971** | 18,647 | 18,892 |
| Discontinued operations | **1,531** | 4,066 | 3,423 | **3,190** | 5,053 | 4,253 |
| Consolidated | **$ 19,475** | $ 21,977 | $ 22,260 | **$22,161** | $23,700 | $23,145 |

| | Tangible Assets | | | Intangible Assets | | |
|---|---|---|---|---|---|---|
| | **1988** | 1987 | 1986 | **1988** | 1987 | 1986 |
| Industrial explosives | **$ 91,520** | $ 84,046 | $ 76,379 | **$ —** | $ — | $ — |
| Specialty industrial coatings | **110,228** | 107,433 | 98,369 | **11,243** | 11,587 | 11,931 |
| Pipe and fittings | **86,264** | 85,097 | 84,653 | **30,374** | 30,374 | 30,374 |
| Other | **18,869** | 7,234 | 7,795 | **—** | — | — |
| Total continuing operations | **306,881** | 283,810 | 267,196 | **41,617** | 41,961 | 42,305 |
| Discontinued operations, net | **—** | 161,715 | 141,679 | **—** | 26,205 | 27,305 |
| Consolidated | **$306,881** | $445,525 | $408,875 | **$41,617** | $68,166 | $69,610 |

| | Identifiable Assets | | |
|---|---|---|---|
| | **1988** | 1987 | 1986 |
| Industrial explosives | **$ 91,520** | $ 84,046 | $ 76,379 |
| Specialty industrial coatings | **121,471** | 119,020 | 110,300 |
| Pipe and fittings | **116,638** | 115,471 | 115,027 |
| Other | **18,869** | 7,234 | 7,795 |
| Total continuing operations | **348,498** | 325,771 | 309,501 |
| Discontinued operations, net | **—** | 187,920 | 168,984 |
| Consolidated | **$348,498** | $513,691 | $478,485 |

REPORT OF INDEPENDENT PUBLIC ACCOUNTANTS

The Board of Directors and Shareholders
of Tyler Corporation

We have audited the accompanying consolidated balance sheets of Tyler Corporation at December 31, 1988 and 1987, and the related consolidated statements of income, shareholders' equity and cash flows for each of the three years in the period ended December 31, 1988. These financial statements are the responsibility of the Company's management. Our responsibility is to express an opinion on these financial statements based on our audits.

We conducted our audits in accordance with generally accepted auditing standards. Those standards require that we plan and perform the audit to obtain reasonable assurance about whether the financial statements are free of material misstatement. An audit includes examining, on a test basis, evidence supporting the amounts and disclosures in the financial statements. An audit also includes assessing the accounting principles used and significant estimates made by management, as well as evaluating the overall financial statement presentation. We believe that our audits provide a reasonable basis for our opinion.

In our opinion, the financial statements referred to above present fairly, in all material respects, the consolidated financial position of Tyler Corporation at December 31, 1988 and 1987, and the consolidated results of operations and cash flows for each of the three years in the period ended December 31, 1988, in conformity with generally accepted accounting principles.

Arthur Young & Company

Dallas, Texas
January 27, 1989.

SUPPLEMENTARY QUARTERLY FINANCIAL DATA

| | First Quarter | Second Quarter | Third Quarter | Fourth Quarter | Year |
|---|---|---|---|---|---|
| Net sales | | | | | |
| **1988** | **$152,446,000** | **$171,628,000** | **$172,826,000** | **$167,745,000** | **$664,645,000** |
| 1987 | 141,957,000 | 161,028,000 | 163,677,000 | 157,455,000 | 624,117,000 |
| Gross profit | | | | | |
| **1988** | **31,781,000** | **39,656,000** | **36,933,000** | **33,637,000** | **142,007,000** |
| 1987 | 31,284,000 | 40,384,000 | 40,258,000 | 36,581,000 | 148,507,000 |
| Income from continuing operations | | | | | |
| **1988** | **2,844,000** | **7,149,000** | **3,823,000** | **759,000** | **14,575,000** |
| 1987 | 2,819,000 | 7,367,000 | 7,605,000 | 5,717,000 | 23,508,000 |
| Income (loss) from discontinued operations | | | | | |
| **1988** | **(1,181,000)** | **874,000** | **6,720,000**[(1)] | — | **6,413,000** |
| 1987 | (1,837,000) | (2,179,000) | (1,914,000) | (729,000) | (6,659,000) |
| Income before extraordinary charge | | | | | |
| **1988** | **1,663,000** | **8,023,000** | **10,543,000** | **759,000** | **20,988,000** |
| 1987 | 982,000 | 5,188,000 | 5,691,000 | 4,988,000 | 16,849,000 |
| Net income | | | | | |
| **1988** | **1,663,000** | **8,023,000** | **10,543,000** | **759,000** | **20,988,000** |
| 1987 | 982,000 | 5,188,000 | 5,691,000 | 157,000[(2)] | 12,018,000 |
| Earnings per common share from continuing operations | | | | | |
| **1988** | **.16** | **.41** | **.20** | **.04** | **.77** |
| 1987 | .16 | .41 | .43 | .33 | 1.33 |
| Earnings per common share from discontinued operations | | | | | |
| **1988** | **(.06)** | **.05** | **.35**[(1)] | — | **.34** |
| 1987 | (.10) | (.12) | (.11) | (.04) | (.37) |
| Earnings per common share before extraordinary charge | | | | | |
| **1988** | **.10** | **.46** | **.55** | **.04** | **1.11** |
| 1987 | .06 | .29 | .32 | .29 | .96 |
| Net earnings per common share | | | | | |
| **1988** | **.10** | **.46** | **.55** | **.04** | **1.11** |
| 1987 | .06 | .29 | .32 | .01[(2)] | .68 |
| Stock trading price range | | | | | |
| **1988** | **13¾-10¼** | **15½-12½** | **18-6¾** | **7-5⅝** | **18-5⅝** |
| 1987 | 15⅛-12⅛ | 15½-11⅞ | 15¾-12½ | 15¾-9¼ | 15¾-9¼ |
| Dividend per share | | | | | |
| **1988** | **.11** | **.11** | **10.00** | **.015** | **10.235** |
| 1987 | .10 | .10 | .10 | .11 | .41 |

(1) *Includes gain on sale of Hall-Mark Electronics of $6,334,000, or $.33 per share*

(2) *After extraordinary charge of $4,831,000, or $.28 per share, relating to early extinguishment of the 12⅞% subordinated notes*

## CORPORATE INFORMATION

*Corporate Offices*

The corporate offices of Tyler Corporation are located at:
3200 San Jacinto Tower
Dallas, Texas 75201
The Company's telephone number is 214/754-7800.

*Securities Listing*

Tyler Corporation common stock is traded on both the New York and Philadelphia Stock Exchanges. The Company's stock symbol is TYL.

The Company's 10½% subordinated debentures are listed on the New York Stock Exchange.

*Common Stock Transfer Agent and Registrar:*

NCNB Texas National Bank
P.O. Box 2964
Dallas, Texas 75221

*Trustee For:*

10½% Subordinated Debentures Due 1998
Continental Bank, N.A.
30 North LaSalle Street
Chicago, Illinois 60697

11% Senior Subordinated Debentures Due 1997
The Bank of New York
21 West Street
New York, New York 10015

*Legal Counsel*

Gardere & Wynne
Dallas, Texas

*Auditors*

Arthur Young & Company

*Annual Meeting*

The annual meeting of Tyler Corporation shareholders will be held at 10:00 a.m., April 19, 1989, in the Plaza of the Americas Hotel, Dallas.

*Additional Information*

The Company's Form 10-K annual report and the Company's Facts & Figures Manual may be obtained without charge by writing or telephoning:
Ms. Lucy B. LeBeau
Tyler Corporation
3200 San Jacinto Tower
Dallas, Texas 75201
214/754-7800

## OPERATING COMPANIES

Atlas Powder Company
15301 Dallas Parkway
Suite 1200
Dallas, Texas 75248
214/387-2400

Reliance Universal Inc.
1600 Watterson Towers
1930 Bishop Lane
Louisville, Kentucky 40218
502/459-9110

Tyler Pipe Industries, Inc.
P.O. Box 2027
Tyler, Texas 75710
214/882-5511

# Index

# Index

## E